# HISTORY OF THE THIRTEENTH REGIMENT OF NEW HAMPSHIRE VOLUNTEER INFANTRY IN THE WAR OF THE REBELLION 1861-1865

*A Diary  
Covering Three Years  
and a Day*

by

**S. Millett Thompson**

Lieutenant Thirteenth New Hampshire Volunteers

HERITAGE BOOKS
2007

# HERITAGE BOOKS
*AN IMPRINT OF HERITAGE BOOKS, INC.*

**Books, CDs, and more—Worldwide**

For our listing of thousands of titles see our website
at
www.HeritageBooks.com

A Facsimile Reprint
Published 2007 by
HERITAGE BOOKS, INC.
Publishing Division
65 East Main Street
Westminster, Maryland 21157-5026

Copyright © 1888 S. Millett Thompson

Originally published
Boston and New York
Houghton, Mifflin and Company
The Riverside Press, Cambridge
1888

— Publisher's Notice —
In reprints such as this, it is often not possible to remove blemishes from the original. We feel the contents of this book warrant its reissue despite these blemishes and hope you will agree and read it with pleasure.

International Standard Book Number: 978-0-7884-1517-3

## DEDICATION.

To my own family, to my Comrades in the Thirteenth Regiment of New Hampshire Volunteer Infantry now surviving, to the memory of the dead, and to the families of all, I most heartily dedicate the historical pages of this book.

S. MILLETT THOMPSON.

Providence, Rhode Island,
April 27, 1888.

# PREFACE.

IN this book the Thirteenth Regiment is treated of as a unit. All personal items, whether concerning myself or any other member of the Regiment, are entered to do an act of justice, to relate an occurrence either of a limited or a general interest, or to fix a date or fact. Eulogies, obituaries, and the making any one person prominent to the disparagement or exclusion of others, have been carefully avoided. Repetitions and duplication of statements have been entered only to make the narrative more clear, or as matters of corroboration; the book, running between a narrative and a diary, must needs be complete with each day, and still maintain the form of a narrative.

I have nothing to say against the collective body of the regular volunteer officers and soldiers of the Southern army as such; though frequently carried out of the right by the external pressure of their own section, they were infinitely better than the order of things which they represented; they were the very best men the South possessed, and I cannot, and would not if I could, detract from or wipe out their bravery, courage and honor.

Adhering to plain facts, I have endeavored to reproduce, as nearly as may be, the affairs, sentiments and spirit of the times of the war; for the spirit of a day, a time or an age is the very soul of its history, without which a string of bald facts is a bit of mere book-keeping.

It is desired that the reader of this book shall gain some idea of what it cost, in labor, fighting and suffering, to re-unite the dissevered States of the American Union; for every regiment in the Northern army had experiences similar to those of the Thirteenth, and many of them suffered more severely and lost more heavily, — and to gain that idea in some measure multiply this Thirteenth Regiment's work and sacrifices by 2,050, the number, equivalently, of regiments in the Northern army engaged in that war.

## PREFACE

Slang phrases, and a sort of camp language, were used in the army immensely; they are not classic, but when a happy phrase, or a slang phrase of a reasonable character, condenses a page into a line and conveys its meaning clear, that phrase should be written until it becomes classic — grammarian dignity is the stage-coach, terse phrase the lightning express. Still, we hold all marred language under protest.

In making the sketches and tracing the maps, the chief aim has been not to be artistic, but by outlines to enable any person, with this book in hand, to find the exact spots where the Thirteenth camped or fought; and nearly all the plats and maps look the way the Thirteenth faced or moved. Both sketches and tracings I made with my pen, and they are reproduced here by photogravure process. The official maps used were those of Brevet Brig. Gen. N. Michler.

No statements have been drawn from cheap newspaper accounts, popular yarns or realms dimesque. The negro is represented without prejudice or favor, and as I saw him; and the broad things said of him, or by him, have been entered merely to show what he was. Swearing enough was done in the army to last any reasonable people until the millennium, and I have seen no need of repeating it here. The ideas and opinions ventured are such as I have entertained for many years, some during the war, and have seen no reason to change.

It was thought best to use the word battle for all engagements inscribed upon the flag. Names are attached to quotations by courtesy, to show whence the statements came. Col. Stevens was applied to for historical data the same as all the other officers of the Regiment and large numbers of the men, but he furnished nothing for this book.

The war was no holiday excursion, and but for the soldiers' fun the army had gone half mad; the few jokes in this book have been put in as a common property; the Thirteenth, as well as the army as a whole, laughed far more than it wept, and will remember its enjoyments far beyond the fading of its woes; but to reproduce the sports of the soldiers, to describe their merry-making and fun, to relate their yarns and stories, to write their laughable anecdotes and jokes with any reasonable degree of clearness and justice, were impossible for any man, and I will not presume to make the attempt, and have carefully avoided all attempts at being funny.

My interest in the war and its results was increased by the fact that when a boy, twelve to fifteen years of age, I had served as a conductor on the Underground Railroad; that is, guiding numerous escaped slaves through New Hampshire woods toward Canada.

## PREFACE.

While temporarily engaged in business in the West in 1877-9, I employed a number of evenings in writing for my family such reminiscences of my army life as came to mind. Upon informing Asst. Surgeon Sullivan of this in 1880, he first of all suggested to me the idea of writing this book, and urged me to do it. I hesitated for a while, but finally undertook the work — not because of any ability of mine to do the subject full justice, but simply because no one else arose to do a much needed work — the meagre early accounts of her Regiments reflecting too small a measure of credit upon our State. Though entering upon the work with hesitancy, I believed it to be the sheerest folly for history to wither upon the stem of any man's modesty — such stems are too dry and dead : modesty was not instituted to choke facts into oblivion, excepting such facts as are most shameful and unfit to print.

The most of this book has been written offhand. I am not a professional writer ; and whether able or otherwise, after examining the many letters, diaries and papers required in the work, after reading every reliable publication that I could obtain bearing upon the particular service in which the Thirteenth took a part. after visiting the fields and camps in Virginia twice for data and measurements, after making all the tracings and sketches, after the necessary correspondence and the arranging and writing of all, and attending to my private business at the same time, I have had no spare time in which to smooth sentences or polish paragraphs, — this book must be taken, as it were, in fatigue dress, there is no attempt at dress-parade about it, and the plain facts must stand as they are in their plain words.

In the compilation of data for this history I have drawn my information from the following sources: Official papers and statements furnished by, and diaries and letters written during the war by, Lt. Col. George Bowers; Lt. Col. William Grantman ; Lt. Col. Normand Smith (letters) ; Maj. Nathan D. Stoodley (diary and letters) ; Capt. Charles O. Bradley ; Capt. George N. Julian (letters) ; Capt. Charles H. Curtis ; Capt. M. T. Betton; Capt. Buel C. Carter ; Capt. James M. Durell (official papers) ; Capt. William J. Ladd ; Capt. Rufus P Staniels (diaries) ; Quarter-master Mortier L. Morrison ; Asst. Surgeon John Sullivan ; Lieut. W. H. H. Young ; Hospital Steward and Lieut. Royal B. Prescott (diaries and letters) ; Lieut. S. Millett Thompson (diary and letters) ; Lieut. Henry Churchill ; Adjt. Nathan B. Boutwell ; Adjt. George H. Taggard (diary) ; Sergt. Major James M. Hodgdon (diary) ; Musicians : James M. Caswell ; Charles W. Washburn (letters). Sergeants : W. G. Burnham ; Charles W. Batchellor (letters) ; Thomas S. Wentworth. Privates : Cyrus G. Drew (diary) ; Albion J. Jenness (letters) ; Horace W. Waldron ; Henry S. Paul ; William B. Luey (diary), and others both officers and men whose names are mentioned in the text. Above diaries and letters were written at the front.

Besides the above, the following named sources of information among others were consulted :

## PREFACE

Gen. A. A. Humphreys' Virginia Campaign of 1864 and 1865.
Capt. Frederick Phisterer's Statistical Record.
New Hampshire in the Rebellion.
Burnside and the Ninth Army Corps.
C. C. Coffin's — 'Carleton's' — writings.
Adjt. Generals' Reports of all the New England States, New York and New Jersey.
Official papers, letters and rolls in State House, Concord.
Lt. Gen. U. S. Grant's Memoirs.
Tenny's Civil War.
Military and Civil History of Connecticut.
Capt. James A. Sanborn's MS. Hist. 10th N. H. Regiment.
Pollard's Lost Cause.
Greeley's American Conflict.
Lossing's Civil War.
Moore's Rebellion Record.
N. H. Adjt. General's Reports.
A bound volume of New Hampshire Newspapers sent by A. S. Batchellor, Esq., of Littleton.
Muster out Rolls of the Thirteenth.

The manuscript, excepting the addition made after the Reunion of 1887, was read before publication by Major Nathan D. Stoodley, Asst. Surgeon Sullivan, Lieut. Royal B. Prescott and Sergeant James M. Woods of the Publication Committee, who were privileged by the writer to correct, amend, add to, or cut from, the text as in their judgment was in the interest of the history. The Thirteenth and the writer are greatly indebted to these gentlemen for their unwearied efforts, painstaking care, and unswerving, hearty fidelity to the best interests of this history, its subject and its writer. We have worked together as one, in the spirit of the belief that the noble acts of each member of the Regiment are the joint property and heritage of all, — nevertheless the writer assumes all responsibilities, and takes to himself all blame that may attach for any inadvertences occurring in the book.

Previous to the committee's examination the writer had revised the manuscript in consultation with Major Stoodley, Lt. Col. Grantman and Lt. Col. Smith, — the purpose being to furnish so far as possible an absolute record to stand as an authority.

S. MILLETT THOMPSON.

# CONTENTS.

AUTHORITIES FOR THE WORK . . . . . . . Preface

## I.

### JULY 1, 1862, TO DECEMBER 10, 1862.

|  | PAGE |
|---|---|
| CALL FOR TROOPS . . . . . . . . . . . | 1 |
| CAMP COLBY, AT CONCORD N. H. . . . . . . | 2 |
| MARCH TO THE SEAT OF WAR . . . . . . . | 9 |
| CAMP CHASE, AT ARLINGTON HEIGHTS . . . . . | 11 |
| CAMP CASEY, AT FAIRFAX SEMINARY . . . . . . | 20 |
| MARCH THROUGH MARYLAND TO FREDERICKSBURG . . . . | 27 |

## II.

### DECEMBER 11, 1862, TO FEBRUARY 8, 1863.

| BATTLE OF FREDERICKSBURG . . . . . . . . | 36 |
|---|---|
| CAMP OPPOSITE FREDERICKSBURG . . . . . . . | 88 |
| MOVE FROM FREDERICKSBURG TO NEWPORT NEWS . . . | 108 |

## III.

### FEBRUARY 9, TO MAY 16, 1863.

| CAMP AT NEWPORT NEWS . . . . . . . . | 111 |
|---|---|
| CAMP NEAR SUFFOLK . . . . . . . . . . | 117 |
| SIEGE OF SUFFOLK . . . . . . . . . . | 126 |
| BATTLE OF PROVIDENCE CHURCH ROAD . . . . . | 139 |

## IV.

### MAY 17, 1863, TO APRIL 18, 1864.

| CAMP IN 'THE PINES,' AT GETTY'S STATION . . . . | 161 |
|---|---|
| 'BLACKBERRY RAID' . . . . . . . . . . | 171 |
| CAMP GILMORE, AT GETTY'S STATION . . . . . . | 195 |
| THIRTEENTH GOES HOME TO VOTE . . . . . . . | 238 |

## V.

### APRIL 19, TO MAY 11, 1864.

| | |
|---|---|
| Spring Campaign of 1864 | 250 |
| March to Yorktown, and Camp there | 251 |
| Move to Bermuda Hundred | 256 |
| Battle of Port Walthall | 259 |
| Battle of Swift Creek | 263 |

## VI.

### MAY 12, TO MAY 27, 1864.

| | |
|---|---|
| Advance on Richmond | 279 |
| Battle of Kingsland Creek | 279 |
| Battle of Drury's Bluff | 284 |
| Camp at Bermuda Hundred | 322 |

## VII.

### MAY 28, TO JUNE 15, 1864.

| | |
|---|---|
| March to Cold Harbor | 335 |
| Battle of Cold Harbor | 338 |
| Move to Front of Petersburg | 374 |
| Battle of Battery Five | 382 |
| Thirteenth captures a Redan with Five Cannon | 387 |

## VIII.

### JUNE 16, TO SEPTEMBER 27, 1864.

| | |
|---|---|
| Siege of Petersburg. In the Trenches | 404 |
| Sketches of Life in a Military Hospital | 405 |
| Mine Explosion and Crater | 431 |
| Return to Bermuda Hundred | 447 |

## IX.

### SEPTEMBER 28, 1864, TO FEBRUARY 28, 1865.

| | |
|---|---|
| Battle of Fort Harrison | 458 |
| Before Richmond | 490 |
| Battle of Fair Oaks | 499 |
| Winter Camp near Fort Harrison | 508 |
| Company C in Redoubt McConihe | 527 |

CONTENTS. xi

## X.

### MARCH 1, TO APRIL 12, 1865.

| | |
|---|---|
| LAST CAMPAIGN | 537 |
| ROSTER OF GEN. DEVENS' 3D DIVISION, 24TH CORPS | 549 |
| SURRENDER OF RICHMOND | 552 |
| FIRST FLAG HOISTED IN RICHMOND | 559 |
| THIRTEENTH THE FIRST REGIMENT IN | 563 |

## XI.

| | |
|---|---|
| CLOSE OF THE WAR — PEACE | 589 |
| ASSASINATION OF PRESIDENT LINCOLN | 589 |
| SCENES IN BOSTON, APRIL 3–16, 1865 | 590 |
| WELCOMING THE HOMING ARMY CORPS | 595 |
| THIRTEENTH MUSTERED OUT AND STARTS FOR HOME | 606 |
| PERSONAL NOTES | 612 |
| BAND OF THE THIRTEENTH | 625 |

## XII.*

| | |
|---|---|
| ROSTER OF THE THIRTEENTH | 638 |
| REUNION AT BOSTON, APRIL 5, 1887 | 686 |
| INDEX | 709 |

# LIST OF ILLUSTRATIONS AND MAPS.

|  | PAGE |
|---|---|
| FLAGS OF THIRTEENTH | Frontispiece |
| REGIMENT OF INFANTRY IN LINE OF BATTLE | 7 |
| CAMP CHASE | 17 |
| PART OF FREDERICKSBURG BATTLE-FIELD | 43 |
| PART OF FREDERICKSBURG BATTLE-FIELD | 47 |
| FREDERICKSBURG | 51 |
| REGION NEAR FALMOUTH CAMP | 91 |
| PROVIDENCE CHURCH ROAD | 149 |
| SUFFOLK AND VICINITY | 155 |
| CAMP GILMORE AND VICINITY | 197 |
| SWIFT CREEK — PLAT | 271 |
| SWIFT CREEK — MAP | 275 |
| DRURY'S BLUFF AND VICINITY | 313 |
| DRURY'S BLUFF | 317 |
| BERMUDA HUNDRED | 331 |
| COLD HARBOR | 353 |
| COLD HARBOR AND VICINITY | 377 |
| CONFEDERATE BATTLE FLAGS | 391 |
| BATTERY FIVE | 399 |
| PETERSBURG FRONT | 411 |
| POSITION OF THIRTEENTH ON PETERSBURG FRONT | 415 |
| FORT HARRISON | 469 |
| FORT HARRISON AND VICINITY | 473 |
| FAIR OAKS AND VICINITY | 505 |
| FORRESTER PAPERS | 561 |
| RICHMOND AND VICINITY — TWO MAPS | 636, 637 |

## FRONTISPIECE — DESCRIPTION.

THE flags at the right — National — and at the left — State — were received by the Thirteenth at Concord, Oct. 5, 1862. These two flags and the two small flags — 'Markers' — were carried by the Thirteenth through its term of service, its camps, marches and battles, until Dec. 27, 1864, when the first flag, the markers being retained, was returned to the custody of the State. The flag in the centre was received Dec. 27, 1864, with the names of the battles inscribed thereon — see page 519; and this one with the old State flag were the two carried into Richmond by the Thirteenth on April 3, 1865. All these flags are now preserved, in a glass case, in the rotunda of the Capitol at Concord.

# THIRTEENTH NEW HAMPSHIRE REGIMENT.

## I.

### JULY 1, 1862, TO DECEMBER 10, 1862.

**July 1. Tues.** At the instance of the Governors of seventeen loyal States, Abraham Lincoln, President of the United States, on this day issues a call for 300,000 volunteers, and under this call enlistments at once commence, and there enlists for three years: —

### THE THIRTEENTH REGIMENT OF NEW HAMPSHIRE VOLUNTEER INFANTRY.

Rockingham, Hillsborough, and Strafford Counties each furnishing two companies, and Merrimac, Grafton, Carroll, and Coos Counties one company each ; assembling from all parts of the State, from Connecticut River to the lakes of Maine, from tide water to Canada line.

Under this call for 300,000 men for three years, New Hampshire furnishes 6,390 men — 1,337 men above its quota. Total enlistments in all the loyal States and Territories are 421,465 men — 86,630 men above all their quotas.

"We are coming, Father Abraham, three hundred thousand more."

**Sept. 1. Mon.** Capt. N. D. Stoodley's 130 men for Company G met, for drill, for the first time, Monday, August 18, in Peterboro', and have since been drilling there. About the same time 104 men, enlisted in and about Littleton for Company D, by Capt. Farr, and Lieutenants Kilburn and Saunders, commenced drilling; and in the other recruiting centres about equally early and speedy activity and preparation have been going on.

**Sept. 6. Sat.** Company E drilling ; a part at New Market, and about sixty men in the Town Hall at Exeter. The writer enlisted as a private, and knew nothing whatever about military drill. Capt. Julian promised to have him appointed First Sergeant of the company, if he would drill the men before they went into camp at Concord. Whereupon the writer purchased a book of tactics, borrowed a gun, shut himself up in a room for a day and a night of hard study, then met his men in the Town Hall, Exeter, and commenced a month of drill — amateur in every respect. The men had assembled, and drilled somewhat, previous to this date.

## CAMP COLBY, NEAR CONCORD, N. H.

**Sept. 11. Thurs.** Company C, enlisted by Capt. Bradley and Lieutenants Curtis and Staniels, goes into camp at Camp Colby, Dark Plains, near Concord. The first company in camp.

Each man of the Thirteenth, on coming into camp, receives a woolen blanket, a rubber blanket, a knife, fork, and spoon, all wofully cheap, a tin plate and a tin dipper.

**Sept. 12. Fri.** Co. G goes into camp at Dark Plains to-day. Co. E leaves Exeter and New Market at 5 p. m., arrives in barracks at Camp Colby at 9 p. m., having been delayed for a time in Concord while waiting to receive blankets. There is much mud in the road, the evening is rainy and very dark, most of the men are merry and full of sport, some can sing, all can yell, and the trip, on the whole, is one not soon to be forgotten.

The Littleton Company, D, arrived in camp to-day, about half an hour after the arrival of Co. G. Every man of Company D can read and write, and there are but few in the whole Regiment who cannot.

Camp Colby is about one and one fourth miles from Concord, near the Chichester road.

**Sept. 13. Sat.** The men of the 13th, in the barracks, last night, represented the entire animal creation, and for six or eight hours nearly five hundred men together howled, crowed, bleated, barked, roared, squealed, yelled, screamed, sung, and laughed to the limit of vocal powers. They lay on boards, "boxy-shelves," having a blanket and about two ryestraws per man for a bed. They are all up at 5 a. m. to-day, the roll is called, and all are set at work to clear, of brush and bushes, the ground for their tents.

The larger part of the Regiment comes into camp to-day, — a total of seven or eight hundred men. A motley company, many in their worst suits of clothes, the most looking as if they had not slept for a week.

Last night's entertainment used up many of the men. Bedlam, Noah's Ark, a Hen Convention, and the Plain of Babel were all sought to be outdone twice over. One more such night would fit all the men for the madhouse. The funny fools were all there, and the drunken fools also; all striving and straining to see who could be the most foolish, and each seemed to exceed all his fellows. A few feathers were the cause of a furious struggle for possession by at least an hundred men. One man found a few straws, cut them up into inch pieces, distributed the pieces to his friends, who solemnly placed them on the boards, under various parts of their bodies, and instantly fell to snoring loud enough to wake the dead. But this only served to provoke numerous contests in the bunks. Bottles were passed around, emptied, and then thrown out of the windows, where they lie this morning, mutely explaining the cause of last night's uproar. General good nature prevailed, however, and scarce an angry word was heard; a night of rough, coarse fun, and boys' wild play.

**Sept. 14. Sun.** Tents are now up, the most of the work done yesterday, and the camp begins to present a very respectable appearance. But we are located on a most unattractive ground. As one man of the 13th writes: "The smutty-est, pitch-piney-est, huckle-berry-est, darnedest, scrubby plains in all New England."

When the men file around with their tin plates and cups this morning for their breakfast, some of them take in a supply of " grumble " that lasts until the end of their term of service; the breakfast is execrable, there is a general storm of hard words, and the food is thrown in all directions to pave the camp, while expressions of resentment and disgust are by no means restrained.

Notwithstanding the rough and much worn clothing of the men, and their generally wearied demeanor, there is ample evidence that we have here a body of men made up almost wholly of the best young men of our State, such as are born to command a reasonable degree of respect even while mere enlisted men.

**Sept. 15. Mon.** Some of the First Sergeants have " A " tents for their own use alone. These tents are about seven feet square on the ground. The First Sergeants and the Adjutant have more work to do than all the other officers put together. Field officers, in new trappings, find a wonderful amount of work in standing, in martial attitudes, near their tent doors; looking at the crowds of visitors of course. They are strangers to our camp.

There are nine companies now in camp, 956 men; and since no company was the last company to arrive here, we must pass the tenth company in respectful silence.

**Sept. 16. Tues.** To those who have lived in houses, the first impression of a tent is that of very close quarters. Some tents have floors, others are provided with straw to cover the ground. The days are warm, nights chilly. Diarrhœa prevalent.

**Sept. 17. Wed.** First Dress-parade. Many have come into camp in their poorest suits of clothes for economy's sake, and the appearance of the line can be better imagined than described. Drill is aching funny. We are all green. Mistakes are corrected by making still worse mistakes. The men in the ranks, grin, giggle and snicker, and now and then break out into a coarse, country haw-haw. We are reminded of the young men squads in the old Militia muster days.

**Sept. 18. Thurs.** Co. G examined by Surgeon Twitchell. He is very critical and careful, but rapid, and completes the examination of the Regiment in a few days. The storm, about our food, that broke out last Sunday, has taught the purveyor of our rations to furnish better material, and to serve it in a more acceptable manner.

**Sept. 19. Fri.** Companies E and G mustered in by Capt. Chas.

Holmes U. S. A. Capt. Stoodley and Lieut. Forbush are mustered in with their company. Capt. Buzzell is taken suddenly ill. (He does not join the Reg. again for nearly two months.)

Sept. 20. Sat. To-day completes the muster-in of the rank and file. In the equalization of companies, Co. E receives several men from Co. I, and among them Royal B. Prescott, of Nashua, on duty in the Hospital Department. The week has been very rainy.

Sept. 21. Sun. The camp is crowded with visitors, an inquisitive nuisance. Patriotism develops early in New Hampshire. A little girl was asked to sing the song beginning, "I want to be an angel," when she answered, "No I don't; I want to be a soldier." Children are beating drums, blowing horns, whistling marches and singing patriotic songs, all up and down the State, from Canada to the sea.

Sept. 22. Mon. Uniforms received. The 10th N. H. leaves Manchester for the seat of war. They number 928 men. Many of the 13th go down to see them depart. The 12th and 14th Regts. are encamped near us.

Sept. 23. Tues. The field officers are mustered in to-day, and the organization of the Thirteenth is now complete.

One night while in camp here, between one and two hundred men manage to elude the guard. A large party of them return from the city to camp, in the small hours of the morning, and plan to enter within the guard lines. Ranging themselves a few yards apart in a long line, tying handkerchiefs around their faces and turning up coat collars by way of disguise, at a concerted signal they make a simultaneous rush past the sentinels. The most of the sentinels cried : " Halt ; who goes there ? " But some of them called out : " Stop ; what's yer name ? " No one of the party halted or stopped, however, but each gave the sentinels a different answer as they rushed past the bewildered fellows to their quarters ; 'Pete,' 'Jim,' 'Dick,' 'Bill,' 'Tiger,' 'Reb,' 'The devil,' 'Spoons,' 'Beans,' and all sorts of names were given ; and one minute later every one of our party was under a blanket in his tent and fast asleep.

Sept. 25. Thurs. Regiment furloughed until Monday evening Sept. 29th.

Sept. 29. Mon. The men and officers are coming in, from their last visit to their friends and families, to-day, and as they assemble it may be well to note a few of the circumstances, and record the "Spirit of the Times," in which this Thirteenth New Hampshire Regiment has been raised all so speedily ; and not only this Regiment, but five others in New Hampshire all within the space of a few weeks, New Hampshire exceeding her quota by over 1,300 volunteers. All these six regiments, with the Thirteenth, are composed of the best material which New Hampshire can furnish. All are entitled to equal credit, but we cannot include in our sketch more than its special subject. As for the Thirteenth, almost every man has received a common school education, and many have advanced much farther. The Thirteenth comprises farmers, manufacturers, mechanics of almost every trade and men of almost every calling, bookkeepers, clerks, tradesmen, the substantial, intelligent, energetic doers of the country's work, and well informed in the country's needs and resources. Its officers comprise lawyers, physicians, students of law, medicine, mining and engineering; and representatives of large wealth and homes of luxury. The Thirteenth is emphatically a body of congenial companions, its companies formed of fellow townsmen, schoolmates, playmates and lifelong friends, and of the entire Regiment there are scarcely a score who cannot read and write. Insult a man of this command, and you will equally insult almost every man in it; offer a worthy purpose, and the most will join in securing its best ends.

Such are our men and officers. Now let us see why such men fly to arms. As for the bounties paid, they are generally regarded merely as means to help care for families and dependents in the absence of principals. Many a man of the Thirteenth gives up from two to five dollars for every dollar which the service yields, counting bounties and all. This is actual fact, and susceptible of proof. Some need the bounties; to some they are a mere bagatelle; while the cravens, to be found everywhere, are with us very few indeed. These men go in to win back a country. They feel that there is a burglar in the house, and either proprietor or burglar must remove. 300,000, 600,000, 1,000,000 men are now wanted. The South is arming every man and boy, and the war is assuming stupendous proportions.

In April and May (the early part), affairs with our army in Virginia turned out badly; before May was out the whole North was in extreme excitement, almost a panic, on account of the dangers to Washington; England, and wavering France, appeared ready to recognize the Confederacy in the event of any apparently decisive disaster to the Union Army; the air was overflowing with discouraging rumors; the very patriotism of some of our prominent generals was in doubt, and June gave its terrible battles before Richmond, its seven days' retreat to Malvern Hill, and rapid changes among the highest commanders in our army. Meanwhile the South moved steadily, determinedly, sternly on in its purpose; every loss it met but seemed to rouse it to more mighty efforts to retrieve them all, with solid gains in addition. The heat of July only increased the heat of the contest, in which the North seemed to make no substantial headway, while its confusion and doubt continued. August came in with the South at the flood tide of confidence, now sure of sweeping away the Northern army like chaff; while the repeated calls in the North for more troops, and in almost countless numbers, threw more and more of burden upon our people and shook the confidence of many. August went out in blood, disaster and retreat; another Bull Run. Alarm for the Capital spread anew, and the calls for lint, bandages, nurses and medical help, coupled with the vast lists of the dead and wounded, sent a shiver of horror throughout the whole North. September found the South magnificently victorious, and our army in Virginia terribly shattered, ending, in short, with the drawn battle of awful Antietam, "The bloodiest day America ever saw." And the far away successes in the Southwest have had but little effect in raising the depression in New England, caused by the terrible disasters nearer home. To cap the whole, Gen. Lee, in these very days, has raised himself apparently above all our Generals, and almost to the level of the greatest military names in history. His prowess and ability are greater causes of anxiety than our country has felt at any time during this war ; while the English aristocrats, using the rebellion sympathizers in the Northern States, the Copperheads, as a cave of echoes, praise and extol him without measure.

Surely the Thirteenth enlisted, and came into camp, on a day, when war, despite all our successes, never in this country wore so grim a visage, and was so monstrous in every aspect; and to sign an enlistment paper seemed like signing one's own death warrant, to be executed by the slow torture of labor, exposure, danger, hair-breadth escapes, fear, sickness, incurable diseases, wounds, pain, dismemberment, and rotting alive ; and after death a burial, uncoffined, in some unmarked hole in the ground, or left above ground to the buzzards, beasts and vermin, our toe and finger bones to be picked up and wrought into necklaces and curios.

The prospect is not Elysian. Still, to-night, our camp is rapidly filling up by our men and officers returning cheerfully from their little furlough; and with them there also rush to arms over 80,000 men in less than one month.

**Oct. 4. Sat. Fair.** All this pleasant week wives and sweethearts, mothers and sisters, fathers and brothers, children and friends have flocked to our camp, and still they come ; while a crowd of all sorts of people has gathered so great that a cordon around camp is a necessity. The Thirteenth feels the first tight grip of a provost guard. To see friends outside of camp, or to receive them within, a pass must be shown. The Thirteenth has the name of being the most orderly regiment that has been organized in this camp. Company D claims the honor of being the only company which came into camp with every man sober. This statement, however, meets the following : "Company G came into camp with 125 or 130 men, all sober. N. D. S." Every company came in remarkably free from intoxicated men. There has been a generous rivalry to see which company would appear the best.

**Oct. 5. Sun. Fair.** Thirteenth marches to Concord from Camp Colby in the afternoon, and receives its colors — a State flag, a National flag and two guidons — from the hands of Hon. Allen Tenney, Sec. of State, in front of the State House, and in the presence of a large assembly of the people. Later in the day the Regiment returns to camp ; sick of buncombe speechifying, and the patting of "our departing heroes" on the back, by the brave homesmen, the men. who do not enlist. The Thirteenth is armed with Springfield rifles, weighing with the bayonet nine and one fourth pounds, calibre 58 ; for a minie bullet weighing 500 grains, and propelled by about sixty grains of powder. The bayonet,

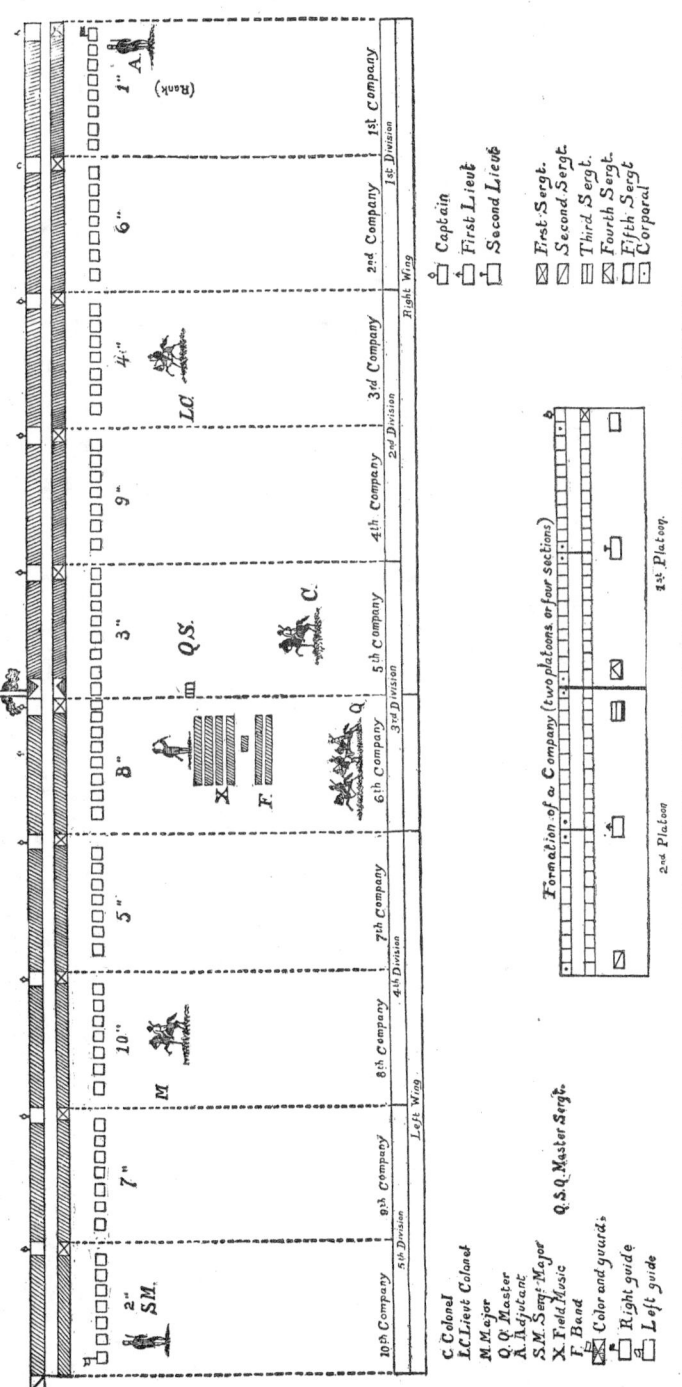

REGIMENT OF INFANTRY—TEN COMPANIES—IN LINE OF BATTLE.

Photograph from U. S. Infantry Tactics.

straight pattern, weighs three fourths of a pound. The Thirteenth holds its first Dress-parade in camp with arms, colors, and uniform complete.

An enterprising Lieutenant in the Thirteenth wants a cook-house, finds an old tool house in a field, has it lugged to camp and fitted up. The owner, after a world of fencing, threats and parley, receives $50 for it. And then the sharp fellow boasts that he will " hev ther tool-howse back 'gin tew, after ther rigimunt er gone." It accidentally takes fire to-night, and will let no more at the fair rental of $25 per week. The whole thing was not worth ten dollars.

## MARCH TO THE SEAT OF WAR.

**Oct. 6. Mon.** Clear, very pleasant. Reg. marches from Camp Colby at 4 a. m., takes cars at Concord depot and moves out at 7 a. m. Breakfast at Nashua, a free gift from the citizens and very fine, in fact a magnificent treat. The men have their haversacks filled for the purposes of lunch later on. Too many canteens are full also.

After marching through the streets, escorted by several bands, and by citizens, cadets, militia and three companies of firemen, and past the residences of Col. Stevens and Lt. Col. Bowers, the Reg. leaves Nashua at 12 noon; arrives at Worcester at 2 p. m. ; stops there about half an hour for sundry errands and for grapes, pears and peaches, which are brought to the cars in large quantities, and given away, or sold for mere nothing; and then proceeds direct to Allyn's Point on the Thames River, arriving and embarking on the steamer " City of Boston " about 8 p. m. It is a beautiful moonlit night, and we enjoy a splendid sail.

**Oct. 7. Tues.** Thirteenth arrives at Jersey City at 4 a. m. about daylight, debarks, breakfasts on soup, bread and coffee, a plenty, but none too good ; and remains about the wharf a long time indulging in an abundance of sunshine, loafing and Jersey peaches. Small teams appearing at the wharf with quantities of the best fruit the country affords. At 10 a. m. we take cars, dirty cattle cars, twenty-nine of them, for Philadelphia, and have a rough, hard ride. One man was severely injured by falling from the car during a brief delay between New York and Philadelphia. E. F. Trow of E was severely hurt in the foot, by the Adjutant's horse stepping upon it, while the horses were being placed upon the cars at Jersey City. This caused his early discharge from the service. We arrive at 6 p. m., landing at the freight depot at the foot of Washington Avenue, then move at once to supper at the Cooper Shop Volunteer Refreshment Saloon, No. 1009 Otsego Street.

Of this famous saloon, Mr. Wm. R. S. Cooper, of Philadelphia, furnishes the writer with the following under date of· Dec. 12, 1884. The saloon was started by his father Mr. Wm. M. Cooper, himself and a few friends, in April 1861. At first they paid all the expenses out of their own pockets, afterwards received contributions for the saloon from citizens of Philadelphia, but not a cent from the United States, the State or the city. They also established a Hospital for sick and wounded soldiers. They could feed half a regiment at a time, and a whole regiment about every hour in the day. During the war they fed over 600,000 men, at an expense of ten to fifteen cents per meal. The affair caused the loss of all of Mr. Cooper's business, and reduced the whole family to severe straits.

After the supper the Thirteenth marches, together with a large body of troops, about one and one half miles through the city, amid the cheers and good-byes of multitudes of the people, who line the streets, and fill the windows, doorways and balconies. Many houses are brilliantly illuminated. We are placed in baggage, cattle and freight cars, near Broad Street and Washington Avenue, 40 men, and in some cases more, in a car, and start for Baltimore at 10 p. m. Crossing the Susquehanna at Havre de Grace, by ferry, the bridge there having been destroyed.

Oct. 8. Wed. Thirteenth arrives in Baltimore at 6 a. m., after a hard night's ride in the dirty, stuffy cars. First, we march about two miles through Baltimore, to the outbound cars, there leave our knapsacks, and then march half a mile to the soldiers' rooms or caravansary; there eat a sort of dogs-fodder breakfast about 9 a. m., and then march back to the cars again, and about 11 a. m. start for Washington, in a mixed train of baggage and passenger cars. While in Baltimore a part of the Reg. have loaded muskets, and we march through the same streets where the Sixth Massachusetts Regiment was mobbed. The citizens are civil now, but many of them look sour and ugly. A large number of U. S. flags are waving from houses as we pass along.

Election at Baltimore to-day. Liquor shops all closed, $500 fine for selling liquor to-day; hence this peace.

On the route to Washington soldiers are everywhere; we pass a large body of them at the Relay House, and at Annapolis Junction. Like our ride last night, our ride to-day is slow, tiresome and jerky. Two of our men were poisoned in Baltimore, and one run over by the cars on the route to Washington; all will survive.

We arrive in Washington at 9.30 p. m., and after a supper of corned beef, bread and coffee at the barracks, we bivouac on the Capitol grounds, north end, in the mud and wet, without tents, shelter, cover or sleep. Less than half the Reg. could be accommodated in the old barracks. This after a nine hours' ride, to make only forty miles, in freight cars, chiefly with forty men in a car. Soldiering thus begins to grow disagreeable.

And here is heard a brogue that is new to us; a man at the station calls out to passengers: "All abode fer Baltemoh!" One man of the 13th writes: "Negroes are here of every shade of color, from the delicate brown seen on a griddle-cake to Japan black, and in such hosts as to astonish us New Englanders."

## CAMP CHASE, ARLINGTON HEIGHTS, VA.

Oct. 9. Thurs. Very warm. "Hot as 4th of July." Our breakfast is bread, beef and coffee, dinner the same. We leave our bivouac at 2.15 p. m., march through Washington, now a rough looking place, via Pennsylvania Avenue, and amid clouds of dust — down near the bridge it is six inches deep in the street. We cross the Long Bridge about 4 p. m., and reach Camp Chase, four or five miles from the city, about 6 p. m. We have no supper worth naming, Another night now, and a very chilly one, is spent on the bare ground of an old cornfield, and without tents. A man in the 13th was sunstruck at noon; our teeth are chattering with the cold to-night.

The thermometer of our experience stood at about 80 degrees, at Concord, rose to 120, in the sunshine, as we came along to Philadelphia, and dropped down towards zero at Baltimore. At Washington, where soldiers are a mere commodity, we struck about 32 degrees, and could not decide whether to thaw or freeze; and now here at Camp Chase, we throw all reckoning away, set our chattering teeth, and resolve to take things as best we may, counting disagreeables as incidents of the service.

From our place of bivouac the Capitol is east, Fairfax Seminary south, and Arlington west; there are two or three forts in the foreground. Camps are seen on every hand, and troops in thousands everywhere.

Oct. 10. Fri. Warm, cloudy. The Thirteenth gathers up its stiff, chilled and dirty ranks, moves a short distance over across the road, the officers and men lugging over the entire equipage and baggage, a comical and amusing caravan, and pitches its tents in open ground, our first camp ground in Dixie. The ground is bare of grass; worn off by the ceaseless tramp, tramp, tramp, of thousands of men, and hundreds of teams, and a little rain suffices to turn the clayey ground into a mortar-trough. Camp Chase, our part of it, is $2\frac{1}{2}$ miles from Fairfax Seminary, in a bee line; $2\frac{1}{2}$ miles from Munson's Hill, and one mile from Gen. R. E. Lee's old home, Arlington Heights. We are encamped on the main road. A visit to Arlington House, very fine, and to the mud-chinked, mud-floored, mud-and-sticks huts of the slaves belonging to the estate, reveals at a glance both sides of the picture of slavery's curse, while the whipping-post near by adds a bold stroke of color to the dark side.

Gen. Casey, in command here, is an elderly man, with a smooth face, a long nose, and white hair, and appears genial. Our rations are chiefly coffee, coarse brown sugar and hard bread, the latter old and wormy. We are now to enter upon a term of severe military discipline and drill.

Oct. 11. Sat. Rainy, cold. We fit up our camp during the day, and have a Dress-parade about sunset. We are much exposed; and there seems to be no need of exposing raw troops after this fashion, and no common sense in it whatever. The nights are exceeding chilly. The Thirteenth looks rather tired and worn out. Oct. 5, Sunday, at Concord, we were up nearly all night; Monday night we slept packed on a stuffy boat; Tuesday night, slept in cattle and freight cars; Wednesday night, slept out doors, indoors, anywhere; Thursday night, slept on the ground; Friday got into tents, but slept on the bare ground. This, added to much eating and feasting, and many hundred miles of travel over bad roads, with rough boards for seats, in cars on poor springs, proves a severe strain upon all the members of the Regiment, and a large number of men are sick. As a whole the Reg. was very sober, quiet and orderly, and did itself great credit, while coming to the front.

Oct. 12. Sun. Showery. The soil here is a clammy, slimy, sticky mass of mud. Regular morning Inspection. The men have lain on the ground so much that their new clothing is very dirty, and arms rusty. Much fault-finding at our first inspection on Virginia soil, and the whole Regiment is ordered to clean clothing and arms before night, which is done. A well filled mail-bag is started for home, and the day closes with a Dress-parade and religious services. These always go together in the army, just the same as in civil life. Very well; one of the greatest civilizing agencies, or influences, in the world is the putting on of nice, new, clean clothes on Sundays, and then keeping them clean. The Thirteenth is in line, the men's and officers' caps are off, the Chaplain reads from the Bible, then reads a prayer, and then the Band plays the tune of a familiar hymn. The scene is martial, spirited and fine, the service impressive.

No one could fail to observe the noble bearing, the strong marks of sterling character, the native independence, honor and manliness, and the high intelligence of this command; the Regiment gives the appearance of men selected, and above the average of New England citizens.

Oct. 13. Mon. Cool, cloudy. Much labor on camp, and drill. Order of the day: Reveille and Roll-call at 5.30 a. m. Breakfast, 6.30. Surgeons' call, 8.30. Company drill, 9 to 11. Dinner, 12 noon. Company drill, 1 to 3 p. m. Battalion drill, 3 to 5. Dress-parade, 5. Supper, 6. Tattoo and Roll-call, 9. Taps, 9.30; all lights out in Company quarters. This gives the officers and men, practically, a drill of seven hours a day. Besides this the officers have a sword drill of an hour in the forenoon, at 8 or 9 o'clock, and a school for an hour at 7.30 p. m.

To-night the men have soft bread for their supper, for the first time since leaving Concord.

Oct. 14. Tues. Showery. Thousands of troops are moving all about us; coming, camping, marching, drilling, breaking camp, leaving. While on parade this afternoon, we are ordered to stack arms and return to quarters, where the most of the men receive 40 rounds of ammunition.

About 6 p. m. we move out, and take arms again, and are ordered to hold ourselves in readiness to march at a moment's notice. Surplus ammunition arrives at 8.30 p. m., when the First Sergeants call the roll again, and every man is supplied with the full 40 rounds required.

The rebels have driven in our distant pickets, and are reported to be in force within one day's march. We have heard to-day a heavy cannonading, and sharp musketry firing. The report comes in that the rebel General Stuart's cavalry are making serious trouble near Centreville.

The flurry is over before the night comes on. The Thirteenth, however, is kept "under arms in quarters" all night.

Our horses are kept saddled and bridled all night ready for immediate use. Mounted horsemen are hurrying in all directions, at all hours till morning. In case of a move we are to support the 9th Mass. Battery. This is our first night of actual war service, we really expect a fight, and every man sleeps half awake, all the time expecting, and desiring for once, to hear the Long Roll.

Oct. 15. Wed. Very warm. The boys begin to indulge in one or two unripe persimmons apiece, "just to try a new thing, you know," and so reduce their capacity for rations fully fifty per cent. The negroes bring them to camp for sale, and greatly enjoy seeing the green Yankees taken in, shriveled, by the extremely puckering things. They are abominable. Our First Brigade, consisting of the 15th Conn., 13th N. H., 142d N. Y. and 9th Mass. Regts., of General Casey's Division — which is known as the Defenses of Washington — is reviewed by Gen. Casey, the review lasting from 8.30 a. m. until 2 p. m.

Six men of the 13th are in regimental Hospital. Their beds are made of barrel staves laid side by side on poles, with blankets spread over all.

Oct. 16. Thurs. Warm day. We have August days, and November nights, and the chill that comes up from the Potomac with its fog, is like the chill from a tomb, as it is. The guarding of Long Bridge is an exceedingly disagreeable business; cold and muddy, wet and windy, and there is no shelter worth the name, and we much prefer our present position in the outer defenses. Again the Thirteenth is ordered to lie on its arms all night.

Orders arrive at 10 p. m. for us to be ready to march at 7 a. m. on the morrow, the 13th and 142d N. Y. to form a brigade under the temporary command of Col. Stevens. Passes have been granted for two men a day from each company to visit Alexandria; these are now revoked, and the grip of camp discipline tightens anew. The fort at Long Bridge is called Ft. Runyon, next Ft. Albany, next Ft. Craig.

Oct. 17. Fri. Very warm. Thirteenth is off in a hurry about 7 a. m., tents and all, for Upton's Hill. The men are heavily loaded with full knapsacks, haversacks, and their arms. We take a roundabout road, and make the distance, six or seven miles, at a dog trot, arriving at 11.30 a. m. The guide selected the wrong road. On the way we pass Ball's Cross Roads and Munson's Hill. There is a fort on almost every hill hereabout. We are, here, two miles from Falls Church (which is about eight miles from Alexandria on the Leesburg Pike) and fifteen miles from the Bull Run battlefield. A large detail from the Thirteenth go out on picket, our *First Picket Duty*, of 48 hours, beyond the earthworks of the outer defenses of Washington; no shelter. Our line of pickets extends about three miles each way from Falls Church.

The portion of the Thirteenth remaining at Upton's Hill receive a few tents, but the most of them are delayed in coming, and so the men rough it, and bid high for chills and fever. Sleeping on the bare ground, in the open air, at this time of year, is a dangerous thing to do, especially for raw troops. One third of the army are continually used up by this ill-considered way of doing the business of war. The camp guard load their muskets for the first time to-night, at "Camp Corcoran," Upton's Hill — an act denounced by men who afterwards deserted!

We do not like the picket diet, principally boiled salt beef cold, and hard bread soaked in water and then fried with salt pork sliced thin, and coffee, made of surface water, and sweetened with cheap brown sugar.

Oct. 18. Sat. Fine weather. Thirteenth fitting up camp at Upton's Hill. The fresh soldier arranges his tent in a very fresh manner. Two companies, about 125 men, are out on the advance picket line near Falls Church, which is just within our picket lines. There is only one pew now left in it and it has been used as a stable for cavalry horses. The pickets have very poor shelter, mere booths made of boards and pine brush, and not enough, such as it is.

There has been a severe skirmish at Falls Church, and we can see, for the first time, how a real battlefield looks. The kinds of bullets and shells that have cut, battered and smashed these trees, buildings and fences, are just the kinds which our bodies must catch! — however, we can give as well as take. Our pickets here are in a very dense growth of small pine-trees, and at night no man can see two rods.

Oct. 19. Sun. Very warm at noon. The picket is relieved about noon, and returns to Upton's Hill. The Thirteenth is put through Inspection, Parade, Drill and Religious services, all to the same tune, nearly, by the new Band, and after a long, busy day, about 5 p. m. receives orders to return at once to Camp Chase. Takes down its tents, packs up, is joined by the incoming picket, and, about 6 p. m., marches off at the top of its speed. Arrives at or near Camp Chase at 8 p. m., having marched the last five or six miles in an hour and a half. The men are too tired to pitch their tents, our old tents which arrive late, about 10 p. m., and make their camp for the night anywhere and anyhow. The night is very cold, raining in the evening and freezing toward morning. About 100 men off duty, more or less sick. The night is enlivened by a magnificent mule-chorus, sung by the Division teams.

Oct. 20. Mon. Very cold. Many men rose this morning very sick. (The writer, and several others, did not recover from the bad effects of last night's exposure until after the march to, and the battle of, Fredericksburg in December. Their discharge from the service was repeatedly offered them, but as often refused.) The Reg. moves this morning about a mile and stakes ground for a new camp, about half a mile from our first camping ground near Arlington Heights. By night our tents are up and we begin to be settled again, but upon an abominable camping ground. About the only fence we have seen standing in Virginia was a few rods of it near Fall's Church. Houses, groves, orchards, shade trees and fences have been destroyed or leveled for miles on miles around.

"We turned in late last night, and after a few hours' rest I was called out about 4 a. m., with all of Company F, and was hurried down with Lieuts. Hall and Dustin to guard the Virginia end of the Long Bridge. We had no rations, and when breakfast time came along, I went to a Sutler's tent near by to purchase something for myself and the men of the Company to eat, but found that I did not have a cent of money with me; I had lost somewhere that morning my pocket-book containing over $800, belonging in part to myself and the rest to the men of my Company. I could not return to camp without a permit, so I hurried across the bridge to Gen. Casey's Hdqrs. in Washington, stated to him the circumstances and obtained permission to return to camp. I then went to our camp with Lieut. Hall, and we hunted for the lost pocket-book for a long time but without success. While we were talking about the matter, and devising plans to recover the money, it incidentally occurred to Lieut. Hall to see if his own money were safe. Thrusting his hands into his pockets, he drew forth not his own pocket-book, but the very one I had lost. We sat down then and there, counted the money and found it all right. Lieut. Hall was surprised beyond measure. While dressing in the morning, in the hurry and darkness, we had exchanged pantaloons. That exchange caused me several hours of worry, and a tramp of nearly ten miles done at the top of my speed. On the whole the hardest morning's work I ever did in my life before breakfast."   LIEUT. YOUNG.

Oct. 21. Tues. Fair. Yesterday's work all for nothing, excepting practice; and the Thirteenth moves half a mile nearer the Potomac, and pitches its tents again; " A " tents, and six men crowded into each tent. The Upton's Hill expedition was very damaging to the health of the men. The experiment is tried to see how quickly the Reg. can assemble, pack and be ready to march; it is accomplished inside of fifteen minutes. There is rarely a more stirring scene in the army; men and officers are moving in every direction; laughter, jokes, commands, inquiries, are heard everywhere; wagons loaded, rations distributed, knapsacks packed. Every one hurries in perfect order, because every man knows exactly what work he has to do.

Oct. 22. Wed. Fair. Thirteenth drilling, seven hours a day. Many men off duty. Lieut. Penrose, Drill-master, is desirous of enforcing a more strict discipline, and threatens to " recommend all officers for immediate resignation," who do not cease from all familiarity with their enlisted men. This caste system is regarded as necessary, and is compulsory. Reg. drawn up in close order and lectured most emphatically. John J. Whittemore is sick, and Royal B. Prescott is employed as Acting Hospital Steward.

Oct. 23. Thurs. Fair. Every one cautioned to be ready for another move. Officers' school in full figure ; they are compelled to study the Tactics very closely, also the Army Regulations, and to perform all to the letter. Assistant Surgeon John Sullivan joins the Reg. He has been in the service since June 1861, as a private in the 2d N. H., and Medical Cadet, U. S. A.

Oct. 24. Fri. Warm. Thirteenth divided between picket, shoveling and camp duties. Officers' messes being organized. A cook stove and mess-chest costs about $35, and a good appetite costs eighteen hours of hard work per day.

Oct. 25. Sat. Cool. About these days an enterprising Lieutenant, in the Thirteenth, discovers a lot of rebels near a neighboring outhouse, and prepares for their capture or annihilation. After creepings and cautions enough to take a city, wonderful generalship and unheard-of strategy, he, with his men, surrounds, surprises and captures them all — and they prove to be men of the Thirteenth making a night raid on a hencoop! The more it is mentioned, the less that Lieutenant is happy. The 13th ordered to furnish a guard for Fort Runyon and Long Bridge, consisting of two officers and 80 to 100 men in all.

Oct. 26. Sun. Very rainy, cold and disagreeable. The Surgeon's tent is much frequented. During a severe shower of rain to-day a large, new regiment marches into camp with their colors flying, and their Band playing "The Campbells are Coming." They make a fine display. Enlistments are being made, among the volunteers, for the Regular Army, and the Navy. None but "No. 1 men" need apply. Inducements: 30 days furlough every year, $50 bounty, $17 per month in pay. The furlough to immediately follow enlistment, transportation free. We have thus far moved five times, and each succeeding move for the worse.

Oct. 27. Mon. A hard rain storm. Cleared toward noon cold and blustering. Camp very wet and muddy. About 80 men sent on guard to Long Bridge, under Capt. Stoodley. An outrageously cold business. Rest of the Reg. in camp and doing nothing. Long Bridge is about $2\frac{1}{2}$ miles from our camp, is about $1\frac{1}{4}$ miles long, and is the only bridge for the passage of teams across the Potomac into Virginia. Immense wagon trains are continually passing, often covering the whole bridge and its approaches as far as we can see. No person is allowed to cross either way without a pass, and the labor of the picket officer in examining these passes is very hard and trying.

Oct. 28. Tues. Fair, very cold. Detachment returns from Long Bridge at evening. Thirteenth reviewed, with eight other regiments, by Gen. Casey. A storm blows tents over and bursts them open, and the rain pouring in makes the ground very wet and muddy. Half the Reg. are thoroughly drenched.

Oct. 29. Wed. Pleasant day, night chilly and cold. Details go to

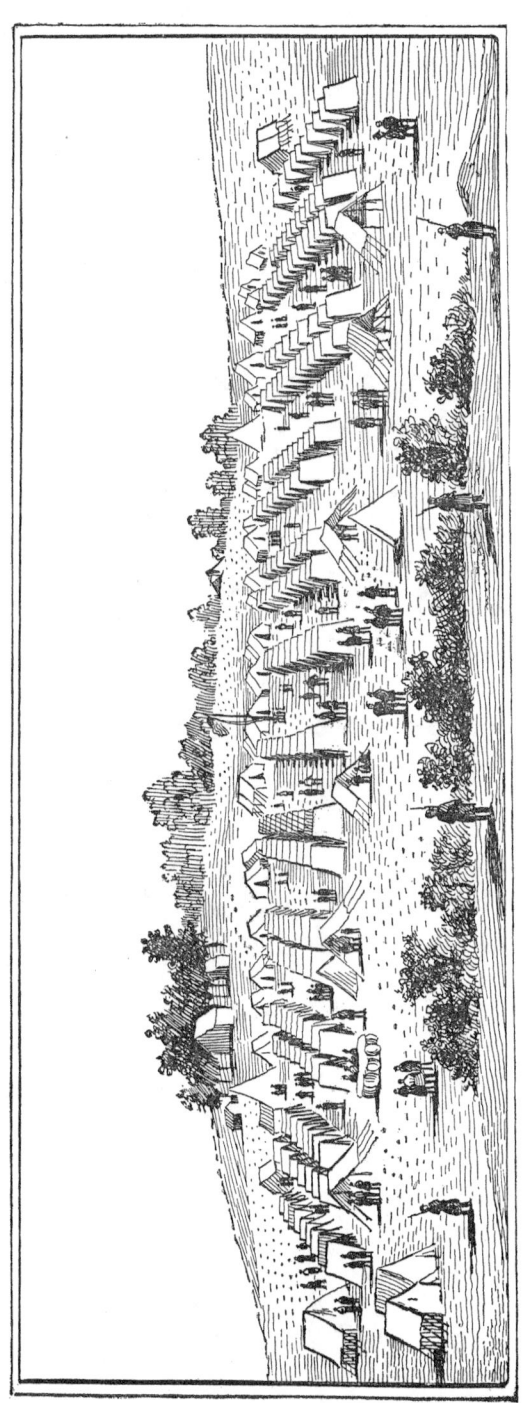

CAMP CHASE, THIRTEENTH REGIMENT NEW HAMPSHIRE VOLUNTEERS.
A. F. STEVENS, Colonel; GEORGE BOWERS, Lieut.-Colonel; J. I. STORER, Major.
From a Photograph.

guard Long Bridge, about 10 men from each company. The guard has headquarters at an old hotel, by some called the " Revere House," just at the Virginia end of the bridge. (What appears to be the same old battered hulk is now standing, May 1885, on the right hand side of the road as you pass into Virginia.)

Oct. 30. Thurs. Pleasant. Monthly Reports now bother the Captains' heads; and to make bad matters worse the wrong kind of rolls are furnished, the work done twice over. A large detail from the Thirteenth are throwing up entrenchments in the rear of Fort Richardson. It is on a high hill, and we can see the country for miles and miles around — a vast camp, a wide region of country laid waste, and hundreds of residences in ruins. The Vermont Brigade marches past camp in grand procession, the soldiers as green as their own native hills. We now begin to feel like Veterans.

Oct. 31. Fri. Pleasant. Thirteenth reviewed, and mustered for pay by Col. Dexter R. Wright of the 15th Conn. Vols., now Acting Brig. General, and commanding our Brigade, consisting of the 15th Conn., 13th N. H. and 142d N. Y. Regts.

During this month the Thirteenth has enjoyed the privilege of unending drill — manual, squad, company, battalion, slow, quick, double quick and run — under Lieut. Penrose of the Regular Army. "He is smarter than a steel trap, and is mounted on a little wiry horse, a double-concentrated combination of git up and git." The 13th had to stand in one position, at " shoulder-arms," for over two hours at one time to-day while on Review. A knapsack-hook set in the gun strap, and allowed to seize the belt, saves much pain in these matters. The forenoon of to-day was occupied by a special drill preparatory to the afternoon's review. The officers have their wit and patience sorely tried now by their first " Monthly Report in the Field."

Reveille is the " Cock-crow " of the army. To one who has risen before the first call, and is in a position to see as well as hear, the scene is most interesting. A single bugle call is heard, when instantly the proper officer, in every regimental camp guard, rouses the Drum-corps; they beat the Reveille, the sound rolling in from every direction, far and near; the First Sergeants are running down the company streets, parting the tent openings, and shouting inside, " Turn out here for Roll-call ! " The men turn out, in every imaginable state of dress, answer to their names in every tone and compass of which the human voice is capable, a perfect Babel, and are assigned their duties for the day, if the First Sergeants can possibly find out beforehand what their duties are to be. Occasionally this is arranged on the previous evening. The whole noisy breeze is past in five minutes, and the work of the day begins. But let us not forget the poor little drummer boy in this noise of Reveille, as he stands at his tent door, or a little away, half awake, half dressed, " mit nottings on sgacely," unkempt, shivering, or half frozen, peddling abroad his unhappy " r-r-rap-tap-tap," cursed by half the Regiment, while the teeth in his unhung jaws can be heard for their chattering nearly half as far as the sound of the drum.

CAMP CASEY, NEAR FAIRFAX SEMINARY.

Nov. 1. Sat. Very fine day. At noon the 13th receives orders to be ready to move in two hours, lively work, but we strike tents, pack, and are ready to move in one hour. We march about five miles to near Fairfax Seminary, arriving at 3 p. m. A detachment of 81 men which has been on duty, under Lieuts. Durell and Forbush, guarding Long Bridge (the Virginia end), and the stores at Ft. Runyon, comes rushing up to camp just in time to join in the march. Reg. much divided; some of Lieut. Forbush's men are left behind to guard the Camp Chase property, others join the Reg. after we reach camp, and 500 men are sent, after arriving near the Seminary, on picket, to a point about four miles distant, in the outer line of defenses. The remainder are settled in camp before dark. We passed the Seminary as we came up and are about half a mile beyond it. This camp is on the south side of a hill, overlooking Alexandria, about one or two miles distant, and a wide valley filled with tents and troops as far as one can see. The Orange Railroad runs along the valley a few rods south of camp, and on it hundreds of cars are continually passing, all in army use. Just south of camp is a brook called Cameron's Run, and the Old Dominion Mill, a weak affair. We have taken the place, duties, and camp ground of Maj. Gen. Daniel E. Sickles's Division, ordered to join the Army of the Potomac; and are on the ground just vacated by the 26th Penn., which with the 1st and 11th Mass. and the 2d N. H. formed Gen. Hooker's old Brigade. The 2d N. H., with colors tattered, faded and shabby, moves away as we come into camp.

A charming story comes to camp. 'T is said that a certain south New Hampshire town possesses a Republican, wealthy very, and closer than the bark to a tree, and a Democrat not very rich but well to do. Between them exists a bitter feud. Inasmuch as the Republican's taxes are far greater than the taxes of any other man, or six men, in the town, this Democrat conceives a brilliant idea to sting this Republican to the inmost quick. The idea is no sooner conceived than executed; and away drives the Democrat with his swiftest team to all the influential men in the town. The result is, that volunteers from that town are surprised by receiving the largest town bounty paid in the State; and the Republican aforesaid, much against his wish, will and exceedingly sensitive pocket, pays the bulk of it all, and the bluff old Democrat is happy.

Nov. 2. Sun. Thirteenth settling in new camp. Usual tiresome inspection, much fatigue work, a Dress-parade, and a little much needed rest. We are still in Col. Wright's First Brigade of Gen. Casey's Division, the Defenses of Washington. Our pickets return to camp about 2 p. m. Hospital Steward J. J. Whittemore is very sick from exposure in sleeping on the ground last night, and Surgeon Twitchell has Royal

B. Prescott of E appointed in his place as Acting Hospital Steward. We hear distant cannon in the direction of Centreville. A raid by the enemy, who succeed in destroying some railroad property, and in causing Aides to gallop about our camp, with orders that all the regiments be held ready to fall in at instant call.

Nov. 3. Mon. Thirteenth receives tents and finishes camp. Expect to spend the winter here, and provide luxuries in the way of stoves, furniture, etc. The men have the huge round "Sibley" tents, and are closely packed in, about 18 men to a tent. The officers have "wall" tents. The writer and Sergt. Van Duzee purchase an "A" tent with floor and bunks; "bought out a leaver." A piece of board nailed to the top of a stake driven into the ground is a table; a small stove furnishes much smoke and some heat; two stools with broken legs are chairs, a potato with a hole in it is a candlestick. Total cost of entire outfit, tent, stove, and all, $3.75. This is a sample of the general job lot. What a come-down from Concord! Rations now: soft bread, salt beef and pork, and occasionally potatoes and rice. Many are sick. Surgeon's call frequently lasts for two hours, and a daily average of nearly a hundred men are prescribed for. The Chaplain's tent is crowded with expectant soldiers when the mail arrives. If the people at home could realize how valuable letters are to the soldiers, and especially to the sick, they would be more generous with their pen and ink and spare time.

Nov. 4. Tues. Cold, very. Thirteenth much driven with drill, picket and labor on the fortifications, has very little rest, and sickness rapidly increases. A part of the Reg. on picket seven miles from Alexandria returns to camp this evening. A large squad of rebel prisoners, nearly 400, are brought in from beyond our lines. We look curiously on these strangers. We have no such men up North. A dirty, sallow, pale-faced, yellow-haired troop, looking over-worked and under-fed.

Nov. 5. Wed. Cold, raw day, with rain at night. Reg. reviewed by Gen. Casey. A Captain, two Lieutenants and ninety men of the Reg. go out on picket about five miles from camp. These picket excursions are usually for 24 hours. The shelter is very poor, or none at all, and the men suffer very much in the rain, snow-squalls and cold. While on picket here the men are placed in a line of squads, three men in a squad. One man of each squad is on guard for two hours, then off four hours, throughout the day and night. A non-commissioned officer has charge of about four squads. A reserve, of fifteen or twenty men, under a Lieutenant, is stationed at a convenient distance to the rear of the main line of pickets. The captain has charge of all. The men of the Thirteenth guard about one mile of the picket line here. Our Brigade of five regiments sends out 450 men for five miles of the line.

Nov. 6. Thurs. Extremely cold. The miserable stoves in the Sibley tents fill them with smoke. Several stoves get overheated and set fire to the tents, wet as they are. The guns and equipments get wet, and the smoke and water together rusts the guns terribly. Such men as are wise roll up guns and equipments in their blankets, and lie down with them alongside.  The men were to-day supplied with straw, to sleep on, the first they have received.

/ Nov. 7. Fri.  Cold, a high wind.  Severe snow storm lasting all day.  About six inches in depth all over the country.  No one of us can remember any Northern snow storm of equal severity coming so early in the season.  It blows into and breaks down tents, and gives no end of trouble.  The Reg. is treated again to-night with an excellent mule chorus, from a "camp" of several hundred of them, near by.  Mules and snow are incompatible.  "For all purposes of discomfort, snow's (hic) snow;" as one philosopher to-day observes.  He drank that expression in, as it were.

Nov. 8. Sat.  Pleasant.  The snow nearly gone by night, and the mud terrible.  There are many houses near our camp, and the natives sell produce at very reasonable prices.  We have an abundance of excellent wood for our miserable, smoky stoves.

Nov. 9. Sun.  Pleasant.  Usual Sunday inspection and parade.  The army is much infested by a lack-lustre set of religious revivalists.  Their zeal is not according to wisdom.  The story goes that one of them pestered a certain New Hampshire Colonel, not of the 13th, out of all patience.  In the midst of a harangue, he informed this Colonel, that he had baptized eight men of a neighboring regiment, recently.  The Colonel at once turned to his Adjutant, and ordered him to "detail nine men to be baptized to-morrow morning;" adding by way of explanation, that he "would n't be outdone by any regiment in the service."  A rough way of expressing a common opinion of the work of some of these harebrained enthusiasts.  Light things are made of light timber.

Nov. 10. Mon.  Pleasant, cool.  Battalion drill under Gen. Casey, the first since we left Camp Chase.  We look upon bare ground at night, and next morning see it covered with hundreds of white tents and thousands of troops.

Nov. 11. Tues.  Very fine day.  Drill, all day.  Fairfax Seminary, now used as a Hospital, contains about 1,700 sick and wounded soldiers, and the deaths among them average eight per day.  The largest and strongest men are the first to break down, while the small and weakly men appear to be benefited by the rough, hard out-door life.

Nov. 12. Wed.  Pleasant.  Drill.  Major Storer, one day along here, has command of the Reg. when on Dress-parade.  Just as he is about to give an order, and has spoken a word or two, he is interrupted by a huge mule near by with a tremendous fit of braying.  The mule's noise times in so queerly as to make a most amusing "annex" to Maj. Storer's remarks, and the Reg. nearly breaks up in laughter.  This, however, is in the early days of discipline, when half of the Reg. act like a lot of country school-boys, as they are.

Nov. 13. Thurs.  Pleasant.  Drill — the most at a double-quick.

Nov. 14. Fri.  Pleasant.  Reg. has the day to fit up camp, and repair clothing.  Rations are short, bad and irregular.

Maj. Gen. Ambrose E. Burnside, under Order of Nov. 14, 1862, assumes command of the Army of the Potomac, relieving Maj. Gen. Geo. B. McClellan. The army is near Warrenton, Va. Gen. Burnside organizes it in three Grand Divisions; the Right under Maj. Gen. E. V. Sumner; the Left under Maj. Gen. W. B. Franklin; the Centre under Maj. Gen. Joseph Hooker. The Union Army numbers about 120,000 men, and soon is in motion toward Fredericksburg.

Nov. 15. Sat. Fair, cold. The whole Reg. goes on picket; that is, all who are able to go. Many of our men are sick. The Band escorts the Reg. out about 2½ miles. The first picket duty of the whole Regiment. We are to do picket duty by regiments, each out for two days. President Lincoln issues an order — read in camp: "Enjoining the orderly observance of the Christian Sunday by the officers and men in the military and naval service of the United States." Hope so!

Nov. 16. Sun. Fair. Reg. all on picket, five miles from camp. The first death in our Reg. occurred last night, Henry S. Sleeper of H, disease, typhoid fever. Was getting well, but had a relapse from eating some bread and cheese. The air here is not so invigorating as in the North, and a man more readily breaks down. Sleeper is buried to-day near Alexandria. Twenty-eight men sick in regimental Hospital.

Charles A. Young, a boy about sixteen years old, came with the Reg. as far as Worcester with his brother, Lieut. W. H. H. Young. There the idea of a boyish venture seized him, and he came along with the Reg. to its Virginia camp. Riding a tractable mule he visited camps, forts, lines and places to his heart's content, and obtained an inside view of the soldiers' life; shared their rations, their marches, and their tents — and especially their shiverings on frosty nights — until the venture lost its charm. He decided to return home. Traveling northward in these days is not so easy as one might imagine. To cross that Long Bridge over the Potomac, down yonder, requires a pass. The affair is explained, and laughed over more or less, and a pass or furlough in full and regular form is made out, and signed by all the officers in rank up to Col. Wright, and armed with this the young gentleman leaves camp for home. Somehow his name, in later days, became identified with the Reg., and Adjt. Gen. Head furnished him with a Discharge from the service, the same as (other) soldiers receive. He has received numerous letters from military sources, and even official communications from the U. S. Pension office. This history could not possibly be complete without a little sketch of "Y" Company, averaging in point of years the youngest company in the military service of the United States.

Nov. 17. Mon. Very cold. The Thirteenth, about 700 men, returns from picket to camp about 3 p. m. Have had a hard, cold piece of work for 48 hours, on a line three and a half miles long, consisting of a line of picket squads at the front, three men together; half a mile in their rear several stations of reserves; still another half a mile farther back the Grand Guard, and many patrols employed between. The picket duty a practical drill, with continual changes. The total strength of the Reg. now fit for duty, is about 700 men, about 200 men are sick in tents. Our Band meets the Reg. on the road to camp and escorts us in. The Band plays well. Another burial, of a member of the 13th, to-day.

Gen. Sumner with his Right Grand Division approaches Fredericksburg. He proposes to cross the river, and to occupy the city and the heights back of it, with his advance, consisting of the 2d Corps under Gen. Couch, and the 9th Corps, under Gen. Wilcox.

Nov. 18. Tues. A heavy rain-storm to-night. Reg. in camp. Many of the men are very sick. The average number of men reported sick, by the Surgeon, every day for a month past, has been nearly twenty men in each company. It is the soldier's privilege to growl and grumble, and now, in this camp and service, there is a plenty of reason for it.

Nov. 19. Wed. Rainy, cold. Reg. in camp. Rations have greatly improved of late. We now have beef, fresh and salt, salt pork, potatoes, beans, rice, hard bread, fresh flour and brown bread, coffee, tea, sugar, molasses and pickles. In the absence of butter, and in the presence of jaundice, the last two items are in great demand and favor. Again the Captains in the Thirteenth are furnished with the wrong rolls in blank, and after expending many hours of labor upon them, receive correct blanks, and, with the proverbial cheerfulness of patriotic soldiers, do the work all over again. The work consists of writing the names of a hundred men, and appending numerous remarks to each name.

Nov. 20. Thurs. Heavy rain-storm. Reg. with the Brigade started out for a Review, but it is postponed on account of the storm. Chess, checkers and cards while away many a dreary, slow hour in a rainy camp. Nearly 300 men to-day on the sick list. The three great " cure-alls " in the army are quinine, mercury and whiskey. Our regimental Hospital is in an old house formerly occupied by overseers or slave drivers. This has been a cold, wet week, and sickness increases so rapidly that the Medical Inspector demands the exercise of greater care of the men, and a shortening of the hours of drill and labor. Dress coats received — made of a sort of blue broadcloth.

Nov. 21. Fri. Clearing. Reg. at work on its camp. Cooking utensils are inspected, and every man is provided with a new tin plate, tin cup, knife, fork and spoon ; and every Company with its full number of kettles and cooking utensils. As a result things look more nicely now when the men file around to the cook's tent for their boil, roast, hash, soup, coffee and bread. After drawing their rations the men go, sit down, and devour them like gentlemen, and hogs. One soldier of the 13th writes home : " When we get home again we will not any more sit at table to eat, but will seize our grub in our fists, and eat it on the wood pile, or in the back yard — like soldiers."

Gen. Burnside's army is concentrating along Stafford Heights opposite Fredericksburg. Generals Hooker and Sumner desire to ford the Rappahannock, the bridges having been destroyed and the pontons delayed in coming. Gen. Burnside regards the attempt too hazardous and refuses to give his consent. Gen. Lee about Nov. 18th reënforced his small garrison in and about the city and is now rapidly occupying the heights beyond. He believes that Gen. Burnside can, and will, cross the river, and proposes to fight him after he has crossed. Gen. Sumner to-day demands the surrender of the city — Gen. Patrick, Provost Marshal General of the Army of the Potomac, crossing the river under a flag of truce with the demand — which is refused.

Nov. 22. Sat. Fair. Reg. expends a great deal of (wasted) labor in grading and turnpiking its Company streets. The "bulge-barrel," the old stubs of brooms, the shovels and an old plantation hoe or two carried by the police gang in procession all about camp, is one of the pictures of camp life not to be forgotten. The police gang is composed of men sentenced to clean the camp as a punishment for small misdemeanors. They almost always behave with the utmost stupidity, mere automatons, never looking up or exhibiting a spark of intelligence while at work. The worst labor in the affair is done by the Corporal, and his guard, who must keep the men at work, whether the camp needs cleaning or not. The "bulge-barrel" has two sticks nailed to the sides, both sticks with long ends extending so that it may be carried upright by two men.

Nov. 23. Sun. Exceeding cold and raw, wind northwest. Reg. goes on picket for 48 hours, beyond the earthwork defenses, and about seven miles from camp, toward the southwest, their position said to be near Falls Church again. Whole Reg. excepting the sick leaves camp at 8 a. m. with two days' cooked rations. The First Sergts. now have to look after the rations, baggage, cooking utensils, etc. This is too much care. Some of the Companies have a non-commissioned officer and four or five men, whose especial business it is to see to these matters, detailed by the First Sergt. and reporting to him. Royal B. Prescott appointed Hospital Steward; and receives $30 per month for doing work enough for two men. He is overworked, and would break down if he had not an exceedingly strong physique; his endurance is wonderful.

Nov. 24. Mon. Very cold. " Water freezes solid in more than a hundred canteens," as the men carry them at their side while on picket. A body of Union horsemen, coming in from a scout, create a pretty little scare in the night. One timid youth declares that he can see "three species of cavalry," and the phrase becomes a by-word. Virginia weather, and mud, is responsible for nine tenths of the profanity in the army. One man in the Thirteenth has suddenly given up the use of profane language; declaring that "no hard words can possibly do the weather and mud here any degree of justice, and he is tired of trying."

Nov. 25. Tues. Cold, raw, rainy. The Band again meets the Reg. a short distance out, and escorts it to camp. Reg. returns from picket about noon, and is soon set at work upon the camp; this is too much labor and exposure after a long march, and the men very tired and wet — it is abominable cruelty and foolishness. Many men are made sick by this needless job. There is much hard talk, and mutiny is threatened.

Nov. 26. Wed. Cold. Reg. drilling all day. Capt. Stoodley is taken down with jaundice, aggravated by the extreme fatigue, exposure and labor of the last three days, including yesterday's useless work on the camp. Many more men than usual require medical treatment this morning. Raised flour bread, from the bakery at Alexandria, sometimes comes hot to our camp, and welcome.

Nov. 27. Thurs. Thanksgiving Day. Reg. at work until 10 a. m., also have a Dress-parade about sundown ; all the rest of the day is observed as a holiday. Many boxes, filled with good things, are received from home, and the officers and men enjoy themselves generally. Some of the men have no home, nor friends, to receive boxes from, and those more fortunate share with them liberally. Capt. Julian entertains, royally, Capt. Rollins, and friends, of the 2d N. H. V., now on their way to Washington from the front.

Nov. 28. Fri. Warm. Reg. drilling, and at work on camp. The stragglers' camp is about one mile distant, of men unfit for duty, but not sick enough for hospital treatment: " Like a dress too clean to wash, but too dirty to wear," as one soldier of the 13th writes. Another writes : " Many men are sick with fowlness of the stomach."

Nov. 29. Sat. Reg. drilling. The most intelligent men give the least trouble. As one soldier puts it, Sergt. Batchellor of D, " The grumblers in the army are chiefly those who never see the inside of a book or of a paper."

Down at Fredericksburg Gen. Lee, his army 80,000 strong, is entrenching on "Marye's Heights," and along the Rappahannock, undisturbed ; and Gen. Burnside prepares unwillingly to cross the river. A battle is to be fought because of political necessity, and after various delays have stolen away the promise of success. " Public feeling demands a movement ; " and the public that entertains that feeling has not enlisted.

Nov. 30. Sun. Pleasant. Orders are received to be ready to march to-morrow at noon ; in heavy marching order, with shelter tents, and two days' cooked rations in haversacks, and five in teams. All is now bustle and hurry. There are tents after tents as far as the eye can see in any direction ; the whole camp, thousands of men, are like ourselves, preparing to move. Many of our men are still very sick. Capt. Stoodley, and several other members of the Regiment are dangerously ill. They are to be sent to Washington. There is a sudden weeding out, and several men are discharged the service. The first, and new, shelter tents issued to the Reg. There is no Sunday in the army. Col. Dexter R. Wright's 1st Brigade of Casey's Division, for the march to-morrow, consists of the 15th Conn., 13th N. H., 12th R. I., 25th and 27th N. J. Regts. We march under sealed orders, and take 100 rounds of ball cartridge per man. The men have been expecting to remain here during the winter, have taken much pains to fit up their quarters, and have been at no little expense besides, and do not at all relish a move ; " all their fixings and expense to be left here free gratis for nothing," as they put it, for the benefit of some one else to them unknown. On the other hand they are very desirous to take a strong hand in putting an end to the war, and their patriotism and devotion to the cause of the Union outweigh all other considerations. The camp resounds to-night with hymns and patriotic songs. Notwithstanding the fact that the Thirteenth are raw troops, and have been put into rough military service at once as if they were hardened veterans, and allowed little rest for many weeks, still in the main they have borne and endured their labors and exposures cheerfully and admirably ; relieving it all by the sport, play and merrymaking common to a camp of young men and boys.

Some person of genius invented a steel vest warranted proof against minie bullets at short range. Hundreds of officers and soldiers have purchased them and worn them until reaching the front, and a few days longer ; but generally with the result indicated by the following remark made in a letter by a member of the Thirteenth : "The soldiers, both of our own regiment and of others, throw away their steel vests, and one can pick up any quantity of them about the camp — too heavy to carry. The men use them for frying-pans with cleft sticks for handles."

## MARCH TO FREDERICKSBURG.

**Dec. 1. Mon.** A warmish day of drizzling rain. The Thirteenth breaks camp at 12 noon, gets fairly in line about 2 p. m., and with the First Brigade marches to Washington over the Long Bridge, and on beyond the Capitol, across the Eastern Branch of the Potomac into Maryland, and bivouacs about 7 p. m. in a field near the village of Uniontown, six miles below Washington, after a march of about fifteen miles from Fairfax Seminary. Many who attempt to march are so sick that they have to give up their arms and baggage to the teams, and follow as best they may, and others weaker still halt along the way.

The writer and three or four other men give up their arms and knapsacks on Long Bridge. On reaching Capitol Hill in Washington about 6 p. m. they are obliged to stop, from sheer exhaustion. They sit down and lean against the trees and fences, feeling forlorn enough, and are taken up by the ambulance about 9 p. m. All of us have been sick for a number of weeks, and as it happened all had been offered their discharge from the service that very morning, and had refused to accept it ; and the ambulance is turned into a debating hall, the question being whether to go ahead or to give up. But the " Ayes " have it, and we decide to go ahead. The writer and one other man were of the Thirteenth, the rest were from other regiments; and one was a pale, thin, but plucky little stripling apparently not eighteen years of age. On reaching the camp the writer is invited to turn in, under a large tent, with the non-commissioned staff of the 13th — the tent crowded full. During the night his bedfellows, being too warm, throw off their blankets upon him, and when he wakes in the morning he is in a proper condition to be run through a wringing machine. But the sweating does more effective service against the chills than a peck of quinine.

The Regiment marches under many disadvantages. Teams are not to be had in sufficient numbers, many stores purchased with the hospital fund, and much needed, have to be left behind, and the men have only what they can carry with them upon their persons. The sick in Hospital and a number of half sick men belonging to the Thirteenth, and to the rest of the First Brigade, 283 in number, are left behind at Camp Casey in charge of Dr. Twitchell and Quarter-master Cheney, the latter having charge of the property of the Brigade which is left behind.

Dec. 2. Tues. Very fine day. Reg. continues its march at 8 a. m., down into Maryland. At Surgeon's call a number of sick men are sent back to Washington. The writer, and others of the sick, who can go ahead, are allowed to march as they please, and where they please; only required, if possible, to keep with the brigade. Our Brigade bivouacs at 6 p. m. on the south side of a large hill, four thousand men on a few acres, and very much crowded together. Distance to-day fifteen miles. We are one mile from Piscataway. The roads are magnificent, the country rich, with pigs, chickens, and other small 'fruits' in plenty.

Dec. 3. Wed. Pleasant, cool. Reg. marches at 10 a. m. and passes Piscataway. We pass Ft. Washington (or Foote) and the men strain their eyes to catch a glimpse of Mount Vernon, said to be in view. The men are heavily loaded with guns, knapsacks, blankets, rations, cooking utensils, shelter tents, and a multitude of things which more experienced soldiers never carry — a heavy marching order indeed. Off they go, however, this morning, half the Thirteenth and as many more men from the 12th Rhode Island, in a wild chase after a large lot of pigs, lambs, hens, turkeys, etc., and they do not come empty away. We have a rush to-day with the 12th R. I. and 89th N. Y. Regts. They were in rear of the 13th yesterday, and pressed us hard, calling us the "New Hampshire babies," and other petty names. To-day we get in their rear, and march straight through the most of them, pushing them as hard as we can, and taking advantage of all their short halts to rush on past them, and leave them straggling all along the roadside. Distance to-day called twenty miles. We encamp to-night about 5 p. m. in an oak grove, six miles northerly of Port Tobacco. Several men have an excellent dinner at a farmhouse for six cents each. The host remarking, when they paid their scot: "'Bout ther cost on 't, er'ekn."

Dec. 4. Thurs. Very fine day. Reg. marches about 9.30 a. m. Our camp last night was a pell-mell huddle, as usual. Plenty of wood, and rail fences feed a thousand fires. An army encamped at night is a fine spectacle. The 13th were close on the roadside, and until very late at night stragglers kept coming in; and when any one inquired for the camp of the 12th R. I. or of the 89th N. Y. they were invariably directed wrong — a touch of soldier's fun. Many of the men this morning practice with their rifles on the numerous gray squirrels in the grove. A man of Co. E brings down two from the top of one of the tallest trees. To-day we march about twelve miles, and encamp at 5 p. m. at a place called Cedar Hill on Robert Ferguson's farm; but on abominable ground, low, wet and muddy, six miles west of Port Tobacco, which tumble-down place we passed about noon. The citizens are not all friendly, if any are. The writer and Lieut. Carter went a little out of the way, to-day, at Port Tobacco, to see the town, and interview a few of the natives whom we saw lounging about. They were so uncomfortable and surly, however, we left them to their meditations.

About midforenoon, the writer, Lieut. Carter, and several men struck across a field to avoid marching around a bend in the road, and as we came out near a house by the roadside, and ahead of the Brigade — a house that we had no notion of approaching, excepting as the path we followed led close by it — two bullets whistled past our heads, and struck the house with a loud noise. Turning quickly we saw, on a hill, some five or six hundred yards distant, three men with guns, and with them two or three women. The house was closed, and the foolish inmates had retreated to the field. We passed on without receiving any more of their cowardly compliments, while a squad of cavalry was seen taking them in hand.

Dec. 5. Fri. Morning cold and cloudy. Reg. marches at 8 a. m. Shelter tents have been scarcely unrolled during the very pleasant weather we have had since we left Camp Casey. The boys have indulged in any amount of fun; and many a camp song, and especially My Maryland, afterwards had this refrain :

> " O how the pigs and chickens suffered ;
> When we marched — down — thar ! "

Tobacco too, tons of it, hanging in the barns to dry, is made use of liberally, "for fear it may spoil." Little or no wanton mischief has been done. The soldiers care for little besides something nice and fresh to eat, and they obtain at farmhouses a great many things by purchase. But there is one black sheep, at least, in every flock. To-day, however, ends all the enjoyment to be had in our march through Maryland. Half the route has been through forests of pine and oak; and "Maryland, my Maryland," has been sung a thousand times, making the woods ring, and ring again. Five or ten thousand soldiers singing together yield a tremendous volume of sound. The whole body on this march numbers about fifteen thousand men. At 11 a. m. a severe storm of rain sets in, and under the tramp of the soldiers' feet, the clayey roads soon become a succession of hillocks and quagmires. A number of men are badly ruptured by slipping on the wet ground. At 2 p. m. the Reg. is halted, in a grove, about two miles from Liverpool Point, "Blue Bank," and preparations are made for the night. Soon after the Reg. is halted, the rain turns to snow. The shelter tents afford but little protection against the driving storm. All the neighboring barns, stables, houses, etc., are turned into temporary barracks.

Albion J. Jenness, Company E, 13th, writes home, grimly, of to-day :

"We went into the woods to camp, on the afternoon of Dec. 5th, and built large fires; beside which we soon got dry — as it began to snow instead of rain." Another writes: "The rain commenced in the morning of Friday, rained until 2 p. m., then turned to snow, and near morning of Saturday cleared very cold."

The writer, and about a dozen other half-sick men, not daring to sleep in tents, after the Reg. encamps push on through the snow a mile or two, and hire lodgings at the house of Mr. —— Childs, near the bank of the Potomac, and enjoy an excellent supper, night's rest, and breakfast in the huge kitchen, where a great, roaring fire is kept burning all night on the ample hearth. There had been trouble here during the day, Dec. 5th, between Mr. Childs's family and some soldiers of a New Jersey Regiment — they of the white leggings, they said — and we mount guard over the family and premises all night. The most the guard has to do, however, is to keep the fire burning, for which purpose one man of the party is awake, a fire guard, gun in hand, and with a bayonet for poker. The night is very cold. The trouble of the day came of a dispute between the "bummers" from the N. J. Regt. and Miss Childs. As near as we could learn, they attempted to burglarize the house, or something of the sort, when Miss Childs, a spare, tall, lithe, spirited lady of perhaps eighteen summers, seized a shot gun and fired upon them. They caught her and took away the gun. There was a fierce struggle, in which nearly all her clothing was torn off, leaving scarcely anything upon her but her dress waist, stockings and slippers. She broke away, and in this light running costume, ran through the snow, rain and freezing air half a mile to a neighbor's house; some of the bummers following and trying to catch her, but they could as easily have run down a deer. She escaped with no further harm than a few slight scratches and bruises. This occurred but a few hours before we reached the house. The bummers, smarting with the well deserved dose of small shot from the young lady's gun, had threatened to return, and Mr. Childs, when we arrived, was preparing to set out for Hdqrs. to procure a guard. We could serve as well, having ten guns, and ammunition for them, and he accepted our offer to protect the house. On the morning of Dec. 6th, we are let off scot free, with the blessing of Mr. and Miss Childs. She is remarkably pretty, and beauty lends a special grace to any young lady's blessing. The cook was set at work early, and each man of our party, on leaving the house to rejoin the Reg., now waiting down on the river bank to cross, is presented by Miss Childs with a fine large "hoe cake," cooked in Virginia's best style, with: "Here, please take these, and may God bless you." The family were not Secessionists.

At one house where we applied for lodgings, we saw a few young slaves, two of them girls twelve or fifteen years old, sweeping snow off the piazza and steps. They had on scarcely clothing enough to cover their nakedness, and were barefooted. We remonstrated with the man of the house in reference to such treatment. He said: "It didn't hurt 'um any, they had n't got their winter clo'se yit, he wur n't treaten 'um hard; and besides, he loved them as well as he did his own children." They were light mulattoes — and we told him we believed all he said, and passed on.

"Hosp. Steward Prescott, Charles W. Green of B, Henry Howard of E, Manson S. Brown of C, and Robert Rand of K, also went to a farmhouse about dark and procured lodgings. The farmer had six very fat hogs, in a pen a little distance from the house, besides other stealable property near by, and wanted a guard. The party were received by the farmer, who dragged in feather beds and spread them upon the floor of his best room, and built a large fire, for his lodgers. They wanted him to drive his hogs up nearer to the house, but he said they were too fat to drive, and they were left in the pen where they were. The lodgers were to stand guard for two hours each, during the night, upon the piazza of the house, having the pen in view. All went well until Green came on at the third watch. He stood for a while, when utterly overcome by weariness he laid aside his gun, came in, threw himself upon the feather bed, and soon was sound asleep. Very early in the morning the whole party were roused by a furious storm of profanity in an adjoining room. It was from the farmer. While the guard slept the wearers of the white leggings had rapped every hog on the head, and carried them all off; not a squeal or a bristle left." PRESCOTT.

Dec. 6. Sat. Very cold. Six inches of snow on a level. Army shoes are poor things excepting upon dry ground. The snow partly disappears in a plenty of mud made by yesterday's rain. The ground being but little frozen, the slushy mixture is knee deep, and scolded about enough, as it fills up, or pulls off, the men's shoes. The Reg. marches at 10 a. m., plunging through the snow and mud, and reaches the Potomac, at Liverpool Point, at 11.30 a. m., after a march of about two miles. Here we have to stand in the slush, exposed to a strong down-river wind, the cold increasing all the while, until near sunset, nearly seven hours, waiting for transportation. Only one regiment can cross at a time, and we are the fourth one in our Brigade to go on board. We go on board the steamer about 6 p. m. Here on the boat we are packed and crammed for over two hours; some are almost roasted, and others, exposed to the sharp north wind, are nearly frozen, while crossing the river, a distance of about five miles. The wind grows very severe, and the temperature falls below zero. We debark at Aquia Creek at 8.30 p. m., stand about on the wharf a while, with no protection from either wind or cold, then march about two miles inland, and bivouac at 10 p. m. just below the railroad on a rough hillside falling to a ravine, among some fallen timber, and in six inches of snow. A part of the Reg. crowd into some old rebel barracks with the roofs off. The Reg. is not fairly settled before midnight. It is a clear, starry, moonlit night, and exceeding cold. The field and staff officers of the Reg. have neither tents nor blankets, messchest nor eatables; all these having been left across the Potomac to follow in the next steamer, which is late, and cannot land on account of the ice. Some of the field and line officers " bunk down " with the men, who have shelter tents, while others tramp, thrash their hands, whistle and scold around the fires all night long. This is the toughest bivouac the Thirteenth ever experiences in all its history.

Just as the 13th approaches the wharf to cross the river, a black boy, about 20 years old, appears and wants to cross to Virginia, and so escape from slavery. He is provided with a suit of Uncle Sam's army uniform, and a gun, by the men of Co. E, dons these honors in a moment, enters the ranks, and passes to freedom unchallenged. He is at once employed as a servant by Capt. Julian ; and a more honest, faithful, true and desirable servant, no man ever had, than this same Charley Bush.

He remained with the Regiment, in Captain Julian's employ for about a year, and then enlisted as a Sergeant of (colored) cavalry. On many occasions he held their watches and large sums of their money, when the officers of the Reg. went on picket or reconnaissance. He learned to read and write very soon after joining his fortunes with the Thirteenth, with the members of which he was a universal favorite.

A squad of four men — Hosp. Steward R. B. Prescott, Privates Chas. W. Green of B, Henry C. Howard of E, and Robert Rand of K — are left behind on the Maryland shore, to guard the regimental baggage, and suffer extremely from the cold. There are but three matches in the possession of the party. Two of these are lighted only to be blown out by the wind ; if the third fails the party will freeze. By using the utmost care they succeed in kindling a small fire, which they keep burning, as there is no wood on the bare plain, only by means of leaves and twigs found by scraping away the snow. Over this wretched little fire they huddle together all night, in the vain endeavor to keep warm. 'T is next to impossible to sleep, even if it be not suicide to allow sleeping at all. And so they brave the night out ; while the water in the canteens at their sides freezes to solid ice. The intense cold causes them to crowd so close to the fire that the clothing and blankets of all are burned and Prescott's boots are ruined.

Dec. 7. Sun. Very cold, clear. Fires roast one side of us while the other side freezes. We present a sorry spectacle this morning. Blankets that we slept on last night are frozen fast to the snow, and many of them are torn while being detached from it. We remain here all day, fix up tents, build fires, munch our half frozen food, and suffer generally. Many of the men are frost-bitten, many are utterly used up. The Potomac is frozen over so far out, that steamers cannot land until the ice is broken. To test its strength, an old horse is driven out, and walks a long distance on the ice before he goes down. An experiment very interesting to the horse ! The snow scarcely melts any. Some of the Reg. are encamped among fallen timber, some in the woods, and some in log huts used by the Confederates last winter. One man of the 13th writes home : " Mail came this morning. Twenty (20) of us slept last night in an old rebel barrack with the roof taken off, a box about twenty feet square. We had a fire in the middle of the room, and also one at each end. They say we have burned up twenty-five miles of rail fence since we left Washington."

Quarter-master Cheney was left at Camp Casey, in charge of 283 men, from all the regiments in our Brigade, who were unable to march because of illness. Surgeon Twitchell was also left at Camp Casey in care of the sick in Hospital. Lieut. W. H. H. Young was left there sick; but on Dec. 5th he was put in command of these 283 men. All were placed on board a steam-tug, and a scow in tow, at Alexandria, and they join the Reg. to-day at Aquia Creek. The care of this large number of half sick men, when sick himself, so prostrated Lieut. Young that he was unfit for duty for several weeks.

The Confederates evacuated Aquia Creek about three weeks ago, destroying everything which they could not take with them.

Lieut. Col. Bowers, in the absence of his mess-chest, revives his experiences in the Mexican war — though he cannot bring those torrid days into this polar atmosphere — by planting himself in front of a fire, and, like a warrior of old, roasting a piece of meat on the point of his sword.

Dec. 8. Mon. Very cold a. m., noon warmer. Huge fires are roaring on every hand, and their smoke fills the land. We thaw out sufficiently to eat a poor breakfast. Civilians can have no idea how inexpressibly *good* to the soldier hot coffee is, on such a morning. Coffee made very strong, sweetened a little with pale brown ' army ' sugar, well stirred in with an icicle, which settles it, is a drink fit for the gods and top royalty. The Reg. receives calls from members of the 6th, 9th, 11th, and 12th N. H. encamped near by. To-night we have another cold bivouac, though less severe than on the 6th and 7th, and the men have learned to make better use of their shelter tents. The writer and two other men have enjoyed a château, made on a sharp hillside by throwing a shelter tent and a few armfuls of pine brush over a fallen pine tree resting securely on a stump, raising it three or four feet from the ground. This tree serves for eight or ten men, who are tucked under it from one end to the other. All sorts of curious and ingenious " coops " are found on every hand ; anything is welcome that protects us from the arctic weather.

The field and staff officers' baggage, tents, blankets, mess-chest, eatables, etc., have waited transportation across the river for nearly two days. Up to this time these officers have had only such blankets and other cover as they could borrow, and have spent two nights in such poor, improvised coops as they could make or get made for them.

All these severities, however, have scenes of relief. Among these are overcoated men in war traps and costumes crouched down and watching the hundreds of little pint and quart tin pots of coffee boiling around the camp fires ; each pot with a green stick laid across it, to prevent its boiling over, the steam curling white and gracefully up alongside the darker smoke of the fires, and the delicious coffee aroma speeding abroad on every side over camp and snow.

Then, too there is Picture No. 20, in this Aquia Creek gallery : A number of cold, hungry and thirsty officers of the 13th gather around a mess-chest, arrived not long since from across the river — open, burglarized, empty. Attitudes, gestures, remarks, plans for detecting the fellows.' Picture No. 21. 'A cosy nook deep under the river bank among dense trees, half a mile from camp. A fire. Three or four private soldiers taking a very private lunch, and something stimulating. Attitudes, gestures, remarks (t' other kind), plans to avoid detection.'

(After nearly twenty-five years, these two pictures are described to the writer by a man who helped enjoy the lunch under the river bank.)

Dec. 9. Tues. Warmer. Snow disappearing. Reg. marches from Aquia Creek, with a large body of troops, at 2 p. m., and after a tramp of six miles or so, straight away for Falmouth, Stafford Heights, across fields and through brush, a rough march, we halt for bivouac about 7 p. m. on fair ground, in a pine grove near Brooks Station, and really pass a comfortable night ; the first comfortable sleep we have had since the night of Dec. 3d, in those Maryland oaks. Our march here from Camp Casey, near Fairfax Seminary, has occupied seven days, marching time, and is estimated at 70 miles, with the few miles from here to Fredericksburg to be marched to-morrow. Col. Wright's provisional Brigade is broken up, and its regiments assigned to other Brigades.

Dec. 10. Wed. Pleasant, warm, hazy. Reg. starts about 10 a. m., and after a march of nearly six miles halts, a little past noon, near and northeast of the Phillips House, the Hdqrs. of Gen. Sumner, and bivouacs among thousands upon thousands of troops quite closely massed. There are a hundred thousand men within a short distance of us to-night. We now become a part of the Army of the Potomac.

The 13th is assigned to the 1st Brigade, 3d Division, 9th Army Corps, in Gen. Sumner's "Right Grand Division" of the Army of the Potomac, organized as follows :

Army of the Potomac, comd. by Maj. Gen. Ambrose E. Burnside.
Right Grand Division, comd. by Maj. Gen. E. V. Sumner.
Ninth Army Corps, comd. by Maj. Gen. O. B. Wilcox.
Third Division, comd. by Brig. Gen. Geo. W. Getty.

First Brigade, comd. by Col. Rush C. Hawkins (9th N. Y.).
    10th N. H.,    Col. M. T. Donohoe.
    13th N. H.,    Col. Aaron F. Stevens.
    25th N. J.,     Col. Andrew Derrom.
    9th N. Y., (Hawkins' Zouaves), Lt. Col. Edgar A. Kimball.
    89th N. Y.,    Col. H. S. Fairchild.
    103d N. Y.,    Col. Benj. Ringold.

Second Brigade, comd. by Col. Edward Harland.
    8th Conn.,     Maj. John E. Ward.

11th Conn.,   Col. Griffin A. Stedman.
15th Conn.,   Lt. Col. Samuel Tolles.
16th Conn.,   Capt. Chas. L. Upham.
21st Conn.,   Col. Arthur H. Dutton.
4th R. I.,    Lt. Col. Jos. R. Curtis.

The 1st Brigade, Hawkins', was organized of four Regiments at Pleasant Valley, Md., early in October, and arrived here Nov. 19th. We go in, with the 25th N. J., as new members of the Brigade family.

Thus organized we are a large Brigade, and great expectations are indulged in because of the special reputation of Col. Hawkins, and of his famous Zouaves, now commanded by gallant Lt. Col. Kimball.

About 9 p. m. the Reg. is ordered to have three days' rations in haversacks, and to take 60 rounds of ammunition. Some companies have 80 rounds. We are warriors now in full feathers and trappings : ten pounds of gun, eighty rounds per man of ball cartridge, one pound of powder, five pounds of lead, heavy equipments ; knapsack, haversack, three-pint canteen, all full ; three days' rations ; rubber blanket, woolen blanket, shelter tent, full winter clothing ; tin cup, tin plate, knife, fork, spoon, spider, *et cetera* too numerous to mention, and too many to carry, and a pound of mud on each shoe. We are a baggage train, freight train, ammunition train, commissary train, gravel train, and a train-band, all in one. Thus handicapped, we are soon to try conclusions with Massa Lee, on his own chosen ground, the high ridges of which, scarcely two miles distant from us, as the crow flies, are plainly visible from this point in the daytime, and also the numerous rebel flags floating over the distant hill-tops.

The day is spent in preparation ; orders are received to be ready to move early to-morrow morning. Prayers are said on the principle of "Trust in God, but keep your powder dry ; " and late at night we bivouac, sleep on the ground, in a long shoal ravine, arms at hand, amid multitude of little smouldering coffee-fires, and in an atmosphere half fog, half smoke, another and larger part, big with terrors undefined — the eve before a battle. A part of the force near us to the northward are in dense woods, but there are only a few scattered trees near the Thirteenth.

## II.

### December 11, 1862, to February 8, 1863.

#### BATTLE OF FREDERICKSBURG.

**Dec. 11. Thurs.** Cool, misty, foggy, damp; sunny and warmish at noon; cold, chilling at morning and night. The day opens with the distant but sharp blows of two Confederate cannon, signal guns located apparently away to our front and left, at five o'clock (5 a. m.), showing that the enemy is on the alert. These guns are fired by the Washington Artillery on Marye's Heights. It is at very early daylight; our whole camp, however, is already astir and a few little fires are burning, and we can never forget the peculiar expression that comes over the faces of both officers and men at the startling, warning, defiant sounds of those two rebel guns. They might be compared aptly with the first short, sharp barks of a disturbed watch-dog. The expression is that of surprise. They are soon known to us all to be rebel guns, and the men near us commence joking about that kind of a rising bell. Some think they are the signal of a commencing battle, others do not understand them at all; no firing follows immediately, and they soon pass out of mind.

The whole scene and surroundings on all hands wear an air very romantic and theatrical, shading down the awful grimness of war, and making its affairs an interesting study for the impressionable and active. War is an immense school, in more senses than one, to the man who lives in it and keeps his faculties alive also.

The Thirteenth, with our Brigade, early moves into a deeper ravine than the one of our last night's bivouac, or rather on the slope of one in front of woods, and about one fourth of a mile to the northward of the Phillips House; and the whole immediate force, after having been massed by divisions, is there formed in order of battle about 8.30 a. m., and remains under arms all the day. We are within a mile of our cannon on the bluffs, the river, and the city of Fredericksburg.

Soon there is heard upon our right much heavy and continuous firing, musketry and artillery, while nearly two hundred heavy guns mounted in line along Stafford Heights — the high bank of the river opposite and overlooking the city — with an increasing and terrific roar, from 7 a. m. until 1 p. m., pour shot and shell by the thousand directly down into Fredericksburg, and high over it upon the hills beyond, where swarm the gray hosts of Gen. Lee's army. We can hear the buildings crash under the awful storm of iron and lead; and are near enough to hear the discharge of almost every cannon fired by the two armies, and the crack of numberless shells marking the sky with hundreds of angry flashes and little ball-like clouds of smoke. Many of the enemy's shells come over far enough to burst near our infantry lines. We are new troops, and have stepped at once from the field of story, out upon the edge, and in full view, of an actual battle in actual war, and that war the most terrible of modern times. For above an hour, from about ten to eleven o'clock in the forenoon, the noise is deafening, the city being battered by the whole fire of the National cannon; the shots frequently counting as high as one hundred per minute, and numbering several thousands in all. Over and over again we try to count the cannon-shots, but always failing, as they mingle in a roar. From the long line of guns on the bluffs opposite the city, from the numberless shells, many of which we can see bursting above the town, and from the burning city itself on our front, the smoke goes up as from an hundred furnaces. The firing continues until about five o'clock in the afternoon, but the worst part of it is over by one. We are waiting for the building of the ponton bridges, and the news comes to us from time to time that the enemy is smashing the bridges, as fast as they are laid, and shooting down the builders by scores. Soon the rumor runs along that we are to be the next Brigade to attempt that dangerous piece of work, but we do not move. It is for us a slow, dragging, tedious, anxious day. We had a hurried breakfast, and now we build our little coffee-fires and have our soldiers' dinner; and again repeat the bill of fare at supper, the air about us heavy, nauseous and thick with the smoke of our fires, the smoke of the burning city, and the smoke of the tons of exploding gunpowder.

Finally, after listening to the ceaseless uproar all day long, about dark, 5 p. m., we fall in and march at a double-quick through the mud for about a mile toward the city, then halt; then retrace our steps to the place of last night's bivouac, and where, for a wonder, our men had been relieved of their heavy knapsacks this morning, and had piled them for future use — by the survivors. We here expect to turn in, and some prepare for bivouac, when at 6 p. m. and now quite dark, we are all suddenly called into line again by the Long-roll. Soon, at 6.20 p. m., the long line of our whole Brigade, defiling to the left from our place of bivouac, and leaving the Phillips House a little distance to our right as we pass it, and marching by fours, by the right flank, moves in a dead silence slowly over the hills where an hour or two before we had double-quicked, then on down the steep river bank, and across the ponton bridge muffled with earth and straw, and thrown across the river near the lower end of the city, and one and a half miles southwest of the Phillips House as we follow the crooked road, and we enter the battered, torn, crushed and burning city, no one opposing. Many will recall the boilers, machinery and other débris of burnt steamers and vessels lying in the river near this ponton bridge as we cross. This ponton bridge is laid from the Washington Farm to the old steamboat and ferry landing — the central ponton bridge. We cross with a slow route-step, every man cautioned to move as quietly as possible, pass up a steep paved way, turn to the left down the street, and about 8 p. m. deploy in line of battle along Caroline street, also called Main street, and is the second street up from the river. The third street is Princess Anne street, leading to Mr. Slaughter's house and grounds. Guards are quickly stationed, and Companies E and B are sent at once as pickets to the rear of the city and along Hazel Run. While these pickets are taking their positions along Hazel Run, the "Taps" are being sounded in the Union Army, and less loudly in the Confederate Army also. With the exception of one or two men in each company who had recently served as guards, the Thirteenth entered the city with unloaded muskets, and loaded them after halting in Caroline street; and about 9 p. m., after standing there a long time in line of battle under arms, the Thirteenth stacks arms along the west side of Caroline street, and bivouacs on the west sidewalk, the side towards the enemy. Other troops similarly occupy the east side. The night is very dark, the streets are filled with the débris of the shattered city and clouds of smoke from the burning buildings, while bummers turn to forbidden pillage. Many houses are entered, blinds closed, fires kindled in stoves and fireplaces, and hot coffee is drank, in the proud, deserted halls of the F. F. Vs., to our own comfort and to the good health of the house-owners — just now absent because of Gen. Burnside's cast-iron hail-storm. The city seems much like a city in the early hours of the morning before the inhabitants are astir. Joseph W. Dickerman of C writes home from Fdsbg.: "We broke camp at 6.20 p. m., crossed the Rappahannock and marched into the city at 8.30 p. m., with unloaded guns; went to the main street, then filed left down some twenty or thirty rods, halted on the right-hand side of the street, and loaded quietly before stacking arms." Lieut. Staniels writes in his diary: "Marched up to Gen. Sumner's Hdqrs. at sunset, then back to camp. Long-roll beat at six. Marched immediately for Fredericksburg. Cross the ponton bridge at eight o'clock. Stack arms and remain in the street over night." [1]

The writer at this time is a First Sergeant. As we cross the city on entering, there lies on the sidewalk as he fell, his gun still held in his hand, a Confederate First Sergeant in a new, clean, Confederate dress uniform, with the regulation chevrons and insignia on the sleeve. His cap held by a loose throat-strap is still on his head, and merely tilted back from a handsome forehead, which alone remains of the whole front part of his head. He was probably instantly killed by a shell or shot, and lies a ghastly object seen in the dim light of a distant fire. Sergt. Chas. F. Chapman of E is the first to see him, and taking First Sergeant Charles M. Kittredge of B and the writer by the arm, Chapman calls out: "Here — see what you First Sergeants are all coming to!" This was the first body of a man killed in the war, that any of us had seen. As soon as

[1] The N. H. Adjt. General's Report, Vol. 2, for 1866, page 785, states that the line was formed about 9 o'clock, reaching the ponton bridge at half past ten; much later than the actual hour — a serious error.

the 13th is in the city, Companies B, Capt. Dodge, and E, Capt. Julian, are hurried forward on picket; and while taking their ground, near Hazel Run, and on the Bowling Green road, several Confederates are seen skittling off in the darkness, and a hunt is instituted among the old buildings for more of them. Soon two of them are found in an old shed by some of the men of Co. E. They raise their guns to fire and threaten to thrash the whole Northern Army if they are molested; but naturally change their minds, as half a dozen loaded muskets are pointed in upon them at the open door, and surrender. Thus Company E has the honor of making the first capture of prisoners for the 13th, and very plucky fellows they were too.[1] One of them, though not very badly wounded, dies before morning of wounds, cold, and loss of blood, despite the best care we can afford him. The other, his comrade, a noble fellow, remained by him to defend him to the last. They both expected to be instantly shot on capture — a common notion among the Confederate soldiers from the far South. These are Mississippians, Barksdale's men. We have crossed the bridge built by the 8th Conn. and other regiments; the 7th Michigan having first crossed and dislodged the enemy's sharpshooters. We cross too from the old Washington plantation, whereon (it may have been) was the garden wherein grew the cherry-tree, whereat the boy, George, went with his little hatchet, whereabout he could not tell a lie; whereof we have all been told, and whereby we all have been, morally, much benefited, of course. Our Brigade, Col. Hawkins, holds the lower part of the city to-night. The enemy on departing piled a dozen or two of his dead in a back yard near the position of the 13th and off Caroline street; they are terribly mutilated, all cut up and battered by bullets, shell, splinters, mortar and brick; many of his dead are also in cisterns and cellars.

With the exception of the special assaulting party, who crossed in boats, and cleared the river bank of the enemy's troops, while the pontons were being laid, our, Hawkins', Brigade are the first troops of the army to cross the river. The assaulting party, excepting a few men of the 89th New York, recrossed, leaving our Brigade to occupy the city; and we hold the lower end of it to-night, while troops of Gen. Howard's Division are coming over and occupying the upper end. Troops are moving all night.

To-night a negro woman occupying the small wooden house, around which the upper brook bends where it first flows into the Bowling Green road (thence following that road towards the river), is seen struggling with a barrel of flour, trying to roll it into her small front door. The door is hardly wide enough to receive the barrel, and the men of Companies E and B help her to put the barrel into the house, and into a back room serving as a store-room. They then go to a grocery store and fill that back room solid with barrels of flour, groceries, etc.; among the lot a box of salt fish that Methuselah had when he first set up housekeeping — at any rate it smelled old enough. Then, in return for their help, Dinah

[1] N. H. Adjutant General's Report for 1866, Vol. 2, page 785.

goes to the brook in the street, gets a pail of water, and sets about cooking griddle-cakes, of plain wheat flour and water, for the men who filled her store-room. The reserve picket is near here, and Dinah is kept busy cooking all night. The writer, and a good many others of the picket, cannot decide to even try the cakes, but they are passed to others in plenty, who eat them with their sugar. They are to-night familiarly called "nigger heel-taps," and probably they merit so good a name.

To go back again to the morning of Dec. 11: Gen. Burnside attempted to lay the ponton bridge opposite the city, the central bridge, this morning about 2 o'clock, but his men were shot down by the 17th and 18th Mississippi regiments of Gen. Barksdale's Confederate Brigade, who with the 8th Florida were posted in the houses and buildings in the city which were nearest the shore of the river. The rest of that Brigade, the 13th and 21st Miss. and the 3d Georgia, were also in the city, in reserve. All together a strong force of about three thousand men. The morning having been spent in fruitless attempts to build the bridge, Gen. Burnside, annoyed, and fretting under the delay, ordered his batteries to open on the town, hoping thus to dislodge the enemy. The river here is about 300 yards wide; and mounted high on the bluffs across the river from Fdsbg., at a distance of half a mile and less, 35 batteries, 179 guns, ranging from 10 lb. Parrotts to $4\frac{1}{2}$ inch siege-guns, opened at once upon the city, about ten o'clock a. m.; continuing their fire for more than an hour, pouring from fifty to one hundred shots per minute directly down into the city, and throwing from 7,000 to 9,000 shells in all, tearing, ripping, cutting, through the buildings of the town. "Houses fell, timbers crashed, dust rose, flames ascended." It was an hour of tremendous thunder, clang, and racket; guns, screams, howls, shells, crashes, echoes, throbs, blows, roars, thunders, flashes, fire, all commingled — but the plucky Mississippians would not budge an inch. Few soldiers ever before kept up such a fire as they did amid such awful surroundings; but out of the din and danger, and the incessant crash and roar, among the buildings about them, there steadily came the little puffs of smoke from their rifles, and their unerring bullets against our men at work near the pontons, on our side of the river.

If Fredericksburg ever raises a monument to anything, it should be a fine one to the memory of these men of Gen. Barksdale's Mississippi Brigade. The terrific bombardment did not dislodge them, and they delayed the pontonniers until 4 p. m., when the 7th Mich., 19th and 20th Mass., of Hall's Brigade, and 89th N. Y., volunteered to cross in boats; which they did, the 7th Michigan leading, and seized the city at 4.30 p. m., clearing it of the Confederate troops; where cannon, shells and rifles were scarcely persuasion, Northern bayonets proved an unanswerable argument. Strange that so many of these men near the river survive the bombardment, while their less fortunate fellows farther back in the city lie headless, armless, legless at every few steps. The city looks as if a huge shell had burst on almost every square rod in all Fredericksburg.

**Dec. 12. Fri.** Foggy morning. Very pleasant day. Companies B and E are relieved on picket by Companies C, Capt. Bradley, and G, Lieut. Forbush; Lieut. Wilson going upon the front line, Lieut. Forbush commanding the reserve. The 13th is called at early daylight, and remains on Caroline st. all day and night. The city streets are the front lines of the army; the rear line is along the river bank. There are two lines (at least) of stacks of arms, ranged as far as we can see, all up and down this and other parallel streets. The city is full of troops, chiefly in bivouac on the sidewalks.

Before the occupation of the city by our troops, an immense quantity of tobacco, in small oak boxes, had been sunk in the river, and our men now fish it out and supply themselves without stint. The city is badly shattered. One double, wooden house, near by the Thirteenth, has over forty holes straight through it, made by shot and shell. A brick house near by was struck in ninety places on the front. The citizens in departing took little with them besides clothing, food and valuables. The soldiers forage everywhere. Not an indiscriminate pillage, but a very free helping of themselves. Stores are cleared out, but there is not much disposition either to destroy or remove anything from houses; aside from a rummaging, scattering and mixing up of things, many a family, on returning to their homes, must find them about the same as when they left.

There is many a concert around a piano or organ. The writer is in one fine parlor where the large piano has just been played by a soldier. The player has scarcely arisen from his seat and stepped aside for a moment, when a solid cannon-ball from the enemy crashes through the chimney near the fireplace, knocking the bricks and mortar about the room; and then taking the piano keyboard diagonally, flings the ivory keys in a shower all about the room, and draws from the piano the most infernal yelp that ever beset human ears — here above. We are covered with dust, bits of plaster and brick, and make a prompt exit down into the street, no one hurt.

The enemy sends no shells into the city, fearing to set it on fire, but a great many solid shot, and chunks of railroad rails from one to two feet in length. The latter rip and tear terrible gaps and holes through the buildings, while the solid shot do but little damage. One solid shot strikes a large stack of muskets, six or eight of them, fairly near their point of union, and sends them 'kiting' and walloping about, end over end, and every way. It is worth going a long journey to see a deserted city occupied by an army. No civilian to be seen, no woman, no child; no person looking from a window; houses, buildings and stores wide open; no citizen going in, none coming out; stables and barns without an occupant, even the dog-kennels and hen-houses are abandoned. Soldiers by the thousand everywhere; long lines of stacks of muskets ranged up and down the streets; infantry, cavalry, artillery, wagons, ambulances, passing continually.

The streets are not paved, and there is little noise save now and then when a solid shot or a chunk of railroad rail escapes from the perpetual growl, noise and smoke within the enemy's lines on the hill, rips through a dozen buildings and drops upon the street or sidewalk. The balls whirl around with great rapidity, like a top, when they first stop from their flight, and if they have crashed through a few buildings, they are often hot enough to set dry wood on fire. We examine them as new curiosities; some are buried by the men, to be recovered after the war is over.

A few men entered an apothecary store. Whiskey was left in several bottles in a very tempting way. Caution suggested a taste before a draught; it is all bitter with poison, or heavily drugged. Crash follows crash. A bayonet run along a shelf tosses off a whole row of medicamentum bottles; the fragrance of rich perfumery fills the air, mingled with smells beyond mention. The floor is flooded. Downstairs and upstairs go the men; and in ten minutes not a breakable thing or vessel in the whole store remains unbroken. The poison in that whiskey cost a thousand dollars an ounce, and was too cheap at that. The story is given as it was heard at the time.

Early this morning there appears on the street a little white girl, three to five years old, alone, and apparently not in the least disturbed by the noise, the smoke, the thousands of soldiers, the rumbling cannon and wagons, and the utterly changed condition of the streets where she had been accustomed to walk and play. She runs along the sidewalk, tripping over the men's blankets and knapsacks lying there, carefully avoids the little fires in the gutter, and looks up at every doorway as if hunting for some particular house. A thousand soldiers see her and are interested. She speaks to none. Soon one stops her. She merely says: "I want to find mamma," and passes on. That is her only answer to every inquiry.

---

### DESCRIPTION OF PLAT.

A. National Cemetery.   B. South wall of same.

C. Superintendent's lodge near where Marye's house stood.

D. New street, made since the battle, from town to Cemetery gate.

E. Telegraph road with stone bank-wall; the stone of the wall is now removed, and built into the Superintendent's lodge. The rebel batteries were on Marye's Hill just west of this road.

F. Steep side of bluff up which the Thirteenth charged into field on the top.   G. Ditch running down to unfinished railroad.

H. Continuation of bluff-side with lone oak tree and spring: * o.

I. Bank and ditches of unfinished railroad.

K. Richmond & Fredricksburg Railroad crossing Hazel Run, L.

M. Low, level field or meadow.

N. Thirteenth and Brigade formed for the assault. The arrow showing nearly the direction of the assault.

P. Brick house, as near as can be located on the plat.

The distances are given in yards.

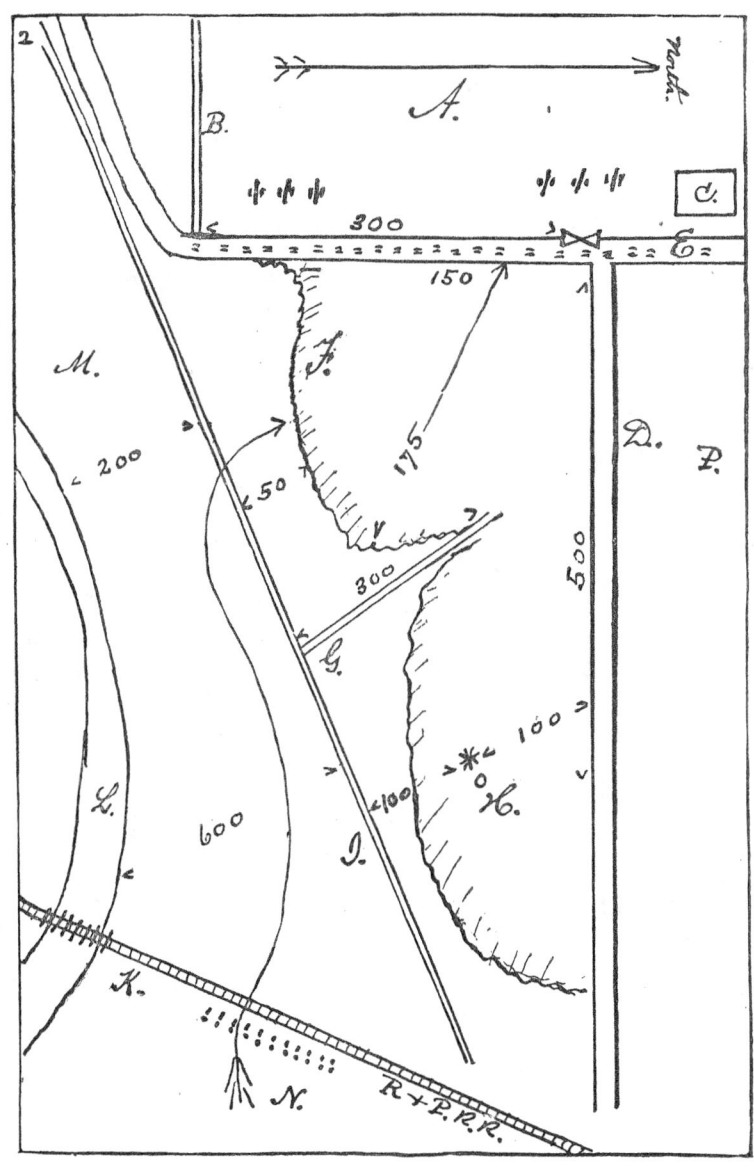

FREDERICKSBURG. — GEN. GETTY'S ASSAULT.

From a sketch made by the writer in May 1885.

After a while an officer cares for the motherless child, and sends her to a place of safety. A more touching little scene rarely occurs.

The remains of the city's destruction are piled and strewn on every hand. Whole fronts of buildings have been torn out and smashed into splinters. Furniture of all sorts is strewn along the streets. Houses are ripped, battered and torn, windows smashed and chimneys thrown down. Every namable household utensil or article of furniture, stoves, crockery and glass-ware, pots, kettles and tins, are scattered, and smashed and thrown everywhere, indoors and out, as if there had fallen a shower of them in the midst of a mighty whirlwind.

To-night Hawkins' Zouaves go on picket to the front. Troops have been pouring into the city for the last twenty-four hours, and to-night we hear the ceaseless tramp, tramp, tramp, through the streets, of the regiments of Sumner's Grand Division, the roll of wagon wheels, the rumble of artillery and the tread of hundreds of horses.

The most of the men of the Thirteenth to-night occupy the houses near their position in the street. The increasing tramping through the streets all night long renders the sidewalks unfit for bivouac, preventing sleep, and wearying the men too much for the hard service before them.

Dec. 13. Sat. Pleasant, but cool. Last night very cold, this morning foggy and dense, clearing bright about mid-forenoon. To-night it is again cold. The 13th furnished details for picket on the night of Dec. 11, as we have said, when we first came into the city, and also for the night of Dec. 12. Since then the Reg. has remained in the city, chiefly along Caroline st., until this morning, and furnished only small detachments for outside work. Early this morning the 13th, with the Brigade, moves from Caroline st. to the river bank near the Gas Works, and just below the ponton bridge which we crossed on the night of Dec. 11. We reach our position on the river bank at eight o'clock.

To plat the scene, draw a north and south line along the city shore of the river and stand upon it, a rod or two south of the Gas Works, and face east. The river runs past you from left to right, that is southward. A part of the 13th are lying about you on the grass at the south side of the Gas Works, the colors of the Reg. are leaning against the south wall of the building near the eastern end, the end towards the river, the color bearers and guard are sitting near by, and perhaps a hundred men are near them. The rest of the 13th are near about, preserving no particular order, some on the grassy bank, some at the river's edge, some sitting on timber, or standing on boards thrown down on the mud of the street and wharf; all making themselves as comfortable as the dirt and mud, the extremely offensive Gas Works, and the clouds of gunpowder smoke will permit.

The rest of the Brigade are near by, and very similarly disposed. The river bank shelves down to a muddy street and wharf all along. Here we remain all day, doing nothing except to watch the constant firing, or to listen to the roar of battle behind us, west, along the front of Marye's Hill, a mile away. (Pronounced Ma-ree.) One mile to your right, south, is Gen. Franklin's ponton bridge, out of sight behind a high bank. One eighth of a mile to your right Hazel Run falls into the river. Directly in front of you, east, and rising high above, across the river, here 300 yards wide, is a long bluff with one hundred or more Union cannon mounted on it, and all in full play. Their shells go over you, and over the city behind you, to Marye's Hill; Marye's Hill replies; and many a shell from both sides bursts in sight; the pieces splash in the river, beat upon the banks, fly among the cannoneers on the bluff, or fall at your own side, and bury themselves in the hard earth. Occasionally a man near you, in the Brigade or Division, is struck, killed or wounded, and a stretcher bears him away. The position is a nervous and a trying one.

Three hundred yards to your left, north, is the central ponton bridge, over which we crossed into the city. The road to this bridge winds down the high, steep Falmouth bank of the river, through the Washington Farm; it is the first road you see on your left. Many soldiers come across the river upon the bridge and go up into the city, through a lane, one hundred feet farther to your left, north of the ponton landing on this side. This lane leads from the old steamboat (now ferry) landing, up into the city. It is provided with a high stone wall on each side, a stone pavement, and is about 150 feet in length. Six hundred yards, or so, to your left, north, is the bridge of the R. & F. R. R. A full mile to your left, north, across the river is the Lacy House; and a mile east of there is the Phillips House.

Here, by the nasty Gas Works, we remain under arms all day. Our po-

---

### DESCRIPTION OF PLAT.

A. Marye's House with rebel batteries to the south of it.
B. Orange Turnpike.   C. Plank road.
D. Telegraph road with stone bank-walls.
E. New street opened since the battle, and leading to Cemetery gate.
F. Bank and ditch of unfinished railroad.
G. Richmond and Fredericksburg Railroad.
H. Hazel Run.   L. Oak tree with Spring near it.
I. Gen. Getty's Division formed for the assault.
K. K. Point near angle in Telegraph road, near which were the rebel batteries A., aimed at by Gen. Getty's men in the assault, and the little field, on the bluff, reached by the Thirteenth.
M. Brick house — as near as can be located.
N. Vicinity of Lee's Hill.

Gen. Getty told the writer that Gen. Hooker's corps was on the right of the Ninth Corps — in which the 13th — and that the place where Gen. Hooker exposed himself during the day was at the cut on the R. & F. Railroad, just to the right of the place where Gen. Getty's Division formed for the assault. This railroad cut was enfiladed by the rebel batteries on Lee's Hill.

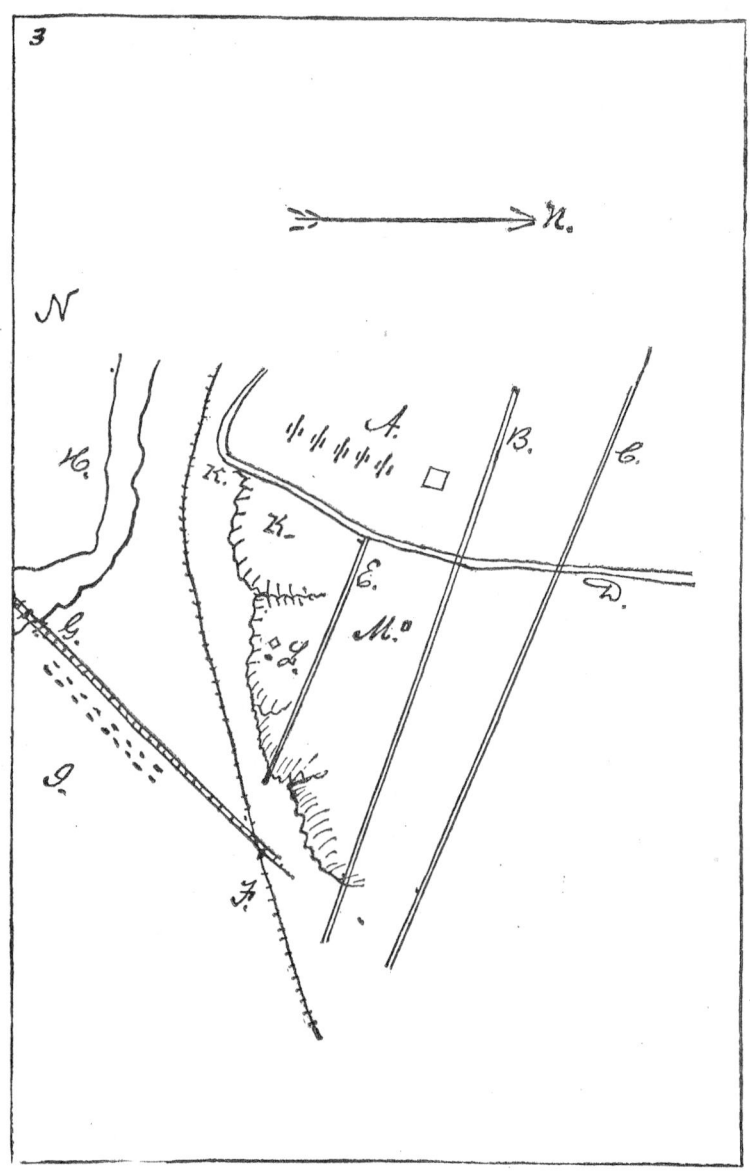

MARYE'S HEIGHTS, December 13, 1862.

From an old print seen by the writer in Fredericksburg in May 1885.

sition on the grassy bank, or on the open ground exposes us to the flying pieces of many of the enemy's shells intended for the cannoneers of our batteries on the Falmouth (or Stafford) bluffs, across the river, but bursting short of their mark; while many shells from our own guns, on those very bluffs, bursting as soon as they leave the guns, pour their jagged pieces down into the river, and upon the hither bank among our men. The water in the river is in a constant state of disturbance made by them. We are about one mile from the enemy's batteries, and within four or six hundred yards, and directly under the muzzles, of our own guns, and are thus exposed to the incessant fire of both. All day long the shells, hundreds of them, pass to and fro over our heads. Many men in our Brigade are wounded here by pieces of shells, and their lead rings.

Peter Smithwick, six feet seven inches in height, the tallest man in the Thirteenth, is severely hurt, while here, by a piece of shell striking his left arm near the shoulder. Many a man with such an ugly bruise, would go to the rear, but he is made of better stuff. He coolly pockets the piece of shell, a rough chunk of iron about the size of a hen's egg, and goes through the battle, though his left arm is practically useless, and is supported much of the time by his cross-belt. Two men are killed and seven wounded here, in our Brigade, by the bursting of one shell, and the men are ordered not to remain massed in dense bodies, but to spread apart and find cover.

From a little hill a few rods from the 13th, westward, we can see the rebel batteries, and lines of battle, and the contest of the day going on in front of Marye's Heights, now wreathed, puffed, lined and festooned with battle smoke, and wide to right and left a similar scene is in view. This hill is near Mr. Slaughter's house, and has a steep bank and cut on one side, which is altogether beyond the range of the enemy's rifles, being nearly a mile distant from them, and, excepting for an occasional shell rushing wide of its proper range, is as safe as any dooryard on a New England farm, incomparably safer than the river bank, and a man might stand here for forty hours unharmed; so we can gaze at ease for the few minutes which we can spend away from the Regiment. Some of those present say that they can count sixteen different points from which the enemy's artillery fire proceeds, each point supplied with four or more guns.

For a part of the day the men of the 13th are obliged to stand in deep mud, in an exceedingly dirty and wet street, and boards are wrenched off the buildings near by to stand upon. At times from early morning till night, we can distinctly hear the din of the battle on the hills west of the city, while our own guns, firing over our heads, keep up a deafening roar, — the sounds sweeping in fitfully, and in gusts, from all sides. As the sounds of louder thunder come in from all around the sky during a violent storm, so amid the general rattle and growl come the sudden outbursts of musketry and artillery, as charge after charge is made by the Union forces upon the enemy's lines along Marye's Heights, and elsewhere, while mingling with the other noises, and topping them all, comes the regular boom and echo of one huge Confederate gun, which we hear but cannot locate. The roar of the furious battle commences about 9 a. m., and continues all the day, until dusk.

So the terrible day wears away, a regiment of men wiped out, a thousand men falling almost every hour, until a little after four p. m., when the rumor runs through our column here like wildfire, that Gen. Getty, with only the two brigades of his Division, is to make a night assault on Marye's Heights; the most formidable position in the enemy's line, a death-dealing semicircle; and on that murderous stone bank-wall, upon which all the assaults of the day have made no impression whatever; and just with the coming to us of that grim rumor, there falls a pause in the rebel firing.

We can scarcely give the rumor any credence whatever, and the movement is roundly condemned on all hands as sheer folly; but there soon rings in our ears the sharp order: "Attention!" The men fall into line along their stacks of muskets, in a stern, dead silence; and soon again follows an order: "Take Arms. Right face — March!"

The sun is now apparently less than half an hour high, and Lieut. Gafney, pointing to its reddish disc just on the edge of the horizon, and seen through the haze and battle smoke, remarks: "I wish I could get up there and kick that thing down!" And the Thirteenth has no braver officer than Lieut. Gafney.

---

DESCRIPTION OF MAP.

A. Rappahannock River.   B. Maj. Lacey's house.
C. Orange Turnpike, passing the Phillips House.
D. Claiborne Run.   F. Ponton Bridge, central.
E. Position near cut on the R. & F. R. R., where Gen. Getty's Division formed for the assault.
G. City Gas Works, around which the Thirteenth remained all the day Dec. 13, on the river bank.   H. Hazel Run.
I. Caroline street (or Main st.), the second street from the river.
K. Princess Anne street; leading to near Mr. Slaughter's house and field, L.   M. Marye's house.
N. Unfinished railroad crossed in the assault; then mere bank and muddy ditches.   O. Union batteries on Stafford Heights.
P. Little hill, or bluff, up which the Thirteenth charged. The same bluff-side continues down towards the city along near the unfinished railroad.   V. Canal.   W. Bowling Green road.
Y. Point aimed at in the charge, as stated by Gen. Getty.
Z. Brick house, about 250 yards east of Marye's, and 150 to 200 yards east of the stone wall on Telegraph road. This brick house was seized by Gen. French's Division about noon, Dec. 13.
R. Telegraph road, with the stone bank-walls, and west of it the rebel batteries and troops on Marye's Heights, the rebel position.
S. Rebel batteries towards Lee's Hill.   T. National Cemetery.

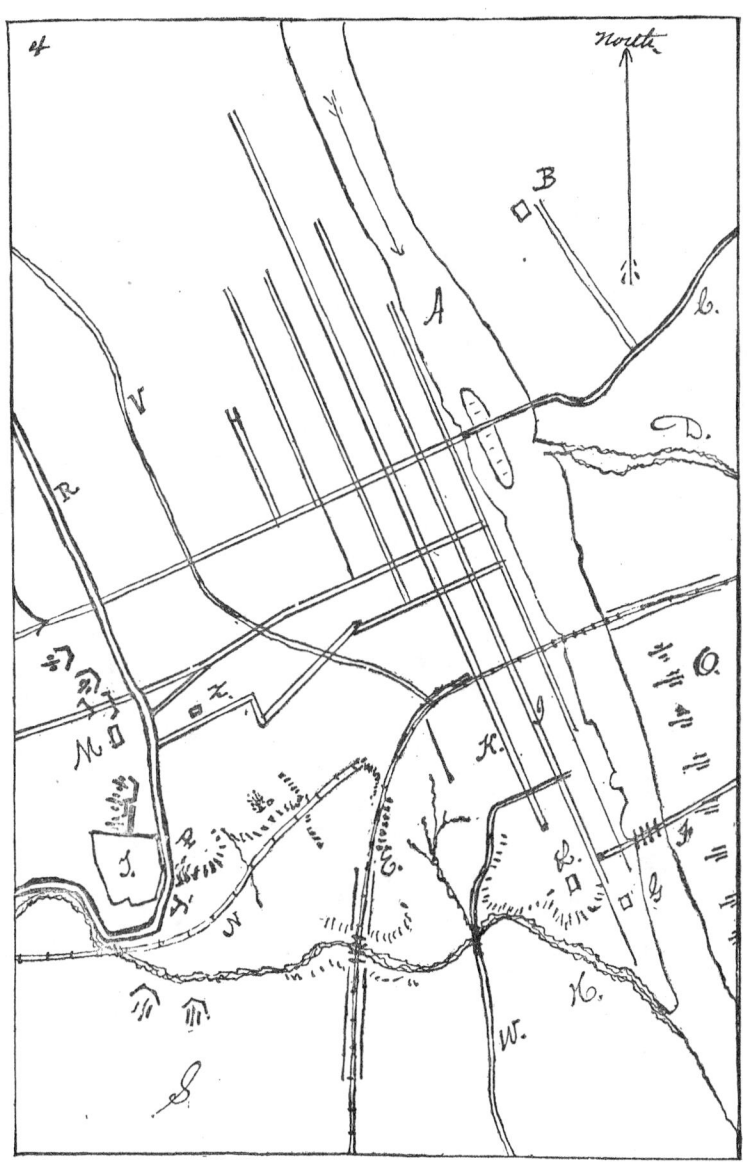

FREDERICKSBURG.

Tracing of Official Map. Scale, three inches to one mile.

The Thirteenth quickly takes its place in the column; but we must say that no one whom we know hankers after a twilight excursion to Marye's Heights on this particular evening. We stand at a terrible disadvantage. They have belched a world of fire, and shot, and shells, and bullets, almost continuously for these last two days; and, within an hour, long columns of the enemy's infantry have been seen by us running over the slopes, and down into position in his front lines under the hill. However, we are new troops, have been anxious for the last fifteen or twenty years, on an average, to 'hear drums and see a battle,' and now our curiosity is to be altogether satisfied. We move off quickly by the right flank, by fours, along the street, landing and wharf, and through an abundance of mud and water. The colors are between the left of Company E and the right of Company C; E being the Color-company.

Hospital Steward Prescott writes that the order, "Forward," was passed to our First Brigade at half-past four o'clock. The prevailing idea and feeling in Gen. Getty's Division is that our assault will be fruitless; but it must be done, and soon the determination rises to do our utmost to win, we desire to strike an effective blow, and we move toward the front growing more and more confident and strong, from the hope we have, that possibly we may now do what our troops have failed to do in all of this day's fighting: break Lee's line at Marye's Hill, which would be a most glorious accomplishment of some of the work for which we volunteered.

To plat the place of our waiting all this long day, you stood on the river bank just south of the Gas Works, and faced due east. Now face about, due west, and follow the north bank of Hazel Run five sixths of a mile, straight west, over ditch, ridge and level, and you will strike the stone bank-wall on the Telegraph road, below Marye's Hill, near the southeast corner of the present National Cemetery grounds. That southeast corner is the point aimed at in this famous night assault of Gen. Getty's Division. (Gen. Getty so informed the writer, May 1885.) Around this corner of the Cemetery, the Telegraph road, now as then, bends sharply from its southward course, and runs almost due west. The corner is sharp, bluffy, steep, rough and abrupt, and was in a still more forbidding condition, in 1862, before the National improvements were made and the Cemetery was walled in. In coming up to this southeast corner of Marye's Hill, from the Gas Works, you cross, first, the Bowling Green road, and afterwards many a ravine, ridge and brook. Second, you cross the Richmond and Fredericksburg Railroad, where it has high banks; right here Gen. Getty's Division formed for the assault. To your left, south, is the Hazel Run bridge. To your right, north, is a deep cut on the railroad; near which cut Gen. Hooker so long and so gallantly bore himself, mounted on a large white horse, during this battle that the Confederate commander, though not knowing who he was, ordered his men not to fire upon him, but to capture him alive if they could.

In May 1885 the writer met accidentally, on a James River steamer, Judge R. L. Henley of Williamsburg, Va., and while in conversation with him, he remarked that during the battle a Federal officer frequently appeared in this railroad cut, which was enfiladed by the batteries on Lee's Hill, greatly exposing himself, and acted so bravely that the Confederate commander gave an order to his riflemen not to shoot him, but to capture him if they could. The Confederates could not make out who this Union officer was, and the Judge inquired of the writer if he knew. The writer did not then know, but told Judge Henley that he was intending to call on Gen. Getty in Washington and would inquire of him concerning the matter. Gen. Getty, when the writer called on him, at his farm a few miles out of Washington, and made the inquiry, answered at once that Gen. Hooker, mounted on a white horse, was riding in and out of that cut on the railroad half the day during the battle of Dec. 13, and that he, Getty, remonstrated with him for exposing himself so much, but Gen. Hooker seemed to care little for the danger or for the remonstrance. This is the writer's authority for the statement concerning Gen. Hooker. Judge Henley served during the battle as a Captain in the 32d Virginia Confederate regiment, Col. Edgar B. Montague commanding.

Third, a little farther west, you cross another railroad, then unfinished and mere banks and ditches, but now completed and used. You cross this new railroad bank, near a low, wet lot of ground, the swampiest place on this railroad along here, and about 500 yards from the Cemetery. As you stand upon this new railroad, at the point marked I. on the map on page 43 and near this low, swampy place; to your right, north, is a long bluff, running southwestwardly toward the Cemetery. On the side of this bluff, about 100 yards northward from you, is a lone oak-tree, and a spring of water called Cold Spring. On the top of the bluff, north of the tree and spring, is a street, opened since the battle, running from the city to near the Cemetery gate. A ditch makes down diagonally from this street, from a point near the Cemetery to the new railroad. We now approach the scene of the assault. Along the southern slope of this long bluff thousands of Union soldiers fell during Dec. 13 ; our night assault was made to the left of nearly all of them. West of this diagonal ditch, between you and the Cemetery, is a very steep bank, marked F. on the same map as above, and is practically the southwest end of the bluff. This bank rises northward some 20 or 30 feet to a little nearly level field, not 200 yards square, lying close up to the Telegraph road, and directly in front of Marye's Hill. This road, and along it also the famous stone bank-wall, bounds this little field for about 150 yards on its west side ; the new street bounds its north side for nearly 200 yards ; the new railroad runs along south of it at a distance of about 50 yards ; while the southeast side of the field falls upon the diagonal ditch, at a distance of about 150 to 175 yards from the Telegraph road, the steep bank sweeping around to that road near the southeast corner of Marye's Hill. There is no better description for this little bluff and field than to call it a flat-top hill.  Up into this little field the First Brigade, Hawkins', of Gen. Getty's Division attempted to rush alone in the night charge. The Second Brigade, Harland's, was held in reserve near the R. & F. Railroad bank, a little north of Hazel Run. It was up the south side of this little bluff that the Thirteenth charged, receiving the first volley of Confederate musketry, most of the bullets flying overhead, and then continued on under the storm of bullets coming from the rebels firing at will, and into the little field on the top until ordered to lie down; and lay there protected by the darkness, and little ridges of land, for apparently a full half hour, and until the worst part of the rebel firing was over. How near to the stone wall they came, will appear farther on. The land falls a little all the way from the road to the bluff, consequently the rebels in the road fire over our heads. The unfinished railroad runs southwestward along near the foot of the bluff, at a wide angle from the R. & F. Railroad, to near the southeast corner of Marye's Hill. The stone bank-wall then standing along the west side of the little field into which the 13th charged, has been removed, and built into the Cemetery lodge, and the surface of the little field furnished the clay for the bricks of the Cemetery wall. It is no stretch to say that the red, in many a brave Union soldier's blood, and of the Thirteenth too, has given its own color to those bricks.

The line of the advance and assault, after the R. & F. Railroad was crossed, was practically along the edge of the southern side of the bluffs, skirting the more level meadow or intervale that forms the north bank of Hazel Run from the Bowling Green road to the southeast corner of the Cemetery. The top of the bluff, and the meadow along Hazel Run, was probably swept by the fire of fifty Confederate cannon and ten thousand muskets; the side of the bluff alone could be made use of by an advancing column.

Now go up on the terrace, at the southeast corner of the Cemetery, reverse this present view, and look east, across the sunken Telegraph road, down upon the little field — this flat-top hill — the level land below it, and down along the bluff sides, and along the north bank of Hazel Run; and you will be ready to stake your reputation and best wits, that no man, knowing the ground, could have sent two brigades, and held back one of them in reserve, to assault this corner; while fifteen or twenty Confederate regiments, and several batteries, knowing every acre of the ground, securely posted behind hill-top and ridge, in ravines and rifle-pits, behind buildings, sunken roads and stone bank-walls, were all ready and waiting to receive them. The Union Generals could not have known and really did not know the extreme difficulties of this assault.

The term flat-top hill is preferred to the word plateau because it seems to more definitely describe the place. The plateau extends eastward from the Telegraph road, and widening, for a quarter of a mile or more, while this little flat-top hill is of but a few acres, and is the extreme southwest end of the plateau where it comes upon the Telegraph road. In all the assaults of the day the troops mounted the plateau, the Thirteenth mounted this southwest end of it.

Now let us return to the river bank and come up with the Thirteenth in the assault, as nearly as we may, the irregularities of the ground, and the necessities of secrecy and cover compelling numerous windings.

Leaving this vicinity, the Thirteenth with its Brigade and Division moves up the wharf northward, then passes into the city, by going through the old lane leading from the steamboat landing near the ponton bridge, westward to the vicinity of Princess Anne street, then turns southward again, and crosses the broad field west of Mr. Slaughter's house. Here in this level field the column of the 13th, as we march by the right flank, is drawn out quite straight, and a solid shot, from the enemy near Lee's Hill, skims with its own peculiar scream along nearly the whole length of the Regiment, and not more than ten or fifteen feet overhead, but harmless. When across this field we go down a steep bank and wade through a little stream of mud and water that empties into Hazel Run ; all the while bearing towards the left, southward, from the point where we emerged from the city. A portion of the 13th crosses a deep ditch upon a few timbers, the rest marches around it at a double-quick. Just before we drop into Hazel Run valley we pass over a part of the day's battle-field. Next we move more directly forward, westward, at an irregular, jerky, rapid pace, quick, double-quick, run, and come upon uneven ground where there is a partial cover, among scant brush and a few low ridges and knolls, from the enemy's musketry fire now coming upon us quite severe from his pickets, evidently at a long range, and from a few small cannon shot. As we pass, the dead of the day's battle are seen lying on the ground to our right in large numbers. The enemy's fire rapidly increases as we move down a slight declivity on nearing the railroad. We next approach the Richmond and Fredericksburg Railroad, countermarch into line of battle along the city side of the embankment, the southeast side, which now affords a little shelter from the enemy's fire. The evening grows dark very rapidly here in the mist or smoke in the valley. The sun set to-day at forty-five minutes after four.

After the line of battle is formed here, the right of the 13th, with Col. Stevens, is towards the city, the left, with Maj. Storer, is towards Hazel Run, Lt. Col. Bowers being in the centre. The Thirteenth is on the right of the second line of Col. Hawkins' (First) Brigade ; the 25th N. J. is on the right of the first line, and in front of the Thirteenth. The 9th N. Y., Hawkins' Zouaves, have the left of the front line of the Brigade. The positions of the 10th N. H., 89th and 103d N. Y. in our Brigade are not distinctly known to the writer.

Gen. Harland's (Second) Brigade is in support, the 4th R. I., 8th, 11th, 15th, 16th, and 21st Conn. ; and this Brigade halts within a few rods of the railroad, and our First Brigade is in all the succeeding part of the charge alone. M. & C. H. of Conn. 294.

The enemy's fire, while we are here at the railroad, is made much worse by a light Union battery, which has taken position to the right and rear of our Brigade, and commences firing furiously, a part of its shells going almost directly over our heads. The enemy's fire, however, thus invited, soon silences this spiteful little snap-dragon; one rebel shell is seen by us to burst directly upon the top of one of these Union guns, others among the guns; and the battery hauls off, or ceases firing, evidently getting the worst of the duel. Soon other Union batteries open, farther to our right, but also firing nearly over our heads as we advance.

Gen. Hazard Stevens, then serving on the staff of Gen. Getty, contributes the following: " Just as Gen. Getty's Division was about to charge, the General sent Maj. Edward Jardine of the 9th N. Y., Hawkins' Zouaves, a gallant officer who had been in action several times before, to assist Col. Stevens in leading the Thirteenth, which had never been under fire. When Maj. Jardine arrived he found the Thirteenth drawn up in line of battle in front of the R. & F. Railroad embankment all ready, and only awaiting the order to advance to the assault. Planting himself in front of the line, he started to make a military speech in order to inspire the Regiment with the necessary ardor for the bloody work before it; but as he looked down the long regular line of glistening bayonets, and saw the determined, resolute faces, and stalwart forms, he realized that any harangue was not needed, and finally burst out with: 'Thirteenth New Hampshire, you love your country, you are brave men, and you came out here to fight for her — now, go in! Forward!!'"

A moment later the Regimental officers give the order to their several commands, and the column moves close up under the railroad embankment to mount it and charge. More than half an hour has been taken up since we left the river bank, but after the dispositions are made our halt and waiting in line of battle along the R. & F. R. R. is but for a few minutes, when the order rings along the line: "Forward!" — at which the most of the Brigade starts, but a part is left lying down flat on the ground. Even with this loss, if the charge had kept on as it started, there might have been some chance for success; but after a little, squads of men halted along the way and commenced firing over the heads of the body of the Brigade which kept advancing. We do not pretend to know where these fools came from — but they were there.

As a whole, however, we quickly cross the railroad in good order, bayonets fixed, and with a rush and a cheer dash forward to the assault on the double-quick. The writer here distinctly remembers seeing the Thirteenth in a fair, good line, in the dusk, when at some distance across the railroad; but soon a part of the left wing of the Reg. plunges into the deep mud of a wet, swampy, ditchy place which extends towards Hazel Run, the right wing and the colors finding better ground. There is much scattering fire upon us from the right and left, but for a few minutes just at the first of our assault there is an ominous silence on our front. The left wing of the 25th N. J. in the front line of our Brigade, and in advance of the Thirteenth, plunges into mud, breaks up, lies down or sinks, and divides, a part only advancing who find solid ground, and the 13th keeping up take their advance position. The order of the right wing of the 25th is better, but this wing soon surges to the right, uncovering the colors of the 13th. and the Reg. springs at once for the advance. This irregularity is soon adjusted to some extent, but the line of the 25th is broken and in squads, and the 13th is up even with them or close behind them from this time.

When the assault first began the Captains of companies in the 13th sprang to the front, all urging their men to the utmost, and the men kept well up in line, dressing on the colors; and followed very close upon the ranks of the Jerseymen. Very naturally, however, the centre of the Regiment bulged forward a little, as the colors directed the course of the assault, and when the 25th N. J. broke up in the mud, its men in front of our colors were in the way of the men of the 13th, who stepped upon them and over them as they fell into the ditch, and before they had time to rise again. Thus our colors easily came to the van; while parts of the line of the 13th were held back by the large squads of the men of the 25th, who kept on in spite of the mud. This mud accident damaged, if it did not destroy, the effective power of both Regiments; but the 13th seeing the 25th in the mud first, had a little better opportunity to avoid it. The assault from this time until we halt near the rebel lines, is all the work of ten minutes and less, and terrible beyond words to describe; and by this time it is so dusky that we cannot see clearly more than a few rods. A part of the right wing of the 25th N. J. extends to the right beyond the extreme right of the 13th; but we are so close upon the men of the rest of that wing that our men could reach them with their bayonets.

As for the colors of the 13th and the centre near them and within view of the writer, we soon clear a stone wall, or broken down fence built partly of stone,[1] the mud and water of a ditch, the enemy for a moment having ceased firing on our front — waiting for us! — move obliquely somewhat to the right, charge directly up a steep bank, and are moving forward, on smooth and nearly level ground, towards a high point on the enemy's line, a great black hill, and said to be his most formidable position in this vicinity; when we hear a rebel order: "Ready, Aim — Fire!" and with a terrific crash, and a long line of blaze and flame lighting up much of the scene, revealing long, dense rows of rebel heads and leveled muskets, and all ripping out at once, right close in our faces, comes a volley of rebel musketry. apparently from three or four ranks of men crowded into one long line of battle and not more than one hundred and fifty feet distant from us and our colors; some members of our Regiment say at less than half that distance, and that they felt upon their faces the heat of the discharge. Anyhow, it was 'pesky near,' as one of our men said of the rebel bullet that blistered the end of his nose without cutting any of it off. The rebel volley seems to pour out of the very ground, and the line of flame appears to be as long as three or four ordinary regimental fronts.

[1] See Carleton, at end of Dec. 13.

After an instant's delay in the firing, of which delay we make the most by advancing, volley after volley follows from the rebels, to the right and left, rapid, solid, crash upon crash, amid a general storm of file firing, or firing at will, more directly in our front ; while shells and grape pour in a shower, from front, from right, from left, from the high hillside and from the lower level, scream through our lines, whirr, purr, and whizz over our heads, and beat and bound on the ground about us, and the enemy's infernal explosive bullets snap, crackle and sparkle on every hand and in the air. The flashes of fire on all sides from musket, cannon and shell are as thousands upon thousands, constant, innumerable, and the roaring indescribably terrific. But for us the enemy fires high, the most of his shots going over our heads. The whole scene is royally magnificent ; and well worth going five thousand miles to see.

At the first terrible volley, a body of men of the 25th N. J. divided into irregular squads, in front of us, suddenly turn and dash to the rear, straight back through the line of the Thirteenth, and create considerable confusion ; but the men of the 13th hold on their way as best they may, give a shout and rush forward a few yards nearer to the enemy's front lines ; when a very deep and hoarse voice, near by to the right, is heard above the din, shouting : " Down, Boys — Down ! " and the order is quickly obeyed. (The writer has been unable to learn who gave this order, the voice unknown to him.) Here the writer must have been near the Thirteenth's colors, for he is nearly knocked down, and is considerably hurt by the staff of the colors hitting him on the left side of the head, as the color-bearer falls towards the front at the word " Down ! " and the colors fall and lie at his left. But after the volley and before the halt, the Captains and other officers are trying to rally the Reg. and to continue the assault. There is a babel of orders and commands in which the writer recognizes the voice of Capt. Dodge, and of Capt. Julian, who stands up for a little time and sends his clear, sharp voice all abroad for Company E to advance ; but wisdom and prudence soon argue for preservation of life, and he lies down on the ground near a rod to the left and front of the colors, and there remains for a long time. Advance now means advance to a grave, or upon scant and bad rations in a rebel prison. We can see the heads of the rebels now and then in the flashes of light, and distinctly hear their officers' words of command. We could easily throw a stone over among them. A few minutes after the halt, and while lying down, the writer receives a hard thump on his side, as a piece of shell strikes Company E's large record book which he carries, and cuts into the leather cover. Peter Smithwick of E hears the blow, and reaching forward, pulls at the writer's foot, and asks in anxious tones: " Orderly, Orderly ; are you killed ? " and receives for an answer : " No ; only jarred."

As the officers and men kept moving forward while rallying from the effects of the first volley, they unconsciously advanced a considerable distance before the final halt. The writer thinks that one of the Regiment's

colors changed hands during the assault. It will be readily seen that the
companies became mingled together, the wings naturally drawing towards
the centre in the closing-up movement as men stopped or fell. Some of our
color-guard, and quite a number of our men, now gather near our colors;
for though the night is now quite dark, we are so near to the muzzles of the
enemy's cannon and muskets, that the wild scene is considerably lighted up
by the incessant flashes of burning powder, and we can see our men lying
about. These, however, eventually all come off the field with us. The
writer moves a little to the right into a sandy depression, or hole made by
a bursting shell. We are so near the enemy that his gun wads, or cartridge bags, fly over us, and some of them fall burning, smoking and stinking
among us, and we feel upon our faces and hands the wind of the discharges of his cannon. Our men here pick up these burning wads or bags
upon their bayonets and toss them away. We constantly hear the rebel
commands. Their cannon are depressed, the muzzles well down, and we
can see them jump back as they are fired. All that saves the portion of
the Thirteenth now directly around the colors is their nearness to the
rebel cannon and rifles, which cannot be depressed sufficiently to reach us
with their fire, and a little dry hollow, dropping less than two feet, in the
surface of the field just where the men are lying. The shelter is just
enough to permit a man to rise a little from the ground, support himself
upon his elbow, and look about him, as some of us do, and have quite a
clear view, for a few seconds at a time, of the near surrounding scene.

We doubt if the enemy can see us, any better than we can see him.
It is too dark to see far, but the flash of a cannon lights up for a moment
quite a wide space near us. The missiles of all sorts fly over our heads
like hail, and with a near, cutting, whizzing hiss, like the sound of a lot
of small buzz-saws, and the cannonading is furious; the shots pouring over
us from all sides, and those from our own batteries, in our rear, as dangerous to us as any. The fire of our batteries is directed upon the huge
black hill rising close in our front. The enemy's aim from his cannon
mounted upon the same great hill seems to be directed upon our troops
on the flat ground nearer the unfinished railroad and Hazel Run than we
are; the missiles from the two fires sweep over our heads, though very
closely, but for those troops a few rods in our rear the situation must be
terrible. There are no Union troops between us and the line of the
enemy's musketry-fire along the sunken Telegraph road in our front, not
a man dead or alive. By the flashes we can see every rod of that space.
Nor are any men with the white leggings to be seen hereabout. We
must needs take the matter philosophically, for there is no way to escape
from our position except to bolt for the rear the instant the firing quiets
down, if it ever does — minutes are hours in a place like this. At some
distance back of us, a little to the right, a scattered line of Union troops
are unwisely firing over us at the enemy's lines; and the enemy is firing
in reply from half a dozen lines high up across our front. There is much
firing also from a lot of houses far to our right, very wild firing and sharp.

We are in the midst of a magnificent exhibition of fireworks, their flashes of flame ranging from the bright spark of a rebel explosive bullet, to the instant glare of a locomotive headlight, as the cannon discharge and the shell burst, the blaze and roaring about the same on every hand and front and rear. The many crazy Union bullets are just skimming over our heads, from the rear, while the flashes of the Union guns only serve to provoke an increasing fire from the enemy on our front, their bullets also just skimming over our heads. The Union bullets are as dangerous for us to face in retreating, as the enemy's bullets are in following us. The situation is a trying one; but our interest in this scene, so new and strange to us raw troops, robs the dangers of half their terrors. And so we lie and wait. Think of spending half an hour in such a place!

The colors of the Thirteenth, and the body of men close about them, are now near the western side of that little field on the southwest end of the bluff; the position is recognizable at a glance, and no other spot on the whole line satisfies the conditions of the charge and halt. To the right and left of the colors we can see the men of the Thirteenth lying upon the ground. While we are here one large Union shell, that comes rushing, screaming, the nearest of all to our heads, plunges into the ground about twenty-five or fifty feet to our front, bursts upon striking, jarring the ground and giving us a shower of gravel; as usual the most of the pieces take the direction of the shell, and we can hear the enemy scream, curse and swear. Since the first volleys, the enemy in dense ranks, in large numbers, and firing at will, have produced a perfect roar of musketry; but as they fire high and about all their shots go over, the result is more threatening than harmful. One thing we note particularly — and it is remarked upon while we lie here, as the firing lulls to fewer bright flashes, and as talk commences about finding and removing all our wounded to the rear — we have not seen and cannot now see any bodies of men, living or dead, lying or standing in front of ourselves, in the narrow space between us and the enemy's nearest line of flashing muskets, though the ground appears smooth and rising a little from us to their line along the sunken road and stone wall. No men of any other regiment are in front of the Thirteenth now and here. We can occasionally, in the flashes of light, see the hands and arms of the rebels working, as they ram their cartridges home; and the multitude of their commands indicate many officers " present for duty." Our interest in the situation is greatly enhanced by knowing that they would instantly shoot us all at sight, if they could possibly do so!

It is officially claimed that the Thirteenth (with the 25th N. J.) gained a point much nearer to the rebel stone wall and batteries here than any other of the Union forces; but as the left wing of the 25th was badly broken up in the mud and its right wing extended to the right considerably beyond the right of the Thirteenth, the colors of the 13th were necessarily uncovered; at any rate they were uncovered, and came up independently to the front line of the assaulting column, and no Union troops, dead or alive, were in front of the colors, and men of the Thirteenth about them, at the final halt; the writer was in a position to know that fact.

We are under fire in the charge about forty minutes. It seems to us that we lie here, where we were ordered down, for a full half hour. On looking about for the wounded, after the rebel firing has slackened, none are found in front of us, and a man now lying near our colors, but to the right of them, remarks : " We will all be captured if we remain here," and suggests a retreat. The word is passed from one to another, and after a little we all rise and move back, crouching low, some creeping on hands and knees, for a short distance, and then march, sweeping around considerably towards the north at first, to the rear of the Richmond and Fredericksburg Railroad, and there find a part of the Thirteenth halted and forming in line; and at the railroad hear a speech going on — some one urging that we charge again — and we are told that the speaker is Col. Donohoe of the 10th N. H. That idea, however, is soon abandoned. Squads of men rapidly coming in join their regiments; the 13th is reformed, withdraws from the vicinity of the railroad about 9 p. m., marches down to the city and bivouacs until morning; having first halted for a long time, in a little field near the city limits, while our wounded are cared for.

Capt. Julian retired from the front with the colors. The writer was directed to look after some of the men who were temporarily missing. When the enemy's first crashing volley struck the Thirteenth, the most of it and the colors had cleared the gully or ditch, had mounted a steep bank, and had advanced some little distance upon the smooth ground beyond the crest, and were aiming towards a big black hill rising high directly in our front, and only a few yards distant.

These circumstantial points are mentioned here only as evidence of what the writer firmly believes, namely : That the colors of the Thirteenth were carried to a point within one hundred feet of the enemy's line and nearer than the colors of any other regiment in the army.

Every Company in the Reg. reached the little field above the bluff, and points about equally distant from the rebel lines; and members of all have about the same experiences to relate of what they met during the charge, and saw and heard while lying down at the front.

While on our way back to the R. & F. Railroad, from the point nearest to the enemy's lines where we finally halted in the assault at the word "Down," and after walking a long distance, we find on the bluff-side, sitting beside a lone tree, apparently an oak, and near a spring of water, an officer of high rank whom we know, and we stop to see whether he needs any assistance. We ask him if he is hurt, and he answers, "No, but I am all bedaubed," and we pass on and leave him there. The writer was startled on seeing this man, and remembers the incident with great vividness. It points a prominent landmark, for now, on visiting the field in May 1885, we find on careful inquiry that but one tree of any considerable size stood during the war on that bluff-side; and that one was the oak-tree near Cold Spring, which stands about 500 to 600 yards eastward from the stone bank-wall and Telegraph road. The tree stands but a few rods from an exceedingly muddy place struck by the column in the assault. Later in the night, water was obtained from this spring by Hosp. Steward Royal B. Prescott, and others of the stretcher-corps and Band, for the wounded men of the Thirteenth. The mud near Cold Spring stopped, short, many members of the assaulting column.

As we leave the field of the assault we pass through a large number of the dead; and at one point not far from the railroad, near the crest of the long bluff and under it, they are so thickly strewn, that if we should try, we could walk a long distance upon the bodies without once stepping upon the ground. The dead lay all along our line of march, most of them to the right, as we went up to the assault, and were very numerous just where the Thirteenth re-formed after the charge, along the bluff, and the R. & F. Railroad nearer the city. Of these Lt. Col. Grantman, then Captain commanding Co. A, on the extreme right of the Reg., states that while the Thirteenth was being re-formed some one inquired what regiment it was lying on the ground under the bluff, and just across our front, and that he, Grantman, went up to them, and spoke to several of them, but received no reply. He supposed them to be asleep, as it was now too dark to see very clearly. Trying to wake one or two of them, he found they were dead — and so of all. As they lay on the ground in a long line conforming to the edge of the ridge or bluff, they had the appearance of a large regiment that had just laid down in a somewhat irregular line of battle — there were hundreds of them.

The New Hampshire Adjt. General's Report for 1866, Vol. II. p. 786, states: About 5 o'clock on the afternoon of Dec. 13, Gen. Getty was ordered to attempt, with his Division of only two brigades, what two Corps had attempted in vain. Hawkins' Brigade was to attack supported by Harland. Hawkins formed his Brigade in two lines, the Thirteenth on the right of the second line. The troops moved across the railroad (R. & F.), under a considerable fire from both musketry and artillery, and nearly to the point where the Telegraph road turns at a sharp angle, about the foot of Marye's Heights, and runs nearly west; when they obliqued to the right, and charged up the steep bank, in hopes of carrying the works which crowned its crest. It was so dark that the line was a good deal confused, and receiving a terrific volley when within a few rods from the enemy, and the point aimed at, the regiments were broken up and retreated in disorder. The lines were re-formed, but the command was ordered to retire to the city.

No language could more perfectly designate the hill close to the Cemetery, and at its southwest corner, and the steep bank of the hill dropping from the little field on the top of it southward towards Hazel Run.

The crest of the bluff not only curved outward generally, but was rough, notched and irregular in outline; so that one company on a part of the crest may have been nearer the enemy than the next company, which advanced into the level-field. The discussion of the question as to who, or what company, of the Thirteenth went nearest to the rebel stone wall is altogether unprofitable — a question of a few feet at most. The writer halted in the field on the top of the bluff; the colors were there also; he saw members of the Regiment to the right and left, and knows them to be so because of the assembly later, and believes that all the companies were about equally represented at the extreme front. The colors were bound to lead and direct, for that is their purpose, the Regiment from right to left dressed on the colors, and any bend in the line was but slight. The honor of the Regiment rests with the colors, and the colors went deep into the level field on the top of the bluff. Though the line of the Thirteenth was somewhat disordered by the deep mud, the first volley from the enemy and the sudden break to the rear made by a small body of troops in our front, all occurring within a few minutes; still every company held its position as a whole, and mounted the plateau, or moved forward into the little field at the top; and this fact is sustained by the positive statements of all the company commanders later made, while discussing the incidents of the charge, each company in the line coming up to about the same point of nearness to the rebel stone bank-wall.

Though quite a number of the men of the Thirteenth were about the colors on the field at the extreme front under the Confederate cannon, the writer has been unable to recall with sufficient clearness the name of any companion who was there at the time excepting Peter Smithwick of E, and he has had no communication with Smithwick since the war closed, till now. To test his memory on the point, the writer requested Quarter-master Morrison to ask C. A. Stiles, Esq., of Wilton, N. H., to interview him in reference to the incidents of the charge, Mr. Stiles being furnished with the items of fact requiring substantiation, but Smithwick not being informed as to them or as to what was the purpose of the interview. This was done about the first of March, 1887. Such personal items well authenticated are very desirable in a history of this form; a history in which the officers and men together tell the story of the Regiment. Smithwick has been an unfortunate man, but is honest to a fault. The following was the result of the interview:

"Wilton, N. H., March 10, 1887.
Lieut. S. Millett Thompson, Providence, R. I.

Dear Sir: When the assault was made on Marye's Heights and the stone wall on the evening of Dec. 13, 1862, by Gen. Getty's Division, I went with the colors of the Thirteenth N. H. V., and also with a number of the men of the Thirteenth, a considerable distance beyond the point where we received the first heavy volley of the rebel musketry fire, and until the firing became so severe and near that we were ordered to lie down; when we did so, falling and lying flat on our faces upon the ground, with our heads towards the enemy; it seems to me we were there nearly half an hour before the firing ceased and we were ordered to retire. While we were lying there on the ground I heard something strike you — S. M. T. — or a book you had, with a hard thump, and I reached forward and pulled at your foot, and asked if you were hurt, or killed, or words to that effect, and you answered ' No.'

I also remember that while we were lying there, the gun wads or cartridge bags from the rebel cannon fell among us burning and stinking, and the men near us tossed them away with their bayonets; we could feel the wind and warmth of the fire of the rebel cannon on our faces and hands, and the place was somewhat lighted up by the flashes of the guns.

I remember too that before we left the field up there on the front where we laid down, we looked about for the wounded, and found no one dead or alive nearer the rebel guns than we were, and we left no one lying there. After retiring, the Regiment was re-formed near the bank, where there was a large number of dead bodies lying about on the ground. Very truly yours,

(Signed) PETER SMITHWICK.
(Signed) Witness, C. A. STILES."

In reference to the above statement and the interview, Mr. C. A. Stiles writes: " Peter Smithwick is very clear in his remembrance. He says it was Orderly Thompson that told him to lie down when in front of the enemy, as he was so tall. It would be impossible for the story to be told so nearly alike unless they (Smithwick and Thompson) were both on the spot. He is very clear in all that he has signed."

It is officially claimed that the Thirteenth was under fire, in the assault, for forty minutes; and that its dead lay within one hundred and twenty feet, officially verified, of the enemy's cannon. Lieut. Staniels writes in his diary: " Our Brigade ordered into action at sunset, charged, withdrew at about nine, and bivouacked on the field." We take the following from Capt. Julian's letters written from the front:

" The Thirteenth was under fire both hot and heavy, for about forty minutes, in the night assault of Dec. 13; and we were for the most of that time within about fifty yards from the enemy concealed behind a stone wall, but they could see every man of us. We labored under a great disadvantage in the assault, having a regiment, the 25th N. J., in front of us, which broke and fled, breaking back through our ranks. Had it not been for this regiment in front, the Thirteenth would have seen the other side of that stone wall. We went nearer to the enemy than any other regiment that participated in the fight at this place. The night was dark, and we were so near the enemy it was impossible to rally the men while at the extreme front. I tried to do so till I found myself standing alone in an open and level space of ground, not many rods distant from the enemy and slightly in advance of the colors ; and then thinking discretion the better part of valor, I laid down as the rest were doing, piled my roll of blankets and haversack in front of my head to protect it so far as they would, and there remained near half an hour between the two fires, and cross-fire, of both the enemy and our own troops.

"Shot, shell and musket balls made merry music around me, and some of them came very near me, but I was not struck. The enemy fired among us an immense number of bullets, or some small contrivance, that exploded as they struck, giving forth little flashes of flame and sounding like fire-crackers, also bounding from the ground and flashing in the air above us and on all sides. Company E was the Color-company. We advanced the colors a number of yards into the field above the top of the bluff and brought them off with us in safety. I took into the fight that night an Enfield rifle captured from a rebel picket, one of the two taken by Company E on the night of Dec. 11. I meant to have preserved this musket and sent it home as a relic of the battle, but intrusted it to the care of one of the men, who lost it, greatly to my regret."

CAPT. JULIAN.

We are also pleased to give the following from Lieut. (then First Sergeant) Charles M. Kittredge of Company B, the second company from the right of the Thirteenth, and commanded by Capt. Elisha E. Dodge:

"It was dusk when the Thirteenth moved over the R. & F. Railroad, and dashed across the level field towards Marye's Heights. The most of the heavy guns had ceased firing; the rebel pickets were troublesome; but without any opposition from the intrenched enemy, we crossed the field, turned to the right, and charged directly up a steep bluff in front of the famous stone wall. The left wing had necessarily the longest distance to go, because of the swing to the right, and before we reached the top of the bluff the ranks of the 13th had become somewhat irregular and broken. The increasing darkness, the mysterious silence of the enemy, and the evidences of defeat and destruction all about us, were by no means inspiring. Repeated orders were heard from the line officers to 'Dress on the Colors;' and all along the line brave officers and men were rallying to the old Flag, and pressing to the front. Company B had hardly reached the crest of the bluff, with a part of the 25th N. J. just in front of us, when a low muffled order was passed along the Confederate line, distinct, firm, deliberate, and dreadful to our ears, 'Ready, Aim — Fire!'

"The next instant came the flash, and by its light we could distinctly see, directly in our front, a solid column of 'Gray Jackets,' behind a wall, in dense ranks, three or four men deep, with guns aiming over each other's shoulders.[1] The terrific volley bowed the men of the 25th N. J., and swayed them, like a swath of grass cut with the scythe, and back down the slope they came, upon and through the ranks of the Thirteenth. Company B was almost literally buried for a few moments, by the terrified and wounded. To add to the confusion, the rebels kept up a rapid fire, which was returned by some of our own men, who were below us and could not discern, in the darkness, friend from foe. We were for a time between two leaden fires.

---

[1] From the contour of the ground Company B must have been well up beyond the general line of the crest of the bluff in order to have seen the rebels' heads at all, and even nearer the wall than Lieut. Kittredge imagines.

"When I succeeded in freeing myself from the heap of the fallen, I was minus my military cap and had a bayonet wound near my right eye, and a war mark across my forehead. Just then I heard the command of that brave and noble man, Capt. Dodge, as he stood above the crest, ringing out clear and sharp above the noise of the musketry, 'Company B — Fall in!' He repeated the order several times, as I stood by his side, but the darkness and confusion were too great to form the broken and scattered ranks. The day's work was done. The battle of Fredericksburg was ended, and only the groans of the wounded and dying could be heard, and the noise of the firing, as in silence and sadness we groped our way back towards the city, and in fragments of companies encamped in the lowlands. We must have gone nearer to the Confederate lines than any other troops. I do not think we were more than from thirty to fifty (30–50) yards from the stone wall when we received that terrible volley. The rebel order to fire was as distinctly heard as though it had been given by our own officers, and it was given in a very subdued tone of voice; and when that flash revealed the mass of slouched hats, and glistening gun barrels and bayonets, it seemed as though we could almost shake hands with the rebels. Certainly their nearness was extremely uncomfortable to us, and I believe that had the order to fire been delayed but a few seconds, and the rebels aimed very low, there would have been a great loss of life, and the happy reunion of the Thirteenth New Hampshire would hardly have taken place on this side of the Rappahannock."

LIEUT. KITTREDGE.

It is also very gratifying to hear from Capt. Betton on these points; he states:

"My Company, K, then having nearly its full number of men, was on the extreme left of the Thirteenth in this charge, being the second ranking company. When the oblique movement to the right was made, Company K was compelled to move more rapidly than the rest, as the Regiment swung to the right, in order to dress on the colors. Just before the enemy fired the first volley at us, Lieut. E. W. Goss, very enthusiastic as usual, sprang to the front of the left of the Company, waved his sword, and called upon the men to follow him, and he was about a rod in front of the Company when the volley came. The bullets flew past him without harm. Many believe that he got nearer the stone wall than any other man in the Regiment, and surely he was among the nearest. The three men on the left of my Company, Henry G. Thompson, John Harmon and John K. A. Hanson, were captured. They approached to a point from which they could not retreat, and were captured when the enemy threw out his skirmish line. We got within about twenty yards of the stone wall. John C. Stevens, who was Thompson's file-leader, says that Thompson was hurt; and Stevens and Henry S. Paul think that the Regiment was not more than three rods from the enemy when they fired the first volley. Robert W. Varrell carried the National colors into the charge. He was a very large man, weighing about 300 pounds. He dropped the colors, and some one else brought them off the field. He claimed that he was hurt. He rapidly fell away to a mere shadow of his former self, and did no duty after the battle."   CAPT. BETTON.

These extracts from letters written at the front and statements clearly indicate the general belief concerning the Thirteenth's nearness of approach to the rebel stone wall. A few incidents of this day, Dec. 13, 1862, which goes into history as the day of chief interest in the Battle of Fredericksburg, may not be out of place.

While we are lying on the bank of the river near the Gas Works this morning, one of the enemy's large shells is seen to burst among a company of a hundred or so of Union soldiers, coming down the road to the ponton bridge, on the Falmouth bank. Many of them fall, some are hurt, but every man rises to his feet, and marches along upon the bridge. The most wonderful instance of hair-breadth escapes the writer ever saw.

While here, too, even in the midst of the shelling, the shells constantly flying each way over our heads, the men enter into a contest of stone throwing for amusement; attempting to throw a stone across the Rappahannock, where it is said that Gen. Washington did, from the Washington farm to the Fredericksburg shore at the ferry landing, just where the central ponton bridge now is. Many make the trial, but only one succeeds, a huge fellow from Michigan.

It is stated on good authority that during the battle to-day about 100 pickets, belonging to a New Hampshire Regiment, not the 13th, while skirmishing, suddenly offered not to fire another shot, if the rebel pickets would not; the proposition was accepted, the men of both sides ceased firing, threw down their arms, met between the lines, shook hands, and mingled together in conversation for some time. Were then severally ordered back to their posts, and soon went on with the work of war as usual.

One reason given for the failure to carry Marye's Heights, and for the awful slaughter attending to-day's assaults upon them, is that "dashes end in fusillades." On coming near the enemy's lines the Union men receive the enemy's close fire, and immediately lie down and commence firing themselves in reply, and there remain without any shelter, right in the focus of the enemy's fiercest fire, until they are cut to pieces; the few survivors having to run back to save their lives, if thus they may. If, instead of this, they had kept straight on, they would it is believed, have captured the enemy's works.

During the charge to-night, a man of the 13th is knocked down the bank of a ditch by the concussion of a bursting shell. He is stunned for a time, and on realizing his situation, finds himself held down in the mud by two men, who lie partly on top of him. He asks them to get off, but they do not move quickly enough to suit him. He struggles out from under them, and upon examination, finds them both dead. He has no idea how long he lay among them. Next morning he finds his clothing so much saturated with blood, which at night he supposed to be water, that he is obliged to throw it all away and obtain a new suit. On the whole, an experience he can never forget, though unhurt.

Maj. Storer loses his sword from the scabbard while on the retreat, and does not discover his loss until he reaches the place of bivouac near the city. He at once starts out upon the field again and recovers it.

The enemy's vicious explosive bullets cracked, flashed and sparkled about us like a shower of fire-crackers in the night, exploding as they struck — hellish little things. The enemy threw samples of all his missiles: grape, canister, shell, minie, round and explosive bullets, and solid shot, and, as the men aver, long pieces of railroad rails.

A large detail goes up on the field to-night, to care for, and to bring off, the wounded. Of course the wounded cannot in many cases be distinguished from the dead, for the night is very dark, and our men must needs carry a lantern. But the enemy fires upon our men with the lanterns, whenever the lights are exposed. Not all in the Southern army are chivalrous! Asst. Surgeon Sullivan worked all night among our wounded men, and was fired at by the enemy while carrying a lantern in looking after the wounded of the Regiment; he was the only regimental Surgeon with the Thirteenth during the assault, Surgeon Richardson having been ordered to remain at the Hospital in the city.

A reliable man of the 13th writes home : " We went so near the mouths of the rebel cannon, in the assault, that the blaze warmed our faces." Another states : " I am unhurt, but the two men next on my right hand, one man next on my left, and the man behind me, were all hurt; one of them having his gun knocked out of his hand by a canister shot."

The Band of the 13th had a very hard night's work. They joined the stretcher-corps, and followed us to the charge, and kept only a few paces in our rear. The volleys meant for us flew over their heads also. After our return from the assault, they hastily removed the wounded; going up within a few yards of the enemy's front line. They were repeatedly fired upon by the enemy, but continued in the work of removing the wounded until after eleven o'clock. One of the Band states that " the fiercest part of the final rush of the Thirteenth and Brigade, and the enemy's worst firing at us, lasted about fifteen minutes." The enemy evidently expected a repetition of our assault, for they threw out no pickets or skirmishers until long after the main body of the Thirteenth had retired from the front, and our wounded had been removed.

The following is copied substantially, as corroborative :

Capt. James A. Sanborn, Historian of the 10th N. H. V., states, that " the plain which we charged across was staked off by the enemy's Engineers before the battle, and the distances marked on the gun-carriages, to cut shell-fuse by." He continues : " The 9th N. Y., Hawkins' Zouaves, were on picket at the front in the outskirts of the city on the night of Dec. 12th, and were relieved by the 10th N. H. on the morning of Dec. 13th. The 10th N. H. drove in the rebel skirmishers, and occupied the railroad and Hazel Run, on the flank. And from their position witnessed the repeated charges, made during the day, upon Marye's Heights.  Just before dark the rest of our First Brigade, excepting Hawkins' Zouaves, came up and joined the 10th N. H. ; and charged just at dark, across the ground where thousands had been repulsed and slain during the day. The Brigade moved across the plain in quick time until the rebel batteries opened, and then at double-quick.  A fence is passed, then a deep ditch, under the tremendous artillery fire, and solid ground is found only to be swept by a perfect monsoon of lead and iron, from the enemy's batteries and lines of battle behind the stone wall.  The Brigade moves forward until the rebel muskets seem to flash in our men's very faces.  Regiments mingle in confusion in the darkness, now only relieved by the flash of the enemy's guns.  Retiring a short distance, the lines of the 10th and 13th N. H. are re-formed, but the attack is relinquished.  The 10th N. H. bivouacked that night in an open field."

The official report of the assault of the 13th on this evening places the losses at two men killed, three officers — Capt. Carter, and Lieutenants Durell and Shaw — and thirty-one men wounded, and six men missing. Total forty-two.  How it was that so many men as there were in the Thirteenth, got into that place, and ever got out again unhurt, is a wonder to all.  It can only be accounted for by the high, wild and excited firing done by the enemy, who "thought that a vastly heavier column was coming upon them."

Six officers of the 13th were absent sick, or on leave.  A few officers, and a number of the enlisted men, the writer among the number, went through the whole battle and on duty all the time, though they had been excused from duty by order of the Surgeon.

After Lieut. M. A. Shaw of Company I was wounded, Lieut. Chas. H. Curtis of Company C was placed in command of Company I on the battle-field.  Sergeant William R. Duncklee of I carried the State colors. He was wounded in the side of the head, but brought his colors off the field, and with them the National colors also, which the other color-bearer had dropped.  Sergt. Amasa Downes of B took the State colors after the return to the railroad.  Sergt. David W. Bodge of B took the National colors.  Duncklee was absent in Hospital about three months.

Our charge is supported by batteries of artillery, which take position about 4.30 p. m. above the town, on the right-hand side of the road to Marye's Hill.  The enemy, however, drive some of these guns away in three minutes.

The writer found a new hatchet in the mud on the wharf, opposite the Washington farm, soon after the column left the vicinity of the city Gas Works for the assault, picked it up, and stuck the handle into his Sergeant's sword-belt.  The hatchet, however, persisted in working out, and to save it he carried it in his left hand most of the way.  As he was off duty, he had to borrow a gun (his own gun having been put on the team at Uniontown, Md., and never seen again).  The bayonet of this borrowed gun fell off and was lost somewhere on the advance to the railroad ; and so he went into the final assault, without a cartridge box or equipments, his Sergeant's straight sword dangling about his legs, the Company's (E) record-book, 14 inches long, 11

The following notes are made from Confederate accounts.

The land rises back of the city like a vast amphitheatre, on whose huge terraced seats is Gen. Lee's Army, occupying parquet, circles, balconies, and far back the highest galleries of all on the crests of the impregnable hills. Gen. Burnside's Army occupying the low arena, or stage, must advance up these semicircling, terraced seats. The chief rebel position near the city is Marye's Hill, located high up between the Plank road and Hazel Run. The next hill to the south of Marye's Hill, and at a distance of about one mile, is Lee's Hill, so called because Gen. Lee's Hdqrs. were established on it during the battle.

The Telegraph road is cut along the east side of Marye's Hill, is about twenty-five feet wide, and is bordered on the side towards the city by a strong stone bank-wall about four feet high — " shoulder high." This road goes around the southeast corner of the hill, turning there at a sharp angle westward. As nearly as can be made out from the rebel accounts, this half a mile or so of stone bank-wall was manned on Dec. 13 by a rebel Brigade and parts of two more, all in the road. They were of Gen. Lafayette McLaws' Division of Gen. Longstreet's Corps, and commanded by Gen. J. B. Kershaw. The 16th and 18th Georgia of Gen. T. R. R. Cobb's Brigade (he was wounded about noon) holding the rebel right. (The writer has been told by Confederate Capt. Henley, referred to on page 54, who was present, that these Georgians fired a volley prematurely,[1] as Gen. Getty's troops appeared above the bank in the night, and that his Regt., the 32d Va., was sent in partly to relieve them, and partly to keep them more steady.) The 24th Georgia of Cobb's Brigade, and the 2d S. C. of Kershaw's Brigade holding the centre. The Phillips Georgia Legion, and the 8th S. C. of Cobb's Brigade, and the 15th S. C. (probably) holding the left. Several other regiments are mentioned, but nothing very definite can be gained as to their distinct positions. The troops on this front were supported by Gen. Ransom's Division, posted not 400 yards to the rear of the stone wall. Gen. Kershaw states officially : " The formation along most of the line (of the stone bank-wall) during the engagement, was *four men deep*." Behind these troops, on both their flanks, and high up all around the sides and crests of the hills, was a very heavy force, a part of it Ransom's Division, supporting McLaws, all within easy rifle shot of the comparatively little space — the stage — in front of Marye's stone bank-wall, where the

---

inches wide and ¾ inch thick, flopping from a strap over his shoulder, a poor gun without a bayonet in one hand, and a shingling hatchet in the other; intending to seize a good gun at the first opportunity, but no other gun came to hand till after the assault. The hatchet did excellent army service for himself, for Sergt. Van Duzee, and for many another man, through the winter camp at Fredericksburg and until after the Siege of Suffolk, when it was sent home, and is still preserved (1887) as a relic. This was the first battle of the Thirteenth !

[1] The line of flame from that first volley was longer than three regiments would ordinarily make, and therefore other troops must have joined in it with the Georgians. — S. M. T.

Union troops charged into the fire of these many thousand rebel muskets, and of the numerous heavy batteries of artillery. The Washington Artillery, Col. Walton, being short of ammunition, had been relieved, on Marye's Hill, before we charged, by Lt. Col. Alexander, with three fresh batteries, who states that he "opened (on us) with canister and case-shot, and this, their last repulse, was said to have been the bloodiest." There were about fifty rebel cannon on and near Marye's Hill.

Gen. McLaws states, officially: "The body of one man, believed to be an officer, was found within about thirty yards of the stone wall, and other single bodies were scattered at increased distances until the main mass of the dead lay thickly strewn over the ground at something over one hundred yards off, extending to the ravine." [1]

We now return again to the account of the Thirteenth.

After the charge the Reg. retires to a field in the edge of the town, halts there a while, and then goes to its old place on Caroline street in the city, and remains there until it goes on picket the night of the 15th.

Sergt. Chas. W. Batchellor of D writes home: "We started to the charge about dark Saturday afternoon. The 13th the second in line, the 25th New Jersey the first. They would not stand fire, and we came upon the field first; and the first thing we knew, we were within about six rods of the rebel battery. We dropped on our faces, after giving them a few shots, and laid there until they ceased firing; when we moved off on the other side of the field, and formed the Reg. once more in line. Our men were brave and courageous. I have lived through one of the most dangerous infantry charges ever made on this continent, as to the best authority we can get from old soldiers."

The remark about moving off "on the other side of the field" is very correct; because in the latter part of the assault the 13th obliqued somewhat to the right, northward, and the men, while coming off the extreme front, first swept northward and then went straight back to the R. & F.

[1] The voice of the man who shouted : "Down, Boys — Down!" to Gen. Getty's men as they approached the Confederate lines, came from our right, was heavy and hoarse, though strong, a strange voice, and the writer has queried many times whether it might not have come from the officer mentioned by Gen. McLaws; and who, realizing our danger in the darkness, shouted to us a word of warning, in the supreme moment before his own life went out. Allowing one yard of space in the line to each man, and making the Confederate lines "four men deep" along the half a mile of stone bank-wall, would make the number of Confederates there about 3,500, exclusive of officers. In an interview with Confederate Gen. Lafayette McLaws, in Boston, on Nov. 17, 1886, he informed the writer that he was unable to locate upon the map the spot where the officer above mentioned was found, though he thought he was not far from the Federal left in front of the stone wall. The space along the wall in the road, he said, would not admit a very large force of infantry without crowding, but every foot was occupied; and as the Federals appeared determined to break the Confederate line there, if they could, re-enforcements were marched in whenever the troops engaged there became wearied or arms became foul, hence many changes occurred during the day and evening. Gen. McLaws stated that the Confederate batteries could have broken up the central ponton bridge very easily, but it was not done, partly because of fear that Gen. Burnside would fire the city in retaliation.

Railroad; the assault and retreat together forming a curve or loop towards the north.

Judge R. L. Henley,[1] previously quoted, stated that the little plain, or intervale along the north side of Hazel Run, and over a part of which our Brigade charged on the evening of Dec. 13, was swept by the fire of more than 10,000 Confederate riflemen, to say nothing of the large force of artillery.

Gen. Getty informed the writer in May 1885, while examining the map of the field, that his assault was directed against the angle at the southwest corner of Marye's Hill, about where the southwest angle of the Cemetery wall now stands. He also corroborated the formation as given above of Col. Hawkins' Brigade, and the statement that Col. Harland's brigade was held in reserve along the R. & F. Railroad. He wished to have the statement made in this history that ' his Division formed for the assault behind the Richmond and Fredericksburg Railroad, and in the course of the assault Col. Hawkins' Brigade crossed over the unfinished railroad; Col. Hawkins' Brigade charged alone, and, after returning from the assault, was re-formed behind the same R. & F. Railroad near the point from whence they entered upon the assault, and also near where Col. Harland's Brigade was held in reserve.'

In the foregoing account we have had no disposition to criticise the 25th New Jersey; many of its officers exerted themselves to the utmost to keep their Regiment in line when the muddy swamp was struck, and a large part of it did hold together. The first volley took more effect among the men of the 25th, and their losses were much larger than in the Thirteenth. They claim to have advanced to within fifty paces of the rebel stone wall, and this establishes our advance to a point still nearer.

The fact that many Confederates moved in and out of the Telegraph road during the day and evening, the reliefs being frequent, will account reasonably for the claim made by such great numbers of them that they fought behind the famous stone wall. A large number have a right to say, "Er'ekn fer shuah, er war thar."

The writer remembers distinctly that the railroad bank, behind (on the city side of) which the Thirteenth and other regiments in our Brigade were re-formed after the assault, had upon it a lot of old railroad ties, and still showed the little hollows from which ties had been removed; and that there was no assembly of, nor attempt to re-form, the Thirteenth behind the unfinished railroad, which at that time was merely an affair of low banks and muddy ditches.

[1] Judge Henley, when holding a Captain's commission in the 32d Va., came near being captured at a farmhouse, where he happened to be one night when a party of Union officers came and occupied a part of the house for the purpose of holding a consultation. Securely hiding, however, he overheard the details of the contemplated raid by Generals Kautz and Wilson against the Danville and other Southern railroads. Succeeding in making an early escape, he at once wrote to Gen. Lee of the contemplated movement. This led to the disasters to the Union cavalry at Reams' Station and vicinity in May 1864; and as a reward for this special service, Gen. Lee promoted him at once to the rank of Major.

Our charge was in and across the ancient bed of the Rappahannock, it is said, now occupied in part by the north bank of Hazel Run. It was noted, both during the day and during the assault, that one huge rebel cannon out-bellowed all the rest. Cannon fired directly at you at a little distance, in the night, look something like instantaneous reddish flashes of the sun while rising. They instantly wink out huge, glaring, dazzling eyes, and the next second shut them in midnight blackness. Then follows the report, and the scream and crash of the shell.

Whoever visits the Fredericksburg battle-field can point to the little field at the extreme western end of the bluff and plateau, and just across the Telegraph road from the south end of the terraced slope of the National Cemetery, and truthfully assert: Deep into that little level field and close to that bank-wall, came the Colors of the Thirteenth New Hampshire Regiment, when Gen. Getty's Division made their night assault on Marye's Heights; reaching a point nearer to the Confederate lines along this front than the Colors of any other regiment in Gen. Burnside's army.

During our charge, says a witness: "The fury of the fire, on both sides, suddenly redoubled, and for half an hour the din was awful, the fighting severe, and the sparkle and flash, of musketry and cannon, a grand display — then all was still."

The best description of the scene of our charge on Marye's Heights, that the writer has met with, is the following:

"At sunset Gen. Sumner made a grand attack: Humphrey, Morrill, Getty, Sykes, or at least a portion of their Divisions, were gathered under the hill. Getty made a flank movement, and forced the rebels to leave the stone wall at the foot of the crest, which they had held all day, and from which they kept up an annoying fire.[1] The sun had gone down, the daylight was fading away. Our own light artillery opened a rapid fire. The hillside, the plain, the thicket, Marye's house, the crest of the ridge, the second range of hills beyond, sparkled, flashed and blazed with the rebel fire. There were twenty thousand flashes a minute; rifles, muskets, cannon, shells. A continuous rattle, and deep, heavy rolls of musketry, with the heavy pounding of two hundred cannon all along the (rebel) line, and our own heavy guns, on the northern (Stafford) side, pouring their heaviest fire upon the rebel positions. The column cleared the wall, the houses, the thicket, almost reached the top of the hill; then weakened, exhausted, were forced to relinquish all they had gained. Of all the battles I have witnessed, I have seen none where the fire equaled that which was poured upon Sumner's command. The new troops, as a general thing, fought as bravely as the veterans." CARLETON.

Dec. 14. Sun. Pleasant. Very cold last night; a bitter, damp, benumbing cold for the wounded left on the field. Reg. comes into the city early to its former place on Caroline street. There is a comparative

---

[1] Not the bank-wall along the Telegraph road — another, a field wall. See page 58. — S. M. T.

quiet all day on our front, excepting occasional severe skirmishing, more noisy than effective. Many buildings are turned into hospitals, and the wounded, dying and dead are all about the city. Many of the wounded are being removed across the river and beyond cannon shot, a constant procession of them. It is a sad, sad Sunday, for there is not an unbroken regiment in the army, and here and there along the lines in the street in our vicinity are little clusters of musket stacks, representing a quarter, third, or half a regiment now surviving; the rest are lying dead along the bloody slopes in front of Marye's Hill, or wounded in the hospitals, or, possibly worse, are on their tramp to a Southern prison. The distant firing nearly ceases by 8 p. m., and the men are allowed to occupy the houses, near by our place on the street, for sleeping; Sergeants being required to know exactly where to find their respective squads at a moment's notice, if they are wanted. To-day Gen. Burnside proposed to head the 9th Army Corps himself, and to rush them, a solid column of 15,000 men, directly upon Marye's Heights. The order was actually given, and the positions assigned, but the scheme was abandoned. The hour was set at 8 a. m., and Col. Hawkins' Brigade, ours, was to lead Gen. Getty's Division; but it is said that Col. Hawkins told Gen. Burnside that it was sheer folly for a dozen or twenty Regiments to attempt to do what sixteen Brigades had tried and utterly failed to accomplish. Other commanders remonstrated so vigorously that Gen. Burnside gave up the idea. Well for us that he did!

"I was on the field of our assault until late last night looking for the wounded of our Regiment. The lantern I carried the rebels fired at repeatedly, and it was necessary to keep it covered as much as possible. We advanced in our search very near to the rebel lines along the stone wall, and I know for a certainty that no Union men, wounded or dead, were lying any nearer to the stone wall than the men of the Thirteenth, all the wounded of whom were found and brought off."

Asst. Surgeon Sullivan.

Dec. 15. Mon. Pleasant, but cool. Heavy firing is heard on the left. The Thirteenth remains in the city on Caroline street during the day. Some heavy siege guns re-opened fire to-day, making a great deal of noise, and in the midst of it a white woman appears in the street, with two small children, coming as unexpectedly among the soldiers as if they had rained down, and all three of them frightened more than half to death. They must have remained in hiding during the bombardment of Dec. 11th and the whole Federal occupation of the city. The sudden opening of the siege guns may have suggested to them the possibility of a second bombardment. They are immediately cared for properly, and sent at once to a place of safety. A number of negroes, men, women and children, for the sake of freedom, hid, remained in the city and braved the terrible bombardment, some of them being killed; but the white population fled, almost every one.

The writer, now a First Sergeant, about half a dozen other men, and two commissioned officers of the Thirteenth, have actually been off duty, by orders of the regimental Surgeon, during all the march through Maryland and all this battle of Fredericksburg, but still have kept with the Regiment; and went into the charge on the night of Dec. 13, hardly knowing what else to do. One of these men was so much used up in the charge, that he returned from it leaning on a comrade for support. All, however, are much benefited by the excitement and activity in the city, since nearly all are suffering, like the writer, from the effects of exposure and malaria. Being thus "off duty," the writer on Friday, Sunday and Monday (12, 14 and 15), visited the various parts of the city.

The city is terribly smashed and shattered. Many buildings have been burned. Houses, in which shells have burst, are a mere heap of rubbish. The Baptist church (said to be) has more than thirty holes through it. Some of the streets are impassable because of the piles of brick, timber, boards and rubbish. There has been some vandalism, but less than one would expect. A large jewelry store has been completely cleaned out of everything worth taking, and the articles scattered. Cheap pins and buttons are just now fashionable in the army. Everything is done, that can be, to prevent pillage and destruction. There is a story that one man on leaving the city buried his valuables, and Western soldiers have been nosing about extensively, hunting for fresh earth and indications.

A lookout posted in the church belfry are visited by a solid shot from the enemy which rings the bell, one loud clang, and scares them half out of their wits for a moment.

The writer takes a fine view far and wide from this church steeple, but is very much winded by the climbing. An officer at the church door tried to prevent the visit, but yielded. The great battle-field is in view from this high steeple. There are puffs of smoke suddenly rising, large and small, from cannon and musket, in the distance, all along the country back of the town; bodies of Union troops are moving towards the front; bodies of Confederate troops are moving in rear of their lines, and away to the right there is heavy musketry firing. In a field, up on the left, a few hundred, apparently about half a regiment, of our cavalry, dash out with glistening sabres, and make a spirited charge. They are in sight but a minute, and raise clouds of smoke and dust. Our batteries along the Falmouth shore are busy and grim, and noisy, in fact there seem to be hundreds of cannon in play. The enemy's lines on the hill show much fresh earth, and the enemy are also active and noisy. A battle is a terrible scene; but a battle-field seen at a distance presents no signs of death. We do not recognize the wounded, and the dead are not distinguishable from the living who are lying still. The writer is admonished that it is time to go down, and leaves a five-minute view never to see the like again. Safely down in the streets again he visits the 6th N. H., and has a long chat with Lt. Col. Pearsons; than whom few better and braver men ever drew sword in America.

Here and there in the yards about the houses, men are lying, in many places half a dozen or more together, with their coat-capes thrown up over their faces — dead. A cellar is shown, where a number of women and children had gone for protection. A shell burst in their midst, not known whether a rebel or a Union shell; but upon the occupation of the city by our troops, it is said that the bodies of ten women and one child were found here, dead, all killed by pieces of shell. Several women and children were found alive hidden in cellars; some in cisterns; one woman was found in a well. The enemy left many of their dead, and a few of their wounded, in the city. A soldier looking for wood in a back yard, in the dark, stumbles over three dead bodies, and not caring to repeat such an experience, secures his wood elsewhere. Another Union soldier, on the same night, looking for wood, finds a long strip of board, places one end upon a log, and is just in the act of jumping upon it, to break it, when the log calls out: "What in — are you at?" This was the night of Dec. 11th, dark as Egypt. The log, a wounded man, spoke just in the nick of time. So are the horrid and the ridiculous jumbled together in the army. About a dozen officers, names not known, sit down to dinner in a small out-door dining-room with many windows. A shell comes down through the roof, down through the table, and down through the floor into a sort of cellar beneath, all done in a twinkling; about as quickly there is a row of boots sticking in at the windows, all around the room, as the officers all scramble out — forthwith. Waiting a little, they reconnoitre, return within, and finish their dinner. The shell is a rebel solid shot. Some of the men of the Thirteenth, together with others in the Brigade, find a spirited Irishwoman, a wild maid of Erin, with huge snaggle teeth, which sometimes indicate a snaggle temper, and finding a kitchen well fitted up, ask her to cook some bread for them. She puts her brawny fists upon her hips, arms akimbo, and swears by all the frogs and snakes out of Ireland that she is not a cook, and will not cook for 'yes blatherin' Yanks.' They threaten to duck her in the Rappahannock, if she does not cook immediately. She cooks; and confesses that she has served as a cook for some skedaddled city nabob. Her biscuit are excellent.

At dark to-night the Thirteenth moves to the front, and is placed on the outer picket line, running along the railroad, and in front of it, and southward on both sides of Hazel Run. Here too the enemy is persistently endeavoring to press our pickets back, and a lively fusillade is kept up all night. We fully realize the fact that we are a part of the rear-guard of Gen. Burnside's army in retreat, and that the responsibility and danger is very great; a sudden dash of the enemy down that little hill can capture us all. There is one important idea that rarely gets a firm lodgment in a soldier's mind, and is a most potent encourager of equanimity: Your enemy is also afraid — of you. More than once during the night, when the little spurts start up in the firing, chiefly with the few U. S. Sharp-shooters near us on the line, our men almost instinctively fix bayonets, in grim determination not to budge an inch if the enemy comes. These sharp-shooters are the last troops to be withdrawn.

A few men who pass the night, where they had been posted by the officer in charge of the picket, under the shelter of a little ridge, where an old fence had stood, on an otherwise smooth hillside, find that they cannot rise, when the order comes to withdraw, on account of the enemy's close fire; and as the only way to save themselves, they throw their rolls of blankets, and everything they have to carry, excepting their guns and the equipments buckled upon their persons, as far as they can down the hill, and then go on hands and knees down after them, gather their effects in a bundle, and move off as best they may. The writer was one of these, and recalls the two or three minutes occupied in gaining the cover of the ridge where the line was waiting, as among the longest minutes he ever experienced. Two or three of the men rolled down the hill, and all have a hearty laugh over the little affair as soon as they are safely beyond the zip, zip, zip of those bullets. Many of our men near Hazel Run have much more difficulty in getting away.

**Dec. 16. Tues.** Pleasant morning; frosty last night. Orders come to the Thirteenth on the vedette and picket line, a little after midnight, to prepare for retreat. Bayonets must be hidden in scabbards, tin dippers and plates must be covered, so that there may not be the least glitter or rattle; guns must be trailed, or carried lower still as held by the strap; the men are to stoop low as they move, and to preserve utter silence, not a word is to be spoken, but orders passed from man to man in whispers; there must be neither sight nor sound of moving. We are finally relieved from picket, a mile or so back of the town, about 3 a. m. Hazel Run is near by. We are near a high broad ridge, and stooping low, trailing arms, and filing in right and left, we soon assemble beneath the ridge and stand there waiting, for some time, in a dead silence. Save for an occasional rifle shot, the whole land is now as silent and still as yonder hideous heaps and windrows of the unburied dead, whose white uncovered faces and torn bodies and limbs fleck the wide, dim and shadowy field of death. 'T is an uncanny hour. The dead are everywhere. We step over and about them. A dozen or two of vedettes,[1] a mere thin fringe of men a rod apart, file towards the left between us and the enemy's lines, where we can now and then see a head as it comes between us and the sky; and where a rebel is occasionally seen to raise his gun, take deliberate aim at some man he sees moving on our line, and to fire, and the badly aimed bullet whistles past, harmless, to the earth. Ticklish business this moving away from the rebel army, now not twenty rods distant, in full force along their chosen lines and strong defenses. The night is just passing into the first gray touches of dawn, a few stars are visible, Gen. Burnside's army is retreating; the greater part of Gen. Lee's army is quietly asleep, but can be roused to action in ten minutes, and throng those near hills and ridges, compelling Burnside to halt, turn back and join unequal fight; two armies, two hundred thousand men, are

[1] U. S. Sharp-shooters from New Hampshire, E Company. See Adjt. General's Report, Vol. II. for 1865, page 748.

now parting company from a terrible and a drawn battle, the Federals — from a field strewn with the mangled bodies of many hundred dead and unburied comrades; each of these two huge armies hourly expects the other to strike again. In the few moments of uncertainty and suspense while we are slipping away, the scene invites the imagination to indulge romance; but the enemy's pickets, who are very near, seeing our vedettes moving, as now and then their heads appear against the sky, open fire with vigor, and their vicious bullets zip, zip, zip to the ground about us, or whistle near over our heads, and we all need our sharpest senses. The enemy probably supposes that we are merely relieving the guards. No serious casualty occurs, and all is still again; a stillness falls that no man feels like breaking even to save his life. Orders are passed in whispers from man to man and we move again, all stepping so softly that not a footfall is to be heard. Soon we catch glimpses of the enemy's long lines of pickets advancing, and firing as they come, then dropping again out of sight, as the few vedettes on our side reply; but we move compactly, cross a muddy brook leading into Hazel Run, breathe freer, march into the city crookedly along the course of a bank of earth, join the Brigade, all done in quick step and in silence, cross the muffled pontons, in a rapid route-step, at 4 a. m., and climb the slippery road up Stafford Heights,— and thus it was all along his line, changing only with circumstance, that Gen. Burnside accomplished one of the most masterly retreats, directly from the face of the enemy, ever made in all history — and that, too, from shore to shore of a rapid river.

In a sudden and severe shower of rain that now comes on, we plod along over the plain in thin mud three to six inches deep, finally entering a bit of brush near the place of our old bivouac, and encamping there at 6.30 a. m., about one fourth of a mile north of the Phillips House. The men of the Reg. were ordered to take sundry supplies with them as they left the city; rations, equipage and stores being piled on the sidewalks where we passed along, with much other army gear; and many a stray roll of blankets, or of old tents, serve them well in the winter camp that follows. Two zealous men of the 13th start from town with a cracker-box between them half filled with sugar. The rain and the sugar find in each other a sweet and juicy affinity, and when the leaky box is opened in camp, there is about a pint of syrup and dregs in one corner. A few boxes of hard tack come into camp, pulp; and as for sundry lots of coffee taken along, it arrives, second-hand — Fredericksburg was an awful failure.

"Companies B, C, and H arrive in camp about 9 a. m. These three Companies were stationed on the outer picket line, on the R. & F. R. R., just where it crosses Hazel Run; Co. B to the right of the railroad bridge, north, and C and H to the left of the bridge, south. Here they held the enemy's pickets back while the rest of Getty's Division evacuated the lower end of the city, and retired across the river. Company H, which I was with and commanding, was the most exposed, and came near being left behind, on their picket posts, after all the other troops had retired, and are now the last Company to rejoin the Regiment in camp."

Lt. Col. Smith.

First Sergeant William H. McConney of C and a few other men stopped in the city for tents and stores to bring to camp, and when they reached the ponton bridge the last boat had swung from its moorings into the stream, and the delayed party had to wade into the river until the water was up to their waists, before they reached the boat and could be pulled into it; the last men of the 13th to leave Fredericksburg.

Our retreat this morning over the central ponton bridge occupies less than two hours for the whole force; in which two hours above 16,000 troops, not to mention unorganized parties, of pioneers, bands and other unarmed men, cross in perfect order. The bridge is muffled with earth three or four inches in depth, and the men march across in the route-step. It must not be forgotten that the enemy's guns have completely commanded this bridge, a portion only being hidden by buildings, none of which are proof against cannon balls.[1] The crossing in retreat is made under the personal supervision of Major Hiram B. Crosby, of the 21st Conn., Provost Marshal of the 9th Army Corps, who has sat on his horse near the bridge, and given the necessary orders to each regimental commander as he passed. "A strong southwest wind blows to-night, 15th, wafting the sound of our army's tramp on this bridge, and the rumble of wagons and artillery, away from the enemy."

Hosp. Steward Royal B. Prescott writes of the battle under date of Dec. 18, 1862, and later (condensed): "The order 'Forward' came to our Brigade, while we were on the river bank, at thirty minutes past four. We went (along the wharf) up the river bank, across the streets, out at the back of the town, down a very steep bank, across a field, up the railroad bank, across the track, on the double quick, with the bullets flying about us. At the railroad we came up in the rear of a regiment, or body of zouaves, lying flat on their faces against the railroad embankment, and we ran directly over them, while they swore at and reviled us without stint, saying, among other things, 'See these countrymen! They have not got the hayseed out of their hair yet.' Their officers cursed them, struck them with their swords, harangued, urged and scolded, but could not get the men upon their feet, and I do not think those men ever crossed the railroad at all.

"Surgeon Twitchell was in Washington, Asst. Surgeon Richardson detailed on the amputating staff to remain in the city, and the Hospital corps was headed by our Asst. Surgeon Sullivan, and halted near the railroad. The Band went forward and returned with some wounded men. Turning for the bag of bandages, brought on the field by our contraband, I discovered that he had skedaddled, bandages and all. I dispatched one of the nurses for him, and the nurse returned with the bandages but not the negro. Our Brigade after crossing the railroad were

[1] See interview with Gen. McLaws, page 72.

ordered to charge on a rebel battery just across the field. Away they went with a yell right up to the earthworks, where they were repulsed by the rebel infantry behind a stone wall. As the wounded were brought back, we were positively forbidden to light a candle or even a match. It was now quite dark. That charge ended the fight of the day. We of the Hospital Dept. remained on the field until midnight, by which time all of our wounded, who could be found, were brought in, carried on stretchers to the ambulances, and thence to the city. I was in charge of the Band and stretcher men all that night, and when the Regiment withdrew from the field, Col. Stevens told me to take a lantern and look among the dead and take the names of any of our Reg. I might find and do what I could for them, and adding that in the morning there would be a flag of truce and ambulances to take them away. Charles W. Green of Company B was alone with me in this work. We found Lieut. Shaw and Capt. Carter, and several men. I finally extinguished the light in my lantern after being sworn at by our wounded men on the field for drawing the enemy's fire. We worked until the morning was well advanced.

"Sunday I was in the Hospitals. Surgeons with sleeves rolled up, with bloody arms and hands, were busy with saw and knife. Arms and legs were scattered about the floor, and streams of blood flowing in all directions. The streets were crowded with troops and hospital flags were flying from the windows of houses. The Surgeons went across the river Sunday noon, and I was left with about fifty sick and wounded men to cross at night. I remained in the city until 4.30 a. m. Tuesday 16th, and then started the nurses, the sick, the Band, and the stretcher men across the river. The rebels stripped all our dead of everything, leaving them lying naked on the ground.

"My experience with the Band of the Thirteenth on this occasion was exciting. The Thirteenth, I believe, was the last regiment (or regimental organization) to re-cross the central ponton bridge, the pioneers waiting for us before taking up the planks and releasing the boats. As we marched through the city our progress was lighted up by the flames of huge stacks of provisions burning in the streets, having been set on fire to prevent their falling into rebel hands. As we neared the river some one cried out, 'Where's the Band?' The question was taken up and ran rapidly through the ranks, 'Where's the Band?' 'Where's the Band?' No one could tell. In the hurry no one had taken any thought of the musicians, and it was certain they were in the city. At length some one remembered seeing the bass drum standing outside one of the negro huts in rear of the house occupied by Col. Stevens. Turning to me, the Colonel ordered me to go back quickly, and hasten the Band down to the river. I flew back with all speed through the deserted city, and as I did so the moon shone brightly out from masses of dark clouds, revealing with horrible distinctness the ghastly faces of the rebel dead strewn thickly about. I finally reached the house, and to my great joy saw the bass drum standing just outside the door of one of the negro quarters. I pounded on the closed door with might and main, and shouted to the sleepers within to arouse and bestir themselves or they would all be taken prisoners. For a little time there was no response, but as the pounding continued, a drowsy voice at length asked: 'What is wanted?' I answered: 'Get up, quick, or you will all be made prisoners. The army is all across the river and you are here alone!' As this was taken as a joke, the sleepy voice replied, requesting me to go to sundry places much warmer than Fredericksburg, and again all was quiet. I then seized a large stone and hurled it with all my strength against the door, which tore it from its hinges and it fell with a loud crash upon the floor. This brought every man at once to his feet; and when the situation was fairly comprehended by their lethargic brains, the 'hurrying to and fro' was lively indeed. A few of them almost forgot to take their instruments, while the time made to the central ponton bridge was one of the quickest on record." PRESCOTT.

And so ends the first battle fought by the Thirteenth — a failure in every respect; and the ranks of the Reg. are thinned by losses, in killed, wounded, and prisoners, of three officers, and thirty-nine men. To add to our vexation, a lot of the men's knapsacks and their contents, left here at the bivouac near the Phillips House while we were in the city, are soaking wet, through and through; and many have been pilfered of articles of especial value to the owners, and there are murmurings loud and deep. Our experiences, all through, are outrageous and exasperating to the last degree, and now we camp, wet, cold, ugly and tired out, in the nastiest of nasty Virginia mud. A third of the men, and eleven officers, are unfit for duty, sick. One thing, however, we shall never forget: We of Gen. Getty's Division and of Col. Hawkins' Brigade made the most hopeless and the last infantry charge in the battle, the closing charge of the Battle of Fredericksburg.

The chief day in the battle was Saturday December 13, when the roar of the firing commenced at 9 a. m. and continued almost unceasing until the charge of Gen. Getty's Division brought on its most furious thunders at early night. After this charge the firing ceased. Meanwhile for over eight hours our Division stood between the artillery fires of the two armies, exposed to much of both. The battle of Saturday raged for ten hours, counting from beginning to close. That the losses in the Thirteenth during the charge in the night were no greater may be counted as one of the fortunes of war; and attributed in great measure to the fact that the rebel infantry fired high and wild. We could see their heads and arms above the stone wall along the Telegraph road, and they worked with the utmost rapidity, as if number of shots, and not accuracy of aim, was the first consideration; and we could hear their officers urging and hurrying them during the whole of their firing.

One writer states (in corroboration) that the Thirteenth with its Brigade held the lower part of the city on the night of Dec. 11; in the charge on the evening of Dec. 13, of Hawkins' and Harland's Brigades,

Hawkins formed his Brigade in two lines, the Thirteenth on the right of the second line; Hawkins assaulted, and Harland remained near the railroad in reserve; a terrific volley was received when our lines, in the charge, came up to within a few yards of the enemy's works at the point aimed at; and on the night of Dec. 15, while Gen. Getty's Division retreated across the river, the Thirteenth held the outer picket line on both sides of Hazel Run and along the railroad, and lively firing was kept up with the enemy's pickets during the latter part of the night.

The following, from Rev. Augustus Woodbury's "Burnside and the Ninth Army Corps," may be of interest. General Burnside organized the Army of the Potomac in three Grand Divisions of two corps each: left, Franklin; centre, Hooker; right, Sumner. (The 13th in Sumner's Grand Division.) On Dec. 10, the morning report gives the force of the army as 111,834 officers and men, and 312 guns. Of these Sumner's Grand Division numbers 22,736 officers and men, and 60 guns, and consists of the 9th Corps, Gen. Wilcox, and 2d Corps, Gen. Couch. Wilcox's division commanders were Generals Getty, Sturgis and Burns. About 100,000 officers and men of the Union army actually engaged in the battle. The battle opened early on the morning of Dec. 11, and after several attempts to build the central ponton bridge had failed, owing to the severe rebel fire, the attempts being made while the bombardment was going on, volunteers from the 7th Michigan, 19th and 20th Massachusetts Regts. crossed in boats, the 50th N. Y. furnishing oarsmen. A party from the 89th N. Y. also crossed. After a half hour's fight, under the eye of Gen. Burnside himself now down on the river bank, the city was captured about four o'clock in the afternoon.

The bridges were now quickly completed, and our 1st Brigade, Col. Hawkins, was the first to cross into the city over the central bridge. Gen. Sumner's Grand Division crossed on the 12th. In the dispositions, our 9th Corps on its left connected with Gen. Franklin's right. During the battle Gen. Sumner's Hdqrs. were at the Lacy House; Gen. Burnside's at the Phillips House, which was Gen. Sumner's Hdqrs. after the battle. Gen. Sumner's Grand Division was to move out on the Telegraph and Plank roads. Gen. Longstreet's Corps occupied Marye's Heights, on which we charged.

On Dec. 13th, the 9th Corps, Wilcox, held the line from the vicinity of Hazel Run south towards Deep Run. Gen. Burns' division on the left, Gen. Getty's in the centre, Gen. Sturgis on the right. Gen. Sturgis' division was sent into the fight about noon, to the right, to support Gen. Couch of the 2d Corps, and advanced and held their ground until night. Sturgis withdrew about 7.30 p. m. About 3 p. m. Gen. Burns' division crossed Deep Run, in support of Gen. Franklin, and could do little but to stand and look on.

Gen. Getty's division, in which the Thirteenth, was held in reserve all day, as a guard to the left of the town; about sundown it moved out, and was formed in two lines under fire, crossed the plain, the R. & F.

Railroad, the canal trench (the unfinished railroad), and some marshy ground, and gained a position on the left of Couch's 2d Corps line, and within less than a hundred feet of the enemy's strongest position. Here a severe fire of the enemy's musketry was added to the artillery, and the first line, Col. Hawkins' Brigade, was forced back under a storm of fire in front and flank. The second line, Col. Harland's Brigade, advanced through a heavy fire of shell and shrapnel to within a short distance from the R. & F. Railroad. Night then settled down. Half a mile beyond the city, the Telegraph road diverges to the left, turning southward. A handsome estate (Marye's) is above this road, near the northern extremity of the first fortified line of hills. The grounds are supported, where they come down to this road, by a heavy bank-wall of stone. On the side (of the road) opposite the same, and toward the city, is a similar wall of stone, in length nearly half a mile. The Telegraph road, after leaving the Plank road, winds along the edge of the second terrace (or ridge of hills) southward, and crosses Hazel Run, thence turns westward into the country beyond. The lawn in front of the Marye mansion was crossed by a line of rifle-pits, and in the southerly part of the grounds was a small redoubt. There were other earthworks on the northerly and westerly side of the Plank road.

At night immediately after Gen. Getty's assault, Gen. Burnside returned to his tent, firmly resolved to renew the battle on the subsequent day. On the morning of the 14th he selected and formed a column of eighteen regiments, of the Ninth Corps, and decided to direct their assault on Marye's Heights in person. Listening to the persuasions and arguments of his Grand Division Commanders, he countermanded the orders, and the attempt was not made.

The losses reported, in these five days of battle, in officers and men, are, killed, 1,339. Wounded, 9,060. Missing and prisoners, 1,530. Total, 11,929. The enemy's total loss, 5,309. The enemy having the advantage in position, and fighting almost wholly behind entrenchments or natural cover, while the Union Army assailed his positions from open ground.

Lossing states that the Confederate army numbered 80,000 strong, with 300 cannon. The Union losses were, in Hooker's Grand Division, 3,548, Franklin's 4,679, Sumner's 5,494, with 50 engineers. Killed 1,152, wounded 9,101, missing 3,234, total 13,487. The Confederate loss was about half that of the Union loss.

Capt. F. Phisterer gives the Union losses: killed 1,180, wounded 9,028, missing 2,145, tofal 12,353. Total Confederate losses 4,576.

The accounts are thus seen to differ somewhat, but the Union loss may be placed roundly at 12,000 men, and the Confederate loss at about one half that number. It may be proper to add here that the items on page 71, drawn from Confederate official reports, were written in 1884, and the maps, and their descriptions, were made in 1885; both long previous to any of the recent (1886-7) popular publications relating to this battle.

Confederate Gen. James Longstreet's account in the *Century* of August 1886, with accompanying map, places the charge of Gen. Getty's Division as follows: from the south side of the R. & F. Railroad, well down towards Hazel Run, across the meadows lying along the north side of that Run, across the trenches of the unfinished railroad (but no canal), to the portion of the plateau southwest of the brick house, and to the southwest end of that plateau where it reaches up to the Telegraph road and the stone bank-wall along the side of it — the course of the south arrow on his map. All this in direct corroboration of the location of the position, as seen by the writer on the night of the charge and remembered clearly, and also recognized by him on visiting the spot in May 1885, and of the statements made to the writer by Gen. Getty.

Gen. Longstreet states that there were over seven thousand Federals, killed and wounded, lying in front of Marye's Hill.

"Nearly all the dead were stripped entirely naked by the enemy. A woman who lived in one of the houses near the stone wall said: "The morning after the battle the field was blue; but the morning after the Federals withdrew the field was white." *Century.*

The legend of poetry, romance and horror will cling in the popular imagination to the battle of Fredericksburg forever, notwithstanding all its failures; for its figures and scenes were large and bold, its actors courageous in the extreme, their experiences pitiable to the last degree, and unfortunate beyond compare; while local superstition peoples the battle-ground with visiting myriad ghosts of the fierce combatants. The Confederate glory, however, of having been behind that stone bank-wall, in comparative safety and unpressed, and in numbers sufficient to overwhelm easily any force of the Union army that could approach, pales into utter insignificance beside the picture of Gen. Barksdale's men fighting among the buildings in Fredericksburg, for many hours on Dec. 11, while Gen. Burnside's batteries were knocking the whole city about their ears, and firing it also in many places. This was courage; only equaled by the repeated dashes of the Union troops against the stone bank-wall at the foot of Marye's Hill.

Dec. 17. Wed. Cold, raw. Reg. in camp, and a miserable camp at that, trying to get dry and warm. There is still considerable firing going on across the river, between the Union and Confederate artillery; and occasionally a stray shell from Marye's Heights flies screaming high and wild over our camp, stirring up the Virginia mud in the distance. We march down near the river about opposite the centre of the city, and support a battery. Pass the night on the frozen ground, without shelter, and in the teeth of the raw, chilling north wind. Two or three Companies from the 13th have this experience every night. The boys find a large potato field, near the batteries, belonging to some careless farmer who harvested only about two thirds of his crop, and we rapidly appropriate what the farmer left. The writer has occasion to visit camp to-day from the batteries, and while going across lots to save distance, observes quite a large white pile of something not far away, somewhat flat and irregular. Curious to see what it is, he goes nearer, and finds it a collection of human legs, arms, hands and feet — one view like that is enough for a lifetime.

"Charles Leathers of Co. F was severely wounded Dec. 13, and lost his gun; but when brought into camp in the ambulance, he had with him about thirty pounds of very excellent tobacco, all of which was purchased by the men of Co. F at a good price."     LIEUT. YOUNG.

Dec. 18. Thurs. Cold, with some snow. Reg. in camp, if we may call it such a nice name. Came here about 4 p. m. to-day. A deep hollow, a long densely wooded ravine, in rear of the Falmouth batteries, and full of soldiers; multitudes of little fires fill the air with smoke, and the boys call this place "Smoky Hollow." This is the headquarters of the pickets, and about one mile nearer the city by the road, than our camp north of the Phillips House. A large detail from the Union army, several men in it from the 13th, one of them George E. Garland of E, unarmed and provided with picks and shovels, go over on the battle-field to-day and bury the Union dead. The men of the 13th help bury about 700 bodies. The enemy have stripped the dead of every article of clothing fit for use, and the bodies are laid away in their last resting place, merely thinly covered with such pieces of blankets or clothing as can be found. So say the men of the 13th burial party.

As a matter of actual measurement some of the dead of the Thirteenth are found, lying where they fell, within forty yards, 120 feet, of the muzzles of the enemy's cannon, Col. Alexander's.[1] A statement is going the rounds of our camp, that the enemy also stripped the clothing from some of our men, who were very badly wounded, while they were still alive, and so left them to die, in the sharp December air, without clothing, shelter, attention or care; as was clearly evident from the marks made by these severely wounded men, in the earth where they lay, after they had been stripped of their clothing. One soldier of the 13th who helped bury the dead says: "Among about seven hundred bodies of our men, who were buried by us, scarcely one had any clothing on which was fit to be worn; all were stripped."

Dec. 19. Fri. Very cold. Thirteenth at work on camp. A large detail on picket near the siege guns on Falmouth bluffs. These men lay on the ground last night while ice formed, over the puddles of water beside them, half an inch thick. The reserve bivouacs in Smoky Hollow. From these guns there is a fine, extended view of the city, and of the

[1] It is claimed that some bodies, of men belonging to Gen. French's Division, were found nearest of any to the stone wall. It should be borne in mind that Gen. Getty's Division charged upon the southwest end of the stone wall, where the road turns the corner westward; while French's Division had charged upon a portion of the stone wall a long way to the north and east of Getty, and near the brick house, and the several roads leading up to the hill where Marye's house stood.

enemy's lines on the hills beyond. Almost every house in the city has smoke issuing from the chimney. More than one family on returning must have found things mixed, even if their house was not smashed to flinders and blown all over the neighborhood.

A great deal of adverse criticism is made upon the bombardment of Fredericksburg, and it is well to state that a demand had been made for its surrender, and had been refused; ample time was given for the removal of all the unarmed people, nearly all of them had abandoned the city, and the city was used by the enemy for direct military purposes; the houses were used to protect the enemy's sharp-shooters, Gen. Barksdale's men, who three or four times drove our pontonniers, with heavy loss, from the ponton bridge they were trying to build, — the fire of our artillery was directed chiefly upon these buildings. Gen. Burnside took unwilling command of the Army of the Potomac, by peremptory order, after he had twice declined; his pontons required for crossing the Rappahannock to the city were delayed until nearly two weeks had passed after Gen. Sumner's advance had reached Falmouth, for which delay Gen. Burnside was in no way responsible; meanwhile the enemy's garrison in the city was largely re-enforced, and Gen Lee, divining Gen. Burnside's purpose, had started his whole army for the heights in rear of the city and vicinity, and a large force had arrived and entrenching begun. The failure of the arrival of the pontons lost to Northern arms the battle of Fredericksburg, " and soaked the streets and lanes of the city with Federal blood."

Gen. Lee had an army present of 80,000 men, and held Marye's Heights with a triple line of works; while the hills, canals, railroad, and the famous Stone Wall, combined, made his position impregnable to assault. The special advantages of his position could not possibly be known to Gen. Burnside. " When our troops found, on the morning of Dec. 16, that Gen. Burnside had retreated across the river, it was a matter of amazement to the whole rebel army." (Confed.)

Dec. 20. Sat. Very cold. Quarter-master Cheney and Capt. Stoodley rejoin the Reg. The Government furnishes a lot of woolen mittens for the men; slack-twisted, loose knit things, consisting of a wrist, a thumb, a hand, a forefinger cot, and a bag, for the other three fingers, shaped like a mule's jaw, and about as large. The men are on short rations now, and have been since the battle.

Dec. 21. Sun. Cold. A part of the Reg., a different detail every night, go out on the bank of the river to support a battery. We lie there on the bleak plain, with no shelter, tents or protection of any kind, and no fires allowed, the weather extremely cold and a high wind blowing from the north. This is our experience these winter nights. A native gives distance in this way : " Right smart go — er'ekn; 'bout three screams and a holler."

Company —, said to be K, loses two kettles of baked beans at Smoky Hollow. In any Regiment except the moral Thirteeeth they would be reported stolen, but here as lost in action. The top joke of the affair is the investigation. A number of men are called up, and have their breath smelled, to detect the odor of baked beans; and this, too, before any of the beans have been eaten. After this conclusive test, the men, who saved the beans after they were lost, warm them over and eat them. It is wickedly reported that Company E loans the fire with which to warm the beans, but no one knows who caused them to be lost. Beans baked with pork always cause trouble.

Dec. 22. Mon. Terribly cold last night. The ground freezes beside the men as they lay, and the pools of water near are covered with ice. Again our pickets have no fires, except now and then a little one, and no shelter at all. Two severe nights. Reg. assembles early this morning at its camp in Smoky Hollow, where we can cook and eat breakfast. We leave this camp for our permanent winter camp this afternoon; arriving there about dark, and too late to see well enough to properly pitch our shelter tents. "We remained in Smoky Hollow, about one mile from camp, near Falmouth depot, three days, returning to our regular camp to-night." ALBION J. JENNESS.

## CAMP OPPOSITE FREDERICKSBURG.

Dec. 23. Tues. Cold, clear. The Thirteenth wakes up this morning in Falmouth Camp, the which no man of the army ever can forget. It soon rejoices in the appropriate names of "Foulmouth Camp," and "Hell-mouth Camp." This morning is very frosty and sharp. Ice formed thick last night, and we make holes through it, on the brook near by, to obtain water for cooking and washing; no other water to be had anywhere near camp this morning. No place here for squeamish stomachs; these pieces of yellow soap (rebel) on these sticks were put here a few months ago, and have been washing into the brook in every rain since that time. That dog's bones have evidently been here in the brook for several months also — pretty white and clean now. That kitchen-midden stuff yonder also improves the water. On the whole a fine place to procure water for coffee, cooking and bathing; rebel soap, rebel dog, rebel wash-tub. Rations poor, quarters poorer, men sick, great discontent, and suffering beyond mention. Our camp rises into a vast city of miserable hovels and tents, containing a hundred thousand inhabitants in every stage of sickness and misery, where for month in and month out no white woman or child is to be seen. Division Inspection, and Review of the 9th Army Corps, is made to-day by Gen. Sumner.

Dec. 24. Wed. Cold, very. We are near the Phillips House, near and on a part of the same camp ground we occupied Dec. 16, and very near where we spent the night of Dec. 10, just before entering Fdsbg. That city is in full view from a point near the camp of the Thirteenth. Almost every night two companies of the 13th go out on picket. No firing on the picket lines. Should the enemy fire upon our men now, our batteries would instantly shell the city. This commands a peace. Here are two huge armies, each of nearly 100,000 men, and each aiming for the other's destruction, encamped side by side, a narrow river only separating them; one is afraid to move, the other dare not, neither can, and so they stay, and keep as quiet as a New England village on Sunday. The pickets frequently cross the river, both ways, and fraternize.

Five or six hundred yards northwest of the Phillips House, that is to the right of the Phillips House as one looks down the road toward Fredericksburg (and directly on the line between the Phillips House and the Clews House situated a mile or two to the northwest of it), a ravine in the field falls to the right, and northward to a brook; the first ravine to the westward and the first brook to the northward of the Phillips House. This ravine was the roadway from camp to the White Oak road running into the city past the Phillips House. Prof. Lowe had his balloon in this ravine a little south of the brook, and we will therefore call it Lowe's Ravine. This brook is the south branch of Claiborne Run; the R. & F. Railroad following the north branch through the bluffs. Go down Lowe's Ravine northward to the brook, turn to the right and follow the brook back eastward up into the country. Just north of the brook is a wide strip of ground sloping southward to the brook and draining into it; really the south slope of the ridge next north of the ridge on which the Phillips House stands. This whole slope is checkered with tent cellars, mixed up, and angling in every direction, as the contour and drainage of the land demanded. Three or four hundred yards up the brook eastward from where Lowe's Ravine and the brook meet is an irregular cluster of tent cellars. The company tents on the north side of the brook looking eastwardly, and the tents of the field and staff on the east side. The brook here turns somewhat towards the north. The ends of the company, or rather division, streets are widest down near the brook, and narrower where they rise upon the slope; though on the whole quite irregular, and thrown upon the curve of the slope something like the ribs of a huge fan. This is the camp of the Thirteenth N. H. Vols.

Company E, the fifth (5th) company from the right of the Regiment, was located on the left, or east side, as one looks towards the brook, of a very deep gully, twelve feet deep at least, extending down towards the brook; the only very deep gully, and the deepest, in the 13th camp, and was called Capt. Julian's 'hole in the ground.' The writer had his tent under a large pine-tree on the east side of this gully, and near the head of it. Capt. Julian's tent was at the head of the gully, across, northward. From the position of Company E on the east side of this deep gully and quite prominent landmark, the huddled tents of the Regiment can be made out. The whole camp-ground is now (1885) covered with a vigorous growth of young trees. The Thirteenth encamped here quite closely massed in divisions, the right of the Regiment to the westward, all facing southward and eastward, and was not crowded upon by the tents of other regiments. Cross the brook eastward and you come upon the cellars of the huts of the field and staff officers, where the earth was ridged up around the log walls of the miserable quarters to keep water out of the cellars, and from the earth floors of the huts. The Hospital tent was on the hill just north of the centre of the line of the company quarters, nearly north of Co. E. Here the many sick men, who could do so, went every morning to receive their allopathic doses ; homœopathic practice being unknown in the army — unless medical supplies ran short. The regimental parade ground was an old cornfield a little northwest, that is to the right and rear, of the camp, and almost exactly due north of the Phillips House. The ground rose gradually northward from the brook, past the camp, to this parade ground, from which a large part of Fredericksburg became visible as the forest fell.

Firewood for camp was obtained from the low ground lying north and west of this old cornfield, some of it brought from a distance of more than a mile on the shoulders of the men. Dry wood was very scarce. The most popular wood was dead laurel, standing densely along the brooks and forks of Claiborne Run ; and hundreds of the roots were carved into tobacco pipes by the men. The Thirteenth was crowded upon a small space near the bend in the brook ; and more than one member of the Reg., and one of the non-commissioned staff in particular, will distinctly remember how an ill-considered leap across this brook resulted in an involuntary and splashing sit-down in it, soiled clothes — and comments on the margin. However, it was a most convenient brook, the water in it perhaps averaging two feet in width by six inches in depth. The men and officers performed their morning toilets here, long rows of them about daybreak ; muddy boots, smutty kettles, and soiled clothing were scrubbed here ; and some huge fools used the water for cooking until strict orders were set to the contrary. 'T was a rich and busy brook of real Virginia water. The camp of the 4th R. I. Vols. was eastward of the field and staff of the Thirteenth, and to the eastward,

---

### DESCRIPTION OF MAP.

A. Rappahannock River.     B. Richmond & Fredericksburg R. R.
C. Orange Turnpike, or White Oak road, passing the Phillips House N.
D. Major Lacy.     H. Hoffman.     N. Phillips House.
F. Ruins of a house.     G. Roy.     K. Claiborne Run.
P. Road to central ponton bridge.
L. Ravine in field where Prof. Lowe had his balloons.
E. Wood road leading from Phillips House and passing north of the camp of the Thirteenth, to Thirstley's house half a mile distant.
M. Camp of Thirteenth, company tents.     R. Tents of Thirteenth, field and staff.     S. Camp of the 4th R. I. Regiment.
T. Fredericksburg.     V. Stafford Heights.

    The whole region about Claiborne Run is rough and timbered, but the timber is most dense near the part of the Run north of the Phillips House.

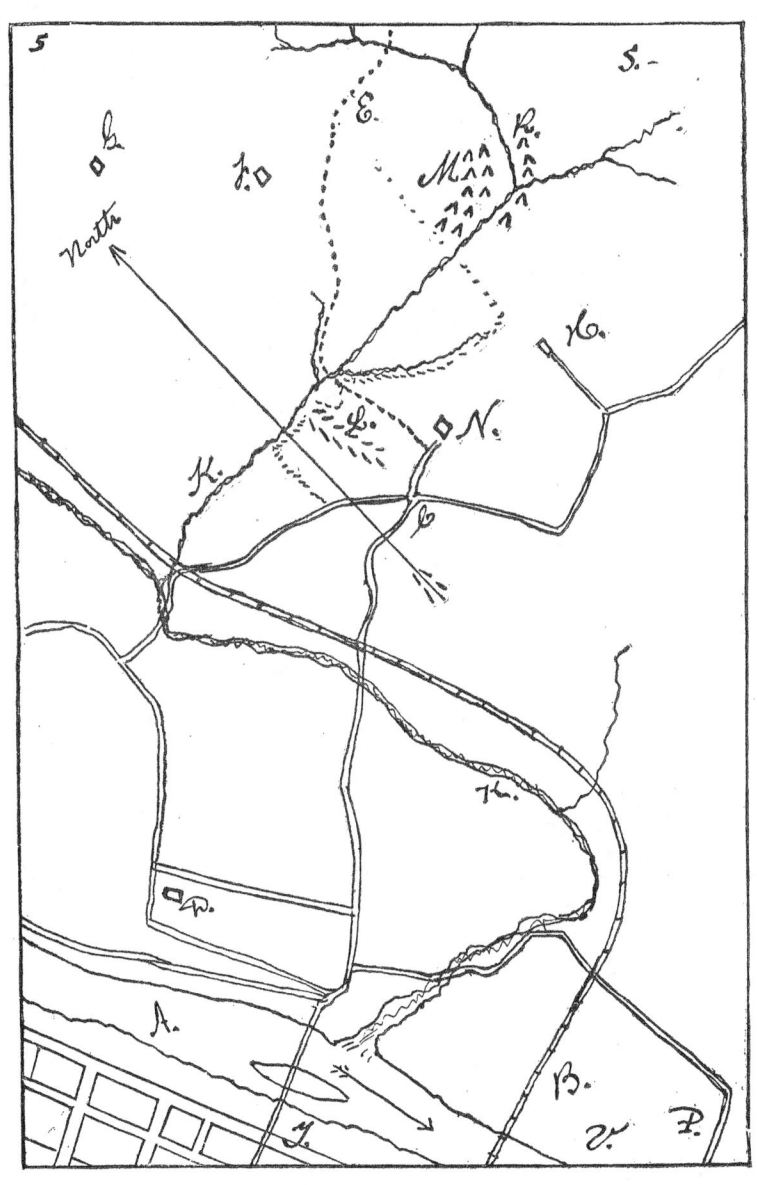

CAMP OPPOSITE FREDERICKSBURG, WINTER OF 1862-3.

Tracing of Official Map. Scale, three inches to one mile. With points located by the writer in May 1885.

rather than northward, of the Phillips House. The land occupied by them being a little higher than the land occupied by the Thirteenth. While visiting the camp, in May 1885, the writer found a mass of iron filings, nails, etc., all concreted by the rust, on the spot where Lowe's balloon was located, and supposed to be some of the ballast or weights used during the ascents of the balloon.[1] It was partly buried in the earth, but after some digging, and pounding with a stone, a piece of the mass was secured, and brought home. Many old pieces of canteens, remains of chimneys, tin cups, and other camp débris are still to be found about our old camping ground, but nearly wasted by the rust and exposure of these many years.

Dec. 25. Thurs. Chilly. The Reg. goes on picket for 24 hours. Yesterday the 13th turned out only about 200 men for Battalion drill, fewer still are fit for active duty to-day. It is fearful to wake here at night, and to hear the sounds made by the men about you. All night long the sounds go up of men coughing, breathing heavy and hoarse with half choked throats, moaning, and groaning with acute pain. A great deal of sickness and suffering on all sides, and little help here, near or in the future. This camp of 100,000 men is practically a vast hospital. Twelve men of Co. G are sick with the measles — now epidemic in camp.

Dec. 26. Fri. Fine day. Cold. The men endeavor to fix up their quarters a little; the day being set apart for the purpose of putting logs under the tents. The mud is everywhere, and we are in it all the day, and not much better situated at night. Our tents are too small for fires inside, though a few manage to have them; the wood is wet or green and the fires smoky. We build large fires outside our tents, and stand around them, in the vain endeavor to get dry and warm. Food is scanty, and poorly cooked at best; smoky, scorched, stewed, greasy. All is damp and cold, and sleep where we will, we wake stiff and rheumatic. New Hampshire is well represented here; her 2d, 5th, 6th, 9th, 10th, 11th, 12th and 13th Regts. are encamped within a circuit of less than two miles, and all very similarly situated.

The Thirteenth left New Hampshire with 1,040 men, but now numbers less than 400 effectives, and few of these are really well men. Disease kills more than bullets. An average of 250 men of the Thirteenth attend the morning Surgeons' call, besides the sick in hospital. Flour is selling in camp at the rate of $25 per barrel. Butter costs 85 cents a pound. A Captain in the 13th closes a letter late to-night with these words, a volume in a sentence, for it is the experience of hundreds, and a picture of the way we live, as there are no fires in our tents: "Good night; I must now go out of my tent to the fire and warm a plate of beans to eat, so as not to go to bed hungry." CAPT. JULIAN.

Dec. 27. Sat. Pleasant. Reg. still at work on camp, and trying to bring it into passable order, a difficult job. The ground is a rough hillside among pines, is much cut up by ravines or gullies, and falls to a dirty,

---

[1] Possibly remains of material used in the manufacture of gas.

muddy brook. One huge gully, 12 to 15 feet deep, directly west of Co. E, is the receptacle for all sorts of camp waste. There can be on this camp ground neither order nor regularity. Capt. Stoodley is selected to straighten out the crooked lines of tents, huts, and does his best, but it is of little use. Lt. Col. Bowers and Chaplain Jones, for the sake of a joke, accuse Capt. Stoodley of adopting, for this camp, the ground plan of Marblehead, Mass.; but the plat of that tangle-jointed town is outdone here in spite of all engineering.

The men of the 13th persist in declaring that many men of the 25th New Jersey laid down early in the assault, on the evening of Dec. 13, and that we ran over them; and the outcome is a decided coldness between the men of these two regiments. There is danger of a fight over the affair. Threats are freely indulged in. An unprofitable squabble.

Dec. 28. Sun. Pleasant. Religious service at 11 a. m. One officer in the 13th writes home: "I never more shall roam; never more shall have a Western, or any other, fever; have come to the conclusion that New England is the Garden of Eden." A private writes home: "Captain Julian, demanding more rations for his men, got into a spat with Col. Stevens, threw down his sword, and threatened to resign."

An old cherry-tree, that was standing on the Washington farm opposite Fredericksburg, has been nearly all cut in pieces and carried away by the Union soldiers. Some one has said that this is the original tree of the famous hatchet story, and there are many credulous enough to believe it. Cherry stones from that locality, to plant at home, are in great demand. The wood of the tree is used to make all sorts of crosses, pipes, rings, etc., that can be sent away by mail.

Dec. 29. Mon. Cold. Reg. drilling all day. At midnight orders are received for the Thirteenth to be ready to move to-morrow morning at daylight, in light marching order, with three days' cooked rations and sixty rounds of ball-cartridge per man. Cooks are hurried out of bed, fires are lighted, and Sergeants are set at work to see that all their squads of men are ready; and there is a busy stir and bustle all over camp for the rest of the night, while the men shout and cheer at the good news of a move from this locality, however temporary the absence may be.

Board at the officer's mess costs from two to three dollars per week — and much serious indigestion; no luxuries are to be had and supplies are scant and poor. All the regimental hospitals in our Brigade are filled to overflowing, and a steamboat load of sick men is sent to Washington in charge of Asst. Surgeon Sullivan.

Dec. 30. Tues. Cold. Reg. ready to move at daylight, but no order arrives; disappointment prevails, and we remain under arms all day. Writes one man of the 13th: "A small amount of wheat flour stole into camp the other day; price of a peep at the stranger, twenty-five cents." A soldier of the 13th, careless of his clothes, remarks concerning an extra smirch of dirt upon them: "Oh, that 'll wash off." A Sergeant in reply delivers a volume of wisdom in a sentence: "The best way, sir, to wash off dirt, is not to get it on."

Dec. 31. Wed. Very cold. Reg. mustered for pay, by Col. A. F. Stevens, in the forenoon. " Mustered for pay " is an agreeable expression, indicating much prospective pleasure, and to some persons whiskey straight, but in the preparation of the muster and pay rolls there is a vast amount of tribulation for the company commanders; as much fuss is made over ten percussion caps, three bullets and a gun-plug, as over a park of lost artillery. In the afternoon our whole Regiment goes down to the river on the picket line at the highway bridge. This bridge, of which only the abutments remain, spanned the river at Brown's Island, on the road leading to Orange Court House.

The writer, who wears heavy boots, wades into the river just south of the bridge to-day to get a shining object seen upon the river bottom. He has not taken five steps into the very shallow water before the rebel picket guard, on the Fredericksburg shore, turns out under arms. He retreats instanter, of course, while our own pickets shout with laughter, echoed in louder tones by the rebel pickets. The shining thing is fished out, however, after night comes on, and proves to be a highly polished brass ornament for some piece of furniture.

### 1863.

Jan. 1. Thurs. Clear, cold and windy. Thermometer near down to zero. Reg. on picket on the banks of the river opposite the city. The men sleep, while here, on the ground close down to the water, and without fires or shelter. While the clock in the old church steeple over in the city struck the hour of twelve, midnight, hard-hearted wags waked the half frozen sleepers; merely to wish them a " Happy New Year," and elicit sundry remarks. We lie about near the abutments of the highway bridge, now destroyed. The enemy's picket is in full sight along the city-side shore and wharves, all within hailing distance, the river here 200 or 300 yards wide. No picket firing now along the line. A deserter from the enemy swam the river last night, and gave himself up to our pickets, and was taken to a house near by, dried and warmed. The Reg. returns to camp about noon, and has the afternoon for rest, excepting time for a Dress-parade about sundown, all the men shivering with the cold.

Jan. 2. Fri. Clear, cold. Reg. in camp, and resting for a day. A Dress-parade is held near night, while it is so cold that the men can scarcely hold their guns. The rebels have been digging rifle-pits, working nights, all along the Fredericksburg bank of the river. A strong line is now seen the whole length of the city. They expect another visit from our side. They are now said to have more than fifty miles of earthworks along their bank of the river. There is fearful suffering among the men in our camp; when the devil first hit upon this Falmouth camp scheme, he must have thrown up his hat in perfect glee.

Jan. 3. Sat. Fair, cold. Company drill on the plain near camp. A walk-round of half frozen men — nonsense. The men make their tents warmer by sprinkling them with water at evening. The water freezes and makes the cloth wind-proof. A little touch of the Esquimaux ice-made hut. A large mail arrives in camp, bringing some letters from New Hampshire now over two months old. Some irreverent persons here think that our old State needs a little toning up.

A great deal of the time a peculiar haze fills the sky here, chilling as a garment woven of icicles and lined with fleecy snow ; the chill seems to grasp every fibre of a man ; while the sun hangs back in the distance as if unaccustomed to the country, afraid to come out, and looking in the cold gray sky like a rounded cake of ice. On such days comfort is out of the question, no matter how well the green pine wood may burn.

Jan. 4. Sun. Very fine day. Regimental inspection, followed by religious services — doleful as seven funerals. Half the Reg. sick with colds, rheumatism and jaundice. Rations of onions cooking ; being roasted in the ashes of little fires all over camp, and they smell to heaven. The men are scattered about camp on the sunny sides of their tents and huts, some reading, some writing, some whittling, some singing, some telling camp stories, some cleaning clothes and equipments, some reading aloud to their fellows, some trying their hands at cooking, some repairing tents, and some merely vegetate. The men have been in common shelter tents all the time since we left Faifax Seminary on December 1st ; a few low, small log huts, with shelter tent roofs, are now being put up.

Jan. 5. Mon. Clear, fine, warm ; heavy rain all night. Lieut. Forbush starts for home on ten days' leave. Company and Battalion drill, the men with their knapsacks on. Any comment would be inadequate. We are so near the city in our camp here, that we can see the church spires pointing upward, among the trees, and when all is still can hear the town clock strike the hours. Funeral this afternoon of a man of Co. B. Several men visit the 6th N. H. Vols., and meet a nearly forgotten stranger — flour bread and butter. Thirteenth placed to-day in 3d Brigade 3d Div. 9th Army Corps.

A teamster driving up from Aquia Creek finds the mules in his team exceedingly frisky ; he can do nothing with them, they run with him up hill and down. He helps other teams through sloughs and up hard hills, but needs no help himself. He has a load of whiskey in barrels. After a while, and quite early in the morning, and after listening to more comments made upon his team than are welcome, he investigates, and finds every whiskey barrel empty. Last night, while halted for the night on the road, some man, or a dozen, had bored holes up through the bottom of the wagon into the barrels, and so wracked off and carried away all the whiskey. All done while the guard slept, or "watched backward," as the boys say.

Jan. 6. Tues. A drizzling cold rain. Too muddy to march troops. Gen. Burnside reviews the Army of the Potomac on the plain, just east of the Phillips House, now Gen. Sumner's Hdqrs., and directly in front, and south, of our camp. The troops, because of the mud and rain, do not march in review past the General, as is customary. There are said to be 75,000 men in line. Gen. Burnside, unwilling to expose his men unnecessarily to the cold storm, cuts the review short; and with bared head, hat in his right hand, and followed by his staff, all dripping with the rain, he rides at a swift gallop up the front and down the rear of the lines — an imperial face and figure. This army will remember him best as he appears to-day; and thus he should be cast in lasting bronze. Few cheers, comparatively, are now heard, for it is stern determination, rather than enthusiasm, which pervades the Army of the Potomac. While on the field we stand where we can see at a glance almost the entire body of troops on review, while many thousands of the men pass where we can see them on their way to their camps. The Thirteenth wears knapsacks; the only regiment present that has them on to-day.

Assistant Surgeon John Sullivan is granted a leave of absence because of sickness; the order of the Medical Inspector certifying: "A change of location, and further treatment, is necessary to save his life."

Jan. 7. Wed. Cold, cloudy. Drilling resumed. The pickets along the river cross and re-cross, so much, in boats, that a special order is needed to put a stop to the dangerous practice. The rebels want good coffee, our men want good tobacco, and the temptation to exchange is hard to resist. There are in use several little 'hand-ferries,' tight boxes drawn back and forth across the river by a small rope running over pulleys, but they are hard to manage in the swift current and among the drift. Many a little toy-like boat is rigged and sent across, by contrivance of sail and rudder, landing far below the place of starting. Scarce a soldier on either side can be induced to give information, being deterred either by honor or fear. We have been in Hawkins' Brigade — 1st Brig. 3d Div. 9th Army Corps — consisting of the 9th, 89th, and 103d N. Y., 25th N. J., 10th and 13th N. H.; but on Jan. 5th were placed in the 3d Brigade, Col. Dutton of the 21st Conn. commanding, and consisting of the 21st Conn., 25th N. J., 13th N. H. and 4th R. I. No change is made in location of camp.

One of the Companies in the Thirteenth had a man of the bow-back species, and who was awkward, and able to strike an erect attitude only at rare intervals. The Reg. came into camp one cold and rainy day, everybody wet, muddy, tired and out of humor, and was to bivouac by divisions. It was "Joe's" off week, and he leaned his shoulders back, and threw his abdomen forward, several inches more than usual. The Captain commanding division was soon out of patience, and called out to Joe to dress up to line. Joe came too far to the front by half of him. Next he was told to fall back; which he did, all out of sight. Back, too, went the centre of the division line. Next came the order to the division to dress up in the centre, and so it backed and filled three or four times, while all in the Regiment grew more and more impatient in the pouring rain. The Captain declared he would keep the division standing there all night if they did not form a good line, and losing the usual words in the order, shouted: "Swell out there — in the middle!" Joe did not come up far enough, and the Captain shouted louder than before : " Swell out there — in the middle — Joe ! " The Regiment roared. The Captain could but laugh too, and ordered his division to stack arms. It was Joe's middle that caused all the trouble.

Jan. 8. Thurs. Cold, cloudy. Reg. drilling in forenoon; afternoon improving camp. New York Heralds ten cents each. That enterprising paper can kill off a regiment or two of soldiers every day. A close computation from its columns would possibly figure up the armies in the field, dead and alive, to about 20,000,000 of men — all for ten cents.

Jan. 9. Fri. Fair. Company drill. Officers mess board $3.00 per week. No luxuries to be had. Two Union pickets cross the river in a boat to Fredericksburg, exchange newspapers, and trade with the rebels. While returning, their boat is upset, and both men are drowned. Men in camp are refitting quarters ; preparing for a threatened storm.

Jan. 10. Sat. Severe rain storm. A detail from the Reg. goes on picket down by the river, near the wire bridge, and has a hard night of it. Pickets now go out in the morning, for 24 hours. Our line is in and near the old Washington garden, not far from the central ponton landing, where we crossed the river into the city on Dec. 11, and re-crossed on Dec. 16. A rebel deserter swims across to our pickets ; a mid-winter plunge for freedom. These determined and bold fellows are usually pulled out of the water about half dead, they are so chilled and benumbed with the cold, and exhausted by their struggles with the river current.

Jan. 11. Sun. Cloudy, rainy. Dress-parade at sundown, with religious services. A detail from the 13th goes two miles from camp for firewood, and brings it in upon their shoulders. They make a bundle of the wood and tie it with ropes, run a pole longer than the bundle through it, and then two men hoist the pole upon their shoulders, the bundle hanging between them, and come staggering back to camp. It must be borne in mind that there is not one man in twenty of the Union Army here, who now enjoys his full normal strength. The writer has borne one half of many such a bundle of wood for one and two miles. and though in better health than the most, he found the labor of it sufficiently severe.

At times last night the rebels in the city, some of them in full sight. were very merry, cheering and singing. This morning the church bells are ringing; but the extremest pietist in all Fredericksburg would not even allow us to attend church in that city — so near and yet so far. But we have a hundred churches here in camp better than any over there to-day. The good old Northern custom of families and friends joining in Christian hymns and pure songs, on Sunday afternoon or evening, is not forgotten here by the suffering but heroic boys in blue. There are many such hours here when the air rings and rings again with the old familiar tunes and hymns, and with many a patriotic song.

Jan. 12. Mon. Fine day. Reg. improves tents and grounds, and the more the grounds are 'improved' the worse they look. The Surgeon

General of our 9th Army Corps states that the Thirteenth has the best camping ground in the Corps. If that be so, Heaven pity the rest! No drill to-day. The Reg. has now 960 men on its rolls, about 440 of them are reported as for duty; of whom scarcely one half are fit for duty, and many are too weak to march in firm order while on drill. The nerveless weakness that comes upon men here is astonishing; strong one day, they are scarcely able to stand erect the next. Regimental Hospital moved to top of hill north of camp. Asst. Surgeon Sullivan goes home on leave. Butter costs in camp 85 cents a pound; cheese 60 cents; potatoes $3.00 per bushel; apples 5 cents each, and everything else in proportion.

A Lieutenant in the 13th temporarily in command of a division on Battalion drill, approaches an extremely dirty, muddy place in the drill ground; puzzled by the situation and not recalling quickly enough the proper order to give, he settles the case off-hand by shouting: "Boys, break up; scoot that hole, and git together on t' other side!" The movement was a quick success. The traitorous Press has been full of remarks about the Union army doing injury while in Fredericksburg. All such malicious stuff may as well take a furlough. There were thousands upon thousands of Union soldiers who did not, and who would scorn to, damage or appropriate the property of citizens; while expressions of sympathy for innocent persons were heard on all hands. Everything was done that could be done to prevent injury to private property, and any Union soldier found offending in this particular was at once arrested.

Jan. 13. Tues. Pleasant. Reg. again takes a day, and makes special endeavors to improve its quarters, for there is much sickness, and great mental depression among the men. Teams are hauling logs to our camp; and shelter tents, which have afforded nearly all the protection that the men have been able to secure, through all the stormy, wet, wintry weather since Dec. 1, are being replaced by low huts. Little cellars are dug seven feet square and one or two feet deep. Log walls are raised about two feet high close around these little cellars on all sides, excepting one. At this side is the doorway, chimney and fireplace. The logs are plastered with mud, and banked up with earth on the outside to keep the water out of the cellars. A fireplace is built of mud and turf at one corner of the hut, and above it on the outside of the hut is raised a chimney of mud and sticks, with a pork or flour barrel placed on the top. Shelter tents are drawn over the hut for a roof. Small poles laid alongside each other a few inches above the cellar floor, and covered with a layer of cedar or pine boughs constitute the bed. The chimney covers nearly all of one end of the hut, and pieces of board, or of tent-cloth, serve for a door. Four to six men are crowded into a hut of this size; and not one in twenty of the huts in Gen. Burnside's army here is really so good as the one above described. The most afford but a poor shelter, and all are miserable lodgings at best; still we can do no better.

Jan. 14. Wed. Pleasant. Battalion drill. Measles suddenly become epidemic in camp. Capt. Stoodley gives up his tent to the sick, and some other officers do the same. Measles under these conditions of tent life are a threatening scourge. We have constant daily drill unless the weather and the condition of the ground is very bad indeed. Lt. Col. Bowers leaves camp for home on a twenty-days' leave granted because of his ill health.

Jan. 15. Thurs. Cold. Rainy at night. Burial of Ira M. Whitaker of Co. G at 3 p. m. Died of the measles. The excitement in camp is now worse and worse indeed. Capt. Stoodley and Private John B. Stevens of G make for Whitaker a coffin of three cracker-boxes placed end to end, and nailed to a couple of saplings. The simple burial of a private soldier is one of the saddest scenes on earth at any time, but here departs a mere boy but sixteen years old. Whitaker's is the first death in Company G. A man's own company forms the usual procession on such occasions, any friends joining who may choose to do so. A bottle well corked and sealed, and containing the man's name, regiment, home address, etc., is usually laid in the grave with his body. The burial is not prolonged: the slow march, the arms reversed, the muffled drum, the piercing fife, the dirge — often the Portuguese Hymn, but more often the Dead March in Saul — the platoon fire over the grave, the quickstep march back to camp, two men left to close the grave, and all is done.

Jan. 16. Fri. Rain storm last night; clears warmer to-day. Orders are received for us to be ready to move on the morrow at daylight, with all camp equipage, three days' rations in haversacks and five days' in wagons, and sixty rounds of ball-cartridge per man. No one sorry to move, almost anything is preferable to this vile camp. The rebels send a small shell at Prof. Lowe's balloon, and it falls within our camp; makes the mud fly where it bursts, and that is all.

Jan. 17. Sat. Fair. Very cold. Reg. remains in camp in suspense all the day. Maj. Storer in command. One Company in the Thirteenth has so far had twelve cases of the measles, but this is above the average number in the several companies. There have been about seventy-five cases in all.

Jan. 18. Sun. Very cold. Clear. Inspection of Reg. by Col. Dutton at 9 a. m. Orders to march to-night. In fact, all along here, for six or eight days, the Thirteenth lives in constant expectation of an immediate march, and in readiness to move at an hour's notice. Rations in haversacks spoil, are thrown away, and re-supplied — waste on waste. Informal inspection of arms; a sure indication of trouble near ahead.

Jan. 19. Mon. Fair. Reg. remains in camp under arms. This long suspense, backing and filling, is a mean business. To-day we have to drill for several hours. The regimental Hospital is too small to receive all the sick, well men are crowded into narrower quarters, and the sick men placed in the vacated tents. The regular hours for drill all winter have been: Company drill 10 to 12 a. m.; Battalion drill 2 to 4 p. m.; Dress-parade at 4.30 p. m.

Jan. 20. Tues. Cloudy, showery. Reg. still in camp under arms.

Orders are received to march to-morrow at 4 a. m. During a break in the rain to-day, the Reg. is hustled out for a Brigade drill, only to get wet in the next shower. Late to-night in almost pitchy darkness, the Reg. is formed in a hollow square, and Col. Stevens makes a fine speech. It is a night of such intense darkness that one remark made by him is taken too literally, and ever after serves as a by-word, when a night comes on that is black enough to make its use seemingly appropriate: " Men of the Thirteenth, the eyes of New Hampshire are upon you!" The Reg. is fairly in their quarters, and settled for the night, when about 10 p. m. the rain again begins to pour furiously.

A barrel of dried apples was drawn for rations, and the apples proved to be mouldy, sour, rotten, black. One man of the 13th upon taking up a bunch of them from the reeking mass, with the hook used to draw things out of barrels, held them up and examined them, while he himself presented a countenance of utter melancholy and disappointment, and remarked : " O if my poor dear mother could only see what her darling son is going to have for his supper to-night! " provoking a general burst of laughter. Melancholy overdone is the most ridiculous of all drollery.

Jan. 21. Wed. Very severe rain storm. The rain commenced last night about dark, rained all night, for many hours literally pouring, and rains all day to-day. The tents leak very badly, and scarce a man in the Reg. can keep dry. The Thirteenth is up and all ready to strike tents at 2.30 a. m. Those having spare shelter tents can leave the roofs of their huts on, all other roofs must be taken off; which order would uncover two thirds or more of the huts. It rains very hard at this hour, the wind has been high all night, and the whole country is flooded. Soon the men are ordered to remain in quarters until orders come to move; officers are going from tent to tent to tell the men what to do to avoid needless exposure to the cold storm. Orders to move do not arrive, though the signal gun was fired at 3 a. m., and the Long-roll was sounded all through the camp. The rain and mud stops all movements of the Union army, excepting concentration. At 4 a. m. it rains like a cloud-burst.

Language cannot describe the scene of this attempted movement. Gen. Hooker's and Gen. Franklin's Grand divisions move off in the mud, and rain, while we look on and await our turn. Orders for us to march are countermanded about 4 a. m. A whole division of one of the Corps laid out in the fearful storm of last night, near our camp, and without any shelter whatever. They kept so still that their presence was known to but few until daylight.

Some little time ago the men received a ration of " desiccated vegetables," and visions of a rare feast danced through ten thousand heads. The ration was cooked, and proved to be some half a dozen different kinds of vegetables and roots cut up in pieces and dried; but they were dirty, sandy, mouldy, and utterly uneatable. The men received them on their plates in liberal quantities, and after one taste threw them away in disgust, not caring where they fell — the camp was paved with them. The men dubbed them "desecrated vegetables." A better surprise was a quantity of "Boston brown bread," fresh and warm when it reached our camp.

Jan. 22. Thurs. Rainy, cold, disagreeable, and the mud almost fathomless. The whole Reg. is hurried off early for picket duty on the river near the Lacy House. A strong, double line of pickets are posted along much of the river bank. The Lacy House was once a splendid place, but is now terribly torn and battered. The storm yesterday and last night was of rain and sleet, the northeast wind at times a gale. The roads were soon bottomless; wagons sunk to the bodies, and hundreds of mules and horses lay stranded and helpless in the clay. Teams are doubled and trebled; even as many as twelve horses harnessed to one twelve-pounder gun, but all in vain. The roadways and paths across the country are strewn with every conceivable kind of army materiel, from muskets and accoutrements to cannon, caissons, supply wagons, lumber, ponton boats and planks, dead horses and mules. Many men, too, enfeebled by the hardships and exposures of this worst camp of all camps, have succumbed in this storm, fallen out, and died by the roadside, from cold, wet and fatigue.

The rebels over the river shouted to our mud-bound pontonniers: "Wait till morning, after it has done raining, and we'll come over and help you build your bridge." It was Gen. Burnside's intention to attempt a crossing at Banks' Ford, and at other fords above the city. Our field-guns posted along the bluffs have been hauled back a little out of sight of the enemy, but many cannot be brought back to camp because of the mud. Even at this time, our pickets near the Lacy House cross the river in a boat to-night, and trade with the rebel pickets.

Jan. 23. Fri. Fair. Reg. returns from picket at noon. Lieut. Forbush returns to camp from home. The recent movement is called the 'Mud March,' and thousands of the mud-larks are coming home in a sorry looking condition. There is any amount of chaffing, and coarse fun, as the muddy columns pass. The storm abates with light showers. The rebels have a large board set up on the Fredericksburg shore, and lettered: "Burnside and his army stuck in the mud." It is read distinctly with the aid of a glass. Little cannon, field-pieces, pass camp drawn by twelve horses to a gun. The mud rolls away from the axles in great chunks, and the horses flounder and plunge; in a word everything, excepting the skies and trees, is mud, mud, mud.

Jan. 24. Sat. Fine. Thirteenth paid off this morning for twelve days, to Oct. 31, 1862, by Maj. S. A. Walker. A detail of 160 men and three or four officers sent on picket. Pedlers about camp; the pedler is a pay-day parasite. Quarter-master Cheney is dangerously sick with dysentery and malarial fever. Thirty-eight sick men, from the Thirteenth, are sent in ambulances to new Hospital at Aquia Creek. A partridge visits our camp, lights on a tree and is shot and eaten. The Corps Surgeon inspects the quarters of officers and men, suggests improvements, and orders that no person must lie on the ground. Beds must be raised at least four inches above the surface. Heretofore hundreds of beds have been made of a few pine boughs thrown upon the ground, which here is a vast sponge, wet with all the water it will hold, and half frozen. All day long straggling soldiers have been passing our camp, muddy, wet, ugly, sour and insubordinate.

Jan. 25. Sun. Rained last night, to-day clear. Usual Sunday inspection and parade. Whiskey rations have been given out to the men liberally — usually about one gill per man. Hot strong coffee is better. A great quantity of quinine is taken ; salt relieves its bitterness. To-day there is formed in the Regiment a Masonic Relief Association having 40 members, one half of them officers. Its purposes are to attend to the wants of the sick, or wounded, to procure for them remedies, food, clothing, and such comfort as can be secured ; and in all cases where practicable to send their remains, if they die, home to their friends.

Jan. 26. Mon. Very warm. Reg. drilling. Non-commissioned officers commence a rigorous term of drill. On one of these warm days the Thirteenth is again drilled, with their knapsacks on, for several hours, and rapidly. A part of our drill ground had been a cornfield, the thawing made the top of the ground very muddy and more slippery than if greased. Many of the men fell to-day and were badly hurt; and some of them return to camp in a complete mud armor. The writer and several other men were laid up for two or three days with sprained ankles. Lieut. Kilburn leaves camp for home.

Maj. Gen. Joseph Hooker assumes command of the Army of the Potomac, Maj. Gen. Ambrose E. Burnside having been relieved at his own request. Generals Franklin and Sumner relinquish their commands.

Jan. 27. Tues. Cloudy, rainy. No drill. Quarter-master Cheney leaves camp for Washington, very sick. Malarial and typhoid diseases very prevalent. Still, notwithstanding the great physical and mental depression here in the army, the old fire of true patriotism, that led these men to take up arms, now burns as bright, strong and hot as ever. This suffering army means brisk business when once again the campaign opens. These sufferings and privations are what patriotism leads a man to meet, and helps him to endure.

Jan. 28. Wed. Cold. A heavy snow storm sets in about 4 p. m. with a severe northeast wind, and causes a great deal of damage to the Thirteenth's frail tents, on the roofs of which it accumulates to the depth of five or six inches. The cloth roofs have been torn and patched, and every seam is strained and leaky. It is next to impossible to keep fires burning in the little fire-places in the tents, and the men have to roll themselves in their blankets to keep warm. There is water in the bottom of half the fireplaces, and but little dry wood can be obtained. Nine tenths of the firewood used is green pine.

Rice is complained of and as rations roundly condemned. The men call it " swamp-seed," and every other vile name imaginable ; and rice is truly a very poor substitute for good food. A board of officers investigating the matter, call in a few of the men, and among them Sergeant Gibbs of E, to learn their opinions concerning rice. They are all loud, and most severe, in their condemnations, excepting Gibbs. He is called upon last, and praises rice in terms fully as emphatic as the others' terms of dislike. He contends that there is no diet so very wholesome, convenient, and desirable; especially for men to have while on a forced march. "And why," they ask, "is it then so very desirable?" "You see," answers Gibbs, "men fed on rice can march right along all day, and all night, they never have to halt for anything — till they drop dead." As a consequence of the investigation, rations of rice give way to something more substantial.

Jan. 29. Thurs. Rain and snow all last night, a hard storm. Above eight inches of snow falls during the night and morning; clears cold about 9 a. m. No drill. The Reg. still have only shelter tents for the roofs of their huts; nothing but cheap cotton drilling, and badly worn at that. Not a tent but what leaks badly, and the men have to get up, every hour or two, and shake the snow off the roofs. Some tents are worthless and break under the weight of the wet snow, and the poor men "double-up" in other tents, already too crowded; and so they suffer — wet, chilled, sick, gloomy, disheartened.

Think of it you able bodied army-shirks, cowards, slinks, sneaks; who are willing to "let the Union slide," and who now let us do all the fighting and hard work to save it, while you stay at home, and will have an equal share and benefit, all for nothing, in our hard won successes. Not one in fifty of you can look a soldier straight in the face. A few hundred of your soulless carcasses set up along the front lines, to shield honorable men from rebel bullets, every one of them fired by better men than you, might have saved to Union arms the Battle of Fredericksburg.

Jan. 30. Fri. Warmer. Snow melting a little. Mud and slush all over camp. No drill. Dress-parade at sundown. O such thinned ranks! In order to keep the men employed, and to divert their minds from their extreme sufferings, discomforts and privations in this winter camp, they have been exercised in some form of military drill on every day during the whole winter, excepting when the weather was very bad indeed, or the ground so very wet and snowy that marching was next to impossible.

The bands are forbidden to play pathetic or plaintive tunes, such as Home, Sweet Home, Annie Laurie, Auld Lang Syne, etc., lest they serve to dispirit, and unnerve our suffering men. While we are here in America's second Valley Forge, the hearthstones of New England are glowing warm and cheerful, and the traditional nuts, apples and cider are passed as when we used to be at home there. Wholesome food in plenty, warm clothing, snug houses, luxurious beds, all are there; and the deserving, and the undeserving, enjoy them alike. We are not envious. Those home comforts could to-day stand between hundreds of us soldiers and death; hence we long for them.

Jan. 31. Sat. Very cold and clear. Ground frozen hard. Picket sent from the 13th to the river near the Lacy House. One post at the highway bridge crossing over Brown's Island. Another picket supporting a battery on the bluffs; an extremely cold job on a wide bare plain. The Thirteenth has taken its turn on the picket line, a little oftener than once a week all the winter.

There has been a serious disturbance over "Regulation Brasses" dealt out to the Thirteenth; a miserable, old-fashioned piece of regular army foolishness. Rightly the Thirteenth rebels, buries or destroys the entire mess of stuff, and then pays the swindle, like honest and indignant soldiers. About a bushel of the brasses, shoulder-pieces, etc., go into one deep hole in the ground, at the hour of twelve, midnight, the writer's with them. "We came down here," the men say, "to put down the rebellion; not to garnish ourselves with old brass, and poor at that, and spend hour after hour in polishing it. We will not submit to such ignominy."

The rebel pickets, over the river, call to us to come over and try them now; and still yell sundry jokes about the mud march. The poor fellows over there have so few jokes, that when they get hold of one they think good, they never know when to drop it.

It is interesting on a sharp, clear morning to go up on the bluff north of our camp, very early, and listen to the bugle and drum calls, the Reveille, of these two great armies. The hour is about the same in both, and if one or the other precedes by a few moments with its first call, the sounds are soon all mingled together, as if the entire country were celebrating in some vast jubilee. But it is far enough from a jubilee; two hundred thousand men are turning out in the cold — shivering, grumbling, growling, and each answering to the roll-call with an angry snap of his jaws, as if he would like to bite a ten-penny nail in two, and chew the pieces. Of course there are some who joke, and even laugh; but both jokes and laughter freeze upon their lips and drop like icicles to the ground, or the jokers are kicked, punched and reviled for disturbing the general tone of the meeting.

Feb. 1. Sun. Rainy afternoon. Reg. came into camp from picket at 10 a. m., all more or less muddy and wet. No Dress-parade, no religious services. Capt. Cummings and Lt. Col. Pearsons of the 6th N. H. visit camp. (Lt. Col. Pearsons laid down his life for his country at the battle on the North Anna river, May 26, 1864.) The people at home should see the men turn out from the tents when the arrival of the mail is announced. Nothing more welcome here than letters from home; nothing more disappointing than their failure to arrive, or more trying than the waiting after they are due.

"The rebels have got a board, still nailed up in Fredericksburg, on which is written in big letters: 'Burnside and his army stuck in the mud.'" PRESCOTT.

**Feb. 2. Mon.** Cold, clear. Company drill in the forenoon; ugly work in the snow. Lt. Col. Bowers returns to the Reg. this afternoon. Arrangements are made for granting furloughs of fifteen days each to two enlisted men in every hundred; and to two line officers in each regiment, leaves of absence for the same period.

**Feb. 3. Tues.** Very cold; snow squalls. No drill. Prof. Lowe's balloons, sometimes three of them, go up almost every day (and have done so all winter), and we soon read what he sees from them, possibly, in the columns of the New York papers; and that is the first and all we know about it, though the balloons are not a quarter of a mile distant from our camp. Our camp is just in range of those balloons and when the enemy essays, as he frequently does, to burst the big bubbles, we take the shells. That fact also conduces to make our camp a pleasant place to sleep and wake in.

Joseph A. Jones of E dies in hospital at Aquia Creek, the first death in the Company. He was a good soldier, keeping up and doing duty just as long as he possibly could, but the deadly malaria slowly destroyed his vitality, and his life ceased as a clock runs down.

Some one in the Thirteenth stepped outside of his hut into the sharp air to-night, and in a magnificent voice opened that favorite song of all songs in the Union army: "Old John Brown." The camp quickly joined in the song; it spread to neighboring regiments and on toward the front, and the grandly swelling chorus must have reached the ears of the rebels over the river. Other patriotic songs followed. It was a cheering and inspiriting hour.

**Feb. 4. Wed.** Stinging cold. No drill. Capt. Grantman starts for home on fifteen days' leave. David Hogan of E has an experience that he can never forget. His round of guard duty takes him near the Regiment's sinks and cesspools. A large shell, intended by the enemy for Prof. Lowe's balloon, falls into one of them, bursts there, and scatters about two cartloads of the vile contents for rods around, nearly burying Hogan out of sight; Hogan is unhurt beyond a scare, but his clothing, and his appetite, are utterly ruined. Another shell strikes a stump near a shelter tent with two men in it. They jump instantly right through the roof, taking cloth, poles and all with them, for a little ravine close to the side of the tent opposite the stump. The shell does not burst, and the two men fit up camp again on the old ground.

Our camp seems to wear a more cheerful face since the return of Lt. Col. Bowers. Within these two days, it is safe to say, he has visited every tent, and has shaken hands with every man in the Thirteenth. He is everywhere, encouraging and cheering the men.

Nearly every street in this camp is named, and in many cases the name is inscribed on a bit of board nailed to a tree or corner of a hut. Hundreds of the huts also are conspicuously marked with names or legends ranging through every grade of notion and idea. Several of the worst sort of huts are labelled Home, Sweet Home. Here is Lincoln

Street and Burnside Avenue ; Starvation Alley and Mud Lane ; Astor House and Swine Hotel ; Dew Drop Inn and We 're Out; Post No Bill Street and Thompson's Chateau. Come Jine Us offsets Git Out, and Happy Family balances with Tiger Den. One street rejoices in the name of Mud Alley, and near it is Sunny Lawn under a huge pine-tree where the sun never shines and grass never grows. An especially muddy place near Chaplain Jones's tent is called Holy Park.

Feb. 5. Thurs. Very cold. Snow in the forenoon, and rain in the afternoon and all night. Another long period of miserable experiences with the shelter-tent roofs of the huts. What with rain, snow, mud, cold, and wind, inside the tents and huts nearly as bad as outside, there has been little comfort for the past two weeks. Fully one half of the huts of the men have broken in, or broken down in parts. The day closes with a severe northeaster. The snow continues until 3 p. m., then the storm turns to rain, which pours heavily all through the night. The mud is washed out of the cracks between the logs, in the walls of the huts, and the rain pours in. The pork or flour barrels on the tops of the chimneys are all blown off, and before morning many of the chimneys, made of mud and sticks, also go down.

Some reader may think that the picture of this winter camp is overdrawn ; but let him inquire of the survivors, or read other accounts, and especially hospital records and death rolls, and he will conclude to discard the vehicle of language to bear to him a true account of this camp's abominations, and depend upon his imagination altogether. The camp and its miseries, discomforts and sufferings are simply indescribably bad. The earth is saturated with water. Men whose tents were set upon the little cellars dug among the roots of trees, have found after a rain storm, a temporary bubbling spring under their bed, or in the middle of their little floor space. One tent in the 13th was for this pleasant reason dubbed " Cold Spring House," and another, " Geyser Number Forty-Two." At most we can give but a few of the facts, and no string of facts can ever do the subject justice. Many of the men in sheer desperation cut the statements of their outrageous experiences short with the roughest of old English and a burst of most vicious profanity, by way of relieving their pent-up feelings of indignation. Frequently the floors of the little cellars, just after a rain storm, are covered with ice-cold water from two to six inches deep, and the water has to be bailed out as from a leaky boat ; such is the house and land we live in. A soldier of the 13th writes home : " We could have no fire in the fireplace in our tent to-day, for the water in it is three inches deep ; so we roll ourselves in our blankets, and lie in bed to keep from freezing." Most welcome orders are received for the Thirteenth to be ready to-morrow morning, with three days' cooked rations, to move to Fortress Monroe. Cheers, such as our army, and especially such as the Thirteenth, never gave before, ring out from regiment to regiment, again and again.

Feb. 6. Fri. Cold, showery ; warm at noon. Reg. ready on time to march — most exceedingly ready ; the men cannot express their readiness to quit this place. The First Brigade of our Division — 3d, 9th A. C. — marches early this morning; the Second Brigade early in the afternoon. The Thirteenth, and the rest of our Third Brigade, are under arms all day, waiting to move. The mud is too deep for army shoes, called in camp language " whangs " and " gun-boats," and tenacious enough to pull them off ; hence the troops move away very slowly, and march in a very irregular order in search of dry ground. Another night in the old camp; with many expressions of disappointment, and much denunciation of the promise of departure as a fable and a sham.

## MOVE TO NEWPORT NEWS.

Feb. 7. Sat. Clear, and quite warm in the sunshine at noon. Very early in the morning the miserable roofs are again pulled off the huts, and the Reg. packs ready to move. Again we wait under arms all day, nearly. The men build fires, by order, for the day at morning and evening is very chilly. There is a large lot of fresh beef in camp, and the men have a splendid dinner. The last dinner in the Falmouth camp is the best one ever known there. We destroy a large quantity of food supplies of every sort, which cannot be moved ; among the rest, a lot of 'old government' Java coffee, of the regular brand used in the army. Fires are built upon it, and then water is poured on. First Sergt. Thompson and Sergt. Van Duzee of E, and others in the Reg., leave their huts standing exactly as occupied all winter, roofs on and fires burning on the hearth. The Thirteenth leaves camp at 4.30 p. m., marches to Falmouth station, distance two miles, takes cars, most of them box freight cars, at 6.30 p. m., arrives at Aquia Creek, after the fifteen mile ride, about 9 p. m., and bivouacs at 10 p. m., at the wharf, in cars, in boxes, on boards, anywhere, everywhere. Some of the men capture a few bales of hay, from cars on a side track, spread it deep on the floor of sundry cattle cars, and thus have a fine clean bed to sleep on. Here they remain until called to go on board the boat.

Good-by Valley Forge Number Two. No place where men can exist at all for three winter months can be much worse, so any change is welcome. Any one desiring to learn how much we have enjoyed this camp can gain experimentally some idea of the matter by taking a sheet off his bed, making a tent of it, pitching the tent in any common swamp in New England, and living in it through the months of February, March and April; the experience will be more nearly similar to ours at Falmouth, if he has about half enough of clothing, and his rations are hard bread, coffee and salt beef, none of it too good and always a scanty supply. This winter camp has been an indescribable mixture of the diabolical, pathetic, laughable, dismal, droll, horrid, funny, sick, picturesque, abominable, comical, damnable, amusing and outrageous, all at once and continually. Men laugh, joke, and die ; men cry, and die ; men suffer the excruciating torments of rheumatism and fever, and die ; men waste away in mind and body without a twinge of pain, and die; all side by side, and in tent by tent. A party of congenial spirits, sick, suffering and almost hopeless, gather in a tent, bemoan, whine and wail, and act like whipped children; in an adjoining tent a party, equal in all points of actual suffering, pour all their miseries into an unending stream of fun, joke, gibe, frolic and glee to drown their sorrows; the next day one or more of each party is dead, or on his way to a Hospital, and is never again able to return to active service; and so it has gone on, week in and week out, all the long winter. Another party look their trials, and even death itself, coolly and deliberately in the face, contrive every possible plan to keep their health, or to regain it if lost, confidently depending upon the eternal truth that God helps them who properly help themselves, and almost every one of these manages to survive. To-day there are not fifty men in the Thirteenth regiment who can call themselves well men, and the same has been true of almost every day since the battle of Fredericksburg; while the good spirits of many of the worst sufferers have been preyed upon continually by the doleful forebodings and scoldings of many of the most vigorous. There is one bright point of relief: practical Christianity — and there is no other — was never more fully at work than here. But as for the whole, write it however you may, language cannot describe this winter camp; and while its denizens survive, they will sing of it, scold it, bewail it, laugh over it, and most roundly denounce it, all in the same breath.

Feb. 8. Sun. Pleasant morning, cold afternoon. Reg. at Aquia Creek. We assemble early, have a liberal morning bath, and go on board the steamer 'George Washington,' about 10 a. m., and are stored as close as cattle; but the boys little mind it: we are going to a better place than Falmouth. Seven companies are on the steamer, the other three on board the schooner 'Pawnee' in tow of the steamer. Occasionally on the trip our Band furnishes fine music. We start at 2 p. m. for Fortress Monroe. Quite a number, about 100, of our men receive boxes here from home, they having been held here to await our coming; and as a consequence almost everything in them is spoiled. Rich and dainty viands, sent to the soldiers by loving hands at home, merely serve to feed a few Potomac fishes, as our boat speeds down the river, and the contents of the boxes go overboard.

The first court martial convened in the Thirteenth was organized Jan. 30, 1863, to try sundry cases of misdemeanor among the men, and the detail for the same was Capt. Smith of H, Lieut. Durell of E, Lieut. Coffin of K, with Lieut. Young of F as Judge Advocate. The condition of the Reg. was such that no larger detail could be made. Maj. Storer was at that time in command. This movement necessarily dissolves the court, and its members reported to the Regiment yesterday for duty.

"Yesterday the sick of the Thirteenth, nearly forty in all, were taken from the regimental Hospital to the station in ambulances before noon, and placed in box cars. About 4 p. m. an orderly galloped up to the Thirteenth Hdqrs., and a moment later the voice of Lt. Col. Bowers was heard ordering : ' Fall in Thirteenth ! ' Never was an order obeyed with more alacrity. The 13th Band struck up ' Marching Along.' And as we passed up over the hill near the Phillips House, we could see our abandoned camp, with its mud chimneys and smoking fires presenting the appearance of a city in ruins. The troops went cheering — glad to get out of that swamp of mud." PRESCOTT.

## III.

### CAMP AT NEWPORT NEWS.

**Feb. 9. Mon.** Fine day. As we move down the bay the air is full of wild birds, small and large, with ducks, geese and gulls by the thousand. The officers and others use their revolvers freely upon the multitude of feathery game. The use of rifles in the same sport is much desired, but altogether forbidden — Uncle Sam's ammunition is not for the feathered bipeds. Many transports and war vessels are passing to and fro on the water, and an enormous fleet hovers around Fortress Monroe, which we pass about 9 a. m.; we lay at anchor two or three hours, and debark at Newport News at 12 noon. About 4 p. m. we are placed in the old barracks nearest the shore, three companies in a building. The whole 9th Army Corps is to rendezvous here, numbering 25,000 to 30,000 men of all arms. The 13th last October had 101 men to a company; now from 36 to 55 men per company are reported for duty. The effective force of the Thirteenth is reduced by more than one half.

**Feb. 10. Tues.** Warm, fine day. Reg. improving quarters, and eating oysters enough for three regiments. Fine camping ground here; a broad, long, sandy plain, running along the bay, clean and dry. Monitors are at anchor in the bay, and almost numberless vessels of various kinds. "Got some soft bread," one soldier in the 13th writes. Another writes: "Letters are as welcome to the soldier as food to the starving beggar."

**Feb. 11. Wed.** Fair, with a few showers. A wonderful change in the appearance of our men, even in these three days: they are cleaner, healthier, more cheerful. This is Paradise to Falmouth. Rather chilly in quarters, however, without fires. Troops are constantly landing in great numbers. We drill for a few hours. The officers have wall tents, the men remain in barracks, which are warmer.

**Feb. 12. Thurs.** Pleasant, breezy, cool. Battalion and Company drill. We have now soft, fresh, nice flour bread; the first the men have had for many weeks. Lieut. Durell of E at home on 15 days' leave. One man of the 13th is sent to the General Hospital, and the first remark made about his case, by the Surgeon, is: "Rub this man down with a brick; let us find him before we attempt to cure him."

**Feb. 13. Fri.** Fair, cold, breezy. "I prescribed for the sick men of two companies this morning for the first time." (PRESCOTT.) Battalion and Company drill all day. The Thirteenth not being considered quite proficient enough in drill, the Brigade commander sets about a reform; and puts us under such strict orders of regularity that we pull off boots, go to bed, sleep, dream, wake, rise, dress, march, drill, eat, drink, and pick our teeth, all in one time and two motions, as the tactics say, One of our Regiment's mules plunged overboard and swam ashore from the transport to-day; the change of camp and the weather have "mettled" man, horse and mule.

Feb. 14. Sat. Fair, cold, windy. No drill. Hawkins' Zouaves are standing in line, and on parade. A sutler's wagon drives by with a load, several barrels, of ginger cookies. A sick zouave near by asks the driver for a cookie, and is abusively refused. Instantly the zouave regiment breaks ranks, drops muskets, and "goes for" that load of cookies, and for several minutes nothing can be seen but a struggling pile of red legs, and flying about the tangled mass a fountain-like shower of cookies. After all is over the sutler is paid for his cookies by the impulsive zouaves, and freely admonished. The writer has just time to see the scrimmage, and gives a zouave's version of the affair. An army cookie is about four inches across and half an inch thick and of the average density of a boot-heel, its color ranging between tan and black; is made of ginger, molasses — and other things, and contains more seeds of biliousness and griping stomach-ache than can elsewhere be found in the same space. They are best eaten with pickles, half and half — by the hogs.

Feb. 15. Sun. Sunshine and shower. Dress-parade and religious services at 5 p. m. The Chaplain is a good man, but a little too solemn. There is of necessity solemnity enough here without any shadow of yielding to it. The fact is Chaplain Jones' sympathies have been exceedingly wrought upon by the sufferings at Fredericksburg, and his health is by no means rugged. The Rhode Island boys receive two schooner loads of fresh vegetables, sent by the State. We are sorry it was ever said that "New Hampshire is a good State to emigrate from;" — what if that very phrase should put it into the head of some one to believe it!

Feb. 16. Mon. Fair. Drill both forenoon and afternoon. A number of men from upper New Hampshire, sent into the woods to chop, say that they never saw such fine timber before. If we stay here six months there will not be one tree left of a thousand.

Feb. 17. Tues. Hard rain storm all last night and all day to-day. Reg. keeps within doors; smokes, jokes, makes merry, sings, plays games, and begins to enjoy life again. There is but little grumbling now, though the weather is cold, we can have no fires, and rations are short and poor with us, while the men from New York and Rhode Island are feasting. When on Dress-parade, we face toward the water, and there is no need to command "Eyes front," for the view is magnificent. Our ammunition remains aboard ship, a fact that makes a long stay in this splendid camp a matter of great doubt.

Feb. 18. Wed. Storm continues and is furious towards night. No work done. A party goes duck shooting, and has great success. There is a slave whipping-post near camp which shows the wear of much use;

a wooden bar nailed across a tree about as high up as a man can reach. The victim's hands were tied to this while the lash was laid on. There is scarce a plantation in all the South without its whipping-post.

Feb. 19. Thurs. Rainy forenoon, a clear and cold afternoon. Dress-parade at 5 p. m., with a turn of poor drilling. It is so very pleasant here that the men refer to the Fredericksburg camp as Camp Misery, and call it many other names too hard to print. Lieut. Holmes resigns, and is honorably discharged the service.

Feb. 20. Fri. Clear and fine, windy. Drill forenoon and afternoon. At Dress-parade the announcement is read that a deserter is to be shot; sending a shiver down men's spines. Our men are ordered to have their shoes blacked, and also ordered not to leave camp "at all;" but when they do leave, to wear their coats buttoned up to the throat, to stand and walk erect, to wear a belt, to have all buttons and brasses shining, and to set their caps on their heads with a try-square, or in words to that effect.

Feb. 21. Sat. Splendid weather, very warm at noon. Reg. fitting up camp and quarters. The 'Congress' and the 'Cumberland,' sunk on Sat. March 8, 1862, by the rebel war-ship 'Merrimac,' are just off-shore, the ends of masts, and a few timbers only appearing above the water. The little monitors lay out in Hampton Roads, waiting to see what may turn up. All the vessels in the stream, and several batteries on the shore, are constantly practicing at target firing; and the shells skimming along the water, or dropping in vertically, burst and throw up handsome fountain-like jets of white water, while we sit, in the sunshine, on the shore, and watch the play. No drill on Saturdays. What would the Base-ballists of the "Great National Game" now, 1887, think to see some thousands of men, representing almost every company in the Ninth Army Corps, engaged in playing base ball? It is safe to say that two hundred games are going on at once, on some of these days, on this plain; probably double that number at times.

Feb. 22. Sun. Snowy, rainy, and the coldest day since we came here. A snow storm commenced last night about 8 o'clock. Four inches of snow fell, and this morning it is flying about in a driving northeast wind. Reg. remains in quarters all day. The barracks leak, are filthy and vile, are crowded, too, with three companies in each building. The men improvise all sorts of crazy contrivances to guard themselves against the cold and the snow; hoping, as the man said when he wrapped himself in a fish net, "to tangle up the cold to some extent." Several vessels are blown high and dry upon the shore. Hundreds of others are tugging at their anchors, and bounding and plunging like a multitude of huge, black, ungainly porpoises.

Feb. 23. Mon. Fair, and very cold. Reg. drills, despite the snow, both forenoon and afternoon. The boys say: "They are fattening us now to kill." At any rate we live well, rations having improved greatly of late, and we have a plenty of healthful exercise called drilling, on a splendid smooth drill ground. Col. Stevens and wife leave camp for home; Col. Stevens has twelve days' leave. Lt. Col. Bowers in command of the Reg. There is much ill feeling now in the army concerning the negro slaves, who, as freedmen, are numerous here and arrogant. Many of the soldiers have an idea that all our sacrifices are forced upon us especially for the benefit of the negroes; the idea being suggested by the newspapers insisting that there must be no peace until slavery has been abolished. A party of officers, who have not seen a white woman for over two months, visit Norfolk — and stare. One of them pretends to be frightened, and wants to know " What those queer creatures are, going about in those Sibley-tent sort o' things."

Feb. 24. Tues. Fine day but cold. The Thirteenth is reorganized, and the Companies take their new places in the line, according to their Captains' rank, determined by the date of their muster-in. Many are extremely dissatisfied, contending that a minute, or an hour, is as good as a day in any such question of precedence. The change in rank is caused by an order, from the Adjutant General of the army, directing that all officers are to rank according to the date of their muster-in, and all mustered-in on the same day are to draw lots for precedence. About as fair, and about as wise, would it be for Gen. Hooker and Gen. Lee to " draw lots " for victories and defeats. But worst of all, orders are set as a wall against all duck-shooting. No more broiled duck, and wild duck broiled is good. Half the Reg. has been under arrest for shooting duck; dead duck and lame duck are all the fashion. A supply of new clothing issued to the men, and greatly needed. Our Brigade go out on review — a frozen review.

Feb. 25. Wed. Fair, sunny. The Ninth Corps inspected and reviewed. A very fine display; the finest review we have yet seen. Very slow, however, occupying upwards of five hours. The men of the 13th stand in line, with arms at a shoulder, for over two hours at a stretch. Hard work to " hold up your gun up " for that length of time, and without changing your position. The review ground is a long, smooth, nearly level plain, about two square miles in extent. There are 37 regiments of infantry, 6 batteries and a small body of cavalry in line — above 25,000 men, forming a line over a mile in length. The thousands of bayonets and the sea of trappings glittering in the sunshine, the dashing horsemen and wheeling columns are all very fine; but the long lines of tattered battle flags tell the tale of many a Ninth Corps field of battle, blood and death, of victory and of defeat. Many of these flags have but a narrow, fringed strip of bunting up and down the staff.

Feb. 26. Thurs. Clouds and sunshine, cold; a heavy rain at night. Reg. resting from their work of yesterday. We start out for a drill, but a thrice welcome shower sends every man to his quarters. Dress-parade at evening. The 103d N. Y. have a fine band, and late last night they played a delightful serenade near our camp.

Feb. 27. Fri. Fair, windy, quite cold. Company and Brigade drill, and rather long hours of it. Wild geese are flying over now in great flocks. Immense numbers of porpoises are sporting in the bay near camp ; and both they and the wild geese overhead go through their evolutions with as much promptness and regularity, nearly, as some of our brigades. A quick-speaking officer on Brigade drill, seeing a muddy place near by, and being proud of the well blacked shoes of his Company, orders : " Forward — don't puddle your boots, boys — March ! "

**Feb. 28. Sat.** Rainy. Inspection in general, camps and all, lasting about five hours. Reg. mustered for pay by Lt. Col. John Coughlin of the 10th N. H. Another day of rest would be most acceptable. On the whole, this month of February has been a time of great gain to this corps of the army, and the last part of the month has been very delightful in most respects. Many officers and men have visited Fortress Monroe and Norfolk, and hundreds of photographs of soldiers have traveled homeward. White collars and gloves are the fashion. The men and officers wear them while on camp and provost guard duty. We have no picket duty of consequence to perform at Newport News ; the enemy not near enough to cause serious concern.

**March 1. Sun.** Fair, with showers, cold. Division guard-mounting, a big show. Company inspection and Dress-parade. Lieut. E. W. Goss placed in command of Company I.

**March 2. Mon.** Fair. Drill forenoon and afternoon. A cold east wind blows all night. This tongue of sand is the wind's playground.

**March 3. Tues.** Fair, splendid day. Drill, drill, drill, Brigade and Battalion. All the members of the non-commissioned staff are required to drill as regularly as their duties will permit. Officers' mess board is good here now at a cost of $2.00 per week. Asst. Surgeon Sullivan returns to camp from home.

**March 4. Wed.** Fair, cold. Company, Battalion and Brigade drill.

**March 5. Thurs.** Fair, " confounded " cold. General Inspection at 9 a. m. Company drill forenoon, Battalion drill afternoon. Dress-parade. The war vessels in the Roads move up the stream into a naval line of battle. We enjoy a wide view of a large fleet. The rebel " new Merrimac " is said to have come down within sight of our fleet.

The burden of the battle of Fredericksburg, and of the winter camp, follows some men even here, and they cannot throw off the incubus, but remain unutterably solemn, doleful and dirty. There is one of them in the Thirteenth, a man who became depressed while burying our dead on the battle-field. Something must be done with this man to break the spell ; kindness, scolding or extra duty has had no effect. So on this exceeding sharp, frosty morning at Roll-call, about daylight, the poor fellow is ordered to step three paces to the front, and then to turn about and face his company in line. A corporal — a grim old sailor — and two strong men are ordered to the front beside him. These take their places, and are then directed to procure sea sand and soap, and to take this man at once to the brook, to strip him, and to scrub him from head to foot, with the soap and sand, as they would scrub a dirty floor. The brook is frozen over, and the water is of course icy cold. They start for their work; but when about half way to the brook, the man offers to keep himself "satisfactorily clean" if he can be spared this disgrace. He is allowed to try for himself, and directed to report within two hours; and as a matter of fact, within a week he is about the biggest dandy in the company to which he belongs.

March 6. Fri. Fair morning, cold. Battalion drill in afternoon broken up by a rain storm. Col. Stevens returns from home. Lieut. Ladd returns to the Reg. from his long sickness at Washington; has been absent since about Dec. 1, 1862.

March 7. Sat. Wet and muddy, no drill. The boys say "they have had enough of drilling, and would like to try a little sheeting for a week or two." A soldier in good health sleeps as soundly as a child. Saturdays are now usually devoted to cleaning camp, arms, etc., not much else done to-day excepting a Dress-parade about 5 p. m., at which sundry promotions are announced.

March 8. Sun. Pleasant. Usual Sunday work. Inspection of arms at 9 a. m., when we all get wet in a shower, our arms, clothing, everything; a thunder shower in March. Surgeon Richardson starts for home on leave ; he has been in poor health for a long time.

March 9. Mon. Fair. Reg. inspected by Capt. Hazard Stevens of Gen. Getty's staff. Drill pronounced good. The Thirteenth is a well drilled and fine appearing regiment. Of late, especially, almost every man has exhibited great pride in doing, and appearing, as well as he can.

The battle between the rebel iron-clad ram Merrimac, ten guns, and the Monitor, two guns, took place, off this shore, March 9, 1862. The Merrimac withdrew, disabled, to near Craney Island, and soon afterwards was blown up, and sunk in shoal water that just covers the hulk.

(July, 1887. The Merrimac has been raised and broken up recently, and sold in Richmond for old iron.)

March 10. Tues. Very stormy, cold. No outdoor work. Reg. votes for N. H. State governor; casting for Harriman 82 votes, for Gilmore 153, and for Eastman 324. (LUEY's diary.) The Reg. being in old and dirty barracks, finds it very difficult to keep arms and clothing clean. Some of the men, a very few, however, are exceeding careless, and vigorous measures have to be adopted to inculcate practical ideas of personal cleanliness.

March 11. Wed. Rainy forenoon Clears, and we enjoy a walk-round of ten or fifteen miles, in a long Battalion drill; something special. The whole 9th Corps is drilling, all up and down the plain as far as we can see, a grand and stirring scene. Sea breezes, clean camping ground, splendid rations, for the most part, and the great change in every respect from the winter camp, has generally transformed the men of the Ninth Army Corps, into fine and magnificent soldiers, self-respecting, erect, strong, healthy and hearty ; the change in the appearance of the troops, in one short month is wonderful indeed, while the common camp sports, frolics, play and entertainment have increased a hundred fold.

March 12. Thurs. Fine day, but cold. Company and Battalion drill. Orders arrive at 11 p. m. for the Reg. to be ready, with two days' cooked rations, to move to-morrow morning at nine o'clock. The cooks and those in care of rations and camp equipage work all night. A soldier in camp is always uneasy — to a live soldier camp life is no life at all. The boys are glad to escape this everlasting, long, hard drilling, let come what may, and greet this move with shouts and cheers. We are going to Suffolk. The enemy, bold and appearing in force, is threatening our outposts on the Blackwater, and driving them in. The Thirteenth are desirous to enter upon an active campaign ; to strike into the business for which they enlisted, to do their part to close this war, and return to the callings of civil life, in a permanent Union.

## CAMP NEAR SUFFOLK.

March 13. Fri. Clear, cold. Thirteenth promptly in line and ready at 9 a. m. (one account states that the Reg. was all ready to march at 8 a. m. — an hour ahead of the specified time), and marches quickly to the 'Landing' — an old ramshackle affair, and an open bid for accidents. Here we embark on the steamer 'Croton,' leave the wharf about 11 a. m., and sail to Norfolk, sixteen miles, arriving about 2 p. m. ; debark here, and the boys have two hours to look about the city. As we sail past the frigate 'Minnesota' her sailors man the yards and cheer. The weather grows colder and is very damp and chilling. A number of sick men belonging to the 13th, taken a few hours ago from the warm Hospital at Newport News upon the comfortable steamer, are led, after we cross to Portsmouth, to some open platform cars. The ride of 20 or 25 miles on open cars would be almost sure death to several of these men, and Asst. Surgeon Sullivan — in whose care they are — protests against such treatment. Protests being of no avail he puts his foot down, and refuses, with all the force he can, to have them put on the open cars at all. A war of words ensues, and a considerable delay is caused, but the thing is settled. Box cars, with a good supply of hay, are found, are attached to the train, the sick men are put in, and we move on toward Suffolk about 5 p. m., the most of the Reg. on open platform cars. After a slow ride of about 21 miles, we arrive, all half frozen, at our designated camping ground, a mile below Suffolk, at 6.30 p. m. Too late and dark to pitch our tents, and the most sleep on the ground in the open air. (" Devilish cold night." LUEY.) Norfolk and Portsmouth are now very much dilapidated, neglected in appearance, and very dirty.

Gen. Getty's whole Division — 3d Div. 9th A. C. — numbering about eight thousand men, comes up here to re-enforce Gen. Peck, who has about eight thousand troops partly entrenched, and is threatened by Confederate Gen. Longstreet with 30,000 men, all so posted to the west and north that they can be concentrated upon Suffolk in twenty-four hours. They call us now the " Army of Suffolk." The Thirteenth in the 3d

Brigade of Getty's Div., Col. Dutton, 21st Conn., commanding. The order was issued for the 1st Division to move from Newport News to this point; but through some mistake our 3d Division was sent here instead.

March 14. Sat. Very cold, clear. Reg. pitches its shelter tents, in order, this morning, and fits up camp generally. The main road from Suffolk to Portsmouth runs very nearly east and west where it passes our camp, and just below camp forks, into Jericho road to the left, and White Marsh road to the right. Our camp, on the north side of the main road, and close upon it, about one mile below Suffolk, is on a strip of low land, some of it very wet, a mere neck, between two swamps. The famous Dismal Swamp is near by on the south side, and on the north side, the Nansemond river, about one mile distant. Brig. Gen. Michael Corcoran, of the old 69th New York, has his "Irish Legion," four or five regiments, encamped about half a mile distant from us, across the road, southward. They have an enormous assembly tent, quite large enough for a huge circus. (Gen. Corcoran was killed by his horse falling upon him, Dec. 22, 1863.)

March 15. Sun. Damp, chilly, hazy. Reg. lays out camp-ground anew and pitches A tents for the officers. Usual Sunday duties. A number of us visit Suffolk, and find a low, mean, dirty place, which has long been wasting in carelessness and neglect. The father of Geo. H. Rollins of E visits camp and tries to obtain a discharge for his son, but without success.

March 16. Mon. Fair. Regimental courts martial are instituted. Drill resumed. On coming up here, the other night, the 16th Conn. were dumped from the cars, half frozen and without officers, tents, rations, guides, or anything — their train having been cut in two somewhere on the road. It was as dark as Egypt, and they knew neither where to go nor where to stay. They started off, however, for somewhere. First they tumbled down the railroad bank five or eight feet, then rolled over in water and mud two or three feet deep, then climbed up a steep bank, smashed through a fence, straggled through brush to clear ground and halted; then they nearly tore down a good house for firewood and built several large fires, and finally a New York regiment, hearing their noise, sent out and took care of them.

March 17. Tues. Pleasant. Reg. not doing much excepting work on the camp. St. Patrick's Day, and Corcoran's Irish Legion celebrate it in a high, barbaric fashion. Gathering all the horses he can, he mounts them with his best riders; mounts all the buglers he can obtain; calls in a battery of mountain brass-howitzers; makes an assembly of this large mounted host — a thousand or two apparently — and parades on the road. Then joined by his whole staff, up somewhere near Suffolk, he brings the whole cavalcade, in full uniform, bugles sounding furiously, and the mounted bands playing "St. Patrick's Day in the Morning," tearing down the road, and through camp, all their horses galloping at their highest speed. A stirring show, a tremendous hullaballoo. Four Irish regiments also turn out and march in grand procession through camp; their banners very numerous and gay. Each man wears a sprig of evergreen in his cap. Three mottoes are — " Erin and Columbia ; " " Irishmen to the rescue; " " Erin go bragh." The volunteer Irish element in our army is generally a magnificent fighting material — brave, reliable, true. The day closes with a torchlight procession, extremely noisy, but all in good nature. The whole day a wild scene from Old Ireland's wild hills and vales, acted more wildly in the wildest swamp of Virginia. Mrs. Stowe in " Dred " describes the Dismal Swamp most admirably ; but she never saw it with the annex of three or four thousand wild Irishmen, all shouting, yelling and cheering at once.

Some of Corcoran's men during the day capture a big negro cook in the 13th, known as "Nigger Joe," take him to their camp, strip him nearly naked, and make a " rainbow nigger " of him ; painting him in patches, bars and stripes, yellow, green, red, blue — every color they can muster, and then turn him loose. He returns to the 13th camp, running as if for dear life, scared half out of his wits, and looking worse than the evil one. This is another phase of the Irish question.

March 18. Wed. Very cold and disagreeable, some rain. Reg. building a bridge across the swamp to rifle-pits. Reg. receives whiskey rations again. Hot, strong coffee is better. The 25th New Jersey, some of whom broke back through the Thirteenth, on the night of Dec. 13, 1862, in the charge at Fredericksburg, are now encamped about half a mile below our camp, and near " Jericho." They are out, or are going out, of our Brigade — Col. Dutton's. We seem to be Brigaded variously, nowadays, for field purposes. One thing sure : wherever there is a ticklish, dangerous and hard place, there they will put the Thirteenth to hold the line firm. Several prisoners brought into our camp last night report the enemy in heavy force, above Suffolk, and about 18 miles distant.

March 19. Thurs. Rainy, snowy, cold. Reg. remains in quarters, the men rolled up in their blankets to keep warm. Heavy hail storm towards night. Reveille nowadays at the break of day, and half the time before daylight. Our cavalry vedettes are about four miles in advance of the infantry, on this front.

March 20. Fri. Snow storm ; nearly six inches in depth falls over all the camp, the wind, very severe, piling the snow in heaps, and driving it into every crack and cranny. The men, in shelter tents only, suffer severely. As one soldier of the 13th writes : " We have to sleep under a cotton sheet drawn over a pole. We keep warm by going to bed and covering up thick." Capt. Stoodley leaves camp for home on fifteen days' leave.

March 21. Sat. Stormy all day. Reg. in quarters, such as they are. This storm — hail, snow and rain mixed — caught us in a very awkward situation. When it commenced, we had just begun to fit up our camp, having taken down our tents for the purpose of putting them up in a better order; and were all in a hubbub. No camp could easily be in a worse condition. Several men crawled into empty barrels, leaving their feet out or heads out, and slept as "short" as nature would allow. The want of proper shelter lays up a large number of men. The compound of snow, hail and mud is nearly a foot deep all over camp. While we are in this mess, the story comes along to-day, that we are going at once to Tennessee! The Colonel of the 89th New York takes pity on the 13th, cleans some barracks, and offers them to Col. Stevens, and our Colonel declines them, for some reason. It is very difficult to keep fires burning out of doors, and none at all can be had in the tents, and all the men have suffered severely from the cold, the snow and the rain.

March 22. Sun. Warm, very muddy. Reg. in quarters. Usual Sunday duties so far as possible. Our three days of storm have made very bad work for the guard and pickets, and the Reg. in camp has been but a little better off. Many men found themselves in the mornings actually blanketed deep in snow. In fact some of the situations are positively laughable as well as pitiable. Three cold, dismal days indeed, and continuous snow, hail and rain for over 48 hours. Warmer to-day, however. A sharp skirmish is reported at the outposts, where we have heard heavy firing to-day. A few rebel prisoners come in to-night, and one of them on being asked what regiment he belonged to, replied: "To Lorngstrit's Ormy Co', er'ekn." ("Co'" for Corps.) One man of the 13th writes of to-day: "It has snowed and rained all the time for 48 hours, and we have had to lie in our tents to keep from freezing. Mud from six inches to six feet deep. Saw an immense host of niggers, and their young ones of all sizes and colors. I killed two snakes to-day." Probably a true mixture! The snakes entered many of the tents for shelter, when the storm commenced.

March 23. Mon. Fine day and warm. It is said that the enemy's troops along the Blackwater have no shelter at all, excepting such as they can improvise out of pine boughs, etc. They would better come down and take our camp — it is a beauty. We would soon be mutually warmed up, and we all need it. A party from the Reg. attended church yesterday in Suffolk. The citizens kept away; none of them will attend church where there are any Yankees. Wags put up signs: "All seats free!" Many officers in the 13th are short of funds, while a recent order deprives them of the privilege of obtaining rations from the Commissary on credit! But where is the officer in the Thirteenth stupid enough to starve for his country? The whole land flows with milk and honey — for those who know where to send a spry forager to procure them.

March 24. Tues. Cloudy; showery afternoon. Dress-parade at sundown. Our pickets go out every morning for 24 hours. A thin line of cavalry vedettes are stationed about four miles from camp; the infantry outposts about $3\frac{1}{2}$ miles from camp. The worst danger is from "Bush-whackers," men who pretend to be farmers in the daytime, and who shoot our pickets at night. Surgeon Richardson returns to the Reg.

to-night. Regimental Hospital moved to a dry piece of ground, and a board floor laid.

March 25. Wed. Fair. Reg. drills all day. Detail cutting logs. We already have quite a strong line of earth-works around our camp.

March 26. Thurs. Fair. Nights very cold. Heavy detail, 200 men, sent out on picket ; squad drill in afternoon. Along here one day a detail from the Thirteenth penetrated the Dismal Swamp for about two miles, making their way at times on floating logs. They came out near a canal, where they passed the night, and then returned to camp, having had enough of that kind of scouting. The reverberations of a cannon shot heard in the swamp are deafening. Lieut. Forbush, officer of the day, has a large quantity of white, clean sand hauled into camp to-day, and dresses the sidewalks with it, covering up the black, vile mud. A very great improvement.

March 27. Fri. Fair. Pickets return. Company drill. Capt. Dodge of B returns from leave. Some of the companies now have quite comfortable quarters, but the camp-ground is very wet. The picket sent to-day from the Reg. numbers 200 men, with Lt. Col. Bowers, Major Storer, Captains Grantman, Julian and Buzzell, and Lieuts. Wilson, Curtis, Sawyer and Saunders. Ten men are sent to work on a bridge, forty are detailed for fatigue, in care of camp, etc., and sixty for guard duty of various sorts. The rest drill, in squads, and on Brigade drill also. Capt. Bradley, in temporary command of the Reg. in camp, holds a Battalion drill with less than five men to a company, and goes through all the movements, strictly according to "Casey." A sample day.

Our "wells" here are made by sinking a flour barrel in the ground. The water tastes as a brick yard, or a new, wet country road might taste. The color a "yellowish-nasty." The reptiles are just now thawing out, and these little wells are their chief delight. A man's coffee of a morning is more refreshing, if, when he goes to his well for water, he first takes a stick, and drives out of the water its last night's occupants — a snake* or two, some toads, and frogs, and lizards, and a multitude of insects ; for then he dips up their bed clothes, so to speak, and makes his coffee out of their unwashed linen. If he has no well, he varies the flavor, by procuring water from a pool, where in addition to the above list of regular boarders, there have bivouacked for a period, some old shoes, rags, bones and a few turtles. This is a little sketch of a No 1 coffee-water well. "You go for a soldier — and you take your chances."

SERGT. GIBBS of E.

March 28. Sat. Cloudy, very windy. Heavy thunder storm about one p. m. "Linen tents slacken when wet, and the wind plays the Dickens with them to-day ; walloping them off the poles, and tearing out the ropes." The men have to turn out under arms at daylight ; no furloughs allowed ; signs of coming trouble. The 11th Penn. cavalry have on exhibition the Confederate "Rocketts Battery," recently captured.

**March 29. Sun.** Fair; very cold at night. Regimental inspection in the forenoon; brigade Dress-parade in the afternoon; both well done. A few members of the Reg. attend church — Episcopal — in Suffolk town. Chaplain Jones at home on leave.

Charles A. Lull, our drummer-boy, has reddish yellow hair. He and Ira E. Wright, the other drummer-boy, greatly enjoy a chat with Lt. Col. Bowers. The writer called at the tent of his most excellent friend Lt. Col. Bowers and found these two boys there. After they withdrew, the Lt. Colonel turned to the writer, and said: "These boys make me feel young again. Wright and that brass-mounted boy are the oldest men in this Division; I am but a mere youth compared with them — but I like these prompt, smart boys."

Surgeon George B. Twitchell went with the Regiment into Virginia and remained with it during the most of the time up to the battle of Fredericksburg, but during that battle he was detained in Washington. His eminent abilities soon led to his being detailed as Brigade Surgeon on the staff of Arthur H. Dutton, Colonel of the 21st Conn. comdg. 3d Brigade 3d Div. 9th Army Corps, in December 1862. He did not again return to the Thirteenth, and was present in no battle where the Thirteenth was engaged. March 24, 1863, he resigned to receive promotion, having been appointed Surgeon U. S. Vols. by commission dated January 7, 1863, and bearing the signatures of President Abraham Lincoln, and Edwin M. Stanton, Secretary of War. On receiving this appointment he was ordered to report to Gen. U. S. Grant, then commanding Dept. of Tennessee, and was assigned to duty as Surgeon in Chief of the 7th Division of the 17th Army Corps, about April 15, 1863. After the fall of Vicksburg, July 4, 1863, he was assigned to duty as Surgeon in Chief of the 6th Division of the 17th Army Corps, at which post he remained until he was honorably discharged the service because of disability, Sept. 15, 1863. He was ever a faithful, true friend to the Thirteenth, both during the war and afterwards.

**March 30. Mon.** Cloudy, cold; showery afternoon. Brigade drill. Dress-parade at sundown. A number of men sent with Descriptions to Battery A, Heavy Artillery, as a permanent detail.

**March 31. Tues.** Rained heavily all last night and this forenoon; afternoon cold and clear. Mud deep; no drill. March is as hard and blustering South as North. The Reg. ordered to send a strong picket to near the small-pox Hospital on Jericho Creek about three miles from camp. The Brigade, all excepting the 13th, are ordered to build and garrison forts. This means any amount of marching-about for our Reg. A large force of cavalry passes camp outward bound.

**April 1. Wed.** Cold, fair, a high wind. Battalion drill, and the wind makes such a noise that we cannot hear the orders. Negroes find their way to our camp — out of slavery, fresh — with steers and cows harnessed to carts just as horses are, bits and all, and are the happiest persons in the whole Confederacy. On picket to-day Wooster E. Woodbury of C climbed a tall pine-tree near the small-pox Hospital, Suffolk, to look within the enemy's lines over the river; one of the bravest acts done in the Regiment, the tree being within easy rifle-shot of the rebels.

April 2. Thurs. Cold. Company drill. It is not an unusual thing here now for a soldier, on rising in the morning, to shake out of his blankets a full-grown snake, a copperhead or moccasin. These cool nights cause the snakes to desire warm bedfellows.

April 3. Fri. Cold and windy. We sign Pay-rolls for four months' pay now due, and draw A tents. Two good things at once. An A tent is small, but when mounted on walls of logs — " stockaded " — it makes a good roof, and holds on better than any other. The amount of shamming, "playing sick," in the Reg. becomes a serious question. Rheumatism is the favorite plea. A hypodermic injection in the region of the muscle complained of works some wonderful cures — especially of all desire for another injection. Our Surgeon is a first-class genius.

April 4. Sat. Rainy, cold, windy, and snow falls to-night to the depth of about six inches. No drill. Heavy detail on picket, a terrible work in this weather. Loud cannonade heard about dark. Our cavalry have a brush with the enemy, a few miles above our camp, and drive him; but four horses, with empty saddles, come slowly back this morning into camp. Capt. Stoodley returns to the regiment from leave. Our pickets leave camp under Capt. Goss at 8 a. m., and go out about five miles on the line that runs from the railroad to the Nansemond, where there are two Union gunboats. The night is very dark, a wet snow falling from 4 p. m. until near morning, then followed by a heavy rain. The pickets have no shelter. Division teams and ambulances come to camp to-day. Ex-Lieutenant Albe Holmes of H, who resigned Feb. 19, 1863, is nominated by Lieut. Gafney for sutler of the 13th, and is to-day elected by a unanimous vote — save one.

April 5. Sun. Cold, some rain. No work outside of quarters, except a Dress-parade at sundown. Last night, an April snow storm, of nearly six inches, gave us the parting blow of winter. It has been cold, wet and generally hard weather for campaigning since we came over here. The weather is a great item in the soldier's life when in the field. He is often confined to one spot for many hours of extreme exposure, while all his life is spent practically out of doors. Pickets are relieved at 11 a. m. and return to camp through snow and mud knee deep. A tents arrive for the men of the 13th.

"I was posted to-day a sentinel in front of Col. Stevens' Hdqrs. There was a continual stream of officers — Generals, Colonels, and others — calling upon the Colonel, and I was kept very busy saluting them as they passed in and out. Just before I was relieved, Adjt. Boutwell came out of Col. Stevens' tent, with paper and pencil in hand, and said that Col. Stevens wished my name and company. Knowing that I had done nothing wrong, and had been prompt and correct in my salutes, I did not feel much worried, but still I was anxious to know what it meant. Well, at

Dress-parade this afternoon, an order was read appointing me to the position of left general guide of the Regiment. As the directions are that: 'The two best drilled Sergeants in the regiment shall act as right and left general guides,' I naturally felt complimented by being selected from nearly a thousand men — or boys as we were then — and placed in such a responsible position. I acted in this capacity until April 24, 1864, when I was detached for duty at Division Headquarters."

WM. H. SPILLER, Co. C.

April 6. Mon. Fair. Reg. paid to March 1, 1863, for four months. Had a review instead of a Dress-parade. Bad — too much mud. Reg. ordered to turn out under arms at daylight; to remain under arms half an hour, then stack arms in line of battle. About a dozen men from each company are daily detailed for picket duty, and remain in camp, armed and equipped for an instant call.

April 7. Tues. Fair. Battalion drill on rough ground. The new greenbacks go largely to Suffolk, and find a poor market. We have seen but few ladies since leaving the vicinity of Washington last December. Some of the men say that for four months they have not set eyes upon a white woman. Under these circumstances men are somewhat excusable for staring when a white woman appears. Two appeared to-day in Suffolk, visiting town, from a distant plantation, on a shopping tour, and elegantly clad. They are young, handsome, and aristocratic in appearance. They are seen to enter a dry goods store, and we naturally wait to see them when they come out — if they don't keep us waiting too long. Presently they appear, take their carriage and drive off. Carriage — a little, old, rickety, country "ding-cart" on two wheels, that go wabble-wabble — the two beautiful ladies sit on straw spread on the bottom of the cart; driver — a little, ragged darkey mounted on a high stool in the front part of the cart; harness — a combination utterly tangled, of strings and ropes, with many ends hanging; team — a small, poor, bony, dirty, yellow-red cow! No "antique and horrible" procession ever had a more ridiculous turn-out. The rebels had taken from the family all movable property of any value, for military purposes, as they said.

April 8. Wed. Fair. Grand Review of the 3d Division by Gen. Peck and Gen. Getty, in the afternoon. Very tiresome in the mud, by which the troops are badly spattered, but still a fine review. Our A tents are now mounted for roofs on log walls about three feet high. Bunks (beds) are made on each side, and across the back end. A bunk is made in this way: four forked sticks are driven into the ground, and left standing about one foot high. In these forks strong sticks are placed crosswise the bunk, and upon these are placed long, small poles, lengthwise the bunk. Spread upon the poles are red-cedar boughs, if possible to procure them, or those of the pine, or leaves, hay, or what best can be had. On the boughs is spread a rubber blanket; the woolen blankets are used to roll one's self up in. The result is a springy, elastic and easy bed fit for the warrior gods themselves; or for a better person — the Union soldier. Red-cedar boughs make the best bed, fragrant and soporific.

April 9. Thurs. Fair. Company and Battalion drill. Reg. works hard and long on its miserable camp-grounds, makes streets, digs ditches, etc., to give it the semblance of dry ground. The whole Dismal Swamp region is a vast peat bog, and is like a sponge full of water. Seven bad men, for doing bad deeds, sit on a rail near the guard-house, for several hours. The contrivance is called the "guard-house mule;" it raises them about ten feet above the ground —a fine perch for human buzzards. There is a class of men in the army who, on the eve of any move, put up a job to make trouble, for the purpose of being placed under arrest, and so escape duty, and, may be, danger. They plan for this weeks ahead. They are caught, occasionally and deserve a severe punishment. A few hundred of them would paralyze a brigade.

Because of the little excitement along the front, the colored people are hurrying within our lines in large numbers. They come in poor, destitute, starved and ragged. Rations are delivered them by the government. While the adults excite some sympathy among the men, it is naturally less than the black children receive. The odd scraps of the soldiers' poorest rations are better food than these little fellows have been accustomed to receiving; and they gather about the men at their meals, watching every motion with their large, pathetic, longing eyes. As a result they receive many a nice fresh lunch; but while their mouths are equally full of food and flooding thanks, both their hands are ready to steal all they can reach and hold — so much for slavery's moral training. The men hire the negroes to sing and dance; it is a source of unending amusement.

## SIEGE OF SUFFOLK.

**April 10. Fri.** Fair, warm. The camp was full of rumors all last night. Many officers kept awake nearly all night, expecting momentarily to be called out, and to meet the enemy. The camp guard were ordered to allow no man to pass out or in without satisfactory papers, and the result was a motley gathering at the guard-house. Early this morning the arms and ammunition of every man in camp are closely examined, and a special muster is made of all the troops in our Division. At 7 a. m. Companies A, H, and G, with Major Storer in command, leave camp and go down on the Nansemond three or four miles, a part for picket, and a part to garrison a fort. The 21st Conn., on the river about four miles below Suffolk, have a very fine camp, and are building their famous "Fort Connecticut." One of these heavy artillerymen of the 21st, as our pickets pass their camp, assumes a contemptuous manner and tone, and asks Lieut. Churchill where — as he was pleased to call us — "this dirty Thirteenth" is going. Churchill replies : "We're going, of course, to relieve the 21st Conn. — who are frightened by the muskrats down here." This ended the conversation. Lieut. Churchill was quick at upsetting sauceboxes.

While the other seven companies of the Reg., left in camp, are on Dress-parade about 5 p. m., orders arrive for them to march. They stack arms, break ranks, go to quarters, pack up, and are in line again in less than fifteen minutes — all ready. The majority were back in their places in eleven minutes. They start about 6.30 p. m. and march until 10.30 p. m., and about nine miles down the Nansemond, before having supper; and then lay on their arms all night — on the bare, wet ground, in thick woods, and in line of battle — prepared for an instant move.

Gen. Longstreet's first regular advance in force upon our lines is made to-day, and he is expected to attempt to force a passage of the river to-night at this point where we lay ; for which purpose he has had a roadway, winding and masked, cut down the sloping bank to the water's edge just opposite our place of bivouac. We hope he will try it. The Thirteenth, the 4th R. I. and the 103d N. Y. occupy to-night a position directly opposite the mouth of Western Branch and are enjoined to be prepared for action ; the night here, however, passes in quiet, though we can hear heavy firing in the distance. Troops ordered to New Berne are held here for a time as a measure of safety. A soldier of the Reg. writes home — and it shows the uncertainty of campaigning life : "The drums to-day beat the call for Dress-parade as usual. On assembling, the men are ordered to hurry to their tents, get one day's rations, their blankets, etc., and to fall in again as soon as possible. This done, we were soon on our way for a place unknown to us, and marched about ten miles."

April 11. Sat. Clear. Now come the shovels. We commence at the first gleam of daylight this morning to dig rifle-pits and trenches, and to build a fort close upon the bank of the Nansemond, working in connection with the 4th R. I. We work all day shoveling, turn in at dark, are again called about 9 p. m., and start on a hasty march back again to our camp near Suffolk, leaving all our provisions, supplies and heavy baggage on the river bank. Some of our men fall asleep while marching, trip their toes, and fall headlong. Companies G and H are relieved, but Company A, Capt. Grantman, is left for two or three days; and when the men of the 13th come again, to relieve them, Company A thinks they may be the enemy, prepares for a fight, and halts them at a long distance, until they find out who are coming. Capt. Grantman has no countersign, hence his extreme caution. The Union troops stationed across the Nansemond are withdrawn to-night, under cover of the gunboat 'Stepping Stones,' Capt. C. C. Harris, and the bridge at Suffolk is destroyed. The Long-roll resounds, twice to-night, all up and down the Union lines.

Gen. Peck is chief in command. Gen. Getty has command of the river defenses. The story in camp is that Gen. Longstreet, counting upon his greatly superior numbers, hoped to cut Gen. Peck's troops off, by crossing the river in overwhelming force, and so capture the entire garrison; and is greatly 'non-plused' when he finds Gen. Getty's troops posted in force all along the river from Hill's Point to Suffolk, and ready to meet him at every point.

April 12. Sun. A pleasant day. Col. Corcoran shot and killed Lt. Col. Kimball, 9th N. Y., on the picket line at 4 o'clock this morning. The cause of the shooting is unknown.

Reg. arrives at camp near Suffolk about 1.30 a. m., and turns in for a little rest — only to be called out again immediately; the enemy attacking on the Somerton and Edenton roads. Many of our men work on a bridge, every available man busy. Before the day is out we form in line in our rifle-pits near the river, two or three miles below Suffolk. Off to our left troops are hastily forming line — a long line of battle — for the enemy has near there driven in our pickets. Things grow decidedly interesting and lively, the muskets rattling, the cannon booming, the shells flying. There is nothing under the sun so exhilarating, inspiriting, and full of life and blood-stirring snap, as a sharp fight, when once you are at it. The day is quite warm, and some very rapid movements cause a number of our weaker men to fall out. The sudden stir involves rather more than a brigade, quite a little army. The enemy in large force is in plain view on the Petersburg Railroad, northward and west of town. Sharp picket firing all day. Night again finds us lying on our arms, on the ground, and as a whole without tents or cover. The citizens are held in Suffolk to prevent the enemy from shelling the city.

April 13. Mon. Rainy a. m., fair p. m. Now comes the tug of war. Reg. in line at 5 a. m. in the streets of their old camp — seven companies, the rest on picket. The Reg. relieves the 10th N. H. on the picket line, along Jericho canal, northeast of town, about 9 a. m., and are set at work on the defenses near Fort Jericho, which commands the railroads to Norfolk. The 10th N. H. go farther down the river. We are on the southeast side of the Nansemond with about 16,000 men, in a long, thin line as a whole. Gen. Longstreet's army, by Gen. Peck estimated at 40,000 men, is on the other side of the river, and threatening in force. He is expected to attack us to-night, and rifle-pits and defenses are being made with all possible dispatch. Houses and buildings are burning on all sides. The enemy disables one of our gunboats, amid a tremendous cannonading near by, and we can hear and see the bursting shells — near enough!

A bridge is built to-day across a creek and marsh — 100 to 150 feet wide — in an incredibly short period of time. The men of the Thirteenth stack arms, cut trees and bring them on their shoulders. Stringers are laid on forked trees set on end opposite each other in the water and mud, the tops inclining inward a very little, and the logs, ten or twelve feet long, are laid on about as rapidly as they can be counted. A layer of brush and earth completes the bridge. Our column, desiring to cross, has merely halted a few minutes, when the bridge is all completed, and the troops proceed on their way. A few men add more supports, and the bridge is ready for artillery, which soon follows. The churches in Suffolk are to be used as hospitals in case of a battle, and Asst. Surgeon Sullivan is ordered to report at the Methodist church when the battle begins.

The entire native population, excepting the negroes, are non-committal, and appear to answer all questions evasively, or dodgingly. They are free with opinions — that always look two ways at once. Their most positive assertions are rendered utterly valueless by their everlasting " er'ekn " appended to every sentence. The Southron's " I reckon " beats the Yankee's " I kalkerlate " all out of time and number. The following expression by a native shows the folly of it: " Jigger my buttons, 'f I ain't tiud of this dog'ond rackit — er'ekn."

April 14. Tues. Fair; a few showers. Reg. returns to the old camp near Suffolk to-night, having been relieved on the picket line; but is called into the front lines again at midnight. Our gunboats and the enemy's batteries make midnight hideous. We have been scattered all along the river and Jericho Creek and canal, for three or four miles; a sort of flying column. Where we are guarding the section of line is considered very important, and we are worked to the limit of endurance. At night detachments from the Reg. march a few miles, then halt and build camp-fires — ten or a dozen fires nearly in a line; when they are well a-burning, we move again for a few miles, halt, and built more camp-fires; then move again, and so repeat the deception over and over again — a deception innocent, excepting in reference to the rail fences burnt up. The zealous enemy shells these mock camp-fires. " We never knew of his hitting but one fire; that was severely wounded by a shell, and died (out) before morning." While the boys were building these mock camp-fires last night, one old fellow stood in his front door-way and for half an hour poured out a perfect 'hypermyriorama' of awful and eternal damnation experiences and places, and scenes most foul and horrid, for every agency under the sun — and above it — that was in any way or degree responsible for this war or was carrying it on. He piled in one promiscuous condemned heap every one he could think of, from a rebel sutler down to the leaders of the Confederacy (as he graded them) and from the meanest Yankee soldier up to President Lincoln — all because the soldiers burned up ten rods of a rickety old rail fence on his paternal acres now too poor to grow wolf-grass.

Col. Corcoran's Irish Legion have a severe brush — on the 11th to 14th — with the enemy on the Edenton road; the 21st Conn. in support. There has been heavy firing all day up to 5 p. m., and Gen. Peck states that the enemy attacks along the Nansemond with 11,000 men. This afternoon, after a four hours' bombardment — from about 1 p. m. — three of our gunboats silence a heavy rebel shore-battery on the river. Many houses are torn down in and about Suffolk, to obtain an unobstructed range for our guns. A large force of Union artillery comes in and passes to the front this afternoon. Company A, 13th, returns to the Regiment.

April 15. Wed. Very rainy. About midnight, last night, the Reg. turned out of camp in great haste and occupied the front rifle-pits (not far from our camp near Suffolk) and at daylight form in line as a support for a battery in action on the river bank, where the enemy is expected to attempt a crossing. Later in the forenoon, for a couple of hours, the firing on our front is very severe, the lines very close; an affair of the pickets and artillery. The gunboats are now, noon, shelling the woods where the enemy is supposed to be — exceeding noisy business. About sunset three companies of the 13th go with the 10th N. H. and a section of the Second Wisconsin Battery, all under command of Col. Donohoe of the 10th, to a point near Fort Connecticut, arriving about 11 p. m., and there work and skirmish all night; are absent 48 hours. A part of this expedition crosses the river, reconnoitres the enemy's camp, have a brush with his pickets, and returns without loss. The Thirteenth is called into line three times to-night, each time by a false alarm. Sergeant Batchellor of D writes: "A solid shot came near Jesse W. Place of D, and knocked him over without breaking the skin. He jumped up, ran as far as he could, and then fell. He will probably recover in a few days."

April 16. Thurs. Showery and sunny. The cannonading brings rain, as it usually does. About 9 a. m. the enemy's batteries and our gunboats have a duel, the pickets and sharpshooters firing continuously all the time during the artillery fire. The Reg. in rifle-pits and busy firing too. The narrow river divides the two armies, and both banks are honeycombed with defenses, and swarming with men. "Show your head — and soon you are dead." When a bullet strikes a man's head, it makes a sound like a blow upon a basket of sea shells, and causes no possible pain. A bullet striking a man's body makes a dull thud, or crack if a bone is struck. There has been an increasing cannonading and picket firing for these last five or six days. Shells and bullets are flying at all times, and in every direction. But the distance disturbs aim, and few are hurt; besides there is much timber for shelter. The larger part of the 13th are moved up the river, about four miles this afternoon. The 9th Vermont comes up as a re-enforcement.

April 17. Fri. Fair, warm. Reg. on picket near Fort Jericho. Lively firing on both sides — we cannot show anything without calling over a rebel bullet. A hat held up on a spade brings several bullets, and two of them striking the spade are elegantly flattened. The firing of muskets and cannon, far and near for many miles, is incessant. Every night picks, shovels and axes, thousands of them, are busy. Forts grow up in a night — and cut full sets of teeth. Jonah's gourd and Jack's beanstalk are fair types of the growth of Gen. Peck's and Gen. Getty's defensive works along the Nansemond. The enemy is equally busy. The constant alarms, watchings, marchings, picket duty, shoveling, chopping, and exposure to rain and cold, night and day, are enough to wear out men of steel. The men of the 13th do their share of the hard work, and some think a little more. Heavy re-enforcements join us, fifteen or twenty regiments in the last twenty-four hours.

"A New Hampshire soldier wearily digging in the small hours of the night, called out to his neighbor: 'I say, Bill, I hope Old Peck will die two weeks before I do.' 'Why so?' asked Bill. 'Because he will have hell so strongly fortified, in that time, that I can't get in.' Then Bill and his neighbor, greatly encouraged, again commence shoveling."

April 18. Sat. Fair, warm. Reg. everywhere; marching, digging, skirmishing, and building mock camp-fires at night. The enemy's shells and bullets thicker than ever. The boys think that the enemy has struck a lead mine. In a short time to-day, one of the Thirteenth's picket posts, entrenched on the river, fires over forty rounds per man. The enemy equally busy in replying. A day of severe picket firing all along the river. The line of the Nansemond is divided between Colonels Dutton and Harland; the Thirteenth to-day holding the position next below the mouth of Jericho Creek. (Official Report.) Two gunboats — one of them aground — have a six hours' contest with the Hill's Point Battery. Both escape, badly riddled. Gen. Dix sends up a dispatch highly complimenting Gen. Peck's troops. Adjt. Boutwell returns to duty. Under date of to-day General Dix commanding the Union forces here says of the enemy: "We have ascertained that the enemy's force is about 38,000 men; they have come for a campaign, and not for a raid or diversion."

Now the writer must again speak of himself — how to-day a necessity was laid upon him. A few men of the Thirteenth are in a rifle-pit, dug in a wide, bare space on the river bank, and flanked by a few trees. The first fort below the mouth of Jericho Creek is situated a few rods to the right, and there is a spring of water a few rods to the left, in a little brush. The men are very thirsty, and Charles F. Gerrish of E volunteers to go for water — for Gerrish scarcely knows what fear is. He takes several canteens, ties the strings together, springs out of the pit, and makes a rush for the spring. He is almost instantly shot in the thigh, and one leg is utterly disabled. He falls, drops the canteens a rod from the pit, and wriggles and scrambles back into the pit, where he must lie until night. His wound is a very bad one, his jacknife being broken in pieces and driven into his thigh with the bullet. Water now must be had — and the writer must go for it. There is no alternative, so he throws off his coat, not thinking of his white flannel shirt sleeves, springs out of the pit, picks up the canteens dropped by Gerrish, and succeeds in reaching the spring, filling the canteens, and returning to the rifle-pit, among many bullets, unharmed. He is now very warm, and keeps his coat off. The pit is so small that a spade must be had to enlarge it; all on account of Gerrish, who is a tall man, lying at full length on the bottom of the pit, and suffering unutterable tortures. The writer must now go to the fort — 50 to 60 yards distant — for a spade, and so he springs again out of the pit, and as swiftly as possible runs the gauntlet of the enemy's fire to the fort; there regains his breath, takes two spades, holds them so as to protect his head with one and his side with the other, and thus returns to the pit. While returning with the spades, he is not aware that the enemy fires at him one single shot — and at night he is told at the fort that the enemy cheered him. The enemy possibly recognized the white shirt sleeves. There is no credit in any of this — the writer had to go.

April 19. Sun. Fair. Capt. Stoodley with about a dozen men from Company G goes out on the 'Neck,' either really or almost an island, in a great bend of the river, where they receive the fire of the enemy from all sides at once. How they ever got safely out of the scrape is a wonder. Until to-day the Reg. has been in the rifle-pits along the Nansemond, a part of the line about two miles below Suffolk, and stretched out for a long distance on 'Jericho Point.' Most of the firing at long range, and a great deal of it; comparatively quiet, however, to-day, and the whole Reg., with the exception of a few pickets who went into the rifle-pits at 2 p. m., is once more together to-night. Col. Stevens has charge of the Jericho Point defenses.

The very brilliant Hill's Point Battery affair occurs about sunset to-night. This afternoon six companies of the 8th Conn. and six companies of the 89th N. Y., in all about 280 men, under Col. John E. Ward of the 8th Conn. (a part of the expedition passing Ft. Connecticut at 2 p. m.), go to the river and embark on the 'Stepping Stones,' and at dusk suddenly attack Fort Huger (pronounced Hu-jee) located on the forks near Reed's Ferry, practically the left of Gen. Longstreet's line, and the last earthwork on his left. Our forces capture two 24-pounders and four 12-pounders, brass cannon (taken from us at Harper's Ferry), and 100 to 150 prisoners. The affair was a combined attack by our sailors and infantry — both of whom seem to have been first in entering the fort; though it appears that the sailors, knowing most of the ground, were a little ahead.

At any rate the affair was very brilliant, and a great discouragement to the enemy, who never afterwards seemed to care much about permanently holding Hill's Point, and gave his attention to the narrower part of the river nearer Suffolk. Hill's Point lies near where the river widens into a bay. Gen. Getty holding the right of Gen. Peck's line, along the river and Jericho Creek — or 'Western Branch,' — had to do with Gen. Longstreet's centre and left. One of these captured brass cannon had a hole scooped out of one side of it by a large grape shot — showing the force of grape. The 10th N. H. had a hand in the Ft. Huger affair, as a reserve. It is said that the rebel commander, seeing himself overpowered, surrendered instanter to save life, calling out : " We cave, we cave, don't fire ; " and upon his exchange was cashiered for losing the fort by such a surprise and capture. A rebel in this captured battery tried to desert this afternoon, was caught in the act and tied hand and foot. When the rebels saw they must abandon their battery, they blew the fellow's brains out ; and so our men found him to-night, nearly headless, still tied, and stretched out on the ground within the fort.

April 20. Mon. Rainy. Reg. on picket day and night about two miles from camp. Re-enforcements coming in all day in large numbers. Our men have a few hours' respite now and then, march back from the rifle-pits into the pines, lie down in some little ravine and take a nap, while the bullets and shells fly across overhead — the sort of angels that sing above and around the soldier's couch. At five o'clock p. m. we are hurriedly moved up to within about twenty rods of our rifle-trenches, and are formed in line of battle in reserve. The enemy seem to act to-day over the Ft. Huger affair like hornets whose nest has received a punch with a pole ; and they are expected to resent it by a dash to-night. One soldier remarks : " Guess Longstreet swared." When the brave expedition with their trophies of captured guns and prisoners — among them a number of very tall Texans — march up through and along our lines, they are cheered to the echo. A soldier of the 13th writes : " Gen. Getty says he can depend on the 13th, and I guess he means it — by the way he makes us hang to these lines."

The labor expended in chopping, shoveling, screen and gambion making is enormous. One of these mornings the 8th Conn. wake up to find their camp-flag replaced by a sheet, on which is painted in large letters : " Peck's Avengers, or the Basket-makers of the Nansemond."

Col. Stevens is fond of trying to gain information from the front, and to learn what kind of land — if any at all — there is in the swamp of Jericho Creek between our lines and the edge of the river toward the enemy ; thinks he may want to run a cannon out there, and therefore desires a brave and trusty man to move out and explore. Upon errands of this sort he has sent, several times, First Sergeant Charles M. Kittredge of B with two or three men. It is like going into the jaws of death, and into the gulf of the bottomless pit, at one and the same time — the whole region is a slough. Nevertheless, Kittredge goes with his men, and managing to return alive, reports each time that there is no dry land to be seen in that vicinity. One of the men, on an occasion like this, reported to the Colonel that: "No man could get a cannon out there on a boat — it was so infernally wet."

April 21. Tues. Showery, cold. Reg. on picket day and night. We have been operating for the most of the time in these last two weeks along the Nansemond river bank, and the shores of Jericho Creek, on the left, to Battery Morris near the island, on the right — space enough, and work enough, for two regiments, the place an intricate succession of creeks and miry swamps. We are relieved by the 21st Conn., which remains on the same line here until May 2d. Some of the men, under the hard strain, become so tired and used up that they go to sleep while marching, trip, and fall headlong into the brush. Officers of the guards and pickets have to be continually moving along the sentry line, both day and night, lest some poor, overworked man shall fall asleep at his post, and invite disaster.

We remain late to-day in line of battle in reserve, and lie on our arms until midnight, when we are all suddenly called up — "routed out in a hurry" — and in great haste go forward into our rifle-pits. The night passes in comparative quiet, however, except for one incident. We are on a tongue of land entering the river northward. On the end of it are two cannon in a little redoubt. To the right of it, sheltered by the bank, is a gunboat, carrying one very large gun. A part of the Thirteenth are in the rifle-pits, a part in the rear of them on the grass and weeds, with no cover but the skies, and nearly all are sound asleep. Now, one man in the Regiment is a little traveling tin-store. He carries an iron spider and more tin dippers and tin plates than any other three men, and sleeps with them all tied upon him. When the night is at nearly the stillest hour the big gunboat cannon is fired not 100 feet distant from us, and the huge shell tears across the tongue of land, directly over our heads, with a terrific roar, and bursts short. Our hero is roused from sound sleep by the hideous noise, springs high into the air with a loud scream, loses his balance and falls back in a heap and with a great rattle and crash of tin. The whole Regiment is waked by the gunboat's discharge, and our hero furnishes the bit of comedy necessary to relieve the unpleasant annoyance. The boys laugh at him heartily while swearing at the gunboat — then all go to sleep again. He is ordered to reduce his stock, both of his tin and his scream. He is joked unmercifully about the affair.

The picket reserve, a part from the Thirteenth, have to lie all of one night within fifty feet of two field-pieces, while they are being fired, alternately, every five minutes. They sleep, however, through the incessant rap — rap — rap, so very tired are they. A constant succession of similar sounds rather conduces to drowsiness. One man said it made him "feel sleepy just the same as good Parson Blank's liturgy used to do, up in Yanktown."

April 22. Wed. Clear, cold. Reg. assembles at 10 a. m., and

returns to our old camp, near Suffolk, arriving at noon, having been relieved in the night again by the 21st Conn. Capt. Goss cheers himself and enlivens the camp by playing his flute. Thirteenth transferred to Gen. Harland's Brigade. This noon ends a period of thirteen days and twelve nights out of camp in the swamps of the Nansemond; all the time under fire, with little sleep, having no shelter worth the name, in very much rain, fording brook, swamp and creek, at constant picket duty, chopping and work on entrenchments, and in hourly expectation of an attack by the enemy. Every member of the Thirteenth has worked from five to ten pounds off his weight, and used up nearly half his effective strength. Rest is imperative. Our clothing, torn and muddy, looks as if it had been run through a threshing machine, been washed in the brickyard pond with ochre for soap, and then dried on a clay-bank.

Every time the enemy laid his plans to surprise Gen. Getty, and to force the passage of the river, Gen. Getty had ready, at that very point, batteries in position and troops in line; surprised the surprisers, and sent them speedily to the cover of their works. We have made strong lines from three to five miles in length; forts, redoubts, and rifle-parapets, with all the appliances of covert way, ditch and abatis. For ten days Gen. Longstreet invested our forces on three sides.

We think that next to Gen. Getty, Capt. Hazard Stevens, on Gen. Getty's staff, has been the busiest man on our part of the line. His horse always gallops. The boys say: "He does not know how to ride that horse at a trot; they look up and there goes Capt. Stevens, on an errand, ten miles down the road; a few minutes later he has returned, and is galloping, on another errand, ten miles up the road; and before there is time to tell it, he is rattling over all the cross-roads in the neighborhood — guess there's going to be a fight."

April 23. Thurs. Rainy. A large detail of our stronger men goes out on picket under Lieut. Forbush; the balance of the Reg. resting. Troops are moving rapidly all about us. We are tired of seeing moving troops — the monotonous tramp, the unchanging scene; all troops look alike, dusty blue in clothing, and dirty gray in blanket and tent, and all heavily loaded. The boys say "There goes another old caravan," as the bodies of troops pass camp. However, our camp seems strangely quiet, the quietest day and night we have seen since the siege commenced. For two weeks we have lived in an indescribable hubbub and rush day and night. We are still under orders to turn out every morning at three o'clock, and to remain under arms until seven a. m., in line of battle on the front street of camp.

April 24. Fri. Very rainy. Reg. in line in camp from 3 a. m. to 5 a. m. A reconnaissance in force this morning. About 10,000 men, including Corcoran's Irish Legion and the Connecticut Brigade, move out on the Somerton road. The advance have some skirmishing, the 16th Conn. having a sharp brush with the enemy's pickets. The Reg. falls in a little after noon, stacks arms in the company streets, and returns to quarters out of the rain; and is again called out in haste about dark as a support for Corcoran's Legion, but is not engaged. The whole force is recalled early in the night. To some extent the men enjoy the rush of the charge, or the ordinary fighting, but thoroughly detest this bushwhacking sort of skirmishing. They call it every sort of name, squirmish, squeamish, skittish, schottische, etc. A detachment of the Thirteenth is sent out to cut down trees and clear the range for our batteries; are ordered to finish the job, and work for nearly twenty-four hours at a stretch. Lieut. Staniels writes in his diary: "Reg. gets under arms at 1.15 p. m. We go over to the rear of Fort Dix at 4 p. m. Remain until 7.30 p. m., when we return to camp."

April 25. Sat. Pleasant. Reg. in camp resting. Heavy firing is heard in the distance, rapid, noisy. Gen. Dix states that the enemy clearly meditated crossing the Nansemond last night between Jericho Creek and Ft. Connecticut. A large prayer-meeting is held this evening. The largest we have ever known in camp.

Like skirmishing, reconnaissances in force are much disliked. A jerky march, frequent halts, distant firing, spent bullets coming over, shells hunting us out; a quiet rest interrupted by a nervous, " Fall in — fall in!"; two or three thousand men jumping hurriedly into line, throwing their rolls of blankets over their shoulders, ordered — every ten minutes — to see if their muskets are properly loaded and capped; and the whole programme repeated over and over again all the day through, and coupled with it all a strong belief that a rebel ' masked battery' or an ambush is just over yonder, 'the woods are full of them,' and an expectation that the next moment will bring in an engagement. After a whole day's work of this sort, a man is used up, disgusted and ugly; and returns to camp angry and indignant all through because there was not a fight.

April 26. Sun. Cold, fair, warm at noon. Reg. in camp near Suffolk. Inspection, Dress-parade and religious services — the first for several weeks; the Reg. listens formed in a square. The Band plays many spirited pieces this morning at guard-mounting and inspection. Out of the fighting for a few hours, all this is a pleasurable relief. The gunboats are quiet for the first day in two weeks. The most of the day passes in rest — not so the night. About 9 p. m. the whole camp is suddenly up and coming like a rush of hornets with a pole in their nest. We are called out by Gen. Peck himself riding into camp like a whirlwind, and demanding that an hour's work be done in two minutes. He is in a terrible hurry, and ' sassy,' and the men scramble into line speedily and march off to the front on the Nansemond river bank, in the chilly darkness, mad; and then shovel all night.

The general plan of this campaign has been for Gen. Getty's Division to occupy the Nansemond front from Suffolk down the river to where it broadens into a bay, and also along the lower part of Jericho Creek; while Gen. Peck occupies the works encircling Suffolk. Fort Connecticut was the first fort built and manned. A very scientific trestle, suggested by Col. Derrom of the 25th N. J., is used for nearly all the bridges required in this campaign.

April 27. Mon. Fair. Thirteenth in rifle-pits at the front, along the bank of the Nansemond. We have shoveled all night, until daylight, when the enemy's pickets commence firing and stop the work; then we take breakfast; after which those who can have cover work at the shovels again until 9.30 a. m.; then the 13th is relieved and marches back a few miles to the old camp again, arriving about noon, and rests for the balance of the day. It is this sort of jerky business that uses men up. We have marched, and fired, and picketed, and shoveled, night and day, in all sorts of weather, in water, in mud, in swamp and brush and timber, up hill and down dale, in this sort of 'hare and hounds' play for nearly three weeks. Very little rest or peace, and no comfort, since April 1st; but it is one of those campaigns which furnish a great deal of rough sport, play and adventure as well as much hard work.

Some men of the 13th on another part of the line, while on picket, arrange with the rebels not to fire, and swim across to a sandy point or an island. Here they are met by men swimming out from the rebel picket, and they have a very friendly meeting, shake hands, swap jack-knives and pipes, have a chat, and then return to their several posts. Strict orders are issued forbidding any more of such useless, dangerous and dare-devil business.

The crookedness, windings, twists, netting, and general tortuousness, in these Nansemond swamps — a part of the Dismal Swamp — of the paths and roads around pool and bayou, boghole and creek ("krik") form a maze baffling the imagination. Sergt. John Pinkham of E, an old sailor, declares: "I can never box the compass after marching all day here; to follow these roads would make a rat sea-sick."

April 28. Tues. Fair and showers. Pay-rolls being made up. The writer (frequently serving as clerk of Co. E), Cyrus G. Drew, clerk of B, and the clerks and Captains of two or three other companies, make temporary desks in an old negro hut near Jericho Point, by driving sticks, at a convenient height, into the log-chinks, and laying rough boards upon them, and work together upon the rolls, for parts of two or three days. Occasionally a rebel bullet whacks against the hut, knocking the dried mud out of the chinks between the logs, and making sudden little wiggles and crooks in the writing's 'lines of beauty'; while two or three of the enemy's shells burst nearer to us than shells ought to do when a man is busy writing his level best. Regimental Hdqrs. are near the old rebel small-pox hospital. Several men of the 13th slept in it recently one rainy night, not knowing its character, but did not contract the disease. They call this "Harland's front." The 13th furnishes a picket for the Norfolk road, also a heavy picket in the front trenches all day, and at 6 p. m. the whole Regiment moves out and joins them. At dark the Reg. goes to work upon a fort near the small-pox hospital. Gen. Longstreet, it is said, has sent word to some citizens of Suffolk that he will dine with them there to-morrow!

April 29. Wed. Warm, fair; a heavy rain last night. The 13th is nowadays called every day at 3 a. m., stacks arms in the company streets, and remains near quarters with accoutrements on, ready for an instant move, until 7 a. m. A large detail from the 13th, under Captains Stoodley and Buzzell, takes a turn on picket far out in the swamp on the Jericho canal — a slough under foot and no shelter from the rain. Company E furnishes 33 poor, forlorn, water-soaked, bedraggled fellows for Capt. Stoodley's command. But the worst is at night. The several picket details assemble at picket Hdqrs. about noon, and then return to Jericho Point. They remain there until about sunset, when all return to camp, and are just fairly at home when a storm commences, the like of which we have never seen. The thunder is a regular roar for over an hour, the skies are all ablaze with incessant and vivid lightning, there is much heavy wind, the rain is in torrents and streams, spattering and pouring through the tents as if they were sieves; and the whole level camp is a sheet of water glowing with the dancing lights in the skies. The camp-guard wade their beats, splash, splash.

April 30. Thurs. Fair; rained all last night. Reg. on picket in the forenoon; about noon returns to old camp near Suffolk. Mustered for pay by Col. Donohoe of the 10th N. H. In the afternoon we remove camp towards Jericho Point, to a clean and dry spot and therefore welcome, near the Nansemond and the small-pox hospital, and about two miles below Suffolk. We move camp to this place in order to be near our picket lines, and to save marching back and forth. Our old camp is set on fire as we leave it, and makes a fine blaze. Nearly the whole Reg. goes again and works nearly all night on Ft. Jericho — the same fort we worked upon on the night of April 26th. First Sergeant Charles M. Kittredge of B has been serving as 'Instructor of the guard;' a new official position in the Thirteenth. His duties, extending to the services of both officers and men, are delicate and difficult; but he performs them to the entire satisfaction of all the parties concerned.

The Nansemond is of an average width of less than 100 yards, a narrow, crooked, shoal, muddy stream, its banks an ever-varying marsh and point and headland, all generally well wooded and supplied with dense underbrush. The gunboats play a very important part in this siege; the 'Stepping Stones,' especially, with its dare-devil crew; what these men will hesitate to venture were best let alone. The gunboats are little river steamers with their sides protected by sheet iron or bundles of hay. Mounting one or two guns, and of light draft, they will sail ' on the dew when the grass is wet,' almost, and have a wide sea in a common creek. They are exceeding noisy. In these woods and swamps one of their cannon discharges in the dead silence of night — all as unexpected and startling as a clap of thunder in a clear sky — booms, roars, reverberates and jars for miles around, while in a few moments the sound of the bursting shell strikes back like an angry echo.

The Confederate soldiers have no high regard for President Lincoln;

to them he stands as the head of the forces suppressing their rebellion. Then, too, they do not all appear to love Jeff. Davis. One of them put it naturally to-day, while exchanging trifles with our Regiment's pickets during a meeting across the river. He said : "Say, Yank, you 'uns bring Abe down heah to the river ; we 'uns will bring Jeff. ; then drown um both 'n go home — er'ekn." They call their scrip 'white-bellies ;' we call ours 'green-backs' — and not even the most patriotic Irishman could express a more instinctive preference for the green than they do.

May 1. Fri. Pleasant. Reg. fits up its new camp, and packs all surplus personal baggage to be sent home, or to be stored at Fortress Monroe. Reg. supplied with new shelter tents, much needed. A large detail hurried out to work on Ft. Jericho. On some parts of the line now the pickets have mutually agreed not to fire upon each other. The rebels complain that their rations now are, chiefly, flour, corn-meal and bacon. All the wounded of the 13th are sent to the General Hospital this forenoon ; they have excellent care here, and dread to leave.

May 2. Sat. Fair. A large detail, about 200 men, go to work on a fort near the river. The 13th builds forts, other troops garrison them as heavy artillery ; that is to say, many of them do the heavy standing around, while we shovel up the earth to protect them. There has been too much favoritism shown among the troops during this siege. Orders are received for the 13th to march to-morrow, at 3 a. m., with two days' cooked rations, and in light marching order. The enemy has fired upon us more or less all the time while we have been building Ft. Jericho, and several men have been hit. The fort was about a week in building and was finished this afternoon. Very noisy about Suffolk to-day. Col. Corcoran is in charge in that direction, and when near the front, he always manages to stir up a breeze. The Confederates say that they have eighty Regiments in our vicinity — an infantry force of near 40,000 men. Regimental Hospital and sick moved to new camp.

Some heavy artillery — infantry serving as such — in the fort here nearest to our camp, were very recently trying to dislodge the enemy's sharp-shooters from a brick house over across the river and what appeared to be an old cellar near by it ; and could not succeed. Sergt. John F. Gibbs of E and other Thirteens were looking on. After a while Gibbs salutes the officer in command, desires to try a shot and is allowed to do so. The ground beyond the river is an almost dead level. Gibbs has just powder enough put into the gun to send the round shell fairly across the river, cuts the fuse himself, sights the gun, and sends the shell rolling over the smooth ground beyond the river. It rolls into the old cellar and bursts there ; and a dozen or so of rebels scramble out, lively, and make the best time on record to the brick house, while the burning brands of a little fire they had in the cellar are flying about with the pieces of shell. Now for the house. Gibbs tries again, with a heavier load of powder, sends his shell ricocheting over there, where it lodges within the house and bursts ; and there is another scattering of Confederates. After firing the two shots, and without saying a word, Gibbs turns, salutes again, and marches off, with the air of an actor leaving the stage.

## BATTLE OF PROVIDENCE CHURCH ROAD.

May 3. Sun. Pleasant as a whole, but very warm at mid-day. The Thirteenth is in line at 5 a. m., and about 6 a. m. marches toward Suffolk, with Col. Stevens in command. Arriving in the city at 8 a. m., after a march of about three miles, we halt on Main street near the Court House, a few rods from the river, and remain here for an hour or two. Here bullets coming over from the enemy's skirmishers fall among our men in the street, or strike against the buildings, altogether too freely. One bullet, seeming to come straight down out of the sky, shaves close to the faces of two men of Company E, and strikes upon the earth sidewalk between their feet with a loud blow — unpleasantly interrupting their conversation. Many have similar experiences with the spent bullets, and a few are hurt by them. In the movement to-day the 103d N. Y. is the first regiment to cross the Nansemond, then follow in order the 25th N. J., 89th N. Y. and the 13th N. H.; the 89th and 103d New York regiments in advance of the whole force as skirmishers. At 9 a. m. the Thirteenth moves down Main street, and soon (Luey writes at 9.30 a. m.) crosses the river at the highway bridge (on canal boats moored and planked over), marching 'by fours' — by the right flank — with arms at 'right shoulder shift,' and rapidly and rather jauntily, Company A leading, and is the fourth regiment to cross, following the 89th N. Y. as a support — and rather too closely. This is done under fire of the enemy's artillery. As soon as we have crossed, and have moved up the bank, past the ruins of Capt. Nathaniel Pruden's house, we swing into line of battle to the left, across a field; the right of the Reg., Co. A, resting on the west side of the Providence Church road; and continue to advance in this field, Co. A keeping close upon the west — left — side of the road during all the day.

When the head of the Thirteenth arrived at the gullies near Capt. Pruden's house, a few minutes after 9 a. m., Col. Stevens was called to some other part of the Brigade, and Lt. Col. Bowers succeeded to the command of our Regiment; and continued in that command until about two hours after the enemy's rifle-pits had been captured, when Col. Stevens returned.

As we come up on the high ground, we can see the skirmishing going on for a long distance to the right and left, and the two long clouds of powder-smoke rolling up above the heads of the combatants. The line of the enemy's rifle-pits appears to be between half a mile and a mile in length along the edge of the woods, a few hundred yards north of us. The firing is very spirited, and we receive an abundance of the spent bullets. A few sneaking cowards are scared, and hide in the gully close to the ruins of Capt. Pruden's house, and so shirk the battle. From the time when we commence crossing the bridge, all through the day, the enemy plays upon our lines with several light field-pieces mounted north of us near the road, and still farther west, but without much effect. Evidently the enemy is seeking to hit the bridge, and the troops as we come up on clear ground, and avoids throwing shells into the city. Our gunboats and batteries are constantly firing over our heads, all the forenoon, with an incessant racket. Company E is detached, and sent forward on the left as skirmishers, and advances through an apple orchard, the trees in full bloom. A part of the left wing of the Reg. also advances through this orchard, which is about half a mile beyond the bridge we crossed. Before the charge, however, Company E is partly merged in the regimental line of battle and with a portion of the 89th N. Y. The right wing of the Reg. advances in open ground.

Lt. Col. Bowers has stated to the writer that he was "particularly directed by Gen. Getty to maintain a distance of 100 to 150 feet between the 89th N. Y. and the Thirteenth; but the men of the Thirteenth would not keep back — they were determined to outcharge the 89th New York." The 89th forming the advance, and the 13th as their support, constitute the left wing of the advancing column; the right wing of the column coming up from under the protection of the river bank, down stream, and extending through the fields for half a mile or more, and all in full view of our more elevated position. A force of dismounted cavalry lying on the ground in a long straggling line, and armed with carbines, are clearing the front of the enemy's skirmishers who are hidden among the weeds and brush along the road, and we move towards the left among these cavalrymen and to their rear. As the men of the 89th N. Y. take the place of this line of dismounted cavalry, they rise up, shoulder their carbines and suddenly disappear, no one knows whither. Our men say they sink into the ground. It may be, for a cavalryman is a most uncertain and mysterious animal.

As the battle line of the 13th comes into clearer view of the enemy, he aims direct for our line over the heads of our skirmishers, and the 13th is ordered to lie down. Two regiments — the 103d N. Y. and 25th New Jersey — now suddenly appear on the right about one fourth of a mile distant from us, down stream, and move directly forward towards the enemy in two splendid lines of battle. Their appearance provokes a spiteful little fusillade, and draws the attention of the enemy's artillery from us. They advance rapidly several rods, in straight battle lines, while quite a number of them are seen to fall under the enemy's fire; and then both regiments drop out of view among the grass and weeds, and the enemy opens again with renewed vigor upon us. As the enemy's bullets, and an occasional shell, cut, rip and tear through the apple-trees, we are showered with apple blossoms, as if in a miniature snow storm — pretty scene, but terribly suggestive bullets. One apple-tree is cut down near us by a rebel shell. From where we now lie, the enemy's line, in the edge of the woods, appears to be about 500 yards distant, and his bullets sink very deep into the wood of the trunks of the trees about us.

To our right is a ruined house (Norfleet's or Northwick's) — seems to be of brick — about which a furious contest is waging, the enemy shelling our lines there very severely. His entire range, however, is too high. Our advance is made, all along the line, as such advances, in open ground, are usually made, with "a lie down and fire, and a jump up and run forward," repeated over and over again. During the whole advance Lt. Col. Bowers is upon his feet, and continually moving, and keeps all the time either with or in front of our Regiment's battle line.

It is perhaps 10 or 11 a. m. when the 89th reaches a rail fence on the northern side of the orchard, and apparently 300 or 400 yards from the enemy, posted in rifle-trenches and behind trees, in the edge of the wood. From this rail fence a brisk fire is kept up with the enemy until the time of the charge. It is a strong, high, zig-zag, 'Virginia' rail fence, made of heavy rails, and affords much better shelter than the small apple-trees in the orchard or the little ridges of ground farther back; and as a consequence, Company E, many of the left wing of the 13th, and of the 89th, are soon mingled together and lying down close behind this fence, in some places as dense as three ranks deep; and the enemy, pleased with this larger target, splinters, clips, chips and batters these rails with hundreds of bullets, not one in fifty of them having any other effect.

Company E of the 13th, a Company of the 89th N. Y., and a few other men, are in the northeast corner of this apple orchard and rail fence, from which point a similar rail fence runs somewhat diagonally down towards the woods, a fence which eventually divides the two wings of the Thirteenth in our final charge. Captain Julian is soon ordered to send a dozen men into the tall weeds along this diagonal fence. They at once take their ground, under a brisk fire, and answer it in earnest. The ground at this rail fence where we now are on the north side of the orchard is a little higher than the rebel position in the woods, a clear field, 300 to 400 yards in width, lying between us and them. The too-inviting rail fence has brought this part of the line up nearer the enemy's line than the right wing of the 13th, which is in more open ground, or our troops farther down towards the right of the main line. This necessitates a delay of more than an hour at this fence.

At one o'clock — 1 p. m. — the order is passed: "Make ready to charge." The little stir in our line brings upon us an increasing rebel fire, from all along their line on our front. An officer — Capt. Hazard Stevens, Adjt. General on Gen. Getty's staff — who has been seen riding and bearing orders to all parts of the field during all the forenoon, and who, after leaving his horse in a safer place, has come up to the line of battle, and has been sitting near the writer, under protection of the fence, for the past few minutes, closely watching the course of affairs, now suddenly rises, mounts the top rail of the fence, steadies himself by a stake, stands there bolt upright — despite the enemy's bullets — waves his hat, and shouts: "Forward!" "Forward!" Another officer, said to be the Lt. Colonel of the 89th N. Y., also mounts the fence. Several officers of the Thirteenth, and men also, are on the fence nearly as soon as they, all shouting at the full strength of their lungs. The right wing of the Thirteenth is also springing up, some fixing bayonets and some not, and all the while the enemy's bullets are coming among us thicker and faster than ever, pounding against the rails of the fence, ripping through the trees, knocking up the dust and earth — a bullet strikes hard — and clipping, chipping, zipping among the dry grass and weeds — whew!

In a moment more almost every man in the Thirteenth is in a wild rush for the woods and the rebel rifle-pits and trenches within them, over fence, ditch, brush and what not, some with bayonets fixed, some fixing bayonets as they run, and all yelling like madmen. The enemy fires into us two quite regular volleys, and follows with a brisk firing at will before the charge is over, and a number of men in the Thirteenth are seen to fall; but the distance, 300 or 400 yards, mainly over the descending and clear ground of a cornfield, is made as quickly as men can run, and just as we enter the woods the enemy takes to his heels, leaving his dead and a few of his wounded in our hands. A number of his men even leave their ammunition and their cartridge-boxes — the latter hanging upon the trees. (The writer still, 1887, has a few bullets taken from one of these cartridge-boxes.) A few prisoners are captured. Quite a number of large pine-trees are standing in front of their rifle-pits, which are a full rod and more within the edge of the timber. Laurel and pine brush is set up thickly in the earth thrown up in front of their pits, quite effectually masking them. The men of the Thirteenth, seeing the trees in front of the rebels, were very desirous to run forward, out of the clear, open ground, to get among these trees and thus have a fair, even chance with the enemy. The charge from the rail fence, and from the position of the right wing, to the woods, does not occupy more than two or three minutes, and we run close upon the enemy in his masked rifle-pits, before we clearly see the enemy's advantage, and before he scrambles out and runs for dear life deeper into the woods. They held their ground bravely and nobly. In less than a minute more, they must all have been captured, or else must have indulged in a little bayonet exercise — or both. At 1.15 p. m. the enemy is in full retreat, the rifle-pits in our hands.

The men of the 89th N. Y. necessarily scatter somewhat — in the rush, and the men of the Thirteenth run among them, and ahead of them, intending to out-charge them on this occasion. When the enemy's rifle-pits and trenches are cleared, the Thirteenth is halted, Company E takes its place in line of battle — having during the most of the forenoon preceded the line of battle as skirmishers — and the 89th N. Y. is moved forward again upon the skirmish line deeper into the woods.

The enemy is found very strongly entrenched, where we dislodged him, along near the edge of the woods, in a line more than half a mile in length, to the right and left of the road, and is driven out by our show of numbers and bayonets alone. Musketry could not have driven him from his pits with the dense and heavy timber around and behind him, and he could have lain with considerable safety under a heavy fire of artillery. The writer heard a rebel prisoner state that our Brigade, in this charge, dislodged two strong rebel regiments backed by a field battery. But it should be borne in mind, that these two rebel regiments were stationed as pickets and not in line of battle, a picket line in large squads a rod or two apart, and though their force was strong, the Thirteenth in their hurried onset pierced and forced back a part of their line first, flanking all the rest, which was compelled to follow, and did so. After a little time, however, the rebels were rallied in the woods and turned upon our advance, fighting it from tree to tree, and so were forced back by the skirmishers of the 89th, after the 13th had been halted in the woods. It was a very pretty little fight, and generally well managed on both sides. The rebels ran only at the moment of inevitable capture.

While the Thirteenth is halted along a little brook in a ravine, about two hours after the short chase into the woods, one of our batteries — a section, as we are informed, of the steel gun battery commanded by Lieut. Beecher, son of Rev. Henry Ward Beecher — comes up near the woods to the right and rear of the Thirteenth, takes position in the field about 200 yards west of the road, and engages in a sharp duel with a rebel battery entrenched a short distance back in the woods and also to the west of the road. Col. Stevens rejoins the Thirteenth, in the woods, soon after this artillery firing begins.

It was the Thirteenth almost alone, who in well closed column on the run broke in the enemy's line, and therefore we lost more heavily than any other regiment. We outcharged the 89th N. Y. deliberately and purposely, and when we halted nine tenths of their men were in our rear, and had to come up and pass through our lines, we parting to give them room to do so, out again upon their skirmish line. Possibly if they had known our intentions they might not have allowed themselves to be outrun in this way. They criticised us at Fredericksburg and without occasion — now we pay back their unfair words with fair deeds. The two regiments, however, are on quite friendly terms, the action of to-day a bit of natural rivalry, and we desire in no way to disparage the 89th N. Y., a very excellent regiment.

Just as the Thirteenth entered the woods, an officer of the 89th N. Y. stepped up behind Capt. Betton and called out, "Hello, Captain; I was just behind you in the charge at Fredericksburg." "So you are now!" replied Capt. Betton, as he hurried forward; and there the colloquy ended.

Lieut. Beecher's battery exchanges rapid shots with the rebel battery in the dense timber and supported by a strong body of infantry, all of which our charge has unmasked. The firing continues until dark, many of the shells, from both friend and enemy, going over our heads, cutting up the trees, treating us to the falling branches, and occasionally bursting near and giving us little rattling showers of the pieces and small shot. The enemy has a few guns of large calibre, and from these come, level, straight through the foliage of the trees, large charges of singing, purring and tree-clipping grape shot; grape makes the most disagreeable noise of any missile used in this war. None of it, however, unless spent, can enter the ravine where we now are.

While the Thirteenth is lying in the ravine along the brook, about two hours after the charge, we are in full view of some of the enemy's sharpshooters — evidently posted in trees. Their bullets, coming from a point to our left and rear, as we have advanced beyond the general line, repeatedly strike a pine-tree on a high bank near by, and also strike the ground about us. Just after one of these bullets has torn a piece of bark off the side of this tree, and hurled it against the head of a man of the Reg. (we think of Co. F), knocking him down, Capt. Buzzell goes up to the tree to find, if he can, the whereabouts of the sharp-shooters. He is too venturesome — there never appeared any fibre of timidity in him — and he does not secure a sufficient cover behind the tree. He has scarcely watched a minute, when he suddenly cries out loudly, "Oh — I 'm killed!" takes a step or two, and instantly falls forward upon his face, dead. At the same moment a spent bullet buzzes close over the heads of First Sergeant Thompson (the writer) and Sergeant Van Duzee, and a few other men of Co. E, who are sitting on a log down near the brook, and drops into the muddy water at their feet. From the time and the direction of its coming, and its spent condition, it is reasonably believed to be the same bullet that passed through Capt. Buzzell; a long search is therefore made for it in the deep, soft mud of the brook, but it is not to be found. The bullet passed straight through his body, and through his heart. When shot Capt. Buzzell is standing near a large pine-tree about twenty feet from the brook, and perhaps ten feet above it; and his death falls upon the Regiment like a cold-blooded murder committed in their midst, and not as a stroke of war.

All our men are soon removed from this dangerous locality. No farther advance into the woods is made, and at dark the Reg. retires, with the rest of the force engaged, to the camp near Jericho Creek, carrying back its dead and wounded; arriving there at 10 p. m., and turning in about midnight. The most of the officers and men are pretty well tired out by this long, hard day's work. Lieut. Curtis has command of the rear-guard as the Reg. retires from the field to camp.

The 89th N. Y. supported by the 13th N. H. formed the left wing of the advance; the 103d N. Y. supported by the 25th N. J. the right wing, the Providence Church road dividing the two wings. The 11th, 15th and 16th Conn. regiments were also engaged farther to the right, while a heavy supporting column moved near the advance. The infantry was accompanied by a small body of cavalry and a field battery; the whole force about 7,000 men. Acting in concert with our force, a body of Union troops crossed the river farther down, at "Sleepy Hole," or Chuckatuck, engaged in a skirmish with Gen. Longstreet's rear-guard, and captured a batch of prisoners. The general movement is made to hasten the raising of the Siege of Suffolk, already begun by Gen. Longstreet — a reconnaissance in force. While we march off in one direction to-night, the enemy calculating that our advance of to-day threatens him with a more persistent pursuit on the morrow, packs and marches off hastily in the other direction.

The advance and charge of the Thirteenth to-day is considered exceptionally brilliant for its dash and steadiness, even though the Reg. was formed somewhat irregularly, in a hurried movement, as the final assault was made — our first bayonet charge on an enemy in view. The honors due to all of its Companies are quite even all along the line. Veterans say that the charge of the Thirteenth, made to-day, was the best one they ever witnessed ; and worthy of special commendation because it was impossible to tell whether the enemy's force was one thousand or five thousand. Besides, after capturing the enemy's line of rifle-trenches, and when lying in the woods, the Reg. holds its place steadily between our own battery and that of the enemy, during their long and sharp engagement, though we were meanwhile exposed to the fire of the enemy's sharpshooters, and stray shells from our own gunboats, all four being about equally dangerous. We were advanced during all the day, beyond the right of our main line of battle, and had much waiting to do, under fire, while the rest of the line was brought forward. The 13th are withdrawn about 8 p. m., and at once return to camp. On the whole the day is one of which the Thirteenth may well be proud. A slow, old-fashioned, regular army charge would have lost us two or three men for every one lost in to-day's most hasty rush. Nine tenths of the Thirteenth made the charge upon the run, as if in a race, their guns held in the right hand, as they would hold a heavy stick by the middle of it when running. Upon the wild racing of our men across the field, the skedaddling of the enemy in the woods was something to laugh at.

A soldier of the 13th writes home : " We crossed the river about 9 a. m., and deployed in line of battle, fronting the wood. In the charge the 89th N. Y. moved rather slowly, and the left wing of the 13th shot by them, and their Lt. Colonel, being in command, ordered the 13th to ' forward,' and let his men stay there if they would ; and the 13th did go forward, making the Johnnies take French leave — some of them leaving their guns and everything else in our possession. We were ordered back about dark, and returned to camp."

The losses of the day in the Thirteenth were about thirty — of killed three and of seriously wounded sixteen. The Reg. went in with less than 500 men. The largest number were hit during the charge. Lieut. Murray was severely wounded, and Capt. Stoodley slightly. Hundreds of men went into the charge wearing button-hole bouquets of apple blossoms, from the orchard ; many of them cut off by the bullets which were ripping through the trees overhead all the time that our men were among them. Quite a natural thing for a man to pick up a twig, covered with fresh blossoms and cut off by a bullet within a few feet, or a few inches, of his head.  A number of the enemy's shells tore through the trees also, cutting off large limbs.  From both causes the petals and blossoms were showering down among us for several hours.  An apple blossom would not be a bad emblem, or badge, for the men of the Thirteenth, but most appropriate.  The writer, and several other men, had their feet and hands badly jarred by bullets hitting the rails of the fence, when they were upon them in the act of climbing over, but are otherwise unhurt.  Lieut. Curtis of C, in command of the Thirteenth's rear-guard in retiring, was ordered back to hurry up some stragglers and narrowly escaped capture by passing the left wing of the Thirteenth, the whole party coming within an ace of going to Libby.

During the charge a part of Co. C slackened their speed a little at the fence which was encountered by the right wing of the Reg., near the edge of the woods.  At this First Sergeant McConney actually jumped up and down with impatience, exclaiming: "Forward, Company C — we'll all get killed if we stop here!"  The slowing was but for a moment, and was caused by the action of two or three men who first reached the fence, and properly enough waited a moment for the rest of the company to come up.  During the action, instead of holding to proper supporting distance, the Thirteenth improved the opportunity, given by the order to charge, to burst through the line of the 89th N. Y., and make a hot race for the fence at the edge of the woods, shouting: "Beat them to the fence, boys," and were the first to reach the fence.  This impulsive action is prompted by accusations of timidity at Fredericksburg, where the 89th followed the Thirteenth, and crowded upon them while their progress was for a moment hindered by the lying down and running back of some men of the 25th New Jersey.  One man of the Thirteenth writes: " The men of the 89th N. Y. were in the front line till the charge, when the men of the 13th passed them at almost every point, and took the matter mostly into their own hands."  The members of the 89th call us the " Granite Thirteenth " — and seem to be glad that we did the work.  Many of the 13th charged without fixing bayonets, there being so much noise as to drown the orders.  The affair on the whole is considered very brilliant, our forces having encountered " a powerful rear-guard of the enemy, which was posted in a position of immense strength," and routed them.

During the most dangerous part of the charge, when John H. Foye of E fell, Albion J. Jenness of E stopped short beside him, gave him water, cut off his belt, and unbuttoned his coat; and remained attending to his wants, amid the pattering, whistling bullets, as coolly and quietly as if beside a cot in the hospital.  A very courageous act.  During the charge, also, a number of men along the regimental line, seeing the enemy firing upon the advance, deliberately halted and fired one shot at them, then joined again in the charge — a sort of independent skirmish line firing over their comrades' heads.  But the most of the Thirteenth fully realized that the only way to secure an even chance with the rebels was to run across the open field and into the woods where the rebels were, and so went for them with a rush. Much of the battle overran gardens. The men never before showed such a fondness for flowers, and especially for apple blossoms.

Col. Stevens advanced with the Thirteenth to a point near the ruins of Capt. Pruden's house just above the river bank ; and there Lt. Col. Bowers took command of the 13th, having received orders, how to support the 89th N. Y., directly from Gen. Getty. Probably no one would be more ready to correct the error made in the N. H. Adjt. General's Reports, Vol. 2, for 1865, page 326, lines 27, 28, and Vol. 2, for 1866, page 787, line 31, than Col. Stevens; for neither the 13th N. H. nor the 89th N. Y. were under command of Col. Stevens during the advance or charge, at any time after the line passed the ruins of Capt. Pruden's house and into the apple orchard near it, until after the capture of the rebel works. Whatever Col. Stevens' duties may have been with the rest of the Brigade — as it was said he was called away — the 89th N. Y. was in command of its Lt. Colonel, and the 13th N. H. was in command of Lt. Col. Bowers, who charged with the 13th upon the rebel rifle-pits, and was overheated by his most energetic exertions on this occasion. Col. Stevens rejoined the Thirteenth about two hours after it had captured the rebel rifle-pits, and while it was halted in the woods.

"The left wing of the Thirteenth charged from an orchard with the 89th N. Y. The 13th generally outran the 89th, reaching the woods first ; all the time exposed to the fire of the enemy from their rifle-pits in the edge of the woods. We fixed bayonets while charging. We advanced into the woods beyond the rest of the line and were halted. The battery that came up in our rear, after we halted in the woods, played over our heads for several hours. We were withdrawn after dark, and arrived in camp about 10 p. m. Capt. Buzzell, when shot, exclaimed, 'Oh — I'm killed!' Lt. Col. Bowers led the Thirteenth after we passed the river bank."
Lt. Col. Smith.

"The Thirteenth has received many compliments for its action to-day ; and has gained a name for bravery which will last as long as any one of its members shall live. Lt. Col. Bowers commanded the Thirteenth, and was forward with the men, when they charged."
Capt. Julian.

Lossing states that Gen. Longstreet's force has reached nearly 40,000 men, and that Gen. Getty's line of defense has been nearly eight miles in length — all held by his Division alone — running down the Nansemond from Battery Onondaga, and sweeping around on Jericho Creek (which forms a large marshy island near its junction with the Nansemond), covering Battery Jericho and Battery Halleck, on the creek farther up.

The most of the foregoing account was written before the writer's visit to the battle-field in May, 1885. We marched up from our camp — two miles below Suffolk on Jericho Creek — between the main Portsmouth road and the Nansemond ; and entered the city by an old lane just south of the Court House, and halted in Main st. near the Court House front.

The river for a little way near the bridge runs nearly due east, but a few rods above the bridge — west — there is a bend sharply around to the northwest between bluffs cut with numerous ravines. Main st. runs down to the bridge nearly due north, and the road beyond continues in nearly the same direction for about two miles from the city, and then a branch runs northwest to Providence church. The field of the Regiment's operations on May 3d lies on the west side of this road, and between the road and the northwest bend of the river — a large, irregular V with the point at the bridge, and the wide part at the line of heavy timber a mile north, the road forming the right hand line of the V. The bank of the river, on the north side, is high and wide, and the road for the first half a mile is quite near the river. As you cross the river and go up the road, and immediately after you have mounted the bank, a deep gully runs from the left side of the road down to the river. A rod or two beyond the gully are the ruins of Capt. Nathaniel Pruden's house; a little farther on is a similar gully, and just north of it is a new house built since the war and now, 1885, owned by a Mr. Nelson. These were the gullies into which sundry cowards crawled and hid, while the Regiment advanced. Mrs. Nelson informed the writer that their house "was built among the stumps of an old orchard." Here is the field of the orchard through which the 89th N. Y. and 13th N. H. advanced; and the north side of this orchard — where the zig-zag rail fence stood — is nearly three fourths of a mile from the bridge, and it is 300 to 400

---

### DESCRIPTION OF PLAT.

A. Portsmouth Road — north branch to Jericho creek, south to white marsh.

B. Camp of Thirteenth near Suffolk, one mile from town.

C. C. Railroads.  D. Old lane on which we entered the town May 3d.

E. Court House.        G. Nansemond River.

F. Main Street, Suffolk, branching two or three miles north of town, west to Providence Church, east to Chuckatuck.

H. Ruins of Capt. Nathaniel Pruden's house, and gullies near by where a few men hid while the rest of the Thirteenth fought the battle out.

I. Apple orchard; with zig-zag rail fence, L, north of it, where the Thirteenth formed line of battle for the charge.

M. Field across which the Thirteenth charged. The course of the advance and charge of the Thirteenth is indicated by the arrow.

N. N. Edge of dense woods, of heavy timber and thick brush, with rebel rifle-pits; the works captured by the Thirteenth.

P. Point near brook R where Capt. Buzzell was killed, about 200 to 300 yards west of the road.    S. Main part of Suffolk.

T. T. Rebel camps, earth-works and batteries.

K. Mr. Northwick's brick house, about one half mile east of road.

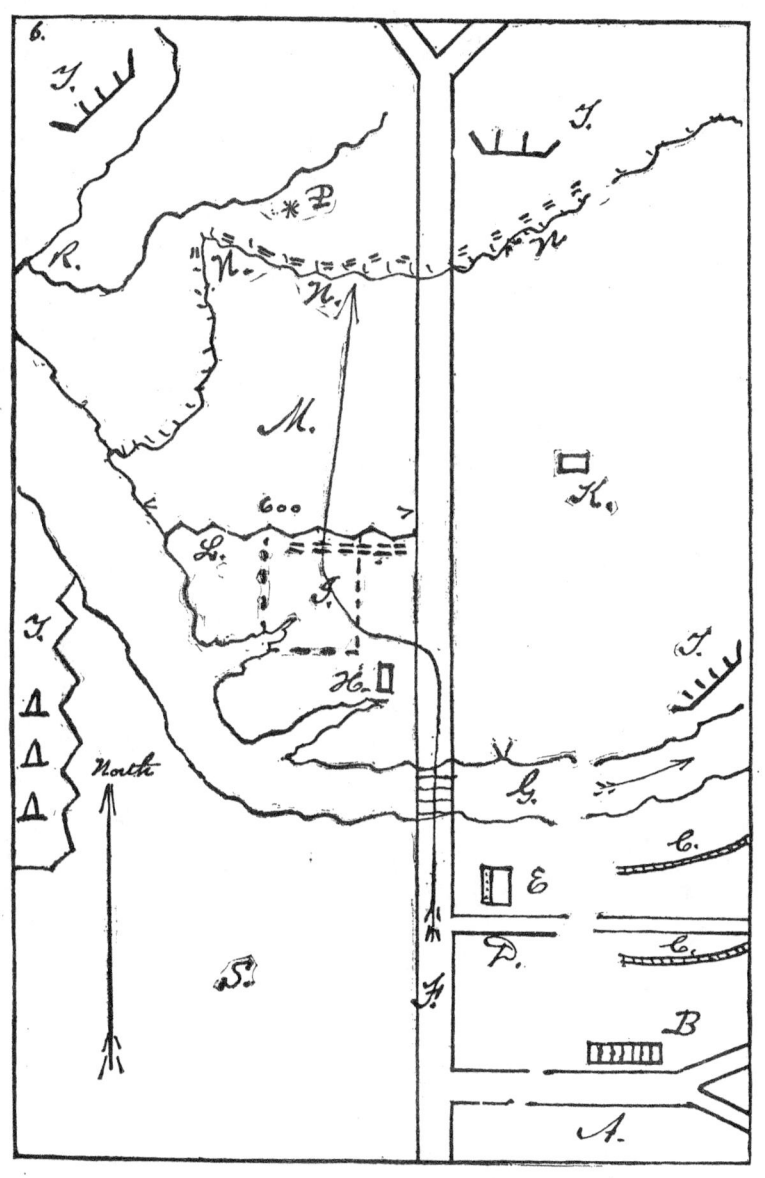

PROVIDENCE CHURCH ROAD.

From a sketch made by the writer in May 1885.

yards farther, northward, to where the edge of the woods was, across the field, beyond the rail fence. The 13th charged across this field to the Confederate rifle-pits and trenches and into the woods, in all not far from 600 yards. The open field is now quite square, and about one fourth of a mile on the road north and south, and about one third of a mile (strong) east and west toward the bend of the river. The field inclines gently northward to the woods. The whole advance of the 13th was about one mile north beyond the river. The wide field containing Mr. Norfleet's, or Northwick's, brick house, on the east side of the road, was the scene of the advance of the 103d N. Y. and the 25th N. J. forming the right of our Brigade.

Hospital Steward Royal B. Prescott writes, May 7, 1863 : " We left camp at 7 a. m., May 3d, and formed, in Main st., Suffolk, a line consisting of the 13th N. H., 89th and 103d N. Y., 25th N. J., 7th Mass. Battery, Battery L 4th U. S. Regulars, and Dodge's Mounted Riflemen. We crossed the bridge about 11 a. m., and the 13th Indiana, 144th N. Y., 11th, 15th, and 16th Conn. remained near the bridge as a reserve. When we came up the north bank of the river opposite the ruins of a house (Pruden's) the rebels opened upon us with a brisk musketry fire from a brush fence, from the woods on our left, and from an open cornfield (in front) where the enemy laid flat on their faces. The 89th N. Y. and 13th N. H. charged through the cornfield to the woods.

" Surgeon Richardson selected a place for a field Hospital ; a fence was torn down to lay the wounded men upon ; lint, bandages, tourniquets, and surgical instruments were prepared ; water brought and everything arranged at hand. A Lieutenant from the 103d N. Y. was the first one brought in, shot straight through his head. Next a man of the 89th N. Y., then another of the 103d, then one of our own 13th boys shot through the body — and so they came all day long. Men were cut, torn and mutilated in every conceivable manner. The day was very hot and we had all we could do until after dark. Captain Buzzell was shot dead, through the heart. We recrossed the river about 10 p. m., and arrived in camp about 11 p. m.[1] A Major of a Michigan regiment having an attack of delirium tremens shot Surgeon Smith of the 103d N. Y. through the bowels. Colonel Ringgold, 103d N. Y., was shot and died. The Chaplain of the 25th N. J. also shot. The 13th N. H. suffered greater loss than any other regiment engaged, losing twenty-three — four killed and nineteen wounded. The original order directed the 13th to leave camp at 2 a. m. May 3d, the bridges being down caused delay." PRESCOTT.

Among the first to bound over the rail fence on the north side of the apple orchard, at the order to charge, was Major Storer, and he was also one of the first to reach the rebel rifle-pits in the woods. He wore boots made of alligator skin, and some of the men who did not know him, but who were referring to his gallant conduct on this occasion, designated

[1] The Hospital-corps followed the Reg., and this accounts for the differences in hours given.

him as 'that high toned gentleman with his boots all marked over with diamonds, squares, figures, and so on.' Major Storer was always elegant and courtly in manner, and very careful in dress and appearance.

May 4. Mon. Fair, showers, warm. Reg. in camp near Jericho Creek, tired, resting, counting noses, cleaning muskets and talking over the incidents and hair-breadth escapes of yesterday. It comes out now that the 89th N. Y. were expected to charge first and alone, upon the enemy, and the Thirteenth were not to charge at all unless the 89th were repulsed. The enemy developed an unexpected strength, the 89th had lost heavily, and when the time to charge came along, the enemy's volleys told severely upon the 89th; and the 13th rather hastily broke through the 89th, and took the van. As a body the 13th actually got into the woods first, running pell-mell over a number of men of the 89th while they were lying upon the ground, and outrunning the most of that regiment. A mixed affair surely. To-day the commander of the 89th said to Col. Stevens: "You may well be proud of that Thirteenth New Hampshire Regiment." One thing is sure: the Thirteenth was well commanded by Lt. Col. Bowers yesterday; it has a number of quick and hot-headed line officers well provided in their companies with men of their own mettle — and there is no such thing as holding the bulk of such a regiment back.

That is one picture; here is another of a different sort: It appears that five men of the Thirteenth sought reputation far in the rear during the battle of yesterday sneaking in Capt. Pruden's gullies. Being proven guilty, they are to-day mounted on barrels near camp and beside the main road. A board is tied to the back of each one, and they are made to turn around every few minutes for four hours. It is pleasant most of the day, and while these five gentlemen are having a holiday and quietly airing themselves, sixteen prisoners — of the 4th Texas — are brought in. The scene amuses the prisoners greatly, and they halt, and laugh and shout at the show like a parcel of school-boys. The boards tied upon the backs of our special exhibition are marked respectively: 'I shirked.' 'I skedaddled.' 'So did I.' 'I did too.' 'DittO.' These are not of New England — that much of disgrace is spared the line of the Thirteenth. But the day gave to us the surprise, and the stinging pain, that we have cowards among us. In the train of cowardice parades every known infamy; to cut it all short: crafty, overbearing, wordy, arbitrary, rascally, deceitful, selfish — spells cowards every time.

The enemy retreated hastily last night, in the intense darkness, from our front along the Nansemond; our troops gave chase and captured a large number of prisoners, and they are coming in to-day. We receive orders to march to the front again, but they are soon countermanded.

The more this siege of Suffolk is studied the more remarkable it appears. The conduct of the Union troops engaged in it has been worthy of the highest praise. Gen. Peck had scarcely 9,000 men all told in the line of works encircling Suffolk, and Gen. Longstreet planned to surprise him, and cut him off by crossing the Nansemond farther down, and then turning to fall upon Portsmouth, Norfolk and the country adjacent. His plans were carefully laid, his force was fully 40,000 men, and with these he swept down like a storm, and spread his forces along for miles upon the north bank of the Nansemond river. Gen. Getty, however, when Gen. Longstreet first began to threaten, was called up from Newport News with a flying column of about 8,000 men, and placed as the right of Gen. Peck's line, along the Nansemond between Jericho Creek — Fort New York — and the bluffs opposite Ft. Huger at Hill's Point; below Hill's Point the river widens into a bay, and is too wide to be crossed safely on pontons while under fire.

Gen. Longstreet planned to cross at several places between Hill's Point and Suffolk, on several days, and at different times in both day and night; but whenever he approached the river for that purpose he found himself confronted at short range by an earth-work fully armed with cannon, and heavily manned by Union riflemen, all ready and waiting to receive him. Within three days — after the arrival of Gen. Getty's troops — all along these rough, swampy, creeky, timbered, bluffy eight miles of river bank strong forts and rifle-trenches grew up, under the sturdy work of the Union soldiers, as it were by magic; and after that continued to grow higher and stronger, until, as Gen. Getty puts it, 'the works were astounding for magnitude.' Fort Connecticut was the first fort, of any considerable size, that was built. The many creeks and swamps demanded bridges, and Col. Derrom of the 25th N. J. devised a peculiar trestle, that was most convenient, and was adopted for use during the siege; Gen. Getty speaks of it in the highest terms, as well as of Col. Derrom its inventor. The investment continued from April 11th to the night of May 3d, when Gen. Longstreet, baffled at every point, withdrew and raised the siege; his retreat, says Gen. Dix, commencing about 9.30 p. m. on the evening of May 3d. Gen. Dix adds that the rebel line of works, ten miles in extent, were immensely strong.

May 5. Tues. Sunshine and showers. Reg. in camp, nothing doing except a Dress-parade. Many men, and several officers, of the Thirteenth, among them Lt. Col. Bowers and Capt. Julian, are suffering from severe sickness caused by the excitement, hard work and heat of May 3d, and from remaining inactive in the damp, chilly woods just after being much heated by the charge. Reg. furnishes a small detail for picket duty, and another detail for labor on a fort near camp. Lieut. Forbush of G assigned to the command of Company F, vice Capt. Buzzell. The camp resounds from end to end with the muffled drum, the fife and the dirge, in the burial of the dead.

Gen. John A. Peck estimates the enemy's losses during this siege at 2,000 men; and the Union losses at much less. Gen. Peck and Gen. Getty together have had about 16,000 or 17,000 men here, and several gunboats, and our lines at all times have been very much extended.

" May 5th. We buried Capt. Buzzell in the woods to-night with only the light of a lantern to see by. A storm is coming up and it is very dark." PRESCOTT.

**May 6. Wed.** Rainy. Reg. in camp. A large detail goes to work upon a fort near by. The pressure of the siege made one or two of the officers of the 13th unduly nervous. One of these on a certain night, when there was not the least danger, was suddenly waked by a man who wished to learn the countersign. The officer sprang to his feet, revolver in hand, exclaiming: "Where! Where! Which way? Which way?" and it was a minute or two before he could be brought to his senses. The watch of the siege was heavy on his mind, and his body tired out.

**May 7. Thurs.** Cold, clear. Reg. in camp. Capt. Smith and Lieut. Staniels with detail go on picket along the river bank. The pickets lodge under some dense pine-trees. It is surprising what a good tent is provided by a scrub pine. Clear away a few of the lower limbs, crawl well under, and make your pillow close to the trunk, your bed of the dry needles — 'pine tags' in pure Virginia lingo — and sleep in the soporific abounding fragrance of the wholesome pine.

A pretty story now comes out in relation to our scouts in the siege. A small body of them penetrated deep into the Dismal Swamp and lost their way. While stumbling about in the thick brush vainly looking for the trail, they were accosted by a similar body of Confederate scouts, in a very similar predicament, who asked where they were going. The Union men replied that they were trying to find the way out of this — very big D — swamp. The Confederates at once answered: "If you 'uns will show

---

### DESCRIPTION OF MAP.

A. Nansemond River, having an average width of less than 100 yards.
B. Dismal Swamp Canal.
C. Fort Halleck on the edge of the swamp, which stretches south.
D. Petersburg R. R.  E. Seaboard and Roanoke R. R.
F. Suffolk.  G. Norfleet or Northwick.
H. Battle-field of May 3, 1863, on Providence Church road N.
Z. Confederate line of rifle-pits and trenches captured that day.
K. Jericho Creek forming an island near the river.
L. Portsmouth Road.  P. Coplin.  R. Council.
M. Hill's Point, Ft. Huger, where the Nansemond widens into a bay.
S. Fort Jericho.  T. Ft. New York (or Onondaga).

Gen. Getty's Division held the line from opposite Fort New York (Union) to opposite Ft. Huger (Confed.) at Hill's Point, a distance of nearly eight miles. The 13th moved April 30th from camp near Suffolk, on the Portsmouth road, to near the point where the S. & R. R. R. crosses Jericho Creek at Ft. Jericho; on which fort (now standing) the 13th did a great deal of work. All the earth-works south of the Nansemond are Union; all north of it are Confederate; and all the forts on each line are closely connected by deep and strong rifle-trenches.

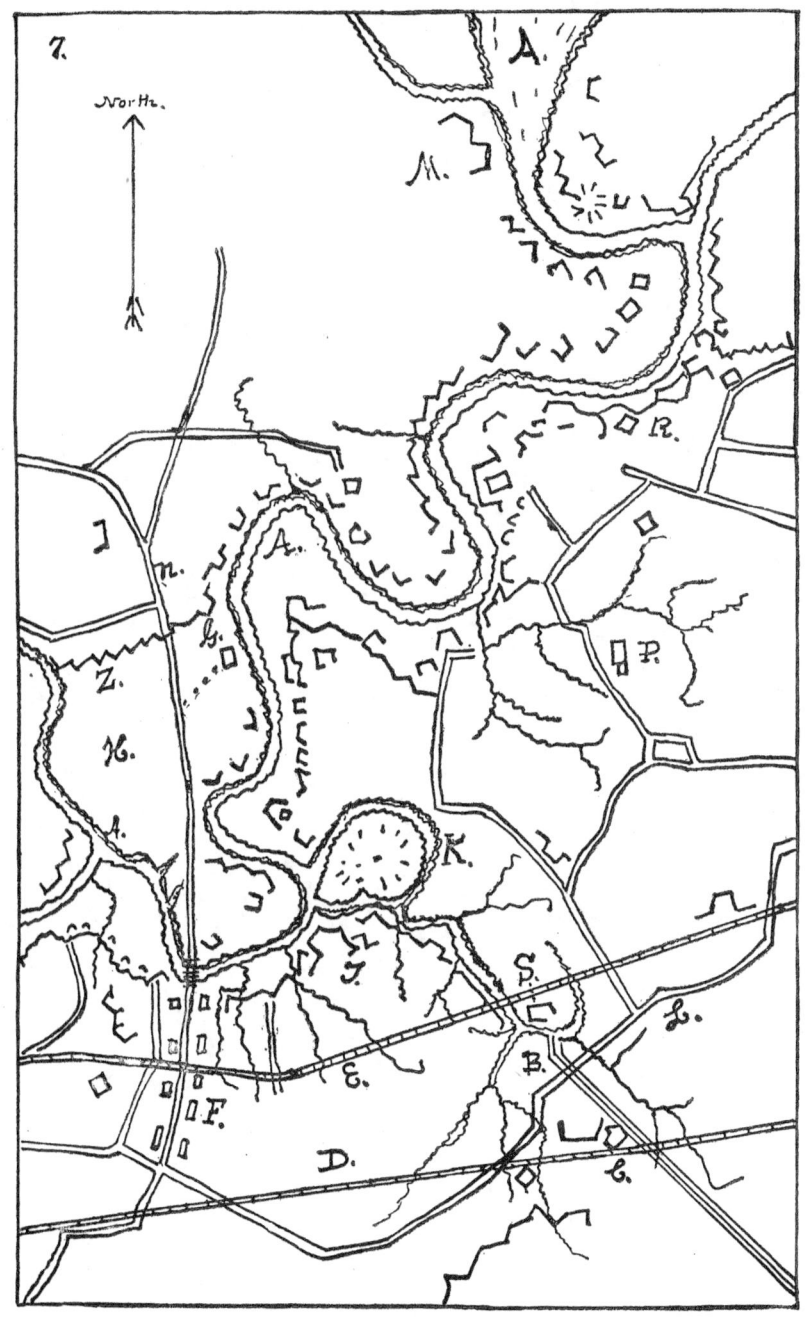

SUFFOLK.

Tracing of Official Map. Scale, one and one half inches to one mile.

we 'uns out, we 'uns will show you 'uns out." The result was a very friendly meeting, an exchange of souvenirs; and a mutual escape from the swamp to their respective commands.

May 8. Fri. Warm, showery. Reg. on picket from Jericho Creek to Battery Kimball. The enemy has gone — that is he no longer threatens, and the siege of Suffolk is ended. The enemy pressed very close for twenty-three days, keeping us working day and night, and then suddenly withdrew. Powder enough has been burned to blow all Suffolk a dozen miles over into the Dismal Swamp. Near about us now are one brigade and two batteries. The rest of the troops, that came up to this point to re-enforce us, have gone; hundreds only remain where thousands were. A part of the camp of the 13th is now in a small orchard sweet with a burden of blossoms. There is much cheering to-day all along our lines.

May 9. Sat. Fair. Reg. in camp. More surplus baggage and winter clothing is sent to Fortress Monroe and home. The Reg. hard at work by details, cutting down trees beyond the river, building earth-works, etc. The rebel earth-works, across the river, are being dismantled, and the river bank cleared of trees. The work has been going on since May 3d. Our picket line is now about three fourths of a mile from camp, and on the river bank; Union outposts and scouts are numerous beyond the river. Asst. Surgeon Small examines the sick of the 13th at Surgeon's call for the first time.

May 10. Sun. Fair. The body of Capt. Buzzell has been embalmed, and is to-day sent out of camp on its way to his old home in New Hampshire. He was a brave man — too brave, and is mourned by every member of the Regiment. Our Band played for the procession while it marched to the railroad station, about three miles from our camp. It costs about $125 to embalm, coffin and transport a soldier's body to New Hampshire.

May 11. Mon. Fair; a few showers. Reg. at work on a new fort near camp; the non-commissioned staff ordered out with the fatigue parties. The writer and the two Van Duzees of E are desiring greatly to take a view of the rebel camp: and 'become separated' — rather too willingly — from a large axe-party sent across the river under Capt. Stoodley. We deposit our three axes in a hollow tree, intending to recover them later on, and return with the other choppers to camp but do not succeed in doing so; alas! what became of those three axes? We are soon off, and make a long tour of the rebel camp, and visit the battle-field of May 3d. We find, where the 13th charged into the woods on that day, two bodies of the rebel dead, and we try to bury them with a couple of old shovels the enemy left near there, but the condition of the bodies is such that we have to desist. The enemy left a large number of his dead unburied. We find the place where Foye of E was killed, and gather as a memento a few leaves of a plant growing on the very spot where his blood was shed, and send them to his family.

The rebel camp is a curiosity; nothing like it under the sun in these last two thousand years. An immense collection of 'dug-outs'— holes made in the banks of earth and covered with poles and brush — small log huts, board shanties, lodges made by lopping the branches of a pine-tree and then piling on still other branches; and every conceivable contrivance that can be made of poles, weeds, hay, straw and brush, all low, dirty, damp and bids for chills and rheumatism; but only a few places can be found where tents have stood. The Union army would mutiny to a man in three days, if subjected to such straits. The enemy's earthworks and trenches are immense. We see where a shell from one of our gunboats had lodged in a large hut, had burst and torn some men into hundreds of pieces, shreds, and scattered them all about — horrible.

After tramping all day — dinnerless — until past mid-afternoon, we get lost in the woods, are followed, as we discover, and are very nearly captured by the enemy's scouts. We start upon the run down toward the river in hopes of reaching the vicinity of a gunboat, and finally reach a point on the river, north side, after dusk, at about three miles below where we crossed in the morning. We see some Union pickets across the river and hail them. They demand our number, and we answer, "Three." Our pickets reply that there are seven; and sure enough on the high bank a few rods behind us are gray-clad men — rebel scouts. We insist that there are but three of our party, and shout to our pickets to "Shoot the rest." This remark saves us, and our pickets send over an armed guard in a large boat to bring us across the river. We institute a hunt for the rebel scouts, but nothing but their tracks can be found. We had previously seen that they were armed with navy revolvers. We were entirely unarmed. They had desisted from firing probably because they thought they could run us down, and effect our capture.

When across the river, to escape arrest, as a ruse we pretend to have returned from a scouting expedition, and ask for a guide, instanter, to show us the way to the General's Headquarters. The guard send a Corporal with his gun. At a convenient point, after we have reached familar ground, we suddenly take to our heels through the low brush — like three genuine scouts! — and leave the Corporal to look on, and whistle, while we run. The last we see of him, he is leaning on his gun, and looking after us — probably expressing his feelings. We arrive in camp just in time for the last Roll-call at night. We report to Col. Stevens, own up, and tell him the story. He excuses us, but says: "This must not occur again." Well, we do not believe it will; we have enough. But Capt. Stoodley is not so easily satisfied. Two other men have left their axes also. And the loss of axes is not so easily managed as the absence of men, and loss of labor. However, the affair is the cause of no further trouble.

May 12. Tues. Fair and warm. There is now much talk in camp about our being 'nine-months men.' Some are even trying to decide whether they will re-enlist or not. Much shoveling at the fort near camp; a fort that has half a dozen names — of which the most prominent is "Fort Jericho" — and looks across the river northward. There is such a demand for men to work that the pickets are not relieved for three days.

*May 13. Wed.* Warm. Every man on duty, who can work. The enemy expected to return upon our front. Reg. at work on the fort. Assembles and has a Dress-parade after its hard day's work. Have orders to prepare to move. The 13th Band serenades Lt. Col. Bowers to-night.

George W. Long of E, a character in the Reg. usually known as "Pud Long," visits Suffolk with the writer, who is sent up there on an errand. Long purchases a quart of molasses, of which he is excessively fond, and carries it in a large open-mouthed glass pickle-bottle. While returning to camp through the woods, by the shortest path, Long discovers a very plump and nearly naked negro girl, perhaps eighteen years old, washing a white garment — possibly her last and only — near a little cabin in the brush, as pretty a brown statuette as her race affords, and wholly unconventional. Long creeps noiselessly up behind her as she bends over the tub, and suddenly pours about a pint of the molasses on the top of her head. When she turned and looked at him, with a most startled expression on her face, her eyes rolled up, and herself frightened half to death, the molasses running down over her neck and shoulders, in streaks lighter than her skin; the whole scene were well worth a painting. She screams: "O bress de Lord — what hab I done?" and rushes into the cabin yelling loud enough to be heard a mile. We hurry from the scene. But Long has only one idea — "I 've sweetened one nigger anyhow," he repeats again and again.

*May 14. Thurs.* Very warm — hot; — showers in the afternoon. We break camp about 9 a. m., and move to the railroad and halt there for a short time, then march down on the Seaboard and Roanoke Railroad about seven miles towards Portsmouth, then halt again; then move about two miles, and encamp in shelter tents at 4.30 p. m., in thick woods at Bowers Hill. While on the railroad to-day, during a short halt, the men lying down upon the grass and weeds under the shade of trees, the whole Brigade still and quiet; suddenly a long, rattling clap of thunder breaks from a clear sky, sounding so much like an irregular volley of musketry that the entire command instinctively springs to arms. There soon follows a heavy shower of rain thoroughly wetting everybody. Such phenomena are said to be quite common here in the Dismal Swamp. The railroad is lined with a thick forest, covered with a tangled matting of brambles and wild vines exceeding dense. The writer usually keeps a considerable number of postage stamps about him, as a supply for the men of his company, and this shower uses up the most of a recent purchase of two dollars' worth. The pickets sent out are unable in many cases to reach their designated posts, because of the water, the mud, and the almost impenetrable jungle of the swamp.

*May 15. Fri.* Pleasant. Reg. fitting up camp at Bowers Hill — but there is here neither hill nor Bowers. The nearest approach to a hill is a half-built fort, and on a knoll near by a huge Scuppernong grape vine giving large promise. Not far away is a large swamp and extremely muddy; the origin of 'Goose Creek,' the head of Western Branch. Close to our camp is a large spring furnishing the best water we have yet found in Virginia. Two flour barrels are sunk near each other to prevent the sides of the spring from caving in. One of our men, not knowing that the heads of the barrels are out, is advised, and at once attempts, to dip one of them dry. After dipping out thirty-two pailfuls — sixty or eighty gallons out of a thirty gallon barrel — he gets warm enough to think himself the victim of a practical joke, quits and goes to his quarters.

May 16. Sat. Warm. Reg. all at work during the whole forenoon on the entrenchments under direction of Col. Dutton of the 21st Conn. who has command of the troops at this point; resting in the afternoon.

# IV.

## May 17, 1863 to April 18, 1864.

### CAMP BOWERS, OR 'THE PINES.'

**May 17. Sun.** Pleasant, warm. While on regimental inspection at Bowers Hill camp about 10 a. m. to-day, orders arrive for us to move; and we march at 12.40 p. m., arriving in this pine grove, which is to be our permanent camp-ground, at 4 p. m. — distance four miles. Col. Corcoran's Irish Legion remains at the front. The army is moved about too much on Sundays.

**May 18. Mon.** Very warm. Reg. at work on our new camp in the forenoon, and on a fort near by in the afternoon; a fort afterwards called Fort Rodman. While on the wing in these last two months, the Reg. has set at work at once on the entrenchments nearest the point where it has happened to light for a few hours. The Thirteenth is the first to break ground here on this new line of earth-works. The 4th R. I. is encamped a short distance to the west of us near Ft. Rodman; details from both regiments are working together 'corduroying' the main road to Portsmouth. The growing cotton on a small field just west of our camp is very soon among the things that were. Our camp here is called Camp Bowers in honor of our loved and esteemed Lt. Col. George Bowers.

Getty's Station — Camp Bowers — The Pines. This camp is between three and four miles from Portsmouth, near a very important point where the railroad and three highroads meet. The course of the Seaboard & Roanoke Railroad where it passes the site of our camp — on the south side — runs a little south of west towards Suffolk. The Portsmouth and Suffolk carriage road runs, parallel with the railroad, on the north side of the camp. Thus the camp is crowded in between the two roads, on a strip of low, level land 750 feet wide — measured. The quarters of the field and staff, and of the line officers, are west fronting east; and the company quarters east. The company streets, running east and west, are parallel with the railroad. The site of Col. Steere's Hdqrs. was pointed out to the writer as between the two roads, and 50 yards east of the lower platform of the present Getty's Station; the quarters of the Thirteenth as commencing about 100 yards farther east. The old Quay road, so called, crosses the railroad, from the southward to the Suffolk carriage road, a little west of our camp.

It is on the whole very difficult to locate the exact site of this old camp. Now, 1885, every tree is gone, and the whole region round about is a cultivated field; scarcely one old landmark is left — even the old Quay road has moved west. Ft. Rodman is located where the Suffolk carriage road and the railroad come very near together, above Getty's Station, and about half a mile west of the camp. See August 20, 1863. The corner below this camp, and the negro camp, about one mile from Portsmouth, where the Suffolk road turns south and crosses the railroad, is called Hall's Corner. Now, 1885, nearly the whole area of all our slashing, and from our old stockade and line of rifle-trenches flanking Fort Rodman, down to Portsmouth, is a vast 'truck' garden, four to six miles square. In 1863 two thirds of this area was forest; the soldiers of the Thirteenth, you perceive, helped to clear this land for cultivation! See June 6, 18, and July 28, 1863.

May 19. Tues. Very warm, uncomfortable, frequent showers. Reg. at work on the entrenchments, which run from the Eastern to the Western Branch of the Elizabeth river — a line about six miles long, all under command of Gen. Geo. W. Getty. He now has here ten regiments of infantry, about 5,000 effective men, with a gunboat in the Branch on each flank; and that small force can hold this short line more easily than three times that number of men could hold the old long line near Suffolk. Hence this new position. Lieut. Kittredge, promoted from First Sergeant of B, receives his commission, and is congratulated. His company makes him a present of an elegant sword.

The following incident did not occur in the Thirteenth, but deserves record. A certain colonel in the Union army was very much annoyed by the incorrigible character of one of his men. He had tried in every way he could by persuasion, argument and punishment to bring the fellow to a sense of his duty, but all in vain. Finally in despair, and in disgust at some new caper, he called the man to him, and asked him what he himself thought should be done with him. The man at once replied: "Well, Colonel, since you ask my opinion, I will give it. Better let me alone to do as I please. You cannot expect to get the cardinal virtues for eleven dollars a month." The man was let alone, thrown upon his honor — what little he had — and gradually reformed himself, and became a good and trusty soldier.

May 20. Wed. Very warm. Reg. at work on the entrenchments. "The boys hallooed for bread when they came in from work." (LUEY.) The men have A tents, which are to be raised on poles in the same manner as at Suffolk. See April 8, 1863. At night now, unless rainy, the tents are all thrown wide open. Our camp here is on the site of an old rebel encampment, a part of it occupied by the 2d Louisiana. The 'Louisiana Tigers,' and 'Wild Cats,' and 'Wharf Rats,' were here also; and when they departed in May of last year, they left an amount of filth amply befitting their names. Norfolk was occupied by Maj. Gen. John Wool on May 10, 1862. The water near camp is abominable, and much that the men use is brought from the swamp, a mile distant; a reddish decoction of cypress and gum-tree, but proves to be wholesome for drinking and cooking.

May 21. Thurs. Hot. Reg. at work on the fort for four and a half hours in the afternoon. Capt. Julian has been sick since the battle of May 3d, when he did work enough for two men. Last night the men of the 13th got up a small bread riot. The affair threatened a considerable mischief. Some say it was specially worked up to draw sundry non-commissioned company officers into possible acts of violence or insubordination, and so spoil their chances for promotion. Others say it was a genuine outburst of indignation on the part of the men, because of really poor bread, and not enough even of that; but there appears to be no possible way to reach the real cause of the affair.

May 22. Fri. Hot. Reg. at work on a fort just west of camp. A fort with four names at least — 'No. 1,' 'Steere,' 'Gilmore,' and finally 'Rodman.' As a result of yesterday's demonstration bread is now hot, when given out as rations, and much better than usual. Lieut. Staniels appointed Judge Advocate of a regimental court martial.

May 23. Sat. Hot. Reg. at work on Ft. Rodman. In the ditch of this fort, and about ten feet below the present level of the ground, are a number of stumps of trees, in a long row, cut off at about the same height — about two feet above the original soil. The trees were evidently cut off with small axes, the marks still visible; but at some prehistoric period, when the level of the country was at least ten feet lower than now, and before the plain was formed which now surrounds the Dismal Swamp. Quite a curiosity, and older than the swamp in its present condition.

May 24. Sun. Exceedingly hot. We rest for one whole day, excepting the usual inspection, parade and religious services. Many letters written home. It is now generally said of the Thirteenth, that no regiment of the force hereabout has done more, if as much, shoveling and slashing. Men cannot make long days, however, in this heat. One detail works from 5 to 11 a. m., another from 3 to 7.30 p. m.

May 25. Mon. Cooler. Detail at work upon the fort and road. The order now is to arrange " uniform tents and bunks ; " the camp is to be put on Dress-parade. Red-cedar boughs are 'prescribed' for beds, as preventive of malaria. Large detail shoveling.

Many letters are written home for the soldiers who cannot write for themselves. Generally the party interested desires the letter written, 'just as I would write it, you know,' and some of the requests are very amusing. They mainly follow one order. First very affectionate words to the wife, then the children are attended to, then items of business, then connections of the family, then a joke or two for old Jake or Sally, then a little final gush, with more or less in special terms, which must be written word for word — because those words were agreed upon when the soldier left home — and they will be fully understood at home, though now worse than Greek to the writer.

May 26. Tues. Cool. Reg. at work on the fort in the afternoon. A large detail at work on a corduroy road near Portsmouth, covering the old roadway with logs laid cross-wise, and then covering them with brush and earth. The army poets are busy. Numerous 'Poems' have been written, and several published 'onto' the wounds and death of the May 3d heroes who fell on the Providence Church road. Bad enough to be shot without these poems. If all the soldiers fallen in this war should at once arise from the dead, and stand exactly as and where they were one second before the fatal stroke came upon them, the view would be wonderful; but still more striking would be their indignation and anger because of the army poets who served them up so fearfully after they were honorably dead.

**May 27. Wed.** Warm. Reg. at work on Ft. Rodman and the military road near it. The nights here usually remain very warm and close till past midnight, before the breeze from the bay penetrates these thick woods of the swamps that surround us. Brigade Hdqrs. are moved down near the west end of the camp of the Thirteenth. Music, dancing, a large assemblage, a fine illumination lighting up the pines and rivaling the brilliant moonlight, and a general jubilee holds the camp late to-night near the Hospital tents.

**May 28. Thurs.** Very warm. Reg. at work on the fort as usual. A great deal of land near by is worked by the contrabands. They are to have half of what they produce. They are coming within our lines in large numbers, and bringing woful tales of their ill treatment by the Confederates. The scenes on their arrival beggar description. Many of them are extremely pathetic, and would draw tears from the most stolid and hard-hearted men, if the monkey-like actions of the negroes were absent, and the negrotesquerie so far laid aside that the scenes could be freely realized as part and parcel of the life and experiences of human beings. You ask them how they feel now that they are free, and they will answer: "'I-golly, Massa, we's feelin' pow'ful good!"

**May 29. Fri.** Very warm. Reg. breaks ground for a new fort near the Western Branch. The walls are to be fifteen feet thick at parapet, twenty-one at base, about ten high. A house is enclosed but afterwards torn down — said to belong to a Mr. Wilson, a Colonel in the Confederate Army, and a member of the C. S. A. Congress. This work is to be hurried both day and night until the fort can be used. The men work in six-hour reliefs. Green peas, costing ten cents a quart shelled ready to cook, are abundant. The negroes bring to camp great quantities of strawberries. Cattle are driven here in large droves, turned to pasture, and killed as they are needed. We have excellent fresh beef in plenty. Lieut. Parker has resigned his commission. His health very poor. (He leaves camp on May 31st.) He is popular in the Regiment, and will be greatly missed; the leave-taking a sad one. The loss of so many officers because of sickness casts a gloom over the whole command. The first case of small-pox occurs in camp to-day.

**May 30. Sat.** Very warm and dry. Reg. at work on the new fort. The dust in the road is about six inches deep, and about one inch deep now upon us. The men are making all sorts of odd things to use and to send home, bone rings, briar-root pipes, cane-brake fifes, buzzard-quill pens, and necklaces of bears' teeth and claws obtained from the natives about the swamp.

May 31. Sun. Warm. Great need of rain. Usual Sunday inspection and parade. The talk that has been going on for nearly a month about our being mustered out on June 19th has arisen because it is claimed that the 12th N. H. filled New Hampshire's volunteer quota. The talk is making many of the men very uneasy. With the exception of fresh beef, rations are very poor now again. The men have had to work so very hard all this spring, that the regular army rations, as served, have not furnished sufficient nourishment; provoking discontent, causing sickness, encouraging secret foraging parties — and filling the sutler's purse. Cavalry and infantry reserves, with a few light cannon, hold the distant Suffolk lines, Corcoran's Legion garrisons the Bowers Hill works, while we run this new line across between the branches of the Elizabeth river. The 9th N. Y. have gone home; the 25th N. J. — nine-months men — go home June 3d, their term of service having expired. The 10th N. H. again a permanent part of our Brigade. The whole force hereabout is kept exceeding busy, building fortifications, leveling forests, building roads, etc. The citizens' children are wearing crape on their arms in mourning for Stonewall Jackson; and these future lords and ladies of the South take especial care to exhibit to the Union soldiers such emblems of rebel sentiment and feeling.

June 1. Mon. Warm, very. Reg. at work on the corduroy road to Portsmouth; commencing work at an early hour in the morning, and continuing but half the day. The 10th N. H., having come down from Bowers Hill, camps near us to-day. The officers of the 13th hold a meeting this evening, and subscribe $5.00 apiece to purchase an elegant gold snuff-box for Lt. Col. Bowers. They desire to make up a purse, for it, of $150. He must resign because of injuries in his shoulder and leg caused by a fall at the battle of Fredericksburg, resulting in severe rheumatism; while added to this are the effects of malaria and this climate, all aggravated by a very severe cold contracted in the fight on May 3d.

A soldier of the 13th writes home : " All happiness in the army here is a matter of the imagination. I am not homesick, but tired of this manner of living. The weather is now as hot as a New Hampshire July. Soldiering loses all the charms it ever had in this place and heat. I have a very depressed opinion of all the Southern cities I have yet seen, neglected, old, broken down, ramshackle affairs." Another writes : " The Thirteenth has shoveled dirt enough this season to make itself immortal, were it possible so to do in this way."

June 2. Tues. Very warm. Reg. at work on fort and road. Fine shower last night. Lt. Col. Bowers receives his resignation papers. Small-pox having made its appearance in camp and among the citizens, a general vaccination is the order of the day. At a recent dinner, one enthusiastic individual offers a toast to Lt. Col. Bowers in these words : " Here 's to Col. Bowers. Jus' 's brave man (hic). Jus' 's brave man — 's any other brave man 's a brave man — (hic), jes' so ! "

June 3. Wed. Cooler. Welcome shower last night. Reg. at work on fort and road. The 25th N. J., nine-months men, leave camp for home this afternoon. They have been in our Brigade since Dec. 10, 1862. A very good regiment as a whole. Gen. Burnside says that we have been merely on detached service since leaving Newport News ('Neuse') on March 13th, and he shall " claim the honor, of defending Suffolk, for the Old Ninth Corps." There is much talk of our joining the Ninth Corps in Tennessee or Kentucky.

Lt. Col. George Bowers leaves the Reg., and camp here, for home, this morning. While he is in a tent at breakfast, the First Sergeants quietly call out the Reg. The men surround the tent, where Lt. Col. Bowers is, and surprise him with three cheers, and then three times three. He comes out and tries to make a speech, but breaks down in tears. The men give him three times three more cheers, and form a line to properly honor him as he leaves the camp.

Extracts from letters written June 3, 1863, and later: " Lt. Col. George Bowers left us this morning — June 3d. We feel very badly to lose him — the best friend the Thirteenth had amongst all of its officers, both field, staff and line. A party of sixteen of the officers of the Thirteenth visited him at Mr. Edward Bunting's house on the evening of June 2d, had a social chat and a serenade by the Band of the Thirteenth. A formal and elaborate reception and supper was planned for him for this evening, all the officers of the Regiment to be present ; but he could not be persuaded to stop, he was so anxious to get home. He was taking breakfast in camp this morning with Col. Stevens, and the Captains had the men of all the companies in the Regiment quietly assembled by the First Sergeants, formed them in line of battle, marched them up to the tent where Lt. Col. Bowers was, and there at once surrounded the tent on all sides, and surprised him by giving three rousing cheers. He left the table, came to the tent door and attempted to address the Regiment, but after a few words he broke down in tears. The Regiment then gave him more cheers, and then returned to their quarters. In the fight at Providence Church road on May 3d, he was forward with the men during all the advance and charge, the day was very warm, and he was much heated by his exertions. After we entered the woods he was chilled by their dampness, and caught a severe cold, which settled in a rheumatic form in his limbs, rendering him unable to perform field duties."   CAPT. JULIAN.

June 4. Thurs. Pleasant. Reg. at work on fort and road. The negroes are coming into our lines in troops. A large camp of them is formed in the woods between our camp and Portsmouth. They regard the Union soldiers as their deliverers, and are unconditional friends to us wherever met. Strawberries cost but three cents a quart now, and they are huge ; to eat ten cents' worth of them is considered a good morning's work.  Chaplain Jones writes to a Northern paper : " Lt. Col. Bowers looked after the needs and wants of the privates.  They love him.  He was very courteous and kindly."

June 5.  Fri.  Warm.  Reg. at work on fort.  Very hard for the men to work in this hot, steamy, sweat-box of a country.  More talk in camp about our being mustered out as nine-months men.

One word more about Lt. Col. Bowers.  The soldiers' letters, that the writer has looked over while preparing this sketch of the Reg., have contained many very pleasant things written of Lt. Col. George Bowers.  He was, in short, the beau-ideal of a soldier, and of an officer, to the members of the Thirteenth — their friend and their brother ; and there could not possibly be a better proof of the affection of the members of the Thirteenth for him than these remarks, written voluntarily and spontaneously to their relatives and friends at home, and in such way that Lt. Col. Bowers would probably never hear a word of them.  He served as a Captain in the Mexican War, and greatly distinguished himself there on many a battle-field.  He was from early youth always prominent in the affairs of the New Hampshire militia.  Was Postmaster at Nashua from 1852 to 1860.  Was twice Mayor of that city, in 1861 and in 1868, and served in numerous minor public offices.  For a year, 1862–3, he served as Major in the Tenth Regiment Veteran Reserve Corps.  Was Department Commander of the New Hampshire Grand Army of the Republic for the years 1879 and 1880, also Junior Vice Commander of the National Department for the year 1881.  His fellow officers in the Thirteenth, a few only excepted, raised a fund sufficient to meet the expenses of his badge and initiation fees, and of his annual fees so long as he lived, in the Military Order of the Loyal Legion of the United States, and he was elected a member of the Massachusetts Commandery on October 4, 1882.  He died February 14, 1884, of heart disease, and chronic diarrhœa contracted in the service at the front while he was a member of the Thirteenth.

June 6.  Sat.  Cool.  Heavy thunder shower this evening flooding the camp.  Capt. Stoodley assigned to the command of the axe-corps — ten men from each company, and each man provided with a sharp new axe.  Their first job, it is said, is the result of a mistake made by a member of Gen. Getty's staff, and a large orchard belonging to one of the enemy's officers is leveled.  The axe-corps goes out to work every morning at 5 a. m. ; 100 men, 10 Non-Commissioned Officers, 2 Lieutenants and Capt. Stoodley.  They return to camp at 11 a. m. and have the rest of the day to themselves.  Capt. Stoodley can, somehow, accomplish more effective work with a gang of choppers than any other officer in the Regiment.  He goes about continually from squad to squad, and plans the felling of nine tenths of the trees.  His lively activity makes him seem able to be in several different places at once — and the whole of him in each of the several places.

June 7. Sun. Cool. Showers at night. Inspection. One Dress-parade a week nowadays; it ought to be with shovels, picks and axes, for the Reg. now works with them all the time. Miss Hozier, residing near Suffolk, a rebel spy, has been captured, while trying to make her way to Richmond. She is found to have, hidden in the handle of her parasol, exact diagrams and descriptions of our whole line of works, on this front. She was captured May 27.

June 8. Mon. Warm, fair. Reg. slashing. The trees are felled and left lying with their tops pointing towards the enemy, the limbs cut off so as to form a sort of abatis, not above five feet high, and the more intricately interwoven the better. Col. Dutton is absent on leave, and Col. Donohoe of the 10th N. H., and formerly a Captain in the 3d N. H., has for some time been in command of our Brigade. Lieut. Young has had charge of building the military road — mostly of corduroy — from Ft. Rodman south to Ft. Tillinghast. The backwoodsmen of Company H are selected to give lessons in felling trees.

June 9. Tues. Warm. Reg. slashing. Albe Holmes, ex-Lieutenant of Company H, opens a fine stock of sutler's goods, and we now have for the first time a sutler of our own. This summer stands of record as the warmest known for many years. So it is always; the last bad is the worst bad of all bads. The Reg. is divided into bands of choppers, shovelers, corduroy road makers, carpenters, etc., every man employed.

June 10. Wed. Warm, fair. Reg. slashing. Under this severe labor in slashing and shoveling, the health of the Thirteenth is again visibly breaking down. Lieut. Curtis has charge of the pioneers cutting ' bramble paths ; ' that is paths through the brambles, where the military roads are to run. The path through the swamp between Forts Rodman and Tillinghast had in many places to be cut foot by foot through thorny tangling vines utterly impassable to man or beast; a most intricate snarl and network, in some places several rods in width and extending to the tops of trees fifty to seventy-five feet high. Some of our pioneers mention this bramble cutting in language quite as tangled, bristling and thorny as these most vicious vines themselves.

June 11. Thurs. Warm, fair. Paymaster in camp. Reg. slashing. The largest pine felled here this summer is a little over five feet in diameter at three feet above the ground, very straight and tall; but thousands of noble trees from two to four feet in diameter have gone down to waste and utter loss. Lieut. Murray returns to camp, but not yet to duty, his wound not sufficiently healed. He is a brave, prompt and efficient officer, and has been greatly missed in the Regiment during his absence. A large force sent from our lines here towards the Blackwater to dismantle the rebel works. They find many skeletons of the unburied rebel dead. Lieut. Staniels has been out, with a squad of soldiers, for three days, picking up contrabands and sending them to the negro camp.

June 12. Fri. Hot. Reg. paid off to May 1st by Maj. G. W. Dyer, in the forenoon; in the afternoon earning greenbacks again at the slashing. The able-bodied negroes, now coming in in great numbers, are employed on the works, receiving rations for themselves and families, and some money also, in the way of payment. Lieut. Coffin leaves camp for home this morning; resigned June 9th, and honorably discharged the service. Lieut. Staniels has charge of the guards posted at citizens' houses to protect their persons and property.

June 13. Sat. Warm, fair. Our whole Reg. slashing every day; clearing a space in front of our works eleven hundred yards wide. Soldiers are out scouring the country in all directions for loafing negroes. Sometimes they bring in large numbers of them. One day two hundred of them were marched in through our camp. When the negroes cut down a tree, they cut into the trunk on all sides alike, showing less sense than a beaver when he gnaws a tree off; while the butt of the log is left sharpened to a central point, with a long 'scarf,' like a fence stake. "The negroes here are filthy and indolent, and freedom to them means perfect idleness; they are brutes in human form, destitute of all ambition, and thieves — stealing everything they can lay their hands upon." So writes truly one member of the Thirteenth.

June 14. Sun. Warm. Inspection in forenoon; Dress-parade in afternoon. The men of the Thirteenth and of the Fourth Rhode Island fraternize on the most friendly terms. Some sort of temporary feud exists, however, between the men of the Thirteenth and Tenth N. H. The 10th were out of our Brigade for a long time between the battles of Fredericksburg and Providence Church road.

June 15. Mon. Warm. Reg. at work. Col. Stevens' wife arrives in camp. It is a fact that the more ignorant people about here have been taught that the Yankees have horns. One of the worst things, which they can think of, is that: "Abe Lincoln will make the negroes equal with the white people, to eat at the same table with them, and to enjoy a social and political equality."

June 16. Tues. Very warm. Reg. at work : so hard at work that we have a Dress-parade only about once a week. Albion J. Jenness of E is on guard at the house of one John Stafford. Unable to catch the idea in the favorite Union army song, Mrs. Stafford wants to know, "Where John Brown's soul is marching to."

June 17. Wed. Hot. Reg. slashing. "A detail from the 13th, including myself, worked on Ft. Rodman, hewing timber for the magazine and unloading cannon, from 6 p. m. yesterday to 1 a. m. to-day." (LUEY.) Signs of a move. The trees stand very close together where the Reg. is now chopping, and it is often exceedingly difficult to make around a tree room enough in which to swing an axe, on account of the masses of tangled thorny vines — greenbrier or bramble. The underbrush and cane-brake form a dense jungle also. The thorns penetrate clothing, and the men are punctured and scratched from head to foot.

June 18. Thurs. Hot, very. Reg. slashing. The trees are so much tangled and tied together by vines that one often stands firmly upright after being cut entirely off. Advantage is taken of this, and the trees are cut nearly off, on one side, over a large space of ground — an acre or more — and then some huge 'bull-pine,' or other large tree, is felled directly into the mass — when down goes the whole 'drive,' with a great noise and crash. The term of labor is increased to eight hours a day, instead of four and a half hours. The men were obliged to work slowly before, in the intense heat; now their work will be "double-slow."

June 19. Fri. Fearfully hot. Showery. Reg. slashing — working eight hours a day. Heavy guns coming down, from the forts nearer Suffolk, and being placed in forts here. Corcoran's Irish Legion remain in the vicinity of Suffolk. Our Brigade transferred from the 9th to the 7th Army Corps. Order read on Dress-parade to that effect.

June 20. Sat. Rainy, warm. A train of army wagons over a mile in length passes down the road to-day. Marked signs of immediate activity. One thing is certain, we are not nine-months men; all bets on that are off. As one man of the 13th writes, " Nine-months stock is flat." The sick are sicker to-day — as a rule. The advance of Gen. Lee's army toward Pennsylvania calls for some movement of the troops in this command, and a hundred rumors are flying.

June 21. Sun. A little rain. Inspection at 11 a. m. Orders arrive this noon for the Thirteenth to leave camp at one o'clock and to be ready to embark at Portsmouth at three o'clock to-morrow morning. Our camp is to be left standing, and a few men left to guard it, and to care for the sick and convalescent. Several men, in view of trouble ahead, are seized with violent fits of vomiting this evening; a powerful emetic and the guard house are prescribed, and work wonderful cures in every case. Corcoran's Irish Legion are to garrison and hold this line in the absence of our troops. Capt. Bradley is very sick, and is forbidden to leave camp. He sits to-day on a stump, the picture of wretchedness, watching the preparation made by his Company to march, and vowing that he will follow. This is plucky.

Extract from a letter written June 21, 1863 : " Rainy. The Thirteenth will take knapsacks for the march to-morrow, three days' rations in haversacks, and forty rounds of ball-cartridge per man. Lieut. Durell is sick and will remain in camp ; Lieut. Murray has not yet returned to duty (recovering from his wound) ; First Sergeant Thompson will act as Lieutenant." CAPT. JULIAN.

An idea occurs to Gen. Dix, to create a diversion in favor of the Union army in Pennsylvania, and to cut off Gen. Lee's conmunication with Richmond on the north. Gen. E. D. Keyes is to move from White House, almost due west along the York River Railroad, via Baltimore Cross Roads, with about 5,000 men, to draw away the enemy from Bottom's Bridges on the Chickahominy river, and to give them battle. He, however, finds the enemy too strong, and is delayed. Gen. Getty is to proceed from White House northwest, with about 7,000 men, nearly his whole Division, directly upon Hanover Junction, and to destroy there the

Virginia Central and Fredericksburg Railroad bridges over the North and South Anna rivers. Both forces are to join as near as possible to Richmond — for advance or retreat, as the case may determine.

### 'BLACKBERRY RAID.'

June 22. Mon. Very warm. Very dark last night. Thirteenth is called at twelve o'clock, midnight, of June 21st, leaves camp at one o'clock this morning, and marches down the main road to Portsmouth. One man of the Reg. writes: "The night was so dark that all the way we could get along, in any kind of order, was by the polished barrels of our guns." In the woods, in the intense darkness, several of our men fall into the deep ditch by the side of the road, and are fished out of the mud and water with poles, and not exactly in a proper condition to appear on a Dress-parade. One man of the Thirteenth somewhat given to stuttering, and who had imbibed a little too freely before he left camp, remarked as he was pulled up from a plunge into the road-side ditch : " I 'm all right; but I doanunner(hic)stand this 'ere moo(hic)oove — it puts my head all into a wh(hic)irl." And his remark becomes a by-word.

We embark at Portsmouth, about 4 a. m., on the steamer 'Maple Leaf,' with the 4th R. I. Arrive at Yorktown about 10 p. m., debark near midnight, march a couple of miles, and bivouac at 3 a. m. on the plain near the Hessian burying-ground. Good place for a patriot camp. The Thirteenth numbers about 400 men now here present for duty. The men of the Thirteenth take their knapsacks for this march, with one change of underclothing in them. The painted things are like huge nonporous plasters upon the men's backs, the straps binding all clothing closely about the chest and shoulders — a most vicious combination for hard marching in hot weather. The side of a knapsack worn next a man's back should be made of something less sweltering than painted canvas ; it should be made of a piece of flannel that could be removed and washed — or of sponge.

June 23. Tues. Pleasant. Reg. called very early. The bivouac last night was irregular, and the first thing done is to bring the tents into the proper order of a regimental camp. Many men take a bath in the river, the water quite clear.

Queer, battered, neglected, dilapidated, little decrepit old Yorktown. Since Oct. 19, 1781, this town has been historic. Gen. Washington then had here a victorious Patriot army of about 16,000 men, and Lord Cornwallis surrendered to him an army of 7,073 men ; the spot is pointed out to us where the commanders, and also the two armies, stood on that occasion. We are of another Patriot army numbering hard upon two round millions of men — so large have things grown in eighty odd years.

June 24. Wed. Showery. Company drill in forenoon, Battalion drill in afternoon. Here are vast deposits of sea shells, mostly scallops, and where Gen. McClellan's troops cut into the hills are very many large springs of water, clear as crystal; and our men, recently from the low, flat, muddy region about the Dismal Swamp, cannot drink enough of it. McClellan's earth-works here are simply immense.

June 25. Thurs. Rainy, cool. Orders received to be ready to move at a moment's notice. Company drill in the forenoon — and a fine scene it is when hundreds of companies can be seen manœuvring at once. Teams at evening are moving off. We are to wait until 3.30 a. m. to-morrow. Thirteenth to march in heavy marching order. Curiosity hunters visit the various places of interest. Among others the tree where 'California Joe,' as a sharp-shooter, concealed himself, and silenced a rebel battery, and also shot the negro Confederate sharp-shooter who had killed and wounded many of our pickets, one year ago. Capt. Grantman, who has been at Norfolk on court martial duty, rejoins the Reg. here.

June 26. Fri. Rainy, warm. Reg. called at 2 a. m., marches at 3.30 a. m., embarks at wharf in town on the steamer 'Hero,' at 6 a. m., with the 10th N. H., and moves at 8 a. m. up the York and Pamunkey rivers to White House Landing, arriving there about 3 p. m.; debarks, moves out half a mile or so, and encamps near a magnolia swamp, at the north side of the York River Railroad. A little, round monitor fort, of the enemy's, mounting one gun, was here rendered useless by one well-directed shot, made yesterday by our gunboat; the enemy, however, got off with his gun about 6 a. m., burned the culverts and bridges on the railroad, and tore up much of the track, behind him, as he retired; he also burned a number of buildings, the ruins of which are smoking when we arrive. The 11th Penn. Cavalry are now clearing our front. The old 'White House' here was the scene of Washington's early married life, and the property of his wife; the house is now in ruins.

June 27. Sat. Fair; rained hard last night. Reg. still in bivouac. In the magnolia swamp near by, the trees in full bloom furnish so much fragrance that many men are made sick, and our camp is moved farther away from it. Inspection and Company drill in forenoon, Battalion drill in afternoon, followed by a Dress-parade. Our picket line is out but a little way — scarce a rifle-shot from camp. Gen. Spear's cavalry come in with a long train of captured wagons, many mules and 120 prisoners, and with them Confederate Brig. Gen. W. H. Lee; trophies of the 11th Penn. Cavalry. Army rations run short, and one soldier of the 13th writes: "A great supply of nothing to eat; fried mutton for supper."

June 28. Sun. Showery. Inspection, parade, and prayers by our Chaplain. The men find a number of Gen. McClellan's unused coffins, and make them do duty for the living, in the form of bedsteads; not at all bad. The bones of a few men, found near camp, are still more suggestive. The ribs and uprights of Gen. McClellan's old army wagons make good shelter-tent poles. Our commissariat appeared last night, and to-day we have fresh beef. Gen. Dix and staff pass along the lines.

Maj. Gen. Joseph Hooker succeeded in command of the Army of the Potomac by Maj. Gen. George G. Meade.

June 29. Mon. Very showery; a clear afternoon. Reg. drills all day and has a Dress-parade at sundown, when orders are read transferring us to the 2d Div. 7th Army Corps. In some places about us the ground is literally blue with a kind of passion flower — the vines are said to grow little gourds called "pop-apples." The rebels collected a large force of negroes here yesterday for work about Richmond; but last night they mutinied, seized boats, made rafts, etc., crossed the river, and came into our lines. They pass our camp to-day in a large crowd; men, women and children all together, each with a bundle. They will be sent to Fortress Monroe. They made a bold dash for freedom, and secured it.

June 30. Tues. Pleasant. Orders to move at call to-morrow morning, with cooked rations, and in light marching order; but the 13th and other regiments in our Brigade take knapsacks — heavy marching order. Reg. mustered for pay by Col. Wm. Keine of the 103d N. Y. Company E has several Kenistons, and Col. Keine has them all stand out until he can muster them beyond a chance for doubt, and causes a laugh in the Regiment by his remarks — wants to know if there are any more "Kan-ee-stones." He is evidently of German extraction.

The general orders upon this raid are that the regiments shall be called out at 3 a. m., have breakfast, and be ready to march at any time from 4 to 7 a. m. — and to halt when the man on horseback gets tired. The scattering of white citizens hereabout, as the Union army approaches, shows their classic tastes — the word 'skedaddle' being excusable Greek. The word seems to be a product of this civil war. Lieut. Young is placed on picket on the York River Railroad, and visits the vedettes of the 11th Penn. Cavalry. They have just killed and cooked a pig, — cooking him almost sooner than he died. The Lieutenant, not knowing the state of the meat, is invited to join in the lunch. He does so. There is no salt to be had, nevertheless all eat heartily of the meat. The result is that all are made fearfully sick. This experience proves that hunger is not always the best sauce.

July 1. Wed. Warm, very. Reg. called at 3 a. m.; crosses the railroad bridge over the Pamunkey to the east side at 7 a. m.; marches to King William Court House near the Mattapony, a march of about nine miles, and bivouacs at 6.30 p. m. on a low, wet, muddy, plowed field about half a mile beyond the collection of buildings. During the day the weather has changed, and a cold rain sets in. The road is an abomination for mud, the field also. The men are very tired, and procure some unthreshed wheat, from the stacks near by, to keep their blankets and themselves out of the mud in to-night's bivouac. We have fairly turned in, when an order comes from the "General commanding," for the men to return "every straw of that wheat" to the stacks. The poor men turn out in the pouring rain, gather up the wheat, and replace it on the stacks — accompanying their action by very many remarks in 'camp language.' About midnight fires suddenly break out among those wheat stacks, and they disappear in smoke, together with a blacksmith shop and a large mill

— the great fires lighting up the entire camp. Instead of a few bushels of wheat with the straw going to a much needed bed in the mud, many hundreds of bushels of wheat, straw and all, go to a useless rest in ashes. Company B of the Thirteenth is rear-guard to-day. They did not burn the wheat — but they believe that a lunch of broiled chicken is just as good for a rear-guardsman as for any other man.

The force now advancing here consists of the 11th Penn. and 2d Mass. Cavalry; 8th, 11th, 15th and 16th Conn.; 10th and 13th N. H.; 3d, 89th, 99th, 103d, 112th, 117th, 118th N. Y.; 13th Indiana; 165th, 166th, 169th Penn., and the 4th R. I. Infantry Regiments, and four Batteries — all under command of Gen. Getty. Occasionally in a turn of the road nearly the whole force comes into view at once, and, as we march compactly in good order, makes a fine appearance among the trees and green fields; the muskets glistening near and far, in long lines and masses, and well mounted horsemen dashing here and there. They call this force the Second Division of the Seventh Army Corps. Our Brigade is under command of Col. M. T. Donohoe of the 10th N. H.

July 2. Thurs. Hot, very. Reg. called between 2 and 3 a. m., and marches from 4.30 a. m. until about 11 a. m. At 3 p. m. the Reg. moves on about half a mile and encamps. Several cases of sunstroke among our troops. Roads abominable. We bivouac near Brandywine. We are marching through the very granary of Gen. Lee's army, and are under the strictest orders to appropriate nothing at all; while at this very hour Gen. Lee, with an enormous army, is devastating the quiet fields and homes of Pennsylvania. Here too are hundreds of acres of wheat, corn and oats, cultivated under the superintendency of Gen. Lee's own soldiers, detailed for this especial purpose — one soldier for every ten or fifteen negroes — and who skedaddle for Richmond as we approach. Our men are even ordered not to go to wells and springs, along the road, for water to drink; in fact, the strictness is exasperating to both men and officers, and necessarily provokes mere wanton mischief from the hands of lawless men among us. Still we will, and we do, to some extent, procure and eat what we want the most — early fruit, chickens, lambs and young beef. They say that in a field, not far from our camp, is a pile of fifty or more lambskins — winter clothing, of course, that the lambs have laid by.

July 3. Fri. A very warm day. Reg. called at 3 a. m. and marches at 6 a. m. We pass through Mongohit and Mechanicsville, so called. Have been put upon the wrong road, and are obliged to countermarch. In crossing a little stream to-day, some men, belonging to a regiment ahead of us, rush into the water, drink deeply, come out, stagger a few steps — and drop dead. The most of this force is moving in light marching order, and such was the order to our Brigade; but the 10th and 13th N. H. Regiments, at least, move in heavy marching order, taking everything with them — knapsacks, blankets, shelter tents, their change of clothing, etc., etc. Some one has made a mistake, and caused our men great loss, and fearful suffering from the heat. We make a long halt about noon. Hot as Tophet. At this noon halt the men enjoy an abundance of blackberries, the ground being covered with them. Cases of sunstroke very common; there is scarcely a worse sight than a man lying dead of sunstroke. The Reg. marches again at 4 p. m., and continues to march, with frequent halts, till 9 p. m. After a march of 18 miles, the Reg. bivouacs at midnight on Confederate Gen. Taylor's plantation, said to be about three miles north of Hanover Court House. The vicinity is called Horn's Quarters. We here liberate 50 or 75 slaves; some of them start at once down upon our line of march, others remain to follow the army. The Thirteenth, and a large part of our Brigade, halts here, while a large force pushes on, across the Pamunkey, for Hanover Junction, eight miles distant to the northward. Taylor's farm is used as a sort of headquarters. Union soldiers have been posted to guard the citizens' property at every house all along the roads; we see them on doorsteps and piazzas, under trees, everywhere.

July 4. Sat. Hot. Reg. called at 3 a. m., but we do not march until after 9 a. m. We march about five miles to Hill's plantation in Caroline County — where we pass through one cornfield said to contain 1,600 acres, the corn up to our shoulders — and halt at Littlepage's bridge between 10 and 11 a. m., and remain during the day and night, along the road and on the river bank. Detachments from the Thirteenth and the Tenth N. H. are sent upon picket along the river. The rest of the Thirteenth, acting as Gen. Getty's body-guard, take the day in ease and peace, along the road and river, among the trees. The force which crossed the river here last night and this morning, moving towards Hanover Junction, said to be nearly the whole Division, has a severe skirmish with the enemy during the day, and we can plainly hear the artillery engagement; at times the firing is very heavy. Roundly speaking, two brigades cross the river, and one (ours) remains here as a reserve.

As the Reg. halts, in an oatfield, to-day just before dinner, Adjutant Boutwell and Asst. Surgeon Sullivan go to the nearest house, take possession and try to have a dinner prepared, but fail. However, by pushing things, they succeed in obtaining an excellent supper for themselves and a number of other officers. After eating the supper, they — like gallant and honorable soldiers — pay for it. Quite a number of our officers sleep, to-night, on the floor of the house.

We celebrate the Fourth of July in a novel fashion. We have here a hundred or more liberated slaves, of all ages, sizes and complexions. One girl about fourteen years old and several boys would readily pass for white children. (This girl was sent North, adopted in a good family, brought up and educated.) These slaves, well aware of the import of July 4th, are induced to give us an exhibition of their plantation melodies and dances. They join hands, form a large circle, and pass around and around for half an hour, bending their bodies and knees with a 'courtesy and a jerk,' as only the negro can; stamping time with their feet, singing melodies that no one of us can understand, and occasionally repeating a yell in every conceivable tone and compass of voice, rapidly and successively round and round the circle, as if each one in turn were suddenly struck mad. They give also a number of duets and solos, and dances for which the music is 'clapped' on the musician's knee. The play is kept up for hours, until they are tired of the show — and we also. Sugar, as a reward for their entertainment, is chiefest in demand. Many of us are emptied of our store. The little darkey will take a handful, fill his mouth, roll his eyes in ecstasy, and then lick his hands and fingers clean — that have not been clean before for three months.

We bivouac here under the protection of a strong picket. There are captured near here, from the enemy, about 150 horses, 50 mules, and 50 head of fine cattle. Our forces across the river are aiming to destroy certain bridges on the Virginia Central and the Fredericksburg Railroads, but find the enemy there in force, and this evening we can hear heavy firing at Hanover Station; the firing commencing at 4 p. m. While the Reg. is broken up, in detachments for picket along the river, Company C, organized as a special guard, under command of Lieut. Curtis, holds Littlepage's bridge — a post of great importance. Companies C and E act as brigade rear-guard in the march and movements of to-day.

The Lieutenant of the Thirteenth who had charge of the regimental Pioneer-corps to-day, which partly tore up Littlepage's bridge and prepared the remaining portion for firing on the retreat of our troops across it from Hanover Station, came into the camp of the Thirteenth late at night thoroughly tired out, and laid him down to pleasant dreams. The Reg. were lying all about him soundly sleeping — a sleep very much needed. The Lieutenant had not been asleep ten minutes when he was seized by a terrible attack of nightmare, and soon brought the larger part of the Reg. to their feet by belching out the most hideous, blood-curdling torrent of howls and screams imaginable. It was several minutes before he could be quieted, while the men near him indulged in much vigorous 'camp language.'

July 5. Sun. Pleasant, warm. The good news from Gettysburg reaches us this morning, and gives occasion for lively cheering.

Heavy firing is heard near very early this morning, and approaching nearer, as our forces retreat from the Junction. Wounded men are coming in on country wagons. The 13th is called about daylight, its pickets are relieved about 7 a. m. and the Reg. at once assembles in the road close down to Littlepage's bridge, ready for anything that may turn up. As the morning and forenoon passes, bodies of infantry march rapidly past us, and form lines of battle in the fields in our rear, all looking as if they had experienced a very rough time of it. It is said, however, that of the force which crossed the river, only the 99th N. Y. and the 165th Penn. engaged the enemy. Detachments from the 13th and the 10th N. H., working together, pile upon Littlepage's bridge a large amount of combustible material. A battery tears across the bridge, rushes past us, the horses galloping, jumping over and crushing down fences, and takes position in our rear, in the field, and prepares for action. Things look decidedly squally. The skirmishing approaches nearer and nearer, the firing sharp. The 13th moves back a little out of the road and forms again in line of battle, across a field, near and in support of the battery. The 10th are to set the bridge on fire and follow. Just as the last of our troops have crossed, and the bridge is well on fire, a man suddenly appears on the roof of his house, off to our right, as we face towards the river — westward — and waves a signal flag to the enemy across the river. Soon a body of our cavalry takes him in hand, and his house joins the bridge — in smoke. His was a piece of treachery.

Now comes the hardest marching that we have ever endured. The 13th lead the whole force on to-night's march, and are ordered to reach Ayletts before one o'clock to-morrow morning. Starting about 9.30 a. m., we first go back to Taylor's plantation, about five miles, at the top of our speed. After a short halt here, near Horn's Quarters, the 13th is joined by the 10th; who come up much out of breath, and minus their knapsacks, for many of these have also joined the bridge in smoke. Our Brigade looks very finely drawn up in the ample grounds of this splendid mansion. Ammunition is here specially examined, extra rations are supplied, and near 1 p. m. we march about one mile, and are assigned position. At 5.30 p. m. is commenced a forced march, that is kept up until we reach White House. Sweeping round northward past the Hebron, or Bethel, church, towards the Mattapony, on a different road from the one by which we came up, our first halt, except for ten minutes or so, is near Ayletts, on the Mattapony River at 1.15 a. m. (LIEUT. STANIELS.) Distance 18 miles since 5.30 p. m. Soon we are off for another mile, and at 2 a. m. we bivouac in an open field for about three hours. We march twenty-four miles in eight hours of marching time; mostly in the dark, with scarcely a halt, and the night damp and warm. On this night march the men suffer terribly from thirst, and actually dip water out of puddles in the middle of the road, and drink it, after hundreds of horses, mules and men have splashed through it — 'horse coffee,' as the boys call it, and with a vengeance!

"Joseph H. Prime of F is a large man. The largest army shoes to be had are too short for him, and on this raid he has been obliged to go barefoot the most of the march; the result is that his feet are very sore, and on this night march his feet are bleeding, and his ankles swollen, rendering him unable to proceed. Rising to march after one halt he is unable to stand, and Lieut. Young, in command of the rear-guard to-night, lifts him by main strength upon his shoulders, carries him to the teams and puts him on one of the wagons. The wagon is crowded, and in order to make room for Prime, Lieut. Young pulls out of the wagon a man — so called — who had no business on the wagon at all, and who wears a Major's uniform. The lifting of Prime, the tussle with the Major, who was merely tired or lazy, the march, the labor in keeping up stragglers and caring for the rear-guard, and the severe cold taken in the morning's bivouac at Ayletts while sleeping on the bare ground without cover, brought on a disability from which Lieut. Young has never recovered, and was the cause of his final resignation of the service. Prime declared on this occasion, that as soon as he returned to camp he would apply for promotion to an official position in a regiment of colored troops. This he did, and received a commission as Captain in the 25th U. S. Colored Infantry, Nov. 4, 1863." LIEUT. YOUNG.

'Ambulance Brown' prefers a black moustache on his amiable face to the huge paler hued one which nature supplies. The color he takes along in his pocket is handy to have in the Thirteenth. For instance : Our excellent Asst. Surgeon Small finds among the captured horses one that suits his fancy. A whining rebel citizen appears and begs for his "dear horse." The Colonel tells this Mr. Secesh to go among the herd and pick out his horse, and he will see about its return. The horse had a white foot or two, a white star in his face and a white nose. Brown, however, the moment he sets his sharp eyes upon this horse, sees that he is a valuable animal, and suspects that he will be demanded. He decides that this particular horse is not the horse he was, and to prove it, he whips out his moustache dye — without the knowledge of the Colonel or Asst. Surgeon Small — and colors all the white marks on the horse jet black. This job has hardly been completed, when Mr. Secesh appears in the herd, and still further proves the horse not the horse he was, by being utterly unable to find his lost property — the work so well done he does not recognize his own "dear horse," and goes his way lamenting. When it is safe to do so the color is washed off — and now he is the horse he was. He does good service in the army, and is brought North at the end of the war. No one but 'Ambulance Brown' would ever have thought of dyeing a horse's moustache — but you see the habit of dyeing moustaches had grown strong upon him.

July 6. Mon. Rainy. Reg. is up and starts again about 4 a. m., is jerked around awhile, and at 8.30 a. m. marches from Ayletts to Ayletts Station, to a field a little beyond King William Court House, in the forenoon, about 10 miles. Encamps here in the afternoon — about 3 p. m. — in a heavy rain. A halt is necessary for the stragglers to come up. The roads are in a terrible condition — awfully muddy. Added to this the men are thoroughly drenched in the rain, and have the extra difficulty of marching in wet clothes. We remain here until morning. Near Mongohit road about midnight last night, the enemy came up with the rear-guard, and threatened mischief; but the scare had an excellent effect in stopping unnecessary straggling. It is reported that guerillas have shot a number of stragglers — and they take no prisoners any way. Several fine horses were taken last night from barns and stables. The writer saw a valuable roan horse taken from a potato hoard, or small cellar, in a field quite a distance from any house. He was awfully hungry, heard somebody coming, called for provender, told where he was, was rescued, fed, cared for and taken along — no brands.

But at the final halt, as the Division is now together again, the scene changes. All the captured mules, horses, teams, carts, wagons, and fat calves led by a string, are filed into a large cattle yard by the Provost Marshal, and there is a general — and many a special — unloading. At King William Court House, where, on the way up, the men could not have straw to sleep on, they are obliged now to relinquish all the 'practical fruits' of this famous raid; to leave their fresh meat on the hoof, and their conveyances, shawls, swallow-tail coats, plug hats, umbrellas, fancy parasols, etc., all so dear to the soldier's heart, and come down to army rations, and the weather, unprotected. They sullenly and slowly strap on their coarser soldier traps, and gear, and then march, and — grumble. The taste for luxuries must hereafter be confined to blackberries and warm water from the wayside-brook. If you ever go on a raid steer clear of King William Court House.

July 7. Tues. Warm, heavy showers. Reg. up at daylight, starts at 7 a. m., marches to the White House, and encamps there at noon. Distance about nine miles. The troops of both expeditions all come together here again. Col. Dutton resumes command of our Brigade, and Col. Donohoe, who is sick, goes by steamer to Norfolk. All sick men are examined to-night by the Surgeons. Many of our men, who are utterly used up, are also put on a transport at 9 p. m. — the 'Juniata' — and sent to our old camp in the Pines. One man of the 13th writes: "We were stowed away on that transport like dumplings in a steam box." The Band also go down by boat. Men have marched with galled and blistered feet, the nails coming off their toes. The fury of the slaveholders, whose slaves we brought off with us, was intense, their threats and curses bitter and deep; but in these days a slaveholder's damn is not worth a tinker's dam — we smile, the darkeys grin, they stamp, swear and howl with impotent fury.

July 8. Wed. Hot; heavy showers. Reg. marches at 6 a. m. to New Kent Court House, and about six miles beyond. Distance twelve miles. Roads one mass of mud. Two wagons are mired in one place, cannot be extricated, and are burned. The worst roads and worst mud we ever saw. As we march to-day over a bad corduroy road, old, rotten and strewn with army waste, a big darkey, leading a mule, gets off the road with his charge and into a deep slough. The darkey is rescued with a pole, but the mule goes down, down until his ears and sorry countenance are alone visible — a sudden struggle, a gulp or two, and a few bubbles are the last signs of the mule. The darkey's sole comment, given with a scared grin, was: "'I, golly! Done gone forebber!" as he plainly saw how he himself might also have gone under, but for that pole and a few strong men. The Thirteenth are all placed on picket, to-night, as rear-guard, and forage far and wide for something good to eat.

During the first halt, near New Kent Court House, of scarcely half an hour and in a pouring rain, some of the men have a lunch of 'quick-pig.' They had caught him a mile or two back, had knocked him on the head and partly dressed him while they marched. Instantly upon halting the pig is cut into very thin slices and distributed, a fire is built — of dry wood found in some wood-shed by the way, rolled in a rubber blanket and lugged may be for a mile or more — the thin slices of meat are rolled in salt, put on a green stick, and broiled in the fire. When a dozen veteran soldiers start upon an affair of this kind, a halt of ten or fifteen minutes suffices to furnish them with a hearty meal.

After this first halt, the 13th moves a little way to drier land near some buildings, and remains there for nearly two hours. Then marches about four hours to make six miles; the teams in the train, we are guarding, sticking fast in the mud at every few rods. We are marching to Hampton as a convoy to the wagon train.

July 9. Thurs. Hot. Reg. marches about 6 a. m., and continues on for 18 miles towards Yorktown; a part of the distance is made at the rate of a forced march. At one halt to-day, after a severe spurt in the march, one company in the Thirteenth actually borrowed a gun to complete a stack of three muskets — in order to strictly obey the order: "Halt. Stack Arms — Rest." At the final halt for the day, about three miles above Williamsburg, at 7 p. m., there are not a dozen men present in some of the companies. The sick and lame of the Thirteenth, who go down on the 'Juniata,' arrive in the Pines at 3 p. m. to-day. Many of them lost on the raid almost everything they had, and come to camp barefoot and shirtless.

July 10. Fri. Hot. Reg. marches into Yorktown, and about 6 p. m. occupies its old camp, that was vacated June 26th. Distance to-day 18 miles; as we wind around about somewhat, the whole distance marched is by some estimated at above 20 miles. The men are terribly tired and stragglers are coming in all night. As we pass through Williamsburg the College of William and Mary, battered and worn, is in a 'vacation' longer than its longest of old. A statue of Jefferson (said to be) also battered and worn, looks down upon us as we hurry through this capital of Virginia's proud old days. How this world does turn over and over as it goes! Now that the men are in camp again, their change of shirts and stockings, thrown away with their knapsacks while on the raid, would be very acceptable; hundreds of men and officers are in the river bathing, and washing their clothing, which they wring out and at once put on again — almost imperative, but a bid for chills and fever.

July 11. Sat. Warm, pleasant. Reg. resting at Yorktown. In passing through the fortifications near Williamsburg we came to one point where we could count 13 rebel forts all in one view; their Fort Magruder is a work of immense strength. The battle-field is terribly torn and broken even now, and strewn with everything used by an army, and not quickly perishable. Over five hundred contrabands have followed our little army down here from the "Up-country," as they call it. Sergt.

James M. Hodgdon of B, who went to the old camp in the Pines, on the 'Juniata,' writes of to-day : "Rainy and warm. The flies bite fearfully. Took out Companies H and K on a Dress-parade, where I acted as Captain, with no shirt on — all right."

July 12. Sun. Very warm; light showers. Reg. marches at 5 a. m., and encamps on the old battle-field at Big Bethel. Distance 14 miles. Here also are very strong fortifications. Now come the huge ripe blackberries in rich abundance. At every halt the men scatter and pick them. Hence the name of this march — 'Blackberry Raid.' One halt of an hour to-day is made especially for blackberries, so it is said ; at any rate several thousand men, in a long line, halt, stack arms, and at once fall to gathering the luscious berries. They whom the berries fail to fill, take a lunch from their haversacks.

The showers to-day — like most summer showers in the South — instead of cooling the atmosphere, fill it with a warm, stifling steam, hard to breathe, clogging the lungs, and really increasing the heat ; a state of the air in which sunshine is not necessary to produce sunstroke, as it is called, several fatal cases of which occur in to-day's march.

July 13. Mon. Fair. Reg. called at 3 a. m., starts about 4 a. m. and marches, via Little Bethel, crossing New Market bridge, to Hampton, arriving there about 9 a. m., rests all the day, and embarks there at 6 p. m. on the steamer 'Express,' crosses to Portsmouth, and arrives at our old camp in the Pines at 11 p. m. Distance marched, besides the sail, 14 miles. The entire tramp, on this raid, is estimated to have been from 160 to 175 miles of actual marching, our marching time twelve days and nights, besides the distance made by steamers.

As the Thirteenth comes into camp, every denizen turns out, and the whole command cheers until the midnight woods ring, echo, and ring again. Now at midnight we stretch our weary limbs upon the welcome bunks in our old quarters, and sleep as only soldiers can — and after the toughest march in their experience. We find our tents remaining exactly as we left them, no knot in string or rope untied ; 'the furniture in our whole absence has not even been dusted.'

While we were waiting at the landing near Hampton to-day, a large water-spout 'spiraled' up Hampton Roads, and broke upon a sandy point near by us. The water came down literally in chunks, for a little while, in the open country, and soon we were treated to a severe shower of rain. As the water-spout approached before it burst — or fell in pieces — there was a lively scattering of the small boats in the bay. An old darkey fishing for soft-shell crabs found himself directly in its track, and being unable to row his boat fast enough to escape the monster, sprang out of it and waded ashore, while his boat soon went up the spout — literally — and in falling again was smashed in pieces. The old fellow, as he came ashore, blubbered out : "Thought I was done gone for, dat time — shuah !" We thought so too.

Somewhere up the Peninsula the medical department of the Thirteenth captured a pair of mules and a wagon, all together worth hard upon a thousand dollars, and used them in the interest of our tired men upon the march. They finally fell to the charge of our Asst. Surgeon John Sullivan; and the 'Doc's mules' are exceedingly handy to have in our regimental family.

A shower came up suddenly one day while we were in the road marching, and instantly the army, stretched along in sight for a mile or more, was changed into a procession with umbrellas and parasols of every style and color — a most ludicrous scene; while gay colored shawls, cloaks, and old plug hats were too numerous to mention. The soldier must have his fun. The writer saw one soldier in the 13th on the march, purchase of a negro woman a dirty, ragged shawl woven in brilliant stripes of red, yellow and green. He washed it, repaired it, brought it to camp, paraded in it upon occasion, and finally sent it home. Many similar purchases were made of old odds and ends as curiosities and relics. The damage done, on this expedition, to private property, was mostly done by rebel guerilla parties, who fell back from district to district, as our forces advanced. Their damage being done to 'fire the Southern heart;' an attempt to blackmail the Union soldiers, who foraged for fresh provisions, and that was about all, excepting for the grotesque or old-fashioned things with which to make sport. One of the amusing features was the conspicuous absence of the native white population. Any inquiry about the man of the house would be answered by the statement that he had ' gone to mill,' ' gone to see a sick brother,' ' gone to town ' — or gone to any indefinite place upon any indefinite errand. The darkey usually said: 'Guess he done goned off somewhere!'—an answer always given slyly and with the negro grinning chuckle, as if the white man's sudden absence was a most amusing thing, but a little dangerous to laugh about just yet.

One dark night a huge deer dashed into the road, over the brush fence, and collided with a mule team. The mules brayed with fright, and that scared the deer more and more. After a short, sharp struggle among the straps and traces, he extricated himself, bounded over the fence at the other side of the road; and his long gallop could be heard for some time, as he made off in the darkness, as fast as his legs could carry him. The orders against firing were so strict that we did not dare to shoot him.

The men of the Thirteenth, and in some cases the officers, when we came to water at convenient places on the march, took off shirts and socks, washed them, wrung them out, put them on again at once, wet, and marched on. When we reached Yorktown almost the whole command took a bath in the river, and washed their clothing. Think of shirts and socks worn in midsummer, for three weeks, without washing!

"It should be understood that the Thirteenth wore their knapsacks on this raid with a change of underclothing in them, but the extreme heat compelled their throwing them away, contents and all; and thus they were scattered all along the roads, from White House to Fontainebleau."

Lt. Col. Smith.

Several of the men hid their knapsacks soon after leaving White House, and recovered them on the return march. Others tried the same experiment farther up, and lost them because of the change in the roads on the return route; and these and their varied contents, snugly tucked under boards, brush and hedges, await the effect of time, or the future collector of useless relics.

Near the wharf at Hampton was a body of raw Ohio troops, hundred-days men, the officers with white kids, and the men with white gloves and collars, while the price-mark was not yet worn off their flag-staffs. One of these asks a man of the Thirteenth: "Are you hundred-days men?" "Yes," answers Thirteen, "One hundred days without a clean shirt — and now it is your turn." Another of these fresh men complained that he had had 'no butter on his bread for more than a week.'

At one aristocratic mansion, near which we halted, when far up on the Peninsula, a number of young ladies had shut themselves in, and refused to be seen. After a little, our Band is drawn up on their lawn; and a grand vocal and instrumental concert, or serenade, is immediately in full chorus, with many fine male voices rendering popular airs, in rich measure. This proves to be more than the pretty girls can resist, and soon the mansion doors are wide open. Later the Band moves up on the piazza, and with their instruments very near the open windows plays our National airs, responded to by the young ladies at the piano with 'Stonewall Jackson,' 'My Maryland,' 'Bonnie Blue Flag,' and other Southern airs.

It is said that Spear's cavalry approached within twelve miles of Richmond, and that they helped themselves pretty freely to abandoned property. Of quite a large body of them, which we saw, no two were dressed alike — a motley cavalcade. We marched over 130 miles in the first ten days of July. Then in two days marched from Yorktown to Hampton, 28 miles; making about 160 miles in twelve days, under a midsummer Virginia sun — and moon. It is regarded as a very severe, and successful march, so far as time, distance and order are concerned. We did not see half a dozen able-bodied white men, between the ages of 18 and 60, in the whole trip above Yorktown. Guards were set at all points to protect rebel property. The excessive rigor of protection made, among the men, a hero of every successful forager, of whom there were a great many. Taking was, by order, confined to military necessity, and military necessities consequently grew every day more and more numerous. The nightly lullaby was the squealing of pigs and the squawking of poultry. The men well knowing that what they did not then eat, the rebel soldiers would eat by and by, for we were on the regular supply grounds of the rebel army; and every fifteen of the negroes had a white overseer, appointed, practically, by the Confederate government. We met negroes everywhere, and in great numbers. They look upon us as their deliverers and are exceedingly friendly. Their intelligence is surprising. Some of them seem to act as if they had been waiting forty years for a chance to free their minds; and the pent-up accumulation of mental and sentimental matter is voided in a flood. Amusing and pitiable — both in the extreme. The enterprising New York Herald, somehow, followed us on the raid. It reaches our camp, here in the Pines, at 9 a. m., on the next day after it is published, and seems to sell ten to one against any other paper that comes to the army.

The opinion prevails throughout the expeditionary force, that if our body of about 12,000 effective men — and that is a very low estimate of our strength — had kept together in one column, and had struck straight for Richmond, disregarding all minor side issues, we could have easily captured that city, done incalculable damage to the rebel army supplies and property of the Confederacy, and returned in safety.

Hospital Steward Royal B. Prescott writes, July 20, 1863: " We had our knapsacks with us on this march — our Brigade only was so burdened; and loud and hearty were the curses of the men upon the officer who issued the order to take them. Manson S. Brown of C carried our Hospital supplies. Strict orders were issued by Gen. Dix against taking anything from the inhabitants along the road; but the inhabitants insulted the men all they could, hence retaliation upon their property. The weather was excessively hot. Knapsacks and blankets were thrown away, collected by the rear-guard, and burned. On the afternoon of July 2d the column reached Mr. Fontaine's plantation. He was gone. His wife and negroes were left at home. The bummers in revenge (for something done or said) smashed everything in his house. The parlor floor was painted with a mixture made of a pot of yellow paint, a pot of black paint, a barrel of flour and a cask of molasses. Gen. Dix was furious when he heard of this mischief, but a drum-head court martial held that night failed to convict any one.[1] The house and buildings were afterwards burned. We saw acres on acres, square miles on square miles, of ripe wheat. Very little damage was done to crops, so they will go to feed the rebel army; and in a land of immense plenty we are confined to army rations, and short at that. Men at night fell like logs, went at once to sleep, in mud, on grass, anywhere, and it was next to impossible to wake them. On July 4th the slaves of Mr. William Carter, about 150 of them (he had 210 in all), came to the road — close down to Littlepage's bridge — where the 13th were, procured boards, laid them in the road, and sang and danced for a long time. They gave a better show than all the 'Original Minstrel' troops that ever traveled. The negroes took all the horses, mules and carts, and followed our troops in retreat. Hundreds of soldiers — on the return march — took off their shirts, (buttoning their blouses close about them for decency's sake), washed them and then slung them over their shoulders, or carried them as banners on their bayonets, and so marched till the shirts were dry again and then put them on. The troops looked more like animated bundles of dirty

---

[1] This court martial was held under a large tree near the house; and it is said that Gen. Dix declared that if the ringleaders in the damage to the house were caught, he would hang them all on that tree and leave them hanging there. — S. M. T.

rags than like anything else. Many marks of the battle of Williamsburg still remain. Major Grantman, of the Thirteenth, was present in that battle, and was severely wounded there, and now graphically describes the scene. We were absent on the raid for 23 days, and accomplished — nothing, or about that. Yes, one thing is certain : that raid has added 2,500 patients to the different Hospitals in this department."

PRESCOTT.

Capt. Smith is bitten or stung on his hand by some small creature while on the return from this raid, and soon shows unmistakable signs of severe poisoning, by the appearance of rapidly spreading blotches and dark spots on his hand and arm. A search is made for whiskey, the best antidote in such cases. After a while some is found which Lieut. Young has saved for an emergency. It is liberally administered, Capt. Smith is placed on an ambulance, and recovers without serious injury. But for that hoarded flask of whiskey, he probably would have died. Moral: The best use to make of whiskey is to save it — for a medical emergency.

A few days after the 13th left the Pines, Lieut. Durell with a Lieut. of the 10th N. H. gathered a squad of volunteers from the 10th and 13th to join their regiments. About half a dozen of the men were of the 13th. On reaching White House a little previous to July 4th this party was not allowed by the Provost Marshal to leave that point because of the rebel guerillas, who would be quite sure to gobble the whole party before they could reach their regiments at the front. The party therefore went into camp, a little apart by themselves, and waited until the regiments returned. While here Lucius Gilmore of the Quarter-master Department of the 10th conceived the idea of obtaining some whiskey. Wearing habitually a blouse with staff-officer's buttons and a tall felt hat, he now assumed his best appearance, took his canteens and proceeded to the commissary's tent. Here the guard at once saluted him as a general officer, and the man in charge of the tent without question filled his canteens with whiskey, which Gilmore paid for with becoming dignity ; returning at once to the camp of the party. he supplied the men without stint, and to the unutterable bamboozlement of half of them.

July 14. Tues. Rainy. Reg. in camp in the Pines. Every man in the 13th is foot-sore and much used up, by these long, rapid mid-summer marches, made when we were either scorched by the southern sun, or stewing in the wet — and almost all the time plunging in the mud. The showers rarely cool the atmosphere. All of Company E, excepting two or three men, are sent on picket to-day ; all are more or less lame, and the Reg. enjoys a hearty laugh as these unhappy men of E limp and hobble out of camp.

July 15. Wed. Showery. A fearful thunder storm to-night — the whole camp a glistening lake. Reg. in camp all day, and doing little or nothing. Inspection of arms and knapsacks ; and of the latter there are very few to inspect. Col. Corcoran's Irish Legion moved last night to join the Army of the Potomac ; while we remain members of the 2d Div. of the 7th Army Corps.

July 16. Thurs. Rainy. Reg. does no work. Dress-parade at evening. Pay-rolls being made out to June 30th, for two months. Many of the men will be obliged to pay for small articles needlessly lost while on the raid. A court martial is organized to straighten out sundry unnecessary irregularities which have occurred in these last three weeks.

July 17. Fri. Fair day; a heavy rain at night. Reg. in camp resting. A number of men have deserted from the 13th to the enemy during the late march. We hope they will be impressed into the rebel service. Tents have to be thrown off the poles almost every day, to dry the ground within. The water we have to use we boil before drinking. Some persons add vinegar to the water to kill the animalculæ; then after the water is cool it is sweetened a little before it is used. The water not only looks repulsive, but it tastes and smells bad; a decoction of surface filth.

July 18. Sat. Pleasant. Reg. in camp. A great deal of sickness in the Thirteenth, and throughout the command; a direct result of the late raid. Almost every man in the 13th is more or less 'broken out' with boils and sores, from overheated blood — some of it, possibly, very bad blood. Capt. Normand Smith and ten officers of other regiments appointed as a General Court Martial to meet at Portsmouth, Col. Donohoe, President, and Lieut. J. D. Mahon, Judge Advocate.

July 19. Sun. Warm, rainy. Usual Sunday duties, Dress-parade and religious services. The waste on the raid, in army supplies and equipage, was scandalous — a heavy total. We have been ready and waiting all day, to turn out, at a moment's notice, and receive Major General Foster.

July 20. Mon. Rainy, hot. Reg. in camp. Reviewed by Maj. Gen. John G. Foster, upon his taking command of this Department of Virginia and North Carolina. Yesterday at 2 p. m. we were in line to receive Gen. Foster, but he did not appear. This morning at 10 o'clock we are in line again, and manœuvre for two hours while waiting his arrival. Again we fall in at 3 p. m., and again exercise for about two hours, when he appears. Gen. Foster is a Nashua man, and the men of the Thirteenth stand at a 'Present-arms,' and with their colors at a 'Dip,' for a very long time. The General notices it, and when he is saluted enough, he passes the order for the men to bring their arms to the shoulder. One of those pretty mistakes that will happen any way. He highly compliments the 10th and 13th — and then makes them work hard to pay for his approbation. "Gen. Foster was the first commander of the 18th Army Corps." (History of the 44th Mass.)

July 21. Tues. Very hot and showery. Reg. in camp. No one busy but the members of the regimental court martial, trying cases growing out of the raid. A heavy thunder shower to-night continuing all night and flooding the camp with water, which is several inches deep under all the tents. The feud between the men of the 10th and 13th N. H., never very serious, has altogether disappeared since the raid.

July 22. Wed. Fair. Reg. in camp. Sergeant James M. Hodgdon of B has been acting as Sergeant Major, and makes a very good one. This land furnishes a little insect nuisance called the pine-tick. He burrows quickly and deeply under the skin of man and beast, and is very difficult to remove — can be picked out only in pieces. A drop of kerosene oil, however, placed upon him, when in the skin, causes him to withdraw himself almost instanter. Everything in Virginia — even a rebel picket — wants to get into a hole, either in whole or part; this propensity is universal. We hope to make the rebel army get into a very big hole — and then pull the hole in after them.

July 23. Thurs. Rainy. Reg. in camp. Detail made for slashing in the swamp — Captain Stoodley's valiant one hundred axemen. A detail of three Lieutenants — Wilson, Staniels and Sawyer — three non-commissioned officers and six privates (the writer has this from a soldier's letter) also leaves camp for Concord, N. H., to bring forward recruits for the Thirteenth. Adjt. Boutwell's wife arrives in camp.

July 24. Fri. Fine, but very warm. Reg. slashing. ' A change in pasture makes calves fat;' but a change in commander makes soldiers lean, as we are now learning to our cost. The hours of labor, and of all other duties, are largely increased since the arrival of Gen. Foster.

July 25. Sat. Very warm, showers. Reg. slashing. The promoted First Sergeants and their Colonel not mutually happy because of sundry due and delayed commissions. We lose our rights — and a hundred or two dollars apiece besides.

July 26. Sun. Very hot. Inspection at 10 a. m., and Dress-parade at sunset. The hottest day any of us have ever seen. A thermometer hanging up on the shady side of a little sapling four or six inches in diameter indicates 108°. It is above 100° in the tents, and 126° in the sunshine. Reg. again begins work on the fortifications to-day; every available man sent out, either chopping or shoveling. More than 1,500 men who went on the raid have been sent to hospital, sick.

The Thirteenth has one man who suffers from attacks of sleeping, and cannot keep awake when under the spell of his peculiar malady. He has been twice caught sleeping at his post while on guard. He cannot help it. The meanest thing in the world is to find a man asleep at his post; the punishment for the offense is very severe, and a desperate man would sooner kill the man who finds him asleep, than run the risk of being shot himself. It is best, therefore — and a sort of general order — to first secure possession of the sleeper's gun, before rousing him.

July 27. Mon. Very hot forenoon, rainy afternoon and night. Reg. out slashing only in the forenoon. Regimental Hospital moved across the road to field north of camp, in pursuance of the Medical Director's orders — the pine grove too close and damp for the sick.

A furious riot with cries of " Kill 'em all," " Murder," " Help — help," oaths, and the shrieks of a hundred or two of black women — the most blood-curdling shriekers under the sun — suddenly breaks out upon the quiet camp to-night; the night pitchy dark and very rainy. A body of teamsters, encamped across the railroad southward of our camp, invade the contraband camp near by, and about twenty of them armed with axes and revolvers are firing and slashing right and left; the whole gang mad with drink. When the disturbance first begins, Captains Julian, Stoodley and Forbush and a few other officers, who are gathered in one of the officer's tents, spring up and hurry to the scene, some armed and some not, and come near having a hand-to-hand conflict with the teamsters before the guard arrives. Major Storer, officer of the day, orders First Sergeant Thompson of E, who is officer of the regimental guard, to proceed out of camp, with about a dozen men of his guard, and to quell the riot; Major Storer remaining in charge of the guard-house and headquarters meanwhile. Only seven men of the guard, however, can be spared. As soon as this guard arrives upon the scene, the teamsters instantly surround Sergeant George H. Van Duzee of E, who is also one of the guard, and threaten him with instant death. He is only saved by the quick orders of Thompson to his guard, to fire. The teamsters quit rioting and haul off under the muzzles of the guards' guns; the purpose of the guard being to scare rather than to kill. A few are arrested, some slink away in the darkness, but the most of them retire to their huge 'Sibley' style of tent, put out their lights, and threaten to shoot any one who approaches. The guard, however, is at once drawn up in line in front of the tent, their guns aimed, the muzzles almost touching the canvas, and the teamsters are called upon to surrender. Thompson's demand is answered by a flood of vile scurrility from the tent. He then gives slowly the order to the guard: " Ready — Aim — ; " the teamsters cave in, the tent is entered, a candle lighted, and two men arrested who had crawled under their bunks. The rest had ripped holes in the back side of their tent, and made good their escape into the deep woods near by. Before the riot was quelled, many of the negroes were badly hurt and several killed, all shot down, or chopped down with axes. This errand should not have fallen to the regimental guard, who on the whole consider it a worse job than attacking rebel pickets at night.

July 28. Tues. Fair, very close and hot, a few showers in afternoon. Reg. in camp, the most writing letters home. The mail leaves camp at 6 a. m. regularly. The order now is to cut down every tree, for a space one mile wide, in front of our works, clear across from river to river, a distance of five miles. A large part of this space is densely wooded. The 100 choppers from the 13th are hard at work on every suitable day; similar parties are furnished by every regiment along the line, while sometimes the 13th in a body, and other entire regiments turn out with axes for the work — five or six square miles of the Dismal Swamp region are thus being rapidly cleared of their dense forest of vines, brush and timber.

July 29. Wed. Afternoon very rainy. Reg. in camp. No work done. Brigade guard-mounting in the morning; very well done. Dress-parade at sundown, at which commissions are given out to sundry Second Lieutenants all promoted from First Sergeants. The commissions dated June 10th, 1863. The recipients mustered on July 29th or Aug. 5th, having first received their discharges as First Sergeants. There was a hitch in the mustering-in and several of them were for two or three days out of the service altogether. The 1st Brigade of our Division leaves camp this forenoon for Charleston, S. C.

The pines in our 'Pines Camp,' are in places dense and tall. The grove has open ground on all sides. During the frequent thunder storms the trees wave and bend, and threaten to snap short off in the heavy wind. Their limbs break off, fall and crush in the canvas roofs of our tents. During the days their closely massed tops shut out the sun, and while affording an agreeable shade, they prevent the evaporation of the water on the ground, and the camp-ground remains soaked like a sponge, and glistening with numerous pools. While fortunately no tree in our camp has been struck by lightning, a cluster of oak-trees an eighth of a mile distant has been struck frequently this summer and some of the trees torn to shreds. One of these thunder storms at night is fearful to witness. The thunder roars, rattles, bellows, resounds and clangs on high continuously, as if the earth was a tremendous battery cannonading all the planets at once. The rain falls in sheets, breaking and pouring in streams from every pine limb; the incessant flashes of vivid lightning are reflected from every rain stream, every wet pine bough, and from the surface of the wide level camp area nearly covered and flooded with water; the guns of the men in their tents are charged with electricity and glow from end to end; the camp guards' guns and bayonets, similarly charged, flash and glisten, and the guards tramp their beats with an incessant splash, splash, like a line of lightning-rod holders, each inviting a hundred strokes of lightning during every storm, while the roar near and far continues without cessation hour after hour.

In the morning after such a night storm, the men and almost everything in their tents are wet, in many cases thoroughly drenched, and the tents must be thrown off the poles; blankets and clothing are hanging on lines all over camp to dry; the water floods the camp, and lies from three to six inches deep in and about all the tents; gradually it evaporates in the hot air, while the whole camp is filled with evil smells, or else the water runs off slowly into the deeper depressions in the ground, and sinks away to form the 'surface water' we must use for drinking and cooking. No sooner is the camp dry, or half dry, than another furious thunder storm causes the whole programme to be repeated — and so on, and so on, without a rest. While therefore we keep an account of the weather, it is because bad weather plays an ugly part in the experiences of the soldier, whether in camp or field.

July 30. Thurs. Showery, more heavy thunder. Reg. slashing. Insects flourish in this warm, damp weather. The camp is pestered with gnats, flies and mosquitoes in numberless swarms. The Surgeons have formally declared this camp in the Pines extremely unhealthy, and that the Reg. must move out of it, and farther away from the negro camp, which threatens a pestilence. The 10th N. H. moves to Julian's Creek.

July 31. Fri. Fine day. Reg. slashing. Quarter-master Cheney returns to camp. At 5.30 p. m. orders come for Companies B and D to be ready to strike tents and march to-morrow at 6 a. m.

One dark and rainy night, near this time, the commissary guard in our Brigade is relieved about ten minutes ahead of the regular time, but apparently in the regular way, and the old relief returns to quarters, having taken 'no note of time.' Ten minutes later the new relief of the regular guard comes around on time, and relieves the relievers — and when the morning dawns the commissary finds that he has been relieved, during the night, of two barrels of whiskey! Now there is a furious storm, that breaks nowhere, and the commissary is advised to report the whiskey as lost in action. It was a job very neatly done.

Aug. 1. Sat. Hot. Reg. in camp. Companies B, Capt. Dodge, and D, Capt. Farr, leave camp at 8 a. m. under command of Major Storer, and march to Fort Tillinghast, about one mile southwest of our camp. They are to garrison that Fort as heavy artillery and to drill all winter. Our Brigade — 3d Brig. 2d Div. 7th Army Corps — a few batteries and a small force of cavalry, are all the troops now left on this line. The Thirteenth has about a mile of line to watch and guard — and half our men are sick. Col. W. H. P. Steere, 4th Rhode Island, commanding our Brigade.

Aug. 2. Sun. Awfully hot. One thermometer indicates 108° in the shade. Usual Sunday duties. We should have been ordered South, but the order was to send the two largest brigades in our Division. Our 3d Brigade was the smallest of the three by over 300 men, so the 1st and 2d Brigades were selected. Diphtheria is very prevalent in camp, caused in great degree by the heat and the bad water we have to use. We are to be transferred to the 18th Army Corps; the 7th Army Corps to be broken up.

Aug. 3. Mon. Hot; 109° in the shade! Reg. stewing in camp. Boys, and young men, 16 to 25 years of age, endure the strain of this army life here in the South much better than men of 35 years and upwards. The Union army averages a little under twenty-two years of age.

Short, thick-set men are more hardy here than the tall men — 'for the purely military reason,' as the boys put it, 'that their forces are nearer their base of supplies.' This Pines camp is a steam-box to-day.

Aug. 4. Tues. Hot. Reg. in camp. Paid off for May and June. Little things, the parts of guns, or parts of equipments or clothing which the men lose or destroy carelessly, or needlessly, are deducted, at stated government prices, from their pay. Officers also have to pay cash for unnecessary losses. It is the only possible way to prevent waste. The pocket rules the world. A negro appears in camp swearing furiously, and gets into trouble. It is a very rare thing to meet a grown-up negro who uses much profane language; and a much rarer thing to meet a Southern white man who does not. Really the best part of the native white population hereabout must now be in the rebel army!

Aug. 5. Wed. Hot and dry. Reg. in camp. Diphtheria very prevalent.' It is a very strange disease. Many men who blistered their feet, while marching on the Blackberry Raid, now have suppurating sores where the blisters were, and very difficult to heal — these are free from diphtheria. Many men have a finger or hand to nurse, where a mere little scratch or bruise will not heal. Diphtheria is organic and wholesale unspeakably repulsive rot.

A corduroy road twenty feet wide — that is, made of heavy logs twenty feet long laid side by side on stringers thrown upon the surface of the morass — extends for near half a mile of the distance between Forts Rodman and Tillinghast; first a strip of the very dense forest was leveled sixty feet wide, and the brush and old timber of fallen trees were thrown into the bog holes. This corduroy road cost the labor of one hundred men working four and a half hours a day for over six weeks. The snakes killed during the time were almost numberless. Disturbing the soil and rotting wood seemed to attract them.

Sundry First Sergeants are mustered in as Second Lieutenants. Every one of the original Second Lieutenants and First Sergeants have received promotion, and some of the First Lieutenants. There is nothing which conduces so much to the honor, stability, efficiency and spirit of a Regiment as the regular promotion of its members as vacancies occur, for that plan alone pays honest dues.

Aug. 6. Thurs. Hot. Reg. slashing, and can work only for a few hours a day. A number of men from the Thirteenth, and others, go out of camp, and make a midnight raid on a lot of hidden theatrical costumes, and other things, and return to camp dressed in the most fantastic fashions that their wit can invent. They departed on foot, they return on mules. Each has a bundle, each has a different style of dress, while the odd hats, bonnets and costumes generally make up a grotesque exhibition indeed. One small mule, ridden by a large man in the costume of the typical Uncle Sam, is dressed up in the fashion — rather pronounced — of a woman of the 17th century, with huge poke-bonnet, bustle, dress, train gathered and dragging at one side, two pairs of white pantalettes, etc. — the head of the mule protruding forward through the division in one pair of the pantalettes, and the tail back through the other pair. A companion mule is gotten up in the costume of a man of the same period. A poke-bonnet and pantalettes look best on a mule. Sergt. Charles F. Chapman of E, and D. Webster Barnabee of K, a right merry pair — though the latter is sick — furnish a deal of amusement to a (ticketless) audience of a thousand or two of men, who line the roadsides. The 'General commanding' laughed at this most ridiculous cavalcade as heartily as any private in the ranks. Fun is the spring of health.

Aug. 7. Fri. Hot. Reg. slashing. Quarter-master Cheney, having resigned his commission, departs for home. Too bad. The climate is too severe for him. He has been sick for nearly seven months, and was one of the last to break down under the effects of exposure and malaria at Fredericksburg. He has taxed his resolution and strength to the utmost to remain with the Thirteenth, and leaves us with profoundest regrets, and only under the pressure of absolute necessity. The members of the Regiment all feel as badly as if parting with a personal friend — as in fact they really are. No man of the Thirteenth has ever complained of him as its Quarter-master; and where the soldier does not grumble the officer is popular indeed.

Quarter-master Person C. Cheney nearly recovers his health in civil life, engages in the manufacture of paper and wood-paper pulp, and is generally understood to have been financially successful in his large and extended business enterprises; he also rises to the position of Governor, of New Hampshire, and Senator in the Congress of the United States, besides filling many minor official positions. It should be said, to the honor of faithful woman, that Quarter-master Cheney owes his life to the devoted, almost superhuman efforts and care of his wife, seconded in every possible way by Mrs. Col. A. F. Stevens, while he lay helpless in Hospital, and wasted by malarial fever and its attendant ills. She found him at the point of death, and succeeded in saving him only as by a miracle.

**Aug. 8. Sat.** Very warm and close. No work done — too hot. Diphtheria increasing in prevalence and becoming malignant in type all through the camp, and also among the native families hereabout.

A Lieutenant of Company E, as a special temperance treat for his new straps, gathered a fine water-melon from the 'Government Farm' last night, at the imminent risk of a bullet from the guard, and this morning calls in a few of his friends to share in the feast. The tent is tied close, and the melon — a large one and a beauty — is produced from the cooler, a hole in the ground under the tent; there is a flourish of knives, and the choicest melon of the field falls open — greener than a summer pumpkin! 'Twixt smiles, regrets, and remarks, the melon finds permanent quarters back in the cooler. It happens to be an old darkey's pet melon, and he is early about camp hotly inquiring, "Who — who got dat ar watermillium?" The Lieutenant and all concerned are doubly sorry, but can give him no information on the subject — that is, not safely. But the old darkey feels so badly (and the harvester also), that he is supplied with sundry rations, worth ten times more than the melon, and returns heavily laden to his ebony Dinah.

**Aug. 9. Sun.** Hot; but cooler — the thermometer indicates only 100° in the shade. Usual Sunday duties. As the wind comes up from the eastward we can smell the negro camp a mile away. They are indescribably filthy; and nothing but ages of civilization will teach them to discard their vile habits. There are a host of them encamped between our camp and Portsmouth, and near by.

**Aug. 10. Mon.** Warm. Reg. slashing. Lieut. Saunders has command of the colored laborers. We have had no drill since April 10th. A man of Company E, and one of another Company, are found sick together in one of Co. E's tents. Lieut. Thompson of E is sent to see what is the matter with them. On opening the tent door the odor from within is so vile that the Lieutenant cannot enter; they are told to cover themselves with their blankets, and he immediately throws the tent off the poles. The Surgeon is sent for and pronounces their disease small-pox; — one already breaking out. Both prove bad cases. The Lieutenant did not catch the disease, however — a narrow escape.

Aug. 11. Tues. Warm. Reg. slashing. A soldier of the 13th, trying to describe the weather of the past week, puts it down as: "Hot, awfully hot, terribly hot, hot as blazes — and several other places — all-fired hot!" A negro religious meeting here at night is a curiosity; generally half fetish and half crazy, utterly and irrepressibly niggerish. The worshipers dance, sing, pray, exhort, yell, scream, shout 'Hallumlooyah,' 'Glory,' 'O — Lord,' and all that sort of thing, and all at once, and all the time. The boys have dubbed these meetings 'solemncholys.' They are much tempered with Voudooism pure and simple, as if direct from Africa. Frequently in the meetings one, or more, of the worshipers loses all control of himself or herself, and commences shouting: 'I'se got it!' 'O, I'se got it!!' and then falls to striking out right and left, slashing about, jumping up and down, and screaming with might and main. They act as if they had got it! These fearful spasms of hysterics are a very important find. The favored ones are usually soon caught and held by three or four other negroes near by, so they may do no special harm to themselves or to any one else, but they are allowed to 'spress demselfs' as loudly and as forcibly as they please. This is all 'git'n glory,' and having a 'pow'ful time — shuah!' To touch a person when thus 'under der infloounce uv de spirit,' is regarded as sharing something with the fortunate possessor. If these Voudoo spasms fail to appear in any meeting, the reason is given, that 'some fool nigger has brought a rabbit foot, to scar 'way de Lord.' It is the same everywhere, the worst ignorance that ever beclouded a people is religious ignorance. The 'Swamp nigger' appears to be of a specially low and degraded class.

Aug. 12. Wed. Hot again. Reg. slashing. The whole force slashing. Down comes the splendid forest. The owner, an old gentleman and a rabid secessionist, who lives near by, looks sadly on; but believes the South will win, and then the 'North will have to pay for all the damages of the war!' This helps him to bear the present waste. Happy thought. Quarter-master Sergeant Mortier L. Morrison appointed Quarter-master of the Thirteenth — an excellent choice.

Aug. 13. Thurs. Hot — very, thunder showers. Reg. slashing. No white man can work all day. The nights, too, are nearly as hot as the days. There has been a great deal of complaint about this camp in the Pines — an old rebel camping ground, and very dirty when we came here. There has been much sickness here, and several deaths from diphtheria, and when news comes to-day that we are to move to a new camp, it is received with much rejoicing by both officers and men. One company in the Thirteenth, whose men were all apparently as well as usual in the morning, had two men, both in one tent, dead at evening; both dying of diphtheria of a malignant form.

Aug. 14. Fri. Hot and dry. The Pines a hot-air box. The Reg. goes out in a body to clear its new camp-ground, just across the road northward, perhaps one eighth of a mile. A large patch of potatoes and an acre or two of growing corn, all come up by the roots. Some of the corn pulled up is twelve feet tall, the ears on it just fit for roasting. Every eatable thing is carefully saved by the darkeys for their camp near by. Lieut. Thompson of E has charge of the men and teams to-day in clearing this new camping ground; and Lieut. Forbush of the men who are digging the ditches and grading the streets. The two equal parties comprise all the men in the Thirteenth who are able to work.

Aug. 15. Sat. Very warm. No slashing. In averaging expenses to-day, it appears that in the line officers' messes, the cost of living is about $4 per week; and surely all live well. The want, that pinches the most, is of ice, of which very little can be obtained.

Aug. 16. Sun. Very warm. Usual Sunday exercises. Numerous boxes come to camp for the officers and men of the Regiment. Lieut. R. R. Thompson of H, a civil engineer by profession, is detailed for service as Lieutenant in the Engineer Corps. Hospital Steward Prescott makes his first medical visit to the contraband camps this morning.

Aug. 17. Mon. Pleasant, cooler. Reg. at work on the new camp-grounds. A furious wind storm blows down hundreds of tents and shanties. All boxes sent here to officers and soldiers are opened and searched at Norfolk, and all contraband articles are confiscated or destroyed. Intoxicating liquors are the things chiefly under ban. This causes disappointment in camp and many emphatic comments. A Lieutenant in the 13th sent to Boston and purchased a lot of liquors, at an expense of $45. A part of the lot was three gallons of brandy at $8 per gallon. The Provost at Norfolk examined the shipment, confiscated the liquor as contraband, and this morning the Lieutenant opens an empty box! The Provost kindly forwarded the box — which of course was not contraband.

Aug. 18. Tues. Cool, fine day. Reg. at work on new camp-grounds. Lieut. Kittredge leaves camp for a visit home.

Aug. 19. Wed. Pleasant. Reg. inspected by staff officer Capt. Dutton. And now, for a change, we are in the 18th Army Corps. A soldier is murdered by a comrade at Fort Rodman, by a bayonet stab in the mouth. Neither are of the 13th.

Hospital Steward R. B. Prescott, on August 16th, was placed in charge of the sick at the contraband camps; one of them two miles distant from the Thirteenth containing about 200 able-bodied men employed on the Government works, another nearer containing 300 or 400 able-bodied men so employed, and both camps containing a host of old men, women and children besides. He goes on his rounds to these camps at 9.30 a. m. every day. His 'horse' is one of the three mules — 'the Doc's mules' — captured at Hanover, on the Blackberry Raid, and he is at times utterly intractable and balky. His favorite method of worrying his rider is to rush suddenly close past a fence or tree; and when whipped, to walk backwards rapidly, darting in every direction for a long time, then halt and suddenly bolt ahead. A most exasperating mule.

### CAMP GILMORE, GETTY'S STATION.

**Aug. 20. Thurs.** Pleasant, very. Reg. moves to new camp, on which all of its available men have been employed for nearly four days, removing growing crops and grading. This is by far the best camp we have ever had, and is laid out strictly in accordance with the Army Regulations and under the personal supervision of Gen. Getty, who has himself located every camp along this line. "Reg. moved into the field — a military necessity." LUEY.

Fort Rodman — the first earth-work west of Getty's Station, and distant from it and our old Pines camp about one half mile, see May 18, 1863, is located close to the south side of the railroad, where the old Suffolk road and the railroad run nearly alongside of each other. The fort is flanked on the left, south, side by a line of rifle-trenches running a short distance to the swamp. The whole line facing westward. At the swamp trenches could not be dug, and log breast-works were thrown up instead. The position of the 13th in case of an attack was assigned, by Gen. Naglee, at the junction of the rifle-trench and these log breastworks — the most of the Reg. having the logs and two or three companies only, on the right, having the breast-works of earth. On the right, north, side the fort is flanked by rifle-trenches crossing the railroad and Suffolk road and running to a little redoubt for two guns, about 125 yards distant. From near this redoubt, on the north side, a log stockade ran northward to Bruce's Creek. The gate of the stockade was 300 or 400 yards north of Ft. Rodman, and near where the new road now crosses the line. A military road ran from north to south along in rear of the stockade, rifle-trenches and Ft. Rodman. The general course of the line of defenses is north and south facing westward, and the railroad and Suffolk road run nearly east and west. Two hundred and fifty yards east and in rear of Ft. Rodman a new road now runs from the old road northwest to Suffolk. This new road leaves the old stockade gate a little to the left of where it crosses the line of defenses. A guide-board at the junction of these roads gives the distances as three miles to Portsmouth, eighteen miles to Suffolk. Five hundred yards down the old road east from Ft. Rodman, a lane with hedges now runs to the north about 400 yards to Mr. J. C. Taylor's house, built since the war upon the old magazine cellar. This lane cuts through the site of Camp Gilmore, so as to leave the ground of the two left companies of the Thirteenth to the east of it, and the other eight companies to the west. The camp faced nearly south, and was about 300 yards north of the road, and west of Mr. Edward T. Bunting's house. "The camp of the Thirteenth," said Mr. Bunting, "was about 100 yards west of my house, and their Hospital stood at the same distance from the Suffolk road as my house, 50 yards due west from it and almost exactly on a line with the quarters of the field and staff officers."

Aug. 21. Fri. Very warm. Reg. at work on new camp. The writer with a party of about half a dozen men recently rowed out to the sunken rebel ram 'Merrimac.' A little flag, on a pole stuck into a hole in the roof, marks her position. The iron roof is about two feet under water at low tide. She lies in the murky water, a huge, black, indistinct mass, of which the form can scarcely be made out — an uncanny morgue.

Aug. 22. Sat. Very hot. Diphtheria increasing all through the command. The forts near Suffolk dismantled, the railroad tracks torn up for many miles, thousands of trees felled across the roads and railroad, the country devastated, and troops of refugees, both black and white, are pouring into our camp from the region well up towards Richmond.

Aug. 23. Sun. Very hot. Reg. all turned out to fell trees along

---

### DESCRIPTION OF PLAT.

A. Road from Portsmouth to Suffolk, with branch K, built since the war — the 'shell road.'

B. Railroad with Getty's Station platforms D, built since the war on the Old Quay road C.

E. Pines Camp, Thirteenth. The space between the railroad and road is 250 yards — narrowed in plat.

F. Lane to Mr. Edward T. Bunting's house, about 300 yards from road, with our regimental Hospital — I — fifty yards due west of house. Next south of hospital was Lieut. Taggard's commissary tent, next the theatre, next the sutler's tent near the road.

G. Camp Gilmore, Thirteenth, about 600 yards northeast of Ft. Rodman.

H. Mr. J. C. Taylor's house, built since the war on the cellar of the old magazine, about 400 yards from the road.

M. Marsh, an impassable slough though small, the mud very deep.

L. Stockade gate, fronting marsh M — a spur of the Dismal Swamp — and leaving only a narrow roadway between.

N. Fort Rodman, enclosing about two acres and having platforms for six guns, and a magazine near the entrance in the rear.

P. Position assigned the Thirteenth, behind the earth-works and log breast-works, by Gen. Naglee on Sept. 6th, and always held when we manned the works.

R. Military road along the works, and to Ft. Tillinghast — 'Fort Till.'

S. Position of Col. Steere's Hdqrs. pointed out by a citizen as at 50 yards east of the eastern platform, D, as it now stands.

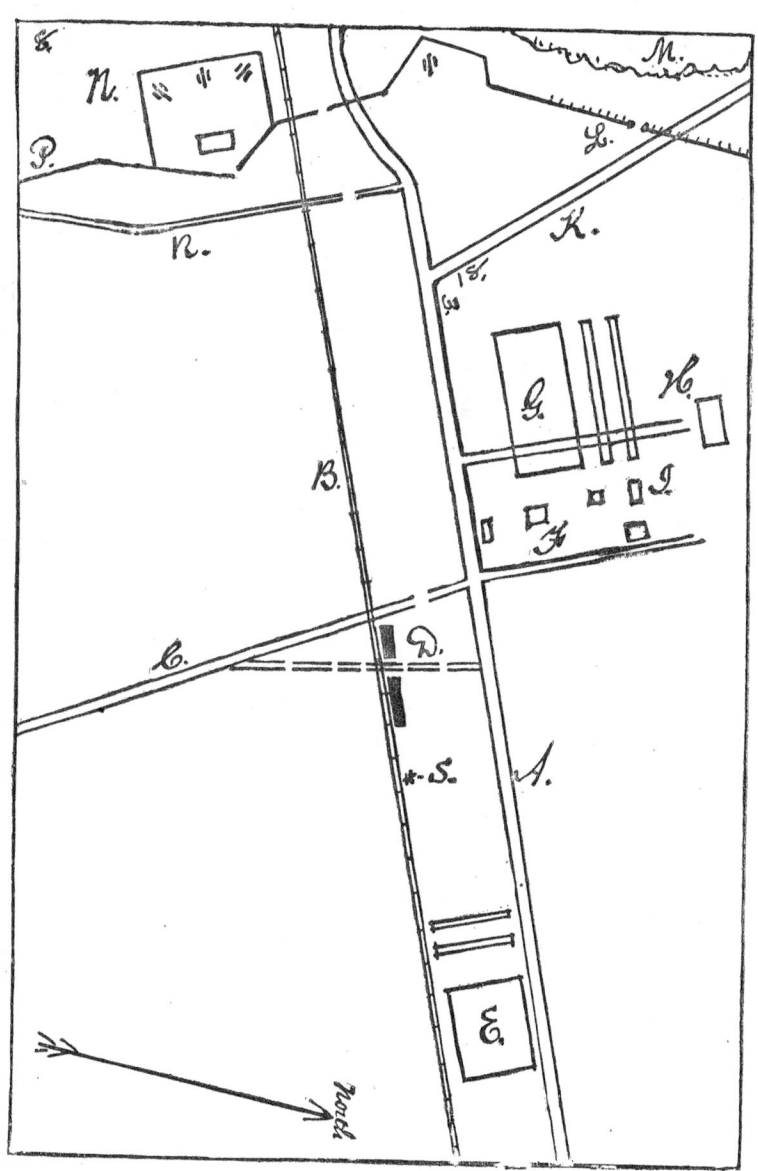

CAMP BOWERS AND CAMP GILMORE.
GETTY'S STATION, 1863-4.
From a sketch made by the writer in May 1885.

the railroad near our camp — the enemy threatening again. The world goes wrong all the time in the region of Bowers Hill four or five miles west; the guards up there are always in trouble, always calling for help, and every few days a force is rushed from our lines here, at a furious speed, for Bowers Hill, to do nothing at all when they get there. One picket post of the 13th at Bowers Hill is at David's mill, a tide-mill, on the creek near Suffolk road. A large body of Union cavalry moves past our camp towards the front.

Aug. 24. Mon. Rainy. Reg. in camp. The dust on all bare and tramped over ground has been at least three inches deep for the last two weeks; rising in clouds with every breeze — enough to choke a horse.

There are teasing boys in all camps. The north-country men — from the upper part of the State — are fond of jokes that will set the south-country men to some disadvantage. The sparring and banter goes on all the time. For one instance: Whenever it is possible to use the name, Nashua is spelled 'Gnash-away,' and in return, Coos appears as 'Coose.'

The men of Company H on Aug. 8th presented to Lieut. R. R. Thompson of H a sword, sash and belt as a testimonial of their esteem. The same thing has been done in whole or part by each Company whose First Sergeant has recently been promoted to Second Lieutenant, excepting in the case of Lieut. S. Millett Thompson of E. The money to purchase a similar present for him had been nearly all raised and pledged, but as soon as he learned of it, he stated his preference to purchase for himself, and the money went back to the kindly contributors. Besides, when his brother, John Ed. Thompson, Adjutant 20th Illinois Infantry, was killed at Pittsburg Landing, Tenn., April 6, 1862, and his sword was sent home, he vowed he would wear it in this war — and is now doing so.

After a few months he purchased for himself a sword with steel scabbard, at Norfolk, and sent his brother's sword home again.

Aug. 25. Tues. Rainy. Reg. in camp. In spite of all precautions a regular mail passes from Norfolk to the rebel army, and our provost-guard lines are being drawn more strictly, all around city and camp. A heavy wind in the afternoon, striking suddenly during a severe shower, blows down the guard tent of the 13th, and does a great deal of damage throughout the camp.

Aug. 26. Wed. Fair. Reg. in camp. Capt. Forbush's wife arrives in camp. Officers at work on Pay-rolls for July and August. Awnings of green brush are being put up in front of tents for shade — not a tree in camp. Charles A. Ames, of G promoted to Quarter-master Sergeant; a most excellent appointment.

Aug. 27. Thurs. Rainy. Reg. in camp all day. Lieut. Young, Lieut. Murray and many of the men are sick at Balfour Hospital, Portsmouth. Weather cooler, the nights very chilly. Salutes being fired to-day all up and down our lines. The men of B and D at Fort Tillinghast find many friends in the 8th Conn. encamped within half a mile of that fort. There are now some nine or ten forts here in line, between the east and west branches of the river, all well armed and manned.

Aug. 28. Fri. Pleasant. Reg. slashing again. A native remarks to-day, and it is a common sentiment among the people hereabout: " As for your Northern copperheads, we, of course, like to have their sympathy — but the sympathy of cowards does not amount to much." A raid is expected from the enemy, extra pickets are sent out, and there is a little fever of excitement — good for our blood.

Aug. 29. Sat. Heavy showers. Reg. out slashing; caught in the rain, and all are drenched. Two men die of diphtheria. Camp hospitals being cleared of the very sick, all of whom are sent to Balfour Hospital, Portsmouth. Gen. Spear's cavalry has been out to find the enemy's raiders — but they had all withdrawn. A darkey says: "Reck'n he done got mad, 'un goned off!"

Aug. 30. Sun. Cooler. Company inspections, and nothing more. Fort Tillinghast, which Companies B and D are garrisoning, receives some new guns — three 18-pounders and three 12-pounders. Every available man in the Reg. is at work on the entrenchments and digging rifle-pits on all week days, excepting during heavy storms.

Aug. 31. Mon. Drizzling, cold rain. Reg. mustered for two months' pay at 7 p. m. by Col. A. F. Stevens. Mrs. Col. Stevens is making a collection of Dismal Swamp butterflies and other insects and curiosities, and the men of the Regiment, at work deep in the swamp, gladly send into camp many specimens for her collection. She is exceedingly popular in the Thirteenth; and — we say it without disparaging her husband in any degree — she can have the Colonelcy at any time by unanimous vote of the Regiment.

Sept. 1. Tues. Cold, stormy. Reg. at work on rifle-pits, and building a heavy log breast-work along the military road, running southward from camp through the swamp, where the Reg. has been slashing. The soil of the swamp cannot be made use of, hence the logs. The swamp stratum is one compact inextricable mass of tangled roots, rotting sticks and logs — peat in process of formation — from two to twenty feet deep. There is so much combustible stuff here above ground on the part of the line held by the 13th, that the enemy can quickly drive us out merely by lighting a fire.

First Sergeant Edwin A. Tilton, of K, promoted to Second Lieutenant in the Invalid Corps. He is ordered to report for duty to Col. Oscar A. Mack, U. S. A., at Concord, N. H., where he is appointed Post Adjutant. He also serves as Department Quarter-master, Ordnance Officer, and Recruiting Officer; commander of the Provost-guard of a detachment of recruits, and of the 168th Company Veteran Reserve Corps. He was subsequently attached to Company G., 11th V. R. C., and assigned to duty at Head-quarters, in Albany, N. Y.

Sept. 2. Wed. Reg. slashing. A large detail at work on rifle-pits. The Officers of the Reg. have purchased and received a library of about

100 volumes — chiefly novels of the better sort. Surgeon Richardson detailed for duty at Brigade Hdqrs.

**Sept. 3. Thurs.** Very warm. Reg. at work all day on rifle-pits and breast-works. Sundays excepted, nine hours' work are done every day — from 7 a. m. to 12 noon, and from 2 to 6 p. m. The whole force are engaged on the works, and all as busy as beavers. Officers of every grade, from Brigadier down, are overseeing the work, and many of them take a turn at the axe or shovel.

**Sept. 4. Fri.** Fair. Whole Reg. at work on the defenses, and driving the work as rapidly as possible.

He was of the no name series — or for convenience' sake he had too many names. A big, slouching, sullen, morose, slovenly old 'Stony Lonesome,' as the boys called him, and regarded as the meanest man in the Thirteenth Regiment. He robbed several men in our Brigade. He tried to kill a tent mate who exposed his crimes. He was caught in the night, attempting to pull the shoes and stockings off the feet of a dead man of the 13th, laid out for burial. He was brought out, after conviction of several crimes — one of them was robbing our wounded men at Fredericksburg — the contents of his knapsack dumped upon the ground, and a small bundle of necessary articles made and given him, and a blanket; all the rest were buried, for they were extremely filthy. Rations were given him. His buttons (U. S. military buttons) were all cut off, and his clothing tied on him with coarse strings, the ends dangling; and he was then drummed through the camp, and out of it, to the tune of 'The Rogue's March,' disappearing forever, so far as we were concerned, in the distance, amid the hoots, jeers, and yells of a thousand or two of men. A dead beat, sham, bummer, and beastly criminal.

**Sept. 5. Sat.** Very warm. Reg. assigned position in the defenses in case of an attack. The enemy reported advancing in force on our lines. Everybody on the qui vive. The Thirteenth is now in excellent fighting condition, and a sharp fight would be quite acceptable.

**Sept. 6. Sun.** Very warm. Inspection, or review, or drill, or all together — or what? by Gen. Naglee and staff at 10 a. m.; and a more formal affair at 12 noon, in the rifle-pits and log breast-works thrown up by the Regiment. A sham preparation for a real fight, with many verbal instructions how to do it — the whole Regiment lectured indiscriminately like an omnibus class by a school visitor. The position assigned to the 13th in the defenses, is to the south of the Seaboard and Roanoke Railroad, a little to the left of Ft. Rodman, at the edge of the swamp, where the line of earth-work trenches ceases and the log breast-works commence. The most of the Regiment have the logs, on low, wet ground, a bad piece of line, a few right companies only have the earth-works to protect them in case of an attack.

**Sept. 7. Mon.** Very warm, rainy in afternoon; Reg. slashing in forenoon. The camp full of rumors about an expected attack. Lieut. Saunders has over 500 negroes under his charge, at work upon the fortifications. A drunken private staggering along on the railroad past the contraband camp excuses his gait by saying: "Million niggers make it so dark — real shober man like me car'nt walk straight (hic), 'thout a lantern in each hand and a head-light on his breast-shtumach — (hic) when the sun shines."

Sept. 8. Tues. Very warm, a thunder storm. Reg. slashing all day, and suffering much from the heat. The 8th Conn. has been increased by about 200 substitutes and conscripts — a bad lot. Many of them are in mischief as soon as they arrive in camp. The common term for all comers, not regular volunteers is, for short, "Subs." "Detail of 48 men from the 13th escorts conscripts (from Connecticut) from Portsmouth to camp." LUEY.

Sept. 9. Wed. Very hot. Reg. at work — so much as we can. Five deserters come in from the region about Suffolk. They say they are members of the Louisiana Zouaves; that they enlisted at the commencement of the war, and that their regiment is now reduced to only nine men of the original organization.

"A man went out of camp of an errand. He returned at night, and throwing down a canvas bag upon my tent floor, went his way without saying a word. Examination revealed a thirty-pound pig. Another man disappeared at early evening, and returned with a peck of new potatoes, combined result: several good dinners. The picket was ordered to allow no one ingress or egress. A hog and two nice pigs appeared to take egress; the hog passed the line — the pigs did not. Result: dinners as before." (Item from a Thirteenth officer's letter.)

Sept. 10. Thurs. Cool, cloudy. Reg. slashing all day. Lieut. Thompson of E and twelve men are sent to-day, for a sojourn of a week, up in the Dismal Swamp at the 9th mile-post from Portsmouth on the Seaboard and Roanoke Railroad. Here a small area of the forest is felled, and the trees left lying every way. Details from the 13th guard this outpost continually, seconded by a small detachment of cavalry vedettes from Dodge's Mounted Rifles — commonly but most unfairly called "The mounted robbers." These men are frequently, if not generally, armed with a sabre, a repeating rifle and two navy revolvers.

To-night the 'rebels' attempt to surprise this post. It is pitchy dark, and one of them comes creeping along on all fours, apparently bent on capturing Warren S. French of E. French is safely ensconced behind a stump and waits the rebel's near approach, determined to give him the bayonet. As soon as the rebel comes near enough, French springs forward and gives him a lunge with his bayonet, when the rebel fetches a most unearthly yelp, and skittles off like a shot — a little black bear! Both he and French are about equally surprised. The incident serves to bring the watchful guard all up standing. French's position was at some distance, and it was reasonable to suppose that some one was trying to get near enough to kill or stun him by a blow, and make too little noise to rouse the rest of the pickets.

The most hideous sound we hear in the Dismal Swamp, and about the worst in point of unutterable viciousness any man ever heard, is said to proceed from a harmless animal called the North Carolina coon — an indescribable screech as if of mingled torture, scorn and defiance. Once heard, however, it occasions little further notice.

Sept. 11. Fri. Cool, pleasant. Reg. slashing all day. Several more deserters come into our lines claiming to have been members of the regiment of Louisiana Zouaves. The natives of the Dismal Swamp assert that the animals here — bears, coons, wild dogs, opossums, wild pigs, deer and jack-rabbits — all turn out to eat at flood tide! These same log-cabined natives, tar-makers, negro-hunters, and poor white trash generally, do not appear as if they ever eat at all; a poor, ragged, patched, faded, sallow, slouchy, lean, lank, dark-eyed, snake-eyed race of vagabonds, more like gypsies than any other people. They look treachery and cutthroat. The term 'poor whites' designates a class who do not own slaves but appear to have a little land and some local standing in the community; while the 'poor white trash' are a class having neither slaves, land, standing or anything else scarcely worth having. Many of these on being asked who their ancestors were, reply: "They war sent over — er'ekn." That means of course that they descended from men who had been deported by England to the colonies, with no credit to either.

Sept. 12. Sat. Clear, very warm. Regimental court martial meets — austere, profound, majestic tribunal! Later on this (sometimes) farcical court is succeeded by a Trial Justice. We must not fail to mention the barrel-coat, which unhandy and sinful men are occasionally sentenced to wear and march in for two or four hours. One head of a barrel is removed, a hole large enough for the culprit's cranium to protrude through is cut in the other head; the remainder of this head rests upon his shoulders, as the barrel is raised and brought down over him. While wearing the barrel-coat the culprit's head rises above the top head of the barrel like a small knob on the top of a huge gate-post, and if the man is short, his legs look queerly enough paddling along beneath, with very short steps. With a few of these well-clad men walking about, and as many more sitting astraddle on a long pole raised ten feet or so above the ground, and called the 'guard-house mule,' each labeled with his special misdemeanor — many regiments advertise the material they are made of. Their choice refrain is: "O why did I go for a military man?"

Capt. Julian and Lieut. Carter learned from many evidences that some one was smuggling whiskey through the Bowers Hill picket line, and also supplying the men on the line. They suspected a woman living near, and whose name we will call Jennie Reb. She soon unwisely sold some whiskey to two officers of the picket, and this stood in proof of her having it in possession. One day she passed the line with her wagon to town, and upon her usual permit, while a negro girl of hers passed the line at another point, joining her mistress later on. Upon Jennie Reb's return to her home in her wagon, Capt. Julian arrested her, and while doing so accused her of having canteens secreted in her clothing. There was no woman about to make an examination, so she was led to her house — the canteens banging about her legs as she walked, and the men of the picket running near to see the fun. She was at once placed in a room by herself alone, a sort of loft, and was ordered to pass out those canteens, while Capt. Julian and others stood outside waiting. There was now no possible escape for her, and presently she began to pass out canteens through the slightly opened door; and soon Capt. Julian had a string of sixteen canteens, which she had managed to fasten and carry upon her person, and all of them brimming full of the best brand of whiskey. As a final result she was fined $75, and imprisoned for six weeks.

Sept. 13. Sun. Rainy afternoon. Col. Steere, 4th R. I., buries his little daughter, seven years old, here to-day. She died of diphtheria here in camp. Of the thirty line officers, eleven are present for duty; of the eight field and staff, four are present for duty; the rest of the officers are sick or detached.

Inspection, at 9 a. m., by Capt. Julian, of each Company in its own street. Arms pronounced in bad condition, by the Inspector, the whole Regiment thoroughly angry, and 'camp language' comes to the front — a language more emphatic than elegant. We are a happy regimental family for one rainy Sunday, and the inspection is to be repeated. In the pressure of work, arms, clothing and equipments have been too much neglected. The Inspector finds grievous fault to the Colonel, and he goes for his staff with severity; they pitch into the Captains; they scold the Lieutenants; they blaze away at the First Sergeants; they harrow up the feelings of the Sergeants of squads; they bury the Corporals in billingsgate; they come down unmercifully upon the Privates; and they with no human object under them upon whom to pour their wrath, kick the first cracker-box or barrel they come to, clear across the camp, rip their shoes, break their toes — and then sit down on a stump and curse the niggers for bringing on this war!

Sept. 14. Mon. Clear. Company inspection forenoon; regimental inspection afternoon. Last Sunday's inspection not satisfactory and had to be repeated. Capt. Julian, Acting Assistant Inspector General on the Brigade staff is exceedingly particular; the ramrods must ring clear in the clean gun-barrels and all the brasses shine. To-day he goes over to inspect Companies B and D at Fort Tillinghast.

Sept. 15. Tues. Fair. A fine looking gentleman visits our outpost at the 9th mile-stone on the S. & R. Railroad in the swamp, plays checkers and cards with the reserve nearly all day, enjoys a good dinner, and makes himself agreeable. He knows little or nothing about the war, or about either army, pretends to be a native of the swamp, but his speech denies it; and finally he takes a walk down along the railroad to Gen. Getty's Hdqrs., in charge of one of Dodge's mounted riflemen, marching ahead of the rifleman's horse, and covered by the rifleman's revolver. His woful ignorance is too suspicious. After examination as a spy, he was detained for a while, and then allowed to depart.

This swamp may indeed be called Dismal in the early part of the night. Thousands of frogs, owls, wild dogs, tame cats run wild, wild cats, coons, bears, and innumerable animals, birds and creatures of every voice, small and large, pipe, trill, boom, bark, howl, growl, caterwaul, yell and scream, until the vile medley grows unendurable; and then atop of all the vocal din, the trees, leaning every way and against each other, when the wind blows will creak, and groan, and grate, and rub, and rustle, till your nerves go mad.

It is an hour or two past midnight, and exceeding dark and cloudy. We arrested to-day and sent to Hdqrs. one suspicious visitor to our outpost; a genuine native of the swamp has also been sent in under guard. At intervals since sundown the rebels have been sending up numerous rocket-signals seen above the trees. Lieut. Thompson of E, in charge of the outpost, does not dare to go to sleep; his trusty right-hand man is Sergt. John P. Haines of C, and both keep awake the entire night. Our cavalry vedettes have reported rebel guerilla parties a short distance to the front. We are five miles from the main line at Getty's Station, in the dense forest of the swamp, and realize that we cannot be too careful and wary. The guard has just changed reliefs, the animals of the swamp are nearly all silent, and all about is quite still. A sentry is a little way up the railroad from the hut which is used as a Hdqrs., another is a little way down the railroad, and two others are among the timber on the side of us towards Suffolk. Suddenly, a few rods to the north of the railroad, a twig is heard to snap. Then all is still. Then the dry leaves on a sapling are heard to rustle, and another snap, and then all is still for a long time. Men are surely lurking about the outpost. The first snap was heard by all the sentries, and all the relief who were awake. The sentries drop on one knee in the brush to be out of sight, and in order to see any approaching person against the sky. After a little time Sergt. Haines and another man are sent out to reconnoitre, and they noiselessly penetrate the timber three or four rods, and drop on the knee behind a well known log. They have been there but a few minutes when two shadowy heads pass a few feet to the front of them and between them and the patch of sky they can see; for it is too dark to see any one passing a rod distant, against the black back-ground of the forest. Haines and his man cock their pieces, and are aiming to fire — for they think these two are part of an approaching squad of guerillas and in such case it would be right to fire, — when Lieut. Thompson, hearing the clicks of their gun-locks, shouts: " Hold!" The two intruders surrender, and come in, each with a bayonet and loaded musket at his back; and prove to be two Union scouts, cleverly disguised as rebels and armed to the teeth, who, having no countersign, were trying to steal, unperceived, through our lines.

That word 'Hold' saved the two men's lives, and possibly rousing half the camp; for two shots heard in the swamp at night might herald an attack, and would be investigated instanter. It was a nervous little incident, and we note it only as an actual occurrence illustrating the thousands of similar, and worse, incidents common to the extreme outposts of an army. Both Sergeant Haines and his companion (name not remembered) were very quick, determined and courageous men, and no one would have found it safe to come prowling around an outpost they were guarding, or attempting to steal past their sentry post. These men are disarmed, and as a measure of surety sent under guard into camp. They tried at first to pass as men out of camp without leave on a foraging expedition, but later gave their true errand.

Sept. 16. Wed. Very hot, showery. Reg. slashing all day. Gov. Andrew of Mass., Gov. Morton of Indiana, Generals Foster, Naglee, and Getty, and a large staff and cavalry escort, ride through camp just at night. An informal visit.

While contemplating the Dismal Swamp in one feature, just imagine yourself walking in a path, and meeting a snake at every few rods, copperheads, moccasins, greens, water-blacks, etc. ; with now and then a tawny half-wild dog, which lies in the path, growling as you approach, and will not move for you until you charge upon him with a cudgel, sword or gun ; or a large wild pig or two — no matter how long or tall, never over six inches thick — which turn aside and hurry away looking by no means amiable ; possibly a jack-rabbit, all legs and ears, crosses your path like a shot, or a little reddish black bear snuffs at you once or twice at a safe distance, and then skittles off into the brush. Then imagine all around you for many miles a forest of large trees with tops densely interlacing ; mingle with them liberally small trees and underbrush, fill every space with cane-brake — a stiff grass with stalks as large as your fingers and ten feet tall — then twist, and tie, and tangle thorny brambles, and vines of a dozen kinds, over and through all up to thirty or fifty feet in the air ; put on the luxuriant twigs and branches mosquitoes, spiders, caterpillars and huge worms grown to a hundred fantastic shapes, sizes and colors ; and still you will not compass half the interesting things to be seen here in mid-summer. Take an axe or hatchet, and slash your best, and there are places where you will be able to cut a straight foot-path for yourself but a few rods in all day. There are hundreds of low, little islets, divided by an intricate maze of watercourse, pool and bog; in the wet season the swamp is penetrable only upon floating logs and fallen trees, and in the dry season many of the depressed areas are a vast carpet of tall, dense luxuriant moss.

Sept. 17. Thurs. Fair. Reg. slashing in the forenoon ; in camp in the afternoon. Pay-rolls being made and signed. Regimental Hospital moved over to our new camp-ground. Salutes being fired all along the lines in honor of Gov. Andrew of Mass., who is cheered to the echo wherever he goes. A magnificent man in most respects. As if to point the sharpest possible contrast to his grand, high patriotism, the execution of a deserter occurs during his visit to this Department — not witnessed, however, by him.

**Sept. 18. Fri.** Very rainy. Reg. in camp all day, — dull, nothing doing. At Ft. Tillinghast Companies B and D drill with artillery from 7 to 8 a. m. ; chop or shovel from 8 to 12 noon ; fire in artillery practice from 12 to 1 p. m., then have dinner ; again chop or shovel from 2 to 5 p. m. Drill again from 5 to 6 p. m. This is working very hard. To-day is followed by a cold, rainy, windy night — almost a gale.

**Sept. 19. Sat.** Very severe rain storm for the past twenty-four hours. Reg. in camp. Half a dozen of us have to tramp to Portsmouth and back — six or eight miles — in a furious rain storm, to attend as witnesses upon a court martial convened there. We have to walk on the railroad, the highroad a mass of mud — an abominable tramp.

**Sept. 20. Sun.** Very cool. Rain ceases — followed by a high wind. Tents go down all over camp. One member of the 13th writes : " We live well here now ; a part of the time on our expectations of what we will have next week, and the rest of the time on sweet potatoes and cold water." Another writes : " Breakfast — baked beans, bread and coffee. Dinner — boiled fresh beef, salt beef, cold beans, bread, coffee. Supper — tea or coffee, cold meat, bread. To-morrow we shall have the same — only have it a little differently."

**Sept. 21. Mon.** Fair, cold. Reg. at work on the defenses in the forenoon ; a part of the Reg. paid off in the afternoon. Lieut. Wilson, Lieut. Staniels, Sergt. Wheeler and others, arrive in camp with 166 recruits — " Subs " — for the 10th N. H.

**Sept. 22. Tues.** Very cold. Balance of the Reg. paid off in the forenoon ; all at work with axes in the afternoon.

**Sept. 23. Wed.** Cool. Reg. slashing all day. Capt. Julian of E is acting Asst. Inspector General of our Brigade ; Lieut. Durell acting Adjutant of the Thirteenth ; Lieut. Murray is at Brigade Headquarters ; and Lieut. Thompson in command of Company E. Lieut. Wilson and his guard start for New Hampshire again to-day, to bring forward recruits.

**Sept. 24. Thurs.** Very cool. Reg. slashing all day. The weather has been very chilling for a week past. Whiskey rations are being served daily to some of our men who are the most exposed to the cold. Strong hot coffee is better.

**Sept. 25. Fri.** Fair. Reg. slashing all day. The 16th Conn. (said to be) has a fancy custom of striking the " Taps " — the last drum-call of the day, signifying that lights must be put out in the men's quarters. After the little drums have rattled out their Taps, in all the regiments hereabout, there rolls down through camp the tremendous " Bum — bum — bum of that big bass-drum."

**Sept. 26. Sat.** Cold. Reg. slashing all day — working nine hours a day. One of the most amusing scenes — at the same time one of the most pitiable — that we ever witnessed, is the coming in of bodies of negro refugees, at our stockade gate. They will appear in the edge of the brush half a mile or so distant, looking back over their shoulders as if expecting pursuit and recapture even there, and within our picket lines. They will also approach the gate with the utmost caution; but once inside, away go their bundles, and all fear and caution at the same time, while they improvise a little jubilee, jumping up and down, and exclaiming: "O bress de Lord — I'se free, I'se free!" Some parties of them just emerged from the brush, in full sight of the gate and perfectly safe, will be seized with a sudden panic, drop their bundles, leave their little children behind, and make a simultaneous rush for the gate, giving every expression of the utmost fear, and running as if Satan himself was at their heels. It is often difficult to induce them to return for their bundles or children without being accompanied by a soldier with his gun.

Sept. 27. Sun. Pleasant. Usual Sunday duties. A Dismal Swamp native, having been asked to give information concerning another native suspected of rebel mail carrying, replies: " He be'nt thar ; right smart chance shet o' that 'ar place, er'ekn."

Sept. 28. Mon. Pleasant. Reg. slashing all day. Dr. Ezekiel Morrill reports for duty as Asst. Surgeon of the Thirteenth. Dr. Morrill's popularity was always great, and his excellent services in the Reg. were always a matter of much credit to himself, and of especial advantage to the personnel of the Thirteenth.

Sept. 29. Tues. Pleasant. Reg. slashing all day.

The rule to joke when you please, provided that you please when you joke, is a very good one. The following toast, drank at a convivial gathering of officers· not long since, was not gauged by that rule : " Here's to your courage, and very good health, ——. Here's hoping that you will go in next time like a man. If you survive, all right. If you are wounded, we will see that your limbs are promptly and neatly cut off ; and if you are killed, we will bury you well and deep." The toast was received by the whole party with the silence that was golden, but with minds that were busy ; the laugh came in later — when there were not so many round.

Sept. 30. Wed. Pleasant. Reg. slashing all day. Mrs. A. F. Stevens, Mrs. C. O. Bradley, Mrs. E. E. Dodge and Mrs G. A. Forbush, wives of officers of the 13th now visiting in camp, have all been ill from malarial causes. No Northern person escapes malaria here. It is sure to visit one sooner or later in some form ; and it has as many open or sly ways of attack as Col. Mosby's guerillas, and all as relentless. Officers' log-houses are now being built. They are all of one story, are about twelve feet by eighteen feet on the ground, and have small glass windows and roomy brick fireplaces. Some of them look oddly enough, with their long, narrow, horizontal windows, made of Mr. Bunting's hot-bed sash loaned or sold for the purpose.

Oct. 1. Thurs. Pleasant. Reg. at work on rifle-pits, and the main line of entrenchments, and much hurried. Capt. Smith departs from camp on fifteen days' leave.

Oct. 2. Fri. Rainy forenoon. Reg. at work on the defenses in the afternoon. Picks and shovels in great demand. The supply of these tools is short, and a special search is made for hidden or misplaced ones, all through the tents of the men. None are found secreted by the Thirteenth. Members of a neighboring regiment, growing tired, are said to have buried several hundred shovels, axes and picks.

Oct. 3. Sat. Pleasant. Reg. slashes all day; and then is called out late in the afternoon for a long, close special inspection followed by a Dress-parade.

Oct. 4. Sun. Pleasant. A part of the Reg'., about one hundred men, sent on picket to Bowers Hill. One hundred and eighty-one recruits arrive for the Thirteenth this afternoon. Only one drafted man in the whole party. They appear to be the 'tag, rag, bob-tail and siftings' of all creation; now and then a good man, generally bad. They come for money — and some of them, we trust, will get their money's worth. No auction sale of a bankrupt stock ever palmed off such a lot of goods as some of these; many of them seem scarcely worth their ticket of leave in powder and ball. The Companies receive them to equalize numbers present; Company E gets twenty, Company B eight, and so on through the Regiment. The 10th N. H. receives 169 recruits of the lot that arrives to-day. They were all escorted together, from the wharf at Portsmouth to camp, by an armed guard with loaded rifles; and as a precaution the camp guard is largely increased, in both the Tenth and Thirteenth.

"Conscripts to the number of one hundred and eighty-one arrived to-day, and are distributed so as to bring every company up to eighty-five men, so that we now number eight hundred and fifty enlisted men present and absent. The new-comers are to be treated in all respects exactly the same as the volunteers in the Regiment. Only eleven of those coming to-day are natives of New Hampshire; the others are from almost every nation on the globe."
CAPT. JULIAN.

Oct. 5. Mon. Very pleasant. Log-houses going up all over the plain — hundreds of them — winter quarters. Last night the Subs were exceedingly boisterous, and half the Reg. were needed to keep them in camp, and to preserve the peace. The line officers remonstrate with Col. Stevens against the using of old soldiers to guard the Subs, in addition to all their regular duties; and those Subs who will not behave take up quarters in the guard-house. The 13th N. Y. Heavy Artillery arrived here yesterday, and are encamped about one fourth of a mile north of our camp. They have among their men fourteen Seneca Indians. One of their men (white) is a giant above seven feet tall. He is employed in mounting cannon and other heavy work. Nine tenths of his regiment can walk erect under his outstretched arms.

Oct. 6. Tues. Pleasant. Reg. in camp. The roofs of our log-houses are made of 'nigger shingles;' a sort of rough boards about five feet long, half an inch thick, and six or eight inches wide, split off from yellow-pine logs — peeled off with the grain like bark round and round the log — and then piled up to be pressed into shape and to dry. A capital roofing material. Some very pretty, quaint, chateau-like houses are made wholly of them in other camps. Musicians from the Reg. mustered into the 3d Brigade Band.

Oct. 7. Wed. Pleasant. Reg. at work on the defenses. Mid-days now are very hot, nights very cold; result many cases of chills and fever. Furloughs are being granted quite freely.

Oct. 8. Thurs. Pleasant. Reg. at work on the defenses. The Lieutenants in command of companies receive $10 per month extra pay — small pay for a great bother. "Had the honor of walking up and down the front street of our camp (as a guard) with a conscript — with a pole on his back." LUEY.

Oct. 9. Fri. Very warm. Reg. at work on rifle-pits west of our camp. Nowadays Reveille sounds half an hour before sunrise; Tattoo at 8 p. m.; Taps at 9 p. m., and the camp is quiet about 9.30 p. m.

Oct. 10. Sat. Pleasant. Reg. at work on the defenses. Battery L, 4th Regulars, goes from our lines near Ft. Tillinghast to Yorktown. Quarter-master Morrison departs for home on leave.

Oct. 11. Sun. Pleasant, cool. Usual Sunday duties. A very particular inspection.

Some regimental officers of the day, with their diagonally worn sash — from right shoulder to waist — and their polygonally worn temper, are the tallest men in the army for their little day. They love to hear: "Turn out the guard — Officer of the Day!!" and to receive their salute of 'present arms.' It is difficult to divide the honors between them and the little corporal with his guard. Every regiment has one, two, or more samples. The boys of the relief waiting about the guard headquarters greatly enjoy making good-natured sport of these pompous gentlemen, and when they see one of them coming, they frequently reverse the above order, and give notice of his approach to their officer, by shouting — "O. T. D.!! Turn out the *day* — Officer of the guard."

Oct. 12. Mon. Warm. Reg. at work on log-houses and tents. Reporters for Northern papers are tramping through the camp all the time. They are supplied with a varied assortment of news by mischievous wags, and over and over again the packages are put up wrong, for the fun of it. Their papers publish the stuff; we read it in a few days, and wonder at credulity. There is, however, a large class of soldiers who manage to visit distant regiments and points in the night, gather reliable information, and exchange it with their fellows. These "camp walkers" will spread any bit of news throughout the command with amazing rapidity. The average soldier is well posted in affairs, as affairs really are; and no barometer ever noted the advance of a coming storm more quickly and accurately than the common soldiers somehow, and almost intuitively, gain the news of coming march or battle. Aggregate mentality is a world of wonders.

Oct. 13. Tues. Pleasant. Reg. improving the defenses. Henry C. Howard of Co. E is detailed as dentist for the Thirteenth — and proves a success in that duty. Inspection by Capt. Julian.

Oct. 14. Wed. Very warm. Reg. in camp. A detail sent as provost-guard to near Portsmouth and on the bank of the creek above the town. The writer, in charge of the provost-guard at Scott's Creek, near Portsmouth, while on his rounds about one o'clock a. m., sees a light burning in a large house not far from the picket line and to the north of Hall's Corner, a house which he knows has no regular tenants. Hoping to find the parties within engaged upon the rebel mail, and approaching cautiously, he succeeds in climbing a high fence that is around the yard, and in getting within a rod or two of the house; when the light is suddenly put out, and two large brown and white dogs make a rush at him, from a shed near by, howling and barking as watch-dogs will. The largest dog was cured by one broadside slash with the sword, and the smaller one with a vigorous lunge, and both went back rehearsing a new tune; while the writer remounted the fence, and 'withdrew for a better position.' He does not like too many dogs. The pickets, hearing the noise, came as soon as possible, but ten or fifteen minutes had passed, and neither dogs nor any other occupants could be found about the premises. It is supposed that all had retreated to one of the underground hiding places, with which this whole rebel region is well provided. And this shows another phase of fighting down the rebellion.

Oct. 15. Thurs. Very warm. Reg. chopping. A detail also cutting logs for our new guard-house; the logs for this building are all to have the bark taken off.

Oct. 16. Fri. Hot. Reg. chopping. Along here work is systematically divided — house-building, chopping, shoveling, etc., according to the capabilities of the men.

Oct. 17. Sat. Pleasant. Officers beginning to be at home in their log-houses. At first it was intended that all the houses should be made of one uniform pattern, but soon that plan was departed from, and the camp presents a pleasing variety of architecture. Colonel Stevens' house is very spacious and well furnished. The line officers' houses are each large enough for a family to reside in, excepting Lieut. Thompson's of Co. E. Owing to his long absence on picket, and the importunate calls of ranking officers upon the labor of the teams, his house is the last one built in camp. The Brigade commander inquiring the cause of this delay, and being informed, orders the teamsters to bring the material at once. This is also the smallest of the officers' houses — 10 feet by 16 on the ground, of one story and of one room. It has two glass windows, a brick chimney and a large fireplace. All the houses are made of logs, partly hewn, chinked with mud, and the most have chimneys of brick — all standing outside. Southern fashion — and wide, open fireplaces. There is any quantity of good dry wood, and great roaring fires give welcome cheer. When a gum-tree has died standing and is thoroughly dried, it makes a fire not surpassed by the best hickory. Half the houses are papered with Harpers, and other pictorial papers, and maps and pictures of all sorts, tacked on all over the inside of walls and roofs.

Oct. 18. Sun. Warm. Companies C, G and H leave camp at 8 a. m. for one week's picketing on the Portsmouth road, a sort of provost-guard. The rebel mail-carrier is the bugbear — and the standing joke — on this whole picket line. Not long since he crossed Scott's Creek in a folding rubber-boat, right under a picket's nose, and was not caught. He could have punched the stupid picket with his pole, he passed so near. Some of the men seem to believe that he is the very Satan, he is so sly and so quick; and they are about as much afraid of a hand-to-hand tussle with him as they would be with that old fellow himself.

Oct. 19. Mon. Very hot, clear. Reg. improving the defenses. The work done by the contrabands is of the poorest sort, and is all done at the snail's pace. They are regularly paid, but their labor does not amount to one third as much as that of the soldiers, man for man. They say: "Dat's de way we work for ole massa; 'i-golly!"

Oct. 20. Tues. Very fine day. Reg. improving defenses; and trying to improve the Subs.

After all is still at night — about 9.30 or 10 p. m. — and the calls of the various regiments around us have been sounded, and even the big bass-drum of the 16th Conn. is at rest; a single bugle, of clear and excellent tone, and in the hands of a skillful player in the N. Y. Heavy Artillery regiment stationed near our camp and to the northward of it, sends wide and full, all through the encampment, its last call of the day. And many a weary soldier of us, just turned in, drops off to sleep, and to dreams of home, while that bugle, in a master hand, rings a hundred changes on that most beautiful, musical and welcome call heard in any army — announcing that the busy day is now done, inviting to sleep, and giving assurance that the camp rests in peace and security.

Oct. 21. Wed. Pleasant. Reg. at work on the defenses. Orders received to be ready to march to-morrow morning at daybreak, with sixty rounds of ammunition; all the troops in light marching order, and with three days' cooked rations in haversacks, and seven days' supply in wagons. Soon countermanded.

Oct. 22. Thurs. Pleasant. Reg. improving the defenses. One Dr. Wright of Portsmouth, Va., is to be hanged for killing Lieutenant Sanborn of the Union army; deliberately shot the Lieutenant while he was drilling negro troops in front of this Doctor's office.

Oct. 23. Fri. Very pleasant. The Reg. is again at work upon Ft. Rodman; the parapets being raised very high to afford a wider range.

Oct. 24. Sat. Rainy, very cold, with a high wind. Reg. resting in camp. To-night some of the officers take the shivering camp-guards in, give them a thorough warming before their big fires — and a glass from the sly canteen. Hot, strong coffee is better.

Oct. 25. Sun. Rainy, cold. Reg. divides picket duties with the 10th N. H. The old soldiers most disgusted of all with the vicious Subs are the volunteer Irishmen. A good Sub is well received, but the bad characters find little mercy at the hands of the Irish Veteran.

Oct. 26. Mon. Cold. Reg. in camp. Drilling talked of; has been very limited in these many months of pick, and axe, and shovel. Lisping patient at Surgeon's call. Surgeon: "Well, young man, what is the matter with you?" Patient: "I have a thick headache — awful thick!" Surgeon: "I know it, I know it, you will die with it; I can only relieve you a little — give him a double-scraper, Steward."

Oct. 27. Tues. Very cold. Reg. in camp. "At the funeral of Lieut. Sanborn, who was shot by Dr. Wright, all the negro troops in the department were in line. They could not get enough of the marching and the music, and our Thirteenth Band played the 'Dead March in Saul' through nineteen times consecutively." CHAS. W. WASHBURN, Band.

Oct. 28. Wed. Fair, cold, windy. Reg. in camp. "The negroes at the contraband camp are suffering severely from the cold. Scarcely any can be found who have a change of clothing of any sort, and a blanket is a rarity among them. The men build large fires out of doors, and sit or lie about them all night to keep warm. They live on bacon and corn meal, and bad meal at that, of which they bake bread after a barbarous fashion. They get rye coffee, and eight pounds of sugar per day for 100 men." PRESCOTT.

Oct. 29. Thurs. Fair. Reg. in camp. Company E and others on outpost picket in the swamp. A party of men of the 13th went into the swamp for wood, and as they were walking along, one of them suddenly disappeared down below. He was fished out with poles. Wondering why a well should be in such a place the men made an investigation. A large pine-tree had died standing, and all but the bark had rotted. During the many years required for its destruction, the brush and peat had accumulated about it to the depth of several feet, so that the bark, remaining in form, made a quite perfect well eight or ten feet deep, and nearly three feet across.

Oct. 30. Fri. Pleasant, warm. Reg. in camp. Pay-rolls being made. The rolls of Company E are made out at the house of a Mr. Bright, a tar-maker, in the swamp. He has a peculiar fancy for naming his children with the names of the Southern States. His eldest — a girl, Louisiana — is about sixteen years old, the youngest a babe; but his family has well-nigh confiscated the entire rebel Confederacy! His house has no glass windows. Square holes are cut, and cotton cloth stretched across to admit the light. All can be closed with heavy board shutters: "To keep the wild-cats from stealing the children," as he says. On the fluid of a sort of thick, 'boiled-dinner' soup, which they had for dinner one day, clear bacon-fat floated to the depth of more than one eighth of an inch — utterly incompatible with the Northern appetite.

During one dinner here — as we 'boarded' — a large pig came in and nosed around familiarly among the children, dogs and chickens on the floor. Soon piggy smelled a large hoe-cake all baking hot in the ashes of the fireplace. Before he could be stopped, his hoof had raked the cake out; and then plunging his nose deep into the scalding hot mass, he gave one hoggish bite, one awful shake of his head, one shower of dough, one most unearthly squeal, one tremendous leap for the door — the gay curl of his tail gone out straight as a candle — and we never saw him more. A sad case of misplaced confidence. The family was sorry to lose the hoecake, but seemed to regard the affair as nothing particularly unusual in their dining-room.

Oct. 31. Sat. Very warm, the warmest day this month. Reg. mustered for two months' pay at 10 a. m. by Col. Chas. L. Upham of the 15th Conn. Orders received for the Reg. to drill six hours a day. Co. E numbers 76 men, a fair average.

All the citizens, as well as all the soldiers, in this part of Dixie have to procure passes from the General commanding, in order to move from place to place. How would Northern farmers like to be stopped at every road-crossing and oftener, by a soldier, with : " Your pass, sir, — if you please ! " No enlisted man can go beyond the regimental guard-line without a pass from some officer. No officer can leave camp without permission ; and to visit the city, three miles distant, a pass is required signed by the Brigade commander, and stating the purpose of the visit. So arbitrarily circumscribed is our soldier life here.

Nov. 1. Sun. Very fine day, cool. Inspection, parade and religious services. It is not probable that one fourth of the Thirteenth have been accustomed at their homes to any form of the Episcopal Church service. This makes its use now quite unpopular among the men. There is no gainsaying that unfortunate fact. Our Chaplain modifies the service somewhat, still many of the men go unsatisfied away, and long for an old-fashioned up-country meeting. Independent religious meetings are frequently held.

This is the way a small society in the Thirteenth came to early grief: It was formed of a few men only, and not with that open and frank independence that should characterize all good endeavors. In trying to avoid 'talk,' they of course invited it. They were called Sons of Temperance. Now the initial letters of those three words are most unfortunate, and soon the sons were dubbed sots — and never heard the last of it. The ridiculous designation practically broke up the little society.

Nov. 2. Mon. Fair. Now comes a griping spasm of drill — squad, company, battalion and brigade; even marching Companies B and D over from Fort Tillinghast to join in the drill, thus adding to their day's labor at drill, a march of over three miles. " The Regiment (to-day) began to drill." Luey.

Nov. 3. Tues. Fair. Reg. drilling; Maj. Grantman drill-master. Details sent far into the swamp on picket.

Nov. 4. Wed. Fair. Reg. drilling. Lieut. Thompson of E, with 30 or 40 men, some from each Company, takes a week of Provost-guard duty near Portsmouth — north of Portsmouth road and along Scott's Creek.

Nov. 5. Thurs. Fair. Reg. drilling. Another simple, impressive, soldiers' burial of the dead.

Nov. 6. Fri. Fair, very dusty. Reg. drilling. An officer in the 13th, given to joking, purchases a yard or two of bright colored calico at Norfolk, hangs it up in his nice log-house, and labels it: "Hands off." He is evidently lonesome.

Nov. 7. Sat. Fair. Rifle practice by the Regiment. Most of the bullets hit the ground — in course of time; a new newspaper covered target will be required about once in three months. We have some fine marksmen, however — "but they're mostly all off on picket duty to-day."

Nov. 8. Sun. Fair. Usual Sunday duties. At Dress-parade — at 5 p. m. — a snow-squall comes up from the rear; and from a handful to a pint of coarse, snowy hail rolls down the back of every man's neck. The loose fitting coat-collars make admirable gutter spouts.

Nov. 9. Mon. Cold, clear; snowy last night. Company drill in forenoon, Battalion drill in afternoon. Lieut. Saunders of D has command of the contraband camp — as the camp of the liberated slaves is called — his Hdqrs. being located within a few yards of the quarters of Co. D at Fort Tillinghast, and Sergt. Batchellor is acting as commissary-sergeant of the contraband camp.

Two deserters are shot to-day near Fort Reno and about a mile from Fort Tillinghast. Sergeant Batchellor of. D thus describes the affair, which he witnessed : " The two deserters were members of the 8th Conn. They were shot at 10 a. m. for their fourth desertion. They had previously been members of the 8th Conn. and at their last re-enlistment were unwittingly assigned to the 8th Conn. again, under their new assumed names — and caught. The Brigade was formed in a hollow square. The deserters rode in a wagon behind their coffins. In the rear of the wagon came their executioners — ten soldiers from the 15th Conn. (one of their guns being loaded with a blank cartridge). When the deserters had arrived in the hollow square, which was open on one side, the coffins were put down and they knelt beside them. The priests performed the Roman Catholic rites. When all was ready, white bandages were tied over the deserters' eyes and their hands were bound. They were then faced toward the men who were to shoot them, and knelt with their backs to their coffins. When shot one of them made no motion, the other moved a little — then all was still. After the surgeons had pronounced them dead they were placed in their coffins with their shackles on their feet."

Nov. 10. Tues. Fair. Major Grantman in command of the Regiment; which is now at work on the rifle-pits near camp. A stupid Sub threatens to shoot Sergt. Chas. F. Chapman of E, while he is making the grand rounds of his guard late at night.

This was the cockney, Reed of E. He was so full of blunders that he had to be placed on some unimportant guard post, and with an empty gun. As Chapman was going the rounds in the night, he came upon Reed, who called out: "Stop," instead of halt, and demanded the countersign. Chapman could not give it at so great a distance, and continued to approach. At every step Reed grew more and more angry, swore, threatened and yelled himself hoarse, and acted more like a mad monkey than like a man. Chapman came within a few feet, when Reed clubbed his musket and broke out with a perfect torrent of profanity; winding up with: " What do you want, anyhow ? " Chapman raised his voice to the loudest pitch, and answered: " I want to know *if you are awake*." Poor Reed fairly danced a pirouette with rage. It was too bad to tease the man; but the scene was very funny.

Nov. 11. Wed. Fair, very cold — coldest day of the season. Regular monthly inspection of the Reg. by Capt. Julian, A. A. I. G. of our Brigade. Asst. Surgeon John Sullivan is now very sick, and is not expected to survive. Has been quite seriously ill for some time past. In general, however, the health of the Reg. has not been so good as it now is, since we were at Newport News last spring. Good food is plenty and cheap. Officers' mess board costs about $3.00 per week.

Nov. 12. Thurs. Pleasant. Reg. improving defenses. Gen. Getty — so the story goes — meets a party of shovelers on their way from work to camp, and asks: " Well, boys, which do you prefer, the axe, the shovel or the gun ? " They reply: " Neither — we want to go home." He answers: " Very good; you can go now, two at a time from each company." And that is the order from Division Hdqrs. Maj. Gen. B. F. Butler succeeds Maj. Gen. Foster, in command of this Department of Virginia and North Carolina.

Nov. 13. Fri. Cold. This afternoon the Reg. is suddenly called out under arms, and marches to Bowers Hill very rapidly — distance near five miles — arrives about sunset, and bivouacs near the fort as a support for the cavalry and pickets. The whole line is under arms all day and night, which is very damp and cold. All quiet where we are, but a rebel force of cavalry is hovering near, said to be 1,800 strong.

Nov. 14. Sat. Cold, rainy last night. Reg. returns to camp to-day about noon, cold, wet and tired. Glad to get away from that front. The Reg. takes a regular fight with some degree of relish, but guerilla warfare is an abomination. One whole regiment is constantly employed in fighting guerillas, on our front lines. At South Mills recently a Lieutenant, riding beyond the lines on a scout, had his horse shot under him and riddled with bullets; while the Lieutenant received nine bullets in his clothing and body, but managed to escape without assistance, and will recover. He came within range of a guerilla band of about fifty men, and they gave him one volley.

Nov. 15. Sun. Pleasant. Reg. in camp. Captain Stoodley takes a detail of about one hundred officers and men for a turn of picket at Bowers Hill. Dress-parade, and particular inspection of arms.

Nov. 16. Mon. Fair. Reg. in camp. The people — natives — in the vicinity of Bowers Hill, are a very peculiar, mixed race, as if the Indian, the white, and the negro were fused together. Some are very handsome, but the most are distant, taciturn, forbidding and repulsive.

**Nov. 17. Tues.** Fair. Reg. at work on the defenses. The Subs are exceedingly troublesome. They get drunk, fight, disturb the camp, break heads, steal, lie, fall asleep at their posts, desert the guard, and serve the evil one generally. The old soldiers are getting angry with them, all through and through. There have been numerous rumors of late that the Subs are planning a mutiny. Many of the regiments have them ; and their plan is for all to suddenly join together, and go over into the Confederacy in an armed body. There will be music when they try it! A search found many navy revolvers among them.

**Nov. 18. Wed.** Fair. The dust about camp is terrible ; when the wind blows, clouds of it shut out all views, blinding and choking everybody and filling the tents and houses. You can write your name in the dust on every coat, cot and table in camp. The country here is sandy, the sand is very fine and filled with the almost impalpable dust of decayed organic matter, light as dry flour.

The swamp natives practice the nastiest custom yet invented — 'dipping.' They pass round a plate filled with snuff, and provided with one or two little brushes. As the dish of snuff goes round, each one present, both young and old, takes the brush, covers it with snuff, and with it slowly swabs the inside of his or her mouth and gums! Read this after dinner ; it is worse than using a family tooth brush — in a boarding-house.

**Nov. 19. Thurs.** Fair. A portion of the Reg., including Company E, are on the Portsmouth road on picket ; we have any quantity of genuine Norfolk oysters, and cook them in every possible style. We guard sundry oyster beds, and take high pay in kind. The creek where they are found is called Scott's Creek.

At Fort Rodman near our camp an ingenious Lieutenant emptied a long Parrott shell of its powder, as he thought, and used the shell for an andiron in the fireplace of his log-cabin. About ten o'clock at night the shell exploded, demolishing the cabin, lifting the roof, knocking the chimney and fireplace all into flinders, hurting the Lieutenant badly and leaving him sprawling on the middle of his cabin floor all out of doors, under the stars, and scared half out of his wits. The explosion was taken in camp to be a signal gun, announcing an attack by the enemy. It roused the whole force, which sprang to arms — an army roused at dead of night. Guns were manned in short order ; regiments got ready to fall into line ; bugle blasts started cavalry and field artillery to ' boots and saddles ; ' the whole camp was all up and coming — and the camp followers gathered their effects for a characteristic skedaddle to the rear. But orderlies soon began to fly about, and to explain the cause of the disturbance. Quiet was then quickly restored, and the men turned in again. Never use loaded Parrott shells for andirons.

**Nov. 20. Fri.** Clear ; extremely windy. This plain — of our camp — a few months ago was a nearly empty field, now there are several hundreds of large houses and buildings, besides all the tents of the men. Quite a city — the snug winter quarters of a lively little army. The Reg. is now all settled in winter quarters, and the duties of guard and picket are quite regular. Regimental court martial convenes, having several hard cases on its list; Lieut. Thompson of E acting as Judge Advocate.

**Nov. 21. Sat.** Fair; a few showers. The part of the line on our front is now held by a company of cavalry, about six miles from our camp: about one mile this side of them are posted two guns and a small garrison near Bowers Hill — where the pickets going out from the Thirteenth are stationed — the Captain of the picket having command of the whole post. A numerous patrol are moving continually between these posts and our camp, and sundry special picket posts at points in the swamp. No firing allowed now on the picket lines, though the outer cavalry vedettes have an occasional brush with guerillas.

**Nov. 22. Sun.** Fair. Dress-parade, inspection, prayers. The picket returns from Bowers Hill to camp about 2 p. m., having been relieved by the 16th Conn. Five officers of the Reg. are now absent on leave. The officers in camp do the work of the absent officers for nothing; while the officers during absence from duty on leave draw half pay. This is hardly a fair proceeding.

**Nov. 23. Mon.** Rainy, cold. Reg. in camp. Francis Wild, a nimble little Englishman, enlisted in Company E, and deserted soon after our Regiment came into Virginia. Now he has the inestimable cheek to write to one of his old comrades in Co. E that he has in all enlisted six times, six times received his bounties, and has just got safely out of his sixth desertion! Where is the Regiment that can excel our own glorious Thirteenth?

**Nov. 24. Tues.** Fair. Capt. Dodge of B is sent away upon some War Department business. The secessionists are growling fearfully about Maj. Gen. B. F. Butler now in command of this Department. Well they may if they do not behave to suit him.

**Nov. 25. Wed.** Pleasant. Reg. drilling. Orders now are that we must drill in all suitable weather. The average soldier prefers to drill when he is shoveling, and to shovel when he is drilling, and, for a change, much prefers — neither.

Just west of our camp, a long stockade stretches straight across the plain, from near Fort Rodman and the Suffolk road, north to Bruce's Creek (so named for a resident landholder). The logs are large, many of them a foot in diameter, they are set deep in the ground, stand exactly vertical, and rise from eight to ten feet above the ground. A deep, muddy swamp lies directly in front of the stockade nearly impassable for infantry. The fortifications on this line are now regarded as completed, and the troops are congratulated in special orders. Fort Rodman is so named in honor of Lt. Col. Isaac P. Rodman, of the 4th R. I., who resigned some months since.

**Nov. 26. Thurs.** Fair and pleasant. Thanksgiving Day in camp

— observed as a holiday. There are all sorts of races; horse-races, sack-races, foot-races, black-races (a black boy will run his legs off for a dollar), white races and wheelbarrow-races. The latter are very funny. About fifty men are in line blindfolded and each with a wheelbarrow. Every nose is set point blank for a barrel a hundred yards distant. At a signal all start at once running toward the barrel; they collide, mix up, tumble over, turn all sorts of curves and circles, some even coming back near where they started — but only one hits the barrel. Almost all of our men have a good dinner to day. The 'plums' for a four quart plum-pudding cost our mess $1.50 in Norfolk. Officers' board in general costs now from $3.00 to $5.00 per week. A Dress-parade at sundown, with religious services, fitly closes the day; and in the evening there is a regular jubilee over the news from Gen. Grant's army about Chattanooga — the whole command cheering.

Nov. 27. Fri. Cold, rainy. Squad drill. For a while this autumn the Reg. is instructed in bayonet exercise by an Italian soldier. The 25th Mass. and 4th R. I. regiments are encamped near the 13th, and all are very fraternal and friendly.

Nov. 28. Sat. Rainy — and our camp is a swamp with all its ditches full of water. To-night one of the darkest nights that man ever saw. The Reg. is ordered to be ready, on Monday next, to witness the execution — by shooting — of three men of our Brigade, for desertion. The whole Brigade is ordered out also. (The writer does not witness this execution — nor any other.)

Copy of a Thirteenth soldier's application for furlough — sent direct to the General commanding:

Nov the 1863 28
Camp Gilmore   Near Portsmouth Va
13 Reg N H Vol

General Sir I Request a furlow of —— days to Visit my home in the State of New Hampshire to arange some unseteled buisness also to make some important famley arangments of Grate impotance to myself and famley        Respectfuly Yours        * * * * *

(He had six children, more or less, the youngest a year old, and 'General Sir' granted him a 'furlow' immediately.)

Nov. 29. Sun. Severe rain storm. Reg. keeps close in its quarters. No Sunday inspection, parade or services.

There is a family named Wood living near our picket post on Deep Creek, consisting of a father, mother, a couple of boys, and several girls nearly grown to womanhood, who spend their winter evenings sitting around their fire, and all smoking together. If one of our pickets gives them a call, it is in good form for one of the girls to take the pipe from her own sweet mouth, and pass it to the guest to smoke, while she proceeds to light another pipe for herself. Dismal Swamp etiquette. Not one of this family can either read or write.

Nov. 30. Mon. Pleasant, cool. Reg. drilling. The guerillas are exceedingly troublesome on the outer lines of this Department. One regiment is almost wholly employed in fighting them. They drive in the outposts repeatedly, and we are all the time under orders to be ready for an instant move. Their style of warfare is diabolical murder.

Dec. 1. Tues. Sudden cold snap; much ice about camp. Reg. drilling. 'Comfort Bags' filled with needles, thread, pins and numerous other little conveniences, now invade our camp in large numbers. They are made by the pretty girls in New Hampshire, and usually contain a letter signed by the maker. Many correspondences are thus begun — with more or less fun, foolishness or mischief.

Dec. 2. Wed. Warmer. Company drill forenoon. Battalion drill afternoon. Capt. Smith writes: "Active service in the army makes strange bed-fellows." Asst. Surgeon Sullivan goes home on leave, granted upon a medical certificate that it is necessary for him to leave the front in order to save his life.

Dec. 3. Thurs. Fair. Reg. drilling; Battalion drill in afternoon with Capt. Dodge for drill-master. Officers' school, in tactics, for three evenings in the week. A canvass reveals the fact that all the officers in the Thirteenth, excepting four, have visited home on leave.

Dec. 4 Fri. Fair. Brigade drill — Col. Steere commanding.

A soldier, very drunk, is seen plodding along the dusty road near our camp, reeling from side to side, and cheering with all his might. Sundry troops, half a mile away, are cheering loudly also. Some one asked him why he was cheering, when he drew himself up as if his dignity was insulted by such a question, and replied: "Hanged if I know. Heard them, Sir, and I, Sir, cheered, Sir — as a 'zample (hic) of discipline, Sir." Swung his cap, cheered again. and reeled along conscious of having done his whole duty. He emphasized ' Sir ' most heavily.

Dec 5. Sat. Pleasant, quite cool. Reg. marches out about a mile and practices at target-shooting, at the usual place, on right hand of road, west of camp, just beyond the stockade gateway. There are 250 guns, and the men fire 20 rounds per gun — 5,000 shots — and the irreverent affirm that the vicinity of the target is the safest place to be found within a circuit of half a mile. The Sub and cockney, Reed of E, wants to show the Regiment, " 'Ow they fire hin the Hold Hinglish Harmy." He steps to the front, holds his gun at arm's length, fires — and doubles up like an old jackknife, a rod back in the brush. The boys have given him a kicking gun. He takes his place in the rear rank again. and at the next fire singes his file-leader's hair and whiskers, and nearly breaks his head. Col. Stevens sends him off to camp; and we turn him into a mess-cook, a good one too, the best in camp. He used to be a cook on a French man-of-war.

Dec. 6. Sun. Fair, very cold. Usual Sunday duties. Company H has a genius by name Blank, a Sub and white-headed war-eagle about eighteen years old. What he does not know he cannot learn — and there is no gainsaying it. The Colonel, between Reed and Blank, could but lose his temper and gravity together yesterday, and was forced to laugh at their mistakes. These with others were put into the awkward squad and drilled in firing; and if all had been drilled for a month at acting the fool, they could not have succeeded better in that rôle. They were honest enough; they cannot learn the manual of arms. Every regiment has a few of these irreclaimable 'awkwards.'

Dec. 7. Mon. Fair, windy. Capt. Stoodley starts for home on a twenty days' leave. Reg. drilled five hours a day every day of last week, and is at it again to-day. Drill now is full martinet. The officers have to study very hard; and, besides, have to drill on extra hours in the Italian bayonet exercise. An Italian, said to be one of Garibaldi's men, is their tutor. The officers are expected to learn the whole exercise in two weeks, and then to drill their companies in it.

Dec. 8. Tues. Fair. Company drill forenoon, Battalion drill afternoon, followed by an hour of bayonet drill — 'bayonet exercise' — for the whole command; the Thirteenth alone requiring a field of many acres. The space occupied by each man at this drill is necessarily as broad as the man can reach with his gun and bayonet in every direction. A body of men drilling with the bayonet look in the distance like a line of beings made up about equally of the frog, the sand-hill crane, the sentinel crab and the grasshopper; all of them rapidly jumping, thrusting, swinging, striking, jerking, every way, and all gone stark mad.

Dec. 9. Wed. Cold, damp, chilly. The sutler has a lot of handsome apples, red cheeked russets, which taste like a mixture of sweet geranium, allspice and lard. They sell readily. Every purchaser protests that they are spoiled. The sutler says: "They are very nice — but I guess that suthin has kinder got onto um." Pud Long smashes one against the head of the sutler's boy, and then visits the guard-house for a few hours; when some one goes and pays over the two cents — the price of the apple — and gets him excused. Those pretty apples, several barrels full of them, nearly raise a mutiny in camp.

Dec. 10. Thurs. Cold. Afternoon drill omitted. Our line of works are highly praised. They demand no labor now excepting for occasional repairs. In front of them a strip of timber, in many places dense and valuable, has been leveled — to rot or burn — nearly a mile wide and three or four miles long. Where the army goes, there goes destruction — the South is being fearfully punished.

Dec. 11. Fri. Clear. Reg. drilling; Capt. Bradley drill-master. It is intended that each Captain in turn shall drill the Regiment.

A couple of soldiers took a walk in the swamp, and finding an unexploded shell, thought to have a little fun in exploding the thing. They built a fire, threw in the shell — a large one — and took position behind convenient trees for protection. The shell was a long time in getting hot enough to burst. One of the men, whose tree was not too large, growing impatient leaned forward, and took a side glance at the shell, on the very instant when it burst. He had in bending, incautiously exposed himself to danger in the rear, and a piece of the shell made away with a considerable slice of his pantaloons, and a piece of himself in addition. He was for several weeks fitted only for election to some standing-committee — the shell chipped him.

Dec. 12. Sat. First Sergeant James M. Hodgdon of B is promoted to Sergeant Major of the Thirteenth — a most excellent appointment. He is six feet tall, straight as an arrow, lean as a rail, popular, thoroughly posted in his duties, sharp, active, quick, prompt, and perfectly cool when under fire. Col. Stevens makes a speech to the Reg. while on Dress-parade. He, his wife and other ladies who have been visiting the Reg. here in camp, are to go North to-morrow.

Dec. 13. Sun. A violent thunder storm to-night; wind, rain, hail, and lightning all at once, and very much of them all. Tents are blown down, chimneys upset, log-houses unroofed, and the earth-work defenses badly washed and gullied. Col. Stevens leaves camp this morning for the recruiting service at Concord. Lt. Col. Storer starts for home on leave; Capt. Dodge succeeding him in command of Ft. Tillinghast. Adjutant Boutwell and wife, and their little boy, also Assist. Surgeon Small, of the 10th N. H., and his wife arrive in camp about 6 p. m.

Dec. 14. Mon. Rainy forenoon. Company drill in afternoon. Capt. Julian of E returns to his company; Adjutant Boutwell returns to duty and relieves Lieut. Durell, who has acted as Adjutant for a long term, and who is now very sick. All this relieves Lieut. Thompson of E from the command of that company, which he has held for about four months. A Lieutenant in command of a company receives $10 per month extra pay for that service — and far more kicks than coppers at that. Lt. Col. Storer is badly hurt, by an accident, in New York city to-day, as we learn by telegraph.

Dec. 15. Tues. Warm, windy.
Dec. 16. Wed. Very chilly, clear. Reg. drilling.
Dec. 17. Thurs. Pleasant; showers. Reg. drilling.
Dec. 18. Fri. Fair, cool. Reg. drilling.
Dec. 19. Sat. Cool. These Saturdays, at noon, are the regular days for target practice — artillery, infantry, cavalry, all together. The big guns make a great deal of noise. The infantry firing is done chiefly in volleys. Frequently it is done about like this: " Fire by battalion; Battalion, ready, Aim — Fire!" Thrrrip-rrip-rip-ip; follows the volley. Next Monday morning the last seven men and a 'half' are drilled at firing, in the awkward squad; and forget all they learn before Saturday comes again. There was one volley well given yesterday by seven regiments; and 2,500 or 3,000 muskets all fired at once reminds us of the opening volley which we received at the hands of the rebels in the night assault on Marye's Heights, Dec. 13, 1862 — a crash.

Dec. 20. Sun. Fair, very cold. Usual Sunday duties. New Hospital of the 13th finished and occupied to-day.

How to bake army beans: Dig a hole in Virginia clay two feet wide, six feet long, and three feet deep, and keep it full of burning wood for several hours. At night — Saturday — put in the camp-kettles full of beans prepared as for an oven, and cover the hole. Sunday morning serve hot. Warranted equal to the best 'Boston-baked' — especially when the whole matter is managed by Andrew Hanou.

Dec. 21. Mon. Fair, very cold. " A $1,000 negro astride a $150 horse makes a colored cavalryman." (Lt. Col. Smith.) As things have changed, however, in Dixie land, the horse will fetch the most money. Reg. at work on military road in rear of forts and trenches.

Dec. 22. Tues. Cold, windy. While the Band is playing at guard-mounting this morning, the valves in the instruments keep freezing, and the music is very bad indeed — a compound of squeaks, yelps and blares. After a little, a small dog — a homely small dog — appears and coolly takes a seat on the ground, a little way to the front of the Band, looks the players full in the face, screws his own face into a most comical, droll and pitiful expression, and begins to whine and howl. He proceeds with his accompaniment all the time while the Band is playing. The scene is a severe strain upon military discipline, nearly causing both Band and guard to break up in laughter. Inasmuch, however, as no one has been specially detailed to kick that particular dog, Army Regulations cannot permit any interference. Later, by special order, this dog is excluded from parades.

Dec. 23. Wed. Snowy, windy, freezing day. Report now has it that we are to visit the south Mississippi country for a campaign this winter. " Lt. Col. Storer was hurt (in New York) — his shoulder broken."

Capt. Julian.

Dec. 24. Thurs. Cold, clear. The men at Fort Rodman dig an opossum out of his hole. He feigns death — plays 'possum — most admirably. He is subjected to very severe handling, almost torture, but cannot be made to exhibit even a sign of life. At last he is laid out on his back on a board, in the sunshine, and we hide behind a pile of lumber to watch him, Presently he opens one eye, then the other — and then in a twinkling there is a streak of opossum a hundred feet long in the midst of a long line of dust. He disappears as if upon the wings of the wind.

No soldier in the army ever hangs up his stocking for the favors of Santa Claus ; the holes in heel and toe so generally comprise the most of that garment, that the leakage would be in excess. One only piece of folly could equal it : that of the Admiral who had his fleet of vessels provided with numerous large casks filled with water, so that if the vessels should run aground, the water could be poured overboard — and lift them off.

Dec. 25. Fri. Fair. Christmas. The 4th R. I. boys celebrate the day with games, races, a banquet and other festivities. The Brigade Band furnishes some excellent music for the occasion. The natives here and the negroes make very much of Christmas ; and they collect in large numbers, and witness to-day's celebration with evident great pleasure.

Dec. 26. Sat. Cold. Sergeant Batchellor of D writes from his commissary tent at the contraband camp : " Darkeys being paid off make a finer show than any circus in the land ; you should see the ivory come in sight as they receive the greenbacks ! Two thirds of them do not know a one from a five dollar bill."

Dec. 27. Sun. Pleasant, warm. A First Sergeant's duties on Sunday are a burden ; and if he ever finds any time for rest, it must be when he is dead, too sick to move — or promoted to a commissioned officer. A part of his Sunday duties are the following, which are the same, and worse, in every infantry regiment in the service :

First. He must manage somehow to wake and get up in the morning before any one else in his company, and before the Reveille sounds.

Second — daylight. Reveille and Roll-call. First Sergeant must call the roll of his company, and find the whereabout of all absentees, no matter where they are ; must notify each man in the company — 50 or 100 of them — as to all that the men are to do on this day ; must make details for camp guard, and half a dozen various other jobs, and set the rogues, under a Corporal, to sweeping and cleaning camp, police duty — where there is no need of it. During this time the whole company stands shivering and grumbling.

Third — six o'clock a. m. Breakfast. First Sergeant must see to it that the men have a good breakfast, whether rations are good or not ; and also see that the men behave well while getting it, for the soldiers are 'passed around' to their victuals, every man his own waiter, and all waiting too long. The men march in single file past the cook's tent, with their plates and cups, get their 'divvy' (portion), and then go eat it where they can. Breakfast done, the men grumble half an hour.

Fourth — 7.25 a. m. Surgeon's call. Tune : " Come and get yer quinine, ye lame, sick and lazy." First Sergeant marches the 'sick' men — often a sorry display of transparent, malingering deceits — up to the Surgeon's tent, to be examined and dosed, and if it be to them possible, to be excused from all duty for 24 hours. Those thus excused are expected to limp slowly back to their tents, close them, and then to stand on their heads, dance a fancy jig, or turn somersaults for ten minutes. First Sergeant in accordance with the Surgeon's order writes on his list of three to a dozen names, what each of these sick men is to do during the day — and he must see that they do it. The Surgeon excuses some from all duty, designates others for light duty, orders some to be put on double duty for shamming, doses several and damns the balance ; after which the men grumble for about twenty minutes.

Fifth — 7.45 a. m. First Sergeant reports the number of men in his company, fit for duty, to the Adjutant. The Adjutant calls all the First Sergeants to his tent several times during every Sunday, by a peculiar tap, made by the drummer. Certain men are wanted at each time, and each First Sergeant must run all over camp to find them. He is now tired, and just as he has parted his coat tails to sit down on a stump and rest a little — the tenth vain attempt he has already made this morning to gain a moment's rest — "rap-tap-tap," sounds the drum for Guard-mounting. Now he has another race all over camp; his temper begins to toss, and he makes a few remarks. Every company has one laggard at least; and in each, also, some men must be substituted for others a few minutes after the last moment — fate and Sunday invariably conspire to this end, and never fail to accomplish it. This causes serious grumbling.

Sixth — 8 a. m. Guard-mounting. First Sergeant has now a half hour's job at this nonsensical show, in which something always goes wrong on Sunday. The regimental Officer of the day can always give sharp points to a Field Marshal of France, and on any Sunday would drum him out of camp. After a time this most pompous and truly 'poppy-cock' ceremony of all in the army is over and done, and the First Sergeant hurries back to his company to prepare for inspection — which is preceded by universal grumbling.

Seventh — 9 or 10 a. m. Regimental Inspection. First Sergeant must get his company at once in line in the company street, or elsewhere, and then he must carefully look all his men over from top to toe; then appears the Inspector; and the men's arms, tents, clothing on and clothing off, are examined, and comments made to most greatly annoy, or to praise, individual cases. All not praised are insulted of course — and ninety-nine out of every hundred commence grumbling.

Eighth — 12 noon. Dinner. A Sunday dinner is the best to be had — banquet is no name for it. First Sergeant marches the men up to the company-cook's tent for their rations. No matter how good the dinner may be, the boys find it 'not half so good as their grandmother used to cook,' and it is not satisfactory. A part of the cook's regular duties is to stand up and be 'camp-lingoed' by seventy-five men; still he is in despair on Sunday, and the more he explains, and the more badly he feels, the worse they belabor him — and grumble. A noted grumbler in the Thirteenth found a mule's shoe snugly tucked into the piece of boiled beef given him for a Sunday dinner. The cook said by way of explanation that 'ther beef-critter must have swallud ther mule.' Still the man grumbled about it! Supper we omit to mention, for it is ten times meaner than the breakfast or dinner — the hash of both re-hashed. After dinner is over First Sergeant goes and writes a lively and cheerful letter home; telling his mother how contented he is, how happy, and what delightful companions the men of his company are, how he is anxious to meet the foe, spoiling for a fight, etc., etc., and stuffs his letter plumb full of patriotism and piety.

Ninth — sunset, Dress-parade. First Sergeant has just had a nap in which he takes a sleigh-ride with his sweetheart — in a dream interrupted in the nicest phase by the malicious drum — and he wakes up, with both eyes shut, and starts to get his company promptly in line. The parade is formed. At the Adjutant's order: "First Sergeants to the front and centre — March!" and when they get there, "Front — Face. Report!" he salutes and reports, with a wonderful elocution and marvelous distinctness, "ComnyJayallpresncounndfor!" and returns to his place, proud of his soldierly appearance, prowess and lofty rank. At Dress-parade religious services are held — when thought necessary. The Thirteenth, however, are all considered so very good, and exemplary, that such services are frequently omitted — and not made very strong at any time. This is as it should be, of course, but, nevertheless, the moment the men break ranks, they all fall again to grumbling.

Tenth — 9 p. m. Tattoo. Roll-call by the First Sergeant; and a few gentle words about the morrow. By this time the men are all sleepy, yawning and grumbling.

Eleventh — 9.30 or 10 p. m. Taps. Lights must be put out in the company tents; but there is no suiting anybody on Sunday. The men want to read or write a little more — like a boy when it is time to go to bed — and the First Sergeant, now three quarters dead, must go from tent to tent, and see that the lights are put out at once. You can hear his persuasive voice shouting — with disgust and wrath — at twenty successive tent doors: "Lights out here — do you hear?" amid unpleasant remarks, and much grumbling, made by the men within them.

Thus the Sundays wear by, turning one after another like the crank of an old up-country cider-mill going slowly round — screak, screak — grumble, grumble — screak: and the First Sergeant falls late to sleep, to dream of home and peace; but to wake before to-morrow's Reveille (if he can) and again hear — though he does the best he may — the daily round of grumble, grumble, grumble. True it is, his lot is not romantic on a Sunday, but he himself never, never grumbles — he is utterly nauseated with it.

There is one other man in the Reg. who never grumbles — the Hospital Steward. He has not had time since he reported for that duty to squeeze a grumble-word in edgewise, besides he is not a grumbling person. He is an overworked man, and how he endures the strain is past comprehension. His horse has been a balky mule, many of his patients are negroes who never saw a physician before in their lives, his duties all done in defiance of weather, while time, place and circumstance have his interests in no regard. The next in order of men of all work, and of unending work, are the Sergeant Major and Adjutant. But these, however harried and hurried, have less of drudgery to perform, and deal more with the few officers than with the many men. The ten First Sergeants in a regiment do more work than any fifty of the other persons in it.

Dec. 28. Mon. Rainy all day. Capt. Stoodley returns to the Reg.

Dec. 29. Tues. Fair. Reg. in camp. The army hard bread — made of flour, salt and water — though a trifle harder, probably more nearly resembles the sunburnt bricks of Babylon than any other modern contrivance. Men at lunch along the roadside, on a halt in their march, or at a short rest in their work, break off small, irregular, jagged pieces of this bread, put them into their mouths, and move their jaws over the unyielding mass — looking for all the world like cattle eating flint corn on the cob, or a lot of cows chewing pieces of brick. Ask any soretoothed Veteran if this is not a true sketch. This is what is meant by "gnawing hard-tack." Once in a while a good fat maggot appears in a hard-tack, and then the lucky owner must encourage his appetite, while he is blamed for cheating the Commissary, that is, procuring fresh meat without orders. Maggots in army bread prove it a good article.

Dec. 30. Wed. Very fine day. Reg. in camp. A long procession of fifty queer little covered carts drawn by cattle and mules, and packed with children, household goods and provisions and accompanied by many men and women on foot, each one with a bundle, plods slowly past our camp — refugees from North Carolina. The most of them white people. Nearly every man, woman and child in the party of two hundred or more is about half naked ; they save their clothing by carrying it in a bundle.

Dec. 31. Thurs. Rainy. Reg. mustered for pay by Lt. Col. Coughlin, 10th N. H. A great deal of drilling has filled nearly all the fair days of this month.

The Subs have taken a new dodge to escape the service : they purposely shoot off the index-finger of their right hands, the finger used to pull the trigger of the gun in firing. After several cases of the kind have occurred, the trick is discovered, and Asst. Surgeon Sullivan suggests to Col. Stevens to give notice to all that the next case of the kind will be punished by having the finger dressed without chloroform or ether. In a few days, however, one of the guard purposely blows off the end of the index-finger on his right hand — it is a clear case. True to the notice given, the finger is properly dressed without the use of any anæsthetic. He is a big fellow with a strong voice, and bawls most vehemently. The job hurt of course, but without doing him any especial injury. No more index-fingers were blown off in the Thirteenth after that noisy case. The majority of these fellows were a pernicious lot. Many were good soldiers ; the rest gave early indications of their unhandy genius.

## 1864.

Jan. 1. Fri. Cloudy, warm morning ; afternoon clear, cold and very windy ; much damage done to tents. "To-day is the anniversary of President Lincoln's Emancipation Proclamation. A review of Gen. Wilde's negro Brigade at Norfolk, and a great time among the negro population."
Taggard.

Jan. 2. Sat. Very cold, windy, clear. Reg. in camp. Suffolk occupied by several thousand Confederates. An extra force sent from our camp to garrison the Union works at Bowers Hill.

Jan. 3. Sun. Fair. Lieut. Thompson of E starts for home on a twenty days' leave of absence.

Jan. 4. Mon. Rainy, cold. Reg. in camp. Whenever a body of troops moves hereabout, the natives — men, women and children alike — ply the men with questions of all sorts. The most prominent of these queries are: "How many air ye?" and "Where ye at, now?" One of a group of half a dozen adult natives asked of us one day: "What rigimunt air ye?" Thirteen replied: "We are the A-Onceters;" and passed on, leaving the group discussing what State that could possibly be.

Jan. 5. Tues. Cold, cloudy. Officers at work on Pay-rolls. A member of the 13th writes: " 'T is a common failing of soldiers to know just what is going to transpire weeks before it never does transpire."

Jan. 6. Wed. Cold, snowy at night. The New Year commences with a rush of re-enlistments in the old regiments. In one of them all the men but five have re-enlisted; in one brigade all but about sixty. "These are the sort of men the Confederates do not wish to meet — trained soldiers and volunteers."

Jan. 7. Thurs. Cold, cloudy; a very stormy night, with hail and snow. Lieut. Saunders goes home on leave. A tent in Co. E takes fire to-night and burns up, with nearly everything in it; no person hurt.

Jan. 8. Fri. Cold, stormy — hail and snow. Too cold for outdoor work; none done nowadays excepting imperative duties. A magnificent theatre has been built in camp — and the amateur entertainments in it are still more magnificent.

Jan. 9. Sat. Cold, clear. The weather reminds us of Fredericksburg; but our quarters are now palaces to the freezing and water-soaked dens of those days.

Jan. 10. Sun. Cold, clear. Reg. in camp. "My house is $11\frac{1}{2}$ feet by $13\frac{1}{2}$ feet (on the ground), and after living in small tents I almost feel lost in it, because it is so large. Asst. Surgeon Sullivan returned to the Regiment to-day. He was married during his absence. Adjutant Boutwell made a sleigh out of a box, hoops, etc., and yesterday took the ladies visiting our camp out sleigh-riding." PRESCOTT.

Jan. 11. Mon. Warmer. Reg. in camp. The 'upper crust,' among the native population we have met, hold themselves aloof with much disdain and haughtiness. The lower million are exceedingly inquisitive and talkative. We soldiers therefore naturally think that the upper tier do not know enough to be civil, and the lower tier do not know enough to keep still; and we turn from both to the great middle class, who, as everywhere, are the honest and honorable people of this great Southern land.

Jan. 12. Tues. Pleasant. Reg. inspected by Lieut. George A. Bruce, Act. Asst. Inspector General on Brigade staff. The 8th Conn. leaves for home on a Veterans' furlough.

Jan. 13. Wed. Warm, cloudy, disagreeable day. Reg. still in camp. Forty-six men sent from the Reg. to join the Invalid Corps.

Jan. 14. Thurs. Cloudy; very muddy. Reg. at work on a corduroy road towards Portsmouth. Lieut. Durell starts for home at noon on leave of absence.

Jan. 15. Fri. Clear, pleasant; toward night rainy. Reg. in camp. Charles W. Green commissioned Captain, and George N. Copp First Lieutenant in the 25th U. S. Colored Regiment.

Jan. 16. Sat. Pleasant. Reg. in camp. Capt. Betton's wife arrives in camp. Many Northern ladies are visiting here this winter, and on pleasant days the many riding parties make the camp attractive. Gen. Heckman assumes command of this line, relieving Gen. Getty. Gen. Weitzel at Norfolk.

Jan. 17. Sun. Very fine day. Inspection in the forenoon. Parade and religious services at sundown. Small-pox breaks out in the contraband camp.

Jan. 18. Mon. Rainy. Reg. in camp. During the whole autumn and winter, detachments from the 13th have been sent on picket duty — for a week at a time — on the Union outposts in the swamp; one of them at the 9th mile-stone on the Seaboard and Roanoke Railroad. The 13th has also supplied men for a long provost-guard line, running across the country west of Portsmouth; from Hall's Corner on the Portsmouth road, about two miles below camp, north to Scott's Creek. Several of the officers take their meals at Mr. Savage Baker's house, at Hall's Corner.

Jan. 19. Tues. Fair, cold, windy. Reg. in camp. Occasionally the boys find a small supply of a fine native wine, made of Scuppernong grapes, at the citizens' houses in the country; the citizens generally realizing a high price for it. The vine is never pruned, and is trained on large trellises, raised six or eight feet above the ground. The boys no sooner visit a new bit of the country here than they begin to interview the citizens about Scuppernong — but where the Confederate soldier has preceded them the demand exceeds the supply.

Jan. 20. Wed. Pleasant. Reg. in camp. Thirty-three recruits arrive in camp for the 13th. Great excitement in the Connecticut Brigade. Many men of the 13th visit their camp, and about thirty are arrested and lodged in the guard-house, for absence from our camp without leave. Lieut. Staniels returns to the Reg. for duty, from absence on recruiting service.

Jan. 21. Thurs. Pleasant. A large detail at work on the defenses. The 15th Conn. leaves our Brigade for New Berne, N. C. The 16th Conn. also departs for the same locality. Last night they burned up their quarters, causing a large conflagration, cut down their flag-staff, and made their camp a scene of desolation. They depart in anger; do not want to go. The whole Connecticut Brigade moves away. Our Brigade would have gone instead, but was too small.

Jan. 22. Fri. Pleasant. Reg. in camp. Hard work now for the troops on this line. It is very lightly manned; not more than 4,000 or 5,000 men all told, for six or eight miles of defenses.

Jan. 23. Sat. Very warm. Thermometer indicates 83° in the shade, 93° in the sun; a January thaw, indeed. The 23d Mass. moves upon the ground vacated by the 16th Conn. The 9th N. J. also moves to ground near the Thirteenth; and for the time Col. Steere's Brigade (ours) consists of the 10th and 13th N. H., 4th R. I., 9th N. J. and 23d Mass. regiments.

There are now but four of the men in our regimental Hospital. All these are convalescing, and are moved into the Dispensary, a large room, and the Hospital is cleared and cleaned for a Military Ball. John A. Bullard the Hospital cook, constructs a gorgeous chandelier of pork-barrel hoops and many-colored tissue paper, and swings it from the centre of the hall, lighted with candles placed in the shanks of old bayonets. Many flags and streamers give color to the walls. The music, by our Band, is as usual very excellent. There are fourteen ladies present, and a large number of officers of all ranks. The writer is absent in New Hampshire, and therefore cannot write very fully of the occasion. One incident, however, makes sport for the entire camp. Some of the visitors, and many outsiders, gain access to Hospital Steward Prescott's medical stores, and find a large supply of cough mixture, new, fresh and strong. Mistaking it for whiskey, they imbibe very freely, and about thirty of them soon enjoy a spry and lively little ball of their own in rear of the building. The chopping seas of the wild Atlantic never saw thirty sicker men than the tartar emetic in that cough mixture furnishes on this occasion. No play is complete without a touch of comedy, and these amiable gentlemen are not slow in furnishing it; while the lookers on nearly laugh their eyes out of their heads, at seeing this large group of victims to misplaced confidence assume postures and attitudes, and "throw up their immortal souls," as Mark Twain says, and swear heartily between the paroxysms at their most ridiculous and humiliating blunder. Rich — rich it was. They dance no more to-night — at our Military Ball — and in the absence of wheelbarrows, a number of them ride home on stretchers — being most seriously wounded from the bottom of their stomachs to the top of their pride. Prescott gives the facts.

Jan. 24. Sun. Pleasant. Many of the men have a day off, along here, and visit Fortress Monroe, Norfolk, Portsmouth, etc. A large party made up of the officers of the Thirteenth, and of other regiments, secure an engine and cars, and make an excursion on the S. & R. Railroad to within three miles of Suffolk. A number of ladies, officers' wives and others, accompany the party, which is supplied with an efficient guard. No accident occurs, and all return much pleased with the expedition. Chaplain Jones holds a prayer-meeting in the regimental Hospital to-night; similar meetings are held nearly every Sunday evening.

Jan. 25. Mon. Pleasant. Reg. in camp. Negro troops doing provost duty in Norfolk; keeping the white people in order. On a visit to Norfolk one can see white Southerners, arrested for sundry misdemeanors, working on the public streets, under negro guards. This punishment is meted out to all who have willfully and maliciously torn up the culverts and bridges, and damaged public property. It is quite a change to see, in Norfolk, negroes forcing white men to work, at the point of the bayonet; calling out to them: "No loaf'n dar!" "Move quicker, Sah!" "Hurry up dar, Old Whitey!" and similar orders. Tables turned!

Jan. 26. Tues. Pleasant. Reg. in camp.
Jan. 27. Wed. Very warm. Thermometer indicates 87° in the sun. A soldier of the Thirteenth writes: " All the one-horse officers and men have a four-horse opinion of themselves."
Jan. 28. Thurs. Hot — for winter. Thermometer indicates 93° in the sun. Reg. at work on the defenses. ' Limpsy ' is the way we feel — and work.
Jan. 29. Fri. Hot. Thermometer indicates 93° in the sun; too warm for the Reg. to work. The negro school established in the contraband camp is largely attended, and in a very flourishing condition.
Jan. 30. Sat. Cooler; a heavy rain at night. Reg. in camp. Order received that all persons in the camp and vicinity must be vaccinated, soldiers, citizens and negroes. Surgeon Richardson leaves camp for Washington, D. C.
Jan. 31. Sun. Cold, cloudy, misty. Reg. in camp. Sixty-four recruits arrive for the Thirteenth, in charge of Lieut. Sawyer of I and Lieut. Thompson of E. Lieut. Thompson was at home on leave, and while there was detailed as part of the escort for this body of recruits, reporting at Concord Jan. 26th. They left for the front on that day. Lieut. Sawyer was taken sick at Baltimore, and for nearly three days the recruits were held without guard in that city. Lieut. Thompson collects them in their quarters, the loft of an old tobacco warehouse, explains the situation, and takes the word of honor of every man of the party, that they will not desert if they have their freedom from a special guard and are not marched out to the fort. They are then allowed to go wherever they may please, only promising that they will assemble in the loft every morning at nine o'clock. They all keep their agreement, excepting one, who deserts. The rest of them scour the city for him, swearing that they will bring him in dead, if he will not come alive; but they are unable to find him. They regard him as having disgraced the whole party. The most of these men made good soldiers.

This incident is noted in the interest of human nature, so called, which none but fools ever attempt to despise. Honesty and honor are the basis — the very spirit — of everything in mankind that is worth having at all; as its measure is great or small in a person, so that person is godlike or satanic, every time and everywhere. Even love and purity must be true and honor bright.

Feb. 1. Mon. Cold, rainy. Reg. in camp. About ten miles from here the rebels make a little stir, by capturing a Union gunboat and about one hundred men. President Lincoln orders a Draft of 500,000 men to serve for three years or for the war; and in the Northern States the cold shivers run down the copperheads and cowards till their boot heels freeze to the snow. " Hospital Steward Prescott taken sick to-day with small-pox." TAGGARD.

Feb. 2. Tues. Cold, rainy; very muddy. Reg. in camp. The recent little movement of the enemy makes orders more strict in our camp. The Thirteenth loses a good officer in the resignation of Lieut. Young.

First Lieutenant William H. H. Young was born in Barrington, N. H., May 15, 1837, and at the breaking out of the war was engaged in business in Roxbury, Mass. He enlisted as a private Aug. 9, 1862, was soon after appointed a recruiting officer for the State of New Hampshire, and proceeding to his old home in Barrington he united with Lewis H. Buzzell and Hubbard W. Hall in recruiting and organizing Company F in the Thirteenth. Sept. 19, 1862, Buzzell was mustered in as Captain of Company F; Young as 1st Lieutenant, and Hall as 2d Lieutenant; their commissions from the Governor bearing date of Sept. 27, 1862. Capt. Buzzell was taken very ill on the day of the muster, and for nearly two months the command of Company F devolved upon Lieut. Young. Capt. Buzzell rejoined the Company at Camp Casey near Fairfax Seminary. When the Thirteenth moved to join the Army of the Potomac under Gen. Burnside before Fredericksburg, Lieut. Young was left at Camp Casey on account of sickness, but five days later he was, by order of Gen. Casey, placed in charge of 283 enlisted men belonging to Col. Wright's Brigade, and sent with them by boat to Aquia Creek. Already broken in health, this care and labor prostrated him for several weeks, and severe illness prevented his engaging in the battle of Fredericksburg and in the movements that followed.

From Jan. 30 to Feb. 7th, 1863, he served as Judge Advocate of a regimental Court Martial. Again, May 26, 1863, he was appointed to the same special duty, and still again, on June, 30, 1863, at Yorktown. The latter was a 'Drum-head' court, short, sharp and decisive. The cases tried at these regimental courts martial were almost all for misdemeanors under the crime of desertion. At Newport News he was for a time placed in command of Company A. Here he had a severe attack of malarial fever, and March 13th was sent to U. S. General Hospital at Hampton, Va., reporting for duty again on May 14th, the Thirteenth then removing from near Suffolk to Getty's Station. Company F had previous to this time united unanimously in a request for Lieut. Young's promotion to the Captaincy, to take the place of Capt. Buzzell killed at the battle of Providence Church Road; but the condition of his health would not warrant his remaining in active service, and the commission was issued to Lieut. Forbush.

Continuing in the service, however, contrary to the advice of friends and Surgeons, he took an active part in Gen. Dix's expedition up the Peninsula to Hanover Junction in June and July 1863, commonly called in irony the Blackberry Raid, but really one of the severest summer marches made by infantry during the whole war. He was placed in command of the rear-guard on the forced march from Horn's Quarters to Ayletts — see July 5, 1863 — and at the halt there laid down from sheer exhaustion, and slept for several hours on the ground of a cornfield with no cover or protection whatever, contracting acute rheumatism and dysentery, which became chronic, and from which he has never fully recovered. On arriving in camp at Getty's Station, he was sent to Balfour

General Hospital, at Portsmouth, Va., for treatment. Here he tendered his resignation, which was not accepted, but he was granted a leave of absence for twenty days, which was afterwards extended to sixty days. Returning to the Hospital at expiration of leave, he was examined by E. B. Dalton, Surgeon in charge, and found unfit for active military service. He again tendered his resignation, and on Feb. 2, 1864, he was honorably discharged the service upon a Surgeon's certificate of disability.

In January 1863, three men deserted from the Regiment and were carried as prisoners to Newport News. Believing that their action was hasty and ill considered, Lieut. Young interested himself in their behalf, visited them and finally succeeded in having them released without trial. All three afterwards made good soldiers, performed their duties well in all the subsequent battles in which the Regiment engaged, were promoted to non-commissioned officers, were mustered out with the Regiment in June 1865, and still bear the scars of wounds received in honorable service.

Feb. 3. Wed. Pleasant, cool. Reg. in camp. Pay-rolls signed, and a part of the Reg. paid off.

Feb. 4. Thurs. Cool, windy. Reg. in camp. Paid off for four months by Maj. R. C. Walker. Hosp. Steward R. B. Prescott sent to small-pox Hospital sick with that disease. Is sick there seventeen days, and finds it a fearful place ; probably he meets with the worst experience of his whole life. The Hospital is located near West Branch.

Feb. 5. Fri. Very pleasant. Reg. in camp.

Feb. 6. Sat. Pleasant. Reg in camp. The 13th furnishes the outpost pickets in the swamp, for this week. Capt. Farr returns to duty. Capt. Forbush officer of the day, Lieut. Sawyer officer of the camp guard. " Guard-mounting ceremony executed as well as in the Regular Army."

It was a negro cabin much frequented by soldiers of the lower type, and the source of much drunkenness, sickness and mischief generally, and finally the decision was reached to break up the affair. In charge of the posse sent to arrest the parties was a young and handsome Lieutenant, but somewhat fat and ruddy, and rather short. He had no sooner entered the cabin than he was seized by a strong and quite good-looking young negro wench, spry and lithe as a cat. She threw both of her arms around him, under his own arms, and gave him a hug like a bear, exclaiming: " O my nice little man ! O my nice little man ! " and much more of the same appreciative sort. In the struggle to be free from her, he fell, and they both came to the floor ; when there ensued an exhibition of Anglo-African wrestling and struggling altogether past description. They waltzed procumbent all over the room, kicking over the chairs and tables, breaking dishes, covering the floor with food, butter, slops and water ; getting into the fireplace, scattering the ashes, and becoming both of them thoroughly bedaubed with the dirt upon the floor. It was a regular cat and dog tussle. Finally the Lieutenant won the battle, and the cabin, its contents and its crew went speedily beyond further opportunities for mischief in our vicinity. On the return to camp the Lieutenant reported the party's success to his Colonel; but requested that some other officer might be sent to "mop up the next old negro cabin that must be cleaned out."

Feb. 7. Sun. Cloudy, lowery, chilly. Usual Sunday morning inspection, and parade at sundown. Chas. H. Tarbell of B discharged to receive a commission in a colored regiment. Eleven men of the Thirteenth have been thus commissioned. Lieut. Murray detailed as aide-de-camp on the staff of Col. Steere commanding our Brigade.

Feb. 8. Mon. Fair. Reg. in camp. The colored men enlist very freely. They often choose the arm of service which they enter from their fancy for certain colors; some preferring one color, some another — choosing the infantry for its blue, the artillery for its red, the cavalry for its yellow. When a young negro has enlisted, and returns in full regimentals, to bid his friends good-bye, he struts like a turkey cock, and bubbles over with grinning chuckles, while the old men and women throw up their hands with a hundred benedictions, the girls languish for a glance of his eye, and the children run after him in wonder, with their mouths and eyes wide open. The whole negro race seems to be governed by instinct, rather than by reason.

Feb. 9. Tues. Fair. Reg. in camp. Very little doing nowadays. A large number of men, however, are to-day at work on the main road from camp to Portsmouth; covering a long piece of the old road bed with heavy corduroy. It is heavy business, we are using large logs and very long ones.

Feb. 10. Wed. Fair. A detail at work on the defenses. A special picket sent to the outposts. There was a rousing Republican political meeting held in camp last night. A man of Co. H confined temporarily in the guard-house is taken sick with small-pox. His misdemeanor is necessarily excused for a season.

Feb. 11. Thurs. Fair. Regular monthly inspection in camp by Lieut. Geo. A. Bruce. "All looked first-rate," he says.

Feb. 12. Fri. Fair, windy. Part of Reg. at work on the defenses. Another case of small-pox in Co. H.

The outpost picket from the Thirteenth located at the 9th mile-stone on the S. & R. Railroad have their reserve tent pitched upon a platform made of railroad ties placed on stringers thrown across the railroad ditch, which is three or four feet deep, nearly dry, and is used as a receptacle for all waste and odd scraps of rations thrown away. One night the reserve were awakened by sundry sounds of snuffing, eating and gnawing beneath their tent, and one of the men went out cautiously to investigate the cause. Just as he had stooped into the ditch to look beneath the tent, there was a short series of grunting growls, and a sudden rush of two animals past him, hitting and nearly knocking him over in their haste; two nearly full grown black bears driven by hunger were having a quiet midnight lunch, that was all — but the investigator's hair went on end, and would scarcely comb down smooth again for a week.

**Feb. 13. Sat.** Fair. Reg. in camp. One man of the 13th writes: "Coming here to camp from home is much like moving from one prominent place, mentioned in Scripture, down to another."

**Feb. 14. Sun.** Cloudy, disagreeable day. Usual Sunday duties.

**Feb. 15. Mon.** Cloudy, rainy. Reg. resumes daily drill. Capt. Betton of K sick in his quarters with small-pox. Small-pox very prevalent at Norfolk; a low type, resembling varioloid, but occasionally violent. The disease has continued among the citizens about here for a year past. Capt. Smith leaves camp for Concord on recruiting service; the wife of Capt. Forbush, and other ladies, leave camp for home, under his escort. Lieut. Staniels placed in command of Company H.

**Feb. 16. Tues.** Cold, a regular gale of wind. The army sings many songs and hymns, but the song of 'Old John Brown' is the favorite song of all; and always sounds best when sung with the extra note at beginning, and one of the best verses is as follows:

"Old John Brown's body lies a-mouldering in the ground,
His soul is marching on.
On John Brown's grave the heavenly stars look kindly down,
His soul goes marching on.
Glory, glory, hallelujah. Glory, glory, halle-hallelujah.
Glory, glory, hallelujah,
His soul is marching on."

**Feb. 17. Wed.** Fair; coldest day of the season. Company drill. The outposts are so far from camp that pickets go out for a week at a time. Some men and officers volunteer to remain, and stay out two weeks; preferable to dull camp life. Asst. Surgeon Morrill thrown from his horse and severely injured.

**Feb. 18. Thurs.** Fair, very cold, a high northwest wind. Snow and dust are having a lively high dance all throughout camp. A little fall of snow to-night.

**Feb. 19. Fri.** Fair, cold. New Berne being invested; Gen. Peck is there; every hour we expect to hear the officers-call, from the Colonel's Hdqrs., and the publishment of orders to proceed at once to New Berne. There is a ripple of excitement every time a mounted aide comes into camp. The Thirteenth prefers to join the Army of the Potomac.

**Feb. 20. Sat.** Fair; very cold. The poor Subs have as many nicknames as characters, and all as ugly. The name applied to them most is the "boughten men," that is men who have been bought with a price in money. There are, however, among them some very excellent soldiers, brave, trusty and prompt.

**Feb. 21. Sun.** Fair, cold. Usual Sunday duties. Five more commissions fall to men of the Thirteenth for positions in colored regiments — sixteen in all. "Prescott returned to Reg. to-day from the small-pox Hospital." TAGGARD.

**Feb. 22. Mon.** Fair, warmer. No drill. Reg. in camp. In reference to rations it may be well to say that they are issued, in accordance with the supply, for periods ranging from one day to ten days. There is an immense amount of waste caused by rations spoiling after they are issued, and before they can be consumed.

Feb. 23. Tues. Fair, fine. Reg. drills forenoon and afternoon. Asst. Surgeon Morrill goes home on sick leave.

Feb. 24. Wed. Fair. Company drill forenoon, Battalion drill afternoon. Dress-parade at sundown.

Feb. 25. Thurs. Fair. Drill all day. Dress-parade at sundown. A case of small-pox in Co. F.

Feb. 26. Fri. Very windy, very dusty. Usual drills all day. George T. Woodward, David E. Proctor, and Charles B. Saunders, all of B, receive their commissions in colored regiments.

Toward evening a fire, fanned by this hard southwest wind, breaks all bounds in the slashing, in front of our works, south of the Suffolk main road in the swamp, and the whole Reg turns out on the double-quick to put it out. The fire, however, soon gets into the logs, which we have piled up for a breast-work, to be manned by the 13th in case of a rebel attack — see Aug. 20, 1863 — and destroys a long stretch of them. After burning over an area of the slashing more than a mile square — near to the front and left of Fort Rodman — the fire, roaring terrifically and unapproachable, suddenly takes a new direction, the wind changing, and surges over into the standing timber also. The slashing is dense, heavy, very dry, and the mass of flame is simply tremendous, and in both the slashing and forest presents a magnificent display as night comes on. Hunting out the huge bull pines, their sides besmeared with pitch, the fire leaps in a moment to their very tops, perhaps a hundred feet, and they become literally pillars of fire.

Feb. 27. Sat. Fair, cold. No drill. Reg. resting — tired from fighting the fire. Lieut. Thompson of E with about 50 men watched all last night by the fire in the swamp; coming into camp about daylight looking like a gang of coal-heavers, and pretty well used up. They could accomplish little, however, in the way of checking the blaze. A great number of unexploded shells, thrown into the timber in the gunnery practice, were bursting, all night, providing showers of chunks of iron; but one man was hit, however, and he more scared than hurt. The fire originated near a white trash cabin; purposely set or not, no one can tell.

Feb. 28. Sun. Very windy. Usual Sunday duties. Many citizens hereabout wish above all things that affairs were now the same as five years ago — sick of secession. Public men, however, do not change; one minister in Norfolk preaches too much in favor of secession, and is sentenced to work as a street-sweeper for three months.

Feb. 29. Mon. Cold, rainy. Reg. mustered for pay by Col. O. Kuse, Jr., of the 118th N. Y. Fight at Deep Creek — a skirmish. The 118th N. Y., 10th N. H. and a force of cavalry sent down this morning. We are ordered to be in readiness to move.

On the whole February has been generally a delightful month, so far as the weather has been concerned. Duties have been light, the men kept busy without any especially hard work. Our quarters are exceptionally fine. If any one is sick, he is removed to our finely arranged and appointed regimental Hospital — built under the immediate supervision of Surgeon S. A. Richardson — and elegant in point of architecture and convenient in plan. If any one is turbulent, he is placed in our log-made guard-house, a roomy and attractive building, to cool off. If any one is "sad and sorry," he has convenient choice of three fine theatres near by, one of them also all our own. If any one is religiously inclined, he will find these theatre buildings well filled by religious meetings assembling on every Sunday. In fact the camp is a model winter quarters for an army. There is a great deal of singing in camp — never so much before. Our regimental Band plays very finely indeed, and serenades are frequent. Many of the officers' families are in camp, and receptions and riding parties are fashionable and numerous. We have had a brother of the actor, Henry C. Barnabee, in the Thirteenth — evidently a chip of the family block. A concert or a play can be put on the boards at a few hours' notice, by our numerous village amateurs and glee clubs; lady visitors in camp often taking parts. In short our winter camp much resembles a New England village, just a little over-stocked with men, and the children away on a visit.

March 1. Tues. Sunshine and showers. Usual drill. A large detail from the Thirteenth works the most of the day repairing the log breast-works burnt out by the late fire in the swamp. These commence a little south of Ft. Rodman and the Suffolk road, and continue, across a very wet place, for half a mile or more. The men, dressed for the work in old cast-off clothing, return to camp as smutty as a regiment of charcoal venders. Applications are made for the legal voters of the 13th and 10th N. H. to go home to vote at the New Hampshire annual election — a twelve days' leave being required. The 8th Conn. return to camp here from Veterans' furlough, having been absent for nearly a month. Half a dozen Connecticut regiments have visited home this winter, and enjoyed a grand good time. While the 8th Conn. has been absent, about 200 of its men, chiefly Subs, have been training in the 10th N. H. It is said that the 13th barely escaped a similar nuisance. Along the front, rebel guerilla parties are numerous and very troublesome. They attacked our troops at Deep Creek yesterday, capturing a Lieutenant and several men. The 10th N. H., 9th and 118th N. Y. and the 8th Conn., are under orders to proceed immediately to that point, and the Thirteenth ordered to keep in readiness to move at once.

March 2. Wed. Fair. Usual drill. At Dress-parade this afternoon the announcement is read that the officers and men named in the applications of yesterday are granted twelve days' leave of absence — from the 4th to the 16th of March — to go home and vote, their transportation free to their homes and return. All are to wear side-arms, and to be on special duty and under military orders; that is, the officers are to take their sword and belt, and the men to take their bayonet and belt, and are to wear them wherever they go, and when they vote. This is done because threats have been made in New Hampshire, that the soldiers should not come home and vote; though each man is a legal voter in the town where he goes to vote. The injustice of this threat is scandalous — characteristic, however, of the copperheads. Lieut. Thompson of E distinctly remembers the satisfaction he experienced — and notes it here merely as a common reminiscence with his comrades in other places — while taking his squad of six men, himself and all armed as per order, up to the polls in Durham, and all voting together the straight Republican ticket. There was no need of arms in Durham, but men were there in the town meeting who indulged in threats, and who would have prevented these seven soldiers from voting — though all of them were legal voters — if they had dared to attempt their threatened opposition. The average able-bodied stay-at-home, army shirk, and copperhead, has no appetite for cold steel taken endwise. This is noted as a picture of the times. Under the caption 'Voters,' we will follow this expedition to their homes and return.

March 3. Thurs. Fair. Capt. Stoodley, being the ranking officer of the Thirteenth, not joining in this voting expedition, takes command of the part of the Reg. remaining in camp. Bullets and ballots are now to shoot at the same target — The Slaveholder's Rebellion.

Voters, 390 officers and men of the Thirteenth and Tenth N. H. Vols. take cars at 6 p. m., and are delayed until 1.30 a. m. of March 4th, when we start for New Hampshire. Cheers and swinging of hats. Inasmuch as the enemy is now threatening our front, there is much hesitancy about sparing these 390 men just now; and we have been nearly all day trying to get out of camp, starting and halting several times. About 4 p. m., however, an orderly appears in camp with the welcome order for us to take cars at once; and we march to the station amid the cheers of several thousand soldiers — and nearly as many of the colored people, who somehow understand the meaning of our journey.

March 4. Fri. Pleasant. Reg. in camp. No drill. Orders arrive for the Reg. to be ready to march at a moment's notice. Troops are being landed at Norfolk and Portsmouth, and hurried forward to the front near Suffolk; including also the 23d Mass., a colored battery, and a regiment of colored cavalry. They are easy and graceful riders; a negro sits a horse as if he and the horse were all in one piece.

Voters after a long delay leave Getty's Station at 1.30 a. m. to-day on cars; go to Portsmouth, and at 7 a. m. embark on the steamer 'Guide.' They pass Fortress Monroe at 10 a. m. The sea very smooth.

March 5. Sat. Very pleasant. Reg. in camp, ready for an immediate move. No passes granted to any one to leave camp. About 200 men only of the Thirteenth are now left in camp, and who are fit for duty. These are consolidated in two companies, by order of our Brigade commander. Capt. Betton commands one company, Capt. Forbush the other; Capt. Stoodley in command of the Reg. and camp. The Subs regard this as their opportunity, and give any amount of trouble ; but are handled with a quick severity that quiets their vicious ardor for a season. We of New England never before saw such men as these.

March 6. Sun. Pleasant, cool. Reg. in camp. Large bodies of troops moving past camp towards Suffolk. Four regiments of colored infantry pass by ; and about 2,000 cavalry with Gen. Judson Kilpatrick at their head, go forward to the front about noon. This movement promises an early spring campaign. Heavy skirmishing last night, several miles this side of Suffolk, with the advance of Stuart's rebel cavalry. Gunboats are shelling the woods ; trains loaded with artillery are moving towards the front. It all reminds us of the siege of Suffolk.

Voters have it a little rough outside. They are due at Boston to-night, but will not get there — too much bad weather. The Captain of the ' Guide ' is suspected by some of disloyalty. There are two opinions, however. At any rate we move too slowly, even for the condition of the sea.

March 7. Mon. Fine day. Reg. in camp. The enemy has retired, and our troops occupy Suffolk again. As quiet returns our troops move back toward Norfolk, and to-day are passing our camp continually, The 23d Mass. return to their camp — our nearest neighbors. The most of the men of the 13th left in camp volunteered to go on the picket lines at the front, during the recent affair with the enemy near Suffolk.

Voters. The 'Guide' comes to a dead standstill in a dense fog and heavy rain storm, near Wood's Holl, this morning, and lays at anchor all day. Out of patience, about 30 officers and men of the Thirteenth — including Capt. Julian and the writer — leave the steamer and go on shore in small boats. There they charter a cranky, schooner-like fishing smack, and sail to Mattapoisett, after a terribly rough little voyage in Buzzard's Bay ; and thence go by cars to Boston, arriving early this evening. The ' Guide ' secures a pilot, gets off about 6 p. m., and reaches Boston about midnight. The Captain of the ' Guide ' is a Democrat, it is said. The fog is very dense, but the delay exasperating. It is said that some of the passengers, who remain aboard the steamer, threaten the Captain towards night, and give him his choice to move at once for Boston, or they will send him to Davy Jones's locker. He prefers Boston ; and moves as soon as he can get up steam. A furious northwest wind soon arises and blows the fog out to sea.

March 8. Tues. Rainy. Reg. all quiet in camp. " In the theatre built by the Thirteenth, at the minstrel performance, about 10 p. m., one of our boys is stabbed in the bowels. Asst. Surgeon Sullivan treats the case in our Hospital."

Voters debark at Boston at one a. m. The ' Guide' ought to have reached Boston Sunday night, March 6th. Those who left the ' Guide ' at Wood's Holl, and came up on the train from Mattapoisett, had a quiet night, last night, with friends, in Boston. All go north on this morning's trains. Those who go via the Boston & Maine Railroad, strike a wash-out at New Market, and are further delayed there, for two hours, and have to walk half a mile or more to reach another train, backed down to receive them, and the other passengers. Seven voters reach Durham at 11 a. m. and go to the polls, as ordered, wearing their swords, belts and bayonets — side-arms. Many belonging to the interior towns of the State lose all opportunity of voting, on account of the delay of the steamer in Wood's Holl. On the whole a hard, close piece of work, only about two thirds of the whole party having an opportunity to vote. All go to their homes for about one week's furlough.

March 9. Wed. Showery. Our pickets again driven in by the enemy, and about twenty of our cavalrymen at the front are killed and wounded. The 2d U. S. Colored Infantry have a severe brush with the enemy near Suffolk. At 11 p. m. to-night the Thirteenth is called out suddenly, is at the Station, a quarter of a mile from camp, in twenty minutes — quick work. Then rides in the cars, over a rickety road at a breakneck speed to Magnolia Station, and then marches back to Bowers Hill, about five miles, nearly using up the night. The road very muddy. The 13th for this trip is commanded by Capt. Stoodley, and is consolidated in five companies of about forty men each, under Captains Farr, Betton, Forbush and Carter, and Lieut. Staniels, and has 60 rounds of ammunition per man. The 13th is joined by the 23d Mass., Col. Chambers, and three companies of the 118th N. Y. Companies B and D are relieved at Fort Tillinghast by a battery from the 13th N. Y. Heavy Artillery, and move forward to the front near Bowers Hill.

March 10. Thurs. Showery. Reg. encamped at Bowers Hill, Companies A, C, E, H, I and K, consolidated in three companies under Capt. Betton, are ordered to the front, and march again to Magnolia Springs. Last night's expedition was a regular rush, using up the night, and as there is much heavy cannonading to-day at the front, the troops are held under arms all day; equipments on, blankets rolled, canteens and haversacks filled — all ready for an instant move.

March 11. Fri. Rainy, cold. Capt. Betton's command returns from Magnolia Springs to Bowers Hill. The rebels have again retired. Their late action is regarded as a mere feint to cover the departure of their immense provision and forage trains. They have stripped, robbed and impoverished a vast extent of their own realm, carrying off everything they could lay their hands upon, that could be of any possible use to an army. Refugees report it a worst devastation than troops usually make even in an enemy's country.

March 12. Sat. Fine day. The rebels have withdrawn from the Suffolk front. The Thirteenth is relieved by the 118th N. Y., and marches from Bowers Hill to camp down the main Suffolk road, now wet, muddy, rough and terribly cut up by teams, cavalry and artillery. We learn that hereafter a larger force is to be maintained in that most uneasy place, Bowers Hill, and that we shall not again be called upon to visit it as guards or pickets.

March 13. Sun. Clear, windy, dusty. Reg. in camp, and resting from their hard jaunt up to the front and back. The Subs behaved very well indeed on this occasion while at the front. Some of them are very fine soldiers. They are most troublesome in camp. The 23d Mass. with artillery is left at the front. During this whole breezy little affair the portion of the Thirteenth left in camp, in the absence of the voters, is divided up arbitrarily into little provisional companies.

March 14. Mon. Pleasant. Reg. in camp. Every man held in readiness for any emergency. President Lincoln calls for 200,000 more men — this makes 700,000 in six weeks. We are a part of a mighty army, one of the greatest ever marshaled in the history of the world — and we could whip the numberless host of Xerxes' barbarians in fifteen minutes, and before we got within a mile of them.

March 15. Tues. Pleasant. Reg. in camp — enjoying squad drill by way of diversion. Surgeon Richardson ordered on duty at our Brigade Hdqrs.

Voters leave Concord this morning at 10 o'clock, and go via Lawrence to Boston, arriving at 2 p. m. Embark on the steamer 'Guide,' at the foot of State street, in the afternoon — a close connection by many and some are left behind — and at 4.30 p. m. cast off for the 'sacred soil' of the Dismal Swamp in Virginia.

March 16. Wed. Clear, cold. Squad drill. Major Grantman returns to the Regiment.

Voters have a lively shaking up while weathering the cape and the island region; stormy, cold, and the sea rough. "Lieutenant, hold up, you swear too much." "No Cap. you misunder-(hic) hear me ; I never use profane l— (hic) liquor." That was what he said, as he walked the deck straight as a bee line. A drunken man and a drunken ship in their union of movement constitute absolute steadiness.

March 17. Thurs. Pleasant. Squad drill, amid clouds of dust.

Voters having a quiet trip. The 'Guide' sails about as swiftly as molasses runs in winter. A story goes the rounds aboard that a rebel cruiser knows of our voyage, and is waiting to swoop down upon us from the high seas, and gobble us all up, or down, as suits his temper best. A delightful nightmare to sleep with, and some there are, who are not a little scared by it. However, we pass Fortress Monroe to-night at midnight in safety.

March 18. Fri. Pleasant. Squad drill. Laura Keene playing at Norfolk. Many soldiers attend. The 10th N. H. goes to Great Bridge, 15 miles distant. They are to engage there in picket and scouting duty, and in fighting guerillas. Asst. Surgeon Morrill reports for duty from sick-leave, though not fully recovered.

Voters leave Fortress Monroe about noon, debark at Portsmouth, and arrive in camp at 3 p. m. — two days late. A furlough of fourteen days ; two splendid ocean voyages ; an enjoyment of the glorious right of suffrage ; a lift at the wheels of Government ; and a smart rap on the copperheads' knuckles — all free of cost to us. Quite a number of the voters are now arrested for absence without leave, when they could in no way avoid it; all passes over, however — and we again settle down to the business of holding the United States together.

March 19. Sat. Pleasant. Reg. is whole again. No drill. Dress-parade at sundown. And now, in the spring sunshine, the former slave-boy, having passed into the Union, through yonder picket line and stockade-gate, stands a Freeman ; dons the waiting uniform — yellow, red or blue — of his choice, becomes a proud Union soldier, and begins to earn greenbacks ; and glowing resplendent — almost — of color, eyes and ivory, well blacked shoes and new shining buttons, salutes you with a jolly " Goo'-mornin' ! " Bless us, how many such a happy one we have seen in these last few weeks ! " Out of the Confederacy " — " Into the Union " means a whole new world to them.

March 20. Sun. Pleasant. Reg. in camp ; usual Sunday duties.

Voters who failed to reach the ' Guide ' before she left the wharf in Boston have come straggling into camp, to be promptly put under arrest for absence without leave, but nothing comes of it. The number is but small. The absentees must needs be regarded as on duty all the time until their return to camp. There is no evidence of their endeavoring to shirk ; and their time is reckoned as 'lost in action.' This is the last item of a very pleasant little journey undertaken to teach copperheads silence and subordination.

March 21. Mon. Cold, windy. Company drill. Half a dozen men and officers tramp to Norfolk, four miles, to serve as witnesses at a court martial.

"Three officers and 113 men sent to Portsmouth last night to serve on provost-guard duty." LIEUT. TAGGARD.

"Receive orders at 11 p. m., March 20th, to take charge of one hundred men, to go to Portsmouth and relieve the 4th R. I., now doing provost-guard duty there. We start at 12 p. m., and relieve the 4th R. I. at 1.30 a. m., March 21st." LIEUT. STANIELS.

March 22. Tues. Severe snow storm with high wind ; nearly eight inches of snow falls. The guards and pickets have to tramp through it, two long hours at a stretch. We never saw a worse snow storm in New Hampshire so late in March. Reg. fortunately in camp. These snow storms appear to come here in local showers (literally streaks). Eight inches in depth of snow falls here ; a mile away fifteen inches are reported, a little farther away, none at all. Companies B, Capt. Dodge, and D, Capt. Farr, which have been serving as Heavy Artillery and garrison at Fort Tillinghast since August 1, 1863, to-day rejoin the Regiment. As Capt. Dodge — ' Old Father ' — puts it : " Returned from exile in Siberia." Capt. Smith, who has been detached on recruiting service at Concord, has been relieved at his own request, and returns to duty in the Regiment.

This region has many very estimable ladies, and the writer may be pardoned for mentioning one of them, a young lady of perhaps eighteen years, Miss Edith Baker, daughter of Mr. Savage Baker, residing at Hall's Corner, a mile or so west of Portsmouth, their home called "Rosedale," a family from Eastern Shore, Md. Inheriting several slaves with an estate, she promptly gave them their liberty. Finding many children in the neighborhood of Portsmouth unable to attend the public school — if there is any — she gathers them into a free private school, and becomes their teacher. Many a sick soldier — Union and Confederate alike — has received aid at her hand; and in return both citizens and soldiers grant the family every possible favor.

March 23. Wed. Stormy, clears at night. The wind has blown a gale for twenty-four hours, upsetting tents and blowing down chimneys. Reg. in camp. Instead of drill, we have snow-balling. Thousands of men at it all over camp. Quarter-master Morrison leaves for home this morning. The voters on their return are put on duty at once to a man, and given the worst places, so as to relieve the soldiers and Subs who remained in camp. Capt. Goss returns to the Reg. to-night.

"My chimney smoked last night so that I could not see; so I took the fire-brands and threw them out of doors, and went to bed." PRESCOTT.

This was the experience of nearly half the entire camp, the driving rain and the water from the melting snow, washing out the mud mortar of the chimneys and rendering them useless, while the water leaked and dripped in through every crack and cranny of the huts and tents.

March 24. Thurs. Clear, cold, windy. Reg. in camp. Nothing doing except repairing quarters injured in the late storm. Too much snow for drill; but the fun at snow-balling is enlisting everybody from drummer-boy to general. Everybody takes a hand, and the soldiers take sides, all up and down on the camp's main street; long lines of active men, so far as one can see — squads, companies, regiments. No school-boy play; but a battle to win in dead earnest, with solid shot at close quarters.

The Thirteenth is gratified to learn that George H. Taggard, its Commissary Sergeant, is to receive a commission as Second Lieutenant in Company F.

All officers and men return from their visits to the North much improved in health, appearance and weight, showing clearly the difference in effect between the Northern climate and good food and shelter, and these army rations, half housings, army life and exposures, and this soft climate and flat, enervating, tide water, stagnant water region of pestiferous forests and generally pervading rot; all together engendering diseases that kill and destroy faster than all the rebel bullets and shells.

From the high tone of bravado and defiance that early characterized much of the Southern war-poetry it has dropped to bitterness and the tone of a desperate and almost hopeless struggle, and to pathos, religion and epitaph strangely mingled. That much of the Southern war-poetry is wonderfully brilliant none can deny.

Of the thousands of Northern war-poems, many of them from the most gifted pens, and marches and songs, not one in a hundred finds a responsive echo in our army, and is sung, repeatedly read or committed to memory. The poetry of a people perhaps exhibits the spirit of the times more clearly and deeply than their prose; but the Northern army needs no stirring up, no special incitement to great deeds, and the poetry written with that end in view falls a dead, flat failure. The patriotism of this army exceeds the patriotism at home, average for average.

March 25. Fri. Pleasant, quite warm, too much snow and mud for drill. Every brigade in the Confederate army has a special corps of sharp-shooters, about 200 men, armed with Whitworth and Enfield rifles. They are the first in an advance, the last in a retreat. Practically a band of robbers; taking all that is of value from every Union soldier whom they kill or capture, and are systematically encouraged in the privilege — guerillas in action, if not in name.

March 26. Sat. Rainy last night, and a cold, windy, disagreeable day to-day. The camp a world of mud, snow and slush.

This is a dull sort of a day in camp, and we may as well tell what happened to a pair of horses — as we hear the tale. Two mounted officers in a near department had spirited and valuable horses; and as they are too smart to stand second anywhere, they want their horses to be in the warmest place on a certain steamer, and so take them well up forward, tie them securely, feed them and leave them. Next in the rear of these two horses come the Government mules. In the morning — by the bright light — when these two fine horses are taken off the steamer, it is discovered that the mules have, during the night, gnawed the hair entirely off the tails of both of them, leaving an ungainly whitish caudal prod sticking straight out behind, not good as against the flies — or for anything at all. Everybody knows that when the spurs are struck to a horse, the first thing he does is to elevate his tail; so these two army horses do duty for one day at least, with their tails working jerky-like, up and down, like a pair of stubby, white pump-handles. Now a horse with a perfectly hairless tail is not a thing of especial beauty, or a joy forever, to any man, on high grand parade in close conjunction with himself a brilliant staff officer — such a bald-headed tail on his horse utterly spoils the generally elegant, bold, centaural effect. There is no way out of it now but a wig, or peeling the entire hide off both horses. Two dead horses' tails are sought, made into rear chignons, or wigs — a false hair show anyhow — are tied on, and so worn until the new hair grows out. But at first the whole camp smiled aloud.

March 27. Sun. Cold. Usual Sunday duties. Lieut. Oliver returns to camp from home: bringing with him a 2d Lieutenant's Commission for Commissary Sergt. George H. Taggard. Capt. Smith returns to the Reg. from New Hampshire.

March 28. Mon. Fair. Squad and Company drill. Three Lieutenants and above 100 men, from the 13th, have been detached as a

Provost-guard in and about the city of Portsmouth. Hardly men enough left in camp to properly guard it. Details called for in every direction.

March 29. Tues. Cloudy morning and rainy night. Cold. Reg. in camp. " Worst rain storm of the season; everything flooded; chimneys blown down; roofs and walls of our houses are like sieves," writes a man of the Thirteenth.

March 30. Wed. Cold, windy and wet. Reg. in camp. Company drill. The 13th furnishes men for an interior picket line, at the junction of the Deep Creek and Gosport roads, two miles from camp and half a mile from Gosport. Capt. Dodge has had much to do on this line, and knows every resident within a wide circuit; and is an authority upon their moral, mental and secessional conditions.

March 31.[1] Thurs. Fair. Reg. in camp. Squad and Company drill — bad. Lieut. Charles H. Curtis of C has been serving for a couple of long terms as Judge Advocate of courts martial; first, in the last part of the summer of 1863, at Portsmouth, Va., followed by a leave of absence to visit home in the fall; second, upon his return from leave, by special order of Gen. Butler, in the winter of 1863-4, at Norfolk, Va. Because of long residence, and extensive acquaintance, in these cities, and eminent fitness for the position, he is placed in command of a Provost-guard, at Portsmouth, consisting of two Lieutenants — Dustin and Sherman of the 13th, excellent men for the place — and one hundred picked men, all of the 13th. The Reg. furnished this detail on March 20th; all the Companies being equally represented in it, after the ranks of the Reg. had been filled by the return of Companies B and D from Fort Tillinghast on March 22d. For an account of the steamship disaster to this detachment, see May 11, 1864.

April 1. Fri. Chilly, foggy, rainy, misty, windy, muddy, sloppy and in general a 'foolish' sort of day. Reg. in camp. No drill. Col. Stevens returns to the Reg. this p. m.; has been absent at Concord, Hilton Head and New Orleans since December, engaged in re-enlisting the 3d, 4th and other New Hampshire regiments. Mrs. Stevens accompanies him to camp. Gen. Grant comes to Norfolk by boat, but does not land.

April 2. Sat. Very rainy. Reg. in camp. No drill. Lieut. Durell returns to the Reg. Has been absent since December; now returns a married man.

April 3. Sun. Cold, raw, cloudy. Morning inspection, and at

[1] It may be well to note some of the rapid changes in this month: February 29th Congress revived the grade of Lieutenant General; March 3d this official title was conferred upon Maj. Gen. U. S. Grant, then at Nashville, Tenn., in command of the Army of the Tennessee. March 9th he arrived in Washington, was duly invested, and on March 11th returned to Nashville, where he assumed command of the Armies of the United States, relieving Maj. Gen. H. W. Halleck. March 19th Lieut. General Grant leaves Nashville, after reorganizing the Western and Southern Armies; and on arriving East, on March 24th he reorganized the Army of the Potomac, Maj. Gen. Geo. G. Meade retaining command. Henceforth Lieut. General Grant is chief in command, next the President, of all the armies of the United States.

evening a Dress-parade. Col. Stevens assumes command of the Regiment. One Captain in the 13th writes: "Two of my 'Subs' are going into the navy, two are in jail, one is locked up wearing a ball and chain, and one is in the small-pox pest-house." This is the sort of timber that represents sundry men in New Hampshire who have more money than courage; and therefore do not volunteer, and when drafted hire this material for substitutes. Not an unfair representation, perhaps.

April 4. Mon. Cold, cloudy. Reg. in camp. Nothing doing. Twenty-four men go to Fortress Monroe for examination — to be transferred to the navy; mostly Subs of the uneasiest kind.

April 5. Tues. Heavy thunder showers. Reg. in camp. Nothing doing. All along here, as usual, regular details go on picket, in the swamp, near Portsmouth, at Deep Creek, Scott's Creek, etc. We have a severe April thunder storm. A part of the pickets near the Gosport road take refuge from the storm in the buildings of one Mr. Ivy. He has one son at least in the rebel army, and a spirited daughter of pronounced secesh opinions, but with a pretty face and name — Nettie Ivy. The Southern people of every station, exhibit great taste in the selection of names for their children.

April 6. Wed. Bad weather. The pickets are having a rough time of it. Not one warm, agreeable, sunny day for a fortnight or more; everything drenched.

April 7. Thurs. Fair. In the Reg. now, turns of special duty come every fifth day — officer of the day, officer of the guard, etc. — all well mingled with jaunts on picket. There is no pleasure in being kept awake all of one night in every four or five, and tramping half the night in the wet and brush and mud.

April 8. Fri. Fair. Fifteen hundred men are being selected from this Department for transfer to the navy. They are allowed to volunteer. The call enlists some of our worst Subs, and a few unhandy volunteers, for whom army life is too tame.

April 9. Sat. Rainy. Reg. in camp. Burwell, photographer, Norfolk, makes a specialty of taking pictures of soldiers for their sweethearts at home, and thrives on the business. Proving Tennyson's line: "In the spring a young man's fancy lightly turns to thoughts of love." On hundreds of passes the line is written, "—— requests a pass to visit the photographer's in Norfolk;" and that is just now a fashionable cover for all errands to the city.

April 10. Sun. Pleasant, showers. Forenoon inspection, afternoon parade. "These inspections are an invention of the Adversary, to cause good men to swear on Sunday." So one soldier writes. Our Brigade is now detached, and doing about all the picket, guard, garrison and provost duty in the entire circuit of this post and camp. Other troops are drilling and preparing for active service. To-day Mrs. Capt. Dodge, Adjt. Boutwell, Musician Critchley and Chaplain Jones make up our 'Theatre Church' choir; so called because the theatre building is occupied by a religious meeting on Sundays.

As the spring advances the prospect of severe contests rises clearer before us, and the Union Army is ready for them. The great will of the North has resolved that the Union shall be restored in peace, that slavery shall utterly cease and be gone; and that the battle shall stay on these alone. The soldiers are in full sympathy and accord with that will, and of course must do the necessary work, hence a stern determination united with enthusiasm pervades the Union Army. The fearful experiences of the Fredericksburg battle and camp are overlooked or out of mind, as well as minor disagreeables; and practical and effective patriotism rules the hour, with strong wills and physiques to back it.

April 11. Mon. Warm. Reg. in camp. Signs of an immediate move. The mail service here is abominable. Three days ought to bring our mail from Boston here; but letters come along anywhere from four to twelve days late — any time that best suits the careless, lazy mail, or the mail-censor at Norfolk.

Nothing can exceed, or describe, the pathetic scenes connected with the soldiers' mail. A letter is opened by a man, and gives the news of his child's, wife's, or near relative's death, sudden and unexpected. He instantly seems to shrink within himself; and goes to his tent in silent, hopeless sorrow, as a man in chains, and mourns for many days. He is not soon, if ever again, the man he was. Another suddenly learns that his wife has been unfaithful to him. He crushes the letter in a nervous grasp, and almost seems to sink into the ground. In a few days he has turned into a dullard or a brute; and he is never again the man he was.

April 12. Tues. Pleasant. Reg. in camp. Quarter-master Morrison returns to camp from home. Our Brigade moves out to the drill ground, west of camp, to drill; but we are driven in by a shower. Just about the time when the Thirteenth is quietly settled down for the night, between 10 and 11 p. m., the 'Long-roll' resounds throughout the camp. In less than half an hour — one says in less than twenty minutes — the 13th is formed in line and arrives at the railroad station, a quarter of a mile distant. A regular rush, but all in perfect order. We go by rail to near Magnolia Springs, there leave the cars and march to near Suffolk, and there lie on our arms all the rest of the night.

To those who do not know what the Long-roll is, we will say that on every drum in camp, great and small, an incessant roll is beaten, as loudly as the drums will bear, and continuing until the troops are all roused and in line. While pouring all through a large camp at dead of night, it would rouse the fabled Seven Sleepers themselves. It is the night call to arms and battle, and the wildest sound known to an army.

April 13. Wed. Fair, warm. The Thirteenth marches early this morning to its old camp-ground near Suffolk — had in March and April 1863 — now looking forlorn enough, and remains there during the day and to-night. Pickets are posted on old familiar ground, but no enemy appears as then. We miss the stir and noise of the siege. Capt. Grantman, on court martial duty at Portsmouth, rode up with our mail last night, and overtook the Reg. on the road beyond Magnolia Station — a long, hard ride. The Thirteenth has never been so healthy as now. The regimental Hospital is almost empty, and the Surgeon's-call is but little attended.

April 14. Thurs. Warm, clear. The 13th breaks camp at Suffolk, at daylight, and in company with the 23d and 27th Mass., and the 8th Conn., all in light marching order, and about 1,700 cavalry, marches up through Suffolk, and 11 miles beyond; then turns to the right toward the Nansemond and moves down until noon; and then returns at night to its old camp of May 1863, near Jericho Creek, two or three miles below Suffolk. A march of about 30 miles. The men endure the long march very well indeed, though in one spurt we march 15 miles in four hours. Many fall out of the ranks. The whole coast, full of inlets, rivers and bays, is infested by smugglers and guerillas, and especially about Smithfield and Chuckatuck; and a combined naval and military expedition is now made to break up their combinations. The outposts report seeing a body of rebel cavalry and infantry, estimated to number some five or ten thousand men, but not near enough to bring about a collision with our immediate force, and we of the Thirteenth serve merely as a support. The 118th N. Y., Col. Keyes, crosses the Nansemond at Halloway's Point.

Lieut. Taggard christened his new shoulder straps by going on his first duty, as officer of the camp-guard, on the morning of April 12th, and remaining in charge of camp during the absence of the Regiment, until this morning — 48 hours.

April 15. Fri. Warm, fair. Thirteenth called at one o'clock a. m. We take cars and return to Camp Gilmore, arriving about 5 a. m.; all pretty well tired out by the long hurried march, and the loss of sleep. The recent expedition might be called a reconnaissance in force by cavalry, supported by infantry; the latter expected to keep up with the horses, and to halt for a rest only when the men on horseback get tired.

"April 12th; called out at 10 p. m., take cars for 'Horse Hospital,' where we laid down for the remainder of the night. 13th; we go up to the old camp-ground and stop over night. 14th; we fall in at 5 a. m., start upon a reconnaissance at 5.30, cross the creek at 7.30, and proceed towards Smithfield. Halt at 11 a. m. for dinner. Start upon return at 12.30 p. m. Arrive at Jericho Creek at 6 p. m., and encamp. 15th; arrive in camp at Getty's Station at 5 a. m."     LIEUT. STANIELS.

"Thirteenth was called by the Long-roll at 10 p. m. April 12th, a dark and stormy night. The Regiment was in line in ten minutes after the alarm was given. Took 60 rounds per man of ball-cartridge. Went aboard open platform cars at Getty's Station. Got off about midnight. Arrived at Magnolia Springs (6 miles east of Suffolk) at 2.30 a. m. Ground very wet. Marched about 7 a. m. — April 13th — to Jericho Creek (1½ miles east of Suffolk). Here the 13th loaded their muskets. We crossed Jericho bridge and went up the hill into Main street, Suffolk, now a deserted town. Passed the night of April 13th on our camp-ground

of a year ago. April 14th went out on the Cross Keys road, crossed Miller's Creek, and marched to within half a mile of Chuckatuck Creek. Passed the quarters of many thousands of Gen. Longstreet's men, of a year ago. Arrived back at Suffolk at night, moved down and camped at Jericho Creek. Men much used up. In a couple of hours or so the bugle sounded : ' Fall in.' We marched to the railroad, mounted open platform cars again, and coming back slowly, with frequent stops, arrived at Getty's Station about daylight. A cold night, following a hot day."
PRESCOTT.

April 16. Sat. Some sunshine and much rain. Thirteenth in camp. Inspected by Lieut. George A. Bruce. Paid off to Feb. 29th by Major Greene. More recruits arrive for the Reg. Asst. Surgeon John Sullivan evidently thinks that the business of the Surgeon is to cure men. He has reduced the sick list in the 13th to a shorter measure here than it ever came before. The sick have been so few, and those few so far convalescent, that our regimental Hospital has been twice cleared this winter, without danger or harm to the patients, and the Hospital used for military balls, at which the Band of the 13th has furnished the music.

April 17. Sun. Showery, cloudy, murky, warmish. Inspection. Religious services in the forenoon. Articles of War read to the Reg. by Adjt. Boutwell at 2 p. m. Dress-parade at sundown. Orders received to march to-morrow morning, with three days' cooked rations. The pioneer-corps of the Reg. has been doubled in number, and provided with axes, shovels and picks. Shelter tents are being issued to-day. Officers are required by order to limit their baggage to a single valise for each officer. Preliminaries to an active spring campaign.

April 18. Mon. Pleasant. Reg. in camp. Orders again arrive this afternoon for the 13th to break camp to-morrow morning at daylight, and to march with three days' cooked rations, and to take all its camp equipage. Rumor has it that we are going to Yorktown. The women visiting in camp prepare to leave for their homes to-morrow. The theatre closed with a stabbing affray, a Spaniard in Company H importing the pleasantries of his native land.

# V.

## April 19 to May 11, 1864.

### SPRING CAMPAIGN.

**April 19. Tues.** Very pleasant day. Many officers and men worked hard all last night. Much labor is required in breaking up a camp occupied for so long a time as the Thirteenth has been in this one. Reg. packs and sends away all its surplus baggage, takes down its tents at 6 a. m., and breaks up housekeeping in all respects. The most of the log-houses remain intact, and are to be occupied by the negroes, or by troops coming in upon this line of defenses. Good-bye, Camp Gilmore, winter homes, and neighbors, gentle and ungentle.

The breaking up of this large camp is a sad scene. We have been on this line eleven months. We know hundreds of comrades in neighboring regiments, and nearly all the citizens far and near. We leave articles of furniture, and household conveniences without number. All must be left or given away, scarcely anything can be sold. Friendly citizens are freely remembered in the forced distribution. But confusion reigns : hundreds of contrabands, all ages, are begging and pilfering, and carrying off all they can hold in their arms, or cram into their capacious bags and pockets; little teams, gathered here from the farms in the vicinity and from Portsmouth suburbs, are all about camp, driven by white natives, and all being loaded with plunder gotten by stealing or begging ; many of the soldiers are drunk ; bonfires are fed with numerous contrivances and conveniences the men have made for themselves ; wives are parting from husbands, while the hot tears fall — many of these partings are the last of earth; there are sweethearts here, too, not to be passed unmentioned ; some of the houses, huts and tents are burning — and amid the bustle, smoke and hot hurrying, the lines are formed, company by company, we shoulder arms, turn our backs upon Camp Gilmore, give three rousing, but not altogether spontaneous cheers, file through Mr. Bunting's well trodden field into Portsmouth road, enter the woods, stumble over the worn-out corduroy, and at 9 a. m. are away.

We arrive in Portsmouth, and embark on the steamer 'Escort,' at noon. There is a great deal of delay with teams and baggage. At the wharf, while trying to straighten out sundry irregular matters, Capt. Forbush is pushed overboard from the boat, has his lip and arm hurt, and is obliged to return to camp for treatment. Lieut. Taggard succeeds to the command of Company F. A man of the 13th, named Anderson, falls into the dock and is badly hurt. Finally at 3 p. m. we are away again, and at 5 p. m. land at Newport News. From there we march into the country about three miles, and bivouac on the edge of the timber, in rear of our old camp here of Febuary 1863 in the barracks.

After all we are glad to be again upon the move. Of the 240 recruits — substitutes and volunteers — received by the 13th last autumn and winter, only about one half — and the best half — now remain with the Regiment. A number of good men also have gone from among them — men whose departure we have regretted.

April 20. Wed. Cool, clear, frosty, a little rain p. m. Last night the water near our tents skimmed over with ice, and we had quite a cold bivouac on the wet ground and in the little shelter tents open at one end. We are called at 5 a. m., the day is clear and bright, and after a busy morning we march at 9 a. m. in the direction of Yorktown, for ten or twelve miles, and at 5 p. m. encamp within the old rebel works at the Run above Big Bethel and near Lee's Mills. Roads very muddy.

Some genius for averages has reached the conclusion, that the people of the earth, in a savage state and out of contact with a higher civilization, would have required six thousand years to reach the level of the refined, educated and best class of the English and American people. This century scale of sixty degrees of civilization — and the want of it — is most convenient to use in judging of the events, the rabble, and the abominations of these last three days in this change of camps. Put the people in their places, when you estimate their graces. The black scion of slavery, the denizen of the Dismal Swamp, the F. F. V., the Union volunteer, the 'Sub,' and the sublimely drunk have struck and mingled after a fashion of their own, and altogether too little restrained.

April 21. Thurs. Pleasant, but quite warm. Reg. called at 4 a. m., marches at 6 a. m., arrives at Yorktown at 10 a. m., and encamps at noon, on the plain about one mile from the town, and near where the Hessians were buried. The roads are very muddy and rough and the men have had to pick their way — for long distances — along Gen. McClellan's 'miles of corduroy,' now badly rotted, broken and worn. A storm of wind and rain comes up this afternoon, slackens our linen tents, rips them off the poles, and scatters them and their contents all about the camp. Papers were afterwards picked up on the plain, blown more than a mile from camp.

The men who are in Hospital, either sick or wounded, are of course not able to eat the coarse army rations. The Government therefore commutes these rations, allowing for such men their full value in money. The Brigade or Post Commissary pays this money to the Surgeon in charge, whose duty it is to see that the money is judiciously expended for such food or delicacies as the inmates of the Hospital can eat. This is known as the Hospital Fund; and in the Thirteenth it sometimes amounted to $150 per month, and all our men while in the regimental Hospital were always fed with the best food that could be obtained for them.

The expenditures from this fund were made, and the whole affair was placed entirely in the hands of Royal B. Prescott, while he served as Hospital Steward; the accounts were carefully audited by the Surgeon, and the Hospital of the Thirteenth was among the best furnished and best provided for in the Brigade or Division.

April 22. Fri. Warm, fair. Reg. in camp; no drill. Lieut. Hall assigned to the command of Company F. Many men foot-sore from marching through the mud and over rough roads. Virginia clay when wet is about as sticky as glue in solution; when dry about as hard as glue in cakes and chunks.

Col. W. H. P. Steere, of the 4th R. I., leaves camp to-night, and is succeeded in the command of our Brigade by Brig. Gen. Hiram Burnham, from the Sixth Corps, and formerly Colonel of the 6th Maine. Our Brigade is now the 2d Brig. 1st Div. 18th Army Corps; and consists of the 10th and 13th N. H., the 8th Conn. and the 118th N. Y. The 18th Corps is commanded by Maj. Gen. W. F. Smith — 'Baldy;' and the 1st Division by Maj. Gen. W. H. F. Brooks. Gen. Burnham received his commission April 15, 1864, and is assigned to the command of our Brigade by special request of Gen. Smith. The 2d N. H. moves to Williamsburg, where there is a large Union force.

April 23. Sat. Pleasant. Reg. in camp; no drill. Lieut. Staniels commences acting as Adjutant of the Thirteenth. We have a Brigade Dress-parade — the first one for more than a year. We are encamped within the largest fort the Confederates had near Yorktown, and the left wing of the 13th rests upon the graveyard of the rebel dead. The boys say that 'neither party now cares to disturb the repose of the other; and they prefer to sleep on the top side of a bed like this!' The ground is liberally strewn with old army-iron — pieces of shell, parts of gun-carriages, and a few huge bursted cannon, with varied and abundant rebel camp-gear; a very fine camp and drill ground, however, and reasonably clean and dry.

April 24. Sun. Pleasant, showery. Reg. in camp. Inspection by Col. Smith of the 8th Conn., and a Brigade Dress-parade. Now comes another reduction in the baggage of the Thirteenth, and the general equipment is cut down to the lightest possible light marching order — one suit, and one change of under-clothing. Extras are packed for storage at Norfolk, and must be sent off within five days. The men are writing many letters home to-day; lying flat on the ground and using their knapsacks for desks. During a march many an order and memorandum is written on a soldier's knapsack, while it is strapped upon his back and as he stoops for a moment and rests upon one knee. One soldier of the 13th writing home to-day hits this expedition exactly, with : " Inspection — all day. It has been Inspection and Dress-parade ever since we came to this camp."

April 25. Mon. Fair, warm. Company and Battalion drill. The way to knock at a soldier's door is to scratch the cloth of his tent. When drawn taut the cloth will respond with a coarse drum-like sound, anything but agreeable to hear, and sure to elicit a response from the party within.

Gen. Burnham writes and distributes a volume of orders. An order compelling officers to wear better clothes would be most acceptable. Too many officers are slouching about in blouse and light-blue pants — a private's uniform. Several officers of the Thirteenth, in disgust, sent their measures and orders to Boston tailors in March last for full dress-suits of dark-blue yacht-cloth. The coats made without lining. No officers in our Brigade are now so neatly and well dressed, for this summer's campaign, as they of the Thirteenth.

April 26. Tues. Fair. Company drill a. m., Brigade drill p. m. Gen. Burnham sits on his horse, mounted upon some convenient knoll, and makes his tremendous voice heard clearly by our entire Brigade of four regiments. We have heard no such power of voice before in the army, and the General understands his business thoroughly. The Brigade is handled as easily as a single regiment. The drill is made very spirited ; is relieved of that too common air of drudgery pertaining to such business; every officer and man does his best, and the General frequently compliments his command. Brigade review this afternoon.

It is not the purpose of the writer to go beyond the martial array of the Thirteenth, excepting so far as may seem to him necessary in order to furnish a general framework, within and upon which to place a reasonably clear tableau of that one Regiment — the subject of our story.

The force now organizing here is called the Army of the James ; and consists of the 18th Corps, commanded by Maj. Gen. W. F. Smith, encamped at Yorktown ; and the 10th Corps, lately come up from Charleston, S. C., commanded by Maj. Gen. Q. A. Gilmore, encamped at Gloucester Point. This army numbers, Infantry, 31,872 ; Artillery, 2,126 ; Cavalry, colored, 1,800 ; and a small body of white Cavalry ; also another body of Cavalry — about 2,900 — now operating about Suffolk and the Weldon Railroad, under Col. A. V. Kautz. Making a total of about 38,000 officers and men of all arms, supplied with 130 cannon.

The objective point of the Army of the James, under Maj. Gen. B. F. Butler, operating from City Point and Bermuda Hundred, is Richmond, by way of the south bank of the James River, and also Petersburg. The orders are very clear to move rapidly and capture Richmond.

The objective of the Army of the Potomac, 100,000 strong, now encamped along the north bank of the Rapidan River, under Maj. Gen. George G. Meade, is the Army of Northern Virginia — 62,000 strong — encamped along the south bank of that river, under Confederate General Robert E. Lee, whose earth-works extend to Richmond and beyond.

Both these Union armies will co-operate under the supreme direction of Lieut. Gen. U. S. Grant. He received his commission March 9, 1864, visited the Army of the Potomac March 10th — Gen. Meade's Hdqrs. being at Brandy Station on the Orange and Alexandria Railroad, about 70 miles from Washington — and established his Hdqrs. with that army at Culpeper Court House, and near those of Gen. Meade.

The Army of the Potomac will move down towards Richmond and the James River, by a perpetual extension of the left flank, and unite with the Army of the James either north or south of Richmond, as the results of the campaign may determine.

In this perpetual extension of the Army of the Potomac by the left, as occasion may require or admit, corps after corps will leave its position on the right of the army, march along the rear of the army, and take a new position on the left; whenever possible forcing in Gen. Lee's lines, wherever these left-swinging corps may strike them. This series of movements by the left, is very clearly described by Gen. Lee, as "Gen. Grant's crab-motion."

It will be seen at a glance that no comparison can be drawn between the positions of Gen. Lee and Gen. Grant. It is all contrast. Gen. Lee is entrenched; Gen. Grant is in the field. Gen. Lee commands a line of a few score of miles in extent in the State of Virginia. Gen. Grant commands not only the troops on the line confronting Gen. Lee at all points, but also the entire armies of the United States, now regarded as one line; the Southwestern army the right wing, the Army of the Potomac the centre, the Army of the James the left wing — the whole vast host stretching wide across the region, of plains, mountain chains and a thousand rivers, in the whole broad land from Mexico to Maryland.

April 27. Wed. Fair. Brigade Drill. The 10th Corps is at Gloucester Point and said to be 18,000 strong. Their camp looks grandly from the Yorktown bluffs.

Gen. Burnham is not always choice in his language. A member of the 13th mistook an order on drill, and the General called him a "leather-head." The member had been a shoemaker. A certain jocular Lieutenant in the Thirteenth could not resist the temptation, the next time he met the member, to inquire of him: "How it was that Gen. Burnham could know, at sight, that the member, an entire stranger to the General, was a shoemaker by profession."

April 28. Thurs. Fair; warm noon, cold night. Brigade drill. As a second instance, Capt. Grantman is relieved from court martial duty, at Portsmouth and Norfolk, and rejoins the Reg. at Yorktown. Lieut. Wilson and Sergeant Wheeler return to camp from Concord.

Cooks, and all detached men, are to be fully armed and equipped and to take their turn at drill — that is, are called upon to do double duty. The absurdity of it will be equaled only when all aides serve in their regiments, and at Hdqrs. too. It is the subject of interminable joke, for none can joke like our Army of the James — or "Army of the Games," as the penny-anti fellows call it.

April 29. Fri. Pleasant. Our Division reviewed this forenoon by Gen. Smith, 'Baldy,' on the plain just out from Fort Yorktown, a mile from our camp. A vast cloud of dust rises and hangs over the review-ground, and blue uniforms turn to whitey-gray on all the troops. We look like an army of millers. A three hours' job. Reviews are a nuisance to the private soldier. The attempt at "splendid marching and wheeling" is exceeding hard work; and the standing with a musket at a shoulder for one or two hours, as frequently occurs, seems like slowly pulling one's arm off. Men have been known to drop their guns, from sheer exhaustion of the muscles of the arm and hand.

Brigade drill in the afternoon. Gen. Burnham is fond of drilling in double-quick time; especially when forming hollow squares, and dropping into the position of "Guard against cavalry." It has been so quickly done on several occasions as to shut the General out of the squares. He usually smiles at such times and says, "Well done!" Rough and harsh as he sometimes is, he is generally very popular in our Brigade.

April 30. Sat. Fair, fine. At 8 a. m. the 13th is mustered for pay by Col. A. F. Stevens. Our Brigade has the only Band in our Division — the Band of the Thirteenth. At 4 p. m. a Grand Review of the whole force here, by Gen. Butler. While moving, the troops raise the dust in perfect clouds, obscuring the lines, and when the review is over — a three hours' job — the men look like an army of millers — the same as we did on yesterday. The review-ground is near Fort Yorktown, a mile from our camp; and on returning this evening Col. Stevens causes numerous rapid evolutions to be made by the Reg. and the companies get mixed up almost inextricably. On arriving at the regimental parade-ground, he dismisses the Regiment by commanding the Captains to take their Companies to quarters. Which order some obey by as many orders, as many 'face abouts,' as much noise, loud voice, and racket as possible — all pretty angry. The trivial affair provokes a hot discussion. The puzzle, however, of how-we-got-there, is solved in peace after a day or two, and ends in good nature all round; clear memories reproducing the large number of evolutions with kernels of corn and pebbles.

May 1. Sun. Quite warm day, showery, cold night. Reg. in camp. No inspection or parade. Masonic Relief Association of the 13th meets and reorganizes. Capt. Stoodley succeeds Col. Stevens as President. Lieut. Wilson, returned to the Reg. from recruiting service on April 28th, and to-day is detailed for duty in the 1st Division Ambulance Corps. At 5 p. m. the Reg. is ordered to have four days' cooked rations, and 100 rounds of ammunition per man. Baggage is again ordered reduced, to one valise for each two officers. On account of the company records the Captains fare much the best in these reductions, reasonably claiming the most of the space; while the Lieutenants, unless they carry a knapsack, are situated about the same as the enlisted men. The 1st Brigade of our Division leaves camp.

May 2. Mon. Fair. Reg. in camp, and has the day for personal affairs. Deserter from the 10th N. H. drummed out of camp. Seven New Hampshire Regiments near here — 2d, 3d, 4th, 7th, 10th, 12th, 13th. The sick of the Thirteenth — five in all — sent to General Hospital. Since we have been in this camp the Thirteenth has drilled every day, unless the weather was very bad indeed. More attention than ever before being given to skirmish drill.

May 3. Tues. Fair, warm. Skirmish and Brigade drill. The number of teams is now reduced to one for each regiment — and this makes over-loaded pack-horses of the men. Thirteenth ordered to turn in its camp equipage at 6 a. m. to-morrow. Medical stores placed on barge 'C. A. Darnfield,' in the river.

A negress at Yorktown happened to see her boy — as black as a boot — playing with some white children, and called to him : " Here, you William Henry Harrison, you; come out o' dar. Git 'way fro' dem white chillen — or you 'll git bad all froo'." Soon he disappears within her cabin amid numerous claps of spanking thunder, and solemn voices from the deep. McH.

May 4. Wed. Pleasant. Reg. breaks camp early in the morning. At 4 p. m. embarks on the steamer 'S. R. Spaulding' with the 10th N. H. While the troops are embarking, each vessel, as soon as loaded, moves up the stream — as if that were the intended direction — and anchors. The whole 10th and 18th Army Corps are hurrying aboard as rapidly as possible. At 9 p. m. we proceed down the river towards Fortress Monroe, where we arrive at midnight, and remain until morning.

Wilde's Brigade of colored troops moves up the James in advance of the main army, and lands at Ft. Powhatan. Gen. Hinks lands with a body of colored troops at City Point. Kautz moves against the Weldon Railroad. The Army of the Potomac plunges into the Wilderness. The spring campaign opens with vigor all along the line.

May 5. Thurs. Warm. very fine day. Reg. passes Fortress Monroe at 1 a. m. Boat lays to for a short time, moves again at 6 a m., and at 7 a. m. enters the James River. The long line of steamers, and the hundreds of vessels in view — transports, gunboats, tugs, sailing craft, dispatch boats, monitors, frigates, iron-clads — make a grand display. Our line stretches for miles, consisting of five armored ships and a large number of gunboats, from Rear Admiral S. P. Lee's North Atlantic Squadron, moving as a convoy in advance to open the way, and protect our transports following in a long procession. As this large fleet, or line, of vessels passes along, among the many ships at anchor, or moving hither and thither, sailors man the rigging and cheer, flags and banners wave, bands play, salutes ring out — and there is glory enough for two days crowded into an hour — a grand holiday excursion, a magnificent gala day. Too much show, theatre, splurge, no touch of war at all. Gen. Butler's steamer passes the whole fleet towards the head, and he is cheered by the men on each transport, as his boat rushes past.

The bay and river are very calm, the shores green and fragrant. As the day wears away, and the river banks approach nearer as the river narrows, batteries begin to appear, and towards night we frequently hear the boom of a distant gun. Squads of cavalry appear, and disappear, on the high ground, and we witness on the right bank what appears to be a sharp cavalry skirmish. We pass Fort Powhatan at 4 p. m., and City Point about dark — between 5 and 6 p. m. — proceed up the James

River, and anchor off Bermuda Hundred. As the darkness increases, many of the men turn in, being advised to sleep while they may.

The Reg. debarks about 10 p. m., at Bermuda Hundred, four miles above City Point, and bivouacs near by a little before midnight. This from the writer's memoranda. There are many things requiring attention, and it is long past midnight before the camp is quiet.

Prescott states that we debarked at 12.30 a. m. May 6th. Lieut. Taggard with Co. F states that we arrived at City Point just at night, and landed two miles above there at midnight. Lieut. Staniels writes that we landed at 2.30 a. m. The differences in hours given are probably caused by the divisions made in the Regiment at the time of debarking.

A foraging party from the Thirteenth discover a nice pig to-night, and a rap on his head quiets all squealing. He is killed and divided, and the men are just preparing to cook a portion, when the order comes to fall in. The meat is instantly cut up in small pieces, convenient to carry, and goes to the front rolled up in paper, pieces of shelter tent, or whatever comes handy in the haste. It is said that the most of it utterly spoiled before an opportunity was found to cook any. A little soldier-scene at a dark night's halt in the woods.

## BERMUDA HUNDRED.

**May 6. Fri.** Very hot and sultry. A reconnaissance in force by our Brigade with other troops. The Thirteenth has this morning scarcely got fairly settled in bivouac, when at 6 a. m. we are ordered to fall in; and we at once proceed in light marching order and rapidly about six miles up into the country to a point from which Petersburg can be seen, and apparently about three or four miles distant; here we halt for a short rest. Soon we move again, and without seeming to approach any nearer to the city make a longer halt a little after noon. Petersburg is now in full view, also the Appomattox river and our gunboats. The men are tired, and fall asleep anywhere and anyhow. Detachments from the force commence work on the entrenchments about noon. In the afternoon heavy firing is heard and regular volleys of musketry, showing that the advance has found the enemy in force. We form line of battle at 2 p. m., and moving slowly come under fire about 5 p. m., the bullets quite plenty. The afternoon wears away amid much noise and smoke, but without any special incident in our Regiment; but at 8 p. m. our Brigade is suddenly ordered to the front, by an aide riding up at a furious pace and apparently in great excitement. This makes our blood tingle a bit, and we hope at last that something is to be done; but the order is soon countermanded, and we turn aside and bivouac for the night, in thick woods, by divisions closed in mass. Col. Stevens has been in command of the 13th about half the time to-day. There has been a great deal of noise at the front all the afternoon, and our sleep is not much aided by what is threatened for the morrow — especially if to-morrow shall prove as vexatious as to-day ; but we take as much rest as veteran soldiers will and can under any circumstances. Our bivouac to-night is about three miles from Port Walthall on the right hand side of the main road from Bermuda Hundred to that place. We are said to be six miles up the Appomattox river, and three miles from the Richmond and Petersburg Railroad. Gen. Charles A. Heckman's Brigade is reported to have had a severe collision with the enemy close down upon the shore of the river.

It seems to us as if we have been all day long on the tail end — the wig-wag end — of a badly managed reconnaissance. While the dense underbrush thick with dead and dry laurel bushes has been tearing our clothing like hooks of iron, and the bushes have switched our faces and hands to bleeding, we have marched and countermarched ; moved to the left, and moved to the right ; advanced with a jerk, 'fetched up sudden,' and retreated in haste ; up hill, and down hill ; in woods, in briers, in vines, in dry reeds, in clear ground ; in mud, in sand, in plowed field, in garden, in small grain ; sent out skirmishers, and called them in ; have run, and have crept slowly ; been called into line, rushed at a double-quick for a minute or two, then halted — as if we had struck a snag ; nobody knew where we were, nobody knew where we were going — and nobody seemed to care a pewter sixpence ; heavy firing sprang up in the distance, and then all was as still as death ; ordered to advance along the whole line, and then ordered to lie down before we had moved three rods ; and so on all day long — jerked, shunted, bobbed and walloped about until every-body became angry all through and through, tired out, and cared not a fig what turned up next. As one Thirteen puts it : " They worked us like a big pickerel-bait."

## BATTLE OF PORT WALTHALL.

May 7. Sat. An exceeding hot day. Reg. breaks camp at daylight; at 8.30 a. m. starts off in light marching order, and moves about two miles, then deploys in line of battle, and proceeds very slowly through a densely wooded swamp. Col. Stevens in command of Reg. The 8th Conn. have the advance of our Brigade as skirmishers; the 13th on the right of the line at first and acting as their support. By 10 a. m. the enemy's pickets are hotly engaged, and when we are about four miles distant from our last night's camp; and the firing continues, along the whole line, from this hour, throughout the day and evening — at times very severe, the 8th Conn. losing heavily, their wounded coming back among us in considerable numbers. We are very close up to their skirmish line, and receive the enemy's over-shot bullets and shells in great plenty. The whole Brigade sweeps across in line of battle, on the right of the main road. A few men from the 13th commence firing upon the enemy's men, as they are seen springing up, and running back, from cover to cover, under the steady advance of the 8th Conn. skirmishers. The action of the day is an advance from our bivouac along the main road from Bermuda Hundred to Port Walthall.

The 13th, as a whole, is not brought to a fire, but men were never more desirous to shoot, or charge, or something else with life in it. The men and officers are exasperated by being mere targets, and jerked about among the brush, up hill and down, through bramble, mire and swamp, among spent bullets and bursting shells, among the dead and wounded, all the day long; when the enemy might, by one sudden dash, be utterly routed in three minutes, captured to a man, or be driven flying off the field. To-day is a repetition of yesterday, only worse if anything. The Railroad — Walthall Branch — appears to be the objective point. Beyond some very sharp skirmishing, the 13th do but little excepting to move hither and thither, to suffer and to fret. It seems to some of us a long drawn day of 'dawdling damphoolishness,' to employ an expression used upon the spot — but we are still quite young.

The 118th N. Y. later in the day reach the railroad, and tear up and destroy a long line of the track. Some of the 13th also take a hand. A huge pile of the iron rails, and dry fencing stuff, is gathered on a bridge, said to be over Swift Creek or a branch of it, and all burned together, the rails warped, twisted and bent in the heat. The enemy set the woods on fire, and many of the dead are burned up — the wounded having been removed and cared for. The fire compelled the Reg. to change position, bringing it out upon more open ground, and under greater exposure to the rebel sharp-shooters; but no reply to them from our line is allowed.

The most nervous incident of the day is the bursting of a large rebel shell high above our heads; every man for a moment expects to catch a piece, or one of the little balls, as they rattle down among the dry leaves — no one hit. About one third of this shell, in one piece, comes down, and strikes the ground with a loud noise, about ten feet to the rear of our colors. The piece falls very near a Lieutenant in the 13th (Lieut. Churchill, the writer believes), and he drops to the ground as if struck dead, but is unhurt. It will not do to laugh at the stories about the 'wind' of a cannon ball; it causes a very disagreeable concussion and enervating shock when passing very near a person, experienced, too, before any sense of danger is realized.

The fight was first opened about 7 a. m. by a body of the enemy who ambushed our advance guard of cavalry in a dense swamp. The cavalry fell back in confusion and haste upon the infantry skirmishers, and the work of the day with them at once began. Later on the 8th Conn. were put in. The 8th Conn. lost 74 men, killed and wounded, having met the enemy in line of battle along the railroad — it was reported on the field that their loss was 105 men; and in the afternoon, when that regiment returned from the front, they were heartily cheered by the whole Brigade as they passed battle-stained to the rear. The 10th N. H. at once moved to take their place at the front.

Lieut. Taggard had been very sick for several days previous to this battle, but he tried his best to keep with the Reg.; after marching a while, however, he was compelled to leave the line and to stop at a house near the battle-field until the evening of May 8th. While he was at this house ninety men of the 8th Conn. were brought there, and the arms or legs of many of them were amputated. The 118th N. Y. also lost heavily.

The 13th, acting as a support and reserve all day, meets with but one severe casualty, though a number are more or less bruised by spent bullets. After remaining near and in view of the line of our skirmishers all day, covered by trees and the ridges of ground as much as possible, the Thirteenth retires some distance to the rear, and bivouacs late at night in deep woods. A large detail is sent on picket, and the balance of the Reg. settles down to rest in pitchy darkness. The excitement, extreme heat, hard work, danger — and fret — together with smoke of powder and of the burning brush, causes several cases of sunstroke. The men left their knapsacks at the place of last night's bivouac, and this relieved the labors of the day very much.

Probably the Thirteenth never saw during its term of service a more unsatisfactory day than this one. There was apparently no head, tail or order to the work — a nebulous fight. Possibly the nearest answer ever made to the questions: 'How to fight without winning?' 'How to advance without going ahead?' The detail from the Thirteenth, and our Band, who were sent together to fight the fire, had a fearfully hot day's work, and the most of them gave out from the heat and exhaustion. Nevertheless they rescued all the wounded.

A singular wound was received to-day by Sergeant Gilman Davis of A. A rebel minie rifle ball passed through his neck from side to side, just back of his windpipe, breaking no bones, and apparently severing no vital part. He died, however, during the night. Davis was wounded about noon, or a little later, and while the Reg. was seated on the ground awaiting orders.

Our Brigade advanced alone, as a body, and drove the enemy back about one and one half miles. At one time we are just on the point of engaging the enemy in full force, expect a severe encounter, and make ready for it, when we are ordered to retire. A day of suspense. We are exposed all day to shells and bullets, without the privilege of action to relieve the tediousness of it; pelted all day, and compelled to endure it without striking back. We go into camp to-night, closely packed in woods deep and very dark. A part of the enemy's troops met to-day are under command of Gen. D. H. Hill. The Union loss to-day is stated to be 250. On the whole a bloody day for the force actually engaged. About our bivouac to-night the dense pine woods are filled with smoke, and are stifling hot and close.

Quite the same as in unrestricted immigration, the Subs import the vices of the nations whence they come. About a dozen of them in the Thirteenth have been in the habit of doing some sort of mischief, on the eve of a move, and thus seeking arrest and escape from duty. They tried it last night; and this morning they are, by order of Col. Stevens, marched into the fight and danger, under arrest, and without muskets or equipments; the neighboring files in their respective companies being ordered to shoot them instantly, if they shirk or run. It being of course understood privately that they were not thus to shoot them — but the Subs, as was intended, took the order to be one made in dead earnest. A more thoroughly scared gang of cowards than these fellows were, when the bullets began to fly, no man ever looked upon. They had to face the music for once. As the Reg. advanced, a gun and set of equipments lay on the ground; and no one who witnessed it can ever forget the expression on the face of one of these Subs, and the tone of his voice, as he said: "Captain — may n't I pick up that gun, and use it?" He was permitted to take the gun and use it — and he did! All of them came out at night unharmed, and each had supplied himself with a gun and set of equipments, off the field, where the dead and wounded had left them. It was too bad to scare men so; but it cured them of their habit of getting up mock riots for the purpose of avoiding duty. Whatever of blame may attach to proposing this plan, the writer will own up to; being in command of the rear-guard the night before he had to settle the special disturbances made by these fellows, to disarm them, and to endure no end of bother with them after they were placed under arrest; they needed a strong medicine to cure them of their bad habits, and he suggested this plan to Col. Stevens.

Hospital Steward Prescott has an ugly experience to-day. He is sent by Col. Stevens to ascertain whether a group of our skirmishers, lying motionless at some distance in advance of the Thirteenth, are dead or alive. He does not return for several hours. Meanwhile Manson S. Brown of C is sent to the front to find him, but cannot. The Regiment is withdrawn, and there is much speculation and anxiety as to the fate of Prescott. No one can penetrate to the point where he was last seen, on account of the rebel fire. Finally very late in the evening he suddenly appears in camp, and is welcomed like a lost boy. He had approached near to the skirmishers referred to, in pursuit of his errand, when he was beset by a severe fire from the rebel line of skirmishers. He dropped at once behind a fallen tree, among dense underbrush — hence could not be seen by Brown — the tree was made a target of during all the afternoon by the rebel sharp-shooters, and he was compelled to lie still, close to the tree, until dark, when he at once made his escape, fortunately unhurt.

May 8. Sun. Very hot, steamy, close, damp. Reg. taking a little rest. Many say that last night was the darkest they ever knew, the blackness being increased by the smoke of the burning forests. When the second picket was detailed the men had to be brought near to the fires to be identified. The Reg. sleeps half the day. Orders are received for the Reg. to be ready to march to-morrow at 4 a. m. with three days' cooked rations. We have been listening to distant firing, the boom of cannon and the rattle of musketry, springing up at times all day ; and have been in readiness, and hourly expecting, to march to the noisy front and take a part in the action. The rest of a Sunday is in no way enhanced by this sort of thing. An old citizen, living near by, says that our camp here is northeast of Petersburg ten miles, and eleven miles from Richmond, by the mile-stones on the Turnpike — we being opposite the 11th mile-stone from Richmond. We have bivouacked for several nights on nearly the same ground — on the right of the main road. See page 259. Lieut. Churchill is lame from some bruise received yesterday, but continues on duty.

The enemy's troops encountered yesterday, and to-day, are known as Brig. Gen. Haygood's South Carolina Brigade, just arrived from Charleston. Gen. Pickett has been in command at Petersburg until recently, when he was succeeded in command by Gen. Beauregard.

The line now being entrenched extends from Trent's Reach on the James to near Port Walthall on the Appomattox ; a distance in a straight line of three or four miles. Gen. Smith on the right near the James, Gen. Gilmore on the left. The Richmond and Petersburg Turnpike is a short distance to the front of this line ; the R. & P. Railroad nearly two miles distant. None of Admiral Lee's boats can now ascend the James above Trent's Reach. Our line is protected on both flanks by gunboats in each river. The distance from Drury's Bluff to Trent's Reach is about five miles by land, and about nine miles by water.

BATTLE OF SWIFT CREEK.

May 9. Mon. Fair, and very hot — 102° in the shade at noon. Reg. called at 3 a. m. and marches at 5 a. m. for the front, on the same road that we moved out upon on May 7th; and said to be the most direct road to Petersburg. Col. Stevens in command of Reg. The men leave their knapsacks in camp. We strike the Richmond & Petersburg Railroad at the 17th mile-stone from Richmond at noon. First we move up the railroad a short distance towards Richmond, and tear up some of the track; and then turn and move down upon the embankment southward towards Petersburg. Here Gen. Butler appears, with a numerous and gay staff, and rides up to the front, close in rear of the skirmishers — consisting of the 81st N. Y. — preceding the 13th on the embankment, as we march along. Some one proposes three cheers. Up goes the General's hand, quick as a flash, and he calls out: "No, no, boys. No cheers now." Soon he and his staff pass off the embankment to the left and disappear. The 13th continues to move down on the railroad — in support of the skirmishers on the left of the Brigade, Company C as flankers on the left of the Reg. — until when near the 18th mile-stone the enemy commences shelling severely, the infantry are engaged, the contest becomes furious, and we move off the railroad bank, to the left, into a field, not far from the position reached by us on May 7th. We pass around, however — sweeping toward the left, and then turn to the right — and gain the railroad at another point farther down, and commence tearing up the track, taking care to keep under cover of the railroad bank as much as possible — the enemy's bullets sweeping the road. We move in line of battle a part of the time, and a part of the time by the flank, as the ground demands. Other troops are moving down on the right hand side of the railroad, and firing continuously. Shells are falling, and bursting, in all directions, and we are treated to clouds of powder smoke. The battle actually commences to be severe about noon.

While crossing a muddy field about this time, near a culvert on the railroad, a flashy Lieutenant, in a fine dress-suit, and wearing new, long kid gloves with gauntlets, appears, and attempts to go up closer toward the railroad bank, but he trips his toe in a vine, and falls headlong into the mud. Rising clumsily, with both hands completely covered with mud, he coolly draws off both gloves and throws them away, remarking in a drawling tone: "Z'easiest way — to clean your hands — (hic) you ever saw." In the afternoon he drew a revolver, and attempted to shoot a Lieutenant in the 13th, whom he claimed that he ranked. The Lieutenant instantly drew sword and chased him off the field; but the half-drunken fellow was able to outrun his pursuer — whose same sword-hand now survives to write this rummy incident. Rum is a curse.

Immense piles of dry wood are heaped on the culverts and bridges, the railroad rails piled on, and then the mass set on fire, twisting and bending the rails all out of shape, and destroying the bridges. We advance rapidly through woods and across fields and amid the dense, blinding smoke, the battle raging on all sides. The enemy steadily falls back, and between 12 and 1 p. m. we come out under fire, into Mr. Thomas L. Shippen's wide field — "Arrow Field" — that surrounds his house, and situated on the left hand side of the railroad; Mr. Shippen's house and other buildings being on the farther side of the field towards Petersburg. (Here we catch a glimpse of Petersburg, some two or three miles distant.) We cross this field and approach the bank of Swift Creek to the left and rear of the house.

Here the enemy's skirmishers are posted in force, and Companies B and E, under Capt. Julian, are sent on the run to the left, to occupy the near bank of Swift Creek among some trees, and where the bank of the creek is high, apparently the highest point along there — perhaps 400 or 600 yards to the rear of the house. It is a risky job, for the enemy appears to be numerous. The charge is made at the top of our speed — say a little faster, at the top of Capt. Julian's speed, for he out-charged half his men — developing a strong line of the enemy, who, being flanked, hastily retreat, followed by our fire while they are in range in and across the creek. Another, heavier, line of the enemy make a stand behind trees, buildings and fences on the flat across the creek. Companies E and B engage these, and George E. Bodge and William F. Staples of B are severely wounded. It is now about mid-afternoon — perhaps a little past — very warm, and notwithstanding the danger we are in, we can but laugh and shout to see the Confederates, not two hundred yards distant across the creek, as they are pushed and flanked, jump up, seize their jackets in one hand and their guns in the other, and make off as fast as their legs can carry them.

Meanwhile artillery has come up and commenced firing, and our lines of battle are formed across the field not far in the rear of the skirmishers. A company from the 118th N. Y. is sent forward to strengthen the skirmish-line. Company E (13th) is divided, and a part sent farther to the left down the bank of the creek (where the first swampy ground is in that direction), under Lieut. Thompson of E, and placed, by the staff officer in charge of the whole skirmish-line, in squads of three or four men each, as flankers, to the left of the skirmish-line, and in a grove of small hard-wood trees. These men are here improperly interfered with by the drunken officer spoken of above, who was rightly refused obedience — with the unpleasant result as stated. These three companies skirmish all the rest of the afternoon — Co. E on the left, a part as flankers — until just at night, when Companies G and F of the 13th, under Capt. Stoodley, relieve E and B and they return to the Reg. now drawn up in line of battle across the open field. Companies G and F are posted as pickets along the near bank of the creek, and on the left of the 10th N. H., and swing away around along the front and to the left and rear of the 13th, until they join the main line of the reserves. A long straggling line, every man of which is required to keep awake all night.

During the afternoon — about 4 or 5 o'clock — an artillery duel opens, and the enemy soon has one of his guns knocked to pieces. The enemy's skirmishers, far across the creek, cannot be dislodged without sending a force across the creek.

A soldier of the 13th writes of May 9th: "On Monday, 9th, we left camp at daylight, and moved directly upon the R. & P. Railroad, striking it at the 17th mile-stone. When we had marched down the railroad, half a mile or more from this point, the rebels began to shell us. They were so troublesome, we sent out skirmishers, formed lines of battle, and so moved forward. We drove back their skirmishers, and followed them up until we came to Swift Creek, the enemy holding both banks of it. We soon dislodged them, when they took position behind trees, fences and houses on the other side. This was about mid-afternoon. In an hour or so the several columns of our troops had joined their lines of battle, and were ready, with artillery, to give the rebels a lively waking up. The artillery connected with our Brigade soon opened, and unmasked a rebel battery. A sharp duel followed, in which the rebels lost one gun. The shells were coming about us, during this little fight, but I did not see a man flinch or turn pale. The enemy's skirmishers were still troublesome, and Companies E and B of the 13th, and a company of the 118th N. Y., were deployed as skirmishers, and running quickly forward, found cover on the near bank of the creek and opened fire on them, and drove them away. In this movement two men of Company B were badly wounded. A part of Company E was placed as flankers on the left of the skirmish-line."

The order of events occurring rapidly is difficult to follow, but the battle continues all day, and until after midnight; chiefly between the skirmishers, though at times the fifing, from both artillery and lines of battle, is very severe. There is no quiet until near morning. Our Brigade is designated to hold the field to-night, and about 6 p. m. is drawn up in two lines of battle across Mr. Shippen's field, now prepared for sowing or planting, very moist and soft. The eight companies of the 13th present acting as a support for the 10th N. H.; which holds the advance and is posted near the bank of the creek, a little northeast of Mr. Shippen's house. A ridge running across the field somewhat protects the line of the 13th. The 8th Conn. have the right of our Brigade line to-night, near the railroad. The enemy assails our lines at various points several times in the night, but with little success. He charges twice furiously, point blank, upon the 10th N. H., with picked men, but each assault utterly fails, and the assailants are driven back across the creek with heavy loss. The first charge on the 10th occurs about 8 p. m., and the several charges are made by fully four hundred men — probably by more than that number.

During one of these charges upon the 10th N. H., accompanied by the usual rebel yell, the contest is so sharp that the 13th expects surely to see the 10th driven back, and our men voluntarily rise and stand with guns loaded, and bayonets fixed, to take a hand in the fray if the 10th is overpowered; but they hold their ground, and the enemy retires, leaving above half of his men dead and wounded. So says a prisoner. The 13th rising voluntarily, and without orders, to help the 10th if need be, is a bit of very fine action, and Col. Stevens thanks the Thirteenth in the name of the State of New Hampshire. The enemy seems to be aiming to capture a little field battery of three or four guns posted near the 10th and not far from Mr. Shippen's house.

The writer is an accidental and unwilling witness to one of these night charges upon the 10th N. H. Everything near the 13th is quite still. Unable to get warm enough to sleep, on the damp ground, because of an 'army chill,' the writer leaves the battle line of the 13th, and walks for exercise, and to see what he may, forward nearer to the line of the 10th, not counting on any danger. Suddenly a sharp, distant voice comes up out of the stillness: "Forward, double-quick — give the Yanks * * * *!" That was hearing enough, and the writer darts back to his place in the 13th, only to hear, in another instant, the rebel yell from three or four hundred throats. Then a few picket shots; and then the volleys of the 10th settle the case in about three minutes. Before all is over, nearly every man of the 13th is up in arms. The rebels charged up within fifty yards of the 10th. Soon it is quiet; the writer keeps his place, and curbs his curiosity for the rest of the night — he is now warm enough.

The night is very noisy. Still the men of the 13th manage to have a few hours of sleep, in short naps. The worst feature of one of these night fights is the sudden calls to arms. Some uneasy officer is very sure, when the picket firing begins to rattle, to call up his men without orders. Each sleeper in turn receives a sudden shake, a hoarse whisper in his startled ears: "Fall in — Fall in!" and so, in a few moments, a straggling line of men mount to their feet, up out of the dust or mud, shivering, swearing and stumbling into their places. Then all lie down again — and try to keep the ground warm. These incidents cause much loss of sleep and rest, and bring no gain.

The incessant whistling of locomotives to-night is for effect; still it is evident that the enemy is re-enforcing his lines, and the citizens are moving away. We could probably have gone straight into Petersburg to-day. Our Brigade is left alone upon the field here to-night; a long night of alarms, giving us no chance for sleep for more than an hour at a time, and the morning opens the contest anew.

To-day about four o'clock in the afternoon, and apparently on the right hand, or west side, of the railroad, and about half a mile from the 13th, is suddenly heard a volley of musketry, then the rebel yell, then five volleys in a regular succession like the striking of a clock — then a loud Northern hurrah. Of this affair the story is told later, on the field, that a rebel regiment of South Carolinians, on coming out of the brush into an open field, suddenly find themselves face to face with the 27th Mass., drawn up in line of battle on the opposite side of the field. The rebels instantly fire one volley, and then yell and charge; the Mass. regiment wait for a close range, and then reply with their Spencer rifles — 'seven-shooters.' The rebels are terribly surprised, turn tail and run, leaving on the field over a hundred of their number dead and wounded. As the Massachusetts men move forward in pursuit, one poor fellow, a rebel badly wounded, points to the Spencer rifle in the hands of a Northern man, who stops to assist him, and asks: "Say, Yank — what yer got thar?" The first experience these men had had with the Spencer rifle, and a bad one. The writer had been sent on an errand from the line to the left; on his return his way led over a high knoll from which a wide view was had of the scenes of the battle, and the country around, and he was taking this view when the volleys were fired.

May 10. Tues. The second day of the Battle of Swift Creek. A very hot day. The pickets commence firing with the very first glimmer of daylight. The enemy seems to surround us on three sides, west, south and east, and the noise is about equally loud in either direction. The enemy shells our lines vigorously. This morning finds the Thirteenth in Mr. Shippen's plowed field, part of a long line of battle, the 10th N. H. a few rods in front of us — all of our line facing south. We are several hundred yards north of Mr. Shippen's house, the 10th a few rods nearer to it, and still nearer is a Union battery, of two or three guns, in full play; and that arrangement brings us, the 10th and the battery, in range of the enemy's fire of both artillery and infantry. We rise from our cosy beds of the dirt and mud of the soft plowed field, and form a dusty line about day-break, then have a poor, damp, mussed and mashed breakfast out of our haversacks; and as no coffee can be had, we wash our so-called breakfast down with the ancient[1] water from our canteens — nectar of swamp-land well flavored with tin. All this puts us into excellent trim, condition and spirit for a vigorous fight.

Early in the day the Thirteenth is moved back a few rods beneath a little ridge, just south of a deep ditch that runs through the field — from the first culvert on the railroad north of Mr. Shippen's house — in order to escape the multitude of bullets coming over from the enemy's pickets and sharp-shooters, and his numerous shells. The 13th being in the second line of the Brigade, and held as a support for the 10th, it is not deemed wise to expose so many men to the fire of the enemy's sharp-shooters and the brisk fire of his artillery; hence an aide appears and talks a while with Col. Stevens, and we are moved to the rear a few rods, and placed beneath the protecting ridge, while the main body of the 10th

---

[1] Water that had been kept in canteens for twelve or twenty four hours the boys called "Old Water" — just as it tasted.

necessarily remains near where they passed the night. They are on the north side of the third ridge south of the ditch, which ridge serves to protect the men of the 10th to a considerable extent if they lie flat upon their faces. It is, however, a very exposed position. Lt. Col. Coughlin sits for a long time in a chair — appears to be a light rattan rocking-chair — in the open plowed field, near his men, and reading a newspaper, while the rebel bullets strike and knock up little puffs of dust on all sides of him and shells scream and crash — as cool as if on the veranda of a summer hotel by the sea. His coolness and courage serve to keep his men steady and firm.

Mr. Shippen left with his family on Sunday the 8th, and if the enemy's pickets had kept out of his house, it probably would not have suffered any damage. Our men found an unfinished letter in the house, written by Miss Shippen, in which she speaks of the Union men as "The Yankee Vandals." A batch of papers is found in the ditch by the men of the Thirteenth, from which we learn that Mr. Shippen's place is called "Arrow Field," and the bank of Swift Creek, where his house stands, is "Violet Bank." Blue violets are very plenty about there just now, rather of a lead color, however, and hurt — the soldiers do not care to pick any of them. The papers were evidently taken from the house by the enemy's pickets, who had fired from the house, and also damaged it before the Union troops got possession of it; probably to make a point against the 'Yankee Vandals.'

We remain in position in the open field, without shelter or cover save this little ridge, until 10 a. m., when we move toward the rear. About noon we move farther back, and near mid-afternoon move off the field into dense woods. As we move off the field, northward, in line of battle faced to the rear, the enemy shells us; many of his shells bursting over, behind, and beyond us, none of us are hurt, however, by these shells. Nearer the railroad several casualties occur from the enemy's musketry fire, our troops there being more exposed than we are; though a man of Co. H (13th) is struck by a rebel bullet, while we are retiring. The ground near the railroad is clear and level, the ground crossed by the 13th, two hundred yards farther east, is more broken and brushy. We retire so slowly, frequently halting and facing about, that it is fully 4 p. m. before we are out of range of the enemy's sharp-shooters, and our camp is but a little beyond the range of his shells. We reach our camp-ground at 5 p. m. While withdrawing to-day, our Brigade — Gen. Burnham's — 2d Brig. 1st Div. 18th Corps — covers the movement as rear-guard, and the last line of skirmishers suffer severely from the enemy's fire. The enemy shells the woods through which we pass, but our position in them is to him so very uncertain, that he can do us but little damage. Before retiring, our troops destroy several miles of the R. & P. Railroad. Besides lying under a dangerous fire, and destroying the railroad, the 13th has had to-day but little to do.

While passing through the brush yesterday and to-day we find the bodies of several Union soldiers stripped, mutilated and lying stark and white on the ground. This mischief was done on May 7th and 8th, and it is said by the Tennesseeans. In one instance a Union soldier's body lay on its back, stripped, and with a bayonet driven down through the mouth and neck, and down into the hard clay beneath. The hands and feet were badly torn and bloody, and the surface of the ground was deeply scratched and broken up within their reach; it being evident that the man had been so pinned down, or impaled, while alive, and had died while struggling to free himself. There were bullet wounds in the legs, and a Union soldier's set of equipments, cut off, and rifled of caps and cartridges, lay near by the body. The scene was unspeakably horrible. The writer and others went some distance from the line of the Thirteenth and saw this case — else he would not record it. The body lay near the railroad a few rods east from the position of the 18th mile-stone. Rumor has it that when the burial party reported these cases of mutilation, the Union organization to which the sufferers belonged swore terrible oaths that they would take no prisoners from the rebel organization to which the perpetrators belonged. See May 16th.

Yesterday and to-day our Brigade has marched about fifteen miles, chiefly in timber and brush, and sometimes in swamps so densely wooded, we could not see clearly fifty yards in any direction. We fought all day yesterday, were under arms all of last night, under fire at least thirty-six hours continuously, and this in weather so hot, much of the time, that sunstrokes have been frequent, therefore to-night rest is welcome. The 13th were not brought to a fire in line of battle, but were engaged in much severe skirmishing on the front lines. Charles Heath of H and James L. Glenville of D are wounded to-day. Many of our men have been struck by spent bullets in these last few days of fighting, but though bruised were not sufficiently hurt to be reported as wounded. The enemy's line has been long and stubborn, but evidently thin.

Capt. Clark, Adjt. General on Gen. Burnham's staff, conducts the withdrawal of our Brigade from the front to-day; moving back one regiment at a time, a short distance, assigning its position in line of battle faced toward the enemy, and then halting it until the other regiments in the Brigade move past and take position in regular order. The general opinion among our troops is that we might have gone straight into Petersburg, in fair marching time, sweeping everything before us, at any time in these last four days, Swift Creek being fordable in many places. There is one gravelly ford a short distance east of Mr. Shippen's house that has been much used by the Confederates. Gen. Kautz arrives at City Point having damaged the Weldon Railroad to some extent, burning several bridges, and seriously delaying the arrival of Gen. Beauregard's troops. Our forces to-day, on this line, have completed the destruction of the Richmond and Petersburg Railroad from Swift Creek, on the south, to Chester Station, on the north — a distance of nearly six miles. The railroad bridge over the creek is high and long.

Lossing states that in the movements of May 9th, Gen. Gilmore commands the right of the advance, Gen. Smith the left; and that Gen. Weitzel, moving directly upon Petersburg, encounters a heavy Confederate force at Swift Creek, three miles from Petersburg.

The foregoing account was written in the main before the writer's visit to the battle-field in May 1885. The best view of the position of the 13th on the battle-field of Swift Creek, as well as of the field generally, is to be had from the north side of a little ridge, or swell, of land, rising a few feet only (6 to 10) above the general level in Mr. Thomas L. Shippen's field, now, 1885, owned by Mr. D. E. Wood of Philadelphia, about 500 or 600 yards north of his house, and running nearly east and west, across the field, from the R. & P. Railroad on the right, to the timber, in the swamps of Swift Creek, on the left. This ridge was the line of the 13th on the afternoon and night of May 9th and on the morning of May 10th; and they advanced to it, from the timber near the 18th mile-stone, down the left — east — side of the railroad, across the wide, level field. They advanced due south to the ridge, their right resting on the railroad for the first part of the way. As you stand here — about mid-way of this ridge — and face south, towards Petersburg, you will have, about 100 yards behind you, a ditch — then deep, now nearly filled up with earth —

---

### DESCRIPTION OF PLAT.

A. Richmond and Petersburg Turnpike, with old mill on the Creek, and a Confederate Battery C, on a hill, about one mile from Mr. Shippen's house.

B. Railroad — here east of the turnpike.     D. Swift Creek.

E. 19th mile-stone from Richmond, one fourth of a mile south of Mr. Shippen's house.

F. First culvert, on the railroad, north of Swift Creek — and house — and about half way between 19th and 18th mile-stones.

G. Ditch leading from this first culvert. Thirteenth placed just south of it on the morning of May 10th.

H. Position of 13th on the night of May 9th, under cover of a little ridge about 100 yards south of the ditch G. The 10th N. H. 150 yards in front of 13th at I.

K. Where Lt. Col. Coughlin sat in a chair for a time, reading a newspaper, on the morning of May 10th.

L. Mr. Thomas L. Shippen's house, 75 yards east from the railroad, and about 400 yards in front of the 10th N. H.

M. Mr. Dunlop's house.

N. Edge of timber bordering 'Arrow Field' on the east.

P. First swampy ground near bank of creek and near a gravelly ford.

S. Wood-road on north bank of creek running from fords to turnpike. Bodge and Staples of B were wounded in this wood-road, a few yards to the right of the edge of the woods.

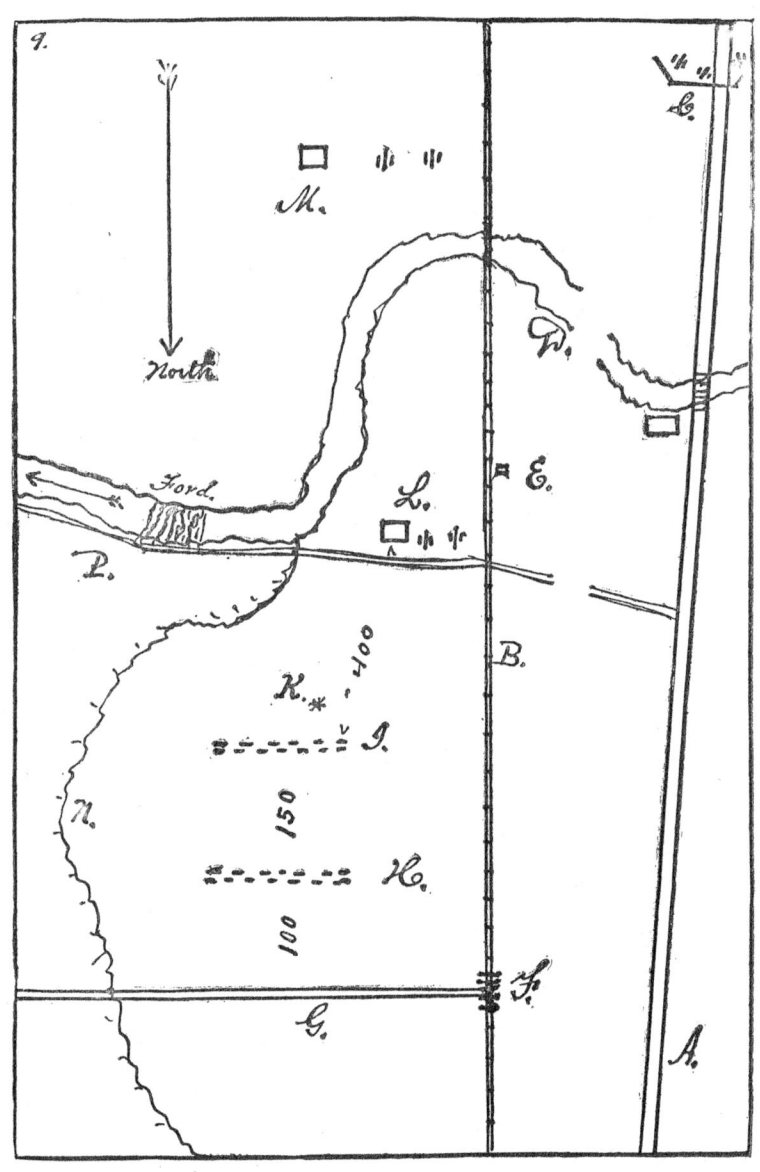

SWIFT CREEK, May 9 and 10, 1864.

From a sketch made by the writer in May 1885.

running east from the first culvert on the railroad north of Swift Creek. During the forenoon of May 10th, it was found necessary to withdraw the 13th line to a position beneath the ridge just south of this ditch for better cover from the enemy's shells and cross-fire of bullets. Members of the Regiment will remember the big fire, of dry wood and fencing stuff, they built on this culvert, and the limp and twisted condition of a pile of railroad rails, after having been suitably roasted in that fire. They will also remember the rails, heated in the middle, and when thus annealed, looped around the trees along the railroad — and also remember how the young trees steamed, smoked and hissed as the sap ran out under the hot hug of the iron.

The 13th were stationed on this ridge, about mid-way the field and 200 or 300 yards east of the railroad, and about half way between the 18th and 19th mile-stones, for nearly 24 hours. On the right — west — of us was the railroad, running nearly north and south, and to the left — east — of us was dense timber — the field of our position and action being nearly one quarter of a mile wide east and west. To the front — south — about 150 yards, is a similar ridge, which was the line of the 10th N. H., and on the crest of it Lt. Col. Coughlin sat in a chair on the morning of May 10th, and read a newspaper for an hour or so — to show his regiment how little danger there was and to keep them steady — while the enemy's bullets frequently struck the plowed ground about him, knocking up little puffs of sand and dust, and the rebel shells screamed and cracked over his head. Lt. Col. John Coughlin, 10th N. H. Vols., had a good head, and heart, as well as great courage — and ought to have worn the Star of a Brigadier General.

To the front, 500 or 600 yards south of the Thirteenth's ridge, is Mr. Shippen's house — now Mr. Wood's — standing about 75 yards east of the railroad. Gen. Butler had his Hdqrs. at this house during a part of the battle. About half a mile from the ridge, still farther south, Swift Creek crosses the railroad, a little south of the 19th mile-stone, and running east; but soon after crossing the railroad bends wide to the north near Mr. Shippen's house. Still farther south, a short distance beyond the Creek, is Mr. Dunlop's house, standing about 150 yards east from the railroad. Here Gen. Lee is said to have had his Hdqrs. during a part of the battle. There was a Union battery in Mr. Shippen's front yard, supported by the 10th N. H.; there was a rebel battery in Mr. Dunlop's front yard, supported also by infantry; and when these two batteries played, the houses were interesting places to live in. Westward of Mr. Dunlop's and a mile or so southwest of the 13th, the rebels had another battery, on a hill, in an earth-work built on the turnpike, south of an old mill. Both of these rebel batteries played severely upon the lines of the 10th and 13th, the most of their shells, however, going over; we thought it all rather bad gunnery practice. A few rods east of Mr, Shippen's house, a wood-road runs down along the high north bank of Swift Creek. Here it was that Companies E and B charged the rebel skirmishers, and drove them from their cover under the bank, across the creek, south, and out of a level field beyond; and were relieved on the picket line, at night, by Companies G and F. It was in this wood-road, where it runs along on the highest part of the bank, that Bodge and Staples were wounded.[1]

"May 9th the Regiment went out at 4 a. m. I was too sick to march and was left in charge of the camp. A very hot day — 102° in the shade. May 10th, 98° in the shade."                      LIEUT. TAGGARD.

May 11. Wed. Very warm. Reg. in camp in thick woods, three miles from Port Walthall, and resting. The woods, chiefly of pine, are so dense that we can see scarcely fifty yards in any direction. It is said to be fully seven miles, by the most direct route, from our camp here to the battle-field of Swift Creek; the road or path winding among impassable swamps. A large mail arrives, and many letters are read and written. The mails for this command have been shamefully irregular for many weeks past; rarely arriving on time, anywhere from one to six days late, and sometimes, like an army Pay-master, never arriving at all.

The Pay-master, as a rule, waits for months, four or six of them, for the army to be ready for a march or a battle. On the eve of the army's departure, he appears and pays off the men. The mail-carrier, as a rule, waits until the march or the battle is over, and all is safe, when he appears, with a nice batch of letters from their homes for the poor men — who have been killed. About the first impulse, and reasonable too, of a soldier, at his resurrection, will doubtless be to grumble about the Pay-master or the mail, — that is if a forced habit can possibly bridge the grave.

Yesterday the writer picked up on the field, near a C. S. A. abandoned knapsack, a New Testament containing the name of Sergeant J. H. Prickett, 25th Eutaw Regiment South Carolina Volunteers. This Testament the writer kept with him, during the rest of his stay in the army, and in the hospital, and brought it home. That was in 1864. On look-

---

### DESCRIPTION OF MAP.

A. Swift Creek.          B. Appomattox at rebel Fort Clifton.
C. R. & P. Railroad          D. Walthall Branch Railroad.
E. Turnpike.          F. Bisby.          G. Boyton.
H. Arrow Field church, badly riddled in the fight, to the right of the Thirteenth, on May 9th and 10th.
K. 'Arrow Field;' position of Thirteenth, fronting Mr. Shippen's house L, and the wood-road along the north side of the creek to ford at T.
M. Dunlop.          N. Confederate batteries on hill.
P. Johnson. Arrow on railroad, D, to Port Walthall. All the earth-works south of the creek are Confederate.
W. W. Confederate earth-works. No Union works near Arrow Field.

---

[1] Even a little repetition is risked, rather than that any person visiting the field with this book in hand should fail to find the exact localities. An attempt is made to furnish a guide for the future, as well as a record of the past. This explanation is made not only for this, but for all similar descriptions. — S. M. T.

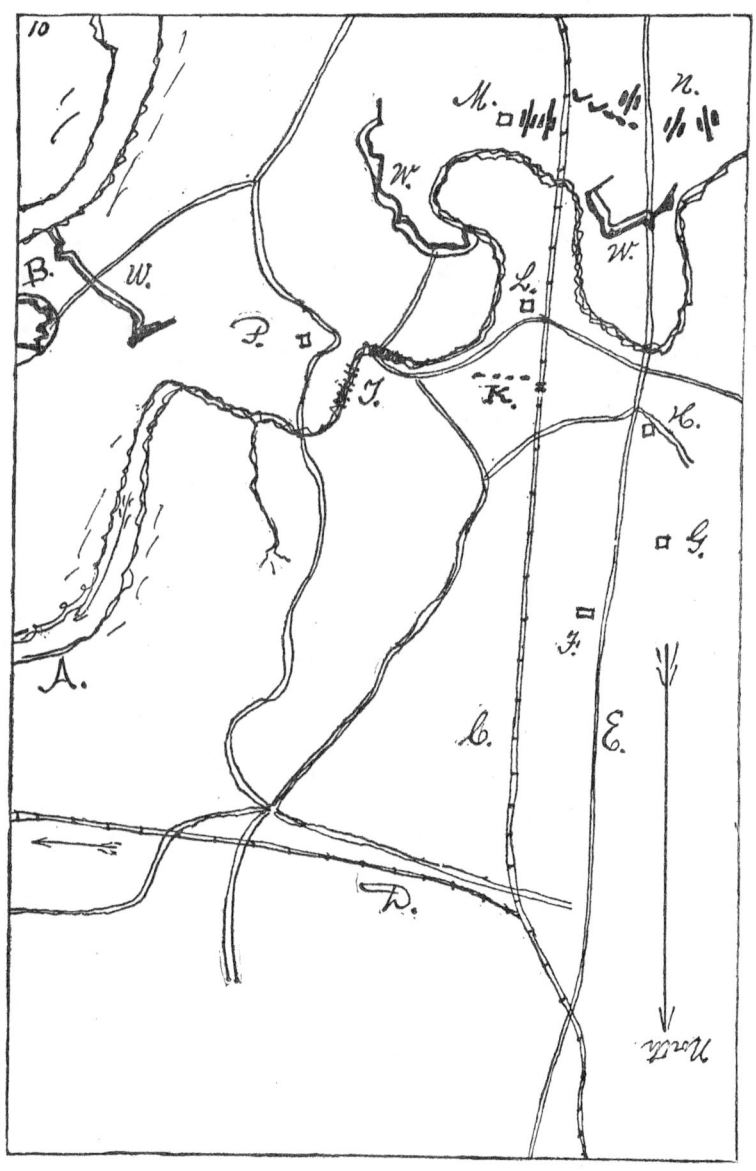

SWIFT CREEK, May 9 and 10, 1864.

Tracing of Official Map.  Scale, one and one half inches to one mile.

ing over sundry packages in 1884, while preparing this Diary, the Testament was found, and the writer decided to find the original owner or his family, and to that end advertised in the Charleston, S. C. *News*. The advertisement was successful, and the Testament was returned to Sergeant Prickett's father, Rev. I. D. Prickett, Orangeburg, S. C., Dec. 1, 1884. Mr. Prickett lost both his sons in the war; Sergeant Prickett, above, died while a prisoner of war at Elmira, N. Y., the other son was killed in battle. This Testament was all that returned to the father.

The Thirteenth are feeling uncomfortable to-day, because they have done several days of hard work, and much fighting, where they felt and knew that the possibilities were immense — and there is plaguey little to show for any and all of it. So we paint the day as no bright one for them. The day closes with a severe thunder shower about 6 p. m.; and we have wet ground to sleep on with our heads full of the order : " Must be ready to march to-morrow at day-break, with two days' cooked rations." That means more slow fighting — " on coffee and hard-tack, salt-horse and brown sugar, chickory-juice and puddle-water." We would like to rush in, have no more dawdling, but one tremendous battle, all along the line from Maryland to Mexico, and close this war. That is the sentiment of this army to-night. The Army of the James is not contented.

Lieut. Charles H. Curtis furnishes the following concerning himself and his men :

" When the Thirteenth moved to Yorktown, April 19, 1864, some twenty-five men of the Reg., who had been detailed as teamsters, and on other duties, were ordered to report for duty to Lieut. Curtis, then in command of the Provost-guard at Portsmouth, Va. See March 31, 1864. Lieut. Curtis with Lieutenants Sherman and Dustin and the (now) 125 men of the 13th, were relieved as Provost-guard there, and not knowing of Gen. Butler's movement upon Bermuda Hundred, left Portsmouth for Yorktown on May 4th, about 11 a. m., and that night, near the mouth of the York River, passed Gen. Butler's fleet moving towards Bermuda Hundred; arriving at Yorktown on the morning of May 5th, to find that the 13th had gone. On May 6th, about noon, Lieut. Curtis and his detachment embarked, at Yorktown, on the steamer ' Fannie,' for Bermuda Hundred, and while approaching the Guard-ship in Hampton Roads, about 8 o'clock that evening, were run into by the steamer ' Cambria,' and cut to the water's edge. Capt. Bradley of the 13th, and Col. Rust of the 8th Maine, who had been left sick at Yorktown, with several other officers and men, were also on board the ' Fannie.' The ' Cambria's ' bob-chains catching in the ' Fannie's ' broken timbers, held the vessels together until most all had left the ' Fannie.' Some men, who, with their wives, were on board the ' Fannie,' in the excitement of the moment, left their wives on board — escaping themselves. A huge Sergeant of the 13th, however, went to their rescue, and soon appearing, with a woman under either arm, strode over the bow of the ' Cambria ; ' and dropping one of the women into the arms of her husband, who was sitting with bowed head bewailing his loss, exclaimed : " Now, blank you, see if you can take care of her." The other woman was also placed in safety by the Sergeant. As the two steamers swung apart, the officer of the deck of the 'Cambria' was informed that men were still on board the 'Fannie.' But no effort having been made to save them, Lieut. Curtis called for volunteers, and without asking permission, lowered one of the 'Cambria's' boats, assisted by the men of Company K — 13th — who responded, and rescued Col. Rust, who was too ill to help himself. He with others filled the boat; obliging Lieut. Curtis with Mr. Grant, who had been in charge of the calcium light on Morris Island, S. C., to remain on the Fannie until rescued by a boat, sent to his aid, from the water-boat plying in the bay. On arriving at Bermuda Hundred, on another steamer, having lost everything, excepting the clothing they had on them, at the time of the disaster, the detachment formed a rendezvous camp, and Lieut. Curtis was placed in command of it. This was located at Bermuda Hundred, some three or four miles from the Regiment. While here Lieut. Curtis made a requisition for arms, and drew them for the parts of the ten Companies of the 13th which formed the detachment. The detachment was taken to the Thirteenth to-day, May 11th, by Capt. Dodge, after having worked for two or three days at the wharf in unloading vessels, and Lieut. Curtis remains at Bermuda Hundred as Post Quartermaster on the staff of Col. Pond of Ohio. No men were lost with the steamer 'Fannie,' but several were badly hurt." LIEUT. CURTIS.

This morning, May 11, 1864, at half-past eight o'clock (8.30 a. m.) Lieut. General U. S. Grant, telegraphs from near Spottsylvania Court House, to Maj. Gen. Halleck, Chief of Staff of the Army, at Washington, these famous words :

" I PURPOSE TO FIGHT IT OUT ON THIS LINE IF IT TAKES ALL SUMMER.
U. S. GRANT, LIEUT. GENERAL."

## VI.

### May 12 to May 27, 1864.

#### ADVANCE ON RICHMOND — BATTLE OF KINGSLAND CREEK.

**May 12. Thurs.** Warm; rainy all day, at times severe showers. Now come several days of hard fighting, and hard work, the scenes very much commingled.

The Reg. is up about daylight this morning, moves at 7 a. m. in light marching order, Col. Stevens in command, and marches through swamp and brush straight for the R. & P. Turnpike, finally striking it near the 11th mile-stone from Richmond, crosses it to the left — west — side, and moves north towards Richmond. Companies H, Capt. Smith, and I, Capt. Goss, are thrown out as skirmishers. We are here fired into, and several men of a battery, near by, are wounded. The 13th deploys at once in line of battle across a field. The skirmishers, however, clear the way and no call to fire is yet made upon the Regiment. We wait here in line of battle a short time and then advance through a swamp. The exceedingly wet and broken ground breaks up the skirmish line, or forces the skirmishers to merge in the regimental line. Companies attempt to pass through the tangled underbrush and swamp by breaking to the right in files of two, but often before the worst places are crossed, the companies are drawn out into a long zig-zag single file, then, on gaining clear ground, run together again in line of battle. Several times the Reg. comes out ahead of all the skirmishers — the Regiment plunging through the bad places in the ground, the skirmishers sweeping around them — and in one instance the Reg. while in line of battle, coming directly upon the enemy's pickets, captures four of them. This was about 4 p. m. In this case Capt. Julian, and several of his men together, pull two Confederates out of a slough, into which they had sunk to their necks, and were holding on to the roots of trees for dear life, and begging us not to kill them — "Please don't kill us" — say they. Julian replies in the language they can best understand: "Hold your tongues — you fools!" They are pulled out; then say that they are hungry, and beg for something to eat — why, they act like children! Capt. Julian and his men supply them with crackers, and coffee from their canteens, and they pass munching to the rear; we warrant, never so happy before. After struggling through one especially bad place, and again coming up into line of battle, the Reg. waits several hours in the edge of a field near the west side of the turnpike, Co. K, Capt. Betton, acting as flankers to protect the left of the Reg.   Company E skirmishes also a part of the day on the left.

From this field the Reg. moves in line of battle through a lot of tangled brush growing in water knee deep, half the companies worming through in single file then running hard to re-form the battle line, swings around and emerges, diagonally, on the turnpike, and halts for a moment in the road, and among the trees on either side of it.   This occurs about 3 p. m.   Many of the men mount a high bank on the left hand side of the road — the crest of the first hill south of Proctor's Creek.   Not a shot can be heard, excepting away off to the right, and we can see nearly half a mile up the road — north.   " Capt. Smith shouts, " Get behind the trees — men ; get behind the trees."   Colonel Stevens promptly sends out a special picket from the 13th, on the run, forward.   In a minute, while we wait to see what is next to be done, two small cannon take position on the hillside, just north of Proctor's Creek, and about one quarter of a mile from us and in the road, north — the guns pointing towards Richmond.   A deep hollow in the road, and a small bridge, intervenes between the Thirteenth and the two cannon.   The guns point right, it seems, and Adjutant Boutwell, mounted on his little ' Kanuck ' stallion, volunteers to interview them — or the gunners.   He has galloped down into the hollow, across the bridge, and about half way to the guns ; when they are both instantly whirled about, and six shells come in rapid succession, over the Adjutant's head, and screaming and crashing among us in the Regiment and among the trees around about — killing Geo. H. Harmon of A, on the high bank beside the road, and wounding Robert Oliver of C, and James Mooney of D, and also giving the Regiment a general stirring up, and a fumigation with rebel gunpowder.   The Reg. is at once moved by the right flank to a place of greater safety.   The shell that killed Harmon burst when just a little past the writer, who stood as high up on the bank as he could get, watching for the result of Boutwell's visit to the guns.   Several men were knocked over by the concussions ; which feel like big sledge-hammers striking both of one's ears at once.   Upon these shots, back comes Boutwell, his stallion screaming [1] and running at the top of his speed, and the shells flying over his head.   The advance skirmish line — not of the 13th — breaking here and there, are to blame for much of this.   The two guns soon disappear by a side path.   Adjutant Boutwell is thus the first man in Burnham's Brigade to cross Proctor's Creek in to-day's advance.

Our advance to-day is now in the turnpike, now alongside of it, now off to the left, straight, diagonal, zig-zag, in line, and out of line : and so we spend the day, skirmishing, wading, and plunging through brush and mud.   Finally, after a hard day's work, in the interminable mud, and rain, and racket, the Reg. bivouacs on high ground, and in line of battle

---

[1] Literally screaming.  He was the most noisy horse in the whole Brigade.  If separated from the other horses of the Reg. for a little time, he would commence calling for company — as a lonesome boy whistles to keep his spirits and courage up.

in the woods not far from the spot where we were shelled and where Harmon was killed. More courage is required for this bushwhacking than for a regular battle. It is full of surprises and tricks of the enemy; as witness their two guns to-day set pointing towards Richmond, then waiting until we are a target at close range — and then instantly whirled around and fired directly into our faces. Besides, there is a pervading feeling all the time that 'The woods are full of them.'

The 10th N. H. made a gallant charge to-day. Fretting under the slowness — it has seemed a double-slow advance for a week past — the 10th suddenly sprang out of the main line of battle like an arrow shot from a bow, and sent a heavy body of the rebels whirling back a long distance, in a hurry. It was very difficult to stop these spirited Irishmen after they were once on the charge; they believed they could cut their way to Richmond. Capt. Betton, on the skirmish line in their vicinity at the time, says their officers had to run before them and beat them back with their swords in order to stop their mad rush.

This morning a division of Confederate troops had preceded us on the turnpike by only about four hours, coming from the south. They left the road heavily marked and tramped as they went along; many of them — or else their negro camp-followers — leaving bare-foot tracks in the mud and sand.

To-night our main line — Gen. Smith's corps on the right, and Gen. Gilmore's corps on the left — bivouacs near Proctor's Creek on the south side. The Confederates fall back beyond Proctor's Creek to the north side.

This advance on Richmond is made by Gen. Smith's 18th Corps on the right, extending from the James River westward to and somewhat beyond the Richmond and Petersburg Turnpike. The Thirteenth, in the 18th Corps, is so situated in the general line of battle as to move along the left side of the turnpike, our right resting nearly on that road. The 10th Corps, under Gen. Gilmore, forming the left of Gen. Butler's line, moves along the railroad, from one to two miles west of the turnpike. The connection between the two corps is faulty, and largely so because of the rough, woody, swampy, jungly, vile country through which the long line must move.

May 13. Fri. Showery. The second day of the battle of Kingsland Creek (which should have been called the battle of Proctor's Creek) opens very rainy and cold. The Reg. is near the edge of open ground, near the turnpike (on the left hand side), and surrounded by woods. Gen. Smith's corps crosses Proctor's Creek early this morning, the enemy retiring before his advance. Companies D, C and A are placed upon the skirmish line; the 13th in support, coöperating with the 10th N. H., also in line of battle, in rear of its skirmishers. We have now advanced within ten miles of Richmond. The firing scarcely ceased all last night, and now, at daylight, it is very heavy on our front. A large lot of the enemy's muster-rolls and camp-paraphernalia is now in our hands. The rolls indicate that these good Southern fighters — and they are good fighters, if they cannot write their names — have enlisted "for life or the war;" and about seven out of every ten of them all sign their names as the rebel battle-flags are made — with a rude cross in the centre.

We are all cold, wet and muddy this morning, and in bad temper. We form line to advance about 7 a. m.; and move forward about 9 a. m. and commence the fight in the rain — rain — rain. Ammunition gets wet, and the men make 'ponchos' of their rubber blankets, wrapping them about their shoulders, and fastening them at the waist with strings and belts. The writer and several other officers limit their entire outfit for this whole summer's campaign to a long rubber overcoat; generally discarding tent and blanket, wearing the coat on rainy days, and sleeping in it on all nights. The whole command is half amphibious. There are jokes about sailing the gunboats up the turnpike. The boys keep calling out: "Where's Kingsland Creek?" And others answer: "Here's Kingsland Creek," as they splash and wade through the innumerable puddles. The country is all creek, above ground and below. The battle line of the Thirteenth halts about noon. The skirmish line — including Lieut. Taggard — moves forward near to Mr. Charles Friend's house, which the rebel skirmishers occupy.

Detachments from the 13th are skirmishing all day long. The lines are very close, the musketry firing severe, and the artillery hammers away unceasingly. Our lines are advanced about a mile and a half, and to a point within sight of the enemy's earth-works, and his strong line of skirmishers behind them, six to eight hundred yards distant. Our men take every possible cover, but the shells are pretty sure to hunt them out, while the bullets seem to drop down out of the sky. The dead and wounded, both Union and Confederate, are very numerous along our lines. The advance is even less rapid than yesterday, but the skirmishers cover every inch of the ground as they move forward. The rebel artillery send their shells crashing through the woods; our own equally busy; an immense amount of noise. Companies D, C and A are kept at the front all day, and Company A, at least, all of to-night. Sergt. Nathaniel F. Meserve of A is killed; Sergt. Charles W. Batchellor, Corp. John E. Prescott and John McCarty of D and Corp. William D. Carr of G are wounded.

In a letter written from Hammond Hospital, Point Lookout, Md., Sergt. Batchellor states: "Company D was thrown out as skirmishers to the extreme front on Friday, May 13th. In the afternoon the enemy charged and drove us back, then we forced them back again. About 4 p. m. I stepped back to speak with Lieut. Sherman, the rebel sharp-shooters got range of me, and shot me in the arm, while my gun was in my hand. The bullet broke my arm between the shoulder and the elbow. Surgeons Richardson and Small operated on the arm, taking out several pieces of bone. They then sent me to Point of Rocks (Corps Hospital) and from there here." SERGT. CHARLES W. BATCHELLOR.

From this wound he never recovered, but died on July 2d from the effects of it. He was a good soldier, brave, efficient and conscientious in performing all his duties, and a universal favorite in the Regiment, which lost in him one of its very best men.

To-night we bivouac on the battle-field; our men lying down without any tents or cover, save their rubber blankets and now and then a poorly-set piece of shelter tent. We have a wet night of it. We are in a little open field, on the west side of the turnpike, on high ground, near to and southwestward of Mr. Charles Friend's house. There is a hard-wood grove on our front and left; and on our right and front near the turnpike is Mr. Friend's. The ground is very wet, but the men are ordered to sleep in the little hollows for protection, for many bullets, and now and then a shell, skims clear across the field just over our heads. A cold rain in the night fills these hollows, and the men have to roll out on higher ground, and so are more and more exposed to the hissing bullets. One man dreams that he is sailing in a boat, the boat capsizes, he is just on the point of sinking, and falls to screaming for help — when he wakes to find himself half buried in water near a foot in depth, and coming up about his ears. Till then the slowly rising water seemed like nice bed-clothing, and in no way disturbed his sleeping.

While the enemy was shelling us in the woods to-day Capt. Julian received a blow on the side, quite a heavy blow but doing him no particular injury. Looking for the cause, he found that a piece of shell weighing several ounces had cut through the side of his haversack and lodged among his rations, mixing them quite thoroughly, grinding the hard bread into crumbs too fine for convenience, and the meat into sausage stuffing.

The general results of the day are an advance along our whole line; Gen. Smith crosses Proctor's Creek, and advances along the turnpike, with Gen. Brooks (our Division) on the west side, and Gen. Weitzel on the east side. Gen. Gilmore has attacked and carried the enemy's works on Woolridge's Hill, about one mile west of the turnpike, near the head of Proctor's Creek. The enemy here repulsed an attack made by Gen. Gilmore, then abandoned his line. Gen. Gilmore captured about one mile of the works, and pressed the enemy back towards Drury's Bluff. Gen. Smith's main line to-night is up within a few hundred yards of the enemy's works on the turnpike, with his pickets at Mr. Charles Friend's house. These pickets are Lieut. Churchill's men of the Thirteenth.

One member of the Thirteenth writes: "Glorious news from the Army of the Potomac to-night — our boys cheer tremendously."

## BATTLE OF DRURY'S BLUFF.

May 14. Sat. Cool, and very rainy most of the day. In order to make the story of this battle as clear as possible, it is necessary to divide it, and give to each part of the regimental organization an account by itself. The Thirteenth — all excepting Company A and a few pickets — is assembled on our place of bivouac about daylight; quite early, for the writer is obliged to make use of a candle in order to read the names of a detachment of men. Our position is on the left, west side, of the turnpike, and on the left of our Brigade. Our line of advance is nearly in the rear of our skirmishers — Company A commanded by Lieut. Churchill. We move forward in support of the skirmish line a little before 6 a. m.; and then hold position in line of battle for a while protected somewhat by the trees from the enemy's numerous shells and bullets.

Leaving the Thirteenth here in line of battle, we turn to Lieut. Churchill's own account of the work of his line of pickets and skirmishers; the following having been furnished to the writer by him a few months before the accident occurred, from the effects of which he died on March 19, 1885:

"On Friday, May 13, 1864, about 11 a. m., Company A, Capt. Hall, with Lieut. Churchill as Lieutenant, and Company C, Capt. Durell, were sent forward on the advance picket, with orders to drive back the enemy's pickets — who had still earlier in the morning driven our line back — and retake the line. This Companies A and C did, retaking the line near the Rev. Mr. Friend's stable (he of the brick house) and held the ground there until dark. About dark Companies A and C made a charge, with the whole line, and drove the rebels beyond a rail fence, and held the line of the fence. Previous to this charge, Sergt. Nathaniel F. Meserve of A while lying behind a log near the rail fence and the edge of the woods, raised his head to look over, was shot, and instantly killed. In the evening pioneers were sent for, who came and threw up a little line of breastworks near the rail fence; soon after this, about 9 p. m., Capt. Durell, who was sick, was relieved by Lieut. Oliver of G. No officer was sent to relieve Lieut. Churchill, and he remained all night alone with Co. A. Early in the night, by some chance, Lieut. Churchill found himself in command of Co. A, and Co. C in command of Sergt. Geo. Burns of C; and they alone remained in charge of these two Companies throughout the night. Lieut. Churchill was tired out, but rallied after a little rest. Having no orders, he established a line of vedettes along the front of Companies A and C; Edwin H. Glidden of A, a boy about 17 years old, being one of them, and having his post in Mr. Friend's pig-yard — a secure place — from which he reported, promptly and in good order, the three charges made by the enemy's pickets during the night, so that the picket line of Companies A and C were ready and repulsed each charge, and held their ground until the morning.

"The rebels were in Mr. Friend's house engaging Lieut. Churchill's pickets, and Major Jesse F. Angell, 10th N. H., commanding the whole picket line, came along at near 11 p. m. (Friday) and told Lieut. Churchill to 'cease firing on the house, for it was occupied by our own men.' But Churchill held that they were the enemy. Major Angell then took off his sword so as to make no noise, but forgot to remove his spurs, and crept toward the house. Soon he was heard to shout vociferously. He was a large man, a rebel bullet from the house struck him, and running round his side under the skin, made a wound about fourteen inches long — this convinced him that the enemy occupied that house. The firm position of Companies A and C, with two Companies of the 10th N. H. on their right, caused the enemy to leave Mr. Friend's house during the night, and about daylight Companies A and C seized the house, when recruit John Burns of A captured a rebel soldier — a man of the 69th Tennessee. Company C was relieved early Saturday morning (May 14th), but Company A was not relieved. The night was rainy and chilly, and by morning Lieut. Churchill and his men were very wet and exceedingly angry at not being relieved as they should have been.

"About 5 a. m. — Saturday — Capt. Reed of Gen. Brooks' staff came along, and said to Lieut. Churchill: 'Captain, who is in command here?' Lieut. Churchill answered: 'I am no Captain, only a Second Lieutenant, and I have not seen any other commissioned officer at all since eleven o'clock last night,' and told him about the wounding of Major Angell at that time. Capt. Reed replied that he would see if he could find any other officer, and went away. Soon he returned without finding any one, and ordered Lieut. Churchill to advance. Lieut. Churchill at this time had Company A and stragglers enough from other companies — with two men from some other regiment — to make his skirmish line up to fifty-four men, with Sergt. George E. Goldsmith of Co. A second in command. Lieut. Churchill at once moved forward, marched his men down around Mr. Friend's house, into the orchard, deployed them again as skirmishers — this time on the left side of the turnpike — and charged; not stopping until they had reached the enemy's earth-works, afterwards occupied by the Thirteenth.

"Company A under Lieut. Churchill reached the line of earth-works at 6 a. m. — Saturday — and then at once formed on the right flank of the rebels a little beyond the first angle in the works to the left of the turnpike; taking the cover formed by the reverse of the works, and continued firing on the rebels off to their right and on their front. In other words, made a breach in the enemy's entrenched picket line and occupied it. Soon Co. A passed over the works, the enemy retiring, and were disposed around and within the rebel barracks within the works. The enemy and our artillery kept up a severe cannonade over their heads. While within one of these barracks, a solid shot, from the enemy's guns on Drury's Bluff — or the large fort on the hill — went through the barrack and knocked down Lieut. Churchill and four of his men; all within the barrack, a log-house, were cut more or less by the splinters, but none severely hurt. Lieut. Churchill soon found it necessary to swing his left around clear of these barracks; later, about noon, a new officer — a Major — now in charge of the picket line, came up, and directed him to fall back under cover of the edge of the woods, near by to the left, and take some rest — which he did, and his men lay down. At near 4 p. m., Lieut. Churchill with Co. A was relieved by Co. I under Capt. Goss of I and Lieut. Thompson of E — all of whom, previous to this, had been skirmishing nearly all day among the barracks and in the brush. This made about thirty hours' uninterrupted advance picket and skirmish duty for Lieut. Churchill and Company A, without relief, rest, or anything to eat, excepting the contents of their haversacks — chiefly hard bread. Lieut. Churchill, half sick, had nothing which he could eat. Sergt. Josiah C. Flanders of A was so pressed by thirst, when no water could be obtained, that he was seen sucking out what moisture he could find in handfuls of mud taken from the road-side ditch." LIEUT. CHURCHILL.

It is related of Lieut. Churchill, when his men complained to him this morning and said they ought to be relieved, that he answered them with: "Well, boys, if they will not relieve us, we will relieve ourselves — by clearing out those rebels yonder." And they did! There was good metal in Lieut. Churchill. Had his health been good, he would have made a large mark. He was brave, prompt, faithful and thorough as a soldier; genial, companionable, quick-witted, and honest to a fault.

Again returning to the Regiment, which enters upon the battle of the day soon after sunrise : Moving in line of battle, straight forward, from our position on the left side of the turnpike, and under a severe fire from the enemy's artillery, we are soon mixed up with a small detachment from some other regiment. As the 13th advances it narrows its front, and passes into the timber bordering on the north the field of our last night's bivouac. Soon passing through this timber, we come out upon lower ground rather rough and broken and having a few stumps and trees, among them large, tall pines. These furnish the men with a little cover. The large fort of the enemy's on the hill — Fort Stevens — is visible during much of our advance, and shells us vigorously, but the rebel aim is bad and little damage is done. They use both shell and grape, and another rebel contrivance that pours out two or three quarts of bullets with a terrible whizz. One large shell cuts off two trees near our line before it bursts. Directly in front of the 13th are the lines of the enemy's earth-works — a long succession of trenches for riflemen — at close range, held in part by our own picket line — Lieut. Churchill's men — and the rest well manned by the rebel skirmishers, who are all firing rapidly. Our own artillery, in our rear, now opens more vigorously; and we spring up and run forward a few yards, then drop on the ground. This manœuvre is repeated over and over again, cover being secured, as best we may, among the little hillocks and stumps. Before the charge is half over our men are firing from the line of battle, over the heads of our skirmishers, at the enemy's pickets wherever seen.

The word is passed for a final rush in line of battle, and a grand charge ensues all along our Brigade line, and by our troops farther to the right and left; quickly occupying the enemy's earth-works while a part of the skirmishers of our Brigade have scarcely time to advance. The enemy clings stubbornly to his works, and the men — Union and Confederate — for a little time fire at each other, at a few feet distance, across the angles. The reverse of the works, however, is soon occupied by the line of battle, and thousands of bullets are at once chasing the enemy's men, now flying in every direction. The Thirteenth captures and occupies its part of the works a little before eight a. m. The whole line is occupied, to right and left, so far as we can see, before nine o'clock a. m. The 13th makes no farther advance, but remains along the reverse of the captured line of earth-works. In the neighborhood of the turnpike, now a little to our right, and beyond there, the firing is terrific — a roar. Soon the enemy is pressed two or three hundred yards back into the brush, followed by our skirmishers of A and I, and the line of the Reg. is no longer in danger excepting from the enemy's shells and spent bullets.

As an incident of the charge this: The writer has in view a large stump, a few yards to the front of the battle line of the 13th, as an objective point for himself in the next little rush. The time soon comes, and just as he is taking cover behind it, a huge fellow, big as two of him, hustles him to one side, seizes the stump for his own protection, and lies flat on his face behind it, while the writer passes over behind another stump perhaps a rod away. The writer's stump is small, but of oak, and though a couple of bullets hit it, they are harmless to him. The big fellow's stump, however, is of pine and rotten — and soon a shell from the enemy sends it flying. The big fellow hugs the ground, but whether hurt or not the writer cannot say, as his attention is called by another incident occurring an instant afterwards. He happens to be looking up, and witnesses the unusual, though occasional, occurrence of two shells colliding in mid-air. The larger, from the rebel fort, overbears the smaller, from the Union battery, but they both burst almost simultaneously, and the pieces rain down in the open field to the left of the turnpike, harmless but suggestive. The mid-air crash is very loud. There are no Union troops in sight to the left of our Regiment, which advances as the extreme left regiment of the 18th Corps; and the infantry firing going on at our left is at a considerable distance from us at this time.

To clear this account a little further it may be well to state that Lieut. Churchill's pickets of last night advanced as skirmishers this morning, and soon found themselves in a very dangerous position, being in comparatively open ground and exposed to the fire of a heavy rebel skirmish line posted behind the rebel earth-works to the left of the turnpike. When ordered to charge, Lieut. Churchill and his men rushed forward and got into the ditch of the works before all the rebel skirmishers had retreated; actually forming on the right flank of a part of the rebel line, while another part faced them on the other side of the ridge of sand that formed the works. As Lieut. Churchill describes the situation, "We and the rebels stood there a few minutes, dodging each other like a lot of boys snowballing over a stone wall." This was but for a short time, however, for the rebels ran along on their side of the works towards the turnpike, the old barracks and the brush, where they again took position. Meanwhile the Thirteenth charged up to the works in line of battle, and occupied the reverse of them, and Capt. Goss with Co. I and Lieut. Thompson of E were ordered forward over the works, and soon united with Lieut. Churchill's line in a sharp skirmish with the enemy. To return:

Immediately upon the capture and occupation of the works by the battle line of the Thirteenth, Capt. Goss is ordered to take his whole Company, I, over the works, drive the enemy back, and establish an advance picket line. Capt. Goss selects Lieut. Thompson of E as an assistant, and deploys his company along the part of the works occupied later (May 15th and 16th) by the Regiment; the right of Co. I resting at the lone apple-tree near the second angle in the works — at the west end of the second trench — behind which tree several men of Co. I take cover from the enemy's bullets, and are called into line by Sergt. W. G. Burnham of I.[1] This is the only tree near the part of the works occupied by the Regiment. After being deployed as skirmishers, Co. I springs quickly forward over the works into the open space in front, charging towards the turnpike, the timber and the old rebel barracks. Previous to this time the rebels had abandoned their line of earth-works, and had taken position among trees, and in and among these old log barracks, near the turnpike. As soon as over the works, Co. I charges directly upon these skirmishers of the enemy, and drives them back from the trees and old barracks, across the turnpike and into the brush beyond; coming upon them so closely that when Capt. Goss's men enter the doors on one side of the barracks, the rebels run out of the doors, and climb out of the windows, on the other side. A few of the enemy are captured. The firing during the charge of Co. I is very sharp on the part of the enemy's pickets, Co. I firing also, skirmishers to the right and left joining in, while a few of the enemy's shells add their noise and danger to the general rush, hubbub, bedlam and excitement, a part of the men — both Union and Confederate — having a stand-up fight in open ground, and a part sharply engaged among the stumps, trees and barracks. Lively! Company A, who had been on this line, and were swinging to the left, are soon out of sight in brush and timber, and Co. I with a few men from other Companies under Goss and Thompson are holding the whole front of the Regiment. Under the circumstances, there is, of course, but a limited opportunity to

[1] In this I am corroborated by Sergt. Burnham himself, 1885. — S. M. T.

take note of time, or of the order of action by detachments other than our own.

Capt. Goss's line, after this sharp bit of skirmishing, is soon posted along the turnpike, in the trees beyond, and to the left of the old rebel barracks. The enemy now shelling these old log-houses makes them of no use to our men as a means of protection, but on the contrary a source of danger from the flying timbers and splinters. The logs of which they are made are small. Besides, the enemy's skirmishers are so near, and so stubbornly contest the ground, that our men are greatly exposed until dark. The enemy fires wild and high, however — in fact we have never seen his men acting more excitedly; but the pickets under Capt. Goss are constantly exposed to a triple danger : the fire of the enemy's skirmishers, his shells from Fort Stevens, and the shells of our own artillery bursting short.

A Union field-battery of ten guns is drawn up during the afternoon in the field, close up in the rear of the Thirteenth and the line of captured earth-works, while a portion of the men of the Thirteenth are moved to right and left to escape the fearful concussions caused by these guns posted about three rods in their rear. The Second Wisconsin Battery furnishes six three-inch Parrott guns for a part of this business. Twenty pieces of Union artillery, in all, are soon playing on Fort Stevens, which replies for a long time with apparently twelve or fifteen guns, and then is silenced by the Union fire. We have seen their flag fall twice during this engagement. It is intensely interesting to witness such a cannonade, though all of our pickets are directly in line between the two fires, and a little over a quarter of a mile from each, and are half deafened by the cannon and the incessant screaming of the shells flying just above our heads. A rumor goes around that this fort is to be stormed; in which case we will advance as skirmishers to a point as near to the fort as we can gain, and work upon the enemy's gunners.

Fury itself is let loose during all the afternoon, and any number of shells, and worse still, the multitudes of pieces, fly over our heads in all directions, smash against the trees and plow up the ground. The stumps and trees, however, afford very fair protection for the most, and we take advantage of every species of cover, and are firing continuously ourselves. The last time the rebel flag falls the halliards only appear to have been cut, the new staff standing uninjured. In place of the flag cut down the rebels run up a new and larger one, bright and almost brilliant in color, which floats throughout the fight of to-day — and was still floating when the sun went down on May 16th, as Company E could plainly see from its position on the picket line. Two or three of the old barracks are blown up and knocked to pieces by the enemy's shells; giving out great clouds of dust, the logs being chinked with clay now dry as flour. Several of our men are in one of them when it is struck near one corner of the foundation by a shell and knocked into a pile of rubbish; and the men crawl out of the débris looking like millers — and scared most desirably, for they had been ordered to keep away from those buildings. All are bruised but none seriously hurt. They run! — one of them, bereft of the ampler part of his trousers, exhibiting sufficient involuntary flag of truce to draw from our pickets a glorious roar of laughter. Responsive, the rebels shout derisively, " Ho ! " " Ho ! "

The enemy's pickets make several attempts to dislodge Capt. Goss's men, but they hold their ground. Capt. Goss is noted in the Regiment as a cool, self-possessed and clear-headed officer when in the face of danger ; a man not to be easily driven. As night comes on our pickets have a little opportunity for rest, but scarcely any for sleep, and nearly every man is awake all night. Under direction of Capt. Goss, Lieut. Thompson and several of the men engage in a considerable scouting during the night, and find that the most of the whole slope, from the turnpike up to Fort Stevens, is covered with a tangled mass of underbrush and slashing. Just after dark two or three of the enemy's most pushing and adventurous men are captured. (For which, by the way, neither Co. I nor the Reg. ever got any credit. The writer now, 1887, has some of the ammunition which he took from one of their cartridge-boxes at that time, and pocketed as a relic ; English make or pattern of bullets having a little, well-greased " expander," a box-wood plug, in a conical depression in the base — a murderous little missile, capable of boring, straight through a man, a hole an inch wide. The prisoners are sent to the rear in the darkness, and may have gone to the 10th N. H. or elsewhere. They were armed with heavy English rifles.)

While we are on the picket line, late in the night, when all is still, the bells of Richmond are heard ringing — we can just hear them. They are either striking time — a great deal of it — or an alarm ; a Long-roll with bells for drums.

On the whole the night is reasonably quiet for an outpost picket line. There are one or two spurts of distant firing, but it merely serves to make the pickets on our line here still more watchful. Capt. Goss has exercised the utmost care, all the time, that the men should protect themselves with the numerous trees and stumps, and as a result only two or three serious wounds are received, among many slight ones. On the whole a fortunate day ; the enemy firing hastily and high — making a great deal of noise, but doing very little execution. A great many bullets may fly, but a man is a small thing on an acre of ground.

A few of the staff of the Thirteenth were directed to avoid exposure to the enemy's fire by keeping back in the rear. Quarter-master Morrison, however, not very easily scared, followed the Regiment in, and with some other member of it came up to the front, the bullets from the rebel sharp-shooters hitting the trees all about them as they came along. On arriving at the line of the Thirteenth then under fire, some one asks him if the rebels fired at him. Morrison replies : " I don't know — we were not hit. The rebels kept firing at the trees where we were as we came along — but we could n't see any sense in that."

Six men in the Regiment are wounded to-day, all severely : Geo. W. Hutchins of A ; Eli Huntoon, Austin Gilman and Henry Lynch of D ; Jerry Morrow of H ; and Joseph F. Lampson of I.

Brev. Maj. Gen. A. A. Humphreys, in his ' Virginia Campaign of 1864 and 1865,' page 147, states : " On the morning of May 14th, Gen. Brooks's Division (in which was the 13th) of Gen. Smith's 18th Corps occupied a part of the enemy's entrenchments on the left of the turnpike. Gen. Gilmore's two Divisions, of the 10th Corps, occupied them on Smith's left. About two and a half miles of the enemy's outer line was thus held by our troops. The Confederates occupied their second line, the right of which was well refused."

May 15. Sun. Rainy last night, and half pleasant to-day. Reg. called at 3.30 a. m. Comparatively quiet on our immediate front ; very noisy on the right towards the river. We of the 13th who are on picket, last night and to-day, in the brush beyond the turnpike — that is to the east of it — have ample evidence that the enemy is strengthening his lines in the rear of his pickets. Staff officers are continually visiting our picket line ; especially about the time when the bells are ringing at Richmond, and just heard for the distance.

No one of us got any rest last night that was worth the name. Toward this morning the enemy try twice, at intervals when all is stillest, to force our pickets back, or to capture them, but are repulsed.

To-day the Reg. prepares the reverse of the captured earth-works for defense, digging a ledge or banquette along the outer (southern) face of them for the men to stand upon, a part of the ditch being filled with water. The final assignment of position is made this afternoon, the line of the 13th stretching along about one man deep, something like a close skirmish line.

Just in front of the 13th is a clear and level space less than two hundred feet wide, and beyond its farther, or northern edge, runs a road with a bank, on its farther side, from one to three feet high, like the bank of a sunken road. On the top of this bank are numerous stumps and trees, and beyond them thick woods. Gen. Burnham to-night stretches along on the edge of this bank a long line of telegraph wire (which had been captured), winding it around the stumps and trees about one or two feet above the ground ; a most excellent contrivance for tripping an assaulting column, and causing it to fall headlong over the bank. Special preparations are made for the night with vedettes, pickets and an extra watch mounted on the top of the works. We are surprised, however, toward evening, to see all the Regiment's baggage, camp and garrison equipage, together with the officers' baggage, Adjutant's and Quarter-master's desks, books and papers, brought up and placed on the grass in the wide, open field in the rear of our line. We have come to stay — alas, too many in a permanent camp !

To-day Jeff. Davis and a body of horsemen have been seen entering and leaving the large fort on the bluff — Fort Stevens. Our batteries opened upon them, and they made off as fast as their horses could gallop, while our shells were cracking about their heads.  Capt. Goss, using his field glass, described some of them as " Uniformed as for a ball."

The worst feature of the day for our pickets in front of the works is the shelling over their heads; the fort engaging our field batteries and many of the shells falling short and bursting near us.  The concussions caused by the guns, and shells bursting so near, disturb our heads severely, and several of the men have to be sent for relief to a more distant part of the line.  The same thing occurs along the regimental line behind the works.  The shelling, however, to-day is of small consequence as compared with that of yesterday.  There is much talk to-night of our storming the enemy's works on the hill in front, on the morrow.  Since the capture of the Confederate works early on the morning of May 14th, the main line of our troops have had little or nothing to do, the work of holding the ground gained, or advancing a little here and there, devolving almost wholly upon the pickets and skirmish lines.

Capt. Goss, Company I, and Lieut. Thompson of E remain on the skirmish and picket line until late this afternoon — thus performing nearly thirty-six continuous hours of severe and trying work — when they rejoin the Reg., posted along the reverse of the captured rebel earth-works. After returning to the Reg. they have barely time to cook and eat their supper, along the edge of the ditch, before the sun goes down ; [1] then they immediately bivouac to gain a little much needed sleep, while Companies H and B guard the front, in their places, along the turnpike and beyond. A shower during the afternoon makes the ground very uncomfortable for bivouac, and the water accumulates in deep pools in the trenches. Fences are torn down, and the water and mud in the trenches are bridged over with rails and boards.

As an incident of the shelling on the afternoon of May 14th, over the heads of Capt. Goss, Lieut. Thompson of E, and the men of Co. I on the picket line, the writer will add this : Rails and a plank were thrown across a pool of water, lying among several large pine-trees close to the turnpike, a little northward from the old rebel barracks, and we sat upon them, for this was the best cover we could find while the artillery duel was going on.  While sitting here, during the worst of the shelling, a shell from our own battery struck a large dead pine-tree, just above the heads of Goss, Thompson and others, with a loud noise and lodged deep, but did not burst. During the visit in May 1885 in company with Lt. Col. Smith, the writer procured a three-inch Parrott shell dug out of the little pile of decayed wood where this very tree had stood.  A fit memento of Capt. Goss, and the battle of Drury's Bluff.  The Second Wisconsin Battery then used three-inch Parrott guns.

May 16.  Mon.  The principal day of the battle of Drury's Bluff. On Sunday afternoon, May 15th, about three o'clock, Lieut. R. R. Thompson of H with Company H and Lieut. Gafney with Company B were

[1] Sergt. W. G. Burnham of Company I corroborates. — S. M. T.

sent to the picket line, relieving Company I, under Capt. Goss and Lieut. Thompson of E, and have remained on the line until this morning.

Rebel pickets, captured last night, report that Gen. Beauregard has 30,000 men; and they threaten terrible things for Gen. Butler's army, the main line of which is here about five miles in length. About 2 o'clock this morning the rebel pickets are heavily re-enforced, the movement being distinctly heard by our pickets.

The Thirteenth is in line ready for action before daylight, and is called into the trenches for battle at 3.30 a. m. At which time Gen. Burnham, Col. Stevens and other officers together pass along in rear of our line, giving minute directions for meeting the possible onslaught of the enemy — matters having indicated some such movement on his part. Gen. Burnham himself, or his aides, was on the outer picket line all last night, so that a surprise of our Brigade is impossible.

Near 4 a. m., and still very foggy, the firing commences on the right, Gen. Heckman's front near the James River, and rapidly approaches along the line towards our front; where long before 5 a. m., nearer 4.30, our pickets are sustaining a heavy fire and replying briskly, and soon are hotly engaged and holding ground and cover as best they may, against double or treble their own number of the enemy.

At 5 a. m., the enemy's skirmish line, now practically a line of battle in one close, heavy rank, charges, and our pickets, being largely outnumbered, fall back and come over the works into the line of the Thirteenth. Gen. Burnham orders Lieut. R. R. Thompson of H, and the part of the picket line that came in with him, out again into the open field, or space, between the works we hold and the enemy; and Lieut. Thompson, as ordered, at once takes his men — the most of them from Company H, but a number from Company B — straight over the works again, neither he nor his men flinching or wavering in the least, deploys the line immediately upon passing the works, and advances with it upon the enemy — practically a little skirmish line going out over open ground to engage a rebel line of battle! By rapidity, however, they succeed in securing a position, the most of them among the trees that hold up the telegraph wire; the right of their line extending out among the stumps a few yards to the right of the standing trees. Sergeant Thomas S. Wentworth of B is the last man on the right of Lieut. Thompson's skirmish line; and he and the men near him find cover among the stumps, and at once commence firing upon the enemy near the turnpike in and among the old barracks, of which they again have full possession.

Soon afterwards Lieut. Thompson is wounded and falls, but succeeds in returning to the Regiment. Not long after he is wounded, the left wing of his skirmish line withdraws, leaving the right wing in position. In a few minutes more the rebel line, now apparently a full and heavy line of battle, fires one volley and charges. The right wing of the skirmish line, remaining in position, receives a portion of this volley; and after the rest of the volley — of bullets and buckshot — flies by, they break cover and come in over the works, into the line of the Reg., in advance of the charging enemy, and in a life and death rush, every man for himself. Sergt. Wentworth is wounded by the volley, receiving three buckshot, one in his arm and two in his leg; and Levi Capen of B is killed. The survivors of the skirmish line, as soon as they are behind the works again, instantly fall to and commence firing with might and main, upon the enemy's skirmishers wherever seen.

The writer has this concerning Lieut. R. R. Thompson's pickets and skirmish line, from Sergt. Wentworth of B; who does not claim, however, to know positively whether it was Gen. Burnham who ordered Lieut. Thompson again to the front upon the skirmish line. The writer, then in the battle line of the 13th, was told at the time that it was Gen. Burnham. Lt. Col. Smith thinks that Lieut. R. R. Thompson happened to retire with his skirmishers to the line of the 10th N. H., and that Lt. Col. Coughlin, commanding the 10th, ordered them out again; but there appears no way of definitely settling the question whether they were sent out at this time by Gen. Burnham or Lt. Col. Coughlin.

Lieut. Gafney with his portion of the skirmish line was not again ordered to the front until after the charge, when they made a very gallant and successful sortie, capturing more prisoners than their own numbers.

Now we turn again to the work of the regimental line: This second, main and last day of the battle of Drury's Bluff is, in the morning, extremely foggy, quite warm, and there is a slight fall of rain. The moon shone brightly during a part of last night, but when towards morning, the fog come up from the James River, rolling in thick and deep, the darkness fell as black as ink; so very dark that the pickets of friend and foe mingled together, passed to and fro, and scouted promiscuously and at will. At daylight the fog is so dense we cannot see distinctly thirty feet. About an hour after sunrise the fog lifts somewhat, so that we can see the enemy's picket lines. The day clears warm, becomes cloudy again at night, when it is again very dark

As this outer line of the enemy's earth-works runs westward across the field to the left of the turnpike, trench after trench and angle after angle, the Thirteenth occupies the third trench, that runs between the second and third angles; the right of the Reg. resting near the second angle, where there is one small apple-tree, the left resting at the third angle, where there is a wide gunway — or passage — through the line of entrenchments, protected by a curtain. This long line stretches the 13th out until it forms a line of battle only one rank deep. The right of the 13th connects with the left of the 10th N. H.; the most of its men being posted similarly along the second trench, between the first and second angles, and in a line curving with the trench, and in a general way forming an obtuse angle with the line of the Thirteenth. This arrangement affords an opportunity for a cross-fire upon the level, open space in front of the two regiments. The 10th N. H. also forms a similar angle with the 118th N. Y., on its right nearer the turnpike. In front of that Regt. is also a wide, open space. (The whole of this long, wide, open space on our Brigade front is now, 1885, covered with a dense growth of young pine-trees.) On the left of the 13th there appear to be no troops excepting pickets, forming the right of the 10th Corps, and but few of them are near us.

Last night the Thirteenth slept, with accoutrements on and arms at hand, in the open field near its baggage and along the reverse of the captured works; preserving its battle line as nearly as possible, and all ready for instant action upon call. About 4 a. m. the Union pickets in front of the 13th commence firing; still earlier a few rebel bullets have come out of the dense fog, and whizzed spitefully over the heads of the Reg. and beaten noisily against the boxes of our baggage, piled on the grass five or ten yards to our rear. The men of the 13th are just eating their breakfast, and do not have time to finish. The officers' breakfast is spread on the top of the baggage boxes, used as tables, and remains there scarcely touched. An extra watch is selected along the line of the 13th, and mounted on the top of the sand that the works are made of. Pretty soon a large rebel shell plunges into the sand under one man of the watch — Jacob Mehel a recruit of E — bursts, throws up the sand, and nearly buries him, jarring him severely. He immediately rolls over into the deep depression made by the displaced sand, and continues his watch as quietly and coolly as if nothing unusual had occurred: and as a reward he is at once appointed a Corporal. Later on he occupies this depression to fire from, Capt. Julian loading muskets rapidly and passing them up to him to fire. He was believed to be a German Jew.

The loud noise of heavy and rapid volleys of musketry now rolls up from the right, nearer the James River. The picket firing in our front rapidly increases, and every officer and man of the 13th takes position, for action, on the earth-works. Dim and undefined lines of the enemy can now and then be seen manœuvring — preparing to assault our right and front. They look like shadows in the fog. Soon our pickets come running in and tumbling over the works among us — some of the 10th N. H. pickets in the party, the enemy's shells plunge, tear and crash all around us, one of them bursting among the Regiment's baggage, while a perfect sheet of bullets flies threatening, but harmless, over our heads. The infernal rebel yell, instantly following the crashing noise of this volley, bursts at once from hundreds of Confederate throats : " Hur-hur-hur " — and a scream — all in a sharp falsetto, and seemingly not two hundred feet distant in the fog, but probably at four times that distance.

We can now see nothing very clearly where they are, in the fog, but instantly commence firing, every man, as fast as our guns can possibly be loaded and fired, straight at the noisy but almost invisible enemy; and the grim business of the battle rages all up and down the lines of our whole Brigade and Division with the fury of desperation and with indescribable noise and excitement. At the same time the men are cool, collected, determined, and do their work with extreme rapidity. The roar of the thousands of musket shots per minute is deafening. We have no support; the enemy, soon coming into view in the edge of the woods, and at very close range, outnumber us four to one — it is a life and death contest. We have approached too near to Richmond. It is credibly reported during the fight, that the enemy is shouting: "No quarter." They charge upon us three times, in rapid succession, each time with three lines of battle — a column six ranks deep — in long, dim, gray lines, with bayonets fixed; a whole rebel Brigade dashing directly upon the front of the Thirteenth at once, and yelling in the half impenetrable fog more like bloodhounds than like men. It is these unearthly yells that make troops nervous sometimes; but they shake no nerves among the men of the Thirteenth this morning; though we stand but one rank deep, we feel sure that we can hold these noisy fellows back, and are going to do it.

Our fire holds them in front, while the 10th N. H., on the line beyond the angle at our right, pours in a cross-fire; a steady, rapid, roaring fire, as if their muskets were being handled by some huge piece of machinery. When the rebels charge upon the 10th N. H., we pour in a cross-fire in turn. Still, but for Gen. Burnham's telegraph wire, the enemy's very numbers would flood our fire, and they would run right over us, in spite of all we can do. Fear altogether vanishes in the excitement, the fierce and hostile array, the boom of cannon, the roar of musketry, the smoke, the dust and the din of the battle. The work, however terrible, is alluring, enticing, awfully magnificent! The enemy's charges, one after another, come up and stop at a certain point; apparently about 100 yards to the front of the 13th — not over 125 yards at most.

They stop, retreat, re-form, then start up with a yell, rush towards us, then stop again; three times this is repeated, and each time we answer their yells with our muskets. We feel as the Quaker did with the burglar, when he said to him: "I bear thee no ill will, stranger, and will not kill thee in spite; but I am going to shoot, and if thy body keeps in front of my gun thou mayest get hurt — thou hadst better run."

Our guns grow very hot, are plugged, and plunged into the water of the ditch to cool them. Officers and sergeants load, while the men fire — a most rapid way. During one of his charges, some of the enemy's men, in their impetuous dash, appear out of the fog, and come straight over the works into our lines, prisoners. Twenty-three come in, in one batch. Still others dash towards our left, to get out of our direct line of fire. Another large squad throw down their arms, rush to our right for the lines of the 10th — and disappear. A number of squads of them run northward into the brush to our left, where they find an easy escape from the front of the 10th Corps picket line; judged to be a thin line from the small amount of its firing this morning. Notwithstanding the noise made by ourselves, we can hear the mingled din of cannon, shells and muskets, in the contest, on the right near the turnpike and beyond, and catch glimpses of the troops and the batteries engaged. We witness the discomfiture of a Union battery in the turnpike, amid a fearful racket, and during apparently a hand-to-hand fight.

As the fog and smoke lift, there is disclosed a most sickening spectacle on our immediate front, and we can fully view the point — a long line — where the enemy's charges stopped and broke; and "where the yell was knocked out of them," as one hard man of the Thirteenth near by remarks. O the damnable horrors of war! All the magnificence of a battle fades out in the unspeakable abominations of its immediate results. We can but pity, for it is a terrible and a most pitiful sight. On our immediate front, along the bank of the sunken road, under the telegraph wire and on this side of it, are lying a large number of the enemy's dead and wounded, in a long row, apparently several hundred of them. As they stumbled over the wire, and plunged down the bank, they bayoneted numbers of their own men, while many of their guns, let fly, are sticking up by the bayonets, at every angle, in the ground.

Now sorties are made. Company B under Lieut. Gafney, numbering 25 men, bring in 26 prisoners, two of them officers — a little Frenchman having two rebels in charge. If we could now send out a regiment, we could capture half a brigade; a strong dash from the left upon his flank could sweep the crippled enemy off our front. But we have no reserves.

A captured rebel officer — seems to be a Captain — as soon as he comes within our lines, and sees how very few there are of us, merely one rank, breaks out into cursing, and begins to shout to the enemy — now scarce three hundred feet distant — to charge again; but the muzzle of a gun placed against his head stops all that, and he marches off to the rear. They say he is a staff officer, and when he was captured demanded of his captors: "Treat me with respect; treat me with respect — I am an Adjutant General!" Fifty-nine prisoners, sure, are brought in to the 13th. There were probably more, as they came in at different times and places, and amid the intense excitement of the battle. Many of our Brigade swore vengeance against the 44th Tennessee, for mutilating our wounded and dead near Petersburg on May 7th or 8th — and execute the vengeance to-day in dead earnest. This item is common report.

John H. Harvey of E is on the works firing, and his curiosity, as the fog lifts, gets the better of his judgment; he rises higher to look over, and a rebel bullet crashes through his head, from forehead to back, and he falls over backwards among the other men, bleeding, dead. His body is laid under the apple-tree at the right of the Regiment.

By 8 a. m. the fog is nearly all dispersed; and by this time too the enemy's fierce charges in force upon our front are over, and he contents himself with firing at us when we show ourselves in any way, sometimes in regular volleys, and with a severe shelling from one of his batteries run down near, or in, the turnpike. We witness the quick silencing of this battery by the 10th N. H. The chief anxiety we now have is that the enemy will flank us on the right, and various plans are discussed for retiring. If a skilled hand could take us off by the left, through the brush, to the crown of the hill in our rear, we could sweep the whole field with our guns, and wholly prevent pursuit. But the 10th Corps there, and the 18th Corps here, are apparently not acting in proper unison, but too independently. Our watch is so sharp that no one of the enemy can show himself within rifle shot and live, so we gain a little respite to look about us ; but every man is ready for instant action, and a constant, at times fierce, contest springs up here and there with the enemy's long lines as he attempts irregularly to push his advance.

We must now go back a little and widen our view of the battle, for as the fog lifts, or rifts, and the scene changes, we can see more and farther, and catch views of the enemy's long, dirty-gray lines of battle, here and there in the brush. The battle first struck Gen. Heckman, near the James — the enemy attacking by the river road — where he is routed and captured. As the enemy sweeps along victoriously towards us, he encounters the 8th Conn. on the right of our Brigade, Lt. Col. M. B. Smith commanding ; the right of that regiment resting at a little redoubt in the line of works, close upon the turnpike. The 8th Conn. is compelled to retire for want of ammunition. Then the 118th N. Y. is attacked, almost in the rear, and forced back after a severe loss in killed, wounded and prisoners. Next the enemy pounces upon the 10th N. H. forming an angle with the 118th N. Y. ; but Lt. Col. Coughlin has sent out two companies of the 10th as flankers on his right and forming a little line nearly at right angles with his Regiment. These flankers check the enemy's advance not far from 7 a. m., and having charged upon him, secure a good position and hold it ; and now for two hours longer, and until 9 a. m. these two New Hampshire regiments alone, both together less than a thousand muskets, receive the brunt of the enemy's strong and fierce attacks, in flank and front and made by at least a whole rebel brigade, and repulse him every time. He brings up artillery to an open space near the turnpike and attempts to shell us out, but before he can fire a dozen shots every gunner is shot down by the men of the 10th N. H., and the guns are not again manned while we remain. They stand there as we leave the field — very quiet and peaceable guns.

We are behind earth-works six to eight feet high, ditch and all, and they afford very fair protection. The few scattered troops on our left — belonging to Gen. Gilmore's 10th Corps — are as yet out of range, but if we retire the enemy will come nearly upon their rear. Lt. Col. Coughlin of the 10th is repeatedly ordered to retire, but in doing so he will expose the 13th, and the other troops to the left, and he bravely objects to moving until their safety is assured ; and so finally he is left to do as he pleases, and it pleases him to act magnificently, as one of the bravest of the brave. The 10th has a little the best position, either to hold or to retire from, for there is a little cover near them ; but in the rear of the 13th there is a clear, open field 400 to 600 yards wide, an almost dead level. The ammunition of the 13th runs very low — about five cartridges left per man — and no possible chance for a further supply.

Finally, nearly or quite two hours after the two right regiments of our Brigade have fallen back, the enemy are again seen massing on our front with flags enough for two brigades, and preparing for a fourth assault upon our position; and the left of the Thirteenth swings around to the rear, through the boxes, valises and bundles of its abandoned baggage, property and records — needless and outrageous shame! a few men and officers here and there seizing what they may conveniently carry, and our whole line sullenly faces about and marches in slow time, in line of battle faced to the rear, and in perfect good order, across the wide, open, level field, south of the works we have occupied, and into the woods beyond the field, all done without any serious casualty, though we are followed by the parting compliments of a few of the enemy's bullets. Troops are also withdrawing on our right, and to our left infantry is retiring in column of fours. The Regiment are all angry, and move with sullen stubbornness. Col. Stevens was present during the battle, and led the Regiment out at the time of retiring. As it was a fight behind breast-works, no great activity was demanded of the field officers.

"It ought to be said here that Col. Stevens had orders two or three times to retreat before he did retreat; as our position was a good one we did not like to leave it."     MAJOR STOODLEY.

No entire page could state the situation more properly than these few words entered as a note by Major Stoodley, while he read the above in manuscript. It was a rapid, determined, stand-up fight, with no need of urging or hurrying; every man was ready and willing to strike, and strike again, and did so.

The whole right flank of these two New Hampshire regiments was, for nearly or quite two hours, exposed without any protection whatever, for a clear space of more than half the distance, along near the west side of the turnpike, from the rebel earth-works to Mr. Charles Friend's house — a distance of full 250 yards.

It is altogether proper, and best, that the Thirteenth should retire first. The 10th could in retiring soon reach cover, the 13th would have to go more than twice as far in open ground. A determined charge by the rebels upon the left of the 13th would imperil both regiments; so that whether by accident or design, this plan of retiring from the rebel front is the best for all concerned that could be devised. The 10th N. H. follows the 13th immediately, and also in line of battle faced to the rear, south, and also in regular order; the enemy, however, follows more closely upon the 10th, and a few men of that regiment become a little too uneasy to please Lt. Col. Coughlin, when they are about half way back from the works to the woods, and still in open ground. Upon this he instantly halts the 10th N. H., faces them to the front, north, dresses them up to line, has their flags unfurled and bayonets fixed; and then after a minute or two faces them to the rear again, south, and marches them off the field, in perfect line, and steady. All this is done in the very eyes and teeth of the enemy's troops, who are so much astounded — or pleased with the boldness of it — that they scarcely fire a shot, and only one man in the 10th is hit by the enemy's fire.

In perhaps half an hour more — and after fighting for nearly six hours — the main body of these two regiments is drawn up in line of battle, in a strong position in the hard-wood grove about 500 yards to the front, south, of the enemy's line of earth-works, and on ground over which they advanced on Saturday morning. Our Brigade line is formed on the crest of the ridge in the woods, on the west side of the turnpike, facing north — left, 13th N. H., 10th N. H., 8th Conn., 118th N. Y., right — the order being the same as when attacked in the morning. They remain in this position until about noon. The front of our Brigade is protected by a small force of skirmishers, consisting of three Companies of the 10th towards the turnpike, and off to their left Company E of the 13th with Capt. Julian and Lieut. Thompson of that Company. Co. E fires but little, being short of ammunition, and at long range, but the three Companies of the 10th, being at closer range, at times fire furiously upon the enemy re-occupying his earth-works. The Union line now again faces north, exactly where it was on the morning of May 14th.

In the afternoon the 13th, leaving Company E on the skirmish line, moves to the right, across the turnpike to the east side, and is drawn up in line of battle in a field and facing north; thus separating the Reg. from Co. E by hard upon half a mile. This movement is unknown to Co. E and it is left without orders, without support, and without any connection with the rest of the skirmish line — a most awkward position; an independent skirmish line, practically, or an outpost picket, a wide space intervening between them and the skirmishers of the 10th N. H.

While the 13th is in this field, on the east side of the turnpike — Co. H deployed as flankers, and a battery in position near by — suddenly a body of the enemy, 200 or 250 men, springs out of the woods, a short distance from the Reg. across the field, and charges, yelling like lunatics. In an instant Co. H and the battery fire one round, and the rebels turn and make for the woods from which they came, rushing pell mell over each other and leaving their dead and wounded on the field. A most foolhardy little charge. Then a rebel regiment appears moving in the same woods. A little later the 13th is moved forward in line of battle, into the woods whence the rebels emerged, but finds no enemy. The 13th remains in this position until nearly night — one of the Reg. writes: "toward night" — when it marches into the turnpike, is placed at the rear of the Brigade to cover the retreat, and without communicating in any way with Co. E, retires with the rest of the forces to Bermuda Hundred. The Reg. arrives there about dark — between 7 and 8 p. m. — and goes into camp, on the old camping ground, after a long, hard, and exceedingly dangerous day's work, dispirited and beaten. Leaves its baggage, records and dead in the hands of the enemy, and Co. E almost as dangerously situated.

The most of the day's fighting is over by 2.30 p. m. Many occurrences of to-day clearly indicate that the connection between our Brigade — Gen. Burnham's — in the 18th Corps, and the Brigade next on our left, in the 10th Corps, has been very faulty indeed.

"May 16th. The rebels opened on us early. They had heavy re-enforcements yesterday. The right and left (of the Union line) broke, and the centre had to retire ; which we did in good order, but with the loss of many good men. We lost (about) all our baggage. I have lost all I have except what I have on me, silk sash and all."   LIEUT. TAGGARD.

When a retreat appeared to be inevitable, the attachés of the field hospital buried the body of an officer of the 103d N. Y., who was killed in the battle, close up beneath one of the parlor windows of Mr. Charles Friend's house, carefully replacing the sods and removing all surface traces of the burial.

Now to return to Company E, Capt. Julian, and Lieut. Thompson, the writer : Our position is to the left of the skirmish line of the 10th N. H. and separated from the men of that line ; we are hard upon a third of a mile due west from the turnpike, on a high knoll among trees, and over 400 yards, and a little south of west, from the part of the works where we fought in the morning. These works we can see, running westwardly back from the turnpike, for quite half a mile ; we can see the first, second, third, fourth and fifth trenches, in the zig-zag course of the line. We can also see all the open ground both north and south of the trenches, the old rebel barracks, a long stretch of the turnpike, and beyond it the slope all the way up to the fort at the top — Fort Stevens, possibly three fourths of a mile distant — a huge affair with very high parapets, and a bright-colored rebel battle flag floating high above it. We have a broad outlook. There are no pickets near to us on our left, and Co. E is posted in a line of squads of three or four men each, a total of about thirty men. The rebels are seen carrying off their wounded, from the scene of their charges of the morning on our front, and they have a large number to attend to, negroes assisting, while their troops in heavy force are marching to and fro and massing in the distance. Half a dozen guns on this knoll could now have for a target five or eight thousand Confederates in full view and within easy range ; it is a wonder that the guns are not here !

Soon a body of Massachusetts troops (said to be) and of Gen. Gilmore's 10th Corps, four or five hundred strong, appears off to our left in the open field between us and the enemy's works, and near the works on the front or south side, and marching up in splendid order takes position on the parapets of the fourth and fifth trenches — those next west of the Thirteenth's position in the morning; the men lie down at full length on the sand of the parapet, their feet towards us, their heads towards Richmond. The short fourth trench is almost exactly due north of Co. E's position. While they lie there the enemy begins to re-occupy his works from which our Brigade has just withdrawn. This is done by two bodies of Confederates acting quite independently. One body of them has passed the works from the north to the south side, and now swings from the enemy's left toward his front and right, coming in from the turnpike westward, and filing along in the very ditch, on the south side of the works, which our Brigade had occupied — nothing could be done more awkwardly by a drove of cattle. But by so doing, four rebel regiments — at least four large, separate organizations, each having a battle flag, the usual stars and bars — come nearly in flank and rear of the Massachusetts men on the parapets of the fourth and fifth trenches. Now comes the other body of the enemy, as skirmishers, approaching the north side of their works from the west side of the old barracks, and with great caution; but pretty soon showing their heads for a long distance close up along the north side of their works, taking a view for a moment, and then dropping down out of our sight behind them. These skirmishers are evidently being handled much better than the rebel regiments moving along the south side of the works. The results of the two movements are to man a long stretch of the recaptured rebel works on both sides at once; a heavy cautious rebel skirmish line in the ditch on the north side with their faces toward us, and a brigade of incautious rebels in line of battle in the ditch on the south side with their backs toward us — and this we presume is what is meant by "holding the fort."

The rebel brigade in the south ditch halt at first and turn their backs toward us and the 10th N. H., and face toward Richmond; soon breaking into a double-quick by the flank, toward the west, along the ditch, and re-forming farther along by file into line — all not only on the wrong side of the works, but wrong side out, and wrong end first! Victory has turned their heads. Every Confederate, however, as he is snapped into place, by the file-into-line movement on the double-quick, halts, raises his musket and fires at the Massachusetts men across the angle; the Confederates forming in the trench which was held by the 10th N. H., firing across the trench which was held by the 13th, upon the Massachusetts men on the parapet of the next trenches westward. The Massachusetts men do not seem to have expected anything of this sort, they have no chance to obtain cover, and before the affair is over, nearly two thousand rebels get a shot at them, and some have time to reload, and to fire a second time; the Massachusetts men are terribly cut up, and at once retreat westward around beyond the left of Company E's position, falling as they go. They seem to be the extreme right regiment of the 10th Corps. It is for us the saddest sight of the whole battle, but we are too far from them either to have given them any warning of their danger or to assist them now. Still the Massachusetts men pluckily re-form to breast the rebel fire, but have to fall back and are soon out of our sight altogether, excepting their dead left behind them on the field. The whole affair is one of but a few minutes, and the range of the rebels too long for our muskets to be used with much effect, even if we had a plenty of ammunition.

But the enemy has done a stupid, foolhardy and most strange and ridiculous thing, and their numbers are rapidly increasing; and the 10th N. H. are now ready to strike them dead in the rear, and at once make the woods ring with volley after volley. These south-ditch rebels receive the fire of the 10th, and possibly of other of our troops nearer the turnpike, directly in their backs as they stand in a long, dense line of battle, and we can see them go down by dozens. We commence firing, but are too far from them for our fire to have much effect, and we have but little ammunition. There are now not far from 3,000 Confederates in plain sight in that long gray line of battle. The whole view, from where we are, is well worth traveling many miles to see. Capt. Julian shouts to his men to fire, and exclaims: "I would give a thousand dollars now for a big cannon chock full of grape!" The Captain has seen service as an artilleryman. But there are no cannon hereabout now. The 10th N. H., however, being nearer than we are, continue a fierce fire ; and the rebels scramble over to the north side of their works in the most hurried manner, but we can see a long line of them lying still on the white sand, their battles o'er, and apparently paying for their rear attack on the Massachusetts men by two or three to one. The survivors of them are soon in the north ditch facing us, but lying low, and scarcely firing a shot.

During this most lively scrimmage, a rebel officer, mounted upon a large white horse, rides up from near the old barracks and the turnpike at a furious gallop, and drives his horse up on the top of the high bank of sand, where the 10th N. H. were in the morning, gesticulating, waving his sword, and shouting like a wild man; and then, in a moment, both horse and rider wilt down and collapse together in the ditch on the south side, struggle a little, and are still. He was evidently endeavoring to hurry the rebels over the works to the north side, where they ought to have been all the time. The whole rebel line now faces south.

Pretty soon the colors of four rebel regiments are planted on the part of the works where the Tenth and Thirteenth fought in the morning ; while still other rebel regiments hurry along past their rear and form, one after another, on their right, until the whole works are manned by them so far as we can see. Now the enemy begins to examine the Thirteenth's baggage, to roll up our blankets, to eat our breakfast, to drink our coffee, to put on our clothes, to handle sundry papers and fling them away ; one fellow coolly sits down, throws off his shoes, and hauls on a pair of our boots — and last, to rob our dead. One of them having just appropriated Capt. Julian's overcoat, proceeds to rifle the pockets, and to strip the clothing from the body of John H. Harvey of E, which we were obliged to abandon lying near the lone apple-tree, at the second angle, near where the right of the 13th rested in the morning. This is a little too much for Sergt. Charles F. Chapman of E, who puts the powder of two cartridges into his gun, rams home a bullet, runs forward a rod or two to the edge of the brush, rests his gun in the fork of a little tree, and fires ; the pilfering rebel lies down and never once moves again — dead or badly wounded. The range is full 500 yards.

By 2 p. m. we have in Co. E an average of less than two cartridges per man. Capt. Julian sends men back twice for more ammunition ; but the men are abused by some Colonel, they say, who thinks they are stragglers, and orders them back to us again. The contest over by the river, now to our right, grows very noisy — there is one tremendous burst of artillery near the turnpike — the enemy's skirmishers are beginning to advance into the field on our front, our position is isolated, the most of our men have but one cartridge left, and that in their guns; and so Capt. Julian resolves to swing his little line around and retire to the next line of our pickets a long distance in our rear, before it is all too late — for it is sheer suicide to remain here without ammunition — and we thus move back a few rods. Capt. Julian soon has a sharp colloquy with an officer, and Lt. Col. Coughlin of the 10th N. H. comes up to see what the matter is. Capt. Julian says that he and his men are perfectly willing to return to his former position, if he is first supplied reasonably with ammunition; but declares: "I will not go back without the ammunition — of which there is a plenty about here." The result is that we get a part of two boxes of the Tenth's ammunition; and then we return rapidly to our former position, distributing the ammunition as we go. We indeed advance our line a little, to better cover, among larger trees; and here we remain until dark, and until after all the rest of the troops on the line have retired.

Our position now is practically an isolated outpost picket. The right front of Co. E looks into nearly clear ground, the left front into a lot of dense small pines and underbrush. Just at dusk a single rebel scout appears about 200 yards to our right in the field, and Sergt. Charles F. Chapman returns him to his friends — wounding him in the arm apparently. Soon a line of men are seen close up on our front, within about two hundred feet, approaching us from the rebel side, all walking backwards, like skirmishers retreating, and firing towards the rebel lines as they back up towards us. We can see that they are dressed in very dark stuff — not gray. They get very close upon the left squads of our line before they are seen; they do not seem to have fired much down there in the brush. Before we can make out what they are, as they come up nearer; suddenly a little rebel field-battery, over near the turnpike, puffs out smoke and fire, and instantly two shells scream and crash through the trees over our heads, and a third shell lodges, and without bursting, in a huge blackwalnut tree, under which Capt. Julian and Lieut. Thompson are, and about ten feet overhead, jarring the tree to its roots. Capt. Julian exclaims: "That's direction — they're going to charge on us" — and orders a retreat; also directs Lieut. Thompson to run down to the left, and to swing the left squads of Co. E around so as to serve as flankers — all to fight as we retire. Lieut. Thompson starts on the run down the line, and just as he is between the two last squads, and within hailing distance of the last squad, on the left and orders them to fall back, that line of dark-coated fellows, now very close, suddenly faces about, and charges with the bayonet on the men of Co. E and fires a few shots. They are the enemy in blue coats stolen from our dead, and more than three to one of us — but are just a little too late for their sharp back-action game. Knowing our isolated position, they had planned to surprise and capture us all; and come within a moment of doing it — the closest sort of a shave.

The right of Co. E gets off safely, but the two squads on the left escape only by clubbing their muskets. Of these seven men, four in the left squad have a hand-to-hand fight. Sergt. John Pinkham breaks his musket over a rebel's head. John Riley — a sturdy Irishman — is seized by two rebels, gets clear, runs, is pursued, cannot get time to load, seizes his musket by the muzzle, swings it around, and lets it fly; the butt strikes one pursuing rebel in his chest and doubles him up like a jack-knife, the other stops and fires, but without effect, and Riley escapes.[1] Owen McMann, a small Irishman, is the only one they capture, or seriously hurt. McMann died in the rebel murder-pen, Andersonville.) Lieut. Thompson, near, and a witness to the most of the scrimmage, expects they will rush upon him, but is merely fired at; and soon sees the escape of all but McMann, whom none could assist without capture.

The first duty is to get all the Company safely out of the scrape and together. Notwithstanding the very close quarters, Co. E soon forms and moves steadily back through the trees, firing with all their might. The enemy fires also briskly, but hits no one — not light enough to take good aim. Company E is now sure that it has for a long time been entirely alone on this advanced line — a nice little arrangement for the regular line of Union pickets; the 10th and 13th are gone, pickets and all, no one in sight. The picket line, of which we formed a part early in the day, has been withdrawn, all excepting ourselves, to a new line nearly or quite half a mile farther back. We have been practically abandoned, or left for capture to draw the rebels on into a trap, and we have no orders!

To say that we are angry, or even furiously mad, is to say nothing at all. The enemy, in a strong line, now presses closer, as Co. E retires, but firing less. Sergt. Pinkham and Riley join the Company, having made a wide détour in the brush, but minus their muskets; and for safety we leave the field in open order as a close line of skirmishers, firing occasionally. As we come into clear ground, some Union men off to our left toward the turnpike fire a few shots at us, all going wild over our heads, and we shout to them to stop. The enemy follows us until he reaches the edge of the brush, and then he halts; we cross a wide level space — a part of the field where the 13th bivouacked on the night of May 13th — pass through a double line of dismounted cavalry acting as vedettes, and then a line of pickets, and form beyond them — the field we have just crossed being soon swept by the bullets of the contending pickets; and then we march out of range amid spent bullets coming over, join the confused, retreating mass of infantry, artillery and cavalry, composed of the 10th Corps, and plunge along the turnpike in the mud and sand, it seems to us about five or six miles, and finally after making numerous inquiries about the way we join the Regiment at Bermuda Hundred between ten and eleven o'clock at night. The first salutation

---

[1] See battles of Battery Five and Fort Harrison.

we receive on arriving in camp is: "Why — you here! We thought you had all gone to Libby." The report having preceded us, that we had all been captured. One account states that we arrived at Bermuda Hundred camp at 11 p. m., and joined the Regiment; which had already been in camp for several hours.

Company E thus remained on advanced outpost picket from about 9.30 or 10 a. m. until after dark, most of the time short of ammunition, without orders and without a single word of communication with the rest of the Thirteenth, no one so far as we know having made any attempt to recall or relieve us. If we were left as a bait to invite the rebels, after capturing us, to advance, there was a chance to exchange us for more than three times our number of the enemy, who by advancing would come upon a double line of dismounted cavalrymen armed with the 'Seven-shooters' — Spencer's carbines. In such a ruse we learn something about the experiences of live bait, when one goes a-fishing. The men of the 10th N. H. were all gone before Co. E retired; all firing along their line had already ceased, and we passed over a part of their abandoned ground seeing none of them. Their historian states that they continued to hold the enemy in check until nearly surrounded, then fell back. Before Co. E retired the enemy's skirmishers had advanced across the field from the line of earth-works to the woods, to the right of Co. E, where Sergt. Chapman of Co. E shot one of them very near by; and on the left of Co. E they had come so near as to capture one man, and to have a hand-to-hand fight with others, who escaped only by clubbing their muskets. But for the darkness the Confederates had not stolen so closely upon us, and but for the darkness, as matters were, they had easily shot half of us. Companies rarely get into a worse place, and then get safely out again. When we first leave our position, there is not a Union soldier within a quarter of a mile of us; for we had advanced, after getting ammunition, to the spur of the ridge or knoll overlooking the field more clearly, and with more safety to ourselves, than our position earlier in the day. Company E retired to Bermuda Hundred with troops of the 10th Corps, not seeing any troops of the 18th Corps. The 18th Corps had gone many hours before, and with our Brigade — Gen. Burnham's — among them.

When men have once been detached from their regiment, they run the risk of falling into the hands of persons who care little what becomes of them. The writer regrets to say so much about Company E, but excuses himself on the plea that it is a matter of history, if not all of a general interest, and, coupled with what Company A had to put up with, shows a proof of reprehensible irregularity somewhere; besides he is writing what he knows about this Thirteenth Regiment. Co. E was probably in charge of the officer of the picket, whoever he may have been, and the space between the pickets on the left of the 10th N. H. and those of Co. E he may have regarded as the space between the pickets of the two corps.

"I arrived with my Company in the old camp at Bermuda Hundred at 10.30 p. m. on the evening of May 16th. We had no rations, and were very hungry, and much exhausted by the long and hard day's work of nearly twenty hours. I succeeded in obtaining two boxes of hard-bread for the men of Company E, about thirty in number, and then Col. Stevens furnished me with a supper. Many in the Regiment supposed that we had been captured by the enemy, and were quite surprised on learning that we had come into camp. When we arrived the Regiment were in bivouac and asleep." CAPT. JULIAN.

We now turn again to the general account of the day: During the morning hundreds of rebel bullets were beating against our regimental baggage, lying in the open field behind us; demonstrating the dangers of a retreat across that broad field all completely swept by the enemy's shells and bullets. The prisoners came in in large squads, at one time constantly passing through our lines to the rear. Many gave themselves up voluntarily. There must be credited to the Thirteenth many more than 59 — chiefly belonging to the 44th Tennessee — as given in the official reports. Possibly some of our prisoners have been accredited to other regiments. Among others the Adjt. General of Gen. Bushrod Johnson was captured by the Thirteenth. One rebel Lieutenant, who was captured, said that his company had already lost sixty men before he was taken, and that most of the companies in his regiment had suffered in about the same proportion. The 44th Tennessee was almost entirely annihilated by the fire of the 10th and 13th, and by prisoners taken. The writer knows for a certainty that Company E of the 13th fired, in the trenches this morning, and before the retreat, nearly eighty rounds per man, besides an extra supply that its provident Captain brought in early from among the Regiment's baggage. The 10th and 13th, together about 1,000 men, must have fired more than 50,000 rounds of ball-cartridge while fighting in the morning behind the earth-works.

Our retreat from the earth-works was made just in the nick of time, when the enemy was preparing, out of range, for his fourth charge upon us; consequently while retiring we receive only the fire of a few of his pickets or skirmishers. The Thirteenth loses all of its baggage, and the most of the officers all of their personal effects. The records, even, of but two or three of the Companies are saved. Company E's records are carried in Lieut. Thompson's valise. During the fight, about 7 a. m., a bullet fills the well eye — he has but one — of James W. Folsom of E with sand, and nearly blinds him. He must go to the rear, and so is directed to take this valise to Bermuda Hundred. He shoulders the valise, placing it on the shoulder towards the enemy to protect his head, joins the escort of a squad of prisoners, and marches off across the field in the rear of the 13th. He succeeds in reaching camp with the valise, and unharmed. Lieut. Staniels, Acting Adjutant of the Thirteenth, also succeeds in saving his valise by furnishing a man, who had to go, with a pass and sending him to the rear carrying the valise with him.

"As the Regiment in retreating passes through its abandoned baggage,

Sergt. Ira A. Spofford of Co. G thrusts his gun through the strap of the valise containing Co. G's records, and Lieut. L. C. Oliver takes hold of one end of the gun to help carry the valise. Lieut. Oliver is not so tall as Sergt. Spofford, and the valise does not ride well between them — giving so much trouble, that they drop it when about half way across the field. When the Reg. is finally halted, Capt. Stoodley inquires about the missing valise. Sergt. Spofford explains; but being a little touched, turns on his heel, marches straight back into the perfectly open field, picks up the valise, and brings it in in safety, amid the cheers of the Regiment. The enemy fire numerous shots at him, but he comes off unharmed. Capt. Stoodley has five dollars and a few cents in his pocket, and gives Sergt. Spofford the five dollars on the spot. The Reg. has furnished few instances of more marked bravery than this act of Sergt. Spofford's. He was always a very brave man." MAJOR STOODLEY.

The fight occurred near Palmer's Creek, about 8 miles from Richmond, on the farm of the Rev. Mr. Charles Friend — owner of the brick house — a secesh of the secesh. His house is more or less battered by shells, but he and his family moved out before we came up.

During the fiercest of the fight, to the east of the turnpike, some rebels boasted that they were of the regiment that mutilated the Union soldiers near Port Walthall. The answer to that boast was: no prisoners from that regiment went to the rear on that side of the turnpike, though quite a number were taken. This is common report.

The battle of Drury's Bluff has been a long, straggling, thin affair, though exceedingly lively in spots; and it is no great honor to Gen. Beauregard to have forced this long and almost single rank of Union men back to Bermuda Hundred. But so the battle has ended, in one of the darkest nights we have ever known, and in a retreat that comes wofully near to a rout. The turnpike is full of troops of every arm, and teams, ambulances, cannon and horses. The troops are very tired, dispirited, beaten, sullen, angry, ugly, silent.

The men of the Thirteenth, many of whom have not slept for the past thirty-six hours, have been constantly under fire, night and day — saving now and then for a few hours of rest — since the morning of May 7th, nearly ten days; have had scarcely enough of fair weather to get their clothing and blankets dry, even for once, during that time; have lost many of their best comrades, and all their regimental records and baggage are in the hands of the enemy. We may properly quote: "We have met the enemy — and all we had is his'n." The losses in these ten days are thirty-one, in killed, wounded and prisoners, the strain has been very severe upon all the Regiment, and many of the men are rendered unfit for immediate service both by exhaustion and slight wounds.

Gen. Humphreys states that from 4.30 a. m. until about 11 a. m. the roar of battle was fearful; no sooner dying down at one point than rising at another, in great successive waves of sound; that the fog cleared about 9 a. m., so that objects could be seen at a considerable distance.

Maj. Stoodley, in a letter written to his wife on May 17, 1864, states that the Thirteenth fired very rapidly from 5 a. m. until 9 a. m., and then retired. The sun commenced shining clear at 8 a. m. Our Brigade — after having retired from the works to the woods — was advanced again about 3 p. m., but not engaged; being sent in merely to cover the retreat of the other forces on the right of the turnpike, that is to the east of it. Everything has been wet for a week, and we lay every night where night happened to find us.

The differences in time, concerning the fog, may be explained by the fact that it was a ground-fog; appearing quite dense when viewed from a low point horizontally, even while the rays of the sun broke clearly through its rifts here and there.

The trench which we occupied was about eight feet wide, and nearly six feet deep, almost a moat, and now containing a considerable amount of water. The trench was on the south or outer side of the works, the earth taken from it having been thrown up to the north — toward Richmond — to form the parapet; showing conclusively that these works were built by men when not under fire — and they were locally reported to have been the work of slaves.

The attack by the enemy in the morning, just as breakfast was prepared, was so sudden that many officers and men of the 13th could get no breakfast at all, excepting what they could snatch in their hands. One mess breakfast was spread upon the baggage boxes, but could not be approached after the firing began. A huge coffee-pot, full of coffee, stood there also, and presently a rebel bullet went straight through it near the bottom, followed by two streams of hot coffee — steaming down to the grass. This coffee-pot is said to have been found in the Halfway House, apparently an old hotel.

Company B took 26 prisoners, and about the time when they were passing along behind the Thirteenth to the rear, one of the captured prisoners received a rebel bullet straight through both cheeks, tearing his face to pieces, and smashing and plowing out half of his teeth. He jogged along to the rear, clearing his mouth of blood and teeth, and — so much as he could — cursing his own careless troops in a perfect rage.

Gen. Burnham had two horses shot under him in to-day's battle.

The withdrawal of Gen. Gilmore's troops of the 10th Corps to near the Halfway House by 12 noon, may in part account for the irregularities on the front picket line to the left of the position occupied by Company E in the afternoon; and for the terrible predicament of the small body of Union troops — the Massachusetts men — on the parapets of the fourth and fifth trenches, when the rebels came firing, and by file into line, while re-occupying their works, from points near the turnpike.

During the fight in the morning, a rebel drum-corps, mere boys, came into our lines as prisoners. The plucky little fellows threw down their drums and stamped the heads in, and threw their fifes as far as they could into the grass of the field in rear of the Thirteenth. The writer went out and secured one fife, a German silver affair, which had been thrown away by one of the boys; and still, 1887, preserves it as a souvenir of the battle. It belonged to the 44th Tennessee.

While Co. E is retiring late at night, Thomas Harrigan of E comes to the writer, and remarks that he has two cartridges in his gun, that he has fallen, gun and all, into a mud hole; and if the charges remain in the gun until morning, they will give him a great deal of trouble, and wants to know what he shall do. The reply is: "Fire it off now." The gun is instantly pointed into the air and the report breaks out upon the darkness almost like the crack of a Parrott cannon; the road is full of troops and horsemen walking in silence on the soft sand and mud, and the startling discharge makes the woods ring and echo, and almost every one near by suddenly turns to learn the cause of it. The writer instantly sees that he has committed an error, and tells Harrigan to take to the woods — which he does as swift as the wind. But none too soon, for a general officer, said then to be Gen. Gilmore himself, not a rod distant, turns quickly in his saddle, calls for the arrest of the man who fired that gun, and declares that he will have him shot. His orderlies soon come around inquiring who fired the gun. Fortunately they cannot inquire of the writer — he removes! — others merely say they "don't know, the man fired and then rushed into the woods." Harrigan is in camp when his company arrives. A few shots like that would have given the enemy too much information. We were at the time about half way down from the front to Bermuda Hundred.

"Chaplain Jones, of the 13th, has written a full Diary of the Regiment's affairs up to date, and it is left, with all his other effects, in the ditch of the rebel earth-works, for the enemy to read. Chaplain Jones stopped in one of Mr. Friend's buildings on Sunday night, and this morning, in the earliest part of the fight, the enemy rings him a call-bell with shot and shell, and the front, where the Regiment's baggage is left, is soon unapproachable." CHAPLAIN G. C. JONES.

In the early morning Maj. Grantman and Capt. Dodge are together on our skirmish line, on the left of the Thirteenth, engaged in making arrangements to send sundry prisoners to the rear. While they are talking together a Confederate officer rides up out of the fog, searching for the Confederate skirmish line. Coming upon Grantman and Dodge, and not recognizing the blue, he inquires of them: "Where is the skirmish line?" Quick as thought Capt. Dodge replies: "The skirmish line is right here, Captain; you may as well get off that nag!" The Confederate dismounts, and proves to be an Adjt. General on the staff of Gen. Bushrod Johnson.

The honors and casualties of the day — omitting numerous slight wounds — are officially given as follows: Col. Stevens commanding the Regiment; Major Grantman Acting Lt. Colonel; Capt. Dodge Acting Major; Lieut. Staniels Acting Adjutant. Adjutant Boutwell present, but sick and not on duty. Sergeant James M. Hodgdon Acting Sergt.

Major. Lieut. Morrison, Quarter-Master. Morrill, Surgeon. Jones, Chaplain. Surgeons Richardson and Sullivan on the operating staff at the 18th Corps Hospital on the field. Prescott, Hospital Steward.

Company A, Capt. Carter commanding, with Lieutenants Hall and Churchill, have Andrew M. Dunsmore wounded. Capture one prisoner.

B, Lieut. Gafney commanding, with Lieut. Favor, have Sergeant Nathaniel E. Dickey wounded. Capture twenty-six prisoners.

C, Capt. Durell commanding, no casualties.

D, Capt. Farr commanding, with Lieut. Sherman, have Corporal John S. Cheney wounded.

E, Capt. Julian commanding, with Lieut. S. Millett Thompson, have John H. Harvey killed, and Owen McMann taken prisoner. Capture three prisoners.

F, Lieut. Dustin commanding, with Lieut. Taggard, no casualties.

G, Capt. Stoodley commanding, with Lieut. Oliver, no casualties.

H, Capt. Smith commanding, with Lieut. R. R. Thompson, have Corporal J. C. Walker killed, and Lieut. R. R. Thompson wounded.

I, Capt. Goss commanding, have Corporal W. B. Lewis wounded. Capture thirteen prisoners.

K, Capt. Betton commanding, no casualties. Capture eight prisoners.

Total: killed two, taken prisoner one, severely wounded five; prisoners captured forty-nine.[1]

Gen. Humphreys — pages 151–156 — drawing from Confederate sources, states concerning affairs near the turnpike, "that the fog suddenly fell, upon a moonlit night, just before day, so dense that a horseman could not be seen at the distance of fifteen paces." The fog cleared away about nine o'clock. He continues: At a quarter before five o'clock a. m. Gen. Ransom advanced in the dense fog, and completely surprised Gen. Heckman's brigade. Gen. Beauregard says that at 10 a. m. his right was still heavily engaged. Gen. Hoke with Johnson's and Haygood's brigades had been hotly engaged on the turnpike. They it was who captured the five guns there. (The affair mentioned on page 297 as witnessed by the Thirteenth.) Johnson's Brigade lost heavily — one fourth of its numbers. Then Clingman and Corse were thrown forward, but both were obliged to draw back. At about 10 a. m. the fighting in front of Haygood and Johnson was stubborn and prolonged. The enemy (Union troops) slowly retiring from Johnson's right, took a strong position on the ridge in front of Proctor's Creek, massing near the turnpike, and occupying advantageous ground at Charles Friend's; and Gen. Humphreys adds in a footnote: "This was the position to which Smith and Gilmore fell back." At 1.15 p. m. Gen. Beauregard telegraphed to Richmond: "We occupy the outer lines; the enemy is still in our front with open ground between us. Some of the Brigades (Confederate) are much cut up."

[1] The account of prisoners captured exhibits an error on the face of it, and cannot possibly be correct — it is much too small. — S. M. T.

Gen. Beauregard's force, engaged in this battle, was about 20,000 men — and his losses are put at 2,184.

Gen. Butler's force, actually engaged in the advance, was about 20,000 men also — his losses about 3,500.

When Gen. Butler's troops landed at Bermuda Hundred, on the night of May 5th, the force of the enemy was so weak about Petersburg that he might have swept everything before him, captured Petersburg, and moved to the very gates of Richmond, and may be entered and held the city. That was possible for several days; but by the time Butler was ready to advance upon Richmond, Gen. Beauregard had collected an army of hard upon 30,000 men, all told. Many thousands of Beauregard's troops came up from the south, passing by the railroad and turnpike, directly in front of Butler's lines, and but a mile or two distant; which avenues should have been closed — and might have been — before night of May 6th by one third of Butler's force.

The writer of 'New Hampshire in the Rebellion' states that the enemy charged upon the 10th and 13th three successive times in columns three lines deep (six ranks); and that each successive wave broke at the line of the telegraph wire, at the edge of the sunken road. Also refers to the rebel battery silenced by the 10th, while trying to shell us out; and relates the incident where Lt. Col. Coughlin of the 10th halts, faces about, and aligns his regiment while on the retreat from the enemy's works.

The foregoing account was written chiefly before the writer visited the field in May 1885, with Lt. Col. Smith. The outer line of Confederate earth-works runs to the left southwestwardly where it crosses the R. & P. turnpike; it crosses here about one mile south of Kingsland Creek, about 350 yards north of Mr. Friend's House (now Mr. Barney's) and about half way between the 9th and 10th mile-stones from Richmond. In this line, on the turnpike, is a redoubt for two or three guns. The first trench in this line of works runs from the left of this redoubt, that is from the west side of the turnpike, nearly west, about one fourth of a mile to, and a few yards across, a lane running parallel with the turnpike, and opened since the war. The second trench is about fifty yards long, a mere southward deflection of the line. At the west end of this trench stood a lone apple-tree, at the second angle. The third trench is about 275 yards

## DESCRIPTION OF MAP.

A. Railroad.
B. Turnpike.
C. Proctor's Creek.
D. Mr. Jordan's house.
E. Half-way House.
I. Mr. Hatcher.
F. Mr. Charles Friend's house.
G. Dr. Woolridge.
H. Clark.
M. Fort Stevens — 16 guns.
K. Position of Thirteenth May 14, 15, and 16, on Confederate works.
L. Sunken road, along which telegraph wire was stretched.
N. Drury's Bluff, or Fort Darling, system of defenses.
P. Kingsland Creek.
R. James River.

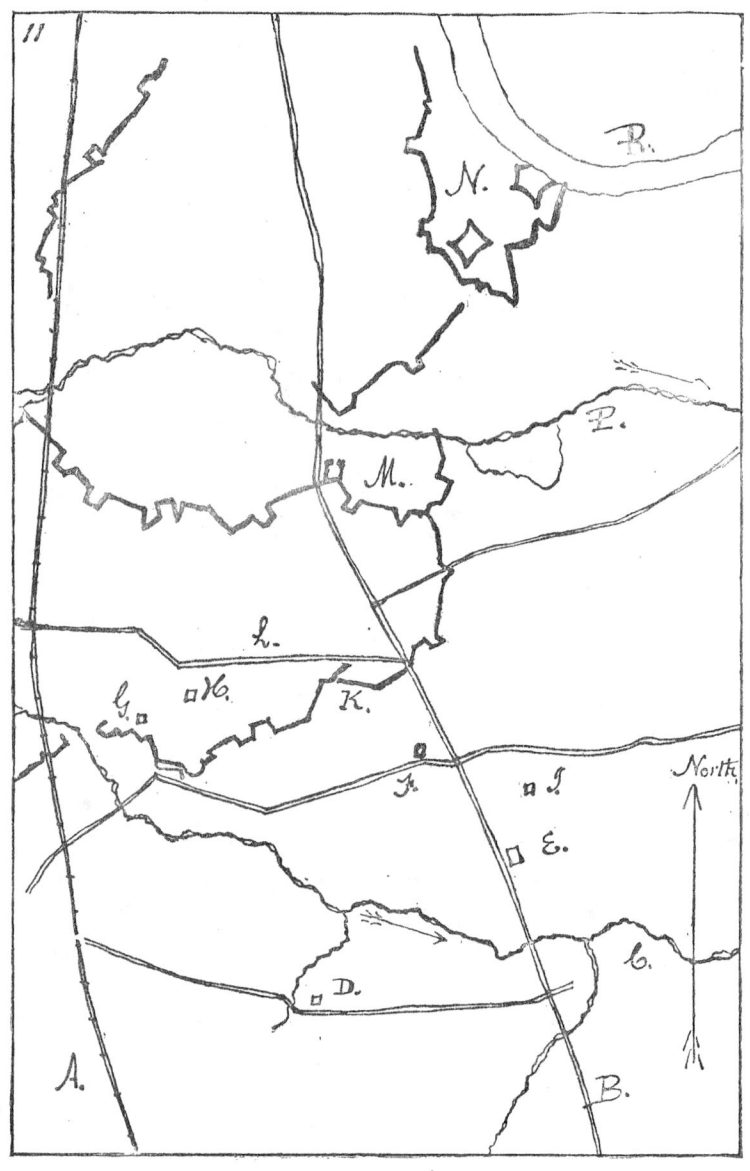

DRURY'S BLUFF, May 14-16, 1864.
Tracing of Official Map.   Scale, one and one half inches to one mile.

long, running nearly east and west, and terminating at a gun-way on the left, provided with a curtain and traverse. The fourth trench is about fifty yards long, sweeping southward, to the left of which the line zig-zags for a quarter of a mile or so until lost to sight in the woods. During the fight, the right of the 10th N. H. rested near where the new lane cuts through the first trench, and about one fourth of a mile from the turnpike. Their line covered the short second trench and sweeping around to the left occupied about one third of the third trench ; hence their effective cross fire. The 13th occupied the left two thirds of the third trench, the left of the Reg. coming to the gun-way between the third and fourth trenches — the only gun-way there is. As this third trench runs nearly east and west, the 13th faced nearly due north during the fight. The apple-tree which stood near the second angle, at the right of the 13th, has been cut down. Traces of the old rebel barracks still remain, near the turnpike, in front of the trench occupied by the 13th.

To the front — north — about three fourths of a mile distant, is a Confederate redoubt for three or four guns, located on a hill to the east of the turnpike. One or two hundred yards to the east of this redoubt, on very high, bold ground, stands the Confederate Fort Stevens, with platforms for sixteen guns. This large fort is about three fourths of a mile northeast from the position of the 13th, and is in the midst of a network of rifle-trenches connected with the famous Drury's Bluff system of fortifications.

There were no Union works. The Union army had turned a portion of the captured Confederate entrenchments, near the turnpike, between M., Fort Stevens, and G., Dr. Woolridge's house, and occupied the reverse or south side of them. See map.

Lt. Col. Smith states that we were attacked at daylight, when we could not see 100 feet for the fog. The first we knew of a general engagement the enemy struck Gen. Heckman's brigade, on the right, with yells. H. B. Gilkey of H fired 84 shots, and the Thirteenth, nearly 500 men, is said to have fired more than 30,000 rounds. The enemy about 40 or 50 rods distant, coming nearer of course, as his charges broke at the telegraph wire stretched along our front. We held the trenches for nearly three hours after the fog began to rise, the enemy on both flanks. We retired about 9 o'clock. While crossing the field in retiring, Col. Abbott of the 7th N. H. — in the 10th Corps — marched his regiment by the flank at a right angle with the Thirteenth in line of battle. As soon as the 13th was halted in the woods Capt. Smith and Maj. Grantman went to the edge of the woods and looked back over the broad field then cleared of troops ; while they were here the rebels began to come out over their works and commenced pillaging among our baggage. They had on blue coats, and Capt. Smith thought they were our own troops ; but Gen. Read, Gen. Smith's Adjutant General, then standing near by, pronounced them to be rebel soldiers.

The Thirteenth is especially indebted to Lt. Col. Smith for his time, team, intense interest in this history, and information given during these visits to its battle-fields. We may add that this visit to Drury's Bluff was made in the midst of a heavy May rain-storm — one of the real old sort — and in the usual superabundance of Virginia mud. During this visit, the writer asked a boy living near Fort Stevens — which is on his father's farm — if he could tell us where we could find some old bullets; he replied: "They're pretty well picked up now — but down by that old road, there used to be just thousands of them!" As he said this he pointed to the sunken road in front of the position occupied during the battle by the 10th and 13th N. H.

To return again to the narrative of the day:

Capt. Stoodley, ever on the lookout for Company G, had succeeded in

---

### DESCRIPTION OF PLAT.

A. Turnpike.   F. Position of Thirteenth in the battle of May 16th.

B. Confederate line of trenches: starting from a small redoubt on the turnpike, and running west nearly one fourth of a mile straight to C, which is a lane cut through the line of works since the war; thence continuing on as indicated, the distances given in yards.

D. Old Confederate barracks near turnpike, in front of 10th and 13th.

E. Position of 10th N. H. in the battle of May 16th.

G. Position of Massachusetts troops when fired upon by the rebels from nearer the turnpike, as they re-occupied their works.

H. Wide, clear field in rear of 10th and 13th, where ten Union field pieces were placed, engaging Fort Stevens — T — during all of Saturday afternoon, May 14th.

I. Position of Co. E, on the picket line after the battle, and until dark on May 16th.

K. Mr. Charles Friend's house, 300 to 500 yards south of the works.

L. Place of Thirteenth's bivouac on the night of May 13th, in a little field south of the line of woods.

M. M. Line of woods where telegraph wire was stretched along, just north of the sunken road Y. (Only a part of the road was sunken, the rest a mere track, now, 1885, very difficult to follow in the dense timber grown up since the battle; the ground was then open between the works and the road.)

N. 10th mile-stone from Richmond.   P. 9th mile-stone.

R. Kingsland Creek, nearly one mile north of the trenches held by the 13th, on May 16th.

U. Columns of rebel infantry, six ranks deep, in woods assaulting. The arrows indicate the advance of the enemy to re-occupy the works — on both sides at once — after the 10th and 13th regiments had retired to the woods L. The arrow V shows the course taken by their careless heavy column of infantry; the other arrow of their extremely cautious skirmishers.

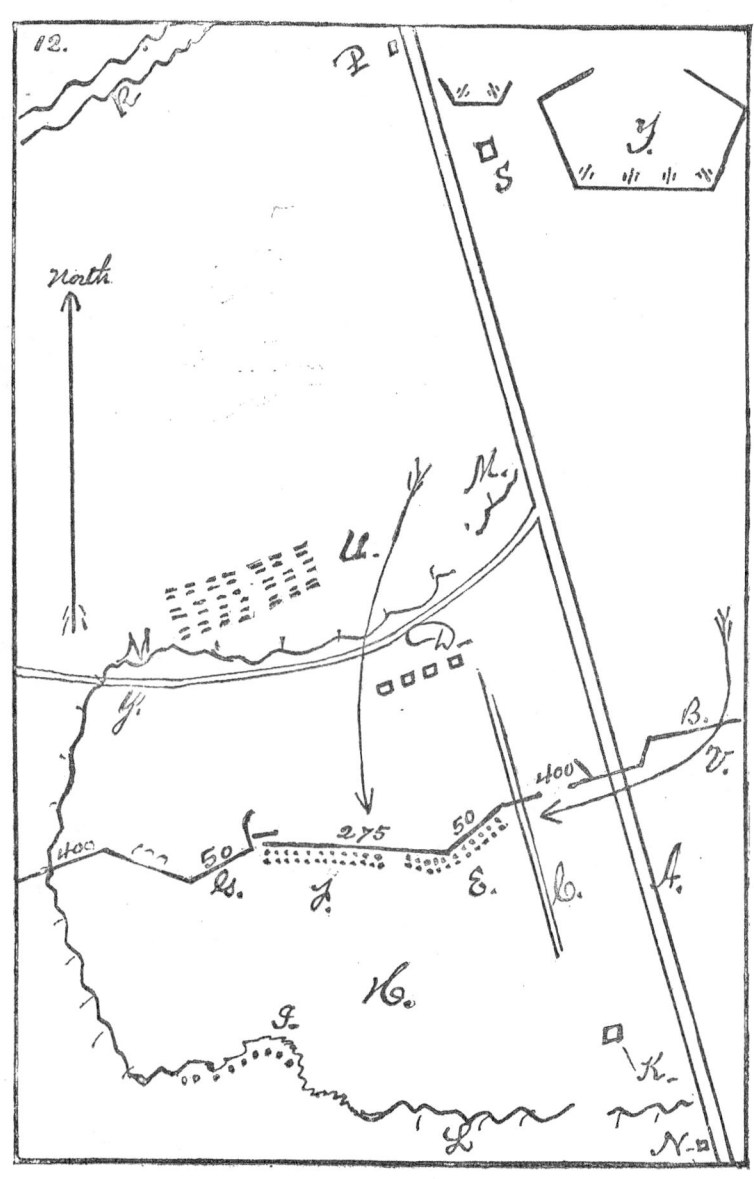

DRURY'S BLUFF, May 14–16, 1864.

From a sketch made by the writer in May 1885.

raising money enough to purchase an extra nest of three iron camp-kettles. These were used exclusively for making coffee, and when the Thirteenth retired, this morning, from the works, these kettles were left full of it. Several years after the war closed, a Confederate officer was lecturing at Reading, Mass., and related, as an incident, the capture here of sundry kettles full of most excellent Yankee coffee. On comparing notes it was made clear and certain that this Confederate officer, and his friends, had enjoyed this morning the coffee made for Company G — and appropriated their kettles. It is, no doubt, very satisfactory to Co. G to know what became of their coffee and kettles on this occasion. The Major adds facetiously concerning this: "Our coffee was on boiling when the rebels came on, and we left it to them, as they were having a hard time — it is not best to be too selfish in this world."

A word here condensed from letters written from the Hospital Department of the 13th: "May 14th. We captured the enemy's out-works within nine miles of Richmond and two of Ft. Darling. We shelled a large fort about three fourths of a mile distant all this afternoon, cut down the flag staff, and silenced the fort, and our troops were expected to storm it. Gen. Butler's Hdqrs. were at Mr. Charles Friend's house. Asst. Surgeon Morrill and I were with the Thirteenth. Surgeons Richardson and Sullivan were at the General Hospital on the field. May 15th. Our artillery shelled the rebel fort and lines. Our baggage and camp equipage was brought up to the front this evening. May 16th. A dense fog prevailed at 2 a. m. About 5 a. m. the enemy massed in large numbers, and with most hideous yells charged upon our troops (Heckman's). Our Brigade, on the extreme left, was not exposed for some time. Our men could see but a few feet ahead. Artillery could not be used with accuracy. The rebels came upon our Brigade, lying safe and silent in the rifle-pits waiting for them, and approached within a few rods, when an awful volley sprang from the Brigade, and as the smoke lifted the rebels lay in windrows; their columns broke and ran. Volley after volley followed. The fog lifted about 8 a. m. Gen. Burnham sent repeated orders for our Regiment to fall back, but the orders were disregarded until a peremptory order came to 'fall back immediately,' which was obeyed. We lost all our personal and regimental property.

"A rebel soldier states — verified by others — that Gen. Beauregard was re-enforced by ten Brigades from Gen. Lee's army on Sunday, 15th, and they were double-quicked six miles on Monday morning, 16th. Whiskey mixed with gunpowder was freely supplied them, rendering them perfectly reckless. I dressed this rebel soldier's wounds. All the rebels I saw were pleased beyond measure to get within our lines as prisoners. I have never seen an instance where a rebel prisoner — well or wounded — was not treated with kindness; while the rebels rob our wounded, and strip and mutilate our dead, as I know from personal observation.

"We have rested but three days in the last ten. Everybody seems tired to death. There has been a great deal of rain. We have had to march through it, fight in it, and sleep on the bare ground under it. As we retreated from the front to-day I assisted in gathering muskets, picking them up by the armful, piling them up against some tree and setting them on fire, to prevent their falling into the enemy's hands. In the afternoon we turned from the road into a field on the east side of the turnpike, lay down flat upon our faces, just on the rear slope of a knoll, while a section or two of a field battery took position behind us. Soon a rebel line appeared emerging from the woods, and when within a few rods they were met with a withering fire which effectually checked their further advance. Then we arose and continued our retreat. I think the Thirteenth covered the retreat from the front. The loss in the 13th (during the recent engagements) has been 5 killed, 19 wounded, 2 missing."     PRESCOTT.

"Rev. Mr. Charles Friend in a conversation with me at his house, after the fall of Richmond, stated that he was an original secessionist, and went around making speeches in favor of secession. Now he knew he was in the wrong, for had the South been in the right, God would have given them the victory. At the beginning of the war he owned about forty slaves, now only their children were left with him, and he asked me, ' What was to become of them?' I replied that that question was not for me to solve."     MAJOR STOODLEY.

During the advance Quarter-master Morrison and others rode beyond the lines, and came to a house which had just been deserted by its occupants and the enemy. The flight was evidently hasty, and the house was found well supplied with dishes, cooking utensils, furniture, etc. Fearing that all this would soon be destroyed, and thinking that many things now in the house would be very serviceable at the Field Hospital near the Half-way House, Morrison hurried back to Surgeon Richardson, obtained an ambulance, proceeded with it to the house, loaded it with beds, bedding, crockery, cooking utensils, etc., and conveyed them to the Field Hospital, where they were used for the comfort of wounded Federal and Confederate alike. On the retreat on May 16th, the most of these things had to be abandoned, but they served an excellent purpose while in our hands. Among the things he found abandoned at this house, was a gray uniform dress-coat belonging to Col. E. C. Brabble of the 32d North Carolina, which he preserved, and still, 1887, has in his possession.

"May 14th. Advance in line of battle at 6 a. m. Gain the enemy's outer works at 8 a. m. Regiment remains on the outside of the works all day and all night. Showery. 15th. Up at 3.30 a. m. Regiment remains on outside of works all day and all night. 16th. Up at 4 a. m. Rebels charge upon our lines at 4.30 a. m.; and at 9 a. m. we fall back, giving up the outer works. Fall back gradually, and at night arrive at our old camp; losing since leaving camp five men killed, nineteen wounded and two missing. Lose all our Headquarters documents."

Diary of LIEUT. STANIELS, Acting Adjutant.

The following extracts from letters, written May 17th–22d from Hospital by Lieut. R. R. Thompson to his wife, are inserted as giving the approximate hour when the first heavy column of the rebel charge struck the Thirteenth, as Lieut. Thompson was wounded at that time. One or two other facts are corroborated also, and after narrating several incidents already entered in this book he continues:

"Chesapeake General Hospital, Hampton, Va., May 22, 1864. On Monday May 9th we went southward towards Petersburg, which was about eight or nine miles distant from our camp. We approached to within two miles of the city and there remained till the next day. We had some fighting, and lost a few men. During the night we lay on our arms in line of battle. Early in the evening of the 9th the enemy attempted to force us from our position; but were repulsed by the 10th N. H., with heavy loss to the rebels. On the morning of the 12th we started on the main object of the expedition — for Richmond. We found the enemy at noon, and drove him back about a mile. During the night the rebels fell back about half a mile, and then seemed to make a stand. It was rainy every day from the 12th to the 16th.

"On the morning of the 16th the enemy opened on us at daylight. The fog was so thick that a man could not be distinguished at a distance of more than ten yards — if so far. The right of the Union line fell back first. The action was very sharp for a while. I was wounded in my left side about six or seven o'clock. The ball just grazed my ribs, nearly opposite the pit of my stomach. When I left the field our forces were retiring.[1] From May 6th to 16th we were under fire more or less every day excepting two, and at night lay on our arms. My wound is not dangerous, though very sore, and I am feeling pretty well. I arrived at this Hospital May 17th."
LIEUT. R. R. THOMPSON.

Extracts from the 10th Corps army correspondence, referring to the battle of May 16th, and the troops of the 18th Corps: "In general the fighting here has been bushwhacking rather than that of pitched battles. The woods have hidden everything not in immediate proximity. The fight of Monday 16th is represented as one of almost unexampled fierceness. Telegraph wire was stretched along the front of Burnham's and Wistar's Brigades, and the rebel prisoners agree in saying they were greatly confused by it. The fog occasioned many mistakes. A rebel Captain went straight in among our pickets while looking for his own men. Rebel soldiers walked into the trenches of the 13th N. H., and were then in an agony of fear lest they should be shot down. A rebel Brigadier it is said, addressed a Union regiment as the 23d Virginia, and requested them not to fire upon their friends. Burnham's brigade lost 339 men. In retiring the Union line went backward from right to left, regiment by regiment, as the bark is peeled from a tree."

While we are thus ringing the door-bell of Richmond, and then running for dear life, leaving our 'May Basket' hanging on the door-knob and filled with all our best camp gear — as children play at the game with flowers; Gen. Sheridan with his cavalry has made the entire cir-

[1] He refers here to our troops to the right of the 10th and 13th. — S. M. T.

cuit of Gen. Lee's army, sweeping around between the rebel host and Richmond. If Gen. Sheridan had commanded these 30,000 and more men of us here, since May 4th, we had swept this entire region clean of the enemy, from Petersburg below to Richmond above, and bagged that lively brace of towns besides. For a number of days — precious days — we were five to one, at least, of all the men the rebels could muster. This is the way we look at the affair.

Gen. Gilman Marston relates, 1887, that some time after the war he met a North Carolinian, who said that he was in one of the regiments which charged upon the Union troops at Drury's Bluff; and the General asked him if he remembered meeting with any telegraph wire during the charge. The North Carolinian replied: "Yes, I remember that wire. It cut my legs." Then he continued with many words, expressive, but not for ears polite; his earnest language and manner giving evidence that he made a very intimate personal acquaintance with that wire.

## CAMP AT BERMUDA HUNDRED.

May 17. Tues. Misty, cloudy, chilly, some rain. The Thirteenth is called at daylight, is moved about a little until a camping ground is selected, and then a large detail is at once set at work on the entrenchments. Earth-works rise up all along the line, more as if they grew than as if they are being made. The pickets are firing briskly all along the line, and artillery is also busy. Many spent bullets come over among us, and now and then a shell. War's music, however, plays loudest far over on the right. Gen. Butler's forces here are being "bottled-up" in very truth — and the cork well driven. The enemy on our front is in very strong force. But see the Thirteenth! The men look as if they had not slept for a week, or washed for a month; their caps are helmets of unburnt brick, their jackets muddy cross-roads, their trousers cylinders of clay, and their feet land's end.

When we approached this line in our magnificent holiday excursion, on May 5th, victory promised us wonderful successes; now she has moved — bag and baggage — across to Gen. Beauregard, who flaunts a hundred rebel flags in our faces — and we cannot help it.

The enemy get the range of our field Hospital and shell it savagely. One of their shells lodges in the ground under the bunk of a wounded man. Expecting it to burst, the man closes his eyes and faints away; then rouses a little, quivers a moment, faints again, and expires — killed by sheer fright. The shell does not burst. The worst dread that ever comes upon a soldier is the fear of another wound, or of being shot to death, after having received the shock of a severe wound and before recovering from that shock. The dread is nervous, when nerves are weakest, as well as mental — a double strain.

Notwithstanding the keenness of indignation and chagrin with which this army feels the defeat of yesterday, it must be borne in mind that an advance upon Richmond from this southern side was beset with numerous and great difficulties. Above Trent's Reach the enemy controlled the James, and re-enforcements could come to the enemy upon both flanks of Gen. Butler's line and straight upon his front; and if in strong force could break through Butler's rear-guard, thrown out towards Petersburg, and come upon his rear. The Army of the James was a mere loop of a line thrust into the enemy's country from the James about Bermuda Hundred and Point of Rocks; extreme celerity of motion, before the enemy could be re-enforced, was the only plan of success.

**May 18. Wed.** Cool, showery. Every available man shoveling muddy earth into long heaps, out of trenches filled with a network of innumerable and almost interminable tree roots. About six o'clock a. m., 100 men, with a shovel in one hand and a gun in the other — the shovel the brighter metal — are sent from the Thirteenth under Capt. Stoodley, with Lieutenants Sherman and Taggard, to the outer picket line, upon some especially dangerous work on the entrenchments. The Reg. worked all last night shoveling and slashing, works all day to-day, and all of this night, without a cessation long enough to call a rest; while the picket firing and shelling is very heavy, and scarcely ceases for a minute day or night. Guns are kept always at hand in momentary expectation of a battle. The Reg. removes a short distance this forenoon towards the right. We are encamped in a wheatfield; and the wheat is getting thoroughly threshed before it is ripe — like the Army of the James. One soldier of the 13th writes home to-day: "We moved camp to-day up on a hill in the woods."

(May 1885: Bermuda Hundred lines not visited by the writer. Neither he nor Lt. Col. Smith could recall any landmark there to point out our camp, excepting a ravine at the left and front of the Thirteenth that was spoken of at the time — May 21, 22, 1864 — as the deepest, worst and least passable from the enemy's side, of all the ravines on the whole line; and that the Union line ran over a very sharp, conical hill near the ravine, the Thirteenth being for a part of the time located on this hill. Lieut. Prescott thinks that we camped, on the night of May 16th, to the left and slightly to the rear of where Fort Dutton now is; moving on the 18th to the right of that fort, a short distance only, and taking position behind a long line of rifle-pits, facing nearly north.)

**May 19. Thurs.** Misty, cloudy, chilly, rainy, muddy, nasty — intolerably nasty. Thirteenth roused at 3 a. m. and posted in the rifle-pits, and from that hour we are hard at work on the entrenchments all the forenoon. In the afternoon we move towards the left, a few rods only, to a new position on the line, and encamp close up under cover of the rifle-trenches. Heavy firing in every direction, the rebels shelling our camp and lines continually all the day. Near us we hear the incessant pounding of heavy guns — big Parrotts; part of the siege train of about one hundred guns, from 100 lb. Parrotts down, and from 10 inch mortars to field-howitzers, requiring twelve schooners to float it, sixty artillery wagons to transport its odds and ends, and 1,700 artillerymen to man it — all under the command of Col. Henry L. Abbott, of the 1st Conn. Artillery.

One angle of the line now occupied by the 13th faces southwestwardly, and looks straight down into a deep and densely wooded ravine, which no troops but infantry or dismounted men can possibly cross to us. Our camp is close to the right and east side of this ravine, in a level wheatfield. About midnight to-night the enemy attacks in force, and an hour's sharp fight ensues both by infantry and artillery — noisy, furious.

The rank and file of this army feel anything but agreeable at the summary defeat at Drury's Bluff, and the humiliating present situation here. The fact cannot be passed. Our soldiers are so inexpressibly angry and disgusted, that they have ceased swearing about the defeat; and they would fight like mad furies if let loose upon the enemy now.

Adjutant Boutwell and Quarter-master Morrison sent to the Hospital, both very sick. The members of the 13th generally have absorbed so much of yellow Virginia mud into the pores of their skin, and have drunk in so much also together with malarial poison in the execrable fluid found hereabout and called water, that their blood appears clogged, and one half of them are sick with the 'yallers,' as the natives call jaundice. There is a mine of yellow ochre not far away, and the faces of many of the men look as if stained with it. The mud is terrible, clay mud mixed with gravel, a thick gruel, yellow mud, ochre mud, infamous mud; mucilage, gum, pitch, glue, cement are all nothing and nowhere compared with this huge Virginia gritty viscous gulf of geological gob and gumbo.

May 20. Fri. Fine day. Reg. at work on the entrenchments; their guns all stacked within reach and ready for instant use. Last night the Reg. was called into line, and prepared for action four times, the enemy attacking each time; Reg. not engaged. Some very severe fighting to-day, and near enough for us to hear the firing and shouting, and to catch a goodly number of the overshot shells and bullets. The Reg. not engaged to-day excepting with shovels, and picks, and in keeping all our heads as low as the work will permit. The chief trouble to-day is on the right near the James River, where the enemy have been attacking all along the line — this forenoon — making three furious charges, but each time repulsed. The Confederate General, W. S. Walker, in command is captured. The 97th Penn. is said to have been badly cut up. Gen. Butler and staff pass along our lines.

Chaplain Jones, of the 13th, takes the position of Chaplain of the Department Hospital, City Point, under Surgeon H. B. Fowler, of the 12th N. H. The 13th loses a good friend — a much better friend than they think. Chaplain Jones deserves a good word at parting. He has always been kindly to a fault. He has cared for the regimental mail with more faithfulness than any regular Post-master. He has written letters home for the men who could not write for themselves. His visits to the sick have been as regular as the day. He has written a full and heartily complimentary history of the Regiment, which was lost at Drury's Bluff. His letters to home newspapers have greatly benefited the Thirteenth, by calling attention to the needs of the men. The chief obstacle to a proper appreciation by the men of his valuable services has been his use of a formal religious written service. Fifty off-hand hearty words, extemporaneously spoken, go farther with them, than fifty pages of set prayers, no matter how well read. Chaplain Jones was greatly missed in the Regiment after his departure; and in the General Hospital, he and the men of the Thirteenth, taken there, at once mutually sought each other.

A soldier of the 13th writes home: "Moved our camp again to-day. Fell into the rifle-pits at 8 p. m., and again at 11 p. m."

Irreverent camp talk: "Say, Tom, I've got a conundrum for you." "Well, Bill, out with it; no gags now." "Why is our General like a Major General?" "Oh — that's easy enough! He has — he has —; Oh fudge — I give it up; ask me something easier than that!"

May 21. Sat. Fine day. Last night the Union gunboats in the James shelled the enemy nearly all night; destroying the sleep of two armies, and sending the frogs to mud — and we guess that is about the full effect of all the firing. The Thirteenth is called before we can clearly see, and sets at work on the entrenchments. The boys say that "early daylight means dark daylight down here in this hole in the mud." Sharp picket firing all the day. To-night, about 10.30 p. m., the enemy suddenly opens a masked battery on our immediate front, a battery that must have been planted very stealthily, and commences a furious shelling, firing with the utmost rapidity, while his pickets, strongly supported, attack our lines with vigor, about one third of a mile to our right, yelling, firing, and raising a general din. Our infantry there replies. Gen. Butler telegraphs orders to give them a drubbing, and our whole line of artillery opens with all its power, and there follows a regular roar of artillery and musketry, continuing for a full half hour, the sky ablaze with brilliant and incessant flashes of fire. The Thirteenth rush out of quarters and man the works, and remain in the front trenches all night.

The contest in all continues for nearly an hour, when the explosion of a magazine, or of an ammunition wagon, near the enemy's battery, silences it, and the general firing soon ceases. The enemy is repulsed, and leaves his numerous dead on the field. The explosion sends the enemy's shells far up into the air, above the top of the tallest trees; exploding there into magnificent fire-works, and a shower of fragments, and giving us a fine opportunity to cheer. The most of the fragments and missiles rain down upon the enemy's own head; but next morning — 22d — many grape shot are picked up in our camp, and kept as souvenirs of the explosion. A prisoner states that the enemy had his infantry massed for a night attack, but our "big guns gave their battery such a terrible pelting," they were forced to give over the purposed attempt.

The line of the entrenchments, now held by the Thirteenth, forms a sharp angle towards the front — or a salient — at the head of a deep ravine, and then trends to the left and rear along the edge of the ravine. During this night melée, the writer is directed to mount the parapet of the works, near the angle, and watch for the inter-line pickets, or vedettes, if they are driven out of the ravine. Taking the position designated, on the parapet, behind a small pine-tree left standing in the works, he becomes a witness to the whole affair. A fight with artillery, in the night, is very grand to see ; but a little pine-tree is small defense against shells.

The general situation of the Army of the James, at Bermuda Hundred, is well down in the crotch formed by the forks of a huge letter Y, formed here by the Appomattox emptying into the James at City Point. The lower part of the Y, is the lower James. The left fork is the Appomattox, with Petersburg at the apex. The right fork is the upper James, with Richmond at the apex. Gen. Butler's line of works crosses the country between the forks, from points on each fork about half way its height; that is from Port Walthall on the left, to Trent's Reach on the right, a line four or five miles in length. Gen. Beauregard's line crosses a little farther up, and only a few rods in front of Gen. Butler's line; and he has both the railroad and the turnpike in his rear, just about near enough for a convenient distribution of supplies along his line. Gen. Beauregard admits that we gave his army a fearful drubbing on May 16th, and he is reported as declaring his success a barren victory.

May 22. Sun. Warm, fair day, rainy at evening. The enemy is pretty quiet to-day, excepting his unending shelling of our lines and camp. This morning while the Reg. is being formed for inspection, Gen. Hiram Burnham commanding our Brigade comes along, and not pleased with the line made by the 13th, the ground being very uneven, draws his sword, and attempts to dress the Reg. up to line. The fault is with the position of one of the markers — too far to the front — which causes the right of the Reg. to stand in the ditch in rear of the works. The General waves his sword several times, motioning the marker back, but the marker does not stir. The General calls to him, but the marker takes no heed ; then the General rounds out his big voice — to be heard half a mile : " Marker ! Are you real estate ? " The marker replies in a lower voice, " No, Sir." " Then," says the General, " if you are not real estate — why don't you move ? " He straightens the line to suit him. Soon he turns to the officer of the picket, Lieut. Thompson of E, standing near by in the trench, and demands pretty roughly, why he does not turn out the camp-guard for a General. Lieut. Thompson explains that these men are the pickets, a special line, not a camp-guard ; the camp of the 13th being placed close to the earth-works for necessary protection from the enemy's continuous fire. The General, upon this, promptly begs pardon for his demand, looks at every man along the picket line, and passes on. This illustrates the man, severity and gentleness strangely combined. As it is the hour of inspection, the General quickly approaches a man of this little picket line, brusquely and sharply demands the picket's gun, and extends his hand to receive it. The picket instantly drops his gun to a ' charge bayonet,' and positively refuses to part with it. The General leaves him, and then tries another man a little farther down the line. This man's gun comes down to a charge with a quick determined snap, and the General receives another refusal, even more emphatic than the previous one. The men of the picket line, this morning, are not generous with their guns; but Gen. Burnham appears greatly pleased. He passes on without examining any guns — but wears a very pleasant smile on his face. Any sentinel while on duty in presence of the enemy will risk less by refusing to part with his musket, no matter who demands it, than by giving it up to any one.

The enemy sends in a flag of truce, desiring permission to bury his dead. Granted. The flag approaches through the deep ravine near the 13th. We are ordered to move up and remain, night and day, as near as possible to the rear of our front trenches; the wide field we are in being continually swept by shell, grape and bullets from the enemy.

"There was a very deep ravine or gulch, in front of a fort, on the Union main line, commanded by Lieut. Day — name of fort not now known — and this fort was built in that part of the wheatfield which the Thirteenth occupied after the return from Drury's Bluff."

Capt. Durell.

May 23. Mon. Warm, clear. Thirteenth at work on the fortifications. Very quiet along the lines, save for an occasional shot. The whole army here is in shelter tents with a few old walls and A's, and every day men are seen patching or sewing up the holes made by the rebel bullets, grape shot and pieces of shell.

A little after midnight last night, Lieut. Thompson of E is recalled from the special picket line, after more than twenty-four hours of service there, and put at the head of thirty-eight picked men of the 13th, of whom several are volunteers, among them Sergt. Charles F. Chapman, and sent under a guide to Gen. Butler's Hdqrs. On the way other detachments, from other regiments, join on, until the expedition numbers about 500 men. The directions were to select 'brave and reliable men,' and 'officers brave, cool and efficient;' and with this pretty send-off we leave camp in a drizzling rain, and in pitchy darkness, expecting never to return alive. On our arrival at his Hdqrs., Gen. Butler appears, receives us cordially, and thanking the little army for their 'commendable patriotism and zeal,' tells them that the enterprise is too hazardous, and orders us to rejoin our regiments. The men give the General three rousing cheers; and then stumble back to their camps, through the rain, the Egyptian darkness, the pools of water, the mud, the brush and stumps. The expedition was a sort of forlorn hope; to go on a gunboat and attack a strong rebel outpost on the Appomattox River. It afterwards came out that nearly a whole rebel brigade were near this outpost; our attacking it would pretty surely have resulted in death or Libby — possibly both.

To-day a large party from the Thirteenth is cutting down trees in front of the fortifications, and another party is in line of battle near by to protect the choppers in case they are attacked. The job uses up nearly all the forenoon, a very dangerous piece of work.

A Pennsylvania Lieutenant sought peace of mind far in the rear during the Drury's Bluff fight, and the charge against him is as follows : " On or about May 16, 1864, he, the said —— First Lieutenant and Adjutant of the —— Penn. regiment, did abandon his post at the first fire, and did run back to the entrenchments — a distance of nine miles more or less." (See June 19, 1864.)

May 24. Tues. Heavy thunder shower with a high wind this morning — the water covering all level surfaces, filling the ditches and paths and turning the earth into gruel. After the water had loosened the pegs and slackened the linen canvas and hemp tent-ropes, the sudden, sharp gusts of wind sent many of the tents flapping and flying, and soon collapsing into tangled heaps of slimy ropes and muddy, wet canvas ; the occupants of the tents left sitting with baggage and arms on the tent sites in a pouring rain. Use cotton ropes and canvas when you go tenting. Afternoon sunny, steamy, very hot. Last night the Reg., and whole camp, was roused by a sudden rattle of noisy picket firing. Quiet all along the lines to-day. The 13th has its tents close up to the front trenches, and the rebel bullets frequently come ripping through the cloth. Boards, logs, barrels and cracker boxes filled with earth, and fence rails or poles are set up on the reb-ward side as a protection.

The enemy for a number of days past has had trains running on the R. & P. Railroad, and sounds the engine whistles merrily as a train runs safely by. Some of our siege guns fire at the rumble of the trains, one or two miles distant. Rations are now somewhat deficient, and one soldier of the 13th writes home : " I have eaten so much pork of late that I expect to speak in grunts."

Many soldiers just previous to a fight, or a dangerous piece of work, fall to praying and talking piety, and — we are obliged to record it — these are not our best soldiers, nor our best men in any place. It is astounding what transparent hypocrites men will sometimes make of themselves by religious pretense, ceremony and sanctimoniousness ; still there are other shams, for instance : " A certain regiment of cavalry has a very prudent Dutchman for one of its captains. Finding himself in a tight place one day, he called a squad of his men to precede him in the dangerous movement, saying to them as he sent them in ahead of himself : ' Go in there, poys — go in sbry ; petter ten men pe killed than me ! ' "

McH.

Let us record the fact right here — of which we have had ample proof in this campaign, as well as previously : Negro slaves of both sexes and of all ages have herded together, occupying quarters promiscuously like pigs, sheep and cattle — a regular Africa in America — and the more rapidly they multiply the more their owners are pleased ; they cultivate the farms and raise produce for the rebel army ; they work in the rebel arsenals, they shovel upon the rebel earth-works ; as soon as the battle is passed they care for the rebel wounded ; none are much risked, and they are not armed, because that means a personal bounty or free contribution by their owners of so much valuable property — a much higher bounty or free contribution than the people of the North have been called upon to give. Relying upon the generally inoffensive and kindly disposition characteristic of the negro, the slave owners leave their families to the care of their slaves, and the safety and peace of the families is almost universally assured. The strangest features, however, of the whole slave affair are the many cases of voluntary devotion of these slaves to their masters, and masters' families now bending all their energies through the aims and issues of this war to rivet upon these very slaves the chains of a perpetual and hopeless bondage.

May 25. Wed. Very warm. Rainy afternoon. Reg. in camp in the front trenches. Not much doing. Jaundice, chills and fever, and diarrhœa have invaded our camp here in force within a day or two, and a large number of our men and officers are sick. Capt. Normand Smith is very sick indeed, far worse off than any other officer. Almost every one who is sick turns to a saffron color. Rev. A. J. Patterson, of Portsmouth, agent of the Portsmouth Ladies' Soldiers' Aid Society, pays a welcome visit to our camp. The wounded are especially well cared for. A strong picket leaves the 13th under Captains Julian and Goss; and are enjoined to prepare for severe fighting.

Unless actually engaged themselves, the men are now so thoroughly tired out that they drop almost mechanically behind a protecting tree, stump or little defense of sand thrown up, and go quietly to sleep, as if altogether unmindful of the whirring, crashing, roaring, unearthly din of the firing going on all around them. The Thirteenth has been called out every morning at 3 or 3.30 a. m., remaining under arms in the front trenches until daylight, has engaged in chopping, shoveling, or fighting during the daytime, and has been frequently called out under arms during the nights — ten days of extremely hard work.

May 26. Thurs. Rainy. Reg. at work on the largest, and nearest, fort in the forenoon. We think this fort was afterwards called Fort Dutton. Move out in the forenoon about one mile along the earth-works to the left, in support of a reconnaissance in force, under command of Col. Arthur H. Dutton of the 21st Conn. While our Brigade is across the deep ravine, near the Appomattox river, Col. Dutton rides forward upon the skirmish line and is severely wounded. (He dies of this wound June 5, 1864.) He was of the Regular Army. His conspicuous uniform presented a too prominent mark for the enemy's sharp-shooters. We return to camp about 2 p. m. Very quiet along the lines during the day. Last night the pickets kept up a continual fire, and many men, unable to sleep soundly and safely in their tents, on account of the danger from the enemy's overshot bullets, took their blankets and laid down in the ditch of the entrenchments. Very sensible.

The 13th has one very nervous six-footer. He was fast asleep the other night, when one of our own batteries near by opened with bang and racket enough to waken the dead. Without stopping to learn that there was no danger whatever, 'Nervy' sprang up, seized his blankets in one hand and his gun and some of his clothing in the other, and ran wildly and half-dressed for the rear. The camp-guard stopped him, and knowing the case, marched him back under guard at once as he was, a picture of utter demoralization and despair. Once engaged he is brave and cool.

Signs of a move; cooked rations ordered to be ready. Maj. Gen. Q. A. Gilmore assumes command of the Bermuda Hundred line. The day closes with a heavy rain storm.

**May 27. Fri.** A hot day. The Thirteenth is in line under arms at early daylight. The officers and most of the men have green peas for breakfast. They are now quite plenty and cheap. An order comes early from Brigade Hdqrs. that the sick will remain here to guard our old camp in the absence of the command! This promises no sport, with the enemy in full force within easy rifle-shot; and every man and officer, who can stand upon his feet, resolves at once to march. The order looks like one of Gen. Burnham's little jokes. Nothing cures malarial disorders like a change in location, or the blood-stirring rush of a battle. We break camp at 8 a. m., start at 11 a. m., march about two miles down nearer the James and bivouac at noon, on a hill on a splendid farm. With the exception of this little march we lie about in the shade of the trees until past noon. Here the rebel shells have plowed and torn through everything, and many are lying about. Negroes have been employed in gathering such of them as have not burst — 'live shells' — 'stuffed shell' — and throwing them into a brook to soak.

On the march through the dense woods and brush, the Thirteenth, alone in the Brigade, from marching by the right flank, in column of fours, on reaching a narrow strip of clear ground swings hurriedly forward into line of battle, at a right angle with the line of march, then breaks by di-

---

### DESCRIPTION OF MAP.

A. Appomattox River at Point of Rocks, with ponton bridge.
B. Port Walthall and railroad.   F. Battery Burpee.
C. Roads to Bermuda Hundred near Mr. Hatcher's.
D. Farrar's Island and James River.
E. Fort Zabriskie and Signal Station.   G. Fort Wead.
H. Battery Walker.   I. Fort Dutton.   K. Battery Pruyn.
L. Battery Marshall.   M. Battery Anderson.   O. Battery Perry.
P. Fort Carpenter.   R. Fort Drake.   T. Battery Wilcox.
U. Battery Parsons.   V. Battery Spofford.
S. Battery Sawyer (near).   Y. Howletts and Confed. Bat. Dansler.
N. Redoubt McConihe; where Company C. with Capt. Durell and Lieut. Prescott served as garrison.

The Confederate lines generally face east, the names of their forts not known; the Union lines face north, west and south.

"The position of the Thirteenth in August and September, 1864, was at the left of the advanced redoubt — McConihe."   Lt. Col. Smith.

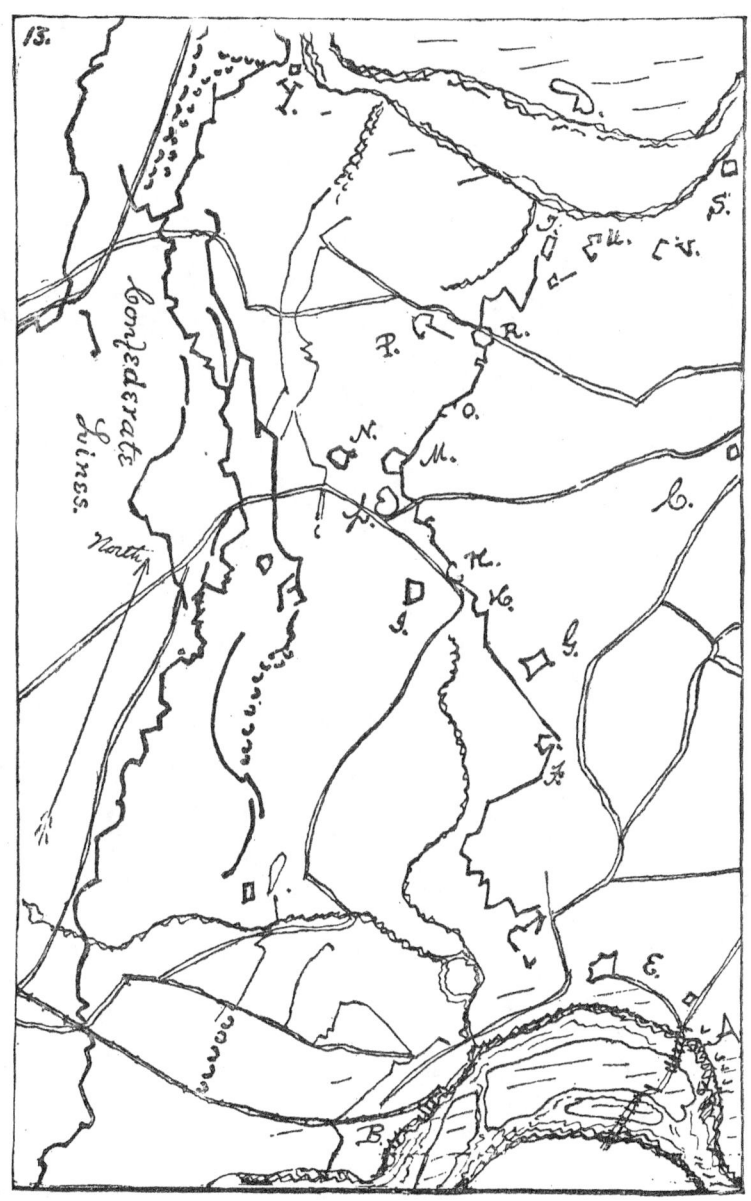

BERMUDA HUNDRED.

Tracing of Official Map.  Scale, one and one half inches to one mile.

visions to the front; the divisions then proceed independently, threading their way through the timber and brush, all the divisions marching side by side and by the right flank — in columns of twos. Gen. Burnham rides back, looks the movement over, and is furious. He orders the change corrected instanter, and the Reg. is re-formed as rapidly as the men and officers can run, and set marching by the right flank as before, and amid a storm and war of hard words. The marching by divisions was by far the easiest method — but the General had not ordered it. The members of the Thirteenth probably never laughed over a movement, and the breaking up of it with a whisk and a gale, so much as over this one, during their whole term of service. Capt. Dodge happened to be on horseback at the time, and declares that his men ran forward, into the column again, faster than his horse could gallop.

At 2 p. m. we move again, and bivouac about sundown nearer Bermuda Hundred, a jerky series of short marches. Gen. Kautz's whole Division of cavalry comes in. A rougher, more torn and battered collection of men, horses and equipments, we have never seen; but the men are jovial, joking and merry, and appear to enjoy thoroughly the staring by our infantry as they pass. Rough riders they. Gen. Butler rides along our lines, but is not so popular as he was a month ago — what a month for the Army of the James!

On the night of May 5th we could have marched straight into Petersburg, and then turning north, have given Richmond itself — only about 22 miles distant — a severe trial, if not at once have captured it. Instead of that, we played at pitch and toss with a rebel skirmish line until Gen. Beauregard organized an army, and thrashed Butler's army out of its boots and baggage, in the four to six foggy morning hours of May 16th, and drove it into that Bermuda Hundred corner, and has held it there ever since. Gen. Butler's losses since May 5th are put at 4,000 men. Gen. Beaureguard's at 3,000 men.

At Bermuda Hundred the advanced forts on the line, from the right, are Carpenter, McConihe, and Dutton. Our first camp after May 16th was to the left and a little to the rear of Ft. Dutton, facing southwest. On the 18th we fell back and towards the right, behind a long line of rifle-pits facing nearly north. This move brought us to the right of Ft. Dutton, but still that fort was very nearly in our front. This change of camp brought the line of the 13th upon a steep, sharp conical hill or bluff in deep woods. It is not very important, perhaps, but our place of operations was within the less than half a mile of space between Forts Carpenter and Dutton, where Gen. Butler's lines swing farthest towards the front, and near the centre of his position. The ravine referred to under May 21st and 22d was said to be the steepest, and deepest, and worst one, on Gen. Butler's whole line between the two rivers, and it then lay at the front and left of the Thirteenth; the left of the line of the Reg. running along it for two or three rods only, the centre of the Reg. being near the head of the ravine. Company E was directly in the sharp angle where the front and main line of rifle-trenches turned to run toward the rear and left along this ravine. This camp of the 13th has been about one mile — along the main line of entrenchments — north of the spot where Col. Dutton was shot.

## VII.

### MAY 28 TO JUNE 15, 1864.

#### MARCH TO COLD HARBOR.

**May 28. Sat.** Warm, fair day, cool, rainy night. Thirteenth called at early daylight, and has an inspection in the forenoon. At noon is ordered to have two days' cooked rations prepared and distributed before 4 p. m. Dress-parade at march. Breaks camp at 5.30 p. m. and marches to Bermuda Hundred Landing; where we arrive a little after 8 p. m. near a cluster of old houses, and 'bunk down' — camp language for a bad bivouac — in the rain, and in the mud vile and knee-deep. We are already as wet and muddy as the mud itself, and the soft mud makes an easy lying bed; but there is no such thing as getting dry again, or gaining much sleep, for our shelter tents pitched in the dark are about as good cover from the rain as so many old cotton umbrellas with the staffs and half the ribs broken. We have a most ridiculous night of it. This is the fifth rainy night in succession. On three fourths of the days in the last two months we have had rain, either in showers or storms. A rumor runs current to-night that we are retreating again, and curses and grumblings are savage and deep. Our army feels that there has been no need of the predicament we have been in, here at Bermuda Hundred, and the men are neither slow nor mild in their expressions of opinion and feeling concerning the vexatious situation. Later on, to quiet the grumbling and disaffection, the word is passed that we are bent upon a secret expedition and are marching under sealed orders. A lively curiosity is thus awakened concerning our exact destination, but the secret of it is well kept.

At whose door lies the faultiness in the recent campaign, broad history must determine — it is not our purpose, and here we leave it. Undoubtedly Gen. Butler did the best he could, as he was known to be thoroughly in earnest to put down the rebellion. The failure appears to have been caused by a lack of celerity; and a want of unity in action, in his army, after the successful attack, in the early morning of May 16th, upon Gen. Heckman. The criticism most common in the Army of the James at this time is: "The two Corps did not work well together."

**May 29. Sun.** Very warm, drizzly, cloudy, windy. The Thirteenth is called at daylight as usual. Breakfast is hurriedly eaten; then we march down to the shore, and immediately embark, at Bermuda Hundred Landing, on the propeller 'Starlight,' with the 10th N. H., and move out into the stream about 8 a. m. At 10.45 a. m. we move down the James River, and arrive off Fortress Monroe at sundown. The propeller is crowded to excess, and is very filthy from long use in transporting horses, mules, war materiel and men. We have in tow an old, leaky barge on board of which is a portion of the men of the 8th Conn., who are in a rage because of their bad accommodations. This barge causes much trouble, as night comes on, when we are near Fortress Monroe. The wind raises quite a sea. About 11 p. m. the propeller runs aground on a sand bar ; the tide and wind drive the barge against the propeller with several hard thumps ; the hawser fouls the propeller's wheel and threatens serious mischief ; so the hawser is cut, and the barge drifts away with its unhappy, noisy crew, to be picked up later by a tug, hauled alongside and again made fast. The remarks of a heavy profane type heard in that barge, as it moved away in the darkness, made us believe that calling Connecticut the " land of steady habits " was no compliment. The men between decks on the propeller, however, fall into a sound sleep, when all at once, as the boat careens, a long line of the overcrowded bunks breaks down, and spills the sleeping men all out sprawling on the deck, and thinking the world has come to an end — for them. They rush up the gang-ways, and almost a panic ensues, but soon quiet is restored below.

A large collection of the officers of the 13th, including the writer, have taken up their quarters and spend the night lying flat on the upper deck, all out of doors. We have sought fresh air, and get a plenty of it, with an occasional dash of salt spray. Sleep is impossible. We laugh at the multitude of mishaps till we cry ; the situation is even more ridiculous than the one we were in last night. As the propeller pitches from side to side we roll to right and left, and sing all the songs in the army hymn and tune book — keep it up for hours. It is cold on the bay, a wild, wild night, and inky black much of the time. After tossing, banging and grating on the sand bar for four or five hours, the incoming tide lifts our little propeller, we move on, and enter the York River about sunrise, the sea now very rough.

May 30. Mon. Very warm, clear. The Thirteenth sails again at daylight — at which time, we can hear a heavy, distant cannonading — reaches West Point about 12 noon, thence moves up the Pamunkey, arrives at White House Landing at 7 p. m., debarks at 8 p. m., and bivouacs on high, clean, dry ground about 9 p. m. The transports have run aground many times to-day, in river mud, but no serious accidents have occurred, so far as we know. Boats seem to be constantly sailing down past us, as we sail up the river, as river bend runs by bend to parallel streams. The name 'Pamunkey' must have been suggested by the innumerable curves, bends, doubles and twists possible to the tail of a prehensile-tailed monkey — though for crookedness the river beats the monkey tail altogether.

The Sanitary Commission have a gorgeous steamer here at the wharf, loaded with supplies — every package tied up in much red tape.  See June 12th.  Our men cheer the Commission to the echo as they pass the steamer.  It is said to be moored to the very bit of shore where Gen. Washington moored his lover's-barge, when he visited here the fair widow, Martha Custis, who became his wife, Martha Washington.

They tell us that our camp to-night is on Confederate Gen. Fitz-Hugh Lee's farm.  Fine camping ground!  The men find an old black man in a hut near by, who claims to be 113 years old — and he looks twice that age.  He also claims to have been chosen to serve Gen. Washington as his special body servant, when he visited this same White House.  The impression is gaining ground that no man in the United States ever had so many colored servants as Gen. Washington; and serving him seems to have had a very salutary effect upon their longevity.

The Thirteenth is now poorly supplied with camp equipage and tents, and some borrowing is the result.  Since our regimental baggage was presented to Gen. Beauregard, on May 16th, we have been deprived of many comforts and conveniences, the officers suffering worst of all.  There is no buncombe splurge and show about this trip, it has, instead of that, a business air which, however trying, inspires confidence.

"While coming up here we have been crowded together, on this nasty steamer, with nothing fit to drink and little to eat, and a broiling sun over our heads.  We got on shore about 8 p. m. to-night, and the first thing I did after landing was to drink about a quart of brook water, and it tasted perfectly delicious."                                               PRESCOTT.

This is the experience of many thousand men on this hasty and hurried expedition.  The rations served out on May 28th ran short, and coffee could not be made on the steamer.

**May 31.  Tues.**  Very warm, clear.  Thirteenth up at 4 a. m., and has breakfast at once — hurried.  At 5 a. m. a large detail, about 100 men, from the 13th, goes to work upon a bridge over the Pamunkey river; works hard until 3 p. m. and then returns to camp.  Three days' rations are drawn, cooked and served during the day.  Col. Stevens in command of the Regiment.

At 4.15 p. m., after having been ready to march for about an hour, the Thirteenth leaves camp and starts inland; marches rapidly until 11 p. m., along roads and through fields, pastures and brush, a terribly rough march in the darkness.  We halt near New Castle, on Washington Bassett's farm near Old Church, and as soon as the column is halted at 11 p. m. our whole Reg. is at once marched to the front of it and placed on picket; Headquarters of the Reg. and reserve of the picket are settled in bivouac about midnight.

The writer is on the picket line at a road bridge over a run a short distance beyond Bassett's, and is awake the most of the night.  We can hear the distant cannonade at times all through the night; the demands of our picket work, in the prospect of a dash by rebel cavalry, allow of little or no rest or sleep for the most of the Reg., while we anticipate a severe battle on the morrow. The reader should experience the situation and witness the scenes in an army on the eve before a battle, in order to properly judge of them, or even imagine them clearly. We are told that we are now only twelve miles from White House, and that we missed the road, and have actually marched more than twenty miles to reach this point. The road has been lined with the bodies of dead horses and mules, relics of recent cavalry encounters and used-up teams.

As the night passes here, in these deep, silent woods and quiet fields, there steals over every one of us the awful sense of coming danger for all, of wounds for many, and of certain death for some. The question comes quick and unbidden, dead home : " Am I to be shot to-morrow ? " Then we contemplate the better side of affairs ; or turn over to dream the brooding nightmare question out of mind — and generally succeed quite soon in doing so. We know now little or nothing of our sudden detachment from the Army of the James and swift expedition here ; but sincerely hope it means a stout and winning fight, and much honor to the Thirteenth — and we are ready to try our fortunes and go in. True courage realizes danger but hesitates not to face it.

### BATTLE OF COLD HARBOR.

**June 1. Wed.** Clear and very warm — very hot about noon, the air dry, dusty, smoky. Maj. Gen. W. F. Smith started from Bermuda Hundred on May 28th, with Gen. Brooks' 1st Division of the 18th Corps, and Gen. Devens' 2d, and Gen. Ames' 3d Divisions of the 10th Corps, a total of about 16,000 men and 16 guns, taking steamers to White House Landing on the Pamunkey River. He left Gen. Ames at the Landing with about 2,500 men, and pushed on, on the night of May 31st, with the rest of his force to join Gen. Meade's army, and arrived at Cold Harbor with above 10,000 men and 16 guns. Gen. Butler's Army of the James thus re-enforces Gen. Meade's Army of the Potomac. The whole force under the supreme direction of Lieut. Gen. Grant.

Gen. Smith marched until 11 p. m. of May 31st, and then halted on Mr. Washington Bassett's farm near Old Church, where he remained until 6 a. m. to-day. By an error in the wording of an order, sent to him this morning by Gen. Grant, New Castle Ferry — ten or twelve miles up the Pamunkey, northwest — was given as the objective point of his march, instead of New Cold Harbor — or Cold Harbor — nearly west. He followed the course indicated by the order, until he discovered the mistake. The error necessitated a long countermarch southward during the forenoon of June 1st, caused a delay of four or five hours, and an extra and rapid march of about ten miles ; making on the whole a march of full thirty-five miles, from White House to our field of battle at Cold Harbor. The roads a mass of dust which every puff of wind and the marching troops raised in clouds, and the weather sweltering hot.

The purpose of this movement, as we learn fully this morning, is to continue the extension of Gen. Meade's army by the left; to seize and hold about one mile of the Bethesda Church road running north from Cold Harbor; also the very important system of roads immediately about Cold Harbor; and to force the passage of the Chickahominy River a few miles south — the 18th and 10th Corps to co-operate with the 6th Corps.

The 6th Corps had come down from the right of Gen. Meade's army, and, during this forenoon, had taken position near Old Cold Harbor. On the arrival of the 6th Corps, Gen. Sheridan's cavalry, in the advance here, moved southward down near the Chickahominy, covering the left of the entire army. The 6th Corps was all up by 2 p. m.

Gen. Smith, with his 18th and 10th Corps Divisions, arriving at Cold Harbor not far from noon (June 1st) passed over, and near 4 p. m., formed on the right of the 6th Corps, getting well into position and ready to advance at near 6 p. m., and is placed under command of Gen. Meade.

To oppose this extension to the left by the 6th, 10th, and 18th Corps, Confederate Gen. Beauregard, retaining upon Gen. Butler's front at Bermuda Hundred about 9,000 infantry, besides artillery and cavalry, sent the rest of his troops, about eight or ten brigades, under Generals Pickett and Hoke, to Gen. Lee at Cold Harbor, while Gen. Longstreet's Corps moves down from Gen. Lee's left wing. A portion of Gen Beauregard's troops, however, were sent here before the 18th Corps left Bermuda Hundred — the portion not required to oppose our army there.

The Confederate line of entrenchments crosses the road from Old to New Cold Harbor, at a right angle, about one half mile west of Old Cold Harbor, thence running southward towards the Chickahominy, and northward towards Bethesda church — a line eight or ten miles in length. The Confederate troops are disposed along this line, near this road, and facing east, with Gen. Hoke on the right, on the road, then Gen. Kershaw, then Gen. Pickett, with Gen. Field on the left, near and beyond the vicinity of Beulah church.

Confronting these troops of the Confederates are Gen. Wright's 6th Corps, on the left, south, the right of the 6th Corps being at the road leading from Old to New Cold Harbor; then Gen. Devens' Division, north of the road, his left connecting with the right of the 6th Corps; next to the right of Gen. Devens' is Gen. Brooks' Division of the 18th Corps, in which is the Thirteenth; while Gen. Martindale is at the right and rear in reserve. That is to say the Confederate line, facing east, is :
Right — Hoke.      Kershaw.      Pickett.      Field.      — Left.

Left — Sixth Corps.      Devens.      Brooks.      — Right.
Martindale — in reserve;
for the Union line, facing west. The right of the 18th Corps, Brooks', crosses the Bethesda church road a little to the front of Mr. Daniel Woody's house near Beulah church, which is about one mile north of Cold Harbor. Being thus in position, our troops merely await the order to open the Battle of Cold Harbor with the first infantry charge upon the

enemy's lines of entrenchments, all within a near view across the irregular tracts of field and brush.

At 6 p. m. the whole Union line — the 6th Corps, and Gen. Smith's 10th and 18th Corps — almost simultaneously, advances to the charge, a dash by more than 25,000 men, breaking in the Confederate line, and capturing their outer line of entrenchments ; and the 6th Corps succeeds in securing a portion of the enemy's main line near the Cold Harbor road. The noise, roar and crash of the musketry and artillery firing is tremendous ; but words are not worth using in the description of such scenes. The whole rush is over in fifteen minutes; the distance covered in the charge varying from three hundred yards to a thousand yards on some parts of the line, chiefly across open and clear ground.

Gen. Smith's leading brigade, on the extreme right, Gen. Burnham's — in which the Thirteenth — of Gen. Brooks' Division, moves up a hill wooded with pines, pushes across an open field on their front, into a thin strip of wood, and then into another strip of wood more dense, capturing the enemy's outer line of rifle-pits, and driving the Confederates before them, until they come upon the enemy's main line of trenches where they receive such a severe fire that they are compelled to halt, and move into pine woods to the left for cover. See pages 344 and 348.

The losses in the 6th Corps are 1,200 and in the 10th and 18th Corps 1,000. They capture 600 prisoners. The result of the day is the complete occupation of Cold Harbor.

The above appears to be about the gist of the various accounts, which differ somewhat in detail. Though the first rush occupied but a few minutes, the battle continued very noisy until midnight. In the Conn. Adjt. General's Reports, the order of Gen. Burnham's brigade at the time of the charge is given as follows : on the left, the 118th N. Y., connecting with the right of the 10th Corps, next the 8th Conn., next the 10th N. H., next the 13th N. H., on the right of the brigade.

Having thus made a general statement of the situation, as near as may be, let us return to the 13th, and accompany it through the battle :

The 13th is now in the 2d Brig. — Gen. Burnham ; 1st Div. — Gen. Brooks ; 18th Army Corps — Gen. Smith ; and consists of the 10th and 13th N. H., the 8th Conn. and 118th N. Y. regiments. To the 13th falls the honor of being the extreme right regiment of the 18th Army Corps, in the front line of the infantry charge that opens the battle of Cold Harbor, Col. Stevens in command of Reg.

To appreciate the extreme severity of the work and battle of the Thirteenth to-day, we must first call to mind the fact that the Reg. was roused at 4 a. m. Tuesday morning May 31st; a large number of the men and officers were kept at work on a bridge from 5 a. m. until 3 p. m. on that day ; the rest of the Reg. also being kept busy all day about one thing or another ; and at 4.15 p. m., all were assembled, and marched rapidly, over rough ground, until 11 p. m., and then at once placed on picket.

By the following it appears that a portion of the 13th were kept moving for even a longer period: "May 31. Left White House at 3 p. m., marched till midnight, then went on picket. Very tired; got a little sleep."   LUEY.

Very little rest could be had while on picket duty; and at 4.30 this morning — June 1st — the Reg. is ordered to assemble, hurries from distant picket posts into line, and about 6.30 is marched off without any breakfast, excepting what the men can eat from their haversacks as they march along. The weather is very hot, the men are suffering much from it, and the actual marching time has been nearly twenty hours, between leaving White House and the charge made to-day — much of the march a series of jerks. The men consequently enter the battle much tired and worn; and with their clothing all gray from the deep, fine dust in the roads, rising in clouds wherever the troops have moved.

When we assemble on Mr. Bassett's farm near New Castle at 4.30 this morning, the noise of cannon is already heard in the distance, and as we march the firing increases in volume and clearness with every mile of our nearer approach, until long before noon there is a continuous roar, as of dull distant thunder; the work of cavalry, skirmishers and cannon. We march by rapid, tiresome spurts, halting now and then for a few minutes only; and near one o'clock p. m. enter the Army of the Potomac in action, and pass over a portion of the field, near the right of the 18th Corps line, where the irregular fighting has already swept. Trees are broken, torn off, blown in pieces, and the ground torn up, by shells, fragments of which strew the ground; while the bullet marks appear everywhere and on everything, beyond numbering or estimating. The dead are lying all about us, chiefly rebel dead; and the wounded Union soldiers are coming back from the front in great numbers, many of them borne on stretchers, or assisted by other men. One General among the number. We cross a wide, open field, and halt among some little oak-trees. Here are quite a number of the rebel dead, and a pile of their knapsacks. One C. S. A. knapsack here, being vigorously kicked, yields to the writer a new, blue and gold, pocket edition of Scott's Lady of the Lake, that is afterwards read by many, and read aloud for the entertainment of many more, in the Cold Harbor trenches. The men of the Thirteenth at this little halt among the oaks commence to lunch, but are moved on before they can finish. We now pass through large bodies of waiting troops of the 6th Corps, who look us over curiously, and several batteries of artillery; a few rebel prisoners pass us going toward the rear, all smiling and jocular, with the air of men just relieved from duty; mounted horsemen are flying in every direction and at the top of their horses' speed — and the care with which a swiftly running horse will avoid stepping upon the body of a man lying on the ground is truly marvelous. On the way we file around the burning ruins of a building, said to be Beulah church, near D. Woody's, on the Bethesda church road.

Soon we enter thick brush close by the roadside, and move along by the right flank — by fours — into a depression in the ground, a shoal ravine, halt, and form close column by divisions, right in front. Here we expect to rest, but soon comes the quick order, given direct by an aide of Gen. Burnham's: "Load!" — a sudden, unexpected and startling order, making eyes to open and nerves to quiver. The order is repeated all along our Brigade, by the regimental and company commanders, and just as we are loading our muskets and calling the roll, and the men are answering firmly: "Here!" "Here!" "Here!" in reply to the call of their names — in many cases their last Roll-call on earth! — a sudden burst of heavy musketry firing rolls in from the near distance and reverberates through the woods; a most belligerent, threatening and suggestive sound, especially when we know by experience just what that sound practically means. There is no flinching, however, the Thirteenth is very ready to take its chances and to go in, never more so than now; and one man of the Thirteenth coolly remarks: "Now that we have loaded, we will give them some more of that!" — the quiet remark provoking an approving smile among his comrades.

The order to load is quickly obeyed and we march on by fours again, by the right flank, into a deep ravine filled with pine-trees, face to the left in line of battle — with a bog-hole or pond and a very wet swamp just behind us, scattered about which are many bodies of dead soldiers, Union and Confederate together — and with the skirmishers from our Reg. preceding us we move forward up a very steep hill or bluff among the trees, and halt at 4.30 p. m., the men being directed to lie down and secure cover for themselves, from the enemy's fire, among the standing and fallen trees. We have been within range of the enemy's shot and shell for a long time, but now we are near his infantry lines, and hundreds of his bullets whistle and whack among the trees about us; while the rebel shells burst over our heads, and the pieces come down among us, or else rip and tear through the trees, favoring us with the falling branches. One large pine-tree is cut clean off, twenty or thirty feet above the ground, and the great branchy top crashes down, and comes near burying or killing Gen. Burnham, who has barely time to escape it.

As we move a little farther up the hill, we see near, before us, a regiment, or a long heavy skirmish line — a part of it at least composed of the men of the 40th Mass — lying along a 'Virginia' rail fence, and hotly engaged; every instant some of them are being killed or wounded, and one officer springs up and dashes back, down among us of the Thirteenth. Gen. Burnham, who is near by, stops him, and orders him back again, as he is unhurt. The officer refuses to go back, when the General raises his sword as if to strike him. At this he turns to go back, and the General follows him up, striking him several times with the flat of the sword, following him through our line, and until he takes his proper place again. We do not know to what Regiment he belongs.

Capt. Goss is struck in his ear by a bullet, and brushes his ear with his hand as if a bee had stung him; and does not discover what the matter is until he sees the blood upon his hand. He finds time to have the ear bound up before we charge. It is now 5 p. m. or a little later, and we keep our position, advancing but little, for nearly an hour, catching glimpses of the enemy here and there across the open field on our front; whence a heavy, long cloud of battle-smoke rolls up and moves towards us, the nauseous and choking compound soon settling over and among us in the dense pine timber and brush.

While we are here and waiting the order to charge, Col. Stevens calls Lieut. Thompson of E to him, and, to use his own words, orders him: "To act as Adjutant in rear of the left wing of the Regiment, in helping to keep the men up in place, as the charge is made." He moves at once to the position indicated, and during the charge he happens to be near to Capt. Farr of D, the eighth Company from the right and third from the left of the 13th, when Capt. Farr is shot. Capt. Farr spins around several times when the bullet strikes him, hitting Lieut. Thompson as he does so; but soon steadying himself he asks Lieut. Thompson to take command of Company D, which he cannot do because of Col. Stevens' order for him to act as Adjutant. Capt. Farr at once disappears — the whole matter is the work of ten seconds — and Lieut. Thompson as quickly as possible runs along the line of Company D, and tells the men to 'stick to their First Sergeant, or whoever shall properly succeed Capt. Farr.' This is done while the Thirteenth is under fire, advancing in the charge, and before any halt is made. Lieut. Staniels until he is wounded serves, in his regular capacity, as Acting Adjutant, in rear of the right wing of the Regiment; Col. Stevens desiring that the Thirteenth shall remain compact, and unbroken in line during the charge, and therefore taking these extra precautions.

After Lieut. Staniels, Acting Adjutant since April 23d, is wounded in the charge, Lieut. Thompson of E is appointed Acting Adjutant of the Thirteenth, at first on the field immediately after the halt in the charge is made and before moving to the left into the point of pines, and afterwards formally about midnight — Col. Stevens then writing the order in a few words in pencil on a scrap of paper torn from a letter which he takes from his pocket — and he serves in that capacity during all our stay at Cold Harbor, and until relieved by the return to duty of Adjutant Boutwell, at White House on June 13th. These are the simple facts of a little vexed dispute, and they in no way or degree disparage any member of the Thirteenth.

Two Divisions — the 2d Division, Devens', of the 10th Corps, on the left, and the 1st Division, Brooks', of the 18th Corps, on the right — now form the front line of the assaulting column; the 3d Division, Martindale's, of the 10th Corps, in reserve to the right and rear of Brooks. Our Second Brigade, Burnham's, has the right of the 18th Corps; the Thirteenth has the right of the front line. This gives the Thirteenth the right of the front line of the Brigade, Division and Corps, and consequently in the charge that follows brings us under both a flank and a front fire from the enemy, as the right surges somewhat forward of the main line. See pages 347 and 350.

While we stand here waiting the order to charge, Gen. Gilman Marston's brigade passes our rear towards the swamp to our right. He finds the swamp nearly impenetrable, and personally leads his men into position in small bodies of a few companies at a time, for no large organization can be safely and readily handled in the dense brush. He finds on advancing that Allerson's road is crossed by several rows of heavy stakes driven deep, standing at a low incline towards the Union lines, and all hewn to a very sharp point. To his right in the field rises a huge rebel earth-work and long rifle trenches.

The artillery fire increases, the skirmishing rattles louder and louder, the smoke rolls towards us heavier and heavier in volume until the sun is obscured, and at six o'clock p. m., and already dusky in the dense pines, we are ordered to charge; and in a minute more we spring out of the pines into the clearer light of open ground, and plunge headlong into the terrible scene of carnage, amid the deafening roar of musketry and artillery — opening the battle of Cold Harbor with the first infantry charge.

Our part of this work is done in less than five minutes — reliable persons have said, in less than three minutes — but in this little turn of time the Thirteenth loses sixty-seven men killed and wounded. We leave our grove of pines, at the crest of the bluff, and dash on the run three hundred yards, across an open field, to a little ridge in the field, and upon our approach the enemy hastily withdraws from his rifle-pits dug near this ridge. Here we are halted, and ordered to lie down and do so, while troops form in our rear, the most of them coming up into the open field in excellent order. We do not here enter the enemy's pits, but take position under cover of the low little ridge, and the scattered piles of sand, thrown out by the enemy when he dug his rifle-pits. It may be well to say here, that the nearest regiment in our rear, when we halt and lie down, is the 40th Mass., forming from their skirmish line and approaching, but not yet so far into the field as the little apple-tree (mentioned below), that is, they are at least 200 yards behind us. Lt. Col. Smith thinks that the 13th charged alone, or else it had no support. The writer is sure that no support has followed us so near as a support should follow on such an occasion. The 40th Mass. could not possibly re-form from the skirmish line, and keep pace with our charge.

Pine timber borders the field of our charge on the left side, but the Thirteenth gains no cover in it at all, our position throughout the charge, and when halted, being in the open field and to the right of all the pines. When the halt in the charge is made, the writer is near the extreme left of the Thirteenth, and would say positively that the whole Regiment halts in open ground; the nearest grove of trees, into which we are afterwards moved, being at some distance to our left. At our left the assaulting line, during the charge, strikes the little grove of pines referred to in the official accounts, where they are halted, and whence they are afterwards moved to the left, to give room for the right of the line, including the Thirteenth, to secure cover from the enemy's fire, coming upon our front and right. The enemy's rifle-pits, two lines of them, run clear across the field from Allerson's road on our right, to and along the pines on our left. The course taken by the Thirteenth in the charge formed a slight curve to the front and left; all the way in a clear, bare, open field.

Capt. Durell, then Lieutenant, furnishes the writer with the following: "Soon after our halt in the charge June 1st and while lying in line of battle on the bare field, the rebel bullets flying over us and their shells cracking about, the rebels just having vacated their rifle-pits, Col. Henry of the 40th Mass., on Gen. Brooks' Staff, rode up to near the left of the Thirteenth, and happening to meet me first, spoke to me, asking where Col. Stevens was. I replied that he was at the right of the Regiment. Col. Henry then directed me to go to the right of the 13th, and ask Col. Stevens to come to the left; remarking that the order was to advance. I passed along the line until I found Col. Stevens, and delivered to him Col. Henry's order, telling him about the contemplated advance. The firing was very severe through which I passed, and I could see the enemy, and the general situation clearly, and I told Col. Stevens that 'to advance two rods into that field meant annihilation for the Thirteenth,' and Col. Stevens agreed with me on that point. At Col. Stevens' direction, therefore, I returned to the left, along the line, and explained the situation to Col. Henry. He directed that Col. Stevens hold his ground, word was passed up the line to that effect, and then he rode away to confer with Gen. Brooks. In about twenty minutes Col. Henry returned, and directed that Col. Stevens should move the Thirteenth by the left flank, into the pines near by, to the left and rear, which was done. The word was passed along the line, and to avoid unnecessary exposure the officers maintained their proper positions, as there was no need of doing otherwise. We were lying on the field — the open, bare field — for nearly an hour, during which the firing was continuous." CAPT. DURELL.

To walk twice the length of the battle line of the Thirteenth, several hundred yards, through and across such a rebel fire as then was going on, was extremely hazardous, and Durell may well be thankful that he was not perforated with a dozen rebel bullets, or blown into minced meat by the shells; but he saved many men of the Thirteenth by the act.

"June 1st. Up at 5.45 a. m. Call in the pickets at 6 a. m. March at 7 a. m. Warm and dusty. Arrive at the front at 4 p. m., halt and rest. Form column by divisions and load. Form line of battle and advance through woods to open field, and ordered to charge across open field at 6 p. m. As we are charging across the field I am pretty severely wounded by a musket ball in my right shoulder. Carried to the Corps Hospital, and wound dressed by Asst. Surgeons Small and Morrill."

Diary of LIEUT. STANIELS.

Extract from a letter:

"At the battle of Cold Harbor I acted, until wounded, as Adjutant of the Thirteenth; and when our Regiment was deployed in line of battle skirmishers were thrown out, and Col. Stevens directed me to advance with the skirmishers, to see that their line was not broken and assist in the movement; the Thirteenth followed in line of battle, and we thus advanced through the woods until we came to the open field, where the men laid down. Soon the order was given to fix bayonets and to charge across the open field in front. When the line first advanced in the charge Col. Stevens was near the Regiment's colors, close in rear of the line, and I was a little to his right. As we advanced I worked farther to the right, and was in the rear of the third or fourth Company from the right when I was hit.

"We had advanced fifteen or twenty rods from the woods into the open field, and many of the poor boys had already fallen, when I received a shock from a missile which seemed to me heavy enough to be a ten-pound shot, it struck me so heavily. It brought me down to the ground, and I realized that I was wounded. My first thought was to avoid being taken a prisoner by the enemy, and I began creeping toward the woods; using my left hand, as my right hand and arm had become useless. I worked gradually toward the woods, and was then helped back to somewhere near the point where the skirmish line was formed, and there Asst. Surgeon Sullivan cut off my coat and vest, examined and probed the wound. He suggested that he had better take my money, watch, papers, and the address of my friends, and said he would telegraph to my friends. I let him have my valuables for safe-keeping, but told him not to telegraph without my consent.

"I was then carried back to the field hospital, and was laid upon the grass in the line of the wounded being brought in. Asst. Surgeon H. N. Small was told that I was there, and he came and spoke to me, saying that I should come upon his operating table, as soon as he was through with Capt. George Farr, whose wound was then being dressed. Soon afterwards I was placed upon the table, and Asst. Surgeon Small — a noble and true friend, and a skillful surgeon — took me in charge, and persevered until he had removed the minie bullet; which he kept for me, and which I now, 1887, have in my possession. The bullet struck my right clavicle, shattering it, and then taking a downward course lodged in the lower part of my right lung. Asst. Surgeon Small told me at the time that it was one of the most difficult cases of wounds that he ever had to operate upon; the bullet going so deep, and lodging finally where it did, was very hard to find, and when found his instruments were not long enough to take hold of it without much effort.

"While charging upon the rebel rifle-pits we advanced upon the double-quick, and would naturally be leaning forward, which position I presume accounts in part for the bullet taking a downward course; striking the clavicle first at a certain angle may also have caused it to change its course somewhat." [1] CAPT. STANIELS.

[1] Personal accounts like this one given by Capt. Staniels — then a Lieutenant — are of vital interest in a history like this; and I doubt not many will regret not having furnished them when I urged them to do so. — S. M. T.

In coming across the field in the charge, the Thirteenth first receives the fire of the enemy's pickets, in a strong line in rifle-pits in a strip of pines a little to our left, and also directly in our front, from his pickets in rifle-pits just behind the crest of the little ridge on which we are finally halted — on the approach of our Brigade these pickets either withdraw or are captured. Before the charge is over, we also receive an oblique fire from a long line of battle, off to our front and right, where the enemy have sprung to their feet, bolt upright, and are standing in line and firing — members of the Thirteenth will recall the blaze and glare of this rebel line of muskets — and also shell and grape from the enemy's batteries, one to the right and one to the left.

Just before the end of the charge, when the rebel bullets were the thickest, Capt. Stoodley's voice was heard above the din, shouting: "Sing, 'Rally Round the Flag,' boys!" A few men, almost breathless from the running and shouting, strike up a note or two — but the song is at once cut short by the order to halt and lie down. Capt. Stoodley, active, quick and enthusiastic, has no fear except that some of the Regiment may break under this terrible fire — but they do not.

We have gained the ground which we started for, and hold it; lying down on our faces, with guns to the front and bayonets fixed, ready to repel a charge if the enemy attempts one, and receiving the fire from a strong line of his men behind another ridge and in other rifle-pits, in the field, still farther to our front and right. A few of our men commence firing upon these, but are ordered to stop. The enemy had two lines of rifle-pits running across this field, and we have captured one of them; but it is harder for us to lie here inactive than it was to dash in upon the charge. While thus lying on the ground under the protection of the little ridge mentioned above, the sheet of bullets flying over our bodies — we would rather be firing, men do not like to lie down and be shot at — several lines of troops form in our rear at some distance, in excellent order and very rapidly, then march into the field in successive lines of battle, halt and lie down. They are much exposed also, and as they lie upon the ground we can see the frequent sudden start, shudder, and struggle, of a man here and there among them, indicating wounds and death. A great number of these inactive men, while lying altogether unprotected in the open field, are killed and wounded. Probably there is no way of avoiding these casualties.

While we are lying here, the writer cannot resist the temptation to raise himself upon his elbow a little and look around, and witnesses the 40th Mass. enacting a most tragic scene. About 100 or 150 yards to the right and rear of the 13th, as we lay, stands a small apple-tree, with two little trunks, both together not one foot in diameter. On coming up into the field the 40th Mass. approaches very near this tree — the writer thinks their line of battle was divided by it — and just then the enemy opens upon them a fearful musketry fire, from the same line of battle that but a few minutes before had been practicing upon us, cutting down many of them. The 40th swing around towards the tree and many of the men huddle together around it, and by so doing become a still better target for the rebels, and they seem to fall by dozens. Their color-bearer is shot down, and their colors lie on the ground; when suddenly a horseman, himself and horse all gray with dust, dashes at a full and furious gallop into the field from the left — Major George Marshall of Chelsea, and of the 40th — reaches down with his sword, and lifts the colors, or attempts to do so. But at this very instant his horse is shot, and plunges fearfully. The Major is unhorsed, or gets off, striking upon his feet, seizes the colors, raises them, and makes most heroic exertions to rally the men of the 40th — never was the action and bearing of a man under fire more gallant than this. Meanwhile his horse turns and gallops off the field, to the left, the way he came, straining every muscle in the frenzy of pain, and going like the wind. He runs straight through and over the line of one regiment of our troops lying on the ground, leaps a high rail fence, and disappears in the distance, with reins, straps and stirrups flying. This fence is the continuation to the left of the same fence over which we charged, on the crest of the bluff, where the 40th Mass. had been skirmishing. The officers of the 40th soon rally that regiment, and bring it forward in line.

After some delay — the evening now quite dusky — the Thirteenth moves off by the left flank, somewhat to the left and rear, out of the open field, into some of the rebel rifle-pits which the charge has captured, and which are situated in a thin strip, or spur, of small pine-trees jutting into the open field on the left side. We have lain on the field nearly an hour. From here men are sent at once to look after our wounded. A rebel fort, or what appeared to be such as we came into the field, rising black and high in a field about half a mile to the right and front of the Thirteenth, fires an occasional shell during the night high over our heads to the lighted bivouac of the Union troops somewhat to our left and rear.

We lie here in these rebel rifle-pits in the pines until some time in the night, hour not definitely known, Lt. Col. Smith thinks until near daylight, when we move nearly a quarter of a mile farther to the left and rear, behind a rail fence, and thence turn towards the right and bivouac in the same woods from which we charged and apparently about an eighth of a mile to the left of the position on the crest from which we charged. A portion of the 13th is thought to have re-occupied the same ground. Here little defenses of sand are thrown up with bayonets and tin dippers, a few logs piled up, and we literally bivouac among the dead — they lie everywhere and in great numbers. More men are now sent over the field to find, care for and bring off the wounded, and to bury the dead, of our Regiment. Capt. Julian and a large detail from the Thirteenth works all night upon the entrenchments near the scene of our charge. Light lines of earth-works rise all along our front.

The 18th Corps thus occupies and holds the ground it gained by the assault, including all of the first line of Confederate rifle-pits; merely extending its lines to right and left to fill the space between the corps on its right and on its left, and co-operating with the 10th Corps.

The foregoing account was written in the main before the writer's visit to the field in May 1885. At that time Lt. Col. Smith went with the writer, located the place of the charge, and the lines afterwards occupied by the 13th, and measured, paced or estimated all the distances.

The National Cemetery is on the main road from Old to New Cold Harbor, and about half way between those places. The first ravine north-northeast of the Cemetery leads down direct to the rear line of the works occupied by the 13th, which were in the ravine, crossing it, and stretching out on the level to the left — westward — of the ravine. The ravine points about southeast toward Old Cold Harbor, and about northwest to our rear line of works. The 13th passed up this ravine on leaving the field of Cold Harbor, noon of June 12th.

Now to find the place where the 13th charged on the evening of June 1st: continuing almost due north from the Cemetery towards Bethesda church, at the distance of about one mile we come to a road, leading from the Old Cold Harbor and Bethesda church road, and from near the old Beulah church, southwest to Mr. Albert Allerson's house, which stood nearly half a mile in the rear of the Confederate front line of rifle-pits which we charged upon and captured. Turning to the left and proceeding southwest up this road, towards Mr. Allerson's house, we soon come to a ravine, and in it a culvert, across the road, over a brook running from a small pond lying some fifty yards to the left of the road, and known as the "Old-Still" pond — a distillery having once been located near here. The only brook, culvert and pond in this vicinity. At the southwest side of this brook and pond is a steep bluff, 30 to 40 feet high, and with a slope of about 50 yards, running along the ravine in a southeastward course for several hundred yards. If the crest of this bluff be taken for the handle of a huge sickle, with the end of the handle resting at the Allerson road, north; a line of woods and a rail fence, sweeping first southeastward and a little to the rear, and then southwestward far to the front, and bordering the east and southeast sides of the field into which we charged, will rather roughly represent the blade — the point of the sickle falling near where the Confederates had a powerful redoubt, in an open field, near a mile to the southwest of the bluff. Here were the cannon that played upon us from the left, during our charge.

On the afternoon of the charge, the 13th came into this ravine from the southeast, marching by the right flank; halted, faced to the left in line of battle, swung around a little, and marched up the slope among large pine-trees, between the Old-Still pond and the bluff west of it, and made the final formation, for the charge, in line of battle, near the crest of the bluff, and facing southwest. The 13th here formed a rod or two in rear of a rail fence, and waited for the order to charge, while the Union skirmishers, a part of them of the 40th Mass., were behind the fence hotly engaging the Confederates in rifle-pits 300 yards to the front

— upon whom we were to charge — and being badly cut up. When the order to charge was given the right of the Thirteenth rested nearly in front of the centre of the Old-Still pond, 150 yards from the road, paced southeast along the crest of the bluff, and 100 yards from the culvert, paced south across the ravine and up the slope, and about 50 feet in rear of the highest part of the crest; the 13th thus occupying the central part of the handle of the sickle. Lt. Col. Smith paced these distances in May 1885. The 13th charged nearly due west, swinging a little to the southwest, and almost directly toward the spot where Mr. Edward Jenkins' house now stands, away over on the farther side of the field toward the left. The charge was for almost exactly 300 yards (the distance measured by a tape line, May 1885) and done as rapidly as the average man can run that distance. The captured rifle-pits have since been leveled, but their line is easily made out from the color of the subsoil thrown up, as the whole is now, 1885, a plowed field.

After halting in the charge, and lying down for about an hour, we moved by the left flank, to the rear and left, about 75 or 100 yards, to the edge of the pines, and into some Confederate rifle-pits among them, and remained there until near morning, the 118th N. Y. on our front. There was a scramble on the part of some of the men when we went into these rifle-pits, and in endeavoring to preserve better order in the sudden rush, after we reached the pits and were ordered into them, the writer had a heavy gold ring pulled off from his finger and lost. It was a present and loose. Bearing upon the crest of the bluff, and upon the whole level field of our charge, with no trees of consequence or other obstruction to their fire, were two rebel batteries at least; one to the right, about one half mile to the northwest of the 13th, and near where Mr. Allerson's house now stands, and the other to the left, about three fourths of a mile southwest of the 13th and a little to the south of where Mr. Jenkins' house now stands. Besides these, and running wide across the field in our front, was a strong system of two lines of rebel rifle-trenches, flanked by similar trenches to the right and left, all occupied by a heavy rebel skirmish and picket line. The charge of the 13th, and of our Brigade, was into a sort of broad inverted V; the Reg. entering at the point, the bar and arms to right and left rifle-trenches, on each end of the arms a battery, and the enemy's gunners and riflemen well manning all. The banks along Allerson's road were also heavily manned by rebels.

"Charles McGaffrey of I carried the National colors through the charge unhurt, and Malachi W. Richardson of G the State colors, and was killed. McGaffrey shook the colors out, and waved them to the front, just as we came upon the crest of the bluff, among the dead and wounded lying along the rail fence. Three of the eight men of our Color-guard were killed. The total loss in the 13th in less than five minutes, during the charge, was seventy in killed, wounded and missing. We moved to the place of our charge by the road that runs from Old Cold Harbor via New Cold Harbor to Gaines' Mill about two miles west;

stopped to load and called the roll in, or near, the road, and straight across, about one half a mile to a mile, from the crest. We next moved along the road a short distance, left it, moved to the right, towards the north, passed around the recent ruins of a building — said to be Beulah church — into a ravine and brush to the right, thence over much rough ground to the position on the crest from which we charged. The 40th Massachusetts were skirmishing on the crest in front of the Thirteenth just before, and at the time of our charge, and Capt. Goss secured nearly enough of Spencer rifles thrown away, or lost, by them, to arm his Company, I, but they were taken away from him by order of the Corps Provost Marshal." LT. COL. SMITH.

The State-color bearer Richardson was struck during the charge, and was found shot through the hips, lying with the colors on the field. He was assisted off the field by Corporal Charles Powell of K, a Swede, who took the colors. As Richardson did not recover from his wound, the colors were placed in Powell's hands as a complimentary reward for rescuing them, and he carried that flag through the rest of the battle.

Lieut. Taggard states that when we fell back after the charge, to the little strip of pines, and went into the rebel rifle-pits, a little to the rear and left of our line of charge and place of halting, Sergt. Van Duzee of E was left in sight, lying on the field. A man of Co. E seeing him there, rose up, reversed his gun, sticking the bayonet into the ground — to indicate that he was bent on a peaceful mission — and advanced towards the rebel line, and towards Van Duzee. The enemy, however, fired at him, and he was obliged to return, leaving Van Duzee on the field.

A rebel prisoner, taken later, so described a man, whom he helped to properly bury, that we believe it must have been Van Duzee.

Asst. Surgeon Sullivan remembers that the Reg. fell back after the charge, and at some hour in the night, to the slope between the little pond and the crest of the bluff, and that night, and the next day, the men obtained water from a spring near the south end of the pond; so that we must have been, during the latter part of the night of June 1st and on June 2d, very near the point whence we charged. As the Reg. passed to the charge he saw quite a number of Union soldiers standing and lying, half sunk in the mud and water of the pond — dead ; all having been shot while attempting to cross to the skirmish line, before the 13th came up.

Under date of June 3d Charles W. Washburn of G, a member of the Thirteenth's Band, temporarily employed at the Hospital, writes home: "Thousands were wounded June 1st. We had poor accommodations. The wounded were brought back to the rear, a mile or so, on stretchers, and laid on the ground in a field, and we put up bushes, the next day, to keep the sun off a little. The Surgeons worked night and day, cutting off legs and arms, and extracting bullets and pieces of shells, from every part of the men's bodies. All had to lie on the ground, both before and after the operations upon them. It rained the night of June 2d, and many of the wounded had little cover, and some of them no cover at all. On the morning of June 3d the ambulances commenced carrying the wounded to White House Landing."

June 2. Thurs. Pleasant, with light showers, hard rain in the afternoon. Last night the enemy made desperate attempts to recapture his works and lost ground, but in vain. The dead of the 13th buried. The Reg. in line of battle and entrenching — along the crest near the point over which we charged, but a little to the left — with bayonets and dippers and now and then a spade, and under a dangerous fire all day. Severe fighting going on to the right and left, in spurts, all night and all day, but no general engagement. We occupy a portion of the crest about 200 yards to the left of Allerson's road, and are fronting a little south of west. The 18th Corps holds the ground which it captured.

Last night Asst. Surgeon Sullivan, and Hosp. Steward Prescott, of the 13th, went out between the lines, looking for the wounded. A man appears on horseback, and demands their business; and they, Yankee like, demand his. And there the interview ends; each parting from the other

---

### DESCRIPTION OF PLAT.

A. Road leading from Mr. Albert Allerson's house H, eastward to Mr. D. Woody's house and Beulah church; with culvert N over the brook from the Old-Still pond B.

C. C. Crest of bluff rising about 40 feet, all along the west side of a deep ravine D, heavily wooded and containing a spring M and pond B. A strong zig-zag rail fence, V, ran along this crest for several hundred yards.

E. Position of Thirteenth, close under the top of the crest, awaiting the order to charge. The right of the Reg. 150 yards from the road, paced along the crest, and 100 yards from culvert N, and almost exactly in front of the centre of the pond B.

F. Thirteenth halted; after the enemy retired from his long outer line of rifle-pits Z. The Thirteenth charged 300 yards. After the charge and halt we moved about 100 yards to the left and rear into rebel rifle-pits in the point of pines at G.

I. Mr. Edward Jenkins's house built since the war. P. Edge of woods.

K. Confederate battery to the right, distant about one third of a mile from the crest.

L. Confederate battery to the left, distant about three fourths of a mile from the crest.

T. Apple-tree where Major Marshall rallied the 40th Mass., about 100 or 150 yards in rear of the Thirteenth when halted and lying down after the charge.

Y. A second line, main line of rifle-trenches, running across the field, and occupied by rebel infantry.

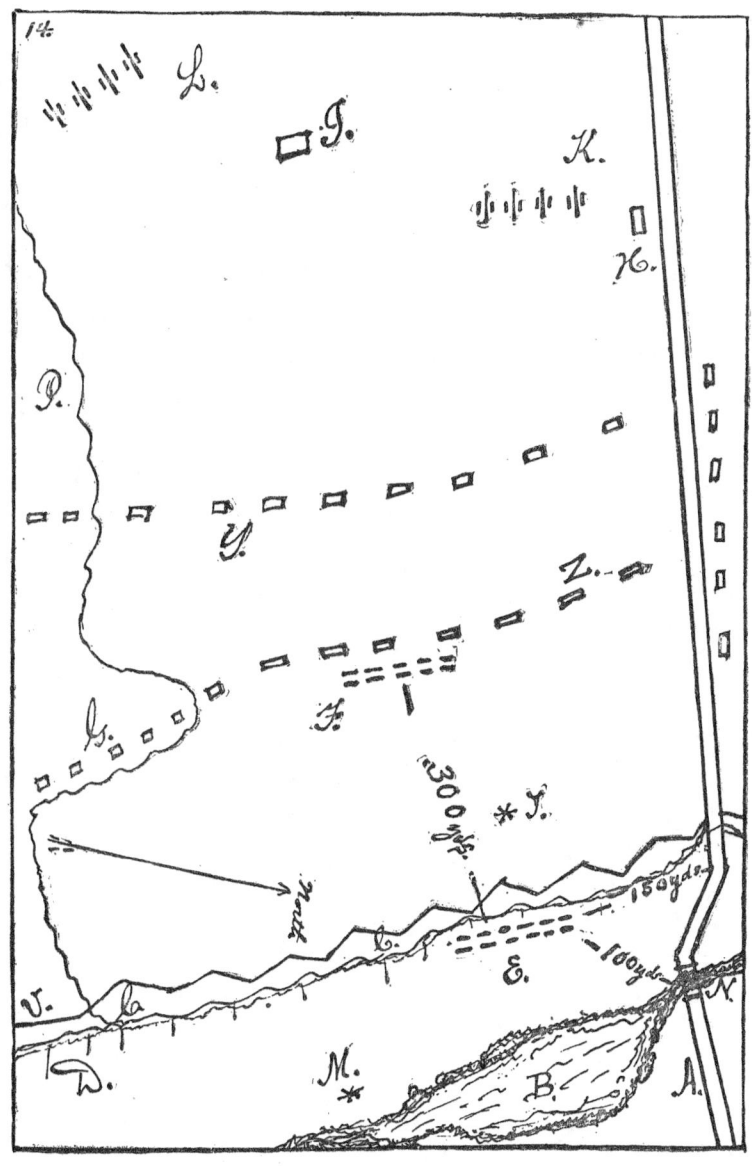

COLD HARBOR, June 1, 1864.
From a sketch made by the writer in May 1885.

full of the suspicion, natural to such an incident, that they had met one of the enemy. As the darkness increased, Sullivan and Prescott were puzzled, and did not know which lines to enter; and remained on the field between the lines until there was enough of daylight to enable them to decide. Both men are courageous, but such an experience no man would care to repeat.

An errand early to-day took the writer about half a mile through the woods to the left, and a more terrible picture of war can scarcely be imagined. The dead are lying everywhere. The bodies show but little evidence of suffering, but the limbs are stretched out stiff and at almost every possible angle. Many bodies are bent backwards, as if the spine were trying to touch ends that way. One body is thus arched up, and is resting upon the shoulders and heels. The coat-capes are turned up over many faces, other faces are bare, others hidden, the bodies lying face down; but the most lie as they fell, and are badly torn — it is a walk of sickening and unutterable horrors. Along the line of a fence, near the ridge, or crest of the bluff over which we charged, one could walk several rods upon the bodies almost covering the ground, lying in every conceivable position, and piled one upon another. Among these are some sitting bolt upright, gun in hand, in a posture almost as natural as life, and appearing as if they had not moved a muscle after being shot. One lies attentively examining the lock of his musket, his head to the foe, and a bullet hole through the lower part of his face. Many bodies of horses, too, are lying among the men.

The scene of our charge presents this morning a strange sight. A man a little apart by himself on the crest, but one of the skirmish line through which we advanced to the charge, had his gun about half way between the position of 'ready' and 'aim,' when he was instantly killed; and there he is this morning, scarcely changed in position, but resting quite firmly and naturally on one knee, his left shoulder against a stump, while he holds his gun raised and cocked, his head leaning a little to one side, peering around the stump as if about to find a good mark among the enemy and to shoot. Those who have occasion to pass in front of his gun, before he is removed, instinctively start, and step quickly out of line of the aim of the dead man's gun. It does not seem possible that any man when dead could retain a position so life-like. But this is not the only case of similar fixed rigidity of muscles after instant death.

The field of our charge bears a little to the right this morning, and contains many bodies of the Union dead lying in full view. The 13th are so badly cut up, that they are not called upon for much duty to-day; are ordered to preserve silence, not to fire a shot, and to remain hidden under the ridge or crest and the trees as much as possible, and avoid betraying their position. Generals Grant and Meade visit our part of the line. About mid-afternoon Gen. 'Baldy' Smith comes up to our line, and seeing the Confederates within close musket range, asks for a gun, and is about to fire, when Lieut. Taggard requests him not to do so; explaining that very strict orders had been given not to fire unless we were attacked. Gen. Smith thereupon quietly returns the gun to its owner without firing — a Major General obeying a Lieutenant's request, and possibly one of his own orders.

The 13th has been practically separated from the rest of our Brigade to-day. After dark orders are received to move farther to the left. This necessitates a hunt for the path through the brush; and the writer, and one or two other officers, can never forget that hunt — stumbling over stumps, fallen trees and brush, and the numerous bodies of the now offensive dead, everything drenched and soaked in the rain. We move about 9 p. m. in pitchy darkness, towards the left, along behind the same rail fence, or what is left of it, abandoning the little defenses thrown up in the twenty-four hours or so since the charge. This move takes us altogether away from the crest, over which we charged — the handle of the sickle — across the short bend in the blade to the rear and left, and along up towards the centre of the blade, as we cross the rail fence, bordering the field, and face more to the northward towards Mr. Allerson's road.

While crossing this fence and moving considerably nearer to the rebel lines, some of the men — probably remembering the fearful experience we had soon after crossing it on the evening of June 1st — hesitated and lay down, or crouched behind the fence. Upon this Lieut. Taggard was obliged to use some quite vigorous measures, to cause these men to continue the advance over the fence, which were witnessed by Maj. Grantman; and the incident may have been the reason for the detail of Lieut. Taggard to the command of Company D, a little later — about midnight. After crossing the fence we take position about one fourth of a mile from the crest, left, in the edge of the woods, and still fronting a portion of the same large, open field into which we charged June 1st. We remain here until nearly daylight on the morning of June 3d, when we move a second time and still farther to the left, across a portion of the open field, without casualty, and among numerous dead, and halt for a short time. While executing this last movement we pass within, apparently, two hundred yards of the enemy's lines, near which are a large busy corps of rebel gray men cutting down trees; swinging their axes as if dear life depended upon their taking down half a dozen trees at every stroke. Our backwoodsmen laugh at the spitefully rapid chip, chip, chip. As it happened they were preparing to cut down 10,000 blue men, two hours later, in ten minutes — the awful Union charge, all along the line, at 4.30 a. m., June 3d. In which charge, however, the 13th do not directly engage.

To-night a rattling musketry fire commences on the line far off to our left — pop, pop, pop — just far enough away to be distinctly heard at first, and then gradually growing louder, as it approaches nearer running along the lines, but without increasing in volume, comes up to the line of the Thirteenth, and there suddenly stops short. The men of the Reg., not seeing anything worth firing at, maintain silence, but with every gun in the line leveled, and held ready for instant use. An affair chiefly of the pickets. We can now, after more than twenty-three years, almost see again in the half-darkness our long, grim line of men, with muskets in hand, all ready and peering from behind trees, over logs and little hillocks of sand, and straining their eyes to catch the first sight of the rebel line — if it dare dash out from yonder works.

Many of the disturbances of last night, to-day, and to-night, are occasioned by changes made in the position of the corps of the Union army. Especially as Gen. Warren's corps appears, to unite with Gen. Smith's corps on the right near Woody's ; a mile or two down on the left also, where it is said that Gen. Hancock's corps is forming on the left of Gen. Wright's corps. We have been momentarily expecting to move, to one scene or the other, but remain undisturbed otherwise than by listening to the din in the near distance. Troops have been moving past our rear for the last eighteen hours, mainly going towards the left, where there is scarcely a minute's cessation of the noise of the firing either in day or night. Gen. Grant is carrying out what Gen. Lee calls "Grant's crab movement" — the perpetual extension of the Union left.

The whole Union line is under orders to attack the Confederate lines of works, rifle-trenches and forts, to-morrow morning, June 3d, at half past four o'clock — a grand charge all along the whole line. The Thirteenth is so much cut up that we will not be put in, unless the situation imperatively demands it, but will form a part of the reserve and support ; and remain in the front line of it, ready for instant advance — a quick reserve. The country all about us, excepting the narrow field, nearly half a mile long, which lies between us and the enemy's entrenchments, is a muddy, thickly wooded, swampy jungle, extending apparently for two or three miles in its worst features toward our right.

June 3. Fri. Warm ; a drizzling rain. The Thirteenth is called at 3 a. m., and near 5 a. m., following close upon the charge, moves across the field to the left, and in support, to an old line of rebel rifle-trenches. Last night the enemy's troops were seen by us, about midnight, moving and massing in rear of their pickets, far across the open field on our front, an occasional distant camp-fire gleaming out upon them ; but nothing comes of it, and the 13th with the Union line near about have a comparatively quiet night, excepting for our moving twice to the left and front in the rear of our picket lines.

At 4.30 a. m., however, there is an earth-shaking roar, as of the united burst of a hundred thunder storms — front, right, left, rear, everywhere ; and then in a comparatively short time all is quite still again save for the usual picket firing and the scattered cannon shots. The contest lasts for about an hour, the noisest and fiercest part for ten or fifteen minutes — the famous charge all along the line at Cold Harbor.

The Thirteenth follows the assaulting columns in, acting as a support, at once occupying a line of rifle-trenches captured in the assault ; the rebel fire still very severe, but ranging too high to seriously damage the support and rear lines.

We remain in these trenches at the front until between 10 and 11 a. m. when we are again moved and formed for an assault, massed in close order by divisions with a large body of infantry, composed in part of Gen. Brooks' Division of the 18th Corps. The column is thirty-two ranks deep where we are; a solid body of men literally covering the ground. The front line of our Brigade is composed of the 118th N. Y., left, and the 8th Conn., right; the 13th in the second line on the right; while the 21st Conn. is in line of battle in rear of our whole Brigade; when deployed in the charge, the 8th Conn. is to lead the column.

We remain thus massed, and lying in timber, and undergrowth with wide, open spaces, from about 11 a. m. until after 4 p. m., when we move back again toward the right, to find cover from the enemy's bullets, which came to us, while massed, over the 6th Corps — a large part of that corps, about 15,000 men, being similarly massed close on our left; while many rebel shells flew over us into the ranks of the 6th Corps — the enemy's infantry being near on the left front of the 6th Corps, and his artillery farther away on the right front of the 18th Corps. The whole body of infantry lying here massed for an assault numbered between 20,000 and 25,000 men.

Capt. Stoodley, with Company G, is acting as provost-guard, on the battle-field, to keep up stragglers, while we are massed for the charge. Lt. Col. Smith thinks that Company I was also absent, not yet having returned from picket duty on the right.

As we have said, we lie here for over four hours, in a lot of dense short weeds and underbrush, and among scattering trees, in full view of the rebel works, high parapets, to be assaulted, not over 350 yards distant, on the other side of an open field strewn with dead men — nothing inviting about that! — and in a ravine, running through the field, we can see the dead lying strewn thickest of all, away up to the rebel line. Caps are removed from the muskets to prevent accidents, bayonets fixed, and the men lie as low as possible upon their faces, in momentary expectation of hearing the order to charge. No order comes; attack considered too hazardous. While thus waiting, two officers and eleven men in the 13th are struck by bullets from the rebel infantry. This is a trying ordeal, but no man flinches.

Lieut. Taggard, now commanding Company D, is severely wounded in the leg about 2 p. m., and Lieut. Durell is slightly wounded across his throat. Lieut. Taggard and the writer are sitting side by side when he is struck. Spending over four hours inactive, as part of such a target, is enough to try the patience of any army of Jobs. Just after 4 p. m. we move back to the right to find cover; and bivouac until near daylight, moving, however, twice during the night, a much disturbed bivouac. While we are massed and waiting the order to charge, it is reported among us as a fact, that some of Gen. Grant's troops flatly refused, to-day, to make any further assaults upon the enemy's lines, when ordered so to do; and this is given on the field as one of the reasons why our column does not charge this afternoon.[1]

This is the chief day of the battle of Cold Harbor ; the 13th is exposed for many hours, in fact about all day, to a severe fire but not engaged. The other two brigades of our Division were in the assault of this morning at 4.30 a. m. Our brigade was then in reserve, excepting the 10th N. H., which charged at daylight — in front of two brigades, one of which was Col. Marston's — and lost 90 men in five minutes.

Again late to-night the writer is sent into the brush, in Egyptian darkness, post haste, to find a path for the Reg. to move in, an old wood-road a short distance to the rear. Before going two rods his foot is tangled in a vine, and he falls flat upon the ground. While getting up he feels cloth upon the ground — an overcoat with a dead body in it. A few steps farther on he runs into a pile of abandoned knapsacks, catching his foot in the straps of one of them by way of introduction to the lot. The owners, a dozen or more, can just be made out, lying in bivouac near a large tree — the bivouac of the dead. The wood-road is soon found, and traced back to the nearest point to the Reg. To travel such a wood-road among the dead, once, is enough for a lifetime. A glimpse of the passing hour. The Reg. retires a short distance to rest near this wood-road, and before daylight again moves to another point on the line — still to the left — and soon relieves a line of our skirmishers who had spent a part of the night here ; this position we take between 2 and 3 a. m., and hold it during our stay at Cold Harbor, daylight on the morning of June 4th exposing us unprepared to a severe front and enfilade fire from the enemy's near rifle-trenches, and from his batteries located about one fourth of a mile to our right front.

The night of June 3d is exceeding dark ; against its blackness there frequently flashes the fire-fly of a picket shot. The picket, possibly seeing against the sky the top of a weed waving in the breeze, imagines it to be one of the enemy, and fires. The weed stops waving ; therefore he knows that he has killed his man, or sent him wounded back to his lines. Brave man. He is a hero next day. Next night the weed wiggles for another shot — and makes another hero. War is a terrible thing in more ways than one.

Lossing states that the Nationals charged upon the Confederate lines at 4.30 a. m., all along the line, and within twenty minutes 10,000 men lay dead and wounded on the field. The battle ended about 1 p. m.

So far as the 18th Corps is concerned in this morning's assault, Gen. Martindale's Division moved down a ravine near the centre of the 18th Corps front ; Gen. Brooks' Division moved in on the left of Martindale,

---

[1] Gen. Grant writes, 1884–5, that no troops under his command ever refused to obey an order given by him. Still the troops may have refused to obey some General on this day ; and the writer will let the report stand as he heard it on the field, not an hour before we moved out of column massed for the charge, as it in no way disputes Gen. Grant's statement. See Greeley's American Conflict, Vol. II. page 582.

connecting with the right of the 6th Corps; Gen. Devens' Division was held in position, on the extreme right, to protect that flank. The assault drove in the enemy's skirmishers, and captured a large portion of his first line of works; but the 18th Corps charged into an angle similar to the one it entered on the evening of June 1st, and was badly cut up, losing a thousand men. The field on our front, into which the 18th Corps plunges, is open, quite level, affords scarcely any cover, and in general is the most exposed piece of ground crossed this morning by the Union troops. From our position in the 13th we can see about half of this field at a glance, and the Union troops rushing, falling or returning, all under a most fearful rebel fire. But the 18th Corps is only a small part of this grand assault. The Tenth, Second and Sixth Corps are in it as well, while along the whole line almost the entire Army of the Potomac takes a hand, the assaulting columns passing forward upon the charge amid the deafening roar of artillery and musketry, and the terrible pelting of thousands of missiles, falling as hail falls in a storm.

Language cannot describe the fearful picture of these assaulting columns, seen here and there — and especially upon the long, open field on our front — rushing in the mad plunge of a battle charge, with muskets in hand and gleaming bayonets fixed, thousands of swords flashing, hundreds of battle-flags waving, many hundreds of officers shouting loud their words of command, and the men screaming and yelling their battle-cries, all mingled with the shrieks of the poor men who are struck down in their wild career — here in ten short minutes ten thousand of them, a thousand men falling in every minute; while along the dense battle lines of more than four miles, huge clouds of gunpowder smoke roll up above the fields and forests, and in addition to the concentrated fire of hundreds of Union cannon and thousands of Union muskets, there roars, bellows, howls, crashes and thunders the awful and tremendous rebel artillery fire and musketry fire that together can stop, short, — and hurl back at once this almost invincible host of Eighty Thousand trained, disciplined Northern soldiers. To witness the scene were well worth rounding the whole world — still may we never see such a scene again. Confederate Gen. Pickett's charge at Gettysburg, most brave and gallant as was that, was small boys' play to this charge all along the whole Union line at Cold Harbor.

Gen. Grant in his Memoirs, Vol. II. page 271, and preceding, refers to us of the 18th Corps, as arriving at Cold Harbor on the afternoon of June 1st, tired and worn out from our long and dusty march; and refers to this field, into which the 18th Corps charged on this morning of June 3d, as an open plain swept by both a direct and a cross fire, and as the most exposed ground of any over which charges were made on this morning.

"June 3, 1864. The Thirteenth up at 3 o'clock a. m. At 5 a. m. started on the advance. Charged across an open field, under fire, into the woods, and rebel rifle-pits. Lay there two or three hours; then moved to the left, and into another wood, and lay on our faces. The order came to uncap pieces and fix bayonets. Moved to the right, and lay down under direct fire; here bullets flew straight over us in great numbers. One tree just behind me had more than forty holes in it. About two o'clock (2 p. m.) the rebels put a bullet through the fleshy part of my right leg above the knee. I left the field, and Surgeon Morrill dressed the wound, which is not at all dangerous. June 4th. I got into an ambulance at noon, passed Gen. Grant's Hdqrs. at 2 p. m., arrived at White House about 1 or 2 a. m. on June 5th. A hard ride. It hurt me, and must have been awful for those severely wounded. A rainy night."

Lieut. Taggard.

"June 3d. While the Thirteenth was massed by divisions in the column for assault, in the afternoon, a bullet wounded me across the throat, not severely though it was a very narrow escape. When the column was dismissed this afternoon, the Thirteenth moved to the right and occupied some earth-works, relieving Col. Marston's brigade. When the Thirteenth moved from there, or from that vicinity, on the morning of June 4th, a Union battery took that place, and commenced firing at once. The rebel battery replied, and the trees were cut and torn in pieces, over our heads, as we moved away." Capt. Durell.

June 4. Sat. Very warm; afternoon rainy. This morning between 2 and 3 a. m. the Thirteenth moves to the left to a new position on the line, as mentioned under June 3d, and as daylight comes on it reveals the enemy's works directly on our front and very near, apparently not more than 500 feet distant — Lt. Col. Smith makes it 30 rods. We should have been in this position and entrenched several hours earlier but for an error in directing our Brigade so as to close the line, and the extreme darkness of last night. The skirmishers and pickets who preceded us on this line, holding it after the charge of yesterday, June 3d, had seized it, had made little pits, but no regular entrenchments excepting a short trench near the left of the Thirteenth. Our men add to these with tin dippers and bayonets; and it is astonishing to see how much earth can be thrown up in this way in an hour. The bodies of the rebel dead lying about, and the bodies of some Union men also, are piled up for a barricade, but separately, also a few logs, and sand thrown upon the whole — anything to keep the rebel bullets back. A rebel shell burying and bursting in one of these horrid heaps makes a scene better imagined than described; the barricade is speedily re-arranged, however. The enemy enfilades a portion of our line as well as attacks the front, and the right of the Regiment is almost wholly unprotected; and in manœuvring, before entrenchments can be improvised, we lose several men.

During this manœuvring and occupation of the ground before commencing to entrench, a piece containing three gilt stars is cut out of our badly tattered flag by the rebel shells and bullets. Capt. Julian, Lieut. Thompson of E and one of the men, as the piece comes fluttering down near them, make a simultaneous rush for it; possession is difficult to determine, all three seizing it at once, and in the moment of waiting before another move is made a jack-knife decides the matter as umpire, by cutting out one star for each claimant. The writer still, 1887, has one of these stars, Capt. Julian has another.

"When we were ordered to move, in pursuance of orders I procured entrenching tools at Gen. Burnham's Hdqrs., and had them ready about dark on June 3d. Later in the night I was directed to turn these tools over to Col. Stedman of the 11th Conn.; hence all the danger, trouble and loss when we appeared on the advanced line this morning, without the means of protecting ourselves against the fire of the enemy posted in force behind their earth-works, and not 200 yards distant."

LT. COL. SMITH.

A little later in the day too, while we are entrenching, the enemy suddenly opens upon us with several field-pieces located off to our right — thus enfilading our line with cannon as well as with musketry — and two Companies [1] of the Thirteenth are extricated only with great difficulty. However, in a few hours our entrenchments are in excellent condition for defense — the most of the bodies of the rebel dead being well covered with high banks of sand, and never removed; and this point, angle, corner is held by the Thirteenth as its advanced line — advanced, too, beyond the general line — until the end of the battle, June 12th, and a red-hot corner it is too!

The right of the Regiment here rests very near a muddy and very wet bit of swamp, called Muddy Run by the natives; a bit of swamp two or three rods wide which is unprotected excepting by a few trees. The centre and left of the Reg. rises and entrenches on a small knoll but quite high — on the whole a very prominent and salient point; the ground in our rear rising still higher than along the line where our works are built, and higher than the parapet of our works at any time while here.

Our entrenchments bend around a large pine-tree standing near the highest point of the knoll, giving room for the trench between the angle of the earth-work in front, and the tree in the rear — possibly it stands fifteen feet in rear of the parapet. This tree is about 75 feet high and $2\frac{1}{2}$ feet in diameter, and the boys of the 13th call it "Our Pine," because we had such a severe fight, to-day, to gain and hold the little knoll on which the tree stands. The colors are to the right of Company E and almost dead in front — a little to the right — of the pine. This pine, so near our angle in the works, is struck by hundreds of bullets, and is the special target for every rebel gunner in this part of the Confederacy. To burst a shell in it, or against it, is esteemed by them a higher distinction than to receive a Colonel's commission — that is, judging from their

---

[1] The writer can vouch for the dangerous and vexatious position of these two Companies, for he was sent post haste down the line with an order for the Companies to remove from the enfiladed trench; and after reaching them was obliged to assist in their removal because of the absence of one Company's commander; the trench at that hour being not more than one or two feet deep, and almost useless as a protection against the numerous rebel shells. It was a full half hour before the rebel field-pieces were silenced by one of the Union batteries.

constant endeavors. The enemy commands the ground in the rear of our trench, a covert way is needed to approach the front line, and is built a few feet to the left of the pine, a cut eight feet deep, and about as wide. Between our angle and the rebel entrenchments is a clear, open field, with a slight valley running across it. The line of the Reg. curves toward the front, but we face nearly west. Before night we render two of the enemy's guns of no use to him, our sharp-shooters allowing no man to approach them; they are quaker-guns for the rest of the day. Muddy Run at our right opens a gap, diagonally to the right, for the enemy's fire and we run traverses across the ditch of our entrenchments for every few men to prevent his enfilading any part of the curving line of our trench. It is very difficult to cross this run, and communications are thrown across tied to sticks and stones.

After our flag is planted on the works this morning it is shot down repeatedly, and the staff split, smashed and splintered so that it will not sustain the flag. Finally, after a very spirited fusillade, it tumbles down, with the staff in a much battered condition. Sergt. David W. Bodge, the color-bearer, ties up the staff with strings, and straps from his knapsack, and mounts the sand to plant it. Just as he strikes the staff into the sand, it is again struck by a rebel bullet, and both flag and bearer come down from the works together. Sergt. Bodge's hand and arm are so much benumbed that he can do no more for some time, and another man volunteers to plant the flag. Watching his opportunity, he rushes up on the sand, and stands the flag up, leaning the staff against some little tree tops rising above the sand in the centre of the embankment, where it cannot again be dislodged. The enemy fires at it a long time, but finally lets it alone. After this affair our tattered colors are less exposed. The fact is, the enemy does his utmost to prevent our occupation of this bold little knoll, sending us bullets and shells in plenty. See the colors in frontispiece.

"The staff of the National colors of the Thirteenth was struck and split just above my hand as I was holding it on the morning of June 4th at Cold Harbor, and would not sustain the flag; I therefore took two pieces of a barrel stave, or of a cracker box, for splints, and tied them to the staff with a piece of rope. That, however, did not make the staff strong enough, and I afterwards added a strap from my knapsack, which is still upon the staff in the Capitol at Concord."

David W. Bodge, Color-Sergeant.

(May 1885. The little tree-tops, mentioned above, of gum or some other hard wood, are now quite large trees; several of them growing together undisturbed in the parapet of our old earth-works, about two rods to the right of where our Pine then stood. The Pine is now a little heap of rotting wood. While standing, a strip, four inches wide and eight inches long, was cut out of the side toward the rebel lines and furnished sixteen rebel bullets.)

To-day we have had one man killed, and six wounded. Capt. Julian receives a bruise on his arm, from a rebel bullet. Aaron K. Blake, of A, is shot through the upper part of his head to-day, a rebel bullet entering and exposing the brain. He is laid near the Pine at first, close to the north side of it, and breathes almost all day. He is utterly unconscious, making no sign when spoken to or touched — every effort being made to revive him — and can suffer no possible pain ; yet he is strangely nervous, breathing more quickly when a shell strikes the tree, or near him, or the noise of the firing increases. Later in the day he is moved to the covert way, a few feet to the south of the Pine, where about 5 p. m. he quietly ceases to breathe ; and dies without showing any sign of consciousness or of suffering from the time when he was struck.

Regular siege operations are commenced to-day, to force Gen. Lee's lines, and shovels, axes, picks and spades are called to the front. Capt. Julian takes cover behind our Pine and acts as a sharp-shooter for several hours, at times firing rapidly, and having a man or two to load the muskets for him. The whole Reg. is hard at work all day either firing or entrenching, and late at night is relieved by the 98th N. Y., and goes to the rear, about one eighth of a mile, to obtain a little rest, moving to the front again just before dawn of June 5th. By night the 8th Conn., the next regiment on our right, also have quite a strong line of earth-works thrown up, and a log breast-work partly protects the line across Muddy Run, lying between our Regiment and theirs.

We are so hard at work both day and night that when an opportunity is given us to sleep, we sleep like logs. The writer completed his duties of the day, as Acting Adjutant, last night — June 3d — about midnight, and well tired out laid down, covered with his rubber overcoat, to take a nap, with the Hdqrs. of the Reg. and with the Reg. in bivouac on the ground in a long line of battle. The night was very dark. The next thing the writer knew, he was waked by the loud rap of a stray bullet against a tree near by him. On looking about, no Hdqrs., no Reg., and at first no person was to be seen. It was now just in the earliest gray of dawn. Rising and looking around in the brush for another person, if any, whom the Reg. departing in the darkness had failed to wake, he finds a number of men lying about, but none will wake — all are dead. Pretty soon, as it grows lighter, he moves out into more open ground, and sees and hears, about 200 yards distant and off toward the rebel lines, a body of men chopping fiercely — clip, clip, clip, go their spiteful axes at the trees of what appears to be an orchard. On approaching nearer them he finds that they are a party of the rebels, and he turns back at once into deeper woods, where he soon comes upon a man on horseback, sitting still and intently watching the rebel choppers. Before the man can see the writer he slips behind a large tree. The horseman is an officer of some sort, looks safe, and after a little the writer inquires of him the whereabouts of Burnham's Brigade. The horseman with an oath answers that he does not know — and his tone indicates no particular interest in Burnham's Brigade. The writer has but one recourse, and without inquiring further, returns towards the rebel choppers, to the place of the Regiment's bivouac, and hunts for a trail. The Union dead are here very numerous, and the rebel dead are scattered among them. Satisfying himself that no one of the 13th is here asleep, he follows the broadest trail he can find, and finds the Reg. halted in the brush, and just before it moves into the place held during our stay at Cold Harbor. The Reg. left the writer asleep in the pitchy darkness an hour or two before he awoke to follow, but how the matter occurred he could never find out. His position, when waken, was between the Union and rebel lines, the man on horseback the only Union soldier he saw. During the first few nights at Cold Harbor the front lines were constantly changing.

June 5. Sun. Warm, rainy. We hear considerable firing to the right and left to-day; but little, however, on our front. The Reg. comes from the front at 3 a. m. and after a little time goes to work on a rear line of entrenchments. This rear line looks west, and is on one side of a belt of timber, in the edge of a wide, open field; on the other side of the belt of timber is our front line also looking west. Many lines of earthworks before this time are built one in the rear of the other, as far as we can see, all up and down the Union lines — right here there are five of them. The enemy's lines, wherever we can see them, are equally well provided. Our rear line is fully one third of a mile from our front trenches. It is said that the effective force of our Brigade has been cut down by more than one half since May 4th — 1,900 rifles to 800.

To-night can be heard, in the distance, the noise and shouts attending a charge upon the Union lines. First a sudden increase of rifle-shots among the pickets, then the crash of artillery and the incessant roar of musketry mingled with the rebel yell follow for a few minutes; soon the din ceases, and we can hear the hoarse hurrahs of thousands of Northern men — then all becomes quiet and still again. The story is told by the cheers! Almost every night attacks are made on one side or the other; often disturbing, and sometimes rousing both armies.

Gen. Gilman Marston relates the following incident: "I was passing along the lines at Cold Harbor one day, and observed that a private had built a fire against a large shell, and was cooking for himself a tin pot of coffee, while he sat near watching it. I had moved on but a few feet when the shell burst with a discharge as loud as a cannon, and sending its pieces, the fire and the gravel in every direction. I was unhurt, and turning saw that the man was also unhurt. He had not moved, and did not appear as if that explosion under his very nose had even caused him to wink; but his face bore an expression of unutterable disgust, as he remarked indignantly: 'There — that cussed thing has upset my coffee!'"

"June 1st. Warm and very dusty. We marched till 4 p. m. Orders to load. At sundown made a charge; Company H had three men killed, and nine wounded including myself. June 4. Some rain. I left the field hospital at 5 p. m., and rode about eight miles. O such roads! Slept to-night under an ambulance. June 5. Arrived at White House at 4 p. m. (Does not again return to the Thirteenth.) Dec. 2, 1864, am assigned to Company E, 14th Regiment Veteran Reserve Corps."

LUEY, in Diary.

June 6. Mon. Warm, very. Reg. at the rear all day, and at 8 p. m. resumes its former position, in the entrenchments, at the front, and relieves the 21st Conn. Our front line, until to-night, has been almost unendurable; some of the rebel dead which we used for a breast-work have been but thinly covered with earth, and had become extremely offensive. Until to-day also, we could count 170 dead bodies — the most of them of the 69th N. Y., of Smyth's 2d Brig., Barlow's 1st Div., Hancock's 2d Army Corps — lying unburied in the open field close in front of our entrenchments, and which had lain there since June 3d; some of them it is said since June 1st, and we came here on the morning of June 4th. There were living men among them then, and some of these were recovered in the night from time to time, by the inter-line pickets; but the rebel commander on our front would not allow them to be visited or helped in the daytime, nor recognize a flag of truce, and this, too, it is said, in accordance with the orders of Gen. Lee himself. To-day however, a flag of truce is respected, and just at night, these dead near us are removed and buried. It is evident that wounded men lived there two or three days, on the hot sand, between the two lines, exposed to the thousands of bullets and hundreds of shells that swept that very field of hell — and lingering on, unhelped, day after day, finally died, and all under conditions too horrible to imagine. One was taken in alive even to-day, but soon died. The dead are buried in a long trench, in the belt of timber, near and north of the path that runs up between our front and rear lines, and we are told that the most of them can be identified by their comrades. Many of the bodies would not hold together so as to be moved in the usual manner, and were rolled upon old shelter tents, blankets or canvas, and so carried to burial.

June 7. Tues. Rainy. Thirteenth came up to the front at 8 p. m. last night, remaining at the front until evening of to-day. There is much shelling and musketry firing. We cannot show our heads for an instant without receiving rebel bullets; and we keep the enemy down also, by shooting through holes made under logs laid along on the top of the parapet. Many men are thus killed or wounded on the lines. Troops can move from front to rear, or return, only at night. The covert way now is a deep trench covered with logs and earth for protection while going back and forth. Our trench is about five feet deep and more than that in width. The main earth-work about eight feet high, and ten or twelve feet thick. One third of the Reg. is constantly on duty. At night the men sleep on their arms, practically in line of battle, and with their clothing all on — ready at a moment's call to spring up and fire.

Muddy Run, on the right of the Reg. is not fortified excepting by a few logs, and to pass up or down the line there requires much care. Jeremiah Murphy of E tries to approach the trench to-day from that direction, and is fatally wounded. Col. Stevens tries to cross Muddy Run to the Reg., and is cornered by the rebels, when half way across, and takes shelter behind a tree smaller in girth than himself. He draws the enemy's fire by exposing his hat — and then runs to cover in safety. He and Lieut. Thompson of E are also brought under fire of the enemy while together in the woods at some distance to the rear of the front line, and engaged in writing a report, and in assorting the mail; they have to draw the sharp-shooters' fire, and then escape.

Asst. Surgeon Sullivan came up to the front, wearing a straw hat. The rebel sharp-shooters took it for a target, and Sullivan removed it — and not a moment too soon.

A log was laid on the top of the works, and little holes made under it in the sand, to shoot through. A man fired through one of these holes, then looked through it to see the effect of his shot, when a bullet came from the enemy straight through the little hole, killing the man instantly.

A very noisy fight occurred about midnight last night, between the enemy and troops of the 9th Corps, at some distance to our right. We were cautioned to be ready to fall in, but were not called into line. It was an attack by the enemy, and was handsomely repulsed.

One of the men behind the works has just loaded his gun, and raised it above the parapet — perhaps a little higher than usual. The gun catches a random Confederate bullet fired at close range, about midway the barrel; it flies out of the soldier's hands, leaving them seriously benumbed, and assumes the shape of the gun that shoots around the corner. It is bent perceptibly, spoiled, and the bullet that struck it falls to the ground, flattened like a silver half dollar, with a rough thick edge. The soldier pockets the relic; and goes, with his spoiled gun, to procure a new one. This caused an order never to hold a gun higher than the works. All shooting being done through holes made in the top of the sand under the logs. At dark the Reg. returns to its old position in the rear trenches.

In reference to the Union wounded Gen. Humphreys states, page 192: "At the close of the day on the 3d of June, there were many of our wounded lying between the lines, and very near the enemy's entrenchments, completely covered by the fire of his pickets and sharp-shooters. Few of these wounded were left, but many dead were unburied, and Gen. Grant proposed an arrangement with Gen. Lee for bringing in the wounded and burying the dead, on the afternoon of June 5th, but no cessation of hostilities for the purpose took place until the afternoon of June 7th, when a truce was agreed upon from six to eight in the evening. Very few wounded were collected. Of those not brought in at night by their comrades the greater number had died of wounds and exposure." [1]

---

[1] There was a flag of truce on both June 6th and 7th; but all accounts, diaries and letters which the writer has seen, including his own, place the burial of the Cold Harbor dead, which were lying on the immediate front of the Thirteenth, on the evening of June 6th — probably the result of a limited and special truce consented to by the

Gen. Grant's Memoirs, Vol. II. page 273, state that the burial of the dead took place 48 hours after Gen. Grant had written to Gen. Lee requesting a truce for that purpose. Gen. Grant first addressed Gen. Lee upon the subject of the burial of the dead and succor of the wounded on June 5th; but delays for which neither Gen. Grant nor any Union officer was responsible covered forty-eight hours, and brought the time of burying the dead to June 7th, on some parts of the line.

A word from the Hospital Dept. of the Thirteenth is in order here : "May 31st. We marched until midnight, and then the Thirteenth went on picket until morning. June 1st. We marched to Cold Harbor. The road was one complete bed of dust as dry as ashes, the atmosphere like that of an oven, and every breath of wind seemed like the blast from a furnace. We were white with dust. We had had little or no sleep for three nights, rations ran short, and when we arrived in the midst of Gen. Grant's army, we were greatly exhausted, but were immediately pushed forward into the terrible battle of Cold Harbor, and the Thirteenth lost seventy men, in killed, wounded and missing, before it was dark.[1] In the darkness to-night, while looking for our wounded between the lines of the two armies, I got lost in the woods with Asst. Surgeon Sullivan and Lieut. Gafney, and finally slept about an hour under a tree, where I was very cold in the chilly air.

"June 3d. Rainy. A terrible battle. Thousands killed and wounded, horrid scenes. June 4th. Our army has suffered terribly, as they have to fight the enemy in entrenchments altogether. I have seen more than a thousand of our men, within the past twenty-four hours, torn, mangled, smashed, disemboweled — every conceivable wound you can imagine — lying about our 18th Corps Hospital, exposed to the rain without shelter, a scene of awful suffering. The 2d and 6th Corps are near us; the 9th Corps two miles to our right. The 2d Corps passed from right to left this afternoon. June 6th. Warm. There was a flag of truce to bury the dead this afternoon, during which the rebels planted a battery so as to shell our rear. We of the Hospital Dept. got shelled out of our position in the woods, and fell back to the rifle-pits. June 7th. The picket line (main, front trench occupied by the 13th) is almost within a stone's throw of the rebels. A flag of truce went out this evening. The rebels, and our boys mounted their breast-works, and advanced out upon the plain between the lines."  PRESCOTT.

"I have it in my record : A flag of truce out both days, 6th and 7th."
ASST. SURGEON SULLIVAN.

June 8. Wed. Fair. Reg. returns and remains in its trenches at

---

Confederate General commanding on our immediate front. The dead lying on the front near the Thirteenth were buried on June 6th between five and eight o'clock in the afternoon; the last bodies being put in and the trench being filled as we moved past at eight o'clock while going from the rear to our front trenches. — S. M. T.

[1] The number lost during the charge proper on June 1st was sixty-seven officers and men killed and wounded. — S. M. T., then Actg. Adjutant.

the rear, last night, to-day, and to-night. The firing is less severe now, than for the first few days. The duel is kept up chiefly by the pickets and the artillery. As we lie here, close to the south side of the main path to the rear, the stretchers — two poles with canvas nailed across them — are constantly coming back from the front with their ghastly freight of dead or wounded. During a battle there is a regular procession of them — then of course bearing only the wounded.

The writer is coming back from the front to-day, and sees a man, carrying two camp-kettles, approaching the rear lines, from the vicinity of the stables — a ravine farther to the rear, where the horses are kept. (The first ravine to the right and rear of the Thirteenth's rear line of works.) The man is coming down hill. Suddenly a random shell, from the enemy, screams over the writer's head, plunges straight through the chest of the man with the kettles, and flying beyond him bursts among the trees in the distance. The man sinks down between his kettles, and then falls over backwards. The contents of one kettle spilled, of the other not. It seems as if there could be no easier death. The kettles and their dead owner remain where they fall all day untouched.

About seventy officers and men of the old Second New Hampshire, on our right, reach the end of their term of service and start for home.

Our work at the front is irregular. We have to furnish special pickets almost every night, besides the regular picket service of the whole Reg. at the front; three fifths of the 13th are awake all night.

A few officers receive a good dinner, and go back out of the front trenches, among the trees, to eat it. They make a fine spread on the ground, using the immense bass-wood leaves and pieces of bark for dishes. As they sit on the ground together eating, one of them reaches out his hand for a large piece of bark lying on the ground near this inviting spread, raises it and turns it over — hair, blood, brains, a piece of skull, maggots! The bark is carefully turned back, with merely the remark: "They're at dinner, too!" — and the officers finish their dinner, without moving. Thus does soldiering make the stomachs of men imperturable.

Again, last night, the enemy attacked our troops on the right most savagely, raising a fearful din, and rousing everybody; but, like all his night attacks, it is a failure.

This evening the Band of the Thirteenth goes into the trenches at the front, and indulges in a 'competition concert' with a band that is playing over across in the enemy's trenches. The enemy's Band renders Dixie, Bonnie Blue Flag, My Maryland, and other airs dear to the Southerner's heart. Our Band replies with America, Star Spangled Banner, Old John Brown, etc. After a little time, the enemy's band introduces another class of music; only to be joined almost instantly by our Band with the same tune. All at once the band over there stops, and a rebel battery opens with grape. Very few of our men are exposed, so the enemy wastes his ammunition; while our Band continues its playing, all the more earnestly until all their shelling is over.

The Band of the Thirteenth becomes very proficient in its long term of service, and enlivens many a dreary and dragging hour with its cheering music, as our Regiment kills its weary time in camp or trenches, or plods along on its muddy, tiresome marches. "And then the Band played — and then the Thirteenth cheered," is the closing complimentary remark in many a story of camp, and march, and field. A good Band. In a battle the men of the bands and drum-corps are expected to help take care of the wounded, and our Band and young drum-corps are very efficient in that delicate and dangerous work.

June 9. Thurs. Very warm ; windy, and the fine dust is flying in huge, dense clouds. Thirteenth remains in the rear through the day, and at dark returns to its entrenchments at the front. There is much firing to-night, and by the light of his numerous fires, the enemy can be seen moving long lines of his infantry towards our right. They are at long rifle-shot from our lines, and cross the open spaces at a double-quick. Occasionally we can see one of them stumble and fall — struck by a bullet from our sharp-shooters it may be. Now and then one of our cannon gives them a shell. They seem carelessly exposed so near our lines.

This afternoon a couple of sutlers, in an open buggy, drove towards the front through our lines, peddling tobacco. They have gone through three or four lines of our entrenchments, winding in and out, in a zig-zag fashion, through the openings covered by curtains, when the rebel bullets wound the horse and kill one of the men. The other man turns to drive back, having his dead companion with him in the buggy. The horse, frantic with pain, starts upon the run, utterly unmanageable, rushes high up over the bank of one of the entrenchments ; and dead man, live man, horse, buggy, tobacco and all, come piling into the ditch in a heap together. The soldiers near there make a rush and scramble for the tobacco — after getting that, they lift out the living and the dead. The horse has to be killed, he is so badly wounded, the buggy is ruined, and the pedler comes back across the wide field alone, carrying the harness on his arm, a poorer and a less careless man.

A man of the 13th comes into the trenches laughing immoderately, and after he is able to speak explains : " That he and this other man with him, had just crossed a bit of ground covered by the rebel fire, when suddenly the man fell to the ground, rolled over, groaned, swore, prayed, and tuned his old organ-pipe a rod above high-C ; but he was n't hurt a bit — a spent bullet had tossed a little gravel in his face, and he thought he was killed, dead sure for sartin." Again he went off in a gale of laughter, while the imaginative sufferer sat by silent, demure, cheap, and unable to see anything amusing whatever.

June 10. Fri. Pleasant. Reg. busy in the front trenches all last night and to-day, and returns to the rear to-night at dark. As this day comes on the enemy's pickets, sharp-shooters and artillery become more and more troublesome ; the changes which he made last night cause increased watchfulness on our part, and there is severe firing all day long.

Some unusual thing struck our Pine to-day, and many men near by are stung by the little splinters; and a dozen or more all at once take to scratching themselves. Examination reveals ground glass on the pine, in a circular depression, and fine bits of glass are found also in the men's clothing and skin. It was a wine bottle from the enemy — and empty, the rascals!

Our Pine is now a shattered monument of war's doings, a mere stub about 30 feet high. The top is a mass of splinters standing out every way — a brush broom. On the sides toward the enemy the bark is gone for two thirds around the tree, knocked off by his front and cross-fire, and the wood is splintered all up and down into a coarse, white fur, full of bullet holes three to six inches deep. A fine mark for the enemy, and they have used it well, burying in it hundreds of bullets.

The writer has been informed that shortly after the war a Government commission cut off a ten-foot section of our Pine, intending to convey it to Washington for the Army and Navy Museum, but the plan failed for want of transportation. The commission estimated — from the average number of bullet holes per square foot in the tree — that a sheet of lead had come over to this knoll from the enemy, about two hundred feet long, ten or fifteen feet wide, and over half an inch thick. This, not to mention the multitude of shells. The 13th were here meanwhile for a period of at least three full days, and three full nights; June 4th day and night, night of June 6th and day of June 7th, night of June 9th and day of June 10th. The writer in 1878 cut several bullets out of this pine, shot by the Confederates, and buried from four to six inches in the wood. A section of the trunk about ten feet long had been cut off and rolled to one side, and was much decayed.

Capt. Julian and Lieut. Thompson of E, having had little breakfast, and no dinner until about 3 p. m. naturally begin to feel hungry. Soon the cook appears with nice steak, potatoes, green peas, bread and coffee. He brings cups, saucers and plates of white earthenware. To tantalize some officers whose cook is less enterprising, this appetizing spread is laid on large leaves in the trench, and the banqueters fall to. About one minute later, and before scarcely anything is eaten, a rebel shell is driven deep into the parapet of the earth-works, behind and above this hungry party, bursts and buries dishes, dinner and all under a cartload or more of sand, sending some quarts of it down inside the coat and shirt collars of the eaters. Instantly a hundred muskets are busy with those rebel canoneers, and their vexatious, dinner-burying cannon stands in full view until dark, silenced, no rebel can approach it. The dishes with what remains of the uneaten repast are left beneath that sand in the trench. They are about twenty feet to the left of where our Pine stood — and there they will lie probably till the crack of doom.

June 11. Sat. Cool. The Reg. left our front trenches at our Pine for the last time yesterday evening at dark, returned to our rear trenches, remaining there through the night and to-day. The cooks are busy to-day preparing extra, cooked rations, and we are on the eve of another march. The front is very noisy to-day at times.

For several nights past, about sunset and later, our bands have played in the front trenches — the rebel bands replying. One man of the 13th describes lying in the trenches to be: "digging holes in the ground from three to six feet deep, and living, eating and sleeping in them all the time."

The enemy gets the range of a large heavy-artillery regiment crossing the bare field in our rear, and higher up than we are, and shells it fearfully. Quite a number of the members of it are killed and wounded, and the rest run for cover at the top of their speed, the shells plowing up the ground, and crashing about them. The whole huge, red-trimmed host — report says there are 1,400 of them — take to their heels spontaneously, and do not stop until they reach the timber.

Bullets come over frequently to our rear lines, after traveling nearly or quite one third of a mile. The hum of a spent bullet is very peculiar, often giving timely warning of its approach. The enemy's Coehorn mortar shells, too, are very plentiful to-day. This is our first experience with them, in any number, while we are within our rear trenches. The enemy fires them high into the air whence they seem to come straight down into the rear trenches, with their threatening "whistle-whistle" — "whistle-whistle," and final crack and whirr of the pieces. Out of two or three dozen, which have come down near us to-day, the one coming nearest burst when about 25 feet above the line of the 13th, causing some dodging but no damage. A large piece of this one proves it to have been a six-inch shell. A great number have burst in the field in our rear. An officer's bomb-proof quarters off to our right receives one of these Coehorns directly on the top; where it instantly bursts, knocking the logs of the roof about, and deluging the parties within with sand and gravel. No one hurt beyond a few slight bruises. When the shell struck the roof of their bomb-proof they, too sure of their safety, were singing the refrain:

"So let the big guns rattle as they will,
We'll be gay and merry still."

— but the song stopped, short, right there and then.

"There came to-day an order for a minute inspection of the Regiment. So by Col. Stevens' orders we were formed in line down in the trenches, several feet below the surface of the ground, where we would have been very safe, as there were some seven or eight lines of earth-works between us and the enemy, a half mile in our front; but the Colonel, for some reason of his own, ordered us up out of these trenches upon the ground in the rear, which brought about one half of our bodies up above the trenches. The Colonel commenced his inspection at the right company of the Regiment, and when he got through with that company had its officers join him and come down the line with him. This was continued to the end of the line, the Orderly Sergeants taking the companies away as fast as they were inspected. When the Colonel was inspecting about the second company on the right, a bullet came over from the enemy and struck James Morris of E on the upper part of his breastbone so hard that it was heard the whole length of the Regiment. Every one heard it; it startled many, and some turned pale. I do not think that Morris himself fully realized who it was that had been hit, the shock of the bullet probably partly paralyzed him. He went into the trenches, however, when ordered to do so. He soon died. We buried him under a tree near by, rolled in his blankets, with his name and company written on a slip of paper and inclosed in a bottle." CAPT. JULIAN.

"I remember this case perfectly. It was not two minutes after he was shot before I was with him. He gasped once or twice, after I came. The hole in his breastbone was large and ragged. A shot at closer range would have made a smaller hole with smoother edges, and would have gone through him." ASST. SURGEON SULLIVAN.

No death in the Regiment ever gave the men a worse shock than this one. It was in every respect a most blood-freezing affair. Morris was a good soldier, and quite a favorite in the Regiment. Lieut. Thompson of E, then Acting Adjutant, was at the time walking along in front of the Regiment, and was nearly in front of Morris, when this bullet came over from the enemy, hummed close by him, and struck Morris with a loud blow. Morris walked into the trenches, some ten or fifteen feet, in a dazed sort of way, but with his gun in his hand, half fell, and half sat down, and soon died. Several other bullets came over before the inspection was completed, but no further damage was done. The bullet that killed Morris[1] must have traveled nearly half a mile, and probably came from some rebel sharp-shooter's double-charged gun.

The general plan at Cold Harbor has been for the Thirteenth to remain at the front for 24 hours, then to rest at the rear for 48 hours; our duties at the front allowing scarcely any rest at all day, or night. But the enemy's shells have completely covered, and swept all the time, both our front and rear trenches, and all the ground between. Besides, several of our men have been killed or wounded, in our rear trenches, the bullets coming over from the enemy's line — a distance of one third to one half a mile. The rebels acting as sharp-shooters, two or three hundred of them in every rebel brigade, double-charge their guns, so that if they miss in their direct aim, the bullets may fly to a random shot among our men in the rear trenches. These bullets come skimming and buzzing over, all the time, at Cold Harbor.

"I was loading my ambulance one day at Cold Harbor with wounded men to send to the Corps Hospital, when a bullet struck the near horse

---

[1] While talking with this man, Morris, a few days before his death, he stated to me that no bodily harm could ever come to him because he wore an "Agnus Dei." Such a thing being new to me, I expressed a desire to see it. After a considerable hesitation, he exhibited to me a leather-covered, heart-shaped affair, some two inches across and half an inch thick, which he wore suspended by a cord upon his neck. It looked like a neat little pin-cushion. His faith in it was unbounded. The bullet that killed Morris struck the edge of that same "Agnus Dei."— S. M. T.

just back of the shoulder, and passed through the horse, which instantly fell dead, then entered the off horse in a like manner and lodged under the skin on the off side ; this off horse stood a moment, then fell dead on the near horse." Asst. Surgeon Sullivan.

Gen. Humphreys states : The 18th Corps — in which is the Thirteenth — receives orders to march as soon after dark as practicable on to-morrow evening, June 12th, by way of Parsley's Mill, Prospect Church, Hopeville Church, and Tunstall's Station, having the right of way over all other troops, to White House, and there to embark for Bermuda Hundred. At Tunstall's our trains and artillery will join the main trains of the army. Gen. Wright with the 6th Corps, and Gen. Hancock with the 2d Corps, with their troops in a new rear line of entrenchments built since June 9th, and running from Elder Swamp on the southward, passing Cold Harbor, and on to Allen's Mill Pond on the north, will protect our lines while we retire. It is expected that the entire Union army will leave the vicinity of Cold Harbor within two days. The expedition of the 18th Corps being secret, the orders to march are retained at its Hdqrs.

June 12. Sun. Clear, cool morning, hot day, warm night. Reg. in its rear trenches, and called at daylight. Do nothing all the morning. We are due, in regular order, at the front trenches to-night, and expect to go there as usual. The writer, and several others, make a last visit to our front trenches near 'Our Pine.' We see fewer troops than usual on the way, but there is little change in affairs. Sharp-shooters and pickets are as busy as ever. The Reg. soon receives orders to march, and makes ready to move, but is not called into line until 10 a. m. Then it rests on its arms for a while, on account of a delay caused by a misunderstanding in reference to the officers' horses, kept in a ravine off to the right, where there is a convenient and appetizing arrangement of cook-tent and livery stable, both under the same tree.

The Reg. leaves its rear line of entrenchments, with the Brigade, about one p. m. (Capt. Stoodley writes, 12.45 p. m.) and marches straight across the wide field in the rear — following the ravine or depression, and going nearly southeast towards Old Cold Harbor ; catching the last glimpses of the battle-field about 1.30 p. m. As we leave the Cold Harbor trenches a large pile of damaged muskets, the muzzles all pointing toward a bluff-side, with much army gear and combustible material, near the right of our Brigade, is set on fire : and furnishes an irregular fusillade heard so long as we are near enough to hear — about the last sound, except an occasional cannon shot, that we hear as we move away in the heat and dust.

A few miles back we pass a body of mounted staff officers and men, by the road-side, headed by two Generals who are pointed out to us as Generals Grant and Meade. Dusty and apparently hard-working men, looking us over intently as we march past them. About 5 p. m., while we are on the march, heated, choked with the deep dust, and thirsty, a boy appears from a little guard-camp by the road-side with a basket full of lemons. The whole are at once purchased, distributed, and eaten down like apples, peel and all — refreshing — good ! At Tunstall's we march through the wagon-trains of the Army of the Potomac, parked in a field : " A hundred acres of wagons." After a hard, hot, dusty march — rarely getting beyond the stench of the very numerous dead horses and mules lying in the brush by the way — a part of the time marching in roads, and a part of the time going straight across-lots, regardless of hills or hollows, woods or waters, for about fifteen miles, we reach White House at 7 p. m. Here the Reg. bivouacs about 9 p. m. on clean, dry ground, free once more from danger and care.

This day ends a period of 35 days, passed by the Thirteenth, almost continually under fire, and covering three terrible battles, and as many more of lighter moment ; nine of the days to be inscribed on our flag — when we get the new one, not space enough on the old ones. Between June 1st and June 12th, all at Cold Harbor, the Reg. has lost fourteen men killed, six officers and sixty-four men wounded and missing — total 84.

The Sanitary Commission representatives exemplified themselves to-night by furnishing freely and liberally of its stores of canned goods, etc., to officers of all ranks, and by refusing to give enlisted men anything at all, unless they came with written requisitions signed by two officers, and in accordance with the strictest red tape. This creates much ill-feeling, and threats of mobbing the concern are freely indulged in. Fair common sense, and Uncle Sam's uniform would have appeared guaranty enough. A rather free distribution would have been less costly, for when the men found themselves wholly refused and the officers bountifully supplied, and afterwards got orders for supplies for themselves, they were harder to satisfy, and demanded more than they needed.

One soldier of the 13th writes : " At the Cold Harbor front for six days the dead and dying men (in front of our lines) could be seen at any time, when a person chose to turn his head and look. The stench arising from the dead was horrible, and mingled with odors from all sorts of decaying matter on every side. On the march to White House, on the 12th, the roads and woods were strewn, all the way, with hundreds of dead horses and mules."

We have several times witnessed the expert work of the Army Telegraph Corps. No sooner is a change made in any part of the line than a small body of men, with a mule or two, a few bundles of wire, and a lot of forked sticks, are seen running a telegraph wire along in the rear ; fence rails, trees, poles, anything that will properly elevate the wire, are brought into use, and long before the soldiers can settle down in bivouac, communications are speeding along the wires to Hdqrs., to Washington, and thence scattering to the world. We might, as it were, halt for a few minutes for dinner, and before the matches can start the little blaze of a coffee-fire, the Telegraph Corps has connected, just back in the rear, and the news flies away on lightning wings : " Blank Brigade at dinner." But they say nothing about our — inexpressible — beef, cooked three days ago and kept in a bag ever since, while the summer heat has ranged at 100° in the shade and above ; how said beef looks, how it smells, and how it tastes — that is no news in this army.

From May 5th to June 10th Gen. Grant's losses are placed at 54,551, and for the same period Gen. Lee's were about 20,000. Cold Harbor being a link in that 40 days' chain of most fearful battles — May 4th to June 15th, 1864 — between the Rapidan and Petersburg. Although the battle of Cold Harbor proper commenced on the morning of June 1st, the preliminary manœuvring for position by the two armies — Grant's and Lee's — appears to have begun soon after the Union army crossed the Pamunkey, say on the morning of May 30th, among the swamps, creeks and innumerable by-roads, a few miles to the northward of Cold Harbor; resulting in cavalry skirmishes and reconnaissances in force by infantry and field artillery, in which the Union losses are put at a total of about 3,022 — 'previous to June 1st and after crossing the Pamunkey.'

Following one of Gen. Humphreys' notes, page 191, quoting the Medical Director, Surgeon McParlin : " The number of killed, wounded and missing after crossing the Pamunkey to the evening of June 12th (excluding the 18th Corps) may be estimated as follows : wounded 7,545, to which Gen. Humphreys adds 900 ; a total of 8,445. Killed 1,420, missing 1,864 ; total 11,729. In the 18th Corps, wounded 1,900, killed and missing 500 ; total 2,400. Grand total 14,129 ; to which he adds 3,000 sick

### DESCRIPTION OF MAP.

A. Old Cold Harbor.  
B. New Cold Harbor.  
C. Mrs. Kelly.  
D. C. Wright.  
E. D. Woody.  
F. G. Williams.  
G. Albert Allerson.  
H. Old-Still Pond.  
K. Field into which the Thirteenth charged on June 1st. No Union earth-works had been built at that time. The Union works near the pond H stand nearly on the crest; those west of them are advanced into the field across which we charged.  
L. Front trench with many traverses occupied by the Thirteenth from June 4th to 12th, facing west.  
M. Rear trench occupied by Thirteenth, also facing west.  
1. 2. 3. Brooks running west to Gaines' Mill pond. The right of the Thirteenth, when in both the front and the rear trenches, rested close upon the second brook, which was called Muddy Run.  
Z. Z. Z. Confederate trenches facing east. The road from D. Woody's to Albert Allerson's crosses a brook over a little culvert, north of Old-Still Pond, referred to in other pages. The many traverses in our front line at L were necessary because the Confederate batteries, to the northward, enfiladed this line as it came up over the knoll.

Lt. Col. Smith writes in reference to this map : " Your recollections of Cold Harbor correspond with mine."

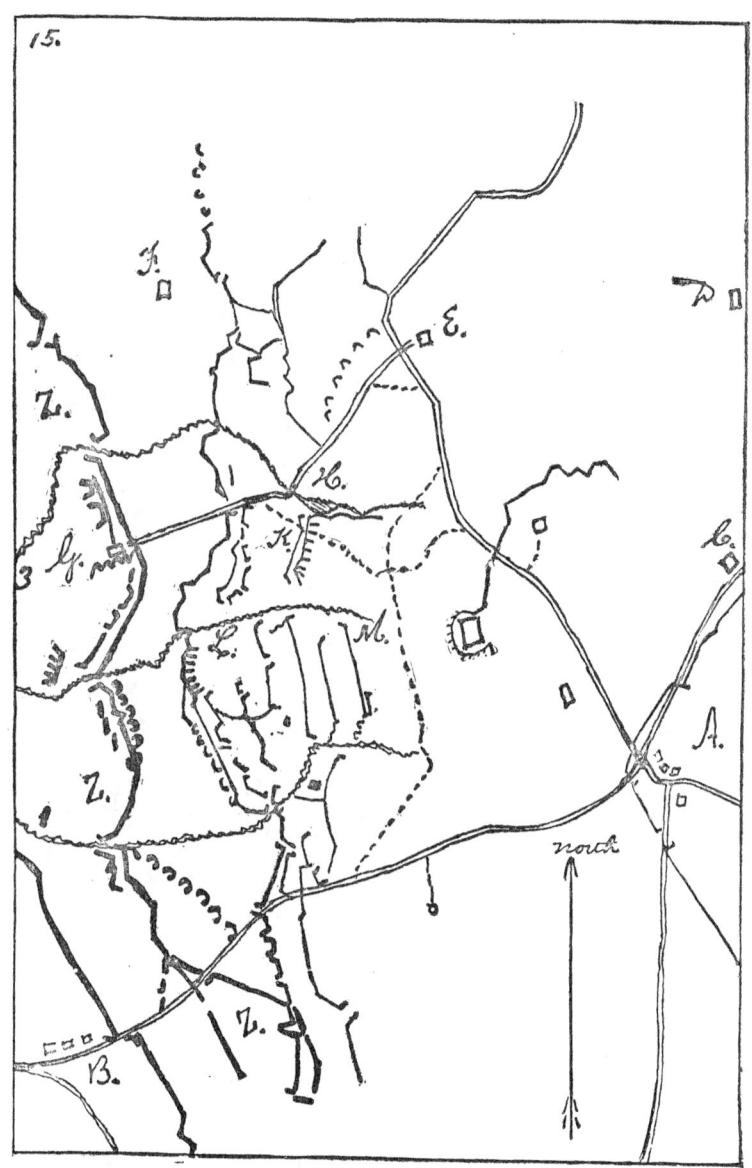

COLD HARBOR.

Tracing of Official Map.   Scale, three inches to one mile.

sent to Hospital = 17,129. Deducting, however, the sick and the 3,022 reported before the morning of June 1st, we have, in killed, wounded and missing between the morning of June 1st and night of June 12th, a total of 11,107, as the Cold Harbor losses.

Capt. Phisterer gives the losses for the same period, killed 1,905, wounded 10,570, missing 2,456; total 14,931. In this he probably includes the losses in the 18th Corps.

Gen. Humphreys says — condensed : "The lines at Cold Harbor were so close they could be advanced only by regular approaches. The daily skirmishing was sharp, and caused severe loss; during the nights there was heavy artillery firing, and sometimes heavy musketry; the men in the front trenches had little water except to drink, and that of the worst kind from surface drainage, were exposed to great heat during the day, had but little sleep, and their cooking was of the rudest character. The army had no vegetables for over a month, the beef was from cattle exhausted by a long march. Dead horses and mules, and offal were scattered over the country, and between the lines were many dead bodies of both parties lying unburied in a burning sun. The country was low and marshy. The exhausting effect of all this began to show itself, and sickness of a malarial character increased largely."

1887. It would be difficult now to find all the front lines of the earth-works, occupied by the 13th at Cold Harbor. The front lines were changed a little by the troops after the Reg. left them for the last time, on the evening of June 10th. The rear line remained unchanged. But the elements have reduced them in height and depth, and rounded all their sharp angles, The most direct way to find them is by the ravine mentioned under June 1st, lying north-northeast of the National Cemetery, and by following that ravine to our rear line of works — which was the extreme rear line of all at that part of the Cold Harbor field and lying to the left of the ravine and abutting on it — then turning slightly to the left, and proceeding a little north of west, straight to the front line, on the left side of a brook starting in that ravine and leading to Gaines' Mill pond ; the second of the three brooks north of Cold Harbor road. By Gen. Michler's official map, our position in the front line was the north end of the most dense system of works shown here on that map, where there is a long succession of little traverses, and about one half mile due north of the point where the Union lines cross the Cold Harbor road. As shown on that map, a line drawn straight across between Mrs. Kelly's house — marked C on the tracing — near and north of Old Cold Harbor, and the north edge of pond, directly north of Gaines' Mill dam, would strike both our front and rear trenches, and near their centres. The right of the Reg. when in the front trench ran to, or near, the muddy brook, in ravine, that drains west into Gaines' Mill pond — the left mounting over the highest part of the knoll. The right of our rear trench was at this muddy brook, near where it first begins. To return :

June 13. Mon. Very fine day. Reg. called at daylight. A large body of rebel prisoners are here near our camp. They say that they have lived for more than a month past, chiefly on dried fish and Indian corn bread. Now, as they have been supplied with Uncle Sam's rations, they have thrown out of their camp the former contents of their greasy, filthy haversacks; forming along one side of their inclosure a windrow of such vile, unsavory compounds as would 'make any respectable hog sneeze the rooter off his nose' — Bah! They are hungry, tired out, and express themselves freely as exceeding glad they have been captured. A rope cordon has been drawn around the plot of ground on which they are, and they make great sport of it — they would not run away if they could. They are done with war, they say. They are exceedingly merry, and full of boyish pranks and jokes. They put on the most doleful faces, and complain of the cruelty of 'fencing them up' in this manner — with a half-inch rope — in such terribly hot weather. Others reverse the idea, and sit on the ground, in the little line of shadow cast by the rope, and thank the guard for such ample protection from the hot sun. They mark a 'dead line' with straws, make their wills on scraps of paper, beg the guard not to shoot them in the head, when they attempt to run away and rejoin the rebel army; and in short, act like a lot of boys just out of school for a vacation.

Adjutant Boutwell returns to duty to-day, relieving Lieut. Thompson of E. To be hustled about everywhere, and at all times of day and night, through such a melée as the twelve days' battle of Cold Harbor, is Adjutant enough for a lifetime — for the writer.

Reg. remains at White House to-day until 10 a. m., when we embark on the steamer 'Ocean Wave,' with the 8th Conn., and at once move swiftly down the Pamunkey and York rivers. After a very pleasant trip we arrive off Fortress Monroe at 9 p. m., move up and anchor off Newport News at 10 p. m., and turn in to sleep. While on the way to the boat this morning, at White House, we pass among some new troops said to be from Ohio. One of them asks what troops we are. Thirteen answers: "One Hundred days' men." Ohio replies: "You cannot fool us with any such nonsense as that — unless your flags have been one hundred days in hell!" — Rough, but not altogether inapt, for neither of our flags can be unfurled, they are so torn and cut up.

We have been through three scenes of terrible slaughter of men, Fredericksburg, Drury's Bluff and Cold Harbor; and now we have a little rest before we again take a hand — shooting and shot at. Such is war; and civil war is the most uncivil war of all.

June 14. Tues. Splendid day save a little rain. The Thirteenth sails at 4 a. m. from off Newport News, moves up the James River, arrives at Point of Rocks, Appomattox River, at 10 a. m., and anchors off Bermuda Hundred at noon; and here we lounge about on the boat and doze away the half-misty afternoon. We have passed many a fine country residence on the Pamunkey, York and James rivers — and many a lonely stack of chimneys. The ruins of Jamestown came partly into view;

nothing left in sight but a few chimneys, a wall or two, one house, and an old vine-covered pile said to be the ruins of a church.  This trip up the James is made like a move in business; our last sail up this river was theatrical.  We debark near Bermuda Hundred at 10 p. m.,[1] march to our old camp-ground of May 28th, and there bivouac.  But we get scarcely any rest.  A large amount of work, which might have been done on the steamer, is now attended to.  Arms and cartridge and cap-boxes are examined by firelight, and deficiencies supplied until every man has sixty rounds of ammunition.  Three days' rations are cooked and distributed.  Finally, very late at night, we turn in, with the most welcome assurance that before daybreak we shall again 'move to the front.'

The query goes the rounds: "Wonder what's up now?"  We must say we care little to-night what is coming provided only that we are victorious.  The fact is that the Thirteenth is now very desirous to take part in another fight here in the neighborhood of Bermuda Hundred, in order to amend the name and fortunes of this Army of the James — or at least make the list of our successes a little more brilliant.  Many of our men have said to-night: 'If we get after the rebels on this front again, we will give them Hail Columbia.'  We have fought hard, done our best, but there is an all-pervading desire now, more than ever, to make a grand mark for The Thirteenth New Hampshire Regiment.  This is the talk of our camp to-night.  The notion of being annihilated as a regiment has never once entered the heads of the members of the Thirteenth — some may fall — the most will survive.

By way of Drury's Bluff, Gen. Lee, at Cold Harbor, is only about twenty-four miles from Bermuda Hundred.

[1] The Thirteenth furnishes details for work on shore, and our steamer — as well as others of the fleet — is moving about a good deal between City Point, Point of Rocks and Bermuda Hundred, as if uncertain where and when to land the troops.  The troops landed in detachments, details of men were made on the boat for guards, pickets, pioneers, etc., who went ashore from time to time.  The writer has, in the above hours given, followed his own record.  A letter written by him while still upon the steamer with the Reg. states: "June 14th, 12 noon, we are now at Bermuda Hundred and about to land.  Rains a little, otherwise pleasant."  But no day has furnished so many and so wide discrepancies in hours as this one.

Sergt. Major Hodgdon states in his Diary: "Arrived at Point of Rocks at 4 p. m."

Prescott states in his Diary: "Reached City Point about 3 p. m., turned into the Appomattox, and landed at Point of Rocks about 5 o'clock and marched to our old camp-ground of three weeks ago."

A soldier of the Thirteenth writes home: "We left Cold Harbor at 1 p. m. on the 12th, and arrived at White House at 7 p. m.  We left White House June 13th on the 'Ocean Wave'; arrived at 'Appomattox Station' at 1.30 p. m., and at our old camp at 2.30 p. m. on June 14th."

## BATTLE OF BATTERY FIVE, PETERSBURG.

**June 15. Wed.** A warm, and very pleasant sunny day. The Thirteenth, with Col. Stevens in command, marches with the Brigade — Burnham's 2d Brig., 1st Div., 18th Corps — from camp near Bermuda Hundred at 2.30 a. m., crosses the Appomattox River on a ponton bridge laid near Broadway Landing, Point of Rocks, two miles below Port Walthall, climbs a very steep bank, and proceeds rapidly to the rear of Petersburg, and halts when about three or four miles from that city. While crossing the pontons, a regiment in our rear takes up the 'cadence-step,' as if marching to music, and soon sets the bridge into a rapid vibration, and a number of its men are seen to lose step, stumble, and plunge off headlong into the mud and water; and as they crawl laboriously up out of the infamous mud, and thoroughly bedaubed with it from head to foot, they are greeted with shouts of laughter from the other troops.

In this day's movements Gen. Smith is sent with a part of his 18th Corps, about 10,000 men, in advance to secure whatever foothold he can, as preliminary to the transfer of Gen. Grant's army to the south side of the James River. Hence our rapid march from Cold Harbor to White House; thence by transports to Bermuda Hundred; and now up here to take Petersburg or ground near it, by surprise, and before Gen. Lee can dispatch troops from about Richmond and Cold Harbor for its defense.

We begin to hear heavy firing in the distance about 5 a. m., but we do not come within range of the enemy's fire until 8.30 a m., when a large solid shot, or a shell that does not burst, strikes with a loud blow in a field near the Thirteenth, but does no harm. Soon after this we come up to the rear of some of Gen. Hinks' colored troops who have just had a sharp skirmish with the enemy posted in rifle-pits near by; driving the enemy out and occupying the ground. This place is on Baylor's farm, about two miles out from the enemy's main line of works. A number of dead negroes are lying about — and a dead negro is the most ghastly corpse ever seen; and their wounded are coming back shot in all sorts of ways, in legs, arms, heads and bodies, but hobbling along and bringing their guns with them. Negroes will keep on their feet, and move on, with wounds that would utterly lay out white men, and they stick like death to their guns. A white man severely wounded throws his gun away. This affair at Baylor's is of but a few minutes, but very gallant and spirited. A little before ten o'clock a. m. Gen. Hinks' negro troops — about 3,700 men — after their first brush here with the enemy, move from our front to the left, and give us the field; and our Brigade advances to the front, and on both sides of the main road to Petersburg. The Union line is now: Gen. Martindale on the right near the Appomattox; Gen. Brooks — in whose Division is the Thirteenth — in the centre; and Gen. Hinks' colored troops on the left.

In brief: Kautz's cavalry about 6 a. m. first cleared the way for Hinks' colored troops, here on the centre of the line, then moved to the left. The colored troops then came up to the front, cleared the enemy from these few rifle-pits, and then they also moved to the left. And now we take the place of the colored troops at the centre front.

About 10 a. m., as we have said, we move forward to the front, the Thirteenth being deployed as skirmishers in front of, and covering the whole of Gen. Brooks' Division, and commanded by Col. Stevens. Our line is consequently very long; the enemy posted in the woods in large squads answers our fire vigorously, and more force is considered necessary to keep him moving back. The Thirteenth therefore narrows its front, moves farther towards the left, connecting with the colored troops, and is joined on the right by 120 men from the 8th Conn. Later the skirmish line is further strengthened by two companies, about 40 men, of the 118th N. Y., and 150 men of the 92d N. Y.; Col. Stevens in command of the Thirteenth and of the skirmish line — a part of the time with his Regiment, and a part of the time called to the right of the line.

The skirmish line, before the day was out, consisted of the 13th N. H., the 8th Conn., two companies of the 118th N. Y. and 150 men of the 92d N. Y. — the 10th N. H. supporting the line at some distance back in the woods.

While we are halted for a moment, among the pines, during some of these changes, an incident occurs that sets a portion of the line roaring with laughter. We unearth about a round dozen of rebels in rifle-pits dug among some thick brush not far away to our right front, and they open fire most spitefully. We are quickly safe behind trees, and they hit no one, excepting a little, wiry Irishman in the Thirteenth; a rebel bullet just glancing across the top of his thumb, a little back of the first joint. The affair is a mere bruise. For a moment the thumb is numb, and Paddy stands still, contemplating it most studiously; and then he suddenly belches out a most diabolical mixture of groan, scream and yell combined and loud enough to raise the dead, throws his gun as far as he can, shoots about six feet into the air, throws his roll of blankets a couple of rods away; and for fully a minute turns himself into a perfect little spinning gyration of sprawling, flying legs and arms, flopping haversack, banging canteen, and rattling tin-cup and cartridge-box, all the time yelling as man never yelled before — in our hearing. He jumped, whirled, laid down, rolled, kicked, struck out, screamed, swore and bawled all at once. Meanwhile the little squad of rebel pickets — either thinking that we have invented a new yell, and are going to charge, or else that we have with us the veritable "Yankee Devil" himself, horns and all — cease firing instant upon the Irishman's first compound scream, seize their loose clothing and blankets in their hands, and make off towards Petersburg, running as for dear life. A most amusing scene to all of the Union troops — excepting Paddy. Soon we move on, and are too busy to note what becomes of him and his little thumb-bump ; but we conclude that he was hurt.

The skirmish line is so long, and the ground so rough, being covered with timber and fallen trees, that Capt. Julian is called to act as Major, and advances the left wing of the Thirteenth a large part of the afternoon. Maj. Grantman being a part of the time in command of the whole Regiment and a part of the time advancing the right wing. It is a crowded, busy day and duty is done wherever duty is demanded, and without much regard to special prerogatives.

As the skirmish line is strengthened by the additions named, our Reg. closes, and narrows its front, until we form a rather close skirmish line ; and in this order, substantially, our line moves forward, constantly skirmishing, through a thick wood, and out of that into a slashing of heavy timber, among the stumps and fallen trees, almost directly in the rear, but somewhat to the right, of Mr. Friend's house ; and in full view of a five-gun battery — Battery Five — with very high parapets and perched on the top of a high hill, to the right, north, of Mr. Friend's house. We reach the slashing about mid-afternoon, after an advance of two miles or more from the scene of the skirmish by Gen. Hinks' colored troops on Baylor's farm ; the line of our advance not only curving, but sweeping to the left, close upon Gen. Hinks' right.

While back in the woods near the City Point road, the enemy gave us many shells, from the front and from the right, and many bullets from his skirmishers, as they retreated before our advance ; but now as he sees us moving about in this slashing, his Battery Five plays on us alone, vigorously, and we receive a great many bullets from an unseen line distant on our front. This makes our advance very slow. We spring forward from stump to stump, and from log to log, drawing the enemy's fire and then gaining ground before he can re-load.

Soon Sergt. Major James M. Hodgdon, who has been acting all day as Adjutant Boutwell's assistant, carrying orders from Col. Stevens on the right to Major Grantman and others — appears, and directs Lieut. Thompson of E to take thirty or forty men of the Thirteenth — taking all of Company E and a few men from another Company — and place them as flankers to the left of the Reg. ; in squads of three or four men each, extending the line of the Reg. toward the left, and swinging back a few yards on the extreme left of the line, in the brush and slashing. This is quickly done, and without accident, though it provokes a lively fusillade on the part of the rebel skirmishers. These flankers are thrown out because the colored troops, not very firm on the skirmish line to the left, might retreat before a heavy charge by the enemy, and imperil the left flank of the Thirteenth.

Battery Five is one of a long line of a dozen or more Batteries — perhaps more properly, Redans — all containing artillery, and connected by rifle-trenches, and protected, a hundred or two yards to their front, by a line of rifle-pits. We can see three or four of these Redans.

As we approach the edge of the slashing, troops are either withdrawn from the skirmish line or closed to the right, for the Thirteenth here widens its front again, by taking more open order towards the right, bringing the main part of the Regiment more nearly in the direct front of Battery Five. After a little further advance, we approach, about 4.30 or 5 p. m., as near to the edge of the slashing as is deemed prudent; and the men are ordered to halt, to find secure cover, to cease firing, and to keep hidden as much as possible. The men are tired from the long day's action, and rest upon their arms, settling down behind the large logs and stumps. The enemy's pickets, however — following the rule of riot at Donnybrook Fair : " Wherever you see a head, hit it " — keep pegging away at us, and Battery Five sends us a goodly number of shells.

We have now nearly two hours of reasonably quiet observation. We are so near to Battery Five, that we can occasionally when the wind serves, distinctly hear the commandant's orders, " Load," " Fire," and can look right into the muzzles of his guns, as they are run up to the embrasures, and fired straight at us, " puff — bang ; " sometimes singly, sometimes all at once. Our cover is so secure, however, that his firing is more interesting than harmful. Away to our left, near to Mr. Friend's house, is a long and strong line of skirmishers — colored troops — working forward over dusty, plowed land, among numerous apple or peach trees. They are in full view, and are having a hard time of it. They rush forward, and are then driven back ; and then try again, and again ; but without success, and quite a number of them are stretched out on the ground, dead. Battery Five shells them severely, and they and the shells drive up a great deal of dust. The scene is very interesting to us ; for a determined charge by the enemy upon those negroes would expose the Thirteenth, and bring Lieut. Thompson's flankers and the left half of the Reg. into instant action. The negroes are doing wretched skirmishing.

Now drums are heard in our rear — a dozen loud taps — and all is still. Immediately a full regiment of colored infantry, with colors flying — that is battle flags — and in a splendid line of battle, moves up toward a rail fence on our left and rear. In a moment Battery Five gives them — over our heads — three or four shells right in their faces. Snap — bang, go the shells among them, and down go their colors into the dirt, and back go they like wild men. Somebody's fool has blundered. A good, thorough, handsome, elegant blunder, too !

There are near us some large piles of stove-wood, cut, split, and thrown up in heaps to dry. Some of our men have unwisely taken cover there. Battery Five drops in a shell ; it explodes, and sends up a beautiful fountain of small stove-wood to rain down among the men. They make the best time on record from that shower. Another body's fool has blundered. None hurt, but all are considerably moved.

From some point away to our right the enemy sends us two or three large shells, Battery Five shells are small, and one of these large shells bursts apparently directly over the right of the Thirteenth, the rest go over. Jordan's and Friend's houses and buildings are used as a cover by the enemy's pickets, and we can see the puffs of smoke there in large numbers; this condemns all the buildings to destruction if need be.

While we are resting on our arms here in the slashing, about twenty field guns — one account says sixteen — take position in our rear and along the edge of the woods, and obtain the range of the enemy's Batteries, or Redans, numbers Five, Six and Seven. The troops of Gen. Brooks' Division, all excepting the Thirteenth and the other detachments forming the skirmish line in front of that Division, are massed near these guns as a support, and also held in readiness for an assault upon the enemy's works. Later on these troops deploy in a long battle line and follow the skirmish line. See Capt. Julian's account page 393.

A little after six o'clock, Gen. Burnham sends for Col. Stevens, Major Grantman and other field officers in our Brigade, now on the skirmish line, and they move back to his Hdqrs. on the wood-road in the timber a short distance to the rear of the front skirmishers. Here they receive instructions concerning the movement about to take place. Capt. Coitt commanding the 8th Conn., and Major Merriman commanding the 92d N. Y. are present at this meeting.

While these field officers are going to Gen. Burnham's Hdqrs., a cannon ball, or shell not exploding, strikes in the wood-road and ricochets, and just at the moment of bounding upwards from the ground strikes Major Pruyn of the 118th N. Y. in his body and tears him fearfully, instantly killing him.

After receiving instructions our field officers return to the skirmishers again; and a little before 6.30 p. m. the skirmish line of Gen. Brooks' Division, now consisting of the 13th N. H., eight companies of the 8th Conn., and small detachments of the 118th and 92d N. Y. regiments, is ordered to make ready to charge. The usual distance is at once taken as skirmishers — about five paces between man and man — and this movement of extending the line to the right — the Thirteenth being on the left next the negro troops — carries the whole skirmish line of Gen. Brooks' Division, excepting the Thirteenth, far to the right of Battery Five, and brings the Thirteenth directly in front of Battery Five, and stretching a considerable distance to the right and left of it.

The 189 men of the Thirteenth deployed as skirmishers, even at a less distance than five paces apart, would make a line more than 400 yards in length, while the east face of Battery Five, the face assaulted, is only about 100 yards in length.

The flankers under Lieut. Thompson of E, on the left of the Thirteenth, are directed to come up on the line, to extend to the right and to deploy as skirmishers in the same manner as the rest of the Thirteenth. As these flankers rise to their feet in the low slashing, and hence come into full view, the rebel riflemen open upon them savagely, and two or three of the men need at first a little encouragement. They come up into line, however, quickly and promptly, and by so doing the most of them are brought to the very edge of the slashing and some of them out of it altogether and into the clear open ground of the field in front, a very exposed position.

The Thirteenth is formed in line as skirmishers and waits but a few moments for orders, when a furious burst of artillery firing opens in our rear from the field guns mentioned above, several loud voices shout "Forward!" there is a rush and a shout; the flankers on the left still moving obliquely to the front and right advance a couple of rods or so into the field, when Lieut. Thompson of E, the writer, is tripped up by a rebel bullet striking through his left ankle and he plunges headlong to the ground falling upon some dry grass or weeds in the field. He is struck while crossing a sort of 'wheel-path' extending from the wood-road — that ran through the slashing crossing a rail fence and out into the open field beyond two large stumps — and goes back upon his hands and knees to one of these stumps for shelter from the severe rebel fire.

(In 1878 the writer, accompanied by young Mr. Jordan, residing near by, readily found this spot when visiting the field, and hence could locate the position of the left of the Thirteenth. Mr. Jordan stated that his father had seventeen buildings destroyed on his farm near Battery Five, by the Union and Confederate armies.)

The enemy's musketry fire is furious — it appears from this fire that counted all along his line the enemy must have near three thousand men — while shell come thick and fast from the enemy's Redans Six and Seven, and still farther to his left from his cannon located nearer the Appomattox river, and the shouting of the Northern men in the charge grows more and more noisy.

The Thirteenth dashes at Battery Five in a long thin line, narrowing front as they advance, striking first a line of rebel 'French rifle-pits' running clear across the middle of the open field, capturing these and above a hundred of the enemy's troops, sending them to the rear, and then advancing again towards the Battery.

In a few moments a little party of the officers and men of the Thirteenth, advancing rapidly, find themselves at the bottom of a deep ravine, now dry but forming a natural moat or ditch for Battery Five, the walls of which loom up above them some thirty or forty feet to the top of the parapet. Capt. Stoodley here remarks to Capt. Julian: "If we follow this thing right up now, we can take this Battery." Capt. Julian answers: "Then we will take it." No sooner said than done. They, Capt. Goss and the few men of the Thirteenth with them in the ravine — the whole party not above a dozen persons — instantly rush for the Battery; some straight up over the front walls, others up the north side, on bayonets stuck in the sand, grasping grass and weeds to assist in climbing, striking their boots into the gravel — anyhow so it be the quickest way in; and as these few Northern soldiers look from the parapet down into the

Battery they see a full hundred of the enemy. These are thrown into a little disorder by a number of their own men who have rushed in hurriedly from their rifle-pits taking refuge in the Battery, and they all appear to be waiting for something — they have not long to wait! Dashing without a moment's hesitation into their midst our officers demand a surrender. Capt. Julian calls upon Lt. Col. Council of the 26th Virginia, commanding the rebel infantry, to surrender, and receives his sword, also receives the swords of several other officers who surrender to him — among them Major Beatty and another Major.

Capt. Stoodley calls upon Capt. Sturtivant, commanding the Battery, to surrender, and receives his sword.

In a few seconds all is over, and the prisoners are forming to march to the rear. Meanwhile the captured guns are found to be loaded, and our men scarcely waiting for orders instantly turn the guns and prepare to fire them upon some of the enemy seen retreating — but the fuse is gone. Capt. Stoodley rather hastily asks Capt. Sturtivant for the fuse, and he replies that he "don't want to be a party in the matter." Capt. Stoodley at once politely acknowledges the right of that.

Soon Sergeant John F. Gibbs of E, who is one of the first to enter the Battery, and is somewhat acquainted with gunnery, finds the fuse, and the guns are fired by Gibbs and others upon the fleeing troops of the enemy which were not in the Battery.

Practically these three officers, Captains Stoodley, Julian and Goss, and less than a dozen men of the Thirteenth, capture Battery Five — an exceedingly daring performance. Affairs move quick at such a time.

Gen. Burnham, commanding our Brigade says, officially: "The Thirteenth N. H. Vols. captured in this work five pieces of artillery and about 100 prisoners; and the prisoners captured in the whole affair, could not have been less than 200."

A General who witnessed the affair, remarks: "It is equal to anything that has been done in the war."

It is said that Gen. Smith — 'Baldy' — commanding the 18th Corps, remarked, as he realized what had been done, that he "felt like giving a commission to the whole regiment that did that gallant deed." One writer calls the affair "startling audacity."

"After the Battery was captured by the Thirteenth, which occurred a little earlier than the taking of the works to the right and left, the Union troops continued firing for some little time; and to stop this firing upon our own men, Capt. Goss tied his white handkerchief to his sword, sprang upon the parapet of the Battery, and stood there waving this white flag until our men ceased their firing, meanwhile the cheers of victory, shouts of battle and firing were all commingled." [1] MAJOR STOODLEY.

---

[1] The writer regrets that he has been unable to learn the names of all these men, for a certainty, who composed this little force which first entered Battery Five. Major Stoodley states that the party consisted of about a dozen officers and men in all, when they started from the ravine to enter the Battery.

"The only Union soldiers who entered Battery Five to-day, before and during its capture, and until after it had been captured with all its guns, equipment and garrison, and had been held for some time, were the officers and men of the Thirteenth New Hampshire Regiment — and this was proved by a careful inquiry that settled the whole matter."

Lt. Col. Smith.

Eight Confederate officers in Battery Five surrendered to Capt. Julian, five of these eight are here accounted for by their arms : Lt. Col. Council, who was in command of the line of works. His sword Capt. Julian still has, 1887, and it bears this inscription : ' Presented to Lieut. Col. Council By the Officers and men of Companies B & C 26th Va. Regt. Jan. 1863.' He received of another officer a sword, apparently a home-made affair, with the edge ground and whetted as sharp as a scythe. This he gave to Sergt. James R. Morrison of K who still, 1887, preserves it as a relic. Of another a revolver — Colt's — which he gave to Lieut. Murray. Of another, a young naval officer, who was at Battery Five merely on a visit to friends for the day, and just down from Richmond, a revolver which he now has. When the officer handed this revolver, with the belt, holster and ammunition-pouch, over to Capt. Julian he remarked : "I will give you this as a special present to Old Abe." Capt. Julian still retains possession of it, however, by prior right. It is a Colt's, of English make, and the ammunition taken with it was made by Ela Brothers, London.

Of another — a Major Beatty — a sword which he still preserves. An incident connected with this sword deserves mention. Sergt. Morrison of K had charge of taking the prisoners to the rear, and just as he was starting with them, Major Beatty said to Sergt. Morrison that Capt. Julian was a very brave man, and expressed a desire to see him again before the party of prisoners was taken away. Morrison sent a man for Capt. Julian, who went over where the prisoners were, carrying with him his special collection of Southern arms. Major Beatty then politely drew out of the collection the sword which he but a few minutes before had surrendered, and turning the hilt, formally presented the sword and belt to Capt. Julian, with the request ' that in future he would wear it as his own, and when doing so would think of him the recent owner.' Capt. Julian accepted the gift, promising to wear it ; and during the rest of his term of service he wore that sword and none other, and still preserves it as a relic of the war having a special history of a particular interest.

The results of the day give to the Thirteenth two rebel colors, one captured by Sergt. James R. Morrison of K, and the other by Corp. Peter Mitchell of K — both of which colors are sent as trophies to the Governor of New Hampshire, and are now, 1887, preserved in the State House, and are the only rebel battle-flags in the custody of the State — about as many prisoners as the Regiment itself numbers ; several ammunition wagons, and five pieces of artillery — four handsome brass cannon, and one iron gun — belonging to Sturtivant's Richmond Battery ; and have broken the enemy's main line on this side of the "Cockade City."

The captured enemy, however, are not so happy. A portion of the men captured are militia, armed with smooth bore muskets — it was a round ounce bullet that struck Lieut. Thompson of E, and others of the 13th received wounds from the same sort of bullets — but the enemy fired with great rapidity. When Capt. Sturtivant, commanding the Battery, finds how few men have caused his surrender, and how matters stand, he is beside himself with anger and chagrin; and exclaims in pure Old Virginia : " Here are my guns double-shotted for infantry, and all of us captured by a —— Yankee skirmish line ! "

When our artillery belched out all at once so heavily, he expected an assault by a strong column of infantry, and prepared for it by double charges in his guns ; while waiting the onset, fuse in hand —about a dozen officers and men of the Thirteenth gobble up the whole of his garrison, pickets, guard, gunners, guns and all! This little party were the first in; but in less than five minutes they are joined within the Battery by nine tenths of the Regiment. The Thirteenth captured in all about 200 prisoners ; and the total loss in the Reg., counting all casualties, were 4 men killed, 5 officers and 44 men wounded.

"The National colors of the Thirteenth were planted by me on the parapet of Battery Five — the first flag planted upon it after its capture."
Sergeant David W. Bodge, Color-bearer.

Capt. Julian says : " During the advance of the Thirteenth as skirmishers, through the pine timber, Lieut. Thompson, the whole of Company E, and some other men of the 13th, were sent to the left of our Regiment as flankers, and this deprived me of a command. I was therefore directed by Col. Stevens to take charge of the general skirmish line on the left;

---

### DESCRIPTION OF FLAGS.

Upon the opposite page is a cut of the two Confederate battle-flags captured in Battery Five. They are the personal property of the brave captors, and are now, 1887, preserved in the Capitol at Concord — the only Confederate battle-flags in the custody of the State.

The upper flag in the cut (worn a little) was captured by Corporal Peter Mitchell of K ; and the lower one (whole) by Sergeant James R. Morrison of K.

At the request of the writer, Gen. A. D. Ayling, Adjutant General of New Hampshire, employed W. G. C. Kimball, Esq., of Concord, to photograph these flags ; the cut is made from the negative, and is accurate in every particular.

Gen. Ayling kindly furnishes the following description : The two flags are practically of the same size (the edge of one being frayed a little), viz.: four feet in length and four feet in width. The body is red ; the bars six inches in width, and blue with white borders ; the stars are white, and three and one half inches from point to point ; the border around both of the flags is two inches in width, and white. The material is bunting.

**CONFEDERATE BATTLE FLAGS.**
Captured at Battery Five.

and practically acting as Major, I spent several hours advancing the left wing of our Regiment. Later on, when the order came to charge, Col. Stevens came along the line, directing the commanders of Companies one after another to charge. The movement hung fire a little, apparently for want of concerted action. It was a dare-devil piece of work at best. After a few moments, when the Colonel was thus ordering a charge, I asked him: 'Colonel, do you want this Regiment to charge?' 'Yes,' answered the Colonel, 'The movement depends on you — every one of you.' This little sting touched me, and I sprang forward and shouted 'Charge!' — with all my might. Whether I was alone in this first shout I cannot tell, but away went the Thirteenth in an excellent line for Battery Five, and captured it and all there was in it.

"After we had taken Battery Five we felt insecure, not knowing but the enemy would soon charge in sufficient force to compel the Thirteenth to relinquish the position. But while we were thinking of this, a body of Union troops marching in one line of battle, apparently a mile long, with all colors unfurled and every officer and man in position, emerged from the woods, through which we had advanced before charging across the field upon the Battery, and bore across the open field rapidly to the front, in support of the Thirteenth and other troops on the skirmish line; they came up near to the captured Battery Five and the rebel works flanking it and halted — then we felt secure, and that no force which the enemy had hereabout could move us from our position."

Few actions ever more thoroughly demonstrated the need of a bugle, in handling a skirmish line too long to distinctly hear one man's voice. Probably Col. Stevens from no point could have made himself sufficiently well heard by every officer in the extended line of the 13th on this occasion. The force of the charge, however, was not in any degree broken, and will be better understood from the fact that while the enemy maintained his position, both on the right and on the left of Battery Five, the Thirteenth, in the centre, broke through one of the strongest, if not the strongest, defenses in his whole line of works — capturing this Battery, its garrison and cannon, and hold all they reach, before our other troops, to the right and the left on the line, capture the works on their fronts. We are the first to break the enemy's main line in front of Petersburg; and were in the front line of the infantry charge that opened the battle of Cold Harbor — that will do.

The results of the day, on the whole line, were the capture of 18 guns, and about 700 prisoners. The Thirteenth thus accomplished close upon one third of the whole day's work in the final dash, besides leading at the front all day. The Thirteenth captures for its Colonel one of the best prizes of the day — the Star of a Brigadier General. The enemy's artillery swept the whole advance, and his rifles all the open ground. The rebels in their 'French rifle-pits' were almost perfectly safe from our fire, and wholly unseen until our men in the charge ran close upon them.

The National colors of the Thirteenth were planted on Battery Five by Color-Sergeant David W. Bodge (of B); and the State colors by Color-Corporal Charles Powell (of K), and no other flags of the Union army were planted on this Battery at all. When the five cannon — one iron gun and four 12 lb. brass guns — captured here were drawn together and turned looking towards Petersburg from the high brow of this bold hill, and the Flags of the Thirteenth were set waving above them, the scene was a happy hour for cheers — three times three and a tiger.

"The prisoners, 125 or more of them, captured with Battery Five were placed in charge of Sergeant James R. Morrison of K, who marched them to the rear; meanwhile Corporal John H. Mawby of K, who had served in the U. S. Navy, with the assistance of other men turned some of the captured guns, which were double-shotted, and fired a couple of rounds at the fleeing rebels who had escaped the general capture."

CAPT. BETTON.

The Thirteenth had on the morning of June 15th, present for duty, fifteen officers and one hundred and eighty-nine men; the night report gives four officers wounded, four men killed, thirty-eight wounded and three missing.

Capt. E. E. Dodge is wounded in the leg just above the knee, the bone badly broken, just before reaching the Battery; Lieut. Charles B. Gafney in the thigh, and Adjutant Nathan B. Boutwell in the shoulder, when in front of and near the Battery; and Lieut. S. Millett Thompson in the left ankle — a round ounce-bullet going straight through it — while he was moving the flankers to the front and right during the preliminary movements in the charge. All these wounds are severe, and caused by round bullets.

The wounded officers and men of the Thirteenth are taken back to the house, buildings and grounds of Mr. Thomas Rushmore, near the Appomattox river, a little over a mile northward from the battle-field. His whole establishment is turned into a hospital. An old piano found about the premises, after having the legs sawed off, is used as an operating table for our Asst. Surgeon Sullivan; and the above named wounded officers and the wounded men are placed on it — while he skillfully plays the instrument! After having their wounds dressed, the officers and several of the men of the Thirteenth pass the night in Mr. Rushmore's house; lying side by side, heads to the north, on the floor along the north side of the room to the left of the front entrance to the house.

Mr. Rushmore and his little son, ten years old, were seized by the rebels a day or two before the battle and imprisoned in Petersburg. His life was threatened, and Mrs. Rushmore and her two daughters were plunged in the depths of worry, fear and despair, never expecting to see father, son and brother again. Mr. Rushmore was from New York city. Mrs. Rushmore and her two daughters — Augusta aged about thirteen or fourteen years, and Virginia aged about ten or eleven years — are up all night caring unceasingly for the wounded — the sweet humanity of it! They tear up all suitable cloth in the house, even to sheets and underclothing, into bandages; and bring milk, coffee and food without stint so long as there is any left to bring. Through the day, and as late as she can see to-night, little Virginia has been all about, up on the field and everywhere, all regardless of flying shells and bullets, carrying a little tin pail and cup and giving water to the wounded and dying; occasionally sitting down and crying bitterly for her little brother, who, as she supposed, had been killed.

The writer fainted from loss of blood at the edge of the woods just on reaching Mr. Rushmore's field, and while being carried back from the battle-field, and had been left lying upon the grass in front of and near Mr. Rushmore's house. The first thing he recalls after leaving these woods — having a long time previously heard the tremendous Northern cheering at the capture of Battery Five — was this little Virginia Rushmore trying to rouse him, and then giving him a draught of nice cold water. This could not have been far from nine o'clock in the evening.

Mrs. Rushmore had charge of the house and a few servants, and Augusta brought to the officers of the Thirteenth a good supper, and next morning a breakfast; and when the ambulance took them away on the morning of the 16th, she appeared with two or three quarts of ripe cherries and handed them up to the officers of the Thirteenth, who soon rode away eating them; and hardly anything could be more refreshing to these suffering men than were those cherries. 'Ambulance Brown,' who was driving, offered some of these cherries to the wounded rebel officer mentioned below, who a little later was placed on the ambulance, but he utterly refused to even so much as look at them. His manners were not those of a hero.

The general movement of to-day is made in this manner: Kautz's cavalry, about 2,400 strong, though not all on this line, precede the Union forces, meeting the enemy's vedettes about 6 a. m. and forcing them back until they came upon a considerable body of the enemy entrenched, about two miles out from Broadway landing, near the City Point Railroad, in an open field on Baylor's farm, and having with them two guns; when Kautz moves to the left, and Hinks' colored division of infantry, which has been following Kautz, moves up, assaults the enemy, and captures one gun and several prisoners, losing about 70 men of the 5th and 22d U. S. colored regiments.[1] This delays the advance until 9 a. m. Hinks now moves to the left, and Brooks' division, in which we are, which has been following Hinks, on the Jordan's Point road, moves up and crosses the ground just charged over and captured by Hinks, passing among his dead and wounded, and into heavy timber beyond, and near the City Point road. Martindale is advancing on the right along the Appomattox.

[1] A negro suffers much less when wounded than a white man; of a lower or less pronounced nervous organization, the wound gives him a less exhaustive shock. To-day the writer saw many negroes moving back with bullet holes in various parts of them, and of such a character as would inevitably have sent a white man upon a stretcher. The negroes walking back using their guns for canes or crutches, and cheerily saying they were not much hurt.

The advance is now made all along the line, through the woods and slashing, driving back the enemy from tree to tree, from stump to stump, until near mid-afternoon, when the skirmishers can advance no farther except by going into open ground. Meanwhile Gen. Brooks' division has moved up and massed near his guns. There now lies directly in front of, and in plain sight of, the Thirteenth, a line of fortifications; "Forming a salient covered by a powerful profiled work, heavily flanked with earth-works and rifle-trenches en echelon." These lines are defended by Wise's Legion, and by citizen militia, home guards, etc. A charge is decided upon at 5 p. m. by Gen. Smith ; and "towards 7 p. m." Gen. Brooks captures these works on the salient with skirmishers. The enemy's lines here being in our hands by 7 p. m.

The foregoing account was written in the main, before the writer's visit to the field, with Lt. Col. Smith, in May 1885.

To find Battery Five, and our positions in the summer of 1864 : Follow the City Point Railroad out from Petersburg, northeast, for about two and one half miles, and we come to a range of bluffs running from near the Appomattox river, southward. On the first bluff we come to, and on the right hand side of the railroad, south, and around which the railroad bends to the north, is Battery Five, mounted high on the very steep bluff, a few yards only from the railroad, and between the railroad and Mr. Charles Friend's house. Battery Five is in the outer line of the oldest Confederate defenses of Petersburg, is the fifth Battery south of the river, while south of it in the next three miles the numbers run up to twenty or more. After this line was broken, on the evening of June 15th, the Confederates retired, on the night of June 17th, to an inner line situated about one mile nearer Petersburg, and running south from the river about two and a half miles to Fort Mahone, then sweeping westward.

Battery Five faces almost due east — the north face 50 yards long, the east face, the front, 100 yards, the south face 50 yards, straight, then curves inward along the edge of the bluff some 25 yards further ; is nearly square with the west side, or rear, open towards Petersburg. The parapet is very bold and high, and the work is protected by a ravine falling 30 to 40 feet on the east and north sides. Due east from the Battery, across a wide, clear field, is a line of woods about 700 yards distant ; and about half way between the woods and the Battery was a line of Confederate rifle-trenches (since leveled) running clear across the field right and left, north and south. The color of the thrown up subsoil marks their position.

Now cross this field due east to the line of woods, turn and face west towards Battery Five. The 13th lay in these woods, stretched out in a long line as skirmishers, on the afternoon of June 15th facing west. Lt. Col. Smith — then Captain of Company H, and commanding that Company, the third from the right of the Reg. — started in the charge from a point (recognized) a little north of east from the centre of the Battery. Lieut. Thompson of E, having with him about 40 men of the 13th acting as flankers on the left of the Reg., started in the charge from a point (recognized) a little south of east; so that the general direction of the charge of the 13th on Battery Five was almost due west, striking the east front of the Battery, the Reg. naturally narrowing front as they came up, and enveloping the Battery as they captured it. The most of the Reg. who entered the Battery mounted the east and north parapets, which were least exposed to a flanking rebel fire.

West from Battery Five, towards Petersburg, lies a generally flat strip of land, wide and cut here and there by ravines draining northward into the Appomattox river. To the right, northward, is Mr. Beasley's house in a broad field running to near the Battery; this field was full of growing corn. Mr. Thomas Rushmore's house — where Dodge, Boutwell, Gafney, Thompson and others were taken, and spent the night of June 15th — is about one and one half miles northward of the Battery. Mr. Charles Friend's house stands about one quarter of a mile south.— to the left — of the Battery; this house became Gen. W. F. Smith's Hdqrs. after the Union line was established.

After the Battery was captured, the Thirteeth were moved to the left and stationed for that night's bivouac on the steep, high bluff-side near and just west of Mr. Charles Friend's house. Their position here — on a steep slope some 40 or 50 feet high, and falling toward the enemy and Petersburg — was directly between Mr. Friend's house and a building on the flat ground in front, and about 500 or 600 yards distant. This building and the vicinity of it, was held by the Confederates, who kept up an annoying fire the next day. The 10th N. H. made a most gallant charge upon them, dislodging them and capturing a number. It was in this movement of June 16th that Capt. James Madden of the 10th was killed.

The next position of the 13th on the line, as we shall see under date of June 21st, was nearly a mile nearer Petersburg, north of the railroad, and in the first ravine crossed by the first bridge on the railroad westward from Battery Five, confronting the enemy's new line of defensive earth-works. To return to the narrative of the day:

During the charge Sergt. George B. Kimball of H got within ten feet of the Confederate rifle-trenches in the middle of the field, and saw a gun being aimed at him by a Confederate soldier, when he instantly raised his own gun and demanded a surrender — and Johnny surrendered like a sensible little man.

Capt. Smith of H during the charge receives a bullet through his blouse pocket, smashing a small vial containing extract of ginger, and cutting ten holes in his folded pocket handkerchief — doing him no harm. Capt. Smith puts it well when he writes: "Two companies of the 117th N. Y. were added to the skirmish line; they took charge of the prisoners we captured in the 'French rifle-pits', and escorted them to the rear — coolly claiming the credit of their capture. Meanwhile the 13th captured Battery Five; the 117th N. Y. took charge of some of the prisoners captured there also — but the Battery they could not take to the rear."

A story went the rounds after the charge, that Capt. Clark, Gen. Burnham's Adjt. General was asked why the assaulting column, then just going in, was made no stronger, and he replied : " There are already men enough in that column to be slaughtered."

Capt. Follett, Chief of Artillery of the 18th Corps, states that the charge was the most splendid sight he ever saw, and he thought it one of the greatest feats of the war.

It is said that the Confederate Chief of Artillery remarked when the Battery was captured : " I expected you to mass your force and advance, and had got the grape ready to cut you to pieces ; but the idea of a skirmish line advancing upon forts never entered our heads."

The following is added as incidental : The writer was shot after having received the order to charge, and after leaving the slashing ; and as soon as he was struck he went upon his hands and knees for a couple of rods or that matter first to the protection of the large stumps, and then still farther back among the slashing where his boot was pulled off and about a tumbler full of blood poured out of it, and a handkerchief was twisted around the ankle to stop further bleeding. The Thirteenth meanwhile shouting and rushing upon Battery Five.

A short time after he was shot, he was being carried — sitting on a musket borne by John Riley a recruit of E, a splendid soldier in every respect, and another man — deeper into the woods for protection from

---

### DESCRIPTION OF PLAT.

A. Road from City Point to Petersburg.

B. Railroad cutting bluff and ravine C C, and crossing Harrison Creek D, by the first iron bridge, about three fourths of a mile west of Battery Five. The creek runs north into the Appomattox.

3, 4, 5, 6, 7. Rebel Batteries, so numbered, in a circuit of nearly two miles. Number 5 is on the end of a steep bluff.

E. Face of long steep bluff looking towards Petersburg.

F. Mr. Charles Friend's house.    G. Mr. Jordan's house.

M. Point near where Capt. James Madden of the 10th N. H. was killed.

L. Negro troops in the slashing an eighth of a mile to the left of the 13th. A line of their skirmishers were at some distance to their front among the trees of an orchard, engaging the rebel skirmishers posted in and in the vicinity of Mr. Friend's and Jordan's houses.

H. Thirteenth deployed as skirmishers near the edge of the brush and slashing I, with flankers thrown out to the left and rear ; the centre of the Reg. in front of the centre of Battery Five and awaiting the order to charge.

K. 'French rifle-pits' running across the field north and south about half way between the slashing and the Battery. The distances are given in yards.

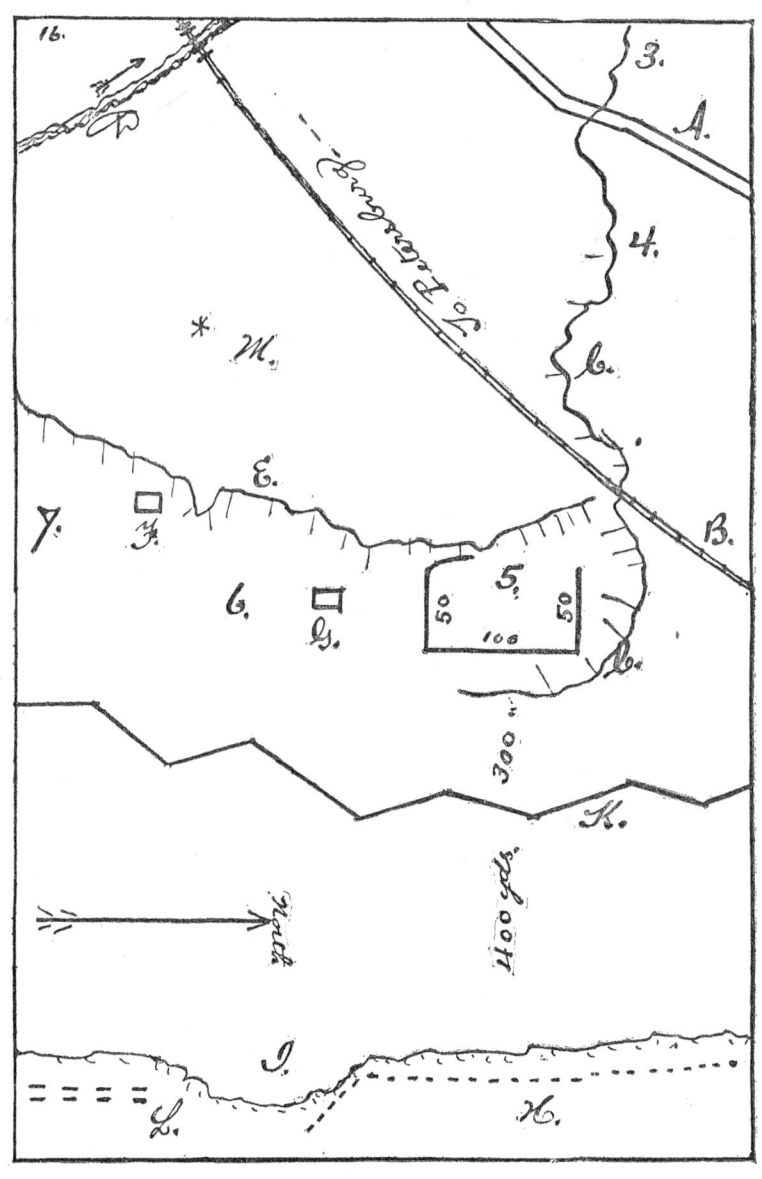

BATTERY FIVE, PETERSBURG, June 15, 1864.

From a sketch made by the writer in May 1885.

the rebel shells and bullets now flying furiously, when he comes upon a man of the Thirteenth standing close — as the bark — to a small pine-tree. He orders the man to join the Regiment. The man replies that he is sunstruck (!), but moves on. He has not moved six feet from the tree, when a rebel percussion shell strikes it at about the height of the man's shoulders, bursts, tears a portion of the tree into splinters and the top comes down with a crash, while the pieces of the shell and tree fly forward and all of us move away as quickly as possible — a close shave for the whole party. The man's eyes stick out and dilate with fright till they 'appear as large as saucers,' and he moves on toward the front, dodging bullets, steering clear of trees, and looking back over his shoulder at Riley, who threatens to shoot him, laughs at his fright and shouts at him a stream of Irish and English expletives, and observations uncomplimentary. Riley appears to have kissed the 'Blarney Stone' on both sides. After the man is well away towards the front, Riley turns to the writer remarking: "He is the only man of the Thirteenth whom I have seen shirking to-day."

Up to this time the shouting and firing of the charge had continued incessantly; and immediately after this affair of the man and the shell and tree we hear the burst of tremendous cheering at the capture of Battery Five. We proceed through the woods, and after seeing the open field and Mr. Rushmore's house the writer remembers nothing further for an hour or two, as previously mentioned. Riley and his companion were now not to be seen, and had probably returned to the front.

The following extracts from Capt. Smith's letters, written from the front a day or two after the battle, clearly state the main facts: "We crossed the Appomattox about 2 a. m. June 15th. Gen. Hinks captured one gun on Baylor's farm; his negro troops walking off with bullet holes in them after their charge. The Thirteenth was deployed as skirmishers about 10 a. m., advanced upon the left side of the City Point road, and went forward into the slashing cut about eighteen months ago. Here the Confederate commander of Battery Five could be heard by the Regiment giving his orders: 'Load — Fire!' Before we charged eighteen pieces of Union artillery opened on Battery Five, and the two Batteries to the left of it. The Thirteenth charged about 6.30 p. m., as skirmishers five paces apart. Capt. Julian was the first man to enter Battery Five. We captured a part of the 28th Virginia Regiment, five guns and ammunition, and turned the guns on the flying enemy. No men were ever so wild as ours were after the capture; and pretty soon three lines of our troops came up, out of the woods, and gave three cheers for the Thirteenth New Hampshire Regiment." CAPT. NORMAND SMITH.

The whole skirmish line numbered about fifteen hundred men, the Thirteenth in front of Battery Five, and stretching wide to right and left of it. The 18th Corps captured, in all for the day, 18 pieces of artillery, and about 700 prisoners. Gen. Burnham, of course, reported for his own brigade only, in giving his number of prisoners and guns. The excitement in Petersburg was most intense. The enemy fired to-day round bullets and buckshot.

Gen. Grant, in his Memoirs, Vol. II. page 295, does the white troops an unintentional injustice, probably following some item of serious misinformation, when he states : " Smith assaulted with the colored troops ; " as if it was the colored troops alone which made the evening assault as skirmishers. The morning assault at 9–10 a. m., upon an out-work on Baylor's farm, when one gun was captured, was made by Gen. Hinks' colored troops; but the evening assault, made about 6.30 or 7 p. m., when the long line of the enemy's works, including Battery Five was captured, with guns and many prisoners, was made by the Thirteenth New Hampshire with other white troops; after which Martindale on the right and Hinks on the left followed up the advantage gained. Gen. Humphreys states that the Petersburg defenses, before our charge, consisted of a line, encircling the city and about two miles from it, of strong redans or batteries, connected by infantry parapets with high profiles, and all with ditches. Gen. Brooks' division moved up along the City Point wagon-road, and advanced to the charge about 7 p. m., after which came the work of Generals Martindale and Hinks; their action also brilliant and successful. The advance was a march of six or seven miles. Gen. Lee, to-day and to-night, is rapidly crossing the James river at Drury's Bluff, 18 miles from Petersburg, and coming down with all dispatch. He adds, page 207, that the force of the enemy in their entrenchments here at this time, besides the artillery, consisted of Wise's brigade, 2,400 strong, the militia, and Dearing's brigade of cavalry.

He further states, page 208, in reference to the colored troops under Gen. Hinks — making the account of the Thirteenth clear, and correcting the error made in Gen. Grant's Memoirs : " About seven o'clock the skirmishers (of Brooks' division) advanced, and the artillery opened upon the salient — Redans 5 and 6 — which made no reply. The skirmishers met a sharp infantry fire, but carried the works, taking between 200 and 300 prisoners and four (five) guns. The lines of battle followed and occupied the entrenchments. Gen. Brooks was formed to resist an attack, while Gen. Martindale on the right, and Gen. Hinks on the left, were following up the advantage gained. Five of the redans on the left, from No. 7 to 11 both inclusive, were captured by Hinks' division, the last, No. 11, at the Dunn house about nine o'clock in the evening."

It will be seen, therefore, that the colored troops followed the white troops in the evening's work ; the white skirmishers first breaking the enemy's line at and near Batteries Five and Six. Battery Five was the first to fall, captured, with its five guns, its garrison, and other Confederate troops who had taken refuge in it from the rifle-pits previously taken, all by the Thirteenth New Hampshire Regiment.

The writer must here — and most reluctantly, for he desired very much to see the war through with the Thirteenth — drop the personal part of the narrative, and hereafter depend altogether upon statements of other officers and men for items from the front, the battle line and camp; while he goes to a military Hospital for four hot summer months, with a bullet hole through a badly smashed left ankle, and the round ounce-bullet, that made it, in his pocket — thanks to Assistant Surgeon John Sullivan; and after those four long and suffering months, to be discharged the service, for disability, and sent home, while still unable to walk a step on the smashed limb and obliged to use crutches. He was laid up for sixteen months. (The wound has never fairly healed.) Since a little sketch of this Hospital life may now be of interest to some one, he will presume to enter an occasional item under the heading Hospital; as of a personal experience similar to that shared by thousands of our comrades in arms.

# VIII.

### June 16 to September 27, 1864.

#### SIEGE OF PETERSBURG.

**June 16. Thurs.** Fair, hot, dusty. Last night the enemy occupied a ravine near Battery Five, and attempted to entrench, but were driven back. The Thirteenth remains in line of battle under arms to the left, south, of Battery Five, on the bluff-side west of Mr. Charles Friend's house and in his door yard. This is a greatly exposed position on the steep slope looking towards Petersburg, which is a little over two miles distant. Details from the whole force here are throwing up entrenchments. The Thirteenth is ordered to lie on its arms night and day. No officer or man is allowed to leave the line beyond a few rods. Attack momentarily expected. The enemy is making almost superhuman endeavors to recover his lost ground here. The Thirteenth is moved into support of a battery of nine field-pieces arranged in a semi-circle on the bluff, thus being a little less exposed. There is a great deal of firing all day, but it nearly ceases at dark.

At this point the country appears to have been at one time the bank and bed of the Appomattox river. In western phrase, we occupy the 'bluffs,' the enemy occupies the 'bottoms.' We are disposed along the ancient river bank, now a line of bluffs thirty to seventy feet high; the enemy at our front is on the ancient river bed, now an immense flat, cut up by numerous small ravines and ridges, with brooks and strips of swampy land. To the left the enemy occupies the hills near Petersburg.

This morning Gen. Grant with his staff, and Gen. Burnside, came up to Battery Five, captured by the Thirteenth, and passed along the line, surveying the position for a considerable time. While standing near him, Capt. Stoodley heard Gen. Grant say: "The taking of this strong line with skirmishers is one of the most brilliant actions in this war."

While all are standing here, a drunken staff officer — of whose staff we do not learn, but not a member of the 13th — dashes out over our lines, rides down on the plain toward the rebel lines, halts, rises in his stirrups, waves his hat at the enemy, loudly bids them defiance, and then rushes back at a break-neck speed, both horse and rider unharmed by the enemy's fire. Gen. Grant orders his arrest, and at once dismisses him from his position as a staff officer.

The forces under Gen. Hancock, having relieved the 18th Corps in a part of the works in our vicinity, make an assault, together with a portion of the 18th Corps, amid a perfect roar of artillery and musketry, forcing the enemy back from the whole length of the line attacked. We have an excellent opportunity to see what a heavy infantry charge means; a grand but terrible spectacle, and especially so this evening when the fighting is exceedingly fierce. Last night, after we captured the enemy's front line, rebel troops in great numbers began to enter Petersburg from Gen. Beauregard or Gen. Lee on the north, and to re-enforce the enemy's lines on our front. The bridges are in the city, and they all appeared to cross there. We could hear their cheering, and the muffled rumble of distant tramping and teams. Gen. Hancock's 2d Corps came up near the front; a part occupying the line we had captured, relieving the 18th Corps, and giving our men a better chance to rest. We could have pushed on, however, if ordered to do so, for the labors of yesterday, though especially severe for a long time, allowed several hours for rest in the latter part of the day. The army of the Potomac is hasting to this front from its fields north of the James.

The whole of last night was thus used up by Clan Grant, and Clan Lee, gathering hereabout, in the darkness, to discuss the question of Petersburg with the arguments of war.

Hospital. The wounded officers and men of the Thirteenth are moved about 10 a. m. to-day from Mr. Thomas Rushmore's house, in the ambulance — 'Ambulance Brown,' driver — and placed on board the steamer 'Hero of Jersey.' Soon after leaving Mr. Rushmore's the ambulance is hailed, and stops to take on a rebel officer, wearing a sort of half-citizen's dark gray suit, and wounded in his arm. The writer, the rebel, and Brown in the centre, occupy the driver's seat outside. He treats those who are aiding him to get up on the ambulance, with the utmost contempt, and scorns to stoop to show the least regard for, or civility to, us his fellow passengers. He is tall, slim, black-haired, black-eyed, frowning and supercilious; a more aristocratic, haughty, snappish, peppery, uncomfortable creature we have never seen prior to this time. He is also extremely dirty, has evidently been in the mud, and his only baggage is an old cotton-cloth bag with strings, something like a haversack, once white, but now a mess of greasy dirt. When he is helped aboard the steamer, Brown, who had shown him several very pleasant and kindly attentions, each rewarded by a snap, a snarl or a sneer, carefully takes up the rebel's haversack and passes it into the boat — taking it up in the most dainty fashion, as if it were poison, or he was fearful of brushing off the tinsel — and hands it over the steamer's rail, with the remark, in mock earnest: "Don't let us forget this *gentleman's baggage*." Brown's courtesy is irresistible, and provokes a general laugh. The rebel's eyes flash fire, but he is too angry to speak, and disappears in silence, looking murder and malice unutterable. He is altogether the most unreasonable and ugly specimen of a Southron we have ever seen. We think he must have been captured by that "Skirmish line of the Thirteenth," now recognizes his captors, and does not like our methods of warfare; or else he is a deserter, and a scoundrel prior to all the rest.

A few miles down the river we are stopped by Gen. Grant's army crossing the James River on a ponton bridge, and here we have to wait until his entire army crosses. The bridge extends from north to south across the James, from Windmill Point, south of Wilcox's Landing, to Fort Powhatan, nearly twenty miles from Petersburg. The river here is 2,100 feet wide, 75 to 100 feet deep in mid-channel, the current strong, and the rise and fall of the tide is about four feet. The ponton boats, 101 in number, are secured to ships anchored above and below. The bridge was commenced at 4 p. m., on June 14th, and finished by midnight. All of Gen. Grant's army and trains, excepting his rear-guard, had crossed by midnight of June 16th.

This immense army crossing the James river here presents a most magnificent spectacle; and as our steamer lies near, those of us who are able to sit up can see it all — a last grand view of war to many a poor fellow on the Union side; while the wounded and other Confederates aboard with us watch the mighty scene with intense interest, their faces betraying no hate but mingled emotions of sternness, dread, wonder and desperation, one of them exclaiming on the last day of our waiting: "Great Heavens! — is there no end to that thing?" We have had no view of an army on the field of a review, which would at all compare with the view of this army hasting here to-day forward to the field of battle. Reviews are shows; this is business, in all the push, stir and energy of war. A living panorama, a vast army in motion, long lines of cavalry, generals with their staffs, infantry in long, dense columns, with all their mounted officers, furled battle flags, knots of camp-followers and teams, wagons, cannon, flying artillery, heavy guns, bands, hundreds of ambulances and countless army gear; all moving rapidly, swiftly over the low, level, floating bridge, in grand procession and all seeming to be as it were down upon the very surface of the water itself.

All day long, and in the hours of night, the bridge, nearly half a mile in length, is full, an unceasing tramp, no break in the column, but steadily, speedily, the great host forges on, as if every organization in it were a huge link in some immense drawing chain, that the God of war was now sweeping irresistibly into place as an impregnable cordon around the presumptuous and turbulent Confederacy — as it is; squadron after squadron, regiment after regiment, brigade after brigade, division after division, battery after battery, train after train, corps after corps, each with all the appliances, ensigns, flags, arms, paraphernalia and materiel of real and tremendous war; all lines and files in perfect order, place and time, moving under the control of the master mind of that one greatest of American men and Captains — Lieut. General Ulysses S. Grant, seconded by his noble Lieutenant, Major General George G. Meade; constantly for hour upon hour appears this huge unbroken stream of men, bursting into full and sudden view from an unseen source in the dense woods on the northern shore, entering low down upon the bridge, crossing with quick route-step the wide level to the southern shore, ascending the river bank, and instantly disappearing as they came, we cannot see whither, apparently inexhaustible in numbers and invincible in power — the fate-holder of our Nation, the strong right arm of our whole People.

June 17. Fri. Fair. Reg. remains in its entrenchments on the bluff side near Mr. Friend's house until 7 p. m.; when we are relieved by troops from the 6th Corps, and march back, with the rest of Gen. Brooks' Division, to our old camp within Gen. Butler's entrenchments at Bermuda Hundred — " Camp near Point of Rocks " — arriving there at 2 a. m. — 18th. To-day a severe artillery firing and skirmishing is engaged in along the Petersburg front, during which the Union forces dislodge a body of the enemy from a ravine near us, which he occupied last night. We witness the affair, without being directly engaged in it. The fighting continues day and night, and our lines are being constantly advanced. This evening the enemy attacked the Petersburg lines in force soon after we left, and were fearfully cut up by the 6th Corps.

Last night about sunset the Union troops — two Brigades of the 18th Corps on the right, the 2d Corps, and two Brigades of the 9th Corps on the left — attacked the enemy's lines, capturing several more redoubts of the same line that Battery Five is on — and drove the enemy back along his whole line. This under Gen. Hancock; and we have a notion that Gen. Hancock would have been a better match for Gen. Beauregard, in all this early business about Bermuda Hundred and Petersburg. In such attacks as our force made on the evening of June 15th celerity and push are the chief causes of success; Petersburg were in our hands then merely by a swift rush into it. However, so far as the Thirteenth is concerned, it is universally conceded in camp that we have done a very fine bit of work — snapping Gen. Lee's line just where we struck it, at its strongest point.

Hospital. The wounded still on the " Hero of Jersey,' and many of us begin to suffer severely for want of care, and from the excessive heat. Cold water freely poured upon gunshot wounds, allays the pain better than anything else, and is now the only means at hand.

June 18. Sat. Fair. Thirteenth in camp -at Bermuda Hundred, and enjoying a much needed rest. During to-day Gen. Lee has made nine assaults on parts of Gen. Grant's lines. While we were moving away last night the enemy withdrew from their old, outer, long line of redoubts, redans and trenches, without the knowledge of Gen. Grant's troops (at least), to a new and much stronger line of defenses, about one mile nearer Petersburg. The enemy in withdrawing leaves many of his recent dead still unburied; and the long trenches, filled with those of his dead which he did bury, tell how very severe his losses must have been.

His old line of works along the bluffs was broken by the capture of Battery Five and others on June 15th, and is indicated by the line accompanied by the numbers 2 to 15, on the east side of map on page 411: their new line is indicated by the line, on the west side of the same map, running between L and S.

Hospital. The wounded officers and men finally pass Gen. Grant's ponton bridge, and a surgeon comes on board the steamer.  Late to-day, nearly night, the steamer arrives at Hampton, and the wounded are carried ashore on stretchers.  We are at once placed in the old Seminary building, now called Chesapeake General Hospital.  (Soldiers' Home, 1887.)  Capt. Dodge, Adjutant Boutwell, Lieut. Gafney and Lieut. Thompson are placed together in the same room — the first room to the right of the head of the main stairway in the third story.  Dodge and Thompson side by side near the window, but on separate cots.  We are told that a number of the wounded died on the steamer, while on the passage down the river and bay.  The nervous fear, experienced by the severely wounded officers while being carried up these long stairways, is so exhausting that many are blindfolded, so that they may see no danger.

Lieut. Gafney carried the bullet that he received at Battery Five until November 8, 1881, when it was extracted by Dr. Horatio N. Small of Portland, Me., formerly Asst. Surgeon in the Thirteenth, and Surgeon of the 10th N. H.  All four of these officers were wounded by round ounce-bullets, the enemy we met using round bullets and buckshot.

June 19.  Sun.  Fair.  Reg. in camp.  Very quiet along the lines. Our Regiment's capture of Battery Five looms up in importance, more and more as the facts come into view.  Gen. Lee regarded the point captured, at and near Battery Five, of such strategic value, that he has since made a move, with over 40,000 troops, to recapture it.

The Adjutant of a Pennsylvania Regiment is drummed out of camp for cowardice — the same man referred to on May 23, 1864.  " The troops are drawn up in line.  The culprit, with a large board fastened upon his back on which is painted, ' Coward,' appears at the right of the line.  Just in front of him are two men with arms reversed — not as at soldiers' funerals, but with the bayonets raised somewhat higher — and two men behind him carrying their guns at a ' charge.'  Preceding the whole is a fifer and drummer.  This melancholy procession, of six men and the culprit, moves slowly down the entire line, the two musicians playing the Rogues' March, then moves back to the point of starting ; when his sentence of dishonorable dismissal, with forfeiture of everything in the way of pay and allowances, is read aloud.  Then a private soldier is called from the ranks, who cuts the straps from his shoulders, and the military buttons from his coat.  After this he is escorted to the limits of the camp and allowed to depart."  PRESCOTT.

June 20.  Mon.  Fair.  Reg. in camp.  Very quiet.  The last four days have been devoted to resting.  Orders received for us to be ready to march to-morrow morning.  Capt. Smith, Acting Major, commanding the Thirteenth.  Major Grantman is commanding the 2d N. H.  Our Brigade has lost 760 men, out of 1,600, since May 8th.

Hospital.  Four months' pay is now due us, and we are much pinched for money to purchase things which we greatly need.  Capt. Dodge's leg is wounded by a bullet just above the knee, a comminuted fracture of the bone.  He suffers but little.  His leg rests in a sort of trough, made of pieces of board, which can be raised or lowered at will. A chaplain so-called, but really a fool and an ass, bores him beyond endurance with a half hour of gloomy talk. Those who are very sick and likely to die soon, are visited by this walking charnel-house of a chaplain — and what little of life is left in them he can soon talk out.

June 21. Tues. Fair. Thirteenth is called at 3 a. m., has a hurried breakfast, and at 4 a. m. again crosses the Appomattox, at Broadway Landing, and marches to the rear of Petersburg. We lie in the road, in the woods, near the front, all the day — a brisk artillery duel going on over our heads all the afternoon — and at dark we move with our Brigade into the front line of the entrenchments. We set at work immediately on the entrenchments, and a covert way required in approaching our front trenches. Co. G is on the right of the Thirteenth, and rests close down on the river bank. The trenches now occupied by us are fully one mile in advance of Battery Five, and on the flat to the westward of it. Col. Stevens again in command of the Regiment. Major Grantman in command of the recruits of the 2d N. H. that are left here after the volunteers have gone home. He retains this command but for a few days, and only until the regular officers of the 2d return again from New Hampshire to the front. The most of these recruits are foreigners, who know but little of the English language.

Hospital. Capt. Dodge dies to-night. His life might have been saved probably, if he had consented to have his leg amputated. His determination to save his leg cost him his life. He died of blood poisoning, and was deceived, by the absence of pain, into believing that he would recover. He died while Lieut. Thompson was asleep. As the patients in the ward awoke, and found that he was gone, they instinctively knew the cause — a shudder ran through them all. The Surgeons and attendants say that he suffered no pain, and passed away without any struggle, and like a person falling asleep.

There are two hospitals here about one fourth of a mile apart, both under one management, with Dr. Ely McClellan Surgeon-in-charge: the old Seminary building, with a high basement and three stories above, with a massively pillared broad veranda in front, and surmounted by a huge dome; and Hampton Hospital consisting of thirty or forty cottage-like buildings 125 feet long, 25 feet wide and 18 feet high, of one story, finished to the roof. Hundreds of smaller buildings and tents are on every hand, the whole constituting almost a city — the city of suffering, pain, dismemberment and death.

The outlook towards Fortress Monroe, Hampton Roads and the sea is very fine; the middle ground a vast collection of army tents, while the training grounds are filled with bodies of troops manœuvring in every measure known to the order of drill. Those of us who can get to the windows, spend hours at a time watching the ever-changing scene. The mind of a wounded man is exceedingly active, and no position for a hospital more desirable and attractive than this could well be conceived.

Again we continue with the notes made in May 1885, when visiting these fields with Lt. Col. Smith : Following the City Point Railroad from Battery Five westward towards Petersburg, about three fourths of a mile will bring us to the first bridge on the railroad, an iron bridge thrown across Harrison Creek, and the ravine in which the creek finds its way northward to the Appomattox. Between this creek and ravine, and the Confederate lines where they come to the river, is, first of all on the Union lines, Fort McGilvery and Battery No. 8 ; and the space here between the creek, the river, the Confederate lines, and the railroad, all together about one half mile square, was the scene of most of the service of the 13th during the summer of 1864. The ravine along the creek served for reserve and Hdqrs. camps. Towards the river to the right of this railroad bridge were the Hdqrs. of our 1st Brigade, Col. Stevens, low down in the ravine, and much exposed to water, mud and mosquitoes, to say nothing of the minor inconveniences of the enemy's continuous fire.

Farther towards Petersburg, where the railroad and the carriage road come close together and run side by side, the last front lines of National and Confederate confronted each other ; neither side budging a rod here for more than nine months. The Union and rebel lines here are a succession of forts, batteries, and innumerable connecting earth-works, run-

---

DESCRIPTION OF MAP.

A. U. S. Military Railroad.     C. Mr. John Hare's house.
D. Alexander Pace.
B. City Point Railroad, crossing Harrison Creek by iron bridge, Y.
E. Battery Five in the old outer Confederate line captured June 15th, This old line faced east. The Confederates soon after retired to the new inner line L. V. S., see June 18th. This new line generally faces east.
W. W. Confederate Batteries north of the Appomattox.
F. City Point road.     G. Thomas Rushmore.
H. Mr. Beasley.     I. Mr. Rowlett.
K. Heavy timber, 13th reserve camp.     X. Appomattox River.
M. Fort McGilvery near Battery VIII. ; next Batteries IX. and X. ; then N, Ft. Stedman, P, Ft. Haskell, R, Ft. Morton, all seven on the Union main line facing west.
S. Elliott's Salient, Mine, Crater.     T. Cemetery Hill.
Z. Union front line from river to railroad, and in rear of it Mr. John Hare's house, C. The Thirteenth held the end of this line on the river bank, between Mr. John Hare's house and the enemy's lines, having its camp in the little ravines shown to the north of Fort McGilvery.
L. A short ravine, but very deep, running between the Confederate line of rifle-pits and their main line of rifle-trenches, in front of the Thirteenth.

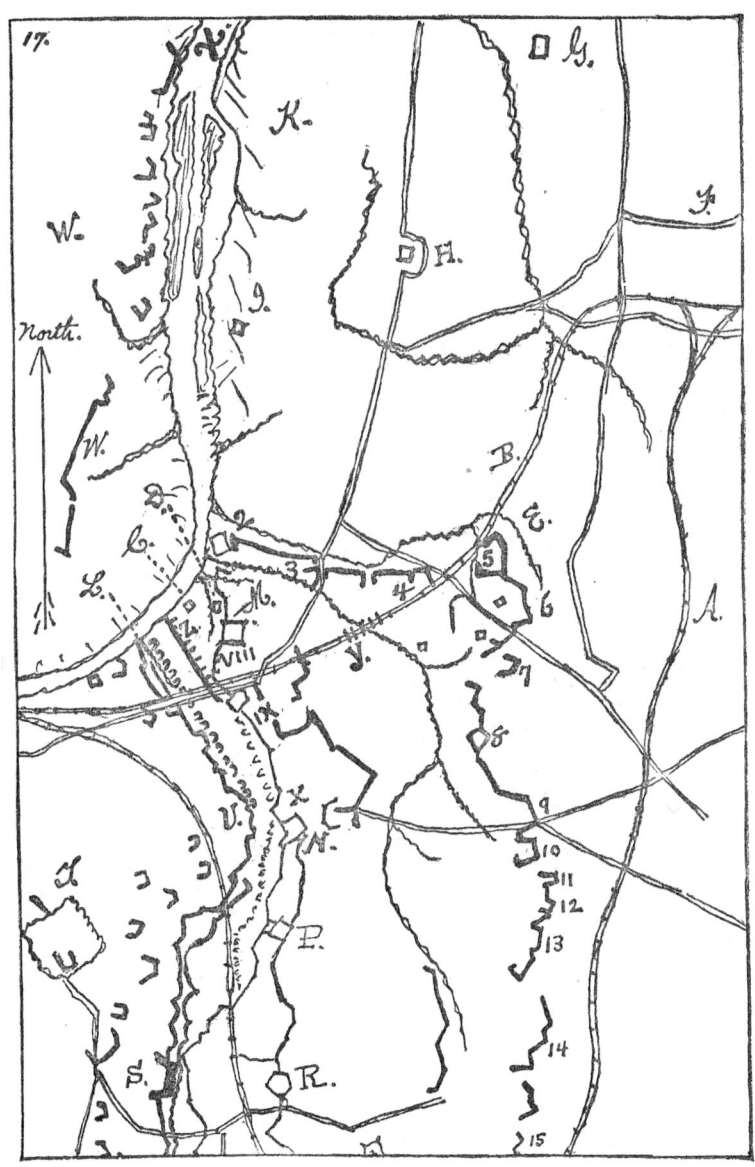

PETERSBURG FRONT.

Tracing of Official Map   Scale, one and one half inches to one mile.

ning from the river side by side southward across the country; a vast double net-work, with bomb-proofs, and traverses, long covert ways, trenches, and high parapets, and the thousands of war's devices framed in timber and iron, cut in earth or piled in sand, and armed to the last point — to save a life, to insure a safe lookout, to secure a night of sleep undisturbed, or to repel an assault.

Moving forward to the vicinity of Fort McGilvery, built on a bluff near the river, we come to the house on the river bank now, 1885, owned by Mr. John Hare — marked C on the accompanying maps — a wooden house built on the same site where his brick house stood during the war. This house is a number of rods towards Petersburg, westward, from Fort McGilvery. The front line held by the Thirteenth, our "Appomattox Line," on the river bank, ran north and south, across Mr. John Hare's field, 200 yards southwest (on the Petersburg side) of his house; and confronting it, west, at a distance of less than 300 yards, was the Confederate front line. Distances paced. This is close down to the bluffy river bank; the extreme right of Gen. Grant's lines south of the Appomattox. Our 1st Brigade picket line extended from the river here up to the City Point road. This narrow, disputed strip of land lying between the Union and Confederate lines and less than 300 yards wide, is cut, close up — almost under — the Confederate line, by a very deep ravine — 50 to 75 feet deep — having very steep sides and extending half way from the river to the road, and is marked L on our maps. While this deep ravine afforded most excellent cover for the Confederates to form unperceived, for a dash at the lines of the Thirteenth, it would have proved an almost impassable barrier to a force attacking the Confederate lines from our side. The Confederates had a high dam built across this ravine near the river, evidently flooding it — a capital moat. The 13th knew little, or nothing, of this ravine during the war.

Long, winding covert ways were made through the bluffs to reach our front lines in safety. The Confederate shells, received here, came mostly from the northwest across the river. Our front lines here were several hundred yards in front of Fort McGilvery, which played over our heads.

Mr. John Hare has leveled all the earth-works, Union and Confederate alike, on his farm, at one time having over three hundred negroes at work upon them. He stated to the writer that he realized money enough from the sale of the wood and timber alone, dug out of the earth-works made by the Union troops on his farm of 125 acres, to pay for all the work of leveling, besides a large sum realized from the sale of the iron and lead recovered, and the railroad rails that he found buried in bomb proofs, and covert ways. Members of the 13th will recall, with much satisfaction, the hard work they did here in order to thus provide the freedmen with employment after the war was over!

Our pickets on the City Point road were often placed as vedettes between the lines at night within 20 feet of the Confederate pickets; and the line of pickets of our 1st Division ran from the river nearly over to the hill where the famous "Hare House" stood, a mile or so southwest of the river.

While the Reg. was here by the river, a 'liver and white' pointer dog used occasionally to get between the Union and Confederate lines in Mr. John Hare's field, and mistaking the flying bullets for bees, would run hither and thither, giving up the chase of one when he heard the hum of another, tacking and darting after them every which way for an hour at a time — a clear case of ignorance proving to be bliss.

Our reserve camp was a long way in the rear of our Appomattox front line, in heavy pine timber to the northwest of Mr. Beasley's house.

Due north from Fort McGilvery about one eighth of a mile, and east of Mr. John Hare's house, on the bank of the river, there stood during the war a story and a half house — marked D on maps — having a brick basement and dormer windows in the roof and belonging to Mr. Alexander Pace. The officers of the 13th found the basement very convenient for cooking purposes, had a covert way dug to it from the main covert way running to the front lines, and constantly frequented the house. Lt. Col. Smith and Capt. Ladd were in this house one day, and had just stepped away from a window, when a rebel shell came in at that window, finding its way out through the side of the house with a crash, but injuring no one.

**June 22. Wed.** Hot. Reg. in front lines all day in a little ravine, and at work on the entrenchments. Enemy very busy, and no one can safely show his head. Our Brigade line rests close down on the river at the right, and much of the line on wet ground. The Thirteenth is the extreme right regiment of our Brigade, Division and Corps. The 2d and

---

DESCRIPTION OF PLAT.

A. City Point Railroad; with City Point road, T, near it.
B. Heavy Union rifle-trench, with many bomb-proofs and traverses, occupied by the Thirteenth at the extreme north end, on the river bank just west of Mr. John Hare's house, C. Dotted line, a long covert way.
D. Mr. Alexander Pace's house, nearly east of Mr. Hare's house.
E. Ft. McGilvery.                VIII. Battery No. 8.
F. F. Old Confederate trenches captured.
G. Battery Five — near as the arrow points — on old Confederate line, captured by Thirteenth June 15th.
H. Harrison Creek, with iron bridge at railroad crossing.
K. Brooks in little ravines where were rear camps.
L. Deep ravine between the rebel trenches and their front rifle-pits.
L. V. S. Confederate lines (new) see June 18th. The Union line faces west; the Confederate line faces east. The Union main line B, and the Confederate main line L. V. S. were less than 300 yards apart where the Thirteenth was on the river bank.

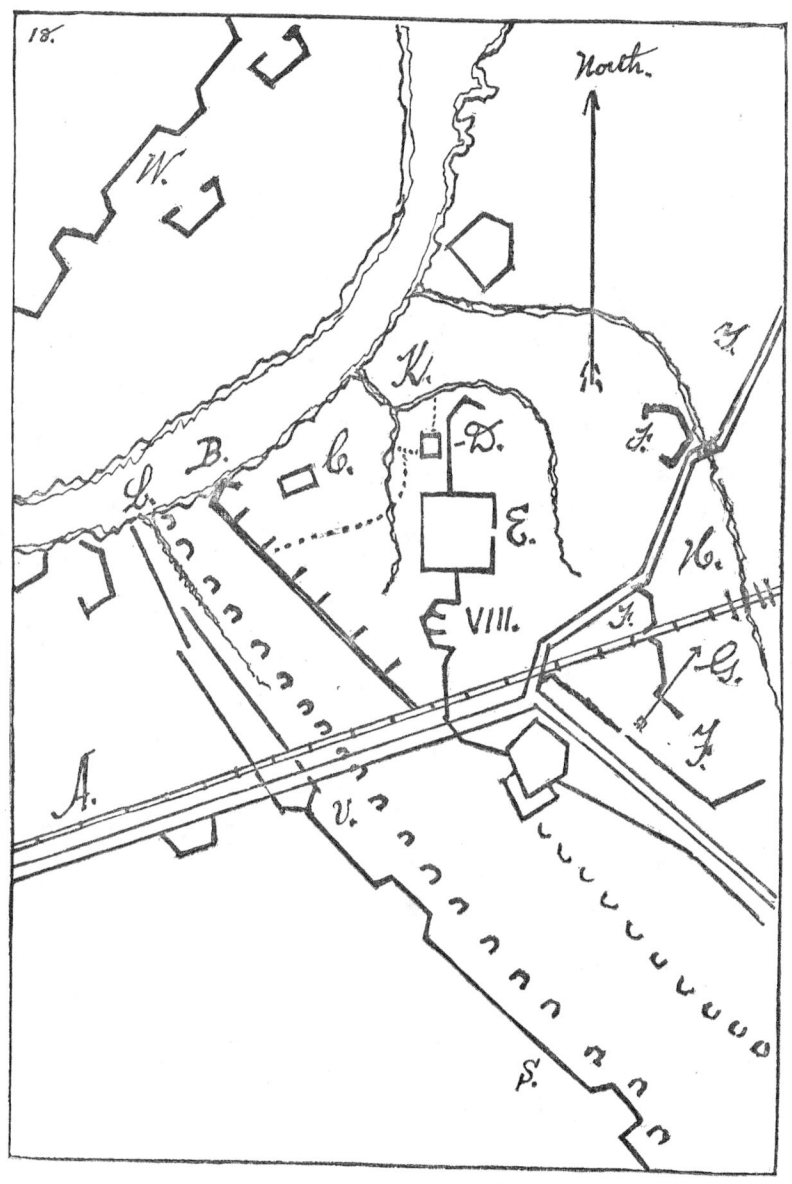

PETERSBURG FRONT.
RIGHT OF GEN. GRANT'S LINE, ABUTTING ON THE APPOMATTOX RIVER.
From a sketch made by the writer in May 1885.

6th Corps, with Wilson's and Kautz's Divisions of cavalry, move to the west of Petersburg and towards the Weldon Railroad. Our Brigade is expected to garrison forts and earth-works as a reserve, and not to engage in any active field operations on the Petersburg front; still retaining our organization with the Army of the James.

Hospital. We all feel very badly about the death of Capt. Dodge. He was a very efficient and brave officer, a kind friend and a genial companion, and in losing him the Thirteenth meets with a very great loss indeed. Capt. Dodge's wife came out here to take care of her husband, and arrived just in time to accompany his embalmed body home. Her sorrow was most pitiful, and she had the sympathy of every person who knew of this terrible bereavement.

All four of us were severely wounded; Adjutant Boutwell's wound is especially severe, the bullet passing through his shoulder and breaking his collar bone. Gangrene makes its appearance in his wound, and he is to-day removed to the gangrene ward, a tent outside. Of these four wounds, Boutwell's did not heal for eleven years, Thompson's has never healed soundly at all, Gafney carried the bullet in his leg for eighteen years, Capt. Dodge died.

June 23. Thurs. Fair, very hot. Reg. in front trenches at work until 11 p. m., when it moves about one and one half miles to the rear and bivouacs in dense pine woods. A great deal of shelling to-day all along the lines. Rev. A. J. Patterson distributes to the 13th sundry stores sent by the Ladies' Soldiers' Aid Society of Portsmouth, N. H.

This afternoon the enemy opens upon our Brigade with three large mortars, dropping the shells almost vertically down behind our trenches. Several men in the Brigade are struck down by the pieces of exploding shells. One mortar shell drops and explodes in Company K's trench, a piece of it severely wounding Sergt. James R. Morrison of K in the head. Col. Stevens' mess — himself, Capt. Smith, Quarter-master Morrison, Capt. Stoodley — a clerk and the Colonel's cook are in Mr. Alexander Pace's house, some of them writing, some reading, and some eating supper. A rebel shell comes down through the roof and bursts in a chamber over their heads, the pieces flying about, knocking the table to pieces, badly smashing the house, scattering the supper, and burying everybody and everything in splinters, plaster, dust and rubbish. Strange to say only one of the party is seriously hurt, the Colonel's cook, George H. Weeks, who is sent to New Hampshire to recover. Andrew Hanou of H is in the house, takes refuge by the chimney and is unhurt. A large rebel shell soon strikes the ground very near the house and explodes heavily jarring the house, but injuring no one.

June 24. Fri. Very hot. Reg. at the rear in thick woods. Heavy artillery firing this morning. In the afternoon the Reg. is employed in cutting abatis. The enemy attacks a portion of our Corps line and captures 300 prisoners. Thirteenth not engaged. The affair provokes a terrific noise, resounding through these deep woods like the roar of continuous thunder. Our troops assault in turn, securing a hold upon a short line of the enemy's front trenches, and capturing 200 prisoners. "Almighty hot — whew! One can hardly breathe." PRESCOTT.

Hospital. Gangrene very prevalent, and the heat of the weather is intense. Wounds all through the Hospital are reported as taking a very bad turn, and a critical examination is made of every case, to detect any possible taint of gangrene. This disease cannot be described better than to say that the flesh immediately in and around the wound dies, turns dark, and rots in the space of a few hours, and when this dead mass is removed, an angry red bleeding pit, or hole, is left, as if a portion of the flesh had been scooped out; a place excessively sensitive, sore, painful and difficult to heal.

June 25. Sat. Very hot. Reg. moves into the front trenches at dark. The enemy's Batteries across the Appomattox, northward, enfilade a portion of our line. Their fire comes upon us from several different points at once. Capt. Smith in command of the Thirteenth. Sergt. Major Hodgdon sick and sent to the Corps Hospital. We open a line of advanced rifle-pits during the night.

Hospital. The difference in the nerve of wounded men is astonishing. There are men here with fearful wounds, and who suffer real torture, but who never utter a sound because of pain, and scarce a sigh ever escapes them, even under its worst twinges. Others cry, bawl and bellow like great hurt boys — make regular asses of themselves. Two of them in an adjoining room groaned, groaned, groaned, and very loudly, a horrid duet, a large part of last night. Two other wounded men not far away, who were suffering probably as badly as they and were kept awake by them for a long time, at last actually laid a wager as to which one of these two special groaners would continue to groan for the longest time.

June 26. Sun. Hot, dusty; rain much needed. Reg. in front rifle-trenches, and firing all day. Andrew J. Smith of I happens to rise straight upright in the trenches this morning, and is instantly shot dead by the rebels. The least exposure of the figure brings half a dozen bullets over from the enemy.

A dispute having arisen about the capture of Battery Five, an investigation is made at Division Hdqrs., and it is formally decided that it was captured by the Thirteenth alone; no Union soldiers excepting members of the 13th entered the Battery at all until long after it was captured; all its garrison as prisoners and all who had taken refuge in the Battery, all its guns, ammunition and equipage, and all the swords of its officers, were surrendered into the hands of the members of the 13th, as also its two battle flags. Besides, the Battery was directly in front of the 13th and was enveloped by them in the assault to the exclusion of all other Union troops. So that gold-headed nail is not only driven in and through, but also officially clinched.

Every ten or fifteen minutes a huge shell, from one of our guns mounted near Battery Five, screams close over our heads with a sound that makes one's nerves crawl, to go hunting the enemy in and near the city — "The Petersburg Express."

June 27. Mon. Very hot. Reg. in the front rifle-trenches all day, and at 11 p. m. returns to the rear. Prisoners captured from the enemy state that the suffering from the heat in the enemy's trenches is far greater than in the Union trenches, and largely because the Confederate earth-works more generally face towards the east, the afternoon sun pouring directly into the most of the ditches in rear of them; while the high parapets of the Union works afford more protection in the way of shade to the men in the ditches in rear of them when the sun shines the hottest and the heat is most oppressive.

To the common reader the following diagram may be of advantage, as showing in a general way the order of the Confederate and Union lines now confronting each other for a stretch of twenty or thirty miles in length. The front rifle-trenches are separated from each other by a clear space from 150 to 500 yards in width; and between them are two ranges — separated by 50 to 200 feet of space — of little rifle-pits for the use of the vedettes, or 'inter-line pickets,' at night. The reserve camps and rear trenches of both armies are ranged along in several lines, one in rear of the other and but a few rods apart, extending back for a mile or more from the front main lines of rifle-trenches and forts.

Confederate side, facing south and east:

Reserve camps.                          Reserve camps.
  Rear trenches.                       Rear trenches.
Forts.              Covert ways.             Forts.
    Front rifle trenches — 'main line' — traverses and bomb-proofs.

      Small rifle-pits for C. S. A. vedettes, inter-line pickets, at night.
      Small rifle-pits for U. S. A. vedettes, inter-line pickets, at night.

   Front rifle-trenches — 'main line' — traverses and bomb-proofs.
Forts.              Covert ways.             Forts.
Rear trenches.                         Rear trenches.
Reserve camps.                      Reserve camps.
        Union side facing north and west.

June 28. Tues. Pleasant, cooler. Reg. in camp at the rear. About 1 a. m. we are suddenly called out, and at once pack ready to march; soon the order is countermanded, and we turn in again. Capt. Bradley takes with him to the Governor of New Hampshire the two Confederate battle-flags captured by the Thirteenth at Battery Five; one of them captured by Sergeant James R. Morrison, and the other by Corporal Peter Mitchell, both of K, and from Portsmouth. See official letter of June 28, 1864, in the Adjutant General's Office, Concord, N. H. These two flags are the only Confederate battle flags now, 1887, in the custody of the State of New Hampshire.

Hospital. We have here, among a generally efficient corps of officers, attendants and nurses, one fool for a surgeon, as well as one fool for a chaplain. They endanger lives and they would do well to start a cemetery in company. This surgeon leaned over Lieut. Thompson's bed, and thrusting a scalpel into his ankle, turned up the white end of a severed tendon, asking with a long, stupid drawl: "Whawt's tha-at?" His answer was a kick with the well foot — or rather a push as he crouched forward off his poise — that sent him over backwards, brains over head, and sprawling upon the floor. The dig he made at that tendon hurt like gouging out a man's two eyes at once. This is one picture of infamous inefficiency. He hurt other patients still worse, and with even less excuse, and met with still more humiliating treatment at their hands. War is bad enough in any event, but no words can depict the horrors and sorrows caused in war by ignorant and careless men, and none can realize them save those who suffer. Some of the hospital attendants and nurses were of such as had proved useless at the front, and so drifted into these rear positions, though by far the most were very fine fellows. Somehow a coward appears to be the very composite of all namable inhumanities, dishonesties and rascalities, meet him where you may.

June 29. Wed. Hot. At dark the Reg. goes again to the front, and into the rifle-trenches close down to the river. Fifteen men of the Thirteenth are sent to the General Hospital to-night, all very sick.

Capt. Charles O. Bradley resigned because of long continued ill health, his resignation was accepted to date June 10, 1864, when he was honorably discharged the service. Before leaving for his home this morning he visits the Thirteenth in the front trenches, and bids the members of it good-by. He was a very efficient officer, expert in drill, courageous in danger, fond of military life, firm and reliable in all places of trial, and remarkable not only for his presence of mind in any emergency but also for his ability to provide almost instant measures of suitable action. His memory was marvelous. The Thirteenth greatly regrets his departure, which is unavoidable, the climate here would soon kill him if he remained.

John A. Tuck, Esq., of Concord, furnishes substantially the following: "Captain Bradley was of a family furnishing a number of military men, and this fact may account in part for his taste for a military life, and his patriotic tendencies. Some of his ancestors served with Gen. Wolfe, and one was killed on the Plains of Abraham. There was one or more also with Gen. Arnold at the Siege of Quebec.

"His great-grandfather on the maternal side was a noted military man, and bore the rank of Captain. His father was a member of the old Concord Artillery until it was disbanded. Capt. Bradley was a close student of history, both ancient and modern, and when quite young was referred to as an authority by both old and young, whenever disputes arose among them as to dates or circumstances connected with the history of our own or foreign countries.

"When the recruiting office was first opened at Concord he with two others left their work at once and enlisted as three months' men; the recruiting office was opened in the morning and he and his two friends had enlisted that morning before nine o'clock — thus being one of the first, if not the first, to enlist as a soldier in the State of New Hampshire to put down the rebellion.

"After resigning his commission in the Thirteenth, he re-enlisted Sept. 17, 1864, as Captain in the First N. H. Artillery, then stationed in Washington, and was mustered out June 15, 1865. Soon after the close of the war he entered the regular army, receiving a commission as Second Lieutenant in the 11th U. S. Infantry, was promoted to First Lieutenant, and on Aug. 25, 1874, was promoted to Captain, and assigned to the 20th U. S. Infantry, which rank he held at the time of his death. He was stationed at different times in almost every fort and station on the frontier from Dakota to Texas; was long on duty at Fort Reno, Indian Territory, later removed to Fort Maginnis, in Montana, where he died May 14, 1887, from the effects of blood poisoning."

Hospital. An indignation meeting is held, and it is resolved that the fool surgeon shall be killed if he ever shows his head in our ward again. We merely mean, however, to literally scare him out. The matter spreads to adjoining wards, where similar resolutions are adopted. One officer declares that this fool surgeon needlessly hurt him worse than the bullet did, when it went through him, and he lays out his revolver to shoot the fool with when he next appears. We will scare him half to death, and so set him flying.

June 30. Thurs. Fair. Reg. in front rifle-trenches on the river bank. Mustered for pay by Col. Stevens. About 5 p. m. the enemy shells our lines severely. For three fourths of an hour his batteries average between forty and fifty discharges per minute. Only one man, however, in the 13th is hit, and he is hurt but little. The rebel fire covers a mile or two of our lines. Our works are now very secure and strong.

"Water suitable for drinking and cooking purposes has been very scarce hereabout during all the summer, and the best to be had at all of late has been obtained from a sort of spring in a swamp among some magnolia-trees. To reach this place our men have had to cross a ravine upon which the enemy's sharp-shooters have a dead range, and therefore have watched their opportunity when the firing has lulled a little, and then ran the gauntlet of the enemy's fire to the spring and return; not always in safety, for a number of casualties have occurred, some wounds severe, some slight.

"Providence came to the relief of our men to-day in a very singular manner. During the heavy firing a large rebel shell lodged in a bank on the bluff-side very near the Thirteenth, exploded and plowed a large hole in the ground, into which almost instantly poured a plentiful supply of excellent water, for the shell had struck a living spring. The shell of an old drum was placed in the ground over the opening to the vein of water, the supply of which was constant, clear and cool; and the boys are decidedly grateful to the iron monster for doing them such excellent good service." HENRY S. PAUL.

The losses in the Army of the James since May 4th have been 6,903, killed, wounded and missing; and in the Army of the Potomac, in the same period, 61,400, of which number the killed and wounded are nearly 50,000 men. Such is war! The whole Union army is tired out, and worn out, by the terribly severe duties of the last two months. The need of rest is most urgent.

The following is given in illustration of the quick native ingenuity of our old commander Gen. George W. Getty : " Early in June 1864, Gen. Getty, who had been wounded at the Wilderness, and having recovered, was about to return to his command in the Army of the Potomac — viz. : the 2d Division of the 6th Corps, then just arrived in front of Petersburg — was ordered to proceed to White House Landing at the junction of the York and Pamunkey rivers, break up the depots there and march across the Peninsula with the immense wagon trains, guarded by the few troops there, to the James River, and thence to the army in front of Petersburg. His force consisted of two one-hundred-days regiments perfectly green and undisciplined, an almost equally raw regiment of colored troops, and about seven hundred dismounted cavalrymen; mostly old soldiers, recovered from wounds, who were returning to the army.

"The second day out, the convoy was assailed by Confederate Gen. Fitz-Hugh Lee with a large force of rebel cavalry. At the first attack, the hundred-days regiments became flurried, one fired into the other, and both scattered and took to the woods. The enemy occupied the road in strong force, and the capture of the entire convoy seemed inevitable. At this juncture Gen. Getty, first handing his watch and valuables to his aide-de-camp Lieut. Murray, with directions to deliver them to his wife in case he fell, personally deployed the dismounted cavalrymen in skirmish order so as to cover the exposed front and flanks; broke up the black regiment, and placed a squad of two or three negroes with each veteran white soldier, and going along the line ordered the negro soldiers to obey the white soldier over them, and the white veteran to hold his ground and to make the negroes fight.

"Every one of these cavalrymen felt like a Brigadier General, and the blacks had no recourse except to stick by the white man, and fight as he did. Every attack of the rebel cavalry was repulsed, and after striving for several hours in vain to drive in this unique skirmish line, and get possession of the trains, Gen. Fitz-Hugh Lee at length gave up the attempt, and drew off. Gen. Getty then collected together his scattered hundred-days men, cared for his wounded, and the next morning continued his march without further molestation."

GEN. HAZARD STEVENS.

July 1. Fri. Hot, dusty. Reg. in front rifle-trenches on the river. The Band of the 2d Brig. 1st Div. 18th Army Corps, and formerly of the 13th, is now at Gen. Smith's 18th Army Corps Hdqrs. at the Charles Friend mansion on Friend's Hill. The 2d N. H. at these Hdqrs. President Lincoln has visited here, and made a long survey of the lines of the rebel army from this hill.

Hospital. A man here has been hurt by the 'wind of a ball,' and has somewhat lost the power of direction. He can walk about, but cannot pursue a direct course for any length of time; is pretty sure, after a few steps, to rush off to the right, or to the left, or to turn short around, and go back whence he came. He acts like a bird shot in the head. He guides himself along the side of the room by his cane, or trails his cane in the cracks of the floor. He is apparently as much amused by his own involuntary antics, as the rest of us are who witness them.

July 2. Sat. Very hot. Muster-rolls being finished in the rifle-trenches. Reg. returns to the rear at 10 p. m. The whole country round about us roars, morning, noon and night, with the almost unceasing battle, battle, battle.

July 3. Sun. Very hot; dust almost suffocating. Reg. goes into the front trenches after dark, and occupies a point farther to the left than before — and about half way between Battery Five, which we captured, and Petersburg — a temporary change from the right of the line.

Hospital. The wounded in our wards get no breakfast at 10 o'clock — they usually have it early — and they send a telegram to Surgeon General McClellan. He soon arrives from Fortress Monroe, having ridden at the top of his horse's speed all the way, and the case of neglect and bad management is laid before him. He calls together before us all the delinquents, and the neglect is proved. He is a thunder storm generally; now he harnesses on a hurricane and cyclone attachment, and makes the ward ring, and ring again, with denunciations and expletives — whew! But that settles it, and we have our breakfast a little before noon to-day; and thereafter enjoy a perpetual promptness on the part of the cooks, waiters, nurses, etc. Surgeon McClellan is very efficient, and is popular among all the patients in the hospital; he can be depended upon to do the right and needed thing, in all cases affecting their health and comfort.

July 4. Mon. Cloudy, cool. Reg. in the front trenches all day. Rather quiet along the lines. The Fourth of July celebrated by a National salute of 34 guns, 30 lb. Parrotts, shotted. We can hear the buildings in Petersburg crash when the shots strike them.

Hospital. Adjutant Boutwell has a very bad case of gangrene in his shoulder. Our Surgeon says that he can see Boutwell's lungs. His wife is here, and her presence and help may save his life. Lieut. Thompson's wound also exhibits symptoms of an attack of gangrene. He is flat on his back, and has not strength enough left to feed himself. Cannot lift his coffee cup with both hands. He has hired a special attendant, who comes in three times a day, and washes his ankle in a strong preparation of soda — finally cleansing the wound with spirits of turpentine at full strength. Hot is a small word to apply to fire of this kind.

July 5. Tues. Fair, warm. Reg. in front rifle-trenches. At night returns to the rear in a grove of pines, near K on map page 411, but not beyond range of the enemy's guns. "The rear camp is in a large grove of dense pines, a long way to the rear of the Appomattox line at Mr. John Hare's house, and near the river, northwest of Mr. Beasley's house." LT. COL. SMITH.

July 6. Wed. Hot, dusty; no rain has fallen for many days. Reg. removes its rear camp across a field into another body of timber.

Hospital. The wounded men here have an excellent Surgeon now; the fool surgeon has disappeared, and the fool chaplain also; the hospital steward who distributed gangrene gratis has also rejoined his regiment in the field. An officer knocked this steward flat upon the floor one day, either for carelessness or malice. He did an immense amount of mischief as a steward; frequently using the same sponge half washed on half a dozen patients, distributing gangrene and blood poison from one to another.

Practice with some huge cannon, the 'Lincoln' and 'Union' guns, on the sand between us and Fortress Monroe, shakes this building we are in very badly, and many patients are seriously injured by the jar.

Wounded rebel enlisted men here receive the same care, food and treatment which our own men receive; there is no difference. In the rebel prisons and hospitals, however, Union prisoners receive only one half or two thirds as much per man, in way of rations, as all rebel prisoners receive in Union prisons and hospitals; while the quality of rations furnished in the rebel prisons and hospitals is far inferior and the variety less. Fearful accounts are told here, of the rebel prisons and hospitals, by the sick and wounded Union officers and men who have been exchanged; and the appearance of the sufferers on arriving here furnish unqualified corroboration of their most hideous and terrible statements.

July 7. Thurs. Very hot; a slightly showery afternoon. Reg. moves at night into its front rifle-trenches on the river. This was done under fire from the enemy's batteries, which opened sharply about sunset. No one hurt.

There is a staff officer in the division who is brave but nervous. He would lead a charge upon the enemy with evident pleasure, but would dodge at a spent bullet. Aware of this nervous trait, Gen. Burnham occasionally amuses himself by slyly sending a nail buzzing past this man's head, just for the fun in seeing him dodge, and step aside to avoid the apparent danger. The General has tried this buzzing-nail experiment on a number of persons besides, and seems to find great amusement in the play, laughing heartily when a man dodges.

Hospital. There is a rebel Brigadier General here who has lost one foot. He has a special servant at Uncle Sam's expense. There are four rebel officers in the ward next to ours, all of them badly wounded. They receive the same care, rations, treatment, everything, that are furnished to the Union officers; and that, too, free, while we pay $1.00 per day for our accommodations here.

This is a long narrow building, and on each floor rooms open out of a long hall-way. This hall is exercising ground, and resounds from morning till night with the stamp, stamp, stamp, of men on crutches. The building is but a few rods from the shore of Hampton Roads, so we have a fine sea breeze for much of the time, and it is especially strong and and welcome at night.

The ward where we are is called the "Happy Family," because we are inexpressibly unhappy and make everybody else so when we are neglected, and will not submit to anything whatever which threatens our interests. We are now having a race neck and neck, with death, and do not purpose to be handicapped with any ill-treatment, on the part of nurses, cooks or any one else, and especially not from cheap surgeons.

July 8. Fri. Excessively hot. Reg. stewing and uncomfortable in the front rifle-trenches all day. 'A sky of brass, an earth of ashes, the air of a furnace,' day in and day out, and scarcely any relief at night. Rumor has it that we are to storm the enemy's works to-night, our Brigade to lead. About 5 p. m. the enemy assaults our lines held by the brigade next on our left, and a furious fight ensues. The enemy there is repulsed, and immediately after the repulse the enemy in front of our Brigade suddenly springs up behind his works and fires one volley — over our heads, of course. A new dodge.

July 9. Sat. Very hot. Reg. in the front rifle-trenches all day. During the whole time along here the enemy's sharp-shooters, pickets, artillery, and mortar-batteries have made our position at the front one of great anxiety, care, and danger; demanding the utmost vigilance. One third of the army is awake all the time, the rest sleep by their guns, ready for work at instant call. The Reg. is called into line at 2 a. m., and remains under arms for about two hours, the enemy expected to make an assault. The Thirteenth can now muster only about 150 men fit for duty, but these are equal to 500 new troops. The troops have made hundreds of holes about as large as barrels, in the banks of earth, into which they can crawl and be secure from enfilading shot and shell.

July 10. Sun. Very hot. Reg. still in the front rifle-trenches on the river, and many are led to repeat the refrain : " O — why did I go for a military man ? " Deserters state that our operations — by regular approaches — upon the enemy's lines, make life in their trenches almost unendurable. They suffer far more than we do. The Confederates are very desirous to exchange newspapers ; on our side orders are very strict against such exchanges. At night our vedettes trade and converse a great deal with the enemy's vedettes ; they stand their hostile watch in friendly attitude, and but a few yards apart.

July 11. Mon. Very hot. A little rain toward night. Reg. relieved in the evening, and returns to its camp in the rear trenches. Enemy shelling the whole camp. Capt. Forbush starts for home on 20 days' leave, going by reason of sickness in his family. We witness some splendid 11-inch mortar practice, and can see the effects of the explosion of these huge shells at points within the enemy's lines, causing a scattering among his troops, and throwing up great clouds of earth and dust in his forts and trenches.

July 12. Tues. Very hot. Reg. in the rear rifle-trenches. Quarterly returns being made up. As we are now in a dense grove, here at the rear, we are for a few hours relieved from the intense heat. It is like a furnace in the trenches at the front. The regular order for our service now is four days in the front lines and two in the rear lines.

Hospital. Lieut. Gafney has suffered exceedingly from an abscess. When it burst he was sleeping, and on waking thought that he was bleeding to death. Hickey was his attendant and a good one, and Gafney roused us all by calling, "Hickey! Hickey! Come! — For God's sake, what am I coming to?" Hickey came on the run, only to find — as all the rest of us had guessed — that Gafney had found the best kind of relief. Gafney was very low, but we all must laugh at his fright. The Surgeon tells Lieut. Thompson, this morning, that he will not be able to take a step for five months!

July 13. Wed. Cooler, with a little rain. Reg. inspected in the morning by Capt. Julian, on the staff of 2d Brigade. We have an unusually quiet day. At night the Reg. goes forward into its front rifle-trenches near the river. The rebel invasion of Maryland creates intense excitement in Gen. Grant's army here.

July 14. Thurs. Pleasant. Reg. in the front rifle-trenches. All quiet along the line here. Many of our men sick. Several of our officers sick in Hospital at City Point. To-night, Capt. Stoodley has command of our Brigade vedettes in front of the works. The rebel vedettes not thirty yards distant, and in plain sight. Men are thus sent out, during the night, between the Union and rebel armies, to insure against a surprise. These inter-line pickets or vedettes rarely disturb each other except in the case of a charge. On moonlit nights the vedettes look like two long lines of rather darkly-clad ghosts. Frequently, however, much chatting and chaffing is indulged in between the vedettes of the two armies here; all limited, however, to commonplace affairs or nonsense; no information can pass.

July 15. Fri. Fair. Reg. in the front rifle-trenches. The enemy shelled our lines furiously last night and this morning after 3 a. m. We have bomb-proofs covered with two tiers of railroad rails, and earth piled deep on top of all — quite safe. No picket firing after dark. We can plainly see the rebels in the clear moonlight to-night. A rebel detail going out on picket. each man carrying a bundle of straw to sleep on, makes an odd procession when marching in single file. Asst. Surgeon Sullivan is very sick, and goes for treatment to Hospital near Point of Rocks.

Hospital. Many of the wounded officers have been trying in vain to obtain leave to visit home. So they enter upon a concerted movement, and about three hundred apply in one list; and they have a promise of approval. Lieut. Taggard called here at Hospital on July 13th, to see Lieutenants Gafney, Thompson and Churchill. The soldier, wounded or sick, while in a Hospital enjoys a call made by a comrade more than at any other time.

**July 16. Sat.** Fair. Reg. still at the front. Hard work in these front rifle-trenches, no sleep at night worth the name, and we are burrowed in the earth like rabbits — no comfort at any time. Deep wells are being sunk for water. The surface water near the army is very bad, the river water also.

**July 17. Sun.** Very hot again. Reg. in the front trenches all day; relieved at night by men of the 3d Brigade, and returns to camp in the rear lines. A little after dark every night the vedettes of both armies go silently and without firing a shot, like long lines of shadows, over their respective works, down upon the plain between the two armies and approach to within a few feet of each other; and there sit down in little rifle-pits, or stand behind protecting trees, and watch each other until near daylight, when all assemble as silently and return. This is done in safety — but a few minutes before, or after, these movements, no person can show his head.

**July 18. Mon.** Very hot. Reg. in camp in rear trenches. Very little firing to-day. There has been no rain of consequence since July came in, and no copious rain for more than a month, and every movement of troops is accompanied by clouds and columns of dust. The huge mortars are thundering all day to-day on every hand. Special watchmen, in each little gathering of soldiers in the trenches, are set to give warning of a coming rebel mortar shell.

Hospital. We are indulging now in liberal quantities of iced lemonade prescribed at our own expense — and no 'stick' allowed in it. We also have all the fruits of the season in great abundance, inexpensive and of excellent quality. The most of us are allowed to eat almost anything we can get to eat.

**July 19. Tues.** Heavy rain all day. Commissions given out, all dated July 15th. Major Grantman promoted to Lt. Colonel. Capt. Normand Smith to Major. First Lieutenants Durell and Saunders to Captains. Second Lieutenants Sawyer and R. R. Thompson to First Lieutenants. First Sergeants Wheeler and Ferguson to Second Lieutenants. At dark the Reg. goes to the front in its old rifle-trenches — and finds them very muddy, and no chance to drain them. In the covert way, approaching the trenches, the mud is knee deep.

Maj. Gen. E. O. C. Ord is to-day assigned to the command of the 18th Army Corps, in place of Maj. Gen. W. F. Smith.

**July 20. Wed.** Clear, hot. Reg. in the front rifle-trenches, and repairing them where damaged by yesterday's rain. The enemy's sharpshooters very busy. Coehorn shells are coming over often.

The effective force of the Army of the James is about 26,000, and of the Army of the Potomac about 48,000; and of Gen. Lee's army about 48,000 according to Confederate reports. The Confederates, while behind such entrenchments as they now have, can resist a siege made by twice the number of Union troops now in front of Petersburg and Richmond. The whole situation is now that of a siege, along lines of huge earth-works twenty to thirty miles in length.

July 21. Thurs. Very warm. The 2d Brigade Band, William Critchley Jr., Leader — formerly 13th — returns to our Brigade from Gen. Smith's 18th Corps Hdqrs. Men of the 2d N. H. and of the 24th N. C. have, to-night, a long bantering confab across the Appomattox, near Mr. John Hare's house. So big words are thrown across the river, as well as big shells. The river here very narrow. Reg. in front rifle-trenches all day and night. Heavy cannonading — at us and over our heads. As one writer says, substantially : " We have a month of siege work ; lying in the trenches ; eying the rebels ; digging by moonlight ; broiling in the sun ; shooting through a knot hole ; shot at if a head is lifted ; shells passing and repassing ; lives endangered by shells from both sides ; officers falling ; comrades dying ; everybody wearied by the monotony, and exhausted by the heat and watching ; numbers growing less, but hope never dying ; constantly under the enemy's fire, whether at the front, or in the rear ; sharp-shooters, shells and mortars busy upon us everywhere ; and in return, we play it all back, and burrow under ground." Chaplain MOSES SMITH, 8th Conn., M. & C. H. Conn. 618.

July 22. Fri. Pleasant. Reg. in front rifle-trenches. Thunder of artillery is continuous, and shells are falling beyond number. The enemy shelled us this morning, between 12 and 1 a. m., most furiously, the shells at times so numerous as to baffle all counting.

Hospital. The dry, hot, clear weather of July helps the wounded men here very much. Lieut. Thompson, the writer, can now sit up ; June 14th weighed 166 pounds, to-day weighs 120 pounds only ; sleeps at night on a cot raised upon another, a quite common arrangement in the Hospital to secure increased coolness, and with his wounded foot on the broad sill of a window that looks towards Fortress Monroe and the sea. Pieces of bone are coming out of the ankle, which has furnished of late about a dozen abscesses for the Surgeon's lancet ; the first output were three abscesses at once where the leg bone was split. Still he cannot complain — his wound is not so bad as hundreds here. Lieut. Gafney has gone home.

When all is still here at night we can hear the cannon at Petersburg, distant sixty or seventy miles ; the water assisting probably in transmitting the sounds. Sometimes the discharges are so distinct we can readily count the throbs ; and we entertain ourselves in trying to learn how many separate discharges we can distinguish before the sounds mingle in a sort of dull distant reverberation.

July 23. Sat. Fine day. Reg. in the front rifle-trenches all day ; relieved at night, and returns to its camp in the rear. This rear camp again shelled by the enemy, between 12 and 1 o'clock this morning. The bursting of these large shells near by makes one feel as if his ears were 'boxed' with a pair of sledge hammers, and his head struck by a pile-driver plump on top — and all at once — and the pieces and small shot scatter with a whirr like a scared covey of partridges. A large shell clips howling and screaming, straight through Lt. Col. Coughlin's tent, in the 10th N. H., just over his head, but does no harm — except to the tent.

One of the rebel mortar-shells bursts near a large beech-tree, tearing the bark entirely off one side of the trunk and limbs, utterly blasting one half the tree, and studding the wood all up and down with many dozen small shot and pieces of shell; besides this the roots are broken and torn up on one side of the tree with the ground about them; a striking exhibition of the destructiveness of mortar shell.

Hospital. Lieut. Thompson can take about ten steps on crutches; and orders are received that he and about fifty others are to report at once at Annapolis, Md., for " light duty ! " We have a meeting, talk the matter over, and decide that our duties will be light — here or elsewhere ; and that we will not be removed from here for any duties whatever, excepting it be by force, so long as the surgeon reports us sick in hospital, and while we are in our present condition. There are not a dozen out of the fifty [1] who can lift ten pounds, or walk a rod; and suggestions and expressions here must sound much like those of a certain army in Flanders. These things may be un-military, but the necessity of saving our life and limb is now our first law — so far as we can enforce it. This ward is filled with a set of very determined men, bound to have the benefit of every advantage ' consistent with the interests of the service.' It is a question of life and death with many of them.

July 24. Sun. Cool day, and a rainy night. Reg. in the rear trenches; where the enemy shells our camp again this morning, beginning soon after midnight and continuing till about 2 a. m. This is the worst shelling we have ever experienced here. They send over every kind of shell, some of them huge. We get behind the trees and any other cover which we can find. Bomb-proofs are now necessary at the rear trenches, and are decided upon. Lt. Col. Grantman's horse is killed by a piece of shell — the only death compassed in our Brigade by all this shelling. No man of the Thirteenth is injured.

The old 2d Brigade 1st Div. 18th Army Corps — 13th and 10th N. H., 8th Conn. and 118th N. Y. regiments — which has held together and fought together through six battles — Walthall Road, Swift Creek, Kingsland Creek, Drury's Bluff, Cold Harbor and Battery Five — is to be broken up and Col. A. F. Stevens is to command a Brigade — the 1st Brig. 1st Div. 18th Army Corps.

The Corps on the Petersburg front have connected from right to left as follows : On the right the 9th Corps, Gen. Burnside, at the Appomattox, relieved the most of the time by men of our 18th Corps; next the 5th, Gen. Warren ; then the 2d, Gen. Birney (Hancock absent because of an old wound breaking out afresh); then the 6th, Gen. Wright, flanking south to protect the left wing.

July 25. Mon. Cool, a heavy rain all last night. Reg. in rear trenches. The 1st Brig. 1st Div. 18th Corps consists of the 13th N. H., 81st, 98th and 139th N. Y. regiments, Col. A. F. Stevens now commanding. The Thirteenth now in command of Major Normand Smith.

[1] After a few days we learned that a clerk made a mistake in sending in these fifty odd names — and then the clerk heard ' a few remarks.' — S. M. T.

The enemy has shelled the camp here severely for three nights, or mornings rather, in succession : 23d, 24th and 25th. Their signal is a huge 'Whitworth screamer' sent over about midnight, immediately followed by a grand shell and cannon chorus for two or three hours, all up and down the line. The main purpose, and effect, being to keep our men awake. Bomb-proofs are being built in our reserve camp ; they are a sort of cellar 10 or 20 feet long as the number of men require, 6 or 8 feet wide and 6 feet deep, roofed over with logs, a few with railroad rails for main stringers, and earth piled deep over all.

Before moving out of the rear camp to-day to take our place in the 1st Brigade, the officers of the 13th make a grand collection of unexploded shells thrown over here by the enemy. Capt. Julian seems to have the largest and most dangerous collection, numbering over forty, of all sorts and sizes. He extracts the powder from a number of these shells, pours it into an old boot, buries the boot in the ground, fires the powder, and enjoys a mine explosion after the most approved miniature style.

Maj. Gen. David B. Birney to succeed Maj. Gen. Q. A. Gilmore, in command of the 10th Corps.

July 26. Tues. Pleasant, warm. Reg. in the front rifle-trenches. Notwithstanding its honors, the Reg. regrets parting with its bluff old commander, Gen. Hiram Burnham, and with its many old and tried friends in the 2d Brigade. Nothing has been too good for the 13th, in Gen. Burnham's opinion, since they captured Battery Five.

The troops have to pass a very exposed and dangerous place while going for water to use in cooking and drinking. Two men of another regiment have been killed there by the rebel sharp-shooters. All the picket posts now consist of a corporal and three men. The vedettes are usually relieved about every hour in the night, to insure wakefulness. Camp and garrison guards stand for four hours at a time.

July 27. Wed. Pleasant, hotter. Reg. returns at dark to its rear trenches. Is very near to its old camp here, and in a position no more secure. Capt. George A. Bruce appointed Actg. Asst. Adjt. General, and Capt. George N. Julian Actg. Asst. Inspector General on Col. Stevens' staff of the 1st Brigade.

July 28. Thurs. Very hot. Reg. remains in camp in the rear trenches ; at work fitting up its new quarters. Furious shelling all night — but not on our front. We can also hear the enemy's cars running all night on the Richmond & Petersburg Railroad.

Long practice in the service brings great skill in sharp-shooting and all gunnery work, but this is counterbalanced in great part by the skill and almost intuitive carefulness gained by long experience under fire. Men know what bullets and shells can do and cannot do, know what risks to venture with them and how to avoid them; while the contrivances for protection against them are numberless, ingenious and sure. With all the skill which experience and practice gains, it may be said, with great truthfulness, that Veterans are not in half the danger of loss by death and wounds, that new and raw troops are. This accounts in large part for the fact that so many men pass unharmed through such terrific storms of rebel missiles as now break upon our lines hereabout.

Hospital. Lieut. Thompson's camp bed — an iron, folding, single-in-width contrivance — is on the shady side of the building, and he has not seen the sun or moon for more than a month. He could not move far enough, excepting in the few first days here, to get a glimpse of them. Has been for the most of that time unable to sit up in a chair — thanks to that fool surgeon, and the lazy hospital steward who peddled gangrene gratis. Moved far enough to see the sun to-day.

Every day and night death has come in among us, and removed his own to the realm of light; and the bed and the ghastly corpse of its occupant have been silently removed, to make space for another suffering soldier-candidate for the spirit land. Men within an inch of death look calmly on, without so much as a visible quiver in eye, face or nerve. Experience has accustomed us. We wake at night and hear the careful footsteps of men in stocking-feet. They approach a cot, they turn the sheet up over the face of the body that lies there, and stepping around, one at each end of the cot, they silently bear all out of the room; a soldier has passed his final muster here — died that his country might live a Nation, the grandest on earth.

### THE PETERSBURG MINE.

July 29. Fri. Very hot. Reg. remains in the rear trenches all day. Lieut. Staniels reports for duty again, though his wound has not healed and his arm is in a sling.

At 3 p. m. we receive orders to march at dark, with two days' cooked rations. At 7 p. m. the 13th is relieved, with the 18th Corps to which we belong, by the 2d Corps, and we march during the night to the rear of the 9th Corps. After marching and countermarching until long past midnight, we finally relieve the 9th Corps, at 3 o'clock Saturday morning, four miles from our camp, towards the left of the line. There is a high crest in the rear of the Confederate lines, the possession of which is desired. The 9th Corps is to charge, as the centre, our 18th Corps is to hold these front lines, in support, with orders to fire all along our line when the mine is exploded.

Lt. Col. Pleasants of the 48th Penn., a regiment of miners in Gen. Burnside's 9th Corps numbering about 400 men, proposed to run a shaft under Elliott's Salient, held by Elliott's Brigade of Gen. Johnson's Division, a fort of the enemy's, near the centre of the 9th Corps front, mounting six guns. The work was commenced June 25th, and mainly completed July 23d, the last work being done about 6 p. m. of July 27th. The shaft is, in round numbers, 5 feet high, 20 feet below the surface of the ground, and 520 feet long, with lateral branches, and having eight magazines beneath the enemy's fort, which is 140 yards from our lines.

The magazines are charged with 8,000 pounds of gunpowder. The earth has been carried out of the shaft chiefly in cracker boxes, and dumped in a neighboring ravine. While the mining was being done the 6th N. H., in the 9th Corps, occupied the trench in our lines where the shaft opened; the men were not allowed to leave the trench at all, and the officers were placed under the strictest orders not to reveal the secret. Gen. Grant has brought up about 100 heavy guns, many of them of the largest calibre, and placed them in commanding positions. The plan is to explode the mine at 3.30 a. m. to-morrow; then immediately to open with every gun along our lines, and in the midst of the confusion to assault the enemy's works.

July 30. Sat. The hottest day of the season. The Reg. is called at daylight, remains in the second line of trenches from the front, and is held with the rest of the 18th Corps as a support to the assaulting columns. The mine was to have been exploded at 3.30 a. m., and our troops were in readiness at that time, but the fuse is damp and must be renewed. The mine explodes at 4.40 a. m., and an immense and exceedingly dusty fountain of earth mingled with cannon, caissons, timber and the 300 men of the garrison, shoots up into the air to the height of 200 feet, spreads abroad there, like an enormous umbrella, into a huge cloud of dust, and in falling throws outward and leaves a 'crater' about 150 feet long, 60 feet wide, and 30 feet deep — "A vast bowl of crumbling earth." The earth jars heavily where the men of the 13th stand, less than half a mile from the crater. Instant upon the explosion our batteries open all along our lines — we can locate about sixty of the guns in full view — and for an hour there is one continual and deafening roar of artillery. After some little delay we can see a portion of the 9th Corps charging into the crater near where they capture a part of the enemy's line; but the enemy has time to rally from his surprise, and our movement miscarries. The negro troops charge, and fall back; the white troops mass together in the crater; the enemy charges upon them; he trains his cannon upon the disorganized crowd, and the crater is turned into a slaughter pen from morning until noon; by which time the most of our troops, who were engaged in the assault, are either killed, wounded or withdrawn. About 2 p. m. the enemy charges in force, captures the remainder of our unfortunate men, retakes his fort and trenches, and the affair is over. Altogether one of the most appalling sights we ever witnessed.

Until after the charge of the 9th Corps, the position of the 13th is in the second line of battle from the front — the 18th Corps being formed in two lines — and behind a little breast-work thrown up in the sand, and acting as the support of the 9th Corps, while they assault. The day is very hot, and our men can get no water. There is no shade, and the sand but reflects the burning heat of the sun. The breast-work held by the 13th is low, and dry as a heap of hot ashes. Here quite a number of men in our Brigade faint from the intense heat, and are carried to the rear. The men are weighed down by their accoutrements, army gear, and sixty rounds of ammunition per man. The enemy's shells are flying over all the time. After the repulse of the 9th Corps, the 13th is moved forward to the front part of the line, remains there until 10 a. m., and is then moved down to the front line of trenches in the support. Here no man can show his head. This forward movement brings our Reg. into the front trench, where the shaft of the mine opens. Capt Stoodley, who has been prostrated for about two hours by the heat, and several men of the 13th who have fainted, are now able to move forward with the Reg. and are all with it again before two p. m., when the enemy's troops make their counter assault.

About 5 p. m. a flag of truce is displayed from this trench, to treat concerning our men wounded in the charge; but the enemy will not allow us to help the wounded, and they are necessarily left to die, or live, as they may. One hundred and seventy bodies of our men, dead and alive, can be seen near our regimental line, and are left to lie there all day. A flag of truce moves out, and while our officers are consulting, the officers from both sides meeting midway between the lines, some of the rebels come down over their works with canteens, and give water to a few of our wounded men — then load themselves with the blankets and effects of our boys, and return to their entrenchments! It was Artemus Ward who called the Confederacy a Conthieveracy.

"Early this morning I was directed to see that certain horses were properly transferred from our Brigade, and while engaged in that duty witnessed the assembly of the 9th Corps, and its formation in the assaulting column. The opportunity was purely accidental and could have occurred to but few that morning besides myself; and this silent gathering of many thousands of men in the dim, early hours of the morning and their movements, all as steady and regular as if on drill or review, and yet for one of the most bloody assaults made in the whole war, was the most grand and impressive scene I ever witnessed. They came up and formed, regiment by regiment, with the precision of machinery. The day was excessively hot. Having little to do, I thought I would see all that I could of what was going on. Near the Brigade were quite a number of our dead, both negroes and white men. I stepped aside to look at them. They had been lying there but a few hours, but the white and black were now scarcely distinguishable in color.

"Soon after this I was looking northward toward the rebel lines near the Appomattox, when a rebel cannon was run out and fired. I had a sort of presentiment that the missiles — they used shrapnel — were coming where I was, and instinctively, or from what cause I know not, crouched or leaned forward, bending both knees considerably. Instantly the balls were flying past me on all sides; and upon looking at my clothing I found that one of the balls had cut two holes in each leg of my pantaloons just back of the knees, merely grazing my legs as it passed through. Had I remained standing upright both of my legs would have been broken, or fearfully cut. It was about the narrowest escape I ever had."

Capt. Julian.

Rev. Mr. Augustus Woodbury, in his 'Burnside and the Ninth Army Corps,' states that — "The mine exploded at precisely sixteen minutes before five a. m. The ground heaved and trembled; a terrific sound, like the noise of great thunder, burst forth; huge masses of earth, mingled with cannon, caissons, camp equipage and human bodies, were thrown up; it seemed like a mountain reversed, and enveloped in clouds of smoke, sand and dust."

The point charged upon by our troops — the crater, where stood the enemy's fort — is in a re-entering angle of the enemy's line, and directly beyond it is Cemetery Hill. The prevailing opinion is, that had the Union charge been more determined, and the deployment within the enemy's lines and about this hill — which were reached — been more prompt, the enemy's works would have been rendered untenable for a long distance both to right and left, and possibly he could have been forced out of his entrenchments altogether. But amid accidents, delays and blunders, there is "A feeble assault; a mournful slaughter — an utter, terrible failure."

Our losses are placed at not far from 5,000; the enemy's at about 1,000. Gen. Humphreys states that the mine was under a redan held by Elliott's brigade of Johnson's division, and opposite the centre of the 9th Corps. The explosion overwhelmed the whole of the 18th and a part of the 23d South Carolina infantry regiments, and the battery in the redan. On our side about 80 heavy guns, and as many field guns opened at once. Our losses he puts at 3,500 to 4,000. The losses in Elliott's Confederate brigade were 677.

July 31. Sun. Very hot. Reg. in the front rifle-trenches, where the shaft opens, all day; and about 500 feet distant from the crater of the mine explosion. A flag of truce is run up to treat for burying the dead; the enemy very slow to answer. The lines quiet to-day. To-night the Reg. is relieved here by the 6th N. H., and returns with our Brigade to its old camp in the rear lines, on the right by the Appomattox; arriving there about 11 p. m. well used up.

The point occupied by the Thirteenth in these two days is in the front trench of the Union works — those nearest to the crater. The 9th Corps farther to the rear in support to-day. When we leave to-night the Union dead and many of the wounded lay on the field of yesterday morning's assault and about the crater, and between the lines of the 13th and the rebel works. The Confederates were seen also to give the wounded negroes water to drink — and then to carry away their blankets and clothes. For a proud Confederate to wear the clothing of dead negroes, is at least peculiar. Lieut. Staniels returns to the front, and visits the 13th, finding it in front of the 9th Corps. His wound is not healed, and he returns to the field hospital again at night.

Aug. 1. Mon. Very hot. Reg. in rear trenches resting — "If men can rest in such weather." Reg. inspected by Capt. Julian. At 10 a. m. under a flag of truce our wounded, who have lain on the battle-field of the Mine explosion uncared for since the morning of the explosion, day before yesterday — over 48 hours — are removed. Out of about 400 only twelve are found alive. The fact is the enemy has removed as prisoners nearly all, excepting those fatally wounded and not likely to recover. The Reg. is now located very near the Appomattox river bank.

Aug. 2. Tues. Hot. Reg. in rear trenches all day. At night resumes its old place in the front rifle-trenches, the right resting on the river. " Expect to be blown up before morning," writes one man of the Thirteenth. The failure of the mine explosion makes a great stir. Everybody is blamed in general, and the Division commanders in particular — " They had better gone in ! "

Aug. 3. Wed. Very hot. Reg. in the front rifle-trenches. Quiet. Deep, large wells have been sunk to obtain water for cooking and drinking. One day a horse accidentally fell into one of these wells, and remained a long time in the water, thrashing about, and otherwise doing after the manner of horses. One of the men came there for water to use for cooking purposes, and seeing the horse at the bottom of the well, merely remarked : " Why — I did n't know that this was a watering-place for horses ; " drew up his pailful of water and went his way, as if nothing in particular had occurred.

Hospital. Many prisoners are sent here from Libby, and it is said that a wounded rebel is occasionally smuggled through with them — of course receiving better treatment here than he could get at home. Some of the cases — of Union men — received here from the rebel prisons present a terrible condition. There is such a case now in the next ward. He is undergoing an operation for the extraction of maggots from a deep wound in his thigh. They have to be scooped out of their comfortable domicile with a spoon-shaped instrument. Nothing that he could possibly bear would kill them, and they must be removed mechanically. He is very low, but will probably recover. He maintains the theory that the maggots saved his life, by neutralizing poisonous matter which his system was not in a condition to expel. Tough theory — tougher practice ! After this when a man complained that his wound was killing him, some cruel wag would suggest, as a remedy, " Put in some maggots — to neutralize the poison."

Aug. 4. Thurs. Very hot and dry. Reg. in front rifle-trenches all day, relieved at night, and moves a short distance to the rear and encamps in a ravine close up to our second line of works. We have shelter tents on poles, and open at the end. Considerable rebel shelling — no one of the 13th is hurt. This reserve camp is much nearer the front lines, and more exposed than the old reserve camp in the pine grove ; we are to occupy this position for quite a period, alternating with the position in the front rifle-trenches, and hence call it our ' Ravine ' camp.

Aug. 5. Fri. Very hot. Reg. fitting up its quarters in the Ravine camp near the second line of works, and five minutes' walk from the front line of the Union works near the river. About 5 p. m. the enemy explodes a 'mine,' a quarter of a mile from the Thirteenth, towards the left. It is a sorry piece of engineering, not being under any work at all, but several rods in front of our works and in an open field — a most ridiculous farce. The enemy follows up his 'explosion' by a demonstration on our lines, but makes no assault. A brisk cannonade ensues. The Thirteenth immediately falls in, and marches to the front; when all is quiet marches back again — not engaged. The affair is not of much consequence, but this matter of mining adds, to the discomforts which the men are already enduring, the imaginary and dreaded horror of being blown to the sky or buried alive. Our camp is now in a depression or ravine in the side of a gravelly knoll, and we have no shade whatever excepting that of our shelter tents. These are stretched on poles, tacked to stakes driven into the ground, drawn over the trench as awnings and set up in every way that ingenuity can devise, to afford a bit of shade into which the men can get, down upon the sand of the trenches, and avoid a literal baking alive in the fierce sunshine.

Aug. 6. Sat. Very hot. This unceasing hot, burning, dry weather makes our army inexpressibly uncomfortable and miserable. Sunstrokes are a matter of every day occurrence among us. The Reg. remains in its Ravine camp during the day, and at night returns to its front rifle-trenches. It is reported that the rebels can be heard mining underneath the front rifle-trenches where we are. Rather a nervous bit of news; but doubted so much that no one appears disturbed by it.

Aug. 7. Sun. Very hot. Reg. in the front rifle-trenches. A flag of truce run up by the enemy's pickets, who want to exchange newspapers — refused. Lieut. Murray goes home, with Gen. Burnham, on 20 days' leave.

Aug. 8. Mon. Very hot. Reg. remains in the front rifle-trenches during the day, and at night returns to the old reserve camp about one mile from the front. There are four principal Union lines of defenses, and camps, along this part of the works abutting on the river. First, the extreme front line, running south from the river across Mr. John Hare's field a little west of his house. Second, in the first ravine east of his house, less than one quarter of a mile from the front — where our Ravine camp is located. Third, in a ravine about one mile from the front, where we are to-night. Fourth, about one and one half miles from the front, a complicated system of earth-works, trenches, rifle-pits and bomb-proofs, in a grove of heavy pine timber.

Hospital. One Abbott, having casually looked in upon these gilded sepulchres of the living dead, writes an article of fulsome flattery for a Northern publication; and we write him a letter, and send him our compliments, inviting him to shoulder his gun, like a true patriot, go to the front, get one or two bullets through him — then come here and take an inside view for himself experimentally. The Hospital does well — Abbott does too well.

Aug. 9. Tues. Exceedingly hot. Reg. moves into the Ravine

camp, nearest to the front line ; and at night 113 men from the Reg. go to work on a new fort just in the rear of our Brigade trenches. The whole force of shovelers is 600 men. During the afternoon, a heavy duel is fought, with large mortars, off toward the right. Two ammunition boats are blown up at City Point, the result of an accident. The explosion is heard, and the jar felt, in our lines, at the front. It destroyed several vessels, and buildings, and killed and wounded a large number of men. Lt. Col. Grantman goes home sick. Has a 20 days' leave. Major Smith in command of Thirteenth.

Aug. 10. Wed. Very hot and dusty. Reg. improves Ravine camp ; at night goes into the front rifle-trenches, and relieves the 81st N. Y. The Union vedettes, sent out between the lines at night, cannot go out farther than 150 feet ; the rebel vedettes come out about the same distance from their front trenches. The Union vedettes are ordered, if attacked, to fire as rapidly as possible, and then to lie down, even at the risk of being captured, and not to attempt to return to our lines. This plan gives a clear field for our lines in front to use their rifles and cannon, and avoids the danger of these vedettes being shot by our own men. Last night a large force of our troops were massed in our rear, the enemy expected to attack us.

From the Hospital Dept. of the Thirteenth : "July 8th. The 13th has four days of service in the front rifle-trenches and two out, alternately ; always going in after dark. The majority of our men who are hit are shot through the head ; along the line of our Division the casualties average fifteen or twenty a day. The mortars on both sides make great havoc and are a terror. I have seen men almost completely torn to pieces by them. When our Parrott shells strike Petersburg, we can hear the bricks crash, we are so near the city. One of our guns — 'The Petersburg Express,' a 100 lb. Parrott — sends a shell into Petersburg every fifteen minutes. The shells from that gun go directly over the Thirteenth's rifle-trenches. Last Sunday night, July 3d, I was in the front rifle-trenches. It was dark. I had just got up to go into another rifle-pit, when a blinding flash rushed past my eyes, and a fierce scream rang in my ears. Then something hit me, with a sharp rap on my leg, bringing me to my knees. Capt. Goss picked me up. No blood could be found. The skirt of my coat was torn badly in several places. I was hit by the lead ring from the shell of 'The Petersburg Express.' [1] My whole thigh was black and blue for a long time afterwards, and I was very lame, but luckily I received no permanent injury.

"There is no Hospital now with the Thirteenth — it is impossible to have one in or near the front rifle-trenches. If a man is sick or wounded he is taken to the Field Hospital about one mile to the rear ; and from

---

[1] The lead ring is used around the base of an iron or steel shell. fired from rifle-cannon, to fit the grooves in the bore, and is thrown off with great force during the early flight of the shell. Many men in Gen. Getty's Division were killed and wounded by these lead rings at Fredericksburg during the day of Dec. 13, 1862. — S. M. T.

there, if in bad condition, he is sent to the base Hospital, at City Point. A Surgeon's call is held once a day in the front rifle-trenches, a Surgeon and Hospital Steward being required to be present. The rebel trenches are but a few rods in front of ours, and they and our boys at once fire when a hat is seen moving about in the opponents' trenches. It is sure death on either side for a man to show his head above the works, which are pierced with numerous small holes to watch and shoot through.

"I was sent for duty in the Commissary Dept. at the Field Hospital by Surgeon Richardson, but do not like the change; would prefer to be with the Regiment. This Hospital is about one mile in rear of the Thirteenth's trenches, in a prominent rebel's house, standing close beside the City Point Railroad. Our troops have here a 13-inch mortar, called the 'Dictator,' mounted on a platform car in a little ravine near this house. To load they pour into the mortar twenty pounds of powder, loose. Then the hollow ball of iron — the sides of it two inches thick — is filled with seven pounds of powder and five hundred and twelve one-ounce rifle balls. The fuse of the shell is then driven in and sawed off at the proper length. The whole weight of the shell when charged is 235 pounds. Four men are required to lift it into the mortar. A fuse is placed in the vent of the mortar, lighted and the men step back. When fired the shell can be seen for quite a long time in its curving up and on through the air; the air resists the sharp rending and shrieks fearfully. Sometimes scrap iron, nails, stones, etc., are put into the shell with the bullets.

"Wednesday, July 20th, a shell from that mortar struck fairly within the rebel fort 'Archer,' making a huge cloud of dust and blowing one angle of the fort away. The rebels say they can stand ordinary shelling, but when we go to throwing at them whole blacksmith's shops, anvils, tools, bellows and all, it is rather too much.

"A terrible disaster occurred at City Point Tuesday. Aug. 9th — a barge loaded with ammunition was blown up. More than 200 persons were killed and wounded. The ground about the wharf and for a long distance back was covered with the débris; which with shells, balls, timbers and mutilated human bodies had been thrown high into the air and falling had scattered far and near. I was there at the time of the explosion. Had gone down to the wharf for ice, in charge of six army wagons and a detail of a Sergeant and ten men. The ice was in a schooner lying at the wharf, and was a gift of the Sanitary Commission to the soldiers in the trenches. I narrowly escaped with my life. My own horse was lost, and several of my men were severely injured. I succeeded, however, in securing several wagon loads of ice, which was delivered at the Field Hospital.

"An old Surgeon here, who has lived in South America, says he never suffered more, from the heat, than he has here during this summer. I went on duty at the Field Hospital on July 4th, and returned to the Thirteenth on Aug. 29th, meanwhile frequently visiting the Regiment."

PRESCOTT.

**Aug. 11. Thurs.** Very hot. Reg. in the front rifle-trenches day and night. Four deserters from the enemy come into our lines. Heavy artillery engagement to-day.

The army salt-beef is anything but appetizing in this fearful heat. The boys call it salt-horse because they say that iron horse shoes and mule shoes have been found in the barrels, with the meat, but never an ox shoe. The salt-beef is generally a fair article.

Hospital. A poor fellow, a Lieutenant, appears in the Hospital temporarily crazed. He was, it is said, a member of Col. Pleasant's 48th Penn., and went into the mine on the morning of July 30th to repair or renew the fuse, just before the explosion. He mistook the sound of some earth falling near him for the explosion, and thought that he was cut off from escape in the shaft and buried alive. The shock unsettled his mind. He walks about the Hospital, wringing his hands in abject fear, and repeating, in a sad, low, frightened, sing-song tone, over, and over, and over again, by the half hour : " Mammy, will the dog bite ? — No, child, no." He will exhibit his usual intelligence for a few moments at a time, and begin a story or statement, breaking off suddenly in the midst of it, and sometimes in the middle of a word, with his regular refrain, mixing things most ridiculously and laughably. He is expected to recover.

**Aug. 12. Fri.** Very hot. Reg. in the front rifle-trenches. A furious artillery duel this morning at 4 a. m. Several men wounded in our Brigade. At night the Reg. is relieved by the 81st N. Y., and goes back to its Ravine camp. Surgeon Richardson's Corps Hospital is an immense spread of canvas, covering two acres or more.

**Aug. 13. Sat.** Very hot. Reg. in Ravine camp, and building bomb-proofs. During our stay here on the Petersburg front, whether in the front rifle-trenches, or in the reserve camps, we, together with the whole force along our lines, are divided in two grand reliefs ; one relief keeping awake and under arms until midnight of every night, then turning in, while the other relief is called up, and kept awake and under arms until the morning. Tremendous shelling to-day ; in the afternoon a regular, incessant roar of artillery.

The troops have access to an excellent spring of water near by, just around the hill, but two or three rods of the path to it are covered by the enemy's sharp-shooters. On some days they molest the water carriers, occasionally shooting one of them, and on other days watch them sharply without firing a shot. The Confederate soldiers appear capricious. Our men go for water and return about as unconcernedly as they would go to the spring or well on the old farm at home.

**Aug. 14. Sun.** Extremely hot. Since July 26th the thermometer has often indicated during the days from 100° to 105° in the shade, and the most of the nights have been but a little cooler. Reg. in Ravine camp — second line from the front ; at 7 a. m. goes into the front rifle-trenches. At inspection, this morning, several men fall out of the ranks, overcome by the terrible heat. The air is a double concentration of all the vile stinks, and of all the unutterable rot, that a camp at the front can possibly be heir to, besides dead men and dead horses not far away.

We have two days at the front, alternating with two days at the rear. Reg. in bad shape for service. Only ten line officers present for duty. Company B has only its Captain and four men present. As many men are detailed for orderlies, clerks, teamsters, special guards, pioneers, sharp-shooters, etc., as are present for duty. An afternoon shower cools the air a little.

Hospital. Gen. Butler's light-duty order, of a month or so ago, not having been enforced, Surgeon Gen. McClellan, a brother of Gen. McClellan it is said, now and sensibly deems it imprudent for the wounded, who are doing pretty well, to remain here while such extremely bad cases are coming in from the rebel prisons; and therefore a large party of us are transferred to-day to Annapolis, Md. We are to travel as we please, and twenty or more of us decide to visit Baltimore for a day or two, and then go down to Annapolis.

One of the party, now rapidly recovering, has had a most singular wound. A minie bullet entered his right eye, and came out at his right ear, demolishing both; and, as it were, "knocked them all out of sight and hearing," as he facetiously describes the affair. He is a merry fellow, and undoubtedly will survive. Among wounded soldiers the rule holds good, almost without exception, that the hopeful and the cheerful men recover, while the man who gives up dies.

Aug. 15. Mon. Warm. Reg. in the front rifle-trenches just west of Mr. John Hare's house, on the river bank. The heavy rain of last night, and a sudden, severe shower to-day, causes much damage to the trenches, flooding the lower parts of them, and several men are drowned in the trenches near us. The lines we occupy are so situated as to be incapable of proper drainage, and nothing at all can be done to them until after dark, and our men are standing in water up to their middle. The water is three feet deep in several places in the trenches now occupied by the 13th. Some of the covert ways are half full of water. A new sutler appears to-day; sutler Holmes has not been with the Reg. since we left Camp Gilmore last April.

Every evening nowadays there is an artillery duel. The huge shells appear like balls of fire flying over our heads in every direction and over the lines as far as one can see, all up and down the two armies — a splendid sight. The most of the shells, which we of the 13th receive, come from the rebel batteries to the northward across the Appomattox. The 9th Corps, next on our left, are and always have been the noisiest on our lines, banging and pounding away almost incessantly.

The men of the 10th N. H. in their trench are standing in mud and water up to their arm-pits, holding their haversacks and cartridge-boxes up over their heads — " in the position of a soldier."

Hospital. The party bound for Annapolis via Baltimore, go up on a small steamer. Lieut. Thompson can walk on crutches for about five minutes, then collapses. Last night, while attempting to go on shore at Baltimore, his crutches slipped, and he fell on the steamer's deck. Attempting to use the lame foot — which had no strength in it — he sat down upon it very heavily. The broken pieces of bone severed an artery, and he would soon have bled to death but for the prompt action of a young surgeon who chanced to be on board the steamer. The artery cannot be tied and a tourniquet is fitted on. A carriage is sent for, and he is taken to the Eutaw House.

This party of twenty or thirty officers makes up a procession almost laughable. Arms in slings, heads in bandages, legs bundled up, feet in white wrappings, crutches stamping, attendants supporting, stretchers here and there, one express wagon packed full; all the officers chatting, joking, laughing and merry as a class of school boys just out for a vacation. The wounded man, as a general thing, is bound to be jolly if he can.

Aug. 16. Tues. Cool, rainy. Reg. in the front rifle-trenches, and repairing them where damaged by the rains. The water cannot be gotten out of the trenches, and the men are in mud and water all the time. No relief to-night. The plan has been for the Reg. to be in the front rifle-trenches two days and then have two days at the rear — that is on two and off two — but now we are on duty in the front rifle-trenches right along day after day and night after night without relief. Heavy shower at 3 p. m. Water three feet deep in the Thirteenth's trenches, and the banks of them caving in; a terrible night, no rest, and the rising water causes the men to expose themselves greatly to the rebel fire. The tents are useless, the roof of our house is the sky, the moon and all the stars are mere holes for the water to run through upon us, there's a rebel shell coming with every gallon, and ten rebel bullets with every pint; the head of our bed is a sand bank, the foot a hole in the ground, the mattress is of mud stuffed with gravel stones, the pillows are a mortar trough, the coverings are sheets of water — we are right in the swim!

Aug. 17. Wed. Cooler, rainy. Reg. in the front rifle-trenches. Every one soaking wet. Rebel batteries shell our lines from 1.30 a. m. until morning, and their sharp-shooters are very busy after daylight. A shell bursts in the soft mud near three men of the Thirteenth, deluges two and literally buries the third; he is hauled out of the mortar blowing, 'spluttering,' and saying several things much nastier than himself. Scene for laughter, and that is all. Hundreds of the situations are most ridiculous. The 18th and 9th Corps on this front; the 2d and 5th Corps are north of the James.

Hospital. Lieut. Thompson at U. S. General Hospital, Naval Buildings, Annapolis, Md. About 20 officers with him in the same ward, containing thirty beds. Surgeons Vanderkieft and Sweet decide that his foot must be amputated. The patient replies: "No, the foot must be saved; else the whole body must go into the same box, all in one piece."

While he was at the Eutaw House the proprietor furnished him an attendant free, deducted one half of his bill upon settlement, sent him to the steamer in a hack and sent two men to carry him aboard, also free. This was commendable generosity, and altogether unsought.

Aug. 18. Thurs. Showery. Thirteenth in the front rifle-trenches, and in the water and mud as usual. Muddier men were never seen, and we cannot show our heads above the works without instantly receiving from one to a dozen rebel bullets. An old felt hat raised on a stick and moved a little — to make it appear as if it contains a head — is perforated with three rebel bullets instanter. The enemy opened his batteries about 10 o'clock last night, and shelled our trenches severely for nearly three hours. A terrific noise, and the crack of multitudes of shells is the result. No one hurt in the Thirteenth.

Assistant Surgeon John Sullivan resigns his commission — much against his inclination, as he would prefer to remain with the Regiment — and is honorably discharged the service. While our Surgeon Richardson has had charge of the 18th Corps Hospital, Assistant Surgeon Sullivan has been doing all the duties of a Surgeon at the front for almost a year.

The severe duties, cares and the climate are surely killing him. He has been granted a leave of absence and sent home from the army twice, under the order that restricted leaves of absence to causes where absence from the front was deemed necessary to save life.

He has always been very efficient and very popular in the Thirteenth, and his place cannot be filled again as well easily, if indeed at all. His great sympathy for, and unwearying, kindly care of such men as really suffer, and his quick and almost intuitive detection of shamming, are decidedly desirable qualities in an army Surgeon. We shake his hand at parting here, with a most unwilling good-by.

John Sullivan, our Asst. Surgeon, recently resigned, was of Exeter, N. H., and the great-grandson of Major General the Hon. John Sullivan, LL. D., of the Continental Army, in the Revolution. He first enlisted as a private in the 2d N. H. Vols., and served in that regiment in the first Battle of Bull Run, July 21, 1861. After the retreat from that battlefield to Centreville, he assisted in performing the first capital operation of the war upon a New Hampshire soldier. The patient was Sergt. Isaac W. Derby of Company A, 2d N. H. V. severely wounded in the arm. No anæsthetics were used. Derby consenting, he was held down by a fence rail, and the arm was cut off. The operation was performed at night, and the only light was afforded by a tallow candle and a brush fire. Derby fought it through manfully, never entered the Hospital at all, and after a few days was attending to such duties as a one-armed man could do about the camp. Sergt. Derby has stated to the writer that: "having one's flesh cut is a small matter, but to have one's bones sawed in pieces is a very serious business." See N. H. Adjt. General's Report for 1866, Vol. ii. page 427.

While serving as a private in the 2d N. H. V., Sullivan was examined in the Surgeon General's office in Washington, and received the appointment of Medical Cadet U. S. A.; in which capacity he served in the army Hospitals in Missouri and Kentucky from September 1861, until October 1862, when he joined the Thirteenth. Here he has served under commission as Assistant Surgeon for nearly two years, but more than half the time as Acting Surgeon. About three weeks after his resignation his services were needed in the U. S. General Hospital at Troy, New York, where he was tendered and received the appointment of Executive Officer. That Hospital contained twelve hundred beds, and was in charge of George H. Hubbard, Surgeon U. S. Vols., who entered the service as Surgeon of the 2d N. H. Regiment.

Aug. 19. Fri. Showery all day. Thirteenth in the front rifle-trenches. Much shelling and picket firing. The only way to dodge the enemy's mortar-shells — which the boys call ' mortal-shells,' as they drop into the trenches and explode — is to rush behind the traverses. The only casualty in the 13th, though many of the enemy's shells have exploded in our lines, is the wounding of Corporal Augustus Boodry of G. His is a very peculiar wound and extremely painful. A piece of shell, $1\frac{1}{2}$ inches long, $1\frac{1}{4}$ inches wide, is driven through his leg below his knee, and between the bones, instantly widening the space between the bones, and tearing the tissues for several inches.

Hospital. A man now here has had a minie bullet driven straight through his head — going in near the right eye and coming out below the right ear. He is doing well. He says he neither saw nor felt anything unusual when the bullet struck him, all was done and over so quickly. The first thing he felt was the blood running down his face and neck, the parts near the wound having been benumbed by the stroke of the bullet.

This is the second case the writer has seen of wounds very similar — a bullet entering the eye or near it.

Aug. 20. Sat. Cool, cloudy. Reg. in the front rifle-trenches by the river bank. The enemy commenced his usual shelling again this morning at one o'clock. We have to lie low in the mud and water, and have not been dry for a week. The Union artillery just in rear of our line opens fire with a terrific din, and keeps it up for half an hour or so, over our heads, and everywhere. A brigade, with the 10th N. H., moves about a mile to the left of our Division, and near the lines opposite the rebel ' Hare House ' Battery.

There are many hours when the men and officers have literally nothing to do, but to ' while away ' the time as best they may. They take old musket barrels, enlarge the vents, load them heavily with powder from some unexploded shell, put in one or two bullets, set the battery up in the sand, and fire it — the bullets falling a third or half a mile away within the enemy's line. Possibly the enemy employs a similar means, for one of the men of our Brigade was killed while sitting with his back leaning against the inside of our earth-works, a bullet penetrating the top of his head in such manner as if it had fallen straight down out of the sky. Our men play with still another ' battery ' where the lines are very close together. A stout stick with a small stone on one end is balanced upon a log, the opposite end of the stick is struck a heavy blow with an axe, and the stone goes far over towards the enemy's line — and sometimes it is claimed that a particularly lucky blow will send a stone within them. A reproduction, for amusement, of a very ancient device.

The following extract from a letter describes one situation of the Thirteenth in the Petersburg trenches :

"In the Trenches near Petersburg, Va.
August 20, 1864.

"We have been in the front trenches here for a week, and are having a hard time of it. It has rained every day. The water is two and a half feet deep in the trenches where the men of the Thirteenth have to stand and wade. About one mile from us the men are in water up to their armpits. It literally floods the trenches. If a man rises up so as to be out of the water, a rebel bullet is sure to be after his head. I have not had my clothing dry for a week, night or day, and am covered with mud from head to foot. The men are still worse off than the officers. The rebels open with artillery between 12 and 1 a. m., and continue shelling for about two hours, and as a matter of course we can get no sleep. We have to lie in the trenches at night, and have no covering except a rubber blanket to shield us from the weather. All the troops that can be spared have now gone to the left, where the 2d and 5th Corps are operating. Rough work this; I feel almost worn out. To be wet, go without sleep, and feel in danger all the time — for there is constant danger of being shot — is anything but pleasant; but I get along so much better than the most of the enlisted men I feel quite satisfied with my lot. If anything will make a soldier think of home, wife and children, this kind of life will do it."
LIEUT. R. R. THOMPSON.

Aug. 21. Sun. Showery. Reg. still in the front rifle-trenches; the right Company, G, in the trench nearest the river, and practically about twelve feet under ground. The enemy shells us as usual, opening to-day, however, at about one o'clock in the morning, and continuing until after five o'clock — over four hours of racket, boom and crash. A soldier of the 13th writes: "It has rained water for a week, and shells for four nights, all along the lines; the rain and the shells do about an equal amount of damage. The boys say of the enemy's large elongated shells : 'Look out ! There comes another pork-barrel with the bung pulled out.' "

About 11 a. m., all along the lines here in our immediate vicinity, our troops in the front trenches — some 3,000 men — commence firing as rapidly as possible. The enemy replies, and soon the discharges of musketry blend in a continuous roar. Pretty soon also the artillery on both sides joins in the fray, and the noise becomes tremendous, continuing for an hour or two in all. During the affair eighty men of the 13th have fired over 4,000 rounds of ball-cartridge — about 50 rounds per man. At the same average the 3,000 men must have fired above 150,000 bullets at the enemy's lines. It is wonderful how very few men are struck amidst the shower of flying lead and iron. This demonstration appears to be made by the Union troops here for the purpose of covering sundry movements on the Union left, to which point a large force has been dispatched from our vicinity, and whose firing we can hear as our own fire slackens. The enemy here replies, scarcely knowing why. Supposing that a general engagement threatens, our camp-followers stampede pell-mell for the rear. They are a spry and amusing people. In a mortar-battery, directly in our rear, a 13-inch mortar is playing upon the enemy; the huge shells rounding high in air through an immense curve above our heads, hissing in a rapidly repeated warning sound: " Ketch you — ketch you," as they go.

"The musketry firing going on about two miles to our left sounds like heavy wagons driven rapidly over very stony ground. The artillery firing sounds like huge bass drums beaten very fast, but without regard to time. After a while the firing settles down to a slow, continuous rumbling and throbbing all along the line." CHARLES W. WASHBURN, Band.

Aug. 22. Mon. Cool — a few showers. Reg. in front rifle-trenches. Enemy gave us no shells this morning. We have been all day momentarily expecting him to assault our lines — but all remains quiet now at 9 p. m.

Hospital. A Major is here from Michigan, who is in a sad state of mind and body. His horse's backbone was cut in two just back of the saddle, on which the Major was sitting at the time, by a large piece of shell which struck upwards from the ground. The Major was not even bruised, but the jar caused a partial paralysis of his spine — and nearly jerked his head off. He is gaining, but very slowly.

Aug. 23. Tues. Fair. Reg. in front rifle-trenches. The enemy fired a few shells this morning, and wounded several men in the 2d N. H. Twenty men of the 2d N. H. are mustered out of the service — a capital time to emigrate from this corner of Tophet. New Hampshire is a good State to emigrate to, just now. The whole Reg. were turned out last night, cooks, clerks, sick and all, and manned the trenches to meet an attack, but the enemy did not appear.

Hospital. The wounded are having the gangrene cut out of their wounds with a 'caustic preparation of iron,' as it is called, and it burns like an iron red hot. One man near by, mad with pain, lost his nerve and actually yelled for half an hour like a teething baby. The Naval band was playing at the same time out of doors, and his yells spoiled the music for the rest of the patients — in fact he overdid it, and in a measure lost sympathy. Possibly thousands have suffered more and not even sighed, for his was not an unusually bad case.

Aug. 24. Wed. Fair, very warm. Reg. in the front rifle-trenches, which are nearly dry now, but we cannot show our heads above them. We are all day, and all night, and all the time, at the mercy of the enemy's front, reverse, and enfilading fire from his river batteries — and how it is that we escape being blown into inch pieces is past our comprehension. Every man in the Reg. seems to have a 'charmed life.' We are in one incessant battle, long and constant, with the men under fire and at close range more than half the time. However, a man is a small thing on an acre of ground, and the swift hare is a hard shot. To-night the enemy is massing on our front, and our line here is very weak. Every available man is at work refitting the trenches, where they have been damaged by the rains; and every man who can lift a musket is ordered into the front rifle-trenches.

Aug. 25. Thurs. Warm, fair, rain at night. Reg. in front rifle-trenches. A great deal of anxiety, enemy expected to attack here. Orders come for us to be ready to move at a moment's notice. Every man at his post. No move to-day. The infernal hubbub prevents. We do not know what is coming next. Now it is proper to call us "Northern Mudsills." We have been in the mud here until we are embedded and fixed. This morning we got all ready to move out of the trenches for a rest, and the teams at camp were loaded with our baggage; then came an order for us to remain, and prepare for action, an attack threatened; and here we are to-night, every man in the trenches, headquarters' guard, cooks, sick and all. We would prefer a fight to this sort of life.

Hospital. Two Brass bands every fair day furnish an abundance of stirring and excellent music. Peaches, berries, melons, tomatoes, and all the fruits of orchard, field and garden abound, and can be had for a trifle, and we live as never before while members of the army.

Lieut. Thompson, much prostrated by a bad turn taken by the wound in his ankle owing to his fall upon it, has lived chiefly on peaches for the past ten days. As he is unable to do much toward feeding himself, he and three others here, all in as bad, or a worse plight, are fed, almost as children are, at every meal, by Miss R. S. Gove, of Elmira, New York, an elegant lady. God bless the women who went down to the army Hospitals as nurses for the suffering soldiers!

Aug. 26. Fri. Foggy and hot. The whole 9th Corps moves out before 9 a. m., and marches to Point of Rocks. Reg. as usual, in the front rifle-trenches.

"Rained water and rebel shells all last night; no sleep, no breakfast — cooks all put for the rear — and the Johnnies shelling us like fury all the morning." SERGT. MAJOR HODGDON.

The Thirteenth has had a hard measure of service here in these front rifle-trenches that run across Mr. John Hare's field; constantly under the enemy's musketry and artillery fire ever since the morning of August 14th — thirteen days and twelve nights — and in very bad weather, generally hot or rainy, wet and steamy, and much of the time we have been half buried in mud and water. And now comes a job that caps the climax of all our misery's worst abominations — an all night march. At 10 p. m. the Reg. is relieved from duty in these front rifle-trenches by troops from the 10th Corps, with which the 18th Corps is to exchange positions; and with our Brigade we march to the rear, and on, and on, in the rain and deep mud, stumbling and groping along anywhere and anyhow, in a darkness where nothing can be seen; tired, drenched, weighed down with guns, equipments, clothing, blankets, tents, they wet and therefore extra heavy, and we bedraggled, chafed, foot-sore, ugly — and finally at 3.30 a. m., arrive within Gen. Butler's fortifications, north of the Appomattox, on the Bermuda Hundred lines, and bivouac near our old camp-ground.

There is no one now hereabout who sings the song, "Tenting on the Old Camp-Ground." That song is especially dedicated to the brave and stalwart home-stayers; while they do furious battle with the ferocious minnow, the deadly trout, the blood-thirsty angle-worm and the awe-inspiring bull-frog, along the bold and dangerous shores of New England summer mill-ponds and meadow brooks. For real soldiers all the color such songs ever had is just now washed out with an ocean of mud and water.

This night march is a fit ending of our "Petersburg Front" experiences, from June 21st to date — 67 days — all the time under fire; our rear camp shelled as furiously as the front, and often more dangerously. For nearly two months we were scarce a day out of the range of the enemy's musketry fire. Still the soldier at the front indulges in many a merry hour, though the big guns may rattle as they will.

### BERMUDA HUNDRED.

Aug. 27. Sat. Fair, warm. We lie down here about four o'clock this morning, and rest an hour or two, when the enemy's batteries open on our lines near by, our batteries reply, and the old play of the Appomattox river bank, in Mr. John Hare's field, is played over again here at Bermuda Hundred. Lieut. Taggard returns to the Reg. late to-night from the Hospital, his wound nearly healed.

The Reg. remains at its place of bivouac until dark, when we move towards the left and occupy an exposed, salient position about midway between the James and Appomattox rivers; our camp is called "Butler's Front above Point of Rocks."

There is one custom in the army that does no little mischief. A is detailed for a bit of hazardous work. He goes to B and hires him to 'volunteer' for this special service. B volunteers to take A's place, is accepted, and A escapes all the danger. The pay for such 'volunteering' substitution among the men is anywhere from fifty cents to five dollars and more. One of these men, with more money than courage, asked a comrade thus to take his place. The comrade felt insulted and replied: "Go in yourself; the sooner rich cowards like you get shot the better." Then turned on his heel with the remark: "Money goes with an awful mean streak." A remark too often proved true.

Hospital. An Adjutant recently arrived here from a four months' sojourn in Libby, has cut out of his shoulder to-day a piece of shell over two inches long, three fourths of an inch wide and half an inch thick, weighing between three and four ounces. He is from West Virginia, by name McLaughlin, and the rebel surgeons refused to take the jagged piece of iron out. He has carried it there, in a festering wound deep near his shoulder blade, for over four hot summer months. He declares that: "It would have killed me long ago; if I had n't been so — awful — mad all the time."

Aug. 28. Sun. Cooler, rainy at night. Since coming from the Petersburg front, we have camped near where we were last May. This morning the Reg. removes and encamps near Battery Six. Later in the day moves again, to a point between Batteries Three and Four, and again encamps. Companies C, Capt. Durell; F, Capt. Forbush; G, Capt. Stoodley; H, Lieut. Ferguson, and I, Capt. Goss; with Lieutenants Wheeler, Churchill and Taggard, remove to Redoubt Dutton, the redoubt nearest to our camp, and which has a garrison of about 100 heavy artillerymen. Capt. Stoodley in command. The 18th Corps Hospital moved across the river, taking the place of the 10th Corps Hospital.

To-day Gen. Grant issues an order offering special inducements to deserters to come in from the rebel army.

Aug. 29. Mon. Warm, fair. The little force of five companies, which went forward to Redoubt Dutton yesterday, rejoins the Reg. this afternoon. They were calculating upon a fine time, had a splendid camp and many conveniences in prospect, and are much disappointed. All quiet on this front. The pickets of both armies mount the front lines of their earth-works, and remain there with impunity. A large number of men rejoin the Reg. from the Hospitals. Capt. E. W. Goss of I detailed to-day as commander of the Division Corps of sharp-shooters. We of the 18th Corps have taken the place of the 10th Corps. A splendid spring of water near the camp of the Thirteenth. No one but a soldier, or a traveler, can fully appreciate good water.

Hospital. A medical board has again decided that Lieut. Thompson's foot must come off; and the owner holds to his decision that it must stay on. This is the third time. These special examinations have a very bad effect. The examiners send a shiver of terror through a ward, the instant they appear; and visions of the 'vivisection' table, or the fearful probing for bullets in old wounds, or a return to the front before recovery — something undesirable is suggested to every patient.

Aug. 30. Tues. Showery, cold night. Reg. in camp, and at work on the defenses. Pay-rolls being made out. The enemy sends one shell straight into our camp, where it bursts among the tents — no one hurt. Quiet on the lines. Dress-parade at evening. Our camp-ground is low and wet. Rebel prayer meeting and band heard all the evening.

Aug. 31. Wed. Cool, fair. Reg. inspected and mustered for pay by Capt. Julian, on Brigade staff. Quarter-master M. L. Morrison detailed as Brigade Quarter-master. There is trouble about rations. The hard bread is wormy; very little of berries, fruit, peas, corn or garden produce can be had; butter is 75c. per pound, ham 26c., cheese 50c.; tea $2.25; eggs 60 cents a dozen, other extras in proportion — and our sutler can clear only $300 per month.

Hospital. A Lieutenant from New Jersey is here, with his mother and sister to take care of him. They fill many orders for us for fruit, etc., in the town, purchasing at wholesale prices. The Lieutenant's wound is sixteen inches long, extending from the hip, along near the bone, to the knee, a bullet hole.

Sept. 1. Thurs. Cool, fair. Reg. moves to a new camp again at the front. Capt. Durell with Company C detailed to garrison Redoubt McConihe — also called Battery Three. Lieut. Taggard commences acting as Adjutant. Quiet along our lines. To-night the pickets from the 13th go out between the lines as vedettes. The lines are so near, that Capt. Stoodley, having some news specially aggravating to the rebels, ties a newspaper to a stick and tosses it over within the rebel picket line. A rebel picks it up — and is at once arrested and marched off to the rear. We came over here to rest, and are now moving our camp for the fifth time since we arrived. We have one night on picket at the front, and one night off. The 2d N. H. leaves for Fort Powhatan on the James.

Sept. 2. Fri. Cool, fair. Reg. in the front trenches all day; at dark is relieved and returns to camp in the rear. Very heavy firing down about Petersburg. Very quiet here.

Sept. 3. Sat. Cold, fair. Reg. in camp. All quiet here. Heavy firing at Petersburg. The sounds come up here a dull, distant, throbbing roar; like a distant railway train crossing a bridge, the wheels striking every sleeper.

Sept. 4. Sun. Pleasant. Reg. in camp. Brigade Inspection from 10 to 12 a. m. Brigade Dress-parade at 4 p. m., and religious services at dark, conducted by Rev. Mr. Herbert of Mt. Vernon, a member of the Christian Commission. Dress-parades are now very infrequent. Capt. Forbush brigade officer of the day. No firing here now on our picket lines. Both our own pickets and those of the enemy are sitting about on the works to-day, staring at each other. The lines about 200 yards apart — in one place not much over 100 yards. The privates, when the officers are absent, have numerous communications, tying scraps of paper to bullets and throwing them across to one another. Circulars, inviting the rebels to desert, are distributed all along our line, and tossed over to the Confederates; they are also rolled in balls and shot over from cannon.

Hospital. Miss Maria M. C. Hall, of Washington, D. C., is Directress of this Hospital. A refined, educated, highly accomplished, beautiful and attractive young lady. A younger sister of hers is often here also.

An officer from Northern New York is here slowly recovering from the work of a minie bullet that bored holes through three parts of him — and then went on its way rejoicing — he says it sang a regular tune. His wounds have six openings. Thirty beds in our room; twenty occupied by wounded men, nearly all of whose wounds are very severe.

Sept. 5. Mon. Pleasant, warm. Reg. in camp. At work on the entrenchments in the afternoon. All quiet here. Our pickets are very near to the enemy; at one point, here at night they have held one end of a fallen tree, and the enemy's pickets held the other end. The reliefs of both, when off duty for three or four hours, have met unarmed, and enjoyed social games of cards together; the reliefs on duty meanwhile preserving the strictest watch. We can hear the rebel officers' commands within the enemy's main lines. The rebel bands were playing to-day, and our men were sitting on the top of the earth-works listening. One of their bands is again playing and delightfully, this evening. This is the way quiet reigns on the Bermuda Hundred front; this big 'bottle' appears to be filled just now with a soothing syrup.

Sept. 6. Tues. Cold, rainy and windy. Reg. in camp. Gen. Grant visits our camp and line. Commissary Sergeant G. W. Ferguson, mustered as First Lieutenant of Co. H, and Sergeant G. Bruce of Company D appointed Commissary Sergeant.

Sept. 7. Wed. Fair. Reg. in camp. Lieut. C. C. Favor of B honorably discharged the service by Special Order 244 (Sept. 5th), from Maj. Gen. E. O C. Ord. commanding Dept. of Va. and N. C. Division review by Maj. Gen. John Gibbon. Dress-parade by 13th after the review. The nights are growing cold, and Capt. Betton is sent to Norfolk, to look after the Regiment's surplus baggage stored there last spring, and to see that it is hurried to the front.

Hospital. Miss Dix, tall and stately, issues an order that the nurses will dress in sombre colors, grays or drabs, and will make no display of ornaments, jewelry, etc. As a proper reply to such an order, Miss Hall and other nurses appear in the wards, dressed as elegantly as they possibly can; and every officer who can rise sits up or stands up, and we all cheer these attractive, pure, beautiful, sensible, human women, as they pass from room to room. That settles it; and Miss Dix retreats with her sombre colors, grays and so on, as best she may. She is a good woman, but sometimes grievously mistaken in some of her notions. Many of these officers and men now in the hospitals were reared among, and have been for a life long accustomed to, all the elegancies and refinements of life in America's best society; why offend them now — and here on the sharpest line between life and death — with a lot of women coming about dressed like cheap house-maids or scullions?

Sept. 8. Thurs. Pleasant, warm. Reg. in camp. Very quiet. Last night the Union vedettes between the lines stood their watch only separated from the enemy's vedettes by about three rods.

Now and then a soldier's letter puts a matter strong and sharp; changing the rough words a bit, we here have a specimen: "Murder is awful, horrid; swindling, theft and cheating are a fearful curse; but of all the crimes known to God or man the worst is the crime of lying, and the basest of all criminals is the liar — I would give more for one good honest man than for all the pious liars the world ever saw."

Sept. 9. Fri. Cold, cloudy. Reg. in camp. Heavy details sent out for work on the trenches, and for picket duty. One of the Reg. writes: "Lieut. —— wet his commission." The rebels suddenly burst out with loud cheering to-night, but we do not know the reason for it.

"The State colors of the Thirteenth were carried by myself continuously from June 1st, at Battery Five, Mine explosion, and in the Petersburg trenches, until we returned to the Bermuda Hundred front — where I thought we were at peace with all nations, and even with the rebels on our front — when I turned in my old flag to Major Smith, then commanding the Thirteenth, and acted as right general guide until we went to the Fort Harrison battle, when I received a new Springfield rifle and went back to the color-guard. Our flags suffered worst of all at Cold Harbor. When turned in at Bermuda Hundred the State colors were useless for field purposes, the bunting a little tattered strip, the staff battered and split, and the pieces I had tied together with strings and straps." CHARLES POWELL, Color Corporal.

Sept. 10. Sat. A fine day. Reg. in camp. A board of survey investigates the matter of a 'Deficiency in the Brigade's commissary stores.' Nearly the whole Reg. has a bath in the James River. "One of them took his swim in a box — pretty full. (Hic!)" The gunboats on the right in the James are booming loudly to-day.

Hospital. A wounded officer — a Union man — from West Virginia, has been in the habit of saying a great many spiteful and bitter things here against the Yankees — the burden of his talk for a month has been against them. One day he received a new dressing-gown, but was feeling unusually bitter and sour, and was more than usually abusive in his talk about the Yankees. The writer thought it was about time, in some good-natured way, to change that current, and commenced by asking him to look and see where the bedstead, that he lay on, was made. New England. He was next asked to look at the sheets, blankets, mattress, a mosquito net, a folding chair, a table, and so on with a dozen articles or more; and all alike were found by him to be from New England — all made by the Yankees. Then last of all he was asked to see where the new dressing-gown was made — for the writer had just received and explored the ins and outs of one like it — and he found that that was also made in New England. Thrusting his hands into the pockets, the officer drew out a letter, written as a random shot by the young lady who made that gown to the soldier in the hospital who might receive it. It was very well written, a very sympathetic, tender and sisterly letter. The officer opened it and began to read. Soon the tears came to his eyes, and before the letter was half read he broke down utterly, and fell back upon his pillow crying like a child. He afterwards read that letter a good many times; but he scolded the Yankees no more.

Sept. 11. Sun. Pleasant. Reg. in camp. Inspection at 10 a. m. Brigade Dress-parade at evening — the whole command caught in a shower. Lieut. Dustin returns to the Regiment. The little circulars containing Gen. Grant's invitation to the enemy to desert and to come within our lines are thrown, bound to a stone, from our lines over within the enemy's lines. Also thrown up into the air to blow across the lines when the wind serves, also passed out by our vedettes. It is said that the enemy metes out very severe punishments to any of his men caught reading these circulars. It does not seem to have entered the heads of the rebel authorities to send a counter invitation to the Union soldiers to desert to the Confederates; they may be rash, but they escape attempting that one impossibility, at least.

Sept. 12. Mon. Pleasant, cool, rains about noon. Reg. in camp. A quiet day. Compared with the Petersburg front, this place is in a perpetual Sunday — or we form a sort of rendezvous camp.

Sept. 13. Tues. Pleasant, cool. Reg. in camp. Battalion drill in the forenoon. Capt. Goss, now commanding the Division sharp-shooters, states that one dark night recently when he was posting vedettes between the lines, he saw a convenient tree, and marched his vedette up to it; just as he was about to give him his instructions a rebel vedette rose up on the other side of the tree and disputed possession, declaring: "This tree belongs to we 'uns. Is'e got here fust — a long time, er'ekn." Capt. Goss concluded that neither would run off with the other and left his man; and there they remained through the night — Confederate on one side of the tree, Union on the other side. Why should n't even a tree laugh, while men thus play the 'awful game of war' around its roots! No 'vexed Bermoothes' this, nowadays.

While speaking of trees it should be added that the deep shade furnished by the dense pine foliage, however pleasant and grateful it may seem during a hot, sunshiny day, is indeed most treacherously unwholesome. The damp ground, the decaying vegetation, in the absence of the sun's purifying rays, produce a dangerous state of the atmosphere under these trees, and half the malaria may well be attributed to shade-aria.

Sept. 14. Wed. Fair, cool. Reg. in camp. Asst. Surgeon Morrill takes a leave of absence. A severe fight on the Petersburg front. Fever and ague becoming prevalent in the Regiment, on account of our swampy camp-ground. Our pickets are now pushed out more than half the distance between the lines. The enemy's sharp-shooters now rarely send a bullet into our lines.

Hospital. 'The flag-of-truce boat' lands at Annapolis, this morning, about 400 Libby prison skeletons — fruits of the rule of Davis & Co. and their infernal gang. These Union prisoners are covered with vermin, ragged, starved, uncared for, rotting alive; have been neglected, treated inhumanly, and made to suffer for months the tortures of the damned. Some of them, from sheer emaciation, cannot move hand or foot, mere skeletons. There are no words to meet the case; one look at them were enough to elicit the sympathies of, and to provoke friendly interposition and kindly offices from the devil himself. Horrible, terrible.

Apropos to this are the resolutions of sympathy for rebeldom freely offered by the New Hampshire copperheads; and their recent distribution up North of 2,000 Enfield rifles among the peace-at-any-price fellows. And the selectmen of one New Hampshire town, at least, were base enough to defraud soldiers of their legal right to vote at home last spring

— and were fined $50 apiece for it. A fitting place for Northern copperheads is found at last: they should go wounded, as common prisoners of war, to Danville, Libby and Andersonville.

Sept. 15. Thurs. Cool, clear. Reg. in camp. Battalion drill. Two rebel deserters come into our lines this morning. Much trading between the pickets. The rebels throw over tobacco — some of it very choice, and our men repay in jackknives, pocket books, pipes, pictorial papers, and such other things as the rebels express a wish for, and are not contraband. Col. Donohoe returns to the 10th N. H., relieving Lt. Col. Coughlin of the command, which he has held for about a year past.

Sept. 16. Fri. Quite warm. Reg. in camp. All quiet here. A regiment of the 9th Corps, on going into action a few days since, held a mock auction of flesh wounds, and the bids ran from $5.00 to $50; a slight flesh wound promising the only relief from constant fighting. This shows how much some of the men hanker after a battle.

Sept. 17. Sat. Very pleasant. Reg. in camp. Details out on work and picket every day. Regular monthly inspection by Capt. Julian. Very quiet here. Now and then a 200 lb. shell from the Howlett House battery screams through the air, making a fearful noise. Lieut. Partridge's signal station received a few of them several days ago. He and his men had to run for shelter. If one of these shells strikes advantageously, it instantly does an immense amount of damage, the concussion feared as much as the fragments.

Sept. 18. Sun. Fair, cool, showers. Reg. in camp. Inspection by Capt. Betton, temporarily commanding the Thirteenth. C. F. Winch, regimental sutler, boards several officers of the Thirteenth.

Sept. 19. Mon. Fair, cool. Reg. in camp. Large detail shoveling. Brigade review by Actg. Brig. Gen. A. F. Stevens. The irreverent, because the Brigade is so small, call it a "Brevet Review." Major Smith and Lieut. Oliver return from Norfolk; a four days' trip made for pay and clothing. The whole army is short of cash; the longer the war lasts the slower are the Government payments. Lieut. M. L. Morrison Brigade Quarter-master. The 13th owe a debt to Quarter-master Morrison, they can never pay. He sees the bright side of everything. With him the moon and stars are never far away on the blackest night, and the days are more than half sunshine through the worst of storms. He must have been born about sunrise on a warm, fair and cloudless morning.

Secretary of War Stanton's order to draft men for the army, in all places where quotas are not already filled, goes into effect to-day.

Sept. 20. Tues. Clear, warm. Reg. in camp. No drill. The Reg. cheers for the news from the Shenandoah valley. The officers start their new 'improved' mess; an attempt to secure the best of supplies at wholesale prices. Exceedingly dull times along here. The 13th has 621 men on its rolls, and draws 273 rations for men present for duty. Eighty men to a Company are necessary to muster a Captain; sixty to muster a First Lieutenant.

Hospital. The most cheerful sufferers a person ever saw are the wounded men and officers. They feel that they have done their duty, and in most cases look upon their wounds as 'glory-marks.' As one Western man puts it: "It is bang-up proof that we have been thar." The Hospitals have their bright sides as well as their dark ones. Cards, chess, checkers, stories, reading, lively chat and songs cheerily while away many an hour, while we wait for nature to rebuild the tissues cut by rebel bullets and shells, and sloughed out by gangrene; all largely a simple matter too of growth and science of materials — why should we fret?

Sept. 21. Wed. Cool, a rainy night. Reg. hurried out this morning and manned the works at an early hour — no engagement. Drill during the day, Dress-parade at evening. Officer's mess board now costs about $5.00 per week. A foraging party from the Thirteenth secure a fat pig, and very muddy, as most pigs like to be. The lucky soldier when he struck the pig down remarked: "Here goes the last Southern dynasty."

Sept. 22. Thurs. Cold, a heavy rain in afternoon. Reg. in camp. All quiet. The men had to-day the first touch of fun for a month, over the misfortunes, antics and 'monkey-shines' of a most stupid negro muledriver, who upset his team and wagon in a heap, in a deep, wet ditch. Negro-like, he made the most of the accident, and entered upon the most childish and awkward methods to extricate his charge. As usual, all the men stand around and laugh — and none volunteer to help. He is left to his own resources, and finally gains the road and moves on with his charge; mules, harnesses, wagon, load, himself and all well bespattered, streaked and plastered with mud.

Sept. 23. Fri. Showery. Reg. in camp. No drill. At work on the entrenchments in the afternoon. On picket at night.

Hospital. Among a boat-load of officers arrived from Southern prisons are several men so fearfully emaciated by their inhuman treatment that now they can scarcely move either hand or foot — mere skin-covered skeletons. One of this large party, however, an officer of the 5th N. Y., by name Leatz, is still quite strong, though badly wounded and suffering severely. He is an elegant personage, a tall, straight Norwegian, with heavy blonde hair and whiskers, and so nobly bears himself that he is called the Count. Soon after his arrival he sees, set up at the end of the room, a pair of boxes hinged together, and provided with sundry shelves and upon them books — so called. Across the top in gilt letters are the words 'Soldiers' Library.' He goes to the pretentious affair, while we curiously watch the result, and selects an elegant volume in covers of blue and gold, and returns to his couch to read it; opens the book, gives it one look, of unutterable disgust, and then throws it as far as he can. We all laugh, of course, for every man in the ward has been similarly cheated by the outward fine appearance of this very book. "These pretty covers will please the soldiers;" probably said some precious piece of stupidity when he sent it. It was written, like many other gilded books of its class, by Miss Antiqua Maiden Pious, of Giggle-hollow, authoress of 'Moon Ray Winglets,' 'Zephyr Wafts of Rill Foam,' etc., is all about some little goody-goody Johnny What's-his-name, who had the world in high consideration and died as young as he could, and the covers of the 'book' are a hundred times the most valuable part of the whole mess of stuff, but a fair sample of the entire lot of books.

Almost the whole 'Library' is juvenile; a lot of books too poor to keep in some generous families or religious Sunday schools, and so sent to the poor soldiers and officers in hospitals, hundreds of whom could write books a thousand times more valuable and not half try. What in the name of common sense do the kid-glove and lace-edging people up North think the Union army is made of? These books are rather too weak for a kindergarten. These outrageous shams weary and pain hundreds of good men. The merry wags here, however, make a deal of sport with this particular 'Library;' reading the silly books aloud, in tones of wrapt admiration, deepest emotion and unending burlesque. One book of 'poetry' in this 'Library' has been set to music, with variations, and the stuff is sung by the patients in unison; each one composing the music and singing the words after his own fashion. A few minutes of this indescribable, horrid medley serves to 'bring down the house,' and the singers also, with roars of laughter.

Sept. 24. Sat. Showery. The whole camp is roused at 2 a. m., to hear the glorious news from Gen. Sheridan — tremendous cheering. At 7 a. m. a salute, with shotted cannon, is fired all along the lines and forts, from every gun and mortar, in honor of Gen. Sheridan's victories in the Shenandoah valley. The enemy replies spitefully with shot and shell. Hurts no one here. The salute is fired from at least 100 guns, aimed with all possible precision at the enemy and his works. Thirteenth on picket all day. For several days past the enemy's pickets have refused to trade, or to exchange newspapers. To-day a paper containing an account of Gen. Sheridan's victories is rolled around a stone by a man of the Thirteenth and thrown within the enemy's lines. A rebel soldier picks it up, and is immediately arrested — an officer seizing the paper.

Sept. 25. Sun. Clear, very cool. Thirteenth in camp. Brigade picket guard-mounting, and Brigade inspection — the whole lasting until noon. Religious services at 2 p. m., conducted by Rev. Mr. Herbert. Brigade review. Brigade Dress-parade at 4 p. m. Too much, altogether too much. If there is ever again, in this country, a necessity for an army to take the field, it is to be hoped that common sense, if nothing else, will so prevail that the common soldiers, when it is possible, may have at least one half a day of rest in each week, and that on Sunday.

We must not pass " Nigger Joe," the man of all work, in the Hospital Dept. of the Thirteenth, big, black and not handsome. Swearing was his especial horror. Hearing any one swear strongly, he would drop on his knees in the road, or wherever he happened to be, and pray long, loud and fervently for the swearer; and of course he had a very constant practice for his faculty. Having done his duty at praying, he would rise to his feet, mingle with the crowd he had collected — and pick the pockets of his hearers.  True type of talky-talky piety.

During the battle of Fredericksburg he found in the city a large trunk, filled it with women's wearing apparel, shouldered it, and presented himself, with his most sanctimonious face, at the ponton bridge ; and representing that he had hospital stores in the trunk much needed across the river, and telling the guard that: "De good Lord would bless de dear guard for not 'taining him," he was allowed to cross.  Once over the river he dumped the contents of the trunk in the nearest clump of pines, took the trunk to the old camp of the Thirteenth, and sold it for $5.00 to a man of the 13th left there in charge, and then returned to the city for more plunder.

"He stretched his mouth so much with his 'prayers,' that his mouth looked like a yard of red flannel drawn across a coal-bin."  This is Lieut. Sawyer's description.  He stole so frequently, and made so much mischief in the Brigade that Col. Stevens had him dismissed ; and thus the Thirteenth lost one of its most unique followers.

Sept. 26. Mon. Quite warm, clear. Reg. in camp. Battalion drill.  Brigade Dress-parade.  Six deserters come in, all direct from Richmond.  They state that there is a great deal of suffering for want of food, clothing and medical care and supplies in that city.  Ponton bridge at Point of Rocks is taken up.  Lieut. Sawyer starts for Norfolk on three days' leave.

Sept. 27. Tues. Very cool. Reg. in camp. Drilling. Dress-parade.  The Bands play all along the line to-night.  A rebel First Lieutenant deserts to our lines.

All the work done by us here on the Bermuda Hundred front, since we came over from the Petersburg front on the morning of Aug. 27th, has been reasonably light, but continuous, and giving little chance for rest. This is considered a very important position, and our Brigade has furnished continually details for outpost picket duty, and for labor on the entrenchments.  These lines. however, have been quiet, there has been but little firing even between the pickets, and we have not been required to be awake and under arms half the night, as we were when in front of Petersburg.  On the whole a stupid, lazy and uninteresting month.  We have drilled for a few days, Company drill in forenoon and Battalion or Brigade drill in afternoon.  The Sundays have been the busiest days of all, crowded with reviews, inspections and parades.

Lieut. Gafney reports for duty, having arrived here from home on Sept. 22d.  The wound in his leg is quite well healed, his robust physique has proved, after a long period of rest, to be in good order, and apparently all right, and so he returns to duty ; but sooner than he ought, for it is a dangerous experiment, the bullet not having been extracted. We think he ought to be written the merriest officer in the Thirteenth.

Extracts from letters written at the front :

"Sept. 18th.  Orders are now made very strict against trafficking with the rebels — pickets with pickets. The rebels are very anxious to get illustrated papers; as I suppose because they want to see the pictures, for few of them can read.

"The rebels cheered tremendously when they received the news of Gen. McClellan's nomination for the Presidency. They tell our boys that he will be elected, and then the war will be over very soon. The enthusiasm was as great in the rebel army as it was in the Chicago convention itself. The rebels cheered, threw up rockets, speechified, their bands played, and they made such a noise nearly all night that we could hardly sleep.

"They have prayer meetings two or three times a week, and we are so near we can almost distinguish the words when they sing. One of their preachers we can hear. He was telling them the other night about the sacredness of their cause, and the necessity for every man to shoulder his musket and drive back the invaders, etc., etc.; and said that if any refused to do so they should be forced to do it, or be shot as recreants and traitors. This apparently did not meet the views of some of their vedettes out in front, nearer our lines than he was, for they hooted at him and hissed him at a great rate.

"A rebel Lieutenant recently offered one of our Corporals $50 in Confederate money, for a dozen cakes of hard-bread. The Corporal gave him fifteen but would take none of his money.

"Sept. 25th. A salute with shotted guns has just been fired. There have been several of them of late. Our troops turn out under arms and take position at their breast-works, the extreme front line, when the cannonade opens first upon the left, then rapidly runs up the line to the right, and then the whole line keeps up the incessant blaze and roar for about an hour. The rebels to-day replied with two shots only, in front of the Thirteenth, their shells going over harmless.

"Lieut. Taggard is acting as Adjutant of the Thirteenth, and makes a very good one indeed."  PRESCOTT.

# IX.

## September 28, 1864, to February 28, 1865.

### BATTLE OF FORT HARRISON.

**Sept. 28. Wed.** Very fine day. Reg. in camp. Last night orders were received to prepare two days' cooked rations, and to be ready, this morning, to march at a moment's notice, and in light marching order. Major Normand Smith is in command of the Thirteenth, and Col. Stevens in command of our Brigade — 1st Brig., 1st Div., 18th Corps — consisting of the 13th N. H., 81st, 98th and 139th N. Y. regiments.

Company C, Capt. Durell, is garrisoning Redoubt McConihe, and remains behind; the balance of the Reg. moves out of the entrenchments at Bermuda Hundred at 8 a. m., with the Brigade, and halts a short distance to the rear while other troops move into our place.

The troops moving in are fresh soldiers from Pennsylvania; some of whom are said to have received $1,500 in bounties to induce them to enlist. One of these freshmen in war college, while we are halted here, asks Andrew J. Robbins of G if the Thirteenth are now going to a battle, and the following colloquy ensues: Robbins in reply. "O yes; we never move without going into a fight." Penn. "Do you suppose that we, too, will be ordered into a battle?" Robbins. "No indeed. They won't put you in — you cost too much to be risked in a battle; we did n't cost anything — so they stick us in everywhere." Penn. thinks he sees the point, and the boys have a laugh with which to begin the day.

At 9 p. m. we move off, and after a rapid march of about three miles bivouac near the James, and nearly opposite Aiken's landing, on a very rough piece of ground but dry and clean. This landing is eight miles above Deep Bottom, and two miles below Dutch Gap. The advance — 10th N. H. and 118th N. Y. — cross the river on pontons, a little after midnight, and move out upon the Varina road as skirmishers. Our Division soon follows.

This movement is for the purpose of surprising and capturing Fort Harrison, the key to a long portion of the enemy's line, situated on Chaffin's farm, about one mile from the east bank of the James River, six miles from Richmond, and nearly opposite Fort Darling on the west bank of the James. The garrison is said to be about 3,000 men. The work consists of one square fort, mounting 8 or 10 guns, the ditch ten feet deep and the sides of it nearly vertical, above which the walls of the fort rise some ten or fifteen feet more. From this strong fort heavy rifle-trenches stretch out to right and left, intersected by numerous small redoubts and redans mounting one or two guns each, commanding and enfilading the approaches in every direction. The works mount 22 guns in all. The approach is also commanded by the rebel gunboats in the James above Dutch Gap. Just about these two bluffs — Drury's and Chaffin's — an area of three or four square miles is closely filled with heavy earthworks; one of the strongest and most easily defended outlying systems of fortifications on the entire Confederate line. The enemy's pontons here bridge the James, and his fleets hold a safe and secure anchorage.

Our assaulting force consists of Gen. George J. Stannard's First Division of the 18th Corps, sixteen regiments, about 2,000 men; co-operating with Gen. Heckman, farther to the right, having also a force of about 2,000 men. All from the Army of the James.

Gen. Birney moves at the same time from the Petersburg front, with about 10,000 men, to invest or attack the Confederate lines north and east of Forts Harrison and Gilmer, both of which are connected by several heavy lines of trenches and numerous redans and redoubts with the Confederate works at Chaffin's Bluff,[1] a mile and a quarter distant on the James. Gen. Kautz, with cavalry, is to move still farther north, along near the Darbytown road.

Sept. 29. Thurs. Fine day, clear, cool. The Reg. is called at 2 a. m., breakfasts, crosses the James river at Aiken's landing about 3 a. m., on a ponton bridge covered with hay and earth to deaden the sounds of tramping men and horses. The 10th N. H. and 118th N. Y. now armed with Spencer rifles, 'Seven-shooters' — the 10th having yesterday received 150 of them — are deployed as skirmishers covering the front of our Division, and under command of Col. Donohoe.

The Thirteenth with the rest of the Division marches by the flank — by fours — up the road above Aiken's house and there forms close column by divisions, the 13th having the right of our Brigade, and the right of the 13th resting on the Varina road.

The firing commences, between our skirmishers and the enemy's pickets, at early daylight, just when we first enter the woods. Our advance is made very rapidly for three or four miles, though the enemy's strong line of skirmishers contest every inch of the ground, and at times most stubbornly. Now and then the contest seems like a regular engagement, as the rapid shots from the Spencer rifles drive the enemy back from cover to cover, until he finally falls back within his entrenchments. The rebels have no language sufficiently strong to satisfy them, while condemning: "That infernal Yankee gun that shoots seven times at once."

The whole distance from Aiken's landing to Fort Harrison is nearly six miles, taking in all the windings of the road, and about four miles as the crow flies. Speaking in general terms, we approach the fort from the south side, driving the enemy up the James river.

---

[1] Though this name frequently appears as Chapin, it is properly Chaffin. A redoubt is a small isolated fort enclosed and defensible on all sides. A redan is a salient angle, or small fort, open and indefensible on at least one side.

Col. Donohoe commanding our Division line of skirmishers, has his horse shot under him, and other mounted men volunteer to carry his orders, and conspicuous among them is Capt. James A. Sanborn of the Tenth New Hampshire.

On arriving at the belt of pine woods running between Henry Cox's and J. K. Childrey's houses, our skirmishers make a splendid charge on the double-quick and run, clearing the timber of the enemy's skirmishers and driving them into the open field and part of the way across it; and secure excellent positions on the flanks, from which they can effectually cut down the enemy's gunners while our Division assaults the works.

The Division halts for a few minutes in this belt of pines, while slight irregularities in the lines caused by the rapid, hurried march are corrected, and the solid columns of the men, massed in divisions, secure the best ground from which to rush upon the assault. It is only the work of a moment, when the column again moves forward, the right of our Brigade resting upon the Varina road. As the column advances and emerges from the wood, all at once the high walls of Fort Harrison come into view, occupying a very high crest of land, a strong natural position, nearly a mile distant. We have already been liberally treated with the enemy's large shells, but at quite a long range; and now, as our skirmishers, moving directly in front of the column, gain the extreme edge of the brush and advance into the open field, and we, in the column, come into view from Fort Harrison, the enemy opens upon us with eight or ten of the most prominent guns in the fort. Whatever we do at all must be done very quickly.

Here we are in brush and slashing, on the edge of a wood. Directly in front of us, and stretching up to the walls of the fort, is a broad, open field nearly a mile wide and swept by the enemy's guns — on the two gunboats in the river, in redoubts to the left, and in Fort Harrison itself, high on our front, surely by guns in one fort and in three redoubts — how many guns in all we know not, but evidently we are in range of more than twenty, besides those on the boats in the James. Added to the fire from all these, comes an occasional and very large shell from the right — the rebel works nearer Fort Gilmer.

Fort Harrison, as the special object of our attack, blazes away at us with all its might. Added to the artillery, are the enemy's sharp-shooters and infantry, manning the long lines of his rifle-trenches, laid in full sight, in long zig-zags, for a full mile and a half, to right and left of Fort Harrison; and we can see the enemy swiftly concentrating, running in together along his lines, upon our front. Their 'saw-horse' battle flags are unfurled, the staffs planted in the sand of their high parapets of fort, redoubt and trench — they have not been surprised.

The prospect is terrible; however, the lines of our skirmishers are pressing forward, our assaulting force — the First Division — advances in close column by divisions; the Thirteenth, the third Regiment from the front of the main column, is steadily leading our First Brigade; caps are removed from all the muskets and bayonets fixed — the bayonet alone is to win this battle ; and in a few moments the Division emerges in a body from the brush, with arms at a 'right shoulder,' and almost jauntily and with confidence and fearlessness — Veterans these ! marches straight through the field for the fort. The men are urged to double-quick, but refuse — saying that they are 'going to keep their wind sound for this job.' The Thirteenth goes in, a little body of only 187 guns.

We are now a special target for every gun which the enemy can possibly bring to bear upon us. Huge shells come tearing and screaming up from his gunboats into our left flank ; the redoubts to right and left plunge in their cross-fire ; while Fort Harrison, directly in our front, plies us with shrapnel, solid shot and shell, and as we approach nearer the rebel riflemen shower upon us their hail of lead ; their severest fire coming from the brush, trees and trenches upon our left. Some of our men fall riddled with bullets ; great gaps are rent in our ranks as the shells cut their way through us, or burst in our midst ; a solid shot or a shell striking directly will bore straight through ten or twenty men ; here are some men literally cut in two, others yonder are blown to pieces — and the horrors of an assault in force, the storming of a fort, are repeated over and over again. Despite the carnage in the ranks, our Division moves forward with wonderful steadiness, though many of our skirmishers and the assaulting column are all merged in a body together ; all our officers, and especially those of the line, being of course more directly among the men, moving and working with almost superhuman courage and energy. The men need no urging, were never more ready for a fight, but the ranks need closing and correcting in line as they are broken by the constant falling of the killed and wounded.

Now our Brigade is deployed in lines of battle, and when we have advanced to within about one hundred yards of the fort, the enemy's fire is so terrific that the wasted and shattered column wavers a little — the task seems impossible. Our column has now marched nearly a mile in the very teeth of the fearful storm, and the worst of the battle is still ahead. A little to our right and front is a ridge of land, within striking distance of the fort on its crest ; and our Brigade, with the rest of the column, now cut down by more than one third already killed or wounded, moves towards the right obliquely in behind this ridge, and for a moment is sheltered from the direct fire of the fort in front. Here we take breath for a minute — the Spencer rifles in the hands of our skirmishers are set at work with all possible rapidity — and this little respite of time and shelter saves to us the day.

The pause of the assaulting column here is but for a little time — estimated at from three to five minutes — when the officers and men of the whole column in a body, almost regardless of organization, mount the ridge with a rush and a shout, make directly for the high front walls of Fort Harrison, again receiving the enemy's full fire, dash rapidly across the intervening space, and all as one, officers and men, plunge together into the deep moat, spread instantly to right and left to secure working space uncrowded on the walls, thrust bayonets into the walls of sand and gravel, and all clamber upon the parapet of the fort — some mounting the high works upon their comrades' shoulders, and then getting firm foothold draw their comrades up after them — and in a minute more the staffs of our battle flags are planted in the sand of the parapet — that of the Thirteenth being among the first. Some claim it was the first. The Thirteenth carries only its National colors in this battle.

The men and officers of brigades and regiments mingle indiscriminately in this last dash, and so near are the contestants, that when we climb up on one side of the walls, the enemy's men are in their places on the other side — we look straight down upon the points of their bayonets, and upon their sallow, savage faces — and a fierce hand to hand conflict ensues ; but we are atop, and at the show and use of our bayonets, the enemy seeks cover within and behind the soldiers' barracks within the fort and to the rear of it. There are from fifty to a hundred of these buildings of all sorts, and here our rifles come into play for the first time ; up to this point the assaulting column has not fired a shot — the bayonet alone has won this battle. The enemy is driven out, or captured, only after a stubborn resistance. The firing is at such short range, that some of our men's faces are actually burned and blackened by the flashes of fire from the muzzles of the enemy's rifles. The enemy is dislodged, however, and our victory is complete by 8 a. m. All his dead and wounded falling into our hands, all the armament of the fort, and a large number of the defenders and garrison as prisoners.

As soon as the contest is over, the works are immediately manned in every direction by our troops, and the guns of Fort Harrison are turned upon the enemy fleeing to right and left, and seeking cover in the distance, while our men make the air ring with cheer upon cheer. A strong skirmish line — made up in part by men of the 13th — at once presses forward, out beyond the rear of the fort, and drives the enemy back quite a distance into the brush, where a sharp contest ensues late in the day, and Col. Donohoe, in command on the left, is severely wounded, when about one quarter of a mile to the left of the fort. The balance of the Union force take position in the fort and trenches, for immediate action in case the rebels make a counter assault.

"When we had captured Fort Harrison, myself and a number of other men of the Thirteenth who were among the first to enter the fort and barracks, found in the rebel officers' quarters an excellent breakfast all prepared and set out ready to be eaten. The rebel officers did not have time to eat their breakfast, and we heated, hungry, begrimed with powder-smoke and dirty, just as we were, sat down at the earliest moment we could and ate their breakfast in their stead, and arose feeling much obliged to them for it."     ERASTUS NEWTON, Company I.

Fort Harrison is a large square work without any walls on the rear side — the side towards the river — being protected here by rifle-pits only; and the enemy continues to shell us, while within the fort, both from his gunboats and from the vicinity of Fort Gilmer. But our men on gaining possession of Fort Harrison at once set at work throwing up entrenchments and defenses across this rear side. The enemy had a quantity of baled hay for his horses stored in the fort, and this is rolled out and placed in line as a breast-work; timber and logs are used also, and barrels and boxes are set up and shoveled full of earth. Every available man is at work all day and all night without rest or sleep, and before morning a strong breast-work is made across the rear of the fort; the works are reversed and put in a state of complete defense, and the troops are stationed to meet whatever may come on the morrow.

"Eight guns are captured in the square fort, two of them 100-pounders." MAJOR STOODLEY.

The track of the advance of our assaulting column, across the field, is thickly strewn with the dead and wounded; and as soon as the fort is taken, details of men are sent to care for our own wounded, and those of the enemy also. Our dead are gathered, and buried within the fort. No one is allowed to leave the fort, and front line, excepting the special details to care for the wounded, and to remove the dead.

While crossing the field in the assault, the Color Sergeant of the Thirteenth, David W. Bodge of B, is severely wounded while the flag is in his hands. When he falls a member of the Color-guard picks up the flag and bears it on. The National colors, only, are carried in this assault. Every one of the men of the Color-guard of the Thirteenth is either killed or wounded in the assault, the most of them being shot in the left side, by rebel sharp-shooters posted in and among trees, and the colors are passed from hand to hand as they come up.[1] It is stated officially, that the Thirteenth at the time of the capture claimed that their colors were the first planted on the fort, but not claiming too much, it is enough that our colors were planted among the very first on a captured fort of the great size and strength of this Fort Harrison.

Col. Stevens, commanding our Brigade, falls in the assault when a few rods from the fort, and lies there until the battle is won, and is then carried from the field. He has commanded the Brigade since July 25th.

Major Smith commanding the Thirteenth is wounded in the head, receiving a scalp wound nearly three inches in length, during the assault and when near the moat, and is assisted in, out of range, by Sergt. Major

---

[1] The writer endeavored to trace the course of our colors through the assault, naming the men, who bore it, in order; but found statements conflicting, the matter mixed, and fearing to do injustice forebore further mention. In the three Brigades were twelve to twenty flags; in the last dash the flags and their bearers were falling, and the flags were being picked up by almost any one who chose to do so. During this last dash Color Corporal Charles Powell of K and an officer of the 98th N. Y. seized the fallen flag of the Thirteenth very nearly simultaneously, a tussle ensued, but Powell got the flag. There are discrepancies in the number of cannon captured, but the field-pieces were turned, run to the rear of the fort and fired upon the retreating enemy; the square fort had at first eight guns. — S. M. T.

Hodgdon; the command then devolving upon Capt. Stoodley. Major Smith's fellow officers state that he bore himself throughout the assault with great gallantry and utter fearlessness, and worked with almost superhuman energy until he was shot down.

On entering the fort the men of the 13th gather at once around their colors, and soon turn two of the enemy's guns and fire them several times upon his troops in retreat. Again, soon after this, the 13th are assembled and posted in line of battle on the left of the fort; that is to say on the right of the Union line at the north end of the fort, where late in the afternoon we commence entrenching. About 10 p. m., we move and join the Brigade in line of battle in the rear of the fort, that is between the fort and the new position taken by the enemy toward the river; but soon return to nearly our former position, and throw out pickets in advance; and the most of the men of the Reg. are at work all night on the entrenchments running from the fort toward the river, and on the line running across the open rear of the fort itself. There is no abatis in front of any part of the fort; the presence of it would have utterly prevented our capturing it at all.

One account states that: "The line officers captured Fort Harrison."

On Gen. Michler's Official Map, the woods near Mr. J. K. Childrey's house, where the Division formed for the assault, nearly a mile southeast of Fort Harrison, are represented as growing along a small fork of Three Mile Creek; and the little hill near the fort where the assaulting column halted to take breath before the final rush, falls upon another small fork of the same creek, both these forks crossing the Varina road. The 13th assaulted on the left — west — side of this road, which runs almost directly towards Fort Harrison until within about one third of a mile from it, when it bends quite short to the right — north.

Sergt. Thomas S. Wentworth of B states that the Thirteenth entered upon the assault formed in column by divisions closed in mass, and was the third Regiment from the front. The first shot received from Fort Harrison struck among the color-guard of the first regiment in the column. The third shell that hit the Thirteenth exploded so closely to Wentworth's face that his eyes were injured by the concussion, flash and glare, and he was knocked over and thrown several feet. During the charge seven men were wounded in Co. B. Sergt. David W. Bodge of B, Color-bearer, carried the National colors into the charge, but was badly wounded soon after the Reg. deployed in line of battle. The colors passed from one man to another in the color-guard, as the bearers were severally shot down, finally coming into the hands of Color Corporal Charles R. Coburn of D, who was the last man of the color-guard shot during the charge. He had climbed upon the parapet of Fort Harrison, where he was severely wounded, and rolled over within the fort.

Thomas S. Wentworth was sixteen years old on February 28, 1862, and enlisted on August 18, 1862. One of the youngest, if not the youngest of the boys in the Reg. who served as soldiers. The drummer boys were a little younger.

Pollard (Confed.) states that Fort Harrison was very strong, and its loss was a serious disaster to the Confederacy; and that Gen. Butler surprised and captured the Fort while a Confederate force was on the double-quick to re-enforce it.

The capture of this fort, with many of the garrison and twenty-two cannon in the fort and lines, is said to have created the greatest excitement ever known in Richmond, and every male between the years of 16 and 60 was hurried into the defenses.

Lt. Col. Normand Smith, commanding the Thirteenth, reports officially: "We advanced, under a heavy fire of musketry, into the outer ditch of the fort without firing a shot. The entire color-guard of the Thirteenth — six in all — were killed or wounded (during the charge), four of them with the colors in their hands. The Regiment claims that their colors were the first planted on the fort, which was carried a few minutes past seven o'clock in the morning."

The evening report of the Thirteenth gives the casualties in the Regiment to-day as two officers killed, and six wounded: six men killed, and forty-one wounded. Total loss 55. The Reg. entered upon the assault with 187 muskets.

Capt. George A. Forbush, and Lieut. R. R. Thompson fall, instantly killed in the assault. Both were exceptionally brave men, and faithful, true soldiers, who have shared in all the Regiment's labors and battles from its first organization.

"I suppose I heard the last words spoken by Capt. Forbush, which were: 'Come on, boys!' It was just as I passed him on my left hand, and he had turned towards some men who had thrown themselves upon the ground, and were apparently unhurt. He fell about two rods from the ditch (during the final assault) and outside of the fort."

EDWIN WARE, First Sergeant Co. G.

Lieut. Robert R. Thompson was born in Rumford, Oxford Co., Me., Dec. 17, 1822. A graduate of Bowdoin College, Class of 1849. A Civil Engineer by profession. He was active in the enlistment of Co. H, in which he enlisted as a private, Aug. 15, 1862. He remained on duty with the Thirteenth until Aug. 11, 1863, when he was ordered to report to Capt. F. M. Follett, 4th U. S. Artillery, Chief of Artillery of the Dept. including Norfolk and Portsmouth, Va. He had served in the ranks, and as First Sergeant of Co. H, excepting when acting as Lieutenant, and was commissioned as Second Lieutenant July 23, 1863.

He remained in the Engineer Corps until April 24, 1864, when he rejoined the Regiment. He was severely wounded in the side May 16, 1864, at Drury's Bluff while performing one of the bravest acts done in the whole war, and again rejoined the Reg. from Hospital about July 1, 1864. See page 293. July 19, 1864, he was promoted to First Lieutenant in Co. D, and from that time acted as Adjutant until about Sept. 1, 1864. At this time the 13th numbered about 140 effective men present for duty.

Capt. Farr being in Hospital, Lieut. Thompson returned to the command of Company D; and led that Company in the assault upon Fort Harrison, when he was killed just in the moment of victory. He was an excellent soldier and officer, and a true man in every relation of life.

Captains Saunders and Bruce, and Lieutenants Ladd, Hall and Wheeler are wounded.

Lossing states that Gen. Ord captured 22 guns and about 300 prisoners. About 700 Union men were killed or wounded in the assault. Gen. Weitzel succeeded to the command of the 18th Corps, after Gen. Ord was wounded.

Gen. Hiram Burnham is mortally wounded by a bullet striking him in the stomach, while within the fort and after its capture. He was at the time giving orders to Sergt. Major Hodgdon of the 13th, to send some men to drive the enemy's sharp-shooters from among the farther barracks. Hodgdon sent two men to carry the General to a more secure place within the fort, where he soon died. This the writer has upon Sergt. Major Hodgdon's own statement.

Some confusion having arisen in the order of casualties, it may be well to say that Col. Stevens, acting Brig. General commanding 1st Brigade, was wounded during the charge across the field, and before reaching the fort; Gen. Burnham was killed within the fort, and after its capture. Each was commanding a separate Brigade in Gen. Stannard's Division.

The force under Gen. Heckman, farther to the right, did not assist in the capture of Fort Harrison, nor join in the assault upon it; but after the capture of this fort he attacked Fort Gilmer, or the works near it, with his Division, and was repulsed with heavy loss.

Gen. Humphreys, page 284, gives the general plan of the attack substantially as carried out: Stannard's Division captured Fort Harrison; Heckman's Division struck the Confederate position to the right of Fort Harrison; and the 10th Corps moved up still farther to the right. Gen. Humphreys states that Gen. Ord had about 4,000 men, in all, from the 18th Corps — 2,000 from the 1st Div. under Stannard, and 2,000 from the 2d Div. under Heckman. He adds: By half past seven (a. m.) Gen. Ord had reached the open ground around Fort Harrison, the strongest work on the enemy's main line, and the artillery of the fort and adjacent works opened upon him. Gen. Stannard's Division, Gen. Burnham's Brigade leading, was to push forward on the left of the Varina road, in column of divisions, over the open ground in front of the works (the south front of course is meant) preceded by skirmishers. The distance it had to traverse was about 1,400 yards. Gen. Heckman was to move his Division, as soon as it came up, along the edge of the wood that skirted the Varina road on the right, until he was opposite Fort Harrison, and then to attack it on the front toward the wood — the east front. Re-enforcements were now seen entering Fort Harrison from the enemy's left.

Gen. Stannard's Division advanced in quick time, and when they reached the foot of the hill which Fort Harrison crowned, Gen. Burnham's brigade ran up the hill under a severe fire of artillery and musketry, and after a sharp encounter captured the work with sixteen guns and a number of prisoners, including the Lieut. Colonel in command of it.[1] Gen. Burnham was killed in the assault; Col. Stevens, the officer who succeeded to the command of the brigade, was severely wounded, and his successor also.[1]

The Division lost 594 killed and wounded during the day. The enemy was next driven from the entrenchments on the right and left of the fort, including two lunettes six hundred yards apart, which were captured with their artillery — six guns. (Total 22 guns.) Gen. Ord now endeavored to sweep down the captured entrenchments to the remaining redan, which was on the river bank (to the left), but the attempt was unsuccessful. In making it, Gen. Ord was so severely wounded in the leg as to completely disable him, and the command devolved upon Gen. Heckman. Fort Gilmer is three fourths of a mile north of Fort Harrison.

The foregoing account was written in the main before the writer's visit to Fort Harrison, with Lt. Col. Smith, in May 1885.

The general line of the James river from Dutch Gap, on the south, to Chaffin's Bluff and a little past and opposite Fort Harrison, on the north, may be called northwest. The general line of the Varina road from Aiken's landing is also northwest, and nearly parallel with the James, and at an average distance of about two miles. The Confederate line of works from the James at the south end of Chaffin's Bluff to Fort Harrison and beyond run generally northeast — diagonally across from the James to the Varina road. The Union troops, therefore, going up from Aiken's landing, approached Fort Harrison from the south-southeast, with the James River on their left — west. Our troops, of Gen. Stannard's Division, in the assaulting column, came up the Varina road, formed on the left of the road, in the edge of a belt of pine timber running between Mr. Henry Cox's house and Mr. J. K. Childrey's house, and, measured by the road, one half mile north of Henry Cox's house. When formed the column of troops faced due northwest, and they rushed straight at the southeast and longest and highest face of the fort.

Fort Harrison is a very irregular earth-work, on the top of a ridge or hill curving outward towards the southeast, the parapet nearly following the curvature of the hill. Commencing at the northernmost point — the extreme left of the work — W in sketch, a strong rifle-trench provided with platforms and embrasures for several guns runs southwest 500 feet,

---

[1] These are both serious errors; and are repeated in Gen. Grant's Memoirs, Vol. II. page 333. The facts were these : Col. Stevens was wounded, disabled, before the fort was captured. Gen. Burnham was shot within the fort, and after its capture. Besides, each of these officers commanded a separate Brigade; and Burnham's 2d, Stevens' 1st, and Roberts' 3d, brigades, having united at the foot of the hill referred to, joined together and moved simultaneously in the final rush that captured the fort and works, spread along the ditch to secure working space, and climbed the parapet man by man indiscriminately — all trying to see who would be the first to enter the works. See account of Lt. Col. Smith. — S. M. T.

and faces southeast, until it reaches the main square fort at a point where there is a gun-way, and a bridge over the deep ditch. For convenience' sake we will call this 500-foot line the first line, and the angle at the gun-way the first angle. With this line for a handle the fort forms a huge sickle, cutting north and west. At the first angle, at the gun-way and bridge, a line, forming nearly a right angle there with the 500-foot line, runs almost due southeast 150 feet, and faces northeast. This we will call the second line, and the angle at the end of it the second angle — K.

At the end of this 150-foot line, at the second angle, commences the principal face of the main fort — the great southeast face, struck and mounted by our Brigade in the assault. This principal face or line commencing at the second angle, runs almost due southwest 435 feet, then sweeps back toward the west in a line 125 feet long, and then again sweeps still farther back toward the west, in a line 150 feet long, thence continuing, as a rifle-trench, more to the southward and toward the river below Chaffin's Bluff.

The principal southeast face of the main fort, 435 feet long, is provided on its inner side with a huge traverse, 30 feet wide at base, 18 feet high, and 10 feet wide on the top, running straight back, from a point 150

---

### DESCRIPTION OF PLAT.

A. Varina Road — shortened. Near the fort the road turns north.
B. Thirteenth with 1st Brigade, and two regiments of the 2d Brigade, leading, formed in pines for the assault — a mile from the fort.
C. Rail fence thrown down by the column while advancing.
D. Assaulting column halted under bluff — 100 yards from the fort.
E. Fort Harrison.   F. Old Confederate barracks.
G. Bridge over ditch, and entrance to the fort.   K. Second angle.
H. Large traverse.   I. Gen. Grant's traverse.
W. Extreme northern point of the fort — a large rifle-trench 500 feet long.
M. Line of Thirteenth in battle of Sept. 30th. The square enclosure, N, was not then built, and the Thirteenth occupied the clear ground of a large open field, the right of the Reg. coming up to the entrenchments, the left thrown a little back — almost the identical ground on which the north wall of the square enclosure, N, was built after the battle.
P. Confederate lines formed in the ravine just before their charge on Sept. 30th.
R. Old Confederate bake-house. Arrow points southward to James River, where the Confederate gunboats were, distant about one mile from the fort.
    Col. Roberts' 3d Brigade moved down on the right of the Varina road ; the arrow indicates the course that brigade followed. The distances marked on the fort are in feet — measured.

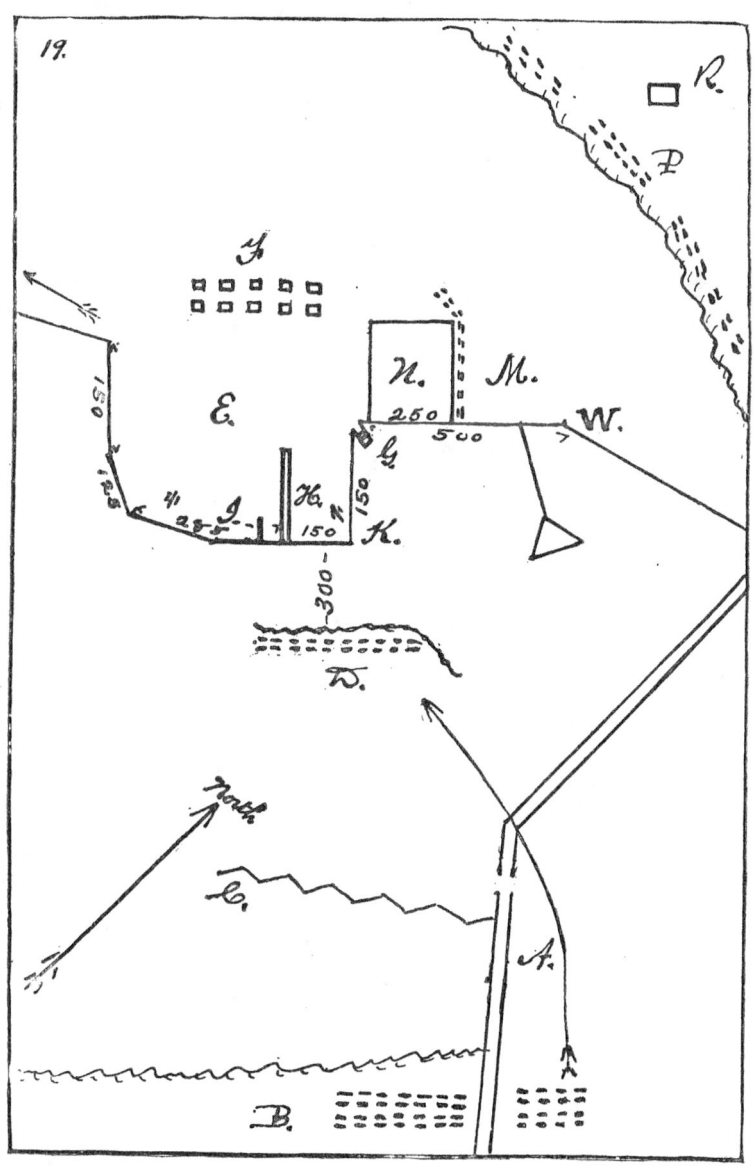

FORT HARRISON, September 29 and 30, 1864.

From a sketch made by the writer in May 1885.

feet south of the northern end of this principal face, for a distance of 100 feet, northwest into and across the fort — leaving about one third of the great square enclosure of the fort to the north of this traverse, and about two thirds to the south of it.

Several days after the capture of the fort a rectangular enclosure was built on the northwest or inner side of the 500-foot first line; and the northern wall of this enclosure starts out from a point about midway of this 500-foot line. On Sept. 30th, the battle line of the 13th was on the ground in the then open field, soon afterwards and now occupied by the north wall of this enclosure, the right resting on the rear — or inner — side of the 500-foot line where the north wall now joins it, their left extending beyond the space now occupied by this north wall, and sweeping back a little to the rear, while the Reg. faced almost due northeast.

Lieut. Taggard, of the 13th, relates the two following incidents, which he witnessed: "I was very near Gen. Burnham when he was shot, the ball penetrating his stomach; he placed his hands over the wound, exclaiming: 'Oh! Oh! Oh!' spun around a moment, and then fell. It is possible, however, that he suffered little beyond the shock that first unnerved him.

"Lieut. Gen. Grant appeared in Fort Harrison within two hours after its capture — about 10 a. m. — the soldiers remarking when they saw him: 'He, for one General, is not far behind his men.' After looking about a little he sat down on the step of the small traverse jutting back from the great southeast, 435 foot, face of the fort — and the nearest small traverse to the south side of the great traverse — took paper and pencil from his pocket, and commenced writing a dispatch on his knee.

"Just then a large shell — the kind the soldiers call a 'three-gallon demijohn' — came up from a Confederate gunboat in the James, passed with a howl very near over Gen. Grant's head, and with a loud thud struck on the side of the great traverse — toward which the General was then facing — directly in front of where he was sitting, rolled down into the open space towards him, and stopped within a few feet of him, the fuse still burning and threatening an instant explosion. There was immediately a lively stampede, and a scattering among the officers and soldiers standing near by, for cover behind various parts of the works, and a number instantly laid flat upon the ground; but Gen. Grant sat perfectly still, merely looked at the shell a moment, and then resumed his writing, all as unconcernedly as if nothing unusual had occurred. The shell, however, did not explode, though there was every reason for expecting that it would do so at any moment."   LIEUT. TAGGARD.

This was undoubtedly the dispatch which Gen. Grant wrote so quietly while the fuse of that rebel shell was hissing at his feet, and while other officers, and the men, were scampering for cover:

"Headquarters, Chapin's Farm,
10.45 a. m. Sept. 29, 1864."

"To Major General Halleck:

"General Ord's Corps advanced this morning and carried the very strongly fortified long lines of entrenchments below Chapin's farm, with some fifteen pieces of artillery and from 200 to 300 prisoners.

"Gen. Ord was wounded, though not dangerously.

"Gen. Birney advanced at the same time from Deep Bottom, and carried the New Market road and entrenchments and scattered the enemy in every direction, though he captured but few. He is now marching on towards Richmond. I left Gen. Birney where the Mill road intercepts the New Market and Richmond road. This whole country is filled with field fortifications thus far.         U. S. GRANT, Lieut. General."

The name of the fort, though changed in honor of Gen. Burnham, to Fort Burnham, remains in general history as Fort Harrison. The men called Gen. Burnham, familiarly, "Old Grizzly," from his heavy iron

---

### DESCRIPTION OF MAP.

A. New Market Heights.         E. Varina Road.
B. Fort on New Market road, D, the main traveled road from Richmond direct to Deep Bottom and to Jones's and Curl's Necks.
C. Laurel Hill church, and Mrs. Pierce's house.
F. Henry Cox.         K. Fort Harrison.         G. J. K. Childrey.
H. Thirteenth with column formed for assault on Fort Harrison.
M. Three Mile Creek. A little brook under the bluff in front of Fort Harrison, where the column halted a moment before the final assault, appears to run into this creek.         L. Fort Gilmer.
S. Cross-way of Union works on New Market road, D.
T. O. Aiken's house, Gen. Devens' Hdqrs. winter of 1864-5.
V. Mr. James's house on road, W, leading due north to Mr. Jordan's house on the Darbytown road, not shown on this map.
Z. Last camp of the Thirteenth at the front, on the line of works leading from Fort Harrison around to Deep Bottom. See April 3, 1865. The arrow at the left points to Chaffin's Bluff on the James about one mile distant.
Y. Y. Y. Confederate earth-works. A portion of the Confederate lines, 2, 3, and 4, near Fort Harrison, were rendered untenable by our capture of that fort, and the enemy threw up a new connecting line to the westward; the Confederate lines being much changed after the official map was made.
X. S. B. The Union line running up to Fort Harrison, and thence curving northward in a huge loop, was all built after the capture of that fort.

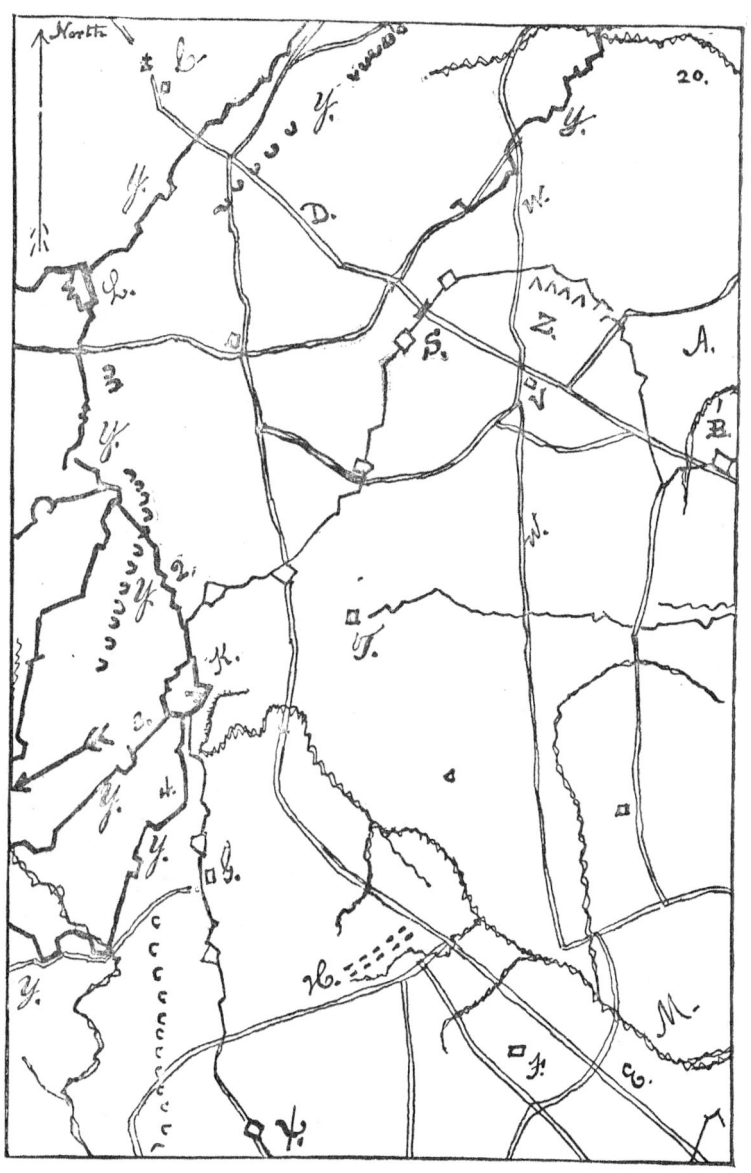

FORT HARRISON, September 29 and 30, 1864.

Tracing of Official Map. Scale, one and one half inches to one mile.

gray hair and whiskers. He was at one time extremely severe with the 13th, for some reason or other, but was never known to use a cross or unhandy word in addressing a member of our Regiment after we captured Battery Five. Capt. Clark, Asst. Adjt. General on his staff, resigned immediately after Gen. Burnham's death.

The wound received to-day by Col. Stevens is of such a character as to make his return to the service very improbable.

He served as Major in the First New Hampshire Infantry, which breaking up early in the war furnished so many officers for succeeding regiments. He had been a prominent lawyer in Nashua, and at the close of his term of service in the 1st N. H. returned there to his legal practice. Commissioned as Colonel of the Thirteenth, he commanded the Regiment, or the Brigade of which it formed a part, in nearly all of its battles up to this battle of Fort Harrison in which he is wounded. He stood well with his personal staff, and was a good officer. His position has been mentioned before, in the body of the book, and needs no repetition here. Major Stoodley was near him to-day when he was hit, which occurred when the Brigade was near the brook, just before the oblique movement was made under the little hill or bluff, a few minutes before the fort was stormed. As soon as he found that he could not recover sufficiently to return to the service, he wrote to the officers of the Thirteenth that he would resign and thus give Lt. Col. Smith and Major Stoodley, and of course other officers, the opportunity of promotion, but these officers, upon consultation, declined to receive promotion at his loss.[1]

It is not the province of this history to follow men into civil life, for space cannot be found for an account of one tenth of the actual services rendered by the members of the Thirteenth in their military life, but a few instances may be pardoned. After the war Col. Stevens — with the honorary title of Brevet Brigadier General — held numerous minor public offices. He was also Post-master at Nashua for several years, and served two terms as Representative to Congress from New Hampshire. He suffered for two or more years from Bright's disease of the kidneys, and from this cause died at Nashua May 7, 1887.

Lewis F. Hanson, Co. G, 10th N. H., relates the following incident of the assault, which he witnessed : " While the first of our men were scrambling into the fort, the rebels trained the gun, at the left angle of the fort near the gunway and bridge over the ditch, directly upon a body of our troops in the field, not fifty yards from the gun, and the rebel gunner already had the lanyard in his hand, ready to discharge the gun ; but a man of Co. I in the 10th had got upon the works, near and within reach of this gunner, and called to him to stop, and not fire that gun. The rebel, however, made the motion to fire — but not quick enough ; the man of the 10th drove his bayonet clear through him, and the gun was not discharged

---

[1] Major Stoodley, having been with the Regiment during Col. Stevens' entire term of service, was requested by the writer to furnish an article upon Col. Stevens, and gave the above. — S. M. T.

at the Union troops, but turned the next minute, and its contents sent crashing among the enemy and his barracks in the rear of the fort."

When the garrisons and gunners of the Confederate army had well learned the hard fact that the Northern bayonet and sabre never hesitated, then the Union cause was more than half won.

Because of the fragmentary and somewhat conflicting accounts, official and otherwise, of the capture of Fort Harrison, the writer asked Lt. Col. Smith, commanding the Thirteenth on that occasion, to make a definite statement of the affair, which with his papers, letters and memoranda condensed, is as follows: "When we started on the morning of Sept. 29, 1864, I looked at my watch as we commenced crossing the ponton bridge over the James at Aiken's, and found it was then 3 a. m. We crossed rapidly in column of fours, myself and Adjutant Taggard on horseback. It is about one fourth of a mile from the ponton landing to Mr. Aiken's house. We left our horses there in care of orderlies. We were formed for the advance very quickly, but of course it takes a little time to put a couple of regiments of skirmishers upon a line in the dark and on wholly new ground. Gen. Ord was not the man to tarry on such occasions; and Col. Donohoe of the 10th N. H., in command of the skirmish line, was another man who never let grass grow under his feet.

"The head of our column was kept close up to the skirmish line. After crossing the wide flats, and reaching the top of the bluff to the second flat, our skirmishers struck the rebel skirmishers. At this time the darkness had in no way decreased, and the firing was rapid, but there were not many bullets from the enemy coming past us. The 10th N. H. and 118th N. Y., on the skirmish line, were armed with Spencer rifles, and they now used them for about ten minutes for all they were worth. We advanced rapidly until we reached the woods a fourth of a mile farther on; and here it began to be light. A good many stray bullets were coming back, and before reaching Mr. Cox's house Lieut. Henry B. Wheeler of I was struck in his foot.

"When the column was advancing on both sides of the Varina road — Col. Roberts' 3d Brigade on the right-hand side, Burnham's 2d Brigade and Stevens' 1st Brigade, with the 13th, on the left-hand side — we came upon a Confederate brigade encamped in an oak grove across the road from Mr. Henry Cox's house. The most of the Confederates were absent, probably on their picket lines, the rest were driven out of their camp by our skirmish line, in view of our main column. They left their camp with their breakfast on the fires.

"We made no halt until we reached the edge of the large wood, when we halted to rest; and here caps were removed from all the muskets in the assaulting column. Here also, about one half a mile beyond — north — of Mr. Henry Cox's house, all irregularities in the column were corrected, and the order of and formation for the assault was arranged as follows: Roberts' 3d Brigade formed on the right-hand side of the road. On the left-hand side of the road were, first, the 10th N. H. and 118th

N. Y., of the 2d Brigade, deployed, in front of the whole Division, as skirmishers with Col. Donohoe in command. The 96th N. Y., of the 2d Brigade, were deployed in line of battle next in rear of the skirmishers. Then came the 8th Conn. in close column by divisions.

"Then came our 1st Brigade also formed in close column by divisions, the Thirteenth leading our Brigade. This brought the 13th the third regiment in the column, after the skirmishers. It may well be described as a column of Brigades, each formed in close column by divisions.

"While we were halted here I went forward to the edge of the pine woods and met there Major Theodore Read, Chief of staff to Gen. Ord. We could see Fort Harrison very plainly, and began commenting upon the situation. Our skirmishers were now slowly advancing into the wide field, but not firing much, and away in the distance the rebel pickets were slowly retreating with their guns at 'right shoulder shift.' A big puff of smoke now appears in Fort Harrison, and a shell strikes near us to the right.

"Near the point where Lieut. Wheeler was hit, Col. Donohoe came riding by, his gray horse covered with foam, and his face lighted up as a man's face can be only when he is in the excitement of battle and everything is going well. As he passed Gen. Ord he exclaimed: 'We are giving it to them to-day, General!' and in an instant more he was out of sight among the leaves and underbrush, as he dashed away.

"The formation above given was first made soon after crossing the ponton bridge, excepting that the troops were then in the road, and was held as nearly as possible, being finally corrected here in the pines fully one and one fourth miles due southeast of the main southeast wall of Fort Harrison. The course of the assault was therefore to be northwest, across an open field a mile wide; sweeping first down a gentle slope, then rising abruptly to the fort on the crest of a bluff.

"We were soon moving again toward the fort, Col. Stevens commanding our First Brigade, myself commanding the Thirteenth, and Capt. Forbush commanding a division (two Companies of the 13th) in front of our Regiment, all three of us marching nearly side by side. About the time when we reached Mr. J. K. Childrey's house our skirmishers left our front — I think going to the left and acting as flank-skirmishers. After leaving the woods behind about one third of a mile, the column came to a heavy zig-zag rail fence leading from the left side of the Varina road along the lane to Mr. Childrey's house, and was halted for a brief moment while the fence was thrown down. After throwing down this fence we advanced without a halt; but at no time at a double-quick, although Capt. Elder on Gen. Stannard's staff came to us ordering us to double-quick. Upon this order came the quick response of the men: 'No; we will not double-quick, it is too far — but we will go all the same!'

"Preserving their formation the men moved over the prostrate fence, and across the open field — under a most furious and murderous rebel fire, of all arms and missiles, raking the whole field — to within 100 yards of the fort, without firing a shot in reply. When they halted here and laid down to take breath, the Thirteenth rested at a point under the hill directly in front of the huge traverse which divides the main fort into two parts; leaving one third north, and two thirds south. In this hollow in the field, under a hill or bluff 15 to 20 feet high the fire from the fort was ineffective by reason of the enemy's inability to sufficiently depress his guns. Up to this point, however, the enemy's fire, rapid and severe, had swept the whole plain across which the assaulting column had advanced.

"Just before we reached the bend in the Varina road Col. Stevens was shot, and at once removed outside of the advancing column, but no halt was made until we were under the little bluff near the fort, when it seems to me every one laid down at once without orders. As soon as we had halted here, I went back at once and told our senior Lieut. Colonel — John B. Raulston of the 81st N. Y. — that he was in command of the Brigade, Col. Stevens having been shot. He turned over the command of the 81st to the senior officer present, and came to the front of our First Brigade with me, lying down close by my side.

"Now as to the final rush and the capture of the fort: The 1st Division of the 18th Corps was formed between 4 and 5 a. m. near Mr. Albert Aiken's house as follows: First, as skirmishers the 10th N. H. and 118th N. Y., covering both sides of the Varina road. Second, the 96th N. Y. in line of battle, the 8th Conn. in column by divisions. Third, our First Brigade, in column by divisions, commanded by Col. Stevens. It was his invariable rule to place his command as follows: commencing with the lowest numerical number and increasing to the rear. This always brought our Reg. to the front being 13, followed by the three New York regiments — 81st, 98th, 139th. So the Thirteenth was the second Regiment in column of divisions behind the 8th Conn., to the left of the road. The 3d Brigade (Col. Guy V. Henry, 40th Mass, in command usually, but at this time absent on leave in Massachusetts) was under command of Col. Samuel H. Roberts of the 139th N. Y. of our First Brigade, and was in column on the right of the road. We thus advanced, and when we came to the bend in the Varina road, the 3d Brigade had crossed from the right side of the road to the left, joining the 1st and 2d Brigades on the right, thus bringing the whole Division together again into a compact column for assault before we reached the little bluff beneath which we laid down to take breath.

"We laid under this little bluff for perhaps five minutes — not more; and it was Col. Samuel H. Roberts who gave the order to advance from this point upon the fort. Our three Brigades were all together lying mixed up on the ground. Col. Roberts was a tall, oldish looking man, apparently fifty years of age, with a thin, dyspeptic looking face — I can see him so plainly even now! He gave the command in a slow, drawling and an even, monotonous voice: 'Come, boys; we must capture that fort — now get up and start!' We all together almost instantaneously obeyed the command, and the column suddenly sprang forward as one man, charged up the hill in a solid body, and rushed straight over ditch and parapet of the long southeast face into the main fort. The advance was made in quick time, all the regiments in the assaulting force being more or less mixed up until the fort was captured. There was no abatis in front of the fort, and the men jumped into the moat, now dry, drove their bayonets into the front side of the walls of the fort up to the muzzles of the guns, then placed the gun-stocks upon their shoulders, and other men climbed upon them up into the fort. Soon we had the fort, garrison and guns — six of them in the main fort, and some say eight.

"Capt. Forbush and Lieut. R. R. Thompson were shot near the moat before entering the fort. I was wounded in the head — a three inch scalp wound, merely such as to compel me to be off duty for four or five days — while trying to cause the Thirteenth to oblique to the left, so as to enter the main fort south of the traverse — which would be nearer the centre of the fort. After being wounded I was very faint for a few minutes, and got into the moat for safety, and there remained and witnessed the capture. Later while returning, wounded and bleeding very badly, down under the little bluff in front of the fort, I found several men loitering behind, and sent them up into the fort. When I was shot the command of the Thirteenth devolved upon Capt. Stoodley. Soon after the capture I was sent back to the rear in charge of the prisoners captured, and when about opposite Mr. J. K. Childrey's house, I met Gen. Heckman's Division advancing northward on the right-hand side of the Varina road, in column of divisions. So that it is impossible for any man of Gen. Heckman's command to claim any share whatever in the capture of Fort Harrison.

"Gen. Hiram Burnham's brigade did not capture Fort Harrison; any more than Col. Stevens' brigade or Col. Roberts' brigade did. These three brigades were mixed together lying on the ground under the little bluff; at Col. Roberts' command these three brigades sprang to their feet simultaneously and almost as one man, and rushed together into the moat of the fort, spread along the moat to the right and left to secure working space, and the men and officers of all the regiments in our First Division in the assaulting column alike and at the same time clambered up the walls and into the fort, all as quickly as they possibly could. Gen. Burnham did not go with his Brigade, Stevens and Roberts led theirs. Col. M. T. Donohoe belonged to Gen. Burnham's brigade, and after Gen. Burnham was killed succeeded him in command of that brigade. Col. Donohoe was wounded in the afternoon when our troops were forced to retire from some captured rebel entrenchments near the James river. Col. Stevens did not belong to Gen. Burnham's brigade at all, but commanded his own brigade until he was shot.

"After the capture, our 1st Brigade turning somewhat upon its right as a pivot swung through the fort and the barracks to the rear of it and advanced, while the Confederates disputed every inch of the ground. This turning movement brought the right of the Thirteenth near the rear, or northwest side, of the 500-foot first line, or face, of the earth-work — the heavy rifle-trench leading **northward** towards Fort Gilmer — the right of the Reg. resting at a point about midway of that trench. About 9 a. m. a heavy skirmish line was sent out from the Reg. which skirmished all day, and remained on picket until the morning of the 30th. Gen. Ord was wounded while standing on the southeast end of the great traverse in the fort. During the night the Reg. was set at work for a time building the line of rifle-trenches that points from the southern part of the fort directly toward Mr. J. K. Childrey's house; this line confronting the rebel line of rifle-trenches running from the southern end of the fort to the James river." Lt. Col. Smith.

**Sept. 30. Fri.** The second day of the battle of Fort Harrison. Rainy, drizzling, chilly. The Thirteenth has been at work all night. Last night it was clearly evident that the enemy was being heavily re-enforced by troops drawn, apparently, from Petersburg; and this threatened renewal of the contest to-day has spurred every man to do his utmost in preparing our defenses.

Last night the Thirteenth was moved into a part of the field which we crossed in the assault, remained there an hour or so, and then was moved back again within the fort. We also moved to the rear of the fort towards the James. Aside from these moves, occupying not much over two hours in all, we worked on the defenses, running across the open rear — the northwest side — of the fort and towards the river, all day yesterday, after capturing the fort between 7 and 8 a. m., all last night, and all this morning up to 11 a. m., without rest or sleep; and all the time, when he could see us, under the fire of the enemy. By this time to-day, we have succeeded in throwing up a strong line of defenses for ourselves — the second line made by us since we captured the fort; when suddenly, at 11 a. m. our Brigade is assembled and moved off towards the right into a wide, clear space next to the colored troops, and posted in line of battle. The movement, and posting the various regiments, occupies a considerable time.

Our right rests now about midway of the 500-foot line of the fort, and on the rear, or northwest side, of this line. We have here no cover whatever, as our line forms a right angle with that 500-foot trench. Capt. Stoodley has command of the 13th to-day, and at his direction we all set at work at once with dippers, bayonets and sticks, each man for himself, throwing up little mounds of earth for protection. A few small logs are also made use of for the same purpose. But we have not been in position here twenty minutes, when, about 12 noon, the enemy opens upon our lines with every gun he can bring to bear from field batteries, forts, mortars and gunboats; the din is terrific. This firing keeps up for about an hour, while our guns scarcely make any reply; but every man in our lines makes ready for what he knows is surely coming — a furious rebel charge. We face northeast, and are out beyond all the improvised breast-works thrown up across the rear of the fort; and are in a smooth, open field, almost entirely unprotected during the whole engagement of the day. The enemy's charges are directed a little west of south, where he strikes our front, and as he comes over from the James river.

Soon the enemy can be seen advancing without skirmishers, in long lines of gray, and as steadily as if on a gala day parade; he emerges from the woods with flags flying, and the swords of his officers waving and flashing, and moves down over a slope into a ravine. He threatens a fierce fight, and our lines and men are placed in the very best possible condition for defense. The 10th N. H., and other troops, having the Spencer rifles are distributed along the weaker parts of our position.

Our flag is at once planted in the sand, unfurled, and all along our lines flag after flag is rapidly unfurled, until every bit of available color and bunting is set waving in the breeze as a challenge to the enemy to come on. These flags spring up like magic; and with them instantly a single loud, strong, clear voice, near by the 13th strikes up 'The Battle Cry of Freedom,' —

" Yes, we 'll rally round the Flag, boys, we 'll rally once again,
   Shouting the battle cry of Freedom,"
— and the whole line takes up the song spontaneously, as it was begun — all joining whether they can sing or not.

An officer, who witnessed this scene of the flags and heard the song, says: " It seemed to me as if the whole rebel army and the devil himself could not have captured those flags."

All is the work of a few swift moments. The enemy re-forms in the ravine, marches steadily up to the crest of the hither slope, in such order as to exhibit his whole long solid columns almost at once, then dashes into a double-quick and run, with bayonets fixed and gleaming, straight for our lines, yelling like an army of demons, and soon is within close range; when, at the sound of a single musket shot fired on our side — apparently an accidental shot and not a signal — the song stops as suddenly as it began, our men drop down behind our hastily improvised cover, and their awful work of the day commences, in dead earnest, with one unbroken blaze and crash of musketry, a solid volley, every man firing after a steady deliberate aim — not a random shot on the whole line. At the first fire the enemy's front lines seem to wilt and sink down into the ground, as if it had suddenly opened beneath them; their columns waver a moment, then fall back in confusion. Our men meanwhile loading and firing at will, and as rapidly as possible.

The firing quiets down. The enemy rallies, forms and charges again; again receives a volley followed by a rapid rattling fire, and is hurled back. Again, and still again — four times — he forms and attempts to advance; the first three charges by the troops of General Hoke and Field, 18 full regiments, under the eye of Gen. Lee himself, and the fourth charge by fresh troops; but all in vain, he cannot recapture the works. His fresh troops cannot be again successfully rallied. A body of his troops have rushed into a depression from which they can neither advance nor retreat. The advantage is seen, and a sortie is made by men of the 10th and 13th, and five hundred prisoners come in at once. Capt. Goss of I, now commanding the Corps of sharp-shooters [1] of our 1st Division, captures the colors of three of Gen. Clingman's regiments, and a large number of prisoners; for which he is specially complimented in General Orders. Lossing states that Clingman's brigade is almost entirely wiped out. Seven rebel battle flags in all are captured by the Union troops.

During these three successive charges, and the less threatening fourth, battle cries, cheers, yells, shouts of command, the crash of volleys of musketry, the thunder of cannon and the crack of shell mingle together in a terrific roar. The enemy charges up very near. No one of our men, in the excessive excitement, feels any sense of fear or danger, and all work together with the utmost coolness and rapidity. The enemy's fourth attempt to rally and charge ends in a complete fizzle, and his men turn and run for cover, every man for himself. They strike a snag.

At the enemy's final discomfiture, our men seize their flags and wave them, swing their caps, scream, hurrah, and shout themselves hoarse, at this most important victory.

One North Carolina brigade — Clingman's — is practically annihilated, either killed, wounded or captured, flags and all. The battle continues from twelve noon until dark; but the severest part, the enemy's fierce charges, covers but a short time, two or three hours.

Fifteen rebel regiments — counted by their flags — were massed on our Brigade front, and in advancing received our front fire, and a sharp and effective fire, from right and left, in both flanks; they dashed into the curvature of the sickle blade, and were cut down. One large batch of prisoners are virtually deserters. They state that Gen. Lee commanded in person, and was willing to sacrifice a large number of his men if he could possibly wrest from us this Fort Harrison — one of the strongest forts upon his entire line, and whose loss is counted a very great disaster to the Confederate cause.

Capt. Stoodley states that after the cannonade the enemy moved to the assault at 1 p. m. Fifteen rebel regiments upon our Brigade front. Gen. Stannard was shot about 1.30 p. m. The battle lasted from 1 p. m. till dark. The enemy charged three times. The officers of the Thirteenth present in to-day's battle are Capt. Stoodley and three Lieutenants. This is the coolest, sharpest, most deliberate, and most 'business-like' battle the Thirteenth has been engaged in. We meet superior numbers in open ground, advancing with desperate courage and dogged determination over and over again; and besides this and the enemy's infantry fire, we are all the time under a severe fire from the enemy's

---

[1] Capt. Goss' men charged with fearful yells into the mass of disorganized rebels; and though it is doubtful, some have it that here began the nickname — 'Sharps'-hooters.'

field batteries, his guns nearer Fort Gilmer, his mortar batteries and his gunboats in the James.

Pollard states that the enemy's assaulting force on us to-day are Anderson's, Bratton's and McLaw's Brigades, of Field's Division.

When these two fearful days are over, our 1st Division of sixteen regiments of infantry numbers but 1,300 men present for duty, and the Thirteenth is cut down by almost one half in dead, severely wounded and disabled. The casualties of these two days in the Thirteenth are two officers and thirteen men killed, seven officers and fifty-nine men wounded; a total of 81, about the same number as the loss in the twelve days at Cold Harbor. Eighty-one out of one hundred and eighty-seven is a severe loss indeed.

One of the most wonderful cases of wounds received in the war was that received to-day by Sergt. Major James M. Hodgdon of the Thirteenth. He was lying down during the enemy's third charge, when a rebel sharp-shooter's bullet — a 'square-ender,' longer, but a trifle smaller than a minie bullet — struck his right eye, entered, and passed downward inside his temple, smashed the end of his jaw, thence down his neck, and finally brought up against his right shoulder blade, breaking it badly. He did not lose consciousness for a moment. Lieut. Curtis gave him a glass of raw whiskey as he lay on the ground, the stimulus of which may have saved his life.

He came very near dying while in the hospital. At one time all hope of his living was given up by the Surgeons; but nothing could damp his own good spirits and hope. When the Surgeon at Hampton Hospital frankly told him that there was but one chance in a hundred for him to recover, Hodgdon tapped the Surgeon on the arm familiarly with his finger, and rather confidentially and good-naturedly replied: "Well, Doc. I will take that chance;" and the brave fellow did! He recovered. Has a wife and fine family now, 1887, and has charge of the weaving rooms at Manchaug Mills, Mass. He says that he can compare the sensation, when the bullet struck him, with nothing but the pleasant feeling experienced when a piece of warm flannel is laid against one's eye.

He was able to leave the hospital for home on Dec. 20, 1864, after being in the hospital but 80 days. The bullet was cut out March 12, 1865, having worked down to the middle of his back, and touching the spine. It is a wonder of wonders that a man could survive such a wound.

Yesterday morning the Thirteenth went into the fight with 187 muskets; this morning Capt. Stoodley, in his field report, reports 89 men as present for duty. Hosp. Steward R. B. Prescott is the only representative of the medical staff of the 13th present in all this expedition — the Surgeons all detached and absent on other duties.

The capture here of the Confederate muster-rolls shows how terribly the 13th and 10th cut up — nearly annihilated — the 44th Tennessee, during the rebel charges in the fog at Drury's Bluff on the morning of May 16, 1864.

A man of the 10th N. H. was sitting down during some part of the battle to-day with his back to the earth-works, and holding his gun between his knees; when a shell thrown from a Confederate gunboat burst near him, and a piece of it broke his gun and cut his spine in two. He merely leaned back a little more, without any show of pain or hurt, and remained sitting against the works nearly as before. The thing was done in a flash. A man instantly killed, if he is sitting or lying down, makes but little change in position.

Gen. Stannard says that the enemy — Gen. Anderson commanding Gen. Longstreet's Corps, and assaulting with Law, Anderson, Bratton, Clingman and Colquitt — opened with twelve guns on his centre and left, the enemy's infantry advancing on his right. That he held his fire, until the enemy emerged from the thick underbrush in front, when he repulsed them with musketry alone. The enemy charged three times. The enemy acknowledges a loss of 2,000 men; and their loss has been estimated at 3,000 and above.

Yesterday, 29th, Gen. Birney with the 10th Corps and a body of colored troops of the 18th Corps carried everything before him at Deep Bottom before 9 a. m; and before noon swept around upon the New Market road, advanced and established communications with the right of Gen. Stannard's Division, north of Fort Harrison, as had been arranged. Gen. Birney, however, could not dislodge the enemy on his front, though his troops, and especially the colored troops who made an assault, behaved with great gallantry. Their charge was witnessed by us from Fort Harrison. Richmond therefore cannot now be entered from this side, as was hoped, by a surprise, and the chief gains of the attack centre about Fort Harrison, captured and held by Gen. Stannard's 1st Division of the 18th Corps. A large force of the enemy is now entrenching on an inner line, on our front, while our lines are being made as strong as possible. Gen. Ord's wound, received after we entered Fort Harrison on the 29th, caused a serious delay in the general movements of the day.

As the line of trenches extended northward beyond the northern end of the 500-foot line, it reached a little redoubt on the main line (not the three-cornered affair now, 1885, seen in that direction) distant 300 to 400 yards from the right of the 13th, as they were placed on Sept. 30th. During the battle the Confederates charged up to this redoubt, captured it, and held it until dark, delivering a very annoying fire upon our lines, at close range.

Almost due north of the front of the 13th, and about 500 yards distant, is a ravine running from right to left across the field, and just beyond it stood an old Confederate bake-house. (The ruins of it now visible, 1885.) About mid-afternoon, Gen. Clingman's brigade charged up into this ravine near the old bake-house, and found it very difficult either to advance or retire from; and Capt. Goss of the 13th charged upon a portion of Clingman's command, with his sharp-shooters, and captured the large number of prisoners and the three battle flags as mentioned.

A Confederate skirmisher used an upper window of this old bake-house for a convenient place to shoot from during the fight, was killed, and his body hung over the window sill for many days after the battle.

The colors of the Thirteenth was planted in the sand to-day, and Color Sergeant Charles Powell, of K, was standing beside it holding the staff in his hand, the most of the Regiment lying down in line of battle, when a rebel sharp-shooter hidden behind a little log-house fired at him, and the bullet cut through his left wrist while the flag staff was in his hand, disabling him for any further service in the army.

Powell was obliged to go to the rear; but with the true courage of a soldier, and of a Color Bearer, too, though under a murderous fire and severely wounded, the wound bleeding profusely and very painful, he calls coolly and carefully upon a comrade at his right to take care of the colors, and after having seen it in safe hands, goes to the rear to have his wound attended to, leaving the colors as he had planted it, the flag unfurled and the staff firmly set in the sand.

During the fight to-day a soldier of the Thirteenth is in the act of putting a cap on his musket, when his arm is suddenly jerked back, and he turns to a comrade near, and commences scolding him, remarking indignantly that 'this is no time to be fooling.' The comrade tells him to look at his hand; he does so, and finds the blood flowing over it from a serious bullet cut in the arm, a flesh wound. Like thousands of other cases, the blow was so instantaneous as at first to cause no pain whatever.

The following is condensed from Prescott's letters from the Hospital Dept.: "The Thirteenth left camp at Bermuda Hundred at 9 p. m. Sept. 27th, marched nearly to the James, then turned aside into the woods and obtained a few hours of sleep. Our 1st Division of the 18th Corps crossed the muffled pontons at Aiken's about 1.30 a. m. Sept. 29th, and reached the crest of a hill about one mile from the river at early daylight. Here a part of the 2d Brigade deployed as skirmishers and advanced, closely followed by the rest of the 2d Brigade, and by the 1st Brigade, in which was the 13th, and also by the 3d Brigade, the most in column by divisions. The enemy retreated, keeping up a brisk fire with our skirmishers. When we emerged from the woods the black guns in Fort Harrison were looking down the road toward us, while the fort was flanked with breast-works interspersed with redoubts mounting other cannon.

"Here a brief halt was made. Gen. Ord surveyed the position, and ordered an assault. While we were waiting the rebels let fly a few shells, one of which struck a gun wheel in our column, glancing and killing three men and four horses. Two brigades moved into the field at the left of the Varina road, and one brigade to the right, and then ensued one of the grandest charges in the history of the war. The troops moved firmly and steadily in close column by divisions, and at a 'right shoulder shift arms' until more than half the distance was gained, when an oblique movement was made, which took the troops partially out of range of the heavy guns of the fort. In a few moments more our men were swarming over the parapet, capturing eight cannon, two of them heavy pivot guns, and about one hundred prisoners. Col. Stevens was struck by a bullet when below the fort (before entering), and was taken away in an ambulance with the body of Gen. Burnham, who commanded the 2d Brigade, and who was killed by a sharp-shooter after the fort was taken. Two rebel iron-clads steamed down the river a few hours after we captured the fort, and threw 200 lb. shell at us all the afternoon, and at intervals during the next day. Some of the rebel barracks were torn down, and the logs piled into breast-works.

"Sept. 30th. Yesterday Gen. Lee, Jefferson Davis and others were plainly seen from the parapet of Fort Harrison; while standing on the parapet with Capt. Goss we both distinctly saw the party. Deserters who came in last night report that Mr. Davis said that this position must be re-taken if it required the entire Confederate army to do it. This forenoon we could see columns of the rebels massing, and working parties apparently planting artillery, on our front. Meanwhile our men were impatiently awaiting the arrival of shovels and picks. It was noon before these arrived, and hardly a shovelful of earth had been moved, before the enemy opened vigorously with artillery, and soon after with their shrill yells, charged down upon us. Our men lying flat upon their faces fired a volley which checked the rebel charge and then repulsed them, cutting them up fearfully. They charged twice afterwards, each time with the same result. They tried the fourth time, then gave it up and retreated to their entrenchments. During the firing our men swung their cartridge boxes to the front and poured a part of their ammunition out in little piles on the ground before them for greater convenience.

"I was at this time Hospital Steward of the Thirteenth, and was the only member of our Medical Department present during the whole two days' fight. Sergt. Major James M. Hodgdon and I took advantage of a small obstacle to the rebel fire, when the enemy charged, but it did not afford sufficient protection for both of us. I was on his right, and left him and went through an opening in the line of trenches — leading northward from the fort — where the colored troops were stationed. Here I found the Hospital Steward of the 8th Conn. While conversing with him he fell, shot in the head. Gen. Stannard, standing but a few feet away, lost his right arm; and in a moment more, poor Hodgdon came through the opening before mentioned, his right eye hanging by a shred on his cheek. I gave him a stimulant, bound up his face, and assisted him to a place of shelter a few rods in the rear.

"First Sergeant John F. Gibbs of E performed prodigies of valor to-day during the rebel assaults to re-take Fort Harrison. The ammunition running short, and the teams being unable to come up by reason of the rebel sharp-shooters killing the mules, Major Stoodley called for volunteers to go back for the boxes. Sergt. Gibbs started instantly, and worked nobly lugging the heavy boxes of ammunition [1] in the face of a heavy fire, for a

---

[1] The boxes contained 1,000 rounds of ball-cartridges, and weighed above eighty pounds each, while Gibbs is a spare man of medium height. — S. M. T.

considerable distance (over open ground) from the wagons to the battle line. He deserved promotion for it." R. B. PRESCOTT.

Some idea of the depletion of the Thirteenth in its term of service may be gained from the following statement made by Major Stoodley: "In the fight to-day, acting as Major commanding the Thirteenth, I stood alone, the only commissioned officer present with the Regiment, of the original thirty-seven officers who left Concord on October 7, 1862."

MAJOR STOODLEY.

Lieut Taggard, acting Adjutant, writes in his Diary: "Thursday, Sept. 29th. We started at 9 o'clock last night; crossed the James at Aiken's. We captured Fort Harrison Sept. 29th, meeting with much loss. Sept. 30th. About noon the enemy made a severe attack on us, but were repulsed with great loss. We took, in the two days, twenty-two guns, 1,500 prisoners (a great number of them wounded men) and four colors. The losses in the Thirteenth were two officers and thirteen men killed, seven officers and fifty-eight men wounded, one missing."

LIEUT. TAGGARD.

"At Fredericksburg on the evening of Dec. 13, 1862, I received a 'clip' in the shoulder, and another bullet through the thigh, when within about four rods of the sunken road at the foot of Marye's Heights, but succeeded in leaving the field. On Sept. 28, 1864, Col. Stevens' brigade was relieved in the Bermuda Hundred trenches by Pennsylvania troops, and at 9 p. m. the entire brigade with the exception of Co. C, 13th N. H., which garrisoned a redoubt of our advanced works, moved in light marching order with its Division commanded by Gen. Stannard to assault Fort Harrison. The 10th N. H. and 118th N. Y. were deployed as skirmishers after we crossed the James on the morning of the 29th. Capt. Goss of the 13th, commanding his corps of sharp-shooters, was also on the skirmish line.

"The column advanced to within about 40 rods of the fort when Col. Stevens was struck. Soon after this the column obliqued to the right, and the enemy, supposing that we were about to attack their left flank, or the open side of the fort, sent a body of their infantry out of the main earth-work to protect that flank. They made another mistake. They had a six-inch Rodman gun mounted a little to the left of the centre of the fort, which had fired upon us repeatedly and with savage execution while we were crossing the open field in the assault; and just as the last of our Division were safe under the cover of the little bluff, that gun double-charged with grape was fired, accidentally or otherwise, and the grape shot tore up the ground and shrieked over our heads without hitting a man. This heavy and harmless discharge dismounted the gun. A moment later the Division with a cheer rushed up the slight rise in the ground. We struck the fort near the left hand corner — the second angle — leaping down into the six-foot moat, and climbing the walls, which were ten or twelve feet high. The fort with the garrison and guns was soon in the hands of our assaulting party. About dark the 13th was moved to the open rear of the fort, where we worked nearly all night throwing up entrenchments.

"There is good reason for my remembering the six-inch Rodman gun above referred to. As we were advancing during the assault, a shot from it had plunged into our column to my left, and I watched the rebel gunners as they re-loaded it; saw them step back, and the puff of smoke as the lanyard was pulled. I was exactly in line, and in the centre of the flame there seemed to be a little black ball coming directly toward me. I gave a warning cry and sprang to the right — a thing that I could easily do, being then in the line of file closers — and a moment later Reuben L. Wood, a recruit in Co. G, who was directly in front of me when the gun was fired, was struck squarely in the centre of the body, the shell passing through him and flying on its way. Strange to say the shell did not knock him over backwards, but cut a round hole in the back of his overcoat (I remember but one other man who wore an overcoat that day); and so true and clean was the circle cut, that apparently there was not a fragment of the cloth half an inch in length left projecting into it. He fell on his left side, terribly perforated.

"I entered the fort a few feet to the right of the second angle, passing the Rodman gun on my left. At that time a squad of rebels at the first angle were firing into the ditch where our men were for a moment before climbing up the walls of the fort. After getting inside the fort the first thing I did was to order two running rebels to halt and surrender, but they seemed to have urgent business elsewhere, and I fired my first shot at one of them. We got into the fort without firing a shot.

"On the 30th the 13th was moved about 1 p. m. to the extreme left — and rear of the main fort, the right of the Reg. resting on the entrenchments — but these were of no use to us in the assaults that followed. Line of battle was formed, guns stacked, and the men set at work building a defense of a few logs about six inches in diameter upon which a little earth was thrown, merely enough to keep them in place and forming a shelter about one foot in height. Presently I heard an officer of the picket line say to Major Stoodley commanding the Thirteenth : 'Your men will have to stand firm ; the enemy are massing on your front, and will charge in a few minutes.' In about twenty minutes from the time when we stacked arms here, the enemy opened on us with artillery. Gen. Field's Division of Gen. Longstreet's Corps, under the supervision of Gen. Lee, soon charged upon us ; and came on four times in succession, but were repulsed each time with a terrible loss. We exhausted the sixty rounds of ammunition per man with which we commenced this day's fighting, and the men were again supplied. The enemy could not recapture the fort. We lost no prisoners.

"The little Confederate redoubt for two guns, on our right towards Fort Gilmer, played a prominent part in this day's fight. From here also a Confederate rifleman had fired several shots at us over the top of the redoubt. Sergt. Albert M. Smith, Daniel W. Osborn and myself rested our guns upon the little log in front of us, and when he raised his head again to fire, we fired simultaneously — and silenced his little battery. It was from the angle, where this two-gun redoubt started from the main line, that another rebel fired later and hit Sergt. Major Hodgdon in the eye. Hodgdon's head when struck was within a foot of my feet. I presume it was the same rebel who fired and hit my right side."

EDWIN WARE, First Sergeant Co. G.

"Lieut. Edwin Ware was mustered as Third Corporal, and rose by promotion to First Sergeant. He was wounded twice at Fredericksburg, Dec. 13, 1862, once at Cold Harbor, June 1, 1864, and again here at Fort Harrison. Unlike many who clung to hospital life, he would return to his Regiment sooner than he ought, after his several wounds. He was commissioned as Lieutenant by the Governor of New Hampshire, but was not mustered as such owing to the early mustering out of the Thirteenth. He was an intelligent, brave soldier, and universally liked by the officers and men of our Regiment." MAJOR STOODLEY.

Capt. Betton states that he entered Fort Harrison during the assault on Sept. 29th, near the bridge at the northeast corner of the main fort, and then climbed up the great traverse; the flag of the Thirteenth lay there and he picked it up and thrust the staff into the sand. The enemy at this time had not all retired from the south end of the fort. Soon after going down from the traverse into the southern part of the fort, John Riley of E stepped up behind Capt. Betton with the Thirteenth's flag in his hand. Capt. Stoodley gave his attention to assembling the men of the Thirteenth, while Capt. Betton, by mutual consent, formed a line of men of the 139th N. Y. and others, it being necessary at this juncture to have every fighting man in hand for immediate and continuous action.

As our troops entered the fort John H. Mawby of K with the assistance of other men turned the captured guns, but having neither fuse nor gun-caps touched the guns off with matches, and in this way fired a number of times at the retreating enemy.

After the fort was captured, Capt. Betton approached Gen. Stannard, who was near the traverse, and requested the use of an ambulance to convey the bodies of Capt. Forbush and Lieut. R. R. Thompson to City Point. Gen. Stannard then ordered Capt. Betton to take an ambulance, put in it these two bodies and the body of an aide to Gen. Stannard who had been killed, and accompany them to City Point. Capt. Betton executed Gen. Stannard's order, arriving safely at City Point; again leaving there he crossed to Bermuda Hundred, procured a horse, and though stopped while on the way by Gen. Heckman was afterwards allowed to proceed, and rode back to Fort Harrison, where he rejoined the Thirteenth in action during the second rebel charge. He had the long ride to City Point and return, and had slept none for nearly forty-eight hours.

Oct. 1. Sat. Cold, a heavy rain falling. The Thirteenth has less than 70 men present for duty this morning. Reg. at work in the rain all the day upon the entrenchments, preparing for defense, all in battle order with arms stacked at hand. The enemy is equally busy on an inner line; and the pickets of both armies are in constant collision all along the lines. The enemy shells us briskly also from mortars, gunboats and batteries. We are suddenly called to take arms at 2 p. m.; the enemy threatening but does not attack. Our skirmishers, advancing to-day, drive in those of the enemy over a portion of the field covered in their assault of yesterday. The rebel dead are not yet buried — 282 bodies now lie in sight in front of our Brigade.

Maj. Gen. Godfrey Weitzel succeeds Maj. Gen. Ord in command of the 18th Army Corps.

Extract from a letter written to-day at the front: "Our Color Bearer was shot yesterday (30th, Charles Powell), being the sixth one this summer. I have now given the colors to a recruit (John Riley of E) in whom I have noticed great bravery. Our colors are but a few tattered shreds any way, but we love it, and shall stick to it." MAJOR STOODLEY.

Oct. 2. Sun. Cloudy, cold. Reg. at work on the entrenchments, every man pressing to his utmost strength preparing to resist attack. We are assigned as a part of the garrison of the captured fort. We have had scarcely any sleep for three days and three nights. Constant shelling is going on between Fort Harrison and the rebel batteries. The enemy must have worked in these last two nights with almost superhuman energy, his earth-works loom up all along in vast banks of sand.

The capture of Fort Harrison plunged the people of Richmond in the depths of despair; the terribly costly attempt to re-capture it, on the next day, anchored them in almost utter hopelessness.

"I have been without sleep so long I am almost used up; to-day seems the least like a Sunday of any day since I have been in the army."

LIEUT. TAGGARD, Actg. Adjutant.

"When Sergt. Major Hodgdon was shot, I detailed Sergt. M. C. Shattuck of B, to act as Sergeant Major. He had passed as best soldier in our Division at the first inspection, and obtained his furlough."

LT. COL. SMITH.

Hospital. To-day in the Hospital at Annapolis, Lieut. Thompson receives a morning paper, in which it is stated that the Army of the James has fought a furious two days' battle, winning at every point; capturing the enemy's Fort Harrison with a large number of guns and prisoners. That the Thirteenth was in the thickest of the fight, and "covered itself with great honor and glory; holding its ground against all odds, though its former Colonel, and Lt. Col. commanding (Major Smith acting Lt. Colonel) were cut down with nearly half of its other officers and men." He is congratulated upon the victory by thirty or more officers present, and three rousing cheers are given for the "gallant Thirteenth New Hampshire." So even a military Hospital has a bright moment now and then; but usually, as in this case, at a terrible cost.

Oct. 3. Mon. Rainy. Reg. filling in with breast-work, ditch and abatis the open space near where we fought on Sept. 30th, and making a regular fort looking towards the enemy. The rebel gunboats send about us many of their huge shells. We, the target's bull's-eye, watch for their coming, dodge when they come too near, and quietly smile while we wait another's coming. If any men dodge too much they are ridiculed, and told to get a new backbone, while the boys shout to them — as to stand up: "Set up them pins!" Our troops bury 260 bodies of the rebel dead, and for want of time leave above ground, on our immediate front, about 100 more, all killed in the battle on Sept. 30th.

Oct. 4. Tues. Showers. Reg. at work on the entrenchments.

Lieut. Jonathan Dustin honorably discharged the service. An exceptionally brave, capable and efficient officer is thus lost to the Thirteenth. We shall see him no more, when called to do any difficult or dangerous piece of work, settle firmly on his feet, straighten up, look his superior officer straight in the eye, listen attentively, catch every syllable of the order, merely answer "Yes, sir;" then go and execute that order to the very letter. As a carpenter might say, he was exactness trued-up.

Hospital. Lieut. Thompson of E, at Annapolis, "Honorably discharged the military service of the United States on account of disability because of wounds received in action." So runs an unwelcome, and in being too early, an unjust document received by him to-day. He cannot bear any weight upon his wounded foot, cannot move about at all excepting upon crutches, and then but a short distance, is hardly in a condition to travel, and therefore must remain here a few days longer.

Oct. 5. Wed. Fair, warm. Reg. at work on the entrenchments and building bomb-proofs. The rebel gunboats about a mile distant have been shelling us severely ever since we captured Fort Harrison; fewer shells came over from them yesterday, and very few to-day. During a little truce between the pickets, our men find in the brush and bring into camp a rebel soldier wounded across his eyes, destroying the sight of both. He had lain there four days. Was from South Carolina. It is believed that he will live.

Oct. 6. Thurs. Cloudy. Reg. at work on the entrenchments. The enemy has concentrated the fire from his mortars on Fort Harrison for several days, but without doing much damage, or deterring our men from their work. Watchmen give timely notice of a coming shell, and the men are generally able to secure cover before it strikes and bursts. These shells plow deep, and spread gravel by the cart-load.

Major Smith, in the absence of Lt. Col. Grantman, who has been at home sick since August 9th, has been in command of the 13th excepting for short periods of absence and for a few days after being wounded on Sept. 29th, and yesterday wrote to the Governor of New Hampshire urging sundry promotions in the Regiment. Only six officers present for duty. No Company has men enough to guarantee the muster-in of a Second Lieutenant, — and there are less than 600 men on the regimental rolls, all told. Major Smith vigorously protests against any idea or plan of consolidation with any other Regiment.

Oct. 7. Fri. Cool, clear. Reg. still at work on the entrenchments, and kept in readiness to move at a moment's notice. During all this forenoon the enemy shells our lines with all the guns he can bring to bear. The colored troops move to the right at noon. We are moved into Fort Harrison in the evening, and our men work all night to-night, tearing down the old front line of works, and building bomb-proofs. Re-enforcements come in. The enemy threatens an attack, but is quiet during the night here on our front.

The enemy attempts to turn the right flank of the Army of the James, but is repulsed with a severe loss near New Market. The Union loss is about 500 men; the enemy's loss much greater, and he abandons the central road. The part of our lines attacked was held by Gen. Kautz's Cavalry; who are said to have been surprised at daylight. Kautz met with a severe loss — nearly all his artillery and many men.

"From one standpoint in front of our Brigade, 280 rebel dead could be plainly counted. (These were killed while assaulting our line on Sept. 30th.) The last of them are buried to day. Twenty-three deserters come into our Brigade lines to-night."   PRESCOTT.

Oct. 8. Sat. Cold. Reg. still entrenching. Move into the fort and work all night upon bomb-proofs. The pickets of both armies join together — a picket truce — and bury all the enemy's dead to be found between the two lines. Sixty-five bodies are buried of those killed on Sept. 30th.

The commencement of this picket truce is thus related : A Lieutenant, said to be a Lieut. Guild of a New York regiment, being on duty on the outer Union picket line, and unable to endure the horrible stench arising from the Confederate dead, takes a newspaper in his hand as a flag of truce, and makes a dare-devil rush towards the rebel picket line. He is not fired upon, parleys with the rebel pickets a little while, and then they and the Union pickets procure spades, join together and bury 560 bodies — all of Confederates. The bodies are scattered here through the dense brush, and but for the stench would be difficult to find. It is believed that fifteen hundred Confederates were killed near our lines on Sept. 30th, to say nothing of a much larger number wounded, as the case usually is.

It will never be possible to tell how many more Confederate soldiers perished in the Rebellion than have ever been reported from the Confederate side; but there must have been very many thousands of such unreported rebel dead, scattered all over the Confederacy.

Oct. 9. Sun. Very cold. Reg. entrenching all day. We are in great exposure and privation ; heavy details at work night and day ; the utmost vigilance and activity are demanded ; the enemy opposes our work in every possible manner ; arms are stacked close at hand at all hours ; and the enemy's fire, chiefly artillery fire, plunges about our heads continually. Deserters say that Gen. Lee and Jeff. Davis came within half a mile of Fort Harrison to-day, examined the ground and discussed the situation for five mortal hours. Ten deserters came into our Brigade lines last night.

"The enemy has shelled us severely from his mortars and gunboats. His 200 lb. shells go screeching overhead, or bursting and plowing great holes in the ground. His lines of works are very near ours. Eleven deserters came in to-night; the most of them belonged to the 'Richmond City Battalion,' and came from there when we took this place. For two days of the past week it rained, and we had no shelter whatever, day or night. Then it cleared very cold, and we had to sleep on the ground under the sky, or walk about to keep warm. We nightly expect to be attacked, and for five nights the men hardly slept a wink. We now occupy the rebel barracks inside of Fort Harrison." PRESCOTT.

Hospital. We live well here. No hotel need be ashamed of such a table as the one set here every day. We have the best the market affords, all generally well cooked and served. The Naval Buildings, where we are, are clean and roomy. The Severn furnishes excellent soft-shell crabs in abundance, and most delicious oysters. The only drawback about the oysters are the numerous pearls, ruinous to the teeth that strike hard upon them. Dr. B. A. Vanderkieft is Surgeon in Charge of Hospital. Dr. Joshua B. Sweet is Surgeon in Charge of Section 3, wards A–B, where the writer is. Both kindly and efficient men. We have interesting religious services Sunday afternoons and evenings. Bible classes on Thursdays. Visitors are admitted to see the patients between 12 noon and 6 p. m. Miss Maria M. C. Hall of Washington, D. C., is Directress. A most attractive and popular young lady. A paper, "The Crutch," is published every Saturday, and contains much matter of interest to the patients. On the whole an excellent Army Hospital.

Oct. 10. Mon. Fair. Reg. at work on the fort, and acting as its garrison. Admiral Farragut, and Generals Grant, Meade and Butler visit Fort Harrison to-day. "They inspect the rebel works, and are inspected in turn by every Union soldier who can get near them."

Firing on the picket line has been much less for a day or two, and excepting for the numerous shells, it is to-day quite safe to go almost anywhere along our lines. Deserters say that the people of the South regard the election of McClellan for President of the United States as the only hope for the success of the Confederate cause. Such a weight of woe to our Nation does now the mere name of Democracy threaten.

Oct. 11. Tues. Pleasant. Reg. on outpost picket. Twelve deserters from the 18th Georgia come in. Since the battle of Sept. 29th and 30th the 13th has been constantly under fire.

Soldiers' food — how to prepare it: Make a little fire on the ground of dry, quick-burning wood — if you can get it. One fire will serve for half a dozen men. Stand on the smoky side, for all sides are about equally smoky. Put a pint of Virginia water — from the wayside brook or puddle — into your tin pint-pot, and boil in it for about ten minutes a tablespoonful of coffee; putting a little green stick across the top of the pot to prevent the rich water from boiling over. When your coffee is nearly done, soak in it for a minute six or eight crackers — 'hard tack'

— and lay them on your tin plate, being careful not to shake the worms out; they eat better than they look, and are so much clear gain in the way of fresh meat. Worms rarely infest poor bread. Next cut off a slice of salt pork, put it on a stick, and broil it over the fire, dripping the scorched lard, yclept gravy, on your hard-bread. When your pork is cooked, your meal is ready to eat. Now take it, while your eyes are smarting with smoke, your fingers smutty and burned and your face no fairer, your clothing and everything begrimed, dirty and greasy; go, sit down in the dirt, and eat your mess like gentlemen and hogs, with a soldier's appetite for your sauce.

Oct. 12. Wed. Fair, cold. Reg. in camp. Inspection. Three deserters come in. Gen. Grant's invitations to desert are being accepted by the enemy's men, in fact growing quite popular — sensible for once in their lives. About 3 a. m. some of the enemy's men attempted to desert, and were fired upon by their comrades. This firing roused our army, and we all turned out under arms in a twinkling — grumbled, and turned in again. Recently a Union man by name Day was wounded in his back, and the boys, hard up for a joke, urged their Surgeon to report Day as wounded in the 'afternoon.'

Oct. 13. Thurs. Cold, rainy last night. Reg. in camp. A general court martial convenes. Three deserters come in, the enemy firing upon them. Last night the 2d Brigade of our Division was sent over to support troops of the 10th Corps. This morning troops of the 10th Corps made a reconnaissance in force on the Darbytown road, and provoked a spirited little fight. The 13th not engaged, but turned out at noon and remained several hours under arms in the front trenches, and ready for action. Gen. Butler tried to dislodge the enemy from a new line of works they were building, and lost heavily.

Oct. 14. Fri. Cold. Reg. in camp. All our baggage and camp equipage is at the old camp at Bermuda Hundred. Our shelter tents are much worn, and the nights are growing very chilly and cold. The enemy captured a lot of negro troops, and set them at work upon the fortifications, whereupon Gen. Butler selected an equal number of white rebel prisoners, and set them at work upon Dutch Gap canal — sending to the rebel commander advice not to fire upon his friends at work there.

Oct. 15. Sat. Clear, warmer. Reg. in camp, in Fort Harrison. Eight deserters come in from the enemy; and one more shot, by the enemy, while running toward our lines. Almost every morning there is held a 'Deserters' Powow' so called, at our garrison camp-fire, where all deserters from the Confederates are welcomed, warmed and fed. The road to the poor rebels' hearts runs through their stomachs — it is a luxury to see them eat. They give hunger's best evidence of short commons in the rebel army.

Hospital. Last item. Lieut. Thompson left Annapolis Hospital Oct. 10th, leaving over thirty pieces of his ankle bones — several of the pieces half an inch across, and one of them still larger — on the banks of the

Severn. Went to Washington and settled up accounts. On Oct. 13th saw President Lincoln, in the White House, for the last time. He stood close by an open window, apparently holding a reception, and occasionally turning and looking out. It was the second window to the left of the front entrance door; and Lincoln stood as it were a full length portrait, the huge window casings serving as a frame. The writer was too lame, and in too much pain to go in. To-day rode from Washington to New York, in the kindly care and company of Mrs. Henry Clay Trumbull and her two little daughters. Chaplain Trumbull is well known as Connecticut's 'Fighting Parson.'

Oct. 16. Sun. Fine day, cool. Reg. in camp. Moves camp from one side of Fort Harrison to the other. The 2d Brigade Band — formerly of the Thirteenth — has remained at Bermuda Hundred until within a day or two; and now the Bands begin here to make our camp life more cheerful.

Lt. Col. Grantman honorably discharged the service. He had command of the Thirteenth, for the most of the time, after Col. Stevens was placed in command of our Brigade on July 26th; but was sick much of the time, when the command of the 13th devolved upon Major Smith. August 10th Grantman went home on sick leave for 20 days. This was extended, but not recovering from his illness — chills and fever — he reluctantly resigns his commission and leaves the service.

Lt. Col. William Grantman was mustered as a Private May 23, 1861, in Co. H, 1st Mass. Vol. Infantry. About the middle of June that regiment went to Washington, and from there found its first engagement in the first battle of Bull Run. Three Companies of the 1st Mass., Co. H among them, opened the action July 18th, at what is known as Blackburn's Ford. In this action Grantman was wounded in the left arm, left side and left groin. After a period spent in Hospital he returned to service in October. His regiment spent the winter of 1861–2 at Buell's Ferry on the Lower Potomac, as a part of Gen. Hooker's Division. The brigade in which was the 1st Mass. was first commanded by Gen. Hooker; afterwards Gen. Sickles' Brigade and the New Jersey Brigade were joined with it, constituting Gen. Hooker's Division. It was on the Virginia side of the Potomac opposite this Division's winter camp, where the rebels established their blockade — so called.

In the first part of April 1862, Gen. Hooker's Division joined Gen. McClellan on the Peninsula, and was engaged upon the fortifications in the vicinity of Yorktown. On the morning of April 26th, three Companies of the 1st Mass. were designated to assault a redoubt held by the enemy. Company H supported by the other two Companies led the assault, which was successful. Here again Grantman was wounded, receiving two bullets in the upper part of his left thigh.

Recovering from these wounds, he was in Wakefield, N. H., when President Lincoln issued the call for 300,000 volunteers, under which the Thirteenth enlisted. The citizens of Wakefield, N. H., came to him and urged him to accept a Captaincy; and as a result of the patriotic endeavors of himself and others, who afterwards became officers in that organization, Company A of the Thirteenth was raised, and Capt. Grantman marched back to the war at the head of it, carrying with him the marks of four rebel bullets and a buckshot.

After the war he returned to his former business — furrier — in Boston, and has expended much of his time and means in assisting the worthy survivors of this war who are sick or reduced in circumstances, and also the families of such, and of the Veterans who have died.

A quiet, gentlemanly man, intensely interested in the good fortunes of the Thirteenth, both when in the service and afterwards, ready for any honorable duty or action, generous, clear and cool headed, brave and firm; his long, faithful services and many battle scars command silence to every verbal enlargement and encomium.

Oct. 17. Mon. Fair. Reg. in camp. A squad of deserters come in retailing, at wholesale, a most doleful account of affairs in Dixie; apparently making all things appear as bad as possible. Like all deserters from the enemy, however, these men are fearfully hungry.

The Southron as a deserter is only too happy when he reaches the Union lines, happy as never before in his life; but he is cautious about making too much of an exhibition of his happiness. Besides, the conscious disgrace of having done a desertion broods over him like a little bluish mist, in which his eye wanders a bit, and the tones of his voice drag a trifle husky. Not so the state of the Southron as a prisoner. Next to bridegrooms in their honeymoons, the happiest men the writer ever set eyes upon (and he has seen many hundreds of them in all), have been the men captured from the Confederate army by the Union army in this war. What they may be in prison he knows not — though none there have been reported as dying of melancholy — but down here in the two years between Fredericksburg and Petersburg, and thence on, these captured fellows exhibit unqualified happiness. Every one of them may have 'spoiled for the fight,' after the description of Southern writers, and no one disputes their bravery when in danger; but he evidently prefers the peace and comfort that Uncle Sam's retirement camp affords, to any battle he has ever seen. The ancient boast was that any Southerner could whip three Yankees, some of them five; but of late it seems as if each Southern soldier would rather live on Union army rations than whip four Yankees, or even half a dozen of them. There may be exceptions, but to the vast majority, evidently, capture is a consummation of battle chances most devoutly to be wished. Southern writers have trussed up and padded a great many paper knights, but the most of the Southern soldiers are wonderfully human after all.

Oct. 18. Tues. Cloudy, cold. Reg. in camp. Paid off for six months. The rebel flag-of-truce boat carries a white flag at her fore; a white flag with the red Union at her top, and the diagonal cross of the Confederacy aft. It is a small river steamer bringing prisoners of war for exchange. A rebel band frequently comes down upon the boat playing Southern airs, to Union and Confederate alike. The boats passing in the James are in plain view from Fort Harrison, for a narrow space. One deserter comes in at noon.

Oct. 19. Wed. Fair, cold. Reg. in camp. The condition of some of the boxes, sent by friends at home to men at the front, when they arrived, after a two or four weeks' trip, would make a pig squeal, and even a soldier swear: Rotten apples, pears, grapes and plums, mouldy cakes, pies past their prime, cheese all wiggle-wiggle, doughnuts rancid; chicken needs no carving, jam fermented and "got loose," cordial weeping, candy in a muss, all mixed topsy-turvy, butter melted and run all over everything, bugs and creeping things holding a grand high carnival — and clothing smelling like the last rose of summer.

Oct. 20. Thurs. Cloudy. The officers of the Thirteenth have for a long time desired to have the Spencer rifles, but doubted if they could obtain them. Gen. Devens sends for Major Smith, without solicitation, and proposes to arm the Thirteenth with Sharps breech-loading carbines — a most agreeable surprise.

A grand salute fired, of five rounds from each cannon on our line all shotted and well aimed at the rebel works, in honor of Gen. Sheridan's latest victory. The enemy feebly replies with only a few mortar shells.

"A few days since I went out with Major Stoodley from our picket line to exchange newspapers with the rebel pickets. I waved a New York Herald, they answered my signal with a Richmond paper. After the usual custom of such errands, each party started to advance half way for a meeting between the lines; and we had nearly completed the distance, when a rebel officer came out and ordered his man back, and we could not make the exchange. Their orders are now very strict against exchanging papers."
PRESCOTT.

Oct. 21. Fri. Cool, clear. Five deserters come in, all fired upon by their own side. Four Subs desert to the rebels from the 2d N. H. Brigade Review — another 'Brevet Review.'

Oct. 22. Sat. Pleasant, cool. Reg. in camp. Gen. Grant visits Fort Harrison. Five deserters come into our lines to-night, and forty more come in at a short distance to the left of us. Our gunners get the range of the rebel gunboats in the James and start them up the river, after a noisy contest. The rebels cheer loudly to-night.

Oct. 23. Sun. Pleasant. Reg. in camp. Usual Sunday duties. For a week or two past our lines here have been very quiet, and nothing of particular note has occurred. Since the fortifications were satisfactorily strengthened, the firing between the pickets — by a sort of common consent — has been discontinued, all along the line here, though in the region about Dutch Gap canal the firing has been continuous. The canal is $2\tfrac{1}{2}$ miles below Fort Harrison. It is about 300 feet long, 75 wide and 40 deep. Saves seven miles of travel. Many rebel prisoners are now at work on the canal, in retaliation for the rebels' treatment of our colored troops when captured by them. The enemy are continually shelling the shovelers, and men and horses are killed almost every day.

Oct. 24. Mon. Cold. Reg. in camp. Our lines here are now protected by a moat and abatis. The enemy has no force to risk in recapturing them. Out in front also our pickets are strongly entrenched. A newspaper exchange is arranged between our Brigade and the enemy — the pickets making the exchanges. Thus we have the Richmond morning papers, and the enemy's men can read the Northern papers, can reflect, grow wiser, and desert to the Union lines, as they are continually doing.

Of the 1,040 men who left New Hampshire Oct. 7, 1862, and of all the Recruits received besides, raising our numbers to nearly 1,300, but 610 men are now on our regimental rolls; 200 of these are absent sick and wounded in various Hospitals, 200 are detailed, the remainder are present. We turn out for duty now about 100 men.

The 8th Conn., our good friends and formerly of our Brigade, now reduced to 90 muskets, Capt. Charles M. Coitt commanding, are headquarters' guard for the 18th Corps. "An easy piece of hard work."

Chills and fever quite prevalent in the Thirteenth, and the force generally; and a man suffering from their 'disintegrating' effects feels, as it were, like an old barrel with the heads half out, the hoops working off, the staves all awry, and the whole thing ready — and infamously willing — to collapse into a shapeless heap of rubbish.

Oct. 25. Tues. Clear, windy, cool. Reg. in camp. Up to this time the Thirteenth has remained in, or in the vicinity of Fort Harrison, strengthening its fortifications, and furnishing the usual quotas for picket and outpost duty, but not engaging in any special battle, service or expedition. The spirits of the men are revived by the period of rest, and their numbers somewhat increased by the return of absentees and convalescents. A body of negro troops moves in to-day, and mans a portion of the line at Fort Harrison. A Union vedette near the 13th is scooped out of his little rifle-pit by a large Confederate shell, which bursts, blows him to pieces, and scatters the pieces all over the field. Asst. Surgeon Morrill returns to the 13th this evening. Six deserters from the enemy came in last night.

Here is a little illustration of the uncertainties of war: "About Sept. 25th I served as a member of a court martial at Gen. Ord's Hdqrs. at Bermuda Hundred. The court adjourned and all the members with one exception went with their regiments to the battle of Fort Harrison. After the fight we finished trying the case that came before us, convening at Mr. Henry Cox's house near Fort Harrison, minus four of our original membership, of whom three had been wounded and one mustered out. I had been wounded also, but was able to attend to my duties after a few days." Lt. Col. Smith.

Oct. 26. Wed. Fine day. Reg. breaks camp at dark, marches about one and one half miles to the rear, halts on Mr. Henry Cox's farm,

bivouacs, and receives orders to prepare three days' cooked rations, and
to be ready to move at 5 a. m. to-morrow. Here we are joined by the
rest of the garrison of Fort Harrison and neighboring works, consisting of
our 1st Division of the 18th Corps, now commanded by Gen. Gilman
Marston of New Hampshire ; and also by a Division of the 18th Corps,
which has come up from the works at Bermuda Hundred ; all together to
form an expeditionary corps under Maj. Gen. Weitzel. Major Smith now
commands the 13th, and our 1st Brigade, consisting of the 13th N. H.
81st, 98th and 139th New York regiments, is in command of Col. John
B. Raulston of the 81st N. Y. Much disturbance and several severe fights
occur to-day among the men of our Brigade, who are made drunk on whiskey obtained from commissaries and sutlers.

To-morrow the whole Union army is to be set in motion, and leaving
only a small garrison along its thirty miles of fortifications is to make the
most powerful demonstration yet attempted on the enemy's present lines ;
if possible, to turn his right flank south of Petersburg, and gain possession
of the Southern railroads. The purpose of our force, now here on Cox's
farm, is to gain the nearest possible point to Richmond, and to prevent
the transfer of Gen. Lee's troops from there toward his Petersburg lines ;
and if his left wing can be turned, to march into Richmond. Among the
men and the lower grades of officers this movement is regarded as of
greater import than any made for many months ; and many a man lies
down for a short rest to-night, in the strong belief that to-morrow will
bring the end of the war in Virginia. More has been said ' at the front '
about this ' general movement,' than of any other since Gen. Grant
crossed the James last June.

The 10th Corps, Gen. Terry, is to make a demonstration on the Charles
City and Darbytown roads ; while Gen. Weitzel's force of the 18th Corps
is to push through the White Oak Swamp at Hobson's crossing, move up
to the Williamsburg pike, and then attack. Consequently the 18th Corps
will pass in the rear of the 10th Corps, and along to the right of it, then
face to the left and advance.

## BATTLE OF FAIR OAKS — NO. 2.

**Oct. 27. Thurs.** Clear and cool a. m. ; rainy p. m. This affair,
however disastrous, deserves a special title ; and is accounted the 2012th
engagement of the war under the above name. At 4.30 a. m. the Thirteenth is assigned to the position of skirmishers leading our 1st Division.
The column moves from Cox's farm at 5 a. m., now about daylight, first
swinging around towards Deep Bottom, then passing over New Market
Heights, then marching across the country by the most direct route, until
we reach the Charles City road near White's Tavern at 10 a. m. Here
a short halt is made, and then the column pushes forward across the country by obscure roads and paths until our Brigade, which leads the column,
comes out upon the Williamsburg pike near that part of the Fair Oaks

battle-field where Gen. Silas Casey was attacked, and driven back, on May 30, 1862, just previous to the great battle of Seven Pines and Fair Oaks. As we come out upon the right of the 10th Corps, its skirmishers are busily engaging the enemy. The order of march this morning was for the troops to march three miles an hour, resting ten minutes in every hour, but this order has been maintained for only one hour — the first. The troops are much wearied by the long, rapid march of some twelve or fifteen miles, and are now unfit for battle. A severe rain storm sets in at noon, continuing all the rest of the day and nearly all night.

On reaching the Williamsburg pike, the Thirteenth is deployed as skirmishers across the pike, and moves along on both sides of it toward Richmond. We first meet the enemy's skirmishers, in any force, on the pike beyond the field known as Seven Pines, where we quickly drive them back, and our Brigade is formed in line of battle across the pike at 1.15 p. m. The Division sharp-shooters, under Capt. Goss of the 13th, with the 118th N. Y. and the 10th N. H. are thrown forward between 1.30 and 2 p. m., all being armed with Spencer rifles. They advance to a position within 100 yards of the rebel earth-works, and there lie down. The Thirteenth is then placed on the right of our Brigade line, as flankers, near and fronting the York River Railroad, north of the pike.

The enemy has hurried up troops, upon the run, from his lines confronting Fort Harrison, and heavily re-enforced his lines within his entrenchments here, rendering them impregnable to any assault that can be made by our force now present on the field. This is not distinctly known, however, and about 3 p. m. our two brigades move forward to the assault; the 13th being held in reserve as flankers in a grove of pines, under fire but not engaged. While we are here the enemy runs a battery of three guns down on the York River Railroad, and shells us severely. Many trees are cut off, and one of them in falling wounds two men. This shelling somewhat draws our attention from the assault, which can be seen only in part, but is extremely noisy, showing that the enemy is present in heavy force. The assault is made most gallantly, but our troops are repulsed, and retire with heavy loss.

The 10th N. H., in the 2d Brigade of our Division, loses eight officers and seventy-four men. It reaches a point within a few yards of the enemy's works, from which it can neither advance nor retreat, and the men lie down and wait for night in which to escape. A sortie from the enemy, before night, captures the most of them. The 10th destroys its colors, and so prevents their capture. The 2d Brigade enters upon the work of the day with about 500 men, and at night is almost among the things that were.

The expedition merely results in preventing re-enforcements from being sent to Gen. Lee's right, south of Petersburg, and at night our troops are all withdrawn. We advance to within less than four miles of Richmond; a mile nearer than Gen. McClellan went, and nearer than any of our infantry have previously gone.

Capt. E. W. Goss commanding the sharp-shooters of our First Division of the 18th Corps was killed while taking part in the assault, and his body fell into the hands of the enemy. His body was never recovered, nor is its resting place known. As near as can be learned, however, Capt. Goss was killed about twenty yards to the left of the Williamsburg road, and about 100 yards in front — east — of the outer line of Confederate works where they cross that road.

A volunteer, a Captain, was wanted last August (29th) by Gen. Devens, to command a corps of 200 sharp-shooters, picked men from the different regiments in our First Division, and Capt. Goss volunteered for the duty. An extremely dangerous position when advancing on the field. The 1st Division, however, contained but few officers of such bold daring, cool courage, sound sense and clear grit, all combined in one individual, as Capt. Goss always evinced.

G. W. Johnson of I states that "he met a Confederate Capt. Catlett, and he stated to Johnson that he was in command of the Confederate skirmishers at Fair Oaks, Oct. 27, 1864; that he saw the commander of the Federal sharp-shooters — Capt. Goss — approach his (Confed.) line and station his men — all the time under a severe fire — as coolly as if on drill; in fact he said he never saw any man act so bravely while under fire as Capt. Goss did on this occasion, and he himself passed the word along the Confederate skirmish line not to shoot this officer because he was so gallant and brave. After posting his men Capt. Goss stepped behind an apple-tree for protection, but in the contest that followed he was killed. This Confederate Captain was one of the burial party, and took for his own use Capt. Goss's gauntlet gloves."

Lieut. Murray on the staff of the 1st Brigade is captured and goes to Libby Prison. He is held as a hostage for a time, for a rebel condemned to be hung by our Government. He is confined in the same cell, and for the same purpose, with Capt. George N. Bliss of the First Rhode Island Cavalry. The cell, in which they were for the most of the time confined, is in the basement, under the northeast corner of the building, and at the corner of East Carey and Twentieth Streets. The same cell in which Dick Turner, commandant of Libby, was afterwards locked up (after the Union occupation of Richmond), and from which he escaped, and was never afterwards captured.

Five men of the 13th are also taken prisoners by the enemy, and two men wounded. Our troops are withdrawn from the front only with extreme difficulty. It is impossible to send orders to the skirmishers on the front, and those of the 13th are necessarily left with the rest to their own resources. As night comes on, they conclude that they must withdraw or be captured, so they come off quietly, as many as are able to do so, and rejoin the Reg. late at night.

The heavy rain renders the roads exceedingly muddy. The night march on the retreat is one of the hardest we have ever had. Everything is mixed together, the very darkness making order impossible. Utter confusion reigns; teams, artillery, ambulances and infantry all jumbled together, and all heavily loaded; mud and water in many places knee-deep in the roads, the night pitchy dark, the rain pouring in torrents, the enemy reported close on our heels, commands are separated, teams are stuck in the sloughs, wagons are tipped over and smashed, the contents scattered and run over, horses and mules ugly, drivers hurrying, noisy, swearing, quarreling, mad, feet of the men blistered, many sitting by the roadside used up; and so the affair goes on for four or five miles, and about midnight the Thirteenth, keeping together as much as possible, but much broken up and drenched through and through, bivouacs in the rain and mud, near the Charles City road, and waits for daylight.

Our men are completely jaded out by the march, the fight, the exposure to the enemy's fire, the excitement, the retreat in the mud, rain and darkness; and also much depressed by the sense of the utterly blasted hope of gaining Richmond, and lie down with very gloomy forebodings for the morrow. The men, probably, have counted upon more success to-day, than those in charge of the movement. The name of this ugly affair should be placed on the colors of the Thirteenth, however, for they did all that was required of them, and were in no way responsible for the result.

A short account of the affair states that while the 10th Corps engages the enemy, the 18th Corps passes along to the Williamsburg road. The rebel skirmishers make a determined stand near Fair Oaks, and the 118th N. Y. drive them back to the entrenchments. The First Division advances to within about 1,000 yards. Now occurs a delay of one and a half hours. After which time the Second Brigade — about 500 men — Col. Cullen commanding, charges through a severe fire, to a point from which it can neither advance nor retreat. The 10th N. H. in this charge loses 74 men out of 100, and 8 officers out of 10.

"On the afternoon of Oct. 26th, we were withdrawn from the works, and encamped near Mr. Henry Cox's house. There was a sharp frost that night, so that when the troops were moving next day — 27th — the ground, as it thawed, was very slippery for marching. We moved over New Market Heights by a cross-road to White's Tavern on the Charles City road, thence past Allen's and Hobson's. At Hobson's we turned to the left and followed the road to Seven Pines. The Thirteenth had the lead, with Capt. Goss's sharp-shooters and the General's staff, only, ahead of us. Spear's 11th Penn. Cavalry had preceded the column, and were out of sight. The cavalry were drawn up in a grove of pines to our right near the Williamsburg road, when we arrived there.

"Capt. Goss moved forward in skirmish line on the left of the Williamsburg road, and the Thirteenth moved by the flank up the road. Gen. Gilman Marston was commanding the Division. The last time I saw Capt. Goss he was in the open field not far from Mr. Kuhn's house. About this time a charge on the right of the road, made by two companies of the 11th Penn. Cavalry, took our attention and I saw or heard no more of Capt. Goss. I think a Richmond paper had his name and Lieut.

Murray's in the list of captured prisoners; and we knew nothing definite about him until the return from Andersonville of some of our sharp-shooters who were captured here. Sharp-shooter Bannister of Co. H was never accounted for, except as missing.

" We marched by the flank toward Richmond, and deployed in line of battle on the right of the Williamsburg road in the woods, where our Brigade remained during the day. The Thirteenth were deployed as flankers, in the edge of the woods, and facing the York River Railroad. The charge on the Confederate works by the other troops was made on the left hand side of the Williamsburg road. The enemy was within his works, and not in his front line of rifle-pits. His large fort, a little south of the York River Railroad (S. on accompanying map), was engaging our field batteries in the Williamsburg road, the shells flying both ways directly over the Thirteenth, cutting the trees in all directions, and some of our men were injured by the splinters. This action should be called ' Williamsburg Road,' and not Fair Oaks, as only colored troops went there. About 3 p. m. it grew very foggy and dark, and although the rebel battery had been in sight it was soon obscured; and it commenced raining hard, the rain continuing nearly all night.

" About 8 p. m., after posting a picket, we were withdrawn, leaving the picket. The cavalry joined us on the right and followed us out, and we retraced the road to near White's Tavern, where we remained during the rest of the night. I never expected to see the men of that picket again, and would have withdrawn them even without orders if I could have taken them without disturbing the pickets of other regiments. It was said that the officer of the day would relieve them but he never came; and they withdrew on their own responsibility about 3 a. m. on the 28th.

" So far as I know, we did not handle spade or pick. If any earthworks were occupied by us, we did not make them, and our Brigade had none I know. It was some time after dark when we withdrew from the Williamsburg road, and we halted for the night, on the Charles City road, at some distance toward the city from White's Tavern. The next morning we were moved into the woods, as this road is almost a straight line to Fort Lee, marked Z on the accompanying map, and we were exposed to a raking fire as we lay in the road. I thought at the time that Gen. Marston expected to entrench at that point.

" The 10th Corps, which had demonstrated here while we were on the Williamsburg road, had their skirmish line between us and the rebels at this time, and were not withdrawn until after we had finally retired to Fort Harrison. There was a garden at the house — W. Jordan's near X on the map — just in front of the cross-road, on the Charles City road, and Quarter-master M. L. Morrison and myself followed up the picket line to this garden, and there filled our haversacks with cabbage, tomatoes, etc. We did not consider ourselves much demoralized that day by the rebel fire; and as we had had no fresh vegetables for a long time, you can imagine what a good dinner we had the next day.

"The east line of my farm is between one and two miles toward the city, up the Charles City road, from Fort Lee; and near this fort is the first station east of Richmond on the Chesapeake and Ohio Railroad, also called Fort Lee."  LT. COL. SMITH.

While we lay in the woods during the shelling by the rebel battery on the railroad, there occurred one of the most singular casualties and escapes known in the war. As a man in our Brigade was lying down upon his face, a large, white, splintered chunk of a tree set flying by a bursting shell, swept along his back from shoulders to feet, like a flash of lightning, carrying everything before it, leaving the man minus the back-side half of nearly all of his clothing. The shock dazed him, but caused him no serious injury beyond a small abrasion. He instantly whirled over upon his back, the rough ground did not feel agreeable, and he turned back as quickly upon his face again; then raised his head and gave himself one glance, swore a fearful oath, seized his gun, sprang to his feet and rushed, a literal tatterdemalion, to brush at the rear. The last seen of him, he was retreating in the distance, in quick route-step, wrapped in a blanket a la Indian. Fair Oaks proved foul oaks to him.

Gen. Humphreys states that Gen. Weitzel, commanding the 18th Corps, having passed through the White Oak Swamp at Hobson's crossing, arrived at the Williamsburg road at 1 p. m., near the Seven Pines battle-field, and came in front of the rebel works after advancing on that road a mile and a half. He assaulted with two brigades, Cullen's and Fairchild's. Col. Cullen's 2d Brigade of the 1st Division was formed on the right of the road, supported by the 1st Brigade (ours) and 3d Brigade of that Division, the Division commanded by Gen. Marston. On the left of the road, in line of battle, was Fairchild's Brigade of the 2d Division, the Division commanded by Gen. Heckman. This force, preceded by skirmishers, advanced over the open ground at 3.30 p. m. They got

---

DESCRIPTION OF MAP.

A. Charles City Road.   C. Allen.   D. Hobson.
B. B. Road followed from New Market Heights to Seven Pines.
E. Old Union earth-works.   F. Seven Pines battle-field.
G. Hilliard.   H. Kuhn.   I. French.   K. King.
L. Williamsburg Road.   M. York River Railroad.
N. Fair Oaks station.   R. Roads leading southward.
P. Pine timber, where the Thirteenth was placed as flankers fronting the York River Railroad.
S. Here was a large fort not shown on the official map.
T. Eacho's Hospital.   V. W. Open ground.
Y. White's Tavern on the Charles City road.
Z. Fort Lee on Charles City road; about two miles eastward of Lt. Col. Normand Smith's farm (1887), which is on the same road.
X. W. Jordan's garden near here visited by Smith and Morrison.
U. U. U. Confederate main lines, trenches and rifle-pits.

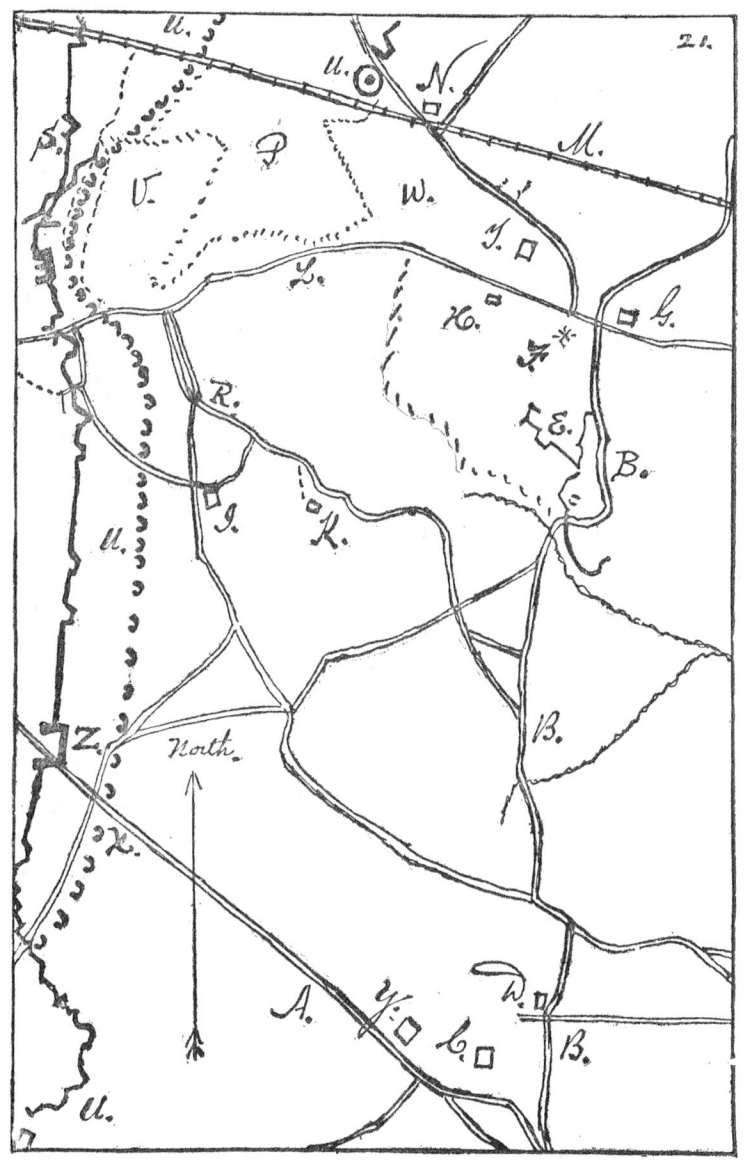

FAIR OAKS, OCTOBER 27, 1864.

Tracing of Official Map. Scale, one and one half inches to one mile.

close to the enemy's works, but were repulsed with a considerable loss, each of the two assaulting brigades losing three colors.

Shortly after dark, Gen. Weitzel began to withdraw to the Charles City road, the rain, darkness, mud and narrow road making the retreat very fatiguing for the troops, who were marching all night. The losses in the whole movement, by the 10th and 18th Corps in killed, wounded and missing, were about 1,100 men. The enemy met here, who had just arrived from Gen. Ewell's lines north of the James, were Gen. Field's Division, assisted by, or co-operating with, Gen. Gary's Cavalry Brigade. The enemy's losses were very small, his defense having been made behind the best of entrenchments, the heavy system of Richmond defenses.

Oct. 28. Fri. "Nice day. Rained last night and did not hold up till morning." In coming down from the front last night, the men were much scattered, a result largely due to the almost impenetrable darkness (there was no rout, we were not pursued) and were arriving at the place of bivouac singly or in small squads all night long. The rain of yesterday and last night has made the roads exceedingly muddy — the glory of this expedition is reduced to mud and water. The Reg. leaves its bivouac on the Charles City road about 9 a. m. When the Reg. arrives at camp a little after dark, we find our old quarters occupied by other troops, and take a new camping ground about a quarter of a mile farther to the right, outside of Fort Harrison, and behind the rifle-trenches.

One soldier writes : " We fugled about in the woods all the forenoon on the Charles City road, in view of a rebel fort. Slashed several trees across the road, then retreated. Reached our old quarters about dark, footsore and thoroughly played out."

From the Medical Department of the Thirteenth (condensed) : " We were called about 4 a. m. Oct. 26th, marched back about one mile and camped in a large field where the entire 18th Corps gathered during the day. At 4.30 a. m. on the 27th we started towards the right, passing the 10th Corps in their rear. We halted on the Fair Oaks battle-field, having gone around the rebels' left flank, leaving many of their works behind us. The 10th Corps was now heavily engaged to our rear and left. Capt. Goss here advanced with his sharp-shooters. Our cavalry charged at a full gallop driving back the rebel pickets — a grand sight. The 10th N. H., armed with Spencer rifles, and under command of Capt. Timothy B. Crowley of Nashua, moved in on our left. This was about 3 p. m., then raining. Our Brigade deployed in the woods to the right, and advanced in line of battle. The musketry firing was already severe, and now the enemy opened upon us with artillery. We laid flat on the ground. The 2d Brigade charged with loud cheers. The firing was awful, a roar. Our men went close up under the rebel guns, but could not penetrate the strong abatis. Then we heard the rebel yell, as the enemy charged down upon the 2d Brigade, gobbling the greater part of it. Capt. Crowley was wounded in the leg, and taken prisoner, but while the rebels went after a stretcher for him, he crawled off and hid. Capt. Goss and all but ten of his sharp-shooters were taken prisoners or killed. We then advanced a few rods and lay down again. The rebels ran a battery down the railroad and shelled us. Here Otis R. Marsh of I was wounded in the head with a piece of shell. It was now dark.

"About 7 p. m. we started to retreat. It was very dark, and raining hard, and the road was soon like pudding. Everybody was wet, tired and cross; the rebels were all around us; the mud almost pulling off boots and shoes at every step; every vehicle, every arm, inextricably mixed together in the road — and how everybody did swear! It beats all description. The men dropped out all along the way. We halted in the woods about midnight, and had four hours to rest. We went on at 4.20 a. m., a little rain still falling. At daylight we were again in the Charles City road, and then we moved up that road toward Richmond a mile or two, when a rebel fort [1] loomed up in the road about half a mile ahead. We moved into the woods (to avoid its fire) and remained there all the forenoon, while details of men felled trees across the road. We finally reached Fort Harrison about dark. Took the position on the right of the fort, formerly occupied by the 2d Brigade, turned in, and were soon asleep." PRESCOTT.

Oct. 29. Sat. Clear. Reg. moves its camp still farther toward the right from Fort Harrison. The negro troops occupy a portion of the line as garrison of the fort; they having furnished a part of the garrison, while our Division was absent on the expedition toward Richmond. The 10th N. H. is this morning commanded by a 2d Lieutenant.

In the 10th N. H., or some other regiment that formed a part of the Fair Oaks expedition, and was much cut up, one of the Companies had an Irishman for its First Sergeant. At the first Dress-parade this First Sergeant came to the front to report the condition of his lost Company. When his turn came to report he hesitated, and scarcely knew what to say. The Adjutant hurried him, when he blurted out in full brogue: "Company G all right, bedad — I'm the only one left!"

Oct. 30. Sun. Clear, cool. Thirteenth on picket all day. "On the eve of a move like the recent one, both officers and men will laugh, joke and appear gay, merry and glad of an opportunity to meet the enemy; but when they take a friend to one side, whose duties do not require him to go into a battle, and pass over to him their watch, money, etc., and say a word to him for the friends at home — the fun of the thing fades out." CHARLES W. WASHBURN, Band.

Oct. 31. Mon. Clear, warm. Thirteenth mustered for pay by Major Normand Smith. In the afternoon we move our camp farther to the right.

Nov. 1. Tues. Clear, cool. Thirteenth in camp, fitting up new quarters.

Nov. 2. Wed. Cold, a little hail turning to rain. Thirteenth in

[1] Lt. Col. Smith writes that this was Fort Lee, the first fort on the C. & O. Railroad below his farm (1887). — S. M. T.

camp. Commissions received to-day, all dated Oct. 28, 1864; Major Smith promoted to Lt. Col.; Capt. Stoodley to Major ; Lieut. Curtis to Captain. Second Lieutenants Taggard and Sherman to First Lieutenants. Hosp. Steward Royal B. Prescott to First Lieutenant. All these officers are mustered for the unexpired term of the Thirteenth's original three years' enlistment.

With the exception of a short absence on account of sickness, and while detailed for a few weeks at the 18th Corps Hospital, Hospital Steward Prescott had served as such with the Thirteenth, during its entire term of service, without so much as a furlough to visit home. In the absence of Asst. Surgeon Morrill, Prescott was the only medical officer with the Thirteenth, in care of the Hospital, the sick and the wounded, for a number of weeks including the two battles at Fort Harrison. His term of medical study had been so limited that the law did not permit of his appointment as Surgeon or Assistant Surgeon, notwithstanding the fact that his long practical experience as Hospital Steward had fitted him excellently for those positions. Major Smith commanding the Thirteenth, and others of its officers, thought that his long, faithful and valuable services should receive a special recognition — hence his commission as First Lieutenant.

At dark orders are received to cook three days' rations, and to be ready to move at a moment's notice. During the night two regiments of our Brigade move out, leaving us to man the works. There has been heavy firing on the left all day.

Nov. 3. Thurs. Rainy, cold. Thirteenth in camp. Transferred, to the 2d Brigade. In the afternoon we again move, to a new campground farther to the right. These successive moves to the right take the 13th away from Fort Harrison, out upon the wide curve in the Union lines that sweeps eastward across the New Market road, and then on southward towards Deep Bottom. The Thirteenth has remained in and near Fort Harrison until to-day.

Nov. 4. Fri. Very stormy last night ; clears this morning. Thirteenth in camp. Drilling resumed. Company drill forenoon ; regimental and brigade drill afternoon. The non-commissioned officers are to meet in school twice a week. Many troops sent North to protect the frontier. The most of the 1st Brigade have gone. The 3d N. H. have also gone. Three men deserted from the Thirteenth last night, scared by the evidences of a movement in the Union lines.

Nov. 5. Sat. Clear, cold. Thirteenth in camp. We are camped in nothing but shelter tents, and our bed is the ground. No fires can be had in the tents, and none outside when it rains. Thirteenth transferred back to the 1st Brigade.

Nov. 6. Sun. Fine, cool. Reg. in camp. Very particular Inspection.

Nov. 7. Mon. Rainy a. m. Reg. in camp. Our Brigade under arms — an attack expected. One third of the army under arms all night. Many of the New York regiments have gone away, we expected to go with our old 1st Brigade, and had orders to prepare three days' cooked rations, but were transferred to the 2d Brigade instead. And then again were put in the 1st Brigade, consisting of two regiments, 13th N. H. and 139th N. Y.

Nov. 8. Tues. Cloudy. Reg. in camp. Voted for President of the United States. The vote in the Thirteenth stands 104 for Lincoln, and 41 for McClellan. The 2d N. H. gives fifty odd votes, four of them for McClellan. The enemy threatened mischief for to-day, but has kept quiet. The 13th under marching orders, but does not move.

Nov. 9. Wed. Cloudy, warm, rainy. Reg. in camp. Log-houses commenced for winter quarters. They are ten feet long, seven feet wide, with walls five feet high, and covered with shelter tents for roofs. Two bunks are placed crosswise, one above the other, at the back end, each bunk for two men. At the front end is a door, and at one side a fireplace, the chimney outside the house, and built up of sticks and mud. The log walls of the houses chinked and plastered with clay. Very comfortable houses. Very heavy and rapid firing below Petersburg heard here this evening. No notice taken of it here.

Nov. 10. Thurs. Cloudy, warm, showery. Thirteenth in camp. A quiet day.

Persistent grumbling in the Northern army is a habit confined chiefly to hirelings. A question principally of character — or of no character. The habit appears to be a sort of relief to an unoccupied mind. There are men who grumble while they eat, or drink, or sleep, or play, or sing, or laugh, or dance, or cheer; and while they imbibe their whiskey rations and while they fight. Grumbling runs in waves; on stormy days the grumble wave runs high, in fair weather the wave is low. But seven out of every ten of the common grumblers are the stuff cowards, bounty-jumpers and deserters are made of.

Once on a time there was born to a certain man's kennels, of a small cross-breed of dogs, a puppy half white and half black, the colors divided along the median line from the end of his nose to the tip of his tail; he was an odd looking scamp with one eye white, the other black. In the daytime it was difficult to tell which half of him was coming first, and in the night he necessarily appeared only half a dog. He grew a solemn, deaconish, long-faced, sorry-eyed dog, and rarely wagged his tail. He knew little, and could be taught little. He was a curious bicolor-dog. But what made him a source of abiding interest was his habit of speech. He rarely or never barked — did not have time — but whether asleep or awake, dozing or dreaming, chasing or sitting in the corner, playing or working, eating or drinking, or whatever he was doing, he kept up an ugly, frequent, almost unending cry, an uncertain mouthing mixture of a growl, a whine of half starvation, and the "Whi — ii!" of a poodle dog stung by two hornets at once. He never let up in that thing for a whole day during the two years or so of his life; and the more he 'grumbled' the healthier he grew. His owner kept him as a curiosity, until he could be endured no longer. We merely mention him as a fair type of the common grumbler, in the army or out of it.

Nov. 11. Fri. Clear. Thirteenth in camp. Fashion invades even a military camp in the field. White gloves and white collars are in demand : " Turn down collars will do — but the garotte, the choker, is by far the most fashionable," writes one member of the Thirteenth.

Nov. 12. Sat. Showery, p. m. clear, cold. Thirteenth in camp. Lieut. Churchill goes home on a twenty days' leave. Gen. Grant suppresses sundry New York papers, ordering a wholesale destruction of all of them that come to City Point. We are thus deprived of our regular daily paper, and probably of some of the most interesting reading of the season. All communication between our pickets and those of the enemy are now strictly prohibited.

Nov. 13. Sun. Very cold, clear. A snow squall in afternoon. Thirteenth in camp. Usual Sunday duties. Cyrus G. Drew of B receives a thirty days' furlough by special order. He has acted as clerk at Hdqrs. for much of his term of service ; and as clerk of Company B whenever with the Regiment. A first class clerk, and an excellent penman. It may properly be said that officers leave camp on a " Leave of absence," while enlisted men go on " Furlough," both terms meaning practically the same thing so far as absence is concerned.

Mess board now costs $5.00 per week, and that for the commonest necessaries, few luxuries are to be had at any price ; an unending round of pork, beef and potatoes, bread, coffee and beans, and none very good.

Nov. 14. Mon. Clear, cool. Reg. in camp, and at work on winter quarters.

Nov. 15. Tues. Clear, sharp, frosty. Reg. in camp. The pinch caused by the scarcity of officers on duty in the 13th is very severely felt. Our officers are practically forced to do double duty.

· Recruiting for the 13th is especially up hill work. Recruits seem to dread the 13th because of its reputation for hard fighting. The average man at home nowadays is more fond of dollars than of war. Lieut. Prescott assigned to the command of Company E this afternoon. New clothing issued to the men of the 13th.

Nov. 16. Wed. Clear. Reg. in camp. Drilling. Log-houses are rapidly going up for winter quarters, all along the line. Six deserters come in ; and all of them who now come in say that there is no danger of a rebel attack on our lines here, they are so strong.

Nov. 17. Thurs. Rainy. Reg. in camp. Capt. Staniels returns to duty. Regular monthly inspection. Asst. Surgeon Morrill commissioned Surgeon of the 1st N. H. Heavy Artillery. Receives his commission Nov. 23d ; leaves the Thirteenth Nov. 26th.

Nov. 18. Fri. Rainy. Reg. in camp. Heavy musketry firing heard this evening on the right of the Bermuda Hundred lines near the Howlett House. The occasion is the attack upon, and capture of, a portion of the Bermuda Hundred line (where the 13th were stationed last

August and September, before coming to Fort Harrison), by Confederate Gen. Pickett's troops. The garrison of Redoubt McConihe — including Co. C — are not driven out, though the redoubt is considerably advanced beyond the main line of our earth-works. A few men of the garrison are pushed out to form a corps of observation, and one of them, John C. Palmer of C, is captured by the enemy. (Palmer was taken to Richmond, afterwards made his escape, and came into our lines near Wilson's Landing.) We are ordered to be in readiness; and turn in at night expecting every minute to hear: "Fall in — fall in!" Turning out in the cold is far more dreaded than any fight we are likely to be called into; to fight (and win) is glorious, to shiver with the benumbing, ague-breeding cold and dampness is a mean experience.

Nov. 19. Sat. Very rainy, cold. Reg. in camp. A very fine camp we now have, with many modern conveniences. The officers' houses are similar to those of the men, only a little larger. See Nov. 9th. This rain, however, washes out the clay between the logs, which had scarcely dried, and all the huts leak badly.

Capt. Staniels appointed Acting Asst. Adjt. General on the staff of the First Brigade, First Division 18th Army Corps.

Nov. 20. Sun. Rainy, all day. Reg. ordered to remain in quarters. Ammunition issued, and special preparations made to resist an expected attack by the enemy. Six deserters came in to our Brigade last night, a fair nightly average. Lieut. Taggard, Adjutant of the Thirteenth, renders himself popular by promptness and efficiency; and by his custom of being particular, exceedingly minute and reliable in all matters concerning rolls, orders and reports. Capt. Farr, absent from the Reg. since his wound was received on June 1st, returns to duty to-day; the wound, however, is only partially healed.

Nov. 21. Mon. Rainy, warm. Reg. in camp. What is left of Confederate Gen. Early's Army of the Shenandoah is now massed on our front. They expect an attack; so do we. We can count three lines of abatis in front of the enemy's works, and the spaces between those lines are reliably reported to be thickly planted with torpedoes. We shall never assault that combination.

Sundry huts built of stakes with brush woven in among them, all well packed with turf and clay — a method of construction known as 'wattle and daub' — in the absence of frost to solidify the structure, are made by this storm most unattractive heaps of twigs and mud. The man who introduced them receives no praises. They prove worse than similar huts did at Fredericksburg — meaner than a musk-rat's nest, shabbier than a broken beaver dam.

Nov. 22. Tues. Very cold. Reg. in camp; everybody and everything soaking wet. We have had a steady rain for four days, clearing to-night cold with a heavy frost. It is most miserable weather, and the Thirteenth is in unfinished quarters — almost a repetition of the Falmouth camp. The mud plastering — 'chinking' — of the walls and chimneys had only partly dried when the rain came on; this soon washed out, and many of the clay-and-sticks chimneys fell down, each leaving a huge muddy hole in the wall, instead of a fireplace, where the storm beat in and no fire could be built. About half the huts in the Thirteenth are in this condition to-night. This evening two deserters from the enemy come in to the Thirteenth.

Nov. 23. Wed. Very cold, clear. Reg. in camp. Our surplus baggage is still at Bermuda Hundred, though very much needed here. The men have recently suffered severely while on picket, and in the frequent changes of camp. All furloughs and leaves of absence have been temporarily suspended, the troops all being needed at the front.

Nov. 24. Thurs. Cool. Thanksgiving Day. Capt. Julian's parents, and with them Miss Charlotte Vinal of Exeter, visit camp.

Gen. Ord has formed a special fund from the savings of the men in the matter of rations, and with it, through Capt. Witherbee, Corps Commissary, has supplied poultry, fruit, nuts, cranberries, etc., in abundance, for the men of the Thirteenth and other regiments, but officers are excluded by special orders from the use of articles purchased by this fund; consequently the men have a good dinner, while the officers are waiting for supplies. One officer of the Thirteenth writes that he had hard bread, butter and a cup of chocolate for his dinner, and that was the best he could get. Another reports having cod-fish and potatoes, as the best that he could muster.

"Pleasant day. Thanksgiving. Cod-fish for dinner."

LIEUT. PRESCOTT.

Nov. 25. Fri. Clear, cool. Reg. in camp. To-day a bountiful supply of turkeys, also crackers, cakes, apples, cranberries and knick-knacks, arrives from New Hampshire for the officers and men of the Thirteenth. A team has waited at the James River landing three days for this shipment; the steamer bringing it having run aground. The poultry now on hand averages about four pounds for every member of the Regiment. "It is Thanksgiving for a week," writes one man of the Thirteenth. The cranberries are a source of much amusement. The ration of sugar, served to the men, is barely enough to sweeten their coffee; and how to make cranberry sauce or pies without any sweetening is a puzzle. One man made a long string of beads of his portion, and wore them around his neck as long as they held together.

Nov. 26. Sat. Cold, clear. Reg. in camp. Many officers are being mustered out on expiration of their three years' term of service. Our Brigade thus loses eight officers this week. Generals Grant, Meade and Butler and the Hon. Henry Wilson visit our camp. The mails average about three days' time in coming from Concord, N. H., to this front. Gen. Grant is very particular about the mails for his command, because, as he puts it: "Regular correspondence with friends at home relieves the soldiers of much fret and worry, and makes them more cheerful, healthy and steady."

Nov. 27. Sun. Clear. Reg. in camp. The officers of the Thirteenth take their Thanksgiving dinner to-day, at the quarters of Lt. Col. Smith, who has charge of the banquet, and all are seated strictly according to rank. Twenty are present besides Lt. Col. Smith, comprising all the field, staff and line of the Thirteenth now in camp. Two fine large turkeys, which have come to camp directed to Col. Stevens, do duty with others on the well spread table.

Nov. 28. Mon. Pleasant, fine. Reg. in camp. Reader — did you ever eat a Thanksgiving dinner while serving as a soldier, in an army, in active service, in the field ? If not, you know not how to eat ; nor how badly a fellow can feel next day !

Nov. 29. Tues. Cloudy, warm. Reg. in camp. The chief speculation in camp is in reference to what will happen when the bulkhead is blown out of the end of Dutch Gap canal. Some there are who expect a furious battle — the final struggle for Richmond. The bulkhead is mined, the rebels have heavy batteries opposite. The work on the canal has been done under the direction of Maillefort, who blew up Hurl Gate in New York harbor.

Nov. 30. Wed. Pleasant, warm. Reg. in camp — "Camp in front of Richmond." And so is England in front of France — but the stormy channel roars between.

The ruins of a house, with chimneys standing, is in front of the picket line on the Varina road (near where Dr. Aiken's house now stands). Major Stoodley wants some brick from these chimneys, and himself and a few men go near the ruins to get them. There is every prospect of success, when a squad of Confederate pickets suddenly rise up by the roadside, uncomfortably near, and show fight. The Major retires with his men, jocularly remarking that "he guesses he don't want any of those brick." One thing is certain, however, when Major Stoodley is forced to give up a dangerous job, all other men will find it for their interest to let it alone.

Dec. 1. Thurs. Very pleasant. Reg. in camp. Lieut. Morrison sick with fever at the field hospital. Lieut. Churchill appointed Adjutant of the ' Substitutes' Camp ' at Concord, N. H.

Dec. 2. Fri. Warm, cloudy. Reg. in camp. An uneasy day. The enemy shells Dutch Gap, and our batteries near it, tremendously with heavy mortars. In the afternoon the Reg. is placed under arms in the front trenches. Orders are issued that neither officer nor man is to sleep, even for a moment, during the night while on picket, and no fires are to be lighted. This is most severe, and on long stormy nights the men and officers suffer greatly. Between 10 and 11 p. m., very heavy musketry firing is heard rolling up from the Bermuda Hundred right, and continuing for nearly an hour, the James river serving as a huge sounding board. "Major Stoodley made a ball-alley to-day." The first in the Thirteenth.

Dec. 3. Sat. Cold with snow. Reg in camp. The 13th assigned

to its new Brigade — 1st Brig. 3d Div. 24th Corps.  The 1st Div. of the 18th Corps becomes the 3d Div. of the 24th Corps. The Thirteenth engaged all day in digging a ditch and in planting abatis in front of the works.  Lieut Sawyer returns to the command of Company E.

Maj. Gen. W. F. Smith — ' Baldy ' — commanded the 18th Corps from May 2, 1864, to July 19, 1864 ; Maj. Gen. E. O. C. Ord from July 21, 1864, to Oct. 1, 1864 ; Maj. Gen. Godfrey Weitzel from Oct. 1, 1864, to Dec. 3, 1864.  To-day the old 18th Corps is broken up, and the white troops of the 18th and 10th Corps are to form the 24th Corps — Gen. E. O. C. Ord commanding, while the colored troops of these two corps will together form the 25th Corps.  The 10th and 18th Corps being discontinued.

Dec. 4. Sun. Clear. Reg. receives orders to move, but remains in camp.  The whole army is turned out before daylight, so as to be ready to repel assaults.  All very quiet along our lines.  Colored troops come in this afternoon.

Dec. 5. Mon. Clear, warm. Reg. moves farther to the right, on account of the reorganization of the corps, to ground previously held by colored troops of the 10th Corps, and encamps.  We thus become the right of the line of the Army of the James.  The negro troops of the 10th Corps holding the left of the line.

The Thirteenth is now commanded by Lt. Col. Normand Smith, and our 1st Brigade, consisting of the 11th Conn., 13th N. H., 19th Wis., 81st, 98th and 139th N. Y., is commanded by Lt. Col. John B. Raulston of the 81st N. Y.

Dec. 6. Tues. Cloudy, cold, stormy. Thirteenth in camp, and fitting up quarters.  The 24th Corps is the right of the entire army in the field, and our 3d Division is the left of the Corps line, bringing the 13th about one mile to the right of Fort Harrison.  We were called this morning at 5.30 a. m., and at daylight exchanged quarters with the colored troops.  The 6th Corps arrives on this front.  The numerous changes of camp subject the men and officers to great inconvenience and discomfort; some of the quarters occupied are filthy beyond description.

Dec. 7. Wed. Cold, rainy. Thirteenth in camp. We, with the rest of our Division, are under orders to remain in readiness to move at an hour's notice, with two days' rations and sixty rounds per man of ammunition.  The Reg. is called into line at 5.30 a. m. as a regular order. The quarters, of the colored troops, now occupied by the Reg. are inferior, and this storm comes on before they can be properly refitted.

Dec. 8. Thurs. Very cold, cloudy. Thirteenth on the front picket line, without fires, and suffering severely from the cold.  The fires on our picket lines have been discontinued, by general order, for about two weeks past, while the enemy's pickets have large, warm fires in plenty, and have had them all the winter.

" I have seen the general officer of our picket going about and extinguishing the tiny fires of a few twigs kindled behind some rock or sheltered nook, around which our poor frozen fellows, on the picket line, were trying to warm their benumbed fingers."      LIEUT. PRESCOTT.

Dec. 9. Fri. Very cold. Snow, rain and sleet at night. About two inches of snow falls, and is covered with a stiff, sharp crust. This cuts the horses' feet to bleeding, and tears the men's army shoes to pieces, as they march through it.

The officers now in charge of our picket lines are required to stay on the picket line for 24 hours, and to keep awake all night. A battle is liable to commence at any hour, and the sleepless vigilance required is ruining the health and vigor of both officers and men. Picketing was never before so strict. The Brigade officer of the day is on the picket line for 24 hours continuously. The Division officer of the day goes along the entire line twice in the daytime, and twice at night; and the Corps officer is constantly on hand to see that all the duties are attended to according to orders. The worst burden, however, falls upon the enlisted men, besides being watched by the eye of every official grade above them — every officer and man is watched by a dozen others.

Dec. 10. Sat. Cold, a little snow, much mud and slush. The Thirteenth suddenly called into line for action; turned out three times during the day, remaining in the front trenches until dark. The enemy again pounding away with heavy mortars, especially about Fort Harrison, and also making a demonstration on the right. Nothing serious occurs near us, but Jourdan's Brigade, on our right, loses 25 men killed and wounded.

The officers of the Thirteenth, and other regiments in the Division, go to Hdqrs. and enter complaint against the order prohibiting picket fires. If attacked, they state, our men could not possibly defend themselves; they could only fire one round and then retire, for their hands are so benumbed they could not possibly re-load their muskets. The result of the complaint is that the picket fires are renewed; and our pickets again have an even chance with the rebels. The pickets go out at 4.30 p. m., and remain on duty for 24 hours; some of them in the front rifle-pits, and some as vedettes on the open ground beyond.

Dec. 11. Sun. Very cold, rainy. Thirteenth called into line in the trenches at 5 a. m.; at daylight returns to camp.

The Thirteenth now has upon its rolls only 21 officers and 580 men, though it has been increased by nearly 300 recruits. We now have 225 men present — less than 200 fit for duty — 125 detached, and over 200 sick and wounded in various hospitals.

Dec. 12. Mon. Very cold last night and to-day. The utmost vigilance is now demanded here. The force is short. As an instance: The Brigade officer of the day is required to remain on the picket line all night, and to keep awake. He must be moving constantly up and down the line during all of both day and night. There are but five officers now in our Brigade who are eligible for this duty; to be awake all of one night in every five is hard work — when added to all other regular duties. All the other officers, and the men, are equally hard pressed. Thirteenth and other troops turn out in line of battle at 5 a. m. every morning, regularly, then stack arms and return to quarters, remaining until late in the morning with equipments on.

Dec. 13. Tues. Clear, cold. Reg. in camp. Gen. Meade and staff visit our lines, and make a most particular inspection of them.

Gen. Butler is on his way, with Gen. Weitzel in immediate command, to attack Fort Fisher at Wilmington, N. C.; by some considered the strongest fort which the enemy has, or which has been attacked during the war. The Army of the James furnishes for the expedition Gen. Ames' Division of the 24th Corps, and Gen. Paine's Division of the 25th Corps (colored), a total of about 6,500 men. Admiral Porter goes with 37 vessels, carrying upwards of 500 guns, the most formidable fleet assembled for any special expedition during the war.

Dec. 14. Wed. Pleasant, some rain. Reg. in camp; turned out only for company drill. Six regiments now in our Brigade, eighteen regiments in our Division — and no Brigadier General.

Dec. 15. Thurs. Pleasant. Reg. in camp. Under arms at 5, or 5.30 a. m. The rebel gunboats and rams, about a mile distant, are blowing their steam whistles far more noisily than usual.

A large pine-tree in front of our works is provided with spikes driven in to facilitate climbing, and serves for signal tower and lookout. Richmond is plainly visible from it.

Dec. 16. Fri. Pleasant. Reg. in camp. A large detail from the Reg. and Brigade — about 300 men in all — at work on the New Market road, now being covered with long stretches of corduroy.

Lieut. Prescott assigned to the command of Company C, and placed in command of Redoubt McConihe on the Bermuda Hundred front. He reports for duty there this forenoon.

Dec. 17. Sat. Pleasant. Reg. again settling down in winter quarters — snug little log-huts. The 24th Corps still holds the right of the line of the Army of the James; and our Third Division holds the left of the Corps line — about one mile to the right of Fort Harrison.

Dec. 18. Sun. Showery. Reg. in camp. Inspection. Under an order granting furlough prizes to the best soldiers, Sergt. M. C. Shattuck of Co. B receives the first furlough granted in our 3d Division of the 24th Army Corps. The Division comprises over 6,000 men. Heavy firing going on near Petersburg all this morning — throb — throb — throb.

Dec. 19. Mon. Pleasant day, rainy night. Reg. in camp. The joke rattles round the camp that the 13th are now "Nine months' men," having nine months more to serve. The 13th has furnished 20 men for musicians in bands; 67 for the navy; 20 for commissions in colored regiments; 15 for heavy artillery — Penn. Battery — and is represented on almost every staff in this Department.

Dec. 20. Tues. Very rainy, chilly. Reg. in camp. Capt. Betton starts for home on 20 days' leave.

Dec. 21. Wed. Rainy, clear in the afternoon. Five deserters from the Union army shot on our right.

Dec. 22. Thurs. Very cold and windy. Reg. in camp.

Dec. 23. Fri. Clear, cold. Reg. in camp. A commissioned officer, a little fellow, appointed to a special duty quite dangerous and important, swelled with confidence and pride, and called for volunteers to accompany him, in these words : " Them as is gwine — g'long with mee ! " He then waited awhile, heard no response — except laughter — and finally was provided with a special detail of men, whom he marched out of camp with the air of a hurt grandee. He was not of the Thirteenth.

Dec. 24. Sat. Pleasant. Reg. in camp. No stockings hung up!

Dec. 25. Sun. Pleasant. Reg. in camp. Usual Sunday duties. A fine Christmas dinner for all. There are, too, the hackneyed sports of the camp ; foot, sack, wheelbarrow, and horse races ; greased pole to climb, greased pig to catch ; mock review, sham parade, etc.

This story of the 13th comes around, condensed : Norfolk plum pudding heated over, large, for fifteen guests. Pint of sutler's best brandy poured over pudding, while the odor fills the tent and all the guests remark upon the waste of good brandy. Brimstone match applied, goes out, then another, then others, all go out ; brandy no burn. Candle, a tallow dip, applied in forty places, rancid tallow dripping over each place ; candle slips out of turnip candlestick and stands head down in platter beside pudding ; brandy no ignite. " I can make that brandy burn," remarks a guest. He brings a torch of pitch-wood with a great smoky flame. Torch applied in twice forty places — black smoke rolls up, pitch and soot rolls down, over each place. Guests make remarks suited to the festive occasion, laugh till they cry, roar themselves hoarse, shout themselves deaf, yell themselves blind ; brandy no take fire. Give it up. Smoke, brimstone, tallow, dirt, pitch, soot, etc., scraped off plum pudding — but the supreme quintessence of all of them had run most liberally into it. Guests served ; one mouthful taken by each, result : a hideous instantaneous explosion of remarks, essence of all of above, expletives and the names of all the high dyked towns in Holland. Guests disperse. All declare that they could not remove the taste of that pudding, etc., etc., out of their mouths for a month ; and the sutler has no further market for his 'brandy.' The pudding was old, mouldy, had soured, a store pudding.

Dec. 26. Mon. Rainy, foggy. Reg in camp. News of the fall of Savannah, Ga., read to the troops this morning at reveille — 5.30 a. m. This dispatch arrived here at 1 a. m., and turned the night into a jubilee. The Thirteenth is the first regiment of our Brigade to be in line at this morning's reveille, to hear the news and to cheer. The men feel that when a rebel prop now goes down, it goes down not to rise again. The cheering sounds right merrily as it runs along the line, taken up by regiment after regiment, repeated rapidly and loudly. It is still very dark at reveille ; invisible troops cheer, and invisible drums, bugles and bands are playing in every direction — save one ; the rebels have gone out of the jubilee business this morning.

Savannah, 150 heavy guns, and 25,000 bales of cotton, is Maj. Gen. Sherman's 'Christmas Present' to the President of the United States. The day is to be observed by the Union army as a special holiday, so far as possible, after the salute is fired this morning with shotted cannon in honor of Gen. Sherman's victory.

Dec. 27. Tues. Cloudy, misty, rainy, foggy; clearing at night.

"On Dress-parade the Thirteenth received its new colors, with its Battles inscribed on them." HIRAM C. YOUNG of H, Color Corporal.

"We drew a flag with a deep, heavy fringe and tassels, elegant lancewood staff, and other appointments complete; but the price demanded for lettering was too high, and we had to return it, and take a much less desirable flag from the State." LT. COL. SMITH.

The old flag of the Thirteenth, which the Regiment has borne through dozens of skirmishes and picket fusillades, hundreds of exposures to the enemy's shell, grape and canister, the hail of thousands of bullets, and a long list of severe battles, now war-worn, torn, tattered, used up, and worthless for further active field purposes, is placed on the retired list, and returned with all the honors of war to the custody of the State of New Hampshire.

A new color — one flag — and none too good, is sent from Concord, Dec. 14th, inscribed by order of Maj. Gen. B. F. Butler with the following list of battles, and terms of constant fighting, and exposure to the enemy's fire:

"Fredericksburg,         Dec. 13, 1862.
Siege of Suffolk,        April and May 1863.
Walthall Road,           May 7, 1864.
Swift Creek,             May 9, and 10, 1864.
Kingsland Creek,         May 12, and 13, 1864.
Drury's Bluff,           May 14, and 16, 1864.
Cold Harbor,             June 1, and 3, 1864.
Battery Five, Petersburg, June 15, 1864.
Battery Harrison,        Sept. 29, and 30, 1864."

Dec. 28. Wed. Very rainy. Reg. in camp. A very strong picket line sent out. The men have no shelter. About noon there falls a breezy bit of excitement. Aides come rushing about camp, and all our troops are hurried into the front trenches. The pickets in rifle-pits are ordered to resist an assault, if made, with all their might, and if compelled to fall back, to dispute every inch of ground as they retire. But the enemy remains quiet, our troops are dismissed, and go back to camp. One man of the 13th writes: "All the blamed rebs wanted was to get us wet."

Dec. 29. Thurs. Snowy, cold. Reg. in camp. Surgeon Richardson was chief operating Surgeon on board of Gen. Butler's boat in the Fort Fisher expedition, and visits our camp to-day. The first intimation we had here of the Fort Fisher fiasco was the cheering of the rebels on our front. They held a jubilee after the fashion of our celebration of the Savannah victory.

The spree is a reversion to animalism and the savage state, a drain upon body, mind and life; and thousands of soldiers have 'spreed' themselves into Hospitals, Invalid Corps or premature graves. The sick from reasonable causes, the wounded and hurt, are to be honorably excepted; but outside of their numbers and the honorably discharged, the present survivors of our Regiment as a rule are of the sober, quiet, steady-going class of men, who exercise the greater care of themselves. As the Thirteenth becomes reduced in numbers, the sport, joviality and fun decreases; and that too even in a greater proportion than the fall in numbers. This is not an evidence of the depression of the spirits of the men; though tired of the war, the Northern army, of which we are a part, is determined to win. The rough, coarse fun, the wild, high times in camp, the 'roaring camp-fires,' the picturesqueness of the Regiment are fast falling away to the stern and sturdy business of the war; while the wide range of personal characteristics, in our original thirteen hundred men, is narrowed to almost the definiteness of one special class — the steady and sober men. Camp life grows dull, and still more dull, with every turning month.

Dec. 31. Sat. Heavy rain, with hail and snow about 10 a. m., and the year goes out with an exceeding cold wave at night. Reg. in camp. Mustered for pay by Capt. Stimpson of the 81st N. Y. Inspection postponed on account of the cold storm. This month has been a quiet one for us, excepting much hard work on the picket lines, and within and upon the entrenchments.

"The work of 1864 is done. An eventful year. God be praised for all his mercies." MAJOR STOODLEY, in Diary.

In the discussion, now so common, of the relative abilities of Gen. Grant and Gen. Lee, it should be said that while no one can do Gen. Grant any credit by disparaging or disputing the great abilities and achievements of Gen. Lee, history can never write them on the same level; Gen. Grant will forever hold the higher place. We must bear in mind that since the Battles of the Wilderness, and that of Cold Harbor in June 1864, Gen. Lee has been operating practically on the defensive, and on inside lines, and shut up in a citadel surrounded by swamps, rivers and high bluffs and made as strong as engineering skill, and the labor of thousands of negro slaves, added to that of his troops, can make its naturally strong walls; while Gen. Grant has been operating on the offensive, trying to enclose, invest or batter down the walls of that citadel, all the time on outside lines, and practically in the open field. The operations have been those of a vast siege.

How these two men would act in an exchange of situations, no one can tell. Their two situations cannot be compared. They are all contrast. The time too for comparing the abilities of these two men ceased before the battle of Cold Harbor — even if not at the first start from the Rapidan, after which Lee swung nearer and nearer to his capital and citadel. At Cold Harbor, at 4.30 a. m., on June 3d, the first attempt to storm that citadel was made — upon Gen. Lee's entrenchments. He had previously entrenched, and had been attacked, when within his defenses, on June 1st, but there was much field work besides. Since that battle he has been, and now is, shut up in a citadel. East central Virginia is a vast pocket or a jug without a handle, and heroic and brave Gen. Lee, and his no less brave and heroic army, is in it, and cannot get out and away. Gen. Lee knows, and every intelligent Southerner knows, that that dash on the early morning of June 3, 1864, at Cold Harbor, was the most tremendous, and effective, Northern threat in this whole war, whether a material gain or not; a threat unmistakable to utterly crush Gen. Lee's army at one blow, if he ever again dares to risk it in the open. A threat that deters lives a near neighbor to the battle that wins. Even the incurred loss of one Union soldier in every eight of the assaulting force on that morning, and the failure of the movement, may be more than compensated by the moral gain: the convincing every Southern soldier, from Gen. Lee down, that he must maintain forever a goodly pile of sand between himself and such bold Union bayonets.

Gen. Grant builded even better than he knew on that morning. Henceforth the Southern soldier must shovel for a living; and the Northern soldier can shovel as fast and as much as he. The Northern troops soon forgot their failure to break through Gen. Lee's entrenchments at Cold Harbor. Twelve days later they hesitated not to assault his heavy entrenchments in front of Petersburg — to do it as skirmishers, and to capture them too, forts, armaments, garrisons and all.

But to turn the story that has no end: The Thirteenth, though so much cut up in the charge on the evening of June 1st that they could not fairly be put into this June 3d assault — less than thirty-six hours later in the battle — still we as a quick reserve held our part of the bloody front bank of the ravine, while our assaulting columns dashed past us out upon the most exposed ground of all covered by the assault of that morning, and over upon the heavy Confederate ranks and trenches a very few short yards beyond; held it while the air resounded and the ground trembled and shook with the awful thunders of that charge, the Union cannon, and the combined artillery and musketry fire of the entire Confederate line; and while the forest all around and over us was crushed and torn, like a field of reeds, with the thousands upon thousands of bullets, grape-shot and shells, amid the roar and crash of one of the most stupendous blows ever struck in modern war; ready, waiting and desirous, if a rebel counter-charge was attempted, to stand up and to do our best part to meet it; and before the echoes of the first Union onset had died away we moved forward over the field of the assault, under fire, as a support — passing nearly over, but a little to the left, of the very crest and field where we charged on June 1st with heavy loss but with success.

Surely the Thirteenth may well claim, and long remember, with just pride and honor, their share in that fearful assault of June 3d, as well as in all the Cold Harbor battle. The simultaneous rush of eighty thousand men, in one combined charge, is no small affair, the hail of bullets, shot and shell from fifty thousand muskets and three hundred cannon, all in full play, is no small storm; and men who will dash through it all upon heavily manned entrenchments, as dashed these Union columns on that June morning, will little hesitate to strike steel on steel in the open field.

The battle of Cold Harbor will grow more and more important in comparison, will have more and more of just credit for its effective results, as the mist of mere bigness and dimension blows off Gettysburg.

"The General Hospital at Point of Rocks was located on a level plat of ground on the north side of the Appomattox, and was about seventy-five feet above the water of the river. I was detailed as master builder of this hospital when it was first established. Surgeon Fowler was Surgeon-in-charge, and Surgeon Munn was executive officer. The bluff of the river bank was very steep and it was very difficult to get supplies for the hospital up from the boat-landing. Having charge of a large number of men, I suggested an inclined railway up the face of the bluff from the landing to the hospital, and to the front of Surgeon Fowler's and other officers' quarters. We had neither rails nor wheels, and consequently laid a double track of trees hewn straight and square and tree-nailed to sleepers imbedded in the clay of the bluff. Two cars were built, with platforms about eight feet long and six feet wide, and so constructed that the platforms would be level when the cars were on the track. The wheels and axles were made of wood.

"On the premises was an old machine, which I suppose had been used for threshing grain, and which had a wheel about six feet in diameter attached to a shaft and frame. This machine we embedded in the earth at the upper end of the tracks; and secured blocks on the wheel for ropes to wind upon, in such manner that when one rope was winding up the other was unwinding. The cars were arranged in such a way that when one was running up the incline the other was running down. The motive power was a mule which traveled first around one way of his path and then around the other, as the car running up demanded. This inclined railway was a success. It was used continuously for freight and passengers until it was worn out. When on visits to this point Gen. Grant and staff and other officers made use of this railway to ascend the river bank, from the steamers on the river. When worn out it was superseded by another arrangement provided with iron rails and wheels.

"My gang of men, numbered from 25 to 200, most of them taken from the convalescent wards, and in addition to these I had a whole regiment of new troops in the winter of 1864. We built three hospital buildings here 50 feet wide and 250 feet long, which were occupied. Other buildings were planned and laid out, but when Gen. Grant began his last campaign, the most of my men were ordered to the front, which put a stop to our work in a great measure. When the war closed of course we did not need any more hospitals, and our work soon ceased altogether. I remained engaged in this work on the hospitals until mustered out with the Thirteenth."　　　　　　　　　　　　　　HENRY S. PAUL, Company K.

## 1865.

**Jan. 1. Sun.** Fair, very cold. Reg. inspected and reviewed by Capt. Stimpson of the 81st N. Y. Dress-parade at 5 p. m.

The last bulkhead of Dutch Gap canal blown out — but the work is not well done. The canal has been dug chiefly by negro troops. The enemy has a strong battery so planted as to sweep the whole canal, rendering it useless, and its completion next to impossible.

**Jan. 2. Mon.** Very cold. Reg. in camp.

Nature has fixed a gulf of prejudice, and generally of mutual personal distaste, between the black man and the white. The less they mix their blood the better. The black stain will revert even after the tenth generation it is said. The blacker the negro the more fitting he seems to be, and the more acceptable, as a rule. The white and negro soldiers are generally good friends. There is little friction between them, and quarrels are comparatively rare. But the negro accepts the superiority of the white man, the white man feels it, and knows it, through and through, and to the last demonstration; and this tough fact utterly knocks out the very keystone of true fraternity even more than color; for the colored soldiers are of every shade from tan to ebony.

Nothing is more natural, and good-natured too, than the chaffing between these two 'arms of the service.' The negroes call the white, 'poor faded men,' 'white livers,' 'cotton-faces,' etc. While the white men call them the 'unbleached,' 'curly-tops,' 'ivory boys,' 'black roses,' 'geranium bottles,' 'silhouettes,' and all that. The latter term is pretty good; for a company of negro troops, standing in line, under the order: 'Eyes right!' were a picture funny enough to make the Egyptian Sphinx laugh four thousand years ago. The average negro on his own ground and level is amiability itself; out of his natural sphere he is quite apt to fail for want of sufficient staying power to hold him through any severe trial. As soldiers they are a great credit to their race. The negro is now led and governed by instinct, rather than by reason. The black man needs education first of all things; it is only upon that foundation that he can build. Ignorance systematically enforced upon a people for many generations breeds one thing; education and mental training breeds quite another thing. To this date the negro has originated nothing.

**Jan. 3. Tues.** Cold. Three inches of snow. Reg. in camp, and trying to keep warm before fires of green pine wood.

The 2d Division of our 24th Corps receives orders to march with five days' cooked rations — destination Fort Fisher. We expect to go also. Confederate Gen. Hoke's Division, which went down and thwarted the former Union attack on Fort Fisher, return to their works on our front to-day. We can hear the rebels cheering lustily.

**Jan. 4. Wed.** Pleasant. Very muddy. Reg. in camp. Officers' mess board averages now $5.00 per week.

**Jan. 5. Thurs.** Cold, clear. Reg. in camp. A Lieutenant in our Division is claiming: "The rebel commander of Fort Harrison offered to me his sword, as I rushed into that fort over the high parapet;" but which end of that sword the Confederate offered to him, the Lieutenant has failed to state. His is not the only claim of the same import. What a swath of grass some men can mow down in January!

**Jan. 6. Fri.** Cold, blustering; rainy afternoon. Reg. in camp. The Reg., however, is constantly cut up by large details for shoveling and picket duty. Tough work soldiering this winter. England expects every man to do his duty; America expects every duty to 'do' its man! The pickets leave camp for the front lines at 10 a. m., and remain out twenty-four hours, and the strictest vigilance is maintained. Little or no drill nowadays. Deserting is quite frequent, and the offenders, if caught, are to have speedy trials, and to be shot within twenty-four hours of conviction of the crime. It rarely or never occurs that a man of any standing or position at home deserts from the Union army. It is the riff-raff that deserts.

**Jan. 8. Sun.** Very cold, clear. Many men frost-bitten. The night work of policemen in cities is mere child's play compared with the work of these winter-night vedettes, standing the long hours of their watch alone, unprotected, unsheltered and without fires, on the open ground, midway between the outer fortifications, earth-works and the lines of the two armies.

One man, and a good soldier, writes: "My application for furlough comes back disapproved — the third time — by Gen. Butler." And then he expresses much indignation, in most vigorous camp language.

Maj. Gen. B. F. Butler is succeeded in the command of the Army of the James by Maj. Gen. E. O. C. Ord. Maj. Gen. John Gibbon to command the 24th Corps, and Maj. Gen. David B. Birney the 25th Corps.

**Jan. 9. Mon.** Pleasant. Heavy rain last night. Reg. in camp. Chaplain Jones visits the Thirteenth from his post at Base Hospital, Point of Rocks. The Reg. had no Chaplain present, in place of Chaplain Jones, after he was detailed for duty at the hospital.

**Jan. 10. Tues.** Very rainy, a thunder storm. Reg. in camp.

A Confederate soldier, captured in a skirmish, said he had no objection whatever to being taken a prisoner; but he cursed the repeating rifle most roundly, and said he would like to see that —— gun which the Yankees loaded up on Sunday, and kept firing off all the rest of the week.

**Jan. 11. Wed.** Fair. Reg. in camp. Much suffering from the cold, scarcely dry wood enough to be found for kindling the fires. Orders received that no more furloughs are to be granted for the present.

**Jan. 12. Thurs.** Pleasant. Reg. in camp. Inspection of arms by Capt. Julian.

**Jan. 13. Fri.** Very pleasant. Reg. in camp. Early in the winter of 1864, after the Thirteenth received the Sharps carbines — breech-loading — Lt. Col. Smith was ordered to drill the Reg. as skirmishers

Not having a bugler in the Regiment, he sent to New Hampshire and after much trouble enlisted Daniel Johnson, a discharged bugler of the 5th N. H. and of Stewartstown. Johnson had been with the Reg. scarcely a week when he was detailed as bugler at 1st Brigade Hdqrs. Hardly a commendable proceeding.

Jan. 14. Sat. Warm, cloudy. Reg. in camp. Lt. Col. John B. Raulston, 81st N. Y., commanding our Brigade, is mustered out.

All veterans will recall the negro camp-follower. A negro appears with nothing to do, and is at once hired as a servant, and greedy devourer of odd and unattractive scraps of rations. Possibly a private hires him for the march, and pays him ten cents in advance, writes his own name, company and regiment on a piece of paper, and gives it to the negro, so that the employer may be found. Then the negro carries the traps of half a dozen men for a while. Within a few hours the negro is gruffly asked whose ' boy ' he is. Now comes the importance, and pomposity of him, in full measure. The negro straightens up, puts on ineffable dignity, and replies : " Dunno, sah. S'pose um Kurnul, sah. May be Brig'dier. Look-out, better not 'pose me, sah! " and starts along. He is stopped, the card is shown, the private's traps are returned to him — the ten cents of course being kept by the negro — and the camp-follower goes into the service of a Lieutenant, with card, but no money in advance — or at any other time. In a few days the negro is promoted — " 'p'moted, sah " — to the service of the Major or Colonel, is dressed up finely, and cannot be touched with a forty-foot pole. But during the various grades of his service he has trudged along, sweating and puffing, with a load of a hundred pounds or more, canteens, haversacks, blankets, odd guns, etc., and the higher grade he serves the less money he gets.

Early in the war we knew one of these black boys whose employer, in a thoughtless moment, gave him a new half-a-dollar. The negro tied it up in a rag, polished it three times a day, and showed it to all his ' cullud f'wends ' for forty days and forty nights; and that mischievous fifty-cent piece cost the Brigade more money than the lucky black owner was worth — the black boys began to ask money for their services. But they are all happy; and that seems to be about all their present life is made for.

Jan. 15. Sun. Pleasant. Reg. in camp.

Jan. 16. Mon. Pleasant. Reg. in camp. The rebel tune of ' Bonnie Blue Flag,' the principal rebel song — unless ' My Maryland ' stands first — is said to be an adaptation of an old air, ' He 's gone to the arms of Abraham.' Its music, however, is flat, and the rebels have worn the stuff in it all to rags. Col. Edgar M. Cullen, 96th N. Y., assumes command of our 1st Brigade.

Jan. 17. Tues. Clear, cloudy, snowy, windy, mixed, disagreeable. Reg. in camp. Review of Division by Gen. Gibbon. News arrives of the capture of Fort Fisher by Gen. Alfred Terry and Admiral Porter; and a salute with blank cartridges is fired all up and down the Union lines.

This most gallant affair is another feather in the cap of the Army of the James. Gen. Terry with the same force from our front that Gen. Butler had in the former attack, and one Brigade more — a total of 8,000 men, with Admiral Porter and the same fleet, captures the fort after a most desperate contest, lasting from 3 p. m. until 10 p. m. The Union army lost 646 men, killed and wounded, and the navy 309. The Confederate garrison of 2,500 men were all killed or captured. The fort mounted 75 guns, the outworks 94, total 169.

Jan. 18. Wed. Cloudy, cold. Reg. in camp.

Jan. 19. Thurs. Fair, cold. Reg. in camp. New quarters being built. A change in the position of Companies. The Thirteenth has recently been highly complimented, for general efficiency, by both our Division and Corps commanders.

In the division of duties one of five officers in our Brigade is appointed each day as camp brigade-officer, to see that the six regiments are promptly in line at 5.30 a. m., at Reveille, that they are all out on the regular terms of drill appointed for the day, and to see to the brigade prisoners and deserters from the enemy. They also act as trial justices; taking the place of regimental courts martial.

Jan. 20. Fri. Cloudy, cold. Reg. in camp. Battalion drill. A great change for the better in the appearance of the troops. New clothing, better rations and quarters work wonders in a few days among the men. Our Reg. and the 139th N. Y. — furnishing together about 160 men besides usual details — are to be consolidated in one battalion for purposes of drill. After the various details are taken out, few regiments have in camp, for drill, so many as ten men in a company.

Jan. 21. Sat. Cold, snowy and rainy, the rain freezing as it falls. In accordance with an order issued by Gen. Gibbon, commanding the 24th Corps, granting one furlough of 20 days, at each inspection, to the best soldier in each Division, the Thirteenth receives a liberal share of the honors. The first furlough granted under this order was given on Dec. 18, 1864 to Sergeant M. C. Shattuck of B; no small compliment in a Division of 20 regiments and over 6,000 men.

The plan is this: Every fourth day, at inspection, each commander of a Company selects the man whom he considers the best soldier he has. These men go before the commander of the Regiment, who selects one man from among them for examination by the commander of the Brigade. The commander of each brigade selects one man from all those sent to him belonging to his brigade of four or five regiments. These men appear before the commander of the Division, who selects one of them to receive the furlough; his name is then announced to the whole Division.

Under a similar order, the best appearing regiment, in the Corps, present at the weekly general inspection is exempt from picket duty for one week, and furnishes the guards for Corps Hdqrs.

Jan. 22. Sun. Rainy. Reg. in camp. Ex-Quarter-master Person

C. Cheney, E. M. Tubbs, A. P. Morrison, J. H. Ames, and Messrs. Scripture, Parker and Spaulding, all from New Hampshire, visit the camp of the Thirteenth. The Reg. receives Quarter-master Cheney with welcoming cheers.

Jan. 23. Mon. Rainy, and exceeding muddy. The entire country, wherever troops move, is a quagmire as soon as the soil is disturbed by the action of feet, hoofs and wheels. The guests of the Thirteenth visit Fort Harrison, our lines of works and the Dutch Gap canal. At night the Thirteenth is suddenly called out into the front trenches, and our whole Union force mans the works.

To-night — or rather, in the early morning of the 24th — in the pursuance of a grand scheme to gobble the entire Army of the James, and to astonish the world, the rebels mass a large body of infantry on our right, and their rams and gunboats steam down the James to the lower end of Dutch Gap, having succeeded in breaking a chain thrown across the river near the Gap. Three of these vessels run past Fort Brady to near the Howlett House Battery. The fleet consists of the iron-clads Richmond, Virginia and Fredericksburg, five gunboats and three torpedo boats. The gunboat Drewry runs aground, is abandoned, and as it keels over, it is blown up by a large shell from Battery Parsons; the rest of the fleet escapes up the river towards Richmond at night. Our shore batteries badly damage the whole fleet, while the huge guns of the iron-clads nearly destroy several batteries. The noise of the contest is tremendous. The rebel infantry make no attack. The whole affair is a failure.

Company C, numbering thirty-two men, has been during all the fall and winter on detached service in Redoubt McConihe on the Bermuda Hundred line. This redoubt is several hundred feet in advance of the main line, and occupies the sharp conical hill on which the Thirteenth encamped on May 18, 1864. It is a little less than a mile from the James. Its position is very exposed, close up to the rebel rifle-trenches; the enemy, however, have no fort on its immediate front. In front of the redoubt is a strong, dense abatis, and a wide, deep ditch encircles it. The enemy has harassed the garrison every night with attacks or feints — making himself as 'unchivalrous and as ungenerous' as possible; but the capture of the redoubt would be of small consequence to him, for a large Union fort near it, to the rear, could knock it all to pieces in a few minutes. The garrison has consisted of Co. C 13th, and a Company from a Pennsylvania regiment of heavy artillery, with four brass 'Napoleon' guns. The total a garrison of about 100 men. The negro troops occupy the positions to the right and left. The whole garrison has turned out every morning at five o'clock and manned the works, the cannon ready to fire, the muskets at the loop-holes, and so remained until daylight. A messenger is sent to the Thirteenth, at Fort Harrison, once a week — a sixteen mile tramp. Capt. James M. Durell took command of this redoubt and garrison on Sept. 1, 1864; but was appointed on the staff of Gen. Graham, and Lieut. Royal B. Prescott was placed in command, in his stead, on Dec. 16, and remained there until Jan. 23. Here is a bit of his experience, given in a letter dated Jan. 7, 1865, a sketch of the pressure on thousands of guardsmen at the front:

"I am under the very strictest orders; am confined to these narrow limits day and night without relief; am responsible for the redoubt and everything in and around it; it is my duty to take every precaution to guard against a surprise; I must employ every means for its defense, and must regulate and determine every feature and movement of all the proceedings, day and night. I hear every little noise that occurs during the night, and am in a half conscious state all night long. I hear the tread of the sentinel at the gate of the redoubt, and startle at the sound of his musket as it strikes the ground at varied intervals; while the sound of a musket-shot on the picket line brings me up in an instant. When I think of the situation here, I almost think I am not myself, but some other fellow. The rebel band played 'Dixie' one evening, when the negro troops on our left struck up 'Rally Round the Flag, Boys,' rendering the chorus with a great deal of vigor." LIEUT. PRESCOTT.

Lieut. Prescott and Company C are relieved to-day, and rejoin the Thirteenth at Fort Harrison, crossing the James over the lower ponton bridge at Deep Bottom. Their whole march of about ten miles is made in a drizzling rain and through almost liquid mud knee-deep, the men heavily loaded with muskets, equipments, tents and camp utensils; and the whole day, from ten o'clock a. m. until five p. m., is required to make the journey. "When they arrived they all looked as if they had been rolled in a brick yard."

Jan. 24. Tues. Pleasant, a little rain. Thirteenth in the trenches all day, and severely shelled — some rebel shells even reaching us from Fort Gilmer. A demonstration is expected from the enemy's left upon our right. The most of the enemy's shells to-day are directed upon Fort Harrison. About dark the Thirteenth, with our Brigade, leaves the front trenches and returns to camp, not having fired a shot. The trenches are wet, however, and the men come in well bespattered with mud.

Jan. 25. Wed. Clear, cold. Thirteenth in camp. Orders received this morning for the 13th to have two days' cooked rations, and everything in readiness to move at a moment's notice. The guests of the 13th go to the Petersburg front; having visited our camp at a most interesting time, when they could enjoy a touch of real war at the front, hear the roar of cannon, the crack of shells and the whistle of bullets as much as they pleased.

The men thoroughly enjoy teasing an unpopular First Sergeant. He calls the roll of the Company morning and evening; often when it is dark he must needs use a candle — a tallow dip — and frequently makes a mess of the roll in more senses than one. The men on such occasions insist on having their exact names called before they will answer: "Here." We must borrow a story to illustrate this kind of sport.

First Sergeant (calling the roll). "Ebenezer Jones." No reply, and Jones stands in his place dumb as an oyster.

1st Sergt. "Jones — why don't you answer to your name, sir?"

Jones. "My name is Eben, not Ebenezer."

1st Sergt. "I see no difference."

Jones. "Well, I do, a heap; and Ebenezer is not my name. Now Sarjunt, your name is Peter Gamble, is it not?"

1st Sergt. "Yes, it is."

Jones. "Well — would you answer to the name of Peternezer Gamble?"

1st Sergt. "Of course not."

Jones. "That settles it; my name is Eben Jones — *Heere!*"

The Company laughs; and that was all that Jones was aiming at.

Jan. 26. Thurs. Very cold. Reg. in camp. Musketry practice with blank cartridges.

Jan. 27. Fri. Cold, snowy. Reg. in camp. Lieut. Prescott starts from camp on ten days' leave; visits Baltimore and Philadelphia, but does not go to New Hampshire. A business trip.

Jan. 28. Sat. Very cold. Reg. in camp. There has been of late a little picket firing near us, the spent bullets coming over. A spent bullet, turned from its course by a twig or other slight obstruction, flies to the earth with a final sharp, spiteful snarl like that of a small hurt cat; but for vicious music in the air a ramrod shot from a rifle surpasses all. They come whirling end over end, and every way, whipping out of the air a multitude of sharp screeches and cutting sounds, which, were their cause unknown. might well be attributed to the infernal imps themselves.

Jan. 29. Sun. Cold, fair. Reg. in camp. Inspection.

Jan. 30. Mon. Fair. Reg. in camp. The rebels the other day struck up 'My Maryland,' when a bad lot of Union men near by answered them loudly with the same air accommodated to a verse composed almost wholly of the vilest possible profanity. The rebels were disgusted and quit. Our men then sang another verse in the sweetest words and terms they could invent. This re-assured the rebels, who were for once outdone in profanity, and they soon renewed the original concert.

Jan. 31. Tues. Pleasant. Reg. in camp. The Reg. has remained in camp the most of this month furnishing details for work on the fortifications, and for picket duty. We have drilled on all days when the weather and mud would permit, and had a Dress-parade on almost every afternoon during the month. Generally quiet along the lines here. On the whole one of the stupidest months since the war began.

Feb. 1. Wed. Cold, clear. Reg. in camp. Battalion drill; 238 men present for duty. Orders are received to prepare four days' cooked rations, and to have sixty rounds of ammunition per man.

Capt. George N. Julian honorably discharged the service because of expiration of his term of enlistment for three years.

When a little over twenty years of age he was mustered as a private,

July 31, 1861, in the Second Battery of Massachusetts Light Artillery — known also as Battery B, and as Nims' Battery, having been organized by Capt. Ormand F. Nims, May 15, 1861. With this Battery Julian enjoyed the privilege of a plenty of sharp artillery practice on that ever memorable occasion when Commodore Farragut ran the rebel batteries at Vicksburg June 28, 1862. Nims' Battery was most hotly engaged at that time behind the levée opposite that city. This was the only important contest this Battery was actively engaged in while Julian was a member of it; but the Battery was in position when Commodore Farragut sailed down past the same rebel batteries.

July 30, 1862, Julian was discharged to receive promotion to a Lieutenancy in an unspecified New Hampshire Regiment. A higher rank awaited him, and co-operating with Dr. William D. Vinall of Exeter he enlisted such of the men of Company E as came from Exeter and vicinity, and was in due time commissioned as Captain of that Company, which he commanded until the summer of 1863, when he received the appointment of Acting Assistant Inspector General on the Brigade Staff, as this history previously records.

In the capacity of Acting Asst. Inspector General, he exercised a most microscopic scrutiny into every bit of war materiel that passed through his hands, while he compelled a thorough cleanliness, and the greatest possible care, of clothing, arms and equipments; gaining the name of being too particular, if he erred in any direction.

No man of the army ever saw this man flinch or quail in the face of danger; on the contrary he kept at the front, was bold and daring to the very verge of rashness, strong, and quicker than a flash. "The quickest officer in the Thirteenth Regiment; and more often too prompt than not prompt enough." Lt. Col. Bowers.

**Feb. 2. Thurs.** Warm, clear. Reg. in camp. Flour and corn meal are now easily obtained, and tin kitchens, or 'Dutch ovens,' are improvised to bake the wonderful cakes upon. Forms are made of boards. A few old fruit cans are unsoldered by heat to furnish a tin covering for the forms. Half the cakes baked upon them before the fires are almost utterly indigestible. A part of them, however, made by skillful hands, are quite an agreeable change in the way of rations. Half a canteen unsoldered by heat, and held in a split stick, makes an excellent little frying-pan; the tin soon burns off, leaving only the thin iron.

**Feb. 3. Fri.** Cloudy, snowy. Reg. in camp. The talk about consolidating the old regiments into five companies each, and mustering out all Colonels and Majors, retaining Lieut. Colonels, causes much uneasiness and mischief. A worse thing could not be done the service than to break up these old regiments.

**Feb. 4. Sat.** Pleasant. Reg. in camp. An ingenious fellow fastens upon his shoes strips of hoop-iron, and enjoys as much of 'skating' on them as the interests of the service will permit.

**Feb. 5. Sun.** Fair. Reg. in camp. For several days and nights an almost continual cannonading has been heard going on in the neighborhood of Petersburg. We remain under marching orders. Inspection today gives us the position of guard for one week at Maj. Gen. Gibbon's 24th Corps Hdqrs.; for which service a Captain, a First Lieutenant, a Second Lieutenant and 100 men are detailed. Lieut. Prescott returns to camp from leave, and is at once detailed with this guard.

Some one chaffing an old negro, among other things asked him when we were again to have peace. The old man answered : " Well, Vol., I rek'n when dey stops de fightin', sah — sartinly not afore, sah."

Another asked an old negro deacon if he thought negroes belonged to the human race. He replied instanter : " Fo' de Lor', yas, sah! Doan de good Book done say to de people, 'Increase de multiply'? I done preaches dat Tol'gy, sah. Dey's people shu' 'nuff! "

Feb. 6. Mon. Fair, cold. Reg. in camp. The pickets were treated to a shower of hail last night. Last week the enemy's forces fell short by 80 deserters at this point, — all of them sick of the Confederacy's war. Brigade drill in the afternoon by Col. Cullen commanding our Brigade.

Feb. 7. Tues. Cold, rainy, snowy, sleety, wretched weather. Reg. in camp. Somehow the negro slaves manage to get past the Confederate lines, and come around our lines here in large numbers. They are generally ill clad, suffering and half starved; and to-day hundreds of them are seeking shelter from the storm, and begging for food and clothing all through the Union camps. The negro question is a terribly tough one.

Feb. 8. Wed. Cold, clear. Reg. in camp. Lt. Col. Smith takes a leave of absence for twenty-five days.

Two substitutes are hanged for desertion and other crimes. One of them selected his grave; merely remarking coolly, as he looked it over : " It is a rather pinched up affair."

The appearance of a regiment which has just received a new outfit of clothing, caps and shoes is most woefully ridiculous. Manufacturers of army clothing stretch a man out upon a sheet of paper, mark around him with chalk, and cut the figure out for a pattern; they all agree that there are no tall men who are lean, and no short men who are fat. Trousers long enough for the lean six-footer give tent room in their amplest parts for the small man too, with more or less of space to spare; while the short, fat man can hardly be squeezed into the pair of trousers that are of the right length for him — his legs looking like two large links of sausage, sky blue, stuck side by side into a larger link. Thus the short men are " tighty," and the long men are ' baggy ; " cloth must be put in, and cloth must be cut out. The pants, too, are often cut preponderous forninst; like the boy's trousers which did not signify whether the wearer was going to school or coming home. Besides, all the clothing, packed like waste paper in huge boxes, comes out wrinkled, creased, puckered, shriveled, twisted, cram-sided and out of joint enough to make a Jew old clo' dealer blush for shame.

No man ever saw a pair of narrow army shoes; they may be short but never narrow. The smaller sizes are nearly square, or a broad oval, so that small feet can almost turn around within them. One little fellow in Company E 13th used, while on drill, to kick the toes of his shoes to the front — after he had got there himself. The army caps — 'skull covers,' as the boys call them — make the men look like natural born fools, growing fooler and fooler every day while they wear them; and pass from man to man, over and over again, in the vain hunt for a head, and a face, caricatured enough to fit them. The poor men, conscious of their grotesque appearance in the general rig, go about looking aslant, downcast, beseeching, shame-faced, and appearing as much as to say: 'We know we look bad — like blue chimpanzees and idiotic baboons; but please don't laugh at us, we are Union soldiers, we cannot dress any better.'

It is the same all through the list. Overcoats 'dress-coats,' blouses and pants must visit the Company tailors — of whom how many takes it to make a man? — to be made over, only to return looking worse than aforetime. The shirts, drawers and stockings are worst of all, past comment, and a scarecrow would play high dandy to any man dressed in them alone, while the rebels would take him for the Yankee devil himself. The prime trouble is that the clothing is all 'theoretical regulation,' while the soldiers had practical, and very many different styles of fathers.

Feb. 9. Thurs. Fair, cold. Reg. in camp. A man of the 13th writes: "At 1 p. m. the 2d Brigade Band escorts a man to his own funeral." A man of the 12th N. H. shot for desertion. The 3d Division of the 24th Corps is formed in a hollow square open on one side. The band precedes, followed first by 20 guards, next the prisoner, next ten men detailed to shoot him, one of their guns being loaded with a blank cartridge. These executions are horrible; but what can be done? Deserters unpunished would soon destroy the efficiency of the army; the bad must go to save the good, and subserve the cause of freedom.

Feb. 10. Fri. Pleasant. Reg. in camp. Brigade drill. Evening schools instituted for officers. The Subs. have been very troublesome of late. They are many of them representatives of a peculiar, a sort of half-abandoned, class of men — a class that the most of us regular volunteers knew nothing about before we enlisted. The better class of recruits are as reliable as volunteers.

Feb. 11. Sat. Cold, clear, muddy. Reg. in camp. Division review this afternoon, on the New Market road, by Maj. Gen. Devens.

News received to-day of the discharge of Brev. Brig. Gen. A. F. Stevens, formerly Colonel of the 13th; honorably discharged on account of disability, caused by wounds received in the charge at Fort Harrison. This discharge was considered premature, and he was afterwards reimbursed in pay and emoluments.

Feb. 12. Sun. Cold, clear, windy. The dust blows through the men's quarters in camp as if they were sieves. Reg. furnishes guards for 24th Corps Hdqrs. for one week. Our 24th Corps reviewed by Generals

Ord and Gibbon on the New Market road at 10 a. m. Wind blowing a gale; the men clad in dress-coats and frozen skins. The review is buried in clouds of dust. One soldier of the 13th writes: " We went without overcoats on, and we nearly froze to death."

Feb. 13. Mon. Fair. Reg. in camp. Our pickets and the rebel pickets are less than 100 yards apart in many places. They indulge in long confabs every day, picket firing being quite generally suspended by a sort of common consent. A part of the 13th, 2d, 10th and 12th N. H. Regiments come on duty together to-day.

Feb. 14. Tues. Fair. Reg. in comp. Drilling again. Company drill forenoon, Battalion drill afternoon.

Feb. 15. Wed. Rainy day and night, rain freezing as it falls. Reg. in camp.

Prisoners tell us that when a deserter or other criminal in the rebel army is executed, his brigade is drawn up without arms, and forming three sides of a hollow square, the fourth open. The deserter with the firing party, marches around the whole line, inside the square, preceded by a band usually playing the 'Dead March in Saul.' The deserter is then tied to a stake in the open end of the square, and shot; and left hanging to the stake. After which the whole brigade file past him to their quarters.

Feb. 16. Thurs. Foggy. Reg. in camp. Capt. Farr — an officer whom all the Thirteenth Regiment likes — leaves camp for Fortress Monroe on a military commission. His wound not having healed sufficiently to enable him to engage in field duties. Very heavy cannonading heard in the neighborhood of Petersburg. A member of the Thirteenth finds a part of an old, broken white marble grave-stone, breaks it in pieces, piles the pieces in the fireplace of his hut and sprinkles them with a little red ink; he says 'they warm him, and cheer him up, just as well as green-pine firewood does.'

When a soldier has a visitor to entertain, he selects hard bread, not broken, and the best he has, soaks it in the best pot of coffee he can make, fries it, then covers it with the moist brown sugar, and places this as the principal dish before his guest. The true soldier serves his coffee in pots; and, by the way, the parade of pots of coffee, and negro attendants, at first class hotels, is after all nothing but an old army custom.

Feb. 17. Fri. Very rainy. Reg. in camp. Inspection at 10 a. m. A Captain in the 11th Conn. says if he ever finds himself desiring to return to the army, he will strap on a knapsack, dig a hole in the ground, get into it, throw up a work, hire a man to shoot buckshot at him if he shows his head above ground; and he thinks one night and one day of it will cure him of the desire. Fifty-one deserters from the enemy have come into the lines of the 25th Corps between the James and Fort Harrison, within the last 48 hours. The Chivalry are thus running for refuge to the "neeg-urs" — as they call the colored people. But neither does the best element in the Southern army desert.

Feb. 18. Sat. Clear, warm. Reg. in camp. The rebel flag-of-truce boat runs afoul of one of their own torpedoes, sunk in the James river just above Fort Brady, and is blown up. Since the meeting of the Peace Commissioners, desertions from the rebel lines have largely increased. Many rebels desert to flee persecution, or to save their lives from danger caused by local feuds perpetuated wherever the inimical parties meet, in the army or out of it — the old vendetta.

Feb. 19. Sun. Clear, warm. Reg. in camp. Inspected by Lt. Col. Kreutzer of the 98th N. Y., now commanding our Brigade. He is teacher of the officers' military school.

Feb. 20. Mon. Clear and very warm. Reg. in camp. Drilling. George H. Pomroy of H receives a 20 days' furlough, as the result of last Wednesday's inspection. At the last Division review the 13th was specially complimented by Gen. Ord; and Capt. Betton, in temporary command, is very greatly pleased. Capt. Betton has high ideas of military matters, and does his best to carry them out. Two hundred and forty-eight men present for duty in the Thirteenth. Lieut. Murray has been exchanged for a nephew of Confederate Vice President Stephens.

A member of the 13th writes home: "Our turn of picket comes once a week nowadays, for 24 hours, on the Varina road. No firing on the picket lines now — which in some places are not over 40 yards apart — except when some one tries to desert, a thing which occurs pretty often on both sides, almost every night. If we stop a man who is attempting to desert, we get $30 reward, and a thirty days' furlough. The rebels desert and come in every day. In one night last week 100 rebel deserters came in. We drill every day when in camp. This is the coldest winter we have seen in the South. The ground is frozen from 12 to 14 inches in depth."

Feb. 21. Tues. Clear. Reg. in camp. Salutes of 100 guns with blank cartridges are fired this noon from every battery on our lines, in honor of the re-taking of Fort Sumter and Charleston, S. C., Feb. 18, 1865. Extremely noisy, and all the Union troops are cheering like men wild with joy. Close to our Regiment is a redoubt mounting eight guns, with two more on the outside. These are numbered 1, 2, 3, etc., and are fired in turn, and then all together, until they fire ten rounds each. The other batteries, including Fort Harrison, are likewise sounding the same high grand pæan of victory. The rebel lines are as dumb as oysters. A member of the 13th writes: "Between the discharges here we can hear the faint boom of cannon away down on the Petersburg front."

Feb. 22. Wed. Cold, rainy. Reg. in camp. The day is observed as a holiday, so far as possible, by the entire Union army; while the roar of cannon fired in salutes fills the whole land. But the rebel army in Virginia do not celebrate Gen. Washington's birthday. Gen. Washington did some noisy work in his time; but he commanded a mere handful of soldiers compared with this modern Union army of nearly three millions of men, divided here and there into masses of 150,000 or so, and armed with thousands of cannon. How the day does always find its man!

Two rebel deserters celebrate the day, as well as they possibly can, by coming over into the lines of the Thirteenth, shouting and cheering like men possessed when they arrive; and soon are well fed and cared for in all their wants and needs.

Quoting from a letter written at the front on Feb. 25, 1865, we have here a scene [1] enacted by the mother of Presidents on her own 'sacred soil,' on the birthday of her most illustrious son: "Wednesday last, Feb. 22d, was the anniversary of Washington's birthday, and a special order from the Hdqrs. of the Union army made it a general holiday. It was a rainy day. About nine o'clock in the forenoon Quarter-master Morrison and myself started off on horseback for Cox's landing on the James river, where the exchange of prisoners takes place every day at ten o'clock. We visited several points, and arrived at the landing a few moments before the rebel flag-of-truce boat, and watched its approach. It had the Confederate flag flying at the stern, and was towing a barge filled with our sick soldiers, the boat itself being a dirty affair.

"In a few moments more, six hundred of our men, half of them commissioned officers, including two Brigadier Generals, were on the shore; and those of them who could walk immediately started for Aiken's landing, at some distance below, where our flag-of-truce boat lay. The rest filled a long line of ambulances, and fully two hours were consumed before they were all transferred to our own boat. Such a looking set of men I never saw before, and hope never to see again. Hatless, shirtless, shoeless, wrapped up in old bed-quilts of as many hues as Joseph's coat; their feet wound with rags, and many of them barefoot (and the wintry, ice-cold mud six inches deep), their clothing in tatters, their hair long and matted, dirty and unshaven, and all looking as pale and thin as though wasted with consumption or fever. Many were carried on board our boat on stretchers, too weak and sick to stand. I talked with numbers of them — one of the Thirteenth, captured Sept. 30, 1864.

"These men left Richmond at eight o'clock that morning, and showed me the day's ration drawn just before they left. It was simply a solid, heavy piece of corn bread, about six inches long, three wide, and one and a half thick. It was made of a sort of meal, ground up, corn, cobs and all together. Whole and partially broken kernels could be seen in it. This with water was all they had. They had tasted salt meat in minute quantities twice since Christmas, and then it was taken from the citizens. Just before our boat moved off, the Naval Band on one of our gunboats struck up the 'Star Spangled Banner,' and the poor emaciated fellows

---

[1] A gentleman, a highly esteemed friend of mine, now a resident of Providence, R. I., then a Second Lieutenant in the 39th Mass. Infantry, Charles Henry Chapman, was a member of this party of exchanged prisoners, and corroborates this sketch in its worst particulars; remarking in addition, that the suffering was too terrible for any language to depict with full justice to the subject. — S. M. T.

tried to cheer. They were too weak to give a very loud one, but I never heard a more impressive cheer in my life." LIEUT. PRESCOTT.

Feb. 23. Thurs. Very rainy all day; heavy thunder at night. Reg. in camp. Regimental or Brigade drill every fair afternoon excepting Saturday. Schools for officers meet on one evening in each week.

Feb. 24. Fri. Cloudy, Reg. in camp. Ordered to prepare to march — but do not move. Salutes fired with shotted guns. A body of colored troops of the 25th Corps, broke camp last night and silently made off in the darkness — an appropriate season. The 3d Brigade is under marching orders. Lively times appear to be in prospect for us.

Feb. 25. Sat. Cloudy, cold, rainy. Reg. in camp. We appreciate a very marked difference in feeling now from that which pervaded our army one year ago. We know not how to express it better than to say, that the light of advancing peace seems to forecast its rays over and around us; while we live in a constantly abiding sense of probably plunging into the final and closing crash of war — our last battle whether we die or live — at the very next hour we see. One describes it as : ' a vast uncertainty full of tremendous good promise sure as to-morrow's sun.'

Feb. 26. Sun. Clear, warm. Reg. in camp. Inspected by Capt. Betton. A host of deserters from the enemy have come in during the past week; 127 came in within one day.

Feb. 27. Mon. Cloudy, warm. Reg. in camp. Three officers and 100 men of the 13th are selected for guard duty at 24th Corps Hdqrs. for one week.

Maj. Gen. Philip H. Sheridan marches from Winchester to-day, with two Divisions and one Brigade of cavalry — a force 10,000 strong; with Generals Merritt, Devin and Custer, to join Gen. Grant's army in front of Petersburg. His orders, and route of march, contemplate sweeping a girdle of waste and devastation, to the northward, all around Gen. Lee's army; and the crossing of a hundred rivers, and a thousand swamps, in the worst season of the Virginian year. The supplies for Gen. Lee's citadel are to be cut off.

Feb. 28. Tues. Rainy. Reg. in camp. Mustered for pay by Capt. Betton. Another quiet month has been passed in our winter quarters. But the camp is full of evidences of terrible business near ahead.

## X.

### March 1, to April 12, 1865.

#### LAST CAMPAIGN.

**March 1. Wed.** Cloudy, cold. Thirteenth in camp. Capt. Hall receives his commission, also Lieutenants Oliver and Hardy. The Thirteenth furnishes a Captain, two Lieutenants and 100 men for guard at 24th Corps Hdqrs. Twenty-seven deserters come in bringing their muskets with them. They are now the jolliest set of men we have seen for many a day. The U. S. Government pays deserters from the Confederacy $10 apiece for their muskets, to induce them to bring them in. Both men and arms are thus a dead loss to the Confederacy, which cannot replace them.

**March 2. Thurs.** Very rainy all day. Thirteenth in camp. Twelve deserters come in — nine of them bringing their guns with them.

Col. Abbott, Chief of Artillery of Gen. Grant's army, reports that the daily average weight of iron — with gunpowder in it, for the most were shells — thrown at the enemy, along our lines in front of Petersburg and along the James, has been: August 1864, 5.2 tons; September 7.8 tons; October 4.5 tons; November 2.7 tons; December 2.1 tons; January 1865 1.6 tons; Febuary 1.1 tons. Aggregating 793 tons in all, or 37,264 rounds. (M. & C. H. Conn. 684.) These are mere initial thunder-figures of Union cannon in action.

"Recently while on picket, one dark night about midnight we were suddenly startled by a loud cry for help from the darkness in our front. Rushing to the spot with one of the pickets we discovered a rebel deserter stuck fast in a swampy place. Reaching out his musket to us, by means of it we soon pulled him out of the mud hole and took him to our line. He was a man about sixty years old, and until forced into the rebel army had been a physician practicing his profession somewhere in North Carolina. He was enormously fat, he wore a wig and spectacles and false teeth, all of which he had lost in the mud hole, was covered with mud and dirt, and you can easily imagine what a ludicrous and pitiable spectacle he presented. After he had wiped the mud from his face and eyes and blown it from his mouth, he drank a dish of coffee, drew a long breath, looked around upon the circle of our pickets and then proceeded in the most deliberate and solemn manner to deliver his opinion of the Confederacy. The Lord Cardinal, in Ingoldsby's little poem the 'Jackdaw of Rheims.' cursing the thief who stole his ring, made a feeble effort compared with the energy with which this North Carolina doctor anathematized the Southern Confederacy.  He cursed it individually, from Jeff. Davis and his Cabinet down through its Congress and public men to the lowest pot-house politician who advocated its cause; he cursed its army from Gen. Lee down to an army mule; he cursed that army in its downsittings and uprisings, in all its movements, marches, battles and sieges; he cursed all its paraphernalia, its artillery and its muskets, its banners, bugles, and drums; he cursed the institution of slavery, which had brought about the war, and he invoked the direst calamity, woe and disaster upon the Southern cause and all that it represented; while the earnestness, force and sincerity with which it was delivered made it one of the most effective speeches I ever heard, and this together with his comical appearance and the circumstance of his capture made the men roar with laughter." LIEUT. PRESCOTT.

**March 3.  Fri.**  Cloudy, cold.  Thirteenth in camp.  Lieut. Churchill honorably discharged the service.  His health is very poor, the climate undermining his constitution.

We may add here, properly, that after suffering for many years from rheumatism contracted in the service, Lieut. Churchill accidentally had his leg broken.  His vitality had been so much reduced that the broken bone would not knit, and he died soon after the accident, on March 19, 1885.  The case was very singular.  He was employed in the U. S. mail service, having charge of the mails at the railway station in Concord, N. H.  Early one evening he went from his work to his home, and sat down to take off his boots.  They were of the 'Congress' pattern, and while removing one of them, the elastic sides clinging somewhat, by a sudden jerk he broke the bone of his leg just above the knee.  The bone was shattered, pieces soon began to come out, and blood poisoning ensued.  Lieut. Churchill said that a shell had come very near, or grazed this leg, and he had always felt a degree of lameness in it after that occurrence.

Adjutant Boutwell also honorably discharged, for disability because of wounds received in the service.  He was detailed as Acting Adjutant of the Thirteenth on the field at the battle of Fredericksburg, afterwards commissioned as Adjutant; in which capacity he served continuously, excepting when sick, until he was wounded at Battery Five, Petersburg.  He has never recovered from this wound sufficiently for him to return to active service.  He was for a time Adjutant of the Substitutes' camp at Concord, N. H., and afterwards held the position of Asst. Adjt. General on the staff of Major Whittlesly commanding rendezvous.

Both were able, brave, prompt and efficient officers, and are a great loss to the Thirteenth.  Both genial, breezy and social, they have contributed no little to the cheerfulness and life of the Regiment.  There seemed to be no tune which the Band of the Thirteenth could play that Boutwell could not accompany with his voice either with words or notes.  He had a very fine tenor voice, loud and clear; and many a time, when the Band was playing in one part of the camp, Boutwell's voice was heard rendering the same air in another part; sometimes he seemed rather outdoing the Band in sound and melody. Generally this accompaniment was a little more agreeable to the camp than to the Band.

A rebel picket boat comes down the James to-night, our pickets along the shore fire upon her, she replies with artillery, and the noise rouses our entire camp. Twenty-seven deserters come in this morning also, bringing their guns, ammunition and equipments with them.

March 4. Sat. Rainy. Reg. in camp. Confederate money has dropped in value to less than two cents on the dollar; $50 in 'White-bellies' (as the Confederates call their money) being nearly equal in purchasing value to a $1.00 Greenback. In Richmond the price of flour is $850 per barrel; corn meal $80 per bushel; chickens $10 to $13 apiece; and everything else in the way of food is in the same proportion, when paid for in Confederate money.

March 5. Sun. Clear, cold. Reg. in camp. Inspected at 4 p. m. by Lt. Col. Kreutzer of the 98th N. Y. commanding our Brigade. Lt. Col. Smith returns from leave.

The average prices paid for supplies by the 'Quarter-master's mess' — Goss, Morrison, Taggard, Sawyer and R. R. Thompson, and others who were members of it — and a fair average for the year ending with to-day, is as follows, the items taken from the account book of that mess and others: cheese 25 cents per pound, butter 44 (sometimes 75), fresh pork $12\frac{1}{2}$, sausage 15, tea 1.60, sugar $14\frac{1}{2}$, corn meal $2\frac{1}{2}$, crackers 20, raisins $32\frac{1}{2}$, lard 8; milk, quart, $17\frac{1}{2}$, eggs, dozen, 28, potatoes, bushel, 80, oysters, quart, 25, condensed milk, pint can, 50, chickens, each, 50. All the officers were limited in their subsistence to bare necessities, for no luxuries could be had; the running expenses for raw materials, as above, amounting to from four to six dollars for each officer per week.

March 6. Mon. Warm, pleasant. Reg. in camp. Brigade drill in the afternoon. About all the firing of late along our lines here has been in the way of salutes in honor of Union victories. The guard furnished from the Thirteenth for 24th Corps Hdqrs. returns to the Reg., having been relieved by men from the 12th N. H.

March 7. Tues. Clear. Reg. in camp. Brigade drill in afternoon; dress-parade at evening.

A regiment prepares to march in this manner: About sunset the regimental drummer beats an officers' call; commanders of Companies gather at once at the Colonel's headquarters; an order is read: "The Thirteenth will march at six o'clock to-morrow morning, in light marching order, with three days' cooked rations and sixty rounds of ball-cartridge per man." Captains inform their men, examine arms and equipments, see that every man has his blankets, his shelter tent and a complete uniform. Lieutenants and Sergeants attend to rations and other matters. Raw rations of beef and pork are drawn by the Commissary, brought to the several company cooks' tents, and at once put over the fires. A few pieces of raw pork are cut up and distributed among the men, for some of them prefer to receive it raw, and to broil it on a stick, or spider, over some little bivouac fire, or at a halt in the march. Boxes of crackers, 'hard tack,' arrive, and a fixed number of the crackers is counted out to each man. Some men need more, some less, and the 'divvying,' and 'evening-up,' is accomplished among themselves. Boxes of ammunition arrive, each box, containing 1,000 cartridges and weighing from 60 to 80 pounds, is lugged by two men. The Captain, if he is wise, will attend to the distribution of the ammunition himself, and see that every man takes his 60 rounds. If possible the camp-guard is changed, weak men and those capable of performing only light duties relieve the strong and able men, so that all who are to march can have a good night's rest before starting. The whole affair of getting ready to march occupies a few hours only of the evening, and the men turn in at the usual hour. No one knows what may come on the morrow, and all prepare for the worst.

Next morning the Regiment is called at 4 a. m. The roll is called. At the Surgeon's call or previously, it is determined what men are able to march, and what men not, and who may be depended upon to guard the camp in the absence of the command. The command is at once made up, a trusty rear-guard selected, breakfast eaten, the cooked rations distributed, an informal inspection made of every man and his belongings, blankets are rolled, each man's blankets in a long roll, the ends of the roll brought together and tied, forming a sort of 'horse-collar,' all is made ready and the muskets are stacked along the several company streets. Servants will carry the line officers' tents and blankets.

Due notice is given, the drums beat a quick assembly, the men fall into line along their musket stacks, the roll is again called; and by this time the name, status and duty of every member of the Regiment has been made a matter of written record. The colors are brought out, markers are placed to designate the line, Companies take their arms, march to the regimental street — 'front street' — and the line is formed. In a veteran regiment an assembly of this kind is made strictly according to Regulations, but to the casual observer appears absolutely informal; and to men and officers all degrees of liberty are allowed within the bounds of promptness and efficiency. If to move in heavy marching order the men take knapsacks and all, the teams carrying the officers' baggage.

When all is ready the Colonel takes command, gives the order to march, places himself with staff at the head of the column, and at the quick step of a lively march played on fife and drum, or by the Band, the command moves out of camp in column of fours, by the right flank, guns on the shoulder, each man with his roll of blankets thrown diagonally across his shoulders; every haversack, canteen and cartridge-box is full — and too many sly flasks also — and the dusty blue column moves away; soon the music ceases, the route-step is taken, the files spread apart till the road is well filled, and the jaunty, joking, merry, laughing host passes out of sight — to fell or to fall.

Whether the numbers of the Thirteenth be large or small, they thus form no holiday pageant strutting across a city square or a village green;

but a body of armed men trained to swing out of marching column into an instant battle line and to fight, and marching, battling in actual war with every energy devoted to its immediate business.

March 8. Wed. Heavy rain, all day and all night. Reg. in camp. The pickets come in drenched by the rain, and bedaubed with mud, the results of a night spent in an old cornfield, without fires, cover or shelter of any kind.

March 9. Thurs. Rainy, clearing about 10 a. m. Reg. in camp. Quarter-master Morrison starts for home on a twenty days' leave. Capt. M. T. Betton assigned to the command of the 81st New York regiment.

This assignment was a very great compliment both to Capt. Betton and to the Thirteenth. The 81st N. Y. was in a demoralized condition, bordering upon open mutiny, and to Capt. Betton fell the task of their discipline. He succeeded not only in satisfying his superior officers, by bringing the discordant elements in this regiment into order and efficiency, but also gained the good will of the members themselves.

March 10. Fri. Rain a. m., hail at noon, clears at night. Reg. in camp. Evening school for field officers continues its sessions.

Lieut. O. M. Sawyer honorably discharged the service by Gen. Ord. Everybody likes Lieut. Sawyer, and it is hard to part with him. A brave, efficient and good officer, always ready, always willing; a genial companion, a true friend — and a right good fellow too.

March 11. Sat. Fair. Reg. in camp. Three officers and one hundred men from the Thirteenth again sent to do the guard duty for a week at 24th Corps Hdqrs. Lt. Col. Smith in command of the Thirteenth says he will gain that position by the Regiment right along, if cleanliness, drill and general efficiency can secure it. As it is, no other regiment receives this honor so frequently as a complimentary reward.

March 12. Sun. Fair, warm. Gen. Grant reviews a Division of troops on our left. One writer says: "Gen. Grant is a business man, of correct methods and a fixed will;" and that is just what he appears to be to-day. Brigade Dress-parade at sunset.

March 13. Mon. Very pleasant. Brigade drill. "Gen. Sheridan set his dogs of cannon barking at Richmond to-day. The people hear them, and are woefully scared." So says a man of the Reg., an exchanged prisoner, who came down on the flag-of-truce boat. A rebel Lieutenant, who deserts to our lines, states that Gen. Sheridan came within eight miles of Richmond; the people expected him to enter the city in force and burn it, and the consternation there was fearful.

March 14. Tues. Pleasant. Reg. in camp. Generals Grant and Ord, and Sec. of War Stanton, visit our camp to-day. Grand Review of the 25th Corps (colored). New Hampshire State election. Legal voters in the Reg. vote for members of Congress — 117 Republican, 10 Democratic. A very particular inspection is made of clothing, equipments, camp, arms, ammunition and men in the 24th Corps. Signs of a battle. The 9th Corps cross the James to our lines on the north side, and a large fleet of Union gunboats moves up the river above the drawbridge. Brigade drill in afternoon. A man of the Thirteenth writes: "If you want to drive the devil, throw him ice — freeze him out."

March 15. Wed. Very pleasant, a little rain, windy. Reg. in camp. Little doing beyond camp and guard duties, inspection, etc., a dull day. Company drill in forenoon. Battalion drill in afternoon.

Army life is rough, hard, forbidding, and still is crowded to the full with almost every species of amusement, singing, playing, fun, jokes, practical and impractical, games, stories and ludicrous incidents and situations. There has been endless sport with words, puns, 'gags' and rhymes. The army laughs far more than it weeps. The soldiers have amused themselves continually by making sport of everybody, and of almost everything, coming in their way. Camp jokes are common property. The fun is frequently rather rough and coarse, but as a rule is made in good nature, and remarkably spontaneous when we consider the terrible strain upon the men — and half of them mere boys — incident to the sudden plunging of these hundreds of thousands of them, from the quiet life and occupations of peaceful citizens, into the wild whirl, abandon and crash of army life in the field, in such times, places, climate and circumstances.

The Thirteenth has had its full quota of nicknames, too, all decidedly pat, but we have space only for one or two: 'Old Bones,' the very strong man. 'Grunty,' the weak man. 'Old Yarn,' the man of too many stories. 'Johnny Spry' and 'Slipper,' quick and lively men, up to all sorts of tricks, pranks and adventures, and rarely or never caught — certainly never caught napping. 'Tommy-Toddler,' the very little short man. 'Lengthy,' between whose legs runs the drummer boy and shouts aloft: 'Say — whawt's the weather up there? Throw us down a chaw-terbakker, will yer?' 'Smellee,' who is seen always to smell of everything set before him before he tastes, drinks or eats. 'Burdock,' whose root is perennial, whose lies are as huge as that plant's leaves, the vicious burs clinging to everything; ill-fortune always catches men of this sort, their stories have loose places like those of the man who declared that cedar bean-poles would last forever — for his father had tried them twice with that result; and last of all 'Quippee,' the manufacturer and rattler of big terms, sometimes disagreeable, who spits out, like a mad cat, 'Ityaal': I think you are a liar; and who calls a Southern thunder shower 'Awaterofluidamskythunderaceouscataractionarydelugination — wet,' and thinks he has said something very funny.

March 16. Thurs. Warm; exceeding windy. Reg. in camp. No drill. The mud has been very deep, and about all the teaming is done on corduroy roads, of which there are miles on miles, all up and down the rear of all the camps and lines. Gen. Grant evidently believes in good roads. The earth is drying now, and to-day the dust is flying in clouds.

Many boxes arriving from home for the men and officers. Twelve hundred boxes in one day, for the 24th Corps, is not an unusual arrival; **one day brought over 2,000 of them.**

**March 17. Fri.** Clear, warm, windy; heavy rain last night. Reg. in camp. Review of the 24th Corps, by Lieut. Gen. Grant, accompanied by E. M. Stanton, Secretary of War, Admiral Farragut, the Secretary of the Navy, and other visitors and ladies. The cavalcade, with nearly a whole cavalry regiment for an escort, passes at a trot. Some of the ladies are in carriages, others on horseback. This review is one of the finest we have ever seen; all the troops in heavy marching order, with knapsacks, blankets, shelter tents and all. Thirteenth at Corps Hdqrs. and not in the review. Capt. Buel C. Carter is Acting Quarter-master on the staff of Maj. Gen. John Gibbon.

**March 18. Sat.** Clear, windy, cold. Gen. Kautz's cavalry left here last night to co-operate with Gen. Sheridan in the region about Cold Harbor. Admiral Porter has a very large fleet of monitors and gunboats in the lower James.

The rebels are on their works in great numbers and in full sight, witnessing the sports in the 10th N. H., now celebrating St. Patrick's Day — the review yesterday causing a postponement of the celebration. "The pole was made so greasy that no one could climb it and get the $25 prize on the top. A darkey and mule race was very funny. Negroes rooted in a half-bushel measure of meal to find a silver half dollar; found the prize, and had their heads and faces white with the meal." So one man of the Thirteenth writes about the sports of the day.

A large detail from the Thirteenth has been at work all day on a corduroy road near the ambulance train. We receive to-night our full complement of Sharps breech-loading carbines, and all the Springfield muskets are to be turned in to the U. S. Government. The badge of the 24th Corps is adopted to-day — a heart within a heart.

**March 19. Sun.** Warm. Thirteenth in camp. The 3d Brigade of our — Gen. Devens' — 3d Division is at White House, on the Pamunkey, to receive Gen. Sheridan on his return from his 'North-of-Richmond' raid, and to replenish his stores. Inspection at noon, Brigade Dress-parade at night.

"Head Quarters Department of Virginia,
Army of the James.
Before Richmond, Va., 19th March, 1865.

"Special Orders No. 78:

The commanding officer of the Thirteenth New Hampshire Volunteers will make requisition for one hundred and twelve Sharps carbines, on receipt of which he will turn in to the Ordnance Depot an equal number of Springfield rifles.

By command of Major General Ord,
THEODORE READ,
Assistant Adjutant General."

The above order was accompanied by another directing the 118th New York Vols. to receive one hundred and twelve Spencer carbines, and to turn in an equal number of Sharps carbines. Lt. Col. Smith states that these 112 carbines were sufficient to arm the Thirteenth, so greatly was the Regiment reduced in numbers at this time. The 13th received the carbines from the 118th N. Y., not new ones. They weigh 10 pounds, the calibre 52, for a one-ounce conical bullet — minie, and the charge of powder is 45 grains. A formidable weapon.

March 20. Mon. "Pleasantest day of the season." Thirteenth in camp. "Sharps breech-loading carbines received by all the Thirteenth;" writes a member.

Orders are received late in the evening for the Thirteenth and other Regiments to be ready to move to-morrow at 8 a. m., with four days' cooked rations in haversacks, and sixty rounds of ball cartridge per man, tents to be struck, and all the troops to move in heavy marching order. Surplus baggage to be packed for storage.

A person must lug his food about in a dirty bag for three or four days, through all the exposures of a military campaign, to realize the condition that rations get into — usually the half is spoiled before the time comes to eat them. Thousands of the enlisted men are made sick by the careless management of the ration supply.

March 21. Tues. Clear a. m., rainy p. m. Thirteenth in camp. Ammunition issued at daylight. Strike tents at 6 a m. and get all ready to move, in heavy marching order, at 8 a. m. Do not move. Eighteen deserters came in last night. A heavy rain sets in about noon to-day.

After loafing about in rain and mud till near night, the men of the Thirteenth are ordered to their old quarters, with permission to spread their shelter tents again over their huts, now thoroughly wet inside and out. About midnight the rain begins to pour in torrents, a heavy gale sets in, blowing the hastily fitted shelter-tent roofs off the huts, and the rest of the night is spent in cold, wet and discomfort.

Gen. William T. Sherman's army is now near Goldsboro, N. C., about 180 miles distant from Richmond.

March 22. Wed. Cloudy, cold, rainy, windy; an ugly day. Twenty-one deserters came in here last night. Thirteenth strikes its tents again this morning, packs up ready to move, and marches up to the "Cross-way" about 9.30 a. m. Here it is announced that our First Brigade is to hold the lines of both the 1st and the 2d Brigades, and we pass the day in the trenches.

The Cross-way is where the Union works cross the New Market road, one and one fourth miles southeast of Laurel Hill church; confronting the Confederate lines crossing that road farther up towards the church. See map, page 473. The Second Brigade marches farther down towards the right and rear. The Thirteenth is assigned position about thirty rods in the rear of the front trenches, in the New Market road, and held as a reserve. All with knapsacks on, and with four days' rations in haversacks. We realize that the spring campaign has opened in earnest — with terrible work in prospect. But the men instinctively feel that Gen. Grant will end the war this year. Large bodies of troops are moving away. At night the Thirteenth goes back to its old quarters, now also all thoroughly wet, and bivouacs in them again.

Col. Edgar M. Cullen starts for home, and Col. Edward H. Ripley of the 9th Vt. assumes command of our First Brigade.

March 23. Thurs. Cold, clear, very windy and dusty. Thirteenth in camp; if we may call it camping where every man is half squat, like a grasshopper, with legs bent, all ready for a spring to arms when the drum beats. "Every man must be kept ready to move at a moment's notice," is the standing order of the day. All surplus baggage has gone to store, or has been sent North. Thirteenth sent to the picket lines at evening in heavy marching order.

A trip along the Union lines reveals an immense region of deep, wide streams and lofty, clayey bluffs; the whole country a succession of hundreds of high-banked creeks, gravelly knolls, sloughy marshes and swamps thickly wooded and filled with brush, briar and vine; long stretches of low, cold, sandy, pine-land flats, here densely wooded and there utterly bare; interspersed by large cultivated farms, with buildings destroyed or half ruined — about the same kind of country all the way from Fort Harrison, here north of the James, to Hatcher's Run south of Petersburg. The vedettes are increased in number. Extending for more than thirty miles, two parallel lines of these wide awake fellows, a few yards apart, stand throughout the nights between the two armies, watching each other. Back of them the pickets, back of them the battle lines, artillery, camps, stores, and the open country.

March 24. Fri. Clear, very windy, a little snow. Thirteenth in camp. The men are greatly pleased with their Sharps carbines. They inspire confidence in defense.

The Thirteenth along at the first of its term of service had few excellent marksmen, and for a year or so less attention was given to individual training in target practice than should have been; but later an interest in the matter was fostered, and the result of practice was to develop great skill, and the men of the Thirteenth soon had few equals as marksmen, with the Springfield rifle, among the infantry regiments. The change to carbines has had but little adverse effect, the men soon become familiar with their use, and the majority are recording good shots made with this new weapon.

In every year, while the Thirteenth has been in the South, they have been treated to a snow storm about this time in March. In 1863, Mar. 20th; in 1864, Mar. 22d; in 1865, Mar. 24th.

Running along in the rear of the Union lines is a wide, straight corduroy road, so constructed as to reach all prominent points on the shortest possible line, and to bid defiance to rain, snow or frost. An aide or courier on horseback, the lightest ambulance, and the heaviest wagon trains, and artillery, can move over this road with equal freedom from mud, slough, accident or delay. An immense amount of labor has been expended on this road, and its branches, and thousands of heavy logs are laid upon it, and embedded as firmly as stones in a city street.

**March 25.** Sat. Cold, cloudy, some rain. We man the works about 9.30 a. m. and about noon return to camp. Reg. strikes tents again this morning, under orders to move in heavy marching order, but remains in camp or along the earth-works all the day. President Lincoln and wife and Gen. Grant visit Fort Harrison, and our line of works.

Gen. Grant wrote yesterday ; " Gen. Weitzel in command north of the James will keep vigilant watch upon his front ; and if found at all practicable to break through at any point, he will do so." This order results in our keeping awake for a week, 'about twenty-seven hours out of every twenty-four,' as the boys have it.

The 'Independent Division,' consisting of Gen. Foster's 1st and Gen. Turner's 2d Divisions of the 24th Corps, Gen. Birney's 2d Division of the 25th Corps, and McKenzie's cavalry, formerly Kautz's, with Gen. Ord chief in command, marches from our front here to-day towards the left of Gen. Grant's army, southwest of Petersburg. Gen. Gibbon goes with Gen. Ord. This movement is made with such secrecy that Generals Longstreet and Ewell on our front, and Gen. Lee, do not learn of it until April 2d. These troops go to find a position near or beyond Gen. Lee's right flank, which, it is expected, he will extend from below Petersburg more and more towards the southwest ; and it may properly be called "Gen. Ord's Flying Corps." They have before them a march of more than thirty miles, to reach the left of Gen. Grant's line below Petersburg.

"Last Tuesday night, March 21st, a substitute in the 81st N. Y. went in company with another fellow. They stole their Quarter-master's and Surgeon's horses, a sash and sword, which one of them put on, and about midnight rode out to the picket line, and in answer to the challenge of the vedette, the one wearing the sword and sash announced himself as 'Corps officer of the day,' and waiting until the vedette turned to walk to the other end of his beat, struck the spurs into the horse, and dashed across to the rebel lines. The other man, who acted as his orderly, was not quite quick enough to elude the vedette, and was caught.

"On Friday morning, 24th, about 8 o'clock a man deserted from the 11th Conn. He was on the vedette line — the outer picket line. His companions probably assisted him to escape. Two shots only were fired after him. The Brigade officer of the picket ordered the vedette nearest the deserter to pursue him, which he did, the officer and myself also joining in the chase. We chased the fellow about a third of the distance between the lines of the two armies, but he escaped to the rebels. While returning from this chase, we found between the lines two skeletons in blue clothing; probably of two Union soldiers killed last September at the capture of Fort Harrison. The 10th Corps charged at that time across this field, where we are picketing, and was repulsed."

LIEUT. PRESCOTT.

**March 26.** Sun. Cold, clear, windy. Inspection at 10 a. m. At 1 p. m. the Thirteenth witnesses the execution of a deserter, a man of the 81st N. Y., the next regiment on our right ; the same fellow who stole the horse and was caught in the act of desertion last Tuesday night.

"Our Brigade was formed on three sides of a square (the fourth side open). The funeral procession entered: a band, six soldiers bearing a rough pine coffin, an ambulance containing the prisoner guarded by six soldiers, three on each side, and the firing party, twelve men of the 81st N. Y. commanded by a Sergeant. They halted, the prisoner stepped from the ambulance, the Provost Marshal read the sentence of the prisoner, who sat down on his coffin, and a cap was drawn over his eyes. The firing party took position, the commands were given by signals of the sword; twelve muskets were fired (in a volley) at the deserter's heart, and he fell over upon his coffin, dead. The whole affair occupied hardly half an hour." LIEUT. PRESCOTT.

This afternoon about 5.30 p. m. our 3d Division, Gen. Devens commanding, is again reviewed by President Lincoln, who is stopping at City Point with Gen. Grant. Gen. Grant takes position just on Lincoln's left. Mrs. Lincoln is present, with her little son "Tad" on his pony. Mr. Lincoln is exceedingly fond of this boy. Many visitors, and an immense cavalry escort, accompany Lincoln and Grant. The country here has been tramped over so much, that there is no grass to cover and hold the soil; and it is either very dusty or very muddy, as the weather serves. To-day the dust blows fearfully, like snow in a gale, blinding every one who has to face it. Nearly all the white troops, excepting our 3d Division, are moving away from this front to-night.

March 27. Mon. Clear, fine. Thirteenth moves farther towards the right, taking the place of the 100th N. Y., Col. Dandy, which marched to the left of Petersburg under Gen. Ord. Major Stoodley, to-day Division officer of the day, has charge of the picket lines to the James at Deep Bottom, a line nearly ten miles in length. He takes Lieut. Prescott with him, and they ride together down over the entire line, and return by it, and the trip uses up nearly the entire day.

There are now on these lines only our 3d Division of the 24th Corps, and a small force of colored troops on our left about Fort Harrison, the whole under command of Gen. Godfrey Weitzel; and he is all up and down the lines and everywhere at once, seeming to neither eat, drink, or sleep. Our 3d Division does all the picket duty from the right of the 25th Corps, near Fort Harrison, to Deep Bottom. Watchfulness, vigilance, has here gone stark mad; 'everything sleeps wide awake, and with both eyes open — men, horses, guns and all.' The order is repeated every hour, day and night: "See that your men are ready to move at any moment."

Gen. Ord's Flying Corps, which commenced moving on the night of March 25th, all leaves our front during to-night; quietly moving away under cover of the darkness, and without the enemy's knowledge.

March 28. Tues. Warm, pleasant. Reg. in camp, fitting up quarters — the same that were abandoned by the 100th N. Y. "We are carefully cleaning around camp," writes one ; " and waiting on our guns under marching orders for a move now — and all the time — expected to occur at any moment."

The lines of troops here are exceedingly thin, and all our fires, and all our calls on both bugles and drums, are kept up as if the whole of the two army corps were present. Mounted buglers dash from Hdqrs. to Hdqrs. sounding call after call, while drum corps run from regiment to regiment and play the same farce. The bands play at their respective stations; their audience a few men, a few mules, a few grinning darkeys, and a wide, barren waste of deserted camps.

March 29. Wed. Very pleasant day — severe rain at night. Reg. in camp. Were our garrison, now garnishing these lines of earthworks north of the James, evenly distributed along our front lines, the men would probably stand about one rod apart. Of course our cares and labor have increased as our numbers have lessened. Our Division does all the picket duty for the 24th Corps, and the turn of the Thirteenth comes around every third or fourth day. Confederate Gen. Ewell's Hdqrs. at Laurel Hill are in full view, one and one quarter miles distant. Two Divisions of the 25th Corps (colored) hold our old lines at Bermuda Hundred.

March 30. Thurs. Showery. Very rainy last night and this morning. Reg. in camp, ready to move at call. All through last night and this morning we have been hearing a very heavy and rapid cannonade going on, along Gen. Grant's lines near Petersburg. Very quiet here on our front. Our camp is now more than a mile to the right of Fort Harrison, and a mile nearer Richmond than that fort is. Our Third Division, Gen. Devens, is scattered along from Fort Harrison to the James at Deep Bottom, a very long line. If we were now attacked by any considerable force of the enemy, we would have but one recourse — that of falling back under cover of the gunboats ; but since our lines run behind strong defenses we could make a stout fight all the way. A peculiar confidence pervades our army ; we somehow feel stronger than the enemy, and are not as doubtful concerning him as we were at the opening of the spring campaign in 1864.

March 31. Fri. Rainy ; has rained almost continually from midnight of Wednesday (29th) until noon to-day, at times pouring down in torrents. Reg. in camp, but almost every man is detailed on guard or picket duty. The Paymaster — appearing as usual on the eve of a move — commences paying off the Reg. ; " all paid off except H, I, and K." All quiet here, but very noisy southward.

Few persons in civil life can appreciate the dangers and severe duties connected with picket duty in the field, especially in the case of vedettes. The extreme front, no one near to consult with, the drenching rain or the blinding snow storm often adding their discomforts to the night of pitchy darkness or benumbing cold ; no fires allowed, no knowing in one minute but that a rebel bullet may crash through one's head in the next, the danger, and dread too of a wound that may cause a lingering death with no one near to help, and may be one's body never found; the awful responsibility that really rests upon the true sentinel's shoulders, possibly the fate of a thousand men, or indeed of the whole army; the waving bushes, in the distance of half darkness, in the dim vision of the sentinel appearing like the enemy advancing in force; or perhaps he comes, with a sudden rush and yell — the pickets are of course struck down first of all. The picket fires his one shot and falls shattered with a dozen bullets, or is captured — for the chief hope of a picket's safety in such case is that the enemy does best to capture and not to kill — and is reported missing, and is next heard from as a prisoner of war, or as having died in a rebel prison. A charge rushes over the pickets as if they were so many worms; fifty of them perhaps run down in a minute by two or five thousand men. Nowhere on earth can a man stand and feel his safety and his danger, his importance and greatness and absolute littleness, and the burden and force of doubt, uncertainty, and the enemy's bitter hate, so very keenly and all at once, as when he thoughtfully stands, at dead of night, alone, an outpost, vedette or picket, between two hostile armies in active campaign in the field. If there is anything at all in him, this work will find it.

Organization of Maj. Gen. Charles Devens' 3d Division, 24th Army Corps, Gen. John Gibbon commanding, on March 31, 1865:

| | |
|---|---|
| First Brigade,[1] | Col. Edward H. Ripley. |
| 11th Conn. | Major Charles Warren. |
| 13th N. H. | Lt. Col. Normand Smith. |
| 81st N. Y. | Capt. M. T. Betton. |
| 98th N. Y. | Lt. Col. Wm. Kreutzer. |
| 139th N. Y. | Major Theodore Miller. |
| 19th Wis. | Major Samuel K. Vaughan. |
| | |
| Second Brigade, | Col. M. T. Donohoe. |
| 8th Conn. | Major Wm. M. Pratt. |
| 5th Md. | Lt. Col. Wm. W. Bamberger. |
| 10th N. H. | Capt. Warren M. Kelley. |
| 12th N. H. | Lt. Col. Theodore E. Barker. |
| 96th N. Y. | Capt. Geo. W. Hinds. |
| 118th N. Y. | Lt. Col. Levi T. Dominy. |
| 9th Vt. | Lt. Col. Val. G. Barney. |

[1] After Col. Stevens was wounded at Fort Harrison, the 1st Brigade passed under the command of Lt. Col. Raulston, then to Col. Cullen, then to Lt. Col. Ripley of the 9th Vt., all without any change in regiments. The 19th Wisconsin came into our Brigade when the white troops were changed from the left to the right — exchanging positions with the colored troops on the Union lines north of the James River on Dec. 5, 1864. — S. M. T.

| | |
|---|---|
| Third Brigade, | Col. Saml. H. Roberts. |
| 21st Conn. | Lt. Col. James T. Brown. |
| 40th Mass. | Capt. John Pollock. |
| 2d N. H. | Lt. Col. J. N. Patterson. |
| 58th Penn. | Lt. Col. Cecil Clay. |
| 188th Penn. | Lt. Col. Geo. K. Bowen. |

| | | |
|---|---|---|
| Engineers. | Mounted Band. | Cavalry. |
| Corps of Sharp-shooters. | | Pioneer Corps. |
| 3d U. S. Battery. | | 1st N. Y. Battery. |
| 5th U. S. Battery. | | 3d N. Y. Battery. |
| | 4th Wisconsin Battery. | |

April 1. Sat. Foggy — clears bright. Reg. in camp. Paid off for four months — up to Dec. 31, 1864. We have to exercise the utmost vigilance day and night, and are so held and disposed as to be ready at any moment for instant action, if these lines are threatened or assailed, or the enemy appears to be evacuating his works on our front. Not knowing what is coming next, we chafe and fret under the strain of forced inaction and anxiety. The lines under our charge are now so extended as to require nearly all of a day, or all of a night, for the general officer of the day, or of the picket guard, to make his rounds. Very quiet along our lines, but Gen. Grant's lines in front of Petersburg are engaged, and making a great amount of noise. The incessant, fearful and hideous din growls, rumbles, jars, and throbs, hour in and hour out. The Bermuda Hundred lines are more quiet; but their guns can be heard mingling with the rest. At night, from high points along our line, the flashes of the cannon and the bursting shells are distinctly visible far down the lines toward Petersburg. The Thirteenth holds a Dress-parade just at night — the last Dress-parade at the front.

The 'Rebel Yell' is probably nothing new, but older than Anglo-Saxon history — as old as the word 'Hur-rah.' As near as can be made out, it is the first syllable of the word hurrah — hur — repeatedly and rapidly given explosively in the roof of the mouth, a high, sharp falsetto note; possibly the sharpest and loudest sound of which the human voice is capable. It is the rapid repetition of the rebel yell, by hundreds and thousands of rebel voices, that gives to it its vibratory, vicious, piercing character. Any one can easily sound this famous yell after a little practice. As a distinguished Southern writer [1] says: "A man can holloa the rebel yell all day; it does not exhaust the voice."

---

[1] Hon. T. W. Dawson, a gallant Confederate officer, now Editor of the Charleston, S. C., News and Courier. The writer had a short correspondence with him in connection with the Prickett affair, see page 277, and made an inquiry of him concerning the rebel yell. He described it so that the writer could 'pick it up;' but added, facetiously, that 'since the war was over he had been "hollering" so much for the old flag and an appropriation, that he had nearly forgotten the old tune.' — S. M. T.

The Northern cheer places the greatest stress upon the deep, broad, last syllable — rah ; and now at last the 'Rahs' are to have it all their own way.

Ten thousand men together, one half screaming, as the rebel yell, hur, and the other half roaring, as the Northern cheer, rah, each man for himself, could probably produce a medley of sounds more hideous and intimidating than by the use of any other two syllables in the English language.

April 2. Sun. Clear, warm. Reg. in camp. "Many men write home, as on the eve of a battle." The morning opens with what seems to us an early, wild, loud alarum on the bells in Richmond, and not like the usual Sunday bell ringing there. We have been flattering ourselves that formerly we were vigilant; but the pressure of strict watching last night, to-day, and to-night along these lines, exceeds anything we have experienced since we have been in the army.

Last night a furious bombardment was kept up all along the Union lines in front of Petersburg and below; a line of hard upon twenty miles of the most severe firing. Shells were dropping in almost every quarter of the city, bursting, and scattering showers of brick and of pieces of shell. No man here can forget the deep, distant rumble, growl, and throb of that night-long, terrific cannonade, by every gun on Gen. Grant's lines; rolling up toward us, as the wind served, continuous, incessant, hour after hour, and boding sure death to the Confederacy.

Such a night it is all around us, while all is very quiet here on our own lines, after midnight. From early evening until midnight, all the bands in Gen. Weitzel's command here, and apparently as many more in Gen. Longstreet's lines on our front, join in a musical contest; 'Dixie' vies with 'Hail Columbia,' 'America,' with 'My Maryland,' and the 'Star Spangled Banner' dips full notes with the 'Bonnie Blue Flag.' All very fine — but exceedingly deceitful.

News arrives in the night that Gen. Grant's army has captured 10,000 prisoners — Cheers! We receive telegrams here about two hours after a movement has been consummated on Gen. Grant's extreme left.

Lieut. Prescott goes out to-night in command of our 1st Brigade picket and vedette lines; a very careful, prompt and efficient officer being required for that most important position at this time.

The last camp of the Thirteenth at the front :

"Last Monday, March 27th, the Thirteenth moved into the abandoned camp of the 100th New York regiment, Col. George B. Dandy, which marched to the left of Petersburg with Gen. Ord's Flying Corps."

Lt. Col. Smith.

The Union line of entrenchments comes up to Fort Harrison, on the left, and thence runs northeast, and toward the right, to and across the New Market road, at a place called the Cross-way, where there is a large curtain on the road. This Cross-way is about one and one fourth miles southeast from Laurel Hill church, one mile due east from Fort Gilmer, nearly two miles north from Fort Harrison, and one mile almost due north from Mr. O. Aiken's house, which was Gen. Devens' Hdqrs. See map on page 473. From the Cross-way the line runs north, east and south, forming a curve, or loop, all north of the New Market road and about two miles in circuit, — re-crossing the New Market road again farther down and sweeping southeastward to Deep Bottom. This curve, or loop, is cut about midway of its circuit by a road (the next road of any importance east of the Varina road) which leaves the New Market road at Mr. James's house and runs north past Mr. H. Jordan's house to the Darbytown road, and is marked W. W. on map.

The last camp of the Thirteenth was close up to the rear, south side, of this curve in the entrenchments, a few rods to the right and the first camp to the right, east, of the point where this James and Jordan road cuts through the line. The camp faced northward and was half a mile northeast of the Cross-way. The camps of the several regiments in our Brigade were very far apart, scattered along the lines north of Fort Harrison and east, and southeast, and south, and on towards Deep Bottom.

### SURRENDER OF RICHMOND.

April 3. Mon. Clear, pleasant, warm. Capt. Hubbard W. Hall regimental officer of the day.

"Broke camp, and marched to Richmond without opposition. Entered the city about 8.30 a. m. — our Regiment leading the column."

Major Nathan D. Stoodley, in Diary.

Few men of the Thirteenth slept last night. South of the Appomattox river there was the usual artillery fire, its deep throbs rolling continuously and incessantly up the misty valley of the James, and heard by us for hour after hour. The enemy's picket fires were burning as usual along his lines on our front, and with undimmed brightness; but all was very quiet on our own lines. There was too much care and curious question, however, among us to make sleep even desirable, the very air seeming to whisper of great events. As we were under orders to move on the morrow at daylight, the night seemed like the night before a battle with most of the anxiety removed, and a strong promise of victory added. But for the sullen boom of huge cannon in the distance, the night were best framed for dreaming wide awake.

Few men, except the pickets and watch, saw anything very unusual going on within the enemy's lines, until well into the night. Every man in the Thirteenth was held in readiness for an instant move, the men turning in under arms, but there seemed less pressure of foreboding and anxiety than we have felt for a week past; and so the night wore slowly away with all excepting the officers and men on the picket lines and outposts; but upon no morning, since the war began, have we felt as we do as this morning comes on. As the pressure of watching and anxiety, experienced for a month past, now falls away, the troops hail with gladness the opportunity to move, and march out of camp with feelings similar to those in which a prisoner indulges when the fetters are struck from his feet.

As telegrams from Gen. Grant's front at Petersburg have been received, and read to the troops here within an hour or two after every one of his successes, cheers upon cheers have rung along our lines until the men are surfeited with cheers; or else they feel the terrible cost in blood, and limb, and life, to their brethren in arms, of those very successes; or else a desire, mingled with impatience, has taken them, to be moving also themselves, instead of playing too much the part of tail to all this most glorious and magnificent kite; or else, and more probable, they have a combination of all these feelings, and so they preserve a stolid, almost sullen silence, most strange in young men, and remarked of all. Their deepest thoughts none may know; but enough of feelings and emotions — now to business!

Suddenly, in the midst of the almost universal stillness, about 4.30 a. m., probably a little earlier, this morning, the strange quiet is broken by a tremendous explosion, occurring on or near the James river, rending the air, and shaking the very ground here beneath our feet, and blazing out a broad noon-day glare over the trees; then another explosion, and a sudden glare of flame, occurs nearer our line, then others upon our front, then others to the right; all following each other in rapid succession from our left, until, growing duller and duller in the distance, the sounds die away in the vicinity of Richmond; only to rise again with louder and more awful thunders, around near the city, and in the city itself, among her arsenals and gunboats, while, soon, immense and steady fires gleam out upon the sky above the woods. A Long-roll of exploding powder magazines, at one and the same time arousing our troops to action, and self-celebrating the downfall and destruction of the Confederacy, its army and its capital; a Long-roll calling to arms nearly two hundred thousand men, Union and Confederate, or causing them to clutch their arms in hand with most nervous grasp; one half of them destined to incomparable victory, the other half to shame and loss and defeat; but ultimately to gain untold, for the American Nation is the Phœnix arising from this day's tremendous flame.

Soon to the southward, and away to the northward again, red flames light up the sky in every direction. Along the James the enemy's fleet is on fire, and there, too, explosion follows explosion, until the earth shakes again and again, and we know that our intimate acquaintance, the famous James river fleet, is no more.

Deserters come in — two from the 12th Virginia, among others — and announce the evacuation of Richmond! Then an aide to Gen. Weitzel dashes along our lines at a breakneck speed, giving orders direct, for our entire force here to be in instant readiness to move at call. Another aide rides wild to the pickets, to order them to advance; but he is a little too late — they have marched toward Richmond. Mounted men, officers, aides and orderlies are flying in every direction, troops are springing to arms; while the camp followers, as usual, prepare to go ahead, or skedaddle, as the case may for them demand. The whole scene is mingled in event, and crowded into the space of a few minutes of time, in the misty, darkly defined hour that just precedes the dawn; and now comes back upon our memories, over the slow and winding road of more than twenty peaceful years, like a fearful and fitful dream, a strange vision, or the sudden, vivid glimpse of a land of chaos and destruction not our own.

But of all the life excited by the events of this morning, the liveliest resides in the negroes. There is scarce a negro antic and caper in all Africa that these overjoyed fellows do not cut up, exclaiming: " Marsa Lee, an' Ole Jeff, done got it now; the whole ting done gone up — I-golly ! "

Lieut. Royal B. Prescott, Co. C, 13th, has command of our First Brigade pickets, and vedettes stationed as usual in front of the main line of works in little semi-circular rifle-pits, and immediately upon the first explosion that is heard he is hurried forward toward the rebel lines. His is the extreme front line, there being no Union troops between his line of men and the enemy. His pickets thread their way through the abatis, and the numerous buried torpedoes, without accident, pass the enemy's works — here immensely strong and impregnable to assault — and continue on without opposition until they reach the top of Tree Hill, and here they halt for a few minutes to view the burning city. Soon they go down the hill, following the turnpike, and halt again near Gillie's Creek. Here they meet the Mayor of Richmond, coming out of the city in a carriage, who tenders to Lieut. Prescott the surrender of Richmond. Lieut. Prescott declines, and refers the Mayor to Gen. Weitzel just then seen approaching in the turnpike. The Mayor rides forward to meet that General. Gen. Weitzel receives the surrender of the city, and then the pickets under command of Lieut. Prescott, move up the streets direct to Capitol Square, arriving there about 7 a. m; having entered the city nearly two hours before the formal entry of the First Brigade led by the Thirteenth.

Lieut. Prescott has kindly furnished the writer with the following statement, as the account of his experiences and duties on this eventful morning; the hours given, and the main points, are those written in his Diary at the time, and in his letters written in Richmond on April 4th 1865, now, 1887, in the writer's hands :

"It was my fortune to go on the picket line in command of the pickets of the 1st Brigade, 3d Division, 24th Corps, on Sunday morning April 2, 1865, about 10 a. m., for the usual term of twenty-four hours. The men under my command were about sixty in all, possibly a few more than that number, all white men, and were from all the regiments in the 1st Brigade. The opening in the Union line of earth-works through which these pickets passed to their line was considerably to the left of the camp of the 13th N. H., and only a few rods to the right of the 1st Brigade guard-house. The position of the pickets on their line was in the woods, tall pines, in front of the Fort Harrison line of Union earth-works ; in a belt of woods continuing from the vicinity of the New Market road, through a marsh to the left, and on toward the James river. This belt of woods was not very wide, nor dense, for we could see, through it, the Confederate picket posts, their main line of earth-works and their camps generally.

" We were to the left of the New Market road, which ran up through the Confederate works to join the Osborne pike nearer the city ; that is to say my picket line extended from a point at some distance from the main works of Fort Harrison to marshy ground that continued down toward the James. My line was the extreme front line of the pickets and vedettes — no Union soldiers being between us and the rebels — and was about 100 yards in front of the main line of fortifications ; and the rebel pickets were very near on our front, being distant less than 200 yards.

" I stationed each one of these pickets and vedettes at night, and as he took his lonely post, transmitted to him the same instructions that had been given to me, viz. : that especial vigilance was to be observed during all the night, and instant report made of any unusual movements occurring within the rebel lines.

" We were daily, hourly, expecting an attack from or to advance upon the enemy, and during the afternoon of Sunday April 2d, we observed a somewhat unusual activity and bustle within the enemy's entrenchments ; we could hear their frequent drum-calls for officers or First Sergeants, and the rumble of their artillery, and many men there were busily loading wagons, which were rapidly moved away as soon as loaded. Upon this, I wrote a note and sent it in to the 1st Brigade Hdqrs., informing Col. Edward H. Ripley of the 9th Vermont, now commanding our 1st Brigade, of what was going on within the Confederate lines. He returned to me a note with instructions to observe unusual vigilance, watching the rebel movements as closely as possible during that night, which we did. There was also an unusual activity in the rebel camp that night. Their religious meetings were continued longer than usual, their singing and praying were louder, their picket and camp fires were kept burning later ; and many means employed to deceive us as to their intentions.

" The first indications I had of the enemy's evacuating his lines, were at half past four o'clock on the morning of April 3d — 4.30 a. m. — when the Confederate gunboat in the James river and their magazines in the vicinity of Drury's Bluff, between one and two miles distant, were blown up. The concussion was terrific. The earth shook where we were, and there flashed out a glare of light as of noonday, while the fragments of the vessel, pieces of timber and other stuff, fell among my pickets, who had not yet moved from the position where they had been posted for the night watch. Fortunately no accidents occurred from the falling pieces.

" Immediately after this explosion occurred, Lt. Col. Bamberger, of the 5th Maryland, acting that night as Division officer of the day, came galloping up ; and his horse, terrified by the explosion, reared and plunged, and gave Lt. Col. Bamberger considerable trouble before he could be controlled, and quieted enough to stand still. He ordered me to advance my pickets without delay, but to use the utmost caution. The men were on the extreme front line, and were all ready to move in a moment; and in a few moments after the explosion my whole picket line was moving through the narrow belt of woods. I had been awake for several hours, in fact all night, and this explosion was the first of the long series that followed along the Confederate lines, and the James, on that morning, each with a similar glare and jar.

"As directed by Lt. Col. Bamberger, my men were held well in line, ready for instant action, and but a few feet apart, forming quite a strong line; and moving in this manner we were soon past the narrow belt of timber, and out of it upon hard, clear, dry ground, much trampled by the Confederate troops. We bore somewhat to the left, as we advanced. While we were moving through this belt of woods the first fires burst out in the direction and vicinity of Richmond, and in the enemy's lines. One of my men here had his thumb blown off by the accidental discharge of his rifle, the lock catching in a bush. This was the only casualty of the day among my pickets.

"On reaching the main Confederate line of earth-works, with its triple line of abatis, I noticed bits of bright-colored cloth attached to little sticks, rising a few inches above the ground, a short distance in front of the rebel works. Suspecting that these marked the location of torpedoes, I halted the line, went down along it, and cautioned the men to step over them very carefully.[1] No accident occurred, and we were soon inside the Confederate works.

"We entered first the fort, the large earth-work, immediately in front of Fort Harrison, having to climb very high walls in so doing. Many heavy siege guns were here in position, unspiked, and the ammunition piled ready for use; and as I passed by I seized a primer from one of these Confederate guns, which I now, 1887, have in my possession as a souvenir of that morning's occupation of Fort Gilmer. I halted my line here within Fort Gilmer, as a measure of precaution, and conversed with several Confederate stragglers, and negroes, who were still lingering about the works, and by them I was informed that Richmond was being evacuated.

"I then advanced my line, formed as before, turning somewhat to the right, until I came to the turnpike; the first highway we met after passing the enemy's main line of works, and leading northward. On coming near this highway, I waited a moment for the stragglers and breathless men to come up, then formed my men, for a rapid march, in a column of fours, obliqued to the right a little, entered the turnpike, and advanced rapidly straight up towards Richmond.

"We saw no Union colored troops, no Union white troops, and no organized Confederate troops whatever, during the whole morning, until we were joined by Lieut. Keener's men after we had reached the high hill near the city, as mentioned below; after a march of about five miles,

---

[1] Only seven pounds weight was required to cause one of these torpedoes to explode.

or more, from my picket line in front of Fort Harrison. We met on the way, however, little knots of Confederate soldiers, all unarmed stragglers, and a few colored people, all of whom reiterated the statement that Richmond was being evacuated; and later on we met some who stated that the city had been already evacuated and abandoned by the Confederate troops and Government.

"Following the turnpike, and marching by the right flank, all the way in, we advanced rapidly until we came upon the crest of the high land known as Tree Hill, sharp and steep, very near to Richmond, and separated from it only by a deep gorge or valley containing a brook or two. Here we halted for a few minutes to take breath, and to look down upon a city in flames. Soon after halting here, we were joined by Lieut. David S. Keener, of the 5th Maryland, and a small squad of his men. They had come up from some point still farther to the left than we had been, between my picket line and the James. His men joined mine, making in all a company of about sixty or seventy men, and I led them all down the hill, all the time marching in the turnpike, until we came to Gillie's Creek bridged by a few planks, on which were stationed three white cavalrymen, who disputed my further progress into the city, and claimed that they were acting under orders of the General commanding.

"We therefore halted at Gillie's Creek, on the south side, and without crossing, stacked arms, and the tired men threw themselves down upon the ground to rest. While we were here, a gunboat in the James, near by, in full sight, blew up; this was the second explosion we had witnessed this morning, the first one being at 4.30 a. m. Another gunboat blew up some time afterwards. A few of the men, who had fallen out because of our rapid marching, joined us here.

"While we were halted here at Gillie's Creek, the Mayor of Richmond came down from the city in his carriage, and I held a conversation with him. This was, as near as I can determine, between six and a half and seven o'clock in the morning (6.30 and 7 a. m.), and the place where I conversed with the Mayor was a few rods south of Gillie's Creek in the turnpike. The Mayor here then tendered to me the surrender of the city of Richmond, and offered to place in my hands a package, in the act of so doing, containing, I presume, papers and the keys of the public buildings. I was about to take the package, but just then I saw Gen. Godfrey Weitzel, with his staff, coming down the hill, riding along the turnpike, and I at once referred the Mayor to him, as the proper officer with whom to treat. The Mayor then proceeded southward down the turnpike to meet Gen. Weitzel.

"A few minutes only after my conversation with the Mayor, Gen. Weitzel came up to the creek where we were waiting, and ordered me to follow him into the city, which I proceeded at once to do, crossing the creek into a wide street, or road, where we immediately came into Richmond. We soon, however, lost sight of Gen. Weitzel in the dense smoke of the burning city, and while he turned off to the right, I deviated to the left toward the river, probably down 29th or 30th street, until I saw a sign 'Main St.' on a lamp post, when I turned my little column of men into that street, and marched along.

"The crowd of people was soon very dense, and we had much difficulty in forcing our way through it. The people pressed their way into the ranks, tried to relieve the men of their loads, of blankets, etc., urged liquors upon them, and testified their joy at seeing them, in every conceivable way, and by the most extravagant expressions and actions. I smashed several vessels of liquor with my sword, to prevent its effect upon the men.

"The heat at the corner of Fourteenth and Main streets was so intense that we were forced to turn aside again to the right toward Franklin street. There was a drug store at this corner, and the proprietor was standing on the steps as we came up. I asked him to direct me to the Capitol, which he did ; and he volunteered the further information that Confederate Gen. Early had just passed up Broad street at the head of a body of Confederate cavalry. The city fire engines were burning in the street, having been abandoned to their fate, the heat being so great that they could not be worked. We had to double-quick as fast as possible, as we passed on, to escape the heat, and our whiskers, hair and clothing were singed by it. It was now near seven o'clock (7 a. m.), and we were almost suffocated with the smoke and heat, were fatigued and hungry. Turning out of Main through Fourteenth street, and then proceeding along Franklin street, in the direction indicated by the gentlemanly proprietor of the drug store, we soon saw the Capitol near by on our left. We marched at once to the Capitol, and I ordered the men to stack arms and rest in the Capitol grounds. Our whole movement in entering the city was very hurried.

"I arrived in the Capitol grounds at seven twenty o'clock (7.20 a. m.), as set down in my diary at the time. There was no flag visible on the Capitol, and no flag of any kind whatever on the flagstaff on the Capitol, when I arrived.

"As we marched into the city behind General Weitzel, the sound of the trains, conveying the last of the rebel troops out of the city was distinctly heard, and they had barely time enough to get away.

"The appearance of the city, and of the people, along our entering line of march, beggars all description. The condition of the poor people was pitiable in the extreme. Women barefoot and thinly clad, with tears streaming down their cheeks, cried 'Thank God!' 'Thank God!' One poor woman, who had four little, pale, starved children clinging to her skirts, herself shoeless, bonnetless, miserably clad, grasped my arm, while the tears ran down her cheeks, and begged for something to eat, saying that her children had tasted no food since Sunday morning, and then only a little meal. She said she was sick, and that she was so was too plainly evident. I gave her the contents of my haversack, others gave of their supply ; and one man in the ranks, William H. Gault of H, a large, brawny man, dashed his hand across his eyes, then gave her his entire three days' rations of hard bread and meat, and then thrust a ten dollar greenback — all the money he had with him — into her hand, swearing like a trooper all the time by way of relieving his feelings.

"The air was full of the cinders, smoke and ashes of the burning city, and the bursting of shells in the arsenals and storehouses of ordnance was incessant for many hours.

"The first body of Union troops that entered the city of Richmond on the morning of April 3, 1865, was my detachment — the pickets from the First Brigade.

"It is customary when troops are advancing, for a line of skirmishers to precede, sweeping the country before them, picking up Confederate stragglers wherever met, but I saw none of such skirmishers. My men were of the picket line and not skirmishers. I was in advance of all the skirmishers, pushing forward with my pickets of the First Brigade in a little solid column of fours, along the New Market road directly toward Richmond. The only Union soldiers that I saw in or near Richmond, excepting my men, Lieut. Keener's, and Gen Weitzel and staff, were the three white cavalrymen at Gillie's Creek; and the only orders I received, during all that morning, were from Lieut. Col. Bamberger of the 5th Maryland at the moment of starting, and later on when just outside the city limits, from Gen. Weitzel himself.

"There was no flag visible on the roof of the Capitol when I entered the grounds, from the point where I entered them — the southward corner; and there was no flag whatever then on the tall staff on the roof; but within a few moments a flag was run up on the Capitol. It suddenly appeared on the flagstaff on the roof, and immediately afterwards I had a conversation with the man who raised it, and took down his name and residence. He was a light colored boy, apparently about seventeen years of age, and he gave me his name as Richard G. Forrester, living at the corner of College and Marshall streets. He was in no way connected with the Union Army. He stated to me that when the State of Virginia passed the Ordinance of Secession, he was a page, or errand boy, employed in the Capitol. The Secessionists then tore down the very flag, which he had just now re-hoisted on the Capitol, and threw it among some rubbish under the eaves, or roof, in the top of the building. At the first convenient opportunity afterwards, he rolled this flag in a bundle, so that he could remove it undiscovered, carried it to his home, and placed it in his bed, where he had slept on it nightly since that time. This morning, he said, as soon as he dared after the Confederates left the city, and — as he put it — 'When I saw you 'uns comin',' — he drew this old flag from its hiding-place, ran to the Capitol with it, mounted to the top, and run this flag up on the flagstaff, whence the Confederate flag had been so lately removed; and this, he claimed, was the first flag hoisted in Richmond after its evacuation by the Confederates.

"After talking with him, I went up through every room in the Capitol and found it entirely deserted, not a person to be seen in it.

"During the few minutes while we waited in the grounds, a few of the men had passed across the street, and were sitting among the trees near the old Powhatan Hotel. Hearing a wordy altercation going on among them, I went across to investigate the cause of the disturbance. Here I found that William H. Gault of H, a quick, impulsive man but withal generous-hearted — the same man who gave the poor woman the ten dollars and his rations as we came into the city — had been listening to a lot of secession talk, made by a citizen, until his indignation could endure such stuff no longer, and he had taken the citizen to task for starving the poor people of Richmond. Hard words ensued. Gault suddenly sprang to his feet, seized his gun, aimed at the citizen, and possibly would have shot him then and there, if I had not interfered and struck up his gun. Gault's indignation, at what he regarded as sheer hypocrisy, knew no bounds.

"Soon after arriving in the Capitol grounds, the men resting themselves at full length on the grass after the fatiguing march and exciting scenes through which they had passed, an orderly rode up with orders for me to report immediately to Gen. Godfrey Weitzel at his Hdqrs. in the house recently occupied by the absconding President of the late Confederacy. Arriving in Gen. Weitzel's presence, he turned to me and in severe tones inquired : 'Are you the officer who was in command of the men I met at the outskirts of the city early this morning?' 'I am, Sir,' I replied. 'And did I not tell you to follow closely behind me on entering the city?' he further inquired. To this I replied that I had done so until the smoke had become so dense and suffocating that I could not follow, and could no longer see clearly in any direction, and that under these circumstances I had deviated somewhat from the course he had taken, and so had failed to keep up with him. I then narrated to him all the circumstances that had befallen me since I had parted company with him, at the close of which he expressed himself as being perfectly satisfied with my explanation, and then inquired where I had left my men.

"After being informed he ordered me to take a squad of from six to ten men, to patrol the streets, arresting every person found in Confederate uniform or bearing arms, and to conduct them to his Hdqrs.; and also to order all colored persons to their homes on pain of arrest. He further ordered me to divide the remainder of my men into small squads of about

---

### DESCRIPTION OF FORRESTER PAPERS.

Lieut. Prescott still, 1887, preserves the two papers received this morning from young Forrester. The larger paper is apparently a piece torn from one of the C. S. A. Government's common blue envelopes; the smaller paper is a leaf from a small pocket memorandum book or diary. The writing is in pencil but clear and legible, though evidently the writing of a person of limited education. The cut opposite is correct and literal in every particular.

THE FORRESTER PAPERS.

From a Photograph.

ten men each, and to dispatch them upon a similar patrol. This I did at once on returning to the Capitol grounds, and while making my first patrol, I came upon a column of Union troops, all white troops, the Thirteenth New Hampshire Regiment at their head, marching up Franklin Street with their colors flying and their drum-corps playing ' Yankee Doodle.' [1]

"Excepting my pickets, these were the first Union troops to enter the city after its evacuation by the Confederates; the Flag of the Thirteenth was the first Flag of the Army to come in. On coming near this body of troops we immediately halted, on the west side of the street, presented arms, and saluted the passing column. There was a mutual recognition, and remarks and cheers naturally incident to such an occasion. After the column passed us, I proceeded on the duties of my patrol. In this duty of patroling the streets of Richmond, I was engaged for the greater part of two days. Changing the men every two or three hours, I collected large numbers of Confederate officers and soldiers alike, and marched them to the place indicated; from whence they were consigned to Castle Thunder and Libby Prison, until those two famous buildings would hold no more — being literally packed from cellar to roof.

"As soon as Gen. Patrick was appointed Provost Marshal, which happened very soon after our occupation of the city, I was ordered to take my prisoners to him, and among the arrests I remember a number of prominent and influential citizens of Richmond and vicinity; among them the Second Auditor of the Confederate Treasury, on April 4th, the two Editors of the Richmond Examiner, on April 8th, and the Editors of the Richmond Times, all of whom were sent to Castle Thunder."

Lieut. Royal B. Prescott.

1887. Lt. Col. Smith has recently looked over the ground with special reference to the incidents of Lieut. Prescott's early morning march toward Richmond on April 3, 1865, and says: "I am sure Lieut. Prescott did not halt at Almon Creek, for the hill is winding and steep beyond there, and he could not have seen any distance at that point. Just above the junction of the Osborne and New Market roads, toward the river and city, and between the road and river, is a depression and another rise beyond, on which stands Tree Hill the residence of Mr. Stearns. This bluff extends with the depression to near the flag of truce bluff — the point where the Mayor of Richmond set up his white flag that morning — where it terminates. This bluff, Mr. Stearns', is nearly in line with the road past the brick yards. The brick yards, where the colored troops were halted by the roadside, are between the flag of truce bluff and Gillie's Creek. When coming round the hill myself, with the Brigade, I saw the explosion of the dispatch boat Allison at Rocketts wharves,

---

[1] Observe that this meeting must have been at some distance from the Capitol toward Rocketts, because it occurred before Major Stoodley had changed the tune to 'The Battle Cry of Freedom.' See page 574.

and at the same time saw the burning bridges across the James. Gillie's Creek bridge is near these wharves, the section was not covered with buildings as it now is, and Lieut. Prescott could have seen a considerable distance to his rear from this point."  LT. COL. SMITH.

To return to the narrative of the day :

Even at the risk of repetition, the following from the pen of Henry A. Pollard, and published by him editorially in his paper, 'The Richmond Times,' in the issue of April 28, 1865, which now, December 1886, lies before the writer, seems appropriate to enter under this day. The copy is given here word for word, and the statement in the article passed unchallenged :

### "THE TROOPS TO FIRST ENTER RICHMOND.

" In the compilation of our narrative of the scenes and incidents attendant upon the late evacuation of Richmond, we purposely refrained from deciding or saying anything as to which were the first troops, or organized body of soldiers to enter the city. The simple fact that it was a matter of dispute, and seemed not to be definitely settled, rendered this the most proper course for us. Since then we have come into possession of information from a most trustworthy and authoritative source, which would appear to decide the question.

" The truth of the matter seems to be about this : On the night before the evacuation, the Federal picket lines opposite the defenses, upon the north side of the James, were respectively held by Lieutenant Royal B. Prescott, commanding Company C, Thirteenth New Hampshire Regiment, of the First Brigade, Third Division, of the Twenty-Fourth Army Corps, and Lieutenant David S. Keener, commanding Company F, Fifth Maryland Regiment, Second Brigade of the same organization. Lieutenant Prescott's line being on the left of the First Brigade joined the line of Lieutenant Keener, who occupied the right of the Second Brigade. The first intimation they received of the evacuation of Richmond was the explosions of the magazines at Drewry's Bluff, as well as the glare of the fires just commencing in the city, about half past four a. m. The Division officer-of-the-day ordered Lieutenant Prescott to advance immediately his picket lines, which he did. On arriving at the Confederate lines he discovered that the pickets had been withdrawn, when Lieutenant Prescott and his men continued to advance until reaching the small bridge over the stream which flows close to Stearns' establishment, just outside the city. They were confronted here by three of the New York cavalry, who informed them that they had been posted there with orders to allow no troops to enter the city until the commanding General came up. Lieutenant Keener with about thirty men here joined Lieutenant Prescott's squad, which numbered about the same. After a halt of some ten minutes General Wilde [1] rode up, attended by his staff, and proceeded to advance into the city — the city having been previously surrendered by the Mayor.

[1] Gen. Wilde probably accompanied Gen. Weitzel. — S. M. T.

"Thus Lieutenant Prescott and his squad of men were the *first*[1] troops to enter the city. Their line of march was up Main street, coming at a 'double quick.' The city was then a sea of flame, and arriving at Fourteenth street, they were compelled, by the intense heat, to turn up from Main street — pressing up Fourteenth street to Franklin. Thence they immediately made for the Capitol grounds, which they reached about 7 o'clock, just as the flag was being raised over the building. Stacking their arms and resting for a short space of time, they were then ordered out to patrol the streets and suppress the pillaging, and aid in subduing the flames.

"The first *body*[1] of troops to enter Richmond was the First Brigade, Third Division of the Twenty-Fourth Army Corps, followed by colored troops. The first regimental organization was the Thirteenth New Hampshire, they holding the right of the Brigade. They entered the city with colors flying and their bands playing 'Yankee Doodle.' These facts are to us narrated with a degree of accuracy which admits of no doubt.

"Lieutenant Prescott, who may be considered one of the first to enter the city, has been on duty of various kinds in and around the city since its occupation by the United States forces, and has commanded the good feelings of the citizens by his general courtesy and considerate demeanor."

Extract from a letter dated Richmond April 29, 1865 : "The Editor of the Times, of which I send the copy of April 28th, is the same Mr. Pollard whom I arrested in April, while he was at supper in the Spottswood Hotel. I arrested him by special order, and have preserved both that order and the receipt I received when I delivered him up to the keeper of Castle Thunder, and propose to keep them as remembrances. Mr. Pollard was released, and allowed to continue his business as Editor of this paper." LIEUT. PRESCOTT.

Gen. Grant in his Memoirs states that Gen. Weitzel took possession of Richmond at about 8.15 a. m., April 3d.[2] That the rebel civil Government left the city about 2 p. m., April 2d; and he does not fix the responsibility of firing the city upon any person in particular.

We will now return to the Thirteenth; the main facts concerning the march to and into Richmond and the route of march have been furnished to the writer by Major N. D. Stoodley, and by Lt. Col. Normand Smith ; with the latter of whom the writer visited the ground, in May 1885, and also with him went over both the route and the account entire and in detail.

The Thirteenth was encamped, on the day and night of April 2d, in its last camp at the front. In the afternoon of April 2d, Lt. Col. Smith read a telegraphic order from Gen. Grant directing Gen. Weitzel to assault the works on this front at daylight of April 3d. With this in mind,

---

[1] The italics are Pollard's in both instances. [2] Probably the "formal surrender" at the Mayor's office, as mentioned in numerous accounts. — S. M. T.

and the Thirteenth having been designated to lead our Brigade, Lt. Col. Smith has the Thirteenth drawn up, in the New Market road at the Cross-way, on this morning of April 3d, all ready to assault, or to march for Richmond, nearly half an hour before the rest of our Brigade comes into line. The Thirteenth are standing in the road, at a rest, close up to the curtain at the Cross-way, and at the head of our Brigade when the final order to march is received. We are now about six miles from the Capitol in Richmond.

As our Regiment is armed with the Sharps carbines, we prepare to form in line of battle in front of the Brigade, or to skirmish, as the case may demand. But Lieut. Prescott has advanced over the ground to the left — west — of the New Market road, and no enemy appears. Of course if no enemy is found to the left of the New Market road, all of his troops must needs have withdrawn from the right front — east of that road — because they were farther from the pontons in the James to be crossed in their retreat.

Our column is fairly in motion about an hour after daylight. The enemy has left many of his torpedoes planted along in front of his works, and our men follow the beaten paths to avoid exploding them — a rebel deserter serving as a guide. Bits of bright-colored cloth are found tied to sticks and set up to mark the location of the buried torpedoes, and a number of the torpedoes are removed to prevent accidents.

We pass the works of Fort Gilmer, which is surrounded by three strong lines of abatis and one line of torpedoes. In his haste to evacuate the works, and to secure secrecy, he has left his camp standing nearly intact; the heavy guns are all in position, and not even spiked; some of his light field batteries are also left intact, and even much of the furniture in the officers' quarters is left undisturbed.

Our line of march is followed up rapidly along the New Market road, in column of fours, until the exceeding strong lines of the Confederate defenses are passed, when it appears that the colored troops may reach the city first. We hurry forward, a part of the time at a double-quick, and the race is kept up until the colored troops, coming in on the Osborne pike, are halted.

While on the march toward Richmond, and after we have passed the Confederate works near Fort Gilmer — about 6.30 or 7 a. m. — Lt. Col. Smith is detailed as General officer of the day, and the command of the Thirteenth devolves upon Major Stoodley. Lt. Col. Smith does not have his sash with him, and hurries about through our whole Brigade, on a fruitless hunt for an officer's silk sash; finally having to borrow a First Sergeant's worsted sash, of some one in the 13th, to wear while caring for the dire needs of the Confederacy's proud capital city, on this awful April morning.

The Thirteenth, followed by our 1st Brigade, hurries along the New Market road, keeping in that road all the way, toward the city, until they come to its junction with the Osborne pike. A strong line of Confederate earth-works crosses these two roads near their junction. Here at the junction, some of the colored troops, probably the best marchers among them, having come up on the Osborne pike, crowd into the road in an unorganized condition, and march along by the side of the white troops; who preserve their own organization compact, and are marching by the right flank — in column of fours — as they have been all the morning.

We press on, now along the Osborne pike, still preserving both our regimental position and organization complete, and the Brigade likewise, despite the colored soldiers scattered along in the roadway beside us, until we reach the brick yards, about half way between Almon's and Gillie's creeks, when Gen. Devens, probably seeing that it is not best for an unorganized body, of any kind of soldiers, to enter the city at this time, halts the colored soldiers at the brick yards, allowing the white troops to pass on toward the city; the 13th N. H. leading our 1st Brigade, which is composed entirely of white troops.[1]

We have marched up all the way by the right flank, momentarily expecting to be deployed as skirmishers, or to swing into line of battle, the deserter's statements concerning the evacuation of Richmond not being fully credited; but our last battle has been fought.

As we come along, the white flag of truce hoisted by the Mayor of Richmond is still flying from a pole set up on a spur of Tree Hill; at the point where the pike bends around it, before reaching Gillie's Creek.

Before starting from camp this morning our Regiment and the other troops expected a hard fight when they should advance, and carefully prepared for it, besides keeping a perfectly compact organization on the whole march. The most dangerous incident of the morning, however, was the passing and removal of the enemy's torpedoes. They were buried about three or four feet apart, between the lines of abatis, in front of the enemy's earth-works, and just merely covered with a thin layer of earth, so that a pressure of seven pounds only was necessary to explode one of them. No accidents occurred with them, however, and their removal merely served to delay the march a very little. We have moved so rapidly that our advance to the city is practically a forced march, and we have not fired a shot this morning.

The city corporation now, 1865, extends only to between Nicholson and Denney streets, where they abut on Rocketts street and Williamsburg avenue.

Capt. Rufus P. Staniels, of Company H, was appointed Nov. 19, 1864, Actg. Asst. Adjt. General on the staff of the 1st Brigade, 1st Div. 18th Army Corps, the Brigade then commanded by Lt. Col. John B. Raulston

---

[1] The colored troops, organized or unorganized, were not allowed to be the first to enter Richmond this morning for many obvious reasons. Collisions would have been almost inevitable; while the state of the city at this early hour demanded the stronger and steadier hand of the white troops, in order to restore order and maintain peace. Some colored troops marched into the city about 10 or 11 a. m. — S. M. T.

of the 81st N. Y. Jan. 15, 1865, Lt. Col. Raulston was mustered out of the service, and on Jan. 16th Col. Edgar M. Cullen of the 96th N. Y. assumed command of the 1st Brigade, and on March 22d Col. E. H. Ripley of the 9th Vt. succeeded him in that command. Capt. Staniels remained in the same position, on the staff of each successive commander belonging to the 24th Corps, and makes the following statement:

"On the morning of April 3, 1865, I was Actg. Asst. Adjt. General on the staff of Col. E. H. Ripley commanding the First Brigade, 3d Div. 24th Army Corps. Our Division, commanded by Gen. Charles Devens, approached the city of Richmond by the New Market road, Col. Ripley's — the First — Brigade leading. As we came to the junction of this road with the Osborne turnpike, the colored troops were seen approaching on that road. Our position, however, was in advance of theirs, and before the head of the column of colored troops arrived at the junction of the two roads, the First Brigade, the Thirteenth New Hampshire leading, had passed the junction by more than half its length.

"A member of Gen. Devens' staff came to Col. Ripley and ordered him to send an officer to remain at the junction of the two roads, and when the commanding officer of the colored troops came up to that point, to direct him not to break in upon our Brigade, but to march parallel with our column in the fields beside the road, and thus prevent confusion, for there was not room enough in the road for the two columns to march side by side. The colored troops were not standing upon the order of their going, but were rushing, while the white troops — of Gen. Devens' Division — were much in advance, and marching in a compact column.

"Col. Ripley sent me to deliver this order. I rode back, took my place at the junction of the two roads, and when the head of the column of colored troops came up, I delivered Gen. Devens' order to the commander of it. After a little hesitation he complied with the order, and I remained in front of his advance until the white troops had all passed the junction. After seeing that Gen. Devens's directions were complied with, I left the colored troops, and again joined Col. Ripley at the head of the Brigade and the column of white troops, which maintained its advance and order in the march, the Thirteenth the leading Regiment, and entered the city alone; the colored troops having been halted outside of the city near Rocketts.

"I had been sent back once before on an errand this morning, and was anxious to be one of the first to enter the city, and my impatience can well be imagined as I sat on my horse waiting for the negroes to be halted and the General's order to be carried out; the instant that was done I galloped to the head of the column of the white troops again, and was in time to enter the city as I had desired, in my proper place in the column."

Capt. R. P. Staniels.

Now comes the final entry into the city — more rapid than formal. The Thirteenth leads our Brigade, and the order to march is given at the point where the Osborne pike passes the brick yards, and we move rapidly straight along into the city. Major Stoodley, commanding the Thirteenth, first orders the drum corps and 1st Brigade Band to play 'Yankee Doodle,' but after a little changes it to 'The Battle Cry of Freedom'; that being, in his opinion, the tune most appropriate for the occasion.

From the brick yards we march along the Osborne pike to near its junction with the present Nicholson and Denney streets, where we turn to the left across 'Old Field,' entering Rocketts street at its junction with Nicholson street. Thence along the following streets: Up Rocketts to Main, up Main to 17th; where the heat of the fire is so intense and the smoke so blinding, that the column is forced to the right up 17th to Franklin; thence we move up Franklin to Governor, up Governor to Capitol, along Capitol to the main entrance to the Capitol grounds opposite 10th Street, where we enter the Capitol grounds, halt and stack arms on the grass plat between the Governor's mansion and the Capitol. The time of arrival here a little after 8 a. m.

As soon as we arrive in Capitol Square, Br. Brig. Gen. Edward H. Ripley, formerly Colonel of the 9th Vt., now commanding our 1st Brigade receives orders to patrol the city, restore order, and to put out the fires. Soon the 13th is sent on Provost-guard and patrol duty, to various parts of the city.

Entering at once upon our duty as patrols, before we have been in the city an hour, we march through the streets, in squads and Companies — the total force of the Reg. present to-day not exceeding 200 men — being neither molested, insulted nor disturbed on the way, and occupy, near the city lines, seven of the roads leading out of the northern side of the city, besides furnishing guards for particular stations. We have orders to allow no one to pass into, or out of, the city. Our posts are all taken on these streets, and stations, some time before 9.30 a. m., and we remain on them until 5 p. m., when we return to Capitol square, and are assigned quarters in the St. Claire Hotel, opposite the northeast corner of the Capitol grounds, and opposite the north end of Capitol street. Many of the men of the Thirteenth are on duty all night.

A few incidents of the entry and occupation of the city may be of interest: As the Thirteenth, leading the 1st Brigade, comes up the street, near the centre of the city, some one in the distant crowd shouts: "The Yankees! The Yankees! God bless the Yankees!" and in thousands of throats the frantic screams of the mob are instantly changed to acclamations of welcome. We are Richmond's saviors this morning. The colored population has turned out and gathered by thousands, and their demonstrations of gladness and joy know no bounds. "God bress de Yankees!" "We's free — we's free!" "Bress de Lord — O bress de Lord!" "O Lord — we knowed you was a-comin'!" and similar shouts are heard on every hand. The negro slave, a little along in years, is the most demonstrative religious specimen of mankind on earth; and like his white over-demonstrative brother in that thing, can lie and cheat, and steal chickens — or anything else — without a single prick of conscience in all his life. But the ex-slave is genuinely happy all over on this April morning, when pops the first spring bud of his new freedom. The negroes offer to carry our men's blankets and knapsacks, their guns — anything, so they may help or favor their deliverers. They offer fruit, food — perhaps their last morsel — and, in many instances, liquor, and the officers have to seize it, and dash the vessels and bottles in pieces on the ground, or with their swords, to prevent drunkenness.

As one writer truthfully says: "The negroes seem to think that the 'Day of Jubilee' has fully come; they shout, dance, sing, wave their rag banners, shake our hands, bow, scrape, laugh all over, and thank God for our coming."

Richmond contains nearly double her usual population, and the half are negroes. A huge, motley crowd, with here and there a scowling son of mischief, but by far the most part in wild ecstasies for joy, lines the streets as we pass along.

Our drum corps and Band play the popular Union airs of the war, as we march along the streets — somehow the Richmond negroes have learned these tunes, and now sing them — and many a little National flag is waved over us from the balconies, windows and house tops. It is a triumphal procession in miniature. The multitude of little U. S. flags is most surprising; hundreds of them not more than a foot long, and many wrought on silk, are fluttering along the streets.

The worser side of life is not wanting here by any means. Hurrying off, along the side streets and alleys, are many vehicles, of every describable variety, filled to overflow with people and goods; drayloads of merchandise; handcarts and wheelbarrows and hundreds of people loaded down with furniture and household goods and stores of every sort; all seeking a refuge from the spreading, threatening fires, or a hiding-place for their plunder.

As we march into Capitol Square, we find it strewn and covered with furniture and household implements of every style and kind, which have been dragged here and deposited, in this most convenient open space, to save them from destruction in the burning buildings; and here, huddled together among these last relics of many a burned-out home, are large numbers of women and children, black and white together, hungry, destitute and helpless.

Lieut. Prescott's pickets, and possibly a few cavalry vedettes, in all scarcely one hundred men, have preceded us; but our Thirteenth is the first organized body of Union soldiers to bring its colors into the city, and our First Brigade are the only troops here.

The fires at this time — between 8 and 9 a. m. — are raging with unabated fury, and the shells are continually exploding in the neighborhood of the arsenal. Our troops organize fire companies, pressing in the white and the black citizens together, to work with them, and succeed in stopping the fires in certain directions — but the task is herculean. Stores, mills, warehouses, bridges, depots, houses, acres upon acres of buildings of every sort, are burning on every hand; dense volumes of smoke, flashing masses of flames, and clouds of fiery cinders, and burning brands, fill the air, which resounds, jars and vibrates, with the incessant explosions of vast numbers of shells, and the stores of gunpowder; so noisy is it all that our troops left behind at Fort Harrison think we are having a fierce battle in the city. By night, however, the fires are under control, or cease in those districts where there is nothing more left to burn.

The enemy in his haste took little care of stragglers from his lines, and we capture above a thousand Confederate soldiers in the city; and in the hospitals, and in private houses here we find about 5,000 of his men, sick and wounded. The able bodied rebel soldiers and officers are packed into Castle Thunder and Libby Prison; which is said to be mined, and the mine charged with gunpowder enough to blow the whole structure, with all its inmates and contents, to the very skies.[1] Our First Brigade are the only Union troops quartered and on duty in the city; but other Union troops are surrounding the city on all sides. The 2d Brigade halted outside the city, and went into camp on the Williamsburg pike near Gillie's Creek. Several batteries of Union artillery follow our troops to the city, and halt in advantageous positions near Rocketts about 9 a. m. The colored troops halted at the brick yards, and went into camp. A small body of them entering the city, and going out again, about ten or eleven o'clock in the morning.

One soldier of the 13th writes home: " We marched into Richmond — and the rebels cleared the way."

The torch was applied to Richmond about daylight, the rebel soldiers were coming into the city all the morning, hundreds of them hiding and deserting the Confederate flag, the balance passing over the James to follow the fortunes of Gen. Lee, and a little after sunrise the bridges over the James were fired.

No language can adequately describe the scenes and incidents of last night, and of to-day, or the woeful appearance of Richmond as we enter it on this pleasant April morning. All through the latter part of last night — after the first crash which occurred near the hour of daylight, about half past four (4.30 a. m.), probably a little earlier, there was an almost incessant series of tremendous explosions; their huge flashes lighting up the country for miles around, while the earth quivered and trembled even at great distances. An explosion may have occurred still earlier near Petersburg, but near us the first note in the awful scale was struck near 4.30 a. m., when the rebel gunboat in the James not far from Drury's Bluff — some think it was the floating magazine or powder-boat — was blown up. That unexpected, sudden and terrible crash burst out upon

---

[1] It appeared, however, upon examination that the powder had been removed before this time; but the excavation for the mine — made and filled with gunpowder about the time of the Dahlgren affair, which occurred March 4, 1864 — remains in evidence of the plot.

the quiet night, resounded, roared and echoed far and wide, and blazed and glared also, like the sudden eruption of a small volcano. Then followed in rapid succession, the explosions of the magazines of numerous forts encircling Richmond, besides many more on the enemy's long lines running out south and west. Then burst the vast stores of powder and fixed ammunition — on board the gunboats, and the iron-clads, in the laboratories, store-houses, and arsenals, and in the outlying places of security — a rapid series of terrific explosions, with the noise of many thunders, following close one upon another, until the fearful and deafening crash of hundreds of tons of powder, and of thousands upon thousands of shells, flashed their blinding glare on every hand, rent the air, and shook the very hills.

"In Richmond, when about 5 a. m. the powder magazine blew up, the earth seemed to writhe as if in agony, houses rocked like ships at sea, while stupendous thunders roared around ; it would almost have awakened the dead." So writes a citizen.

Large buildings were crushed to ruins by the concussion, as an eggshell can be crushed in the hand. Block after block went down, blown to shapeless piles, and strong walls of brick and stone, at great distances, were cracked and rent from eave to foundation. Many houses were piled bodily in the streets, others tipped over at every angle from their foundations ; while hundreds of chimneys fell over, and went rumbling down the roofs to the ground, thousands of glass windows crashed, rattled, rang and fell throughout the city, and the air was filled with huge volumes of blinding smoke, and choking dust. Rarely in civil life are people so exposed, or so dangerously threatened by countless objects falling everywhere along the streets, and a more direful din never pelted human ears. This explosion was the first great gun in the city. Then followed the arsenal, said to have contained 750,000 loaded shells, their incessant explosions continuing for several hours, and sounding at times like a grand battle of all the nations of the world in arms ; while the thousands of pieces of the shells rained down, over the whole contiguous district, like the countless drops from some huge fountain — if such a simile can be used. Great fires instantly ensued, and hundreds of the people dashed out and ran for their lives, scarcely knowing which way to run, and a large number were killed. Soon one third of Richmond's finest edifices, and hundreds of outlying buildings, were huge, roaring and unapproachable masses of flame ; the smoke of which rolling up in dense masses of black covered the city and near vicinity like a vast pall, and shutting out the light of the sun.

In the very midst of this scene of indescribable confusion, noise and destruction, Lieut. Prescott of the Thirteenth, with his sixty or more pickets from the 1st Brigade, was hurrying into the city. About an hour, a little more, after Lieut. Prescott came in with his pickets, the Thirteenth followed, while the storm of fire and shell was scarcely any abated, and amid the heat, smoke and flying cinders.

But as the Thirteenth came into the city, notwithstanding the fearful and terrific noise, fire and confusion, there were, in the outskirts of the city, cattle quietly browsing in the pastures, men at work in the gardens, and digging in the fields, and women hanging clothing upon their lines to dry ; the cattle, the women and the men, all apparently about equally moved by the awful events of the morning — that is, not moved at all; a most laudable case of strict attention to business !

All through the night, too, before the Union troops came in, the city had been given up to sack and pillage, and the fury of the mob. Stores were gutted, and their contents strewn in the streets. The militia and city police seem to have broken all bonds of order and restraint, and joined hands with the worser remnant of Gen. Lee's army left straggling in the city ; and all three together appear to have vied with the meanest rascal and the lowest slave, in the hell and license of indescribable mischief — all filled and crazed alike with the abundant liquor, that was seized and poured out like water, to be dipped up and drank without stint. The Confederate military authorities had in retreating — between daylight and sunrise — caused to be fired the huge flouring mills and warehouses, among the most extensive in the world, the vessels in the James, and the bridges over the river ; in short almost everything combustible that could be of use to the Union forces. There was no fire brigade fit for duty, and the fires, from the huge mills and warehouses, spread unchecked on every hand, in the densest parts of the city, until five or six hundred buildings were destroyed.

We will now add a few special statements made by officers of the Thirteenth, and by other persons who held positions of authority in the city, at the time of its surrender and occupation. Lt. Col. Smith acting during April 3d as General officer of the day.

Lt. Col. Smith writes as follows : " Before Richmond April 2d. I have just seen a dispatch, of to-day, from Gen. Grant to Gen. Weitzel, in which he says : ' A heavy battle is going on to-day. The 6th and 9th Corps are inside the enemy's lines. The 2d and 5th Corps are sweeping around to the west. Everything is working gloriously. If any weakness is exhibited near you, *push*. U. S. Grant.' "

And again, the next day, Lt. Col. Smith writes : " City of Richmond, April 3, 1865. We fell in at daylight this morning. The Thirteenth had the lead. The picket lines advanced, and found the enemy were gone. Excepting the picket lines, my Regiment was the first in the city; and we marched in with my drum corps playing ' Yankee Doodle'. I have posted the first picket and patrol in the city of Richmond. No troops but this (1st) Brigade are in the city. It is now 11 p. m. The city is quiet. The explosion of shells, in the burning buildings, yesterday, was incessant. Our troops, left behind us in Fort Harrison, thought we were having a battle. Jeff. Davis's Ordnance and Quarter-master's accounts are pretty well settled." Lt. Col. Smith.

Lt. Col. Smith also states : " Color Sergeant Van R. Davis of H carried our colors into the city on the morning of April 3d." This was the new flag with the list of battles inscribed upon it; the other color of the Thirteenth — the old State flag — was carried into the city this morning by Color Corporal Hiram C. Young of H.

The passage through the streets, on entering, was necessarily slow, and we halted in Capitol Square some time before 9 a. m., so that the Thirteenth must have crossed the city line very near to 8 a. m.; one account states that the Brigade reached Capitol Square at 8.30 a. m.

Maj. Gen. Charles Devens, in a letter written by him to Governor Smyth of New Hampshire, and dated at Richmond, Va., June 22, 1865, speaking of the Tenth, Twelfth and Thirteenth Regiments of N. H. Vols. states: "On the formation of the Twenty-Fourth Corps, all these Regiments formed a part of the Third Division, to which, they have, until now, belonged; and were of the first column that entered Richmond on the morning of April 3, 1865 — the Thirteenth New Hampshire being the first Regiment of the army whose colors were brought into the city."

In a letter written to his wife, from Richmond, under date of April 5, 1865, Major Stoodley states: "While entering Richmond on the morning of April 3, 1865, our Thirteenth Regiment led the column of troops, and was the first Regiment in. Some few cavalry, and a part of our picket line were in before us (Lieut. Prescott's pickets as related above) — but Ours was the first Flag. I caused the drum corps to play 'Yankee Doodle,' thinking that the best tune for the occasion, and from that changed to 'Down with the traitor and up with the Star' — the good old 'Battle Cry of Freedom.'

"The sides of the streets were crowded with people, mostly negroes. They shouted, they danced, cried, prayed, sang, and cut up all manner of wild capers. The most common expression was 'Thank God, thank God, deliverance has come.' I state what was a literal fact, the people were in a state of starvation. The rebels had set fire to the warehouses and workshops, and the fire had got under great headway before we entered the city, and we heard one rebel ram blow up, after we came into the city. It is estimated that 600 buildings were destroyed. No warning at all was given of the purpose to fire the buildings, and the explosion all day of large quantities of shells and ammunition sounded like a grand battle. Many of the people were burned to death. In one place lay three bodies of little girls, five or six years old, burned to a crisp. In a house near by, seventeen persons were killed by the explosion of the powder magazine — which was (also) fired without giving any warning at all. Destitution prevails here to an alarming extent.

"Ours is the only Brigade in the city, and keeping order is no play. (1st Brig. 3d Div. 24th Army Corps.) We are doing provost duty. Lt. Col. Normand Smith of the Thirteenth was Division officer of the day, the first day, April 3d, and I relieved him, and took it yesterday, April 4th.[1] I patrolled the streets myself the most of last night, taking what I

[1] This was a very unusual proceeding, and a great compliment to Lt. Col. Smith,

considered the worst districts under my own eye. Very many of the best citizens have told me, yesterday and to-day, that the city has been more quiet and orderly since we have been here, than for many weeks before, and that they feel safer under our rule than they did under their own. Capt. M. T. Betton of K has command of Libby Prison. Gen. Weitzel occupies Jeff. Davis' former Hdqrs. Gen. Devens occupies the Government House where Gov. Smith resided.

"While marching into the city we were greeted, from many and many a window, with the waving of the Old Flag, and our troops cheered whenever one was displayed. As soon as our column halted in front of the Capitol, on the morning of April 3d, I was ordered to take the Thirteenth through the city, and occupy the roads leading from it. And our little Thirteenth, with less than two hundred men, marched alone through the principal streets unmolested, and without any insult being offered to us. I put our little force so as to control seven roads, and on the principal one, on that (north) side of the city; and held them from nine thirty o'clock a. m. (9.30 a. m.) till five o'clock p. m., allowing no one to pass out or in. Scores of wealthy citizens came to me for protection, — 'From what?' I asked them; but they did not seem to know. But to sift all down, I found their fears grounded in a dread of the lower orders of their own population, and perhaps, a very natural one, of the colored troops.

"President Lincoln visited this city yesterday, April 4th, the next day after we took possession. He looked very much gratified. The display made by the negroes, on seeing 'Marsa Abraham,' was very amusing. Some of our gunboats got up here yesterday.

"April 6th, morning. All quiet here now. I go alone around all parts of the city in perfect safety, and unmolested. Gen. Lee's family is here. We have a guard (a part of the time from the Thirteenth) at his house, to protect his family from any rudeness or molestation."

MAJOR STOODLEY.

"April 3d. Receive orders at 4 a. m. to be in readiness to move at a moment's notice. March through breast-works at 6.15 a. m.[1] March into Richmond at 8.10 a. m., and immediately post men, and commence doing Provost duty. The Thirteenth N. H. V. the first Regiment to enter." CAPT. STANIELS, in Diary.

The Richmond Whig of Thursday April 6th states that by 7 a. m. on April 3d nearly the whole of the city south of Main Street, between 8th and 15th streets and 20th and 23d streets, was one great sea of flame. Gen. Gary, in command of the Confederate cavalry (rear guard of Gen. Lee's army), passed up Main Street not five minutes ahead of the Federal troops.[2] The fire was under control — so far as further spreading was concerned — by three o'clock in the afternoon.

---

Major Stoodley and the Thirteenth. Usually this duty passes, from day to day, among the field officers, around from regiment to regiment; but Lt. Col. Smith and Major Stoodley were the right men in the right place, and the day demanded strong hands and level heads. [1] Meaning the Cross-way on the New Market road. [2] By these the Editor must needs mean Lieut. Prescott's pickets. — S. M. T.

A writer of the time states, possibly of April 3d: "As a large body of colored cavalry approached the Capitol Square in Richmond, amid the dense throngs that crowded the streets, they suddenly, as by a common impulse, rose in their stirrups, their white eyes and teeth gleaming from their lines of dark visages, waved their flashing sabres in exulting frenzy, and rent the air with wild huzzas; a scene of barbaric fury savage enough to make one's blood chill in his veins."

In the conflicting statements that have been made about the surrender and first occupation of Richmond, and about the 'hoisting of the first flag upon the Capitol,' Lieut. Prescott's account must be accepted as the true one (see page 554 et seq.); among other reasons because he was the first of all to meet the Mayor of Richmond, was the first Union officer on the ground at any hour near the time of raising the first flag, has no personal interest whatever in the raising of any flag, and was in the Capitol grounds before any flag was to be seen on the Capitol.

C. C. Coffin, in his 'Four Years of Fighting,' pages 506-7, states that a little past four a. m. Maj. A. H. Stevens, 4th Mass. Cavalry, moved over the entrenchments [1] and toward the city, and a mile and a half out of the city met a party — the Mayor of Richmond in a barouche, and five men mounted and bearing a white flag — and these tendered the surrender of the city.[1] He went into the city. He proceeded to the Capitol, ascended the roof, pulled down the State flag which was flying, and raised the two guidons of Companies E and H, 4th Mass. Cavalry, upon the building. Mr. Coffin adds, of himself, that he did not enter the city until the afternoon.

Mr. Coffin was not in the city at the time when the guidons were raised, and must have given here the report of some other person. But note particularly here that a 'State flag' is said to have been pulled down, and that act done, too, after the surrender had been made at Tree Hill, and probably after the more formal surrender in the City Hall at 8.15 a. m. Mr. Coffin states that he left Petersburg this forenoon arriving at City Point at noon, and from there proceeded on horseback via Broadway on the Appomattox, and Varina on the James, approaching the city by the New Market road, overtaking the 25th Corps (colored) on the outskirts of the city, and reaching the rebel capital at five o'clock in the afternoon. (Correspondence Boston Journal.)

Gen. Humphreys states, page 372, that the formal surrender of Richmond was made to Gen. Weitzel, at City Hall, at 8.15 a. m; and that Lieut. Johnston De Peyster, a young man eighteen years old, had carried a U. S. flag on the pommel of his saddle for several days, for the purpose of hoisting the same on the Capitol in Richmond, when the city should be captured; and he with the assistance of Capt. Loomis L. Langdon, U. S. Artillery, raised that flag on the Capitol this morning; the hour is not given.

---

[1] The Union entrenchments are meant, necessarily, for the Mayor on his way from the city had already passed Lieut. Prescott before meeting Capt. Stevens. — S. M. T.

Gen. Weitzel telegraphed to Secretary of War Stanton : " We entered Richmond at 8 a. m." In Gen. Grant's Memoirs, Vol. II. page 462, it is stated that Gen. Weitzel telegraphed to Gen. Grant that he took possession of Richmond " at about 8.15 o'clock."

The sum of the matter is undoubtedly this: Lieut. Prescott with his pickets had advanced to Gillie's Creek, and there had halted at the instance of three white cavalrymen. About 6, or 6.30, a. m. the Mayor of Richmond appears there, and would surrender the city to him, but Lieut. Prescott refers him to Gen. Weitzel, and the Mayor proceeds farther down the road from Richmond, to near Tree Hill, sets up his white flag — still flying an hour or two later when the Thirteenth comes up the road, as Lt. Col. Smith has informed the writer — and there surrenders the city to the U. S. military authorities. After the surrender the General and his staff, the Mayor, Capt. Stevens of the 4th Mass. Cavalry, and it matters not who else, forming, however, but a small party in all, turn and enter the city. As they enter the city, the General and his party turn to the right; while Lieut. Prescott is forced to separate from them by the heat and smoke and turns to the left, hurrying with all speed to the Capitol grounds by the more direct route, and arrives there at 7.20 a. m. A more formal surrender is now consummated at the City Hall at 8.15 a. m ; and Gen. Weitzel fixes upon the hour of 8 a. m. as the hour of entering the city.

Lieut. Prescott with his pickets reaches the Capitol grounds at 7.20 a. m., at which time no flag whatever is on the Capitol ; and soon after Lieut. Prescott's arrival young Forrester hoists his flag there — which must have been the old State flag, a modification of the United States flag. Lieut. Prescott is then called away. The cavalry commander now appears, and seeing Forrester's flag, and supposing it to be the " State flag which was flying," as if left flying by the retreating Confederates, hauls it down, and ties up somehow his two cavalry guidons. Next rides up Lieut. De Peyster, and taking little note of cavalry guidons, or not seeing them at all, goes upon the Capitol and hoists his flag, that he had carried on his saddle.

Each of these in turn appears to have hoisted flags, or what should pass as such ; each doing his work independently and unknown to all the rest, and each departing as soon as it was done — in order to give the next comer a fair chance undisturbed ; while the hoary old Capitol once more begins to feel good, at home, at peace with all the world, and smiles all over in the morning sunshine at the thought of better days a-coming ; and the colossal statue of Gen. Washington, near by in the grounds, rises in his stirrups, and sternly points out the course, down through old Chesterfield, taken by the Confederates in their hopeless retreat.

The whole thing seems to work like a play managed by a master hand, and is one of the best arranged affairs on record. Since Capt. Stevens with his cavalry did not enter the city, or hoist his two guidons on the Capitol, until after he had met the Mayor a mile and a half out of the city, the few scattered cavalrymen who first entered the city were probably men out of organization for the time being, adventurous men moving upon their own account, or else a few scouts or cavalry vedettes, preceding Capt. Stevens by a considerable time.

The facts put the Thirteenth ahead; and in at this point properly falls an incident of the occupation, that still further honors the old Thirteenth Regiment in the person of Capt. William J. Ladd, the first Union soldier to enter Richmond on the morning of April 3, 1865 : "It was the custom of Gen. Devens to have one of his staff officers on the picket line all night; and Capt. George A. Bruce of the Thirteenth was the staff officer of the picket in front of the 3d Division on the night of April 2d. Capt. Bruce sent for me, at that time at Gen. Devens' Hdqrs., to come out to the picket line where he was, about 3 a. m. on the morning of April 3d. I believed that Richmond was already evacuated by the Confederates; and soon after going out to the picket line, Major Joseph C. Brooks of the 9th Vt., myself, and a few other mounted officers and men, a party of about half a dozen in all, started by the most direct route for Richmond, and arrived there several hours before the Mayor surrendered the city to the Union military authorities. As Richmond came into view we began to run our horses to see who would be the first to reach the city. My horse outran the rest, and I finally entered the city without molestation or opposition; and entirely alone rode directly up the streets and entered the Capitol grounds through the street in rear of the Governor's house. Near the grounds was a bridge running across the street from an old hotel, the Ballard, I think. At this bridge was a squad of Confederate soldiers on the sidewalk. One of them drew an old navy cutlass, ran out and made a lunge at me as I came up. I drew my sabre, in defense, and charged upon him, when he retreated, and his companions merely laughed without assisting him or opposing me. I think he was intoxicated.

"I was in the Capitol grounds as early as 5.30 a. m. I saw no flag on the Capitol at that time. After looking about the grounds and vicinity for a few minutes, and realizing that I was alone in the city, I rode back toward Rocketts, and when near there met a white Union cavalryman — the first Union soldier I had seen in Richmond that morning. We tied our horses, took a skiff and rowed out to a rebel war ship in the James, and captured the two Confederate flags then flying upon her. I pulled down the larger flag, the cavalryman the smaller one, and we rolled them up and tied them to our saddles. These were the first and only flags of any kind — Federal or Confederate — that I saw in Richmond that morning. I still, 1887, have this flag. Soon after we secured these flags the vessel blew up." CAPT. LADD.

Capt. Ladd was at this time serving as a member of Gen. Devens' staff.

Our last campaign may be regarded as occupying one hour : one half of that time while the Thirteenth was massed in rear of the Cross-way curtain on the New Market road, this morning, and waiting for the Brigade to assemble, all preparing for an assault on the enemy's lines ; the other half in finding out and realizing that there was no enemy to assault — and cheers to match the situation.

April 4. Tues. Clear, warm.

"Richmond, Va., April 4, 1865.

Dear Mother, — Richmond is ours without the loss of a man. I had the honor of commanding the first Company of troops that entered the city (yesterday morning) — two hours in advance of any other troops.

(Signed) ROYAL B. PRESCOTT."

Thirteenth in Richmond, and quartered at the old St. Claire Hotel. Major Stoodley relieves Lt. Col. Smith as Division officer of the day, by special order of Maj. Gen. Devens — a very marked compliment — and has charge of the guards throughout the city. Quiet is now restored. The citizens say that Richmond has not been so quiet in two years past as it is to-day. The fires are out or confined. The citizens appear more pleased than otherwise with Northern occupation, and are for the most part very friendly.

Lt. Col. Normand Smith is appointed Acting Asst. Provost Marshal of the First District of Richmond — about the centre of the city — with his Hdqrs. in Picinis' Building on Broad st. between 8th and 9th streets.

The Hdqrs. of the Thirteenth is in the same building, and the flag of the Thirteenth — the National Stars and Stripes — floats from a window out over the street. A few of the rebel army officers, having openly and contemptuously scorned to pass along the sidewalk under this flag, are put under guard, and marched backward and forward under the flag, until they learn to treat the flag of the United States with due respect. Dangerous now, in Richmond, to turn off the sidewalk, with a sneer and a scowl, just before coming under that little flag ; and besides that, the act shows a very bad spirit, and small common sense, on the part of such persons as must needs receive the U. S. army rations or starve.

"Yesterday morning, April 3d, a lady came to me in Capitol Square, in deep distress because of the insolent behavior of her colored servants. She inquired the whereabout of Gen. E. O. C. Ord, saying that she was his relative, and desired him to give her a guard. (Gen. Ord was with Gen. Grant south of Petersburg.) I could render her no assistance then, but took her card promising to do what I could to assist her later. When I met Lt. Col. Smith that evening at supper, I related to him the incident, and received permission from him to call upon her. Lieut. Taggard requested to accompany me. We were most heartily welcomed. We served as a guard for the house, and met with no disturbance. The family were evidently wealthy and respectable, and resided in a large brick house on Grace st. The family name was Maben. This morning on being invited to take breakfast with the family, we were offered the best the house could afford : nothing but plain flour biscuit, crust coffee, and a little fried pork — no butter, no sugar, no milk, no sauce. The straits to which this family have been reduced differ but little from what the best families have suffered in all Richmond, the fearful deprivations of the poor passing all description." LIEUT. PRESCOTT.

President Lincoln is being cheered in the streets of Richmond! Such a whirligig is time. On learning of the fall of Richmond, President Abraham Lincoln, at City Point, embarks on a gunboat, with Admiral D. D. Porter, and steams rapidly up the James to Rocketts, a mile below the city, and is rowed thence in a small boat to the wharf in the city. Here he lands, and proceeds on foot to Gen. Weitzel's Hdqrs. — Jeff. Davis' mansion — in this wise: First, six sailors armed with carbines precede; next, President Lincoln leading his little son "Tad" by the hand, and accompanied by Admiral Porter and a few officers; next C. C. Coffin, army correspondent, then six more sailors armed with carbines — twenty persons in all.

Not much triumphal buncombe about that way of a " conqueror's entering the capital city of a great and conquered people;" but the route of this little procession, from one end to the other, literally roars with welcoming cheers and shouts, and in that welcome, most thoroughly genuine as it is, lies the grandest of human triumphal honors.

After obtaining a carriage, President Lincoln rode somewhat about the city. Great was the desire to see him on the part of the colored people. They crowded about the carriage by hundreds at one point where it stopped, and the little fellows unable to see through the press, climbed upon the top of the carriage, laid flat down and peered in upon the President. On looking up and seeing the row of woolly heads — little fuzzy reddish-black knobs, with the usual supply of white from teeth and eyes — festooning the front of the carriage, the President settled back in the carriage and laughed almost immoderately in spite of himself.

April 5. Wed. Pleasant, rather cloudy. The Thirteenth enjoys its visit to Richmond very much indeed. Major Miller, 139th N. Y., officer of the day, relieving Major Stoodley. Capt. M. T. Betton, with his 81st N. Y., has charge of Libby Prison and Castle Thunder; where he receives cordially, and with a becoming, quiet, dignified smile of genuine welcome; and places in their vile and filthy lofts all Confederate soldiers and officers found in Richmond. They indulge in the experience of — "Now you know how it is yourself." The tables are turned; but are not so outrageously empty as our poor boys have always found them in this same Libby. These Confederates are now supplied with full U. S. army rations well cooked and served.

The defensive works around Richmond consist of a circle of field forts, seventeen in number, mounting about three hundred heavy guns, and placed from one to two miles out from the city. No. 1 is down on the James river, east side, a little below Peyton's Creek, two miles south of the city; No. 2 on the Osborne pike; No. 3 on the Williamsburg road; and thence the line of them runs around the city, by the east, north and west, to No. 17, near Ward's Race-course, on the west side of the James, a mile below Manchester, on the Richmond and Petersburg turnpike.

Outside of this circle of forts, in an irregular belt, nearly two miles in width, run various lines of interlacing defenses, with rifle-trenches and small redoubts. A very strong system of fortifications. 'Not a knoll for miles around but mounts a cannon. Every avenue of approach is strongly fortified, and an immense number of cannon has fallen into our hands.'

Jeff. Davis, down at Danville to-day, sets up the Confederate nine pins, by proclamation — a tremendous foundation, that! As Gen. Lee's army is now so near, and yet so far, and the Confederate capital is in Union hands; Jefferson's proclamation, so long, limber and furry, with now and then a bristle, much — and some may think he, likewise — much resembles a tail with the cat cut off.

"Our soldiers are glutted with Confederate money. Thousands of dollars of it were found, and it is as common as dirt. The baggage of the Thirteenth will be brought up from our Fort Harrison camp this morning. I saw Libby Prison yesterday, April 4th, and the sufferings of our men there have not been one whit exaggerated. I saw there the hole where the rebels planted the mine of many tons of gunpowder to blow all the prisoners to atoms. Richmond contains about 40,000 inhabitants. Our soldiers here have behaved like gentlemen, I have not heard a word of complaint concerning them. The Richmond ladies will not pass under the United States flag, if they can help it, but turn into the middle of the street." LIEUT. PRESCOTT, April 5, 1865.

"Head-Quarters U. S. Forces,
Richmond, Va., April 5, 1865.

"By command of Major General Godfrey Weitzel the following rules, regulations and orders are established for the government of the city of Richmond, and the preservation of public peace and order.

Par. IV. — Extract.
District Provost Marshals.
For the First District,

"Lieut. Col. Normand Smith, commanding Thirteenth New Hampshire Volunteers.

G. F. SHEPLEY,
Brig. Gen. U. S. Vols.,
Military Governor of Richmond."

April 6. Thurs. Very pleasant. Reg. doing provost duty. A guard from the Reg. protecting the house and family of Gen. Lee; and other squads of its men are scattered, as guards and patrols, all over the city.

A Confederate officer, arrested for wrong enthusiasm, claims immunity on the ground that he is re-constructed all over; and that the "Confed-(hic)-rebcy has done goned to th-(hic)under." And he is sent carefully to his home in a carriage, the first, or among the first of the re-constructed in Richmond. His method, however, places him in the minority.

**April 7. Fri.** Rainy. Reg. in Richmond, on provost duty. President Lincoln again visits Richmond, with Mrs. Lincoln, Vice President Johnson, and a large party.

It is enough to melt a heart of stone to look over this once beautiful and delightful city, the home of many of the best people the world ever knew. Now battered, burned, blackened, marred, neglected, blown to pieces, torn up and torn down, rent and plowed; its good people starved, despoiled, beggared, half murdered, sick, hungry, destitute, discouraged and humiliated to the last degree ; and now coming, in the flood tide of their unspeakable misfortunes, to the United States authorities for food, medicine, clothing, care and protection. Thank God, they go not empty away!

Gen. Grant has between twenty and thirty thousand rebel prisoners at City Point — several acres of them.

**April 8. Sat.** Cool, windy, very warm at noon. Reg. in the city engaged in provost duty. The destitution here is appalling, and sickness rapidly follows the half starvation. Medical supplies and Government rations are distributed free, and almost without limit; and to all classes and colors, rich and poor alike. A procession, made up exclusively of citizens, gathered in honor of deliverance, marches through the principal streets ; a gay and stirring affair, with music, banners, flags, mottoes, and cheers, ad libitum — ad infinitum.

Gen. Devens this afternoon reviews the 3d Div. of the 24th Corps at 2 p. m. — 17 regiments, a corps of sharp-shooters, 5 batteries — in front of Jeff. Davis' mansion, now Gen. Weitzel's Hdqrs. The first review of Federal troops here. The 10th, 12th and 13th N. H. Regiments are in the line. About 12,000 troops present. One soldier of the Thirteenth writes : "All Richmond turned out to see it." Another : "We marched all over the city of Richmond." Another : "The citizens said they thought we had a 'master heap of cannon in the city.'"

**April 9. Sun.** Fine, a little rain. Reg. in the city, and inspected this morning in the Capitol grounds, surrounded by an immense collection of the citizens and people — a curious, motley, staring, gaping crowd.

It is proposed by way of a joke that a goodly number of these knocked-up Confederate bonds and bank bills, thousands upon thousands of 'dollars' of which are now being kicked and wind-blown about the streets of Richmond, like so many scraps of waste paper, be put up in packages and sent up North to notorious copperheads and rebel sympathizers, with the request that they cash them at sight at their face value, and that the proceeds be applied to assisting, feeding and educating the ex-slaves ; the copperheads ought to do something for their fellow countrymen.

After Aug. 28, 1864, there came into the lines of the 13th, and near by, over five hundred rebel deserters, and probably as many more uncounted by the person who tried to keep the account of them.

Gen. Lee surrenders the Army of Northern Virginia to Gen. Grant. The parole includes 28,356 officers and men — the rest are scattered everywhere. News of the surrender is received to-night. The troops cheer. The negroes are wild with delight. Hundreds of the citizens express their satisfaction at the result, but as a rule the sympathies of the citizens are with Gen. Lee's army, and most naturally.

April 10. Mon. Rainy. Reg. in the city. Dr. J. C. Emory joins the Thirteenth. A salute of 100 guns is fired in the Capitol grounds this morning in honor of Gen. Grant's final victory : " The capture of Gen. Lee's army, and the surrender of all Virginia." The citizens begin to take the oath of allegiance, and many are very anxious so to do.

A Provost Marshal's office is a mixed-up affair — the city dumping-ground. Here is a sample morning job: A party of a dozen or more citizens come in to take the oath of allegiance ; soldiers want passes to go into the country for duty as guards ; rows in the street to be quieted ; landlord and tenant differences (on account of the change in the currency) to be settled offhand ; liquor stores to be closed ; houses of ill repute to be shut up ; the inmates to be fed ; stolen goods to be found ; a stolen mule found, an order wanted by the owner to take it ; sentences to be passed on persons arrested for sundry misdemeanors ; guards to mount ; a man wants some non-paying tenants ejected ; a poor woman appears begging for something for her starving children to eat ; some one has thrown a dead negro baby into a back yard, and it must be buried at once ; paroled Confederate officers asking for rations ; Confederate soldiers to be sent with suitable orders to Libby ; man wants a guard to protect his property (more probably he is afraid of his " neeg-urs," and wants his head protected) ; Northern visitors want to be escorted to all " points of interest " at once ; a bevy of beautiful young women (and Virginia girls are passing beautiful) come in asking for a guard for their houses, and to see what sort of creatures these Yankees are ; a permit to sell goods (and bads) wanted by a man-looking thing from Judea, via New York, and mostly nose ; fifty-one negroes, with one hundred and two complaints ; several persons with quarrels to be settled ; all callers impatient with waiting — and all wanting to be attended to first — and this pile is about half the deposit ; while the office is packed and jammed with people half the time, and occasionally smelling like the Black Hole in Calcutta.

There is an awful state of society in Virginia now. The negroes are almost in open insurrection, idle, indolent and insolent. There are numerous cases where the wives of absent Southern soldiers, and the wives of negroes also, have thought their husbands dead, and have married again, some having children by this second marriage. The original Benedict now turns up, blue ; and Enoch Arden is played again, with peace or with war.

Wm. H. Spiller of Company C was one of the very few men of the Thirteenth who went with Gen. Ord's Flying Corps sent to head off Gen. Lee in the Appomattox valley. He states : " The column had a plenty of marching and some hard fighting. I was very tired on the night of April 1st, having been in the saddle for a large part of three days in succession, but slept soundly through the fearful cannonade that pounded all that night upon Gen. Lee's works surrounding Petersburg. About daylight on the morning of April 2d an advance was made all along our front, on the rebel works. Gen. Gibbon, commanding the 24th Corps contingent, had two very serious fights, first he captured Fort Alexander with a rush, but his first attack upon Fort Gregg was repulsed; but he finally took it with thirty or forty of its brave defenders, some one hundred and fifty of them having been killed or wounded. Gen. Gibbon lost about 500 men that morning. Our troops now held the outer line of the Confederate works.

"On the morning of April 3d I saw our troops preceded by skirmishers advance upon the Confederate inner line — but the enemy had fled. We expected a triumphal entry into Petersburg; but Gen. Grant was in command, and there was to be no picnic so long as Gen. Lee's army held together. The advance was stopped, breakfast was eaten, and an hour later the chase commenced, Gen. Lee having the start by several hours. Gen. Ord's column advanced along the Southside Railroad, and Gen. Meade south of the river, while Gen. Lee was north of the river.

"I was at this time serving as Orderly to Brev. Brig. Gen. Theodore Read, Asst. Adjt. General Army of the James. The first incident, that I recall, of this day's march, occurred about noon : Gen. Ord and staff had left the head of the column, and had ridden into a grove of pines by the roadside to rest, and allow the troops to pass ; as was his custom while on the march, in order, I presume, to see for himself that they kept well closed up. Gen. Ord and staff formed one group, we orderlies another, and the cavalry escort a third — all quite close together. All were dismounted. Soon cheering was heard from far down the line, and rapidly coming nearer and louder, when Gen. Ord said : 'Gen. Grant must be coming. Gentlemen mount, and give the General three cheers!' All mounted, and a few minutes later Gen. Grant and staff rode into the grove. Three cheers were given him with a will; Gen. Grant acknowledged the salute, talked a moment with Gen. Ord, and then turned to one of his staff and asked him to read a dispatch — it was from Gen. Weitzel announcing the fall and his occupation of Richmond! We instantly made the woods ring with our hurrahs; the troops now marching past caught up the glorious news, passed it along, and we could hear their loud cheers pass to right and left, ringing up and down the line, until the sounds were lost in the distance.

After hearty congratulations had passed between the parties, Gen. Grant took his leave. When Gen. Grant rode out of the grove into the road, a baggage wagon was going by, from the rear end of which a turkey had flopped out, and was fluttering and struggling along, with one of its legs fastened to a rope that hung from the ribs of the wagon. As Gen. Grant rode past he smiled, and jocularly remarked to the men on the wagon : 'Boys, everything is lovely — but your goose hangs low.'

"A few moments after this Gen. Ord and staff mounted, and started on a gallop toward the head of the column.

"During these rides from the rear to the head of the column when on the march, we used (when possible) to take to the fields and woods along near the road so as not to bother the troops with dust or crowding, and to save time. We had to jump fences and ditches, dodge trees and duck under low hanging branches. I rode a little black Kentucky mare, captured from a rebel Major, near Fort Darling, by Gen. Read, that was equal to any emergency — she was a 'daisy' and could run like a deer.

"We halted at Nottaway Court House for about two hours to rest, and I wandered down the street on a foraging expedition. I was about to open the door of a small building on my left, apparently unoccupied, when I saw Gen. Grant sitting alone, on the piazza of a house on the opposite side of the street. His staff were in the house, their orderlies and horses at the rear; but there sat the grand hero Grant, the commander of all our armies, and at that hour at the head of a victorious one, close upon the heels of an enemy, and in one of the most exciting pursuits known in modern warfare, quietly smoking his cigar as usual, and apparently as unconcerned as any private in the ranks. I can never think of Gen. Grant without developing this picture, all as vivid as I saw it then. I saluted him, he recognized it, and then I quietly withdrew.

"On the evening of April 5th we reached Burkesville, and there encamped for the night. The next morning at an early hour I called Gen. Read, and he made preparations to perform a duty assigned him the previous evening by Gen. Ord; and that was to take a small body of about 500 infantry and cavalry, and proceed with dispatch towards Farmville, either to cut off Gen. Lee's retreat in that direction, or, if too late for that, to save the bridge for our pursuit. As Gen. Read mounted his horse to depart upon this expedition, I asked him if I was to go also, and he replied : ' No — you follow with Head-quarters.' Little did I think, as he rode off, that that would be the last time I should ever see him.

"We moved an hour or so later, and were met by the rumor that Gen. Read had been killed, and his force all captured or killed. I hurried forward to the spot where the engagement took place, and there met an old colored man, a slave on the plantation where the fight occurred, and he told me the story of the fight as he saw it. He said that Gen. Read attacked the enemy very gallantly — ' but dar was a heap mo' rebels dan of de Yankees.' Gen. Read had struck the advance brigade of Gen. Lee's army. He fell while at the head of his men, and being outnumbered and overpowered, those who were left of them had no recourse but to surrender. The old colored man told me where the General's body was. He said that the rebels stripped the body; and I heard afterwards, from the parties who removed the body, that such was the fact. Some of Gen. Ord's staff came up, and the body was sent at once to City Point. I felt very sad at the General's death, for I had been with him a year, and he had always treated me with great kindness and courtesy.

"I recently (Nov. 4, 1887) met John Atkins, who was Orderly Sergeant in the battalion of cavalry stationed at Gen. Ord's Hdqrs., and who was taken prisoner at the time Gen. Read was killed. Atkins says: ' Gen. Read was shot while making a speech to his troops. His body fell into the rebels' hands, and they stripped the body of everything, as also the body of Col. Washburne, who was killed a few minutes after Gen. Read fell. They also stripped me (Atkins) of all I had on me except my shirt and drawers, and on the night of my capture by them I nearly froze in the chilly air.'

"Gen. Read was brave to rashness. One afternoon, just before sunset, a few days before the Mine explosion, at Petersburg, he mounted his large white horse, lighted a cigar, rode out to, and up on the top of the Union earth-works, and sat there smoking for several minutes, oblivious of both shells and bullets, and I stood watching him (at some distance to the rear), fearing that he would be shot, and indignant at such a risk. He seemed to feel that he was going to be killed, and courted death at every chance. He had been married but a short time before he was killed, and I think he left his bride at City Point, when he started upon this, his last campaign.

"After the death of Gen. Read, I was ordered to join Gen. Ord's private orderlies, as one of them, and we proceeded, as soon as troops enough came up, to drive the rebels from our front. We moved with great rapidity during the whole pursuit, and marched nearly all of the night of April 8th. On the forenoon of April 9th we maintained a rapid pace. Evidences of Gen. Sheridan's work were plenty all along the road. I rode up to one abandoned rebel caisson, behind which lay a dead Confederate officer, and upon opening the ammunition chest found a Sharps carbine, which I now have, 1887. It had probably been captured from our cavalry.

"As we were going forward at a good pace on April 9th, suddenly Gen. Custer came riding up to Gen. Ord in great haste, and pointing with his sword off a little to our front and right, said in a kind of triumphant shout : ' Go in, General, and give it to them ; General Sheridan has got them sure ! ' and wheeling his horse, was off again to the front like a flash of light. Gen. Ord instantly hurried staff officers and orderlies to different parts of the column ; and in an incredibly short period of time solid ranks of our infantry were forming in rear of our line of dismounted cavalry. When all was ready, Gen. Sheridan withdrew his cavalrymen, and there stood the Veterans of the old Eighteenth Corps, now 24th Corps, and the gleam of their sharp bayonets made the now discouraged and beaten Army of Northern Virginia ' Stop, short, — never to go again.'

"The day was fine, and that afternoon this famous Confederate army was massed in a large field, with woods on either side of it, on a hillside north and east of Appomattox, while our army lay upon the hills overlooking, and to the south and west of the place. Generals Ord and Gibbon rode down to the McLean house, where the surrender was made. While the surrender was taking place, the officers and men on our side — not knowing what was going on — commenced talking of the situation, and were speculating how long it would take to clean the rebel army out just as it now lay, and wondering what was coming next. For an hour or so everything was quiet; then suddenly a long, loud shout went up, which was quickly echoed from hill to hill by our exultant troops, and several bands began to play; but in a few moments this all ceased and quiet reigned again. Whether this cessation of outward jubilation was from a spontaneous desire on the part of our men to show respect and pity for their fallen but brave foe, or was caused by an order from Gen. Grant, I know not.

"The rest of that eventful Sunday afternoon was passed in quiet; in congratulations, letter writing, telegraphing and in sending dispatches and accounts of this Last Campaign.

"After the many years of war it seems reasonable that the Northern army should have gone nearly wild with joy — but we did not. I remember how our men sat there on the high hillside, after the surrender was made known to us, and looking over where the remnant of Gen. Lee's army was lying, their artillery and teams parked for the last time; I remember how we sat there and pitied, and sympathized with those courageous Southern men, who had fought for four long and dreary years all so stubbornly, so bravely and so well, and now whipped, beaten, completely used up, were fully at our mercy — it was pitiful, sad, hard, and seemed to us altogether too bad.

"After musing upon, and talking of the situation for a time, I rode down to the McLean house. I saw quite a number of Confederate officers there, and among them Gen. Pickett. I regarded him rather the most of all, because, no matter where our Division (Getty's) was — at Fredericksburg, Suffolk, Cold Harbor, or at any other place — it was always Gen. Pickett's Division of Gen. Longstreet's Corps that confronted us.

"I had but little time to look about, for Gen. Grant at once ordered Gen. Ord to Richmond, to take command of the Department. Starting immediately we reached Richmond on Wednesday April 12th, and took up our quarters in Jeff. Davis' house; where I slept that night on a mattress, for the first time in three years. I remained as a private Orderly for Gen. Ord until mustered out with the Thirteenth in June 1865. Gen. Porter's article, 'Grant's Last Campaign,' published in the November *Century*, 1887, which I have read since writing the above, confirms my statements in many particulars."   WM. H. SPILLER, Company C.

**April 11. Tues.** Cloudy, misty, rainy. Reg. still doing provost guard duty in Richmond. While Richmond is as quiet, and possibly much stiller than most New England cities, suddenly there bursts from Capitol Square a salute of 200, guns shaking the city, and making the rebel element turn pale. These tremendous salvos of artillery are repeated in every military Department, post and arsenal, within the authority of the United States, all over land and sea, in honor of Gen. Grant's recent victories.

A white scamp whom the Provost Marshal cannot make behave himself is punished by having his head, face, neck and hands smeared all over with molasses, then he is tied to a post in the public square, while the flies eat off the molasses. He is a sight to behold — but it cures him; and certainly such punishment does him no bodily harm.

April 12. Wed. Cloudy, rainy. Reg. doing provost duty in the city. Capt. M. T. Betton in command of the remnant of the 81st N. Y. still has charge of Libby Prison, and has had within it nearly 3,000 rebel soldiers as prisoners; all taken in and about the city, and held awaiting parole. These are mostly stragglers, 'beats' and skulkers. Gen. Lee's best troops stuck to him like men, in the retreat.

Praise of Gen. Lee may be regarded by some persons as out of place here, but simple justice wrongs no man. This afternoon, with a few members of his staff, he rides on horseback into Richmond, and goes undisturbed and unmolested to his house, where his family await him. A special guard, a part from the Thirteenth, has protected his property and family ever since we have been in the city.

He appears dispirited — a disappointed man; but the great chieftain though beaten, preserves all his dignity. The weather is wet, cloudy, gloomy, and the burned, blackened, battered and dirty city necessarily appears to him as in its worst estate. However, under no form of procession, escort, or parade could Gen. Lee have returned to Richmond and to his home, with such exquisite dignity, good taste, and manly honor, as in this way that he does; his great army lost, his cause gone forever, himself under a military parole; now a Southern gentleman and a private citizen, though the first citizen of Virginia, he simply and quietly rides from his camp to his home with a few of his friends.

Peace is now reasonably assured, and the Union army agrees profoundly with the Confederates in the feeling that the war is practically over, though collisions farther south may still occur; and ninety-nine out of every hundred soldiers, on both sides, are brimful and running over with unspeakable gladness, that this huge and terrible war is ended. This is unreserved, free and common remark. Surely Virginia now stands free; and the Southern army confronting Gen. Sherman and still others farther south must soon furl their banners.

## XI.

### CLOSE OF THE WAR — PEACE.

April 13. Thurs. Rainy. Thirteenth moves from the city to Confederate Battery Number Ten, and bivouacs for the night. This Battery is on the inner line of the rebel earth-works, on the north side of the city, on Deep Run turnpike, and beyond Camp Lee (Confederate). Up to this time the Reg. has been quartered in the city, at the old St. Claire Hotel — quarters dingy and dirty.

The better element in Gen. Lee's army, all who were able so to do, clung to his fortunes to the last. But it contained a class gathered from the worst, and which grew still worse when free from all social and civil-law restraints. They are numerous now in Richmond as laggards, skulkers and stragglers, and we have seen enough of them : " Men with sallow, dirt-begrimed faces ; dull, fishy eyes ; long, yellow, uncombed hair ; meaningless expression of countenance ; clad in rags ; at home in filth ; " huddled together about the Provost Marshal's offices. Poor white trash in very fact ; descendants of England's outlaws and criminals deported to her American colonies, and always the rangers and curse of Southern mountain, forest and swamp.

April 14. Fri. Clear, warm. Hdqrs. of the Thirteenth moved from St. Claire Hotel at 5.30 a. m. to the camp near Battery No. 10 ; then the Thirteenth goes into the Hospital Barracks at Camp Lee, two miles north of the city, on the Fair grounds ; but finding a most populous army of gray-backs in possession — and which did not retreat with Gen. Lee's army, but waited here for United States rations — the officers decide that any open ground is far preferable to a house with such hosts for entertainers, and we therefore move out, speedily, and bivouac near by, on the road-side. We furnish numerous guards for houses on the outskirts of the city.

Confederate Gen. Johnston, in North Carolina, sends a flag of truce to Gen. Sherman, upon an errand of surrender or parley, and hostilities between their two armies are suspended.

The Flag of Fort Sumter hauled down Sunday April 14, 1861, is again hoisted to-day, April 14, 1865 ; also on the same eventful Sunday in 1861, President Lincoln himself penned the proclamation calling 75,000 militia men into service for three months.

This night about ten o'clock, Abraham Lincoln, President of the United States, was assassinated by J. Wilkes Booth, with a pistol, in Ford's Theatre, Washington, D. C.

**April 15. Sat.** Forenoon very rainy, afternoon clear. Thirteenth still in bivouac by the roadside near Camp Lee. On the whole we have been enjoying our Provost duty in the city, and would prefer to continue it. One Brigade of our Division is now in Manchester, three miles from Richmond; one on the road to Fort Harrison, three miles out; and ours here north of the city, two miles out. Col. Mosby, the guerilla chief, and his band are reported to be near Richmond. The Thirteenth during to-day temporarily occupies the old rebel barracks at Camp Lee, as they afford a better protection from the storm, but they are exceedingly dirty, and unfit for use. The men protect themselves against the numberless vermin by applying to their clothing the medical mercurial preparations, even pulverizing the 'blue pill' and using that — the mercury an absolutely efficacious protection.

A heavy picket line is sent to-night to the main line of the old Confederate earth-works, and cavalry vedettes farther out.

A member of our Band writes: "Band in the city. Officers are too fond of music. They want us to blow, blow, blow."

**April 16. Sun.** Very pleasant. Thirteenth moves about half a mile from Camp Lee, to Robinson's grove, on Grove Street leading toward Hollywood Cemetery, and about one mile from the city.

We had just staked off ground for a camp, and pitched a few tents at the grove, this afternoon, when orders came for us to march into Richmond. We march in at 6 p. m., and are quartered in the City Hall. The officers of the Thirteenth take up quarters in the Council Chambers. The city guard is increased by 700 men as a precautionary measure. Col. Mosby is expected to attempt a raid into Richmond. The paroled officers and men who have come in from Gen. Lee's disbanded army far outnumber all the Union troops in the city, and mischief is feared. The most, however, are orderly.

The rebel officers go about in full Confederate army uniform, many of them with much swagger and importance of manner. The result is a closer watching and less freedom. The first overt act will precipitate a fearful riot, in which offenders will enjoy but short respite, for the Union soldiers are roused to the utmost stretch of indignation by the assassination of President Lincoln, for which they instinctively hold the Confederacy in some way responsible.

The writer was in Boston in April 1865, and finds among his notes an item or two that may not be out of place here, as glimpses of the day:

**April 3d.** Boston very excited at the news of the fall of Richmond, and the hasty retreat of Gen. Lee's army; and the fever of excitement increases hour by hour as Gen. Grant chases the swift fugitives up the Appomattox valley.

**April 10th.** All places of business closed at noon, and the day and night given over to one vast, grand jubilee. Processions marched, bands played, cannon roared, people shouted, steam whistles blew, bells rang — until the din became a nuisance, and at night the entire city was a brilliant blaze of illumination.

April 15th. A paper published about daylight gave the news of the murder of President Lincoln; and copies of the paper sold faster than they could be handed out. Boston quickly put on the deepest mourning. As the news flew through the city, it seemed as if the tremor and shudder, running through the minds of the people, could be felt in the very air and surroundings, so deep and terrible was it. The principal streets were soon an endless succession of black-bordered flags, festoons and drapings, and long floating streamers in black and white.

Amid the profusion of its drapings, the front of the Boston Theatre presented a large white sheet, with these words in great black letters — from Shakespeare, Macbeth, Act 1, Scene VII.:

> He "Hath borne his faculties so meek, hath been
> So clear in his great office, that his virtues
> Will plead, like angels trumpet-tongued, against
> The deep damnation of his taking off."

Sunday April 16th. Attended church in the Old South. Dr. Manning came into the pulpit, as usual, wearing the black gown of his service. He opened a book and was about to read, when glancing up he saw no emblem of mourning whatever in the church; nothing to relieve the dead uni-color of the whiting finish. He laid down the book, and in the most deliberate and dignified manner unclasped the large gown at the neck, and then swung it gracefully, broad over the whole pulpit, threw his white handkerchief upon it, and again taking his book proceeded with the service. Possibly a more impressive scene never took place in the Old South church; and rarely a scene when man, manner, time, place, circumstance and act so aptly combined for effect. — S. M. T.

April 17. Mon. Pleasant, clear. Reg. remains in quarters in City Hall during the day. Among the citizens this is a season of stupid rest. There is no business; everything is at a dead stand-still; few have any money; there is nothing to do; and many spend the most of their time sitting on the door-steps, and discussing the past, the present and the future. To a large number all is equally blank and promiseless; choking down whatever rising pride they may feel, they form an endless procession to and from the places where U. S. army rations are distributed.

April 18. Tues. Clear. Reg. returns from the city at 1 p. m., and fits up a permanent camp, at Robinson's grove on the ground we staked off last Sunday. Just before arriving in camp we are thoroughly wet in a shower. We are here ordered to make use of unoccupied sheds, etc., and to pick up other suitable lumber, wherever it may be found; and we make for ourselves roomy and comfortable huts, with shelter tents for roofs. We are in an oak grove, about half way between the city limits and the inner line of rebel earth-works, where we have stationed a strong line of pickets.

Col. Ripley goes home on fifteen days' leave, and Col. Nichols assumes command of our 1st Brigade.

April 19. Wed. Pleasant, a very warm afternoon. Reg. at work on new camp at Robinson's grove. The assassination of President Lincoln spreads a gloom over the Union army, as well as over the entire North. The citizens of Richmond for the most part also feel very badly about it. All honorable men condemn it. The people here are very severe upon Jeff. Davis. Gen. Lee keeps at his house, closely shut in. Several of our men have been poisoned since we came into the city. Minute guns fired in Richmond during the funeral of President Lincoln. Duties suspended as far as possible.

April 20. Thurs. Pleasant a. m., showery p. m. Reg. in camp. All food supplies are high in price. Some of the people have lived on corn bread and water, month in and month out. Mr. Robinson, the wealthy owner of this grove, states that he has not had coffee, for use in his family, half a dozen times in these last two years.

April 21. Fri. Very warm. Regular monthly inspection by Capt. Curtis of the Thirteenth, acting Asst. Adjt. General on the staff of our 1st Brigade. The Thirteenth was sent on picket to the outer lines yesterday, returning to camp about 10 a. m. to-day.

Col. Mosby, to-day, holds a formal review of his rebel guerilla band of about 600 men; tells them that disbanding is preferable to surrender; and simply saying: "I am no longer your commander,"—he and they depart, no one knows whither. He remained in hiding until Gen. Grant succeeded in sending him word that he might avail himself of the privileges of parole extended to the soldiers of Gen. Lee's army.

April 22. Sat. Cloudy, cold. Reg. in camp. Richmond is very quiet, but the unstable element is immense. The larger number appear, however, to be exceeding glad that the war is over, and are peaceful and quiet. They all need watching though, for the paroled soldiers by this time outnumber three times over all our white troops hereabout, on duty as provost guard.

April 23. Sun. Windy, chilly. Reg. in camp. The Mayor of Nashua, H. T. Morrill and other guests of the Thirteenth, visit Fort Harrison, and other points on the line, in company with Quarter-master Morrison, Adjutant Taggard, Lieut. Prescott and other officers of our Regiment. Gen. Lee's paroled troops have been passing our camp all day; and Falstaff's nondescripts were beaus, fops and dandies to these dirty, ragged, sour, whitey-yellow, thin, haggard, dejected creatures. The poor fellows have had a hard time of it. Our soldiers entertain for them a genuine sympathy, and extend to them a great many kindly courtesies.

April 24. Mon. Clear. Reg. in camp. There is no Brigade stationed in the city now. Our 1st Brigade 3d Div. 24th Corps is about one mile out, on the Fredericksburg road; the 2d is in Manchester about one mile from Richmond; the 3d is scattered to various points around the city, sending in detachments every day for Provost duty.

April 25. Tues. Very warm. Thirteenth called at 4.30 a. m., leaves camp at 6 a. m., and with the 3d Division of the 24th Corps, assembling from the various Brigade camps around the city, receives the other two Divisions — 1st and 2d — of the same Corps on Broad Street in Richmond. They arrive and march into the city about noon to-day. The reception lasts for several hours, while arms are presented, colors dipped, cheer follows cheer, crowds gather and stare, and negroes shout. After the reception, the whole Corps moves together to a new camp in Manchester, about two miles from Richmond, on the Broad Rock road, near the race-course.

We venture to say that no corps of the army will enjoy a more enthusiastic reception than these men who marched to the left with Gen. Ord. These 1st and 2d Divisions of the 24th Corps constituted a part of Gen. Ord's 'Flying Column,' which marched from Fort Harrison March 25th, to head off the retreating columns of Gen. Lee's army, accomplishing the feat at Appomattox Court House. In their final rush in that most exciting chase, they marched April 6th, 18 miles ; 7th, 22 miles ; 8th, 27 miles ; 9th, 37 miles.

On April 9th Gen. Sheridan had thrown a thin line of cavalry across Gen. Lee's route of retreat, and just as these men of the 24th Corps swept around into line of battle in rear of the cavalry, Gen. Lee was about to continue his retreat. Our troops had not an hour to spare. As Gen. Lee's advance guard approached the cavalry vedettes, they withdrew from before his front ' as a curtain is drawn aside,' revealing the long lines of Gen. Ord's infantry, which now no present rebel power could pass, and the surrender immediately followed. Surgeon Richardson of the Thirteenth had charge of the field Hospital, and he states that ten hundred and sixty wounded men, belonging to these two Divisions and the Flying Corps, passed through his hands during the expedition, to say nothing of the killed, and of the men who fell out, used up by the forced march.

In returning to Richmond the two Divisions marched by way of Lynchburg, a distance of 120 miles, and arrive exceedingly dusty, bronzed, dirty and ragged. A few days in camp, however, will repair all that; and greetings are now cordial and congratulatory beyond description. The 24th Corps is to perform the agreeable office of 'mine host,' and receive in Richmond all the visiting corps, as they march through the city on their way to Washington.

The homeward march, along Virginia's chief thoroughfares, of these two or three hundred thousands of dusty, bronzed and war-worn Veterans, moving in huge, solid masses from their two thousand and more of battle-fields, is no inconspicuous scene in the large, grand moving panorama of this eventful month of April. While hasting away, to every town and hamlet in the South, there spreads the constantly dividing stream of the beaten, dispirited and unfortunate men in gray ; organized, unorganized, troops, bands, companies, squads, twos, singly, they pass off the broad stage of their awful drama — and disappear.

April 26. Wed. Warm, clear. Thirteenth fitting up a camp two miles southwest of Manchester, on the Broad Rock road, near the race-course, and the rebel Battery No. 16, a little west of the Petersburg turnpike. A very pleasant camp in shelter tents pitched on an open, grassy plain. The ground, however, is a trifle low and damp. Dry weather will soon remedy that difficulty.

Sundry officers of the Thirteenth call, in a friendly way, upon the family of Mr. Lipscomb, a farmer living near our camp, and his daughter-in-law, to entertain the visitors, regales them with music on the piano, and sings a few secession songs — 'Bonnie Blue Flag,' 'Farewell to the Star Spangled Banner,' and others. Major Stoodley, as well as the others, fails to appreciate this kind of entertainment, and all the officers leave the house. Now, of course, the Confederacy is a mere matter of history, but it is hard for the people to realize that fact. We note this circumstance as a mere indication of the popular feeling.

General Joseph E. Johnston to-day, at Durham's Station, North Carolina, surrenders, to General W. T. Sherman, his army numbering about 30,000 men.

April 27. Thurs. Pleasant. Thirteenth in new camp. The ladies of Richmond give an entertainment for the city's poor. Tickets $2.00. Tableaux are the chief feature. The 2d Brigade Band — formerly Thirteenth — furnishes the music for the occasion. A large building has been fitted up for homeless negroes, hundreds of whom are flocking into the city. They find no employment, and are soon in a destitute and starving condition. A hungry negro is apparently as void of delicate taste as an animal; he will eat almost anything that is eatable, and not wince at taste, condition or appearances. The blacks will fatten where white people would starve.

April 28. Fri. Pleasant. Thirteenth in camp. After the excitement of the last six weeks, this camp life falls exceeding quiet, monotonous, stale and flat. Our troops are scattered all through the country, as guards to protect property and life and to preserve order.

It cannot be denied, the evidences are too exact and too numerous, that a deep-seated and ever-abiding dread pervades the whole ex-slaveholding class — with scarcely an exception — that somehow, in the darkness of night or in the light of open day, they know not when or how, the ex-slaves will avenge their wrongs, will resent their stripes, will claim their rights so long denied, and may plunder, destroy, burn, maim or assassinate. The ability resides in this now mixed race — and the half white are the worst — to do an incalculable amount of mischief. Will they strike? Will they not strike? Where? When? How? These are the fear-born questions, and common talk everywhere about here among the white people.

April 29. Sat. Rainy, windy and fair. Thirteenth in camp.

April 30. Sun. Pleasant. Showers last night, and very much needed. Thirteenth in camp, and mustered for pay at 9 a. m. Dress-parade at evening. The boys have a cool way of quieting the yarn-spinner. If any story does not meet their approval, they express their opinion, at the close of it, by remarking sarcastically: "Then the Band played — and then the Thirteenth cheered!"

**May 1. Mon.** Clear, cold. Thirteenth in camp. Capt. Betton returns to the Thirteenth, from his command of the 81st N. Y. and charge of Libby prison. By orders of Gen. Devens, Capt. Betton has sent to Gov. Andrew of Massachusetts the lock and key of the outer door of Libby, and they are preserved in the State House, Boston.

News received that the War Department has issued an order relating to the reduction of the Volunteer army. The men are very jubilant at the prospect of a speedy return to their homes.

**May 2. Tues.** Very cold and chilly. Thirteenth in camp. Company drill in afternoon and a Dress-parade. We have recently had hundreds of evidences of what has been previously noted in these pages, viz : the Southern people are the more religious : talk, ceremony, devotion, prayerfulness and all that ; the Northern people the more Christian : kindly work and sympathy, practical help, human nature Christianized.

**May 3. Wed.** Clear, cold. Thirteenth in camp. These are the days when great mails go North — everybody writing letters.

**May 4. Thurs.** Windy, rainy and clear. Reg. in camp. A disgusted teamster appears to the commander of the Thirteenth, and wants to go back to the ranks. He says he has been kicked, by the mules, upon every part of his body excepting one spot about an inch square just over his heart — ' if a mule should kick him there, he would be instantly killed.' He is relieved.

Gen. Richard Taylor surrenders, to Gen. E. R. S. Canby, all the Confederate forces remaining in arms east of the Mississippi River, at 7.30 p. m. to-day, at Citronelle, Alabama.

**May 5. Fri.** Rainy. The Reg. with other troops of the 24th Corps, leaves camp about 7 a. m. ; moves as far as the Ponton bridge, on the way to Richmond, to receive the 2d and 5th Corps, of the Army of the Potomac ; but the reception is postponed on account of the weather, and the troops return to camp. A six-mile march for nothing, save a drenching in the cold rain, and a liberal coating with the mud.

The 5th Corps encamps near us. These two Corps passed the camp of the Thirteenth while coming in, and presented for two days an almost uninterrupted stream of cavalry, artillery, infantry, teams and ambulances. A war-worn and weather-beaten host. About 40,000 troops are in Richmond to-day.

Many of these troops having no arms march with old brooms, and hundreds of little broom-corn clothes brushes are stuck in the muzzles of the muskets and borne aloft — the broom the emblem of a clean sweep. War songs are sung in the very grandest of choruses — by the victorious warriors themselves.

**May 6. Sat.** Very warm. Reg. turns out at daylight, and at an early hour assembles with the 24th Corps, goes to Richmond, and receives the 2d and 5th Corps of the Army of the Potomac. The column is seven hours — from 9 a. m. to 4 p. m. — in passing a given point. There are about 50,000 troops in all, and the movement is very slow.

Our receiving column stands in line, the 24th Corps extending along Broad Street for nearly a mile, and as each General passes at the head of his troops, our men give three cheers, present arms, and dip their colors. Occasionally several thousand voices join in some loud chorus, or grand old army song. We also cheer every regimental flag that passes; at least two hundred sets of three cheers each, though some are considerably flatted. A long, hard, noisy, hoarse job.

One soldier of the 13th writes home : " While the troops were passing Gen. Lee's house, the house was kept closed."

May 7. Sun. Very pleasant. Reg. in camp. Inspection a. m. Everybody hoarse and sore, from giving orders and cheering yesterday. Lieut. Murray returns to the Reg. from parole camp. Dress-parade at evening. The Thirteenth not so large, now, as three of its companies were when the Regiment first entered Virginia. The 14th Corps, in Gen. Sherman's army, are passing our camp to-day.

May 8. Mon. Fine day. Reg. in camp. Regimental drill in afternoon. " The men take no interest in drill, camp duties or anything connected with a soldier's life, they are simply almost crazy to go home," — writes a man of the 13th.

May 9. Tues. Showery — afternoon. Reg. in camp. Drilling now is voted a nuisance, and declared off. The men go through a few manœuvres, then are allowed to stack arms and rest; and they rest very slowly because they are very tired of drilling. They sit on the grass, and toss pebbles at the stalks of dead weeds; which exercise they now regard quite as important as the drilling for a war that is over and done. It is like singing that old song : ' Rally Round The Flag,' now that there is no need to ' Rally once again,' or ' Shout the battle cry.'

May 10. Wed. Pleasant; rainy at night. Regimental drill. Gen. Custer's cavalry pass through Richmond.

May 11. Thurs. Very warm, thunder showers. Reg. in line at 4.30 a. m. and with the 24th Corps goes to Manchester and receives the 14th and 20th Corps, of Maj. Gen. Wm. T. Sherman's army, while they are marching into Richmond, on their way to Washington. The Thirteenth stands for six hours on Main Street, in the intense heat, while these two Corps march past. His whole army passes through the city, occupying three days in the passage. They have marched up from Raleigh, N. C., since April 30th, a distance of 150 to 175 miles. They have many pack mules with them carrying the men's baggage, as well as that of the officers. On one of these mules are riding two little girls, with light hair, blue eyes and fair complexion — liberated slaves, to be taken North and educated. The chief interest of the day centres in Gen. Sherman — ' Old Tecumseh ' — as he rides at the head of his army. At 2.30 p. m. the Thirteenth returns to camp.

Of the war songs now sung in the armies of the Potomac and James, ' Old John Brown,' and in Gen. Sherman's army ' Marching Through Georgia,' are by all means the favorites. Both have spirited, stirring music, and have a roll, swing, rhythm and general sentiment good for all time, war or peace, and both are magnificent, though simple, tunes for troops to sing while marching.

May 12. Fri. Pleasant; heavy rain last night. Regimental drill this afternoon — for a few dull minutes; then we stack arms and toss pebbles.

The 15th and 17th Corps, of Gen. Sherman's army, pass through Richmond, followed by two Divisions of Gen. Sheridan's cavalry. These now are surely rough riders. Our Brigade does not go into town to receive them, and so escapes an exceedingly fatiguing piece of work.

May 13. Sat. Very warm. In compliance with the request of Major Stoodley, commanding the Thirteenth, Gen. Devens gives our Regiment a holiday. He furnishes us with transportation, and we visit Fort Darling, and our old battle-field at Drury's Bluff; leaving Richmond at 7 a. m., and returning about 6 p. m. We find the lines about Drury's Bluff but little changed. It is a year since our severe engagement there on May 14th, 15th and 16th, 1864. The field of that affair is still deeply marked with the evidences of the conflict. Trees battered, ground dug up; shells, shot, army gear, and human bones scattered about in plenty. The rebel dead were poorly buried, and the bones have in many cases been dug out and scattered by animals.

May 14. Sun. Very fine day. Inspection at 9 a. m. We talk over the trip of yesterday, and vote a perpetual thanks to Gen. Devens.

A battle is a mere incident in the soldiers' life, often an accident, their real work is to drill. Turn to the right, turn to the left; face this way, face that way; dress up, align, touch elbows; eyes front, toes square; move forward, sidewise, backward, oblique; turn about, wheel about, and do just so — then do it all over again, four thousand times; 'hold up your gun up, plunk it down'; manualize, evolute, quick, slow, double-quick, inextricably commingled. Drill is a shirky business; dryer than chips, more lifeless than the awkward squad and duller than army stories told the fortieth time. The boys say, 'drill begins with a big, big D, and has more l in it twice over than the whole universe calls for.'

May 15. Mon. Pleasant. Reg. in camp. The troops of Generals Grant's and Sherman's armies, in passing through Richmond northward, march up to Manchester through Chesterfield County, cross the James on pontons below Mayo's bridge, into 17th Street, pass through the city along Main or Broad Street, and out on the Brook turnpike, toward Charlottesville, going to Fredericksburg. Immense crowds of citizens, of all classes, pack the sidewalks, fill the windows and balconies, and cluster upon the roofs of buildings, while the trees are full of boys, black and white together.

Many of these organizations now passing shout sundry 'war-cries,' or what serve as such. The Thirteenth, to the writer's knowledge, never formally adopted any war-cry, for use in battle or elsewhere. Whenever roused or excited in the natural love of combat, adventure or danger, the men have frequently shouted to one another, and even to the enemy, after the common manner of using slang phrases : "Set up them pins!" — and this call, in its various applications, probably comes about as near to a war-cry as the Thirteenth ever had any need of approaching.

May 16. Tues. Pleasant. Reg. in camp. Chills and fever again very prevalent here among the troops. First — freeze and shake; second — burn with fever; third — perspire like rain; fourth — feel used up for a week; then repeat. New clothing issued to the men. Drill, all day. Dress-parade at evening.

May 17. Wed. Very warm; thermometer indicates 90° in the shade. "I saw, at Hollywood Cemetery to-day, the skull of one of our soldiers, on which was written : 'The skull of a Yankee — may his soul rest in hell.' Signed by three rebels." LIEUT. PRESCOTT.

May 18. Thurs. Rainy, warm. Reg. in camp. The custom continues in war, and in peace the same: The bands play 'Smith's March,' or the 'Dead March in Saul,' on the way to a soldier's burial; and 'Pickerel Reel,' or some other tune equally lively, on the return.

Many of the men are now so uneasy that discipline necessarily grows very strict. No one is allowed to visit the city, or even leave camp, without a pass, which is scrutinized by three or four lines of guards between the camp and the city. Passes are granted with caution, and only to men regarded safe, and as a reward for good behavior.

May 19. Fri. Showers, warm. Reg. in camp. Monthly inspection at 8 a. m. A short term of drill.

Visit the fields, and woods, have nothing to do, and nothing to trouble you, and you will not find, in all the wide world, anything so inexpressibly inviting to exquisite, delicious, ineffable laziness as the gentle, mild, soft, sunny, Virginia May day. This climate clips the wings of all push and energy. As a wordy free negro puts it: "When de warm spring comes on, I 'sperience a degree of drowsy lassitude; but when de cool autumn 'proaches I begin to recuperate."

May 20. Sat. Warm, showers, thunder, wind. Reg. in camp. No drill nor parade. Congress advanced the price of rations from 30 cents to 50 cents per day, and a servant's pay from $10 to $16 per month, to date from March 1, 1865, thus materially advancing the pay of officers. All officers, also, who serve until the end of the war, are to receive three months' additional pay.

An Irishman in the Thirteenth inquired of a negro what part of the country he came from. The negro replied "The Island" — naming some island along the coast. The Irishman misunderstood him, and thinking that the negro said he came from Ireland, fired up instantly and exclaimed: "Out wid yes! There's niver a nagur in all Ireland, — an' did n't St. Patrick druv um all out, begorra — wid the snakes, frogs and sich?" Refusing to listen for a moment to any explanation, he forthwith chased the negro out of camp.

May 21. Sun. Clear, cool. Reg. in camp. Inspection a. m. The

Thirteenth was never so uneasy, and so impatient to return home, as now. Discontent is very outspoken, too. Farmers are especially uneasy, for they are losing their spring's work on the home farm. The citizens here, however, feel so insecure that they terribly dread the departure of the Union soldiers. Dress-parade at evening. The day closes with a heavy and windy thunder storm, drenching everything, and everybody, in tents and out — a shower well worthy of Quippee's longest word.

May 22. Mon. Showers. Reg. in camp. Dress-parade at evening. For about a week past, we have really done little besides eating and sleeping. Drilling is exceedingly unpopular. Our Reg. is blamed for not drilling with all its might. Our argument and feeling against much drilling now is that we have completed all the work which we enlisted to do, have done that work well, and there is not even a shadow of use or sense in preparing for that which surely is not coming; having thus decided the whole case in our own favor, we stack arms and rest — toss pebbles — until the drill hour is up. Then return to camp, brush off the dust, read the papers, write home, and plan for civil life, when once more we reach our New Hampshire homes.

Jeff. Davis, partly disguised, was captured at Irwinsville, Irwin County, Georgia, 75 miles southeast of Macon, on May 10th; and goes to a casemate in Fortress Monroe, to meditate upon the mischief he has done.

May 23. Tues. Clear. Thirteenth in camp. Company drill in afternoon. Dress-parade at evening. So many Northern people are now visiting Richmond that the streets present much of the appearance of a Northern city. It is as quiet as a country village.

May 24. Wed. Clear, cool. Thirteenth called at 4 a. m., goes to Manchester and Richmond with the Third Division, and receives the 6th Corps on its march to Washington. More standing in line for hours, more presenting arms, more dipping colors, more repetition of orders, more cheers, and more hoarseness. Nevertheless, it is on the whole a most glorious sport. There is a meaning now to the tune and words of 'Hail to the chief who in triumph advances,' that we Veterans can feel. Thirteenth returns to camp at 11 a. m.

While these two days pass, dull enough here at the best, 200,000 of our fellow Veterans in this war pass in Grand Review, in Washington, before Gen. Grant and the President. Gen. Meade's Army of the Potomac on May 23d, and Gen. Sherman's Army on May 24th. These armies each require about six hours in passing a given point.

May 24, 1861, at Fortress Monroe, Gen. B. F. Butler first gave to the escaped slaves a legal status as ' Contraband of War ' — hence their name 'Contraband.' Now at the tap of every Union drum they literally swarm. All questions between the races in America are to be settled in the times when the questions rise. Now the ex-slaves are Freed-men enveloped in a sort of halo, but they multiply most rapidly; and we are thinking that on some coming day, here in the South, the negroes will prove a band contra to peace, or provocative of war. No state half white and half black can maintain a perpetual peace. The white man, as nature's highest and best type of man, must rule, should rule — and will rule, or both fire and wool will fly.

**May 25. Thurs.** Showery. Thirteenth in camp. A large detail, the first from the 13th, at work repairing Mayo's Bridge over the James — leading from Hull Street, Manchester, to Fourteenth Street, Richmond. The men most heartily despise this job, and grumble about it exceedingly. 'They declare they did not enlist to work out road-taxes here; nor to repair the enemy's highways and bridges for his use again. Better compel the disarmed enemy to do this work. This is one of the three bridges over the James that the rebels burned on the morning of April 3d, after their troops had crossed in retreat. A vast host of the rebels late in arms are this day straggling, loafing, begging, stealing, all over the late Confederacy, from the head of it in Virginia to the tail of it in Texas, and there are several thousands of them here within easy call — the devil take their bridge.' And so the men grumble, for now they want to go home. The Union army is now using two ponton bridges near this highway bridge, but they are being so frequently damaged by the swift current of the river and hard usage, that it is deemed best to repair this bridge of Mayo's.

Lieut. Prescott, Quarter-master Morrison and Adjutant Taggard to-day visit the old lines of the two armies, below Petersburg. They find many of the rebel dead still lying unburied; in one place are fifteen or twenty of them with clothing and equipments on, lying just as they fell. The works which they visit are scarcely changed in any way. Little has been done to repair the breaches and damages done to the city of Petersburg.

**May 26. Fri.** Very rainy last night and to-day. Reg. in camp, about four miles from the city, doing nothing but a little guard duty.

Gen. E Kirby Smith, at New Orleans, surrenders to Maj. Gen. E. R. S. Canby his forces in Texas; and the last armed force of the Confederacy disbands and disappears. After the rebels cease to be rebels, the term Confederate is the more appropriate.

The War of the Slaveholders' Rebellion is concluded. Slavery, the 'Corner Stone of the Confederacy,' is no more. The Union army line from Mexico to Maryland is assembled and assembling to the north and east as a curtain is drawn aside. The Confederate line, lately confronting it, is scattered and scattering to the four winds. As they all withdraw, the wide country opens to light and freedom, and peace resumes her true vocations.

**May 27. Sat.** Very cold, rainy and gloomy day. Reg. in quarters. One soldier of the 13th writes: " We are within three miles of Drury's Bluff; but now we are on the other side of the breast-works, and the rebels are not so plenty hereabout as they were last year at this time."

**May 28. Sun.** Pleasant, cool. Reg. at work on the bridge. The

13th has about 100 men sick in hospital. One of Col. Mosby's guerilla Captains wants to sell to Lt. Col. Smith a thorough-bred horse — former owner not cited!

May 29. Mon. Pleasant, warm. Inspection in the morning. Reg. at work on the bridge. A visit to Belle Isle reveals a horrid scene of filth, and shows how terribly our men must have suffered when confined there as prisoners ; at times as many as 13,000 of our soldiers were there crowded upon about two acres of land, and some of them so poorly housed and cared for that they froze to death.

We are asked to describe a ' Copperhead,' but the task is extremely inconvenient if not altogether impossible ; we recall no good word in the English language that roundly applies to him, scolding is out of our line, and we are morally persuaded not to use such awfully bad words as would properly meet his case — if indeed any such competent words there be. He is a little or big politician, of marked double-dealing propensities, living in the North, but wiggling for the South, and still too big a coward to go down there and fight for it — hence thoroughly despised by both sections. He not only sits ' upon the fence ' so as to save his head by jumping either of two ways, as personal danger may suggest, but he mounts a fence-crossing, that he may have four ways to jump ; and sits hissing at freedom. Union and everything Northern, glowing all over in happy resplendency with slavery and everything Southern, and snapping his venomous jaws at the back of every Northern patriot and soldier.

May 30. Tues. Pleasant, warm. Reg. at work on the bridge. Orders have been issued for the muster-out of all Union troops whose terms expire before Oct. 1st — about 500,000 men. One member of the 13th writes : " Soon we shall all be citizens, and forget that the war ever existed."

May 31. Wed. Reg. moves down near Mayo's bridge at the James River early this morning, so that the men may more conveniently work on the bridge. Detail at work.

The 2d Brigade Band goes on a serenading tour in Richmond this evening. Plays at six different places. The Richmond papers speak of it as : " The very splendid Band attached to Gen. Devens' command." So the boys of the Thirteenth, now remaining in this old Thirteenth Band, are complimented. Here at the bridge the Thirteenth occupies the camp of the 188th Pennsylvania regiment.

June 1. Thurs. Clear, hot. Reg. in camp. A detail of about one third of the Reg. at work on Mayo's bridge. National Fast Day. Very quiet in Richmond. Captain Lewis P. Wilson returns to the Reg. from the charge of our 3d Division Ambulance Corps.

June 2. Fri. Very warm. Detail from the 13th at work on bridge ; and the weather is so hot our men can work but half the day. The officers have to go in charge of the work every day.

June 3. Sat. Very warm. Reg. in camp. Our 3d Division of the 24th Corps reviewed this afternoon by Gen. Devens.

The last review of his Division. He makes a fine speech, his farewell address. The Division is soon to be broken up. The affair closes with three rousing cheers for Gen. Devens, whom the soldiers have always liked. After our troops are dismissed, the officers of each regiment in the Division are invited to a reception at Gen. Devens' Hdqrs. The 2d Brigade Band furnishes the music. Five other bands in this Division.

" Because of the work on Mayo's bridge, the Thirteenth do not appear on this review. Prices are enormous here now, and we have to pay fabulously for everything we eat." LIEUT. PRESCOTT.

June 4. Sun. Very warm. Reg. in camp at the bridge. Inspection a. m. Dress-parade p. m. Major Stoodley, Captains Betton and Hall, Lieutenants Ferguson, Wheeler, Taggard, Hardy, Prescott, Sherman, Quarter-master Morrison and Dr. Emory visit Belle Isle, and witness evidences of the intense suffering and awful misery of the Union prisoners who were confined there.

June 5. Mon. Clear, hot. Reg. in camp. Lieut. George H. Taggard mustered in as First Lieutenant and Adjutant.

He was first mustered September 19, 1862, as Commissary Sergeant. It ought to be said of him, though he would prefer no particular mention, that the Thirteenth is greatly indebted to him for his conscientious and efficient care in seeing that the Thirteenth was not imposed upon in the many distributions of rations. There were those who would show favoritism if they could, but any attempt to do this against the interests of the Thirteenth was sure to arouse Taggard's indignation, and to meet with his instant denunciation and exposure. His efficiency was constant, positive as well as negative, and day, night, cold, heat, fair weather or storm found him on hand all the same, with his busy pencil and memorandum — and his two and two always counted plump four. He was as quick to speak for the Thirteenth to a Major General as to private Bangs; and in his position as Commissary he was an unqualified success.

On March 16, 1864, he was promoted to Second Lieutenant in Co. F; and on November 3, 1864, he was promoted to First Lieutenant in the same Company. He commenced acting as Adjutant of the Thirteenth on Sept. 1, 1864, and on May 30, 1865, he was commissioned by Gov. Joseph A. Gilmore as First Lieutenant and Adjutant, in place of Adjutant Nathan B. Boutwell resigned, and discharged on account of disability because of wounds received in action.

In Taggard's position as Lieutenant and Adjutant he is mentioned in the body of the history; but it is fair to add that the commanding officers of the Thirteenth have mentioned him with unstinted praise.

June 6. Tues. Cloudy. Reg. in camp. The Reg. as a whole has not worked on the bridge continuously day after day, but has furnished large details for that work for nearly two weeks, when the weather has been suitable for men to work in at all. The labor is hard and the materials heavy to handle.

It is astonishing how very brave some men are now that the war is over!

Surprising, too, to see how great a thing can be made of a little — and that little borrowed. Steep reminiscences began to sprout within three seconds from the moment of Gen. Lee's surrender at Appomattox, and before the ink he wrote with was dry ; and have since grown and flourished like a Japanese yam, and are about as bodiless and brittle. The boasting rear brave is the front coward. In the theatre of this war has been presented the drama in which the noble have played the noble parts, and these other amusing gentlemen the bits of comedy and roaring farce.

June 7. Wed. Very warm. Our 3d Division reviewed by Generals Ord and Gibbon on the Fairfield race-course, about one mile northeast of Richmond. All together a very long march. Much suffering from the heat. Thirteenth relieved from work on the bridge that it may appear on the review ; and receives a special commendation from Gen. Ord, 'as one of those Regiments that become prominent and useful in every position where they are placed.' All Richmond turns out. An immense crowd of people.

Men of the Thirteenth on guard, at city residences and farm houses, report many instances of provisions laid by for the day when the very worst should occur. A barrel of flour, a small quantity of corn meal, or other edible that would not readily spoil, packed carefully away among old boxes and bundles in a store-room, out of the probable reach of Confederate searching parties ; all awaiting the hour when starvation should make their use an absolute necessity.

June 8. Thurs. Very warm. Thirteenth is relieved from the work on the bridge, by the 40th Mass., this morning, and at once moves back to its old camp-ground on the Broad Rock road. As the Thirteenth passes through Richmond nowadays, the crowds that line the streets often cheer us as we pass along. The negro especially cannot be demonstrative enough in his own peculiar way. His oil-polished ebony face lights up with white of eyes and white of teeth, while he gives a most hearty negro chuckle, and a " Goo' Mornin'," as he meets a familiar face among us. The negroes point to the Thirteenth and remark : " Dere goes the fus' Reg'munt dat done came inter Richmond." We have a high standing in their regard. He is a rare and a bad darkey who ' goes back ' (as his expression has it) on a Northern soldier. The writer has never heard of a case of the kind.

The old plantation negroes have a peculiar chuckle, a guttural, rolling, deep-toned sound, brimming over with good nature, just as if they were literally too full for utterance, in selected words, and so break out all over in nature's own expression, a hearty, whole-souled, bubbling-over chuckle. Letters cannot express it, though it is something like " Er-hurckh ! " given in the lowest possible tones of the voice, and accompanied with good-natured laughter. When some old black couple have first found themselves safe within the cordon of Uncle Sam's bayonets, that chuckle invariably follows the first wild expression : " We 's free — bress de Lord, we 's free ! " Freedom means a whole new world to them ; but in less than two generations that hearty chuckle will disappear, as something smacking too much of "Ole Slave'y times, you know, sah."

June 9. Fri. Very warm. Thirteenth in camp, and the men resting. The muster-out rolls are received to-day with orders to fill them out at once; and the commanders of Companies and their clerks spend the entire day upon them.

The occasion for having so many First Lieutenants in the Thirteenth was this: After the fall of 1864 no Second Lieutenant could be mustered in a Company having less than 80 men on its rolls, hence some First Sergeants and members of the non-commissioned staff were mustered in as First Lieutenants, in order to have a proper number of line officers in the Regiment. An irregular proceeding, but unavoidable under the circumstances.

June 10. Sat. Stormy, cool. Thirteenth marches from camp at 7.30 a. m. to the review ground — the same Fairfield race-course — arriving about 10 a. m., but the review is postponed on account of the storm. The whole 24th Corps assembles here, and the men lounge about in the woods until 3 p. m. A heavy thunder shower then comes up, drenches every one of us to the skin, and spoils every new suit in the command. The rain continues to pour for over two hours. Such a streaked and bedraggled crew — the very darkies laugh at us! The march is full ten miles to go and return, and the Thirteenth does not arrive in camp again till about 8 p. m. "The men are as ugly as dogs, and do a good deal of hard swearing about this day's work," writes an officer of the Thirteenth.

June 11. Sun. Warm, murky. Inspection at 9 a. m. Dress-parade at 6 p. m. No troops are to be mustered out until after a review of the Corps. Gen. Patrick is relieved from the duty of Provost Marshal, succeeded by Gen. Turner.

As one of the many proofs that familiarity breeds contempt, the following has been observed by Adjt. Gen. A. D. Ayling, who has served in this war in both the artillery and infantry: Artillerymen are most disturbed by and most dislike bullets, while infantrymen are most disturbed by and most dislike shells; a curious illustration of the desire of men to meet a foe armed with their own familiar weapons.

June 12. Mon. Cloudy, close. Thirteenth in camp. We have furnished, all along, a large number of guards for the plantations hereabout. A pleasanter position is not easily found, if the proprietors are agreeable. A horse-race to-day at the Broad Rock course is attended by all who can get out of camp.

June 13. Tues. Very hot, showers in afternoon. Thirteenth leaves camp at 12 noon, marches to the review-ground, appears on the review with the 24th Corps, and returns to camp, arriving at 9 p. m. The review is held at 5.30 p. m. on the Fairfield race-course, Mechanicsville, by Maj. Gen. John Gibbon, who to-day delivers his farewell address to his troops — the 24th Army Corps. We form a straight line, when in line of battle, over a mile in length, and are on a splendid field. Our last Grand Review ; and a very fine display notwithstanding the heavy rain. On arriving in camp at night the men are bespattered with mud, and there is scarcely a dry thread in the clothing of any of the troops.

The 9th Vt. and 118th N. Y. are mustered out to-day, and will start for home to-morrow morning. Brev. Brig. Gen. E. H. Ripley bids our 1st Brigade adieu, and will go home with his regiment.

June 14. Wed. Hot. A heavy thunder shower at night. Thirteenth in camp, and everybody half used up. Reviews are quite as laborious as the average of battles. The entire Union army is still in mourning for President Lincoln. The officers wear on their left arms a crape rosette about two inches across, the men a similar rosette but smaller. These emblems of mourning are to be worn by members of the army, for six months from the date of President Lincoln's death.

June 15. Thurs. Hot, misty. Thirteenth in camp. Lt. Col. Normand Smith returns to the Thirteenth from his special duty as Provost Marshal of the First District of Richmond. He was appointed April 4, 1865, and has served until to-day. The chief officers of the Confederate army, and the more prominent citizens, have taken their oaths of allegiance before him. In his absence the command of the Thirteenth devolved upon Major Stoodley, who has held it ever since we came into the city. Cyrus G. Drew of B and Sergt. John P. Haines of C have been serving as clerks for Lt. Col. Smith in the Provost Marshal's office.

June 16. Fri. Rainy, sultry. Thirteenth in camp. Captains Farr and Durell return to the Thirteenth from detached service.

June 17. Sat. Warm, rainy. Reg. in camp. The 40th Mass. and 21st Conn. start for home this morning.

June 18. Sun. Very warm. Inspection by Lt. Col. Smith, Company by Company. No Dress-parade — weather too hot. Reg. in camp — and the uneasiest set of do-nothings who ever sat and waited for something to turn up. A little guard duty in camp ; no drill, no picket, no war ; the most onerous duty that falls to us is to eat our army rations, of which we are thoroughly tired, and to do the heavy standing around. We are prisoners of war. We play cards and other games from morning until night. Cannot go anywhere, have nothing to do ; and so we lounge about the camp and merely exist, and wait for the muster-out. While the men are idle, the officers are compelled to employ all the time they can get upon the muster-out rolls.

The departures of regiments are quite informal. Not much parade about it. The men pack up, fall into line as if to start upon an ordinary march, and move off, amid more or less cheering, and many hearty farewells from the soldiers who remain in camp, and who gather informally at the roadside while the departing regiment passes by. Thus the Veterans part, probably never to meet again.

June 19. Mon. Showery, very warm. Reg. in camp. The Thirteenth assembles now, officers and all, about 300 persons.

It is due to the fair history of the Thirteenth to say that in no case were the men of this Regiment ever plied with whiskey, or any other intoxicant or stimulus, to specially nerve them to duty or to battle. They have been too brave, too willing, too patriotic and too efficient in all respects to need anything of that sort. Whiskey rations were issued in camp to counteract the effects of climate, over-work or malaria, but never for any other purpose; and even for those medical purposes hot, strong coffee would have been better.

The 139th N. Y. mustered out, and starts for home this afternoon. Capt. William J. Ladd visits our camp this afternoon, and examines the muster-out rolls of the Thirteenth.

June 20. Tues. Very warm. Thirteenth in camp. Rolls are being prepared for the final muster-out, a very slow and difficult piece of work. Ten separate rolls are required for each Company. Every officer and man who ever belonged to the Thirteenth must be entered with his entire military history; battles, wounds, pay, arms, ammunition, and equipage of each man, and the entire accounts of each officer must be squared up; in short the rolls cover everything concerning the military life of each officer and soldier, and all army gear to him pertaining.

Our Broad Rock camp is located close up to the race-track, and the road to camp runs southwest from Manchester, and west of the Richmond & Petersburg Turnpike and Railroad. Our First Brigade Hdqrs. are at Mr. David McDaniel's house.

June 21. Wed. Very warm. The Thirteenth Regiment of New Hampshire Volunteer Infantry is this evening, at Broad Rock camp, mustered out of the military service of the United States by Capt. Ladd.

"Battalion drill this afternoon. After which the mustering officer came over (from the city), and during the evening we were mustered out of the United States service." LIEUT. PRESCOTT.

The Reg. has been in that service thirty-three months; a long, hard term. Those who are unfortunate enough to read this Diary through may have some realizing sense of that length and hardness; though, may be, less as to that, than as to this.

The war is over — now for Home. The mustered-out officers and men are now war Veterans — the American Nation's truest noblemen. They may pass down no gorgeously emblazoned coats-armorial, but better far, an American soldier's name, and honor too, all untarnished.

It takes about three hours time to muster out a regiment; and our Regiment is one of a total of 2,050 regiments who have served in this war — if all organizations were reduced to infantry regiments.

The Thirteenth has been in the First Brigade — consisting of the 13th N. H., 11th Conn., 19th Wis. and 81st, 98th and 139th N. Y. regiments — and in the 3d Division of the 24th Corps, since Dec. 3, 1864.

The Thirteenth is to report to the State authorities at Concord, and therefore retains its organization, arms and equipments complete. Many purchase their guns at $6.00 apiece, to preserve at home as souvenirs of the great civil war.

The Recruits of the 10th, 12th and 13th N. H. V., about 400 men, whose term of service will not expire until Sept. 30, 1865, will go into the 2d N. H., which remains near Richmond in the 2d Brigade, 3d Div. 24th Corps. When these Recruits of the 13th were transferred to the 2d N. H. they did not want to go, and it required strong nerves, on the part of the guard and its commanding officer, to carry out the order transferring them. They naturally and properly desired to go home with the Regiment, and threatened hard things, but finally yielded.

Our sutler, for a number of months past, Charles F. French, of Peterboro, remains in Richmond.

June 22. Thurs. "A splendid day." The Thirteenth breaks camp — our last camp in Virginia — on the Broad Rock road, at 4 a. m ; at 5 a. m. forms line ; is joined in Manchester by the Tenth and Twelfth N. H. Regiments ; marches to Richmond ; embarks, together with the 10th and 12th, at Rocketts, on the Steamer ' State of Maine ; ' and starts from the wharf at 8 a. m. for home ; arrives at City Point at 11 a. m., at Fortress Monroe at 5.15 p. m., stops half an hour, then sails north.

We form a provisional — Homing — Brigade, consisting of the 10th, 12th and 13th, N. H., under command of Brevet. Brig. Gen. Michael T. Donohoe, Colonel of the Tenth.

As we sail quietly and slowly down the James River, this clear summer morning, among these many frowning forts and batteries, we can hardly realize our own identity. A few days ago we saw them swarming with hostile soldiers, and belching a murderous fire of shot and shell ; now they are mere Virginia clay banks, half buried in rank grass, weeds and trailing vines ; are dilapidated, weather-worn, silent, uncared for, and of no possible use — as worthless as the mud at the river bottom. While the soldiers who manned them — and are now surviving at all — are scattered to the four corners of the late Confederacy, having thrown away four years or more of the best part of their lives. Much difficulty is experienced in working the boat through the obstructions placed by the rebels in the James, but we pass through them without accident.

The James River is now a curiosity. Here are boats scuttled and sunk, the masts standing above water, while funnels and smoke-stacks point to other wrecks down below ; there the broadside of a large vessel ; yonder on the shore a huge piece of a blown-up gun-boat or iron-clad ; higher up a cannon, sent toward the skies and then crashing down among the trees, lies half buried in the sand, with the muzzle end up ; picket pits, and huts of the river guard, tucked in like rabbit warrens, or crows' nests, all along the banks ; embrasures, cut as low as possible for depressed cannon, look straight down at us from the forts ; now we come to a grove of trees battered and torn with shells, as if a lightning storm had swept through them ; log-barracks of numerous camps in the fields and great numbers of shed-roofs over ledges or holes dug in the bluffs ; a few huge cans stranded on the shore — once floating torpedoes ; ponton bridge landings, and wharves, thrown deep into the stream to navigable water, their innumerable piles in long rows, cribbed and ballasted with stone; their shore ends flanked with remains of large camps, and pointing to roads leading up among the bluffs — roads so infernally rough and bad that the rebel teamsters' profanity must have continued to rumble and echo along them for several weeks after Gen. Lee's army had left these parts; the whole region speaking of an immense amount of human labor expended, of property destroyed to a value untold, and of unnumbered animals and men dead and wasted — but the anguish cry of the slave is heard here no more forever.

Our boat winds in and out among the rows of piles set to block any rapid navigation in the channel, dodges the sunken hulks, crosses the river over and over again, and brings us off Fortress Monroe about 5 p. m., and we soon leave there for the open sea and home.

June 23. Fri. Fine day. True to the pursuing instinct — to chase everything that appears to be running or retreating — that has ruled all Virginia for the last four years and more, a school of porpoises follow our boat, like a body of skirmishers, far out to sea from Hampton Roads — all and the last we can see of Hampton's Black Horse Cavalry.

After a pleasant sail up the coast, we arrive in New York harbor at 7 p. m., and drop anchor at 8 p. m. Many of the officers go on shore, having permission to remain in the city until 2 a. m.

June 24. Sat. Fine. This morning the steamer hauls up to the Government coaling station in Jersey City. Nearly the whole force aboard are here detailed to wheel coal on board the vessel. Many of the men, however, leave their barrows at the coal-bunkers, go up town, and take aboard another abundant means of getting up steam — 'Jersey lightning.' The steamer leaves Jersey City at 4.45 p. m. for Boston — "All hands drunk," one soldier writes.

Gen. Donohoe in command of our Homing Brigade is presented this evening with an elegant sword, sash and belt suitable to his rank.

June 25. Sun. Fine day. "Was officer of the guard to-day. Had a good deal of trouble with some of the men who were drunk. Lt. Col. Smith ordered me to search the boat for two of the men, and to tie them up on deck. The Regiment swore that it should not be done, and violence was offered. The men were found, however, and secured from doing further mischief."        LIEUT. PRESCOTT.

There are, among all gatherings of men, a few who make trouble for all the rest. After some of these of ours are secured so they can do no further mischief, the voyage proceeds quite agreeably to the end. We enter Boston harbor about sunset. We arrive in Boston about 9 p. m., proceed to Faneuil Hall, and there pass the night.

All are sober now; the Jersey lightning flashed, and was expended in the deep. Many friends, and ex-members of the 13th, as also of the 10th and 12th, are present to receive our Homing Brigade. The officers are quartered at the City Hotel.

While in Boston the men of the 10th, 12th, and 13th are free to go about as they may please, and the Jersey City programme is not repeated. At night, while our Brigade is quartered in Faneuil Hall, it is very hot, and the most of the men of the Thirteenth go out and spread their blankets upon the steps and passage ways and sleep there. About two o'clock next morning the employees of the market appear, and rouse the whole command with their noise, and of course the men must get up and remove from the steps. The men of the Thirteenth take the matter good-naturedly, however; but remark: "This is the only position from which the Thirteenth New Hampshire, when alone, has ever been driven."

The soldier is proud to return home bearing his shield; and is received in this gold-capped, brown old city by the sea with every token of honor, respect and welcome.

When the Great Father of nations and of men resolved to bring about the settlement of America by the Northern white men — the best people He had on the earth for that purpose — He decided to have the very best city in all America's broad commonwealth, founded and controlled by that race who had English for their language; and to have it located far eastward on the Atlantic sea-coast, whence that city's good and grand influence, life, moral and educational jurisdiction and power might pass free and be felt throughout the entire Nation — and He called that choice city's name, BOSTON.

**June 26. Mon.** Fine day. Reg. leaves Boston at the Lowell Station with the Brigade, at 9 a. m., goes to Nashua by rail, arriving before noon, has a public reception, and remains in Nashua all night. Here the Reg. enjoys a splendid entertainment. The officers of the Brigade assemble at the Indian Head House, and Brev. Col. Geo. A. Bruce, on the staff of Gen. Donohoe, in behalf of the assembled officers of the 13th presents to Brevet Brig. Gen. A. F. Stevens, formerly Colonel of the Thirteenth, a sword, sash and belt suitable to his rank. Gen. Stevens appropriately replies.

In the afternoon the Reg. and Brigade is reviewed on Main street by Col. Stevens. No picture of war's work can be more striking than the one presented by these three veteran Regiments, as they march, at full regimental distance and company distance, along Main street, Nashua, to-day. Now thirty broken, straggling, squads, a few hundred men in all — the 10th, 12th and 13th having been depleted each in about the same proportion; three years ago, while on their way down to the war, thirty full companies, of a round one hundred men each, a total of three thousand strong.

The Thirteenth comes home numbering 321 officers and men all told — Officers, 24; Non-commissioned staff, 4; Musicians, 9; Company A, 27 men; B, 35; C, 31; D, 25; E, 26; F, 29; G, 24; H, 30; I, 33; K, 24 — a Regiment whose ranks have numbered, volunteers, recruits and all, a total of nearly 1,300 men.

While waiting at the station in Boston this morning, an officer, not of high rank, in one of these regiments, gives the following order: "Say —

Sarjunt! You hold on to this eend of ther Rig-ermunt — while I go down to ther bottom of ther colyum."

The following is said to have occurred while our Division was marching from Fort Harrison to Williamsburg pike on Oct. 27, 1864 : A few bummers from a regiment preceding the Thirteenth had entered a house a little off the road, seeking forage. The good old woman of the house said to them : "There is nothing in my house that can be of any use to you, the soldiers have already taken all they could ; but there is one thing I have which no one can ever steal from me — that is my religion." " Don't be too sure of that," replied the awful bummer, "the Thirteenth New Hampshire is coming along just behind us — and they need religion more than anything else! " The good woman threw up her hands with an expression of despair, immediately fled to her attic, barricaded the door and hid herself until the column of troops had passed the house.

June 27. Tues. Reg. leaves Nashua at 10 a. m., goes to Manchester by rail, arriving before noon. Here we have a very fine dinner at the grove, followed by many congratulatory speeches. Reg. leaves Manchester for Concord at 3.30 p. m. The cars run off the track a little below Hooksett, and the Chaplain of the 12th and several men in the Brigade are injured. Two hours' delay here. The Reg. arrives in Concord a little before sunset — between 6 and 7 p. m. An immense crowd of citizens have here gathered at the depot, and welcome the Veterans with cheers on cheers. The regiments form at the depot, and are escorted by the Veteran Reserve Corps, and the Concord Brigade Band, through Main Street to the front of the Capitol, where they are addressed by Gov. Frederick Smyth, and others.

Lt. Col. Smith has eight men in the Thirteenth who have no guns; in fact having been detailed on sundry special duties — all, however, necessary and honorable — the most of them have scarcely ever used gun, pick or shovel during their entire term of service; so the Lieut. Colonel enjoys a little sport, and makes these eight men useful and ornamental at the same time, by forming them into a pioneer corps and providing them with picks and shovels ; and now they come marching home, and parading in the reviews and processions, with these arms — all doubtless enjoying their position as much as any men in the Regiment.

The Brigade keeps together ; and the citizens of Concord receive all the men and officers with the most flattering attentions, courtesies and honors. The most of the men and the officers find entertainment with friends or at the hotels.

Probably an extract from Gen. Devens' letter to Gov. Smyth would be most appropriately entered here :

" Headquarters Third Division, 24th Corps.
Richmond Va. June 22, 1865.

" Sir :
The Tenth, Twelfth and Thirteenth New Hampshire Regiments are

temporarily organized as a provisional Brigade under command of Brev. Brig. Gen. M. T. Donohoe. . . . The Thirteenth New Hampshire being the first Regiment of the Army whose Colors were brought into the city of Richmond.

"You will see by their thinned ranks the terrible ravages war has made. Their tattered ensigns will recall the many night marches, the wet and dreary bivouacs, and the fierce and desperate conflicts. These men return inured to the rugged toils of war, and bronzed with the smoke of battle. . . .

"CHARLES DEVENS,
Brig. and Brev. Maj.
Gen. U. S. V. Comdg."

Some time after the war closed, by direction of the State authorities there were inscribed on the window of the cabinet containing all the flags of the Thirteenth, in the State House at Concord, New Hampshire, the names of the battles placed on the flag of the Thirteenth, and given on page 519 of this book, and these two in addition:

"Fair Oaks,      Oct. 27, 1864.
Richmond,      April 3, 1865."

And also this legend:

"The 13th N. H. headed the column that entered the city of Richmond, April 3, 1865; and their colors were the first carried into the city."

To these there should be added:

Siege of Petersburg — in the trenches sixty-seven days in the summer of 1864. Burnside Mine Explosion, July 30, 1864.

June 28. Wed. Clear. Thirteenth early this morning moves out to the barracks of the Substitutes' Camp. Returns to the city again at 11 a. m. with the Brigade, and turns over its colors to the custody of the State during a review held by the Governor at 12 noon, after which the men receive a furlough until the night of Friday, 30th. Gov. Smyth holds a reception this evening, a very crowded but brilliant affair.

June 14, 1864, John M. Woods of I was detailed at Point of Rocks in charge of a dozen or more of men of the Thirteenth to guard and take care of a park of cannon. Soon afterwards he was appointed to take charge of commissary supplies, under direction of Capt. Geo. C. Witherbee, Division Commissary, and was engaged in this duty until Aug. 15th, when he returned to the Regiment.

Again, a few days after the battle at Fair Oaks, Oct. 27, 1864, he was called to the same post to attend to the proper shipment of the fresh bread for the army, and remained there until he was mustered out of the service. The Thirteenth and other regiments may know now, if not before, who attended to their fresh bread supply, a very important duty, and saw it properly and timely forwarded to the several commands in our Division. When it rained shoulder-straps what an immense body of the most faithful and best men in the army were not to be caught in that shower!

The Army of the Potomac is disbanded to-day.

June 29. Thurs. Very warm. Reg. quartered at Substitutes' camp, but the men are scattered everywhere.

When the Thirteenth went to the front in October 1862, the citizens of Nashua presented Col. Stevens, and Lt. Col. Bowers, each with a fine horse — both large, dark bays. Both these horses served their term in the war, always with the Regiment, and returned to Nashua; and both have lived there since the war, and died of old age. Col. Stevens kept his horse, so long as he lived, in his possession at Nashua. Lt. Col. Bowers' horse, while in the army, passed successively from his possession to Major Storer, Lt. Col. Grantman, Lt. Col. Smith and Major Stoodley. After the war, Col. Bowers hunted up this old war horse, and kept him at Nashua until he died of old age. Here indeed were a pair of strong, excellent, noble war horses, worthy of a better mention, and a more extended history. In the most of the severe engagements, where the owners of these horses for the time being were present, they fought dismounted after reaching the immediate field of action.

June 30. Fri. Pleasant. Reg. quartered at Substitutes' camp. Camp and garrison equipage of the Thirteenth turned in to-day.

When at Richmond, the key of the office, or Hdqrs. of the rebel commandant of Libby prison, came into Major Stoodley's possession, and he now keeps it as a souvenir. An old-fashioned iron key of medium size.

Ex-Governor Gilmore holds a reception at the Phenix Hotel this evening — no copperheads present.

The Northern copperhead is hated and condemned in the North, and thoroughly despised in the South; but that class of persons in the North known as War Democrats deserve an especial praise. When the Union and the Flag were assailed, they broke away at once from the political and social affiliations and sympathies nurtured and prized by them for their whole life long, and by their fathers before them, and turned their entire interests without reserve to the cause of the Union. American history in these last five years finds hundreds of these worthy citizens rising high in the army and in the State. They deserve a place of great honor, and will receive it without stint or qualification, when the passions and bitterness of the day have run out.

The following personal items it seems best to enter here. Many persons have been quite fully mentioned in the body of the book. Accounts of living persons are open to pit-falls and objections, and the writer here, as well as in other pages of the book, acting impartially and from good-will, presumes upon the considerate lenience of his comrades.

Capt. George Farr enlisted as a private and with Lieutenants Edward Kilburn and Marshall Saunders recruited Company D. Lieut. Kilburn was, however, the chief recruiting officer of the Company.

Capt. Farr was present in all the marches and battles of the Thirteenth until the battle of Cold Harbor June 1, 1864, when he was severely wounded in the shoulder, during the charge upon the enemy's rifle-pits, and while commanding Co. D.

In January 1865, he was, by order of Gen. Ord, placed upon a Military commission at Norfolk, Va. He served upon this commission or as a member of courts martial until the close of the war, crossing every day to the military hospital at Portsmouth to have his wound dressed. The wound did not heal sufficiently to allow of his return again to active duty with the Regiment.

After the war he served in numerous important public positions, and was Department Commander of the Grand Army of the Republic in New Hampshire for the year 1886.

"Phenix Hotel, Concord, N. H., June 8, 1887.

Dear Thompson : — I send within a biographical sketch of Major Carter. Sincerely Yours, CHARLES B. GAFNEY."

"Buel Clinton Carter was born in Ossipee, N. H., January 20, 1840, he attended the common school, 'The Old Academy' at Wolfboro, fitting for college at Phillips Academy, Exeter. He entered Yale in 1858, graduating in 1862. He was a classmate with the Rev. W. H. H. Murray, Joseph Cook, and D. H. Chamberlain of South Carolina. On his return home from College his services were offered in organizing Company A, 13th N. H. Vols., and he was mustered into the service as a First Lieutenant. At the battle of Fredericksburg Dec. 13, 1862, he was severely wounded. In July 1863, he was commissioned as Captain, and in 1864 as Captain and Acting Quarter-master, and assigned to duty in the Artillery Brigade of the 18th Army Corps. In 1865 he was brevetted Major, and was mustered out of the service at the close of the war; and was subsequently Deputy Collector of Internal Revenue for Southwestern Virginia.

"He was married May 16, 1866, to Ellen F., daughter of Hon. James M. Burbank of Saco, Me.

"On his return from the army and his official duties in Virginia, he commenced the study of his profession in the office of his father Sanborn B. Carter Esq., a prominent lawyer in northern New Hampshire, and after admission to the Bar, located at Wolfboro, where for ten years he had a lucrative and successful practice, holding for several terms the office of prosecuting attorney for Carroll County.

"In 1878 by reason of failing health — 'the sequence of exposure in army life' — he was compelled to relinquish business temporarily, and removed to Rollinsford (to a farm two miles northeast of Dover) where he sought to regain his health and strength by devoting his time to out of door pursuits. In 1879 he became a member of the law firm of Carter and Nason, and practiced his profession in Dover. In 1881 he was appointed Bank Commissioner, and held that office at the time of his death, which occurred, at his home in Rollinsford, Dec. 11, 1886.

"Major Carter was an officer who merited and received the esteem and friendship of his comrades ; he was beloved by the men under him, and while exacting in matters of discipline he was courteous in his deportment and forgiving in his disposition. He was a prominent Mason, and in religious belief a Congregationalist, but in this as in all other matters he was broad in his views and exhibited great liberality and honesty of purpose in reasoning with those who did not agree with him.

"His comrades, and those who associated with him in civil life in the active duties of an honored profession, will remember him as a faithful soldier, a sincere friend, an able lawyer and an honest man. Noble and generous in all the acts of an active and useful life, this brief tribute from a friend adds but a leaflet to the bright laurel that rests on his name."

Brev. Lt. Col. George A. Bruce served with the Regiment until Jan. 9, 1863, when he was appointed Acting Asst. Adjt. General on the Staff of Col. Dutton, commanding 3d Brigade, 3d Division, 9th Army Corps. July 1863, appointed Actg. Asst. Inspector General in the same Brigade then commanded by Brig. Gen. W. H. P. Steere. January 1864, appointed Asst. Inspector General of all the troops defending Norfolk and Portsmouth, Va., then commanded by Gen. George W. Getty. April 1864 appointed aide to Brig. Gen. Hiram Burnham commanding 2d Brigade, 1st Division, 18th Army Corps.

July 1864, appointed Asst. Adjt. General on the staff of Col. A. F. Stevens commanding 1st Brigade, 1st Div. 18th Corps. September 1864 appointed Asst. Adjt. General on the staff of Gen. Gilman Marston commanding 1st Div. 18th Corps, and continued in the same position while that Division was subsequently commanded by Gen. J. B. Carr and Maj. Gen. Charles Devens. While that Division, as the 3d Div. 24th Corps, was commanded by Gen. Devens he served as Judge Advocate on his staff.

After the occupation of Richmond he served as Recorder of the commission appointed to try all criminal offenses in that city. He was promoted successively from First Lieutenant of Co. B to Captain of Co. A May 30, 1864 ; to Major by brevet April 3, 1865 ; and to Lieut. Colonel by brevet April 3, 1865.

Since the war he has held numerous civil offices, and among them that of Judge of the Police Court of Somerville, Mayor of Somerville for 1878, 1879 and 1880, Massachusetts State Senator from First District for 1882, 1883 and 1884, and was President of the Massachusetts State Senate for the session of 1884.

Capt. James M. Durell was mustered in as First Lieutenant in Co. E, having assisted in recruiting that Company. He acted as Adjutant of the Thirteenth for a time in the latter part of 1863, previous to his promotion to the position of Captain. He commanded Co. C from the time of his promotion until he was detached with his Company, and placed in command of Redoubt McConihe on Sept. 1, 1864. This Redoubt is six or eight hundred yards from the James, on the Bermuda Hundred line.

About Sept. 15th, Capt. Durell was appointed a member of a General Court Martial convened at Gen. Stannard's Hdqrs. There were about ten officers in this court, which was adjourned on account of the battle of Fort Harrison. Capt. Durell was ordered back to Redoubt McConihe; the rest went into that battle, and eight or nine of the number were either killed or wounded. The smoke could be seen, and the cannonade heard at Redoubt McConihe, while the battle was going on.

Nov. 27, 1864, Capt. Durell was appointed Acting aide de camp on the Staff of Brig. Gen. C. K. Graham, commanding Defenses of Bermuda Hundred, and afterwards in command of the Naval Brigade.

Gen. Graham and Staff were invited by Gen. Butler to accompany him while on the first expedition to attack Fort Fisher, and did so, Capt. Durell being one of the party.

A flag of truce appeared from the rebel lines in front of a fort, built in the corner of the wheat-field where the 13th were encamped May 22, 1864, and now commanded by Lieut. Day. Capt. Durell was sent to meet the rebel officer bearing the flag, between the lines, and to do so passed through the deep ravine in front. On this occasion Capt. Durell received a letter from Gen. Lee to Gen. Grant, concerning an exchange of prisoners, and returning with it to Gen. Grant's Hdqrs., gave it to a member of Gen. Grant's staff, who read it, and then passed it to Gen. Grant, who happened to come into the tent while he was reading it. Gen. Grant at once read the letter, and then referring to the second attack upon Fort Fisher remarked : " Terry is going to take Wilmington — but we will allow the exchange to be made." He then replied by letter to Gen. Lee, and Capt. Durell again passed through the lines, and this ravine, and delivered the letter to the member of Gen. Lee's staff appointed to receive it.

March 3, 1865, Capt. Durell was ordered to proceed on board the gunboat 'Chamberlain,' and notify the commanders of gunboats ' Moss Wood ' and ' Jessup ' to report at Fortress Monroe. The three boats were to move from Fortress Monroe by noon on March 4th, upon an expedition to Fredericksburg, under command of Gen. Roberts. Capt. Durell then proceeded in the night to the mouth of the Rappahannock to notify the commander of the naval forces there that the troops for the expedition would be up by midnight that night. As Capt. Durell's gunboat was approaching the guard-boat, on duty there, within hailing distance, the commander of the guard-boat trained his guns and made ready to fire, thinking that Durell's gunboat was approaching a little too near, and shouted that he would blow them out of the water if they advanced another fathom, or less polite words to that effect, and communication had to be made from an open row-boat approaching under the rifles of the guard-ship's ' marines.' Capt. Durell, as aide, represented

Gen. Graham on this expedition, which proceeded to Fredericksburg, destroyed twenty car loads of tobacco, tore up a portion of the railroad, and burned a large amount of supplies collected for the rebel army.

From this expedition Capt. Durell was ordered to report at White House Landing, to Gen. Sheridan by 10 a. m., on March 24th. Here Gen. Sheridan ordered Durell to remain in the river until his entire force of cavalry was out of sight, then to return to Bermuda Hundred. While at White House Gen. Sheridan and his staff, and other officers in his command, were very short of provisions, and Durell's boat steamed to Yorktown and procured supplies, and among the lot were several barrels of oysters procured especially for Gen. Sheridan and his staff.

April 2d Capt. Durell was appointed Actg. Asst. Adjt. General on the staff of the Naval Brigade, where Capt. Nathaniel Low Jr. was serving as Asst. Quarter-master.

May 9th he was appointed a member of a board of three officers convened to examine the list of indigent persons receiving Government aid at Portsmouth and Norfolk, Va., from which duty he was relieved on June 8th.

Having served on several other special duties, in boards of survey, appraisal, etc., Capt. Durell was relieved from his position on the staff of Gen. Graham and the Naval Brigade, in order to be mustered out of the service; and being furnished with letters of high commendation, was ordered on June 14, 1865 to report to the Thirteenth.

Capt. Lewis P. Wilson was mustered into the service as Second Lieutenant of Co. G. He served with the Regiment through the Battle of Fredericksburg, Siege of Suffolk, and the Battle of Providence Church Road. Here he was severely bruised by a spent bullet, but continued on duty and was not reported as wounded.

In July 1863 he was ordered to report with a detachment of three officers and six men for duty at the draft rendezvous at Concord, N. H., Gen. Hinks commanding the Post. Here Lieut. Wilson had a varied series of duties, on court martial and guard duty, as Post Adjutant and Commissary of recruits, etc., until April 16, 1864, when he was ordered from there to report for duty to Gen. Devens at Galloup's Island. On the 23d he was ordered to proceed to Fortress Monroe with a party of recruits. He then reported for duty to the Regiment at Yorktown.

May 3, 1864, he was by order of Gen. W. F. Smith, commanding 18th Corps, appointed Chief of Ambulance Corps of the First Division 18th Army Corps, in which duty he served until the end of the war. He had about 150 men. Acting for a long time in this capacity in the 1st Div. 18th Corps, which afterwards became the 3d Division of the 24th Corps, Capt. Wilson had the pleasure and honor of serving in succession on the Division staffs of Generals Brooks, Marston, Stannard and Devens commanding Division, and on Acting Corps staff with Generals Smith, Ord, Terry, Gibbon and Weitzel, commanding Corps, and was with the command in every fight the Corps had. He took his ambulance corps also into Richmond at the earliest moment.

During the more than a year of this service, Capt. Wilson states that he was enabled to avoid leaving a single wounded man on the battle-field over night, excepting once. On October 28, 1864, in the flank movement to Fair Oaks, though he had over forty ambulance wagons and also used all the baggage wagons there were to be had, he could not transport all the wounded; and left two hospital tents standing, and many wounded men in them, in charge of a Surgeon, who was captured, taken to Richmond, and in a few days released and sent within the Union lines.

Capt. Wilson was specially commended by Surgeon General Barnes, who inspected his ambulance train, while the Corps was operating in front of Petersburg. Turning to Dr. Sukely, Medical Director of the 18th Corps, Surgeon Gen. Barnes remarked that "Capt. Wilson's Ambulance Corps and train was the best one in the whole army;" and this was considered a well deserved compliment.

On June 20, 1865, he rejoined the Regiment, was mustered out with it the next day, and placed in charge of all the muster-out papers, blanks and records of the Companies and Regiment, and turned them over to Major Silvey, chief mustering officer, in New Hampshire.

Capt. Charles H. Curtis of C served with that Company in the Battle of Fredericksburg Dec. 1862. When Lieut. M. A. Shaw of I was wounded Dec. 13th, Lieut. Curtis was placed in command of Co. I on the battle-field, and retained the command until some time in January 1863, when he was relieved at his own request, and rejoined Co. C. He remained on duty with Co. C until Sept. 1863, meanwhile commanding it on the raid up the Peninsula in June and July, and serving frequently as Judge Advocate of regimental courts martial. In September 1863, by order of Gen. Getty, commanding 3d Div. 9th Corps, he was detailed as Judge Advocate of a General Court Martial convened at Portsmouth, Va. On completing that duty and shortly after rejoining the Regiment, he was detailed by order of Gen. Butler as Judge Advocate of a General Court Martial convened at Norfolk, Va. On completing that duty in February 1864, he was granted a leave of absence, and went home to New Hampshire to vote.

On the day the leave expired, he was detailed to command the provost guard stationed at Portsmouth, Va., the guard being composed of about one hundred men and Lieutenants Sherman and Dustin, all of the Thirteenth. The accident to this detachment while on its way to Yorktown is mentioned under date of May 11, 1864. While on his way to rejoin the Thirteenth he was by order of Gen. Burnham detailed as Actg. Asst. Quarter-master on his staff. This service continued until the Brigade was reorganized in July 1864, when he was appointed temporarily as acting regimental Quarter-master by Lt. Col. Smith, then commanding the Thirteenth. Soon after this he was promoted to Captain, and assumed command of Co. F.

He was appointed Actg. Asst. Inspector General by order of Col. Edgar N. Cullen, commanding 3d Brig. 3d Div. 18th Army Corps, taking the position vacated by Capt. Julian's expiration of term of service. His services were continued in this position by Brig. Gen. E. H. Ripley, who succeeded Col. Cullen in command of the Brigade, until his muster-out on June 21, 1865. Capt. Curtis says — as well he may : " The greatest satisfaction I have in thinking of my army experience is from the fact that I was always in good health, ready and able to do any duty when my services were required, during my entire term of service."

Capt. William J. Ladd, when Second Lieutenant of Co. K, was appointed Ordnance Officer on the staff of Gen. Getty, at Suffolk, Va., in April 1863.

Just before Gen. Getty was succeeded in the command of the Third Division of the 9th Corps by Gen. Heckman, Lieut. Ladd was appointed assistant Commissary of Musters by the Secretary of War, and held that office until the close of the war.

May 30, 1864, he received a commission as First Lieutenant.

He was appointed aide on the staff of Gen. Brooks, commanding the 1st Div. 18th Army Corps, in place of Capt. Parsons, who was killed in the Battle of Cold Harbor, and served on Gen. Brooks' staff until he resigned.

He was promoted Captain United States Volunteers by brevet, for gallant and meritorious services, to date from March 13, 1865.

First Lieut. Milton H. Hardy, Co. G, was mustered as a private, and rose through the several non-commissioned grades, while serving with his Company, to First Sergeant, being appointed as such August 20, 1864. In October 1864 he was detailed from his Company to act as Sergeant Major of the Thirteenth, and served in that capacity for a considerable time, in place of Sergt. Major Hodgdon, who was wounded Sept. 30 at Fort Harrison. March 9, 1865, he was commissioned as First Lieutenant of Co. G, and immediately took command of that Company in the absence of Capt. Wilson ; and retained that position until mustered out of the service with the Regiment.

Jan. 16, 1864, he was, by command of Gen. B. F. Butler, detailed to report to Capt. Brown, at Norfolk, Va., and by him placed in charge of the famous Sylvester Farm, bordering on the Dismal Swamp. Here his duties were to look after and provide for the colored people, about fifty in number, an irregular band who were quartered upon the farm, and also to cultivate the farm as much as possible. The work was done, mostly, by colored help and condemned horses. With this irregular sort of help, however, Sergt. Hardy succeeded in bringing about 300 acres of the farm under a luxuriant crop of corn and grain, when August 16, 1864, he was relieved and joined his Company in the trenches before Petersburg ; thereafter remaining with the Regiment until mustered out of the service.

Lieut. Nathan D. Chapman was mustered in as a private in Co. B, and served through all the grades of Corporal and Sergeant to First Sergeant of his Company, and while First Sergt. of Co. B he served for seven or eight days as commander of Co. D, during the Battle of Cold Harbor. He served with his Company and Regiment in every one of its battles and marches during its term of service, and commanded Co. B after the occupation of Richmond, in the absence of Capt. Marshall Saunders, who was detailed on special service. June 15, 1865, he received a commission as Second Lieutenant of Co. B, but owing to depletion in the numbers of the Regiment he could not be mustered.

At the first competitive examination for prize furloughs under the orders of Gen. Gibbon, Sergt. M. C. Shattuck of B received the prize due to the Thirteenth. See Jan. 21, 1865. At a later examination an amusing scene took place at Division Hdqrs. Sergt. Nathan D. Chapman of B, the subject of this sketch, and another soldier in the Division, were sent there on March 5, 1865, to compete for the prize furlough. They were a well matched pair, and had already baffled the discrimination of the Brigade commander. Arriving at Division Hdqrs. the General commanding put them through the entire manual of arms several times apiece, stood them up together and turned them to all views while they drilled, and in his puzzled frame of mind would probably have ordered them to stand upon their heads, if that had been regarded as a military exercise ; finally after a long drill and examination, the lookers on being as much puzzled as he was, in sheer desperation at his inability to justly decide between the two, the General cut the knot by passing out a twenty days' furlough to each competitor, and directed them to report to their commanders forthwith.

The Medical and Surgical, or Hospital, Department of the Thirteenth, from the beginning to the end of its term of service, was honorably officered and ably managed, and never referred to as second to that of any other regiment. This Department was organized with Dr. George B. Twitchell of Keene as Surgeon, Dr. Samuel A. Richardson of Marlboro as 1st Asst. Surgeon, Dr. John Sullivan of Exeter as 2d Asst. Surgeon, and John J. Whittemore of Nashua as Hospital Steward. Whittemore was the first to withdraw — having been taken seriously ill on the first day the Reg. spent in Virginia. His place was filled soon afterwards by Royal B. Prescott, of Nashua, as Hospital Steward. Dr. Twitchell was called to a higher position early in 1863, and his place was taken by Dr. Richardson as Surgeon ; Dr. Sullivan moving up to First Assistant.

Of Surgeon Richardson, Prescott — Hospital Steward — writes as follows : " He was detached from the Regiment a great deal, both as Brigade Surgeon, Surgeon of special expeditions, and as Surgeon-in-chief of the Corps Hospital at Point of Rocks, on the Appomattox, but he made frequent visits to the Reg., and was always glad to extend to it whatever privileges and favors it was in his power to bestow. There is not a survivor of the Reg. who does not remember that jovial soul with feelings of the liveliest gratitude and pleasure. He was as a father to all of the 'boys,' and his interest in them never wavered nor abated. The sick looked forward to his visits with pleasure, and took fresh hope and courage from his inspiring words ; his expansive smile was in itself sufficient to light up the entire hospital. He was universally beloved for his geniality, his deep and ready sympathy, and his boundless charity and generosity."

In the absence of its own Surgeon while Surgeon Richardson was near, either at Brigade or Corps Hdqrs., he interested himself in all severe cases of wounds or sickness occurring among the members of the Thirteenth, and thus a feeling of confidence was inspired. The men believed that somehow " Dr. Rich " would take care of them. His promotion to Surgeon took place April 1, 1863. On April 25, 1864, he was appointed Acting Medical Director of the 2d Brigade, 1st Division, 18th Army Corps. Dec. 6, 1864, he was assigned to duty at the Corps Hospital, following in the same position in the 24th Corps, and on June 8, 1865, was appointed Surgeon-in-charge of the same. He died at Marlboro, N. H., June 19, 1884.

Surgeon Richardson had a most remarkable faculty for story telling, and for finding and 'drawing out' the odd characters among the citizens, soldiers and negroes; they were always ready to talk with him, and to exhibit to him their peculiar traits without reserve.

He enjoyed repeating his side-splitting accounts of this or that affair, to the patients in Hospital — declaring that a hearty laugh would do a patient more good than a pint of medicine.

Dr. Horatio N. Small came to the Reg. in May 1863. Upon his leaving the Reg. in the following August, to accept promotion as Surgeon of the 10th N. H., his place was supplied by Dr. Ezekiel Morrill, of Concord, until Nov. 1864, when he was promoted to Surgeon of the 1st N. H. Heavy Artillery. Meanwhile, in August 1864, Asst. Surgeon Sullivan had resigned because of long continued ill health.

Hospital Steward Prescott received promotion Oct. 28, 1864, to a First Lieutenancy, after over two years of incessant toil, and care of wounds, breaks, burns, cuts, smashes, crushes, perforations, amputations, and all the ills that the flesh of thirteen hundred soldiers can possibly be heir to — to say nothing of the special gratuities ; and the only furlough, vacation or respite he had in all that time was a brief detachment as patient in the small-pox pest house. Even after his promotion as Lieutenant, he was called upon to prescribe in numerous cases of sickness, in the absence of Surgeons.

The Thirteenth in the changes and losses in its Medical Department was deprived of medical service, for long periods, by its own skilled and experienced medical men, and had to 'borrow' from other regiments. However, by this time the survivors present for duty were so tanned, inside and out, and callous on all surfaces, like hand-palms inured to constant contact with rough and hard materials, that it mattered little what the doses were, or whether the drugs were taken allopathically or homœopathically ; at retail or at wholesale ; it was safe to practice on the rule that " A pint is a pound the wide world round." One member of the Quarter-master's department (13th) could with impunity take quinine by the spoonful, and wash it down with any fluid that first came to hand.

Daniel W. Butterfield succeeded Prescott as Hospital Steward (and we think his family, to this day, somewhere, has possession of the medical chest and its apparatus belonging to the Thirteenth Regiment, and several books and records besides). Butterfield had a long experience as assistant about the hospital, and as nurse, and became very proficient, and far better qualified than many Hospital Stewards.

Prescott writes of him in this capacity : " A man was brought to the hospital sick. Butterfield took the first prescribed dose of medicine to him. The man inquired what it was ; ' 'T ain't none o' your b-b-b-usiness what it is,' stammered Butterfield, taking his short black pipe out of his mouth, 'that is the d-d-doctor's affair. All you have got to do is to t-t-t-take it.' ' I won't have it,' retorts the man, ' it smells nasty and I won't take it,' and he set down the cup in a determined manner and laid his head wearily on the pillow. In a moment more he raised his head and said : ' I 'd like some of that gruel, though.' ' All r-r-right,' said Butterfield, and taking up the rejected cup of medicine he started for the cookhouse for the gruel.

" Arriving again at the hospital door, Butterfield slyly poured the medicine into the gruel and advanced briskly to the bedside stirring the villanous mixture vigorously with a spoon as he went. ' H-h-here you are now ; drink it right down while it is h-h-ot,' remarked Butterfield, and the man drank it to the last drop without a word. Receiving the bowl again, Butterfield turned away, a smile of triumph lighting up his face, remarking : ' T-t-there 's more than one way to k-kill a c-c-cat. The c-c-country would go to the d-d-dogs pretty quick, if these fellows were allowed to h-h-have their own way about things.' "

Butterfield served as Hospital Steward to the end of the Regiment's term of service, and was mustered out with it. He had small mercy with 'playing sick '— malingering. One morning at a Surgeon's call the writer heard a man — a malingerer — say that he was too sick to be in his tent and ought to be sent to the hospital, and went on describing his diseases, a long list of them. Butterfield near by remarked : " Y-y-yes, Doctor, send him in. Any man who w-w-w-wants hospital, ought to have all the h-h-h-hospital he wants — that 's m-m-military."

Manson S. Brown of C carried the Hospital knapsack upon all marches and battle-fields. He represented a traveling drug store, stocked and provided, from the inside of his boot legs up through all his pockets to the lining of his cap, with medical materials and appliances of every description known to the army practice. No one would have been much surprised at any time to see him pull a stretcher, or a hospital cot-bed of some folding pattern, out of his capacious pockets. What he carried with him no one knew — but whatever was wanted he could somehow produce at once; straps, strings, bandages, bottles, paper, thread, twine, needles, plates, knives, spoons, tumblers, surgical instruments, and drugs in almost any variety.

Surgeon Horatio N. Small first entered the United States military service as Asst. Surgeon in the 17th New Hampshire, which was consolidated with the 2d N. H., April 16, 1863. He was commissioned Asst. Surgeon in the 13th N. H. May 7, 1863, and served with the Thirteenth until August 20, 1863, when he received a commission as Surgeon in the 10th N. H. For a part of the time while the 13th was in the 9th and 18th Corps, he acted as Brigade Surgeon. He was also a member of the operating surgical staff of the 24th Corps until the close of the war.

During the hard work and exposure of the spring and summer of 1864, he contracted the prevalent malarial disorders in a severe form. Early in September 1864 he was ordered upon a tour of Hospital inspections, with orders to report to the Surgeon General at Washington. On his arrival there he was suffering from chills and fever to such a degree that he was granted a leave of absence for twenty days from September 8th, instead of being ordered upon any service. He went home to Lancaster, N. H., but had been at home only a few days, when the news came of the two battles at Fort Harrison, and the severe losses in the 10th and 13th Regiments. His leave had already been extended, as he was still unfit for duty; nevertheless, he resolved to start immediately for the front, and did so as soon as he could. It troubled him greatly that he was not there. To use his own words: "The boys at the front need me. I have promised to look out for them. I must go back at once." He left home for the front about October 8th, and before the extension of his leave had expired. He was really unable to travel, had to take short distances, and did not reach the Regiment until October 17th. He remained with the 10th Regiment and Brigade nearly all the time after this until the end of the war; and after leaving the Thirteenth he was many times called upon in the interest of sick and wounded men in the 13th, always responding with a willing hand.

After peace was restored he settled in Portland, Maine, where he soon acquired an extensive medical practice, and to the day of his death justly occupied a foremost place among the practitioners in that city and vicinity. In 1866 he was appointed one of the United States Pension Examiners, which office he held until 1885, when he resigned. In 1874 he was appointed Instructor in Portland Medical School, which position he held until he died. In 1878, when the Marine General Hospital was established, he was elected Attending Physician on the Hospital staff, which position he also always retained. He was also Asst. Surgeon on Gov. Connor's staff.

He was intensely devoted to his profession, and to the interests of his

patients, quickly winning the confidence of all persons with whom he
came in contact. The cheerfulness of his face and voice was but the outward manifestation of his happy disposition, and this with his sterling
qualities made him always welcome in every company. He maintained
a most lively interest in all his old army comrades and acquaintances,
with ever an open and helping hand and heart for all who needed his
aid or assistance. His conduct through all was marked by the qualities
which ever distinguish a pure, noble and exemplary life. As his work
grew harder with the incessant calls of his ever extending practice, and
of his public position, the malarial infirmities contracted in the army
increased, and he died, in Portland, December 29, 1886, from a brain
disease caused by malarial poisoning and excessive hard work.

Lieut. S. Millett Thompson was born in Barnstead, N. H., April 27,
1838, the son of Stephen Jones Thompson and Nancy (Griffin) Thompson,
of Durham, and Lee, N. H. Besides the families here mentioned, he is
descended from Hon. Thomas Millét, of Dover, N. H., prominent in Col-
onial affairs, Capt. William Gerrish of Berwick, the Emerson, Waldron,
and several other families of Dover district; and it may be proper to
add is a lineal descendant of David Thompson, Gent., Scotchman, the first
permanent white settler in Massachusetts Bay, he having settled there
on 'Thompson's Island,' in Boston Harbor, in the spring of 1619, and
in 1623 was leader of the Laconia Colony settling at Piscataqua, New
Hampshire.

On both the paternal and maternal sides his ancestors were officers and
soldiers in the Indian wars, the war of the Revolution, and later on in
the New Hampshire militia organizations; besides others his father (S.
J. T.) having between 1832 and 1835 risen from private to Captain in
the Sixth Company of the old Tenth Infantry; and his great-grandfather
John Griffin having served as an officer in the Continental Army under
Gen. Greene, and later holding commission in the New Hampshire
militia, with rank of Lieut. Colonel, under Maj. Gen. John Sullivan.
See also page 199.

Lieut. Thompson fitted at Phillips Exeter Academy for the Sophomore
class at Harvard, studied medicine for a year with Dr. Ira Allen, at Roxbury Mass., and then enlisted as a private in the Thirteenth. Four
months' sojourn in a military hospital so utterly disgusted him with the
medical profession, that after his discharge from the service he went to
work as a book-keeper, being unable from lameness caused by his wound
to engage in any more active calling. Later he engaged in business connected with machinery and steam work, still later in Insurance and as
Treasurer of a Western Land Company.

He was present in every march, skirmish and battle in which the Thirteenth was engaged until wounded, and then compelled to leave the service much against his will. Some time before this, sympathizing strongly
with Capt. Charles O. Bradley, who did eventually join the regular ser-

vice, he had commenced a course of study with a special view of joining the regular army. Though having, previous to the battle at Battery Five, received three bullet holes through his clothing, and a small slit in his cap from a piece of shell, he somehow felt almost as sure he would not be killed in battle as if he had received a special revelation to that effect. With the exception of taking the compulsory whiskey rations two or three times while an enlisted man, he let intoxicants alone while in the army; and to this day feels that he owes his life to his temperate habits and strict abstention from intoxicants and alcohol in every form; he would under no other circumstances have recovered from the wound received at Battery Five, and the severe attack of gangrene while in hospital.

The Band of the Thirteenth was first organized at Concord, by selecting the two musicians belonging to each Company, which gave a membership of about twenty men to commence with. There were many changes. The Band remained with the Reg. until Jan. 20, 1863, when it became a Brigade Band, with the understanding that the Band should always remain in the same brigade with the Thirteenth. This was done in justice to the 13th, who had contributed about $700 for the original purchase of the instruments. The Band thus remained with the Reg. nearly all the time, and came home with it at the last.

William M. Critchley was Band Master and Leader during the three years. Charles E. Graham served as Sergeant of the Band for the first year and a half; he received a commission as Second Lieutenant in a colored regiment, and for the balance of the three years Charles W. Washburn served as Sergeant. Henry G. Parshley, by some considered the best musician in the Band, died of diphtheria. Henry Snow, Albion K. P. Shaw, and one or two others, were discharged the service because of sickness. A few members of the Band were supplied by other regiments in the brigade.

The Dirge most frequently played at funerals was the 'Dead March in Saul.' The Band played that march through nineteen times at the funeral of Lieut. Sanborn, who was shot by Dr. Wright of Norfolk. His remains had been sent home several days before this funeral was celebrated. All the colored troops in the Department were present at the funeral and our Band was engaged to play by the First Regiment of U. S. colored troops.

The above items about the Band were furnished to the writer by Sergt. Charles W. Washburn, who adds: "We had the good fortune to be in the first Division to enter Richmond, and to blow our horns."

"When the Band was mustered out of the service each man was given the instrument which he had used, and I have mine to-day" (1886).

JAMES M. CASWELL.

## PERSONAL NOTES.

### BAND ROSTER.

| Co. 13th. | | |
|---|---|---|
| K | Wm. M. Critchley, Jr., Leader, | First Eb Cornet. |
| K | Thomas Critchley | Tenor Drum and Solo Alto. |
| " | John Harrison | Bb Bass. |
| " | Abel Jackson | Bass Drum. |
| " | Nathan Whalley [1] | Second Eb Cornet. |
| " | Robert B. Welch | |
| H | Charles E. Graham, Sergt. | Second Alto. |
| " | Daniel G. Ripley | Second Eb Bass. |
| G | C. W. Washburn, Sergt. | First Bb Tenor. |
| F | Henry G. Parshley | Second Eb Cornet. |
| " | John H. Parshley | Solo Bb Cornet. |
| E | Stephen H. Brown | |
| " | James M. Caswell | First Alto. |
| D | Henry W. Burnham | Solo Alto and Tenor Drum. |
| " | John W. Palmer | Third Eb Cornet. |
| C | Horace D. Carter | Third Bb Cornet. |
| " | Gilman F. Chase | Eb Bass. |
| B | Albion K. P. Shaw | |
| " | William H. Peckham | Second Bb Tenor. |
| " | Frank Sanborn [2] | Bass Drum. |
| | Albert Nelson (10th N. H.) | Tenor Drum. |
| | John H. Peckham | |
| | Henry Snow. | |

"Company K, Thirteenth, was organized in Portsmouth, N. H., in the months of August and September 1862; 135 men enlisted for this Company, 115 of whom went to Concord to be mustered into the service. It was intended at first that the Company should join the Ninth Regiment, but Jacob I. Storer having obtained a commission as Major of the Thirteenth requested that these men be retained for that regiment, which request was granted, and 98 men of the 115 were assigned to Company K in the Thirteenth. Of the remaining number William J. Ladd was mustered as Sergeant Major, Edwin Lesley was appointed Corporal, afterwards Sergeant, in Company F, five or six were assigned to Company E, and the rest returned to their homes.

"Of the 101 officers and men who constituted this Company, 42 were enlisted by Capt. Betton, 22 by Lieut. Goss, 18 by Lieut. Coffin, 2 by George W. Towle and 1 by J. N. Brown; 77 went from Portsmouth, 17 from Rye, 6 from Newington, and 1 from Seabrook.

"Sergeant Robert M. Spinney and Corporal Jacob Ormerod were pro-

---

[1] Took Henry G. Parshley's place after he died.

[2] After Abel Jackson was discharged. There may have been other members of the Band, but this is the most authentic list that can now be found. — S. M. T.

moted to commissioned officers of colored troops. Benjamin F. Winn was promoted to First Lieutenant of Co. B, but was not mustered because of the early muster-out of the Regiment. William M. Critchley Jr. was appointed leader of the Band of the Thirteenth — afterwards a Brigade Band — and Nathan Whalley second leader; six men in all from Company K, were members of this Band.

"Company K was a good Company, second to none; and I always felt highly honored by having been the commander of such a patriotic, brave and efficient body of soldiers." CAPT. BETTON.

Three men of Company B — Corporal Charles B. Saunders, Sergt. David E. Proctor and Sergt. George T. Woodward — occupied the same tent, or hut, in the winter camp at Fort Tillinghast. Proctor proposed that all the three apply for commissions in colored regiments. The other two 'sat down' upon the proposition — heavy. Then one of them repented and proposed the same thing in return to Proctor; the result of their plans was an earnest study for examination. All three were successful, and received commissions, Sanders as First Lieutenant, Proctor and Woodward as Captains. The three were assigned to the 30th U. S. C. T.

Capt. Proctor left the Thirteenth and joined the 30th C. T. March 3, 1864, two days before he was twenty-one years of age. The 30th with other colored regiments had charge of the wagon trains on the march from the Rapidan to the James, arriving in front of Petersburg June 18th. It belonged to the 4th Division of the 9th Army Corps. It was engaged continuously in the operations carried on in front of Petersburg during the summer.

"At the explosion of the Mine July 30th," writes Capt. Proctor, "we went in three hours after the mine was fired. The 30th was the leading regiment. I had command of the first division of two companies, and such position brought me in the advance of the whole charging column. It was bloody work. My Company went in with 58 men, and 33 of that number were killed, wounded or missing."

The 30th did duty with the 9th Corps until Nov. 27, 1864, when it was transferred to the Army of the James, in the 3d Div. of the 10th Corps. Also took part in both of the Fort Fisher expeditions. Then joined Gen. Sherman's army in North Carolina. Was mustered out Dec. 10, 1865.

Nov. 28, 1864, Capt. Proctor was severely wounded in his right hip, while in command of the picket of the 30th near an old mill upon a creek which flows into the Appomattox — Proctor's Creek (but so named anciently). — and rejoined his Regiment, after many weeks of suffering and hospital life, May 28, 1865. He was promoted Major by brevet, to date from March 13, 1865, for gallant and meritorious conduct.

Charles B. Saunders served with the Thirteenth in all of its marches and engagements until March 1, 1864, when he was discharged, and commissioned a First Lieutenant in the 30th U. S. C. T. He served with this regiment until mustered out on Dec. 10, 1865. During the march from the Rapidan to the James the 30th was frequently hurried out of column into battle order to repel rebel attacks, but did not come to any engagement, except at Old Church, Va., where the picket line alone was attacked by a small force of rebel cavalry, which was easily repulsed.

The 30th was brought under fire frequently, during the summer, on the Petersburg front, up to July 30th, when it engaged in the charge succeeding the Mine explosion. Here Lieut. Saunders was captured, and with the exception of about a week at Petersburg and Danville, Va., was held as a prisoner of war at Columbia, S. C., until March 1, 1865, when he came into the Union line at Wilmington, N. C., under parole.

When Richmond was surrendered he was on a leave of absence as a paroled prisoner, and completely broken in health. After his return to his regiment in May 1865, he was urged by its Colonel to accept a Captaincy, his health, however, was very poor, and not feeling equal to the additional duties necessarily demanded in that higher position, he declined. He served as Adjutant of the 30th from June 1865 to the time of muster-out Dec. 10, 1865. He received no wounds while in the service, but suffered in health severely for a long period because of the rigors of the southern prison life and from starvation, exposure and chronic diarrhœa. He is now, 1887, a physician of extensive and lucrative practice in Acton Centre, Massachusetts.

Sergt. George T. Woodward served with the Thirteenth until March 1, 1864, when he was mustered out, receiving a commission as Captain in the 30th U. S. C. T. He followed the fortunes of the 30th with his compatriots Proctor and Saunders, the three also always tenting together, up to the Mine explosion, when he was severely wounded in the arm. Recovering and rejoining his regiment, he was present in both the Fort Fisher expeditions. At the capture of that fort he commanded the courier line established by Brev. Maj. Gen. Charles J. Paine commanding 3d Div., 10th Corps, in which position he earned and received the highest commendations of that General and of the other officers. He received promotion as Major by brevet, to date from March 13, 1865, for gallant and meritorious conduct.

July 1. Sat. Rainy. The Thirteenth is paid off for six months by Paymaster Henry McFarland, and the members receive their final discharge from the service in the forenoon. In the afternoon they turn in their guns and equipments, form their last line of battle in the rear of their stacks of arms, hear — and obey — their last military command : " Break Ranks — March ! "

Just three years and a day have passed since the call of President Lincoln for volunteers was issued under which enlistments immediately commenced for the Thirteenth, the survivors of which at the close of this day are speeding to their homes.

The members of the Thirteenth now form part of a body of 800,000 men, who like themselves have been discharged the military service of the United States within a few recent weeks; men, who have fought in hundreds of battles — 2,261 the record runs — some of them ranking high among the greatest battles of history; men, who are now hurrying homeward to every city, town and hamlet in the whole East, North and West; men, who are passing at will, without guard or escort, without violence or jar, and all as quietly as if their immediate four years of tremendous war were but a natural and commonplace incident of an American citizen's life; men, who but a few short hours ago stepped from out the most grim, terrible and destructive lines of battle the world has ever seen, to enter at once upon all the quiet paths, vocations and industries of profoundest peace, — in the land they have freed, in the Union they have saved, in the mighty NATION their hard blows have welded when never so hot; and men who now as citizens will sternly but kindly hold all they have so firmly welded, until it cools. Of such another scene history is dumb.

"The only National Debt we can never pay, is the Debt that America owes to these victorious Union Soldiers."

New Hampshire Adjt. General's Report. Vol 2, for 1865, page 339: "The Thirteenth bore an honorable part in fifteen engagements, the names of which are inscribed on its colors. No officer of the command has ever been cashiered or dismissed the service. One half or more of its officers are on detached service in various capacities in the army, while the general intelligence and honesty of its men have won for the Regiment a character for trustworthiness, efficiency and integrity in the discharge of their duties, second to none in the service. It has captured five pieces of artillery in one charge, and with its Division taken sixteen pieces more; has captured three battle flags, and taken more prisoners from the enemy than the number in its own ranks; and has never been driven from the field, or from its positions by the enemy."

The following, of a bold personal act, is furnished at a late date: "In the Band of the Thirteenth (see Roster) who were awakened by Prescott on the night we left Fredericksburg, were Charles E. Graham and myself. When we went to sleep, in the basement of a brick house — on Caroline Street — in that city, we left a large pot of beans cooking, in the fire-place of the house, well covered up with coals and ashes in approved army style. On reaching the street, after being called up, we began to discuss with much disgust the unfortunate necessity of leaving those Yankee baked beans for the rebels to eat in the morning. Graham, fleet of foot, suddenly left us, and a few minutes afterwards returned with the pot of beans in a piece of shelter tent, which he had gathered at the four corners. They were nicely done and steaming. We took turns in carrying those beans the several miles we marched; and astonished all who saw us by eating hot baked beans that morning in the chilly pine woods near Falmouth."

CHARLES W. WASHBURN, BAND.

ADDENDA. 629

## OFFICIAL MONTHLY REPORTS BY COMMANDERS OF THE THIRTEENTH.

| End of Month. | COMMISSIONED OFFICERS. | | ENLISTED MEN. | | COMMISSIONED. | ENLISTED. |
|---|---|---|---|---|---|---|
| | Present for duty. | Sick. Present and absent. | Present for duty. | Sick. Present and absent. | Total Comd. Present and absent. | Total Enlisted Present and absent. |
| **1862.** | | | | | | |
| Oct. | 30 | 4 | 640 | 137 | 39 | 974 |
| Nov. | 34 | 3 | 590 | 320 | 38 | 953 |
| Dec. | 29 | 7 | 587 | 291 | 37 | 933 |
| **1863.** | | | | | | |
| Jan. | 24 | 7 | 468 | 361 | 36 | 892 |
| Feb. | 22 | 6 | 493 | 299 | 35 | 860 |
| Mar. | 27 | 4 | 454 | 274 | 37 | 816 |
| April | 30 | 4 | 485 | 219 | 36 | 788 |
| May | 23 | 5 | 438 | 229 | 36 | 766 |
| June | 22 | 4 | 376 | 258 | 33 | 756 |
| July | 18 | 3 | 365 | 244 | 33 | 742 |
| Aug. | 20 | 6 | 326 | 227 | 37 | 710 |
| Sept. | 18 | 5 | 329 | 191 | 39 | 675 |
| Oct. | 23 | 4 | 463 | 163 | 39 | 806 |
| Nov. | 23 | 4 | 463 | 158 | 38 | 787 |
| Dec. | 22 | 3 | 421 | 149 | 39 | 763 |
| **1864.** | | | | | | |
| Jan. | 25 | 3 | 448 | 148 | 39 | 783 |
| Feb. | 24 | 3 | 518 | 137 | 38 | 806 |
| Mar. | 19 | 5 | 506 | 131 | 38 | 791 |
| April | 17 | 5 | 307 | 161 | 39 | 728 |
| May | 15 | 9 | 394 | 168 | 37 | 695 |
| June | 10 | 10 | 213 | 283 | 35 | 650 |
| July | 9 | 8 | 210 | 280 | 35 | 642 |
| Aug. | 10 | 7 | 197 | 285 | 35 | 625 |
| Sept. | 5 | 10 | 170 | 289 | 33 | 602 |
| Oct. | 10 | 7 | 183 | 267 | 30 | 595 |
| Nov. | 10 | 3 | 168 | 265 | 30 | 583 |
| Dec. | 10 | 2 | 205 | 225 | 30 | 571 |
| **1865.** | | | | | | |
| Jan. | 10 | 2 | 215 | 211 | 30 | 560 |
| Feb. | 8 | 2 | 219 | 189 | 29 | 543 |
| Mar. | 7 | 1 | 215 | 156 | 28 | 520 |
| April | 8 | 3 | 228 | 142 | 29 | 520 |
| May | 9 | 2 | 178 | 130 | 26 | 502 |

The Thirteenth served all its term in Virginia, excepting the few days' march through Maryland. It was present in engagements where nearly 50,000 Union soldiers were officially reported killed or wounded.

From the best information the writer can obtain, it appears that the average age of the officers and men of the Thirteenth was a little under twenty-five years; average height, five feet eight inches; a great majority of the members having blue eyes, darkish hair and light complexion.

The Thirteenth was in :

The Defenses of Washington, Gen. Silas Casey's Division, from our arrival in Virginia on October 9th, up to the march to the Battle of Fredericksburg on Dec. 1, 1862.

Ninth Corps during the Battle of Fredericksburg, and until June 19, 1863. Badge: Shield with anchor and cannon crossed.

Seventh Corps from June 19, 1863, to Aug. 1, 1863. Badge: Crescent, the horns enclosing a five-pointed star.

Eighteenth Corps from Aug. 1, 1863, to Dec. 3, 1864. Badge: 'Clover-leaf' cross, with two small triangles.

Twenty-fourth Corps from Dec. 3, 1863, to close of the war. Badge: Heart enclosing a heart.

The First Division of a Corps wore the badge in red; the Second, in white; the Third, in blue.

The total number of enlistments in the Union army were, according to the Century, 2,778,304. Capt. Phisterer, in his 'Statistical Record,' states that the total number will exceed 2,850,000.

The South, with a population nearly half as large as that of the North, and pressing into the Confederate army every boy and man it could between the ages of 16 and 60, probably had a force more than half as large as that of the North, all acclimated and fighting on its own soil.

It is stated that the Union army which put down the Rebellion was, as an average, not quite twenty-two years old — the Boys did it!

## VISIT SOUTH.

Having been provided by the Secretary of War, Hon. Robert T. Lincoln,[1] and later by Hon. William C. Endicott, with a 'Letter of introduction to Commanders of Departments and Posts, and Superintendents of National Cemeteries,' I went to Virginia in May 1885, and spent several weeks among the old camps and battle-fields where the Thirteenth was during the war. I stopped at Lt. Col. Normand Smith's house for a week, and with him visited the fields of Cold Harbor and Fair Oaks, Petersburg Front, Battery Five, Drury's Bluff, Fort Harrison, and the place of entry into Richmond, April 3, 1865, following that march from the front into the city.

He assisted in locating places and in measuring, pacing or estimating

[1] Robert T. Lincoln was my classmate at Phillips Academy, Exeter, and I had the pleasure of being the first person to inform him of his father's first nomination for the Presidency. — S. M. T.

distances. The Thirteenth is greatly indebted to him for his time, his team, his numerous notes and facts, and for the assistance that made the sketches in this book possible. All was done by him with the whole-hearted and generous cheerfulness characteristic of the man. His farm is on the Charles City road, two or three miles below Richmond. When Fort Harrison was captured the Union cavalry penetrated to this farm, for the purpose of attacking a large earth-work situated about one third of a mile northward from where Lt. Col. Smith's house now stands. While clearing the farm of brush after the war, he found several human skeletons, but could not tell whether they were of Federals or Confederates. A portion of his land was occupied as a camp by Gen. Wade Hampton's famous Black Horse Cavalry. This old cavalry camp is now Lt. Col. Smith's favorite garden tract, where his plow frequently turns up sundry bits of Confederate army gear, together with saddle iron, mule and horse shoes, and soldier's clay tobacco pipes — and now and then an arrow head, an ancient memento of the dusky warriors of the famous old Indian, King Powhatan.

From Richmond I went on a steamer down the James to Norfolk, and from there visited the Soldiers' Home at Hampton — in war time the Chesapeake Hospital — where now 1,500 Veterans are provided for; saw them all seated at dinner, the most of them gray-haired men. In the Cemetery, connected with this Home, are buried thirty-one members of the Thirteenth, twenty-nine of them buried there in 1863-4. From Norfolk I visited Fortress Monroe, obtaining there several convenient maps. Afterwards visited Suffolk and vicinity, and went thence by rail to Fredericksburg and Washington ; at the latter place receiving from Maj. Gen. John G. Parke, for a long term commander of the 9th Corps, the official maps traced in this book.

While in Virginia I talked freely with the citizens, and, with one exception, met with no one who in any way or degree appeared at all crossgrained ; and this fellow was a mere little upstart of about twenty summers. All others were perfectly cordial and gentlemanly ; in fact the Southern soldiers, and people generally, are very agreeable for the Northern soldiers to meet. The most expressed themselves as glad that the war turned out just as it did. Several said expressly : "We now see it was all for the best." One citizen of Richmond said: "The South was educated to the States' rights idea, the North to the National idea ; now we are all one, that root of evil, slavery, is gone, and we are all glad of it. Before the war and during it here, the poor white man of the non-slaveholding class had little or no redress for mischiefs, insults or wrongs done by the rich man's negro — but now any white man is just as good as any nigger." The people were very free with reminiscences of the war — and quite impartial as to which side they would talk upon — but the most are quite out of place here.

The men I met discussed the war freely, holding that the Cold Harbor battle was very important and the chief turning-point, forcing the war into a hopeless siege. Several held that the South should have established a frontier, the one most easily defensible as against the North, and then bent every energy to maintaining it; keeping within its own territory, leaving losses of domain here and there for final treaty adjustment in the event of Confederate success. There were similar mistakes made, where in all the South lost 50,000 men beyond her legitimate borders, but Gettysburg was the crowning blunder of all — the great Confederate mistake. I will venture to add: Whenever a person shall ask the historical conundrum: "At what battle did Gen. Lee surrender?"— answer: At Cold Harbor.

It seemed to me that the South has a most troublesome and a fearfully dangerous legacy inherited from slavery. There are good negroes, but there are also great numbers whose life is dominated by their animal propensities, immoral to the last degree; we have no class like them here in the North, and can form little idea of actual affairs from the press of the South. The negroes swarm; every bullet planted in the war seems to have sprouted into a little negro; and every shell, case and canister shot turned into a dirty negro hut, ready and willing to burst with a numerous tribe of more little negroes. One remark made to me by a respectable native white man near Suffolk, I will give as a notion of trouble ahead: "Neeg-urs here are gwine ter git erbuv 'emselfs fore soon, er'ekn — 'f ther don't look-out."

Of the present condition of the old camps, battle-fields, forts and lines of trenches, I may say they are as tame as the gorilla that was 'starved to it' a day too long — heavy, dead, limp, flat and uninteresting. They are like champagne and soda, with all the 'sizz' off. Their stillness is positively painful. Trees, underbrush and vines have covered them, and all their steep sides and sharp angles are rounded into huge ridges and banks of earth; they need forty cannon, two dozen drum corps and ten thousand muskets, all in full snap, to make them seem at all natural.

On the whole my journey was to me very agreeable and interesting, as was a similar but shorter trip in 1878; and I would earnestly advise every Veteran, who can avail himself of the privilege, to visit the old camp-grounds and battle-fields where he served while a soldier.

---

It seems best to the writer to add one fair, plain word in closing this book. Altogether too much has been claimed for the Union army, in the way of representing it, or parts of it, as all the time spoiling for a fight, anxious to meet the foe, eager for battle, cheering on the eve of an opportunity to wipe out the rebel army, enthusiastic heroes, glorying in gore, tremendously given to 'chewing flint and steel and spitting fire' — and all that sort of bosh; thus painting us as an army of ancient Jews, Arabs, Bazouks, heathen and savages, and not as Christian soldiers. All that is neither courage nor a commendable bravery, it is all a mere gross animalism, the way of dogs and bullies — any brute can act like that. Better leave all that kind of stuff to those who love to write thus about the men of the Southern army — and they would better quit; it is no praise, but the worst possible detraction from their manliness. Bloodthirstiness and hate is no patriotism.

To fight for the sake of fighting was contrary to the spirit and genius of the Northern army in this struggle — to build a Nation was the real issue; there was no instance, however, where combativeness was required where our Regiment, at least, failed to furnish it in abundance; and such instances were extremely rare in the army in general. Beware the hand of a man, slow to anger, when once you have roused him.

Excepting a few men, and they for the most part the floating 'soldiers of fortune,' who were thrust in among the regular volunteers, the men of the Union army were sustained by a high patriotism, and by the consciousness of the justice, honor and right of their cause — they felt it through and through; and went into battle with the same cool, stern feelings with which any sane and good man encounters danger to his life and limb: because the honorable necessity is laid upon him. With all its faults, the Northern army as a whole was good, honest, honorable and of clean grit. There was much loud cheering over victories, no matter what the cost to either side; but no cheers, not one, that army ever gave over the rebel wounded or dead, and no jeering at or insulting prisoners taken. A clear sense of danger and a high purpose is necessary to a noble courage — this can face danger down; this characterized the Northern army.

Curiously enough, after making the final copy of this page for the press, the writer's attention was called to Maj. Gen. W. T. Sherman's contribution to the Century Magazine for February 1888, in which he writes (condensed):

"We veterans believe that in 1861–5 we fought a holy war, with absolute right on our side, with pure patriotism, and achieved a result which enabled the United States of America to resume her glorious career in the interest of all mankind."

Of himself and Gen. Grant he adds: "We were as brothers — I the older man in years, but he the higher in rank. We both believed in our heart of hearts that the success of the Union cause was not only necessary to the then generation of Americans, but to all future generations. We both professed to be gentlemen and professional soldiers, educated in the science of war by our generous Government for the very occasion which had arisen. Neither of us by nature was a combative man; but with honest hearts and a clear purpose to do what man could we embarked on that campaign."

He also adds a description of our old campaigning methods, that is too good and clear to be passed by: " A regiment, brigade, division or corps, halting for the night or for battle, faced the enemy; moved forward to ground with a good outlook to the front; stacked arms; gathered logs, stumps, fence-rails, and anything which would stop a bullet; piled these to their front, and, digging a ditch behind, threw the dirt forward, and made a parapet which covered their persons as perfectly as a granite wall."

As to the Thirteenth the writer does not act as a critic; does not draw any invidious comparisons between man and man; does not decry one nor exalt another; he merely endeavors to give the facts with the utmost possible exactness, and with an impartial hand. There was a remarkable evenness among the officers, and also among the enlisted men. It is fortunate that no pet hero stands for the Thirteenth, that no mere individual name overshadows this organization with a great, a buncombe or a bounceful personality. This is no one-man regiment; any member of this regiment is mentioned only as the incidental, fortunate or unfortunate part of the one grand whole. The Thirteenth is a historic Regiment, in which 'I' goes to the rear, and 'We' stands at the front.

Of the members of the Thirteenth each one had his own natural way of acting his part; all could not excel in any one direction, but all found a useful place — and take them for all in all it is doubtless safe to assert that thirteen hundred better men and soldiers did not fill any regimental organization in the Union service in the war of 1861–5.

In civil life the worst enemy the Union Veterans have among themselves is General Blab — the big talker who does not talk truly; the worst enemy outside of their own numbers, the meanest opponent, the least trustworthy and shabbiest person generally, whom the Union Veteran soldier now meets, knows, or has anything to do with, is the Northern man of near his own age, who was then able-bodied for military service, but who ignobly, cowardly, and without honorable cause or reason shirked the war of 1861–5, — in anything whatever trust him not at all. The writer speaks from a long and a most unsatisfactory personal experience with, and observation of, many persons of this class, native born, but still unworthy of American citizenship.

Widening our view again, the men of the Southern army were of the same race as the Northern, differing only in training, education and in the hotness of temperament that a hot climate seems to provoke in English stock; and nine out of every ten men of both armies now, 1888, meet as friends, and are as proud as can be of mutual prowess, honor and grit. This now national kindliness and fraternity of spirit, that comes of kin, as well as from other sources, is increasing wherever persons of the two sections meet, at home or abroad, and the old soldiers of both armies, and of all grades of rank, take the lead in it; and the schemer for personal ends who works against it, should be held as unworthy of public official place, should be reckoned a consummate fool, a mischief-maker, and no American — he ought to be pitched ignominiously head-foremost into the nearest goose-pond, and there be left to cool off. In the language of our noble old commander, the world's first General, Ulysses S. Grant: "Let us have peace."

## ADDENDA.

This book is no place for a sermon, but the oft repeated remark that, comparatively speaking, the Southern army was more religious than the Northern army — as if that were any great credit — ought not to be passed in silence, for religion may be this thing and may be that thing, from Confucianism to Voudooism, or better or worse, and Christianity be altogether another thing; and it is always far better than all else combined.

The South was led wrong. Bring together in like circumstance, custom and habit the white people of the North and of the South, and they of the two sections would scarcely be separable.

There was a fearful bar to unity between these English peoples; and when God, the father of us all, found slavery as the political corner-stone, and the economical and social corner-stone, of the Southern Confederacy, standing as a determined bar to the Gospel of Jesus Christ in this great American commonwealth — and there is no disputing that — He gathered, in the free Northland, ninety-nine out of every hundred of her best young men, formed them into a compact body, and hurled them at a stroke against this system of human slavery, crushed that Confederacy's corner-stone to powder, and scattered it to the four winds; and all the world, and gradually this very Southland also, rose up and said Amen! The Old South passed out into history and tradition.

That the most of those ninety-nine out of every hundred of the best young men of the entire North were Christians needs no proof. Their life before, during and since the war, their every thought, word and act of truth, honor, kindliness and right, is proof direct to the point — they are our fellow citizens. He must be a blind, narrow and bigoted person indeed who cannot, or will not, see the workings of the providence of God, and the advance of Christianity and the best interests of mankind — and these two are a unity — in the events and issues between 1860 and 1888, this one generation, nearly, of the white people of these United States. Probably the most of the story of the differences in and between the peoples of the two sections in 1860–5 can be written in one sentence — the South was the more religious, the North was the more Christian. The New South is now free to build upon a new foundation, hand in hand and heart in heart, with the free North.

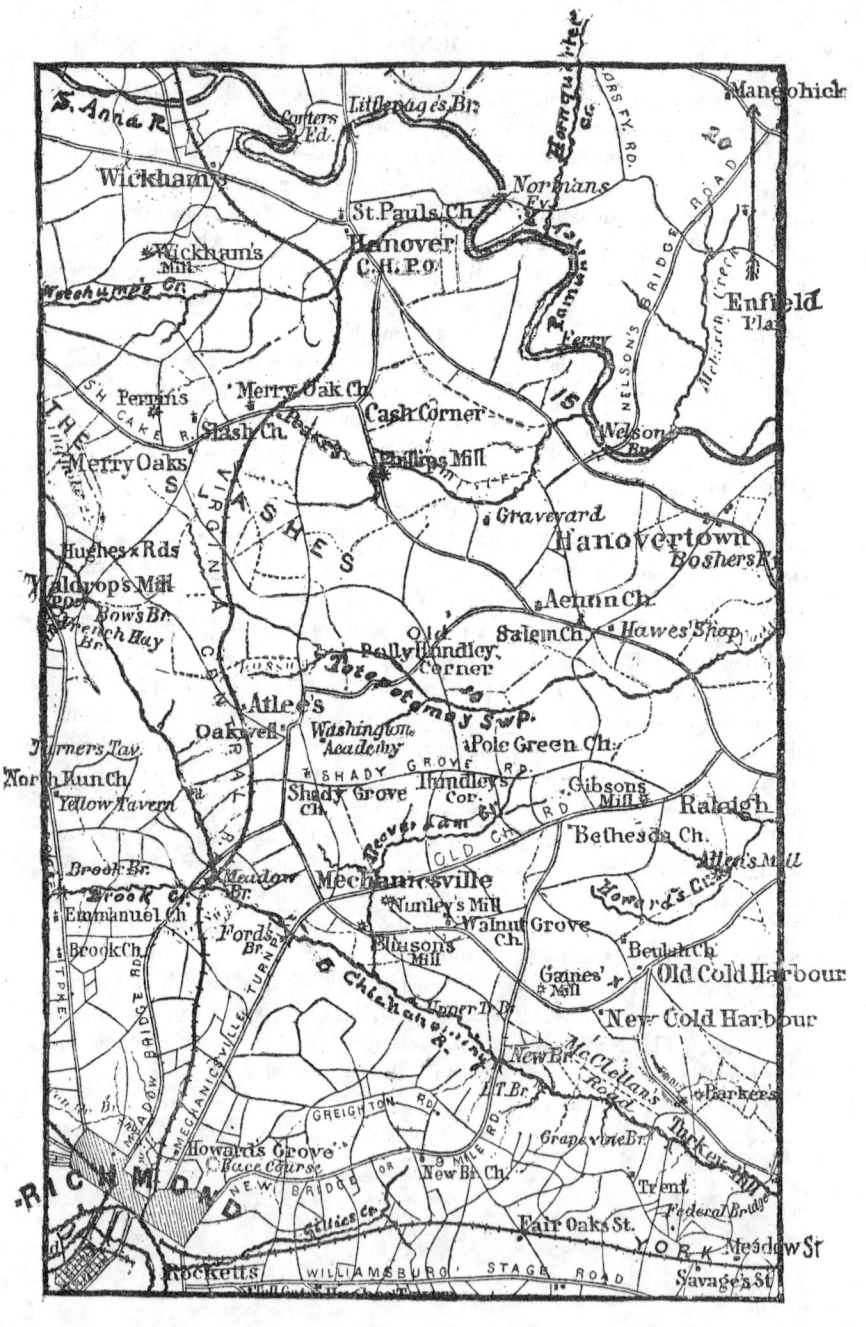

SECTION OF MAP, 'THIRTY-FIVE MILES AROUND RICHMOND.'

Scale, five sixteenths of an inch to one mile.

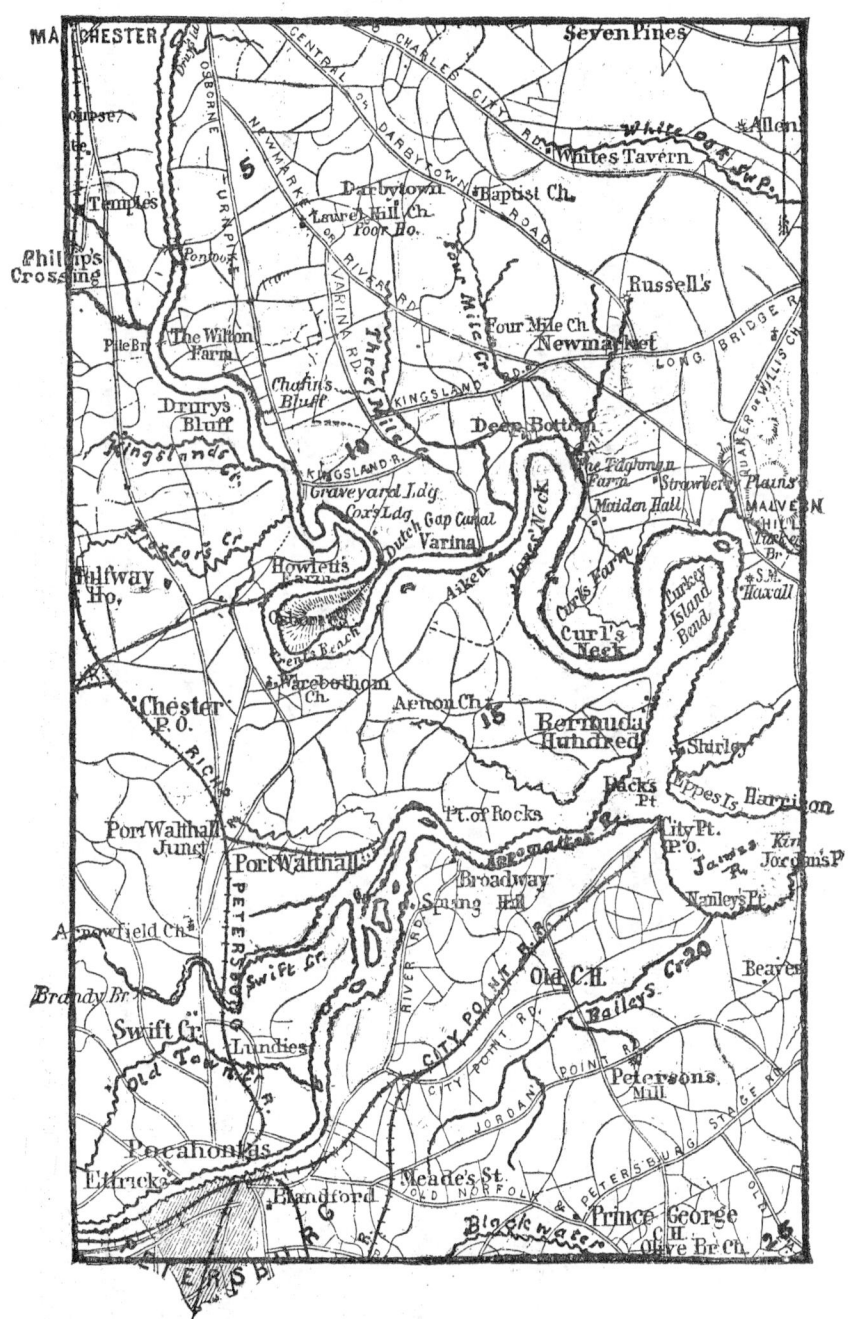

SECTION OF MAP, 'THIRTY-FIVE MILES AROUND RICHMOND.'

Scale, five sixteenths of an inch to one mile.

# ROSTER.

This Roster of the Thirteenth was first copied by me from the New Hampshire Adjutant General's Report, Vol. II, for 1865; then was corrected as far as possible from the same Report, Vol. I, for 1866; then Adjutant General Augustus D. Ayling took the Roster, in my manuscript, and thoroughly revised it from end to end and compared it in exhaustive detail with the rolls and papers in the State archives; so that it is complete and correct so far as it goes, but is unavoidably brief in the personal histories of the men. The ages given are the ages of the men at the date of their enlistment. It is quite necessary to state here, in order to save space, that the men were recruited, or gathered by enlistment, in each Company, respectively, by the first Officers — the original Captains and Lieutenants — of that Company. — S. M. T.

| | Age. | Residence. | Rank. | Date of Commission. | Remarks. |
|---|---|---|---|---|---|
| Aaron F. Stevens | 43 | Nashua | Colonel | Aug. 26, '62 | Wounded sl. June 1, '64. Wd. sev. in leg Sept. 29, '64. Discharged Feb. 4, '65. Discharge suspended. App. Brig. Gen. U. S. V. by Brevet to date Dec. 8, '64. Mustered out as Colonel June 21, '65. |
| George Bowers | 45 | Nashua | Lt. Col. | Aug. 26, '62 | Dis. for disability May 31, '63. |
| Jacob I. Storer | 36 | Portsmouth | " | June 1, '63 | Dis. for disability May 29, '64. |
| William Grantman | 23 | Wakefield | " | July 15, '64 | Dis. for disability Oct. 16, '64. |
| Normand Smith | 32 | Stewartstown | " | Oct. 28, '64 | Mustered out June 21, '65. Wounded at Ft. Harrison Sept. 29, '64. |
| Jacob I. Storer | 36 | Portsmouth | Major | Aug. 26, '62 | Pro. Lt. Col. June 1, '63. |
| William Grantman | 23 | Wakefield | " | June 1, '63 | Pro. Lt. Col. July 15, '64. |
| Normand Smith | 32 | Stewartstown | " | July 15, '64 | Pro. Lt. Col. Oct. 28, '64. |
| Nathan D. Stoodley | 39 | Peterborough | " | Oct. 28, '64 | Mustered out June 21, '65. |
| George H. Gillis | 28 | Nashua | Adjutant | Sept. 3, '62 | Dis. for disability Mar. 23, '63. |
| Nathan B. Boutwell | 29 | Lyndeborough | " | March 24, '63 | Wounded sev. June 15, '64. Dis. for disability May 5, '65. |
| George H. Taggard | 26 | Nashua | " | May 30, '65 | Mustered out June 21, '65. Wounded sev. June 3, '64, at Cold Harbor. |
| Person C. Cheney | 34 | Peterborough | Qr. Master. | Sept. 3, '62 | Dis. for disability Aug. 8, '63. |
| Mortier L. Morrison | 26 | Peterborough | " | Aug. 12, '63 | Mustered out June 21, '65. |

| Name | Residence | Age | Rank | Mustered in | Remarks |
|---|---|---|---|---|---|
| George B. Twitchell | Keene | 42 | Surgeon | Sept. 15, '62 | Dis. for pro. as Surgeon U. S. Vols. Mar. 21, '63. |
| Samuel A. Richardson | Marlborough | 31 | | April 1, '63 | Mustered out June 21, '65. |
| Samuel A. Richardson | Marlborough | 31 | Asst. Surgeon | Sept. 16, '62 | Pro. Surgeon April 1, '63. |
| John Sullivan | Exeter | 22 | " | Sept. 16, '62 | Dis. for disability, Aug. 16, '64. |
| Ezekiel Morrill | Concord | | " | Sept. 7, '63 | Pro. Surgeon 1st Regt. N. H. H. Arty, Nov. 17, '64. |
| Horatio N. Small | Lancaster | | " | April 16, '63 | Pro. Surgeon 10th N. H. V. Aug. 20, '63. |
| Jeremiah W. White | Unknown | | " | Sept. 3, '62 | Declined Sept. 3, '62. |
| Rockwood G. Mather | Marlow | | " | June 27, '64 | Declined. |
| Levi P. Sawyer | Nashua | | " | Jan. 2, '65 | Declined Jan. 10, '65. |
| John C. Emory | Hudson | | " | March 1, '65 | Mustered out June 21, '65. |
| George G. Jones | Nashua | 40 | Chaplain | Sept. 3, '62 | Hon. dis. May 9, '65. |
| William J. Ladd | Portsmouth | 18 | Sergt. Major | Sept. 30, '62 | Pro. 2d Lieut. Dec. 30, '62. |
| Charles C. Favor | Boston | 25 | " | March 7, '63 | Pro. 2d Lieut. Nov. 28, '63. |
| James M. Hodgdon | Rollinsford | 26 | " | Dec. 12, '63 | Wounded sev. Sept. 30, '64. Pro. 2d Lieut. Co. A June 15, '65. |
| Mortier L. Morrison | Peterborough | 26 | Qr. Mr. Sergt. | Sept. 26, '62 | Pro. Quarter-master Aug. 12, '63. |
| Charles A. Ames | Peterborough | 23 | | Aug. 26, '63 | Mustered out June 21, '65. |
| George H. Taggard | Nashua | 26 | Com. Sergt. | Sept. 30, '62 | Pro. 2d Lieut. Co. F March 16, '64. |
| George W. Ferguson | Monroe | 33 | " | May 1, '64 | Pro. 1st Lieut. Co. H July 15, '64. |
| George Burns | Concord | 21 | " | Sept. 6, '64 | Pro. 2d Lt. Co. K June 15, '65, not mustered; mustered out as Com. Sergt. June 21, '65. |
| John J. Whittemore | Nashua | 27 | Hosp. Steward | Sept. 30, '62 | Dis. for disability Nov. 22, '62. |
| Royal B. Prescott | Nashua | 23 | " | Nov. 22, '62 | Acting Asst. Surgeon 1864. Pro. 1st Lt. Co. C Oct. 28, '64. |
| D. W. Butterfield | Nashua | 33 | " | Nov. 28, '64 | Mustered out June 21, '65. |
| Charles Lull | Strafford | 23 | Musician | April 28, '64 | Died of disease in Hospital at Point of Rocks, Va., Jan. 22, '65. |
| Charles C. Hall | Campton | 26 | " | March 1, '65 | Mustered out June 21, '65. |
| Manson S. Brown | | | " | | |

## A.

| | Age. | Residence. | Rank. | Muster in. | Muster out. | Remarks. |
|---|---|---|---|---|---|---|
| William Grautman | | Wakefield | Captain | Sept. 27, '62 | | Pro. Major. |
| Buel C. Carter | | Ossipee | " | June 1, '63 | | App. A. Q. M. Volunteers May 17, '64. |
| George A. Bruce | | Mount Vernon | " | May 30, '64 | June 21, '65 | Wounded sl. Sept. 29, '64. |
| Buel C. Carter | | Ossipee | 1st Lieut. | Sept. 27, '62 | June 21, '65 | Wounded sl. Dec. 13, '62. Pro. Capt. Co. A. |
| Charles B. Gafney | | Ossipee | " | June 1, '63 | | Wounded sev. June 15, '64. Pro. Capt. Co. I, not mustered; mustered out as 1st Lieut. |
| Benjamin F. Winn | | Portsmouth | " | May 30, '65 | June 21, '65 | Pro. Lieut., not mustered; mustered out as 1st Sergt. |
| Charles B. Gafney | | Ossipee | 2d Lieut. | Sept. 27, '62 | | Pro. 1st Lieut. Co. A. |
| Henry Churchill | | Brookfield | " | June 1, '63 | | Dis. for disability March 1, '65. |
| James M. Hodgdon | 28 | Rollinsford | " | June 15, '65 | | Pro. Lieut., not mustered. Dis. for disability at Concord, N. H., as Sergt. Major June 14, '65. |
| Luke Nickerson | 38 | Madison | Sergeant | Sept. 18, '62 | | Died of disease Jan. 7, '63. Malarial fever. |
| Henry Churchill | 28 | Brookfield | " | " | | Pro. 2d Lieut. June 1, '63. |
| Charles H. Smith | 18 | Wakefield | " | " | | Dis. for disability Jan. 13, '63. |
| George E. Goldsmith | 30 | Tuftonborough | " | " | | Pro. 1st Sergt. Wounded sev. June 1, '64, at Cold Harbor. Died of wounds July 29, '64. |
| Mark W. Roberts | 21 | Effingham | Corporal | " | | Died of disease Aug. 15, '63. |
| Josiah C. Flanders | 24 | Madison | " | " | June 21, '65 | Pro. Sergt. Wounded sl. at Cold Harbor, June 2, '64. |
| Jasper H. Warren | 31 | Brookfield | " | " | | Pro. Sergt. Hon. dis. March 1, '64, by order. Pro. Capt. U. S. C. T. Feb. 29, '64. |
| Gilman Davis | 21 | Wakefield | " | " | | Pro. Sergt. Wounded sev. near Petersburg May 7, '64. Died of wounds May 13, '64. |
| Enoch D. Elwell | 29 | Eaton | " | " | | Pro. Sergt. Wounded sev. at Cold Harbor, June 3, '64. Died of wounds June 5, '64. |
| E. Hewitt Vining | 21 | Wakefield | " | " | June 21, '65 | Des. July 3, '63. Returned. Red. to ranks. Again pro. Corp. March 1, '65. |
| Leander B. Abbott | 21 | Ossipee | " | " | | Dis. for disability Jan. 16, '63. |
| Robert C. McDaniels | 44 | Wakefield | " | " | | Dis. for disability Sept. 8, '64. |
| Nathaniel F. Meserve | 19 | " | " | " | | Pro. Sergt. Wounded near Petersburg May 13, '64. Died of wounds. |
| Stephen H. Jackson | 18 | Madison | Musician | " | | Died of disease in N. H. Jan. 8, '64. |
| Theodore G. Allard | 23 | Eaton | Private | " | | Des. at Camp Chase, Va., Oct. 20, '62. |
| George Abbott | 24 | Bartlett | Private | Sept. 18, '62 | | Des. at Concord, N. H., Sept. 25, '62. |
| William Abbott | 38 | Jackson | " | " | | Dis. June 10, '65. |
| Lewis Abbott | 26 | Bartlett | " | " | | Des. from Gen. Hosp. Willett's Point, N. Y., July 20, '64. |

| Name | Residence | Age | Rank | Enlisted | Discharged | Remarks |
|---|---|---|---|---|---|---|
| Levi M. Ames | Wakefield | 18 | Private | Sept. 18, '62 | June 21, '65 | Dis. for disability Feb. 28, '63. |
| James O. Applebee | " | 18 | " | " | | Pro. Corp. Nov. 12, '64. |
| John H. Beacham | Wolfborough | 20 | " | " | | Hon. dis. Dec. 21, '63, by order for pro., at Portsmouth, Va. |
| Andrew Berry | Brookfield | 41 | " | " | | Dis. for disability Nov. 11, '63. |
| Aaron K. Blake | " | 19 | " | " | | Pro. Sergt. Wounded at Cold Harbor. Died of wounds recd. June 5, '64. |
| Jesse G. Berry | " | 25 | " | " | | Transf. to V. R. C. July 1, '63. Dis. for disability at Concord, N. H., Dec. 4, '63. |
| Elijah B. Baxter | Effingham | 30 | " | " | June 21, '65 | Transf. to V. R. C. July 1, '63. |
| Henry J. Bean | Eaton | 26 | " | " | June 21, '65 | Dis. for disability April 15, '63. |
| Jeremiah Q. Brown | Ossipee | 34 | " | Oct. 4, '62 | | Des. while on march July 3, '63. |
| Roswell J. Brown | Unknown | 34 | " | Sept. 18, '62 | | Transf. to V. R. C. April 28, '64. |
| David Connor | Ossipee | 19 | " | " | | Pro. Sergt. Wounded at Battery Five, June 15, '64. Died of wounds July 31, '64. |
| John B. Connor | " | 44 | " | " | | Transf. to V. R. C. Nov. 30, '63. |
| John J. Curtis | Brookfield | 18 | " | " | | Dis. for disability Sept. 29, '63. |
| Joseph Gilley | Ossipee | 21 | " | " | | Dis. for disability at Portsmouth, Va., Feb. 20, '64. |
| Mark A. L. Colbath | Brookfield | 35 | " | " | | Des. at Concord, N. H., Sept. 25, '62. |
| Daniel F. Drew | Wakefield | 24 | " | " | | |
| Charles E. Davis | Eaton | 19 | " | " | | |
| John L. Drew | " | 44 | " | " | June 21, '65 | |
| Elijah M. Dinsmore | Jackson | 23 | " | " | | Wounded sev. at Cold Harbor June 1, '64. Dis. May 27, '65. |
| George E. Dearborn | Tuftonborough | | " | " | | Transf. to V. R. C. Oct. 15, '64. |
| Daniel W. Emerson | Wakefield | 29 | " | " | | Dis. by order of War Dept. May 10, '65. |
| George W. Ferrin | Madison | 37 | " | " | | Dis. for disability March 28, '63. |
| George S. Frost | " | 18 | " | " | | Pro. Corp. Wounded sev. at Battery Five, June 15, '64. Died of wounds June 18, '64. |
| William K. Fellows | Wakefield | 20 | " | " | June 21, '65 | Wounded sev. at Cold Harbor June 1, '64. Pro. Corp. May 1, '65. |
| Walter Ford | Effingham | 18 | " | " | | Transf. to Navy April 27, '64. |
| Andrew J. Ford | " | 35 | " | " | | Des. from Gen. Hosp., March 15, '63. |
| Edwin H. Glidden | Wakefield | 18 | " | " | June 21, '65 | |
| Nathaniel W. Gray | Madison | 29 | " | " | June 21, '65 | Wounded sl. at Fredericksburg Dec. 13, '62. |
| Ansel B. Greene | " | 44 | " | " | | Dis. for disability May 30, '63. |
| George W. Gray | " | 27 | " | " | | |
| James F. Gerals | Wolfborough | 18 | " | " | June 21, '65 | Died of disease, Feb. 26, '63. Typhoid Fever. |
| Timothy Gilman | Madison | 40 | " | " | | Dis. for disability at Concord, N. H., Nov. 30, '63. |

| Name | | | Rank | Enlisted | Mustered Out | Remarks |
|---|---|---|---|---|---|---|
| William H. Glidden | 18 | Effingham | Private | Sept. 18, '62 | | Wounded sev. at Battery Five June 15, '64. Dis. for disability at Concord, N. H., Nov. 3, '64. |
| Harold Hardy | 18 | Ossipee | " | " | June 21, '65 | Pro. Corp. Oct. 1, '64. |
| John W. Hodsdon | 27 | " | " | " | June 21, '65 | Dis. for disability Nov. 27, '63. |
| Samuel Harvey | 28 | Effingham | " | " | | Dis. for disability March 18, '63. |
| Charles H. Hurd | 21 | Freedom | " | " | | Wounded sl. May, '64. Pro. Sergt. Dis. by order June 3, '65. |
| George W. Hutchins | 41 | Wakefield | " | " | June 21, '65 | Pro. Corp. May 1, '64. Pro. Sergt. Sept. 1, '64. |
| Jeremiah G. Hodgdon | 20 | " | " | " | June 21, '65 | Pro. Corp. Aug. 18, '63, — Sergt. Sept. 1, '64. |
| Charles P. Hanson | 18 | Jackson | " | " | | Dis. for disability May 12, '63. |
| Luther H. Harriman | 31 | Effingham | " | " | | Killed on Richmond and Petersburg Turnpike, by a shell, May 12, '64. |
| George F. Harmon | 21 | Madison | " | " | | Dis. for disease Jan. 19, '63. |
| Charles A. Hammond | 18 | Ossipee | " | " | | Died of disease Aug. 7, '63. Diphtheria. |
| Charles A. Hawkins | 21 | Eaton | " | " | June 21, '65 | Pro. Corp. Aug. 18, '63, — Sergt. May 1, '64; 1st Sergt. Sept. 1, '64. |
| Orren W. Harmon | 18 | Madison | " | " | | Dis. by order Nov. 15, '62. |
| George A. Homestead | | Unknown | " | Oct. 4, '62 | | |
| John Johnson | 27 | Effingham | " | Sept. 18, '62 | June 21, '65 | Dis. by Gen. Order No. 77 A. G. O. May 3, '65. |
| George A. Kennison | 19 | Ossipee | " | " | June 21, '65 | Des. at Falmouth, Va., Jan. 26, '63. |
| Diamond Littlefield | 37 | Madison | " | " | | Died of disease March 9, '63. |
| William Milliken | 22 | Effingham | " | " | | |
| Daniel E. Meserve | 19 | Wakefield | " | " | June 21, '65 | |
| Freeman Nute | 23 | Bartlett | " | " | | Transf. to V. R. C. March 31, '64. Dis. Sept. 18, '65. |
| James Nute | 23 | " | " | " | | Transf. to Navy April 4, '64. |
| Francis Peters | 28 | Wakefield | " | " | | Dis. May 3, '65. |
| Thomas L. Pickering | 42 | " | " | " | | Des. from Hosp. April 2, '63. Apprehended. Pardoned on condition of re-enlistment for 3 years. Transf. to 2d N. H. V. June 21, '65. |
| Charles Pike | | Ossipee | " | " | | Transf. to V. R. C. Sept. 30, '63. Dis. July 6, '65. |
| Lafayette Place | 22 | Barnstead | " | " | June 21, '65 | Pro. Corp. May 1, '65. |
| Asa Pray | 18 | Ossipee | " | " | | Killed in action June 15, '64, at Battery Five. |
| George Z. Ricker | 22 | Brookfield | " | " | June 21, '65 | Pro. Corp. July 1, '64. |
| Abraham Roberts | 21 | Eaton | " | " | | Dis. for disability Jan. 16, '63. |
| Mark Remick | 23 | Wakefield | " | " | June 21, '65 | |
| Turner N. Seward | 28 | " | " | " | June 21, '65 | Pro. Corp. Jan. 24, '63, — Sergt. Sept. 1, '64. |
| George W. Sawyer | 33 | " | " | Sept. 18, '62 | | Dis. for disability Feb. 9, '63. |
| Henry E. Sias | 18 | Ossipee | " | Oct 4, '62 | | Transf. to Co. B Oct. 4, '62. Dis. May 24, '63. |
| Henry E. Spaulding | | Unknown | " | | | |

| Name | Age | Residence | Rank | Mustered in | Remarks |
|---|---|---|---|---|---|
| Henry K. Shattuck | 21 | Mount Vernon | Private | Sept. 18, '62 | Transf. from Co. B Oct. 4, '62. Died of disease Nov. 23, '63. |
| Timothy C. Taylor | 18 | Effingham | " | " | Pro. Corp. May 19, '64. Wounded sev. June 15, '64. |
| Charles W. Thompson | 18 | Ossipee | " | " | Wounded sl. in head Sept. 29, '64; wounded June 10, '65, Alexandria, Va. Dis. July 5, '65. |
| James H. Thurston | 36 | Eaton | " | " | |
| Henry C. Wentworth | 18 | Great Falls | " | " | On detached service Wilmington, N. C. |
| Andrew J. Wentworth | 27 | Wakefield | " | " | |
| John E. Witham | 19 | " | " | " | Pro. Corp. Aug. 18, '63, — Sergt. July 1, '64. Wounded sev. Sept. 29, '64. |
| Stephen A. Wentworth | 24 | " | " | " | Dis. for disability Nov. 25, '63. |
| George E. Wentworth | 20 | " | " | " | Pro. Corp. July 1, '64. Wounded sl. in arm Sept. 29, '64. |
| John C. Waldron | 39 | " | " | " | Transf. to V. R. C. Aug. 17, '64. Dis. Aug. 11, '65. |
| Cyrus Whitten | 36 | " | " | " | Transf. to Navy, April 4, '64. |
| Myron D. Young | 18 | " | " | June 21, '65 | Dis. for disability Feb. 21, '63. |

## RECRUITS.

| Name | Age | Residence | Rank | Mustered in | Remarks |
|---|---|---|---|---|---|
| Caspar Alback | 23 | Unknown | " | Aug. 11, '63 | Wounded sev. June 15, '64. Transf. to 2d N. H. V. June 21, '65. |
| William G. Atkins | | " | " | " | Wounded sev. June 1, '64. Mustered out May 12, '65. |
| George Andrews | | " | " | Aug. 10, '63 | Transf. to 2d N. H. June 21, '65. |
| Edward Austin | 22 | " | " | Aug. 11, '63 | Transf. to 2d N. H. June 21, '65. |
| William Ashton | 24 | " | " | Aug. 12, '63 | Transf. to U. S. Navy, April 4, '64. |
| John Burke | | " | " | " | Des. April 18, '64, regained May, '64. Wounded sev. June 4, '64. Dis. for disability March 25, '65. |
| Charles Bone | | " | " | Aug. 11, '63 | Wounded sev. June 15, '64. Transf. to 2d N. H. June 21, '65. |
| John Brown | 25 | " | " | " | Wounded sev. June 15, '64. Died of wounds at Hampton, Va., June 21, '64. |
| Andrew Bean | | " | " | " | Transf. to 2d N. H. June 21, '65. |
| Philip Bendelnagle | | " | " | Aug. 12, '63 | Transf. to 2d N. H. June 21, '65. |
| George P. Bennett | 36 | Wakefield | " | Dec. 31, '63 | Pro. Corp. Killed at Battery Five June 15, '64. |
| Martin Brandon | 32 | Unknown | " | Aug. 12, '63 | Transf. to Navy April 27, '64. |
| Edward Bishop | 36 | " | " | Aug. 11, '63 | Des. Oct. 10, '63, Portsmouth, Va. |
| Thomas Burke | 27 | " | " | Aug. 12, '63 | Des. Oct. 10, '63, Portsmouth, Va. |
| Joseph Byerd | 23 | " | " | " | Transf. to Navy April 27, '64. |
| John Brannon | 28 | " | " | " | Des. from Hospital Nov. 24, '64. |
| George Blake | 21 | Unknown | " | Aug. 10, '63 | Transf. to Navy April 4, '64. |
| Albert P. Craton | | Albany | " | Feb. 3, '64 | Died of disease April 13, '64. |
| John Cox | 33 | Unknown | " | Aug. 25, '63 | Transf. to Navy May 4, '64. |

| | | | | |
|---|---|---|---|---|
| Patrick Coleman | 21 | Unknown | Private | Aug. 10, '63 | Des. Feb. 17, '64, Portsmouth, Va. |
| Timothy Collins | 21 | " | " | Aug. 11, '63 | Killed at Ft. Harrison Sept. 29, '64. |
| Timothy Cronan | | " | " | | Transf. to 2d N. H. V. June 21, '65. |
| Thomas Collins | | " | " | | Killed at Ft. Harrison Sept. 29, '64. |
| George Emerson | | Ossipee | " | Dec. 29, '63 | Volunteer. Wounded sl. June 15, '64. Transf. to 2d N. H. V. June 21, '65. |
| William H. Geralls | | " | " | Jan. 5, '64 | Transf. to 2d N. H. V. June 21, '65. |
| John A. Nichols | | " | " | Dec. 9, '63 | Pro. Corp. Dis. for disability at Concord, N. H., May 20, '65. |
| George W. Woods | 23 | Nashua | Musician | Dec. 31, '63 | Volunteer. Transf. to 2d N. H. V. June 21, '65. |

## B.

| Name | Age. | Residence. | Rank. | Muster in. | Muster out. | Remarks. |
|---|---|---|---|---|---|---|
| Elisha E. Dodge | 34 | Rollinsford | Captain | Sept. 27, '62 | | Wounded sev. June 15, '64, at Petersburg, Va. Died of wounds June 22, '64, at Chesapeake Gen. Hospital. |
| Marshall Saunders | 29 | Littleton | " | July 15, '64 | June 21, '65 | Wounded sl. Sept. 29, '64. |
| George A. Bruce | 22 | Mount Vernon | 1st Lieut. | Sept. 18, '62 | June 21, '65 | Pro. Capt. Co. A May 30, '64. |
| William J. Ladd | 18 | Portsmouth | " | May 30, '64 | | Wounded sev. Sept 29, '64. App. Capt. U. S. V. by brevet, for gallant and meritorious service, to date from March 13, '65. |
| Nathan B. Boutwell | 29 | Lyndeborough | 2d Lieut. | Sept. 27, '62 | | Pro. Adjt. March 24, '63. |
| Charles M. Kittredge | 24 | Mount Vernon | " | Mar. 26, '63 | | Hon. dis. Nov. 3, '63, on Surgeon's certificate of disability. |
| Charles C. Favor | 25 | Boston, Mass. | " | Nov. 28, '63 | | Hon. dis. Sept. 5, '64, on Surgeon's certificate of disability. |
| Nathan D. Chapman | 29 | Rollinsford | " | June 15, '65 | | Pro. Lieut., not mustered. |
| Charles M. Kittredge | 24 | Mount Vernon | 1st Sergt. | Sept. 18, '62 | June 21, '65 | Pro. 2d Lieut. March 26, '63. |
| James M. Hodgdon | 26 | Rollinsford | Sergeant | " | | Pro. 1st Sergt. June 10, '63; Sergt. Major Dec. 12, '63. Wounded sev. in eye at Ft. Harrison Sept. 30, '64. |
| Hiram W. Muzzey | 20 | Antrim | " | " | | Transf. to V. R. C. Nov. 20, '63. Dis. for disability March 1, '65. |
| George F. Shedd | 23 | Rollinsford | " | " | | Dis. for disability Feb. 7, '63, at Philadelphia, Pa., by Gen. Montgomery. |
| James M. Pierce | 36 | " | " | " | | Transf. to V. R. C. March 31, '64. |
| Marcellus C. Shattuck | 19 | Derry | Corporal | " | June 21, '65 | Pro. Sergt. Jan. 21, '63; 1st Lieut. May 30, '65. |
| Amasa Downes | 29 | Francestown | " | " | June 21, '65 | Color Bearer in Battle of Fredericksburg. |
| Benjamin J. Boutwell | 22 | Lyndeborough | " | " | | Dis. May 25, '63. |
| Levi J. Bradley | 38 | Rollinsford | " | " | | Dis. for disability April 13, '63. |
| George E. Cochran | 18 | New Boston | " | " | June 6, '65 | Wounded Dec. 13, '62. Dis. for disability May 6, '63. |
| John M. Dore | 22 | Rollinsford | " | " | June 21, '65 | Pro. Sergt. Sept. 7, '63. |
| Nathan D. Chapman | 29 | " | " | " | | Pro. Sergt. March 12, '63; 1st Sergt. Jan. 1, '64; 2d Lieut. June 15, '65. |
| William H. Sythes | 20 | " | Musician | " | June 21, '65 | Pro. Sergt. March 1, '64. |
| Albion K. P. Shaw | 33 | " | " | " | June 21, '65 | Transf. to Brigade Band June 20, '63. |
| Solomon Jones | 25 | Mount Vernon | Private | " | June 21, '65 | |
| William H. Aspinwall | 27 | Rollinsford | " | " | June 21, '65 | |
| Charles F. Averill | 18 | " | " | " | June 21, '65 | Appointed Musician. |
| George G. Averill | 29 | Mount Vernon | " | " | June 21, '65 | |
| Irving A. Bedell | 18 | Rollinsford | " | " | June 21, '65 | |
| George E. Bodge | 20 | Madbury | " | " | June 18, '65 | Wounded sev. May 9, '64. Dis. for disability caused by wounds Nov. 12, '64. |

| Name | Residence | Age | Rank | Mustered in | Mustered out | Remarks |
|---|---|---|---|---|---|---|
| David W. Bodge | Rollinsford | 31 | Private | Sept. 18, '62 | June 21, '65. | Pro. Corp. June 10, '63; Sergt. June 6, '64. Wounded sev. Sept. 29, '64. |
| Charles H. Bodge | Madbury | 20 | " | " | " | Died of disease at Falmouth, Va., Jan. 14, '63. |
| John Blanchard | Bennington | 26 | " | " | " | Dis. May 29, '65. |
| Milton Bartlett | " | 23 | " | " | " | Des. at Falmouth, Va., Feb. 9, '63. |
| Reuben Boutell | Antrim | 26 | " | " | " | Transf. to V. R. C. Feb. 11, '64. Mustered out July 14, '65. |
| Jackson Boutell | " | 29 | " | " | " | Dis. for disability Sept. 28, '63. |
| David W. Boutell | " | 25 | " | " | " | Dis. for disability Dec. 5, '62, at Columbia College Hospital, Washington. |
| William Boutell | Unknown | 27 | " | " | June 21, '65 | Wounded sl. Sept. 29, '64. |
| William T. Boutwell | Lyndeborough | 21 | " | " | " | Transf. to V. R. C. Aug. 10, '64. |
| Henry A. Belcher | Francestown | 20 | " | " | June 21, '65 | Died of disease at Portsmouth, Va., Nov. 9, '63. |
| Albert Burnham | Mount Vernon | 22 | " | " | " | Wounded sl. June 1, '64. |
| Israel Burnham | " | 24 | " | " | " | Dis. for disability May, '64. |
| Andrew Cochran | Antrim | 37 | " | Sept. 19, '62 | " | Hon. dis. Jan. 19, '64 to accept an appointment as 1st Lieut. in 30th U. S. C. T. |
| George N. Copp | Mount Vernon | 36 | " | Sept. 18, '62 | " | Wounded sev. Sept. 30, '64. Dis. June 6, '65. |
| Jesse F. Colby | Francestown | 24 | " | " | " | Wounded sev. June 15, '64. Died of wounds at Hampton, Va., June 23, '64. |
| Richard Doherty | Rollinsford | 36 | " | " | " | Transf. to V. R. C. Sept. 30, '63. Mustered out July 6, '65. Pro. Corp. Jan. 1, '65. Clerk at Hdqrs. of Brigade. |
| John Drew | Strafford | 25 | " | " | June 21, '65 | |
| Cyrus G. Drew | Rollinsford | 27 | " | " | June 21, '65 | |
| John A. Dawson | Antrim | 39 | " | " | June 21, '65 | |
| James B. Decatur | " | 28 | " | " | June 17, '65 | |
| George D. Dresser | " | 21 | " | " | June 21, '65 | |
| Nathaniel E. Dickey | Bennington | 30 | " | " | " | Pro. Corp. March 12, '63; Sergt. March 1, '64. Wounded sl. May 16, '64; wounded sev. June 1, '64. |
| Charles H Dodge | Antrim | 18 | " | " | " | Died at Concord, N. H. (date unknown). |
| Charles W. Dodge | Mount Vernon | 18 | " | " | June 21, '65 | Pro. Corp. March 12, '63. Dis. by order Dec. 22, '63, to accept app. in U. S. C. T. |
| Cyrus P. Douglas | " | 26 | " | " | " | |
| Lewis Emery | Brookline | 27 | " | " | " | Dis. for disability Feb. 12, '63. |
| James W. Eaton | Antrim | 44 | " | " | June 21, '65 | |
| Franklin Grant | Rollinsford | 40 | " | " | June 21, '65 | |
| Charles W. Green | New Market | 20 | " | " | June 13, '65 | App. Capt. in 25th U. S. Colored Troops Jan. 19, '64. |
| Charles E. Hartford | Rollinsford | 18 | " | " | " | Wounded sl. June 1, '64, at Cold Harbor, Va. |
| James O. Hanscom | " | 26 | " | " | " | Died of disease at Portsmouth, Va., Oct. 4, '63. |
| John Hanscom | " | 44 | " | " | " | Dis. for disability Nov. 29, '63, at Portsmouth, Va. |

| Name | Age | Residence | Rank | Mustered in | Mustered out | Remarks |
|---|---|---|---|---|---|---|
| James F. Hayes | 21 | Rollinsford | Private | Sept. 18, '62 | | Died at Washington April 5, '63. |
| David J. Hodsdon | 25 | " | " | " | June 21, '65 | |
| David A. Hill | 29 | Brookline | " | " | June 21, '65 | Wounded June 3, '64. Pro. Corp. Aug. 23, '64. Wounded sl. Sept. 29, '64. |
| Albion A. Lord | 28 | Rollinsford | " | " | June 21, '65 | Pro. Corp. March 1, '64. Wounded June 5, '64. |
| William E. Lord | 19 | " | " | " | June 21, '65 | Transf. to Navy, May 4, '64. |
| Tenny Major | 30 | Derry | " | " | June 21, '65 | |
| John McKenzie | 31 | Rollinsford | " | " | June 21, '65 | Killed at Chapins Farm, Va., Sept. 30, '64. |
| Dearborn W. McGregor | 23 | Londonderry | " | " | June 21, '65 | Wounded July 4, '64. |
| David McGroty | 18 | Rollinsford | " | " | June 21, '65 | Pro. Corp. Jan. 1, '64. |
| Charles E. Morrows | 22 | Antrim | " | " | June 21, '65 | |
| Edwin S. Marden | 21 | Francestown | " | " | June 21, '65 | Dis. for disability June 6, '63. |
| Charles H. C. Otis | 18 | Rollinsford | " | " | June 21, '65 | Transf. to V. R. C. Nov. 15, '63. |
| William C. Powers | 20 | " | " | " | June 21, '65 | Transf. to Brigade Band, Jan. 19, '63. |
| John Pindar | 20 | " | " | " | June 21, '65 | Died of disease at Falmouth, Va., Jan. 5, '63. |
| Smith C. Page | 26 | " | " | " | | |
| Alonzo F. Pierce | 30 | " | " | " | June 21, '65 | Pro. Corp. Missing in action June 1, '64. |
| William H. Peckham | 18 | Antrim | " | " | | |
| Peter F. Pike | 36 | Mount Vernon | " | " | June 21, '65 | Pro. Corp. March 1, '64. Wounded sl. May 16, '64. |
| John H. Parker | 18 | Derry | " | " | June 21, '65 | Pro. Corp. March 12, '63; Sergt. Jan. 1, '64. Dis. by order Feb. 24, '64, to receive app. as Captain in 30th U. S. C. T. |
| Thomas S. Pease | 22 | Strafford | " | " | June 21, '65 | |
| John T. Perkins | 23 | Mount Vernon | " | " | June 21, '65 | |
| David E. Proctor | 19 | Lyndeborough | " | " | June 21, '65 | |
| Oren Rollins | 23 | Rollinsford | " | " | June 21, '65 | |
| Orenzo Rollins | 37 | " | " | " | June 17, '65 | |
| Tobias Roberts | — 22 | Strafford | " | " | June 21, '65 | |
| Charles H. Robinson | 21 | Mount Vernon | " | " | | Died of wounds at Milford, N. H., May 23, '64. |
| James C. Richardson | 28 | Antrim | " | " | | Dis. April 18, '63. |
| Reuben Randell | 25 | Rollinsford | " | " | June 21, '65 | |
| Daniel F. Shedd | 19 | New Boston | " | " | | Dis. for disability April 6, '63. |
| William F. Staples | 32 | Rollinsford | " | " | | Wounded sev. May 9, '64. |
| Henry K. Shattuck | 21 | Mount Vernon | " | " | | Transf. to Co. A Oct. 4, '62. |
| Charles B. Sanders | 18 | Rollinsford | " | " | | Pro. Corp. June 10, '63. Dis. by order March 1, '64, to accept app. as 1st Lieut. in 30th U. S. C. T. |
| John H. Smith | 27 | Mount Vernon | " | " | | Dis. for disability at Newport News, Va., March 12, '63. |
| William S. A. Starrett | 24 | " | " | " | | Dis. for disability March 21, '63. |

| Name | Age | Residence | Rank | Mustered in | Mustered out | Remarks |
|---|---|---|---|---|---|---|
| Charles F. Stinson | 21 | Mount Vernon | Private | Sept. 18, '62 | | Dis. by order Dec. 8, '63, to accept app. in U. S. C. T. Pro. Capt. and Brev. Major. |
| Henry E. Spaulding | 18 | Lyndeborough | " | Oct. 4, '62 | | Transf. from Co. A Oct. 4, '62. Dis. May 24, '63. |
| Albert C. Thompson | 21 | Rollinsford | " | Sept. 18, '62 | | Pro. Corp. June 6, '64. |
| Charles H. Tarbell | 27 | Dublin | " | " | June 21, '65 | App. 2d Lieut. 30th U. S. C. T. Feb. 2, '64. |
| Henry C. Willard | 25 | Rollinsford | " | " | June 21, '65 | Pro. Corp. March 1, '64. Wounded sl. June 1, '64. |
| Horatio H. Warren | | | " | " | June 21, '65 | Pro. Corp. March 12, '63. Wounded sev. June 3, '64. Pro. Sergt. June 6, '64. |
| Joseph Wiggin | 32 | " | " | " | June 6, '65 | Wounded sev. May 16, '64. Wounded sev. Sept. 29, '64. |
| Thomas S. Wentworth | 18 | " | " | " | June 21, '65 | Transf. to V. R. C. Sept. 1, '63. Mustered out July 10, '65. |
| Charles H. Wilson | 24 | Antrim | " | " | June 21, '65 | Pro. Corp. Jan. 1, '64. Wounded sl. Sept. 29, '64. |
| Henry F. Warren | 18 | New Boston | " | " | June 26, '65 | |
| William H. Wilson | 23 | Antrim | " | " | | |
| George T. Woodward | 22 | Lyndeborough | " | " | | Pro. Corp. March 12, '63; Sergt. June 10, '63. Dis. by order Feb. 24, '64, to accept app. as Captain in 30th U. S. C. T. |
| Levi M. Wines | 33 | Gorham | " | Sept. 19, '62 | June 28, '65 | Wounded sev. Sept. 29, '64. |

RECRUITS.

| Name | Age | Residence | Rank | Mustered in | Mustered out | Remarks |
|---|---|---|---|---|---|---|
| James Breme *alias* John Valiere | 24 | Kensington | " | Aug. 11, '63 | | Des. while on picket Nov. 3, '64. |
| Harrison Capen | 23 | Barrington | " | Feb. 19, '64 | | Des. while on furlough March 1, '65. |
| Levi Capen | 21 | " | " | Feb. 23, '64 | | Killed at Drury's Bluff, Va., May 16, '64. |
| John H. Carr, Jr. | | Unknown | " | Aug. 11, '63 | | Transf. to 2d N. H. V. June 21, '65. |
| John Connors | | " | " | " | | Transf. to 2d N. H. V. June 21, '65. |
| Thomas Collins | 20 | " | " | " | | Transf. to Navy April 10, '64. |
| James Clancey | 22 | " | " | " | | Des. at Portsmouth, Va., Oct. 5, '63. |
| John W. Cornell | | " | " | " | | Transf. to 2d N. H. V. June 21, '65. |
| John Clark | 23 | " | " | " | | Des. at Portsmouth, Va., Oct. 5, '63. |
| Henry Cole | 22 | " | " | " | | Des. while on picket Nov. 3, '64. |
| Charles Nute | | Bartlett | " | Feb. 6, '64 | | Transf. to 2d N. H. V. June 21, 65. |
| Fabri Candido | 26 | Portsmouth | " | Aug. 12, '63 | | Transf. to Co. C Jan. 28, '64. |

## C.

| Name | Age | Residence | Rank | Muster in. | Muster out. | Remarks. |
|---|---|---|---|---|---|---|
| Charles O. Bradley | 30 | Concord | Captain | Sept. 19, '62 | | Dis. June 9, '64, on Surgeon's certificate of disability. |
| James M. Durell | 20 | New Market | " | July 19, '64 | June 21, '65 | |
| Charles H. Curtis | 23 | Farmington | 1st Lieut. | Sept. 27, '62 | June 21, '65 | Pro. Captain Co. F Oct. 28, '64. |
| Royal B. Prescott | 29 | Nashua | " | Oct. 28, '64 | June 21, '65 | |
| Rufus P. Staniels | 35 | Concord | 2d Lieut. | Sept. 27, '62 | | Pro. 1st Lieut. Co. H Feb. 20, '63. |
| William H. McConney | 35 | Windham | " | Feb. 20, '63 | | Pro. 2d Lieut. Feb. 20, '63. |
| William H. McConney | 23 | Concord | 1st Sergt. | Sept. 19, '62 | | Pro. 1st Sergt. Dis. to receive app. in U. S. C. T. Dec. 5, '64. |
| Levi W. Curtis | 23 | Newcastle | Sergeant | " | June 21, '65 | Transf. to Brigade Band Jan. 25, '63. |
| Horace D. Carter | 24 | Concord | " | " | June 21, '65 | Pro. 1st Sergt. Jan. 1, '65. Pro. 1st Lieut. Co. E May 30, '65 not mustered. |
| John P. Haines | 21 | Chichester | " | " | | Wounded sl. June 15, '64. Pro. Com. Sergt. Sept. 6, '64. |
| George Burns | 21 | Concord | " | " | | Pro. Sergt. Dis. May 9, '65, at Hospital, Manchester, N. H. |
| Alvin D. Batchelder | 32 | " | " | " | | Transf. to Navy April 29, '64. |
| William S. Davis | 38 | " | " | " | | Pro. Sergt. Pro. 2d Lieut. 18th N. H. V. Nov. 30, '64. |
| Robert K. Flanders | 20 | " | " | " | | Captured May 25, '64. Died of disease at Andersonville, Ga., July 17, '64. Grave No. 3472. |
| Lucius F. Smith | 26 | Farmington | " | " | | |
| Moses Ladd | 24 | Concord | " | " | June 21, '65 | Pro. Sergt. May 9, '65. |
| Charles E. Putney | 22 | Bow | " | " | June 21, '65 | Dis. for disability at Portsmouth, Va., Nov. 30, '63. |
| George W. Wingate | 32 | Farmington | Corporal | " | | Killed at Cold Harbor, Va., June 1, '64. |
| Charles H. Dorr | 21 | Gilmanton | " | " | | |
| Henry W. McMichael | 15 | Concord | Musician | Sept. 20, '62 | June 21, '65 | |
| Jeremiah B. Roberts | 22 | Farmington | Wagoner | Sept. 19, '62 | | Dis. for disability at Concord, N. H, July 29, '63. |
| John L. Amazeen | 19 | Newcastle | Private | " | | Transf. to Navy April 29, '64. |
| William Anderson | 28 | Windham | " | " | | Dis. for disability at Fortress Monroe, Va., June 7, '63. |
| John W. Austin | 18 | Bow | " | " | June 21, '65 | |
| Josiah Batchelder | 28 | Concord | " | " | June 21, '65 | Pro. Corp. April 25, '64. |
| Justin S. Batchelder | 18 | Loudon | " | " | | Killed at Suffolk, Va., May 3, '63. |
| Asa Bean | 28 | Windham | " | " | | Des. at Aquia Creek, Va., Feb. 7, '63. |
| Manson S. Brown | 26 | Campton | " | " | | Pro. Principal Musician, March 1, '65. |
| George H. Butler | 36 | Bow | " | " | | Died of disease at Portsmouth, Va., Nov. 9, '63. |
| George F. Butters | 22 | Concord | " | " | | Dis. for disability at Fort Schuyler, N. Y., Feb. 28, '63. |
| George V. Card | 21 | Farmington | " | " | June 21, '65 | |
| Weston M. Carter | 21 | Concord | " | " | June 21, '65 | |
| Michael Casavaint | 23 | " | " | " | June 21, '65 | Pro. Corp. Nov. '63. |

| Name | Age | Residence | Rank | Enlisted | Discharged | Remarks |
|---|---|---|---|---|---|---|
| Gideon Casavaint | 18 | Concord | Private | Sept. 19, '62 | June 21, '65 | Pro. Corp.; Sergt. March 1, '65. |
| Charles H. Clay | 24 | Farmington | " | " | June 21, '65 | Wounded Dec. 13, '62. Des. Feb. 9, '63. Apprehended Sept. 13, '64. Returned to Co. Jan. 18, '65. Transf. to 2d N. H. V. June 21, '65. |
| Harris Clough | 18 | Bow | " | " | | |
| George W. Colburn | | Windham | " | " | June 21, '65 | |
| John J. Cook | 26 | West Milton | " | " | June 21, '65 | Pro. Corp. Jan. 1, '65. |
| Dudley P. Corson | 21 | " | " | " | | Dis. for disability at Portsmouth, Va., Dec. 4, '63. |
| Gilman F. Chase | 24 | Hudson | " | Sept. 20, '62 | June 21, '65 | Transf. from Co. I Sept. 25, '62. Transf. to Brigade Band Jan. 25, '63. |
| John F. Davis | 20 | West Milton | " | Sept. 19, '62 | | Dis. at Richmond, Va., May 30, '65. |
| Thomas J. Davis | 24 | New Castle | " | " | | Killed near Petersburg, Va., June 15, '64. |
| Joseph W. Dickerman | 25 | Concord | " | Sept. 20, '62 | June 21, '65 | |
| Orrin B. Dudley | 24 | Farmington | " | Sept. 19, '62 | June 21, '65 | "Was with us all the time we were in the service."—MAJOR STOODLEY. |
| Isaac H. W. Dodge | | | | | | |
| Samuel E. Dudley | 28 | Farmington | " | " | June 21, '65 | Died of disease at Newport News, Va., Feb. 24, '63. |
| Woodman B. Durgin | 22 | Thornton | " | " | June 21, '65 | Dis. May 21, '65. |
| Henry Dwinnells | 21 | Bow | " | " | | Killed near Petersburg, Va., July 1, '64. |
| Jason Elliott | 38 | Campton | " | " | | Transf. to V. R. C. Sept. 7, '63. |
| Simeon T. Elliott | 18 | Windham | " | " | | |
| David B. Fessenden | 40 | " | " | " | | |
| Harris K. Frost | 23 | Bow | " | " | June 21, '65 | Pro. Corp.; Sergt. Sept. 5, '64. |
| James Gallagher | 18 | Concord | " | " | June 21, '65 | Dis. by order at Washington, D. C., April 16, '63. |
| William G. Gilman | 20 | Thornton | " | " | June 21, '65 | Pro. Corp. Wounded sl. June 1, '64. Pro. Sergt. Jan. 1, '65. |
| Charles F. Glover | 20 | Concord | " | " | June 8, '65 | |
| George A. Glover | 20 | " | " | " | | |
| Ivory H. Glover | 29 | Woodstock | " | " | | Dis. by order at Philadelphia, Pa., Sept. 2, '63. |
| John F. Guild | 34 | Bow | " | " | | Transf. to V. R. C. Sept. 7, '63. Dis. by order, July 6, '65. |
| Nathan Hardy | 40 | " | " | " | | Died of disease in New Hampshire, Jan. 15, '65. |
| William Hodgdon | 44 | New Castle | " | " | | Wounded Dec. 13, '62. Dis. by order at Washington, D. C., Feb. 5, '63. |
| Oscar O. Hodgdon | 18 | " | " | " | June 21, '65 | Pro. Corp. March 1, '65. |
| William T. Holbrook | 19 | " | " | " | | Dis. for disability at Ft. Wood, N. Y., Jan. 23, '63. |
| Micajah B. Kimball | 39 | Windham | " | " | | Dis. for disability near Portsmouth, Va., Oct. 18, '63. |
| Austin L. Lamprey | 21 | " | " | " | | Dis. at Hampton Gen. Hospital, Va. |
| John A. Lane | 35 | Concord | " | " | June 6, '65 | Dis. for disability at Concord, N. H., Aug. 5, '63. |
| Everett W. Leighton | 42 | Farmington | " | " | | Dis. for disability at Newport News, Va., March 4, '63. |

650

| Name | Age | Residence | Rank | Date | Remarks |
|---|---|---|---|---|---|
| Frank Leighton | 34 | Farmington | Private | Sept. 19, '62 | Dis. for disability at Philadelphia, Pa., Jan. 15, '63. |
| Charles Libbey | 21 | Concord | " | " | June 21, '65 |
| George W. Libbey | 28 | New Castle | " | " | June 21, '65 |
| Hiram E. Lock | 25 | Chichester | " | " | June 21, '65 |
| John C. Lull | 18 | Concord | " | " | June 21, '65 |
| John E. Lull | 40 | " | " | " | Transf. to V. R. C. Aug. 17, '64. Mustered out Sept. 19, '65. |
| Leander C. Lull | 42 | " | " | " | Dis. for disability at Concord, N. H., March 3, '65. |
| Carter S. Morgan | 21 | Bow | " | " | Dis. for disability Sept. 7, '64, at Lovell Gen. Hospital, R. I. |
| Henry B. Neally | 35 | Concord | " | " | Wounded Dec. 13, '62. Died of wounds at Washington, Jan. 5, '63. |
| George W. Nichols | 31 | Hopkinton | " | " | Dis. by order near Portsmouth, Va., Oct. 18, '63. |
| Robert Oliver | 20 | New Castle | " | " | Wounded sl. May 12, '64. Transf. to Navy to date April 28, '64. |
| George A. Nute | 20 | Farmington | " | " | June 21, '65. Captured near Petersburg, Va., May 25, '64. Released. |
| John C. Palmer | 19 | Concord | " | " | June 8, '65. Captured Nov. 18, '64. Paroled. Dis. at Patterson Park Hospital, Baltimore, Md., June 8, '65. |
| Robert K. Peavey | 34 | Farmington | " | " | Wounded sev. June 15, '64. Transf. to V. R. C. March 10, '65. |
| Reuben O. Phillips | 38 | Windham | " | " | Des. at Aquia Creek, Va., Feb. 7, '63. |
| Nathan Pierce | 20 | Campton | " | " | Des. while on furlough at Portsmouth, Va., Sept. 2, '63. |
| Liberty Richards | 43 | Farmington | " | " | Died of disease at Fredericksburg, Va., Dec. 26, '62. |
| Silas F. Richards | 18 | Thornton | " | Sept. 20, '62 | June 21, '65. Pro. Corp. May 1, '64. Wounded sev. June 1, '64. |
| Charles E. Robie | 18 | " | " | Sept. 19, '62 | June 21, '65. Dis. by order at Portsmouth, Va., Sept. 29, '63. |
| David P. Robie | 21 | " | " | " | June 23, '65. Pro. Corp. May 1, '65. |
| John M. Rowe | 34 | Woodstock | " | " | Sick at Hampton Gen. Hospital since April 20, '64. Probably dead. |
| Edwin Sanborn | 26 | Concord | " | " | June 21, '65. Pro. Corp. May 9, '65. |
| Frank Sargent | 18 | " | " | " | June 21, '65 |
| Edward Schanks | 44 | " | " | " | June 21, '65. Dis. by order at Portsmouth, Va., Nov. 3, '63. |
| William M. Sargent | 28 | Thornton | " | " | June 21, '65 |
| Lewis Silver | 42 | Bow | " | " | June 3, '65. Dis. at Richmond, Va. |
| William H. Spiller | 20 | Chichester | " | " | Des. near Washington, D. C., Jan. 21, '63. |
| Andrew J. Stackpole | 29 | New Castle | " | " | June 21, '65 |
| Zimri Stearns | 28 | Woodstock | " | " | June 21, '65. Wounded sl. June 15, '64. |
| John F. Varney | 33 | Farmington | " | " | June 21, '65 |
| William W. Virgin | 35 | Concord | " | " | Died of disease, diphtheria, at Portsmouth, Va., Sept. 4, '63. |
| James H. Wakeham | 30 | West Milton | " | " | Wounded June 3, '64. Transf. to V. R. C. Feb. 10, '65. |
| William H. Watson | 19 | Farmington | " | " | Dis. at U. S. Gen. Hospital, Fortress Monroe, Va., June 6, '65. |
| George H. Weeks | 21 | Concord | " | " | |

| Name | Age | Residence | Rank | Mustered in | Remarks |
|---|---|---|---|---|---|
| Alfred Webster | 24 | Campton | Private | Sept. 19, '62 | Des. at Washington, D. C., March 12, '65. |
| George A. Wilder | 19 | Concord | " | " | Transf. to Navy April 29, '64. |
| William Williamson | 32 | Pelham | " | " | Dis. by order at Portsmouth, Va., Sept. 29, '63. |
| Wooster E. Woodbury | 26 | Campton | " | " | Wounded sev. June 3, '64. Pro. Corp. May 1, '65. |

### RECRUITS.

| Name | Age | Residence | Rank | Mustered in | Remarks |
|---|---|---|---|---|---|
| Fabri Candido | 26 | Unknown | " | Aug. 12, '63 | Des. April 18, '64. Returned Nov. 18, '64. Des. May 1, '65. |
| Michael Corbett | | " | " | Aug. 10, '63 | Wounded sl. June 1, '64. Transf. to 2d N. H. V. June 21, '65. |
| Frank Dudley | 28 | " | " | Aug. 27, '63 | Des. while on furlough from Hospital Aug. 27, '64. |
| Andrew M. Dunsmore | | " | " | Aug. 11, '63 | Wounded sl. May 16, '64. Transf. to 2d N. H. V. June 21, '65. |
| Albert Denacre | | " | " | " | Transf. to 2d N. H. V. June 21, '65. |
| John Drew | 27 | " | " | " | Transf. to Navy April 28, '64. |
| Isaac Dodge | 21 | " | " | Aug. 12, '63 | Transf. to Navy April 28, '64. |
| John Denison | 23 | " | " | Aug. 11, '63 | Transf. to Navy April 28, '64. |
| John Devine | 24 | " | " | " | Transf. to Navy April 28, '64. |
| Franklin Dent | 22 | " | " | " | Des. at Portsmouth, Va., Oct. 19, '63. |
| Thomas Dudley | | " | " | " | Volunteer. Dis. by order June 1, '65, on Surgeon's certificate of disability. |
| George Philbrick | 19 | Boscawen | " | Dec. 8, '63 | Dis. May 28, '65, at Richmond, Va. |
| James Delaney | 28 | Unknown | " | Aug. 11, '63 | Des. at Portsmouth, Va., May 7, '64. |
| George Dunn | 27 | " | " | Aug. 10, '63 | Des. at Portsmouth, Va., Oct. 6, '63. |
| John Donovan | 22 | " | " | Aug. 12, '63 | Volunteer. Dis. by order June 3, '65, for disability at Hospital in Manchester, N. H. |
| Edward G. Glover | 24 | Bradford | " | Dec. 3, '63 | Volunteer. Dis. for disability July 29, '64. |
| Edwin A. Hoffman | 23 | Pittsfield | " | Dec. 7, '63 | Transf. to Navy May 4, '64. |
| Henry F. Pettigrew | 21 | Farmington | " | Dec. 29, '63 | Volunteer. Pro. 2d Lieut. 1st N. H. Cavalry March 18, '64. |
| George H. Smith | 29 | " | " | Jan. 5, '64 | June 21, '65 |

## D.

| | Age. | Residence. | Rank. | Muster in. | Muster out. | Remarks. |
|---|---|---|---|---|---|---|
| George Farr | 26 | Littleton | Captain | Sept. 19, '62 | June 21, '65 | Wounded sev. June 1, '64, at Cold Harbor. |
| Edward Kilburn | 32 | " | 1st Lieut. | Sept. 27, '62 | | Resigned June 24, '63. |
| Marshall Saunders | 29 | " | " | Jan 25, '63 | | Pro. Captain Co. B July 19, '64. |
| Robert R. Thompson | 39 | Stratford | " | July 15, '64 | | Killed at Ft. Harrison, Sept. 29, '64. |
| Andrew J. Sherman | 30 | Bethlehem | " | Oct. 28, '64 | June 21, '65 | |
| Marshall Saunders | 29 | Littleton | 2d Lieut. | Sept. 27, '62 | | Pro. 1st Lieut. Co. D Jan. 25, '63. |
| Andrew J. Sherman | 30 | Bethlehem | " | Jan. 25, '63 | | Pro. 1st Lieut. Co. D Oct. 28, '64. |
| Augustine C. Gaskill | 27 | Littleton | " | June 15, '65 | June 21, '65 | Pro. Lieut. not mustered. |
| Andrew J. Sherman | 30 | Bethlehem | 1st Sergt. | Sept. 19, '62 | | Wounded Dec. 13, '62. Pro. 2d Lieut. Jan. 25, '63. |
| George W. Ferguson | 33 | Monroe | Sergeant | " | | Pro. Commissary Sergt. May 1, '64. |
| Francis D. Sanborn | 28 | Littleton | " | " | June 21, '65 | Transf. to Brigade Band Oct. 7, '63. |
| William A. Crane | 24 | Bethlehem | " | " | | Dis. for disability near Portsmouth, Va., Oct. 8, '63. |
| Edwards Clark | 23 | Landaff | " | " | | Dis. for disability at Washington, D. C., Nov. 20, '62. |
| Marcus A. Taylor | 38 | Littleton | Corporal | " | | Wounded, Dec. 13, '62. Dis. at De Camp Hospital, N. Y., Aug. 6, '64. |
| John S. Cheney | 24 | Bethlehem | " | " | June 21, '65 | Pro. Corp. March 12, '63. Wounded sev. May 16, '64. |
| Joel E. Hibbard | 24 | Haverhill | " | " | June 21, '65 | Dis. for disability at David's Island, N. Y., Feb. 9, '63. |
| Jonathan M. Rix | 28 | Dalton | " | " | | Dis. by order at Newport News, Va., Feb. 19, '63. |
| Benjamin W. Kilburn | 34 | Littleton | " | " | June 21, '65 | Pro. Sergt. Dec. 12, '64. |
| Edwin Bowman | 20 | " | " | " | June 21, '65 | |
| Murray Scott | 28 | Bethlehem | " | " | | Pro. Sergt. Wounded sev. May 13, '64. Died of wounds at Point Lookout, Md., July 2, '64. |
| Charles W. Batchellor | 23 | " | " | " | | |
| Henry B. Burnham | 20 | Littleton | Musician | " | June 21, '65 | Transf. to Brigade Band Jan. 20, '63. |
| John W. Palmer | 28 | " | " | " | June 21, '65 | Transf. to Brigade Band Jan. 20, '63. |
| George M. Hardy | 23 | Bethlehem | Wagoner | " | | Died of disease at Falmouth, Va., Feb. 6, '63. |
| Stephen W. Atwood | 30 | Littleton | Private | " | June 10, '65 | |
| Ezra B. Bean | 21 | Landaff | " | " | June 21, '65 | Dis. for disability March 4, '64, at Columbia Hospital, Washington, D. C. |
| Jerome B. Beane | 18 | Bethlehem | " | " | | Dis. for disability at Portsmouth Grove, R. I., June 10, '63. |
| Kimball E. Beane | 29 | Franconia | " | " | | Dis. for disability near Portsmouth, Va., Oct. 14, '63. |
| Edwin Belville | 38 | Monroe | " | " | | Dis. for disability at Portsmouth Grove, R. I., Aug. 5, '64. |
| Almon R. Blandin | 18 | Bethlehem | " | " | | Wounded sev. June 4, '64. Died of wounds at Washington, D. C., July 6, '64. |

| Name | Age | Town | Rank | Date | Remarks |
|---|---|---|---|---|---|
| Harvey W. Bishop | 19 | Landaff | Private | Sept. 19, '62 | Dis. for disability Feb. 26, '63. |
| Josiah Brown | 35 | Littleton | " | " | Wounded sl. June 15, '64. |
| Nathan Burns | 40 | Dalton | " | " | Wounded sl. June 1, '64. Transf. to V. R. C. March 8, '65. |
| Albert Carpenter | 33 | Landaff | " | " | Killed at Fort Harrison, Va., Sept. 30, '64. |
| Francis G. Carpenter | 18 | Littleton | " | " | App. Musician. Dis. for disability April 6, '65. |
| Albee B. Carter | 18 | " | " | " | Des. at Littleton April 2, '63. |
| John D. Chandler | 36 | " | " | " | |
| Dudley Chase | 19 | Monroe | " | June 10, '65 | Wounded sev. June 15, '64. Died of wounds at New York Aug. 13, '64. |
| Frank Chase | 20 | " | " | " | |
| Daniel M. Clough | 21 | Littleton | " | June 21, '65 | Died of disease at Falmouth, Va., Feb. 6, '63. |
| Frank Clough | 21 | Landaff | " | " | Pro. Corporal. |
| Samuel J. Clough | 25 | Littleton | " | June 10, '65 | Dis. May 6, '65. |
| George W. Cleasby | 18 | " | " | " | Died of wounds at Suffolk, Va., May 11, '63. |
| Alanson F. Classon | 22 | " | " | " | Pro. Corp. June 10, '64. Wounded sev. Sept. 29, '64. |
| Charles R. Coburn | 18 | " | " | June 21, '65 | Pro. Corp. Dis. for disability at New York July 28, '64. |
| Calvin P. Crouch | 18 | " | " | " | Transf. to V. R. C. Aug. 1, '63. Mustered out June 28, '65. |
| Dearborn Davis | 22 | Franconia | " | " | |
| Isaac F. Dodge | 30 | Lyman | " | June 21, '65 | Des. from Hospital Nov. 4, '64. Gained from desertion April 16, '65. Dis. May 15, '65. |
| Henry H. Elkins | 23 | Bethlehem | " | " | Transf. to V. R. C. Sept. 30, '63. |
| Francis W. Fitzgerald | 25 | Littleton | " | " | Pro. Corp. Jan. 6, '63; Sergt. March 12, '63; 1st Sergt. Aug. 15, '64; 2d Lieut. June 15, '65. Wounded sl. June 1, '64. |
| Augustine C. Gaskill | 27 | " | " | " | Pro. Corp. |
| Austin Gilman | 27 | " | " | June 21, '65 | Wounded sl. May 14, '64. Pro. Corp. Dec. 12, '64. |
| Loveren L. Gilman | 29 | " | " | " | Pro. Corp. Killed at Cold Harbor, Va., June 1, '64. |
| Alburn G. Goddard | 19 | " | " | " | Killed at Cold Harbor, Va., June 1, '64. |
| Otis B. Harriman | 20 | Lancaster | " | June 21, '65 | Transf. to V. R. C. Dec. 21, '63. Mustered out June 25, '65. |
| George O. W. Hatch | 18 | Bethlehem | " | " | Died of disease at Washington, D. C., March 13, '63. |
| David G. Hatch | 21 | " | " | " | Des. at Whitefield, N. H., Jan. 14, '64. |
| Harlow Hall | 26 | " | " | " | Pro. Corp. Dis. for disability at Washington, D. C., April 30, '63. |
| Alexander Hinman | 29 | Monroe | " | June 21, '65 | Wounded Dec. 13, '63. |
| Charles H. Hoit | 18 | Bethlehem | " | " | Wounded May 13, '64. Died of wounds at Point of Rocks, Va., May 18, '64. |
| Eli Huntoon | 31 | " | " | " | |
| William J. Huntoon | 29 | " | " | June 8, '65 | |
| John W. Hutton | 18 | Monroe | " | " | Died of disease at Portsmouth, Va., Sept. 30, '63. |
| Joseph J. Hutton | 27 | " | " | June 21, '65 | Wounded sev. June 15, '64. |

654

| Name | Age | Residence | Rank | Date of enlistment | Remarks |
|---|---|---|---|---|---|
| Frederick L. Kendall | 26 | Franconia | Private | Sept. 19, '62 | Killed at Chapin's Farm, Va., Sept. 29, '64. |
| John M. Little | 21 | Monroe | " | " | Pro. Corp. Sept. 1, '63; Wounded sl. Sept. 30, '64. |
| Elijah B. Lovejoy | 45 | Landaff | " | " | Dis. for disability at Washington, D. C., March 26, '63. |
| E. B. Matthews | 20 | Monroe | " | " | Died of disease at Monroe, N. H., Nov. 15, '64. |
| Milo S. Matthews | 18 | Littleton | " | " | Dis. for disability at Washington, D. C., April 24, '63. |
| Robert L. Merrill | 19 | " | " | " | Died of disease at Fairfax Seminary, Va., Nov. 24, '62. |
| David B. Moffatt | 19 | " | " | June 21, '65 | Wounded sev. Sept. 30, '64. |
| Elmer C. Moulton | 39 | " | " | June 21, '65 | Pro. Corp. Jan. 6, '63; Sergt. Oct. 28, '63. Wounded sev. Sept. 29, '64. |
| Jabez B. Nelson | 29 | Monroe | " | " | |
| George W. Nourse | 19 | Littleton | " | " | Died of disease Aug. 1, '63. |
| Anthony F. Nutting | 22 | " | " | June 21, '65 | Died of disease at Portsmouth, Va., March 1, '64. |
| Horace Palmer | 26 | " | " | " | Pro. Corp. May 1, '65. |
| Benjamin F. Parker | 19 | " | " | June 21, '65 | Dis. for disability at Washington, D. C., March 12, '63. |
| Robert Petree | 24 | Lisbon | " | " | |
| Lorenzo Phillips | 18 | Bethlehem | " | " | Died at Fredericksburg, Va., Dec. 14, '62, of wounds rec'd in action Dec. 13, '62. |
| Jesse W. Place | 18 | Littleton | " | June 21, '65 | Wounded sev. June 15, '64. |
| Oscar H. Presby | 18 | " | " | " | Transf. to V. R. C. Sept. 30, '63. |
| Jonathan Place | 18 | " | " | " | Killed at Cold Harbor, Va., June 1, '64. |
| John E. Prescott | 25 | " | " | June 21, '65 | Pro. Corp. March 12, '63; Sergt. Dec. 12, '64. Wounded sl. May 13, '64, and Sept. 30, '64. |
| Charles W. Parker | 19 | Lyman | " | " | Wounded sev. Sept. 29, '64. |
| Thaddeus Quimby | 33 | Lisbon | " | June 21, '65 | Wounded sev. Dec. 13, '62. Dis. for disability at Washington, D. C., Feb. 17, '63. |
| Zadoc B. Remick | 19 | Littleton | " | " | Dis. for disability at Willett's Point, N. Y., Jan. 28, '63. |
| Charles H. Russell | 19 | " | " | " | Dis. by order at Washington, D. C., April 2, '63. |
| Thomas E. Russell | 26 | " | " | June 21, '65 | Transf. to V. R. C., Aug. 10, '64. Dis. for disability May 29, '65. |
| Levi W. Sanborn | 38 | " | " | " | |
| William S. Shattuck | 22 | Bethlehem | " | " | Dis. for disability at Washington, D. C. March 15, '63. |
| William S. Simonds | 18 | " | " | " | Transf. to V. R. C. Sept. 30, '63. |
| Riley S. Simpson | 25 | Littleton | " | " | Wounded sl. Sept. 29, '64. Pro. Corp. May 1, '65. |
| Chester Simpson | 24 | " | " | June 21, '65 | Pro. Corp. Jan. 6, '63; Sergt. Nov. 22, '63. |
| James M. Streeter | 37 | " | " | June 21, '65 | Died of disease at Newport News, Va., March 7, '63. |
| William W. Scott | 30 | " | " | " | Dis. for disability at Fortress Monroe, Va., May 27, '65. |
| John L. Taylor | 18 | Landaff | " | " | Pro. Corp. Died of disease at Portsmouth, Va., Aug. 2, '63. |
| Silas P. Taylor | 20 | " | " | " | Died of disease at Portsmouth, Va., Aug. 28, '63. |

| Name | Age | Residence | Rank | Mustered In | Mustered Out | Remarks |
|---|---|---|---|---|---|---|
| Norman Towns | 18 | Littleton | Private | Sept. 19, '62 | | Died of disease at Portsmouth, Va., Aug. 3, '63. |
| Andrew M. Wallace | 20 | " | " | " | | Died of disease at Aquia Creek, Va., Jan. 27, '63. |
| Mason M. Wallace | 18 | Franconia | " | " | | Pro. Corp. Dec. 12, '64. |
| Silas Wheeler | 25 | Littleton | " | " | | Pro. Corp. Died of disease at Fairfax Seminary, Va., Nov. 17, '62. |
| Luke A. Whitcomb | 21 | Bethlehem | " | " | | Killed at Chapin's Farm, Va., Sept. 30, '64. |
| William H. Woodward | 19 | Monroe | " | " | | Dis. by order at Fairfax Seminary, Va., Nov. 9, '62. |
| Theodore F. Wooster | 18 | Littleton | " | " | | Wounded Dec. 13, '62. Dis. for disability at Concord, N. H., July 17, '63. |
| James J. Young | 29 | " | " | " | June 21, '65 | Transf. to 2d N. H. V. June 21, '65. |
| | | | | | June 21, '65 | Des. at Portsmouth, Va., Dec. 18, '63. |

RECRUITS.

| Name | Age | Residence | Rank | Mustered In | Mustered Out | Remarks |
|---|---|---|---|---|---|---|
| Almon Eaton | 25 | Unknown | " | Aug. 12, '63 | | Des. near Portsmouth, Va., March 10, '64. |
| Daniel Fogarty | 22 | " | " | Aug. 11, '63 | | Wounded sev. June 15, '64. Dis. for disability May 28, '65, at Point of Rocks, Va. |
| John Frank | 36 | " | " | " | | Des. at Portsmouth, Va., March 10, '64. |
| John D. Gibson | | " | " | " | | Wounded sev. June 15, '64. Transf. to 2d N. H. V. June 21, '65. |
| James Gulien | 23 | " | " | " | | Pro. Corp. Wounded sl. May 10, '64. Dis. for disability Feb. 20, '65. |
| Thomas Gilman | | " | " | " | | Transf. to Navy April 29, '64. |
| James L. Glenville | 22 | " | " | " | | Dis. May 13, '65. |
| Robert Howill | 22 | " | " | " | | Dis. by order of G. C. M. April 28, '64. |
| Edward Ealy | 23 | " | " | " | | Des. at Bermuda Hundred, Va., May 20, '64. |
| Thomas Igo | 30 | " | " | Aug. 10, '63 | | Dis. for disability Sept. 7, '64, at Willetts Point, N. Y. |
| Daniel Keating | 21 | " | " | Aug. 11, '63 | | Transf. to 2d N. H. V. June 21, '65. |
| James S. Kempt | 36 | " | " | Aug. 12, '63 | | Transf. to 2d N. H. V. June 21, '65. |
| Jacob Korn | | " | " | Aug. 11, '63 | | Transf. to Navy April 29, '64. |
| John Kneen | | " | " | Aug. 12, '63 | | Killed at Fort Harrison, Va., Sept. 30, '64. |
| Nicholas Kelley | 24 | " | " | Aug. 10, '63 | | Wounded sev. May 14, '64. Des. from Hospital at Point Lookout, Md., Sept. 11, '64. |
| Andreas Lopf | 31 | " | " | Aug. 12, '63 | | Transf. to Navy April 29, '64. |
| Henry Lynch | 26 | " | " | Aug. 11, '63 | | Wounded sl. May 13, '64. Transf. to 2d N. H. V. June 21, '65. |
| Philip G. Lord | 23 | " | " | Aug. 27, '63 | | Wounded sl. June 1, '64. Transf. to 2d N. H. V. June 21, '65. |
| John McCarty | | " | " | Aug. 10, '63 | | Wounded sev. May 12, '64. Dis. by order June 13, '65. |
| James McNeil | | " | " | Aug. 11, '62 | | Transf. to 2d N. H. V. June 21, '65. |
| James Mooney | | " | " | Aug. 10, '62 | | |
| Engelbert Hensler | | " | " | | | |

## E.

| | Age. | Residence. | Rank. | Muster in. | Muster out. | Remarks. |
|---|---|---|---|---|---|---|
| George N. Julian | 21 | Exeter | Captain | Sept. 27, '62 | June 21, '65 | Hon. dis. at expiration of term of enlistment, 3 years, Feb. 1, '65. |
| Hubbard W. Hall | 33 | Strafford | " | March 9, '65 | | |
| James M. Durell | 30 | New Market | 1st Lieut. | Sept. 27, '62 | | Wounded Dec. 13, '62. Wounded sl. June 3, '64. Pro. Capt. July 19, '64. |
| Oliver M. Sawyer | 23 | Nashua | " | July 15, '64 | | Hon. dis. March 10, '65. |
| Henry H. Murray | 21 | New Market | 2d Lieut. | Sept. 27, '62 | | Pro. 1st Lieut. Co. K July 29, '63; Wounded sev. May 3, '63. |
| S. Millett Thompson | 24 | Durham | " | June 10, '63 | | Wounded sev. June 15, '64, in assault on Battery Five, Petersburg. Hon. dis. on account of wounds Oct. 4, '64. |
| John F. Gibbs | 31 | New Market | " | June 15, '65 | June 21, '65 | Pro. Lieut., not mustered. |
| S. Millett Thompson | 24 | Durham | 1st Sergt. | Sept. 19, " | | Pro. 2d Lieut. June 10, '63. |
| John F. Gibbs | 31 | New Market | Sergeant | " | | Pro. 1st Sergt. Aug. 1, '63, — 2d Lieut. June 15, '65. |
| Fernando Gerrish | 26 | Durham | " | " | | Killed by Railroad accident in New Jersey April 8, '63, while returning to duty. |
| George H. Van Duzee | 23 | Exeter | " | " | | Killed at Cold Harbor, Va., June 1, '64. |
| Charles F. Chapman | 23 | New Market | " | " | | Wounded sev. Sept. 30, '64. Died of wounds April 7, '65. |
| Orrin Dow | 27 | Lee | Corporal | " | | Pro. Sergt. Wounded sl. June 1, '64. Wounded sev. Sept. 29, '64. Dis. May 12, '65. |
| Stephen H. Brown | 27 | Kensington | " | " | | Transf. to Brigade Band Jan. 20, '63. Dis. July 10, '63. |
| Ossimus T. Smith | 28 | Exeter | " | " | | Dis. for disability at Washington, D. C., March 9, '63. |
| William West | 21 | Exeter | " | " | June 21, '65 | |
| John Pinkham | 36 | New Market | " | " | | Pro. Sergt. Killed at Fort Harrison, Va., Sept. 29, '64. |
| Nathaniel S. French | " | " | " | " | June 21, '65 | |
| Frederick Bearse | 42 | Exeter | " | " | | Transf. to Navy April 24, '64. |
| Newton Cram | 41 | " | " | " | | Transf. to Navy April 28, '64. |
| Ira E. Wright | 13 | Hampton | Musician | " | | Dis. for disability May 26, '63. |
| John C. Brown | 32 | Exeter | Wagoner | " | | Ambulance driver. Died of disease at Exeter, N. H., Jan. 19, '65. |
| Charles F. Adams | 34 | Portsmouth | Private | Sept. 23, '62 | June 21, '65 | Pro. Sergt. Sept. 6, '64. Wounded sl. Sept. 30, '64. |
| Horatio P. Abbott | 28 | Durham | " | Sept. 19, '62 | June 21, '65 | Wounded sl. June 1, '64. |
| Job C. Allard | 31 | Exeter | " | " | June 21, '65 | Pro. Corp. Feb. 13, '63. Wounded sl. June 1, '64. Wounded April 3, '65. |
| Joseph N. Austin | 21 | Kensington | " | " | June 21, '65 | Dis. for disability March 10, '63. |
| George Black | 34 | New Market | " | " | June 10, '65 | Pro. Corp. May 1, '65. |
| Samuel P. Brackett | 25 | " | " | " | June 10, '65 | |
| David Brackett | 40 | " | " | " | | |

| Name | Age | Residence | Rank | Mustered in | Mustered out | Remarks |
|---|---|---|---|---|---|---|
| Alanson Cram | 18 | Exeter | Private | Sept. 19, '62 | June 10, '65 | Pro. Corp. Transf. to Navy April 28, '64. |
| David A. Blake | 32 | New Market | " | " | " | Transf. to Navy, April 28, '64. |
| George R. Cilley | 38 | Kensington | " | " | " | Dis. for disability near Portsmouth, Va., Oct. 7, '63. |
| George K. Caswell | 29 | New Market | " | " | " | Dis. for disability at Philadelphia, Pa., Feb. 5, '63. |
| Moses E. Colby | 26 | " | " | " | June 21, '65 | Transf. to Brigade Band, Jan. 20, '63. |
| James M. Caswell | 25 | " | " | " | " | Des. June 21, '63. Gained from desertion April 16, '65. Pro. Sergt. June 1, '65. Transf. to 2d N. H. V. June 21, '65. |
| Joseph H. Chapman | | Durham | " | " | " | |
| David W. Chapman | 32 | New Market | " | Sept. 30, '62 | June 21, '65 | Wounded Dec. 13, '62. Pro. Corp. May 1, '65. |
| William Chapman | 34 | " | " | Sept. 19, '62 | " | Des. at Camp Chase, Va., Oct. 14, '62. |
| Augustus H. Davis | 21 | " | " | " | June 21, '65 | Pro. Corp. May 1, '65. |
| Jesse L. Dolloff | 29 | Nottingham | " | " | June 21, '65 | Pro. Corp. Aug. 26, '62; Sergt. March 1, '65. |
| Bradbury C. Davis | 32 | Durham | " | " | June 10, '65 | Dis. by order March 21, '65. |
| George M. Dowe | | | | | | |
| William H. Dockum | 19 | New Market | " | " | " | Dis. for disability at Fort Schuyler, N. Y., March 10, '63. |
| Rufus Eastman | 34 | Kensington | " | " | June 21, '65 | |
| James W. Folsom | 24 | Exeter | " | " | " | Dis. May 16, '65. |
| Charles A. Fernald | 24 | Lee | " | " | June 10, '65 | Pro. Corp. Feb. 13, '63; Sergt. Nov. 10, '64. Wounded sl. Sept. 30, '64. |
| Robert W. Francis | 31 | Durham | " | " | " | Des. at Fredericksburg, Va., Feb. 7, '63. |
| Charles A. French | 25 | New Market | " | Sept. 30, '62 | June 21, '65 | Killed at Battle of Providence Church Road, near Suffolk, Va., May 3, '63. |
| Warren S. French | 28 | " | " | " | " | |
| John H. Foye | 21 | Rye | " | " | " | |
| Henry V. Freeman | 28 | Claremont | " | " | June 9, '65 | Wounded sev. May 3, '63. |
| Alfred J. Gilman | 26 | Exeter | " | " | June 21, '65 | Pro. Corp. May 1, '65. |
| George E. Garland | 18 | " | " | " | June 21, '65 | Pro. Corp. June 9, '64. Wounded sl. June 15, '64. |
| John B. Greene | 21 | New Market | " | " | June 24, '65 | Wounded sev. April 18, '63, in Siege of Suffolk. |
| Charles F. Gerrish | 39 | Nottingham | " | " | June 21, '65 | |
| Warren Glover | 31 | New Market | " | " | June 21, '65 | |
| Joseph Gould | 43 | Unknown | " | | | Killed at Fort Harrison, Va., Sept. 30, '64. |
| Bernard Gunning | 25 | Durham | " | Sept. 30, '62 | | Des. at Camp Chase, Va., Oct. 14, '62. |
| John Goodrich | 23 | Durham | " | Sept. 19, '62 | | Transf. to Navy April 28, '64. |
| Benjamin F. Horn | 29 | New Market | " | " | | Transf. to Navy April 28, '64. |
| George W. Hanson | 21 | Lee | " | " | June 21, '65. | Wounded Dec 13, '62. Dis. for disability Feb. 8, '65, at Belfour Gen. Hospital. |
| David Hogan | 43 | New Market | " | " | | |
| John H. Harvey | 45 | " | " | " | | Killed at Drury's Bluff, Va., May 16, '64. |

| Name | Age | Residence | Rank | Mustered In | Mustered Out | Remarks |
|---|---|---|---|---|---|---|
| James Hughes | 18 | New Market | Private | Sept. 19, '62 | June 21, '65 | Des. at Concord, N. H., June 10, '64. Gained from desertion. Mustered out May 16, '65. |
| Henry C. Howard | 25 | " | " | " | | |
| Thomas Harrigan | 30 | Littleton | " | Sept. 20, '62 | June 21, '65 | Des. near Portsmouth, Va., June 22, '63. |
| George A. Jenkins | 20 | New Market | " | Sept. 19, '62 | | Died of disease at Aquia Creek, Va., Feb. 3, '63. |
| Joseph A. Jones | 18 | Lee | " | " | | Died of disease at Portsmouth, Va., Aug. 8, '63. |
| Albion J. Jenness | 18 | Rye | " | Sept. 30, '62 | | Dis. for disability at Portsmouth, Va., Sept. 15, '63. |
| William S. Keniston | 45 | New Market | " | Sept. 19, '62 | | Transf. to V. R. C. July 1, '63. Dis. at New York, Dec. 14, '63. |
| Edward F. Keniston | 33 | " | " | " | | |
| James F. Keniston | 27 | " | " | " | June 21, '65 | |
| Charles Keniston | 38 | " | " | " | | Died of disease at Portsmouth, Va., Sept. 5, '63. |
| George O. Keniston | 27 | Durham | " | " | | Des. at Fort Schuyler, N. Y. |
| Charles A. Kent | 26 | " | " | " | | Transf. to V. R. C. April 10, '64. Mustered out July 21, '65. |
| Rufus Lampson | 18 | Exeter | " | " | June 21, '65 | |
| George W. Long | 19 | Durham | " | " | June 21, '65 | |
| John Leavitt | 25 | Exeter | " | Sept. 24, '62 | | Transf. to V. R. C. Sept. 18, '63. Mustered out July 13, '65. |
| Lewis Little | 28 | South Hampton | " | Sept. 19, '62 | | Des. at Concord, N. H., Sept. 25, '62. |
| Howard M. Moses | 21 | Exeter | " | Sept. 30, '62 | June 18, '65 | Wounded sl. May 3, '63. |
| Alexander Mulligan | 38 | " | " | Sept. 23, '62 | June 21, '65 | |
| Henry Nutter | 26 | Portsmouth | " | " | | Wounded Dec. 13, '62. Dis. for disability at Washington, D. C., Feb. 5, '64. |
| Lawrence G. Otis | 26 | Lee | " | Sept. 19, '62 | | Dis. for disability at Concord, N. H., May 14, '64. |
| Edmund P. Palmer | 44 | Hampton | " | Oct. 2, '62 | | Dis. for disability at Alexandria, Va., Jan. 1, '63. |
| Royal B. Prescott | 23 | Nashua | " | Sept. 30, '62 | | Pro. Hosp. Steward Nov. 22, '62. Pro. 1st Lieut. Oct. 28, '64. |
| Daniel S. Randall | 43 | Lee | " | Sept. 19, '62 | | Transf. to V. R. C. Feb. 16, '64. Mustered out June 28, '65. |
| Richard Randall | 38 | " | " | " | | Dis. for disability at Portsmouth, Va., Sept. 29, '63. |
| Charles H. Robinson | 21 | Stratham | " | " | | Transf. to V. R. C. Sept. 1, '63. Mustered out July 13, '65. |
| George F. Rollins | 19 | Exeter | " | " | | Transf. to V. R. C. Sept. 30, '63. |
| William M. Richardson | 22 | New Market | " | " | | Transf. to Navy April 28, '64. |
| George K. Smart | 33 | " | " | " | | Pro. Corp. Dis. for disability at Falmouth, Va., Feb. 6, '63. |
| Frederick W. Sawyer | 21 | Exeter | " | Sept. 24, '62 | | Dis. for disability at Philadelphia, Pa., Dec. 14, '63. |
| David C. Smith | 23 | Kensington | " | " | | Dis. for disability at Fort Schuyler, N. Y., March 5, '63. |
| Peter Smithwick | 39 | Hollis | " | Sept. 26, '62 | | Wounded at Fredericksburg, Va., Dec. 13, '62. Transf. to V. R. C. May 30, '64. Six feet seven inches tall. Tallest man in the Regiment. |
| Andrew J. S. Tuttle | 18 | Durham | " | " | | Des. at Fredericksburg, Va., Feb. 7, '63. |
| Elbridge F. Trow | 26 | Mount Vernon | " | " | | Dis. for disability at Washington, D. C., Oct. 23, '62. |

| Name | Age | Residence | Rank | Mustered in | Mustered out | Remarks |
|---|---|---|---|---|---|---|
| John C. Van Duzee | 18 | Exeter | Private | Sept. 19, '62 | | Pro. Corp. Dis. for disability at Point of Rocks, Va., Jan. 27, '65. |
| Joseph Watson | 31 | New Market | " | " | | Dis. by order of G. C. M. and sentenced to hard labor at Norfolk, Va., May 14, '64. Sentence remitted by Special Order No. 379, War Dept. Adjt. General's Office, July 18, '65. |
| Francis Wild | 25 | Hampton Falls | " | " | | Des. at Camp Chase, Va., Oct. 14, '62. |
| Joseph Warren | 21 | " | " | Sept. 30, '62 | | Dis. for disability at Portsmouth, Va., Sept. 29, '63. |
| Charles J. Woods | 18 | Barrington | " | Oct. 1, '62 | | |
| Horace W. Waldron | 21 | Wilton | " | " | | Wounded sl. June 15, '64. Dis. May 16, '65. |
| George W. Williams | 19 | Littleton | " | " | | Dis. for disability near Portsmouth, Va., Oct. 27, '63. |
| Lowell H. Young | 19 | Exeter | " | Sept. 19, '62 | June 21, '65 | |
| John T. Young | 19 | New Market | " | " | June 21, '65 | |

RECRUITS.

| Name | Age | Residence | Rank | Mustered in | Mustered out | Remarks |
|---|---|---|---|---|---|---|
| George Conklin | 24 | Unknown | " | Aug. 20, '63 | | Transf. to Navy April 28, '64. |
| Charles A. Lull | 36 | " | Musician | June 9, '63 | | Volunteer. Transf. to 2d N. H. V. June 21, '65. |
| George W. Myers | 22 | " | Private | Aug. 11, '63 | | Transf. to Navy March 30, '64. |
| George A. Marshall | | " | " | " | | Des. at Portsmouth, Va., Oct. 9, '63. Apprehended. Des. from Norfolk Jail, Va., Oct. 11, '63. |
| Jacob Mehal | 31 | " | " | " | June 21, '65 | Pro. Corp. June 1, '64. Transf. to 2d N. H. V. June 21, '65. |
| John Martin | 22 | " | " | " | | Transf. to Navy April 28, '64. |
| Owen McMann | | " | " | " | | Captured at Drury's Bluff May 16, '64. Died of disease at Andersonville, Ga., Oct. 20, '64. Grave No. 11,207. |
| James McCloy | 23 | " | " | Aug. 12, '63 | | Des. at Portsmouth, Va., Oct. 9, '63. |
| Jeremiah Murphy | 29 | " | " | Aug. 10, '63 | | Killed at Cold Harbor, Va., June 7, '64. |
| James Morris | 21 | " | " | Aug. 11, '63 | | Killed at Cold Harbor, Va., June 11, '64, while on regimental inspection. |
| William Moore | 26 | " | " | " | | Des. at Portsmouth, Va., Oct. 5, '63. |
| Patrick Norton | 31 | " | " | " | | Wounded sl. June 1, '64. Des. from Hospital at Washington, D. C., Jan. 4, '65. |
| Patrick O'Neil | 29 | " | " | " | | Des. at Chestnut Hill, Pa., Aug. 2, '64. |
| John O'Reilly | 35 | " | " | Aug. 11, '63 | | Dis. by Special Order No. 429 War Dept. Dec. 3, '64, to accept an appointment as Hospital Steward U. S. A. |
| Peter E. Plumpton | 30 | " | " | " | | Transf. to Navy April 24, '64. |
| Richard Proctor | 39 | " | " | Aug. 14, '63 | | Transf. to Navy March 30, '64. |
| Benjamin F. Peters | | " | " | Aug. 20, '63 | | Transf. to 2d N. H. V. June 21, '65. |
| Gamaliel Rose | 27 | " | " | Aug. 11, '63 | | Des. at Portsmouth, Va., Oct. 9, '63. |

| | | | | |
|---|---|---|---|---|
| John Riley | 23 | Unknown | Private | Aug. 12, '63 | Pro. Corp. Transf. to 2d N. H. V. June 21, '65. |
| John Reed | 28 | " | " | " | Transf. to Navy April 28, '64. |
| Philip Smith | | " | " | " | Des. near Portsmouth, Va., Oct. 6, '63. |
| Charles Steinburg | | " | " | " | Transf. to 2d N. H. V. June 21, '65. |
| John Sullivan | 21 | " | " | Aug. 11, '63 | Des. at Fort Harrison, Va., Nov. 3, '64. |

## F.

| Name | Age | Residence | Rank | Muster in | Muster out | Remarks |
|---|---|---|---|---|---|---|
| Lewis H. Buzzell | 30 | Barrington | Captain | Sept. 27, '62 | | Killed at Battle of Providence Church Road, Suffolk, May 3, '63. |
| Gustavus A. Forbush | 21 | Peterborough | " | May 5, '63 | | Killed at Ft. Harrison Sept. 29, '64. |
| Charles H. Curtis | | | " | Oct. 28, '64 | June 21, '65 | Pro. Capt. Co. F. |
| William H. H. Young | 25 | Farmington | 1st Lieut. | Sept. 27, '62 | | Hon. dis. Feb. 2, '64, on Surgeon's certificate of disability. |
| Jonathan Dustin | 41 | Barrington | " | March 16, '64 | | Hon. dis. Oct. 1, '64, on Surgeon's certificate of disability. |
| George H. Taggard | 26 | Nashua | " | Nov. 3, '64 | | Pro. Adjt. May 30, '65. |
| Hubbard W. Hall | 30 | Strafford | 2d Lieut. | Sept. 27, '62 | | Pro. 1st Lieut. Co. I July 29, '63. |
| Jonathan Dustin | 41 | Barrington | " | May 1, '63 | | Pro. 1st Lieut. Co. F March 16, '64. |
| George H. Taggard | 26 | Nashua | " | March 16, '64 | | Wounded sev. June 3, '64. Pro. 1st Lieut. Nov. 3, '64. |
| M. C. Shattuck | | | " | May 30, '65 | June 21, '65 | Pro. Lieut., not mustered. |
| Charles A. Woodman | 21 | Strafford | " | June 15, '65 | June 21, '65 | Pro. Lieut., not mustered. |
| John D. Parshley | 41 | Barrington | 1st Sergt. | Sept. 19, '62 | June 21, '65 | Pro. 2d Lieut. May 1, '63. |
| Charles A. Woodman | 33 | Strafford | Sergeant | " | | Wounded sl. June 3, '64. Pro. 1st Sergt. July 1, '63; 2d Lieut. June 15, '65. |
| Goodhue Ceorim | 21 | Brookfield | " | Sept. 24, '62 | | Died of disease at Hampton, Va., March 5, '63. |
| Elisha E. Locke | 18 | Barrington | " | Sept. 19, '62 | | Wounded Dec. 13, '62. Dis. for disability at Portsmouth Grove, R. I., March 19, '63. |
| Alpheus D. Evans | 33 | Strafford | Corporal | " | | Died of disease at Newport News, Va., March 8, '63. |
| Joseph H. Prime | 21 | Barrington | " | " | | Dis. by order Nov. 4, '63. |
| William H. Gilpatrick | 25 | Nottingham | " | " | | Transf. to V. R. C. March 31, '64. Mustered out Sept. 18, '65. |
| Edwin H. Leslie | 21 | Portsmouth | " | Sept. 24, '62 | | Pro. Sergt. March 1, '63. Wounded sev. June 3, '64. Dis. by order at Washington, D. C., May 29, '65. |
| John D. Daniels | 23 | Nottingham | " | Sept. 19, '62 | | Dis. May 12, '65. |
| Charles C. Hall | 23 | Strafford | " | " | | Pro. Principal Musician April 28, '64. |
| Samuel S. Morrison | 18 | Barrington | " | " | | Transf. to V. R. C. Sept. 30, '63. Mustered out Sept. 18, '65. |
| Augustus S. Parshley | 22 | Strafford | " | " | | Transf. to V. R. C. Nov. 13, '63. Mustered out June 26, '65. |
| Charles Morgan | 18 | Concord | Musician | Sept. 23, '62 | | Transf. to Navy May 4, '64. |
| George W. Arlin | 22 | Barrington | Private | Sept. 19, '62 | June 21, '65 | |
| Jeremiah Arlin | 37 | " | " | " | | |
| James W. Buzzell | 23 | " | " | " | June 21, '65 | Des. at Concord, N. H., Sept. 30, '62. |
| Charles O. Buzzell | 19 | " | " | " | June 17, '65 | Pro. Corp. May 6, '64; Sergt. June 1, '64. Wounded sev. June 15, '64. |
| Daniel R. Berry | 20 | " | " | " | | Dis. for disability at Fairfax Seminary, Va., Dec. 4, '62. |

| Name | Age | Residence | Rank | Enlisted | Discharged | Remarks |
|---|---|---|---|---|---|---|
| Sherburne K. Burnham | 36 | Nottingham | Private | Sept. 19, '62 | June 21, '65 | Pro. Corp. Nov. 8, '63; Sergt. June 1, '65. Wounded sev. June 1, '64. |
| Aaron Bridge | 43 | " | " | " | " | Died at Washington, D. C., Feb. 14, '63. |
| George P. Blake | 21 | Brookfield | " | " | June 21, '65 | Dis. for disability at Portsmouth Grove, R. I., May 11, '64. |
| William F. Berry | 22 | Strafford | " | " | | |
| Charles H. Berry | 27 | " | " | " | June 21, '65 | Wounded sl. Sept. 29, '64. |
| Charles Burt, Jr. | 18 | Littleton | " | " | June 21, '65 | Transf. to V. R. C. Nov. 15, '63. Dis. for disability May 17, '65. |
| Addison F. Bean | 19 | Nottingham | " | " | | Pro. Corp. March 1, '63. Wounded May 3, '63. Died of wounds May 5, '63. Interred at Suffolk, Va. |
| Nathaniel Caverly | 18 | Barrington | " | " | | Dis. for disability at New York Jan. 29, '63. |
| Samuel E. Caswell | 37 | " | " | " | | Dis. for disability at New York Dec. 31, '62. |
| James Clark | 38 | " | " | " | June 21, '65 | |
| Joseph G. Clay | 24 | " | " | " | | Dis. for disability at Philadelphia, Pa., March 24, '63. |
| George F. Demeritt | 20 | " | " | " | June 21, '65 | Pro. Corp. Jan. 14, '65. |
| Albert W. Demeritt | 18 | Nottingham | " | " | | Dis. for disability at Portsmouth Grove, R. I., May 29, '63. |
| Lorenzo D. Drew | 29 | Newington | " | " | | Died of disease at Portsmouth, Va., Aug. 22, '63. Interred at Suffolk, Va. |
| George W. Dame | 19 | Barrington | " | " | June 21, '65 | Pro. Corp. June 1, '65. |
| Wright T. Ellison | 21 | " | " | " | " | Dis. for disability at Concord, N. H. June 6, '63. |
| John W. Emerson | 18 | " | " | " | | Dis. for disability at Philadelphia, Pa., April 2, '63. |
| True Emerson | 33 | Lee | " | " | June 21, '65 | Wounded sev. June 1, '64. |
| Joseph S. Evans | 18 | Strafford | " | " | | Died of disease at Washington, D. C., March 8, '63. |
| Charles E. Edgerley | 19 | " | " | " | | Wounded May 3, '63. Died of wounds at Suffolk, Va., May 7, '63. Interred at Suffolk, Va. |
| Amariah J. Foss | 23 | " | " | " | | Transf. to V. R. C. Feb. 15, '64. |
| Ira Foss | 44 | " | " | " | June 28, '65 | |
| Lemuel P. Foss | 20 | " | " | " | " | Died of disease at Concord, N. H., Oct. 15, '64. |
| George W. Foss | 22 | " | " | " | June 21, '65 | |
| Samuel I. Furbur | 18 | Nottingham | " | " | | Dis. for disability at New York Dec. 31, '62. |
| William G. Grey | 18 | Barrington | " | " | June 21, '65 | |
| Thomas Goodnue | 18 | Brookfield | " | " | June 21, '65 | Pro. Corporal. |
| William F. Holmes | 23 | Nottingham | " | " | | Dis. for disability near Portsmouth, Va., Oct. 3, '63. |
| Noah W. Holmes | 31 | " | " | Sept. 23, '62 | June 21, '65 | |
| John L. Holmes | 20 | " | " | Sept. 19, '62 | June 21, '65 | |
| Charles F. Hall | 26 | Barrington | " | " | | Wounded Dec. 13, '62. Dis. for disability at Portsmouth Grove, R. I., May 29, '63. |
| Gilman Hall, Jr. | 21 | " | " | " | | |

| Name | Age | Town | Rank | Date | Notes |
|---|---|---|---|---|---|
| Daniel D. Hall | 28 | Strafford | Private | Sept. 19, '62 | June 21, '65 | Pro. Corp. Aug. 1, '63; Sergt. May 6, '64. Wounded sev. Sept. 29, '64. |
| George H. Hanscom | 21 | " | " | " | | Pro. Corp. Wounded sl. June 15, '64. Dis. May 19, '65. |
| John Hubbard | 24 | " | " | Sept. 23, '62 | | Dis. for disability at Portsmouth Grove, R. I., Jan. 15, '63. |
| Ai C. Hall | 24 | " | " | Sept. 19, '62 | | Dis. for disability at Philadelphia, Pa., May 11, '64. |
| Charles H. Jackson | 18 | Barrington | " | " | | Wounded sev. June 15, '64. Pro. Corp. Jan. 14, '65. Dis. May 23, '65. |
| Thomas E. Kilroy | 22 | " | " | Sept. 20, '62 | June 21, '65 | |
| John C. Locke | 34 | " | " | Sept. 19, '62 | " | Dis. for disability at New York June 29, '63. |
| True W. Lovering | 29 | Nottingham | " | " | June 21, '65 | Dis. for disability at Washington, D. C., March 30, '63. |
| Charles Leathers | 21 | " | " | " | | |
| Daniel A. Lee | 32 | Barrington | " | " | June 21, '65 | Wounded Dec. 13, '62. |
| Elisha E. Locke | 18 | " | " | " | " | Pro. Corp. June 1, '64. |
| Irving C. Locke | 18 | " | " | " | June 21, '65 | Dis. for disability at Philadelphia, Pa., April 13, '63. |
| Wainwright M. Locke | 34 | " | " | " | | Pro. Sergt. Transf. to Navy May 4, '64. |
| George F. Locke | 21 | " | " | " | | Died of disease at New York Oct. 16, '64. |
| Andrew Lovering | 25 | Nottingham | " | " | | Transf. to Navy April 28, '64. |
| Llewyllyn D. Lothrop | 26 | Madbury | " | " | June 21, '65 | |
| Patrick McGrath | 40 | Barrington | " | " | June 21, '65 | Pro. Corp. Sept. 28, '63; Sergt. Jan. 14, '65. |
| Joel H. Morrison | 30 | " | " | Sept. 24, '62 | June 21, '65 | Wounded and missing at Fredericksburg, Va., Dec. 13, '62. Gained from missing. Dis. May 29, '65. |
| William Morgan | 18 | Bow | " | Sept. 19, '62 | | Dis. for disability at Portsmouth, Va., Sept. 23, '63. |
| John P. Mulligan | 18 | Barrington | " | " | | Died of disease at Portsmouth, Va., March 19, '64. |
| John P. Neal | 42 | " | " | " | | Transf. to Brigade Band Jan. 27, '63. Died Nov. 15, '63. |
| Eliphalet B. Peavey | 27 | Strafford | " | " | | Transf. to Brigade Band Jan. 27, '63. |
| Henry G. Parshley | 33 | Rye | " | " | | Died of wounds at Fredericksburg, Va., Dec. 9, '62. |
| John H. Parshley | 24 | " | " | Unknown | | |
| Lorenzo Phillips | | Bethlehem | " | Sept. 19, '62 | June 21, '65 | Wounded sev. June 1, '64. Died of wounds at Washington, D. C., June 17, '64. |
| Stephen H. Richardson | 21 | Madbury | " | " | | |
| Daniel Smith | 44 | Barrington | " | " | | |
| Joseph W. Smith | 18 | " | " | " | June 21, '65 | Pro. Corp. June 1, '64. Wounded sev. Sept. 30, '64. |
| Nathaniel H. Seavey | 32 | " | " | " | | Pro. Sergt. July 1, '63. Transf. to Navy May 4, '64. |
| Albert F. Seavey | 18 | " | " | " | June 21, '65 | |
| Austin F. Seavey | 18 | " | " | " | June 21, '65 | Pro. Corp. May 6, '64. |
| Alfred H. Stephenson | 24 | " | " | " | | Wounded Dec. 13, '62. Transf. to V. R. C. Nov. 20, '63. Mustered out Aug. 11, '65. |

664

| Name | Age | Residence | Rank | Mustered in | Mustered out | Remarks |
|---|---|---|---|---|---|---|
| Joel D. Seward | 44 | Strafford | Private | Sept. 19, '62 | | Dis. for disability at Portsmouth, Va., Sept. 23, '63. |
| George A. Seward | 21 | Nottingham | " | " | | Dis. for disability at Portsmouth Va., Dec. 1, '63. |
| James W. Smith | 23 | Strafford | " | " | | Dis. for disability at Philadelphia, Pa., April 13, '63. |
| David Thompson | 32 | Barrington | " | " | | Died of disease at Washington, D. C., Dec. 30, '62. |
| Jonathan D. Thompson | 20 | Strafford | " | " | | |
| Hiram S. Thompson | 35 | " | " | " | | Wounded sl. June 3, '64. Wounded sl. Sept. 29, '64. |
| Darius Tuttle | 27 | Nottingham | " | " | | |
| Levi C. Tuttle | 27 | " | " | " | | Dis. for disability at Washington, D. C., Dec. 25, '62. |
| Albert H. Tuttle | 24 | " | " | " | | Pro. Corp. Feb. 1, '63. Wounded sev. June 1, '64. |
| John M. Tuttle | 19 | " | " | " | | Died of disease at Portsmouth, Va., June 27, '63. |
| Joseph A. Tuttle | 26 | Strafford | " | " | | Pro. Sergt. Killed at Cold Harbor, Va., June 1, '64. |
| John H. Twombly | 18 | Barrington | " | " | | Dis. for disability at Portsmouth Grove, R. I., Jan. 19, '64. |
| Miles B. Tibbitts | 34 | " | " | " | | Dis. for disability at Concord, N. H., March 12, '63. |
| James H. Witham | 32 | Strafford | " | " | | Dis. for disability at Camp Casey, Va., Nov. 8, '62. |
| Charles F. Wentworth | 25 | " | " | " | | Drummed out of the service Sept. 4, '63. |
| Samuel S. Willey | 43 | Barrington | " | " | | Transf. to V. R. C., July 1, '63. |
| George W. Young | 19 | Strafford | " | " | | |

RECRUITS.

| Name | Age | Residence | Rank | Mustered in | Mustered out | Remarks |
|---|---|---|---|---|---|---|
| Charles D. French | 33 | Peterborough | " | Sept. 2, '63 | | Dis. May 9, '65. |
| John Smith | 21 | Unknown | " | Dec. 24, '63 | | Volunteer. Transf. to 2d N. H. V. June 21, '65. |
| Dennis Shea | | " | " | Aug. 11, '63 | | Wounded sev. June 3, '64. Died of wounds June 25, '64. |
| John Schmidt | 22 | " | " | Aug. 10, '63 | | Transf. to 2d N. H. V. June 21, '65. |
| Louis Stadelmars | 25 | " | " | Aug. 11, '63 | | Des. at White House, Va., May 30, '64. |
| Auguste Schaffer | 21 | " | " | Aug. 12, '63 | | Wounded June 1, '64. Des. at Chester, Pa., Aug. 31, '64. |
| James Smith | 25 | " | " | Aug. 11, '63 | | Des. near Portsmouth, Va., Oct. 6, '63. |
| Robert Scott | 22 | " | " | " | | Transf. to Navy May 4, '64. |
| George Scott | 26 | " | " | | | Des. near Portsmouth, Va., Oct. 8, '63. |
| James Smith | 23 | " | " | Aug. 12, '63 | | Des. near Portsmouth, Va., Oct. 8, '63. |
| John Smith | 44 | " | " | Aug. 11, '63 | | Transf. to Navy May 4, '64. |
| William Smith | 36 | " | " | | | Died at Portsmouth, R. I., July 27, '64. |
| John Taylor | | " | " | | | Des. near Portsmouth, Va., Oct. 19, '63. |
| George W. Taylor | | " | " | Aug. 12, '63 | | Captured at Fair Oaks Oct. 27, '64. Transf. to 2d N. H. V. June 21, '65. |
| James Taylor | 21 | " | " | Aug. 11, '63 | | Transf. to Navy April 28, '64. |
| James Thompson | 26 | " | " | Aug. 10, '63 | | Des. near Portsmouth, Va., Oct. 12, '63. |
| John P. Webster | 32 | " | " | Aug. 11, '63 | | Transf. to Navy April 28, '64. |

| | | | | |
|---|---|---|---|---|
| Wm. J. G. A. Waters | 22 | Unknown | Private | Aug. 12, '63 | Transf. to Navy April 28, '64. |
| James Waddell | 24 | " | " | Aug. 11, '63 | Des. near Portsmouth, Va., Oct. 5, '63. |
| Thomas Williams | 22 | " | " | " | Transf. to Navy, April 28, '64. |
| James B. Williamson | 26 | " | " | " | Transf. to 2d N. H. V. June 21, '65. |
| Frank Wilson | 21 | " | " | " | Transf. to Navy April 28, '64. |
| Joseph Wright | 28 | " | " | " | Des. at White House, Va., May 30, '64. |
| William Warren | | " | " | " | Transf. to Navy April 28, '64. |
| Edward F. White | | " | " | " | Des. from Hospital, Oct. 3, '64. |
| Charles E. Wells | 28 | Francestown | " | Oct. 5, '64 | Volunteer. Des. at Manchester, N. H., June 5, '65. |

## G.

| | Age. | Residence. | Rank. | Muster in. | Muster out. | Remarks. |
|---|---|---|---|---|---|---|
| Nathan D. Stoodley | 39 | Peterborough | Captain | Sept. 27, '62 | | Pro. Major Nov. 2, '64. |
| Lewis P. Wilson | 33 | Greenfield | " | Jan. 11, '65 | June 21, '65 | Detached in charge of Division Ambulance Corps. |
| Gustavus A. Forbush | 30 | Peterborough | 1st Lieut. | Sept. 27, '62 | | Pro. Captain Co. F June 1, '63. Killed at Ft. Harrison, Sept. 29, '64. |
| Lewis P. Wilson | 33 | Greenfield | " | July 29, '63 | | Pro. Captain Co. G Jan. 11, '65. |
| Milton H. Hardy | 27 | Mason | " | March 1, '65 | June 21, '65 | |
| Lewis P. Wilson | 33 | Greenfield | 2d Lieut. | Sept. 27, '62 | | Pro. 1st Lieut. Co. G July 1, '63. |
| Lucius C. Oliver | 22 | New Ipswich | " | May 5, '63 | | Pro. 1st Lieut. Co. I March 8, '65. |
| Edwin Ware | 20 | Hancock | " | | June 21, '65 | Pro. Lieut. not mustered. |
| Lucius C. Oliver | 22 | New Ipswich | 1st Sergt. | June 15, '65 | | Pro. 2d Lieut. May 5, '63. |
| Nathaniel Eaton | 38 | Greenfield | Sergeant | Sept. 19, '62 | | Pro. 2d Lieut. 39th U. S. C. T. March 1, '64. |
| Henry B. Wheeler | 28 | Peterborough | " | " | | Pro. 1st Sergt. Pro. 2d Lieut. of Co. I Aug. 4, '64. |
| Milton H. Hardy | 27 | Mason | " | " | | Pro. 1st Sergt. Aug. 20, '64. Pro. 1st Lieut. March 1, '65. |
| Daniel F. Pratt | 22 | New Ipswich | " | " | June 25, '65 | Dis. for disability at Philadelphia, Pa., Jan. 28, '63. |
| Oliver H. Brown | 34 | Peterborough | Corporal | " | June 21, '65 | Pro. Sergt. March 1, '63. |
| Ira A. Spofford | 37 | " | " | " | June 21, '65 | Pro. Sergt. March 1, '63. |
| Edwin Ware | 20 | Hancock | " | " | June 21, '65 | Wounded Dec. 13, '62. Pro. Sergt. July 29, '63. Wounded at Cold Harbor. Wounded at Fort Harrison. 1st Sergt. April 1, '65; 2d Lieut. June 15, '65. |
| John G. Blood | 23 | Mason | " | " | June 21, '65 | Pro. Corp. Oct. 1, '64; Sergt. April 1, '65. |
| George D. Chapman | 25 | Greenfield | " | " | | Died at Portsmouth, Va., Aug. 25, '63. |
| Herbert E. Follett | 25 | Temple | " | " | June 21, '65 | Wounded sl. Sept. 29, '64. |
| Nathan C. Forbush | 24 | Peterborough | " | " | June 21, '65 | Pro. Sergt. Aug. 20, '64. |
| Albert M. Smith | 25 | " | " | " | June 21, '65 | Pro. Sergt. Jan. 1, '65. |
| Jeremiah D. Smith | 20 | " | Musician | " | | Dis. for disability at Philadelphia, Pa., May 21, '63. |
| Charles W. Washburn | 23 | Hancock | Wagoner | " | June 21, '65 | Pro. to Brigade Band Jan. 20, '63. |
| John H. Whitney | 24 | New Ipswich | Private | " | June 21, '65 | |
| Eugene F. Appleton | 23 | " | " | " | | Dis. for disability at Portsmouth Grove, R. I., May 5, '63. |
| James E. Avery | 23 | " | " | " | | Dis. for disability at Washington, D. C., Feb. 28, '63. |
| Charles A. Ames | 23 | Peterborough | " | " | | Pro. Q. M. Sergt. Aug. 26, '63. |
| Luther Blood | 26 | New Ipswich | " | " | June 21, '65 | |
| Joseph Ash | 21 | Greenfield | " | " | June 21, '65 | Pro. Corp. May 1, '65. |
| Willis W. Bailey | 30 | Mason | " | " | June 21, '65 | Wounded sev. June 3, '64. Pro. Corp. Feb. 1, '65. |
| Charles W. Bailey | 23 | Peterborough | " | " | June 21, '65 | |
| Joel E. Boynton | 18 | Mason | " | " | | Died Feb. 25, '63, at Washington, D. C. |

| Name | | Age | Town | Rank | Enlisted | Discharged | Remarks |
|---|---|---|---|---|---|---|---|
| Augustus Boodry | | 18 | New Ipswich | Private | Sept. 19, '62 | | Wounded sev. June 1, '64. Pro. Corp. Transf. to V. R. C. Jan. 24, '65. Mustered out July 13, '65. |
| Rodney M. Brackett | | 25 | Peterborough. | " | " | | Dis. for disability July 23, '63. |
| Thomas W. Blanchard | | 18 | New Ipswich | " | " | | Pro. Corp. Wounded sev. Sept. 29, '64. Dis. by order at Manchester, N. H., May 31, '65. |
| John A. Bullard | | 38 | Peterborough | " | " | June 21, '65 | Detailed as Hospital Nurse Nov. 22, '62, and served in that capacity during his term of service. |
| William D. Carr | | 38 | Mason | " | " | " | Pro. Corp. Wounded sev. May 13, '64. Died of wounds at Point Lookout, Md., June 22, '64. |
| George A. Currier | | 21 | Bennington | " | " | " | Dis. for disability at Concord, N. H., April 28, '63. |
| Joseph A. Crosby | | 22 | Peterborough | " | " | " | Pro. Corp. Killed at Chapin's Farm, Va., Sept. 29, '64. |
| Abner P. Cragin | | 23 | New Ipswich | " | " | " | Dis. for disability at Camp Bowers, Va., May 26, '63. |
| Hiram Cram | | 18 | Bennington | " | " | June 21, '65 | Missing at Cold Harbor, Va., June 1, '64. Gained from missing. |
| William H. Clark | | 21 | Hancock | " | " | May 12, '64 | Wounded sl. Sept. 29, '64. |
| John Clark | | 34 | Greenfield | " | " | | Killed at Chapin's Farm, Va., Sept. 29, '64. |
| Wallace Clark | | 18 | Peterborough | " | " | | Wounded sl. Sept. 29, '64. Transf. to V. R. C. April 17, '65. Mustered out July 29, '65. |
| Jacob Chamberlain | | 36 | " | " | " | | Wounded Dec. 13, '62. Died at Portsmouth, Va., Nov. 4, '63. |
| Arthur C. Decatur | | 18 | Bennington | " | " | June 21, '65 | Pro. Corp. May 1, '65. Injured by the sinking of the Steamer 'Fanny,' in Hampton Roads, May 6, '64. |
| Luther M. Davis | | 21 | Sharon | " | " | " | Dis. for disability at Washington, D. C., April 8, '63. |
| Edward W. Davis | | 18 | Mason | " | " | " | Wounded Sept. 29, '64. Died of wounds at Hampton, Va., Oct. 12, '64. |
| John W. Edwards | | 18 | Temple | " | " | " | Dis. for disability near Fredericksburg, Va., Jan. 29, '63. |
| Harrison D. Evans | | 26 | Peterborough | " | " | June 26, '65 | |
| Benjamin F. Eastman | | 30 | Dublin | " | " | June 8, '65 | Pro. Corp. Wounded sev. June 15, '64. Died of wounds at Hospital, Hampton, Va., June 22, '64. |
| Charles Foot | | 18 | Bennington | " | " | | Died at Hampton, Va., June 12, '64. |
| Eugene G. Farwell | | 29 | Peterborough | " | " | | Transf. to V. R. C. Sept. 30, '63. Mustered out Sept. 18, '65. |
| Benjamin N. Fletcher | | 35 | New Ipswich | " | " | June 21, '65 | |
| Andrew Z. Fuller | | 29 | " | " | " | June 21, '65 | |
| Rufus R. Frair | | 18 | Peterborough | " | " | | Killed near Petersburg, Va., June 15, '64. |
| Henry H. Frair | | 28 | " | " | " | | Dis. for disability at Fortress Monroe, Va., June 6, '63. |
| Sherwood A. Freeman | | 23 | New Ipswich | " | " | June 21, '65 | |
| Daniel W. Goss | | 20 | Temple | " | " | | Transf. to V. R. C. Sept. 1, '63. |
| E. Q. S. Greenwood | | 42 | Peterborough | " | " | June 21, '65 | |
| Charles W. Gould | | 20 | " | " | " | | |
| Jacob Gannett | | 18 | Greenfield | " | " | | Died at Greenfield, N. H., May 13, '64. |

| Name | | Age | Residence | Rank | Enlisted | Remarks |
|---|---|---|---|---|---|---|
| Perkins W. Hopkins | | 23 | Greenfield | Private | Sept. 19, '62 | |
| Samuel Hadley | | 44 | Hancock | " | June 21, '65 | Died at Portsmouth, Va., Aug. 21, '63. |
| Henry H. Holt | | 21 | Dublin | " | June 21, '65 | Dis. May 22, '65. |
| John W. Herrick | | 40 | Greenfield | " | " | |
| John J. B. F. Hardy | | 30 | Peterborough | " | June 21, '65 | Dis. for disability at Concord, N. H., March 10, '65. |
| Ahira Z. Jones | | 19 | Greenfield | " | " | Died at Washington, D. C., Feb. 9, '63. |
| John C. Knowlton | | 25 | Windsor | " | " | Died at Newport News, Va., March 4, '63. |
| John F. Knowlton | | 19 | New Ipswich | " | " | Died at Portsmouth, Va., Aug. 31, '63. |
| Herbert Lee | | 26 | Peterborough | " | " | Wounded at Suffolk May 3, '63. Dis. for disability at Camp Lee, Va., May 29, '65. |
| Charles H. Lee | | 18 | Greenfield | " | " | |
| John Leathers | | 44 | Peterborough | " | June 21, '65 | Died at Point of Rocks, Va., March 25, '65. |
| Henry K. McClemming | | 20 | " | " | " | Detached in Ambulance Corps Nov. 13, '62. Returned to Reg. June 17, '65. |
| Jonathan McConnell | | 38 | New Ipswich | " | June 21, '65 | Died at Suffolk, Va., April 12, '63. |
| George J. Moore | | 21 | Greenfield | " | " | Dis. for disability at Camp Gilmore, Va., Nov. 30, '63. |
| George W. Matthews | | 32 | Hancock | " | " | Pro. Corp. Wounded sev. June 1, '64. Dis. by order at Manchester, N. H., May 31, '65. |
| Robert M. McGilvary | | 18 | Peterborough | " | " | Killed at Cold Harbor June 1, '64. |
| Warren C. Nicholas | | 28 | New Ipswich | " | " | Wounded sev. June 1, '64. Died of wounds at Washington, D. C., July 4, '64. |
| George H. Nutting | | 25 | " | " | " | |
| Daniel W. Osborn | | 22 | Peterborough | " | June 21, '65 | Pro. Corp. April 1, '65. |
| Cortiee S. Osborn | | 18 | " | " | " | Died of disease at Hampton, Va., Oct. 31, '64. |
| William H. Powers | | 21 | Greenfield | " | " | Pro. Corp. Pro. 1st Lieut. 31st U. S. C. T. March 1, '64. |
| Charles H. Pratt | | 24 | New Ipswich | " | Sept. 20, '62 | Transf. to V. R. C. Sept. 30, '63. Mustered out Sept. 18, '65. |
| Amos J. Proctor | | 31 | " | " | Sept. 19, '62 | Dis. for disability at Providence, R. I., May 28, '63. |
| Malachi W. Richardson | | 19 | Dublin | " | " | Pro. Corp. Wounded June 1, '64, at Cold Harbor, Va. Died of wounds June 2, '64. |
| Charles H. Russell | | 29 | Mason | " | June 21, '65 | Pro. Corp. Oct. 1, '64. |
| Collins C. Robbins | | 29 | Dublin | " | " | Dis. for disability at Philadelphia, Pa., April 2, '63. |
| George D. Reed | | 31 | Mason | " | " | Dis. for disability at Portsmouth, Va., Nov. 29, '63. |
| Andrew J. Robbins | | 26 | Peterborough | " | June 21, '65 | Pro. Corp. May 1, '65. |
| Ambrose W. Stearns | | 21 | Greenfield | " | " | Died at Richmond, Va., May 29, '65. |
| Thomas S. Stewart | | " | " | " | " | Pro. Corp. Pro. 1st Lieut. 19th U. S. C. T. Dec. 12, '63. |
| John E. Spaulding | | 20 | " | " | " | Wounded sl. June 1, '64. Pro. 2d Lieut. 116th U. S. C. T. Aug. 12, '64. |
| Samuel G. Stearns | | 23 | " | " | " | Died of disease at Portsmouth, Va., Aug. 11, '63. |

| Name | Age | Residence | Rank | Date | Remarks |
|---|---|---|---|---|---|
| Sewell P. Stearns | 18 | Greenfield | Private | Sept. 19, '62 | Killed at Cold Harbor, Va., June 1, '64. |
| John B. Stevens | 30 | Peterborough | " | " | Died at Portsmouth, Va., May 18, '63. |
| Myron R. Todd | 21 | Hancock | " | " | Died at Hampton, Va., March 21, '63. |
| Ralph Weston | 39 | Mason | " | " | Transf. to V. R. C. Sept. 30, '63. Mustered out Sept. 18, '65. |
| William H. Wilson | 21 | New Ipswich | " | " | Dis. for disability at Fredericksburg, Va., Jan. 16, '63. |
| Mark A. Wilder | 19 | Peterborough | " | " | Dis. for disability at Camp Gilmore, Va., Sept. 21, '63. |
| Seth B. Wheeler | 29 | Temple | " | " | Died of disease at Falmouth, Va., Jan. 15, '63. |
| Ira M. Whitaker | 18 | Mason | " | " | Dis. for disability at Fortress Monroe, May 26, '65. |
| Porter B. Weston | 29 | Hancock | " | " | |
| William H. H. Wilder | 22 | Peterborough | " | " | Transf. to Navy April 28, '64. |
| Samuel M. Woods | 31 | " | " | " | Wounded sev. June 1, '64. Died of wounds at White House, Va., June 6, '64. |
| Daniel P. Wilson | 26 | Sharon | " | " | |

RECRUITS.

| Name | Age | Residence | Rank | Date | Remarks |
|---|---|---|---|---|---|
| James Anderson | 30 | Unknown | " | Aug. 19, '63 | Dis. May 19, '65. |
| Dominic Burns | 26 | " | " | " | Transf. to Navy April 28, '64. |
| Charles Bauer | 22 | " | " | Aug. 20, '63 | Transf. to Navy April 28, '64. |
| George Brown | 19 | " | " | Aug. 19, '63 | Transf. to Navy April 12, '64. |
| Henry R. Brown | 24 | " | " | Aug. 20, '63 | Des. from Chester Gen. Hospital, Philadelphia, Pa., Sept. 10, '64. |
| John Bissett | | " | " | " | Dis. for disability April 6, '65, at Central Park, N. Y. |
| Fred. R. Boyle | | " | " | Aug. 19, '63 | Transf. to 2d N. H. V. June 21, '65. |
| James Burns | | " | " | " | Wounded sl. June 15, '64. Transf. to 2d N. H. V. June 21, '65. |
| Willis B. Beaver | | " | " | Sept. 2, '63 | Transf. to 2d N. H. V. June 21, '65. |
| Charles Baker | 26 | Temple | Musician | Jan. 1, '64 | Des. at Portsmouth, Va., Nov. 3, '63. |
| Charles W. Edwards | 29 | Brookline | Private | Sept. 1, '63 | Volunteer. Transf. to 2d N. H. V. June 21, '65. |
| Lewis L. Emery | 36 | Greenfield | " | Dec. 5, '63 | Wounded sev. Sept. 29, '64. Dis. May 30, '65. |
| Antoine Goddard | | | | | Volunteer. Wounded sev. Sept. 29, '64. Died of wounds at Hampton, Va., Feb. 23, '65. |
| George Jencks (alias H. B. Horne) | | Dover | " | Aug. 14, '63 | Transf. to 2d N. H. V. June 21, '65. |
| Ervin L. Lee | 18 | Greenfield | " | Dec. 5, '63 | Killed at Cold Harbor, Va., June 1, '64. |
| Charles F. Lakeman | 18 | Peterborough | " | Aug. 19, '64 | Volunteer. Died of disease at Point of Rocks, Va., March 10, '65. |
| Joseph E. Wilde | 22 | Unknown | " | Aug. 10, '63 | Transf. to Navy April 3, '64. |
| Charles Welch | 22 | " | " | " | Des. near Portsmouth, Va., Oct. 26, '63. |
| Reuben L. Wood | 24 | " | " | Aug. 11, '63 | Killed at Chapin's Farm, Va., Sept. 29, '64. |
| Edward F. White | 22 | " | " | " | Des. from Hampton Gen. Hospital Oct. 3, '64. |

## H.

| | Age. | Residence. | Rank. | Muster in. | Muster out. | Remarks. |
|---|---|---|---|---|---|---|
| Normand Smith | 32 | Stewartstown | Captain | Sept. 27, '62 | June 21, '65 | Pro. Major July 21, '64. |
| Rufus P. Staniels | 29 | Concord | " | July 15, '64 | | Resigned Feb. 19, '63. Pro. Captain Co. H July 15, '64. |
| Albe Holmes | 31 | Stratford | 1st Lieut. | Sept. 27, '62 | | Wounded sev. June 1, '64. Pro. 1st Lieut Co. D July 19, '64. |
| Rufus P. Staniels | 29 | Concord | " | Feb. 20, '63 | | |
| George W. Ferguson | 33 | Monroe | " | July 15, '64 | June 21, '65 | Resigned May 31, '63. |
| Edward Parker | | Nashua | 2d Lieut. | Sept. 27, '62 | | Wounded sev. May 16, '64. Pro. 1st Lieut Co. D July 19, '64. |
| Robert R. Thompson | 39 | Stratford | " | June 1, '63 | | Pro. Lieut., not mustered. |
| George C. Kimball | 28 | " | " | June 15, '65 | June 21, '65 | Pro. Capt. U. S. C. T. Jan. 30, '64, later to Major. |
| Frederick K. Fletcher | 22 | Colebrook | 1st Sergt. | Sept. 19, '62 | | Pro. 1st Sergt. March 1, '64. Dis. for disability Jan. 8, '65. |
| Paul C. Davis | 44 | Columbia | Sergeant | " | | Pro. 1st Sergt. Pro. Capt. U. S. C. T. Feb. 29, '64. |
| William A. Graham | 20 | Stewartstown | " | " | | Pro. Corp. May 1, '65. |
| Ira Quimby | 40 | Colebrook | " | " | June 21, '65 | Pro. 1st Sergt. Pro. 2d Lieut. June 1, '63. |
| Robert R. Thompson | 39 | Stratford | " | " | | Pro. Sergt. Jan. 23, '64. |
| Van R. Davis | 31 | Colebrook | " | " | | Pro. 1st Lieut. U. S. C. T. Dec. 28, '63. |
| Cyrus R. Blodgett | 21 | Stratford | Corporal | " | | Dis. for disability at Concord. N. H., May 18, '65. |
| John A. T. Perham | 33 | Northumberland | " | " | June 21, '65 | Wounded sev. June 3, '64. Dis. on account of wounds May 12, '65. |
| William Heath | 36 | Pittsburg | " | " | | |
| Oliver H. Stark | 35 | Northumberland | " | " | | Pro. Sergt. Wounded sev. Sept. 29, '64. Died of wounds at Philadelphia, Pa., Jan. 13, '65. |
| Sidney A. Elmer | 36 | Stewartstown | " | " | | Killed in action June 3, '64. |
| Ferrin A. Cross | 33 | Clarksville | " | " | June 21, '65 | Wounded sl. Sept. 29, '64. |
| Augustus Osgood | | Columbia | Musician | " | June 25, '65 | Transf. to Brigade Band, Jan. 20, '63. |
| Daniel G. Ripley | 37 | Stewartstown | " | " | June 21, '65 | Dis. for disability Feb. 9, '63. |
| Frank Snow | 38 | Stratford | Wagoner | " | | Dis. for disability Feb. 25, '63. |
| Roberson S. Gamsby | 35 | Columbia | Private | " | | Wounded June 1, '64. Dis. on account of wounds at New York Oct. 25, '64. |
| Elbridge G. Arlin | 20 | Colebrook | " | " | | Des. July 1, '63. |
| Franklin B. Annis | 27 | " | " | " | | |
| Erastus S. Atherton | 27 | " | " | " | June 21, '65 | Pro. Corp. Jan. 13, '63; Sergt. March 1, '64. |
| Elias Anderson | 17 | Stratford | " | " | June 21, '65 | |
| Arnold Aldrich | 37 | Stewartstown | " | " | June 21, '65 | |
| Charles W. Brown | 33 | Colebrook | " | " | | Died Sept. 21, '63. Interred at Norfolk, Va. |
| Sherman H. Barnett | 27 | Columbia | " | " | | Transf. to V. R. C. Sept. 1, '63. Mustered out July 13, '65. |
| Truman D. Barnett | 21 | " | " | " | | Transf. to V. R. C. Sept. 1, '63. |

| Name | Age | Residence | Rank | Mustered In | Mustered Out | Remarks |
|---|---|---|---|---|---|---|
| John F. Bennett | 30 | Colebrook | Private | Sept. 19, '62 | | Died of disease at Colebrook, N. H, Nov. 23, '64. |
| Albert C. Blodgett | 23 | Stratford | " | " | | Died Dec. 11, '62. |
| Leander Babb | 31 | Clarksville | " | " | | Des. from Hospital July 22, '64. |
| George Brown | 32 | Stratford | " | Sept. 30, '62 | | Dis. for disability Feb. 27, '63. |
| Jesse M. Colby | 22 | Colebrook | " | Sept. 19, '62 | | |
| James Carr | 22 | " | " | " | June 21, '65 | |
| James C. Carleton | 29 | " | " | " | June 21, '65 | |
| Benjamin R. Corbett | 38 | Clarksville | " | " | | Dis. for disability Nov. 10, '62. |
| William Chappell | 24 | Colebrook | " | " | | Died June 29, '63. |
| Caleb T. Cleveland | 20 | Colebrook | " | " | | Des. on furlough Nov. 4, '63. |
| Alma M. Cross | 26 | Stewartstown | " | " | June 21, '65 | Dis. for disability Feb. 23, '63. |
| Chester W. Cilley | 35 | Pittsburg | " | " | June 21, '65 | Wounded Dec. 13, '62. Dis. for disability March 12, '63. |
| Addison Chase | 18 | Stewartstown | " | Sept. 30, '62 | | Pro. Corp. May 1, '65. |
| David Clement | 18 | Colebrook | " | Sept. 19, '62 | | Dis. for disability March 8, '63. |
| Patrick Doorley | 43 | Stewartstown | " | " | June 21, '65 | |
| Caleb S. Dalton | 18 | Colebrook | " | " | June 21, '65 | |
| Joseph B. Eastman | 18 | " | " | " | | Wounded June 1, '64. Pro. Corp; Sergt. Jan 14, '65. |
| Carlos R. Fletcher | 25 | Northumberland | " | " | | Des. at Fort Schuyler, N. Y., July 4, '63. |
| Charles Forbes | 21 | Stratford | " | " | | Killed at Fort Harrison, Va., Sept. 29, '64. |
| Carleton C. Fuller | 26 | Boston | " | Nov. 27, '62 | June 21, '65 | Pro. Corp. March 1, '64; Sergt. May 1, '65. |
| Charles C. Favor | 25 | Colebrook | " | Sept. 19, '62 | | Wounded Dec. 13, '62. Dis. for disability Aug. 5, '64. |
| Henry B. Gilkey | 25 | " | " | " | | Pro. Sergt. Major March 7, '63. |
| Abiel B. Glines | 28 | Stewartstown | " | " | June 21, '65 | Pro. Corp. Wounded June 1, '64. Dis. on account of wounds April 11, '65. |
| Charles E. Graham | 18 | " | " | " | | Transf. to Brigade Band Jan. 20, '63. Commissioned in U. S. C. T. June 25, '64. |
| Emery Hibbard | 24 | Colebrook | " | " | June 21, '65 | Dis. for disability May 19, '65. |
| Orrin Hibbard | 26 | " | " | " | | Des. from Hospital Nov. 1, '64. |
| Charles J. Hilliard | 22 | " | " | " | | Dis. for disability Jan. 27, '63. |
| Albert Harris | 23 | Stratford | " | " | June 21, '65 | Wounded sl. June 15, '64. Rec'd two other wounds not of this record. |
| David Holbrook | 20 | " | " | " | | |
| Oliver B. Huggins | 22 | Pittsburg | " | " | | Transf. to V. R. C. Sept. 30, '63. Mustered out Sept. 19, '65. |
| Edwin Holbrook | 18 | Columbia | " | " | | Dis. on account of wounds at Concord, N. H., Oct. 10, '64. |
| Francis G. Haines | 30 | Pittsburg | " | " | | Died of disease at Fortress Monroe Nov. 15, '64. |
| Nathan Heath | 19 | " | " | " | | Transf. to V. R. C. July 1, '63. |
| Almanyo Heath | 23 | Clarksville | " | " | | Des. Sept. 30, '62. |

| Name | Town | Age | Rank | Enlisted | Mustered out | Remarks |
|---|---|---|---|---|---|---|
| Augustus A. Heath | Clarksville | 28 | Private | Sept. 19, '62 | | Des. Sept. 30, '62. |
| Nelson Haines | Stewartstown | 24 | " | " | | Dis. Jan. 8, '64. |
| John W. Heath | Pittsburg | 32 | " | " | | Pro. Sergt. Transf. to V. R. C. Sept. 1, '63. Mustered out July 13, '65. |
| John A. Hodge | Stewartstown | 21 | " | " | June 21, '65 | Pro. Corp. Jan. 1, '64. |
| Andrew Hanon | Colebrook | 25 | " | " | June 21, '65 | |
| William R. Jordan | Columbia | 27 | " | " | | Dis. for disability Dec. 1, '63. |
| Abel Jordan, Jr. | " | 21 | " | " | | Wounded Dec. 13, '62. Des. from Hospital July 12, '63. |
| George C. Kimball | Stratford | 28 | " | " | | Wounded sev. June 15, '64. Pro. Corp. Jan. 13, '63; Sergt. July 1, '63; 1st Sergt. Jan. 14, '65; 2d Lieut. June 15, '65. |
| James Knights | Stewartstown | 30 | " | " | | Killed at Fredericksburg, Va., Dec. 13, '62. |
| John R. Little | Colebrook | 21 | " | " | | Dis. for disability Sept. 29, '63. |
| Joseph D. Little | " | 29 | " | " | | |
| Philip Ledoo | Stratford | 35 | " | " | June 21, '65 | Des. Sept. 30, '62. |
| William B. Luey | Columbia | 30 | " | " | | Wounded June 1, '64. Transf. to V. R. C. Sept. 16, '64. Mustered out June 28, '65. |
| James Legro 2d | Colebrook | 36 | " | " | | Dis. May 30, '65. |
| William McKinnon | " | 22 | " | " | June 21, '65 | Wounded Dec. 13, '62. Dis. for disability Feb. 16, '63. |
| Ephraim H. Mahurin | Columbia | 42 | " | " | | Dis. for disability Dec. 9, '62. |
| Milo Mahurin | " | 44 | " | " | | Dis. for disability May 8, '63. |
| Jeremiah Morrow | Stratford | 19 | " | " | June 21, '65 | Wounded sev. May 14, '64. |
| William Merrill | " | 26 | " | " | | Dis. for disability Nov. 10, '62. |
| Edwin Patterson | Colebrook | 28 | " | " | | Des. from Hospital Aug. 27, '64. |
| Daniel W. Patrick | " | 21 | " | " | June 21, '65 | |
| George R. Pomroy | Errol | 19 | " | " | June 21, '65 | Pro. Corp. May 1, '65. |
| William Rowe | Colebrook | 32 | " | " | June 23, '65 | |
| Daniel Renton | Stewartstown | 27 | " | " | | Wounded sl. June 3, '64. |
| Selden J. Stacey | Colebrook | 24 | " | " | | Died of disease Jan. 16, '63. |
| James Spreadby | Stratford | 21 | " | " | June 21, '65 | |
| David Spreadby | Northumberland | 21 | " | " | June 21, '65 | Dis. for disability Jan. 13, '63. |
| Charles C. Stoddard | Columbia | 27 | " | " | | Pro. Corp. Wounded sev. June 1, '64. Died of wounds June 30, '64. |
| Fred. Shorey | " | 18 | " | " | | |
| Thomas Smith | Pittsburg | 21 | " | " | June 21, '65 | |
| Gardner W. Smith | Stewartstown | 26 | " | " | June 21, '65 | |
| Henry S. Sleeper | " | 18 | " | " | | Died Nov. 15, '62. |
| Alvah Warren | Northumberland | 23 | " | " | | Killed at Fredericksburg, Va., Dec. 13, '62. |

| Name | | Residence | | Date | Remarks |
|---|---|---|---|---|---|
| Jeduthan F. Warren | 25 | Northumberland | Private | Sept. 19, '62 | Dis. for disability Feb. 5, '63. |
| Henry M. Woodbury | 26 | Pittsburg | " | " | Killed at Fredericksburg, Va., Dec. 13, '62. |
| John C. Walker | 32 | Stratford | " | " | Pro. Corp. Killed at Drury's Bluff, Va., May 16, '64. |
| James W. Weeks | 34 | Columbia | " | " | Dis. for disability March 17, '63. |
| Hiram C. Young | 27 | Stewartstown | " | " | Pro. Corp. June 9, '64. |

RECRUITS.

| | | | | | |
|---|---|---|---|---|---|
| George B. Abbott | 25 | Stewartstown | " | Jan. 4, '64 | Volunteer. Wounded sev. June 1, '64. Des. while on furlough Dec. —, '64. |
| Arthur R. Aldrich | 18 | Clarksville | " | " | Volunteer. Transf. to 2d N. H. V. June 21, '65. |
| Albion C. Aldrich | 28 | Columbia | " | Jan. 5, '64 | Volunteer. Killed at Cold Harbor, Va., June 3, '64. |
| George H. Bannister | 20 | Stewartstown | " | Jan. 4, '64 | Killed in action Oct. 27, '64. |
| James H. Bacon | | Clarksville | " | " | Volunteer. Des. while on furlough from Hospital. |
| Edward Bumpkin | | Unknown | " | Sept. 1, '63 | Transf. to 2d N. H. V. June 21, '65. |
| Charles G. Crawford | 20 | Colebrook | " | Jan. 1, '64 | Des. at Fort Harrison, Va., Oct. 26, '64. |
| William H. Clark | 42 | Columbia | " | Jan. 4, '64 | Volunteer. Wounded June 1, '64. Mustered out May 12, '65. |
| John Clark | 24 | Unknown | " | Aug. 20, '63 | Killed at Cold Harbor, Va., June 1, '64. |
| George Cook | 20 | " | " | Sept. 2, '63 | Des. April 26, '64. |
| Charles Carle | 23 | " | " | " | Des. at Portsmouth, Va., April 19, '64. |
| Cornelius Covanney | 40 | " | " | " | Dis. for disability March 3, '65. |
| James Durgin | | " | " | Aug. 20, '63 | Wounded sl. Sept. 2?, '64. Transf. to 2d N. H. V. June 21, '65. |
| John F. Delaney | 21 | " | " | Aug. 19, '63 | Killed at Cold Harbor, Va., June 1, '64. |
| Patrick Driskill | 22 | " | " | " | Des. at Portsmouth, Va., Dec. 6, '63. |
| Daniel Fletcher | | Stewartstown | " | Jan. 4, '64 | Wounded June 1, '64. Transf. to V. R. C. April 17, '65. Mustered out June 7, '65. |
| William Ferry | 27 | Unknown | " | Sept. 1, '63 | Des. at Portsmouth, Va., Nov. 18, '63. |
| Bernard Gannon | 39 | " | " | " | Dis. for disability April 7, '64. |
| W. H Granville | 27 | " | " | Aug. 19, '63 | Des. at Portsmouth, Va., April 19, '64. |
| Charles F. Ham | 22 | " | " | " | Wounded sev. June 15, '64. Died of wounds near Petersburg, Va., June 17, '64. |
| George Hess | 21 | " | " | Sept. 7, '63 | Des. while on furlough from Hospital. |
| Peter Holland | 22 | " | " | Sept. 2, '63 | Des. April 30, '64. |
| Charles Hill | 21 | " | " | Aug. 19, '63 | Transf. to Navy April 30, '64. |
| James M. Jordan | 19 | Colebrook | " | Jan. 4, '64 | Wounded sl. June 15, '64. Transf. to V. R. C. March 8, '65. |
| Benjamin Knights | 38 | Stewartstown | " | " | Volunteer. Wounded sev. June 15, '64. Transf. to V. R. C. March 17, '65. |
| Lemuel Lafo | 24 | Pittsburg | " | | Volunteer. Des. in 1864 while on furlough from Hospital. |

| Name | Age | Residence | Rank | Date | Remarks |
|---|---|---|---|---|---|
| Walter Lawson | 43 | Unknown | Private | Sept. 2, '63 | Dis. for disability at New York Sept. 29, '64. |
| Daniel McAllister | 32 | Columbia | " | Jan. 4, '64 | Volunteer. Died of disease at Point of Rocks, Va., Sept. 18, '64. |
| Dana R. Moody | 27 | Clarksville | " | Sept. 2, '63 | Volunteer. Des. while on furlough from Hospital Oct. 30, '64. |
| James Moran | 28 | Unknown | " | Aug. 20, '63 | Des. Feb. 8, '64. |
| John Mason | 25 | " | " | Sept. 2, '63 | Des. from Provost Guard May 7, '64. |
| John Merritt | 20 | " | " | Sept. 1, '63 | Des. at Fort Harrison, Va., Oct. 26, '64. |
| William Morris | 35 | " | " | Sept. 2, '63 | Killed at Cold Harbor, Va., June 1, '64. |
| John McMann | 45 | " | " | Aug. 19, '63 | Dis. for disability Dec. 27, '64. |
| Henry Nuttell | 24 | " | " | Jan. 4, '64 | Transf. to Navy April 30, '64. |
| John Paul | 31 | Pittsburg | " | " | Volunteer. Wounded sl. Sept. 29, '64. Dis. for disability Jan. 27, '65. |
| Charles Perry | 37 | " | " | " | Volunteer. Wounded sev. June 15, '64. Dis. for disability March 2, '65. |
| George A. Rowell | | Colebrook | " | Jan. 2, '64 | Volunteer. Transf. to 2d N. H. V. June 21, '65. |
| David Rowell | | Pittsburg | " | Jan. 4, '64 | Volunteer. Pro. Corp. Wounded sev. June 15, '64. Transf. to 2d N. H. V. June 21, '65. |
| William H. Gault | | Stewartstown | Musician | " | Transf. to 2d N. H. V. June 21, '65. |
| Daniel Johnson | | Columbia | Private | Dec. 30, '63 | Transf. to 2d N. H. V. June 21, '65. |
| Henry A. Keach | | Stewartstown | " | Jan. 4, '64 | Volunteer. Dis. by order June 3, '65. |
| Robert Knight | | Unknown | " | " | Volunteer. Transf. to 2d N. H. V. June 21, '65. |
| Thomas Keenan | | Colebrook | " | Sept. 2, '63 | Transf. to 2d N. H. V. June 21, '65. |
| Lewis Tashro | | Pittsburg | " | Jan. 4, '64 | Volunteer. Transf. to 2d N. H. V. June 21, '65. |
| Amasa F. Huggins | | | " | March 31, '65 | Volunteered for one year. Transf. to 2d N. H. V. June 21, '65. |

I.

| Name | Age | Residence | Rank | Muster in. | Muster out. | Remarks. |
|---|---|---|---|---|---|---|
| Luther M. Wright | 35 | Nashua | Captain | Sept. 27, '62 | | Resigned Dec. 28, '62, at Falmouth, Va. |
| Enoch W. Goss | | Portsmouth | " | Dec. 30, '62 | | Wounded June 1, '64. Killed at Fair Oaks Oct. 27, '64. |
| Charles B. Gafney | 44 | Ossipee | " | May 30, '65 | June 21, '65 | Pro. Capt., not mustered. |
| Alfred S. Smith | 29 | Pelham | 1st Lieut. | Sept. 27, '62 | | Resigned Nov. 14, '62, at Camp Casey, Va. |
| Major A. Shaw | | Nashua | " | Nov. 15, '62 | | Wounded sev. Dec 13, '62. Resigned April 29, '63, at Suffolk, Va. |
| Hubbard W. Hall | 30 | Strafford | " | May 1, '63 | | Wounded sev. Sept. 29, '64. Pro. Captain Co. E March 1, '65. |
| Lucius C. Oliver | 22 | New Ipswich | " | March 9, '65 | June 21, '65 | Pro. 1st Lieut. Co. I Nov. 15, '62. |
| Major A. Shaw | 29 | Nashua | 2d Lieut. | Sept. 27, '62 | | Pro. 1st Lieut. Co. E July 15, '64. |
| Oliver M. Sawyer | 23 | " | " | Nov. 15, 62 | | Wounded sl. Sept. 29, '64. |
| Henry B. Wheeler | 28 | Peterborough | " | Aug. 4, '64 | | Pro. 2d Lieut. Nov. 15, '62. |
| Oliver M. Sawyer | 23 | Nashua | 1st Sergt. | Sept. 20, '62 | | Dis. for disability at Washington, D. C., Feb. 25, '63. |
| James M. Greeley | 41 | Hudson | Sergeant | " | | Pro. 1st Sergt. April 1, '63. |
| John B. Burton | 22 | Nashua | " | " | June 21, '65 | |
| William T. Burton | 22 | " | " | " | June 21, '65 | |
| Henry G. Cameron | 28 | Hollis | " | " | | Dis. for disability at Falmouth, Va., Jan. 14, '63. |
| Alfred Willoughby | 39 | Nashua | Corporal | " | | Dis. by order at Washington, D. C. Jan. 22, '63. |
| Willis G. Burnham | 19 | Pelham | " | " | June 21, '65 | Pro. Sergt. Feb. 20, '63; 1st Sergt. Nov. 14, '64. |
| Nathan M. Blodgett | 24 | Hudson | " | " | | Dis. by order at Portsmouth, Va., Nov. 30, '63. |
| William R. Duncklee | 30 | New Boston | " | " | June 21, '65 | Wounded Dec. 13, '62. |
| Charles Wheeler | 22 | Pelham | " | " | | Dis. for disability at Fortress Monroe, Va., May 2, '63. |
| J. P. Marden | 26 | Nashua | " | " | | Des. from General Hospital, Philadelphia, Pa., Jan. 13, '63. |
| Charles W. Hobbs | 18 | Pelham | " | " | July 5, '65 | |
| Frank E. Butler | 32 | " | Musician | " | June 21, '65 | Pro. Sergt. Nov. 14, '64. |
| Reuben Cummings | 42 | Hudson | " | " | June 21, '65 | |
| Alden M. Jones | | " | Wagoner | " | June 21, '65 | |
| John L. Bennett | 32 | Nashua | Private | " | | Dis. for disability at Concord, N. H., Feb. 18, '65. |
| John H. Arbuckle | 19 | Bedford | " | " | June 21, '65 | |
| Charles A. Austin | 44 | Mason | " | " | | Dis. for disability at Philadelphia, Pa., April 27, '63. |
| George Batchelder | 20 | Hudson | " | " | | Captured Oct. 27, '64. Died of disease at Salisbury, N. C., Feb. 12, '65. |
| George F. Boyson | 33 | Nashua | " | " | June 21, '65 | |
| George W. Badger | 30 | " | " | " | | Dis. for disability at Philadelphia, Pa., April 19, '63. |
| George Bartlett | 40 | " | " | " | | Dis. at Balfour U. S. Gen. Hospital Portsmouth, Va. |
| G. H. Buswell | 34 | " | " | " | June 7, '65 | Dis. at Camp Lee, Va., May 15, '65. |

| Name | Age | Residence | Rank | Date of enlistment | Date of discharge | Remarks |
|---|---|---|---|---|---|---|
| Henry Butler | 35 | Pelham | Private | Sept. 20, '62 | June 21, '65 | Wounded Dec. 13, '62. Pro. Corp. April 1, '63. |
| Warren J. Bright | 21 | " | " | " | June 21, '65 | Pro. Corp. Feb. 20, '63; Sergt. Dec. 1, '63. |
| Benjamin F. Bean | 25 | " | " | " | | Pro. Corp. Feb. 20, '63. Wounded sl. Feb. 29, '64. Dis. by order Aug. 24, '65. |
| Edwin S. Burnham | 21 | " | " | " | June 21, '65 | Pro. Corp. June 7, '64. |
| John G. Bradford | 32 | Windham | " | " | June 21, '65 | Pro. Corp. April 1, '63; Sergt. June 7, '64. |
| Daniel W. Butterfield | 33 | Nashua | " | " | | Pro. Hospital Steward Nov. 28, '64. |
| Bradford Campbell | 18 | Hudson | " | " | June 21, '65 | |
| Henry F. Colburn | 26 | " | " | " | | Dis. for disability at Concord, N. H., July 20, '63. |
| Andrew Conant | 39 | Nashua | " | " | | Dis. for disability Sept. 30, '63. |
| Gilman F. Chase | 27 | Hudson | " | " | | Transf. to Co. C Sept. 25, '62. |
| Benjamin Chase | 34 | Pelham | " | " | | Transf. to V. R. C. Sept. 30, '63. |
| Kimball J. Chaplain | 25 | Windham | " | " | June 21, '65 | Wounded Dec. 13, '62. Transf. to V. R. C. May 12, '64. |
| Henry W. Chellis | 19 | New Ipswich | " | " | June 21, '65 | Pro. Corp. May 24, '64. |
| Edward J. Carr | 30 | Nashua | " | " | | |
| Alonzo L. Decatur | 22 | " | " | " | June 21, '65 | Dis. at Brattleboro, Vt., Dec. 8, '64. |
| Lucien R. Dunham | 24 | Pelham | " | " | | Pro. Corp. April 1, '63. |
| Isaac H. Daniels | 27 | Greenfield | " | " | | Died at Camp Casey, Va., Nov. 22, '62. |
| J. S. Draper | 18 | Pelham | " | " | | Wounded sl. June 15, '64. Dis. by order June 1, '65. |
| Frank M. Ellenwood | | | | | | Wounded May 3, '63. Dis. for disability at Portsmouth Grove, R. I., May 20, '64. |
| E. S. Elliott | 37 | Mason | " | " | | Dis. May 27, '65. |
| Joseph Elliott | 24 | " | " | " | June 21, '65 | Dis. for disability at Concord, N. H., Jan. 19, '65. |
| M. V. B. Elliott | 21 | " | " | " | June 21, '65 | |
| Erastus E. Elliott | 18 | " | " | Sept. 23, '62 | June 21, '65 | |
| Alonzo Ellenwood | 19 | " | " | Sept. 20, " | | |
| Daniel Flanders | 36 | Nashua | " | " | June 21, '65 | Dis. for disability Feb. 16, '63. |
| Rufus M. Fletcher | 25 | Hudson | " | " | June 21, '65 | |
| Myron B. Fields | 18 | Nashua | " | " | June 18, '65 | |
| James G. Fields | 40 | " | " | " | June 21, '65 | |
| Daniel B. Fox | 26 | Pelham | " | " | June 17, '65 | |
| Lorenzo Fuller | 18 | Hudson | " | " | June 21, '65 | |
| Arthur C. Gordon | 27 | Nashua | " | Sept. 23, '62 | | Pro. Corp. Nov., '63. |
| Ezekiel C. Gage | 18 | Pelham | " | Sept. 4, '62 | | Dis. for disability at Bedloe's Island, N. Y., Dec. 19, '62. |
| Lucius Gilmore | 18 | Portsmouth | " | " | | Transf. to Co. G 10th N. H. V. Oct. 31, '62. Mustered out May 25, '65. |
| Richard Henson, Jr. | 34 | Merrimack | " | Sept. 20, '62 | | Des. while on March Dec. 3, '62. |
| William R. Hanaford | 34 | Nashua | " | " | | Des. while on March Dec. 3, '62. |

677

| Name | Residence | Age | Rank | Mustered In | Mustered Out | Remarks |
|---|---|---|---|---|---|---|
| Frederick F. Hickcox | Hudson | 38 | Private | Sept. 20, '62 | May 12, '65 | Wounded sl. June 15, '64; wounded sev. Sept. 29, '64. |
| Albert F. Hall | Amherst | 18 | " | " | June 21, '65 | Pro. Sergt. Jan. 20, '63. |
| John W. Hall | Windham | 30 | " | " | June 21, '65 | |
| Seth N. Huntley | " | 28 | " | " | June 21, '65 | |
| Napoleon E. Jones | Hudson | 18 | " | " | | Dis. May 19, '65. |
| George C. Jackman | Pelham | 18 | " | " | | Wounded sl. May 16, '64. Pro. Corp. April 1, '63; Sergt. June 7, '64. |
| William B. Lewis | Hudson | 25 | " | " | June 21, '65 | Dis. Sept. 25, '62. |
| Francis M. Lewis | Unknown | 35 | " | " | | Wounded sl. May 14, '64. Des. near Petersburg July 1, '64. |
| Joseph F. Lampson | Pelham | 22 | " | Sept. 23, '62 | | Dis. for disability at Washington, D. C., May 25, '63. |
| Sydney J. Lyon | " | 18 | " | " | | Pro. Corp. Feb. 20, '63; Sergt. April 1, '63; 1st Sergt. June 7, '64. Dis. for disability at Point of Rocks, Va., Nov. 13, '64. |
| Charles McGaffey | Nashua | 30 | " | Sept. 20, '62 | | |
| Jacob Marshall | " | 19 | " | " | | Died of disease at Portsmouth, Va., Aug. 21, '63. |
| Otis R. Marsh | Hudson | 30 | " | " | | Wounded sev. Oct. 27, '64. Dis. by order May 27, '65. |
| Michael Murray | Pelham | 35 | " | " | | Dis. by order at Newport News, Va., March 12, '63. |
| Erastus Newton | Nashua | 21 | " | " | June 21, '65 | |
| James Ordway | Bow | 18 | " | " | | Dis. for disability at Washington, D. C., March 26, '63. |
| L. C. Parker | Nashua | 23 | " | " | | Wounded Dec. 13, '62. Transf. to V. R. C. Oct. 20, '63. Mustered out July 3, '65. |
| Daniel Parker | Mason | 18 | " | " | June 21, '65 | |
| Albert M. Putnam | Antrim | 23 | " | " | June 12, '65 | |
| James A. Reed | Nashua | 21 | " | " | | Pro. Corp. Nov. '63. Transf. to V. R. C. Mustered out Aug. 7, '65. |
| David G. Robbins | Hollis | 26 | " | " | | Pro. Corp. Wounded, and died of wounds Sept. 30, '64. |
| Daniel T. Roby | " | 43 | " | " | | Wounded sl. Sept. 30, '64. |
| A. H. Randall | Londonderry | 19 | " | " | June 21, '65 | Dis. for disability at Washington, D. C. March 14, '63. |
| Alexander Sharkey | Nashua | 29 | " | " | | Des. while on furlough from Hospital, Sept. 25, '62. |
| Andrew J. Smith | Hudson | 32 | " | " | | Killed at Petersburg, Va., June 26, '64. |
| James G. Smith | Pelham | 20 | " | " | | Died of disease at Portsmouth, Va., Oct. 3, '63. |
| John B. Smith | Mason | 18 | " | " | | Died of disease at Washington, D. C., March 14, '63. |
| Charles P. Titcomb | Pelham | 26 | " | " | June 21, '65 | Wounded sl. June 15, '64. Pro. Corp. Nov. 14, '64. |
| Wm. Henry Titcomb | " | 24 | " | " | | Dis. for disability at Washington, D. C., Nov. 20, '62. |
| Oscar W. Towns | Nashua | 26 | " | " | June 21, '65 | |
| Michael Tulley | Pelham | 23 | " | Sept. 23, '62 | June 21, '65 | |
| Frank E. Titcomb | " | 18 | " | " | | Wounded Dec. 13, '62. |
| George W. Wilson | Nashua | 22 | " | Sept. 20, '62 | June 21, '65 | Dis. by order at Washington, D. C., Jan. 18, '63. |

| Name | Age | Residence | Rank | Date | Status | Remarks |
|---|---|---|---|---|---|---|
| John M. Woods | 22 | Pelham | Private | | | Wounded Dec. 13, '62. |
| Gilman H. Woodbury | 18 | " | " | June 21, '65 | | |
| John F. Wetherbee | 34 | Brookline | " | June 21, '65 | | Dis. for disability at Philadelphia, Pa., Feb. 26, '63. |
| Mark H. Webster | 18 | Pelham | " | June 8, '65 | | Dis. at Point Lookout, Md. |
| A. J. Willard | 26 | Nashua | " | Sept. 23, '62 | | |

RECRUITS.

| Name | Age | Residence | Rank | Date | Status | Remarks |
|---|---|---|---|---|---|---|
| Charles Anderson | 23 | Rochester | " | Dec. 28, '63 | Volunteer. | Transf. to Navy March 13, '64. |
| Charles Brown | | Henniker | " | Aug. 18, '64 | Volunteer. | Transf. to 2d N. H. V. June 21, '65. |
| Fred. R. Boyle | | Unknown | " | Aug. 20, '63 | | Wounded sl. Sept. 29, '64. Dis. for disability at |
| Edwin R. Cilley | | Colebrook | " | Jan. 1, '64 | | Concord, N. H., June 5, '65. |
| Timothy Covil | 19 | " | " | " | Volunteer. | Des. while on furlough June 19, '64. |
| David S. Chandler | | " | " | " | Volunteer. | Transf. to 2d N. H. V. June 21, '65. |
| Carlton Fay | | " | " | " | Volunteer. | Transf. to 2d N. H. V. June 21, '65. |
| Nathaniel W. Folsom | | Nashua | Musician | Dec. 31, '63 | Volunteer. | Transf. to 2d N. H. V. June 21, '65. |
| Henry Gleason | | Colebrook | Private | Jan. 2, '64 | Volunteer. | Dis. May 6, '65. |
| Charles D. Garnsby | 38 | Stratford | " | Jan. 4, '64 | Volunteer. | Transf. to 2d N. H. V. June 21, '65. |
| Loren D. Hemphill | | Henniker | Musician | Jan. 1, '64. | Volunteer. | Wounded sev. Sept. 29, '64. Died of wounds at Hampton, Va., Oct. 15, '64. |
| Gustavus E. Hardy | 30 | Colebrook | Private | | Volunteer. | Wounded sl. Sept. 29, '64. Transf. to 2d N. H. V. June 21, '65. |
| Levi Hicks | | " | " | | Volunteer. | Dis. May 12, '65. |
| John Hogue | 40 | Stewartstown | " | Jan. 25, '64 | Volunteer. | Wounded June 4, '64. Missing near Petersburg, Va., June 15, '64. Gained from missing. Transf. to 2d N. H. V. June 21, '65. |
| Guy W. Johnson | | Stratford | " | Jan. 4, '64 | Volunteer. | Transf. to 2d N. H. V. June 21, '65. |
| John J. Johnson | | Londonderry | " | " | Volunteer. | Des. Apprehended, Mustered out June 17, '65, with loss of all pay and allowances from Jan. 17, '65. |
| John Little | | " | " | Jan. 2, '64 | | Wounded sl. Sept. 30, '64. Transf. to V. R. C. Jan. 2, '65. |
| Terrence O'Brien | | Unknown | " | Aug. 20, '63 | | Dis. for disability Feb., '65. |
| Augustus H. Penfold | 21 | " | " | Aug. 19, '63 | | Des. near Portsmouth, Va., Oct. 21, '63. |
| Evan Pollard | 22 | " | " | " | | Transf. to Navy April 3, '64. |
| Charles W. Randall | | Colebrook | " | Jan. 1, '64. | Volunteer. | Wounded sev. Sept. 30, '64. Transf. to 2d N. H. V. June 21, '65. |

| Name | Age | Residence | Rank | Date | Remarks |
|---|---|---|---|---|---|
| James Reid | 29 | Unknown | Private | Aug. 20, '63 | Wounded sev. Sept. 30, '64. Transf. to 2d N. H. V. June 21, '65. |
| Thomas Reis | " | " | " | " | Transf. to Navy April 3, '64. |
| Simon S. P. Smith | " | " | " | Aug. 19, '63 | Volunteer. Transf. to 2d N. H. V. June 21, '65. |
| Ira Sweatt | " | Colebrook | " | Jan. 1, '64 | Volunteer. Missing near Petersburg, Va., June 15, '64. Gained from missing. Transf. to 2d N. H. V. June 21, '65. |
| R. B. Shattuck | 20 | Unknown | " | Aug. 20, '63 | Dis. for disability July 28, '64. |
| Thomas Smith | 27 | " | " | Aug. 19, '63 | Transf. to 2d N. H. V. June 21, '65. |
| John Smith | 21 | " | " | Aug. 20, '63 | Transf. to Navy May 4, '64. |
| John Sohns | " | " | " | Aug. 19, '63 | Des. while on furlough Oct. 22, '64. |
| Thomas Shannon | 23 | " | " | " | Transf. to Navy April 28, '64. |
| John Schneider | 25 | " | " | Sept. 2, '63 | Des. while on furlough from Hospital March 23, '65. |
| James Scott | 28 | " | " | " | Des. while on furlough from Hospital Nov. 8, '64. |
| Henry G. Sangar | 34 | " | " | Aug. 20, '63 | Des. near Portsmouth, Va., Oct. 7, '63. |
| John W. Snare | 28 | " | " | Aug. 19, '63 | Transf. to Navy March 30, '64. |
| Charles Scott | 36 | Colebrook | " | Jan. 1, '64 | Transf. to Navy March 30, '64. |
| John Titus | | " | " | | Volunteer. Des. in New Hampshire July 18, '64. Reported under the President's Proclamation of March 11, '65. Mustered out May 15, '65. |
| William H. Tibbitts | | " | " | | Volunteer. Transf. to 2d N. H. V. June 21, '65. |

## K.

| Name | Age | Residence | Rank | Muster in | Muster out | Remarks |
|---|---|---|---|---|---|---|
| Matthew T. Betton | 25 | Portsmouth | Captain | Sept. 27, '62 | June 21, '65 | Pro. Captain Co. I Dec. 30, '62. |
| Enoch W. Goss | 26 | " | 1st Lieut. | Sept. 27, '62 | | Resigned June 9, '63, at Portsmouth, Va. |
| Nathaniel J. Coffin | 35 | " | " " | Dec. 30, '62 | | |
| Henry H. Murray | 21 | New Market | " " | June 10, '63 | | Taken prisoner Oct. 27, '64, at Fair Oaks, Va. Paroled Feb. 15, '65. |
| Nathaniel J. Coffin | 35 | Portsmouth | 2d Lieut. | Sept. 27, '62 | | Pro. 1st Lieut. Co. K Dec. 30, '62. |
| William J. Ladd | 18 | " | " | Dec. 30, '62 | | Pro. 1st Lieut. Co. B May 30, '64. |
| George Burns | 21 | Concord | " | June 15, '65 | June 21, '65 | Pro. Lieut. not mustered. Mustered out as Com. Sergt. |
| Edwin A. Tilton | 28 | Portsmouth | 1st Sergt. | Sept. 20, '62 | | Dis. by order Sept. 1, '63, to accept app. as 2d Lieut. in Invalid Corps. |
| Thomas Fairservice | 32 | " | Sergeant | " | June 21, '65 | Transf. to V. R. C. Sept. 17, '63. Mustered out July 6, '65. |
| Robert W. Varrell | 37 | " | " | " | | Dis. by order at Manchester, N. H., June 12, '65. |
| James R. Morrison | 22 | Rye | " | " | | Dis. for disability at Fredericksburg, Va., Feb. 6, '63. |
| Daniel J. Spinney | 23 | Portsmouth | " | " | | Pro. Sergt. Dis. by order at Portsmouth, Va., March 1, '64. |
| Joseph N. Danielson | 23 | " | Corporal | " | | Dis. for disability at Philadelphia, Pa., Jan. 12, '63. |
| Benjamin F. Winn | 30 | " | " | " | June 21, '65 | Pro. Sergt. May 17, '63; 1st Sergt. Nov. 1, '64; 1st Lieut. May 30, '65, not mustered. |
| Alfred P. Dearborn | 26 | Newington | " | " | | Pro. Sergt. Transf. to V. R. C. Aug. 10, '64. Mustered out July 10, '65. |
| Samuel Taylor | 35 | Portsmouth | " | " | | Dis. for disability at Portsmouth, Va., Sept. 19, '63. |
| Robert B. Welch | 36 | " | " | " | | Pro. Sergt. Transf. to Navy April 3, '64. |
| Abel Jackson | 20 | " | " | " | June 6, '65 | Transf. to Brigade Band Jan. 20, '63. |
| John L. Randall | 39 | " | " | " | | Pro. 1st. Sergt. Transf. to V. R. C. March 15, '64. Mustered out July 26, '65. |
| Wm. M. Critchley, Jr. | 26 | " | Musician | " | June 21, '65 | Transf. to Brigade Band Jan. 21, '63. |
| Martin Moore | 18 | " | " | " | June 21, '65 | Transf. to V. R. C. Nov. 15, '63. Re-transf. to Reg. June 20, '64. |
| Storer E. Stiles | 25 | " | Wagoner | " | | Transf. to V. R. C. Sept. 1, '63. Mustered out Sept. 19, '65. |
| Samuel P. Abbott | 25 | " | Private | " | | Dis. for disability at Washington, D. C., Feb. 23, '63. |
| Henry Bean | 32 | " | " | " | June 21, '65 | |
| Joseph B. Brown | 30 | " | " | " | | Des. at Portsmouth, N. H., Sept. 29, '62. |
| John W. Brown | 28 | " | " | " | | Dis. for disability at Bermuda Hundred, Va., May 18, '64. |
| Charles Bragdon | 44 | " | " | " | | Transf. to V. R. C. Nov. 23, '64. |

| Name | Age | Residence | Rank | Mustered in | Mustered out | Remarks |
|---|---|---|---|---|---|---|
| Ferdinand Barr | 23 | Portsmouth | Private | Sept. 20, '62 | June 21, '65 | Dis. May 28, '65. |
| George W. Brown | 32 | Unknown | " | " | " | Dis. for disability at Portsmouth, Va., Sept. 23, '63. |
| D. Webster Barnabee | 24 | Portsmouth | " | " | " | Pro. Corp. June 1, '65. |
| Joseph Berry | 18 | Rye | " | " | June 21, '65 | Des. at Portsmouth, N. H., Nov. 20, '64. Apprehended. |
| Lyman Clark | 23 | Portsmouth | " | " | June 21, '65 | Captured Oct. 27, '64. Exchanged March 1, '65. |
| Joseph H. Cochey | 19 | " | " | " | June 3, '65 | Transf. to Brigade Band Jan. 21, '63. |
| Thomas Critchley | 18 | " | " | " | June 21, '65 | Pro. Corp. June 1, '65. |
| Augustus Caswell | 18 | Rye | " | " | June 21, '65 | Wounded sl. Sept. 29, '64. |
| Henry N. Caswell | 31 | " | " | " | " | Dis. for disability at Washington, D. C., Dec. 11, '62. |
| Charles R. Caswell | 42 | " | " | " | " | Dis. May 12, '65. |
| Nathan Clough | 26 | Portsmouth | " | " | " | Des. from hospital at Portsmouth, N. H., Feb. 10, '63. |
| George David | 33 | " | " | " | " | Pro Corp. Dis. for disability at Portsmouth, Va., Oct. 7, '63. |
| James Davidson | 19 | Unknown | " | " | " | Dis. for disability at Georgetown, D. C., Nov. 10, '62. |
| A. P. De Rochment | 31 | Rye | " | " | " | |
| Robert S. Foss | 18 | Portsmouth | " | " | June 21, '65 | Died of disease at Portsmouth, N. H., Jan. 10, '64. |
| Nathaniel Gunnison | 23 | " | " | " | June 21, '65 | Captured Dec. 13, '62. Released May 20, '63. |
| James Gilchrist | 35 | " | " | " | June 21, '65 | Captured Dec. 13, '62. Released May 20, '63. Wounded sl. Sept. 29, '64. |
| John K. A. Hanson | 38 | " | " | " | " | |
| John Harmon | 18 | " | " | " | " | Died of disease at New York Dec. 3, '62. |
| Henry C. Hodgdon | 23 | " | " | " | " | Wounded Dec. 13, '62. Transf. to Navy April 18, '64. |
| Henry A. Hunnefield | 27 | Unknown | " | " | June 23, '65 | Transf. to Brigade Band Jan. 21, '63. |
| John Harrison | 25 | Portsmouth | " | " | " | Des. at Portsmouth, Va., June 30, '63. |
| Michael Hoy | 29 | " | " | " | " | Transf. to Navy April 3, '64. |
| Martin Johnson | 30 | " | " | " | " | Transf. to V. R. C. March 8, '65. |
| Ephraim Jackson | 20 | " | " | " | June 21, '65 | Pro. Corp. June 1, '65. |
| Francis R. Johnson | 26 | " | " | " | " | Dis. May 26, '65. |
| Daniel M. Jellison | 25 | " | " | " | " | Dis. for disability at Washington, D. C., Feb. 3, '63. |
| William H. Jellison | 21 | " | " | " | " | Transf. to V. R. C. Sept. 1, '63. Mustered out July 6, '65. |
| William H. Lear | 39 | Rye | " | " | " | Killed at Fort Harrison, Va., Sept. 29, '64. |
| David Locke | 23 | Portsmouth | " | " | June 21, '65 | Pro. Corp. July 1, '64. |
| John H. Mawbey | 30 | Rye | " | " | " | Dis. May 16, '65. |
| William Mitchell | 23 | Portsmouth | " | " | " | Pro. Corp. May 17, '65. |
| John Moore | 36 | " | " | " | June 21, '65 | |
| John Motfram | 18 | Rye | " | " | June 21, '65 | Wounded sl. Sept. 20, '64. Pro. Corp. Jan. 1, '65. |
| James McIntire | 18 | " | " | " | June 21, '65 | Pro. Corp. Jan. 20, '64. Wounded sl. Sept. 30, '64. |
| Peter Mitchell | 23 | Portsmouth | " | " | June 21, '65 | |
| John McMillan | 33 | Portsmouth | " | " | June 21, '65 | Des. at Portsmouth, Va., June 30, '63. |

| Name | Age | Residence | Rank | Mustered In | Mustered Out | Remarks |
|---|---|---|---|---|---|---|
| John May | 32 | Portsmouth | Private | Sept. 20, '62 | June 21, '65 | Dis. for disability at New York Jan. 14, '63. |
| Daniel H. McIntire | 28 | " | " | " | June 21, '65 | Pro. Corp. Jan. 21, '63; Sergt. April 5, '64. |
| Jeremiah L. McIntire | 36 | " | " | " | | Dis. for disability at Philadelphia, Pa., Jan. 10, '63. |
| George Manning | 27 | " | " | " | | Dis. for disability at Philadelphia, Pa., March 13, '63. |
| Charles J. Mace | 29 | Rye | " | " | | Pro. Corp. Wounded sev. June 15, '64. Dis. on account of wounds Dec. 14, '64. |
| Woodbury N. Mace | 27 | " | " | " | | |
| Edward Miller | 21 | " | " | " | | Des. at Portsmouth, N. H., Sept. 29, '62. |
| Charles H. Morse | 21 | " | " | " | | Dis. for disability at Philadelphia, Pa., March 11, '63. |
| William T. Matthews | 43 | " | " | " | | Killed at Cold Harbor, Va., June 1, '64. |
| Jacob Ormerod | 21 | " | " | " | | Pro. Corp. Commissioned in U. S. C. T. Sept. 1, '64. |
| Daniel H. Plaisted | 24 | Portsmouth | " | " | | Dis. for disability at Washington, D. C., Feb. 5, '63. |
| Thomas Parks | 19 | " | " | " | | Dis. for disability at Washington, D. C., Feb. 23, '63. |
| William J. Pierce | 35 | " | " | " | | Dis. for disability at Philadelphia, Pa., April 8, '63. |
| Henry S. Paul | 20 | " | " | " | June 18, '65 | Master Builder of Hospitals at Point of Rocks, Va., at Hdqrs. Army of the James. |
| Charles Powell | 35 | " | " | " | | Pro. Corp. Wounded sev. Sept. 30, '64. Dis. for disability April 20, '65. |
| Oliver B. Philbrick | 44 | Rye | " | " | | Dis. for disability at Portsmouth, Va., Oct. 7, '63. |
| Reuben G. Randall | 29 | Portsmouth | " | " | | Transf. to Navy April 18, '64. |
| Isaac H. N. Pray | 19 | " | " | " | June 21, '65 | |
| Ezekiel C. Rand | 22 | " | " | " | | Transf. to Navy April 18, '64. |
| Charles W. Randall | 25 | " | " | " | | Dis. for disability at Fortress Monroe, Va., May 27, '65. |
| Owen H. Roche | 19 | " | " | " | | Transf. to V. R. C. Sept. 1, '63. Mustered out Sept. 19, '65. |
| Judson P. Randall | 22 | Rye | " | " | | Wounded sev. June 1, '64. Dis. May 28, '65. |
| Robert Rand | 45 | Portsmouth | " | " | | Dis. for disability at Fortress Monroe, Va., May 24, '63. |
| Moses Rowe | 44 | " | " | " | | Transf. to V. R. C. Sept. 1, '63. |
| William Rowe | 35 | " | " | " | | Pro. Corp. Sept. 1, '63. Dis. for disability at Concord, N. H., May 29, '65. |
| John C. Stevens | 18 | " | " | " | | Dis. for disability at Washington, D. C., Feb. 20, '63. |
| Enoch F. Smith | 18 | " | " | " | | Dis. for disability at Washington, D. C., March 6, '63. |
| Charles G. Smith | 35 | " | " | " | | Transf. to Navy, April 3, '64. |
| Edward W. Sides | 19 | " | " | " | June 21, '65 | Died at Fredericksburg, Va., Dec. 19, '62. |
| George L. Sides | 21 | " | " | " | | |
| Patrick Sullivan | 38 | " | " | " | | Dis. for disability at Concord, N. H., Jan. 15, '64. |
| Horace S. Spinney | 24 | " | " | " | | |
| William H. Shapley | 31 | Rye | " | " | June 21, '65 | Transf. to V. R. C. July 1, '63. |
| George Stott | 43 | Portsmouth | " | " | | Dis. for disability at Portsmouth, Va., April 16, '64. |

| Name | Residence | Age | Rank | Mustered in | Remarks |
|---|---|---|---|---|---|
| Henry G. Thompson | Portsmouth | 21 | Private | Sept. 20, '62 | Transf. to V. R. C. Feb. 15, '64. Mustered out June 26, '65. |
| George Taylor | Rye | 26 | " | " | Pro. Corp. Wounded sev. Sept. 29, '64. Dis. for disability at Manchester, N. H., May 10, '65. |
| Stephen B. Tarleton | " | 29 | " | " | Pro. Corp. Feb. 14, '63; Sergt. March 1, '64. Wounded sl. June 1, '64. |
| Wm. Warburton 1st | Portsmouth | 42 | " | " | Des. at Portsmouth, Va., Jan. 22, '64. |
| Wm. Warburton 2d | " | 36 | " | " | Pro. Corp. Killed at Cold Harbor, Va., June 1, '64. |
| John F. Welch | " | 18 | " | " | Pro. Corp. Died of disease at York, Me., April 19, '64. |
| RECRUITS. | | | | | |
| John Adams | Unknown | 21 | " | Aug. 19, '63 | Transf. to Navy April 27, '64. |
| John Burke | " | " | " | " | Transf. to 2d N. H. V. June 21, '65. |
| George W. Berry | " | 21 | " | Aug. 14, '63 | Wounded sev. June 15, '64. Died of wounds at Petersburg, Va., June 16, '64. |
| William Brennan | " | 22 | " | Aug. 11, '63 | Des. near Portsmouth, Va., Oct. 10, '63. |
| Francis N. Burns | " | 21 | " | Aug. 19, '63 | Transf. to 2d Mass. Cavalry Oct. 5, '64. |
| David Curry | " | 21 | " | " | Des. at Portsmouth, N. H. Aug. 15, '64. Gained from desertion. Wounded sev. Sept. 29, '64. Des. at Point of Rocks, Va., Oct. 15, '64. |
| William H. Gray | " | 25 | " | " | Wounded sev. June 1, '64. Died of wounds at Alexandria, Va., June 25, '64. |
| Henry Gardner | " | 26 | " | " | Transf. to Navy April 3, '64. |
| Thomas Green | " | " | " | " | Wounded sl. Sept. 29, '64. Pro. Sergt. Transf. to 2d N. H. V., June 21, '65. |
| Joseph Labelle | " | 34 | " | Sept. 1, '63 | Des. at Fort Harrison Nov. 3, '64. |
| George H. Throop | " | 45 | " | Aug. 19, '63 | Des. while on furlough at Washington, D. C., March 5, '64. |
| George S. Tufts | " | " | " | Dec. 15, '63 | Transf. to 2d N. H. V. June 21, '65. |
| Nathan Whalley | Portsmouth | 34 | Musician | " | Transf. to Brigade Band, 2d Brig. 3d Div. 24th A. C., Feb. 1, '64. Mustered out July 17, '65. |
| Marshall R. Watson | Unknown | 32 | Private | Aug. 19, '63 | Transf. to Navy April 18, '64. |
| Ammi Woodbury | " | 27 | " | " | Died of disease at New York Sept. 5, '64. |
| Harry Watson | " | 22 | " | Sept. 2, '63 | Des. near Portsmouth, Va., Oct. 11 '63. |
| Bartlett F. Wentworth | " | 28 | " | " | Wounded sev. and died of wounds Sept. 30, '64, at Fort Harrison, Va. |
| John Wilson | " | 25 | " | Aug. 19, '63 | Des. at Portsmouth, Va., Oct., '63. [29, '64. |
| Rudolph M. Zeller | " | 31 | " | " | Wounded sev. and died of wounds at Fort Harrison, Va., Sept. Wounded June 1, '64. Des. from hospital at Philadelphia, Pa., Aug. 10, '64. |

RECRUITS NOT ASSIGNED TO COMPANIES IN THE ADJUTANT GENERAL'S REPORTS.

| | | | | |
|---|---|---|---|---|
| Richard Hill | Unknown | Private | Aug. 11, '63 | Supposed to have deserted while en route to the Regiment. |
| William Henry | " | " | Aug. 10, '63 | Supposed to have deserted while en route to the Regiment. |
| Henry McDonald | Portsmouth | " | Dec. 28, '63 | Volunteer. Supposed to have deserted while en route to the Regiment. |
| James Smith | Unknown | " | Jan. 4, '64 | Supposed to have deserted while en route to the Regiment. |

## REUNION OF 1887.

In view of the dislike entertained by many members of the Thirteenth for the crowded reunions at Weirs, in view of the residence of many members near Boston, in view of having a downright good time without a single drawback, or an incident to mar the occasion, and in view of publishing a history of the Regiment, Assistant Surgeon John Sullivan, John M. Woods of Company I, and Sergeant Thomas S. Wentworth of Company B, all residing in or near Boston, were appointed at Weirs, on August 26, 1886, to arrange for a Reunion in Boston on April 3, 1887 — the twenty-second anniversary of the Thirteenth's entry into Richmond. As this anniversary fell upon Sunday, the following Tuesday, April 5th, was fixed upon.

A spirited circular was issued in September 1886, by the gentlemen of this committee, to every surviving member of the Thirteenth whose address could be found. The addresses of the members had previously been found in considerable numbers by Lieut. Thompson, the writer of this account, by advertising in newspapers, by circulars, and by sending to nearly every Postmaster, and to every Grand Army Post, in New Hampshire, a conspicuous poster to be put up and read of all men — this while gathering data for the history. He had also in May 1885, while in Washington, made arrangements with Gen. John C. Black, Commissioner of Pensions, for an exchange of addresses of the Thirteenth. A few days before the Reunion, Asst. Surgeon Sullivan in Boston copied his list of addresses which he sent to Lieut. Thompson at Providence, who added sundry names and then sent the full list by special-delivery post to Quarter-master Cheney, then U. S. Senator and in Washington; the list was immediately placed by him in the hands of Gen. Black, and the result was a speedy addition of nearly one hundred addresses, received in time for those members to be notified of the Reunion, and for some of them to attend.

Over five hundred invitations had been sent out to as many surviving members of the Thirteenth. The most of them could not accept, many because of sickness; the early morning trains, however, centring in Boston, brought in numerous happy groups of members, and at the hour of reception, ten o'clock, parlors numbers one and two at the Revere House were crowded by our Veterans, and there was heard repeated on every hand the good old salutation of army days — 'How are you?'

Sheets of paper had been provided, and as each Veteran of the Thirteenth arrived the clerk secured his signature. There were present among others:

William Grantman, Lt. Colonel.
George N. Julian, Captain.
Rufus P. Staniels, Captain.
Charles H. Curtis, Captain.
Hubbard W. Hall, Captain.
William J. Ladd, Captain.
Nathan B. Boutwell, Adjutant.
Person C. Cheney, Quarter-master.
John Sullivan, Asst. Surgeon.
Charles M. Kittredge, Lieutenant.
Nathan D. Chapman, Lieutenant.
James M. Hodgdon, Sergt. Major.
John M. Woods, of Co. I.
Charles W. Washburn, Band.
James M. Caswell, Band.
David W. Bodge, Color Sergeant.
D. E. Proctor, Major, C. T.

Nathan D. Stoodley, Major.
George Farr, Captain.
Lewis P. Wilson, Captain.
George A. Bruce, Captain.
James M. Durell, Captain.
Royal B. Prescott, Lieutenant.
George H. Taggard, Adjutant.
Mortier L. Morrison, Quarter-master.
W. H. H. Young, Lieutenant.
S. Millett Thompson, Lieutenant.
Benj. F. Winn, Lieutenant.
Thomas S. Wentworth, Sergeant.
Manson S. Brown, Principal Musician.
William Critchley, Band.
Nathan Whalley, Band.
Charles Powell, Color Corporal.
Charles B. Saunders, Captain, C. T.

Co. A, 6 Veterans; B, 15; C, 6; D, 2; E, 6; F, 7; G, 16; H, 6; I, 18; K, 15; total (with a few whose names were not obtained) 140.

Invited guests:

Maj. Gen. Charles Devens.
Gen. Hazard Stevens.
Lt. Col. W. H. D. Cochrane.

Gen. M. T. Donohoe.
Gen. A. D. Ayling, Adjt. Gen. N. H.
Chaplain Alonzo H. Quint.

Col. George H. Patch (Representing also the Boston Globe).

At 11 a. m. the Business Meeting was opened by Asst. Surgeon Sullivan, who called the gathering to order, and read this address of welcome:

"Comrades: The committee appointed at the Weirs to arrange for a Reunion here have sought the address of Comrades, and sent circulars to them, in the East, South and West. We hope no Comrade has been omitted, or has failed to receive a notice of this Reunion. The number present make glad the hearts of your committee. There are to be with us to-day one hundred and thirty-five Comrades, gathered from the Canada line to Washington, D. C., and from the great lakes to the Atlantic.

"Now, instead of a Reunion at the Weirs, where but few of us ever assemble, and are soon lost among the thousands of civilians who congregate there, we have arranged for the use of these elegant apartments, where we can meet as gentlemen as well as Veterans, and enjoy ourselves in a manner impossible at the Weirs. At one o'clock we shall have a Revere House banquet — how different it will be from the 'banquets' we existed upon from 1862 to 1865!

"Never since we returned from the war in 1865, have we had so many Comrades together. Some will meet here to-day who have not shaken hands for twenty-two years — hands that when last they grasped, were mere skin and bones, bronzed with a Southern sun, or begrimed with gunpowder ; young men whose waists were no larger round than the waist of a young lady, poor, emaciated, reduced by hardship, sickness and misery known only by those who have lived for months and years in the Southern climate and in the face of a deadly foe.

"To-day we meet as Veterans of a terrible war. The empty sleeve, the single eye, the limb which never moves but with a twinge, the wounds which often break out afresh, the diseases contracted in the rifle-pits, the deep trenches, or on the borders of the Dismal Swamp in Virginia, the gray hairs and grizzly beards which have come to us with the two decades and more that have passed since we returned to the peaceful vocations of civil life, all go to make up the reality of the Veterans that we are.

"The once familiar faces and voices of many members of our Regiment who returned with us are not to be with us to-day ; our old commander, Gen. Stevens is an invalid in Florida ; Lt. Col. Smith is sick at his home in Richmond.

"There are others, noble fellows, who have been transferred to another department : Lieut. Churchill, always ready for a fight or a frolic ; Surgeon Richardson, whose burly frame was scarcely large enough for his big heart ; Capt. Carter, a good soldier and a model citizen ; Surgeon Small, always so kind and considerate with the sick and wounded ; these and others have been transferred.

"But we still have with us some whose fingers are not drawn out of shape with rheumatism, and whose voices are as strong in tone as they always were. I see among you Comrade Critchley, who can still blow his horn ; and Adjutant Boutwell, whose voice was not shot away with the bullet that went through his shoulder ; Lieut. Kittredge, just from his position in charge of the Insane Asylum on the Hudson ; Manson S. Brown, whose grip would subdue the best business leg of an army mule ; and Webster Barnabee, who used to sing so sweetly and so well; they are all here with us to-day ; and with these to lead us, we want first to salute the Old Flag by singing, ' Rally 'round the flag, Boys.' "

This song then rang out with a will — reminding us all of the old war-scenes in the forests of Virginia. After the song came three rousing cheers. The meeting then organized with Asst. Surgeon Sullivan as President, and Lieut. Prescott as Secretary. Quarter-master Cheney was chosen to preside at the banquet.

Lieut. Thompson was then called upon to present the matter of the regimental history, which he did briefly, and substantially as follows :

"Comrades : Thinking it not necessary, I did not prepare any elaborate speech concerning the history, and upon the whole think I will not say much about that ; or anything else, in a general way, beyond congratulating you all most heartily upon your continued life, health and prosperity which together have made this Reunion possible, and upon the pleasures, enjoyments and genuine fraternal spirit of this meeting.

"Nearly a quarter of a century ago you were engaged in making American history — volumes of it — far more volumes of it than can ever be written by the pen of mortal man. Of your part in the life and death struggle which took place in those days — the great South War — I have gathered a Diary covering nearly every day of your term of service. Our amiable friends, Stoodley, Sullivan, Prescott and Woods, who have read the manuscript, call it a History; it is not for me to say much about it. The writing thus done for you should speak for itself; and there appears but one way to gain that end, and that way is to publish the work; and I now come squarely to the point: I wish a few of you, who can afford the use of the money as well as not for a little time, to place in my hands the sum of fifteen hundred dollars to use toward publishing that work in book form. It is thought that with that sum, and the sales that may be made meanwhile, the work can be carried through. We have calculated the whole affair, amounting to about 600 pages $4 \times 7$ of print — the size of the pages of the circular distributed here — as closely as possible, and to the members of the Regiment and their families, and to the families of deceased members, the price is placed at $3.50 per copy carriage paid; there are to be no free lists, no deadheads, no go-betweens — the whole business is to be managed upon a cash basis."

The call was then made for subscriptions, and in about thirty minutes the sum named for the fund was subscribed, and several hundred dollars paid in.

This done, the Veterans at once formed by Companies and marched into the dining-room in order — forming there in single rank behind the chairs at table as we formed behind the sand of the captured rebel parapets at Drury's Bluff just before daylight began to break on the foggy morning of May 16, 1864, — in both cases the Veterans 'meant business.' After a fervent prayer and grace, said by Chaplain Quint, the banquet began. A temperance banquet it was, as befits Veterans; there were numerous courses, and all served in the best style that pertains at the Revere House. There stood beside each Veterans' plate a colored engraving, printed upon heavy card-board, of the Thirteenth's battle flags (the same as the frontispiece in the history) and bound with it, by a bit of ribbon, the menu of the banquet together with a bivouac scene highly suggestive of the straits of campaigning life.

After the banquet was concluded Quarter-master Cheney rose and spoke as follows : —

"Comrades: We all feel that the pleasure of this occasion is very much lessened by the absence of our Colonel and Lieutenant Colonel, both of whom are detained at home by severe sickness. Resolutions of sympathy have been prepared by Lieut. Thompson, and I will now ask him to read them."

The resolutions were then read and adopted, and the meeting rose and stood for a few minutes in silence; an impressive act of respect for the memory of our departed Comrades.

Quarter-master Cheney proceeded : " I am much pleased and gratified by meeting the large number present. In recounting as briefly as possible the early and eventful days of the Thirteenth New Hampshire, I may say at this time, that the impressions made upon my mind, during that trying ordeal, are lasting, and can never be effaced. This Regiment, like others from the North, was an offering in response to a summons from a Government that had exhausted every peaceful method to preserve intact the Unity of the States. Not until it had been humiliated beyond measure by foes without and traitors within ; not until a defiant foe had proclaimed starvation for, or the surrender of the loyal band at Fort Sumter, followed by actual hostilities, did our Government and the Nation awake to the fact, that if it would longer exist, it must continue only by an appeal to arms. A hostile Government had been formed and large armies organized. We had been attacked and our Flag captured. There was absolutely no other alternative left us — we must fight in self-defense, or cowardly surrender.

" If this peril had come to us through a foreign enemy, to be repelled by a united people, as in the earlier days of our history, this struggle would have been divested of its very worst features ; but this was not so to be. This Republic, founded only upon God-given rights, was to receive a baptism of blood flowing from the arteries of a people who had shared a common inheritance — sealed by the blood of the Fathers. We had received and enjoyed this bequest; would we regard it as sacred and hand it down to our children's children unimpaired ? This was the question of the hour, and one which was uppermost in the minds of the people, when the call was made for ' Three Hundred Thousand More.' Never did a people respond with greater alacrity. The emblem of our Nationality, although riddled with shot and shell, must not trail in the dust, but must be borne triumphantly into the very citadel whose pride it was to bring it dishonor. Could we at that time have lifted the veil that obscured our vision from a glance at the Thirteenth Regiment's future glories, we should have discerned at the very top of the roll of honor the enchanting and soul inspiring words : ' Thirteenth Regiment of New Hampshire Volunteers ; the first in Richmond April 3, 1865,' under a picture of its battle-flag torn in shreds, but forgivingly resuming its old time place of Talisman for a re-united and suffering people.

" It was a bright October day, just twenty-four years and six months ago to-day, when we bade adieu to our loved ones, and left home for Washington and the seat of war. The heart-struggles, the tears and convulsive sobs, together with the fervent prayers that rose heavenward for divine aid, even now cause the heart to swell with emotion. In Washington we were presumably received with open arms. We were consigned to a Tentless Field for our first night's experience. We had arrived too late to make a requisition for our supplies, and we kept our first 'night-watch' amid the fog and miasma that arose from the turbid Potomac.

"At early dawn your Quarter-master was in the saddle to make a fight for the best of 'what there was left.' As a whole we were reasonably successful. The matter of securing good teams was important. Our choice lay between the rattling wild mule, who assumed the defiant airs of his native heath, and whom we found in process of taming by being securely fastened at one end of a long rope, while playing away at the other end were a group of laughing, singing darkies. These mules, like their former owners, were for 'Secession,' and were trying to kick themselves into a greater freedom, but they also had failed to count the cost, and the colored man took the advanced position. We could take our pick from these wild mules, or from the broken-down horses and mules that had been turned back into the Department as unfit for service. We made our selection from this last class; the mules predominating in number. We had heard that mules never wore out nor died from old age. We got our teams into camp and commenced a more careful inspection. We found almost every conceivable ailment quite evenly distributed among them; and I suppose it was the length of the requisition for medicines, with which to treat these ailments, that brought from the bluff old Quarter-master General the emphatic declaration: 'That it was the first time he had ever seen so much doctoring for a mule.' But we had chosen wisely. We were not kicked; and their evening lullabies, and early dawn echoes, were in harmony with the music of the Union. They were loyal to the flag, and if the stripes were sometimes too conspicuous, it was that the stars might twinkle all the more brightly.

"On Dec. 1, 1862, we broke camp at Fairfax Seminary to take position in the great Army under Gen. Burnside in front of Fredericksburg. The efficiency of the Thirteenth had been recognized, and it was classed as veteran, although it had scarce received two months' drill. I joined you a few days later at Aquia Creek, being obliged to remain behind to care for what we could not take with us. The lamented Chaplain Arthur B. Fuller of the 16th Mass., and known to many of you, was my companion on the steamer down the river. The next Saturday week there entered into the heavenly rest one of the brightest and purest of spirits that ever blessed earth or heaven. This brave Chaplain, with musket in hand, had fallen on the field of Fredericksburg.

"The impregnable position of the rebel centre, and Gen. Sumner's attack upon it, I will not dwell upon, for its results carried consternation to every heart in the loyal North. On the twenty-second anniversary of this battle, Dec. 13, 1864, in company with two other New Hampshire officers I visited this historic ground under the escort of a Confederate officer now a resident lawyer in Fredericksburg. He wondered at the reckless bravery of Meagher's Irish Brigade, and their mid-day dash in an unbroken line of attack through an open field upon the rebel infantry.

It was a matter of interest to us all, that, as he pointed out to us the most advanced spot where our men fell in their assault upon Marye's Heights, to hear him say it was their (the rebels') general belief that Meagher's Irish Brigade, who held the post of honor (at the Union centre, in the daytime assaults), must have become reckless by whiskey, so foolhardy did it seem to them to rush into the very gates of death. By our own measurements they had come within 24 paces of the rebel infantry, who were massed in the highway between the stone walls, and covered by heavy guns in their rear on Marye's Heights. But how absurd the rebels' conclusion! These brave men of Meagher's had received their inspiration from the fountain of a fearless manhood. Their consecration to duty had been through the revered symbols of a patriotic ancestry ; and most nobly did they honor the call of their adopted country. Their lips are sealed in death, but their memories will ever be sacred in the hearts of a grateful people.

"The Thirteenth delights to bear testimony to their gallantry, they being among its supporters in that famous night assault of Dec. 13th, when the Thirteenth bore its own flag nearest to those walls, on the left, along the sunken Telegraph road under Marye's Heights; there it was where its members received their first baptism of fire. Its ranks were decimated, but it did not waver.

"The intervening days that elapsed, before the Union army again advanced, were indeed dark and gloomy. In addition to our military reverses was the threatening aspect of the business situation. Gold at a price that suggested National bankruptcy; the market excited by the mutterings of a large class of people who did not believe in the wisdom of President Lincoln's Emancipation Proclamation, which took effect January 1, 1863; the doubt and uncertainty of the action of England and other foreign nations; all conspired to a feeling of great anxiety.

"Almost a quarter of a century has since passed, and still we wonder at the mysterious way in which a higher type of manhood was forced upon the American Nation.

"I have made reference to what followed the disastrous battle of Fredericksburg. We were still in camp at Falmouth almost imbedded in its fathomless mud; and our shelter nothing but the little 'shelter tent' such as is used while on a march. The weather cold, wet and disagreeable in the extreme. The Army was in constant expectation of being ordered to advance, and supplies had been graded accordingly, although we had a fair supply of hard bread, coffee and pork. No class of men, no matter how great their endurance, could without acclimation resist such exposure and the insidious climatic diseases which were inhaled with every breath. Our Hospitals were full. Our officers' tents were visited by anxious Surgeons, while the line officers of each Company found abundant opportunity for a cheering word to the afflicted private. Your Quarter-master was among the last to yield. That awful chill (that creeps through every fibre of a man's frame till at last it clutches at his very vitals) with all of its attendant horrors, came in its turn. The slow, dull, flickering fire from the unseasoned pine offered little hindrance to the piercing midnight frosts which gathered upon the hard couch of the stricken sufferer, — but I will not recite tales of personal suffering. I only desire to acknowledge the most tender and careful attention from those nearest me. The skill of the Surgeons, the watchfulness of Quartermaster Sergeant Morrison was only excelled by the brotherly ministrations of the Colonel, who personally secured permission from Headquarters to send me to Washington there to be cared for by Mrs. Col. A. F. Stevens until my own family could reach me. This sickness I did not recover from for a long series of months. The following August, under the advice of my physician, I tendered my resignation, and received my discharge from the service.

"I may say in closing that I have never lost my interest in the Regiment, and always have felt an intense pride and satisfaction in its hours of triumph as well as being a sympathetic mourner in all its sorrows. I congratulate you one and all upon the pleasures and enjoyments of this Reunion, and trust that the ties that bind us together will be strengthened by the lapse of time."

President Cheney next introduced Maj. Gen. Devens. On rising he was greeted with hearty cheers by every one present, and was visibly moved by the genuine outburst of respect, honor and affection; the General was always exceeding popular with the Thirteenth and much loved by every member of it. As soon as quiet was restored, he spoke as follows:

"Mr. President, friends and comrades of the Thirteenth New Hampshire Regiment: Ordinarily I can trust myself to speak a few words to old comrades without any fear of giving way too much to feeling and emotion. I am not sure to-day that I can preserve the requisite calmness in presence of the friends who have so cordially received me, and in memory of all the recollections that are evoked in looking back to a day such as was April 3, 1865: a day which ended the long and terrific struggle of our civil strife; a day which by the capture of the city which had been the seat of its power, foreboded the rapid destruction of the Confederacy.

"The words which have first been read and which I wrote twenty-two years ago to his Excellency the Governor of New Hampshire, I have no occasion to alter or qualify, far less to take back. They were true then, they are true now, and will always be historically true. The Thirteenth New Hampshire was the first Regiment to bring the colors of the Union into Richmond. This does not rest on my authority. In the most explicit terms Gen. Weitzel, who was the commander of the 25th Army Corps, to which the 3d Division of the 24th Army Corps was temporarily attached, and Gen. Shepley who was his Chief of Staff, have asserted that it was from me, as the commanding officer of the 3d Division that they learned that the skirmishers of the Division with whom was Capt. G. A. Bruce, then on my staff, were in possession of all the fortifications which so long had frowned in front of us; and that it was but justice to this 3d Division of the 24th Corps to say that it was the first to occupy Richmond.

"When Mr. Greeley published his history of our civil conflict, and stated that the colored troops were the first to occupy the city of Richmond, I deemed it proper, through Capt. Bruce, to address Gen. Weitzel, urging him to do the justice to this 3d Division to which it was entitled. He did it in a manful, soldierly and direct way, and stated that although the troops of this Division were not his except temporarily they were the first to occupy Richmond, and that it was from me in the early dawn of the morning that he knew that it had occupied the fortifications of the city. I trust justice has been done in the later editions of that work.

"In that 3d Division the First Brigade commanded by Gen. Ripley (who I hope will be with us here before the day is done) was on the morning of the 3d of April the leading Brigade, and the Thirteenth New Hampshire was the leading Regiment of that Brigade. There were no colored troops to precede us or accompany us, and none there at all until the arrival of a regiment of colored cavalry at nine or ten o'clock (that morning), after the city had been in our hands at least two hours.

"When any fact stated as history assumes a poetical shape, nothing is harder than to confute it by evidence, however positive. As it was once asserted without any authority and as it seemed a sort of poetical justice to the controversies of the great civil war that at the conclusion colored men and soldiers should take possession of the rebel capital, even the evidence of the distinguished corps commander with whom we served and who would and ought to have claimed this honor for his own corps (had it been justly entitled to it) is ignored and disregarded. Poetic imagination is allowed to supplant well-attested facts in order that some one may round an impressive period or make a brilliant antithesis. I trust I am not one of those who would willingly detract from the just claims of any body of troops, whether white or black, or whether they were under my command or not, but I cannot allow the men I have commanded to be deprived of the honor rightfully their due, in order to please those who would prefer what is fanciful and imaginative to that which is accurate and correct.

"Undoubtedly in taking possession of Richmond the 3d Division was reaping what others largely had sown in the success which had attended the operations of the left wing of our army. But the occasion and the opportunity came to us, we availed ourselves of it promptly and vigorously and were entitled to whatever of credit there may have been in it. It was accidental that your Regiment (the 13th N. H.) was the one to lead our column, it came in the regular order of assignment to march, but you did your work gallantly and well. It was accidental also in a certain sense that this Division was the one nearest Richmond, yet this was not altogether so, for by its gallant fighting on the previous 29th of September the troops of this Division substantially (although then a Division of the 18th Corps) had won the nearest point ever taken to Richmond and had held it through the winter of 1864 and 1865 ; and through its lines all the communications by flag of truce between the contending armies had been conducted. On that day your Regiment was in a Brigade gallantly commanded by Gen. Stevens whose absence and the ill health which is the cause of it we profoundly regret, and Gen. Donohoe whom we are all glad to see won for himself deserved credit at the head of the Regiment he then commanded.

" None of us will ever forget the sight that met our eyes as we reached the last range of hills above Richmond. We had been so long near it yet never able to capture it that it had seemed almost like a fairy city that would never appear to our sight. Dead on the battle-fields, fortifications and trenches around it were thousands of our brave companions who were never to know the joy of final victory. But Richmond at last was ours and without a conflict, for the losses of the whole Division were but six or seven men and these among the skirmishers with what were hardly more than the stragglers of the retiring forces. No sight will ever be seen by any of us more majestic or more illustrative of the horrors of war: The lurid flames springing up from the warehouses, the magazines of ammunition rending the air with their explosions, the three great bridges across the James burning to prevent our pursuit of the retreating force, six gunboats on fire in the river (from one of which before the magazine exploded, my energetic aide, Lieut. Ladd, rescued its flag, which I have long kept as a most interesting memento), all presented a scene of terrific grandeur. But beyond this external view there was a moral aspect which might well excite the profoundest emotion. The great bell of time had struck one of those hours by which the progress of nations and peoples is marked. It had marked the preservation of the American Union and it had marked the redemption from slavery of a whole race of men.

"' There was some small satisfaction in filling Libby Prison and Castle Thunder with the two thousand Confederate soldiers belated in their retreat whom we gathered up, there was much wider and higher satisfaction in bringing again to the city so long the stronghold of rebel power the great Flag under which our columns so long had marched and fought. Even in Richmond, there were eyes that were wet with tears of joy and gratitude as they looked again upon its shining folds.

" The day after the capture I called upon Mrs. Van Lew and her daughter, two ladies well known for their unflinching devotion to the Union cause. They had been substantially prisoners in their own house although not treated with personal indignity. I stood with the elder lady on the piazza of the river front of her mansion from which the New Market road is seen over which our troops advanced that morning. ' We knew,' she said, ' last night that they were going, the sentinel disappeared from our street. All night we heard the rattling of the army wagons and the rumbling roll of the artillery and when morning dawned we came out here to watch the coming of our troops.' 'Soon after it was light,' she continued, 'we saw them coming, at first seeming to straggle along both sides of the New Market road; why was this?' I replied that 'those were the skirmishers who are always thrown out in front of every moving column to ascertain if its march was to be opposed.' She then said, 'We waited a few minutes longer and it then seemed as if a whole wall of bayonets came up over the hill, flashing in the rising sun and above them waved the American Flag. General, it was four years since I had seen the American Flag and my daughter and I sank down upon our knees and thanked our God that He had permitted us to see it come again and come in triumph.'

"The Flag which sent those true Christian, Union women down upon their knees in gratitude and which was the first to enter Richmond waved above the Thirteenth New Hampshire and was sustained by the strong hands and stout hearts of its men.

"The good conduct of the Division that day made two Brigadier Generals, my friends Donohoe and Ripley, and one Major General; of the latter I will not speak except to say that I thank you and all its men for their good service.

"It was twenty-two years ago: many of those who were with us then are gone before us now; we recall them as we ourselves should wish to be recalled in the hours of kind and social intercourse, and we pay them the tribute of our tenderest memory. Of those who survive I congratulate you that so many have been allowed to gather here on this most interesting Anniversary. Heads are somewhat balder, beards and moustaches are very much grayer, but hearts are unchanged still and courage yet remains. We could not, I fear, march quite so far or so fast as in the old days, especially with rifles in our hands, with knapsack and blanket across our backs, with haversacks containing five days' rations slung over our shoulders and besides our cartridge boxes with forty extra rounds of ammunition in our pockets for immediate use. But even if this were so and if we could not manœuvre so smartly or move so quickly, post us along a sunken road or behind a low stone wall or by the edge of a wood and we could convince any troops who might attempt to drive us from such a position that they had undertaken a very serious contract indeed, and that it would be better on the whole to let us alone.

"Comrades: I thank you sincerely for the cordial welcome you have given me. Nothing is more grateful than the regard and respect of brave men. I trust you will live long to celebrate the anniversary of a day of which you have a just right to be proud."

Gen. Devens was followed by Gen. Donohoe with a few remarks upon the friendly relations of the Tenth and Thirteenth; Gen. Ayling gave a hearty congratulatory speech; Chaplain Quint spoke quite at length;

next followed Maj. Cochrane with expressions of much feeling and interest eulogistic of his friend Lt. Col. Bowers; Capt. Bruce read a very interesting paper concerning the Fredericksburg campaign; but of the remarks of these gentlemen no notes were taken.

Gen. Hazard Stevens was introduced as the first Drill-master of the Thirteenth, and among other matters related the incident occurring at Fredericksburg on the evening of Dec. 13, 1862, which he afterwards wrote out and which has been embodied in the History on page 57.

Lieut. Prescott read a valuable paper on the Medical Staff of the Thirteenth, much of which has been entered on page 619 and elsewhere as historical matter. He then read this letter from Lt. Col. Smith:

"Comrades of the Thirteenth: When Asst. Surgeon Sullivan first wrote to me that we were to have a Reunion in Boston, I fully intended to be present; but a long-continued illness decrees otherwise. To yourselves I leave the fitting words expressing our appreciation of the Comrades who have been finally mustered out.

"It seems to me I had less opportunity of becoming acquainted with the men than any other line officer. I was frequently detailed to serve on Courts Martial — serving as a member of one for three months continuously in 1863. When promoted to Major in July, 1864, I almost at once succeeded to the command of the Regiment, Lt. Col. Grantman being sick in camp. He was soon sent home on leave of absence because of sickness; and until we were mustered out, either Major Stoodley or myself were always in command. I began to more fully appreciate the good qualities of our men soon after the command of the Regiment devolved upon me. The first and only time I ever doubted them was at Cold Harbor. I was a Captain then. When we fell back from that desperate charge on the evening of June 1st, and were lying upon the ground while the rebel bullets were singing so constantly and closely just over our heads, I said to Capt. Julian: 'Well, it has been our boast that the Thirteenth New Hampshire never ran away, but many of them seem to have left us this time.' Pointing to our depleted ranks and to the front, Captain Julian quickly responded: 'You are mistaken, they are out yonder among the dead and wounded.'

"Comrades, I now ask your forgiveness for ever having expressed such a suspicion.

"That we were appreciated beyond other regiments in the First Division of the 18th Corps, and in the Third Division of the 24th Corps, the following incidents will show: First in the matter of details. It was an officer here and a soldier there, until at times we had less than a full Company of men present for duty in the whole Regiment with two or more of our Companies in command of Second Lieutenants. We supplied officers for both Brigade and Division staffs: Lieut. Murray, Lieut. Gafney, Capt. Curtis, Capt. Julian, Capt. Ladd, afterwards appointed by President Lincoln Asst. Commissary of Musters; Capt. Bruce, Capt. Staniels, Capt. Carter — appointed later Actg. Quarter-master by President Lincoln; Surgeon Twitchell appointed Surgeon of Volunteers; Surgeon Richardson appointed 24th Corps Surgeon at Appomattox; Quarter-master Morrison Brigade Quarter-master; Quarter-master Cheney Brigade Commissary; Asst. Surgeon Small detailed to attend the 10th N. H., and soon thereafter appointed Surgeon of that Regiment; Capt. Betton commanding the 81st New York; when Richmond was evacuated Lieut. McConney in charge of an Ambulance train; Capt. Durell, with Company C, detailed to command the advanced redoubt — Redoubt McConihe — on the Bermuda Hundred front, and to protect a force of green Pennsylvania troops; Capt. Durell soon placed on the staff of Gen. Graham, being succeeded at Redoubt McConihe by Lieut. Prescott; Asst. Surgeon Morrill promoted Surgeon of the 1st N. H. Heavy Artillery; Capt. Farr, wounded at Cold Harbor and past doing active service, detailed on General Court Martial; Capt. Wilson in charge of Division Ambulance Corps — and these are not all, — where is there a regiment with a list of details like this one?

"The Corps commander was continually growling at me, on paper, about our details; and asking where and what the details were; for whom Adjutant Taggard, our able clerk Cyrus G. Drew of B, and myself had to hunt up all this information at least twice a month — but never was a detailed man or officer returned to the Regiment. At last, when an aide-de-camp came to me and asked me to assign an officer as Brigade Commissary, I vigorously protested, and said to him: 'Go on, and detail the balance of us. If you will do that it will be all right; but if you do not do that, I will not designate an officer for that position, nor assent to having one of us assigned to that position, without making a vigorous protest to Gen. Ord.' The aide went away with a pretty good sized flea in his ear; and that was the last of it.

"Again when Gen. Gibbon issued orders for Wednesday and Saturday inspections, the best soldier in our Division received the first furlough granted under that order, eighteen regiments competing for this honor. Were we not proud when Sergeant Shattuck received that first furlough? We did not stop there; but of the fourteen furloughs granted under the order, the Thirteenth captured four.

"Again, in the winter of 1864–5, when Col. Cullen, commanding our Brigade, had resigned and was going home, there were left only Lt. Colonels in the Brigade; the Lt. Colonels of both the 98th and 139th New York regiments being my seniors in rank. While at Division Hdqrs. one evening, Gen. Devens tapped me on the shoulder, saying: 'Young man, if you had your Eagles, we should not be sending out of this Brigade for a commander.' So it seems, that if I had been the senior officer in our Brigade, when we entered Richmond, the unprecedented incident would have occurred, of a brigade and two of its regiments commanded by the officers of one regiment — our own old Thirteenth.

"When at Nashua on our return home, I was invited to spend the evening with Brevet Brig. Gen. Stevens. Said he to me: 'Can you not arrange it so that we can camp in my field to-night — I want so much to camp with the boys once again?' My response was: 'General, you forget that all our tents were turned over to Quarter-master Cochrane at Richmond; and we cannot go in the rain to spend the night in your field.' So you see I am not the only commander who was proud of the Thirteenth.

"Again, when we were ordered to the post of honor: to lead our Brigade in the final 'advance on Richmond;' its commander was made general officer of the day, and the first picket and guard in Richmond was posted by him; to be followed the next day by our Major Stoodley.

"We were very curious to learn the exact reason for this double detail and special honor. Now if any of you, Comrades at the Reunion, happen to have noses biggest at the end, and of the color of a blood-beet (as I know there are none of you in this predicament) — just put your finger tips in your ears while whoever reads this whispers to the rest: 'It was because we knew that neither of you ever touch spirituous liquors.'

"Well, boys, I can only say in conclusion that I am proud of you all your entire record through. Yours faithfully,

NORMAND SMITH.

HENRICO COUNTY, VA., March 29, 1887."


Lieut. Prescott also read a paper, written for the occasion by Lt. Col. Smith, concerning the ability of the Thirteenth to take care of itself, from which the following extracts are made:

"Scene first: A bleak hillside near Falmouth, Va., soon after the Battle of Fredericksburg, Dec. 13, 1862. A Regiment of as honest, sturdy and patriotic men as the Granite State was capable of producing, the men and officers, however, almost perfectly green so far as military affairs were concerned. The Colonel, Stevens, sick and half-crazed with the effects of malaria; the Lt. Colonel quite an invalid and always averse to assuming command; the Major, Storer. ordered to lay out a camp. The camp-ground so small we scarcely had room to walk between the terraced sleeping places of the men. Rations supplied: the stringiest kind of 'mule-beef,' rancid pork, hard bread full of maggots — many a time myself and the boys taking a stick, knocking these inhabitants out of a piece of a cracker of the proper size to bite off, and while masticating that piece, depopulating a space for another bite, and so on; the boxes of bread marked 'B. C.,' which the boys interpreted as meaning a vague prehistoric date of manufacture, preceding Anno Domini. Where in those days were the West Point officers whose duty it was to care for and instruct us? Quarreling, and in a state of general insubordination. We then roused and took care of ourselves; and had the credit of having the best quarters for men and officers in our Division.

"Well, the Ninth Corps was declared ready to mutiny, and was ordered to Newport News. There we had ample quarters, plenty of room in which to walk about — and in ten days what a change! Here and in the few succeeding months we had educated ourselves as soldiers, and were ready for the campaigns in the years which followed. We educated ourselves in the best ways to preserve our own lives and limbs, and in the best ways to make the lives and limbs of our enemy's men of the least possible use to them — except to run. Was there ever a regiment who, when under fire, could get under cover more quickly, or return the fire more sharply, than we? None. Did we ever fail our commanders anywhere? Never. Who could upon the shortest notice put up a finer camp than we? No one.

"Last scene — though I could have written many more — in the winter of 1864: Our line officers had long before this time got all accounts of picks, spades, shovels and axes off their returns, and did not intend to receipt for any more,[1] but we had to cut our fuel, and needed axes; and when the teams brought wood to our camp nearly every one of our men had a good axe to swing. So the First New York Engineer regiment — perhaps with reason — accused us of getting their axes. Now, boys, I understand that Gen. Devens is to be your guest at this Reunion; but his authority to put you under arrest has departed, and we will proceed with our story. Gen. Devens' first move in the matter of those axes was to order a search for axes in the camp of the Thirteenth. Was that search a success? Twice our camp was thoroughly searched, but never an axe was found.

"These two searches were not a success, and Gen. Devens tried another move. He ordered me to furnish one hundred men, with axes, for fatigue duty. I immediately complied, sending twelve axes. When the hundred men reported, they were ordered to return to our camp, but to leave their axes — every axe. Our men saw the point at once. They came back to our camp, and reported to me, directly, that they had left all their axes, twelve of them, at Gen. Devens' Headquarters — but had returned to our camp with thirteen!

"Were our men reprimanded? To you I leave the answer. Ever after that time, when I was called upon to furnish a detail of men with axes, I returned answer that we could not furnish the axes, for Gen. Devens had taken them away from us. What could the General do? We had a plenty of vim and snap, ready for anything favorable to the interests of the service, soldierly qualities that a commander always likes, and he could never catch any of us napping. But did we not all love him, and try to please him in every way? Indeed we did."

---

[1] Accounts of these tools were vexatious in the extreme. There was no such thing as theft in the soldiers' appropriating a few axes or other tools to use about camp; it was at the worst a mere minor breach of discipline, for the tools belonged to one soldier as much as to another, and the most of the exchanges and seizures, however annoying, were much regarded in the light of practical jokes. — S. M. T.

Col. George H. Patch was the next speaker; his remarks were brief, but during the meeting he took such notes as were required for the extended account of the Reunion furnished by him to the Boston Globe, of which he was the military editor.

Major Stoodley then read the following, which he had written for the occasion:

### "Our Place in the War.

" 'T is well to meet at times and bring anew
  Our loyal men and their great work to view;
  To live again those trying times and scenes
  That wear too oft the drapery of dreams;
  To clear away the dark and shadowy maze
  That time and distance gather o'er those days,
  And picture forth, in colors clear and true,
  The things these faithful men did dare and do.

" Go back with me and let us trace with care
  Those dark, eventful days when called to bear
  Our part in all the work then just began;
  The most stupendous work e'er wrought by man.
  The thunder of Treason's cannon, booming forth
  O'er fated Sumter, woke the slumbering North.
  Aroused at last, the North looked forth to see
  How best to meet the great emergency.
  The time for idle talk had passed away;
  To act was now the duty of the day.
  The grim old giant, War, his hand had shown,
  And we must now make manifest our own.
  In the first war-meetings one could trace
  An anxious heart in every honest face;
  Men said but little; but their words, well weighed,
  The deep, strong feelings of the heart betrayed.
  They saw the crisis, aye, and met it too,
  As only brave and loyal men can do:
  There for their bleeding country pledged their all.
  No unmeaning phrase, nor light affair, this ' All.'
  'T was everything by man held dear —
  His home, his friends, his health, his limbs, his life,
  All these he pledged, if needed in the strife.

" I looked with reverence on those noble few
  So ready for the work I too should do.
  I envied them what seemed a God-like stand,
  As proffered saviors of a dying land;

Or else as martyrs to the glorious cause
Of human freedom, just and righteous laws.
I honored them as never men before ;
I saw them standing at the very door
Of death for me and mine ; my heart was filled
With worship, and the moistened eyes distilled
The deep, embodied feelings of the soul
In glistening tears that would not brook control.
I wished their noble spirit had been mine,
That I might offer at my Country's shrine
All that I was, or ever hoped to be,
To aid her in her hour of agony.
These wishes were prophetic of the end,
As all true wishes must forever tend.
Whate'er our souls, in their deep longings, crave,
Will come at last to purify and save, —
For pangs and throes must always shadow forth
The nobler, purer, and the grander birth ;
And untold thanks are due those noble men,
For helping others to be ' born again ; '
And in that grand, unmatched, historic day,
Stand forth as men, in manhood's best array,
To follow in their footsteps and to share,
For God and Country, all that men could dare.

" Then came that first great battle — and defeat ;
The shattered columns and the long retreat ;
The list of killed and wounded, — how it fell,
With crushing weight, nor tongue nor pen can tell !
That day a mother, in our street, I met ;
And never, while life lasts, can I forget
The deep and bitter anguish of her tones,
As reeling, most distracted, she bemoans
Her young son's early death with voice of dread,
And wrings her hands, and cries : ' My boy is dead ! '
How many mothers then, and since, have felt
The crushing blows this fearful war has dealt !
Our land was filled with mourning as the grave
Received its thousands of the young and brave.

" The price was costly, but the glorious end
Will to all coming time the means commend.
Our Country's life, with all her future good,
Was cheaply purchased with the nation's blood.
Naught else less precious could make good its place,
Bequeath such treasures to the human race ;

For not to us alone shall these fruits be,
But every land shall share the legacy.
For, under God, what blesses us, we find
The seed to disenthrall and bless mankind.
The world itself shall know a better life
For what we suffered in that fearful strife.

" How little thought we then, we e'er could boast,
Our little band, of all the Union host,
The first to enter Richmond, and to show
The dear old Flag to the rebellious foe!
Not trailing in the dust, nor spit upon in scorn,
But highest honored; and by victor Veterans borne.
The Flag that was from thence, henceforth to be,
To them and us, the emblem of the free.
Its glorious stars, as pure as Heaven's own,
Reflect the justice that surrounds God's throne, —
Its consecration came anew in slavery's fall,
And now it means: ' Protection true to all.' "

Lieut. Staniels related the incident occurring at the surrender of Richmond, which he afterwards supplied for the History, and which is entered on page 568. He was followed by Sergeant Woods, Capt. Farr, Lieut. Thompson, Corporal Card, Lieut. Kittredge, and others, with very brief remarks, of which no notes were taken.

Adjutant Taggard then read a paper, written by him, as follows:
" The organization of the non-commissioned staff of the Thirteenth was:

| Rank. | Original. | Subsequent. |
|---|---|---|
| Sergt. Major. | William J. Ladd. | Charles C. Favor, James M. Hodgdon. |
| Qr-mr. Sergt. | Mortier L. Morrison. | Charles A. Ames. |
| Comm. Sergt. | George H. Taggard. | George W. Ferguson, George Burns. |
| Hosp. Steward. | J. J. Whittemore. | R. B. Prescott, D. W. Butterfield. |
| Prin. Musician. | C. C. Hall. | Manson S. Brown. |

" In the limited time allotted I can hardly do justice to these men, but am very glad of an opportunity to give expression to the respect and esteem with which I remember them. I will speak of them in the following order.

" C. C. Hall was a quiet, unassuming, conscientious man, whose greatest anxiety was lest he should not discharge his whole duty; and still his duties were so done as to secure for him the respect and good will of the men under his command, and the cordial commendation of his superior officers. He had been a Corporal in Company F, and was promoted for merit. His death in the service, on Jan. 22, 1865, was deplored by all his comrades.

" Manson S. Brown, who carried the knapsack containing the medical supplies, provided for the Thirteenth while marching or fighting, was a man whose physique was such as to make him our beau-ideal of a 'Drum Major,' as seen in the volunteer militia of ante-bellum days. His every qualification enabled him to fill the position chock-full; and we shall never forget his genial face and cheerful voice.

"John J. Whittemore was a whole-souled, jovial fellow, who made the life of every company, and was a prime favorite with all. An experienced Pharmacist he bid fair to be a most valuable factor in the medical department; but his physical system was not equal to the changed conditions, and the hard racket of army life. An early and very severe sickness was soon followed by his discharge for disability. His uprightness of character, and business ability, coupled with his genial spirit, secured for him a reasonable success in business, and great popularity in social life. He died several years ago, mourned by his friends and lamented by all.

"Daniel W. Butterfield, the last to hold the position, was in the hospital corps during his whole term of service. He had a slight limp in his gait — and a more pronounced one in his speech when laboring under excitement. There was never discovered any halt, however, in his efforts to smooth the feverish pillow or to relieve the aching wound of his unfortunate comrade. He discharged all his duties with the full measure of his ability, and for his kindness to them he will be long remembered by his comrades in the Regiment. He came home with us, and filled an honorable position in the community where he resided; but the hardships of the service resulted in ruined health and a broken constitution. He ultimately found quarters in the Soldiers' Home, at Hampton, Va., where he was finally mustered out, and now is with the majority.

"George Burns was the last to hold the position of Commissary Sergeant. His round, cheery face, and frank, cordial manners made a loud call, upon all who met him, for their friendship. His association with the boys had given him a complete knowledge of their wants. His generous nature was in sympathy with them; his energy and force of character was always exerted in their behalf, and through his efforts I think they always received their full share of the best of the supplies. He came home with us, and I hope may live long and prosper.

"George W. Ferguson, the immediate successor of Burns, was a man whose character and manners were a happy medium between 'grave and gay,' always dignified, always cheerful, his companionship a pleasure, his influence good. He earned his higher promotion by faithful services. He also has gone to answer the Roll-call above; his memory is sacred in the hearts of widow and children, and we to-day mingle our tears with theirs.

"Charles A. Ames was a scholarly young man, in whose bosom the fires of patriotism burned so brightly that the peril of his country drew him from the fields of learning to the fields of strife. He left college, his books, and the hope of success in the paths of peace for a suit of blue, scant rations, a bed on the ground, a knapsack, a gun, and a fight. The responsible duties of the position he was called to fill were faithfully, ably and well done. He has since the war turned his attention, with success, to milling and mining in the far West.

"James M. Hodgdon was tall and slim, with a quick, active step and movement, and the air of a man born to command. We all remember his incisive voice, and the snap with which he brought the color-guard into line for Dress-parade. We remember, too, his cheerful, happy spirit and manner — a detail for fatigue or picket lost half its disagreeables by the way in which he made it, and if the boys growled the sound of the growl was lost in a laugh. Where his post of duty was, there we always found him. That he was brave goes without saying. Look him in the face, and you will see, in the track there made by the rebel bullet, that he has faced even death without flinching. The duties that he so faithfully did, the suffering he has so patiently endured, and the scar he so honorably wears, prove him the hero of the Non-commissioned staff.

"Charles C. Favor preceded Hodgdon. He had apparently been favored with the influences of polite society, and had received such impress therefrom that he could not, or did not, readily become assimilated with the unconventional surroundings of camp and army life. With a somewhat haughty manner it was but natural that he should only slightly attract men to himself. He probably did not enjoy his army associations and experience. He early received a commission, and after a limited service returned to civil life, and died many years ago.

"William J. Ladd came among us in an elegant uniform, and had an air of nicety about him that led some of us to be a little shy of him for a while, but we soon learned that he was every inch a soldier, cordial, gentlemanly and a good fellow. His military instincts and qualities soon gained him a commission; his abilities and bravery won rapid and merited promotion. The scars he wears prove his fidelity and courage; they are his badges of service, and we all heartily unite to do him honor.

"Mortier L. Morrison had an individuality all his own; was large of frame, strong of limb, and possessed great force of character; and an intimate and close acquaintance with him developed the fact that he had a very large heart, and as tender as a woman's; while the strength and firmness of his friendship was only equaled by the strength and firmness of his character. He was early promoted to regimental Quarter-master, and every officer and man will attest the remarkable energy and success with which he discharged his arduous duties. His reputation and popularity were not confined to the Regiment and Brigade in which we served, but were universal, and were to us all a source of pride.

"Royal B. Prescott was probably the most scholarly man on the staff, at any rate he was undeniably the most studious. Many and many an hour that the rest of us spent in 'simple sociability,' he spent in poring over books on flesh and bones. Nor were his studies confined to medical science, but extended to literature and art. We well remember how, drawing upon a good memory, he would fling at us quotations from the highest English authors — and, when occasion demanded, a little Latin or Dutch.

"The refinement of his nature found illustration in his quarters, order being everywhere visible, and such frequent little artistic touches of taste as could be wrenched from his surroundings.

"He studied 'Casey,' too, exhaustively. A commission finally came as a reward for his faithful services; but while as an officer and soldier he always maintained the honor of his commission, his heart was with the hospital department, and his sympathies were with the sick and suffering, among whom he had ministered so long and so well. In his studies and practical experiences while in the Thirteenth, he laid the foundation of his medical profession, which to-day he so nobly adorns.

"George H. Taggard needs but little said of him, you all know him. But there was a time when he was a stranger among you; it was then while on the march from Aquia Creek to Fredericksburg that Lewis Silver, the teamster, mistook him for an army Chaplain — he saw his mistake later. The issuing of rations in the streets of Fredericksburg he never recalls without a smile, and the persistency with which he urged the men to put a good supply of tea in their haversacks; telling them they had started for Richmond, and it was probably their last chance to obtain any tea until they got there.

"Yes, we had started for Richmond, but we took a round-about route, and were many long months in traveling it; and very many of our good fellows became weary and worn, and fell out by the way, giving up themselves and their lives to make it possible for some few of us to reach that goal; and we here to-day record our meed of affection and honor for the memory of the men in the ranks of the Thirteenth, and in the army, who dared, and were glad 'to do and to die' for their country.

"Twice during his term of service he confesses to having been considerably scared. Once when the 'bread riot' arose in the Thirteenth while we were in the 'Pines' camp at Getty's Station in 1863. He had not had much experience with hungry soldiers, and when the tumult was at its height, he thought war had begun in earnest, and did not know but he was to be 'hanged, drawn and quartered.' As he looks back upon the affair, he guesses the Colonel was in quite as much danger as himself.

"The next time was during the rebel Coehorn mortar shelling, on the evening of the day when we captured Fort Harrison. He was Acting Adjutant of the Thirteenth then. As he moved along the line to the right the shells came thickest there; going to the left the shells were still thicker there; again arriving at the right he found the fire redoubled and concentrated there — each particular shell with its little tail of fire seeming to be aimed directly at his head. Indifference, however, soon seized him, as the danger, though made more terrible by our forced inaction, seemed to be about as great in one place as in another, and he remained on the right and received no harm.

"As a body the non-commissioned staff of the Thirteenth comprised a set of men of more than ordinary intelligence, education and character, comparing very favorably with the staff of any regiment we met with in the service and one which any Colonel might reasonably be proud to have under his command."

The expenses of the Reunion, itself, aside from individual traveling expenses, were a total of above four hundred and fifty dollars. In addition to this, and on his personal account, as a fitting incident to the Reunion, though at a later date, Asst. Surgeon Sullivan presented to John A. Andrew Post, G. A. R., of Boston, the colored cut of the Thirteenth's battle-flags richly and appropriately framed, the Post acknowledging the gift in most complimentary terms.

The meeting extended a vote of thanks to the committee — Sullivan, Woods and Wentworth — who had so ably and acceptably managed the entire affair; after which at about 6 p. m. the meeting closed with a song and cheers. No incident occurred to mar the enjoyments of the Veterans or their distinguished guests, — and this was unanimously voted the best Reunion ever held by the Thirteenth Regiment.

These Veterans now part temporarily, with cheerful word, benison and outlook and with high hope and confident step, to march — and may weather be fair, roads broad, grades rising, stages easy, reunions many, rations full, bivouacs merry, pay-day frequent and the march be long — to march through their own good land to that greatest and best of all countries; where slavery is not, conspiracy unknown, secession most undesirable, rebellion without a place, and war an impossibility though its heroes assemble, but where union, peace and freedom abide without discord, interruption or an end.

# INDEX.

A. — Company. 63, 126, 127, 129, 139, 240, 281, 284, 496.
Abbott, Henry L., Col. 323, 537.
Abbott, Joseph C., Col. 315.
Alexander, C. S. A. Lt. Col. 72, 86.
Allerson, Albert. 349.
Alexandria, Va. 11, 18, 19, 21, 24.
Ames, Charles A., Qr.-mr. Sergeant. 199, 704.
Ames, J. H. 527.
Ames, Adelbert, Gen. 338, 517.
Anderson, R. H., C. S. A. Gen. 483.
Andersonville, Ga. 305, 453.
Andrew, John A., Gov. of Mass. 206, 595.
Annapolis, Md. 440.
Angell, Jesse F., Major. 285.
Antietam, Va. 6.
Appomattox. 587, 593.
Aquia Creek, Va. 31, 33, 34, 96, 102, 106, 108, 109.
Arlington Heights, Va. 9, 13.
Arms, Thirteenth. 6, 497, 543.
Army of the Potomac. 21, 34, 87, 96, 97, 103, 254, 406, 422, 427, 612.
Army of the James. 254, 422, 427, 459, 515.
Armies of Grant and Sherman. 597, 599.
Atkins, John. 585.
Ayletts, Va. 178.
Ayling, Augustus D., Adj't. Gen. N. H. 390, 604, 687 et seq.

B — Company. 31, 32, 38, 39, 41, 66, 67, 70, 79, 81, 96, 190, 199, 207, 214, 240, 242, 245, 264, 265, 292, 297, 309, 440.
Bamberger, William W., Lt. Col. 549, 555 et seq.
Band, Thirteenth. 10, 12, 21, 22, 24, 63, 69, 80, 81, 135, 179, 183, 210, 223, 249, 369, 370, 422, 428, 590, 601, 602, 624. Roster of, 625, 628.
Baltimore, Md. 9, 440.
Bannister, George H. (of H). 503.
Batchellor, Charles W. (of D), Sergeant. 24, 72, 129, 215, 224, 282.
Barksdale, William, C. S. A. Gen. 39, 85, 87.
Barlow, Francis C., Gen. 366.
Barker, Theodore E., Lt. Col. 550.
Baker, Savage. 229, 243.
Barnabee, D. Webster (of K). 191, 237, 687 et seq.

Barnabee, Henry C. (Brother of above — Actor). 237.
Barney, Val. G., Lt. Col. 549.
Bassett, Washington. 337, 338.
Beatty, , C. S. A. Major, 388, 389.
Beasley, , Mr. 397, 410.
Betton, Matthew T., Captain. 67, 68, 143, 235, 239, 240, 281, 311, 394, 450, 453, 489, 517, 534, 536, 541, 549, 575 et seq., 580 et seq., 595, 602, 626, 698 et seq.
Belle Isle — Prison. 601 et seq.
Beauregard, G. T., C. S. A. Gen. 262, 293 et seq., 312, 339, 407.
Birney, David B., Gen. 430, 459 et seq., 524, 546.
Big Bethel, Va. 181.
Blake, Aaron K. (of A). 364.
Black, John C., Gen. 686.
Bliss, George N., Capt. 501.
Bodge, Daniel W. (of B), Color Sergeant. 70, 363, 390, 394, 463 et seq.
Bodge, George E. (of B). 264.
Boutwell, Nathan B., Adjutant. 7, 123, 175, 222, 246, 249, 280, 324, 343, 380, 384, 394, 408, 417, 423, 538, 602, 687 et seq.
Bowers, George, Lieut. Colonel. 8, 33, 56, 94, 100, 106, 109, 113, 121, 122, 139, 141, 147, 165, 166, 167, 530, 612, 697 et seq.
Bowen, George K., Lt. Col. 550.
Booth, J. Wilkes. 589.
Boodry, Augustus (of G). 444.
Bounty. 5, 18.
Boston, Mass. 590, 609.
Brooks, Joseph C., Major. 578.
Brooks Station, Va. 34.
Brooks, W. H. F., Maj. Gen. 252, 291 et seq., 338 et seq., 345, 383 et seq.
Brabble, E. C., C. S. A. Col. 320.
Brown, Manson S. (of C). 31, 184, 262, 621, 687 et seq.
Brown, James T., Lt. Col. 550.
Brown, John C. (of E). 'Ambulance Brown.' 178, 395 et seq., 405.
Brown, John, Song of. 235.
Bradley, Charles O., Captain. 2, 41, 121, 170, 221, 277, 419, 420, 421.
Bratton, John, C. S. A. Gen. 482.
Bright, John. 213.
Bruce, George A., Captain. 228, 249, 430, 466, 578 et seq., 609, 614, 687 et seq.
Bruce, G. (of D). 450.
Bush, Charles, 32.

Bullard, John A. (of G). 230.
Buzzell, Lewis H., Captain. 4, 121, 137, 144, 147, 153, 157, 232.
Burkesville, Va. 585.
Bull Run, Va. 5, 442.
Burnside, Ambrose E., Maj. Gen. 20, 22, 24, 34, 36, 39, 40, 71, 72, 74, 75, 77, 78, 79, 83, 87, 96, 97, 102, 103, 404, 691 et seq.
Burbank, James M. 613.
Burns, John (of A). 285.
Burns, W. W., Gen. 83.
Burns, George (of C), Sergeant. 284, 704.
Bunting, Edward T. 196.
Butler, Benjamin F., Maj. Gen. 216, 253 et seq., 263 et seq., 312, 333, 407, 440, 447, 465, 494, 517, 519, 524, 599, 615.
Burnham, Hiram, Brig. Gen. 252, 254 et seq., 291 et seq., 326, 342, 362 et seq., 386, 388, 398, 424, 436, 466 et seq., 479, 486, 614.
Burnham, W. G. (of I), Sergeant. 288, 292.
Butterfield, Daniel W. 621, 704.

C — Company. 2, 38, 41, 53, 70, 79, 80, 146, 176, 212, 240, 281, 284, 448, 458, 487, 512, 517, 527, 554, 614.
Caswell, James M. (Band). 687.
Canby, E. R. S., Gen. 595, 600.
Casey, Silas, Maj. Gen. 9, 11, 13, 14, 18, 19, 20, 500, 630.
Catlett, , C. S. A., Capt. 501.
Carter, Buel C., Captain. 25, 70, 81, 203, 240, 311, 543, 613, 688 et seq.
Carter, Sanborn B. 613.
Carr, J. B., Gen. 614.
Carr, William D. (of G). 282.
'Carleton' — C. C. Coffin. 58, 74, 576 et seq.
Capen, Levi (of B). 294.
Centreville, Va. 11, 19, 442.
Chapman, Charles Henry, Lieut. 535.
Chapman, Nathan D., Lieut. 619, 687 et seq.
Chapman, Charles F. (of E), Sergeant. 38, 191, 215, 303, 304, 327.
Charleston, S. C. 534.
Chuckatuck, Va. 144.
Chichester, N. H. 2.
Churchill, Henry, Lieutenant. 126, 260, 262, 284 et seq., 426, 448, 511, 514, 538, 688 et seq.
Cheney, Person C., Quarter-master. 26, 87, 102, 103, 190, 192, 527, 686 et seq.
Childrey, J. K. 460 et seq.
Christian Commission. 449.
Childs, Mr. and Miss. 28.
City Point, Va. 438.
Clark, , Capt. 269, 398, 475.
Clingman, , C. S. A. Gen. 311, 482.
Clay, Cecil. Capt. 550.
Coitt, Charles M., Capt. 386, 498.
Corse, M. D., C. S. A. Gen. 311.
Cold Harbor, Va. 335 et seq.
Copp, George N. (of B). 228.

Coburn, Charles R. (of D). 464.
Cochrane, W. H. D., Lt. Col. 687 et seq.
Colquitt, , C. S. A. Gen. 484.
Contrabands — Negroes. 599.
Copperheads. 452.
Cobb, T. R. R., C. S. A. Gen. 71.
Cox, Henry. 460 et seq. 498.
Cooper, Wm. M. 7, 8.
Cooper, Wm. R. S. 7, 8.
Couch, D. N., Maj. Gen. 22, 83.
Concord, N. H. 1, 6, 7, 10, 19, 610.
Coffin, Nathaniel J., Lieutenant. 109, 169.
Corcoran, Michael, Brig. Gen. 118, 127, 129.
Coughlin, John, Lt. Col. 115, 227, 268, 273, 294, 299, 428.
Council, , C. S. A. Lt. Col. 388, 389.
Colors of Thirteenth. 6, 70, 74, 361, 393, 394, 462 et seq., 519, 565 et seq., 574.
Critchley, William, Jr. (Band). 246, 428, 687 et seq.
Crosby, Hiram B., Major. 80.
Crowley, Timothy B., Capt. 507.
Cullen, Edgar M., Col. 502 et seq., 525, 545, 568, 698.
Cummings, Capt. 105.
Custer, George A., Gen. 536, 586.
Curtis, Charles H., Captain. 2, 70, 121, 144, 146, 168, 176, 245, 277, 483, 509, 592, 617, 687 et seq.

D — Company. 1, 2, 6, 31, 72, 190, 199, 207, 214, 240, 242, 245, 281, 282, 343, 356, 466, 613.
Dahlgren, Ulric, Col. 571.
Dandy, George B., Col. 547, 551.
Dalton, E. B., Surgeon. 233.
Davis, Gilman (of A). 261.
Davis, Van R. (of H). 573.
Dawson, T. W. 550.
Davis, Jefferson, President C. S. A. 138, 291, 452, 486, 492, 573 et seq., 581, 592, 599.
Devin, Thomas C., Gen. 536.
Derby, Isaac W., Sergeant. 442.
Derrom, Andrew, Col. 34, 136, 153.
De Peyster, Johnston, Lieut. 576.
Devens, Charles, Maj. Gen. 338 et seq., 359, 472, 497, 501, 532, 547, 548, 549, 567 et seq., 597, 601, 610, 614, 687 et seq.
Defenses of Washington. 18.
Dickerman, Joseph W. (of C). 38.
Dix, John A., Maj. Gen. 130 et seq., 170, 184.
Dix, Miss Dorothea. 450.
Dodge, Elisha E., Captain. 39, 59, 66, 67, 121, 190, 218, 220, 222, 242, 245, 278, 310, 333, 394, 408, 409, 417.
Donohoe, Michael T., Brig. Gen. 34, 62, 129, 137, 168, 174, 179, 186, 459 et seq., 479, 549, 607, 608, 610, 687 et seq.
Dominy, Levi T., Lt. Col. 549.
Downes, Amasa (of B). 70.
Drew, Cyrus G. (of B). 136, 511, 605, 698.
Durell, James M., Captain. 18, 70, 109, 170, 185, 207, 222, 228, 245, 284, 327,

## INDEX. 711

345, 358, 361, 427, 448, 449, 458, 527, 605, 614, 687 et seq.
Dustin, Jonathan, Lieutenant. 13, 18, 311, 451, 491, 617.
Duncklee, William R. 70.
Durham, N. H. 238.
Dutch Gap Canal. 497, 522.
Dutton, Arthur H., Col. 35, 100, 118, 122, 130, 160, 179, 329, 614.
Dunlop, , Mr. 274.
Dyer, G. W., Major. 168.

E — Company. 1, 2, 3, 4, 32, 39, 41, 53, 66, 88, 89, 137, 139, 140, 141, 176, 185, 193, 240, 264, 265, 279, 300 et seq., 384, 390, 396, 511.
Early, Jubal A., C. S. A. Gen. 511.
Elmira, N. Y. 277, 446.
Elder, , Capt. 477.
Emory, J. C, Asst. Surgeon. 583, 602.
England, 5.
Endicott, William C. 630.
Ewell, R. S., C. S. A. Gen. 507, 548.
Exeter, N. H. 1, 2, 442, 530.

F — Company. 15, 86, 232, 236, 250, 252, 257, 264, 448, 602, 617, 703.
Farr, George, Captain. 1, 190, 233, 240, 242, 311, 343, 346, 466, 511, 533, 605, 612, 687 et seq.
Fairfax Seminary, Va. 9, 18, 20, 25, 34, 96.
Falls Church, Va. 11, 12, 13, 23.
Fairchild, H. S., Col. 34, 504.
Falmouth, Va. 86.
Farragut, David G., Admiral. 493, 530.
Favor, C. C., Lieutenant. 311, 450, 703 et seq.
Ferguson, George W., Lieutenant. 427, 448, 450, 602, 704.
Ferguson, Robert. 26.
Field, C. W., C. S. A. Gen. 339, 481, 507.
Flanders, Josiah C. (of A). 286.
—Forbush, Gustavus A., Captain. 4, 18, 41, 96, 102, 121, 134, 153, 188, 194, 232, 239, 250, 425, 448, 465 et seq., 479, 489.
Folsom, James W. (of E). 307.
Foye, John H. (of E). 146
Foster, John G., Maj. Gen. 186, 216, 546.
Fowler, H. B., Surgeon. 324, 522.
Follett, F. M., Capt. 398, 465.
Forrester, Richard, G. 559 et seq.
France. 4.
Franklin, W. B., Maj. Gen. 21, 83, 101, 103.
French, Wm. H., Gen. 50, 86.
French, Warren S. (of E). 202.
Fredericksburg, Va. 21, 36 et seq., 40, 99, 113, 380, 456.
Friend, Charles. 384, 397, 404, 422.
Friend, Rev. Charles. 282 et seq.
Fuller, Arthur B., Chaplain. 691.

G — Company. 1, 2, 3, 6, 41, 93, 100, 126,

127, 131, 212, 264, 319, 358, 409, 444, 448, 616, 618.
Gafney, Charles B., Captain. 50, 123, 292, 297, 368, 394, 408, 417, 426, 428, 456, 613, 697 et seq.
Gault, William H. (of H). 558 et seq.
Gary, , C. S. A. Gen. 507, 575.
Garland, George E. (of E). 86.
Gaines' Mill, Va. 350 et seq.
Getty, George W., Maj. Gen. 34, 46 et seq., 54, 63, 73, 74, 75, 82, 83, 84, 85, 86, 117, 124, 127 et seq., 162, 170, 229, 422, 614.
Gettysburg, Pa. 522.
Gerrish, Charles F. (of E). 130.
Gilman, Austin (of D). 291.
Gilkey, H. B. (of H). 315.
Gilmore, Lucius. 185.
Gilmore, Q. A., Maj. Gen. 254, 279 et seq., 330, 430.
Gilmore, Joseph A., Gov. N. H. 602, 612.
Gibbs, John F. (of E). 104, 121, 138, 388, 486.
Gibbon, John, Maj. Gen. 450, 524, 526, 549, 584 et seq., 603, 604, 698.
Glenville, James L. (of D). 269.
Glidden, Edwin H. (of A). 284.
Goss, Enoch W., Captain. 67, 115, 123, 243, 279, 286, 288, 292, 329, 342, 351, 387 et seq., 437, 448, 452, 482 et seq., 501 et seq., 507.
Goldsmith, George E. (of A). 285.
Gove, Miss R. S., Hospital Nurse. 446.
Grant, Ulysses S., Lieut. General. 122, 245, 278, 333 et seq., 355, 358, 359, 368, 374, 402, 404, 406, 413, 450, 451, 467, 471, 493, 497, 511, 513, 520, 522, 541, 544, 546, 551, 565 et seq., 582 et seq., 592, 615, 633, 634.
Grant, Mr. 278.
Grantman, William, Lieut. Colonel. 63, 121, 127, 172, 185, 214, 241, 247, 254, 310, 356, 384, 408, 409, 427, 429, 491, 495, 612, 687 et seq.
Graham, C. K., Gen. 528, 615 et seq., 698.
Green, Charles W. (of B). 31, 81, 228.
Greeley, Horace, Hon. 359, 694.
Guild, , Lieut. 492.

H — Company. 79, 126, 127, 108, 212, 234, 240, 249, 268, 292, 365, 3.6, 448, 465, 548.
Hall, Hubbard W., Captain. 13, 232, 252, 284, 466, 537, 552, 602, 687 et seq.
Hall, Miss Maria M. C., Directress of Hospital. 449, 450, 493.
Hall, C. C., Principal Musician. 703.
Hancock, W. S., Gen. 357, 374, 404, 407.
Hawkins, Rush C., Col. 34, 63, 73, 75, 82, 83, 84.
Hare, John. 410 et seq., 446.
Harrigan, Thomas (of E). 310.
Harris, C. C., Capt. 127.

# 712 INDEX.

Harland, Edward, Col. 34, 56, 63, 73, 82, 83, 84, 130.
Hardy, Milton H., Lieutenant. 537, 602, 618.
Harmon, George H. (of A). 280.
Harmon, John (of K). 67.
Hanson, John K. A. (of K). 67.
Haines, John P. (of C). 205, 605.
Harvey, John H. (of E). 297.
Hanou, Andrew (of H). 223, 417.
Hanson, Lewis F. (10th N. H.). 475.
Halleck, H. W., Maj. Gen. 245, 278, 471.
Hampton, Va. 180, 409.
Hagood, J. R., C. S. A. Gen. 262, 311.
Heath, Charles (of H). 269.
Heckman, Charles A., Brig. Gen. 229, 258, 293, 298, 459 et seq., 504.
Head, Natt, Adjt. Gen. N. H. 23.
Henley, R. L., C. S. A. Major. 54, 71, 73.
Henry, Guy V., Col. 345 et seq.
Herbert, Rev. Mr. 449.
Hinks, E. W., Gen. 256, 382 et seq.
Hinds, George W., Capt. 550.
Hill, D. H., C. S. A. Gen. 261.
Howard, Henry (of E). 31, 32, 211.
Hogan, David (of E). 106.
Hodgdon, James M., Sergeant Major. 181, 187, 222, 310, 381, 384, 418, 446, 464 et seq., 483, 486, 490, 513, 687 et seq.
Holmes, Albe, Lieutenant. 113, 123, 168, 440.
Holmes, Charles, Capt. 3.
Hoke, R. F., C. S. A. Gen. 339, 481, 523.
Hooker, Joseph, Maj. Gen. 18, 21, 22, 46, 54, 83, 84, 101, 103, 172, 495.
Hospital, Chesapeake — Sketches at. (405 –7), 408, 409, 417, 418, 419, 421, 423, 424, 426, 427, 428, 429, 431, 435, 436, 439, 440.
Hospital, Annapolis — Sketches at. 440, 441, 443, 445, 446, 447, 448, 449, 450, 451, 452, 454, 490, 491, 493, 494.
Humphreys, A. A., Maj. Gen. 74, 308, 311, 367, 374, 376, 402, 434, 466 et seq., 504, 576 et seq.
Hubbard, George H., Surgeon. 443.
Hutchins, George W. (of A). 291.
Huntoon, Ely (of D). 291.

I — Company. 4, 70, 115, 240, 286, 292, 358, 448, 548, 617.

Jardine, Edward, Major. 77.
Jenness, Albion J. (of E). 28, 88, 146, 169.
Jenkins, Edward. 350.
Jersey City, N. J. 7.
Jones, George G., Chaplain. 10, 19, 94, 107, 112, 122, 230, 246, 310, 324, 524.
Jones, Joseph A. (of E). 106.
Johnson, G. W. (of I). 501.
Johnson, Bushrod, C. S. A. Gen. 307, 310, 311.
Johnson, Daniel (of H). 525.
Johnson, Andrew. 582.
Johnston, Joseph E., C. S. A. Gen. 589, 594.

Jordan, Mr. 398.
Julian, George N., Captain. 1, 24, 32, 39, 59, 62, 65, 89, 93, 94, 121, 141, 147, 163, 170, 188, 203, 207, 209, 223, 239, 264, 279, 283, 295, 300 et seq., 307, 348, 361, 364, 371, 373, 384, 387 et seq., 390, 401, 426, 430, 433, 453, 513, 529, 687 et seq.
Julian, Luke. 513.

K — Company. 31, 32, 67, 68, 87, 240, 278, 279, 417, 548, 618, 625.
Kautz, A. V., Maj. Gen. 73, 253, 256, 269, 333, 383 et seq., 417, 459 et seq. 492, 543.
Kershaw, J. B., C. S. A. Gen. 71, 339.
Keener, David S., Lieut. 556 et seq.
Keyes, E. D., Gen. 170.
Keine, William, Col. 173.
Kelley, Warren M., Capt. 550.
Kittredge, Charles M., Lieutenant. 38, 66, 67, 132, 137, 162, 194, 687 et seq.
Kimball, Edgar A., Lt. Col. 34, 127.
Kimball, W. G. C. 390.
Kimball, George B. (of H). 397.
Kilburn, Edward, Lieutenant. 1, 103, 612.
King William Court House, Va. 178, 179.
Kilpatrick, Judson, Gen. 239.
Kreutzer, Lt. Col. 534, 539, 549.
Kuse, O., Col. 236.

Ladd, William J., Captain. 116, 414, 466, 578 et seq., 606, 618, 625, 687 et seq.
Lamson, Joseph F. (of I). 291.
Langdon, Loomis L., Capt. 576.
Lee, W. H., C. S. A. Gen. 172.
Lee, Fitz-Hugh, C. S. A. Gen. 422.
Lee, S. P., Rear Admiral. 256, 262.
Lee, Robert E., C. S. A. Gen. 6, 9, 23, 24, 35, 36, 71, 73, 87, 253, 339, 357, 366 et seq., 402, 407, 408, 427, 481, 486, 492, 500 et seq., 520, 546, 582 et seq., 592, 615.
Leathers, Charles (of F). 86.
Leatz, Lieut. 454.
Lincoln, Abraham, President. 1, 21, 122, 129, 137, 169, 231, 495, 510, 546, 547, 575 et seq., 589 et seq., 605.
Lincoln, Robert T., Hon. 630.
Littleton, N. H. 1, 2.
Liverpool Point, Md. 25, 31.
Libby Prison. 453, 501, 563, 580 et seq., 595, 612, 695 et seq.
Lossing, B. J., Historian. 84, 260, 359, 466.
Long Bridge, Va. 9, 12, 14, 17, 18, 21, 25.
Low, Nathaniel, Jr. 616.
Lowe, Prof., 'Balloonist.' 89, 93, 100, 106.
Longstreet, James, C. S. A. Gen. 71, 83, 85, 117, 126 et seq., 145, 339, 488, 551.
Long, George W. (of E). 159, 221.

## INDEX.                                                          713

Luey, William B. (of H).   116, 117, 139, 162, 195, 210, 341, 366.
Lull, Charles A., Drummer.   122.
Lynch, Henry (of D).   291.

Martindale, John H., Gen.   339, 359, 383 et seq.
Mawby, John H. (of K).   489.
Madden, James, Capt., 10th N. H.   397, 398.
Malvern Hill, Va.   5.
Manning, J. M., Rev.   591.
Manchester, N. H.   7, 610.
Manchester, Va.   7, 593.
Maryland.   25 et seq.
Maryland, My Maryland, Song.   25, 529.
Marblehead, Mass.   94.
Marston, Gilman, Maj. Gen.   322, 359, 361, 365, 499 et seq., 614.
Marsh, Otis R. (of I).   508.
Marshall, George, Major.   348.
Mack, Oscar A., Col.   200.
Mayor of Richmond.   554 et seq.
Manchaug, Mass.   483.
McCarty, John (of D).   282.
McClellan, George B., Maj. Gen.   21, 172, 457, 493, 500, 510.
McClellan, Ely, Surgeon.   409, 423, 440.
McGaffrey, Charles (of I).   350.
McMann, Owen (of E).   305.
McConney, William H., Lieutenant.   80, 146, 698 et seq.
McDaniels, David.   606.
McKenzie, R. S., Gen.   546.
McLaws, Lafayette, C. S. A. Gen.   71, 72, 80, 483.
McLaughlin, Adjutant.   448.
Merrimac, C. S. A. war-ship.   113, 116.
Merriman, Major.   386.
Merritt, Wesley, Gen.   536.
Meade, George G., Maj. Gen.   172, 253, 338 et seq., 355 et seq., 374, 406, 493, 517.
Meserve, Nathaniel F. (of A).   282, 284.
Mehal, Jacob (of E), Corporal.   295.
Michler, N., Gen.   379, 464.
Mitchell, Peter (of K), Corporal.   389, 419.
Miller, Theodore, Major.   549, 580.
Morris, James (of E).   373.
Morrison, James R. (of K), Sergeant.   389, 417, 419.
Morrison, Mortier L., Quarter-master.   64, 193, 243, 290, 311, 320, 324, 417, 448, 453, 503, 514, 535, 539, 541, 592, 600, 602, 687 et seq.
Morrison, A. P.   527.
Mount Vernon, Va.   26, 449.
Montague, Edgar B., C. S. A. Col.   54.
Monitor, U. S. war-ship.   113, 116.
Morton, Oliver H., Governor of Indiana.   206.
Morrill, Ezekiel, Asst. Surgeon.   208, 235, 241, 311, 361, 452, 498, 509, 511, 620.
Morrell, Gen.   74.
Morrill, H. T.   592.

Mooney, James (of D).   280.
Morrow, Jerry (of H).   291.
Mosby, C., C. S. A. Col.   590, 592.
Munn, Surgeon.   522.
Murphy, Jeremiah (of E).   366.
Murray, Henry H., Lieutenant.   145, 168, 170, 199, 207, 234, 389, 436, 501 et seq., 534, 697 et seq.

Naglee, Maj. Gen.   195, 201.
Nashua, N. H.   4, 7, 610.
New Market, N. H.   2.
New England.   2, 6, 10, 451.
New Berne, N. C.   126, 235.
Newport News, Va.   111.
New Kent Court House, Va.   179.
Newton, Erastus (of I).   462.
Nims, Ormand F., Capt.   530.
Nichols, Col.   591.
Norfolk, Va.   114, 117.

Oliver, Lucius C., Lieutenant.   244, 308, 453, 537.
Oliver, Robert (of C).   280.
Old John Brown, Song.   106, 596.
Orange Court House, Va.   95.
Ord, E. O. C., Gen.   427, 450, 466 et seq., 498, 513, 514, 524, 546, 579, 583 et seq., 603, 698.
Osborn, Daniel M. (of G).   488.

Parker, Edward, Lieutenant.   164.
Palmer, John C. (of C).   512.
Partridge, Lieut.   453.
Pace, Alexander.   410 et seq.
Patrick,        , Gen. Provost Marshal General.   23, 563 et seq., 604.
Patterson, A. J., Rev.   329, 417.
Patterson, J. N., Lt. Col.   550.
Patch, George H., Col.   687 et seq.
Parke, John G., Gen.   631.
Paul, Henry S. (of K).   67, 421, 522.
Pearsons, Henry H., Lt. Col.   76, 105.
Penrose, Wm. H., Lieut.   13, 17.
Peck, John A., Gen.   124, 127 et seq., 153, 235.
Peterboro, N. H.   1.
Phisterer, Frederick, Capt.   84, 379.
Philadelphia, Pa.   7.
Piscataway, Md.   26.
Pinkham, John (of E), Sergeant.   136, 305.
Pickett, George E., C. S. A. Gen.   262, 339, 360, 512, 587.
Pittsburg Landing, Tenn.   199.
Pleasants, Lt. Col.   431, 439.
Pleasant Valley, Md.   35.
Place, Jesse W. (of D).   129.
Porter, Horace, Gen.   587.
Pollock, John, Capt.   550.
Pomroy, George H. (of H).   534.
Porter, D. D., Admiral.   517, 526, 543, 580.
Powell, Charles (of K), Color Corporal.   351, 394, 451, 463 et seq., 485, 687.
Pollard, Henry A.   563 et seq.

# INDEX

Potomac River. 11, 24, 25, 31, 32.
Port Tobacco, Md. 26, 27.
Portsmouth, Va. 117.
Pond, , Col., of Ohio. 278.
Pollard's 'Lost Cause.' 465, 483.
Prescott, Royal B., Hosp. Steward, Lieut. 4, 14, 19, 23, 31, 32, 53, 63, 80, 105, 109, 111, 151, 184, 194, 213, 228, 229, 231, 233, 235, 243, 249, 252, 257, 261, 320, 337, 352, 368, 381, 408, 418, 438, 457, 483, 487, 492, 493, 498, 508, 509, 511, 513, 516, 517, 528, 529, 531, 535, 538, 546, 551, 554 et seq., 579 et seq., 592, 598, 600, 602, 606, 608, 619, 687 et seq., 705.
Prescott, John E (of D), Corporal. 282.
Prime, Joseph H. (of F). 177.
Prickett, J. H. 274.
Prickett, I. D. 277.
Pratt, William M., Major. 549.
Proctor, David E. (of B). 236, 626, 687.
Providence, R. I. 64.
Pruden, Nathaniel, Capt. 139, 148.
Pruyn, , Major. 386.

Quint, Alonzo H., Chaplain. 687 et seq.

Rand, Robert (of K). 31, 32.
Raleigh, N. C. 596.
Raulston, John B., Lt. Col. 478, 499 et seq., 515, 525, 567 et seq.
Ransom, , C. S. A. Gen. 71, 311.
Reed, John (of E). 215, 220.
Read, Theodore, Major. 477, 543, 585 et seq.
Reams Station, Va. 73.
Reveille. 17.
Richardson, Samuel A., Surgeon. 69, 80, 116, 120, 151, 201, 231, 237, 241, 282, 311, 438, 439, 442, 519, 593, 619, 688 et seq.
Richardson, Malachi W. (of G). 350.
Ringgold, Benjamin, Col. 34.
Riley, John (of E). 305, 398, 489.
Ripley, Edward H., Col. 545, 549, 555, et seq., 591, 605, 696 et seq.
Roberts, Samuel H., Col. 468 et seq., 479.
Rosters: Getty's Division. 34.
Troops on Blackberry Raid. 174.
Burnham's Brigade. 340.
Stevens' Brigade. 429.
Officers Thirteenth N. H. V. 310, 311, 697.
Gen. Devens' Division. 549.
Band of Thirteenth. 625.
Roberts, Samuel H., Col. 550.
Robbins, Andrew J. (of G). 458.
Rollins, , Capt. 2d N. H. 24.
Rollins, George H. (of E). 118.
Rodman, Isaac P., Lt. Col. 218.
Rust, , Col. 8th Maine. 278.
Rushmore, Thomas, Augusta and Virginia. 394 et seq., 405.

Saunders, Marshall, Lieutenant. 1, 121, 192, 201, 215, 427, 466, 612.
Saunders, Charles B. (of B). 236, 626, 687.
Sanborn, James A., Capt. 69, 460.
Sanborn, , Lieut. 212, 213.
Sanitary Commission. 336, 375, 438.
Savannah, Ga. 518.
Sawyer, Oliver M., Lieutenant. 121, 187, 231, 427, 456, 539, 541.
Shattuck, M. C. (of B), Sergt. Major. 490, 517, 526, 698.
Sherman, Andrew J., Lieutenant. 277, 311, 323, 509, 602, 617.
Sheridan, Philip H., Maj. Gen. 321, 339, et seq., 455, 497, 536, 541, 586, 597, 616.
Shaw, Major A., Lieutenant. 70, 81, 617.
Sharpshooters. 77, 78, 448, 482, 500 et seq.
Shippen, Thomas L. 264.
Sickles, Daniel E., Maj. Gen. 18, 495.
Sherman, William T., Gen. 519, 544, 588, 589 et seq., 596, 633.
Shepley, G. F., Brig. Gen. 581, 693 et seq.
Sleeper, Henry S. (of H). 21.
Slaughter, , Mr. 38, 49, 56.
Smith, Andrew J. (of I). 418.
Smith, Normand, Lieut. Colonel. 80, 109, 147, 182, 185, 186, 208, 220, 223, 235, 242, 244, 279, 280, 292, 294, 312, et seq., 323, 329, 348, 361 et seq., 389, 396, 397, 401, 408, 414, 417, 418, 424, 427, 429, 450, 453, 458 et seq., 476, 480, 490, 491, 497, 498, 499 et seq., 504, 508, 509, 514, 519, 524, 531, 539, 541, 543, 549, 551, 563 et seq, 579 et seq., 605, 608, 610, 612, 630.
Smith, W. F., Maj. Gen. 252, 279 et seq., 338 et seq., 355 et seq., 382 et seq., 388, 397, 422, 427, 514, 616.
Smith, M. B., Lt. Col. 298.
Small, Horatio N., Asst. Surgeon. 157, 178, 222, 346, 408, 620, 622, 688 et seq.
Smyth, Frederick, Gov. of N. H. 610.
Smyth, Thomas A., Gen. 366.
Smith, Moses, Chaplain. 428.
Smith, Albert M. (of G). 488.
Smith, E. Kirby, C. S. A. Gen. 600.
Smithwick, Peter (of E). 49, 59, 64, 65.
Smoky Hollow, Va. 86, 88.
Spear, Samuel P., Gen. 172, 200, 502.
Spiller, William H. (of C). 124, 583 et seq.
Spofford, Ira A. (of G), Sergeant. 308.
Soldiers' Libraries. 454.
Staniels, Rufus P., Captain. 65, 135, 168, 177, 187, 207, 229, 235, 240, 242, 248, 252, 257, 307, 320, 343, 345, 346, 431, 434, 512, 567 et seq., 687 et seq.
Stafford Heights, Va. 22, 32 et seq.
Stanton, Edward M., Sec. of War. 122, 453, 541, 577.
Staples, William F. (of B). 264.
Stannard, George J., Gen. 458 et seq., 486, 489 et seq., 615.
Stephens, Alexander H. 534.

## INDEX. 715

Stedman, Griffin A., Col. 34, 362.
Steere, W. H. P., Brig. Gen. 190, 196, 204, 252, 614.
Stevens, Aaron F., Colonel. 7, 11, 34, 56, 57, 81, 94, 95, 101, 113, 116, 119, 123, 131, 132, 139, 143, 147, 169, 211, 222, 227, 245, 255, 257, 259, 261, 263, 266, 267, 279, 280, 293, 299, 307, 337, 340, 343, 345 et seq., 368, 372, 382, 386, 390, 409, 410, 417, 421, 429, 453, 456, 458 et seq., 475, 479, 486, 514, 532, 609, 612, 614 et seq., 688 et seq.
Stevens, Mrs. A. F. 192, 200, 693.
Stevens, Hazard, Gen. 57, 116, 134, 141, 422, 687 et seq.
Stevens, John C. (of K). 67.
Stevens, John B. 100.
Stevens, A. H., Major. 576 et seq.
Stimpson, , Capt. 520, 523.
Stiles, C. A. 64, 65.
Storer, Jacob I., Lieut. Colonel. 20, 56, 69, 100, 109, 121, 126, 151, 188, 190, 222, 223, 612, 625, 699 et seq.
Stoodley, Nathan D., Major. 1, 4, 6, 14, 87, 94, 99, 100, 119, 123, 131, 137, 146, 158, 167, 188, 221, 226, 238, 255, 264, 299, 308, 309, 316, 320, 323, 347, 358, 374, 387 et seq., 404, 417, 426, 433, 448, 463 et seq., 480 et seq., 487, 489, et seq., 497, 509, 514, 520, 547, 552 et seq., 579 et seq., 597, 602, 605, 612, 687 et seq.
Stowe, Mrs. Harriet Beecher. 119.
Sturgis, S. D., Gen. 83.
Suffolk, Va. 117.
Sturtivant, , C. S. A. Capt. 390.
Sullivan, John, Maj. Gen. 442.
Sullivan, John, Asst. Surgeon. 14, 69, 75, 80, 94, 97, 99, 115, 128, 175, 182, 216, 220, 227, 228, 239, 249, 311, 346, 351 et seq., 367, 368, 373, 374, 394, 403, 426, 442, 619, 686 et seq.
Sumner, Edwin V., Maj. Gen. 21, 22, 34, 38, 74, 83, 87, 88, 96, 103, 691 et seq.
Sunday in the Army. 21, 24.
Sweet, Joshua B., Surgeon. 441, 493.
Sykes, , Gen. 74.

Taggard, George H., Adjutant. 196, 227, 231, 242, 244, 250, 260, 274, 301, 323, 351, 355, 356, 358, 361, 426, 447, 448, 449, 457, 471, 487, 490, 509, 512, 539, 592, 600, 602, 687 et seq.
Tarbell, Charles H. (of B). 234.
Taylor, Richard, C. S. A. Gen. 595.
Tenney, Allen, Sec. of State of N. H. 6.
Terry, Alfred, Gen. 499 et seq., 526, 615.
Thompson, Robert R., Lieutenant. 194, 199, 292, 294, 320, 427, 444, 465 et seq., 479, 489, 539.
Thompson, Henry G. (of K). 67.
Thompson, John Ed., Adjt. 20th Illinois Vols. 199.
Thompson, S. Millett, Lieutenant. 38, 41, 58, 59 et seq., 70, 76, 130, 157, 170, 188, 192, 199, 207, 218, 231, 239,

264, 266, 286, 292, 300 et seq., 326, 343, 364 et seq., 384 et seq., 387, 390, 394, 423, 428, 441, 491, 494, 590, 623, 686 et seq.
Tilton, Edwin A. (of K). 200.
Tolles, Samuel, Lt. Col. 35.
Trow, Elbridge F. (of E). 7.
Tubbs, E. M. 527.
Turner, Dick, Commandant Libby Prison. 501.
Turner, John W., Gen. 546, 604.
Trumbull, Henry Clay (Chaplain), Mr. and Mrs. 495.
Tuck, John A. 420.
Twitchell, George B., Surgeon. 3, 18, 22, 26, 80, 122, 619, 698 et seq.

Uniontown, Md. 25, 70.
Upham, Charles L., Capt. 35.
Upton's Hill, Va. 11, 12, 13.

Van Duzee, Hezron (of E). 19, 71, 108, 144, 157, 188, 351.
Vanderkieft, B. A., Surgeon. 441, 493.
Varrell, Robert W. (of K). 67.
Vaughan, Samuel K. 549.
Vicksburg, Tenn. 122, 530.
Vinall, William D., M. D. 530.
Vinall, Miss Charlotte. 513.
Virginia. 5, 23, 535.

Washington, George, Gen. 68, 171, 337, 534, 535, 577.
Washington, D. C. 5, 8, 9, 25, 33, 94.
Warrenton, Va. 21.
Walton, , C. S. A. Col. 72.
Walker, S. A., Major. 102.
Walker, W. S., C. S. A. Gen. 324.
Walker, R. C., Major. 233.
Warren, Charles, Major. 549.
Warren, G. K., Gen. 357.
Ward, John E., Col. 34, 131.
Ward, Artemas (C. F. Browne). 433.
Washburn, Charles W. (Band). 213, 351, 445, 508, 687.
Washburne, Col. 586.
Ware, Edwin, Lieutenant. 465, 489.
Wakefield, N. H. 495.
Weeks, George H. 417.
Wentworth, Thomas S. (of B). 293, 464, 686 et seq.
Weitzel, Godfrey, Maj. Gen. 229, 283 et seq., 490, 499 et seq., 514, 517, 546, 547, 553 et seq., 693 et seq.
Whalley, Nathan (Band). 687.
Wheeler, Henry B., Lieutenant. 207, 254, 427, 448, 466, 476, 602.
Whittaker, Ira M. (of G). 100.
White House Landing, Va. 336, 375, 422.
Whittemore, John J. 14, 18, 619, 703 et seq.
Whittlesly, Major. 538.
Wilson, , Gen. 73.
Wilton, N. H. 64, 65.
Wilde, , Gen. 256.
Wild, Francis (of E). 218.

Willcox, O. B., Maj. Gen. 22, 34, 83.
Wilmington, N. C. 517.
Williamsburg, Va. 54, 180.
Winn, Benjamin F., Lieutenant. 626, 687 et seq.
Winch, C. F. 453.
Wistar, , Gen. 321.
Wilson, Lewis P., Captain. 41, 121, 187, 207, 254, 601, 616, 687 et seq.
Wilson, Hon. Henry. 513.
Witherbee, George C., Capt. 513, 611.
Woods, John M. (of I). 611, 686 et seq.
Wood, D. E. 270.
Wood, Reuben L. (of G). 488.
Woody, Daniel. 339, 352.
Woodbury, Rev. Augustus. 83, 434.
Woodbury, Wooster E. (of C). 122, 123.
Woodward, George T. (of B). 236, 626.
Wool, John, Major. Gen. 161.
Worcester, Mass. 7, 21.
Wright, Dexter R., Col. 17, 18, 21, 24, 34.
Wright, Ira E., Drummer. 122.
Wright, Horatio G., Gen. 357, 374.

Young, W. H. H., Lieutenant. 13, 21, 86, 109, 168, 173, 177, 185, 199, 231, 687 et seq.
Young, Charles A. 21.
Young, Hiram C. (of H). 519, 574.
Yorktown, Va. 171, 180, 251 et seq.

New Hampshire Troops: — 2d. 14, 18, 24, 93, 252, 255, 369, 409, 422, 428, 442, 445, 449, 497, 510, 533, 550, 607.
3d. 255, 509.
4th. 255.
5th. 93.
6th. 33, 76, 93, 96, 105, 432 et seq.
7th. 255, 315.
9th. 33, 93.
10th. 4, 34, 56, 62, 69, 70, 93, 97, 127 et seq., 165, 169, 174 et seq., 209, 229, 236, 237, 252, 255, 259 et seq., 335, 340, 359, 383 et seq., 397, 408, 428, 429, 439, 443, 458 et seq., 481, 484, 500 et seq., 533, 574, 582, 607.
11th. 33, 93.
12th. 4, 33, 93, 165, 255, 324, 532, 533, 539, 574, 582, 607, 610.
14th. 4.
1st Heavy Artillery. 421, 511.
Troops of Northern States: —
Connecticut. — 8th. 39, 56, 131, 174, 215, 228, 237, 248, 252, 259 et seq., 336, 340, 358, 380, 383 et seq., 428, 429, 486, 498, 549.
11th. 34, 56, 144, 174, 362, 515, 533, 546, 549, 606.
15th. 11, 17, 24, 34, 56, 144, 174, 215, 229.
16th. 34, 56, 118, 134, 144, 174, 207, 218, 229.
21st. 34, 56, 80, 97, 126, 129 et seq., 329, 358, 549, 605.
1st Heavy Artillery. 323.

Indiana. — 13th. 151, 174.
Illinois. — 20th. 199.
Maine. — 6th. 252.
Maryland. — 5th. 550 et seq.
Massachusetts. — 1st. 495.
6th. 8.
9th. 11.
16th. 691.
19th. 40, 83.
20th. 40, 83.
23d. 229, 239, 241, 248.
25th. 219.
27th. 248, 267.
30th. 535.
40th. 342, 344, 347 et seq., 351, 549, 603, 605.
2d Battery — B— or Nims'. 530.
7th Battery. 151.
9th Battery. 11.
4th Cavalry. 576 et seq.
Michigan. — 7th. 39, 40, 83.
New York. — 3d. 174.
9th. 34, 35, 45, 56, 57, 69, 70, 97, 112, 165, 237.
50th. 83.
69th. 366.
81st. 263 et seq., 429, 439, 458 et seq., 499 et seq., 515, 520, 541, 546, 549, 580, 595, 606, 698.
89th. 26, 34, 39, 40, 56, 83, 97, 112, 120, 131, 139 et seq., 152, 174.
92d. 383 et seq.
96th. 549.
99th. 174, 176.
98th. 429, 458 et seq., 499 et seq., 515, 534, 549, 606, 698.
100th. 547, 551.
103d. 34, 56, 97, 114, 126, 139 et seq., 174, 301.
112th. 174.
117th. 174, 397.
118th. 174, 236, 237, 248, 252, 259 et seq., 340, 358, 383 et seq., 429, 458 et seq., 500 et seq., 543, 549, 605.
139th. 429, 458 et seq., 499 et seq., 510, 515, 526, 549, 606, 698.
142d. 11, 17.
144th. 151.
Corcoran's Irish Legion. 129, 134 et seq., 170.
Dodge's Mounted Rifles. 151, 202.
1st Battery. 550.
3d Battery. 550.
13th Heavy Artillery. 209, 212, 240.
New Jersey. — 9th. 229.
25th. 24, 34, 35, 56, 57, 65, 66, 72, 73, 94, 97, 119, 139 et seq., 165.
27th. 24.
Pennsylvania. — 26th. 18.
48th. 431.
58th. 550.
97th. 324.
165th. 174, 176.
166th. 174.
169th. 174.
188th. 550, 601.
11th Cavalry. 121, 172, 502.

## INDEX.                                                          717

Rhode Island. — 4th. 34, 56, 90, 97, 112, 126, 127, 161, 174, 219, 223, 229.
  12th. 24, 26.
  1st Cavalry. 501.
Wisconsin. — 19th. 515, 549, 606.
  2d Battery. 129, 289, 292.
  4th Battery. 550.
Vermont. — 9th. 130, 569 et seq., 605.
  'Vermont Brigade.' 18.
United States Regular Army.
  11th Infantry. 421.
  3d Battery. 550.
  4th Battery. 151, 210, 465.
  5th Battery. 550.
Veteran Reserve Corps: Co. E, 14th. 366.
Meagher's Irish Brigade. 691.
Colored Troops. — U. S. C. T.
  2d. 240.
  25th. 228.
  30th. 626.
Army Corps: Second. 22, 360 et seq., 366, 374, 405, 407, 417, 441, 444, 595.
  Fifth. 441, 444, 595.
  Sixth. 339, 341 et seq., 358 et seq., 374, 407, 417, 515, 599.
  Seventh. 170, 173, 185, 190, 630.
  Ninth. 22, 34, 75, 80, 83, 84, 88, 96, 97, 113, 114, 116, 166, 367, 407, 431 et seq., 441, 541, 630, 699.
  Tenth. 252 et seq., 256, 281 et seq., 339 et seq., 446, 448, 459 et seq., 494, 499 et seq., 514, 546.
  Fourteenth. 596.
  Fifteenth. 597.
  Seventeenth. 122, 597.
  Eighteenth. 186, 190, 194, 252 et seq., 256, 281 et seq., 339 et seq., 348 et seq., 358 et seq., 374, 376, 382 et seq., 401 et seq., 404, 422, 427, 428, 429, 431 et seq., 441, 446, 448, 459 et seq., 490, 499 et seq., 514, 522, 586, 630, 695 et seq.
  Twentieth. 596.
  Twenty-Fourth. 515, 526, 531, 532, 536, 537, 539, 542, 543, 548, 549, 554 et seq., 574, 592 et seq., 604, 630, 693 et seq.
  Twenty-Fifth. 515, 533, 541, 548, 576, 693 et seq.
Confederate Troops: Florida. — 8th. 40.
  Georgia. — 3d. 40.
    16th. 71.
    18th. 71, 493.
    24th. 71.
  'Georgia Legion.' 71.
  Louisiana. — 'Tigers.' 162.
  Mississippi. — Barksdale's Brigade. 39, 40, 86.
    17th. 40.
    18th. 40.
    21st. 40.
  North Carolina. — 32d. 320.
    24th. 428.
  South Carolina. — 2d. 71.
    8th. 71.
    15th. 71.
    23d. 434.
    25th. 274.
    18th. 434.
  Texas. — 4th. 152.
  Tennessee. — 44th. 297, 310, 483.
    69th. 285.
  Virginia. — 12th. 553.
    32d. 54, 70, 73.
    28th. 401.
  Washington Artillery. 36.
  Richmond City Battalion. 493.
  Wise's Legion. 396, 402.
  Dearing's Cavalry. 402.
  Elliott's Brigade. 434.
  Army of Northern Virginia. 582 et seq.

www.ingramcontent.com/pod-product-compliance
Lightning Source LLC
Chambersburg PA
CBHW071212290426
44108CB00013B/1170